CONGRATULATIONS!

50 NOT OUT.

Keep your eye on the ball.

Best wishes,

Richard + Norma,

BENSON *and* **HEDGES**

Cricket Year

Sixteenth Edition

September 1996 to September 1997

Editor **David Lemmon**

Foreword by **Ian Botham**

BLOOMSBURY

Editor's note

The aim of *Benson and Hedges Cricket Year* is to give the cricket enthusiast an opportunity to read through the events in the world of cricket from each October until the following September (the end of the England season), although one must admit that it becomes increasingly difficult to draw lines of demarcation for seasons which tend to overlap. India toured Sri Lanka in August, and Zimbabwe engaged in a Test series with New Zealand just as the England season drew to a close, yet these must remain within the province of next year's book.

The structure of the book, as in the past, offers a three-dimensional look at twelve months of cricket – narrative, pictures and statistics. This year's foreword is written by the mighty Ian Botham, and there is a fascinating contribution on the return of the legspinner from Trevor Bailey. The greatest post-war English all-rounders air their views in these pages.

There is, too, an interview with Tim Lamb who explains the aims and structure of the England and Wales Cricket Board.

The symbol * indicates not out or wicket-keeper according to context.

Once more I would like to give thanks to those friends whose help and encouragement make this book possible. Les Hatton is a mine of information on the Sunday League and meticulous in all that he does. Sudhir Vaidya continues to supply information and immaculate work on Indian cricket, while this year we have a new colleague in Gamini Senadhira who has made possible a full Sri Lankan section for the first time. Anthony Lalley is wonderfully quick and precise in supplying information from Australia and his research is exemplary. The same must be said about Ian Smith in New Zealand. My thanks are due, too, to Charlie Wat in Australia whose publications offer a wealth of information concerning the Sheffield Shield and Australian Test cricket. Andrew Samson of South Africa, Qamar Ahmed of Pakistan, Vic Isaacs, Phil Bailey and Jo King are others who are unstinting in their assistance. I remain eternally grateful to county secretaries who are never too busy to give me a moment of their time to answer queries.

Above all, I should like to record my appreciation of the work done by my dear friend Brian Croudy. He labours tirelessly, and I must be responsible for 90% of his telephone bill.

A word, too, in praise of Melanie Porte of Book Creation Services who is ever patient and good humoured in her dealings with me and without whom this book would never be published as quickly as it is.

The world of cricket is a wonderful place in which to meet good people and make good friends.

David Lemmon

First published in 1997 by
Bloomsbury Publishing Plc
38 Soho Square
London W1V 5DF

Copyright © David Lemmon

The right of David Lemmon to be identified as the author of the work has been asserted by him in accordance with the Copyright, Designs and Patents Act 1988

A copy of the CIP entry for this book is available from the British Library

ISBN 07475 3106 4

10 9 8 7 6 5 4 3 2 1

Designed by Carroll Associates
Typeset by Book Creation Services, London

Printed by Bath Press, Great Britain

Contents

Sponsor's Message

We are delighted to bring you the sixteenth edition of *The Benson and Hedges Cricket Year*. It is a major feat of publishing by Bloomsbury and, of course, a 'tour de force' by the Editor, David Lemmon, to ensure that all cricket enthusiasts have a complete record of the English county season within weeks of it ending.

This season has been an interesting one in many respects, not least for the fact that the future structure of the game has been under scrutiny in Lord MacLaurin's *Raising the Standard* proposal. Naturally, these discussions have a direct effect on us at Benson and Hedges with the proposed abolition of the Benson and Hedges Cup after 1998. While we understand the need for change we are sad that our 27 year association with cricket may be at an end.

Benson and Hedges is, in fact, the longest supporter of cricket in this country. Our sponsorship of the Benson and Hedges Cup began in 1972 when Peter West suggested to the then Test and County Cricket Board that they might like to consider introducing a second domestic one-day knock-out cup competition to county cricket. At that time one-day cricket was in its infancy, but was gaining credibility and an increasingly enthusiastic following. Indeed the first international one-day series, between England and Australia, was played in 1972 and the first World Cup not until 1975. It was, therefore, important for English cricket to develop this side of the game and we at Benson and Hedges were delighted to be able to support it.

We have thoroughly enjoyed our 27 years and, not only have we developed wonderful friendships and associations in cricket, but we have contributed significantly to the sport during that time, both financially and in terms of supporting the game at domestic level. As well as the competition itself, Benson and Hedges has been committed to supporting county player's benefits and assisting development of media facilities at county grounds through the Media Grant.

The structure of the English game is tackled by our foreword writer this year, Ian Botham, and no doubt he will have some forthright comments to make on the proposals. We are also grateful to Tim Lamb for talking to David Lemmon about the structure of the new England and Wales Cricket Board, with its brief to bring all cricket under one umbrella, and Trevor Bailey for his article on the return of the leg-spinner.

Whether it is reading the views of our contributors or simply using the book as a reference point, I hope you will find this latest edition of *The Benson and Hedges Cricket Year* an interesting and useful addition to your collection.

Jim Elkins
Special Events Director
Benson and Hedges

Comment

by David Lemmon

The twelve-month period covered by this book saw more than a hint of sadness. Tragically, the Surrey wicket-keeper Graham Kersey died following injuries sustained in a motor accident in Australia. He was a county cricketer in mid-career, and he was one who loved every minute of the game, a team-man in every good sense that that term implies. He is mourned and much missed.

The year, too, embraced the death of Denis Compton shortly before his 79th birthday. For the generations brought to cricket in the war and in the seasons immediately after the war, he inspired a love and passion for the game which will never be extinguished as long as his memory lives. There was joy in all that he did, and that joy was infectious. One wonders what Denis would have thought of the schemes and suggestions that have been made for the restructuring of the game. In his later years, he was, by nature, very conservative, but then he was of an age who believed in the intrinsic worth of the county championship as a competition in its own right. His commitment to the county game was as total as was his commitment to Test cricket.

In this he was at one with a great cricketer of our own time, Graham Gooch, who retired in 1997. They differed in style, but they shared an attitude which brought health to the game. Perhaps the greatest problem that faces the ECB in their most worthy efforts to raise the standard is that it is not possible to legislate for attitudes. There are those who have moved from positions in the theatre or the business world to take up administrative posts in cricket and have been astonished to identify as what they see as a lack of ambition among some players. Surely, among the most important of recommendations in the blueprint presented by Lord MacLaurin and his committee is that county staffs should be substantially reduced.

"While a reduction in staff numbers may be seen as depriving a number of young men of cricketing opportunities, the truth is that the current system often leaves 25–26 year olds who have not made the grade without any relevant qualifications for further employment. The new system should lead to better qualified cricketers with better post-cricket employment prospects."

As the blueprint also points out, those who are released but who maintain their appetite and ambition to play at the top level will strengthen the top tier of the *recreational* game and have the opportunity to develop their game and earn the right to make a return to first-class cricket.

That several counties have staffs which are too large is undeniable. In 1997, a season during which their captain resigned and departed and their best batsman was released, Derbyshire used 26 players in their county side. This would suggest that Derbyshire are able to field two teams of first-class standard, which, on the evidence of results, is patently untrue. The ECB's blueprint requires that counties take on the responsibility of making professional judgements as to who has the temperament and ability to succeed at the top level. This will not only help to raise standards, it will also make sense economically.

A sound economic structure is an essential for any sport, and cricket is putting its house in order in this respect. The game has been more than fortunate in its sponsors, who have been both generous and supportive, but nothing should be taken for granted. There is a popular myth that commerce and industry are full of companies clammering to sponsor anything and everything. Nothing could be further from the truth as *The Cricketer* magazine will verify.

The Cricketer has organised the National Village Championship for the past 27 years. Village cricket is a foundation stone of the game, and the competition is a worthy one, but the most recent sponsor, once a building society now a bank, has lost interest. In 1997, they declined to host the traditional pre-match dinner and are to withdraw completely at the end of the 1998 season.

The first-class game has been luckier in its sponsors who now wait to see what is required of them as cricket faces restructure. The plans have been many and varied and have not pleased all, but the idea of a super cup for which qualification is to finish in the top eight of the county championship is an idea that has much to commend it. It will keep alive ambition and competition to the end of the season, and it will still provide us with a July final which has been one of the great delights of the season.

There are those who have said that it would have been better to have replaced this final with an extra one-day international which would generate as much income. That is a narrow attitude. There are cricketers who know now that they will never appear in a Test match, but they hold on to the dream that one day they could play in a Lord's final. Their supporters, too, cherish that ambition, and if we ignore their passions and desires, we lose everything.

In his foreword to *Raising the Standard*, Lord MacLaurin writes, "There is no quick fix to addressing the issues in cricket." He is right. Too frequently do we clutch at straws. In the past few years, young men like Lenham, Roseberry, Lathwell and now the Hollioakes have been heralded as instant saviours. This is fair neither to them nor to the game itself. Cricket is based on the virtues of patience and humility, and we must be ever conscious of both.

A few days before his death, Denis Compton should have spoken at Lord's and made presentations to young cricketers at a function organised by Neil Burns. He was too ill to attend, and his place was taken by Peter Parfitt whose career overlapped with Compton's. Parfitt's closing words were to quote what Compton had said to him as a young player.

"Enjoy it while it lasts, son. It doesn't last long."

Perhaps that should have been included in the blueprint.

David Lemmon

Foreword

by Ian Botham

On Monday, 14 September 1997, the chairmen of the eighteen first-class counties plus representatives of MCC met at Lord's to vote on Lord MacLaurin's blueprint for the future of the English domestic game, *Raising The Standard.*

That day they had the chance to usher in the first meaningful change to cricket in this country for more than a century.

They had the chance and they blew it.

The counties did vote for the majority of the points proposed by MacLaurin and his England and Wales Cricket Board chief executive Tim Lamb, formulated after months of consultation with almost everyone connected with the game.

But the crucial question raised in the (revised) document concerned how county championship cricket should be played now and into the next millennium and in this respect the majority of the counties failed pitifully in their obligation as trustees of the first-class game, by putting the interests of the few (i.e. themselves) ahead of the needs of the many.

On the table were four proposals, as follows:

1. *Conference Scheme*: The county championship to be divided into three equal conferences with end-of-season play-offs to decide all eighteen placings, starting in 1998. Sunday League and Benson and Hedges Cup to be scrapped in 1999, to be replaced by a two-division, 50-overs competition with promotion and relegation. As with the other proposals, the NatWest Trophy to become the "FA Cup of cricket", expanded to 60 teams.

2. *Two Divisions*: A two-division county championship with nine teams in each, every side playing the others twice; three promoted, three relegated. A two-division 50-overs league, along identical lines to the championship. NatWest Trophy to remain 60-overs per side. Whole programme to be introduced in 1999, with the make up of divisions decided by finishing positions in 1998.

3. *The "Radical" Status Quo*: All-play-all county championship, with 18 teams playing the others once for enhanced prize money. Top eight finishers qualify for a new knock-out cup ("Super Eights") to be played in the first half of the next season: top four receive home ties. Bottom four participate in following season's NatWest Trophy at earlier stage. A two-division 50-overs league and 60-overs NatWest Trophy. Programme introduced in 1999, with 50-overs divisions, Super Eights and NatWest seedings decided by 1998 positions.

4. *The "Actual" Status Quo*: God help us.

Shortly after 5.30 pm on D-Day, Lord MacLaurin announced the verdict. Option 3 was preferred. D-Day became Dog's Dinner-Day.

In the days leading up to the vote Lord MacLaurin made it plain which option he favoured. Indeed you could almost hear the tut-tutting among the more conservative counties at his clear call for revolution.

"There is no doubt in my mind that we need to give championship cricket a shot in the arm. Two divisions with promotion and relegation would send out all the right messages in terms of increased competitiveness and commercialisation.

"Without money from the centre raised by sponsorship and television revenue, cricket in this country would be bankrupt.

"The county clubs need to understand that sponsors and television companies will only put money into something they believe is worth supporting. Unless the fortunes of the England team take a decisive upturn they could easily look elsewhere.

"All sports are moving ahead. Cricket has to keep pace with a changing market place. I absolutely do not accept that the status quo is a viable option. People must wake up to the real world."

Those observers who tallied up the likely votes in advance knew that the chairman of the ECB was, to borrow Graham Gooch's memorable phrase, "farting against thunder".

Nonetheless, the eventual outcome was a huge disappointment not only for MacLaurin but for all those like him who felt that a golden opportunity to take steps to arrest England's decline to the second division of Test-playing nations had been wasted.

The adoption of the so-called "radical status quo" – sounds a bit like Rick Parfitt and co. in mohican haircuts to me – was like a kick in the stomach to all those who had campaigned, pleaded and begged for real progress. Quite what the benefit of the Super Eight one-day knockout will be to England's development at Test level remains to be seen, or even explained.

I made my own thoughts on promotion and relegation clear in my book *The Botham Report*, published a fortnight before the fateful Lord's meeting, setting them out in a Ten Point Plan for the future of English cricket thus:

"The benefits are clear; raising the level of the competition and toughness required among county players for too long stuck in the mire of mediocrity and increasing interest by making every game mean something. For those who believe that this would not happen, try the following thought for size. Imagine if you now announced that, as of the season after next the championship would be split into two divisions of nine clubs each and that your position in Division One or Two would depend on where you finished in next season's championship. Now imagine how competitive that contest would be.

"We do produce some talented young players, but by the time they have been put through the process of playing uncompetitive county cricket for two or three seasons their mental edge is dulled. Then, when they come into Test cricket, the toughest examination of all, most of them simply do not know what it is like to confront and deal with the intense pressure involved because they have never experienced it at county level."

Quite apart from the benefits to England of increasing the competitive element in our domestic cricket, to me there are sound commercial reasons for a two-division championship. With promotion and relegation affecting six teams each season, not to mention the fight for the championship itself, almost every team would be playing for something tangible every match. That would increase the level of interest dramatically whether your club was in the first or second division. Not only would revenue be increased through the turnstiles but the heightened media interest would mean local sponsors would be far more likely to see value for money.

The second main proposal in my Ten Point Plan, contracting an elite squad of international players to the central board, didn't even warrant a serious mention in *Raising The Standard* when Lord MacLaurin gave it its first public airing, but it did have widespread support, not least from David Lloyd, the England coach. My argument is simply this: bearing in mind the seemingly ever-growing list of casualties among England bowlers, isn't it about time we concentrated on making them fit for England at all times? If county clubs wish to survive in anything like their present form, the bottom line is that England must win and their best chance of winning comes from looking after the players, not forcing them to play second-rate cricket.

I am not advocating that contracted players should play no county cricket, but that the amount should be controlled and determined by the national selectors in order to make sure that every single time an England player sets foot on the field to represent England he is fit and ready for the challenge of facing the best players in the world, and capable of excelling.

How sadly typical of the current state of our game it was when, just days after their inclusion in England's squad for the winter tour to West Indies, three of the five pace bowlers chosen, Darren Gough, Dean Headley and Ashley Cowan, suffered injuries. In the case of Darren Gough and Dean Headley, their ailments were serious enough to keep them out for the rest of the season.

And how fitting it was that Mark Taylor's Australians and Alistair Campbell's Zimbabweans should have spent the 1996–97 international season reminding everyone of the A to Z of reasons why change should have been considered so necessary in the first place.

However much they were maligned back home for their performances in Zimbabwe, with rent-a-quote Tory politicians calling for the tour to be abandoned and the players to be sent home in disgrace and, however much the team's performances improved in New Zealand thereafter, the fact is that, given five opportunities to beat the newest entry to international cricket in two Tests and three one-day international matches, they failed to do so once. Indeed their 3–0 defeat in the one-day series was a frightening indictment of the English game.

What is more, their entire approach to touring Zimbabwe left an awful lot to be desired. Too often the most pressing question occupying the thoughts of some players seemed to be "when do we get out of here?"

Inspired by the wind of change suggested by MacLaurin at the start of the summer Ashes action, England did manage to catch Australia cold early on and followed their Test series victory over New Zealand with an impressive 3–0 whitewash in the Texaco Trophy series.

Then, glory be, came Edgbaston and the ecstatic scenes after England completed a well-earned Test win against all expectations. And the scenes were repeated in the final Test of the series at The Oval when Phil Tufnell and Andrew Caddick bowled England to an equally unlikely victory.

It was what happened in between that offered a more accurate reflection of the current state of the English game.

When Australia confirmed their series victory by winning the fourth Test at Trent Bridge, England were left to reflect on their fifth Ashes defeat in succession and their failure to win a five-Test series against anyone for ten years.

Some counties proved they were not afraid of innovation. And how Warwickshire were rewarded when the first competitive floodlit match, versus Somerset at Edgbaston, attracted a crowd of more than 15,000, earning more in one evening's takings than the club took through the gate for the entire 1997 championship season; a profit of some £70,000.

This was a clear indication to the more conservative counties that some changes really can be for the better. I believe that it is only when that concept is embraced by all that the English game will begin to take the first steps towards re-establishing itself as the national summer sport and the envy of world cricket.

Of all forms of bowling, wristspin is the most fun to bowl, the most fun to face, and the most fun to watch. It provides a fascinating duel between bat and ball, and, like putting in golf, is almost a game within a game. My long love affair with wristspin began during those five summers I spent in the Dulwich College XI. The master in charge of cricket was "Father" Marriott, who was still a class legbreak bowler, had taken 11 for 96 in his only Test in 1932 and was still good enough to play for Kent in the school holidays. He taught me how to play both slow legbreak bowling of the type which so often destroys, and still does, school teams, and also high class legspin, which has been causing England's best batsmen so much trouble in recent years.

At least three times a week I would face (in the nets) slow, well flighted, and gentle legbreaks, plus a rather obvious googly from "Father", exactly the type of bowling I would encounter in school and senior club cricket. It was ideal practice, as he was constantly posing the problem of whether to go down the pitch and try to hit the ball on the full toss, or half volley, or to play it off the back foot. The most important lesson I learned was not to panic when he deceived me in the flight and I was down the track. Out in the middle for practice sessions and in three or four matches against the school, he bowled as he did in first-class cricket, faster, flatter and making the break much sharper. I quickly realised that it was fatal to play back, because he would have me lbw with his top spinner, while the half-cock shot also invited disaster. To last any length of time it was essential to be able to employ the full forward defensive stroke.

The hours spent practising against legspin gave me confidence against this form of attack, which was just as well, because when I began playing for Essex immediately after the war most counties had a legbreak bowler in their side and many, including Essex, had two. Although I always fancied the challenge of batting against wristspin, it did cause me many problems, as illustrated by the first time I faced Jack Walsh, a chinaman and googly bowler. I played his deliveries, which pitched just outside my off and turned into me (with the middle of my bat). The next pitched on my leg stump and I attempted a delicate leg glance to find myself looking into the equally astonished face of the Leicestershire keeper, Paddy Corrall, who had also failed to pick the googly, while the ball went over the top of my off stump for four byes.

The forties were ideal for the wristspinner in county cricket, because he helped to provide the fun, the entertainment and the excitement that the large cricket-starved crowds wanted. It was a time when the results were considered to be of less importance and pitches were more user-friendly. Our selectors also believed it was essential to include a wristspinner overseas, often two: Doug Wright and Peter Smith to Australia, "Roly" Jenkins to South Africa and Doug Wright and Eric Hollies to Australia. Despite the successes of the Australians Bruce Dooland, the finest legspinner I batted against, and George Tribe the gradual decline of the English legspinner began in the fifties and this is what I wrote in 1955.

"A regrettable feature of modern cricket is the surprising lack of legbreak bowlers. There are indeed only three English born legspinners who regularly capture more than 100 wickets in a season, Doug Wright, Eric Hollies and "Roly" Jenkins. All three are pre-war cricketers. Since the war not one top-class post-war English legbreak bowler has come to the scene."

Trevor Bailey was reunited during the summer's series against Australia with Willie Watson, with whom he fought a famous rearguard action at Lord's in 1953. (David Munden/Sportsline)

Although we did produce Tommy Greenough, Robin Hobbs and Bob Barber, who were all capped by England, none could claim to be great wristspinners at the highest level.

There were a number of reasons for the gradual disappearance of English wristspinners from the county circuit. First, the game itself had become less carefree and more ruthless. There was a marked increase in defensive fields and economic bowling, which suited the fingerspinner far more than the wristspinner, though Eric Hollies was an exception. The emphasis was on the denial of runs, while buying wickets, which the legbreaker employed, was going out of fashion.

Secondly, it normally takes a wristspinner a long time to reach his peak, while in his novice period he is bound to be expensive. As a result the counties gradually gave up carrying one, let alone giving him sufficient opportunities to bowl, which was absolutely vital if he was to improve.

Thirdly, the wristspinner is at his most valuable on a true, firm, fast pitch, on which the fingerspinner is unable to achieve much, if any, turn, and a seamer is unable to make the ball deviate. In the next three decades there was a marked decrease of that type for county matches, but a marked increase in what might be described as "result wickets" on which the seamers and fingerspinners were far more effective than a legbreak bowler.

Fourthly, the large number, and the importance of limited-over matches was yet another nail in the wristspinner's coffin, because it was believed, quite incorrectly as it turned out, he would always be too expensive.

Fifthly, young cricketers have always needed a role model for them to try to emulate, so it was hardly surprising that with no legbreak bowler included in any county team, let alone the England side, that nobody should consider becoming one.

The gradual demise of the English wristspinner continued throughout the sixties and seventies, although there were still some outstanding practitioners from other parts of the world, including Abdul Quadir and Intikab, Pakistan, Gupte and Chandresekhar, India, while Australia continued to produce a few, including John Gleeson. The West Indies were becoming more and more pace committed, possibly because the majority of their cricket grounds are not big enough to suit legbreak bowling, which is why they have so often been suspect against it. However, in the eighties there were no serious legbreak bowlers operating in the county championship and it began to look as if my love affair with wrist-spin was over, and, like the lob bowler, he had become an extinct species. It saddened me, as I had experienced the pleasure of seeing the best wristspinners in the thirties, Bill O'Relly, Clarrie Grimmett, "Chuck" Fleetwood-Smith and "Tich" Freeman, faced all the finest in the twenty-five years following the War, and watched their successors for T.M.S. As a result I was delighted when Shane Warne burst on to the international scene in 1993, capturing 34 wickets and playing a major part in Australia retaining the Ashes. He has continued to cause problems throughout the world and, providing he does not break down again, could well become the highest wicket taker in international cricket, as at the present moment he is averaging nearly 5 wickets per Test and there are an enormous amount of Tests these days. Although Shane was the catalyst which caught the imagination of the cricket world, a gradual revival of wristspin, due to several different factors, had commenced before he hit the headlines.

There was a marked increase in the number of county pitches which gave no assistance to fingerspin and seam, but on which a wristspinner could turn the ball. The normal, if somewhat monotonous tactic for the four-day county game is for the team batting first to make four or five hundred runs, declare sometime on the second day and hope to dismiss the opposition twice; a situation which is tailor-made for any good legbreak bowler. In addition to being able to make the ball break even on a true batting surface, he should possess four other weapons to deceive batsmen: flight, a late dip, a topspinner or flipper, and a googly. In sharp contrast the unfortunate offbreak bowler has been heavily handicapped by covered pitches and the artificial limitation of fielders and where they cannot be placed on the legside.

Back in 1988 I chanced to watch an Essex match at Ilford against Sussex, who had shown considerable imagination by including Andy Clarke in their team. I would have termed him no more than an experienced club legbreak bowler and it was therefore not surprising that on a good pitch both Gooch and Border should make centuries. But Andy did worry the middle order, far more than I believe he would have done me when I was still at school, for the very good reason that they had never encountered the problems he posed. This was borne out by the 42 wickets he captured in first-class cricket that summer, while he also met with considerable success in the Sunday League. Sussex began with two legspinners next season, Clarke and Ian Salisbury, who spun the ball far more and went on to become the first bowler of this type to be capped for England since Robin Hobbs back in 1971, while the former simply faded from the scene. I still feel that with better advice at the start of his career about field placing and the realisation that it is not necessary to spin every ball, Salisbury would have done much better. However, more important, and also before the arrival of Warne, was the fine legspin bowling, both entirely different in method, of Mushtaq Ahmed for Pakistan and Anil Kumble for India, who both did, not surprisingly, very well against England. Much later this was also true of Paul Strang from Zimbabwe. All three were a success in county cricket and their presence has certainly provided our batsmen with some much needed experience against legbreak bowling, but, alas, apart from Salisbury, no other English legbreak bowler has yet appeared, though the need is obvious.

An Interview with Tim Lamb
Tim Lamb on the England and Wales Cricket Board and the future administration on English cricket.

Tim Lamb was a right-arm medium pace bowler who won his blue at Oxford in 1973 and again in 1974, the year he first played for Middlesex. In 1978, he joined Northamptonshire for whom he played until 1983 when he returned to Middlesex as secretary and general manager. As a cricketer, he was noted for his commitment, endeavour and passionate love of the game, and it was soon recognised that he was a man who would give outstanding service to cricket as an administrator.

In 1988, he was appointed cricket secretary of the Test and County Cricket Board, and nine years later he became Deputy Chief Executive of the TCCB. When the England and Wales Cricket Board came into existence in January 1997, Tim Lamb was named as Chief Executive, the most important and powerful job in English cricket. In him lie most of our hopes for the future of the game in this country. We put to him some of the concerns which are being voiced by cricket lovers.

It was only in 1968 that the Test and County Cricket Board came into existence, replaced the Board of Control and, in effect took over the administration of much of the game from the MCC. Why is it now necessary to create another body?

That is simple. Cricket is one game. I think it was Arlott who said that all cricketers are cricketers and that the only distinction between them is statistical. With the ECB, we have something that we have never had before – one organisation to manage and administer the game at all levels from, as we say, the school playground to the Test arena. In the past, cricket has had the most fragmented of set-ups. There are more than 20 national representatives organisations at various levels. They speak for schools cricket, youth cricket, the clubs and the leagues, women's cricket, for umpires and scorers, cricketers with disabilities and a host of other associations who are concerned with a specified area of the game. It is a recipe for disunity. The aim of the ECB is to bring everything under one umbrella, to make the whole organisation and administration of the game more cohesive. We want to reduce the levels of bureaucracy while maintaining an awareness of the needs and aspirations of all those who have a concern for the game.

One remembers that when the MCC gave way to the TCCB as the game's governing body there were former Test cricketers who were excited by the change but who felt that the same people were in charge, only the initials of the organisation had changed. Is this not what has happened this time?

No, not at all. There must be some of the same personnel. You cannot sever a link with the past, but we have a completely different structure which is, in effect, a partnership between all concerned with cricket. There is a voice for everybody through the 38 county boards and MCC which make up the ECB. The ECB will act for the good of the game as a whole.

You mention personnel, and you have in Lord MacLaurin a new chairman. What exactly is his role?

Ian MacLaurin is in a non-executive position. He receives no salary, but his experience in business is invaluable to us and he combines the qualities that we need. He is an all-round sportsman of considerable ability, and he has a wealth of business expertise. He believes that the ECB must be run along the lines of a plc, with delegated authority being given to the Board's executives at the centre, as applies at Tesco, but with the necessary operational checks and balances put in place. It is that type of governance which is necessary if the game is to progress.

You use the term business and talk of a organisation along commercial lines. Where does this leave the member of a county club, the individual who has been at the heart of the game and has been its very life blood?

I made it very clear from the moment that I was appointed Chief Executive of the ECB that I believed that cricket must be run as a business *within* a game, not as a game within a business. We recognise that the county member is, and always will be, the core of the game. But we must also face realities. Membership of county clubs now account for less than ten per cent of the game's overall income. The average attendance at the majority of county matches – there are obviously exceptions in the case of certain counties – amounts to just a few hundred. The game will not survive on income from that. We are very largely dependant on the revenue generated on the back of international cricket and the money that comes from television rights, sponsorship and gate receipts.

To many people there seems to be too much emphasis on the England team and upon Test matches to the exclusion of other levels of the game.

There is certainly an emphasis on the Test side, but not to the detriment of other levels of the game. Quite the reverse, for the money that is brought in by international cricket supports and nurtures the game at its lower levels. The emphasis on the England side is because their performance sets the tone for the whole game and they themselves are role models, especially for the young. We need to impress upon the players that their successes and their behaviour will excite enthusiasm for and interest in the game. Look at the reaction to England's victories in the Texaco Trophy and in the Edgbaston Test. The whole country got a huge lift. When that happens more youngsters want to play and more people want to watch. That can only be good for cricket as a whole.

Bob Bennett has been named as the England manager for the West Indies. Does this mean that he will manage the England side wherever they tour?

No, Bob's position is chairman of the England Management Committee, and as such his responsibility, in a non-executive role, is to oversee the smooth running of all matters relating to the England Senior, 'A' and Under-19 Teams in conjunction with the newly appointed International Teams Director. His appointment as Manager of the England side in the West Indies is separate to that and is only for one time at this stage.

With regard to the England side, you have been accused of neglecting countries like Sri Lanka where, in the past, England always took the lead in encouraging the younger cricketing nations. Is this a fair criticism?

I can understand how some people can see it that way, but we were supportive of Sri Lanka, and we have maintained a close association with them over the years. They have acknowledged the reasons for our giving them only one Test match on their previous visits to the UK, and they understand that this was born of commercial and financial necessity during their years of development. They are now a much more established cricketing country, and in 1998, they will play both a Test and up to three one-day internationals. It has also been agreed that they will not be expected to play just a single Test when they come to England in 2002.

There have been suggestions that the TCCB was over-sensitive to criticism and weak in man-management. Would you accept this observation?

Not entirely. People often criticise when they are not fully aware of the facts of a case, and there is frustration on both sides

when this occurs. It is not easy to please everybody, although we are aware that our media relations in particular have not always been as good as we would have liked them to be. An immediate aim of the ECB is to improve in this area and to develop a much more effective corporate affairs and communications strategy that provides the media with a better service and raises the profile of both the Board and cricket as a whole. The more people who read and hear about the game, the better.

When the TCCB came into being it seemed to many of us that it consisted of Donald Carr and Peter Lush in upstairs broom cupboards in the Pavilion at Lord's. The ECB have impressive modern offices at the Nursery End, and you speak of an umbrella system of organisation that encompasses every facet of the game. In this high-powered new management structure where does the social cricketer fit in, the man who wants to play on a Sunday afternoon and never be part of a league?

He will, I hope, continue to play and enjoy his cricket. We are totally aware of the fact that the enthusiastic amateur is at the roots of the game. It is he who so often encourages youngsters, and it is he who invariably becomes a county member and supports his county team. He is one of that vast band of men, and women, who sustain the game, like the teachers and club cricketers who give hours of their time to coach young players, prepare pitches and organise school and youth matches. They have never been paid for what they do, and there is no way we could ever pay them realistically, but within the framework of the ECB we at least need to make them feel that they matter and that we appreciate and value what they do. The game will not survive without their enthusiasm.

As I have said, we are running a business, but we are a sport first and foremost. If we lose sight of that, we lose sight of everything.

International Rankings

It is encouraging to note that several other publications are now following the lead we set some years ago in trying to establish an order of merit in international cricket. What we offer is a statistical assessment of countries' achievements at international level during the period covered by this book. The method employed is simple – two points are given for a win and one for a draw or tie. Points obtained are divided by points possible to arrive at a percentage.

The rankings should be treated with some caution. Pakistan played three two-Test series and won only one of them, against Zimbabwe. Australia were victorious in Test series against West Indies, South Africa and England. Two of these series were on foreign soil and three of the six matches in which they were beaten were when the series was 'dead'. Statistically, they are second; in reality, they are undisputed world champions.

The limited-over rankings are a truer picture with Sri Lanka gathering more trophies to add to the World Cup.

There were 43 Test matches played in the period covered by this annual, an increase of 14 on the previous year, while the number of one-day internationals went from 103 to 113 even though there was no World Cup in 1996–97. It is time to consider that we may be in danger of wringing the neck of the golden-egg-laying goose.

David Lemmon

Test Rankings

	P	W	L	D	Pts won	Pts poss	%
Pakistan	6	2	1	3	7	12	58.33
Australia	15	8	6	1	17	30	56.66
England	11	4	3	4	12	22	54.54
West Indies	12	4	3	5	13	24	54.16
South Africa	9	4	4	1	9	18	50.00
New Zealand	7	3	3	1	7	14	50.00
India	12	3	4	5	11	24	45.83
Sri Lanka	8	2	3	3	7	16	43.75
Zimbabwe	6	–	3	3	3	12	25.00

Limited-Over International Rankings

	P	W	L	T	Pts won	Pts poss	%
Sri Lanka	28	20	7	1	41	56	73.21
South Africa	26	19	7	–	38	52	73.07
West Indies	15	9	6	–	18	30	60.00
Pakistan	42	25	17	–	50	84	59.52
England	11	5	5	1	11	22	50.00
New Zealand	18	6	10	2	14	36	38.88
India	33	11	21	1	23	66	34.84
Australia	27	9	18	–	18	54	33.33
Zimbabwe	20	6	13	1	13	40	32.50
Kenya	3	–	3	–	0	6	0.00
Bangladesh	3	–	3	–	0	6	0.00

Four new faces appear in this year's World XI, and they appear at the expense of Mark Waugh, Nathan Astle, Gary Kirsten and Mushtaq Ahmed. Mark Waugh played one of the very greatest of Test innings to bring Australia victory over South Africa at Port Elizabeth, but he had an inconsistent year and a very disappointing Ashes series. Potentially, he is, one feels, the best batsman in the world, and the most profligate.

Nathan Astle has continued to perform nobly. Memorably, he played an innings which kept England at bay in Auckland, and he scored heavily in domestic cricket and did well for Nottinghamshire, but the return to form of Lara squeezes him out. Astle is a most dedicated professional, and he will serve New Zealand impressively for many years to come.

Mushtaq Ahmed, like the great Waqar Younis and Wasim Akram, missed much international cricket and even carried an injury in his last weeks with Somerset, while Gary Kirsten fell away, and it is probable that his successful partnership with Hudson is at an end.

It was hard not to find a place for the ever improving Chanderpaul and for Mohammad Azharuddin. Azharuddin was something of a loner in a bitterly disappointing Indian side, but he played innings against South Africa both in India and in the Republic which were of exceptional merit.

Below: Saeed Anwar (Ben Radford/Allsport)
Top right: Brian Lara (Shaun Botterill/Allsport)
Bottom right: Sanath Jayasuriya (Mike Hewitt/Allsport)

Sachin Tendulkar (David Munden/Sportsline)

Aravinda de Silva (David Munden/Sportsline)

Had he maintained form and discipline in the Caribbean, his inclusion in the World XI would have been automatic.

For the future, one would look to Elliott, Blewett, Ponting and Gillespie, all Australian, and to Fleming of New Zealand and Kallis of South Africa. There will be concern that no England player has found his way into the side. What of Thorpe, second in the Coopers and Lybrand Ratings, and Hussain?

Both had good years, Thorpe in particular, but he still remains something of a peripheral figure, unable to assert and take command when necessary. Interestingly, of the Coopers and Lybrand top nine batsmen, his Test average would place him ninth although he is rated second.

It is interesting to consider, as we note elsewhere, that members of the Australian party that toured England asserted that, were he English, Stuart Law would replace any one of the top six in the England order, and he has not been given a Coopers and Lybrand Rating.

Saeed Anwar (Pakistan)
(9) Saeed Anwar threw off the effects of illness to establish a new record in a one-day international, a form of cricket in which he now has 12 centuries to his credit and more than 4,000 runs. His successes in the limited-over game have tended to obscure the fact that he is a Test opener of dynamic quality and that he has a Test average in excess of 48.

Sanath Jayasuriya (Sri Lanka)
(5) Jayasuriya was named as the most valuable player in the 1996 World Cup and for long he was looked upon simply as an aggressive batsman and a useful slow left-arm bowler in limited-over cricket. In1996–97, he matured into a Test batsman of the highest quality, displaying both consistency and discipline. His triple century against India heralded the start of the 1997–98 Sri Lankan season.

Brian Lara (West Indies)
(6) After twelve months of indifferent form, Brian Lara fought his way back to somewhere near his former glories. The burden of record-holding had not rested easily upon him, but 1996-97 saw him make his peace with the West Indian authorities (although he was still fined for arriving late for one match) and to show a greater discipline in his approach to batting without losing his powers of free-scoring. He led West Indies against India with intelligence and distinction.

Sachin Tendulkar (India)
(3) No batsman in the world has so much responsibility thrust upon him as Sachin Tendulkar. Now captain of India, he often carried the side upon his shoulders, and if he failed, India failed, whatever the form of cricket. In spite of these burdens, he played some brilliant innings and

Steve Waugh (Clive Mason/Allsport)

Ian Healy (Clive Mason/Allsport)

maintained a Test average in excess of 52. It is difficult to remember that he is only 24 years old.

Aravinda de Silva (Sri Lanka)

(11) Arguably, Aravinda de Silva is the most exciting batsman in world cricket, and in 1997 he became a record holder. He hit three centuries in successive innings against Pakistan and became the first batsman in Test history to make two undefeated hundreds in a match. He failed only in New Zealand, but even there, in domestic cricket, he scored the fastest century recorded in the limited-over competition. He dominated one-day international competitions as Sri Lanka added more trophies to their collection.

Steve Waugh (Australia)

(1) Steve Waugh shared a record with Greg Blewett in South Africa and hit two centuries in a Test against England. He remains a model of consistency and a batsman capable of dealing with any crisis. He was vice-captain of the Australian side in England and his contribution to the series victories over West Indies, South Africa and England was enormous.

Ian Healy (Australia)

(44) Ian Healy has been the best wicket-keeper in the world for the past six or seven years. One would now consider that

cricket has not seen a better wicket-keeper since the Second World War and that he must rank alongside Tallon, Evans, Knott and the other great keepers. Indeed, one would go as far as to say that his keeping in the Ashes series surpassed anything that we have seen before. As a bonus, he topped the Australian batting averages in the series against the West Indies.

Shane Warne (Australia)

(4) Recovering from a finger operation and troubled by a shoulder injury, Shane Warne still bemused the best batsmen in the world. He has now taken more Test wickets than any other Australian spinner in history and more than any bowler in the world he is capable of turning the course of a match in the space of a dozen deliveries. To see him in action is one of the joys of the modern game.

Curtly Ambrose (West Indies)

(1) One suggested last year that the great fast bowler's career may be nearing its end. This may be true, but he still topped the West Indian bowling averages in the series in Australia and passed 300 Test wickets during the series in the Caribbean. His pace, height and control allow him to remain among the most feared bowlers in the world.

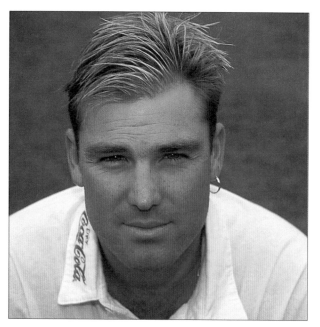

Top left: Shane Warne (Clive Mason/Allsport)
Top right: Curtly Ambrose (David Munden/Sportsline)
Bottom left: Allan Donald (David Munden/Sportsline)
Bottom right: Glen McGrath (Clive Mason/Sportsline)

Allan Donald (South Africa)

(3) Firmly established as one of the greatest fast bowlers of his generation, Allan Donald found success in all countries and on all surfaces in 1996–97. He topped the bowling averages against India in India and against India in South Africa, and he was South Africa's leading wicket-taker against the Australians. In county cricket, he was a potent force for Warwickshire.

Glenn McGrath (Australia)

(2) Glenn McGrath took 26 wickets against West Indies in Australia and topped the Test averages. He then went to South Africa where he took 13 cheap wickets in three Tests. In England, he captured 36 Test wickets and was named Man of the Series. He is now recognised as at the forefront of a new generation of fast bowlers.

The numbers in brackets are the Coopers and Lybrand Ratings of Test cricketers. The first seven refer to batting ratings (there are no ratings for wicket-keepers) and the last four are bowling ratings.

Zimbabwe

Zimbabwe cricket came of age in 1996–97. It was as if the Test status attained in 1992 was given its final recognition and blessing with the agreement of England to play two Test matches and three one-day internationals against Zimbabwe prior to their tour of New Zealand. England's visit to Zimbabwe was welcomed not simply for the prestige it brought, but because it also had significant financial advantages for cricket in the country.

Harare South Country Club where England began their tour of Zimbabwe.
(Stu Forster/Allsport)

England Tour
Logan Cup
Miscellaneous Matches

The Zimbabwe Cricket Union has never been blessed with riches, and money coming from television rights attendant on the England tour was welcome in that it would help to put the game in Zimbabwe on a more professional basis.

By the time England arrived in Zimbabwe, the national side had been toughened by their experiences in Test series in Sri Lanka and Pakistan. England, one felt, would be most unwise to underrate their hosts.

England Tour

For personal reasons, Dominic Cork missed the tour of Zimbabwe. He was to join the party later in New Zealand. There were no surprises in the chosen 14. Tufnell had been forgiven for past misdemeanours and was back in favour – though possibly on probation – and Silverwood, the Yorkshire pace bowler and Young Cricketer of the Year, was a wise and deserved choice.

30 November 1996
at Harare South Country Club
Country Districts 198 for 9 (G.J. Whittall 58) v. England XI
Match abandoned

England's opening match of the tour was abandoned after 45.3 overs because of rain. This was hard on the local side who had to raise some six thousand pounds to stage the match, but a crowd of 2,000 helped them to recover much of their money. Mullally and Irani each took three wickets.

1 December 1996
at Harare Sports Club
England XI 211 for 5 (A.J. Stewart 105, N. Hussain 50)
President's XI 215 for 5 (D.N. Erasmus 67)
President's XI won by 5 wickets

Danie Erasmus hits out as England suffer a surprise defeat at the hands of the President's XI. (Stu Forster/Allsport)

England suffered a shock and a warning when they lost to a strong President's XI in a 50-over match. The home side reached their target with 25 balls to spare. The England side had recovered from 24 for 3 through Stewart and Hussain, who added 133 in 33 overs. Brandes took the first three wickets in the space of 15 balls, and Stewart's assured century was much needed to steady the innings. There was no such steadiness in the England bowling where Caddick delivered nine wides and conceded more than six runs an over. Mullally and Croft were the only members of the England attack to suggest control and discipline.

3, 4, 5 and 6 December 1996
at Harare Sports Club
England XI 197 (R.D.B. Croft 80 not out, R.J. Kirtley 5 for 53) and 180 (J.P. Crawley 74, G.B. Brent 5 for 22)
Mashonaland 280 (D.L. Houghton 110, A.D.R. Campbell 55, P.C.R. Tufnell 5 for 78, R.D.B. Croft 4 for 65) and 98 for 3 (A.D.R. Campbell 53 not out)
Mashonaland won by 7 wickets

The only consolation that England could draw from their defeat at the hands of Mashonaland was that most of the damage inflicted on their batting was done by James Kirtley, the Sussex pace bowler who was coaching in Zimbabwe. England fielded what they deemed would be their Test side, which meant Stewart keeping wicket and no place for Russell, but their vaunted batting line-up failed miserably, succumbing in the first, and most difficult, session of a hot day. Atherton had survived two balls in the one-day game. Against Mashonaland, he made his first runs of the tour, two, before touching the third ball he received to the wicket-keeper. In the next two overs, both Stewart and Hussain played on. Knight then had a difference of opinion with Thorpe over a third run and was beaten by Paul Strang's throw to the bowler Brent. Thorpe, who made 30, drove to cover where Houghton took a good catch, and the tourists lunched at 78 for 5.

Crawley was needlessly run out in early afternoon, and the enthusiastic Croft was left to salvage something from the wreckage as England closed on 175 for 9. Croft's last wicket stand with Tufnell was not ended until it was worth 52. Tufnell, having survived bravely for 71 minutes, was finally caught behind for six to give Kirtley a deserved fifth wicket. Croft's 80 came off 164 balls and included two sixes and nine fours. One dreads to think what England would have done without the Welshman.

Skipper Alistair Campbell hit a brisk 55, and Mashonaland passed the England score with three wickets down. The substance of the innings was provided by Houghton and Wishart who put on 116 for the fourth wicket. Houghton was outstanding. He is a batsman of immense stature, and his 110 off 144 balls in under three hours was as entertaining as it was positive. He hit two sixes and 14 fours, and once he and Wishart, 45, were dismissed, Mashonaland crumbled. The pitch encouraged spin, and

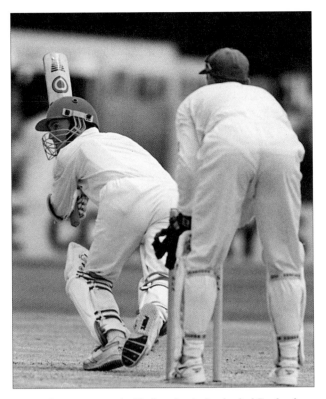

Grant Flower in action for Mashonaland who shocked England and the cricket world with their seven-wicket victory over the tourists. Grant Flower hit the only double century of the Zimbabwe season when playing for Mashonaland against Matabeleland. (Clive Mason/Allsport)

Croft and Tufnell exploited it to the full as the last six wickets of the home side's innings went down for 14 runs.

England's second innings followed a pattern very similar to their first. Knight was first out, caught behind off Kirtley in the third over. Three balls later, Stewart diverted a fast delivery into his stumps, playing as if his feet were in concrete. When Atherton was caught behind off the medium pace Brent England were 27 for 3, and only two runs had been added when Thorpe suffered a fate similar to Atherton's. Hussain and Crawley suggested survival in a stand of 76, but once Hussain was leg before to Paul Strang, a fine cricketer, the end was nigh.

Needing 98 to win, Mashonaland started uncertainly. Mullally sent back both openers for 11, but Houghton and Alistair Campbell added 84 to take their side to the brink of victory.

Defeat for England was seen as a humiliating experience, and they were subjected to the severest criticism. Not for the first time they had undervalued their opponents with an arrogance that bordered on contempt, and they had suffered the consequences. Not for the first time, too, the side appeared to be lacking in grace, and their reluctance to socialise in the most hospitable of countries made them an unpopular party of poor ambassadors for cricket and for England.

8 December 1996
at Bulawayo Athletic Ground
England XI 210 for 9 (N.V. Knight 58, G.J. Whittall 4 for 45)
Matabeleland 151
England XI won by 59 runs

England's problems had been compounded by the news that Atherton's back troubles had resurfaced, but he was given injections that relieved the pain and certainly helped him to bat more freely and confidently. He hit 28 off 29 balls as England claimed their first win of the tour. Mullally and Gough bowled well at the start of Matabeleland's innings.

10, 11, 12 and 13 December 1996
at Bulawayo Athletic Ground
England XI 334 (N.V. Knight 114, J.P. Crawley 63) and 230 for 5 dec. (G.P. Thorpe 65, M.A. Atherton 55)
Matabeleland 188 (W.R. James 62, D. Gough 6 for 64) and 261 (M.H. Dekker 104, H.H. Streak 67, D. Gough 5 for 75, R.D.B. Croft 4 for 65)
England XI won by 115 runs

Remarkably, after a deluge that came 90 minutes into the first day, play was possible, and England closed on 199 for 3 with Nick Knight unbeaten on 100. It was an important innings, for England had needed a boost, and Knight had provided it. There was also encouragement in that Stewart and Hussain batted well while Crawley contributed a fine 63 on the second day as the tail lost momentum and wickets fell.

Caddick soon dismissed Rennie, and Gough accounted for Guy Whittall with successive deliveries. Gough produced another spell later in the innings, which took his number of wickets to six, but Matabeleland just saved the follow-on.

Victory at last as England beat Matabeleland in the first-class fixture in Bulawayo. Gough bowls Olonga for 8. (Stu Forster/Allsport)

Half-centuries from Thorpe and Atherton, and confident innings from Stewart and Hussain, gave England further cause for pleasure on a rain-affected third day.

England duly completed victory on the fourth day but not without some worries. Gough, who again bowled impressively, sent back Guy Whittall and Ranchod with 20 scored, but Dekker and Streak added 156 in the next three hours. It looked as if this pair would thwart England, but once Streak was bowled by Caddick wickets began to tumble. Mark Dekker reached his century shortly before tea and shortly after the left-hander was leg before to Croft. Vaghamaria was out at the same total, 204, but skipper Rennie kept the tail together, and there were just 11.1 overs remaining when Croft had Mbangwa caught to win the match for England.

The most encouraging aspect of the game from England's point of view was the bowling of Darren Gough who returned match figures of 11 for 139.

First Test Match

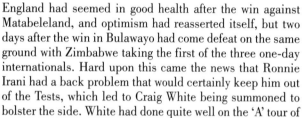

Zimbabwe *v.* England

England had seemed in good health after the win against Matabeleland, and optimism had reasserted itself, but two days after the win in Bulawayo had come defeat on the same ground with Zimbabwe taking the first of the three one-day internationals. Hard upon this came the news that Ronnie Irani had a back problem that would certainly keep him out of the Tests, which led to Craig White being summoned to bolster the side. White had done quite well on the 'A' tour of

Australia, but past performances had seemed to prove conclusively that he was not of international standard. For the first Test, England named Silverwood ahead of the erratic Caddick. The young Yorkshireman had made his international debut in the first one-day international and now he won his first Test cap. More romantically, perhaps, Zimbabwe gave a first Test cap to the 37-year-old Andy Waller who had made his limited-over international debut nine years earlier. Campbell won the toss, and Zimbabwe batted.

There was early success for England. In his first over, Gough persuaded Carlisle to touch the third ball he bowled into the hands of short-leg, but the euphoria was soon over. Mullally was astray in line and length and was punished accordingly. Campbell hit him for three fours in one over, and Silverwood was similarly dealt with when he joined the attack. The Zimbabwe captain scored 50 in 70 minutes, and, at lunch, his side was 109 for 1, and he had scored 70.

The second wicket partnership was broken when Hussain took a magnificent diving catch at third slip to remove Grant Flower 40 minutes into the afternoon. The catch gave Silverwood his first wicket, and the Yorkshireman was involved in the removal of Campbell, who mishit a Croft delivery high to backward point.

At tea, Zimbabwe were 200 for 3 with Houghton and Andy Flower looking well set. In the cooler last session, England clawed their way back into the game. Immediately

Robert Croft takes the wicket of debutant Andy Waller. Croft bowled with great maturity in what was only his second Test match. (Clive Mason/Allsport)

after the break, Croft had the vital wicket of Houghton, and he added debutant Waller as he and Tufnell bowled in tandem, looking threatening and curbing the flow of runs. It was Silverwood, however, who took the final wicket of the day: Guy Whittall driving to cover just before the close, which came at 256 for 6, Andy Flower unbeaten on 58 after three hours at the crease.

The former Zimbabwe captain batted for more than three hours on the second day. He did not offer a chance and hit 112 off 331 deliveries and was eighth out, having hit 12 fours. Zimbabwe strengthened their position when Paul Strang trapped Atherton leg before with his quicker ball just on tea, which heralded the advent of rain. Play was over for the day.

If Zimbabwe had commanded the first two days, the third belonged to England. Knight fell to the quick but erratic Olonga before lunch after hitting 56 off 79 balls, and Stewart and Thorpe were out in the afternoon, but by the close, with Hussain on 101 and Crawley on 51, England were 306 for 4 and growing in confidence.

Hussain's rehabilitation into a Test cricketer had been the major gain for English cricket in 1996, and the increasing maturity and technical improvement in the batting of John Crawley had not been far behind in importance. Hussain had added only 12 to his overnight score when he hooked a Streak bouncer to long-leg where Bryan Strang took a rather speculative catch above his head. Crawley was 59 at this point, and when Croft was out

Andy Flower on his way to a century in the first Test Match. (Stu Forster/Allsport)

half an hour later there was not much left to help. When the eighth wicket fell he was on 72, but Mullally and Tufnell defended solidly as the Lancastrian moved towards his second successive Test century. Crawley reached three figures when he hoisted a Streak bouncer over mid-wicket for six. He also hit nine fours and faced 297 balls in his 374-minute accomplished and intelligent innings.

First Test Match – Zimbabwe v. England
18, 19, 20, 21 and 22 December 1996 at Queen's Sports Oval, Bulawayo

Zimbabwe

Batsman	First Innings		Second Innings	
G.W. Flower	c Hussain, b Silverwood	43	lbw, b Gough	0
S.V. Carlisle	c Crawley, b Gough	0	c Atherton, b Mullally	4
A.D.R. Campbell (Capt)	c Silverwood, b Croft	84	b Croft	29
D.L. Houghton	c Stewart, b Croft	34	c Croft, b Tufnell	37
*A. Flower	c Stewart, b Tufnell	112	c Crawley, b Tufnell	14
A.C. Waller	c Crawley, b Croft	15	c Knight, b Gough	50
G.J. Whittall	c Atherton, b Silverwood	7	(8) c Croft, b Tufnell	56
P.A. Strang	c Tufnell, b Silverwood	38	(9) c Crawley, b Croft	19
H.H. Streak	b Mullally	19	(10) not out	8
B.C. Strang	not out	4	(7) c Mullally, b Tufnell	3
H.K. Olonga	c Knight, b Tufnell	0	c Stewart, b Silverwood	0
	lb 4, w 3, nb 13	20	b 4, lb 6, w 2, nb 2	14
		376		**234**

	O	M	R	W	O	M	R	W
Mullally	23	4	69	1	18	5	49	1
Gough	26	4	87	1	12	2	44	2
Silverwood	18	5	63	3	7	3	8	1
Croft	44	15	77	3	33	9	62	2
Tufnell	26.5	4	76	2	31	12	61	4

England

Batsman	First Innings		Second Innings	
N.V. Knight	lbw, b Olonga	56	run out	96
M.A. Atherton (Capt)	lbw, b P.A. Strang	16	b Olonga	4
*A.J. Stewart	lbw, b P.A. Strang	48	c Campbell, b P.A. Strang	73
N. Hussain	c B.C. Strang, b Streak	113	c Carlisle, b P.A. Strang	0
G.P. Thorpe	c Campbell, b P.A. Strang	13	(6) c Campbell, b Streak	2
J.P. Crawley	c A. Flower, b P.A. Strang	112	(5) c Carlisle, b Whittall	7
R.D.B. Croft	lbw, b Olonga	7		
D. Gough	c G.W. Flower, b Olonga	2	(7) not out	3
C.E.W. Silverwood	c Houghton, b P.A. Strang	0		
A.D. Mullally	c Waller, b Streak	4		
P.C.R. Tufnell	not out	2		
	b 4, lb 4, w 1, nb 24	33	b 2, lb 13, w 3, nb 1	19
		406	(for 6 wickets)	**204**

	O	M	R	W	O	M	R	W
Streak	36	8	86	2	11	–	64	1
B.C. Strang	17	5	54	–				
P.A. Strang	58.4	14	123	5	14	–	63	2
Olonga	23	2	90	3	2	–	16	1
Whittall	10	2	25	–	2	–	10	1
G.W. Flower	7	3	20	–	8	–	36	–

Fall of Wickets
1–3, 2–130, 3–136, 4–206, 5–235, 6–252, 7–331, 8–372, 9–376
1–6, 2–6, 3–57, 4–82, 5–103, 6–111, 7–178, 8–209, 9–233

Fall of Wickets
1–48, 2–92, 3–160, 4–180, 5–328, 6–340, 7–344, 8–353, 9–378
1–17, 2–154, 3–156, 4–178, 5–182, 6–204

Umpires: I.D. Robinson & R.S. Dunne

Match drawn

One of the most thrilling finishes ever seen in Test cricket. The hero Nick Knight hits Streak for six in the last over of the match, but England fall one run short of their target. (Stu Forster/Allsport)

Unexpectedly, Zimbabwe faced a deficit of 30 runs, and they lost both openers before clearing those arrears. Carlisle was taken at silly mid-off, and Grant Flower offered no stroke to Gough's in-swinger and was adjudged leg before. The spinners came into operation and Croft knocked back Campbell's leg stump in his first spell. Tufnell had immediate success and had Andy Flower taken at short-leg off a lifting delivery in his first over. The prize scalp came in the penultimate over of the day when Houghton made a hash of a leg-side shot and skied the ball to mid-on. Zimbabwe closed on 107 for 5, and England appeared to be on the brink of victory.

That, it transpired, was a false illusion although it had appeared even more certain when Tufnell dismissed Bryan Strang four runs into the morning. Guy Whittall joined Andy Waller in a stand worth 67 that frustrated England and did not get the praise it earned. Waller hit two sixes and five fours in his two-and-a-quarter-hour innings while Whittall kept England at bay for more than three hours. The outcome was that England were left 37 overs in which to score 205 to win the match.

Atherton was out after facing ten balls, but this brought Stewart to the crease to join Knight, and the Surrey man announced his arrival by hooking Streak for six. At tea, England were 36 for 1 in five overs.

Stewart's strength is that he can score quickly without resorting to the grotesque. He hits crisply and cleanly and he runs avidly. By the halfway mark, England had scored 106,

and victory seemed a formality. Having made 73 off 76 balls, Stewart was leg before to Paul Strang, who is rapidly becoming a world class leg-spinner to be mentioned in the same breath as Warne and Mushtaq. Strang had Hussain caught second ball, a major setback for England, and Crawley and Thorpe both went cheaply. The compensation was that Nick Knight was now well into his stride. His batting is flawed, and his means of scoring quickly were far from aesthetically pleasing, but he has enthusiasm, energy and a good temperament. He had to plunder an attack that mostly concentrated on a line wide of the stumps, too wide on many occasions in the opinion of some judges. That attack was supported by athletic fielding of the highest quality, but Knight brought England close to a remarkable victory.

When Streak began the last over England needed 13 to win, but a massive six over square-leg brought the target down to five off three balls. Streak bowled wide of the off stump – too wide? Umpire Robinson decided not. Three were needed from the last ball, and Knight hit hard through the off side. Carlisle cut the ball off inside the boundary rope, and his return to the keeper left the batsman short of his line. The match was drawn with the scores level.

Knight took the individual award for his 96 off 117 balls in three hours, and extravagant claims were made for England's performance. In some quarters, Zimbabwe were criticised for adopting tactics that any Test side would, and has, adopted in an effort to save the game, and England's failings were forgotten: their slow scoring on the fourth morning; their inability to remove the last four Zimbabwe batsmen in the second innings until 127 runs had been scored and 56 overs used; and their intimidating appealing, which had brought a rebuke from the referee.

Second Test Match

Zimbabwe v. England

The newly arrived Craig White was preferred to Silverwood, while Zimbabwe made two changes: Dekker, with a century against the tourists to his credit, came in for Carlisle, and Brandes, who had been unfit for the first Test, reclaimed his place from Bryan Strang.

Campbell won the toss and asked England to bat first on a seemingly lifeless pitch with a sluggish outfield. The first day belonged entirely to Zimbabwe. In the first hour, England lost Knight, who touched a ball down the leg side to the wicket-keeper. Two more wickets fell before lunch as Atherton and Stewart drove unwisely in successive overs and were caught at slip and at gully. Thorpe was duped by Streak, who had him caught at short square-leg immediately after lunch, and Hussain perished in the same manner as Atherton and Stewart had done. Crawley alone showed the necessary technique and composure, but White looked as much out of his depth as ever in a Test match, and England went to tea at 108 for 6. Croft was caught driving, Gough was bowled by Paul Strang, and Mullally gave Guy Whittall figures of 4 for 12 in 13 overs when he plopped the ball

Second Test Match – Zimbabwe v. England
26, 27, 28, 29 and 30 December 1996 at Harare Sports Club

England

	First Innings		Second Innings	
N.V. Knight	c A. Flower, b Olonga	15	c Campbell, b P.A. Strang	30
M.A. Atherton (Capt)	c Campbell, b Whittall	13	c Campbell, b Streak	1
*A.J. Stewart	c G.W. Flower, b Streak	19	not out	101
N. Hussain	c A. Flower, b Streak	11	c Houghton, b P.A. Strang	6
G.P. Thorpe	c Dekker, b Streak	5	not out	50
J.P. Crawley	not out	47		
C. White	c Campbell, b Whittall	9		
R.D.B. Croft	c G.W. Flower, b Whittall	14		
D. Gough	b P.A. Strang	2		
A.D. Mullally	c and b Whittall	0		
P.C.R. Tufnell	b Streak	9		
	b 1, lb 5, w 1, nb 5	12	lb 5, w 1, nb 1	7
		156	(for 3 wickets)	**195**

Zimbabwe

	First Innings	
G.W. Flower	c Crawley, b Gough	73
M.H. Dekker	c Stewart, b Mullally	2
A.D.R. Campbell (Capt)	c Thorpe, b White	22
D.L. Houghton	c Stewart, b Gough	29
*A. Flower	lbw, b Gough	6
A.C. Waller	lbw, b Tufnell	4
G.J. Whittall	b Gough	1
P.A. Strang	not out	47
H.H. Streak	c Crawley, b Croft	7
E.A. Brandes	c Gough, b Croft	9
H.K. Olonga	c Hussain, b Croft	0
	lb 8, w 2, nb 5	15
		215

	O	M	R	**W**	O	M	R	**W**
Streak	24.1	7	43	4	18	5	47	1
Brandes	16	6	35	–	21	6	45	–
Olonga	9	1	23	1	7	–	31	–
Whittall	16	5	18	4	14	6	16	–
P.A. Strang	18	7	31	1	26	6	42	2
G.W. Flower					7	2	49	–

	O	M	R	**W**
Mullally	23	7	32	1
Gough	26	10	40	4
Croft	15	2	39	3
White	16	4	41	1
Tufnell	25	3	55	1

Fall of Wickets
1–**24**, 2–**50**, 3–**50**, 4–**65**, 5–**73**, 6–**94**, 7–**128**, 8–**133**, 9–**134**
1–**7**, 2–**75**, 3–**89**

Fall of Wickets
1–**5**, 2–**46**, 3–**110**, 4–**131**, 5–**136**, 6–**138**, 7–**159**, 8–**197**, 9–**211**

Umpires: K.T. Francis & R.B. Tiffin

Match drawn

back to the bowler. England were thankful that bad light cut 17 overs off the day when they were 137 for 9.

Crawley's patience was rewarded with an unbeaten 47 in 218 minutes. He saw England past 150 before Tufnell was bowled by Streak who, like Guy Whittall, had four wickets in the innings. Whittall's figures were the best of his Test career.

In contrast to the first Test, England's new ball bowling was disciplined, and there was early success when Dekker nibbled at a Mullally out-swinger. Campbell was positive, and Zimbabwe reached lunch at 36 for 1. Six overs into the afternoon, Campbell steered a long hop to first slip, but there was no more joy for England as Grant Flower and Houghton demonstrated the application needed to bat on such a pitch. They had taken the score to 93 when, four balls after tea, the rains came and the last 29.2 overs of the day were lost.

Gough, initially, and Croft, ultimately, bowled England back into the game on the third day. Gough had Houghton caught down the leg side in the 13th over of the day, and he beat Andy Flower with a full length delivery 12 overs later. Waller was leg before offering no shot, and Guy Whittall was yorked. When Grant Flower chipped Gough to mid-wicket, Zimbabwe were only three runs ahead with just three wickets remaining. Grant Flower had held the batting together. His 73 had occupied 354 minutes, and he had

Guy Whittall, 4 for 18 in 16 overs in the second match of the series, his best figures in a Test. (Clive Mason/Allsport)

Alec Stewart saves England with an unbeaten 101. It was his first century as England's wicket-keeper.
(Clive Mason/Allsport)

One-Day International Series
Zimbabwe v. England

The first of the limited over matches was played two days before the first Test, and the second match was played two days after the second Test. The first game marked the international debut of Silverwood and represented a disaster for England, who suffered their third defeat in 15 days.

Campbell asked England to bat when he won the toss, but there was no immediate success as England reached 40 for the loss of Knight in nine overs. The innings then began to stutter with Stewart removed by the aggressive Streak and Thorpe, totally out of form, bowled by Brandes. Atherton had not scored at this stage, so he and Hussain were faced with a repair job in difficult circumstances. Atherton was not at his best and, had the television replay system been in operation, would have been run out when he was 15, but he stayed to add what turned out to be the major stand of the innings.

Zimbabwe bowled a tight line, never wavered from the task and England fretted and fell in consequence. They were bowled out with 21 balls of their quota unused, and Hussain was left unbeaten on 49 from 86 balls with one four to his credit.

Atherton marshalled his forces, and Zimbabwe were at a disadvantage because Campbell had a finger damaged in practice and sustained a gashed cheek and did not want to bat. Waller, opening as pinch-hitter, gave the innings

Nasser Hussain attempts to hold the England innings together in the first one-day international in Bulawayo. (Stu Forster/Allsport)

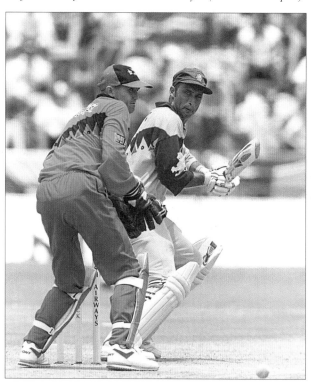

faced 255 deliveries. He hit a six and five fours and gave positive proof, if any more were needed, that he has the Test match temperament.

To England's chagrin, that delightful cricketer Paul Strang made an unbeaten 47, which took Zimbabwe to a first innings lead of 59. With Atherton failing again, caught low at first slip, England ended the day on 17 for 1, still 42 runs behind.

On the fourth day, Knight got a thick edge that rebounded from wicket-keeper to slip, and Hussain drove low to cover so that, at 89 for 3, England were in crisis. Thorpe responded with his first positive and meaningful innings of the tour, but the hero of the hour was Alec Stewart who reached his ninth Test century, his first as wicket-keeper. He reached his hundred with two crashing boundaries off Olonga. It had taken him more than six-and-a-half-hours of self-discipline and came off 259 balls. His commitment is total, and he was England's saviour. No play was possible on the final day, and the match and the series were drawn.

Much criticism was levelled at England, most of it totally just, but too little praise was given to Zimbabwe, whose attitude and enthusiasm could not have been bettered. They are learning fast, and they have much to commend them.

necessary substance, being fifth out at 97 after hitting 48 off 71 balls with eight fours. His departure brought in Campbell who quickly lost Guy Whittall and Paul Strang, but the Zimbabwe captain took charge. He hit 32 off 40 balls with five boundaries and had good help from Streak and Brandes as Zimbabwe won with 37 balls to spare.

1997 proved to be no better for England than 1996 had been. The New Year had begun well with Gough and Mullally reducing Zimbabwe to 38 for 4, but Zimbabwe are as resourceful as they are committed, and Andy Flower and Craig Evans began the reparation with 49 in 64 minutes. Andy Flower's 63 off 114 balls gave the innings some backbone, and Streak chanced his arm and enjoyed good fortune in making an unbeaten 43 off 53 deliveries. Even so, Zimbabwe failed to bat out their 50 overs although a score of 200 was considerably more than they can have expected earlier in their innings.

Rain fell shortly after Zimbabwe had finished batting, and, under the new, highly mathematical system for calculating revised targets, England were left to make 185 off 42 overs. Knight helped no one in trying to hit every ball out of sight and was totally off balance when he hit Brandes to cover. Stewart and Crawley showed a sharp contrast to the Warwickshire man, batting with style and confidence to add 66 in 10 overs. Guy Whittall removed Stewart and Hussain, but Crawley and Atherton kept the runs flowing and 74 were needed from the last 14 overs.

The advent of Paul Strang changed matters. It was judgement on the part of Campbell to introduce his leg-spinner for the climax of the match, and Strang was as confident in himself as his skipper had been in him. England

Ronnie Irani is caught and bowled by Rennie for 7. (Clive Mason/Allsport)

were 137 and needing 48 runs from the last eight overs when Atherton pulled Strang to deep mid-on. The leg-spinner was so demanding, so accurate, that first Crawley and then Irani were drawn down the pitch by him and stumped. From the last two overs, 19 were needed and White perished almost immediately. Rennie bowled the last over with 16 wanted, but this was a task well beyond Croft and Gough.

This victory sealed the series for Zimbabwe, but the final humiliation for England was still to come. Atherton asked Zimbabwe to bat first when he won the toss. By the

A wicket for England as Alec Stewart runs out Andy Waller in the third match of the one-day series. (Clive Mason/Allsport)

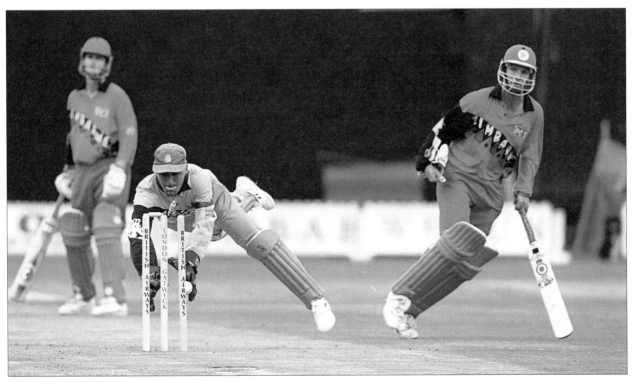

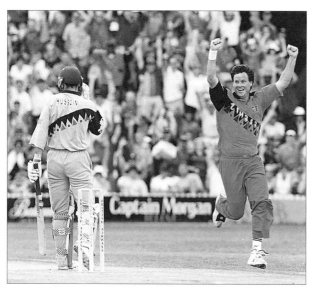

Eddo Brandes raises his arms in joy as Nasser Hussain is caught behind. This wicket gave Brandes the hat-trick, the first taken by a Zimbabwe bowler in international cricket. (Stu Foster/Allsport)

30-ball innings, and, at the death, Houghton and Paul Strang plundered runs. Houghton hit two sixes, and Strang a six and a four to take Zimbabwe to dizzy heights.

It was soon apparent that these were heights that England could not scale. With the last ball of his second over, Eddo Brandes had Knight caught behind down the leg side. With the first ball of his third over, he trapped Crawley leg before, and with his next delivery, a superb late away-swinger, he had Hussain magnificently caught by Andy Flower diving far to his right. Brandes had accomplished the first hat-trick for Zimbabwe, and, in the process, had virtually decided the match.

Stewart and Atherton added 32 in 10 overs before Brandes removed them both in successive overs. Irani and White were unable to score before becoming victims of Streak, and Croft, 30 off 37 balls, and Mullally, 20 off 23 balls, brought only light relief to the funeral rites.

Zimbabwe were worthy of their success in every aspect of the game. Brandes was not flattered by his 5 for 28, and Andy Flower's five catches would have earned him the individual award on another day. In the field, Zimbabwe were light years ahead of England.

England moved to New Zealand, bruised by defeat in the limited-over matches and by drawing a Test series they had been expected to win comfortably. They had reacted badly to the adverse criticism that they received for their cricket and off-field behaviour and had withdrawn into themselves. All this tended to detract from the achievement of Zimbabwe and from the boost that the national side's

time Waller was run out for 19, 58 runs had come in just over an hour, and Campbell and Grant Flower increased the momentum. The opening batsman hit 62 off 87 balls, and the skipper made his fourth half-century of the tour against England. His 80 included a six and four fours and came off 103 deliveries. Andy Flower hit a six and three fours in his

First One-Day International – Zimbabwe v. England
15 December 1996 at Queen's Sports Club, Bulawayo

England				Zimbabwe			
N.V. Knight	lbw, **b** Streak	13		G.W. Flower	**b** Silverwood	14	
*A.J. Stewart	c A. Flower, **b** Streak	26		A.C. Waller	run out	48	
M.A. Atherton (Capt)	c sub (A.R. Whittall), **b** G.W. Flower	23		*A. Flower	c Knight, **b** Silverwood	10	
				D.L. Houghton	c Crawley, **b** Gough	2	
G.P. Thorpe	**b** Brandes	1		C.N. Evans	c Stewart, **b** Gough	1	
N. Hussain	not out	49		G.J. Whittall	c Stewart, **b** Mullally	13	
J.P. Crawley	c Campbell, **b** Rennie	10		A.D.R. Campbell (Capt)	not out	32	
R.C. Irani	c and **b** Rennie	7		P.A. Strang	c Stewart, **b** Mullally	0	
A.D. Mullally	c and **b** Rennie	0		H.H. Streak	c and **b** Croft	11	
R.D.B. Croft	c G.W. Flower, **b** Streak	0		E.A. Brandes	not out	8	
D. Gough	run out	9		J.A. Rennie			
C.E.W. Silverwood	c Houghton, **b** P.A. Strang	1			lb **9**, w **4**, nb **1**	14	
	lb **6**, w **3**, nb **4**	13					
	45.5 overs	**152**			**43.5 overs (for 8 wickets)**	**153**	

	O	M	R	**W**		O	M	R	**W**
Brandes	8	2	28	1	Mullally	10	2	24	2
Rennie	8	1	27	3	Gough	10	2	31	2
Streak	9	1	30	3	Silverwood	10	–	27	2
G.J. Whittall	5	–	17	–	Croft	5	–	32	1
P.A. Strang	9.5	1	27	1	Irani	6.5	1	25	–
G.W. Flower	6	–	17	1	Thorpe	2	1	5	–

Fall of Wickets
1–**28**, 2–**41**, 3–**47**, 4–**96**, 5–**124**, 6–**134**, 7–**134**, 8–**135**, 9–**150**

Fall of Wickets
1–**33**, 2–**58**, 3–**73**, 4–**87**, 5–**97**, 6–**106**, 7–**106**, 8–**137**

Umpires: Q.J. Goosen & R.B. Tiffin *Man of the Match:* A.D.R. Campbell

Zimbabwe won by 2 wickets

Second One-Day International – Zimbabwe v. England

1 January 1997 at Harare Sports Club, Harare

Zimbabwe

G.W. Flower	b Hussain, b Gough	4
A.C. Waller	b Mullally	0
A.D.R. Campbell (Capt)	c Stewart, b Gough	14
D.L. Houghton	c Croft, b Mullally	5
*A. Flower	c Stewart, b Mullally	63
C.N. Evans	lbw, b Croft	32
G.J. Whittall	run out	14
P.A. Strang	c Atherton, b Croft	1
H.H. Streak	not out	43
E.A. Brandes	c Atherton, b Gough	0
J.A. Rennie	b Gough	0
	lb 11, w 10, nb 3	24
	48.5 overs	**200**

	O	M	R	W
Mullally	9	1	29	3
Gough	8.5	1	43	4
Silverwood	6	–	30	–
White	10	1	39	–
Croft	10	2	33	2
Irani	5	–	15	–

Fall of Wickets
1–2, 2–14, 3–26, 4–38, 5–97, 6–125, 7–126, 8–200, 9–200

England

N.V. Knight	c Houghton, b Brandes	0
*A.J. Stewart	c A. Flower, b G.J. Whittall	41
J.P. Crawley	st A. Flower, b P.A. Strang	73
N. Hussain	lbw, b G.J. Whittall	7
M.A. Atherton (Capt)	c G.J. Whittall, b P.A. Strang	25
R.C. Irani	st A. Flower, b P.A. Strang	5
C. White	lbw, b Streak	4
R.D.B. Croft	not out	10
D. Gough	not out	2
A.D. Mullally		
C.E.W. Silverwood		
	b 2, lb 5, w 5	12
	42 overs (for 7 wickets)	**179**

	O	M	R	W
Brandes	6	2	25	1
Rennie	5	–	26	–
Streak	8	–	41	1
G.J. Whittall	8	–	30	2
Evans	2	–	6	–
P.A. Strang	9	–	24	3
G.W. Flower	4	–	20	–

Fall of Wickets
1–1, 2–67, 3–95, 4–137, 5–157, 6–165, 7–169

Umpires: G.R. Evans & I.D. Robinson *Man of the Match:* P.A. Strang & J.P. Crawley **Zimbabwe won on faster scoring rate**

Third One-Day International – Zimbabwe v. England

3 January 1997 at Harare Sports Club, Harare

Zimbabwe

G.W. Flower	c Mullally, b White	62
A.C. Waller	run out	19
A.D.R. Campbell (Capt)	not out	80
*A. Flower	c Stewart, b Irani	35
C.N. Evans	c Stewart, b Gough	1
G.J. Whittall	b Croft	1
D.L. Houghton	c Stewart, b Mullally	19
P.A. Strang	run out	13
H.H. Streak		
E.A. Brandes		
J.A. Rennie		
	b 4, lb 5, w 8, nb 2	19
	50 overs (for 7 wickets)	**249**

	O	M	R	W
Mullally	10	3	39	1
Gough	10	1	42	1
Silverwood	5	–	27	–
White	7	–	39	1
Irani	10	–	39	1
Croft	8	–	54	1

Fall of Wickets
1–58, 2–131, 3–181, 4–183, 5–190, 6–220, 7–249

England

N.V. Knight	c A. Flower, b Brandes	3
*A.J. Stewart	c A. Flower, b Brandes	29
J.P. Crawley	lbw, b Brandes	0
N. Hussain	c A. Flower, b Brandes	0
M.A. Atherton (Capt)	c A. Flower, b Brandes	18
R.C. Irani	c G.J. Whittall, b Streak	0
C. White	c A. Flower, b Streak	0
R.D.B. Croft	not out	30
D. Gough	c Streak, b P.A. Strang	7
A.D. Mullally	b G.J. Whittall	20
C.E.W. Silverwood	c Evans, b G.J. Whittall	0
	w 8, nb 3	11
	30 overs	**118**

	O	M	R	W
Brandes	10	–	28	5
Rennie	3	–	11	–
Streak	10	–	50	2
P.A. Strang	5	–	18	1
G.J. Whittall	2	–	11	2

Fall of Wickets
1–9, 2–13, 3–13, 4–45, 5–54, 6–55, 7–63, 8–77, 9–118

Umpires: R.B. Tiffin & I.D. Robinson *Man of the Match:* E.A. Brandes **Zimbabwe won by 131 runs**

One-Day International

Zimbabwe v. India

Following their tour of South Africa, India were scheduled to play two one-day internationals in Zimbabwe. The second match, in Harare, had to be abandoned without a ball being bowled because of rain, and the first, in Bulawayo, was also affected by the weather.

India introduced medium-pacer Doddanarasiah Ganesh of Karnataka to international cricket.

The visitors batted first, but their top order fell apart against Zimbabwe's pace attack. Six wickets fell for 95 runs before Singh and Kumble added 64. Streak returned to dismiss them both as the last four wickets went down for nine runs.

Rain reduced Zimbabwe's target to 136 in 38 overs, but they romped to victory with 12.1 overs to spare.

Zimbabwe had the satisfaction of winning all four of their home one-day internationals in 1996–97.

A fine season as Zimbabwe's captain – Alistair Campbell.
(Stu Forster/Allsport)

One-Day International – Zimbabwe v. India
15 February 1997 at Queen's Sports Club, Bulawayo

India

V. Rathore	c Campbell, b G.J. Whittall	34
S.R. Tendulkar (Capt)	c G.W. Flower, b Brandes	13
S.C. Ganguly	run out	2
M. Azharuddin	c A. Flower, b Brandes	24
A.D. Jadeja	c A. Flower, b Streak	0
R.R. Singh	c A. Flower, b Streak	45
*N.R. Mongia	c Waller, b Evans	4
A.R. Kumble	c Campbell, b Streak	21
S.B. Joshi	lbw, b Streak	0
D. Ganesh	c and b Streak	4
Venkatesh Prasad	not out	0
	b 6, lb 2, w 11, nb 2	21
	43.5 overs	168

	O	M	R	W
Brandes	8	1	34	2
Rennie	9	2	38	–
Streak	8.5	–	32	5
G.J. Whittall	8	–	29	1
Evans	8	1	20	1
P.A. Strang	2	–	7	–

Fall of Wickets
1–**23**, 2–**33**, 3–**68**, 4–**72**, 5–**84**, 6–**95**, 7–**159**, 8–**159**, 9–**168**

Zimbabwe

G.W. Flower	not out	61
A.C. Waller	b Ganesh	25
A.D.R. Campbell (Capt)	c Azharuddin, b Kumble	24
G.J. Whittall	not out	19
*A. Flower		
D.L. Houghton		
C.N. Evans		
P.A. Strang		
H.H. Streak		
E.A. Brandes		
J.A. Rennie		
	b 4, lb 2, w 3, nb 1	10
	25.5 overs (for 2 wickets)	139

	O	M	R	W
Venkatesh Prasad	6.5	1	35	–
Ganesh	5	–	20	1
Ganguly	2	–	10	–
R.R. Singh	4	–	31	–
Kumble	6	2	18	1
Joshi	2	–	19	–

Fall of Wickets
1–**31**, 2–**96**

Umpires: Q.J. Goosen & I.D. Robinson   *Man of the Match:* H.H. Streak

Zimbabwe won on faster scoring rate

The Logan Cup

When Lord Hawke's side visited South Africa in 1898–99 they played several matches in Rhodesia. The matches were watched by Mr J.D. Logan, a member of the Cape Legislative Council and a noted patron of cricket. He asked Lord Hawke to buy a cup on his behalf when he returned to England, for Logan wanted to present a trophy for inter-town competition. The cup was first presented in 1903–4, and it became the trophy for the first-class competition in 1993–94. In 1996–97, it was awarded to Mashonaland for winning a best of three competition with Matabeleland.

4, 5 and 6 October 1996
at Bulawayo Athletic Club
Matabeleland 118 (P.A. Strang 5 for 45, B.C. Strang 5 for 50) and 279 (M.H. Dekker 90, M. Ranchod 56 not out, P.A. Strang 5 for 103)
Mashonaland 314 (A.D.R. Campbell 76, D.L. Houghton 67, A. Flower 61) and 85 for 2
Mashonaland won by 8 wickets

The leg-spin of Paul Strang was quickly introduced into the Mashonaland attack, and only the left-handed Mark Dekker seemed able to cope with him. The left-arm medium pace of Bryan Strang was also effective, and Matabeleland lost their last seven wickets for 50 runs. Grant Flower fell to Olonga at 17, but Viljoen and Campbell added 80, and Houghton, who hit a six and eight fours, put on 103 with Campbell. Batting a second time, Matabeleland were wonderfully served by Dekker who made 90 off 197 balls with 13 fours, but Paul Strang again tore the heart out of the Matabeleland innings, and Mashonaland won with ease.

15, 16 and 17 November 1996
at Alexandra Sports Club, Harare
Mashonaland 503 for 4 dec. (G.W. Flower 242 not out, A.C. Waller 104, S.V. Carlisle 96)
Matabeleland 448 (G.J. Whittall 159, M.H. Dekker 55, W.R. James 52, E.A. Brandes 4 for 107)
Match drawn

Grant Flower shared stands of 231 with Carlisle for the first wicket and 233 with Waller for the second wicket. Flower hit a six and 25 fours in his 369-ball innings while Waller reached a maiden first-class century after 12 years in cricket. Guy Whittall faced 351 balls for his 159, and Matabeleland were dismissed just before the close of the third day.

Paul Strang, an outstanding cricketer of world class. He averaged more than 47 with the bat, captured 36 wickets and fielded brilliantly. (Clive Mason/Allsport)

22, 23 and 24 November 1996
at Bulawayo Athletic Club
Mashonaland 477 for 6 dec. (S.V. Carlisle 131, C.B. Wishart 110, P.A. Strang 103 not out, A. Flower 73 not out) and 0 for 0 dec.
Matabeleland 69 for 4 dec. and 195 (W.R. James 74, G.M. Fellows 50, R.J. Kirtley 5 for 56)
Mashonaland won by 213 runs

Three centuries in an innings put Mashonaland in an impregnable position. Carlisle laid the basis with his patient hundred, and Wishart raised the temperature with 110 off 117 balls. He hit four sixes and 14 fours. The real fireworks came at the end when Paul Strang dominated a stand of 161 in 128 minutes with Andy Flower. Strang hit 14 fours and faced just 97 balls for his 103. Matabeleland declared their first innings while well in arrears and Mashonaland forfeited their second innings in an attempt to compensate for time lost to rain. Matabeleland never really recovered from the loss of Guy Whittall and Madondo for 16, and Kirtley and Paul Strang bowled Mashonaland to victory and the Logan Cup.

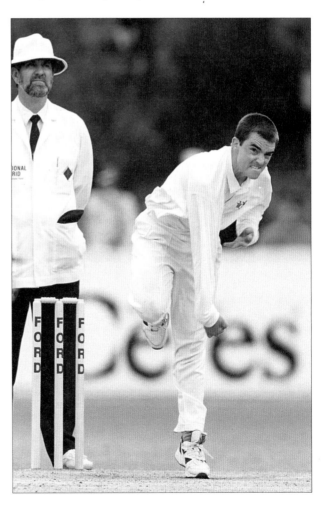

Miscellaneous Matches

26, 27 and 28 September 1996

at Alexandra Sports Club, Harare

Western Province 303 (M. de Villiers 84, S.G. Koening 67, P.A. Strang 4 for 111) and 237 for 9 dec. (J.B. Commins 104, P.A. Strang 4 for 110)

Mashonaland 276 for 8 dec. (B.C. Strang 68, C.B. Wishart 53, A. Martyn 4 for 46) and 74 for 4

Match drawn

Zimbabwe has become a favourite pre-season touring venue, and Western Province warmed up with a match against Mashonaland. John Commins hit the 10th century of his career.

28, 29 and 30 March 1997

at Bulawayo Athletic Club

Worcestershire 145 (H.H. Streak 4 for 20) and 263 for 8 dec. (V.S. Solanki 61)

Matabeleland Invitation XI 168 for 9 dec. and 222 (G.A. Hick 4 for 59)

Worcestershire won by 18 runs

Graeme Hick returned to his homeland and bowled his adopted county to a narrow victory. Streak took a wicket in each of his first three overs in the first innings. The start of the match was brought forward by 24 hours because members of the local side had to fly to Sharjah with the national team.

First-Class Averages

Batting

	M	Inns	NO	Runs	HS	Av	100s	50s
A. Flower	5	6	2	271	112	67.75	1	2
J.P. Crawley	4	6	1	328	112	65.60	1	2
A.D.R. Campbell	5	8	2	370	84	61.66		4
G.W. Flower	7	11	2	476	242*	52.88	1	1
M.H. Dekker	4	6	–	309	104	51.50	1	2
C.B. Wishart	5	8	3	250	110	50.00	1	1
P.A. Strang	7	7	2	236	103*	47.20	1	
A.J. Stewart	4	8	1	324	101*	46.28	1	1
D.L. Houghton	6	7	–	311	110	44.42	1	1
A.C. Waller	3	4	–	173	104	43.25	1	1
W.R. James	4	7	1	255	74	42.50		3
N.V. Knight	4	8	–	328	114	41.00	1	2
S.V. Carlisle	4	6	–	243	131	40.50	1	1
G.J. Whittall	6	10	–	316	159	31.60	1	1
N. Hussain	4	8	–	249	113	31.12	1	
H.H. Streak	6	9	2	204	67	29.14		1
R.D.B. Croft	4	5	1	112	80*	28.00		1
M. Ranchod	4	7	3	109	56*	27.25		1
G.P. Thorpe	4	8	1	187	65	26.71		2
J.A. Rennie	5	8	2	153	57*	25.50		1
D.P. Viljoen	5	8	–	155	47	19.37		
M.D. Abrams	5	9	–	134	45	14.88		
M.A. Atherton	4	8	–	102	55	12.75		1

(Qualification: 100 runs, average 10.00)

Bowling

	Overs	Mds	Runs	Wks	Av	Best	10/m	5/inn
R.J. Kirtley	71.1	19	172	14	12.28	5/53		2
D. Gough	124.2	26	367	19	19.31	6/64	1	2
R.D.B. Croft	153.2	40	349	16	21.81	4/65		
P.A. Strang	365.3	92	906	36	25.16	5/45	1	3
H.H. Streak	180	41	476	17	28.00	4/20		
P.C.R. Tufnell	157.3	38	407	14	29.07	5/78		1
H.K. Olonga	125	22	458	15	30.53	3/38		
B.C. Strang	173.4	51	436	12	36.33	5/50		1

(Qualification: 10 wickets)

Leading Fielders

16 – A.D.R. Campbell; 11 – J.P. Crawley; 10 – A. Flower, G.W. Flower and W.R. James; 9 – D.J.R. Campbell; 8 – A.J. Stewart; 7 – G.J. Whittall

(Contrary to our usual practice these figures include records of the England touring team)

New Zealand

New Zealand began a full season in good heart. They had drawn the Test series in Pakistan where they had also won a limited-over international, and the team appeared to be responding well to new coach Steve Rixon, the former Australian Test wicket-keeper, and to the intelligent leadership of Lee Germon. Astle was confirming his position as an international, and Doull had made a pronounced advance as a fast bowler.

The discovery of the season, left-arm spinner Daniel Vettori. The 18-year-old claimed 36 wickets in his debut season, won four Tests caps and took 18 Test wickets.
(Clive Mason/Allsport)

England Tour, Tests and One-Day Internationals
Sri Lankan Tour, Tests and One-Day Internationals
Shell Cup
Shell Trophy

Much depended on Cairns's form and attitude. New Zealand were further encouraged by England's poor showing in Zimbabwe, so the arrival of Mike Atherton's men held no fears.

The first problem that confronted the New Zealand selectors was the announcement by Roger Twose that he would not be available for selection for the national side for business and personal reasons. Twose, the former Warwickshire player, had been appointed captain of Wellington and was to lead them to the Shell Cup Final with distinction, but he was to take no part in the matches against England or Sri Lanka.

The Shell Cup was in its final stages when England arrived in New Zealand.

England Tour

Dominic Cork joined the England party after missing the Zimbabwe leg of the tour. The team remained under fire. There was still speculation concerning Atherton's position as captain while Caddick had voiced his disappointment at having played no part in the international matches in Zimbabwe. There was added woe for Atherton. Shortly after his arrival in New Zealand, he agreed to play in a benefit match for the pace man Danny Morrison. It took place at Ericsson Stadium, home of Auckland rugby league club, and was a gently amusing affair in which many celebrities took part. Facing the bowling of Ofisa Tonu'u, a rugby league player, Atherton slogged the ball into the outfield where he was caught by Emily Drumm, a member of the New Zealand Women's cricket team and the only woman playing in the match. The event did, of course, give further ammunition to those who considered Atherton a figure of fun following the happenings in Zimbabwe, but he was to have time to recover.

Stephen Fleming hit a maiden Test century in Auckland and by the end of the season was New Zealand's youngest captain.
(Graham Chadwick/Allsport)

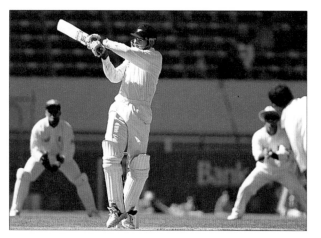

10 January 1997
at Pukekura Park, New Plymouth
New Zealand Academy XI 201 (C.D. McMillan 58, G.R. Loveridge 54)
v. **England XI**
Match abandoned

England could not have had a more disappointing start to their tour as rain caused the opening match to be abandoned after the home side had been bowled out in 40.4 overs. Cork took a wicket, Caddick three, and Silverwood, Gough and Irani two each. In one of his rare outings, Russell held five catches.

13, 14, 15 and 16 January 1997
at Fitzherbert Park, Palmerston North
New Zealand Select XI 138 (C. White 4 for 15) and 176 (P.C.R. Tufnell 5 for 58)
England XI 427 for 7 dec. (A.J. Stewart 153 retired hurt, N. Hussain 139, D.K. Morrison 4 for 81)
England XI won by an innings and 113 runs

After some weeks of turmoil and criticism England could draw comfort from a day's cricket. The New Zealand side of Test hopefuls were led by Mark Greatbatch, whose days as an international cricketer may well be behind him, but it was a strong side with Morrison anxious to prove his fitness and Kennedy keen to show the selectors that they should not have left him out of the party that went to Pakistan. Pocock and Spearman, too, were fighting to impress and began with a stand of 48, which was broken when Caddick had Pocock taken at slip. The most impressive English bowling came from White, who took a wicket with his first ball in New Zealand: a gentle loosener that Spearman dragged into his stumps. In 58 balls, White took four wickets, three of which were front-line batsmen. Atherton went cheaply, but England ended the first day on 106 for 3. The real substance of the England innings was provided by Stewart and Hussain. Rain restricted play on the second day so that the score advanced only to 154, but the pair eventually added 215 with some confident batting. Others, Thorpe in particular, were less confident, but the bowlers grabbed their chance. Greatbatch hit Tufnell for six and four in one over before being run out, and Tufnell then took over, ably supported by Silverwood. Pocock alone offered serious resistance.

18, 19, 20 and 21 January 1997
at Trust Bank Park, Hamilton
Northern Districts 69 and 259 (M.E. Parlane 74, B.A. Pocock 69, A.D. Mullally 4 for 52)
England XI 294 (G.P. Thorpe 71, J.P. Crawley 65, A.R. Tait 5 for 96, S.B. Styris 4 for 110) and 38 for 0
England XI won by 10 wickets

England needed only three days in which to beat Northern Districts instead of the scheduled four. Atherton asked the home side to bat first when he won the toss, and in 28.4 overs, his bowlers shot them out for 69. Cork accounted for the New Zealand opening pair, Young and Pocock, and then had Bailey caught at slip while White and Gough each claimed three wickets. England's worry was that Atherton was again dismissed for a low score, falling to Scott Styris, the 21-year-old highly promising medium pace bowler. Most heartening for England was the form of Thorpe and Crawley, while all their main bowlers save Croft and the under-used Irani went into the international series with wickets and confidence behind them.

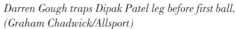

First Test Match

New Zealand v. England *at Auckland*

England chose Mullally ahead of Caddick and Croft and banked on Cork's fitness, while White was preferred to Irani, whose opportunities, like those of Russell, had been few. New Zealand left out Haslam and decided on Patel as their front-line spinner. Atherton won the toss and asked New Zealand to bat, a policy which had been found effective in the preliminary matches. On this occasion it was not. Young and Pocock negotiated the seamers with ease and went to lunch at 72 for 0 from 29 overs.

Darren Gough traps Dipak Patel leg before first ball.
(Graham Chadwick/Allsport)

Cork was aggressive, but Mullally was wayward, and Tufnell was introduced as early as the 11th over. Stewart injured a finger, and nothing seemed to be going right for England. It came as something of a surprise when Young played round an inswinger and was leg before to Mullally, a wicket the bowler had scarcely deserved. A thin leg-glance to the keeper saw the end of Parore and gave Cork his first wicket. Considering that a back injury had caused him to withdraw from the match against Northern Districts and that he had originally been given no chance of playing in this Test, Cork's performance was remarkable.

Fleming was at ease from the start, and his shots flowed smoothly and menacingly. It was not until later that England claimed their third wicket, Pocock falling to a Gough yorker. White accounted for Astle, who drove wastefully at a wide delivery and edged to the keeper, while Cork took the new ball and trapped the left-handed Vaughan to leave New Zealand 233 for 5 at the close, bringing England right back into the game.

Near the end of play on the first day, Cairns had been dropped by Gough at mid-off, and on the second morning he made England suffer. Cairns and Fleming took their partnership to 118 in 33 overs and Cairns had hit two sixes and seven fours before he slashed at a wide ball a quarter of

New Zealand heroes Morrison and Astle leave the field after their match-saving last wicket stand. (Clive Mason/Allsport)

an hour before lunch and paid the penalty. Fleming reached a maiden Test hundred by lunch and New Zealand were well in command at 338 for 6.

In the afternoon, Gough swung the game back towards England. A bouncer brought about the end of Germon, and Patel was out first ball, victim to a yorker. Doull edged a four and then edged to slip, and Cork finally ended Fleming's outstanding innings with a low catch off his own bowling.

Fleming had batted with majesty and mastery for 368 minutes and had hit a six and 18 fours, facing 254 balls – but he had played with such grandeur that New Zealand should have accorded him better support and reached a higher total.

Knight was soon out to Doull, but Atherton gave the first indications of a return to form as Stewart immediately took command. By the close, England were 123 for 1, Atherton 48, Stewart 67.

There was a sense that England would attain supremacy. Stewart ran to his second Test hundred in succession in 215 minutes, and he was without blemish, troubled only by Patel. Atherton had dropped anchor and had moved out of the doldrums that had been gripping him for so long. He batted 291 minutes and faced 213 balls for his 83, which was an innings to be cherished both for its

determination and for the relief of rehabilitation. The stand between captain and former vice-captain was worth 182 when, just after lunch on the third day, Atherton drove the ball to short mid-on where Vaughan diverted it into the hands of the bowler. Patel had bowled his off-breaks tidily and well deserved the wicket. He immediately claimed another, a smart bat and pad catch to account for Hussain.

Stewart's imperious innings, which included 23 fours and a six, finally came to an end when Doull, who had bowled well, stooped to take a low return catch. Stewart had played some lavish strokes and had been at the crease for 364 minutes, during which time he never lost concentration or authority.

Some of the very fine work that Stewart and Atherton had achieved was wasted when Thorpe ran out Crawley and White was out first ball. At 366 for 6, Thorpe had only the bowlers left to help him if England were to confirm their superiority on the fourth morning.

Thorpe made ample amends for his lapses when he and a restrained Cork batted throughout the first session on the fourth day to take England into the lead at 448 for 6. Thorpe reached an admirable third Test hundred before falling early in the afternoon to the inconsistent Cairns. Cork showed great resolve for 238 minutes, and there were exciting and unexpected flourishes from Mullally and Tufnell. England led by 131 runs and captured the wickets of both openers and, vitally, Fleming before the close, by which time New Zealand had scored 56 and faced a worrying last day.

By lunch, the home side faced defeat. They were 105 for 8. Astle had 7 and only Doull and Morrison remained. What followed was one of the greatest rescue acts in the history of cricket. Doull chose to hit, 26 in 37 minutes off 40 balls in a stand of 37, which made sure that at least England would have to bat again. Doull was bowled by Gough, and in came Morrison with a Test batting average under nine and with a record number of Test cricket ducks to his credit (or debt). For the next 165 minutes, Morrison stood firm. Every ball he stopped was applauded, and he even scored 14 runs. Tufnell had looked to be the match-winner. Now he was frustrated. The pace men returned with the second new ball and the score on 170. It made no difference. At tea, New Zealand were 207 – Astle 64, Morrison 13. When the game was accepted as drawn 15 overs into the final session Astle had reached the third century of his infant Test career of which this was only the seventh match. He had batted for 279 minutes, faced 214 balls and hit 13 fours, a wonderful effort. Even more miraculously, Morrison had survived 133 deliveries.

It was easy to hurl criticism at England for not finishing off the game, which was all but won – but far better to praise two cricketers who showed a strength of character that most would envy. They shared the second longest match-saving last wicket stand in Test history, and, rightly, they were national heroes.

Astle and Stewart shared the Man of the Match award, which was probably right in a game where honours were even.

First Test Match – New Zealand v. England
24, 25, 26 27 and 28 January 1997 at Eden Park, Auckland

New Zealand

	First Innings		Second Innings		
B.A. Young	lbw, **b** Mullally	44	(2) **c** Hussain, **b** Cork	3
B.A. Pocock	lbw, **b** Gough	70	(1) lbw, **b** Gough	20
A.C. Parore	**c** Stewart, **b** Cork	6	**st** Stewart, **b** Tufnell	33
S.P. Fleming	**c** and **b** Cork·	129	**c** Crawley, **b** Tufnell	9
N.J. Astle	**c** Stewart, **b** White	10	(6) not out	102
J.T.C. Vaughan	lbw, **b** Cork	3	(7) lbw, **b** Tufnell	2
C.L. Cairns	**c** Stewart, **b** White	67	(8) **b** Mullally	7
*L.K. Germon (Capt)	**c** Stewart, **b** Gough	14	(5) run out	13
D.N. Patel	lbw, **b** Gough	0	lbw, **b** Mullally	0
S.B. Doull	**c** Knight, **b** Gough	5	**b** Gough	26
D.K. Morrison	not out	6	not out	14
	b **5**, lb **12**, w **2**, nb **17**	36	lb **11**, nb **8**	19
		390	(for 9 wickets)	**248**

England

	First Innings		
N.V. Knight	**c** lbw, **b** Doull	5
M.A. Atherton (Capt)	**c** and **b** Patel	83
*A.J. Stewart	**c** and **b** Doull	173
N. Hussain	**c** Fleming, **b** Patel	8
G.P. Thorpe	hit wkt, **b** Cairns	119
J.P. Crawley	run out	14
C. White	lbw, **b** Vaughan	0
D.G. Cork	**c** Young, **b** Morrison	59
D. Gough	**c** Germon, **b** Morrison	2
A.D. Mullally	**c** Germon, **b** Morrison	21
P.C.R. Tufnell	not out	19
	b **2**, lb **12**, w **2**, nb **2**	18
		521

	O	M	R	**W**	O	M	R	**W**		O	M	R	**W**
Cork	32.5	8	96	**3**	16	3	45	**1**	Morrison	24.4	4	104	**3**
Mullally	27	11	55	**1**	26	11	47	**2**	Doull	39	10	118	**2**
Gough	32	5	91	**4**	22	3	66	**2**	Cairns	30	3	103	**1**
Tufnell	25	5	80	**–**	40	18	53	**3**	Astle	14	3	33	**–**
White	15	3	51	**2**	10	2	26	**–**	Vaughan	36	10	57	**1**
									Patel	44	10	92	**2**

Fall of Wickets
1–**85**, 2–**114**, 3–**193**, 4–**210**, 5–**215**, 6–**333**, 7–**362**, 8–**362**, 9–**380**
1–**17**, 2–**28**, 3–**47**, 4–**88**, 5–**90**, 6–**92**, 7–**101**, 8–**105**, 9–**142**

Fall of Wickets
1–**18**, 2–**200**, 3–**222**, 4–**304**, 5–**339**, 6–**339**, 7–**453**, 8–**471**, 9–**478**

Umpires: S.A. Bucknor & R.S. Dunne

Match drawn

30, 31 January, 1 and 2 February 1997
at Victoria Park, Wanganui
New Zealand 'A' 181 (M.J. Horne 64, C.E.W. Silverwood 6 for 44) and 288 (C.Z. Harris 71, L.G. Howell 66)
England XI 107 (H.T. Davis 4 for 22, G.I. Allott 4 for 44) and 272 (R.C. Russell 61 not out, N. Hussain 57, G.I. Allott 4 for 76)
New Zealand 'A' won by 90 runs

In their last match of any kind outside Tests and one-day internationals, England began well. Silverwood sent back Spearman and Chandler with only 12 on the board, but by lunch Murray and Horne had taken the score to 109. Murray was out immediately on the resumption, caught behind off Tufnell. Wickets continued to fall regularly as Silverwood returned the best bowling figures of his career, a just reward for an aggressive spell. Matthew Horne enhanced his chances of a Test call-up with 64 off 109 balls.

England were soon in trouble, losing both openers for 17. Crawley quickly followed, and they closed on 23 for 3. There was no respite on the second morning as England collapsed against the pace duet of Geoff Allott, left-arm, and Heath Davis. Bowled out before lunch, England would have been in dreadful straits but for Ronnie Irani's 40 off 68 balls. With a comfortable if unexpected lead of 74, the New Zealanders batted with more confidence and purpose in the second innings. They ended the second day on 187 for 4,

Geoff Allott bowled himself into the New Zealand Test team with his performance for New Zealand 'A' at Wanganui. (Graham Chadwick/Allsport)

and Chris Harris and Llorne Howell were very much in charge. Their fifth wicket partnership was eventually worth 117, and by lunch the home side had advanced to 266 for 7. Caddick and Irani quickly brought the innings to a close after the interval, and England had the best part of five sessions to score 363 to win. This time both openers were out for 6. Atherton was leg before third ball, and there was increasing pressure on him from such people as Ray Illingworth to relinquish the captaincy. Failure to win in Auckland had not been well received.

At the end of the day, England, 166 for 6, had lost hope of victory. Inevitably it was Russell who fought the brave fight for 130 minutes, but then he was not even in consideration for a Test place.

Second Test Match

New Zealand v. England at Wellington

New Zealand sprang a surprise when they selected a slow left-arm bowler Daniel Vettori in their eleven for the second Test. At 18 years 10 days, Vettori, who had two first-class games to his credit and who had just finished exams, became the youngest player to represent New Zealand in Test cricket. He replaced Vaughan while Allott came in for Morrison, whose brave batting had not been enough to compensate for some poor bowling.

England brought in Caddick for Mullally and Croft for White. Silverwood had suffered an injury in training and could not be considered. England started the match with

their reputation at the lowest ebb. They were criticised not simply because they were losing matches, but because of their general lack of grace and charm. There was much repair work to do.

Play was delayed for four hours because of rain, and only 30 overs were possible on the first day. New Zealand won the toss, chose to bat and must have regretted it. Their batsmen were far too eager to play their shots on a pitch that demanded initial caution, and they perished in consequence. Pocock was the first to go when he steered the ball into the hands of the finer of two gullies in Caddick's fourth over. Gough replaced Cork and took two wickets in his first 10 balls, both catches behind. Fleming was caught and bowled by Caddick when he was deceived by a late inswinger. Cairns edged Gough to third slip, and New Zealand were 23 for 5.

Germon and Astle lived dangerously, but they doubled the score and were not separated until Caddick, having taken a breather, returned to beat Germon with an outswinger which the batsman touched to the keeper. England took much comfort from a day that ended with New Zealand 56 for 6.

New Zealand were all out 40 minutes before lunch on the second day. In his fifth over of the morning, Gough had Astle well held at mid-off off a fierce drive, and Doull was caught behind two balls later. Allott was subjected to unnecessary intimidation by Gough who otherwise had

A danger removed – Fleming, caught and bowled Caddick, 1. (Clive Mason/Allsport)

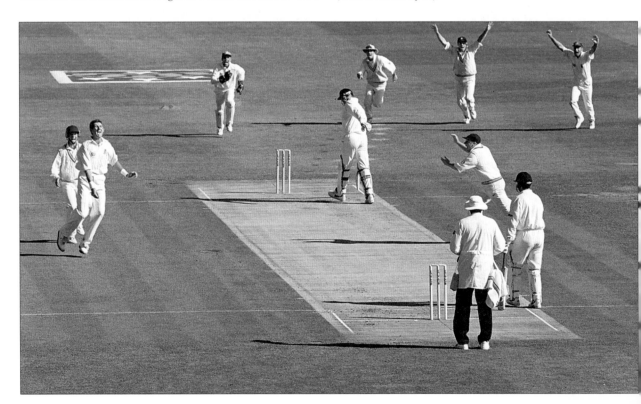

bowled so well. Allott survived half an hour before giving Cork his only wicket of the innings, and Patel's brave resistance ended when he miscued to mid-off.

Nick Knight's technical weaknesses were again apparent when he was soon caught in the gully, and England went to lunch a little uncertainly at 20 for 1. That uncertainty disappeared in the second session. Atherton and Stewart gave a firm foundation, and although both fell, Hussain and Thorpe took England serenely to 204 by the close.

Hussain added only four to his overnight score before edging to slip to give young Vettori his first Test wicket. It was well deserved. The left-arm spinner flighted the ball intelligently and obtained considerable turn, but New Zealand were handicapped by the absence of Cairns with a bruised hand. Thorpe and Crawley now settled into a stand worth 118 in approximately three hours. It was broken immediately after a drinks interval when Thorpe went down the pitch to Patel, who turned the ball sharply past the outside edge. Once again Thorpe had provided the rock of the England innings with his second century in successive Tests. He batted for 331 minutes and hit 12 fours. There were chances that were not taken, but Thorpe's poise and temperament looked to be so vital to England's healing process.

Sadly, Thorpe's dismissal signalled an England collapse. In the next over, Crawley cut at Doull and was caught behind. Croft hung out his bat to the same bowler and was taken at slip. Three wickets had fallen at 331. The

Centuries in successive Tests for Graham Thorpe.
(David Munden/Sportsline)

Second Test Match – New Zealand v. England
6, 7, 8, 9 and 10 February 1997 at Basin Reserve, Wellington

New Zealand

	First Innings		Second Innings	
B.A. Young	c Stewart, b Gough	8	(2) c Stewart, b Tufnell	56
B.A. Pocock	c Cork, b Caddick	6	(1) c Stewart, b Gough	64
A.C. Parore	c Stewart, b Gough	4	lbw, b Croft	15
S.P. Fleming	c and b Caddick	1	c and b Croft	0
N.J. Astle	c Croft, b Gough	36	(7) c Stewart, b Gough	4
C.L. Cairns	c Hussain, b Gough	3	(8) c Knight, b Caddick	22
*L.K. Germon (Capt)	c Stewart, b Caddick	10	(6) b Gough	11
D.N. Patel	c Cork, b Caddick	45	(5) lbw, b Croft	0
S.B. Doull	c Stewart, b Gough	0	c Knight, b Gough	0
G.I. Allott	c Knight, b Cork	1	b Caddick	2
D.L. Vettori	not out	3	not out	2
	lb 5, nb 2	7	b 5, lb 4, nb 6	15
		124		**191**

England

	First Innings	
N.V. Knight	c Patel, b Doull	8
M.A. Atherton (Capt)	lbw, b Doull	30
*A.J. Stewart	c Fleming, b Allott	52
N. Hussain	c Young, b Vettori	64
G.P. Thorpe	st Germon, b Patel	108
J.P. Crawley	c Germon, b Doull	56
D.G. Cork	lbw, b Astle	7
R.D.B. Croft	c Fleming, b Doull	0
D. Gough	c Fleming, b Doull	18
A.R. Caddick	c Allott, b Vettori	20
P.C.R. Tufnell	not out	6
	b 3, lb 9, nb 2	14
		383

	O	M	R	W	O	M	R	W
Cork	14	4	34	1	10	1	42	–
Caddick	18.3	5	45	4	27.2	11	40	2
Gough	16	6	40	5	23	9	52	4
Croft					20	9	19	3
Tufnell					23	9	29	1

	O	M	R	W
Doull	28	10	75	5
Allott	31	6	91	1
Vettori	34.3	10	98	2
Cairns	4	2	8	–
Astle	14	5	30	1
Patel	24	6	59	1
Pocock	2	–	10	–

Fall of Wickets
1–14, 2–18, 3–19, 4–19, 5–23, 6–48, 7–85, 8–85, 9–106
1–89, 2–125, 3–125, 4–125, 5–161, 6–164, 7–175, 8–175, 9–182

Fall of Wickets
1–10, 2–80, 3–106, 4–213, 5–331, 6–331, 7–331, 8–357, 9–357

Umpires: S.A. Bucknor & D.B. Cowie

England won by an innings and 68 runs

Darren Gough has Adam Parore caught behind for 4.
(Clive Mason/Allsport)

tail wagged merrily, but England must have been disappointed at being out for under 450. Doull, not always having the confidence of his captain, claimed five worthy wickets.

Pocock and Young took New Zealand to 48 in 21 overs, and, on the fourth morning, rain denied any play before lunch and frustrated England. When the rain finally relented there was time for one lengthened session in which 52 overs were bowled. England's pace bowlers could make no inroads into New Zealand's second innings, and it was Tufnell who broke a competent and worthy opening stand when Young tried to force the ball off the back foot and was adjudged caught behind. Parore, suspended by his association for the rest of the season for disciplinary reasons but still playing for his country, was leg before to Croft when he offered no shot, and Patel suffered the same fate. In between these two, Fleming had hoiked across the line and skied the ball to the bowler. Croft had 3 for 12 in 16 overs, New Zealand were 125 for 4, and England joyfully anticipated the final day. The Welsh off-spinner's three wickets in 14 deliveries had turned the match conclusively towards an England victory.

There were still frustrations to be endured. Play began half an hour late, and it was an hour before Gough provided the desired breakthrough. He found a way through Germon's defence, and four balls later took the vital wicket of Pocock, caught above his head at slip by Knight. Astle was spectacularly caught by Stewart diving to his right, and two balls later Doull perished at second slip. At lunch, New Zealand were 177 for 8.

Half an hour into the afternoon the game was over as Caddick got just reward for his consistently good bowling. England had won their first 'away' Test for two years. Thorpe was named Man of the Match. Atherton was relieved and applauded. New Zealand now suffered the slings as rumours of late-night drinking and lack of commitment circulated.

Third Test Match

New Zealand v. England at Christchurch

New Zealand lost the services of skipper Lee Germon, who was injured in training. Stephen Fleming took over as captain for the first time, and Adam Parore, who had originally been dropped from the side, came back as wicket-keeper. Fast bowler Heath Davis replaced Dipak Patel, and Matthew Horne was rewarded for a fine season with his first Test cap. England were unchanged.

For the second time in the series, Atherton asked New Zealand to bat when he won the toss. There was early success when Cork bowled with the first ball of his second over, but Cork's opening spell of six overs cost 33 runs and contained six no-balls. Pocock, having played the pace bowlers with confidence, hit Croft into the hands of mid-on. Horne had looked totally at ease until he was taken at first slip, and Nathan Astle's characteristic impetuosity led to him edging low to the same position where Hussain took a stunning catch. He is an outstanding fielder in any position.

Fleming and Parore showed style and authority just as New Zealand threatened to crumble. Fleming, having showed a sound defence and utmost concentration, began to play his shots, but he was drawn forward by the enthusiastic Croft and stumped when he had made 62. Parore and Cairns took New Zealand to 229 by the close.

If the New Zealand innings had been flagging, the sixth wicket pair did much to put it right. They repelled with ease England's attack with the second new ball. The obsession with short-pitched bowling aided their cause. Parore batted for 216 minutes and displayed unflinching concentration. It took a very good ball to account for him. Croft deceived him with an away drifter that caught the edge of the bat and was taken by Hussain at slip.

Cairns, too, batted well, but he was guilty of running out Doull, and he remains an enigma, flawed in temperament, application and ability. Vettori was impressive, looking a veteran in his second Test, but when Cairns was caught behind he took one risk too many. Eventually, England were

Stewart stumps Fleming off Croft for 62. (Clive Mason/Allsport)

glad to be facing 346, as the score could have been much bigger. Croft was well worth his first five-wicket haul in Test cricket. He kept the right length and a line on off stump that allowed the ball to drift away on occasions like the delivery that accounted for Parore, and he was always thinking.

England quickly lost Knight who, not for the first time, was too eager to make the big hit. Stewart also perished through over-indulgence, 15 off 10 balls with three fours, and Hussain was the third batsman to fall to a forcing shot off the back foot. Thorpe played on to Astle, and Crawley, a somewhat shadowy figure at number six, sliced a ball slanted across him. Atherton quietly gathered runs while suicides abounded at the other end, and he was still there at the close with 66 of England's 145 runs and five leading batsmen gone.

Cork had shown good sense on the Saturday evening, but he pulled wildly at Davis in the first over on Sunday and was caught behind. England were 145 for 6, sinking fast. Croft batted with more composure than in his previous Test innings, and he and the resolute Atherton shared the first 50 partnership of the innings. It was broken by Astle, grossly underrated by opponents, who deceived Croft with a slower ball of full length, which the Welshman skied to mid-on. Gough was immediately beaten by Vettori, and England lunched at 210 for 8. Caddick was out on the resumption, and Tufnell hit 13 off 15 balls while failing to let his captain have enough of the strike. So, after 345 minutes at the crease, Atherton, who had faced 235 balls and hit 10 fours, found himself the seventh English batsman to carry his bat

Another wicket for Croft as Hussain catches Astle at slip.
(Clive Mason/Allsport)

Third Test Match – New Zealand v. England
14, 15, 16, 17 and 18 February 1997 at Lancaster Park, Christchurch

New Zealand

	First Innings		Second Innings	
B.A. Young	b Cork	11	(2) c Knight, b Tufnell	49
B.A. Pocock	c Atherton, b Croft	22	(1) b Cork	0
M.J. Horne	c Thorpe, b Gough	42	(8) c Stewart, b Caddick	13
S.P. Fleming (Capt)	st Stewart, b Croft	62	c Knight, b Tufnell	11
N.J. Astle	c Hussain, b Croft	15	c Hussain, b Croft	5
*A.C. Parore	c Hussain, b Croft	59	(3) c Stewart, b Gough	8
C.L. Cairns	c Stewart, b Caddick	57	(6) c Knight, b Tufnell	52
S.B. Doull	run out	1	(7) c Knight, b Croft	5
D.L. Vettori	run out	25	not out	29
H.T. Davis	c Hussain, b Croft	8	b Gough	1
G.I. Allott	not out	8	c Stewart, b Gough	1
	b 1, lb 16, nb 19	36	lb 8, nb 4	12
		346		**186**

England

	First Innings		Second Innings	
N.V. Knight	c Fleming, b Allott	14	c Davis, b Vettori	29
M.A. Atherton (Capt)	not out	94	c Parore, b Astle	118
*A.J. Stewart	c sub (Harris), b Allott	15	c Pocock, b Vettori	17
N. Hussain	c Parore, b Cairns	12	(5) c Fleming, b Vettori	33
G.P. Thorpe	b Astle	18	(6) c and b Vettori	2
J.P. Crawley	c Parore, b Allott	1	(7) not out	40
D.G. Cork	c Parore, b Davis	16	(8) not out	39
R.D.B. Croft	c Davis, b Astle	31		
D. Gough	b Vettori	0		
A.R. Caddick	sub (Harris), b Allott	4	(4) c Fleming, b Doull	15
P.C.R. Tufnell	c Young, b Doull	13	b 2, lb 8, w 1, nb 3	14
	lb 4, w 1, nb 5	10		
		228	(for 6 wickets)	**307**

	O	M	R	W	O	M	R	W
Cork	20	3	78	1	6	2	5	1
Caddick	32	8	64	1	10	1	25	1
Gough	21	3	70	1	13.3	5	42	3
Croft	39.1	5	95	5	31	13	48	2
Tufnell	16	6	22	–	28	9	58	3
Thorpe	1	1	0	–				

	O	M	R	W	O	M	R	W
Allott	18	3	74	4	12.4	2	32	–
Doull	17.4	3	49	1	21	8	57	1
Davis	18	2	50	1	18	6	43	–
Vettori	12	4	13	1	57	18	97	4
Cairns	8	5	12	1	10	1	23	–
Astle	11	2	26	2	28	10	45	1

Fall of Wickets
1–14, 2–78, 3–106, 4–137, 5–201, 6–283, 7–288, 8–310, 9–337
1–0, 2–42, 3–61, 4–76, 5–80, 6–89, 7–107, 8–178, 9–184

Fall of Wickets
1–20, 2–40, 3–70, 4–103, 5–104, 6–145, 7–198, 8–199, 9–210
1–64, 2–116, 3–146, 4–226, 5–226, 6–231

Umpires: R.S. Dunne & D.B. Hair

England won by 4 wickets

Test Match Averages – New Zealand v. England

New Zealand Batting

	M	Inns	NO	Runs	HS	Av	100s	50s
D.L. Vettori	2	4	3	59	29*	59.00		
S.P. Fleming	3	6	–	212	129	35.33	1	1
C.L. Cairns	3	6	–	208	67	34.66		3
N.J. Astle	3	6	1	172	102*	34.40	1	
B.A. Pocock	3	6	–	182	70	30.33		2
B.A. Young	3	6	–	171	56	28.50		1
A.C. Parore	3	6	–	125	59	20.83		1
L.K. Germon	2	4	–	48	14	12.00		
D.N. Patel	2	4	–	45	45	11.25		
S.B. Doull	3	6	–	37	26	6.16		
G.I. Allott	2	4	1	12	8*	4.00		

(Played in one match: M.J. Horne 42 & 13; H.T. Davis 8 & 1; J.T.C. Vaughan 3 & 2; D.K. Morrison 6* & 14*)

England Batting

	M	Inns	NO	Runs	HS	Av	100s	50s
M.A. Atherton	3	4	1	325	118	108.33	1	2
A.J. Stewart	3	4	–	257	173	64.25	1	1
G.P. Thorpe	3	4	–	247	119	61.75	2	
D.G. Cork	3	4	1	121	59	40.33		1
P.C.R. Tufnell	3	3	2	38	19*	38.00		
J.P. Crawley	3	4	1	111	56	37.00		1
N. Hussain	3	4	–	117	64	29.25		1
R.D.B. Croft	2	2	–	31	31	15.50		
N.V. Knight	3	4	–	56	29	14.00		
A.R. Caddick	2	3	–	39	20	13.00		
D. Gough	3	3	–	20	18	6.66		

(Played in one match: C. White 0; A.D. Mullally 21)

New Zealand Bowling

	Overs	Mds	Runs	Wks	Av	Best	10/m	5/inn
D.L. Vettori	103.3	32	208	7	29.71	4/97		
S.B. Doull	105.4	31	299	9	33.22	5/75		1
N.J. Astle	67	20	134	4	33.50	2/26		
G.I. Allott	61.4	11	197	5	39.40	4/74		
D.N. Patel	68	16	151	3	50.33	2/92		
C.L. Cairns	52	11	146	2	73.00	1/12		
H.T. Davis	36	8	93	1	93.00	1/50		

(Bowled in one innings: B.A. Pocock 2–0–10–0; D.K. Morrison 24.4–4–4–104–3; J.T.C. Vaughan 36–10–57–1)

England Bowling

	Overs	Mds	Runs	Wks	Av	Best	10/m	5/inn
R.D.B. Croft	90.1	27	162	10	16.20	5/95		1
D. Gough	127.3	31	361	19	19.00	5/40		1
A.R. Caddick	87.5	25	174	8	21.75	4/45		
A.D. Mullally	53	22	102	3	34.00	2/47		
P.C.R. Tufnell	132	47	242	7	34.57	3/53		
C. White	25	5	77	2	38.50	2/51		
D.G. Cork	98.5	21	300	7	42.85	3/96		

(Bowled in one innings: G.P. Thorpe 1–1–0–0)

New Zealand Fielding Figures

7 – S.P. Fleming; 4 – L.K. Germon (ct 3 / st 1) and A.C. Parore; 3 – B.A. Young; 2 – H.T. Davis, D.N. Patel and sub (C.Z. Harris); 1 – B.A. Pocock, S.B. Doull, D.L. Vettori and G.I. Allott

England Fielding Figures

16 – A.J. Stewart (ct 14 / st 2); 9 – N.V. Knight; 6 - N. Hussain; 3 – D.G. Cork; 2 – R.D.B. Croft; 1 – M.A. Atherton, G.P. Thorpe, J.P. Crawley and A.R. Caddick

through a completed Test innings. It was an heroic performance, but the skipper must have gained little comfort, for his side trailed by 118.

Yet comfort did come. Where the batsmen had failed, the bowlers succeeded. Cork bowled Pocock with his fourth ball, and Young was dropped by Knight at slip off Caddick.

Michael Atherton – 94 not out and 118 at Christchurch – Man of the Match and the series. (David Munden/Sportsline)

Parore was far from happy and was caught behind off Gough in the last over before tea. It was in the final session that the spinners Croft and Tufnell operated in tandem and brought England right back into contention. They bowled with aggression and intelligence and were supported by some excellent close catching. The fifth wicket to fall was that of Young who had been batting for 165 minutes when he was caught at silly point. He stood his ground and made obvious his disagreement with umpires and catcher Knight. It was a sad altercation with which to end the day, but the sides had been simmering for superiority throughout the series.

For New Zealand, worse followed. Doull lasted 22 minutes before falling to Croft, and Horne, batting with a broken hand in his first Test, was in obvious pain as he played out time with Cairns. When stumps were drawn New Zealand were 95 for 6.

Horne battled bravely for half an hour, and when he was caught behind Vettori joined Cairns in a stand worth 71 in as many minutes. Cairns had completed his second fifty of the match before falling to Tufnell, and he had seen that England would face a target of 297. Vettori, whose innings included five fours, made sure that the target would be beyond 300.

England chose the occasion to provide their first opening partnership of fifty or more of the winter. Knight is quite plainly too technically flawed to be considered a Test batsman, but he stayed for 107 minutes while he and Atherton put on 64. Stewart batted longer with restraint and patience. He was not at ease, and he enjoyed some fortune against Vettori, for whom, surely, the future is bright. Stewart was out as soon as the young left-arm spinner went round the wicket to him, taken at short leg off bat and pad. England closed on 118 for 2, Atherton 65, and a last day of tension and drama beckoning.

Caddick did all that could be expected of a night-watchman, batting for more than an hour and scoring an invaluable 15. His was the only wicket to fall before lunch, by which time Atherton was unbeaten on 105.

In the first innings, only Croft had offered Atherton adequate support, but now Hussain stayed with him for ten minutes under two hours while 80 runs were added and England moved to within 79 runs of victory. Having batted for 399 minutes, faced 311 balls and hit 11 fours in his 11th Test century, Atherton pushed wearily at Astle and was caught behind. In the next over, Hussain was caught at silly point as he tried to avoid playing a shot to Vettori, who bowled with accuracy, intelligence, stamina and guile. Eleven balls later, Thorpe gave the same bowler a simple return catch, and England had lost three wickets for five runs.

Cork had been less than impressive since joining the England party for the New Zealand leg of the tour and even Crawley had been something of a peripheral figure. Now the pair faced their greatest challenge. They responded magnificently. In 144 vigilant minutes they scored 76 runs and took England to victory and to their first overseas series win for five years.

For Atherton, Man of the Match, this was the sweetest of moments. Never can a captain have done more off his own bat to bring victory to his side.

One-Day Internationals

New Zealand v. England

England began the one-day series with a confidence born of their success in the Tests. Mullally came in for Caddick while Germon returned to lead New Zealand, who included one-day specialists Harris and Larsen.

The first match was played on the pitch used for the third Test, and England wisely fielded both spinners. The Lancaster Park lights were used for the first time, and music of sorts accompanied batsmen to the crease and allowed no breath between overs. The circus was in town. New Zealand began well enough and reached 76 for 1 after 15 overs. Astle was out to the fourth ball of the 20th over, caught at cover, having hit 50 off 62 balls. Tufnell then deceived Parore in the flight and accounted for both Fleming and Cairns to take the heart out of the New Zealand innings. Harris made 48 off 51 balls, mainly

Man of the Match in the first one-day international, Phil Tufnell celebrates the removal of Adam Parore. Tufnell's figures of 4 for 22 were his best in a limited-over international. (Clive Mason/Allsport)

with some deft running, but New Zealand fell short of expectation.

Their hopes were raised by the early fall of Atherton, who batted rather fretfully, and the demise of the troubled Knight at the same score, but Thorpe and Stewart were soon in serene command. They added 170 in 34 overs, and when Thorpe played on to Davis, a much improved fast bowler from the one seen in England in 1994, the visitors needed only 25 from 10 overs.

The innings now wobbled. Stewart was caught at deep square-leg, Crawley played across the line and paid the price, and Cork clouted impetuously to mid-wicket. Croft joined Hussain to restore sanity, and England won with seven balls to spare. Tufnell deservedly took the individual award for his best analysis in a limited-over international. His bowling had tilted the game in England's favour, and a long line of 12 defeats was halted.

Atherton stood down for the second match because of a slight back strain, and Hussain led England for the first time. Irani, a forgotten man, came into the side, and

Chris Harris bowls Nasser Hussain in the match at Napier. Harris took the individual award. (Clive Mason/Allsport)

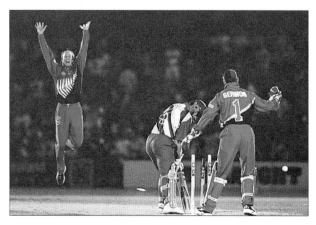

First One-Day International – New Zealand v. England
20 February 1997 at Lancaster Park, Christchurch

New Zealand

B.A. Young	c Thorpe, b Mullally	14
N.J. Astle	c Thorpe, b Tufnell	50
A.C. Parore	c and b Tufnell	26
S.P. Fleming	st Stewart, b Tufnell	34
C.L. Cairns	c Mullally, b Tufnell	15
C.Z. Harris	not out	48
*L.K. Germon (Capt)	b Cork	19
D.N. Patel	not out	1
G.R. Larsen		
S.B. Doull		
H.T. Davis		
	lb 9, w 4, nb 2	15
	50 overs (for 6 wickets)	222

	O	M	R	W
Cork	9	–	52	1
Mullally	5	2	21	1
Croft	10	1	41	–
Gough	10	–	45	–
Tufnell	10	1	22	4
Thorpe	6	–	32	–

Fall of Wickets
1–24, 2–87, 3–100, 4–134, 5–148, 6–203

England

N.V. Knight	c Germon, b Doull	8
M.A. Atherton (Capt)	b Patel	19
*A.J. Stewart	c Astle, b Davis	81
G.P. Thorpe	b Davis	82
N. Hussain	not out	11
J.P. Crawley	b Doull	0
D.G. Cork	c Young, b Davis	5
R.D.B. Croft	not out	8
D. Gough		
A.D. Mullally		
P.C.R. Tufnell		
	lb 6, w 6	12
	48.5 overs (for 6 wickets)	226

	O	M	R	W
Doull	10	–	33	2
Patel	7	–	43	1
Astle	4	–	26	–
Cairns	4	–	25	–
Davis	8.5	–	44	3
Larsen	8	–	23	–
Harris	7	–	26	–

Fall of Wickets
1–28, 2–28, 3–198, 4–204, 5–207, 6–218

Umpires: C.E. King & D.M. Quested   *Man of the Match:* P.C.R. Tufnell

England won by 4 wickets

Second One-Day International – New Zealand v. England
23 February 1997 at Eden Park, Auckland

New Zealand

B.A. Young	c Stewart, b Irani	46
N.J. Astle	c Stewart, b Mullally	4
A.C. Parore	run out	2
S.P. Fleming	c Caddick, b Gough	42
C.L. Cairns	run out	79
C.Z. Harris	c sub (White), b Caddick	14
*L.K. Germon (Capt)	b Caddick	1
D.N. Patel	run out	24
G.R. Larsen	not out	12
S.B. Doull		
H.T. Davis		
	lb 9, w 16, nb 4	29
	50 overs (for 8 wickets)	253

	O	M	R	W
Cork	10	–	51	–
Mullally	7	–	36	1
Caddick	6	–	33	2
Gough	10	–	65	1
Irani	7	–	26	1
Croft	10	1	33	–

Fall of Wickets
1–24, 2–44, 3–96, 4–138, 5–189, 6–202, 7–219, 8–253

England

N.V. Knight	not out	84
*A.J. Stewart	lbw, b Davis	30
D.G. Cork	c Young, b Larsen	4
R.C. Irani	c Astle, b Doull	0
G.P. Thorpe	c and b Doull	4
N. Hussain (Capt)	not out	9
J.P. Crawley		
R.D.B. Croft		
D. Gough		
A.R. Caddick		
A.D. Mullally		
	w 3	3
	19.3 overs (for 4 wickets)	134

	O	M	R	W
Davis	6	1	39	1
Doull	5	–	39	2
Larsen	5	–	31	1
Harris	2	–	8	–
Astle	1.3	–	17	–

Fall of Wickets
1–86, 2–91, 3–92, 4–100

Umpires: B.F. Bowden & D.B. Cowie   *Man of the Match:* N.V. Knight

England won on faster scoring rate

Third One-Day International – New Zealand v. England
26 February 1997 at McLean Park, Napier

New Zealand

B.A. Young	b Caddick	53
N.J. Astle	c Stewart, b Gough	34
*L.K. Germon (Capt)	st Stewart, b Croft	22
S.P. Fleming	run out	12
C.L. Cairns	c Cork, b Caddick	11
A.C. Parore	c and b White	24
C.Z. Harris	c Stewart, b White	19
G.R. Larsen	c Stewart, b Gough	19
S.B. Doull	b White	22
H.T. Davis	b White	1
G.I. Allott	not out	1
	lb 11, w 4, nb 4	19
49.4 overs		237

	O	M	R	W
Cork	9	1	42	–
Caddick	10	2	43	2
Gough	10	–	34	2
Irani	5	–	28	–
Croft	10	–	42	1
White	5.4	–	37	4

England

N.V. Knight	c and b Allott	39
M.A. Atherton (Capt)	b Harris	23
*A.J. Stewart	b Harris	17
G.P. Thorpe	c Germon, b Doull	55
N. Hussain	b Harris	13
R.C. Irani	c Doull, b Larsen	4
C. White	run out	38
D.G. Cork	not out	31
R.D.B. Croft	b Allott	4
D. Gough	not out	0
A.R. Caddick		
	b 2, lb 4, w 5, nb 2	13
50 overs (for 8 wickets)		237

	O	M	R	W
Doull	9	–	53	1
Allott	9	2	49	2
Davis	10	–	46	–
Harris	10	3	20	3
Larsen	10	–	50	1
Astle	2	–	19	–

Fall of Wickets
1–50, 2–102, 3–125, 4–140, 5–145, 6–178, 7–191, 8–233, 9–234

Fall of Wickets
1–67, 2–82, 3–87, 4–114, 5–127, 6–174, 7–232, 8–236

Umpires: C.E. King & D.M. Quested   *Man of the Match:* C.Z. Harris

Match tied

Fourth One-Day International – New Zealand v. England
2 March 1997 at Eden Park, Auckland

New Zealand

B.A. Young	c and b White	16
N.J. Astle	c Stewart, b Irani	51
*L.K. Germon (Capt)	lbw, b Gough	0
S.P. Fleming	c Hussain, b Croft	37
C.L. Cairns	run out	2
A.C. Parore	c Croft, b Caddick	13
C.Z. Harris	c Hussain, b Croft	0
G.R. Larsen	run out	2
S.B. Doull	not out	13
H.T. Davis	b Caddick	0
G.I. Allott	b Gough	3
	b 2, lb 3, w 11	16
39.5 overs		153

	O	M	R	W
Caddick	8	1	29	2
Silverwood	5	–	20	–
Gough	5.5	–	29	2
White	5	–	21	1
Croft	9	1	26	2
Irani	7	–	23	1

England

N.V. Knight	not out	1
M.A. Atherton (Capt)	b Harris, c Allott	9
*A.J. Stewart	b Astle	42
G.P. Thorpe	c Parore, b Allott	7
N. Hussain	b Davis	3
R.C. Irani	c Fleming, b Davis	0
C. White	c Parore, b Harris	32
R.D.B. Croft	run out	20
D. Gough	c and b Larsen	5
A.R. Caddick	b Larsen	0
C.E.W. Silverwood	c Allott, b Larsen	12
	lb 6, w 7	13
41.3 overs		144

	O	M	R	W
Davis	6	–	32	2
Allott	5	1	21	2
Doull	6	1	15	–
Larsen	8.3	1	20	3
Harris	9	–	26	1
Astle	7	1	24	1

Fall of Wickets
1–53, 2–54, 3–113, 4–116, 5–120, 6–120, 7–129, 8–136, 9–141

Fall of Wickets
1–22, 2–32, 3–41, 4–41, 5–91, 6–113, 7–132, 8–132, 9–133

Umpires: D.B. Cowie & R.S. Dunne   *Man of the Match:* N.J. Astle & G.R. Larsen

New Zealand won by 9 runs

Fifth One-Day International – New Zealand v. England

4 March 1997 at Basin Reserve, Wellington

New Zealand

B.A. Young	c Russell, **b** Caddick	11
N.J. Astle	c Atherton, **b** Caddick	94
S.P. Fleming	lbw, **b** Croft	17
C.L. Cairns	c Russell, **b** White	1
A.C. Parore	lbw, **b** Caddick	18
C.Z. Harris	c Stewart, **b** Gough	36
*L.K. Germon (Capt)	lbw, **b** Silverwood	2
D.N. Patel	not out	16
G.R. Larsen	run out	0
H.T. Davis	not out	7
G.I. Allott		
	lb 10, w 14, nb 2	26
	50 overs (for 8 wickets)	228

	O	M	R	W
Caddick	10	1	35	3
Silverwood	10	–	53	1
Gough	10	1	48	1
White	10	–	44	1
Croft	10	1	38	1

Fall of Wickets
1–**28**, 2–**84**, 3–**87**, 4–**122**, 5–**197**, 6–**200**, 7–**206**

England

M.A. Atherton (Capt)	run out	43
A.J. Stewart	**b** Patel, **c** Allott	18
N. Hussain	st Germon, **b** Harris	20
G.P. Thorpe	st Germon, **b** Larsen	55
C.E.W. Silverwood	**b** Patel	4
J.P. Crawley	lbw, **b** Larsen	11
*R.C. Russell	c Germon, **b** Astle	2
C. White	c Germon, **b** Astle	0
R.D.B. Croft	run out	2
D. Gough	c Fleming, **b** Davis	16
A.R. Caddick	not out	12
	lb **8**, w **8**, nb **1**	17
	47.5 overs	200

	O	M	R	W
Allott	8	–	40	1
Davis	7.5	–	44	1
Larsen	10	–	31	2
Harris	10	2	22	1
Patel	7	–	29	1
Astle	5	–	26	2

Fall of Wickets
1–**43**, 2–**77**, 3–**107**, 4–**119**, 5–**136**, 6–**139**, 7–**139**, 8–**158**, 9–**173**

Umpires: R.S. Dunne & E.A. Watkin   *Man of the Match:* N.J. Astle

New Zealand won by 28 runs

Mullally replaced Tufnell. Germon decided to bat first when he won the toss, a decision that delighted England, for rain was forecast and duly arrived. The ball swung prodigiously, so much so that England conceded 16 wides, but they also took wickets. The dangerous Astle was quickly dismissed, and Irani ran out Parore. After 15 overs, New Zealand were 81 for 2 with Young going particularly well. The momentum was halted by Croft and by Irani, who bowled a tight spell and had Young caught behind. Cairns hit 79 off 74 balls with three sixes and five fours, and Patel also batted with adventure, but, once again, New Zealand's total was short of expectation.

Knight and Stewart went off at a blistering pace, and they had made 47 in six overs when the rain arrived. After much debate the umpires concluded that play could restart and that the match could be finished, but England now faced the moderate task of reaching 132 in 26 overs, or, quite simply, 85 from another 20 overs. When Stewart was adjudged leg before the score was 86, and it was only the 11th over. There was some unnecessary juggling with the batting order, which brought a tumble of wickets, but when Knight hit Astle for three consecutive fours to bring England victory there were still 6.3 overs unused. Knight's 84 came off 69 balls.

Atherton returned for the match in Napier, and White was included for the first time. Germon again won the toss, and New Zealand again batted first. They began well. Astle hit seven fours in his innings of 34, which came off 32 balls,

and Young scored just 12 of the opening partnership of 50. After 15 overs, New Zealand had reached 75, which was becoming par for the course, and although there were several useful cameos, there was no innings of substance. White finished with two wickets in four balls, and New Zealand committed the crime of not batting out their fifty overs.

Atherton and Knight took 52 runs from the first six overs, and by the end of the 15th over, the score was 77 for the loss of Knight. It was the introduction of Harris that changed the mood of the game. Keeping a very full length, he bowled his 10 overs in one spell, conceded only 20 runs and claimed three major prizes, Atherton, Stewart and Hussain, all bowled. When Larsen dismissed Irani England were still 111 short of victory with 19 overs remaining.

Thorpe was now joined by White, and the pair added 47 to revive England's hopes and bring the target within quite comfortable reach. Thorpe was caught behind, and White was partnered by Cork, whose 31 came off 34 balls. They maintained a good momentum, and 34 were needed from five overs, and, eventually, eight from the last over, bowled by Geoff Allott, who frustrated attempts to score off his first delivery. A frantic single was scrambled off the second ball, and White was run out off the third when he attempted an optimistic second run. Croft heaved his first ball for four through mid-wicket, but his second, the penultimate ball of the match, spreadeagled his stumps. Gough swung at the last ball, missed, but ran a bye to the keeper, which meant the match was tied.

Lee Germon stands exultant as Craig White is run out in the last over of the tied match in Napier. Germon was to be dropped at the end of the series. (Clive Mason/Allsport)

The tied match at McLean Park kept the one-day series alive and maintained the interest and excitement of the New Zealand public, for whom the limited-over game is of far more importance than any Test match. The fourth game of the series saw a return to Eden Park, where rain not only put the fixture back a day but reduced it to 43 overs after a late start. England had Silverwood in for Cork, who was resting a hamstring strain. Atherton won the toss and asked New Zealand to bat. It was a most important toss to win, and the home side should have been in considerable trouble. As it was, they began with a blaze. Astle hit 51 off 68 balls, and the first wicket realised 53 in 11 overs. Young hit two fours, Astle six, and, after Germon had fallen second ball, Fleming two. Thereafter, New Zealand could not muster a single boundary. Croft bowled a very fine spell, but the batting was dreadful, and the last eight wickets went down for 40.

One-day expert Gavin Larsen traps John Crawley leg before in the final match as New Zealand go on to draw the series. (Clive Mason/Allsport)

England seemed to face an easy task, but the first ball of their innings brought disaster. Davis struck Knight on the finger, and examination revealed that it was broken in three places. Knight was to return at the fall of the ninth wicket, his left hand strapped as he attempted to bat one-handed. It was a brave gesture, but it could not save England from a humiliating defeat. At the end of 12 overs, England were 53 for 4. Tidy, nagging bowling from Allott and Davis had seen the first four wickets go down for 41 runs. Stewart and White put on 50 in 20 overs before Stewart was bowled when he offered an ugly pull at Astle. Harris now produced the mesmeric effect he had produced in Napier, and White was strokeless until, frustrated, he drove into the hands of mid-off.

Croft raised spirits with 20 off 33 balls. He hit Astle for six and appeared well set with 23 needed from four overs when he essayed a second run and was beaten by Astle's arrow throw. Larsen caught and bowled Gough in the same over and bowled Caddick first ball. Silverwood shielded Knight from the strike and hit lustily. His 12 off 11 balls took England to within 10 of their target, but he drove Larsen high to Allott, who took a splendid catch on the run just in front of the sightscreen.

New Zealand were now set to draw the series and went to Wellington in good spirits. They won the toss and were once more greatly indebted to Nathan Astle, who flayed at everything, hit 10 fours and made 94 off 129 balls before being acrobatically caught low at mid-wicket. Caddick had taken the first wicket, having Young caught behind by Russell, recalled to the colours after a tour in the shade. The wicket-keeper also held Cairns off White after Fleming had been bemused by Croft. It was not until the arrival of Harris that the New Zealand innings acquired any substance. He and Astle added 75 in 17 overs for the fifth wicket, after which New Zealand subsided.

England began purposefully enough. Stewart and Hussain were out when looking set, and Atherton enjoyed much fortune in reaching 43 off 82 balls before being run out by Harris when Thorpe called him for a sharp single. From 107 for 2, England melted into obscurity. Silverwood was needlessly promoted and was bowled, and Thorpe watched from the other end as batsmen departed. Finally, with the score on 173, he was stumped, having hit 55 off 82 balls, and a spirited last wicket stand could not rectify the errors of the senior batsmen.

So, to New Zealand's relief and credit, the series was drawn, but after the misery of Zimbabwe, England could leave for home in the knowledge that much had been accomplished on the second leg of their tour. They had won the Test series, and won well. Problems remained, not the least of which was to find an opening batsman to partner the skipper, but the future looked brighter than it had done for a long time, and the challenge of the Ashes beckoned.

Sri Lankan Tour

The omens were not good for Sri Lanka. They had arrived in New Zealand without Gurusinha, whose relationship with the Sri Lankan Board seemed to be such that his Test career could well be at an end. The Sri Lankan schedule was for a first-class match against New Zealand 'A' at Gisborne, two Test matches, a one-day game against Central Districts and then two limited-over internationals. Rain completely washed out the match at Gisborne so that Sri Lanka entered the Tests without any first-class practice to aid them.

In contrast, New Zealand, elated by their revival in the one-day series against England, welcomed the Sri Lankans in good spirits. Sadly, Lee Germon had been dropped at the end of the one-day series against England. He had taken over the captaincy at a most difficult time when New Zealand was at a particularly low ebb. He had done much to improve morale and had achieved remarkable results in the Caribbean, in Pakistan and, to the surprise of many, in the World Cup. The matches against England, however, had emphasised that whatever his qualities as a man and as a captain, his own form was below Test standard. Ironically, the man to benefit most from Germon's

Bryan Young – 267 not out in the first Test against Sri Lanka, the second highest score by a New Zealand batsman in Test Cricket. (Andrew Cornaga/Sportsline)

dismissal was Parore, the maverick who had run into trouble with his own association and with the Test selectors, but who now found himself restored to the wicket-keeping post. Fleming, who had led New Zealand in the third match against England, succeeded Germon as captain.

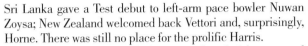

Test Series

New Zealand v. Sri Lanka

Sri Lanka gave a Test debut to left-arm pace bowler Nuwan Zoysa; New Zealand welcomed back Vettori and, surprisingly, Horne. There was still no place for the prolific Harris.

Ranatunga followed the example of Atherton and asked New Zealand to bat. His decision had much less success than Atherton had enjoyed. By the end of the first day, New Zealand were 343 for 4. The Sri Lankan attack, patently short of match practice, could command neither line nor length on a pitch favourable to batsmen and suffered in consequence. After 64 minutes, Pocock was taken at slip off Vaas, but Horne played fluently in a stand of 140 at a run a minute with Young. Fleming and Young added 76 in 69 minutes, and Young and Astle made 66 in 54 minutes in the final session. Young reached his century in 272 minutes off 203 balls, and he was unbeaten on 154 at the close.

Vaas had Vettori caught at slip without addition to the score at the start of the second day, but this brought no relief to Sri Lanka. Cairns, who hit a six and nine fours in his 123-ball innings, joined Young in adding 123 before becoming Zoysa's first Test wicket. The young left-arm bowler had performed well but was devoid of any luck. When Fleming declared, New Zealand had reached 586, the second highest score in their Test history. Bryan Young was undefeated for 267, the highest score of his career and second only to Martin Crowe's 299 as a New Zealand Test record. He had faced 422 balls, batted for 605 minutes and hit 37 fours.

New Zealand had lost Allott with a back strain shortly before the start of the match and had included two spinners, but it was the quick bowlers who influenced the early damage on Sri Lanka. Doull bowled Jayasuriya off an inside edge, and, after what seemed to be a recovery, he trapped both Atapattu and Mahanama leg before. When Aravinda de Silva chased a wide delivery from Heath Davis and was caught in the gully Sri Lanka were in dire trouble.

They closed on 78 for 4, and Ranatunga was caught at slip after adding a single on the third morning. The only hint of resistance came from Tillekeratne and Kaluwitharana who put on 56, but Kaluwitharana and Vaas were out in quick succession. Tillekeratne played with unrelenting concentration for 246 minutes while Wickramasinghe hit six fours in his aggressive 43. Doull and Davis returned to bring an abrupt end to the innings, and Doull finished with his second five-wicket Test haul of the summer. Following on, Sri Lanka were 37 for 0 at the close.

The match was over on the fourth day. Once the opening pair were separated, wickets began to tumble to a varied attack aided by some indisciplined batting. At 133 for

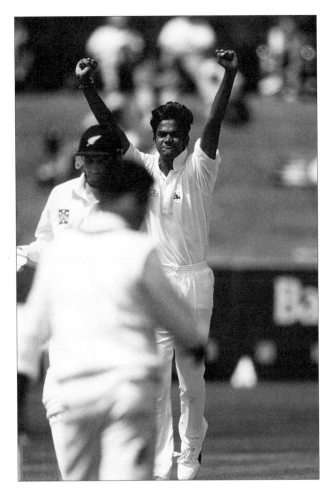

Sri Lanka's new left-arm pace bowler Nuwan Zoysa celebrates a wicket. (Andrew Cornaga/Sportsline)

6, the game was heading for an early finish, but Vaas joined Kaluwitharana in a stand that brought 137 in 130 minutes. Kaluwitharana reached his second Test century, and his 103 came off as many deliveries in 134 minutes. He hit two sixes and 13 fours. It was a brave, defiant gesture in an inevitable defeat.

New Zealand were unchanged for the second Test while Sri Lanka brought in Dharmasena for Atapattu and Sajeewa de Silva came in for his Test debut at the expense of Wickramasinghe. The inclusion of de Silva, who had played in limited-over internationals, meant that Sri Lanka fielded four left-arm bowlers. Fleming won the toss and New Zealand batted.

The first day belonged to Sri Lanka as New Zealand were bowled out for 222. There was early success when Young, the hero of Carisbrook, was run out for four, and, after again suggesting that he was a quality batsman, Horne played a loose shot at young Zoysa and was bowled. Fleming was caught at slip, and Astle, strangely ill at ease, soon fell to Zoysa.

First Test Match – New Zealand v. Sri Lanka
7, 8, 9 and 10 March 1997 at Carisbrook, Dunedin

New Zealand

	First Innings	
B.A. Young	not out	267
B.A. Pocock	c Mahanama, b Vaas	18
M.J. Horne	c Mahanama, b Ranatunga	66
S.P. Fleming (Capt)	c Zoysa, b Wickramasinghe	51
N.J. Astle	b Vaas	27
D.L. Vettori	c Mahanama, b Vaas	1
C.L. Cairns	c Mahanama, b Zoysa	70
*A.C. Parore	c Wickramasinghe, b Vaas	19
D.N. Patel	not out	30
S.B. Doull		
H.T. Davis		
	b 14, w 2, nb 21	37
	(for 7 wickets) dec.	586

	O	M	R	W
Vaas	35	6	144	4
Zoysa	40	6	112	1
Wickramasinghe	25	4	117	1
Muralitharan	33	6	136	–
Ranatunga	5	–	29	1
Jayasuriya	8	–	34	–

Fall of Wickets
1–**55**, 2–**195**, 3–**271**, 4–**337**, 5–**343**, 6–**466**, 7–**512**

Sri Lanka

	First Innings		Second Innings	
S.T. Jayasuriya	b Doull	0	c Parore, b Doull	50
R.S. Mahanama	lbw, b Doull	26	b Doull	21
M.S. Atapattu	lbw, b Doull	25	b Patel	22
P.A. de Silva	c Patel, b Davis	3	lbw, b Astle	0
A. Ranatunga (Capt)	c Young, b Doull	14	c Horne, b Vettori	13
H.P. Tillekeratne	not out	55	run out	8
*R.S. Kaluwitharana	c Fleming, b Patel	43	c and b Vettori	103
W.P.U.J.C. Vaas	c Horne, b Patel	2	c and b Davis	57
G.P. Wickramasinghe	c Parore, b Davis	43	c Doull, b Astle	9
D.N.T. Zoysa	c Young, b Davis	0	not out	16
M. Muralitharan	c Cairns, b Doull	0	c and b Doull	26
	lb 10, w 1	11	lb 9, nb 3	12
		222		328

	O	M	R	W	O	M	R	W
Doull	21.2	5	58	5	20.3	5	82	3
Davis	19	6	34	3	22	2	79	1
Horne	6	5	4	–	4	2	18	–
Astle	3	–	11	–	15	3	51	2
Patel	22	4	67	2	10	3	36	1
Vettori	14	5	38	–	15	3	53	2

Fall of Wickets
1–**4**, 2–**55**, 3–**58**, 4–**58**, 5–**79**, 6–**135**, 7–**141**, 8–**214**, 9–**215**
1–**49**, 2–**82**, 3–**85**, 4–**99**, 5–**115**, 6–**133**, 7–**270**, 8–**271**, 9–**285**

Umpires: C.E. King & I.D. Robinson

New Zealand won by an innings and 36 runs

Second Test Match – New Zealand v. Sri Lanka
14, 15, 16 and 17 March 1997 at Trust Bank Park, Hamilton

New Zealand

	First Innings		Second Innings	
B.A. Pocock	c Tillekeratne, b Muralitharan	85	(2) c Mahanama, b Zoysa	7
B.A. Young	run out	4	(1) c Ranatunga, b Dharmasena	62
M.J. Horne	b Zoysa	21	st Kaluwitharana, b Muralitharan	16
S.P. Fleming (Capt)	c Mahanama, b Zoysa,	2	b Muralitharan	59
N.J. Astle	lbw, b Zoysa	0	c Mahanama, b Vaas	52
C.L. Cairns	c Ranatunga, b Dharmasena	10	c sub (Chandana), b Muralitharan	4
*A.C. Parore	run out	25	run out	2
D.N. Patel	c Dharmasena, b Muralitharan	13	c P.A. de Silva, b Dharmasena	4
D.L. Vettori	b Muralitharan	4	b Zoysa	6
S.B. Doull	c P.A. de Silva, b Vaas	20	c Mahanama, b Zoysa	25
H.T. Davis	not out	8	not out	2
	b 11, lb 9, nb 10	30	b 9, lb 11, w 7, nb 7	34
		222		273

	O	M	R	W	O	M	R	W
Vaas	12.4	1	32	1	15	3	34	1
Zoysa	18	3	47	3	22.4	7	53	3
S.C. de Silva	15	4	36	–	10	2	29	–
Dharmasena	22	7	39	1	24	5	75	2
Muralitharan	22	4	43	3	26	7	62	3
Jayasuriya	1	–	5	–				

Fall of Wickets
1–**19**, 2–**88**, 3–**96**, 4–**100**, 5–**126**, 6–**172**, 7–**172**, 8–**178**, 9–**203**
1–**14**, 2–**64**, 3–**108**, 4–**183**, 5–**198**, 6–**201**, 7–**211**, 8–**239**, 9–**243**

Sri Lanka

	First Innings		Second Innings	
S.T. Jayasuriya	c Astle, b Davis	20	run out	3
R.S. Mahanama	lbw, b Vettori	45	lbw, b Doull	65
H.P. Tillekeratne	c Young, b Doull	2	b Vettori	10
P.A. de Silva	c Parore, b Vettori	1	(5) lbw, b Doull	5
A. Ranatunga (Capt)	lbw, b Davis	4	(6) c Doull, b Vettori	33
*R.S. Kaluwitharana	c Parore, b Davis	11	(7) lbw, c Doull	13
H.D.P.K. Dharmasena	c Fleming, b Davis	27	not out	38
W.P.U.J.C. Vaas	c Pocock, b Vettori	28	(1) c Patel, b Vettori	8
D.N.T. Zoysa	c Doull, b Vettori	14	c Parore, b Vettori	13
S.C. de Silva	not out	0	c Young, b Davis	7
M. Muralitharan	c Parore, b Davis	5	c Cairns, b Vettori	0
	lb 9, w 1, nb 3	13	b 4, lb 5, w 1	10
		170		205

	O	M	R	W	O	M	R	W
Doull	13	4	19	1	15	4	34	3
Davis	20.2	3	63	5	17	4	35	1
Astle	3	1	8	–	3	1	9	–
Vettori	24	8	46	4	29.2	8	84	5
Patel	8	2	25	–	12	5	34	–

Fall of Wickets
1–**39**, 2–**57**, 3–**58**, 4–**76**, 5–**87**, 6–**93**, 7–**144**, 8–**154**, 9–**165**
1–**5**, 2–**16**, 3–**40**, 4–**50**, 5–**129**, 6–**147**, 7–**152**, 8–**185**, 9–**186**

Umpires: D.B. Cowie & Mahboob Shah

New Zealand won by 120 runs

Cairns held out for more than an hour before falling to Dharmasena, and Parore and Pocock were out at the same score. Pocock had kept the innings together for 288 minutes and hit five fours, but Muralitharan was obtaining considerable turn and dismissed Pocock, Patel and Vettori in quick succession. Defiance came from Doull, 20 off 30 balls, but the day belonged to Sri Lanka.

The second day however, did not. There was a sound opening stand between Jayasuriya and Mahanama, which was broken by Davis. The fast bowler was to have an outstanding game, capturing five wickets in a Test innings for the first time, but Vettori's spin also played a major part in the demise of Sri Lanka. Six wickets went down as 54 runs were scored before Kaluwitharana and Dharamsena temporarily halted the slide with a stand of 47 in an hour and a half, but New Zealand had seized an advantage that should not have been theirs. The usually dependable Pocock was caught at slip off the impressive Zoysa, but Young and Horne advanced the score to 53 by the close, a lead of 105.

New Zealand displayed a professional approach on the third day, attempting to build solidly against spinners who were favoured by the conditions. Young, Fleming and Astle took them to a strong position at 198 for 4 before there came a clatter of wickets. Again it was Doull who brought life to the tail with 25 off 30 balls, and Sri Lanka were left more than two days in which to score 326 to win. They had enjoyed one moment of history in that, when he bowled Fleming, Muralitharan became the first Sri Lankan bowler to take 100 wickets in Test cricket.

Sri Lanka's bid for victory had the worst of starts. In the second over of the innings, Jayasuriya turned Davis behind square-leg and went for an unwise second run. Doull's fierce and accurate return to Parore found Jayasuriya short of his ground. Worse followed, for in the ninth over of the innings, Vettori bowled Tillekeratne round his legs so that Sri Lanka limped to 20 for 2 in 11 overs by the close.

Blair Pocock, a durable opener, grinds his way to 85 in the second Test. (Andrew Cornaga/Sportsline)

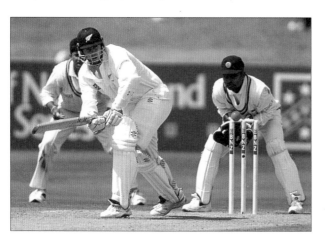

A five-wicket haul for Heath Davis against Sri Lanka at Hamilton. (David Munden/Sportsline)

Vaas and, vitally, Aravinda de Silva were soon out on the fourth morning. Mahanama, who batted for four-and-a-quarter hours, and Ranatunga shared an encouraging stand of 79, but there was no real resistance after that. Daniel Vettori, the 18-year-old left-arm spinner, confirmed his immense talent with his first five-wicket haul in Test cricket. He bowled with intelligence, variety and accuracy, and his coming has helped transform the New Zealand side, which is starting to look as if it is emerging from a troubled time.

Sri Lanka were a bitter disappointment. They not only failed to do themselves justice, but, for the most part, they played some poor cricket and lacked their usual spirit.

It was certainly not a tour they will remember with much pleasure, for the one-day international scheduled for Auckland was abandoned without a ball being bowled.

20 March 1997
at McLean Park, Napier
Central Districts 227 (M.S. Sinclair 67, C.M. Spearman 56, S.T. Jayasuriya 5 for 37)
Sri Lankans 228 for 4 (A. Ranatunga 96 not out)
Sri Lankans won by 6 wickets

In the warm-up match before the limited-over series, the Sri Lankans were sped to victory by skipper Ranatunga who steered his side home with 6.3 overs remaining.

One-Day Internationals

New Zealand v. Sri Lanka

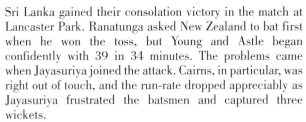

Sri Lanka gained their consolation victory in the match at Lancaster Park. Ranatunga asked New Zealand to bat first when he won the toss, but Young and Astle began confidently with 39 in 34 minutes. The problems came when Jayasuriya joined the attack. Cairns, in particular, was right out of touch, and the run-rate dropped appreciably as Jayasuriya frustrated the batsmen and captured three wickets.

It was Jayasuriya the batsman who then took over. He hit four sixes and eight fours and dominated an opening stand of 68 in 40 minutes. Two wickets fell quickly, but Aravinda de Silva hit 66 off 70 balls, and Sri Lanka won with 19.1 overs to spare. Jayasuriya, who took 24 off one over from Doull, reached 79 off 63 balls.

New Zealand introduced medium-pacer Andrew Penn to international cricket in the match at Basin Reserve, but, like Daniel Vettori, he found the initiation in limited-over contests rather difficult. Sri Lanka again asked New Zealand to bat first with much the same result as in the first encounter. Cairns found form with 56 off 79 balls but runs were never easy to come by, particularly against Vaas, who was in fine form. Davis struck an early blow for New Zealand when he bowled the dangerous Jayasuriya third ball. Kaluwitharana was sparkling, but Aravinda de Silva was surprisingly subdued in spite of hitting a six and five fours, and his 36 occupied 75 balls. He was forced on to the defensive because none of his colleagues could master the bowling of Davis and Astle, and New Zealand won with surprising ease to level the series.

So New Zealand could gain some satisfaction in the end. New captain Stephen Fleming had certainly started his career on a high note, and there was confidently quiet optimism.

Chris Cairns, who had been unable to bowl against Sri Lanka, underwent surgery at the end of the season.

First One-Day International – New Zealand v. Sri Lanka
25 March 1997 at Lancaster Park, Christchurch

New Zealand

B.A. Young	b Zoysa	21
N.J. Astle	c Mahanama, b Zoysa	23
M.J. Horne	b Muralitharan	13
S.P. Fleming (Capt)	run out	31
C.L. Cairns	c Dharmasena, b Jayasuriya	27
*A.C. Parore	c and b Jayasuriya	19
C.Z. Harris	not out	38
G.R. Larsen	c de Silva, b Muralitharan	13
S.B. Doull	c and b Jayasuriya	1
D.L. Vettori	b de Silva	4
H.T. Davis	not out	4
	lb 1, w 2, nb 4	7
	50 overs (for 9 wickets)	201

Sri Lanka

S.T. Jayasuriya	c Larsen, b Harris	79
*R.S. Kaluwitharana	c Cairns, b Harris	15
R.S. Mahanama	c Cairns, b Larsen	4
P.A. de Silva	b Astle	66
A. Ranatunga (Capt)	not out	19
H.P. Tillekeratne	not out	13
H.D.P.K. Dharmasena		
U.U. Chandana		
W.P.U.J.C. Vaas		
D.N.T. Voysa		
M. Muralitharan		
	b 1, w 3, nb 2	6
	30.5 overs (for 4 wickets)	202

	O	M	R	W
Vaas	7	–	45	–
Zoysa	7	1	29	2
Dharmasena	10	–	32	–
Muralitharan	10	1	42	2
Jayasuriya	10	–	26	3
Chandana	4	–	22	–
de Silva	2	–	4	1

	O	M	R	W
Doull	5.5	1	38	–
Davis	8	–	58	2
Harris	10	–	38	2
Larsen	5	–	23	1
Vettori	2	–	21	–
Astle	5	–	23	1

Fall of Wickets
1–39, 2–49, 3–68, 4–104, 5–124, 6–142, 7–157, 8–164, 9–176

Fall of Wickets
1–68, 2–73, 3–137, 4–183

Umpires: D.B. Cowie & Mahboob Shah *Man of the Match:* S.T. Jayasuriya **Sri Lanka won by 6 wickets**

Second One-Day International – New Zealand v. Sri Lanka
27 March 1997 at Basin Reserve, Wellington

New Zealand

B.A. Young	lbw, **b** Vaas	2
N.J. Astle	**c** Muralitharan, **b** Zoysa	12
M.J. Horne	**c** Kaluwitharana, **b** Muralitharan	14
S.P. Fleming (Capt)	**c** Tillekeratne, **b** Zoysa	9
C.L. Cairns	**b** Vaas	56
C.Z. Harris	**b** Muralitharan	5
*A.C. Parore	run out	39
G.R. Larsen	run out	26
S.B. Doull	**c** Chandana, **b** Vaas	18
A.J. Penn	**c** de Silva, **b** Vaas	1
H.T. Davis	not out	1
	lb **8**, w **8**, nb **2**	18
	49.2 overs	**201**

	O	M	R	**W**
Vaas	9.2	1	26	4
Zoysa	10	1	47	2
Dharmasena	10	–	41	–
Muralitharan	10	1	32	2
Jayasuriya	5	–	30	–
Ranatunga	5	–	17	–

Fall of Wickets
1–**17**, 2–**17**, 3–**28**, 4–**71**, 5–**91**, 6–**125**, 7–**156**, 8–**199**, 9–**199**

Sri Lanka

S.T. Jayasuriya	**b** Davis	0
*R.S. Kaluwitharana	lbw, **b** Davis	23
R.S. Mahanama	**c** Young, **b** Doull	10
P.A. de Silva	**c** Fleming, **b** Davis	36
A. Ranatunga (Capt)	**b** Harris	16
H.P. Tillekeratne	**b** Astle	8
H.D.P.K. Dharmasena	**st** Parore, **b** Harris	2
U.U. Chandana	lbw, **b** Astle	3
W.P.U.J.C. Vaas	**c** Doull, **b** Astle	0
D.N.T. Zoysa	not out	3
M. Muralitharan	**b** Davis	2
	lb **13**, w **16**	29
	38.1 overs	**132**

	O	M	R	**W**
Penn	2	–	14	–
Davis	8.2	–	35	4
Doull	5	–	21	1
Larsen	7	5	9	–
Harris	10	2	31	2
Astle	6	1	9	3

Fall of Wickets
1–**10**, 2–**49**, 3–**57**, 4–**87**, 5–**113**, 6–**116**, 7–**121**, 8–**125**, 9–**126**

Umpires: R.S. Dunne & E.A. Watkin   *Man of the Match:* H.T. Davis

New Zealand won by 69 runs

Shell Cup

The Shell Cup competition dominated the early part of the New Zealand season with each team playing the other on a home and away basis. Canterbury were clear leaders in the qualifying rounds, winning seven of their ten matches. In the opening game, Craig McMillan showed his all-round strength with 5 for 38 and 74 not out off 72 balls against Northern Districts. Canterbury also provided the first centuries of the season's competition when Murray and Fleming scored hundreds against Central Districts. Fleming's 105 came off 86 balls and included 13 fours.

Auckland's Chris Brown had remarkable figures of 5 for 16 in 10 overs in the victory over Otago at Eden Park. Otago finished bottom of the table. Cairns, Penn and Wisneski all took six wickets in an innings.

Matthew Hart (Northern Districts), 100 off 101 balls, Chris Cairns (Canterbury), Scott Weenink (Central Districts), Nathan Astle (Canterbury), Mark Richardson (Otago), twice, Llorne Howell (Central Districts) and Roger Twose (Wellington) twice, were the century-makers, but they were eclipsed by Aravinda de Silva who, playing for Auckland against Canterbury at Eden Park, hit 106 out of 141. His runs came off 66 balls and included three sixes and 16 fours. It was the fastest century recorded in the competition. On this occasion, Canterbury were beaten, but they went on to win the final, beating Wellington at Basin Reserve by 123 runs.

Shell Trophy

25, 26, 27 and 28 November 1996
at Victoria Park, Wanganui
Otago 227 (M.J. Horne 124, A.J. Penn 4 for 47) and 271 (M.J. Horne 90, A.J. Penn 6 for 54)
Central Districts 263 (M.S. Sinclair 85, P.J. Wiseman 5 for 80) and 236 for 7 (M.S. Sinclair 83)
Central Districts won by 3 wickets
Central Districts 12 pts, Otago 0 pts

at Basin Reserve, Wellington
Auckland 119 (R.G. Petrie 4 for 32, S.J. Hotter 4 for 33) and 246 (S.M. Lynch 79 not out)
Wellington 365 (P.J.B. Chandler 177, R.G. Twose 63, C.J. Drum 4 for 51) and 1 for 0
Wellington won by 10 wickets
Wellington 12 pts, Auckland 0 pts

at Lancaster Park, Christchurch
Northern Districts 518 for 4 dec. (G.E. Bradburn 148 not out, M.E. Parlane 142, B.A. Pocock 137)
Canterbury 549 (C.D. McMillan 159, D.J. Murray 153, M.W. Priest 67 not out)
Match drawn
Canterbury 4 pts, Northern Districts 0 pts

With the national team away on active service, there was an opportunity for young players to bring themselves to the notice of the selectors and for more experienced players to reassert their claims. It was one of the more mature players, Matthew Horne, who was the first to make a mark. He had played little in 1995–96, but he was the first first-class centurion of the new season. It was his batting that saved Otago from total disaster, but it was the bowling of Andrew Penn, ten wickets in a match and five wickets in an innings for the first time, and the batting of the 21-year-old Matthew Sinclair that won the game for Central Districts. Sinclair, playing his fourth first-class game, reached fifty for the first time.

Wellington destroyed Auckland inside three days. Philip Chandler, who had never before reached fifty, hit 177 in six hours. His innings included 29 fours, and he and Twose scored 160 for the third wicket.

Northern Districts made their highest ever score against Canterbury as Bradburn and Parlane made career-best scores, and skipper Pocock, too, hit a century. In spite of these achievements, it was Canterbury who took first innings points in this run-saturated game. They made their highest ever score against Northern Districts with Murray returning after a year's absence to hit 153 and McMillan making a career best.

30 November, 1, 2 and 3 December 1996
at Eden Park Outer Oval, Auckland
Auckland 109 (A.J. Penn 6 for 36) and 198 for 4 dec.
Central Districts 61 (C.M. Brown 5 for 21) and 77 for 7
Match drawn
Auckland 4 pts, Central Districts 0 pts

at Harry Barker Reserve, Gisborne
Northern Districts 474 (M.E. Parlane 104, R.G. Hart 78, A.R. Tait 70, B.A. Pocock 53)
Wellington 238 (J.D. Wells 52) and 213 (P.J.B. Chandler 69, S.B. Styris 6 for 42)
Northern Districts won by an innings and 23 runs
Northern District 12 pts, Wellington 0 pts

at Centennial Park, Oamaru
Canterbury 162 (B.J.K. Doody 79, J.W. Wilson 5 for 34) and 303 (G.D. McMillan 129, P.J. Wiseman 5 for 88)
Otago 191 (R.A. Lawson 98, G.I. Allott 6 for 60) and 152 (J.W. Wilson 69 not out, W.A. Wisneski 4 for 37, G.I. Allott 4 for 49)
Canterbury won by 122 runs
Canterbury 8 pts, Otago 4 pts

There was no play on the second day in Auckland, and only 32.2 overs were possible on the fourth day. There was enough time for medium-pacer Andrew Penn to return career-best bowling figures for the third innings in succession.

Northern Districts scored heavily for the second match in succession and beat Wellington by an innings. Michael Parlane hit his second century of the season, but

the outstanding performances came from Robert Hart and Alex Tait, who made career-best scores and shared a ninth wicket partnership of 139. Scott Styris, who made an excellent impression in two matches the previous season, returned the best bowling figures of his career.

Lawson's 98 off 165 balls took Otago to a first innings lead over Canterbury, but Craig McMillan responded with three sixes and 12 fours in his second century in as many matches. Geoff Allott then completed ten wickets in a match for the first time as Otago crumpled. Jeff Wilson, 69 off 54 balls with three sixes and seven fours saved Otago from total humiliation after they had slumped to 57 for 6.

17, 18, 20 and 21 January 1997
at Basin Reserve, Welllington
Wellington 147 (S.B. O'Connor 5 for 43) and 135 (P.J. Wiseman 8 for 66)
Otago 250 (M.J. Horne 103, M.H. Richardson 59, S.J. Hotter 6 for 69) and 36 for 0
Otago won by 10 wickets
Otago 12 pts, Wellington 0 pts

20, 21, 22 and 23 January 1997
at Dudley Park, Rangiora
Central Districts 347 (M.J Greatbatch 141, M.W. Priest 4 for 92) and 185 (C.M. Spearman 96, M.W. Priest 5 for 57)
Canterbury 543 for 8 dec. (C.Z. Harris 251 not out, M.E.L. Lane 61, M.W. Priest 56)
Canterbury won by an innings and 11 runs
Canterbury 12 pts, Central Districts 0 pts

With the England tour under way and the New Zealand side back from their travels, the Shell Trophy matches had an added urgency. Matthew Horne's second century of the season helped Otago to their first victory, but the most notable feature of the match at Basin Reserve was the bowling of Paul Wiseman. Nearing his 27th birthday, the off-spinner took 10 for 107 in the match, and his second innings figures of 8 for 66 were the best of his career. Left-arm medium-pacer Steve Hotter also returned the best figures of his career but finished on the losing side.

Mark Greatbatch returned to lead Central Districts and celebrated with a century, but his side lost to Canterbury by an innings. This was due mainly to Chris Harris hitting the first double hundred of his career. The all-rounder faced 531 balls and hit 29 fours in his unbeaten 251, which occupied 13 minutes under ten hours. Craig Spearman hit 96 off 115 balls, but the game was over early on the fourth day.

27, 28, 29 and 30 January 1997
at Trafalgar Park, Nelson
Northern Districts 386 (M.D. Bailey 101, M.D. Bell 66, A.J. Penn 5 for 89) and 194 (C.J.M. Furlong 7 for 72)

Central Districts 245 (M.D.J. Walker 84, D.L. Vettori 5 for 61, A.R. Tait 4 for 50) and 180 (M.S. Sinclair 70, G.E. Bradburn 4 for 12)
Northern Districts won by 155 runs
Northern Districts 12 pts, Central Districts 0 pts

at Lancaster Park, Christchurch
Wellington 212 (J.D. Wells 69, J.M. Aiken 50, C.Z. Harris 4 for 22) and 245 (R.G. Petrie 80, M.W. Priest 4 for 59)
Canterbury 489 (C.D. McMillan 157, C.Z. Harris 93, M.A. Hastings 52, G.R. Jonas 4 for 49, R.G. Petrie 4 for 78)
Canterbury won by an innings and 32 runs
Canterbury 12 pts, Wellington 0 pts

at Carisbrook, Dunedin
Auckland 272 (S.M. Lynch 85, S.J. Peterson 71, R.J. Kennedy 4 for 44, S.B. O'Connor 4 for 83) and 307 (R.A. Jones 99, A.C. Barnes 52, R.T. King 52, S.B. O'Connor 6 for 55)
Otago 548 for 8 dec. (C.B. Gaffaney 194, M.J. Horne 112, C.J. Drum 4 for 102) and 34 for 0
Otago won by 10 wickets
Otago 12 pts, Auckland 0 pts

What was for four of the associations the fourth round of matches in the Shell Trophy was an offence to the traditions of the game and brought no credit to those who administer cricket in New Zealand. The last two days of the first Test match between England and New Zealand coincided with the first two days of this round of Shell Trophy matches, and the last day of the Trophy matches coincided with the first day of the game between England and New Zealand 'A'. Such chaotic fixture scheduling could surely have been avoided, and what it led to was an insult to cricket. Players were withdrawn from Trophy sides to appear in the 'A' side even though they had batted and bowled on the first two days. They were replaced by others who had not started the match so that 13 men represented Central Districts and Wellington, 12 appeared for Auckland and 14 for Otago.

From this confusion several things emerged. Off-break bowler Campbell Furlong produced the best bowling figures of his career for Central Districts against Northern Districts, but Northern won the match comfortably, and the bowler to catch the eye was a young left-arm spinner named Vettori who took 8 for 142 in his debut match.

Craig McMillan hit his third century of the season and shared a fifth wicket stand of 183 with Chris Harris as Canterbury beat Wellington. Both fell to Jonas who did not join the game until the third day.

Otago gained their second victory in succession. Left-arm fast medium bowler Shayne O'Connor, 23 years old, had career best figures for innings and match, and Chris Gaffaney and Matthew Horne both hit centuries. For Horne it was the third of the season. Gaffaney, just turned 21, had played four times in 1995–96, his debut season, and had managed just 119 runs. Now he hit three sixes and 27 fours as he plundered 194 off 234 balls in four-and-a-half hours.

Matthew Horne, a century for Otago in the opening round of the Shell Trophy and later a place in the New Zealand side. (Graham Chadwick/Allsport)

3, 4, 5 and 6 February 1997
at Trust Bank Park, Hamilton
Auckland 126 (A.R. Tait 9 for 48) and 245 (A.C. Barnes 89, R.A. Jones 54, A.R. Tait 7 for 82)
Northern Districts 127 (C.J. Drum 4 for 33) and 32 (C.J. Drum 4 for 13)
Auckland won by 212 runs
Auckland 8 pts, Northern Districts 4 pts

Medium-pacer Alex Tait had never taken six wickets in an innings nor ten wickets in a match before Northern Districts' game against Auckland. His 9 for 48 in the first innings and his match figures of 16 for 130 were both records for Northern Districts. In spite of Tait's remarkable performance, Northern, who led by one run on the first innings, were comprehensively beaten. They were bowled out for 32 in 24.5 overs in their second innings, the lowest score in their history, and the match was over before lunch-time on the fourth day.

10, 11, 12 and 13 February 1997
at Eden Park, Auckland
Auckland 293 (H.D. Barton 76 not out, S.M. Lynch 68, W.A. Wisneski 4 for 83, M.W. Priest 4 for 104) and 100 (M.W. Priest 5 for 31, W.A. Wisneski 4 for 37)
Canterbury 301 (C.D. Cumming 60, M.W. Priest 50) and 93 for 4 (D.K. Morrison 4 for 19)
Canterbury won by 6 wickets
Canterbury 12 pts, Auckland 0 pts

their own bowling hero in David Sewell, left-arm medium fast, 19 years old, with one match to his credit in 1995–96. Sewell bowled Otago to victory with match figures of 10 for 130. He also showed he knew how to use a bat, hitting 22 off 40 balls with a six and two fours at number 11.

Another young man to gain plaudits was Matthew Sinclair, whose maiden first-class hundred in what was only his second season set up Central's victory over Wellington. Sinclair hit a six and 32 fours in his 293-ball innings. Penn, too, added to his growing reputation with another nine-wicket haul.

Heath Davis left the match at the end of the third day to join the New Zealand side, and he was replaced by Hotter, who took the two Central wickets that fell in the second innings.

23, 24, 25, and 26 February 1997
at Trust Bank Park, Hamilton
Wellington 247 (S.J. Blackmore 78, D.L. Vettori 5 for 82, A.R. Tait 4 for 59) and 212 (R.G. Petrie 56, D.L. Vettori 4 for 79)
Northern Districts 244 (D.J. Nash 76, S.B. Styris 56, S.J. Hotter 6 for 77) and 201 (J.A. Yovich 78, S.J. Hotter 5 for 48, G.R. Jonas 4 for 51)
Wellington won by 14 runs
Wellington 12 pts, Northern Districts 0 pts

at Lancaster Park, Christchurch
Auckland 172 (S.M. Lynch 55, S.E. Bond 5 for 59) and 233 (S.M. Lynch 94, M.A. Hastings 4 for 37)
Canterbury 223 (B.J.K. Doody 93, C.J. Drum 6 for 47) and 184 for 3 (C.M. Cumming 90 not out)
Canterbury won by 7 wickets
Canterbury 12 pts, Auckland 0 pts

at Queen's Park, Invercargill
Central Districts 74 (D.G. Sewell 8 for 31) and 348 (C.M. Spearman 87, M.S. Sinclair 66, L.G. Howell 63)
Otago 347 (C.B. Gaffaney 100, M.H. Richardson 98 not out) and 77 for 5 (L.J. Hamilton 4 for 26)
Otago won by 5 wickets
Otago 12 pts, Central Districts 0 pts

Chris Harris, the first Canterbury player to score two double centuries in the Shell Trophy in one season. He also hit 198 in the Trophy final. Batsman of the season. (David Munden/Sportsline)

at Queen Elizabeth Park, Masterton
Wellington 263 (G.R. Larsen 76, A.J. Penn 4 for 43) and 166 (A.J. Penn 5 for 55)
Central Districts 411 (M.S. Sinclair 189, L.G. Howell, 66, H.T. Davis 4 for 88, G.R. Jonas 4 for 113) and 19 for 2
Central Districts won by 8 wickets
Central Districts 12 pts, Wellington 0 pts

at Molyneux Park, Alexandra
Northern Districts 141 (D.G. Sewell 6 for 58) and 236 (D.G. Sewell 4 for 72)
Otago 304 (S.A. Robinson 50, A.R. Tait 6 for 104) and 74 for 5
Otago won by 5 wickets
Otago 12 pts, Northern Districts 0 pts

Canterbury's fourth win in five matches placed them emphatically at the top of the Trophy table, eight points ahead of Otago, who beat Northern Districts. A week earlier, Alex Tait had become the first bowler to take 16 wickets in a first-class match in New Zealand, and he took another nine wickets for Northern Districts against Otago to bring his total to 25 wickets for 267 runs in four innings. Tait, 24 years old, had appeared in only seven matches in two seasons prior to 1996–97. In spite of his record-breaking feats, he again finished on the losing side, and Otago found

The sixth round of matches confirmed that Canterbury and Otago would meet in the Shell Trophy final. Although two rounds of matches were still to be played, neither side could be caught. Wellington's narrow win over Northern Districts had come too late to bring them into contention, and they could muse that their victory had been brought about by opening bowler Stephen Hotter who, having spent much of the season in reserve, returned career-best figures for match and innings.

Auckland offered only limp resistance to Canterbury, while Central Districts never recovered from the first day trauma against Otago. Sewell followed his fine performance of ten days earlier with the best bowling figures of his career, and Gaffaney showed maturity and rich promise in an innings of 100 off 156 balls.

15, 16, 17 and 18 March 1997
at Basin Reserve, Wellington
Wellington 285 (G.J. Wilkinson 77, G.R. Larsen 56) and 317 (S.J. Blackmore 102, G.J. Wilkinson 96, R.J. Kennedy 4 for 55)
Otago 292 (R.A. Lawson 79, C.B. Gaffaney 58, G.R. Larsen 5 for 33) and 311 for 7 (C.B. Gaffaney 74, R.A. Lawson 63)
Otago won by 3 wickets
Otago 12 pts, Wellington 0 pts

at Eden Park Outer Oval, Auckland
Auckland 229 (A.C. Barnes 81, J.A. Yovich 5 for 66) and 180 (R.A. Jones 79, G.E. Bradburn 4 for 40)
Northern Districts 351 (G.E. Bradburn 88, M.N. Hart 61) and 59 for 0
Northern Districts won by 10 wickets
Northern Districts 12 pts, Auckland 0 pts

at Horton Park, Blenheim
Central Districts 285 (L.G. Howell 91) and 392 (M.S. Sinclair 78, M.D.J. Walker 63, G.P. Sulzberger 56, M.W. Priest 6 for 146)
Canterbury 537 (C.Z. Harris 206, G.R. Stead 124, C.E. Bulfin 5 for 111) and 142 for 6 (C.E. Bulfin 5 for 53)
Canterbury won by 4 wickets
Canterbury 12 pts, Central Districts 0 pts

Openers Lawson and Gaffaney began Otago's innings against Wellington with partnerships of 145 and 131 and played a major part in their side's fifth consecutive win. Blackmore's patient maiden century and his fifth wicket stand of 145 with Wilkinson served only to delay the inevitable.

Auckland's miserable season continued when they were soundly beaten by Northern Districts, for whom Grant Bradburn and Matthew Hart had outstanding all-round matches. Canterbury, too, had a resounding victory, their sixth of the season. Facing a total of 285, they were struggling at 35 for 4 when Gary Stead joined Chris Harris. The pair added 290 in 282 minutes, and Harris became the first Canterbury player to score two double centuries in the Shell Trophy. Central Districts' consolation was in the bowling of Bulfin who took five wickets in an innings and ten wickets in a match for the first time.

22, 23, 24 and 25 March 1997
at Trust Bank Park, Hamilton
Northern Districts 353 for 9 dec. (M.D. Bell 73, B.A. Pocock 69, M.N. Hart 60) and 0 for 0 dec.
Central Districts 34 for 2 dec. and 320 for 4 (M.S. Sinclair 99 not out, M.J. Greatbatch 72, C.M. Spearman 57)
Central Districts won by 6 wickets
Central Districts 8 pts, Northern Districts 4 pts

at Molyneux Park, Alexandra
Otago 126 (J.T.C. Vaughan 8 for 27) and 179 (M.H. Austen 50, D.K. Morrison 5 for 66)
Auckland 137 (R.A. Jones 54, A.J. Gale 4 for 43) and 169 for 7 (S.M. Lynch 60)
Auckland won by 3 wickets
Auckland 12 pts, Otago 0 pts

at Basin Reserve, Wellington
Wellington v. **Canterbury**
Match abandoned
Wellington 2 pts, Canterbury 2 pts

Rain badly interfered with the last round of matches and caused one to be abandoned completely. There was no play on the first two days in Hamilton and a result was reached only by a freak declaration and a forfeiture. Matthew Sinclair ended an excellent season with the bat in fine style, being unbeaten one short of his second century when the winning hit was made.

There was no play on the first day at Alexandra. The second day saw two bowlers gaining the limelight. Vaughan produced the best bowling figures of his career, and Morrison was fined for unacceptable behaviour when an appeal for caught behind against Gaffaney was rejected. In spite of this, Auckland gained their second win of the season, but still held the wooden spoon.

Shell Trophy Final Table

	P	W	L	D	Ab	Pts
Canterbury	8	6	–	1	1	74
Otago	8	5	3	–	–	64
Northern Districts	8	3	4	1	–	44
Central Districts	8	3	4	1	–	32
Wellington	8	2	5	–	1	26
Auckland	8	2	5	1	–	24

Shell Trophy Final

29, 30, 31 March and 1 April 1997
at Lancaster Park, Christchurch
Canterbury 777 (C.Z. Harris 198, N.J. Astle 160, C.D. McMillan 94, S.P. Fleming 66, D.J. Murray 59, C.L. Cairns 57, M.W. Priest 56, P.J. Wiseman 4 for 172)
Otago 189 (M.J. Horne 98, N.J. Astle 6 for 22) and 306 for 8 (M.H. Austen 100 not out, P.J. Wiseman 73)
Match drawn

Having dominated the qualifying games, Canterbury won the Shell Trophy by virtue of having finished top of the table and having the better of a draw in the final against Otago. The final was a match of records.

Canterbury batted for the first two days to reach the highest score ever made in first-class cricket in New

Zealand. They made 777 off 1348 balls in 808 minutes, and the innings included ten sixes and 96 fours.

In scoring his third century of the season, Harris joined McMillan and Walter Hadlee with the record number of centuries in a season for Canterbury. McMillan's 809 runs in the competition established a Canterbury record.

Stead, Murray and Fleming gave Canterbury a sound start, and when McMillan joined Harris the score was 183 for 3. The pair added 124 in 113 minutes. McMillan's 94 came off 106 balls and included three sixes and 12 fours.

Harris was on 69 and Astle on 64 when Canterbury ended the first day at 415 for 4, and next day they were not separated until the score was 543. Their stand of 236 was a fifth wicket record for Canterbury against Otago. Astle hit

five sixes and 23 fours in his 221-ball innings while Harris hit two sixes and 21 fours.

Nathan Astle confirmed his status as Man of the Match when he returned the best bowling figures of his career as Otago were shot out on the third day and forced to follow on. Astle took 6 for 22 in 8.4 overs with only Horne's three-hour innings offering real resistance. Batting a second time, Otago could hope only to achieve a draw, and for saving the match they had to thank Michael Austen, born in Cape Town and formerly of Wellington and Western Province. He scored an unbeaten century that occupied 487 minutes and during which he faced 413 balls. His century came off 390 balls and was the slowest ever century in domestic first-class cricket in New Zealand.

First Class Averages

Batting

	M	Inns	NO	Runs	HS	Av	100s	50s
C.Z. Harris	5	7	1	835	251*	139.16	3	2
C.D. McMillan	8	12	1	809	159	73.54	3	2
B.A. Young	6	11	1	510	267*	51.00	1	2
M.J. Horne	10	17	–	843	124	49.58	3	4
M.S. Sinclair	8	16	1	722	189	48.13	1	6
N.J. Astle	6	10	1	411	160	45.66	2	1
J.W. Wilson	2	4	1	135	69*	45.00		1
M.W. Priest	8	11	3	357	67*	44.62		4
M.D.J. Walker	5	9	1	340	84	42.50		2
G.R. Stead	8	12	2	405	124	40.50	1	
C.B. Gaffaney	9	18	2	642	194	40.12	2	2
S.P. Fleming	6	10	–	390	129	39.00	1	4
B.A. Pocock	11	18	–	682	137	37.88	1	6
C.D. Cumming	6	9	1	287	90*	35.87		2
S.M. Lynch	8	16	1	536	94	35.73		6
L.G. Howell	10	19	2	604	91	35.52		4
G.R. Larsen	3	6	–	211	76	35.16		2
M.E. Parlane	9	14	–	489	142	34.92	2	1
C.L. Cairns	6	10	–	349	70	34.90		5
R.A. Lawson	9	18	2	549	98	34.31		3
M.A. Hastings	4	4	1	101	52	33.66		1
P.J.B. Chandler	8	15	1	466	177	33.28	1	1
G.E. Bradburn	8	12	1	362	148*	32.90	1	1
M.J. Greatbatch	6	10	–	321	141	32.10	1	1
S.J. Peterson	4	8	1	224	71	32.00		1
M.D. Bell	8	13	1	380	73	31.66		3
A.C. Barnes	8	16	1	438	89*	29.20		3
R.G. Petrie	7	13	1	347	80	28.91		2
C.M. Spearman	8	15	1	401	96	28.64		3
R.A. Jones	8	16	–	455	99	28.43		4
M.H. Richardson	9	16	1	423	98*	28.20		2
M.H. Austen	5	10	1	252	100*	28.00	1	1
B.J.K. Doody	7	11	–	295	93	26.81		2
M.P. Maynard	4	6	1	129	47*	25.80		
D.J. Murray	9	14	–	355	153	25.35	1	1
S.B. Styris	7	11	3	202	56	25.25		1
R.G. Hart	9	13	1	299	78	24.91		1
D.J. Nash	6	10	–	248	76	24.80		1
S.J. Blackmore	6	12	1	272	102	24.72	1	1
S.B. O'Connor	7	11	3	196	47	24.50		
M.R. Jefferson	7	13	5	186	35*	23.25		
C.J.M. Furlong	6	9	1	179	39	22.37		
A.R. Tait	9	13	1	268	70	22.33		1
M.D. Bailey	9	14	–	306	101	21.85	1	
C.J. Nevin	7	13	2	238	42	21.63		
J.D. Wells	6	11	1	208	69	20.80		2
M.N. Hart	7	12	–	227	61	18.91		2
R.G. Twose	7	13	–	245	63	18.84		1
D.K. Morrison	7	14	6	150	30	18.75		
H.D. Barton	7	14	3	198	76*	18.00		1
G.R. Loveridge	5	10	1	158	49*	17.55		
M.E.L. Lane	6	7	–	121	61	17.28		1
R.T. King	4	8	–	137	52	17.12		1
A.C. Parore	6	11	–	184	59	16.72		1
J.M. Mills	8	14	3	165	40*	15.00		
P.J. Wiseman	11	17	2	221	73	14.73		1
W.A. Wisneski	7	8	1	103	40	14.71		

Batting

	M	Inns	NO	Runs	HS	Av	100s	50s
A.J. Gale	7	11	2	132	44	14.66		
M.G. Croy	6	12	1	157	35	14.27		
G.R. Sulzberger	8	16	1	212	56	14.13		1
J.T.C. Vaughan	7	14	–	192	38	13.71		
J.M. Aiken	5	8	–	107	50	13.37		1
D.L. Vettori	7	13	5	100	29*	12.50		
J.C. Forrest	6	12	–	133	34	11.08		

(Qualification: 100 runs, average 10.00)
(G. Wilkinson, one match, 96 & 77)

Bowling

	Overs	Mds	Runs	Wks	Av	Best	10/m	5/inn
A.J. Penn	237.1	79	552	36	15.33	6/36	1	4
A.R. Tait	377.2	120	865	53	16.32	9/48	1	4
C.J. Drum	198.4	56	523	30	17.43	6/47		
D.L. Vettori	350.5	111	762	36	21.16	5/61		3
D.K. Morrison	203.2	46	574	27	21.25	5/66		1
J.T.C. Vaughan	178.2	55	425	20	21.25	8/27		1
S.J. Hotter	229.5	52	641	30	21.36	6/69	1	3
C.M. Brown	88	20	257	12	21.41	5/21		1
S.B. O'Connor	190.5	43	602	28	21.50	6/55	1	2
M.A. Hastings	105.1	30	221	10	22.10	4/37		
R.J. Kennedy	208.1	50	563	25	22.52	4/44		
G.I. Allott	224	44	689	30	22.96	6/60	1	1
N.J. Astle	121.4	36	280	12	23.33	6/22		1
S.B. Doull	175.3	49	492	21	23.42	5/58		2
P.J. Wiseman	365.1	80	968	40	24.20	8/66	1	3
D.G. Sewell	234.3	47	851	35	24.31	8/31	1	2
C.Z. Harris	126.3	40	244	10	24.40	4/22		
C. Bulfin	129	27	420	17	24.70	5/53	1	2
M.W. Priest	451.5	133	1023	41	24.95	6/146		3
S.E. Bond	175	43	530	21	25.23	5/59		1
H.T. Davis	276.2	69	769	29	26.51	5/63		1
G.R. Jonas	113.5	20	401	15	26.73	4/45		
R.G. Petrie	180.5	49	458	17	26.94	4/32		
W.A. Wisneski	257.5	79	745	27	27.59	4/37		
G.E. Bradburn	208.5	66	435	15	29.00	4/12		
A.J. Gale	228.4	65	595	20	29.75	4/43		
L.Hamilton	131	23	429	14	30.64	4/26		
S.B. Styris	196.2	42	617	18	34.27	6/42		1
G.R. Loveridge	149.3	23	472	11	42.90	4/23		
M.R. Jefferson	239	73	575	12	47.91	3/41		
C.J.M. Furlong	248.4	43	775	16	48.43	7/72		1

(Qualification – 10 wickets)

Leading Fielders

27 – J.M. Mills; 24 – M.G. Croy and R.G. Hart (ct 23 / st 1); 22 – M.E. Austin (ct 20 / st2) and C.J. Nevin (ct 20 / st 2); 14 – M.J. Horne and M.E.L. Lane (ct 13 / st 1); 12 – G.E. Bradburn and A.C. Parore; 11 – M.D. Bell and R.A. Jones; 10 – S.P. Fleming, C.B. Gaffaney, C.Z. Harris and M.S. Sinclair

Canada

The claim that cricket is a world game gained more credibility when Pakistan and India ventured to Canada to play a  five-match limited-over international series for the Sahara Cup. Both sides relied mainly on the players who had toured England only a few weeks earlier, although India recalled Kambli who had missed the trip to England for disciplinary reasons.

Man of the Series – Anil Kumble, 14 wickets in the Sahara Cup Tournament.
(David Munden/Sportsline)

Match One – India v. Pakistan
16 September 1996 at Toronto Cricket, Skating and Curling CLub

Pakistan				India			
Saeed Anwar	c and b Kumble	46		*N.R. Mongia	b Waqar Younis	9	
Aamir Sohail	c Dravid, b Srinath	12		S.R. Tendulkar (Capt)	not out	89	
Ijaz Ahmed	lbw, b Srinath	35		R.S. Dravid	c Aamir Sohail, b Salim Malik	39	
Inzamam-ul-Haq	c Kumble, b Venkatesh Prasad	5		M. Azharuddin	not out	30	
Salim Malik	c Joshi, b Kumble	3		V.G. Kambli			
Shadab Kabir	c Azharuddin, b Kumble	0		A.D. Jadeja			
Wasim Akram (Capt)	run out	9		S. Ganguly			
*Moin Khan	c Tendulkar, b Srinath	2		S.B. Joshi			
Azhar Mahmood	c Joshi, b Venkatesh Prasad	6		A.R. Kumble			
Saqlain Mushtaq	not out	22		J. Srinath			
Waqar Younis	not out	6		Venkatesh Prasad			
	lb 13, w 9, nb 2	24			lb 2, w 3, nb 1	6	
	33 overs (for 9 wickets)	170			29.5 overs (for 2 wickets)	173	

	O	M	R	**W**		O	M	R	**W**
Srinath	7	–	23	3	Waqar Younis	6	–	30	1
Venkatesh Prasad	7	–	38	2	Wasim Akram	6.5	–	37	–
Jadeja	4	–	30	–	Azhar Mahmood	4	–	19	–
Joshi	6	–	22	–	Aamir Sohail	3	–	25	–
Kumble	7	–	32	3	Saqlain Mushtaq	6	–	39	–
Tendulkar	2	–	12	–	Salim Malik	4	–	21	1

Fall of Wickets
1–**44**, 2–**80**, 3–**91**, 4–**98**, 5–**108**, 6–**123**, 7–**131**, 8–**135**, 9–**148**

Fall of Wickets
1–**18**, 2–**108**

Umpires: L.H. Barker & D.R. Shepherd *Man of the Match:* S.R. Tendulkar

India won by 8 wickets

The weather was not kind to the competition. The opening match should have been played on 14 September, but it had to be put back 48 hours because of rain, while the final match in the series was also delayed 48 hours due to rain.

Pakistan gave an international debut to Azhar Mahmood, a medium-pace bowler from Islamabad, and the match was reduced to 33 overs because of further rain. Venkatesh Prasad and Kumble tore out Pakistan's middle order, and with Tendulkar in his best form, India won with ease.

Pakistan gained revenge in dramatic fashion the following day. Dravid and Azharuddin added 161 for India's third wicket, and, facing a stiff target of 265, Pakistan slipped to 221 for 8. Saqlain Mushtaq joined Salim Malik in a stand that won the match, Salim hitting the fifth ball of Joshi's last over for four to bring victory. Salim Malik's 151-ball innings rightly earned him the individual award.

In the third match, the individual award went to Dravid, although Kumble and Venkatesh Prasad must have been strong contenders. India lost their last five wickets for 12 runs, but Pakistan were 16 for 3 after six overs. Saeed

Anwar and Salim Malik added 47, but three wickets then fell for three runs. Saqlain Mushtaq helped Moin Khan to add 33 for the eighth wicket, but, in spite of Moin's heroics – he was last out for 42 – Pakistan were well beaten.

Needing to win to level the series Pakistan, having been put in to bat, faltered and lost four wickets for 91 in the fourth match. Inzamam-ul-Haq then joined Ijaz Ahmed in a partnership worth 86 which transformed the game. Tight bowling by Wasim Akram and Saqlain Mushtaq saw India tumble to 64 for 6. Jadeja and Kapoor stopped the rot with a stand of 54, but this only delayed the inevitable.

Pakistan took the series by three matches to two when they won the final match by 52 runs in spite of a tendency to self-destruct. Three run outs took them from 195 for 6 to 197 for 9. Facing a target of 214, India began comfortably enough with a stand of 46, but Mushtaq Ahmed then wrought havoc and they collapsed to 99 for 7. There was no effective recovery, and Pakistan took the Sahara Cup.

The Man of the Series award went to Anil Kumble, who captured 13 wickets for 160 runs in the five matches.

Match Two – India v. Pakistan
17 September 1996 at Toronto Cricket, Skating and Curling Club

India

*N.R. Mongia	c Wasim Akram, b Azhar Mahmood	18
S.R. Tendulkar (Capt)	c Wasim Akram, b Azhar Mahmood	20
R.S. Dravid	b Saqlain Mushtaq	90
M. Azharuddin	c Azhar Mahmood, b Mushtaq Ahmed	88
V.G. Kambli	c Aamir Sohail, b Mushtaq Ahmed	3
A.D. Jadeja	not out	21
J. Srinath	c Wasim Akram, b Saqlain Mushtaq	0
S. Ganguly	not out	11
A.R. Kumble		
S.B. Joshi		
Venkatesh Prasad		
	b 4, lb 5, w 3, nb 1	13
	50 overs (for 6 wickets)	264

	O	M	R	W
Wasim Akram	10	1	52	–
Waqar Younis	6	–	37	–
Azhar Mahmood	9	2	38	2
Mushtaq Ahmed	9	–	47	2
Saqlain Mushtaq	10	–	39	2
Aamir Sohail	5	–	33	–
Salim Malik	1	–	9	–

Fall of Wickets
1–32, 2–44, 3–205, 4–214, 5–245, 6–245

Pakistan

Saeed Anwar	c Joshi, b Tendulkar	80
Aamir Sohail	c Mongia, b Venkatesh Prasad	0
Ijaz Ahmed	c Mongia, b Venkatesh Prasad	13
Inzamam-ul-Haq	c Dravid, b Kumble	29
Salim Malik	not out	70
*Moin Khan	c Azharuddin, b Joshi	14
Wasim Akram (Capt)	c Ganguly, b Srinath	20
Azhar Mahmood	run out	1
Mushtaq Ahmed	c and b Srinath	4
Saqlain Mushtaq	not out	11
Waqar Younis		
	b 4, lb 11, w 9	24
	49.5 overs (for 8 wickets)	266

	O	M	R	W
Srinath	10	–	53	2
Venkatesh Prasad	10	–	54	2
Jadeja	3	–	20	–
Joshi	9.5	1	57	1
Kumble	10	–	32	1
Tendulkar	7	–	35	1

Fall of Wickets
1–10, 2–44, 3–115, 4–144, 5–169, 6–213, 7–215, 8–221

Umpires: L.H. Barker & D.L. Orchard *Man of the Match:* Salim Malik

Pakistan won by 2 wickets

Match Three – India v. Pakistan
18 September 1996 at Toronto Cricket, Skating and Curling Club

India

*N.R. Mongia	lbw, b Wasim Akram	2
S.R. Tendulkar (Capt)	c Aamir Sohail, b Wasim Akram	2
R.S. Dravid	c Salim Elahi, b Saqlain Mushtaq	46
M. Azharuddin	st Moin Khan, b Aamir Sohail	38
V.G. Kambli	st Moin Khan, b Mushtaq Ahmed	29
A.D. Jadeja	b Wasim Akram	23
S.B. Joshi	run out	31
J. Srinath	c Saqlain Mushtaq, b Wasim Akram	3
A.R. Kapoor	c Mushtaq Ahmed, b Saqlain Mushtaq	0
A.R. Kumble	run out	2
Venkatesh Prasad	not out	0
	lb 8, w 7	15
	50 overs	191

	O	M	R	W
Wasim Akram	9	–	35	4
Waqar Younis	7	1	15	–
Azhar Mahmood	5	1	28	–
Mushtaq Ahmed	10	2	29	1
Aamir Sohail	9	1	31	1
Saqlain Mushtaq	10	–	45	2

Fall of Wickets
1–5, 2–14, 3–88, 4–103, 5–133, 6–179, 7–189, 8–189, 9–189

Pakistan

Saeed Anwar	c Tendulkar, b Kumble	28
Salim Elahi	c Kambli, b Srinath	4
Aamir Sohail	c Mongia, b Venkatesh Prasad	1
Ijaz Ahmed	c Mongia, b Venkatesh Prasad	0
Salim Malik	lbw, b Kumble	27
Azhar Mahmood	b Kumble	10
Wasim Akram (Capt)	st Mongia, b Kumble	0
*Moin Khan	c Mongia, b Srinath	42
Saqlain Mushtaq	c Tendulkar, b Venkatesh Prasad	9
Mushtaq Ahmed	st Mongia, b Joshi	1
Waqar Younis	not out	0
	b 1, lb 10, w 3	14
	42.4 overs	136

	O	M	R	W
Srinath	7.4	–	20	2
Venkatesh Prasad	9	3	22	3
Kapoor	6	–	27	–
Joshi	9	1	27	1
Kumble	7	2	12	4
Tendulkar	4	–	17	–

Fall of Wickets
1–9, 2–12, 3–16, 4–63, 5–66, 6–66, 7–91, 8–124, 9–131

Umpires: D.L. Orchard & D.R. Shepherd *Man of the Match:* R.S. Dravid

India won by 55 runs

Match Four – India *v.* Pakistan
21 September 1996 at Toronto Cricket, Skating and Curling Club

Pakistan

Aamir Sohail	c Srinath, b Joshi	23
Saeed Anwar	b Venkatesh Prasad	35
Salim Elahi	lbw, b Srinath	1
Ijaz Ahmed	b Kumble	90
Salim Malik	run out	1
Inzamam-ul-Haq	run out	40
*Moin Khan	st Mongia, b Tendulkar	33
Wasim Akram (Capt)	c Venkatesh Prasad, b Kumble	10
Saqlain Mushtaq	not out	10
Waqar Younis	not out	0
Mushtaq Ahmed		
	b 3, lb 8, w 4	15
	50 overs (for 8 wickets)	258

	O	M	R	W
Srinath	9	–	51	1
Venkatesh Prasad	10	–	50	1
Jadeja	1	–	8	–
Kapoor	8	–	34	–
Joshi	9	1	45	1
Kumble	10	–	37	2
Tendulkar	3	–	22	1

Fall of Wickets
1–**42**, 2–**43**, 3–**84**, 4–**91**, 5–**177**, 6–**214**, 7–**235**, 8–**248**

India

*N.R. Mongia	c Ijaz Ahmed, b Wasim Akram	0
S.R. Tendulkar (Capt)	c Salim Malik, b Wasim Akram	3
R.S. Dravid	c Moin Khan, b Saqlain Mushtaq	25
M. Azharuddin	c Salim Elahi, b Saqlain Mushtaq	16
V.G. Kambli	run out	6
A.D. Jadeja	st Moin Khan, b Salim Malik	47
S.B. Joshi	c Moin Khan, b Saqlain Mushtaq	1
A.R. Kapoor	c Moin Khan, b Waqar Younis	19
A.R. Kumble	c Aamir Sohail, b Salim Malik	16
J. Srinath	c Saqlain Mushtaq, b Waqar Younis	10
Venkatesh Prasad	not out	0
	b 8, lb 7, w 3	18
	39.2 overs	161

	O	M	R	W
Wasim Akram	6	2	11	2
Waqar Younis	8	–	51	2
Saqlain Mushtaq	7	1	9	3
Aamir Sohail	10	–	36	–
Mushtaq Ahmed	7	–	33	–
Salim Malik	1.2	–	6	2

Fall of Wickets
1–**4**, 2–**9**, 3–**41**, 4–**58**, 5–**63**, 6–**64**, 7–**118**, 8–**148**, 9–**160**

Umpires: L.H. Barker & D.R. Shepherd *Man of the Match:* Ijaz Ahmed

Pakistan won by 97 runs

Match Five – India *v.* Pakistan
23 September 1996 at Toronto Cricket, Skating and Curling Club

Pakistan

Aamir Sohail	c Jadeja, b Kumble	44
Saeed Anwar	c Dravid, b Kapoor	14
Ijaz Ahmed	c and b Kumble	27
Shadab Kabir	c Dravid, b Kumble	0
Salim Malik	b Venkatesh Prasad	43
Inzamam-ul-Haq	c Venkatesh Prasad, b Kapoor	9
*Moin Khan	run out	15
Wasim Akram (Capt)	run out	17
Saqlain Mushtaq	run out	0
Waqar Younis	not out	12
Mushtaq Ahmed	not out	5
	b 1, lb 21, w 4, nb 1	27
	50 overs (for 9 wickets)	213

	O	M	R	W
Srinath	10	–	40	–
Venkatesh Prasad	10	–	32	1
Kapoor	10	–	36	2
Joshi	10	1	36	–
Kumble	10	–	47	3

Fall of Wickets
1–**44**, 2–**95**, 3–**99**, 4–**108**, 5–**135**, 6–**174**, 7–**195**, 8–**195**, 9–**197**

India

A.D. Jadeja	b Mushtaq Ahmed	20
S.R. Tendulkar (Capt)	run out	23
R.S. Dravid	c sub, b Mushtaq Ahmed	20
S.B. Joshi	c Salim Malik, b Mushtaq Ahmed	2
M. Azharuddin	c Inzamam, b Mushtaq Ahmed	2
S. Ganguly	lbw, b Aamir Sohail	12
J. Srinath	run out	2
*N.R. Mongia	c Wasim Akram, b Saqlain Mushtaq	10
A.R. Kapoor	c Ijaz Ahmed, b Mushtaq Ahmed	18
A.R. Kumble	not out	8
Venkatesh Prasad	c Saeed Anwar, b Saqlain Mushtaq	19
	b 7, lb 3, w 15	25
	45.5 overs	161

	O	M	R	W
Wasim Akram	8	1	16	–
Waqar Younis	8	–	27	–
Saqlain Mushtaq	7.5	–	34	2
Aamir Sohail	10	1	27	1
Mushtaq Ahmed	10	–	36	5
Salim Malik	2	–	11	–

Fall of Wickets
1–**46**, 2–**62**, 3–**66**, 4–**70**, 5–**92**, 6–**96**, 7–**99**, 8–**127**, 9–**128**

Umpires: L.H. Barker & D.L. Orchard *Man of the Match:* Mushtaq Ahmed

Pakistan won by 52 runs

Kenya

Kenya's victory over West Indies in the sixth World Cup was one of the greatest sensations in international cricket. In celebration, a four-nation tournament was staged in Nairobi towards the end of 1996. The hosts invited World Champions Sri Lanka, near neighbours South Africa, and the perennial travellers of international cricket, Pakistan, who were on the third leg of a world tour that would take them to five continents.

Shahid Afridi established a new world record when he scored a century off only 37 deliveries for Pakistan against Sri Lanka, 4 October 1996. Shahid was appearing in his second one-day international, and it was alleged that he was short of his 17th birthday. (David Munden/Sportsline)

Pakistan's journeying had taken its toll. Aamir Sohail, Inzamam-ul-Haq and Mushtaq Ahmed had been forced to remain in Toronto for treatment to injuries, and Wasim Akram returned to Pakistan after one match because of his father's illness. Saeed Anwar took over the captaincy and Rameez Raja, Saeed Azad and Shahid Afridi were the replacements.

Shahid Afridi was reputedly 16 years 217 days old when he played against Sri Lanka on 4 October 1996, but his age was later challenged by the Pakistan Board who suggested it was closer to 19. These mistakes occur because it is often difficult to judge exact dates of birth in Pakistan where it can take many months for a birth to be registered.

Shahid Afridi was one of five players to make his international debut during the tournament. The others were Gupta and Suji of Kenya, Sri Lanka's Sajeeva de Silva, a left-arm medium-pace bowler with a good record in domestic cricket, and Herschelle Gibbs, who had made a great impression with the South African 'A' side in England.

The competition was highly successful, with teams fully committed and spectators matching their enthusiasm to such an extent that the Gymkhana ground proved too small for the event. Heartened by the response of players and public, the Kenyan authorities set about organising another Sameer Cup competition for 1997 with India and Australia as likely participants.

Man of the Series – Allan Donald, the South African fast bowler who took 14 wickets in four matches, including his best performance in a one-day international, 6 for 23 against Kenya. (Alan Cozzi)

The inaugural tournament opened with Sri Lanka gaining an expected easy win over the hosts. Modi and Gupta did well, but they were overshadowed by a blistering 100 off 89 balls by Kaluwitharana. He hit a six and 10 fours, and his first 50 came off only 34 deliveries.

A fourth wicket stand of 232 in 206 balls between Cullinan and Rhodes was the main feature of South Africa's victory over Pakistan. Cullinan faced 117 balls for his 124, which included 12 fours, while Rhodes's 121 came off 114 balls and contained 11 fours. Pakistan were never really in the hunt although Waqar's successive sixes off Symcox allowed them to die bravely.

Sri Lanka maintained their winning sequence in one-day internationals when they beat South Africa with 9.2 overs to spare. It was the World Champions' 13th win in succession. Off-spinner Muralitharan took four wickets in an innings for the second time in the tournament.

With Wasim Akram departed, Pakistan made rather hard work of beating Kenya who, the following day, were shattered by Allan Donald. Consistent batting took South Africa past 300 so that Kenya faced a difficult task that became more difficult when Brian McMillan removed three batsmen within seven overs. Donald joined the attack as second change and brought havoc with bowling of infinite variety in pace and movement. His 6 for 23 were his best figures in a one-day international, and he also reached 100 wickets in this kind of cricket.

There were even greater sensations on the same ground the following day. Put in to bat, Pakistan lost Salim Elahi at 60 before Shahid Afridi joined Saeed Anwar in a stand worth 126. The partnership was dominated by the teenager who had joined the Pakistan side as a spin-bowling replacement for Mushtaq Ahmed. In only his second international match, Shahid Afridi established a world record by hitting 100 off 37 balls. His innings included 11 sixes and six fours, and he beat the record set up by Jayasuriya only six months earlier. Ironically, Shahid destroyed the previous record holder on his way to his century, taking 43, including five sixes, off two overs bowled by the slow left-armer.

Sri Lanka did not surrender easily. The magnificent Aravinda de Silva hit 122 off 116 balls with two sixes and 12 fours, and Vaas hit Waqar Younis for a six and a four in the last over. Had he scored one more run, Sri Lanka would have qualified for the final, but Waqar bowled him with the penultimate ball. The 600 runs scored in the match was a record for a one-day international, as was Pakistan's 371 for 9.

Qualifying Table

	P	W	L	Pts
South Africa	3	2	1	4
Pakistan	3	2	1	4
Sri Lanka	3	2	1	4
Kenya	3	–	3	0

Match One – Kenya v. Sri Lanka
28 September 1996 at Nairobi Gymkhana Ground, Nairobi

Kenya

D. Chudasama	b Vaas	0
*K. Otieno	lbw, b S.C. de Silva	2
S. Gupta	b Muralitharan	41
S. Tikolo	lbw, b S.C. de Silva	5
M. Odumbe (Capt)	c Kaluwitharana, b Ranatunga	3
H. Modi	not out	78
T. Odoyo	b Muralitharan	9
M. Suji	c Gurusinha, b Muralitharan	0
E. Odumbe	b Muralitharan	5
Asif Karim	run out	24
Rajab Ali	not out	1
	lb 8, w 11, nb 1	20
	50 overs (for 9 wickets)	188

	O	M	R	W
Vaas	10	2	40	1
S.C. de Silva	8	–	27	2
Ranatunga	3	–	10	1
Dharmasena	10	1	39	–
Muralitharan	10	4	18	4
Chandana	5	–	22	–
Jayasuriya	4	–	24	–

Fall of Wickets
1–0, 2–7, 3–14, 4–31, 5–65, 6–83, 7–85, 8–93, 9–182

Sri Lanka

S.T. Jayasuriya	lbw, b E. Odumbe	5
*R.S. Kaluwitharana	not out	100
A.P. Gurusinha	lbw, b E. Odumbe	0
P.A. de Silva	c E. Odumbe, b M. Odumbe	55
A. Ranatunga (Capt)	not out	25
H.P. Tillekeratne		
H.D.P.K. Dharmasena		
S.C. de Silva		
W.P.U.J.C. Vaas		
U.U. Chandana		
M. Muralitharan		
	lb 1, w 4	5
	30.4 overs (for 3 wickets)	190

	O	M	R	W
Rajab Alib	4	–	23	–
E. Odumbe	4	1	29	2
Suji	5.4	–	48	–
Asif Karim	7	–	42	–
Odoyo	6	–	34	–
M. Odumbe	4	–	13	1

Fall of Wickets
1–5, 2–7, 3–128

Umpires: I.D. Robinson & R.B. Tiffin *Man of the Match*: R.S. Kaluwitharana   **Sri Lanka won by 7 wickets**

Match Two – South Africa v. Pakistan
29 September 1996 at Nairobi Gymkhana Ground, Nairobi

South Africa

A.C. Hudson	lbw, b Waqar Younis	2
G. Kirsten	lbw, b Wasim Akram	15
D.J. Cullinan	c Salim Malik, b Waqar Younis	124
P.L. Symcox	lbw, b Wasim Akram	0
J.N. Rhodes	run out	121
W.J. Cronje (Capt)	c Ijaz Ahmed, b Saqlain Mushtaq	11
B.M. McMillan	lbw, b Saqlain Mushtaq	4
*D.J. Richardson	not out	11
P.S. de Villiers	b Saqlain Mushtaq	3
C.D. Matthews	not out	0
A.A. Donald		
	b 1, lb 18, w 8, nb 3	30
	50 overs (for 8 wickets)	321

	O	M	R	W
Wasim Akram	10	–	42	2
Waqar Younis	9	–	48	2
Shahid Nazir	7	–	54	–
Azhar Mahmood	9	–	73	–
Saqlain Mushtaq	10	–	42	3
Salim Malik	3	–	26	–
Ijaz Ahmed	2	–	17	–

Fall of Wickets
1–12, 2–37, 3–38, 4–270, 5–299, 6–305, 7–312, 8–316

Pakistan

Saeed Anwar	run out	1
Salim Elahi	c Richardson, b McMillan	54
Saeed Azad	lbw, b de Villiers	14
Ijaz Ahmed	c Cronje, b Donald	88
Salim Malik	run out	0
*Moin Khan	run out	31
Wasim Akram (Capt)	b Donald	8
Azhar Mahmood	b Symcox	15
Saqlain Mushtaq	b Donald	2
Waqar Younis	b de Villiers	28
Shahid Nazir	not out	5
	b 5, lb 4, w 4	13
	42.3 overs	259

	O	M	R	W
de Villiers	8.3	–	39	2
Matthews	6	–	44	–
Donald	8	–	29	3
McMillan	8	–	49	1
Cronje	2	–	21	–
Cullinan	1	–	8	–
Symcox	9	–	60	1

Fall of Wickets
1–1, 2–48, 3–115, 4–117, 5–189, 6–200, 7–210, 8–210, 9–229

Umpires: R.B. Tiffin & S.K. Bansal *Man of the Match*: J.N. Rhodes   **South Africa won by 62 runs**

Match Three – South Africa v. Sri Lanka
1 October 1996 at Nairobi Club Ground, Nairobi

South Africa				Sri Lanka			
A.C. Hudson	c Mahanama, b Vaas	7		S.T. Jayasuriya	c Cullinan, b Symcox	45	
G. Kirsten	c Muralitharan, b Dharmasena	28		*R.S. Kaluwitharana	b Symcox	27	
P.L. Symcox	c Ranatunga, b S.C. de Silva	9		A.P. Gurusinha	run out	22	
D.J. Cullinan	b P.A. de Silva	51		P.A. de Silva	c Cullinan, b Donald	3	
J.N. Rhodes	c Gurusinha, b Muralitharan	7		A. Ranatunga (Capt)	lbw, b Crookes	11	
W.J. Cronje (Capt)	b Muralitharan	15		R.S. Mahanama	lbw, b de Villiers	10	
D.N. Crookes	c Vaas, b Jayasuriya	10		H.P. Tillekeratne	c McMillan, b de Villiers	13	
B.M. McMillan	not out	25		H.D.P.K. Dharmasena	not out	18	
*D.J. Richardson	run out	1		W.P.U.J.C. Vaas	b Donald	13	
P.S. de Villiers	c sub (Chandana), b Muralitharan	5		S.C. de Silva	not out	4	
A.A. Donald	b Muralitharan	0		M. Muralitharan			
	lb **5**, w **6**	11			lb **1**, w **1**, nb **2**	4	
	42 overs	**169**			**40.4 overs (for 8 wickets)**	**170**	

	O	M	R	W		O	M	R	W
Vaas	5	1	13	1	de Villiers	8	1	37	2
S.C. de Silva	7	–	28	1	McMillan	6	–	38	–
Dharmasena	8	–	36	1	Donald	9.4	2	35	2
Muralitharan	10	1	35	4	Symcox	10	1	20	2
Jayasuriya	8	–	29	1	Crookes	7	–	39	1
P.A. de Silva	4	1	23	1					

Fall of Wickets
1–**16**, 2–**33**, 3–**45**, 4–**69**, 5–**105**, 6–**132**, 7–**136**, 8–**137**, 9–**167**

Fall of Wickets
1–**69**, 2–**82**, 3–**85**, 4–**110**, 5–**113**, 6–**130**, 7–**144**, 8–**166**

Umpires: I.D. Robinson & R.B. Tiffin *Man of the Match*: S.T. Jayasuriya

Sri Lanka won by 2 wickets

Match Four – Kenya v. Pakistan
2 October 1996 at Aga Khan Ground, Nairobi

Kenya				Pakistan			
D. Chudasama	c Saeed Azad, b Salim Malik	51		Saeed Anwar (Capt)	c Otieno, b M. Suji	27	
*K. Otieno	c Rameez Raja, b Waqar Younis	25		Salim Elahi	b Odoyo	14	
S. Gupta	c Moin Khan, b Waqar Younis	0		Ijaz Ahmed	lbw, b M. Suji	3	
S. Tikolo	run out	6		Rameez Raja	b Odoyo	0	
M. Odumbe (Capt)	b Saqlain Mushtaq	1		Salim Malik	b T. Suji	27	
H. Modi	c Salim Malik, b Saqlain Mushtaq	3		Saeed Azad	b Odoyo	1	
Asif Karim	run out	0		*Moin Khan	not out	50	
T. Suji	c Shahid Afridi, b Saqlain	4		Saqlain Mushtaq	not out	8	
T. Odoyo	c and b Salim Malik	32		Shahid Afridi			
M. Suji	not out	6		Waqar Younis			
E. Odumbe	b Shahid Nazir	2		Shahid Nazir			
	lb **3**, w **15**	18			b **4**, lb **5**, w **6**, nb **4**	19	
	47 overs	**148**			**40.2 overs (for 6 wickets)**	**149**	

	O	M	R	W		O	M	R	W
Waqar Younis	10	2	31	2	M. Suji	10	–	42	2
Shahid Nazir	9	2	31	1	E. Odumbe	2	–	13	–
Saqlain Mushtaq	10	1	27	3	Odoyo	10	2	25	3
Shahid Afridi	10	–	32	–	Asif Karim	10	1	32	–
Salim Malik	8	–	24	2	M. Odumbe	4	1	12	–
					T. Suji	4.2	2	16	1

Fall of Wickets
1–**38**, 2–**40**, 3–**51**, 4–**54**, 5–**58**, 6–**58**, 7–**62**, 8–**129**, 9–**142**

Fall of Wickets
1–**39**, 2–**45**, 3–**45**, 4–**52**, 5–**61**, 6–**115**

Umpires: I.D. Robinson & S.K. Bansal *Man of the Match*: T. Odoyo

Pakistan won by 4 wickets

Match Five – Kenya v. South Africa
3 October 1996 at Nairobi Gymkhana Ground, Nairobi

South Africa

A.C. Hudson	lbw, **b** Onyango	27
G. Kirsten	c Chudasama, **b** Asif Karim	66
P.L. Symcox	c Odoyo, **b** Asif Karim	35
H.H. Gibbs	**st** Otieno, **b** M. Odumbe	17
J.N. Rhodes	run out	54
W.J. Cronje (Capt)	not out	63
D.N. Crookes	lbw, **b** Odoyo	1
B.M. McMillan	run out	1
*D.J. Richardson	run out	3
P.S. de Villiers	not out	20
A.A. Donald		
	lb **5**, w **12**, nb **1**	18
	50 overs (for 8 wickets)	305

	O	M	R	W
M. Suji	9	–	47	–
Odoyo	9	–	54	1
Onyango	3	–	45	1
T. Suji	6	–	38	–
Asif Karim	10	–	44	2
M. Odumbe	10	1	53	1
Tikolo	3	–	19	–

Fall of Wickets
1–77, 2–116, 3–158, 4–161, 5–262, 6–264, 7–266, 8–276

Kenya

D. Chudasama	**b** Donald	29
*K. Otieno	lbw, **b** McMillan	0
S. Gupta	c Crookes, **b** McMillan	2
S. Tikolo	c Crookes, **b** McMillan	9
M. Odumbe (Capt)	lbw, **b** Donald	19
H. Modi	c sub (Boje), **b** Crookes	14
T. Odoyo	lbw, **b** Donald	0
Asif Karim	lbw, **b** Donald	1
T. Suji	**b** Donald	10
L. Onyango	**b** Donald	4
M. Suji	not out	0
	lb **6**, w **8**, nb **1**	15
	25.1 overs	103

	O	M	R	W
McMillan	4	–	17	3
de Villiers	3	–	25	–
Symcox	4	–	18	–
Donald	9	–	23	6
Crookes	5.1	–	14	1

Fall of Wickets
1–20, 2–20, 3–42, 4–68, 5–75, 6–77, 7–79, 8–93, 9–103

Umpires: I.D. Robinson & R.B. Tiffin *Man of the Match:* A.A. Donald

South Africa won by 202 runs

Match Six – Pakistan v. Sri Lanka
4 October 1996 at Nairobi Gymkhana Ground, Nairobi

Pakistan

Saeed Anwar (Capt)	c Mahanama, **b** Muralitharan	115
Salim Elahi	c Muralitharan, **b** Dharmasena	23
Shahid Afridi	c Muralitharan, **b** S.C. de Silva	102
Rameez Raja	c Gurusinha, **b** Muralitharan	7
Salim Malik	c Ranatunga, **b** P.A. de Silva	43
Ijaz Ahmed	**st** Kaluwitharana, **b** Jayasuriya	6
*Moin Khan	c Dharmasena, **b** Jayasuriya	18
Waqar Younis	c Dharmasena, **b** Jayasuriya	12
Azhar Mahmood	run out	0
Saqlain Mushtaq	not out	13
Shahid Nazir	not out	6
	b **7**, w **17**, nb **2**	26
	50 overs (for 9 wickets)	371

	O	M	R	W
S.C. de Silva	6	–	47	1
Vaas	7	–	44	–
Dharmasena	7	–	48	1
Jayasuriya	10	–	94	3
Muralitharan	10	–	73	2
P.A. de Silva	10	–	58	1

Fall of Wickets
1–60, 2–186, 3–207, 4–299, 5–314, 6–322, 7–335, 8–336, 9–364

Sri Lanka

S.T. Jayasuriya	c Shahid Nazir, **b** Waqar Younis	2
*R.S. Kaluwitharana	c Moin Khan, **b** Waqar Younis	19
A.P. Gurusinha	**b** Waqar Younis	1
P.A. de Silva	**st** Moin Khan, **b** Saqlain	122
R.S. Mahanama	lbw, **b** Waqar Younis	0
A. Ranatunga (Capt)	c Moin Khan, **b** Shahid Afridi	52
H.P. Tillekeratne	**b** Saqlain Mushtaq	3
H.D.P.K. Dharmasena	c Saeed Anwar, **b** Saqlain Mushtaq	51
W.P.U.J.C. Vaas	**b** Waqar Younis	16
M. Muralitharan	**st** Moin Khan, **b** Saqlain Mushtaq	0
S.C. de Silva	not out	0
	lb **10**, w **12**, nb **1**	23
	49.5 overs	289

	O	M	R	W
Waqar Younis	8.5	–	52	5
Azhar Mahmood	5	2	39	–
Shahid Nazir	2	–	32	–
Saqlain Mushtaq	10	2	33	4
Salim Malik	10	–	58	–
Shahid Afridi	10	–	43	1
Saeed Anwar	1	–	8	–
Ijaz Ahmed	3	–	14	–

Fall of Wickets
1–4, 2–26, 3–26, 4–27, 5–151, 6–160, 7–270, 8–279, 9–279

Umpires: I.D. Robinson & R.B. Tiffin *Man of the Match:* Shahid Afridi

Pakistan won by 82 runs

Sameer Cup Final – Pakistan v. South Africa

6 October 1996 at Nairobi Gymkhana Ground, Nairobi

Pakistan

Saeed Anwar (Capt)	c Richardson, b Donald	32
Salim Elahi	c Kirsten, b de Villiers	30
Shahid Afridi	c Richardson, b Donald	14
Ijaz Ahmed	c Richardson, b McMillan	47
Salim Malik	c and b Symcox	24
Rameez Raja	c and b Crookes	3
Saeed Azad	c Cronje, b Donald	31
*Moin Khan	b McMillan	2
Azhar Mahmood	lbw, b Crookes	3
Waqar Younis	c Donald, b Crookes	3
Saqlain Mushtaq	not out	2
	lb 3, w 9	12
	46.2 overs	203

	O	M	R	W
McMillan	10	–	55	2
de Villiers	8	–	40	1
Donald	8.2	–	32	3
Cronje	1	–	8	–
Symcox	9	–	35	1
Crookes	10	–	30	3

Fall of Wickets
1–**58**, 2–**78**, 3–**90**, 4–**138**, 5–**143**, 6–**170**, 7–**174**, 8–**185**, 9–**195**

South Africa

A.C. Hudson	c Saqlain Mushtaq, b Shahid	42
G. Kirsten	not out	118
P.L. Symcox	c Shahid Afridi	0
D.J. Cullinan	c Saqlain Mushtaq, b Shahid	17
J.N. Rhodes	not out	16
W.J. Cronje (Capt)		
D.N. Crookes		
B.M. McMillan		
*D.J. Richardson		
P.S. de Villiers		
A.A. Donald		
	b 1, lb 2, w 6, nb 2	11
	39.2 overs (for 3 wickets)	204

	O	M	R	W
Waqar Younis	9	–	49	–
Azhar Mahmood	6	–	31	–
Saqlain Mushtaq	10	1	42	–
Shahid Afridi	10	–	48	3
Salim Malik	3.2	–	25	–
Saeed Anwar	1	–	6	–

Fall of Wickets
1–**77**, 2–**77**, 3–**125**

Umpires: I.D. Robinson & S.K. Bansal *Man of the Match*: G. Kirsten

South Africa won by 7 wickets

Final

A capacity crowd of 14,000 watched the final and saw South Africa win comfortably, thanks to a gritty century by Gary Kirsten who survived two early chances to reach his sixth one-day international century.

Salim Elahi had given Pakistan a good start with 30 off 26 balls, but the innings faltered, and only Ijaz Ahmed produced the necessary briskness in scoring.

Hudson and Kirsten put on 77 for the first wicket before Shahid Afridi struck twice, but Kirsten stayed calm and reached his century off 114 balls with 14 fours.

Allan Donald was named Man of the Series for his 14 wickets, and South Africa claimed the Sameer Cup and prize money of 50,000 American dollars.

Most applause went to the Kenyan Cricket Association for their splendid organisation, and they were warmly praised by all four sides.

Gary Kirsten hit a century for South Africa against Pakistan in the final and was named Man of the Match.
(Paul Sturgess/Sportsline)

Sri Lanka

Proud and confident as World Champions, Sri Lanka engaged in a full programme in 1996–97. They hosted a four-nation one-day international competition, played two Tests at home to Zimbabwe and travelled to Kenya and Sharjah for limited-over tournaments. They journeyed to New Zealand for a Test series, and the ultimate challenge came with a trip to the West Indies. Their international season extended from August 1996 until June 1997.

The first batsman to score an unbeaten century in each innings of a Test match, Aravinda de Silva, brilliant and belligerently dominant in all forms of cricket. (David Munden/Sportsline)

The Singer Cup
Test Series – Sri Lanka v. Zimbabwe
Test Series – Sri Lanka v. Pakistan
Asia Cup

Sri Lanka were not without their problems. Dav Whatmore, who had achieved much as national coach and who had masterminded the World Cup triumph, resigned his post to become coach at Lancashire, while, in contrast, Arjuna Ranatunga, who had expressed a wish to relinquish the captaincy, continued to lead the side.

In manners and demeanour, Sri Lankan cricketers continue to be a model to others. They wear the world crown with dignity and grace.

Singer Cup

India, Zimbabwe and Australia were enticed to Sri Lanka for the Singer Cup, the timing of which deprived Essex and Yorkshire of their overseas players at a crucial time towards the end of the English season. However, with the increasing demands of international cricket, this is likely to become a growing problem.

The start of the Singer Cup was hampered by rain, which caused the abandonment of one match. It finally began with Australia's comprehensive win over Zimbabwe, who were led by Alistair Campbell. Australia gave a one-day international debut to Brad Hogg, the left-handed Western Australia all-rounder, but it was Steve Waugh who was the mainspring of the Australian victory, with 82 off 70 balls.

Sachin Tendulkar celebrated his appointment as India's captain with a fine century, but he was powerless to prevent Sri Lanka claiming victory with remarkable ease. Jayasuriya was again in devastating form. He hit Kapoor for 17 in one over, and he and Kaluwitharana scored 129 in 22 overs for the first wicket. Aravinda de Silva then joined Jayasuriya in a match-winning stand of 101.

Australia presented Sri Lanka with stronger opposition, and, chasing a target of 229, the hosts slipped to 81 for 5 before Mahanama gave de Silva the necessary support in a stand of 115.

Zimbabwe batted well at the outset against India and reached 201 for 4, but the last six wickets crashed for 25. India made a spirited reply with Jadeja and Tendulkar scoring 91 for the first wicket in 15 overs, and victory came with 37 balls to spare.

Craig Evans's highest score in international cricket helped Zimbabwe to 227 for 5 against Sri Lanka, and when Olonga sent back both openers with only 25 scored, the Africans were in a strong position. Once more it was the great Aravinda de Silva who rallied the home side. He hit a six and 13 fours and faced 123 balls for his unbeaten 127. Andy Whittall, the former Cambridge University all-rounder, made his debut for Zimbabwe.

With Sri Lanka having qualified for the final, the match between India and Australia became the decider as to who would be their opponents. India and Australia had been scheduled to meet on the fifth but rain had put the game back a day. India collapsed to 89 for 6 before Ganguly and Joshi kept the game alive with a partnership of 100.

Sanath Jayasuriya, 120 not out in the Singer Cup match against India, a Test century against Pakistan and a powerful force in world cricket at all times. (David Munden/Sportsline)

Australia, too, stumbled at first, but Steve Waugh and Law virtually decided the issue with a stand of 113.

Qualifying Table

	P	W	L	Pts
Sri Lanka	3	3	–	6
Australia	3	2	1	4
India	3	1	2	2
Zimbabwe	3	–	3	0

Singer Cup Final

Rain reduced the final to a 35-over contest, but Sri Lanka, put in to bat, scored at a blistering pace and set Australia the hardest of tasks. Again, Sri Lanka's star was Aravinda de Silva, whose 75 came off 64 balls. In four matches in the tournament he scored 334 runs without being dismissed and was indisputably Man of the Series.

Needing to score at 6.7 runs an over, Australia started bravely, but they quickly found the pace too much for them. In fairness, they had been without Taylor and Warne for the series, but the dominance of Sri Lanka was undeniable.

Four wickets in the Singer Cup Final for Upul Chandana.
(David Munden/Sportsline)

Test Series

Sri Lanka v. Zimbabwe

Triumphant in the Singer Cup, Sri Lanka continued their dazzling form in the two-Test series against Zimbabwe. Neither match lasted the full five days, and Sri Lanka did not lose a second innings wicket. Zimbabwe were unable to call upon David Houghton, while Sri Lanka enjoyed the luxury of a settled and confident side. For the first Test, Zimbabwe introduced Andy Whittall to their team, although his form at Cambridge University had hardly suggested that he was an international cricketer.

Sri Lanka won the toss and batted, but they were soon in trouble, losing both openers with only four runs scored. Aravinda de Silva hit a brisk 35, but lunch came with the score on 77 for 3.

Gurusinha had been rock-like. He hit six fours and batted for 197 minutes, but he and Tillekeratne fell in quick succession to leave Sri Lanka in trouble at 128 for 5. Salvation came in the form of Ranatunga and Kaluwitharana, who hit ten fours and a six. Ranatunga scored seven boundaries, and the pair added 142 runs in 152 minutes. Streak returned to dismiss them both, and it was left to Dharmasena and Vaas to take Sri Lanka to 290 for 7 by the close.

The eighth wicket pair continued to score freely on the second morning before Paul Strang brought the innings

Match One – Australia v. Zimbabwe

26 August 1996 at Premadasa Stadium, Colombo

Australia

M.J. Slater	c P.A. Strang, b G.J. Whittall	50
M.E. Waugh	c P.A. Strang	18
R.T. Ponting	c and b G.J. Whittall	53
S.R. Waugh	c Campbell, b G.J. Whittall	82
S.G. Law	b Streak	20
M.G. Bevan	c Campbell, b Brandes	9
*I.A. Healy (Capt)	b Brandes	5
G.B Hogg	not out	11
P.R. Reiffel		
D.W. Fleming		
G.D. McGrath		
	b 1, lb 8, w 3, nb 3	15
	50 overs (for 7 wickets)	**263**

	O	M	R	W
Streak	10	1	50	1
Brandes	10	1	47	2
P.A. Strang	9	–	41	1
G.W. Flower	6	–	28	–
G.J. Whittall	10	–	53	3
Dekker	3	–	17	–
Omarshah	2	–	18	–

Fall of Wickets
1–**48**, 2–**92**, 3–**167**, 4–**230**, 5–**240**, 6–**242**, 7–**263**

Zimbabwe

A.H. Omarshah	c M.E. Waugh, b Hogg	41
G.W. Flower	c Ponting, b Fleming	7
*A. Flower	lbw, b Fleming	0
A.D.R. Campbell (Capt)	lbw, b McGrath	9
C.B. Wishart	c Healy, b Reiffel	0
G.J. Whittall	b Reiffel	11
C.N. Evans	c Healy, b S.R. Waugh	15
M.H. Dekker	not out	8
P.A. Strang	b M.E. Waugh	9
H.H. Streak	b M.E. Waugh	0
E.A. Brandes	c Hogg, b M.E. Waugh	17
	lb 4, w 10, nb 7	21
	41 overs	**138**

	O	M	R	W
McGrath	7	2	13	1
Fleming	7	–	24	2
Reiffel	6	1	23	2
S.R. Waugh	7	2	24	1
Hogg	9	2	26	1
M.E. Waugh	5	1	24	3

Fall of Wickets
1–**16**, 2–**16**, 3–**33**, 4–**35**, 5–**56**, 6–**98**, 7–**100**, 8–**120**, 9–**120**

Umpires: K.T. Francis & W.A.U. Wickremasinghe   *Man of the Match:* S.R. Waugh   **Australia won by 125 runs**

Match Two – Sri Lanka v. India
28 August 1996 at Premadasa Stadium, Colombo

India

A.D. Jadeja	run out	0
S.R. Tendulkar (Capt)	run out	110
S. Ganguly	c de Silva, b Dharmasena	16
M. Azharuddin	st Kaluwitharana, b Jayasuriya	58
V.G. Kambli	run out	18
R.S. Dravid	not out	7
J. Srinath	not out	1
*N.R. Mongia		
A.R. Kumble		
A.R. Kapoor		
Venkatesh Prasad		
	b 1, lb 3, w 9, nb 3	16
	50 overs (for 5 wickets)	226

	O	M	R	W
Vaas	9	2	35	–
Pushpakumara	6	–	23	–
Dharmasena	10	–	59	1
Muralitharan	10	–	42	–
Jayasuriya	10	1	39	1
de Silva	5	–	24	–

Fall of Wickets
1–4, 2–57, 3–186, 4–217, 5–218

Sri Lanka

S.T. Jayasuriya	not out	120
*R.S. Kaluwitharana	b Tendulkar	53
P.A. de Silva	not out	49
A.P. Gurusinha		
A. Ranatunga (Capt)		
H.P. Tillekeratne		
R.S. Mahanama		
H.D.P.K. Dharmasena		
W.P.U.J.C. Vaas		
M. Muralitharan		
K.R. Pushpakumara		
	lb 3, w 2, nb 3	8
	44.2 overs (for 1 wicket)	230

	O	M	R	W
Srinath	8	–	33	–
Venkatesh Prasad	6	–	47	–
Kapoor	10	2	51	–
Kumble	10	1	40	–
Tendulkar	6	–	29	1
Jadeja	2.2	–	13	–
Ganguly	2	–	14	–

Fall of Wickets
1–129

Umpires: S.A. Bucknor & C.J. Mitchley   *Man of the Match:* S.T. Jayasuriya

Sri Lanka won by 9 wickets

Match Three – Sri Lanka v. Australia
30 August 1996 at Premadasa Stadium, Colombo

Australia

M.E. Waugh	c and b Jayasuriya	50
M.J. Slater	run out	9
S.G. Law	c Tillekeratne, b Dharmasena	13
M.G. Bevan	c Vaas, b Chandana	56
S.R. Waugh	b Muralitharan	22
R.T. Ponting	not out	46
D.S. Lehmann	st Kaluwitharana, b Chandana	2
*I.A. Healy (Capt)	c Ranatunga, b Muralitharan	8
J.N. Gillespie	st Kaluwitharana, b Chandana	6
D.W. Fleming	c Chandana, b Jayasuriya	3
G.D. McGrath	not out	8
	lb 3, nb 2	5
	50 overs (for 9 wickets)	228

	O	M	R	W
Vaas	7	–	29	–
de Silva	4	–	25	–
Dharmasena	9	–	49	1
Muralitharan	10	–	41	2
Jayasuriya	10	–	43	2
Chandana	10	–	38	3

Fall of Wickets
1–21, 2–52, 3–97, 4–149, 5–157, 6–163, 7–178, 8–198, 9–203

Sri Lanka

S.T. Jayasuriya	c Healy, b Fleming	44
*R.S. Kaluwitharana	b S.R. Waugh	8
A.P. Gurusinha	run out	16
P.A. de Silva	not out	83
A. Ranatunga (Capt)	lbw, b Fleming	0
H.P. Tillekeratne	lbw, b Fleming	1
R.S. Mahanama	b McGrath	50
U.U. Chandana	not out	14
H.D.P.K. Dharmasena		
W.P.U.J.C. Vaas		
M. Muralitharan		
	lb 3, w 7, nb 6	16
	45.5 overs (for 6 wickets)	232

	O	M	R	W
S.R. Waugh	5	1	36	1
Law	2	–	23	–
McGrath	9.5	–	44	1
Fleming	8	1	26	3
Gillespie	6	–	27	–
M.E. Waugh	5	–	29	–
Lehmann	6	–	26	–
Bevan	4	–	18	–

Fall of Wickets
1–22, 2–78, 3–78, 4–78, 5–81, 6–196

Umpires: S.A. Bucknor & C.J. Mitchley   *Man of the Match:* P.A. de Silva

Sri Lanka won by 4 wickets

Match Four – India v. Zimbabwe
1 September 1996 at Sinhalese Sports Club, Colombo

Zimbabwe

A.D.R. Campbell (Capt)	c Tendulkar, b Venkatesh Prasad	10
P.A. Strang	st Mongia, b Joshi	19
*A. Flower	c Venkatesh Prasad, b Kumble	78
C.N. Evans	c Mongia, b Joshi	4
G.W. Flower	b Kumble	26
C.B. Wishart	c Joshi, b Kumble	53
G.J. Whittall	run out	1
M.H. Dekker	c Kumble, b Srinath	3
H.H. Streak	b Kumble	2
A.H. Omarshah	c Azharuddin, b Venkatesh Prasad	6
B.C. Strang	not out	1
	lb 12, w 9, nb 2	23
	49.4 overs	226

	O	M	R	W
Srinath	10	2	42	1
Venkatesh Prasad	7.4	–	42	2
Joshi	10	1	37	2
Jadeja	5	–	20	–
Kumble	4	–	20	–
Tendulkar	10	2	33	4
Ganguly	3	–	20	–

Fall of Wickets
1–22, 2–50, 3–61, 4–117, 5–201, 6–204, 7–217, 8–218, 9–220

India

A.D. Jadeja	c A. Flower, b Evans	68
S.R. Tendulkar (Capt)	c B.C. Strang, b Streak	40
S. Ganguly	c B.C. Strang, b P.A. Strang	36
M. Azharuddin	not out	40
V.G. Kambli	not out	29
R.S. Dravid		
*N.R. Mongia		
S.N. Joshi		
A.R. Kumble		
J. Srinath		
Venkatesh Prasad		
	lb 1, w 9, nb 6	16
	43.5 overs (for 3 wickets)	229

	O	M	R	W
Streak	10	1	46	1
B.C. Strang	7.5	–	52	–
P.A. Strang	10	–	73	1
G.J. Whittall	9	–	28	–
G.W. Flower	2	–	10	–
Evans	5	–	19	1

Fall of Wickets
1–91, 2–148, 3–161

Umpires: B.C. Cooray & T.M. Samarasinghe   *Man of the Match:* A.D. Jadeja

India won by 7 wickets

Match Five – Sri Lanka v. Zimbabwe
3 September 1996 at Sinhalese Sports Club, Colombo

Zimbabwe

G.W. Flower	c Kaluwitharana, b Pushpakumara	0
P.A. Strang	c Kaluwitharana, b Pushpakumara	24
A. Flower	c Kaluwitharana, b Wickremasinghe	11
A.D.R. Campbell (Capt)	st Kaluwitharana, b Muralitharan	54
C.B. Wishart	c Chandana, b Ranatunga	7
C.N. Evans	not out	96
G.J. Whittall	not out	15
*W.R. James		
H.H. Streak		
A.R. Whittall		
H.K. Olonga		
	lb 7, w 13	20
	50 overs (for 5 wickets)	227

	O	M	R	W
Wickremasinghe	9	1	32	1
Pushpakumara	6	–	28	2
Muralitharan	10	1	36	1
Ranatunga	5	–	22	1
Chandana	10	–	48	–
Jayasuriya	10	–	54	–

Fall of Wickets
1–13, 2–48, 3–48, 4–66, 5–180

Sri Lanka

S.T. Jayasuriya	b Olonga	5
*R.S. Kaluwitharana	c Wishart, b Olonga	12
A.P. Gurusinha	run out	15
P.A. de Silva	not out	127
A. Ranatunga (Capt)	c Olonga, b A.R. Whittall	20
H.P. Tillekeratne	not out	34
M.S. Atapattu		
U.U. Chandana		
G.P. Wickremasinghe		
K.R. Puchpakumara		
M. Muralitharan		
	b 1, lb 2, w 8, nb 4	15
	47 overs (for 4 wickets)	228

	O	M	R	W
Streak	8	–	24	–
Olonga	6	–	47	2
G.J. Whittall	5	–	26	–
A.R. Whittall	10	1	30	1
P.A. Strang	10	–	50	–
Campbell	4	–	24	–
G.W. Flower	1	–	10	–
Evans	3	–	14	–

Fall of Wickets
1–18, 2–25, 3–100, 4–129

Umpires: S.A. Bucknor & C.J. Mitchley   *Man of the Match:* P.A. de Silva

Sri Lanka won by 6 wickets

Match Six – Australia v. India
6 September 1996 at Sinhalese Sports Club, Colombo

India

*N.R. Mongia	c Bevan, b McGrath	38
S.R. Tendulkar (Capt)	c S.R. Waugh, b McGrath	7
R.S. Dravid	b Reiffel	13
M. Azharuddin	c M.E. Waugh, b Reiffel	3
V.G. Kambli	c Healy, b McGrath	1
A.D. Jadeja	c and b S.R. Waugh	6
S. Ganguly	lbw, b Bevan	59
S.B. Joshi	b Bevan	48
J. Srinath	run out	2
A.R. Kumble	c S.R. Waugh, b M.E. Waugh	0
Venkatesh Prasad	not out	6
	lb 4, w 11, nb 3	18
	41 overs	**201**

	O	M	R	**W**
McGrath	9	1	33	3
Fleming	6	–	25	–
Reiffel	5	–	37	2
S.R. Waugh	6	–	20	1
Hogg	5	–	33	–
M.E. Waugh	7	–	35	1
Bevan	3	–	14	2

Fall of Wickets
1–**32**, 2–**64**, 3–**67**, 4–**68**, 5–**72**, 6–**89**, 7–**189**, 8–**191**, 9–**194**

Australia

M.J. Slater	c Azharuddin, b Venkatesh Prasad	29
M.E. Waugh	c Tendulkar, b Joshi	23
R.T. Ponting	lbw, b Joshi	0
S.R. Waugh	st Mongia, b Kumble	55
S.G. Law	c Dravid, b Venkatesh Prasad	67
M.G. Bevan	not out	12
*I.A. Healy (Capt)	run out	4
G.B. Hogg	b Kumble	2
P.R. Reiffel	not out	1
D.W. Fleming		
G.D. McGrath		
	lb 2, w 4, nb 3	9
	44.3 overs (for 7 wickets)	**202**

	O	M	R	**W**
Srinath	6	–	32	–
Venkatesh Prasad	9	–	53	2
Joshi	9	1	23	2
Kumble	8.3	1	36	2
Tendulkar	8	–	38	–
Jadeja	4	–	18	–

Fall of Wickets
1–**50**, 2–**50**, 3–**69**, 4–**182**, 5–**185**, 6–**194**, 7–**197**

Umpires: B.C. Cooray & K.T. Francis   *Man of the Match:* S.R. Waugh

Australia won by 3 wickets

Singer Cup Final – Sri Lanka v. Australia
7 September 1996 at Premadasa Stadium, Colombo

Sri Lanka

S.T. Jayasuriya	c Law, b McGrath	27
*R.S. Kaluwitharana	c and b Lehmann	58
A.P. Gurusinha	c Bevan, b McGrath	29
P.A. de Silva	not out	75
A. Ranatunga (Capt)	not out	39
H.P. Tillekeratne		
R.S. Mahanama		
U.U. Chandana		
H.D.P.K. Dharmasena		
W.P.U.J.C. Vaas		
M. Muralitharan		
	b 1, lb 1, w 2, nb 2	6
	35 overs (for 3 wickets)	**234**

	O	M	R	**W**
McGrath	7	–	35	2
Fleming	7	–	53	–
Reiffel	4	–	43	–
Lehmann	5	–	29	1
S.R. Waugh	7	–	31	–
M.E. Waugh	5	–	41	–

Fall of Wickets
1–**42**, 2–**104**, 3–**131**

Australia

M.E. Waugh	run out	9
M.J. Slater	c Chandana, b Vaas	8
R.T. Ponting	c Jayasuriya, b Vaas	17
S.R. Waugh	c and b Chandana	55
S.G. Law	c Muralitharan, b Dharmasena	31
M.G. Bevan	b Dharmasena	7
D.S. Lehmann	st Kaluwitharana, b Muralitharan	15
*I.A. Healy (Capt)	c Muralitharan, b Chandana	20
P.R. Reiffel	c Mahanama, b Chandana	12
D.W. Fleming	not out	1
G.D. McGrath	c Mahanama, b Chandana	0
	lb 3, w 4, nb 2	9
	33 overs	**184**

	O	M	R	**W**
Vaas	5	–	23	2
Gurusinha	2	–	17	–
de Silva	3	–	18	–
Muralitharan	7	–	28	1
Jayasuriya	5	–	27	–
Dharmasena	5	–	33	2
Chandana	6	–	35	4

Fall of Wickets
1–**17**, 2–**26**, 3–**48**, 4–**104**, 5–**129**, 6–**145**, 7–**151**, 8–**183**, 9–**183**

Umpires: S.A. Bucknor & C.J. Mitchley   *Man of the Match:* P.A. de Silva

Sri Lanka won by 50 runs

Centuries in Test matches against both Zimbabwe and Pakistan for Hashan Tillekeratne. (David Munden/Sportsline)

A tower of strength in Sri Lanka's batting against Zimbabwe, but disagreement with the Sri Lankan Board has probably brought an end to Gurusinha's international career. (David Munden/Sportsline)

to an abrupt close with three wickets in four balls. The leg-spinner claimed his best figures in Test cricket.

Having had success as a batsman, Vaas now took control with the ball. He had Grant Flower caught behind with the first delivery of the Zimbabwe innings, and he soon accounted for Dekker and Campbell, so taking 3 for 31 in an 11-over spell. Dharmasena sent back Andy Flower, and Zimbabwe were in deep despair at 45 for 4. Guy Whittall and Craig Wishart added 58, but two wickets fell for two runs, and the visitors closed on a perilous 105 for 6.

The third day was decimated by rain. Play was possible only in the afternoon session. The last four Zimbabwe wickets fell for the addition of 40 runs, with left-arm spinner Jayantha Silva taking 3 for 10 in 14.4 accurate overs, his best figures in Test cricket. One of his victims was Craig Wishart, who hit two fours and a six in his patiently defiant 157-ball innings. Zimbabwe, following on, were 20 for 0 when rain returned.

The rain also delayed the start of play on the fourth day by two hours, but once the opening stand was broken the Sri Lankan spinners took over and hurried their side to victory. Muralitharan and Silva both finished with their best figures in Test cricket as Sri Lanka gained their first innings win in their brief life in international cricket. It was a thoroughly deserved triumph, and skipper Arjuna Ranatunga was named Man of the Match. In defeat, Zimbabwe retained both dignity and chivalry. They are

courteous and warm people, and one wishes that all Test matches were played in the spirit in which this game was fought.

The second Test followed hot upon the first, and the margin of Sri Lanka's victory was only slightly less emphatic than the innings win in the first encounter. Zimbabwe made two changes. Bryan Strang replaced the injured Streak, and Ali Omarshah, the 37-year-old left-hander, returned in place of Evans. Sri Lanka made one change, Pushpakumara replacing Dharmasena.

Campbell won the toss, and Zimbabwe batted on a grassless pitch that looked destined to aid the spinners. The visitors began well enough with Grant Flower batting three hours for his 52 and hitting six fours. He and Campbell put on 65 for the third wicket before the Zimbabwe skipper rushed at Silva and was stumped. This brought a cascade of wickets as Muralitharan and Silva again dominated. The last eight wickets went down in an hour for 22 runs. For the third time in succession, Silva bettered his previous best Test figures. Both spinners were again splendidly served by the catching of Mahanama at slip.

Mahanama was less impressive with bat, edging a cover drive to Andy Flower behind the stumps. Jayasuriya was caught at cover, and Paul Strang took a one-handed return catch to account for Aravinda de Silva. Sri Lanka ended the first day on 86 for 3.

They took complete control on the second day when Gurusinha and Tillekeratne shared a fifth wicket stand of 114. Gurusinha batted resolutely for 294 minutes and hit a six and eight fours before offering a simple chance to short

First Test Match – Sri Lanka v. Zimbabwe
11, 12, 13 and 14 September 1996 at Premadasa Stadium, Colombo

Sri Lanka

First Innings		
R.S. Mahanama	lbw, **b** Streak	4
S.T. Jayasuriya	**c** Evans, **b** Olonga	0
A.P. Gurusinha	**c** Olonga, **b** P.A. Strang	52
P.A. de Silva	**b** P.A. Strang	35
H.P. Tillekeratne	**c** A. Flower, **b** Olonga	20
A. Ranatunga (Capt)	lbw, **b** Streak	75
*R.S. Kaluwitharana	**c and b** Streak	71
H.D.P.K. Dharmasena	not out	42
W.P.U.J.C. Vaas	**b** P.A. Strang	34
M. Muralitharan	**b** P.A. Strang	0
K.J. Silva	**c and b** P.A. Strang	0
	lb **6**, w **2**, nb **8**	16
		349

	O	M	R	**W**
Streak	20	6	54	3
Olonga	17	3	57	2
G.J. Whittall	12	1	43	–
P.A. Strang	34.3	3	106	5
A.R. Whittall	13	3	40	–
Evans	6	–	27	–
G.W. Flower	4	1	16	–

Fall of Wickets
1–4, 2–4, 3–53, 4–105, 5–128, 6–270, 7–271, 8–345, 9–349

Umpires: S.A. Bucknor & B.C. Cooray

Zimbabwe

	First Innings		Second Innings	
G.W. Flower	**c** Kaluwitharana, **b** Vaas	0	**b** Muralitharan	27
M.H. Dekker	lbw, **b** Vaas	10	**c** Jayasuriya, **b** Dharmasena	20
A.D.R. Campbell (Capt)	**c** Mahanama, **b** Vaas	12	(4) **c** Mahanama, **b** Muralitharan	26
*A. Flower	**c** Ranatunga, **b** Dharmasena	2	(5) **c** Mahanama, **b** Muralitharan	0
G.J. Whittall	lbw, **b** Silva	39	(6) **c** Mahanama, **b** Silva	13
C.B. Wishart	**c** Vaas, **b** Silva	51	(3) **b** Silva	3
H.K. Olonga	**c** Tillekeratne, **b** Muralitharan	1	(9) **c** Mahanama, **b** Silva	0
C.N. Evans	**c** Kaluwitharana, **b** Vaas	9	(7) lbw, **b** Silva	1
P.A. Strang	**b** Muralitharan	6	(8) **c** Vaas, **b** Muralitharan	8
A.R. Whittall	**c** Dharmasena, **b** Silva	1	**b** Muralitharan	11
H.H. Streak	not out	0	not out	3
	b 4, lb **4**, w **2**, nb **4**	14	b **6**, lb **4**, w **1**, nb **4**	15
		145		**127**

	O	M	R	**W**	O	M	R	**W**
Vaas	22	3	73	4	12	1	34	–
Gurusinha	3	3	3	–	2	–	4	–
Dharmasena	9	3	23	1	14	7	19	1
Muralitharan	24	9	28	2	20.3	4	33	5
Silva	14.4	9	10	3	19	12	25	4
de Silva					2	1	1	–
Jayasuriya					4	3	1	–

Fall of Wickets
1–0, 2–15, 3–21, 4–45, 5–103, 6–105, 7–123, 8–138, 9–145
1–35, 2–42, 3–65, 4–65, 5–98, 6–99, 7–101, 8–102, 9–113

Sri Lanka won by an innings and 77 runs

Second Test Match – Sri Lanka v. Zimbabwe
18, 19, 20 and 21 September 1996 at Sinhalese Sports Club, Colombo

Zimbabwe

	First Innings		Second Innings	
G.W. Flower	**c** Mahanama, **b** Muralitharan	52	lbw, **b** Silva	13
M.H. Dekker	**c** Mahanama, **b** Muralitharan	18	lbw, **b** Vaas	4
A.H. Omarshah	**c** Kaluwitharana, **b** Pushpakumara	1	**c** Vaas, **b** Pushpakumara	62
A.D.R. Campbell (Capt)	**st** Kaluwitharana, **b** Silva	36	**c** sub (Atapattu), **b** Silva	4
*A. Flower	run out	3	**c** Gurusinha, **b** Muralitharan	31
C.B. Wishart	**c** Kaluwitharana, **b** Silva	2	**c** Kaluwitharana, **b** Jayasuriya	25
G.J. Whittall	**c** Silva, **b** Muralitharan	0	**c** Gurusinha, **b** Jayasuriya	3
P.A. Strang	not out	2	(9) **c and b** Vaas	50
A.R. Whittall	**c** Gurusinha, **b** Muralitharan	3	(8) **b** Muralitharan	12
B.C. Strang	**c** de Silva, **b** Silva	3	**b** Muralitharan	2
H.K. Olonga	**c** Mahanama, **b** Silva	3	not out	3
	b 3, lb **10**, nb **5**	18	b **2**, lb **6**, w **1**, nb **17**	26
		141		**235**

	O	M	R	**W**	O	M	R	**W**
Vaas	10	1	31	–	26.3	11	34	2
Pushpakumara	11	3	34	1	8	–	24	1
Muralitharan	20	5	40	4	41	9	94	3
Silva	10.1	4	16	4	26	7	49	1
de Silva	2	–	7	–	5	1	10	–
Jayasuriya					7	3	16	3

Fall of Wickets
1–44, 2–54, 3–119, 4–121, 5–123, 6–125, 7–126, 8–133, 9–136
1–9, 2–30, 3–34, 4–91, 5–135, 6–144, 7–167, 8–193, 9–201

Umpires: C.J. Mitchley & K.T. Francis

Sri Lanka

	First Innings		Second Innings	
R.S. Mahanama	**c** A. Flower, **b** B. Strang	3	(2) not out	12
S.T. Jayasuriya	**c** A. Whittall, **b** P. Strang	41	(1) not out	18
A.P. Gurusinha	**c** Wishart, **b** B. Strang	88		
P.A. de Silva	**c and b** P. Strang	16		
A. Ranatunga (Capt)	**c** Wishart, **b** B. Strang	6		
H.P. Tillekeratne	not out	126		
*R.S. Kaluwitharana	**c** A. Flower, **b** G. Whittall	27		
W.P.U.J.C. Vaas	**st** A. Flower, **b** P. Strang	8		
K.R. Pushpakumara	**c** B. Strang, **b** P. Strang	23		
M. Muralitharan	not out	1		
K.J. Silva				
	lb **4**, w **3**, nb **4**	11		0
	(for 8 wickets, dec)	**350**	(for no wicket)	**30**

	O	M	R	**W**	O	M	R	**W**
Olonga	26	6	81	–	3.4	–	17	–
B.C. Strang	20	6	63	3				
A.R. Whittall	31	7	75	–				
P.A. Strang	38	11	66	4	3	–	13	–
G.J. Whittall	17	4	48	1				
G.W. Flower	2	–	13	–				

Fall of Wickets
1–19, 2–58, 3–86, 4–102, 5–216, 6–267, 7–276, 8–340

Sri Lanka won by 10 wickets

square-leg. Tillekeratne remained and was unbeaten on 100 at the close with Sri Lanka 317 for 7. The left-hander had hit 12 fours and batted for 335 minutes in reaching his fifth Test century, his first on home soil.

Sri Lanka batted for just over an hour on the third day before Ranatunga declared. Tillekeratne added 26 to his overnight score and hit one more boundary.

Zimbabwe began disastrously, as had become their custom and were 34 for 3. Omarshah and Andy Flower put on 57, but, at the close, with Jayasuriya claiming two wickets, Zimbabwe were 162 for 6. Omarshah had batted with great determination to record his first Test 50, but he was brilliantly caught in the gully without addition to his overnight score early on the fourth morning. There was further resistance from Paul Strang, who hit his first Test 50 in a 98-minute innings in which he hit five fours. He and Olonga put on 34 for the last wicket and so forced Sri Lanka to bat again.

It was small consolation. Sri Lanka had totally dominated both Tests, but the matches had been played in the best possible spirit, and cricket was the winner.

Tillekeratne was named Man of the Match, and the triumphs of Sri Lanka under Arjuna Ranatunga continued.

Sara Trophy

29, 30 November, and 1 December 1996
at BRC Ground
Kurunegala Youth CC 153 (A.W. Ekanayake 82, D. Ekanayake 5 for 33) and 220 (R.R. Jaymon 51)
BRC 142 and 103 for 0 (A. Ranaweera 61 not out)
Match drawn

at Tyronne Fernando Stadium, Moratuwa
Sebastianites 302 (S.K. Silva 111, U.C. Hathurusinghe 4 for 61) and 312 for 7 (M.S. Mendis 100, S.K. Silva 83, C.N. Bandaratilleke 6 for 95)
Tamil Union 180 (M. Perera 5 for 49)
Match drawn

at Colts Ground, Havelock Park
Bloomfield C & AC 262 (N. Bopage 81, I. Bahiwitarachchi 70, W.P.U.J.C. Vaas 4 for 65) and 178 for 4 dec. (S.K. Perera 83, I. Bahiwitarachchi 51 not out)
Colombo Colts CC 185 and 1 for 0
Match drawn

at Panadura Esplanade
Panadura Sports C 138 and 107 for 3
Nondescripts CC 253 for 6 dec. (R.P. Arnold 70)
Match drawn

at Galle Ground
Galle CC 109 (A. Priyantha 6 for 30) and 187 (C.K. Hewamanne 54, M.M. de Silva 53)
Police SC 176 (N. Soyza 64, A. Rideegammanagedera 4 for 37) and 111 for 6
Match drawn

Three days of poor weather made it impossible for any of the first round of matches to produce a definite result. S.K. Silva scored the first century of the season, and, in Sebastianites' second innings, shared an opening stand of 171 with Manoj Mendis.

The sensation of the season was that reigning champions Colombo CC were suspended from the competition and matches that they played were discounted.

6, 7 and 8 December 1996
at Tyronne Fernando Stadium, Moratuwa
Kalutara TC 142 (H.S.S. Fonseka 70) and 249 (T.M. Dilshan 91, R. Herath 5 for 96)
Kurunegala YCC 334 (S.K.L. de Silva 108, R.R. Jaymon 102) and 58 for 2
Kurunegala YCC won by 8 wickets

A century against West Indies 'A' by Marvan Atapattu and a recall to the Test side for this aggressive batsman. (David Munden/Sportsline)

at P. Saravanamuttu Stadium, Colombo
Tamil Union 312 (U.U. Chandana 83) and 97 (K.J. Silva 6 for 42)
Sinhalese SC 334 (M.S. Atapattu 106, R.P.A.H. Wickramaratne 77, M. Muralitharan 5 for 120) and 76 for 0 (D.R.M. Jayawardene 54 not out)
Sinhalese CC won by 10 wickets

at Panadura Esplanade
Bloomfield C & AC 403 (P.B. Dassanayake 119, I. Bahiwitarachchi 109, B. de Silva 66, I.S. Gallage 5 for 100) and 250 for 8 dec. (S.K. Perera 53)
Panadura SC 295 (D. Ruwan 58, S. Kumara 58, P. Wickramasinghe 4 for 52)
Match drawn

at Colts Ground, Havelock Park
Colombo Colts 194 (A. Perera 4 for 67) and 300 for 8 dec. (M.C. Mendis 80, D.K. Liyanage 60 not out)
Sebastianites 242 (M.S. Mendis 70, A. Perera 51, D.P. Samaraweera 4 for 55) and 171 for 9
Match drawn

at Galle Esplanade
Singha SC 173 (A. Rideegammanagedera 4 for 42) and 117 (A. Rideegammanagedera 4 for 31)
Galle CC 137 (B. Ranjith 8 for 50) and 135 (B. Ranjith 7 for 48)
Singha SC won by 18 runs

at Police Park
Police SC 158 (J.A. Mahindaratne 4 for 29) and 300 for 8 dec. (I.D. Gunawardene 93, J.A. Mahindaratne 4 for 78)
BRC 123 (N. Soyza 5 for 44) and 175 for 9 (N. Soyza 4 for 61, P. Serasinghe 4 for 65)
Match drawn

Lanka de Silva and Roshan Jaymon put on 157 for Kurunegala's fourth wicket to set up victory over newcomers Kalutara.

Led by Arjuna Ranatunga, Sinhalese Sports Club proved too strong for Tamil Union. Atapattu reached his century in under three hours, and left-arm Test spinner Kelaniyage Silva destroyed Tamil Union's second innings.

A fifth wicket stand of 212 between Dassanayake and Bahiwitarachchi formed the substance of Bloomfield's large total against Panadura while Bandula Ranjith returned the season's best bowling figures as Singha beat Galle in a low-scoring match.

13, 14 and 15 December 1996
at Nondescripts Ground
Sinhalese SC 57 for 4
v. **Nondescripts**
Match abandoned

at Tyronne Fernando Stadium, Moratuwa
Sebastianites 196 (D. Bodiyabaduge 55)
Panadura SC 159 for 3 (S.N. Liyanage 51 not out)
Match abandoned

at Colts Ground, Havelock Park
Tamil Union 232 (U.U. Chandana 67, S.I. de Saram 54, T.T. Samaraweera 5 for 50)
Colombo Colts 413 for 9 (R.S. Kaluwitharana 162, T.T. Samaraweera 56)
Match drawn

at Moors Ground
Galle CC 205 (G.H. Perera 4 for 37)
Antonians SC 105 for 6
Match abandoned

at BRC Ground
Kalutara TC 160 (D. Madurapenuma 6 for 45) and 257 (H.S.S. Fonseka 60, C. Hettiarachchi 52, T.M. Dilshan 51, S. Madanayake 5 for 36)
BRC 332 (E.M.I. Galagoda 117, C. Hettiarachchi 5 for 51) and 19 for 4
Match drawn

The third round of matches was badly hit by rain. Test wicket-keeper Kaluwitharana hit 162 in just over three hours for Colts while another wicket-keeper, Indika Galagoda formerly of Bloomfield, hit a maiden first-class century for BRC.

27, 28 and 29 December 1996
at Welagedara Stadium
Singha SC 128 and 187 (S. Jayantha 56, A. Wewalwala 53, R. Madurasinghe 4 for 67)
Kurunegala YCC 147 (A. Wewalwala 5 for 40) and 170 for 8 (S.K.L. de Silva 59)
Kurunegala YCC won by 2 wickets

at Police Ground
Police SC 138 (R.C. Liyanage 66, G.H. Perera 4 for 20) and 300 for 7 dec. (N. Soyza 73, R.R. Wimalasiri 66)
Antonians 145 (P. Serasinghe 6 for 38) and 156 for 6 (P.N. Wanasinghe 56)
Match drawn

at Sinhalese SC, Maitland Place
Bloomfield C & AC 161 and 300 for 5 (S.T. Perera 102 not out, S.T. Jayasuriya 89)
Sinhalese SC 352 for 9 dec. (R.P.A.H. Wickramaratne 84, D.R.M. Jayawardene 60, R.S. Kalpage 4 for 72)
Match drawn

at Tyronne Fernando Stadium, Moratuwa
Sebastianites 172 (S.K. Silva 58, K.R. Pushpakumara 6 for 64) and 102 (K.R. Pushpakumara 5 for 26)

Nondescripts 300 for 9 dec. (R.P. Arnold 116)
Nondescripts won by an innings and 26 runs

at P. Saravanamuttu Stadium, Colombo
Tamil Union 310 (A. Jayasinghe 95, G. Wijekoon
92 not out, U.U. Chandana 53, I.S. Gallage 4 for 64) and
15 for 0
Panadura SC 144 (M. Muralitharan 5 for 28) and 177
(C.M. Hathurusinghe 6 for 72)
Tamil Union won by 10 wickets

at Galle Esplanade
Galle CC 235 (D.D. Wickramasinghe 81, P. Silva 4 for 82)
and 218 for 6 dec. (N. Shiroman 53)
Kalutara TC 112 (M.M. de Silva 6 for 27) and 218
(P. Perera 63)
Galle CC won by 123 runs

Sri Lanka's pace bowler Ravindra Pushpakumara took ten
or more wickets in a match for the first time as Nondescripts
crushed Sebastianites. Slow left-arm spinner Malaka de
Silva returned his best bowling figures as Galle beat
Kalutara while another left-arm spinner, Pushpakumara
Serasinghe produced his best bowling figures for Police
Sports Club against Antonians.

3, 4 and 5 January 1997
at P. Saravanamuttu Stadium, Colombo
Antonians 81 (B. Ranjith 9 for 29) and 295 (P. Perera 57,
N. Devarajan 53, B. Ranjith 4 for 101)
Singha SC 268 (A. Wewalwala 62) and 112 for 3
Singha SC won by 7 wickets

at Police Park
Kurunegala YCC 76 (V Ranaweera 5 for 39) and 208
(A.W. Ekanayake 67, A. Priyantha 4 for 29)
Police SC 133 (R.K.B. Amunugama 5 for 61) and
152 for 4 (R.C. Liyanage 53 not out)
Police SC won by 6 wickets

at Sinhalese SC, Maitland Place
Sinhalese SC 453 for 4 dec. (A. Ranatunga 200 not out,
R.P.A.H. Wickramaratne 104 not out)
Sebastianites 222 (W.D.J. Abeywardene 75,
S.B. Dodanwela 4 for 42) and 207 (A. Perera 90,
G.P. Wickramasinghe 6 for 82)
Sinhalese SC won by an innings and 24 runs

at Nondescripts Ground
Bloomfield C & AC 364 (R.S. Mahanama 111,
S.T. Jayasuriya 75, R.S. Kaplage 71) and 212 for 6 dec.
(M.N. Nawaz 84, S.T. Jayasuriya 72)
Nondescripts 316 (A. Gunawardene 108, R. Peiris 85,
H.P. Tillekeratne 71, S.T. Jayasuriya 4 for 54, R.S. Kalpage
4 for 110) and 73 for 3
Match drawn

at Colts Ground, Havelock Park
Colombo Colts 446 for 5 dec. (R.S. Kaluwitharana 150,
M.C. Mendis 102, D.P. Samaraweera 100, T.T. Samaraweera
50 not out)
Panadura SC 105 (D.P. Liyanage 5 for 26,
K.E.A. Upashantha 4 for 48) and 151
Colombo Colts won by an innings and 190 runs

at Galle Esplanade
Galle CC 267 (A. Rideegammanagedera 71) and 232
(N. Shiroman 55)
BRC 353 (D. Arnolda 129 not out, S. Madanayake 110,
A. Rideegammanagedera 5 for 87)
Match drawn

Having claimed the best match analysis of the season,
Bandula Ranjith added the best innings performance
with nine wickets for Singha against Antonians. Arjuna
Ranatunga hit the season's first double century and shared
an unbroken fifth wicket partnership of 317 in 235 minutes
with Hamintha Wickramaratne.

There was another sensational partnership at Galle.
When Madanayake joined Arnolda, BRC were 95 for 7.
When they were separated the score was 322 and BRC had
claimed first innings points.

*Reigning captain of Sri Lanka and the only batsman to hit a double
century in the Sara Trophy, Sinhalese SC v. Sebastianites, Arjuna
Ranatunga. (David Munden/Sportsline)*

Dulip Samaraweera and Chaminda Mendis began Colts innings with a stand of 188, and Rumesh Kaluwitharana followed with his second century in succes-sive matches.

Jayasuriya played innings of 75 off 81 balls and 72 off 51 balls for Bloomfield against Nondescripts. Mahanama, skippering the side at number five, hit a more patient century.

10, 11 and 12 January 1997
at Colts Ground, Havelock Park
Colombo Colts 295 (D.P. Samaraweera 90, R.S. Kaluwitharana 52, P. Serasinghe 4 for 60) and 302 for 7 dec. (J. Kalatunga 89, T.T. Samaraweera 68)
Police SC 57 (T.T. Samaraweera 5 for 8) and 156 (S.I. Fernando 4 for 35, B. Perera 4 for 43)
Colombo Colts won by 384 runs

at Panadura Esplanade
Panadura SC 294 (S.N. Liyanage 77, S. Kumara 74, J.C. Gamage 4 for 34) and 150 for 4 dec. (D. Ruwan 61 not out)
Galle CC 188 (S.D. Anurasiri 6 for 36) and 45 for 1
Match drawn

at Tyronne Fernando Stadium, Moratuwa
Antonians 275 (P.N. Wanasinghe 70, N. Devarajan 50, A. Perera 4 for 40) and 137 for 5
Sebastianites 260 (A.P. Dalugoda 52, K.G. Perera 6 for 64)
Match drawn

at P. Saravanamuttu Stadium, Colombo
Tamil Union 448 for 9 dec. (G. Wijekoon 117, U.U. Chandana 104, C.N. Bandaratilleke 77)
Singha SC 133 (M. Muralitharan 4 for 26) and 119 (U.U. Chandana 6 for 25)
Tamil Union won by an innings and 196 runs

at Welagedera Stadium, Kurunegala
Bloomfield C & AC 411 for 7 dec. (H.D.P.K. Dharmasena 155 not out, R.S. Kalpage 74, M.N. Nawaz 57) and 113 for 6 dec.
Kurunegala YCC 264 (R.R. Jaymon 60, D. Hunulumhura 54, P.W. Gunaratne 6 for 71) and 126 (P.W. Gunaratne 4 for 40)
Bloomfield C & AC won by 134 runs

at Nondescripts Ground
Nondescripts 412 for 8 dec. (H.P. Tillekeratne 143, P.K. Rajapakse, C.I. Dunusinghe 50 not out) and 188 for 1 dec. (C.R. Peiris 100 not out)
BRC 326 (D. Rajapakse 67, D. Arnolda 61, S. Tennakoon 53) and 127 for 3
Match drawn

at Sinhalese SC, Maitland Place
Kalutara TC 109 (D.N.T. Zoysa 5 for 33) and 74 (D.N.T. Zoysa 4 for 16, S.B. Dodanwela 4 for 49)

Sinhalese SC 350 (R.S. Jayawardene 89, R.P.A.H. Wickramaratne 52, D.R.M. Jayawardene 51, M.N. Perera 50, P. Perera 5 for 70)
Sinhalese SC won by an innings and 167 runs

Colts bowled out Police for 57, the lowest score of the season, and won an overwhelming victory. Upal Chandana followed a century for Tamil Union against Singha with the best bowling performance of his career. His leg-breaks brought him 6 for 25. Test bowler Dharmasena hit a maiden first-class century for Bloomfield against Kurunegala, while young fast bowler Nuwan Zoysa edged close to the Test side with match figures of 9 for 49 as Sinhalese conquered Kalutara.

17, 18 and 19 January 1997
at Nondescripts Ground
Kalutara TC 114 (K.R. Pushpakumara 5 for 65) and 165 (R. Kottachchi 52, K.R. Pushpakumara 6 for 43)
Nondescripts 301 (R. Peiris 125, A. Gunawardene 68)
Nondescripts won by an innings and 22 runs

at Reid Avenue, Colombo
BRC 283 and 141 (H.D.P.K. Dharmasena 5 for 27)
Bloomfield C & AC 410 for 9 dec. (R.S. Mahanama 94, H.D.P.K. Dharmasena 94, H.M.L. Sagara 4 for 131) and 17 for 0
Bloomfield C & AC won by 10 wickets

at Tyronne Fernando Stadium, Moratuwa
Sebastianites 307 (S. Silva 129, A.P. Dalugoda 50, M.M. de Silva 5 for 72) and 315 for 7 (S.K. Silva 59, M.S. Mendis 53, M.M. de Silva 5 for 109)
Galle CC 349 (N. Shiroman 103, D.D. Wickramasinghe 91, D. Sudarshana 64, G.R.M.A. Perera 4 for 62)
Match drawn

at P. Saravanamuttu Stadium, Colombo
Tamil Union 370 (V.S.K. Warangoda 138, U.U. Chandana 56, Y.N. Tillekaratne 4 for 65)
Antonians 179 (T.P. Kodikara 54, M. Muralitharan 7 for 55) and 136 (C.N. Bandaratilleke 4 for 41)
Tamil Union won by an innings and 55 runs

at Colts Ground, Havelock Park
Singha SC 328 (S. Jayantha 77, S. Sanjeewa 72 not out, S.I. Fernando 5 for 45) and 281 (S. Jayantha 73, S. Sanjeewa 54, K.E.A. Upashantha 4 for 66)
Colombo Colts CC 380 (M.C. Mendis 131, T.T. Samaraweera 117, B. Ranjith 6 for 132) and 136 for 6
Match drawn

at Panadura Esplanade
Panadura SC 156 and 230 for 6 dec. (S. Kumara 58, P.K. Serasinghe 4 for 69)

Police SC 84 (S.D. Anurasiri 5 for 21) and 121 for 9
(S.D. Anurasiri 5 for 21, I.S. Gallage 4 for 36)
Match drawn

For the second time in the season, Pushpakumara took 11
wickets in a match when Nondescripts beat Kalutara, and
Malaka de Silva of Galle had ten wickets in a match for the
first time. Muralithan was another bowler to claim ten
wickets. He had match figures of 10 for 78 for Tamil Union
against Antonians. A fourth bowler to capture ten wickets
was Don Anurasiri, the former Test left-arm spinner.

24, 25 and 26 January 1997
at Galle Esplanade
Sinhalese SC 196 (U.N.K. Fernando 71, M.M. de Silva 6
for 47) and 335 for 8 dec. (M.S. Atapattu 135,
U.N.K. Fernando 77)
Galle CC 225 (D. Sudarshana 57, S. Kodituwakku 52) and
172 (A. Rideegammanagedera 64, D.N.T. Zoysa 4 for 46)
Sinhalese SC won by 134 runs

*Prolific scoring for Colts CC in the Sara Trophy – Rumesh
Kaluwitharana. (David Munden/Sportsline)*

at Reid Avenue, Colombo
Bloomfield C & AC 432 for 3 dec. (R.S. Mahanama 176,
M.N. Nawaz 101, P.B. Dassanayake 55, R.S. Kalpage 52 not
out) and 250 for 8 dec. (R. Palliyaguru 73, N. Bopage 57)
Kalutara TC 125 (H.D.P.K. Dharmasena 4 for 27) and
141 (N. Tilakaratne 64, R.S. Kalpage 7 for 37)
Bloomfield C & AC won by 416 runs

at BRC Ground
Sebastianites 340 (A. Fernando 92 not out,
A.P. Dalugoda 51, W.C. Labrooy 4 for 102) and 161 for 5
(W.C. Labrooy 4 for 71)
BRC 433 for 9 dec. (D. Rajapakse 101 not out,
E.M.I. Galgoda 81, M. Rajapakse 66, S. Tennakoon 62,
A. Perera 6 for 87)
Match drawn

at Welagedara Stadium
Tamil Union 350 (G. Wijekoon 81, V.S.K. Warangoda 75,
A.W. Ekanayake 4 for 88) and 287 for 4 (D.N. Nadarajah
102, A. Jayasinghe 100)
Kurunegala YCC 261 (S.K.L. de Silva 109,
C.M. Hathurusinghe 4 for 42)
Match drawn

at Colts Ground, Havelock Park
Antonians 303 (P.N. Wanasinghe 110, T.P. Kodikara 68)
and 241 (M. Prasanga 73, E.F.M.U. Fernando 67,
W.P.U.J.C. Vaas 4 for 57)
Colombo Colts CC 364 for 4 dec. (R.S. Kaluwitharana
149, S.I. Fernando 144 not out, S. Janaka 62)
Match drawn

at Panadura Esplanade
Panadura SC 169 and 176 (B. Ranjith 4 for 63)
Singha SC 90 (K.C. Silva 5 for 41) and 129 (S.D. Anurasiri
6 for 42)
Panadura SC won by 126 runs

Test opener Roshan Mahanama shared stands of 153 for the
first wicket with Dassanayake and 154 for the second with
Nawaz as Bloomfield overwhelmed Kalutara. Another Test
cricketer, Ruwan Kalpage had match figures of 10 for 75.
Sajith Fernando and Romesh Kaluwitharana, a batsman in
sparkling form, shared a third wicket stand of 267 for Colts
against Antonians.

---

31 January, 1 and 2 February 1997
at BRC Ground
Sinhalese SC 394 (M.N. Perera 106, A. Ranatunga 88,
M.S. Atapattu 61, R.S. Jayawardene 60, W.C. Labrooy
5 for 90) and 67 for 3
BRC 204 (D.N.T. Zoysa 4 for 61) and 255 (W.C. Labrooy
65 not out, D. Rajapakse 50)
Sinhalese SC won by 7 wickets

Former Test opener Chandika Hathurusinghe excelled as an all-rounder in the Sara Trophy and produced the best bowling performances of his career. (David Munden/Sportsline)

at Nondescripts Ground
Galle CC 326 (D.D. Wickramasinghe 103,
A. Rideegammanagedera 100, D. Samarasinghe 4 for 47)
and 44 for 1
Nondescripts 401 for 5 dec. (A. Gunawardene
120 not out, H.P. Tillekeratne 110 not out, S. Ranatunga 80,
R. Peiris 61, S.M. Faumi 4 for 111)
Match drawn

at Tyronne Fernando Stadium, Moratuwa
Kalutara TC 229 (H.S.S. Fonseka 91, A.P. Dalugado
4 for 65) and 322 for 8 dec. (P. Perera 133, T.M. Dilshan 111,
A.P. Dalugado 5 for 42)
Sebastianites 412 for 9 dec. (A. Fernando 113,
S.K. Silva 71, R. Yasalal 54) and 46 for 3
Match drawn

at P. Saravanamattu Stadium, Colombo
Police SC 197 (N. Soyza 53, M. Muralitharan 4 for 44)
and 206 (A. Driyantha 56, R.C. Liyanage 51, M. Muralitharan
6 for 75)
Tamil Union 236 (V.S.K. Warangoda 84, V. Ranaweera
4 for 67) and 168 for 3 (U.U. Chandana 104 not out)
Tamil Union won by 7 wickets

at Colts Ground, Havelock Park
Colombo Colts CC 413 for 6 dec. (R.S. Kaluwitharana
179, J. Kulatunga 118)

Kurunegala YCC 197 (C.P. Handunettige 82,
H. Liyanage 50 not out, D.K. Liyanage 5 for 42) and 110
(W.P.U.J.C. Vaas 6 for 12)
Colombo Colts CC won by 106 runs

at Panadura Esplanade
Panadura SC 384 (S. Kumara 142, B.P. Perera 67)
and 183 for 6 (R.C. Galappaththi 69, S. Kumara 57 not out,
D. Surendra 5 for 95)
Antonians 214 (Y.N. Tillekeratne 67, E.F.M.U. Fernando
61 not out, S.D. Anurasiri 7 for 84)
Match drawn

Needing 66 to beat BRC, Sinhalese hit off the runs in
seven hectic overs. There was lightning batting, too,
by Tamil Union, for whom Chandana hit a century off
82 balls in 118 minutes, the fastest of the season.
Kaluwitharana was again in the runs with a brisk 179.
He and Kulatunga put on 203 for Colts' fourth wicket.
Tillekeratne and Gunawardene shared an unbroken
sixth wicket stand of 239 for Nondescripts against
Galle.

7, 8 and 9 February 1997
at Colts Ground, Havelock Park
Colombo Colts CC 403 (S. Janaka 85, D.P. Samaraweera
82, S.I. Fernando 65, J. Kulatunga 65) and 179 for 8 dec.
(S. Janaka 58)
BRC 302 (E.M.I. Galagoda 93) and 179 (W.P.U.J.C. Vaas
6 for 48)
Colombo Colts CC won by 101 runs

at Tyronne Fernando Stadium, Moratuwa
Kurunegala YCC 258 (R.J. Jaymon 57, I.S. Gallage
5 for 72, K. Kaynaweera 4 for 95) and 172 for 8
(S.K.L. de Silva 60, I. Amithakeekthi 4 for 50)
Panadura SC 193 (M.W. Kumara 6 for 64)
Match drawn

at Reid Avenue, Colombo
Galle CC 172 (A. Rideegammanagedera 77) and 104
(P. Wickaramasinghe 5 for 26)
Bloomfield C & AC 401 for 6 dec. (S.T. Jayasuriya 129,
R.S. Kalpage 92 not out)
Bloomfield C & AC won by an innings and 125 runs

at P. Saravanamattu Stadium, Colombo
Tamil Union 357 (U.C. Hathurusinghe 121,
V.S.K. Warangoda 55, R. Perera 5 for 66)
Kalutara TC 119 (C.N. Bandaratilleke 6 for 50) and 160
(R. Perera 55)
Tamil Union won by 78 runs

at Sinhalese SC Ground
Singha SC 136 (H. Premasiri 51, S.B. Dodanwela 5 for 39)
and 143 (D.N.T. Zoysa 7 for 58)

Sinhalese SC 405 for 7 dec. (M.S. Atapattu 91, R.S. Jayawardene 67, D.R.M. Jayawardene 54)
Sinhalese SC won by an innings and 126 runs

at Nondescripts Ground
Police SC 102 (C.D.U.S. Weerasinghe 6 for 32) and 142 (S.C. de Silva 6 for 48, R.P. Arnold 4 for 38)
Nondescripts 272 for 9 dec. (R.P. Arnold 131, V. Ranaweera 5 for 83)
Nondescripts won by an innings and 28 runs

Zoysa confirmed his growing reputation with nine wickets in Sinhalese's victory over Singha, while Russell Arnold had an excellent all-round match for Nondescripts.

14, 15 and 16 February 1997
at Sinhalese SC Ground
Antonians 206 (G.P. Wickramasinghe 4 for 61) and 197 (V. Sittamige 53, D.N.T. Zoysa 4 for 68)
Sinhalese SC 417 for 6 dec. (A.A.W. Gunawardene 158, R.P.A.H. Wickramasinghe 130, P.N. Wanasinghe 5 for 131)
Sinhalese SC won by an innings and 14 runs

at Welagedera Stadium
Kurunegala YCC 189 (S.K.L. de Silva 80, K.R. Pushpakumara 5 for 50) and 250 (S.K.L. de Silva 104, R.P. Arnold 7 for 84)
Nondescripts 153 (A.W. Ekanayake 5 for 41) and 177 (M.A.W.R. Madurasinghe 5 for 49)
Kurunegala YCC won by 109 runs

at Reid Avenue, Colombo
Bloomfield C & AC 417 for 7 dec. (R.S. Kalpage 160, H.D.P.K. Dharmasena 93)
Police SC 204 and 63 (M. Villavarayan 9 for 15)
Bloomfield C & AC won by an innings and 150 runs

at Tyronne Fernando Stadium, Moratuwa
Singha SC 101 (A. Perera 5 for 34) and 182 (S. Jayantha 69 not out, A. Perera 4 for 49, A.P. Dalugoda 4 for 31)
Sebastianites 307 (A.P. Dalugoda 80, C. Mahesh 59, M.S. Mendis 51)
Sebastianites won by an innings and 24 runs

at Colts Ground, Havelock Park
Colombo Colts CC 453 for 5 dec. (S.I. Fernando 178 not out, R.S. Kaluwitharana 157) and 258 for 6 dec. (R.S. Kaluwitharana 107)
Galle 176 (W.P.U.J.C. Vaas 4 for 50) and 233 for 8 (D. Sudarshana 57, B. Perera 4 for 113)
Match drawn

at Panadura Esplanade
BRC 213 (D. Rajapakse 55) and 235 for 6 (M. Rajapakse 61, S. Tennakoon 53)

Panadura SC 420 (I. Amithakeerthi 137 not out)
Match drawn

Two splendid innings by Lanka de Silva helped Kurunegala to victory over Nondescripts, but Bloomfield moved closer to the top of the table with a crushing win over Police. Ruwan Kalpage hit the highest score of his career, but the main honours went to medium-pacer Mario Villavarayan, whose 9 for 15 was a career best performance and the best bowling performance of the season, bettering Ranjith's 9 for 28. Kaluwitharana's astonishing batting success continued with a century in each innings against Galle.

21, 22 and 23 February 1997
at Panadura Esplanade
Kalutara TC 203 (N. Thilakaratne 78, I. Amithakeerthi 5 for 6) and 231 for 8 (T.M. Dilshan 93, P. Perera 56, K.P. Rathnaweera 4 for 63)
Panadura SC 115 (P. Perera 6 for 41)
Match drawn

at P. Saravanamattu Stadium, Colombo
Tamil Union 285 (U.C. Hathurusinghe 85, S.P. Herathge 60, A. Rideegammanagedera 5 for 54) and 197 (M.M. de Silva 4 for 60)
Galle CC 282 (U. Samarawickrama 66, D.D. Wickramasinghe 63, C.N. Bandaratilleke 8 for 78)
Match drawn

at Moratuwa Stadium
Police 284 (N. Soyza 70, A. Priyantha 57, A.P. Dalugoda 4 for 50)
Sebastianites 302 for 8 (S. Silva 135)
Match drawn

at Air Force Ground, Katunayake
Antonians 107 (B.N. Saranasekera 4 for 22) and 197 (S. Jayawardane 120)
Nondescripts 118 (P.N. Wanasinghe 6 for 42) and 190 for 2 (S. Ranatunga 84 not out, D. Maiarachchi 79)
Nondescripts won by 8 wickets

at Reid Avenue, Colombo
Bloomfield C & AC 419 for 8 dec. (P.B. Ediniweera 82, S.K. Perera 69, S. Abeynaike 62, B. de Silva 62)
Singha SC 216 (R. Palliyaguru 4 for 45, B. de Silva 4 for 47) and 143 (W.G.S. Wijenayake 5 for 38, R.L. Perera 4 for 38)
Bloomfield C & AC won by an innings and 60 runs

at Sinhalese SC Ground
Kurunegala YCC 263 (S.S. Guruge 66, H. Liyanage 56, S.K.L. de Silva 50, S.B. Dodanwela 4 for 46) and 191 (K.J. Silva 6 for 78)
Sinhalese SC 392 (C. Fernando 107, U.N.K. Fernando 92, T.M.C. Boteju 53 not out) and 63 for 0
Sinhalese SC won by 10 wickets

Rain affected several matches, and Damith Maiarachchi and Sanjeeva Ranatunga took Nondescripts to a thrilling victory by adding 175 in under two hours. Ranatunga hit 14 fours. Both Bloomfield and Sinhalese SC gained their sixth victories in succession and remained locked together at the top of the table.

28 February, 1 and 2 March 1997
at Nondescripts Ground
Nondescripts 382 (R.P. Arnold 104, S. Ranatunga 97, C. Chrisnantha 4 for 106)
Singha SC 193 (G. Sanjeewa 55, C.D.U.S. Weerasinghe 5 for 66) and 187 (C.D.U.S. Weerasinghe 5 for 69)
Nondescripts won by an innings and 2 runs

at Reid Avenue, Colombo
Bloomfield C & AC 389 (R. Palliyaguru 117, P.B. Ediriweera 64) and 180 for 6 dec. (S.K. Perera 54 not out, P.N. Wanasinghe 4 for 74)
Antonians 265 (T.P. Kodikara 88, W.G.S. Wijenayake 4 for 66) and 54 (R.L. Perera 5 for 26)
Bloomfield C & AC won by 250 runs

at Colts Ground, Havelock Park
Tamil Union 444 for 6 dec. (A. Jayasinghe 183, G. Wijekoon 73, D.N. Nadarajah 52 not out, M. Perera 52)
BRC 291 (D. Rajapakse 79, E.M.I. Galagado 72, D. Madurapperuma 59 not out, U.C. Hathurusinghe 7 for 158) and 136 (U.C. Hathurusinghe 8 for 29)
Tamil Union won by an innings and 17 runs

at Panadura Esplanade
Kalutara TC 133 (B. Perera 4 for 21) and 200 (T.M. Dilshan 67, N. Thilakaratne 55)
Colombo Colts CC 405 for 7 dec. (S. Janaka 148, J. Kulatunga 61, M.T. Sampath 50)
Colombo Colts CC won by an innings and 75 runs

at Welagedera Stadium
Kurunegala YCC 329 for 7 dec. (S.K.L. de Silva 109, H. Liyanage 82)
Sebastianites 275 (S. Silva 69, M.S. Mendis 57, R. Kariyawasam 4 for 102)
Match drawn

at Police Park
Sinhalese SC 345 (A.A.W. Gunawardene 135, A. Kapilaratne 58, C. Fernando 54)
Police SC 293 for 7 (R.C. Liyanage 83, A. Priyantha 79, K.J. Silva 5 for 80)
Match abandoned

Rain caused the abandonment of the game at Police Park and allowed no play on the second day at Welagedera Stadium. With the national side in New Zealand, the strength in depth of the leading teams became important. It was a former Test player, however, who stole the headlines. Chandika Hathurusinghe, opening batsman and medium pace bowler, still short of his 30th birthday, took ten wickets in a match for the first time. The Tamil Union all-rounder twice bettered his previous best bowling performance.

7, 8 and 9 March 1997
at Colts Ground, Havelock Park
BRC 265 (E.M.I. Galagoda 77, B. Ranjith 4 for 53)
Singha SC 64 (S. Madanayake 4 for 15) and 128 (A.S. Wewalwala 74)
BRC won by an innings and 73 runs

at St Antonians School
Kurunegala YCC 148 and 70 (S. Jayawardene 5 for 40)
Antonians 276 (Y.N. Tillekeratne 135 not out, A.J. Ekanayake 5 for 86)
Antonians won by an innings and 58 runs

at Police Park
Kalutara TC 166 (C. Hettiarachchi 68) and 160 (N. Thilakaratne 63, P.K. Serasinghe 7 for 55)
Police SC 311 (R.C. Liyanage 86, I.D. Gunawardene 52, R. Kottachchi 5 for 60) and 19 for 0
Police SC won by 10 wickets

at Nondescripts Ground
Nondescripts 257 (D. Maiarachchi 74, A. Weerapuli 50 not out, C.N. Bandaratilleke 6 for 78, U.U. Chandana 4 for 55) and 194 (S. Ranatunga 82, U.C. Hathurusinghe 7 for 63)
Tamil Union 410 (S.I. de Saram 105, A. Jayasinghe 65, D.N. Nadarajah 63, S.P. Herathge 52, S. Jayaratne 5 for 106) and 42 for 2
Tamil Union won by 8 wickets

at Tyronne Fernando Stadium, Moratuwa
Bloomfield C & AC 424 for 5 dec. (M.N. Nawaz 124, P.B. Dassanayake 96, S.K. Perera 87, P.B. Ediriweera 68)
Sebastianites 121 (S. Dissanayake 4 for 26, R.S. Kalpage 4 for 46) and 238 (R. Yasalal 139, S. Dissanayake 4 for 73)
Bloomfield C & AC won by an innings and 65 runs

Bloomfield gained their eighth successive victory and became virtually assured of the title while Antonians and BRC both won for the first time.

14, 15 and 16 March 1997
at Colts Ground, Havelock Park
BRC 278 (C. Perera 74) and 322 (E.M.I. Galagoda 64, D. Rajapakse 56, A. Ranaweera 56, K.G. Perera 4 for 58)
Antonians 254 (E.F.M.U. Fernando 105, V. Sittamige 62, S. Madanayake 5 for 47) and 11 for 1
Match drawn

at Colts Ground, Havelock Park
Nondescripts 256 (S. Ranatunga 61) and 331
(A. Weerapuli 65, G.R.P. Peiris 62)
Colombo Colts CC 349 (S.I. Fernando 80, S. Janaka 72,
N. Ranatunga 57, S. Weerasinghe 8 for 77) and 239 for 6
(J. Kaltunga 52)
Colombo Colts CC won by 4 wickets

at Panadura Esplanade
Kalutara TC 191 (B. Ranjith 5 for 68, K. Jayalath 4 for 26)
and 145 (B. Ranjith 5 for 30)
Singha SC 193 (G. Sanjeewa 58, A.S. Wewalwala 51,
P. Perera 4 for 57) and 146 for 5
Singha SC won by 5 wickets

at Air Force Ground, Katunayake
Galle CC 248 (D. Sudarshana 61, C. Vithanage 60) and
266 (S. Kodituwakku 74, A.W. Ekanayake 5 for 66,
R. Kariyawasam 4 for 95)
Kurunegala YCC 204 (R. Kariyawasam 87) and 198 for 4
(R.J. Jaymon 74, S.K.L. de Silva 61)
Match drawn

at Reid Avenue, Colombo
Bloomfield C & AC 303 (M.N. Nawaz 95, R. Palliyaguru
76, U.C. Hathurusinghe 5 for 129) and 224
(U.C. Hathurusinghe 4 for 91)
Tamil Union 190 (G. Wijekoon 56, B. de Silva 5 for 88)
and 99 (B. de Silva 6 for 22)
Bloomfield C & AC won by 238 runs

Bloomfield clinched the title with a convincing win over
Tamil Union.

28, 29 and 30 March, 1997
at Police Park
Singha SC 126 (P. Serasinghe 5 for 38, A. Priyantha 4 for
38) and 103
Police SC 226 (R.R. Wimalasiri 59, B. Ranjith 5 for 76,
W. Kusamsiri 4 for 53) and 4 for 1
Police SC won by 9 wickets

29, 30 and 31 March 1997
at St Antonians School
Antonians 167 (P. Silva 4 for 68) and 228 (U.N.K. Fernando 83)
Kalutara TC 189 (K.G. Perera 7 for 49) and 71 (K.G. Perera 5 for 31)
Antonians won by 135 runs

at Reid Avenue, Colombo
Panadura SC 374 (B.P. Perera 110, I. Amithakeerthi 105)
and 190 (C. Fernando 5 for 25)
Sinhalese SC 270 (A.A.W. Gunawardena 83, V.W.
Gunawardena 74, R.P.A.H. Wickramasinghe 64 not out,
K.P. Rathnaweera 4 for 59) and 295 for 6 (C. Fernando 99,
P. Viswanath 61)
Sinhalese SC won by 6 wickets

4, 5 and 6 April 1997
at Colts Ground, Havelock Park
Colombo Colts CC 336 (M.C. Mendis 86, B. Perera 59,
D.R.M. Jayawardena 5 for 72) and 233 (S.I. Fernando 54,
S. Janaka 50, S.H.S.M.K. Silva 4 for 35)
Sinhalese SC 190 (D.R.M. Jayawardena 100 not out) and
222 for 4 (D.R.M. Jayawardena 106 not out)
Match drawn

Final Table

	P	W	L	D	Ab	Pts
Bloomfield C & AC	13	9	–	4	–	255.50
Sinhalese Sports Club	13	9	–	2	2	223.00
Colombo Colts CCC	13	6	–	7	–	221.50
Tamil Union	13	7	2	4	–	197.50
Nondescripts CC	13	5	3	4	1	169.00
Kurunegala Youth CC	13	3	6	4	–	122.50
Police Sports Club	13	3	4	5	1	115.00
Burgher Recreation Club	13	1	3	9	–	112.00
Sebastianites C & AC	13	1	3	8	1	100.50
Antonians Sports Club	13	2	5	5	1	99.50
Panadura Sports Club	13	1	3	8	1	99.00
Singha Sports Club	13	3	9	1	–	97.00
Galle CC	13	1	3	8	1	83.00
Kalutara Town Club	13	–	10	3	–	44.50

Colombo Cricket Club, winners in 1995–96, were expelled
from the competition for failing to play their game against
Sinhalese Sports Club on the scheduled date. Panadura and
Kurunegala were both deducted two points for failing to
submit score cards within three days of the completion of a
match. Kalutara were deducted four points for twice failing
on this count. Galle and Colombo Colts were both deducted
0.5 points for submitting incomplete score cards.

The all-rounder Ruwan Kalpage. (Paul Sturgess/Sportsline)

West Indies 'A' Tour

Under the management of Joel Garner, West Indies 'A' toured Sri Lanka from late October to early December. The tour was a success for both sides although West Indies, ably led by Roger Harper, could take more comfort from the first-class international matches than their hosts. Opening batsmen Philo Wallace and Stuart Williams were outstandingly successful, and Cameron Cuffy gave indication that he could still become a regular fast bowler in the Test side.

30 and 31 October 1996
at Police Park, Colombo
Sri Lanka Colts XI 373 for 6 dec. (S.I. de Saram 100 not out, R.P. Arnold 85, V.S.K. Warangoda 50) and 27 for 0
West Indies 'A' 240 (S.C. Williams 159)
Match drawn

A fine century by Tamil Union's Indika de Saram was followed by a sensational 159 out of 240 from Stuart Williams. The West Indian opener hit 20 fours and four sixes.

2, 3 and 4 November 1996
at Colombo CC, Maitland Crescent, Colombo
Sri Lankan Board President's XI 340 (S. Jayantha 97, S.I. Fernando 56, D.R.M. Jayawardene 50)
West Indies 'A' 343 for 6 (P.A. Wallace 125, D.R.E. Joseph 93, T.O. Powell 50)
Match drawn

Philo Wallace followed the example of Stuart Williams by hitting a blistering century in the second match. He faced 189 balls and hit eight sixes and ten fours. Kalpage bowled most economically for the home side.

7, 8, 9 and 10 November 1996
at Welagedara Stadium, Kurunegala
Sri Lanka 'A' 269 (M.S. Atapattu 104) and 204 (C.E. Cuffy 7 for 84)
West Indies 'A' 470 for 9 dec. (P.A. Wallace 124, F.L. Reifer 96, T.O. Powell 87, R.A. Harper 51) and 5 for 0
West Indies 'A' won by 10 wickets

Put in to bat, the home side were 25 for 3 and were saved from total collapse by the aggressive batting of skipper Atapattu. Williams and Wallace gave West Indies a fine start with a stand of 87, and Reifer, the left-hander, then joined his fellow Bajan Wallace in a stand worth 111. Another left-hander, Tony Powell also batted well, and the visitors took a commanding lead of 201. It proved to be a

winning lead. On a good pitch, Cuffy bowled at a great pace and had match figures of 10 for 132. It was the first time he had claimed ten wickets in a match.

13, 14, 15 and 16 November 1996
at Sinhalese Sports Club, Maitland Place, Colombo
West Indies 'A' 220 (P.A. Wallace 56, S.C. Williams 52, R.S. Kalpage 6 for 51) and 231 (P.A. Wallace 71, R.S. Kalpage 6 for 62)
Sri Lanka 'A' 287 (D.P. Samaraweera 73, R.A. Harper 5 for 61) and 95 (R.N. Lewis 4 for 23, R.A. Harper 4 for 26)
West Indies 'A' won by 69 runs

The match was dominated by some outstanding spin bowling. Ruwan Kalpage dominated the West Indies with his off-breaks, but Roger Harper and Rawl Lewis, the leg-spinner, conjured up a remarkable victory for the visitors. Sri Lanka lost their last seven second innings wickets for 24 runs. Sri Lanka had made seven changes for this second match.

20, 21, 22 and 23 November 1996
at Uyanwatte Stadium, Matara
West Indies 'A' 523 for 9 dec. (S.C. Williams 170, R.D. Jacobs 100 not out, F.L. Reifer 60)
Sri Lanka 'A' 108 (N.B. Francis 4 for 32) and 118 for 2
Match drawn

With the 'Test' series already won, West Indies continued their domination into the final game. Stuart Williams played another fine innings, and wicket-keeper Ridley Jacobs, given his one opportunity, reached his century when the last man was at the wicket. Cuffy brought his total of wickets to 16 in three games while Kalpage had 17 for the series.

25 November 1996
at Moors Sports Club, Colombo
Sri Lankan XI 208 for 9 (O.T. Gibson 5 for 28)
West Indies 'A' 209 for 7 (D.R.E. Joseph 65)
West Indies 'A' won by 3 wickets

The tourists won this practice match with ten overs to spare.

27 November 1996
at Tyronne Fernando Stadium, Moratuwa
West Indies 'A' 138
Sri Lanka 'A' 140 for 4 (M.S. Atapattu 51)
Sri Lanka 'A' won by 6 wickets

Sri Lanka won the first of the one-day internationals with ease. They bowled out West Indies in 46.2 overs and reached their target in 34.1 overs.

29 November 1996
at P. Saravanamuttu Stadium, Colombo
West Indies 'A' 131
Sri Lanka 'A' 134 for 6 (G.R.P. Peiris 51,
M.V. Nagamootoo 4 for 31)
Sri Lanka 'A' won by 4 wickets

Sri Lanka clinched the one-day series with some ease in spite of
some impressive bowling by leg-spinner Mahendra Nagamootoo
of Guyana. He caused a fright as Sri Lanka went from 83 for 2
to 94 for 6 before Nawaz and Jayawardene steadied the innings.

1 December 1996
at Sinhalese Sports Club, Colombo
West Indies 'A' 238 for 6 (F.L. Reifer 69, D.R.E. Joseph 58)
Sri Lanka 'A' 197 (M.S. Atapattu 64)
West Indies 'A' won by 41 runs

*Sri Lanka's leading bowler in Test cricket, Muttiah Muralitharan, 6
for 98 in the first Test against Pakistan. (David Munden/Sportsline)*

The West Indians ended their tour with a victory and
announced themselves well satisfied with events. Certainly
Wallace and Williams had emerged as a potent opening
pair, and a good future was seen for Lewis. Sri Lanka had
unveiled a six-foot-five left-arm fast bowler Nuwan Zoysa,
and he, too, seemed destined for a big future. At 18 years
old, he was to make his Test debut some four months later.

Test Series

Sri Lanka v. Pakistan

Sri Lanka returned from New Zealand chastened by their
defeats. The Caribbean lay ahead, but they faced the
immediate problem of two Test matches against Pakistan. It
is difficult to understand why these games were arranged.
Both countries had exhausting programmes, and the only
preparation for the Tests was a two-day practice match that
turned out to be a disaster. Pakistan had arrived in Sri
Lanka without Saeed Anwar, who was suffering from viral
fatigue syndrome, and Aamir Sohail, who was beginning a
two-year suspension, which was later lifted when he offered
an unreserved apology to the Pakistan Board. To add to their
woes, Wasim Akram announced that an arm injury was still
troubling him and that he was not fit for the series. Rameez
Raja took over as captain.

The practice match saw Waqar Younis break down
after a long spell of bowling and Mohammad Zahid sustain a
muscle injury to the spine which was to erupt in the second
Test. Sri Lanka had a more positive outcome from the
match. They had lost Mahanama because of a foot injury
sustained in the nets, but Russell Arnold, a left-handed
opening batsman, performed well in the game at Police Park
and won his first Test cap.

Ranatunga won the toss, and Sri Lanka batted,
but the moissture in the pitch on the first day gave aid to

the bowlers, and, with Mushtaq Ahmed in top form, the
home side were soon in trouble. They were rescued by
Ranatunga and Tillekeratne who added 89, and Hashan
Tillekeratne found another able partner in wicket-keeper
Kaluwitharana. The pair added 75 in the last 90 minutes of
the day so that Sri Lanka closed on 254 for 5.

Kaluwitharana fell to Saqlain Mushtaq early on the
second day, and the off-spinner, a most impressive young
cricketer, claimed his first five-wicket haul in Test matches.
There was little support forthcoming for Tillekeratne, whose
sixth Test hundred came off 228 balls and occupied 349
minutes. He hit ten fours.

There was a sensational start to the Pakistan innings
with Vaas trapping Salim Elahi leg before first ball.
Rameez Raja and Ijaz Ahmed effected an immediate
recovery by adding 102. The pitch had now dried under the
hot sun and gave no help to the bowlers. Ijaz Ahmed and
Salim Malik took Pakistan to a strong position with a stand
of 117. There was some confusion on the third day when,
following a mix up, umpire Shepherd gave Ijaz run out. He
reversed his decision after consultation with the third
umpire, K.T. Francis, and Salim was the one who had to go.
Ijaz was on 90 at the time, and he went on to complete his
seventh Test hundred.

Muralitharan brought about a mid-innings collapse,
but Pakistan ended the day on 370 for 9, a comfortable
position, but one which suggested an inevitable draw.

Jayasuriya was suffering from tonsilitis, and Zoysa
had left the field after bowling ten overs. He had a strained
leg muscle and took no more part in the series. Atapattu and
Arnold scored 38 for the first wicket, and Ranatunga and
Aravinda de Silva 129 for the third. Sri Lanka ended the
fourth day on 206 for 3. There was little prospect of a result
and they batted throughout the final day. The feature of the
day was the batting of Aravinda de Silva who scored his
ninth Test century. His 168 came off 383 balls and included
a six and 14 fours. Tillekeratne and Jayasuriya also batted

well, and Saqlain and Mushtaq continued to bowl accurately and tirelessly.

Pakistan fielded an unchanged side for the second Test while Sri Lanka made three changes. Kalpage and Sajeewa de Silva came in for Muralitharan and Zoysa, both of whom were injured, and left-arm spinner Jayantha Silva came in for off-spinner Dharmasena. Ranatunga again won the toss and batted.

Sri Lanka began confidently, but the advent of spinners Mushtaq and Saqlain brought about a collapse, and they suddenly found themselves struggling at 144 for 5. Salvation came in the form of Aravinda de Silva who added 60 with Kaluwitharana and had useful support from Vaas. Sri Lanka ended the day on 281 for 7.

The blot on the day was Ijaz Ahmed's crude behaviour when Ranatunga was dismissed. It earned him severe punishment from match referee John Reid.

Sri Lanka scored 50 more runs on the second morning, and Aravinda de Silva was left unbeaten on 138, his tenth Test century.

Salim Elahi was out to the fourth ball of Pakistan's innings, and Vaas and fellow left-arm seamer Sajeewa de Silva reduced the visitors to 83 for 4. Inzamam and Asif Mujtaba stopped the rot and took Pakistan to an uneasy 146 for 4 by the close, but Inzamam was out on the third morning without adding to his score. It was left to Moin Khan, one of the most improved batsmen in Test cricket over the past three years, to restore pride to Pakistan. He decided that attack was the best form of defence and hit 98 off 109 balls. His innings included nine fours and three sixes, and it took Pakistan to within 39 runs of Sri Lanka.

Moin was unable to keep wicket when Sri Lanka batted a second time because of injury, and Salim Elahi took over behind the stumps. Neither Mohammad Zahid nor Shahid Nazir was fit to bowl, and Salim Malik and Ijaz Ahmed took the new ball. Jayasuriya and Arnold responded by reaching 102 by the close and eventually their partnership was worth 157. Jayasuriya reached a most responsible century and laid the foundation for the excitement that followed. Pressing for an early declaration, Ranatunga hit 66 off 62 balls with three sixes and nine fours while he and Aravinda de Silva added 105 off 107 deliveries. Aravinda de Silva hit a six and 11 fours, and his 103 came off 99 balls. He became the first batsman in Test history to score an unbeaten century in each innings, and Sri Lanka declared on 386 for 4.

Vaas sent back both openers before the close, and Pakistan faced defeat, but the last day saw Salim Malik play an outstanding innings to deny Sri Lanka. His defence was impeccable and his concentration never wavered. He and Ijaz Ahmed added 127, and, with Inzamam, Salim put on 121. Sri Lanka fielded poorly and were too defensive in their tactics, but Salim Malik's batting deserved to save the match.

First Test Match – Sri Lanka v. Pakistan
19, 20, 21, 22 and 23 April 1997 at Premadasa Stadium, Colombo

Sri Lanka

	First Innings		Second Innings	
S.T. Jayasuriya	b Mushtaq Ahmed	31	(7) c Elahi, b Saqlain	62
R.P. Arnold	b Mushtaq Ahmed	24	c Shahid, b Saqlain	15
M.S. Atapattu	c Elahi, b Saqlain	0	(1) c Shahid, b Saqlain	25
P.A. de Silva	st Moin, b Mushtaq	23	(3) c Saqlain, b Mushtaq	168
A. Ranatunga (Capt)	c Elahi, b Asif	49	(4) c Rameez, b Mushtaq	58
H.P. Tillekeratne	c Asif, b Saqlain	103	(5) c Rameez, b Saqlain	54
*R.S. Kaluwitharana	b Saqlain Mushtaq	57	(6) c Moin, b Shahid	17
H.D.P.K. Dharmasena	b Saqlain Mushtaq	1	not out	11
W.P.U.J.C. Vaas	c Moin Khan, b Mohammad Zahid	17	c sub (Momammad Hussain), b Mushtaq Ahmed	1
D.N.T. Zoysa	lbw, b Saqlain	0		
M. Muralitharan	not out	8		
	b 3, lb 9, w 1, nb 4	17	b 3, lb 4, nb 5	12
		330	for 8 wickets	423

	O	M	R	W	O	M	R	W
Mohammad Zahid	17	2	44	1	11	1	60	–
Shahid Nazir	18	6	37	–	12	–	61	1
Saqlain Mushtaq	44.2	10	89	5	63	13	137	4
Mushtaq Ahmed	34	2	123	3	39.1	9	94	3
Asif Mujtaba	9	2	25	1	30	5	64	–

Pakistan

	First Innings	
Salim Elahi	lbw, b Vaas	0
Rameez Raja (Capt)	c Ranatunga, b Dharmasena	50
Ijaz Ahmed	c Dharmasena, b Muralitharan	113
Salim Malik	run out	58
Inzamam-ul-Haq	c sub (Kalpage), b Muralitharan	12
Asif Mujtaba	c and b Muralitharan	21
*Moin Khan	b Muralitharan	0
Saqlain Mushtaq	run out	58
Mushtaq Ahmed	b Muralitharan	26
Shahid Nazir	c Ranatunga, b Muralitharan	2
Mohammad Zahid	not out	6
	b 11, lb 7, nb 14	32
		378

	O	M	R	W
Vaas	32	6	75	1
Zoysa	10	–	55	–
Dharmasena	52.5	19	93	1
Muralitharan	53	19	98	6
Jayasuriya	3	–	15	-
de Silva	4	–	16	-
Ranatunga	3	1	5	-
Arnold	2	1	3	-

Fall of Wickets
1–61, 2–62, 3–64, 4–90, 5–179, 6–268, 7–280, 8–322, 9–322
1–38, 2–53, 3–182, 4–265, 5–315, 6–390, 7–420, 8–423

Fall of Wickets
1–0, 2–102, 3–219, 4–247, 5–248, 6–248, 7–298, 8–336, 9–349

Umpires: W.A.U. Wikremasinghe & D.R. Shepherd

Match drawn

Second Test Match – Sri Lanka v. Pakistan
26, 27, 28, 29 and 30 April 1997 at Sinhalese CC, Colombo

Sri Lanka

	First Innings		Second Innings	
S.T. Jayasuriya	c Mushtaq, b Saqlain	72	c sub (Abdul Razzaq), b Saqlain Mushtaq	113
R.P. Arnold	run out	37	b Mushtaq Ahmed	50
M.S. Atapattu	c Elahi, b Mushtaq	14	run out	4
P.A. Silva	not out	138	not out	103
A. Ranatunga (Capt)	c Elahi, b Saqlain	4	st Elahi, b Mushtaq	66
H.P. Tillekeratne	b Mohammad Zahid	10	not out	24
*R.S. Kaluwitharana	b Asif Mujtaba	22		
R.S. Kalpage	c Elahi, b Saqlain	5		
W.P.U.J.C. Vaas	c Elahi, b Saqlain	17		
S.C. de Silva	st Moin, b Mushtaq	0		
K.J. Silva	run out	0		
	b 6, lb 3, nb 3	12	b 12, lb 6, w 1, nb 7	26
		331	(for 4 wickets, dec.)	386

Pakistan

	First Innings		Second Innings	
Salim Elahi	c Tillekeratne, b Vaas	0	(2) c Arnold, b Vaas	14
Rameez Raja (Capt)	c Arnold, b S.C. de Silva	36	(1) c Kaluwitharana, b Vaas	0
Ijaz Ahmed	c Arnold, b Vaas	4	c Vaas, b Silva	47
Salim Malik	b Ranatunga, b S.C. de Silva	24	c Kaluwitharana, b Silva	155
Inzamam-ul-Haq	c Kaluwitharana, b Vaas	43	not out	54
Asif Mujtaba	c P.A. de Silva, b Vaas	49	c Ranatunga, b Atapattu	6
*Moin Khan	b Atapattu, b Silva	98	(7) not out	5
Saqlain Mushtaq	b S.C. de Silva	23		
Mushtaq Ahmed	b Atapattu, b S.C. de Silva	1		
Mohammad Zahid	b Kaluwitharana, b S.C. de Silva	0		
Shahid Nazir	not out	0		
	b 4, w 4, nb 6	14	lb 3, nb 1	4
		292	(for 5 wickets)	285

	O	M	R	W	O	M	R	W
Mohammad Zahid	12	1	44	1				
Shahid Nazir	8	1	50	–				
Mushtaq Ahmed	32	6	90	2	33	4	113	2
Saqlain Mushtaq	45	12	115	4	42.5	4	171	1
Asif Mujtaba	15	3	23	1	6	–	33	–
Salim Malik					9	2	33	–
Ijaz Ahmed					5	–	18	–

	O	M	R	W	O	M	R	W
Vaas	27	7	60	4	16	7	40	2
S.C. de Silva	24.2	5	85	5	19	2	73	–
Silva	25	5	91	1	28	10	71	2
Kalpage	23	8	42	–	20	6	60	–
Ranatunga	4.1	1	8	–				
Arnold	5	3	2	–	6	–	26	–
Atapattu					4	–	9	1
Tillekeratne					2	–	3	–

Fall of Wickets
1–95, 2–124, 3–124, 4–129, 5–144, 6–204, 7–224, 8–300, 9–321
1–157, 2–171, 3–203, 4–308

Fall of Wickets
1–0, 2–13, 3–59, 4–83, 5–147, 6–238, 7–276, 8–283, 9–283
1–0, 2–19, 3–146, 4–267, 5–279

Umpires: P. Manuel & I.D. Robinson

Match drawn

Asia Cup

Just as one might be forgiven for believing that the Sri Lankan season was over, there was still the Asia Cup to be played. Saqlain Mushtaq had played for Surrey in the Benson and Hedges Cup Final on the Saturday, on the Monday he found himself playing for Pakistan against Sri Lanka in Colombo. In spite of the arrival of Saqlain, Pakistan remained weakened by the absence of Waqar Younis, Mushtaq Ahmed and the injured Wasim Akram. Aamir Sohail's ban had been lifted, but the side was well below full strength.

Winning the toss, Rameez Raja asked Sri Lanka to bat first on a damp pitch. The move was partly successful in that Sri Lanka were restricted to 78 for the loss of Jayasuriya in the first 15 overs. Aravinda de Silva raised the tempo with 34 off 42 balls before falling to a fine diving catch. In spite of the loss of their top batsman, Sri Lanka looked set for a big score when they reached 160 for 2, but their last eight wickets went down for 79 runs in 94 balls. They suffered three run-outs in the space of 17 deliveries.

Pakistan slipped to 51 for 3 in 12 overs before Rameez and Inzamam doubled the score. Inzamam and Salim Malik were building a useful partnership when Inzamam, responding to Salim's call, was beaten by substitute Chandana's direct hit on the stumps from square-leg. Moin was out at 205 and when Salim, having hit 57 off 79 balls, went for a big hit off Dharmasena and was bowled Pakistan's last hope disappeared.

They were predictably successful two days later in the same stadium when a total in excess of 300 proved far too much for Bangladesh. Saeed Anwar hit 11 fours as he made 90 off 94 balls, and Inzamam-ul-Haq scored 77 off 68 balls. The compensation for Bangladesh was that Athar Ali Khan, who employed a runner for much of his innings, hit a six and eight fours in compiling his country's highest score in a one-day international.

Sri Lanka introduced a new wicket-keeper for their second match in the tournament, Lanka de Silva who had enjoyed a wonderfully successful season for Kurunegala Youth. He performed well on his debut. Facing a target of 228, Sri Lanka were 9 for 2, but skipper Arjuna Ranatunga played a storming innings of 131 off 152 balls, and victory came with 32 balls to spare.

Having been beaten by Sri Lanka, India, the holders, desperately needed to beat Pakistan to keep alive their chances of reaching the final. They began happily, reducing Pakistan to 30 for 5 in nine overs, four of the wickets falling to Venkatesh Prasad. Rain then forced the game to be abandoned and struck from the record books with a replayed match scheduled for the next day, but the rain was unrelenting.

Sri Lanka duly demolished Bangladesh to claim a place in the final. Jayasuriya blasted 108 off 103 deliveries.

He hit three sixes and 14 fours and took 26 off 5 deliveries from Akram Khan.

Sri Lanka had temporarily lost the services of their coach, Bruce Yardley. The former Australian Test spinner had returned to Australia for an operation for the removal of his left eye. He had been complaining of sight problems for some time. Sri Lanka were well satisfied with his work and looked forward to welcoming him back as soon as possible.

For India, the sixth match in the competition was vital. They needed to beat Bangladesh and score at such a rate as to move ahead of Pakistan. Rain caused a late start that reduced the match to 47 overs, but more rain brought an end to Bangladesh's innings after 43 overs. The Indian bowlers did their job well in restricting Bangladesh to three runs an over, but to win a place in the final, the reigning champions needed to reach their target of 131 inside 20 overs. Tendulkar and Ganguly began with 54 in seven overs, and Azharuddin kept the momentum going with 23 off 20 balls. It was Ganguly who took the major honours, however, with 73 off 52 balls. His innings included two sixes and eight fours, and India reached their target in 15 overs.

A capacity crowd saw the final and were delighted as Sri Lanka brought home yet another trophy. India began badly, but Tendulkar and Azharuddin added 109 off 140 balls for the fourth wicket to restore order. Sri Lanka fielded brilliantly. Kalpage and Muralitharan took outstanding running catches to account for India's two leading batsmen, and Aravinda de Silva held two diving chances.

A target of 240 never looked likely to trouble Sri Lanka, and Jayasuriya and Atapattu began with a flurry of boundaries. After four overs the score was 49, and the weakened Indian attack had conceded 98 by the tenth over. Jayasuriya hit two sixes and seven fours in his 63 off 52 balls, and when he was caught off debutant left-arm spinner Kulkarni the score was 137 in 18 overs. Aravinda de Silva went cheaply, but Atapattu stood firm, and Arjuna Ranatunga hit three sixes and five fours as his 62 came off 67 balls. The Sri Lankan captain was named Man of the Series, and his side won the Asia Cup with 13.1 overs to spare.

Postscript

It is often difficult to know where the Sri Lankan season ends and when it begins. Officially, the Asia Cup brought an end to the season, 1996-97, but within a month, the Indians had arrived for a two-Test series and three one-day internationals. This marked the beginning of the 1997–98 season. The first Test caused a sensation. There were three centuries in the Indian innings, and in the Sri Lankan innings, Mahanama made 225, Aravinda de Silva 126, and Jayasuriya 340, the fourth highest score in Test cricket. Sri Lanka reached 952 for 6 so establishing a new record in Test cricket.

These events will be reported fully in the 1998, 17th edition of *Benson and Hedges Cricket Year*.

Match One – Sri Lanka v. Pakistan
14 July 1997 at Premadasa Stadium, Colombo

Sri Lanka

S.T. Jayasuriya	c Rameez Raja, b Kabir Khan	33
M.S. Atapattu	run out	80
P.A. de Silva	c Saqlain Mushtaq, b Aamir	34
A. Ranatunga (Capt)	c Rameez Raja, b Arshad Khan	28
R.S. Mahanama	lbw, b Shahid Afridi	3
*R.S. Kaluwitharana	lbw, b Kabir Khan	1
R.S. Kalpage	run out	15
H.D.P.K. Dharmasena	st Moin Khan, b Saqlain	25
W.P.U.J.C. Vaas	run out	0
M. Muralitharan	not out	2
S.C. de Silva	b Aqib Javed	6
	lb 4, w 7, nb 1	12
	49.5 overs	239

Pakistan

Saeed Anwar	b Vaas	27
Aamir Sohail	c Ranatunga, b S.C. de Silva	6
Shahid Afridi	c Muralitharan, b S.C. de Silva	16
Rameez Raja (Capt)	st Kaluwitharana, b Jayasuriya	29
Inzamam-ul-Haq	run out	48
Salim Malik	b Dharmasena	57
*Moin Khan	c Kalpage, b Jayasuriya	14
Saqlain Mushtaq	c Kalpage, b Jayasuriya	5
Aqib Javed	c Kalpage, b Jayasuriya	0
Arshad Khan	not out	6
Kabir Khan	not out	1
	b 3, lb 2, w 9, nb 1	15
	50 overs (for 9 wickets)	224

	O	M	R	W
Aqib Javed	7.5	–	37	1
Kabir Khan	8	1	49	2
Saqlain Mushtaq	10	–	38	1
Shahid Afridi	4	–	25	1
Arshad Khan	10	–	48	1
Aamir Sohail	10	1	38	1

	O	M	R	W
Vaas	6	1	30	1
S.C. de Silva	6	–	26	2
Dharmasena	10	–	33	1
Muralitharan	10	–	44	–
Jayasuriya	10	–	49	4
Kalpage	8	–	37	–

Fall of Wickets
1–46, 2–111, 3–160, 4–168, 5–169, 6–199, 7–209, 8–216, 9–232

Fall of Wickets
1–31, 2–36, 3–51, 4–102, 5–165, 6–205, 7–214, 8–216, 9–216

Umpires: S.K. Bansal & Venkataraghavan   *Man of the Match*: M.S. Atapattu   **Sri Lanka won by 15 runs**

Match Two – Pakistan v. Bangladesh
16 July 1997 at Premadasa Stadium, Colombo

Pakistan

Saeed Anwar	c Habibul, b Enamul Hoque	90
Aamir Sohail	c Khalid Masud, b Hasibul Hussain	0
Rameez Raja	c and b Minhajul Abedin	52
Inzamam-ul-Haq	c Habibul Bashar, b Sheikh Salahuddin	77
Salim Malik	c Aminul Islam, b Saiful Islam	62
*Moin Khan	not out	21
Shahid Afridi	not out	4
Saqlain Mushtaq		
Aqib Javed		
Arshad Khan		
Kabir Khan		
	b 1, lb 2, w 9, nb 1	13
	50 overs (for 5 wickets)	319

	O	M	R	W
Hasibul Hussain	4	–	47	1
Saiful Islam	7	–	45	1
Athar Ali Khan	5	–	27	–
Sheikh Salahuddin	10	–	50	1
Aminul Islam	8	–	49	–
Minhajul Abedin	10	–	51	1
Enamul Hoque	6	–	47	1

Fall of Wickets
1–13, 2–136, 3–166, 4–275, 5–315

Bangladesh

Athar Ali Khan	st Moin Khan, b Saqlain Mushtaq	82
Naimur Rahman	lbw, b Kabir Khan	8
Habibul Bashar	lbw, b Kabir Khan	0
Aminul Islam	c Kabir Khan, b Saqlain	14
Akram Khan (Capt)	c Rameez Raja, b Saqlain	59
Enamul Hoque	c Aamir Sohail, b Aqib Javed	8
*Khalid Masud	c Moin Khan, b Saqlain Mushtaq	4
Hasibul Hussain	b Aqib Javed	10
Saiful Islam	c Moin Khan, b Saqlain Mushtaq	7
Sheikh Salahuddin	not out	0
Minhajul Abedin	absent ill	–
	lb 7, w 9, nb 2	18
	49 overs	210

	O	M	R	W
Aqib Javed	9	3	18	2
Kabir Khan	5	1	23	2
Saqlain Mushtaq	9.3	1	38	5
Shahid Afridi	9	–	36	–
Arshad Khan	7	–	24	–
Aamir Sohail	6	–	35	–
Salim Malik	4	–	29	–

Fall of Wickets
1–13, 2–13, 3–61, 4–171, 5–184, 6–188, 7–199, 8–209, 9–210

Umpires: S.K. Bansal & B.C. Cooray   *Man of the Match:* Saeed Anwar   **Pakistan won by 109 runs**

Match Three – Sri Lanka v. India
17 July 1997 at Premadasa Stadium, Colombo

India

S.R. Tendulkar (Capt)	b Vaas	21
S.C. Ganguly	c Dharmasena, b S.C. de Silva	11
*S.S. Karim	c S.K.L. de Silva, b Dharmasena	12
R.S. Dravid	b Jayasuriya	69
M. Azharuddin	not out	81
R.R. Singh	c P.A. de Silva, b Vaas	10
A.D. Jadeja	st S.K.L. de Silva, b Jayasuriya	3
A.R. Kumble	not out	16
N. David		
A. Kuruvilla		
Venkatesh Prasad		
	w 3, nb 1	4
	50 overs (for 6 wickets)	227

	O	M	R	W
Vaas	8	1	35	2
S.C. de Silva	7	–	30	1
Muralitharan	10	1	30	–
Dharmasena	10	1	52	1
Jayasuriya	10	–	52	2
Kalpage	5	–	28	–

Fall of Wickets
1–32, 2–35, 3–51, 4–168, 5–189, 6–201

Sri Lanka

S.T. Jayasuriya	c Dravid, b Venkatesh Prasad	0
M.S. Atapattu	lbw, b Singh	31
P.A. de Silva	c Karim, b Venkatesh Prasad	6
A. Ranatunga (Capt)	not out	131
R.S. Mahanama	c Karim, b Singh	5
S.K.L. de Silva	not out	37
R.S. Kalpage		
H.D.P.K. Dharmasena		
W.P.U.J.C. Vaas		
M. Muralitharan		
S.C. de Silva		
	lb 6, w 12, nb 3	21
	44.4 overs (for 4 wickets)	231

	O	M	R	W
Venkatesh Prasad	8	–	44	2
Kuruvilla	7	–	35	–
Kumble	10	–	38	–
David	8	–	36	–
Ganguly	3	–	19	–
Singh	4	–	29	2
Jadeja	4	–	18	–
Tendulkar	0.4	–	6	–

Fall of Wickets
1–0, 2–9, 3–117, 4–125

Umpires: Salim Badar & Mohammad Nazir   *Man of the Match:* A. Ranatunga   **Sri Lanka won by 6 wickets**

Match Five – Sri Lanka *v.* Bangladesh
22 July 1997 at Sinhalese Sports Club, Colombo

Sri Lanka

Batsman	Dismissal	Runs
S.T. Jayasuriya	c Mafizur Rahman, b Salahuddin	108
M.S. Atapattu	c Aminul Islam, b Minhajul Abedin	60
P.A. de Silva	c Khalis Masud, b Minhajul Abedin	15
A. Ranatunga (Capt)	c Naimur Rahman, b Salahuddin	51
R.S. Mahanama	not out	39
*S.K.L. de Silva	not out	10
U.U. Chandana		
D.K. Liyanage		
R.S. Kalpage		
S.C. de Silva		
M. Muralitharan		
	lb 4, w 9	13
	46 overs (for 4 wickets)	296

Bowler	O	M	R	W
Saiful Islam	6	–	34	–
Habibul Bashar	8	–	50	–
Mafizur Rahman	6	–	37	–
Akram Khan	2	–	34	–
Sheikh Salahuddin	8	–	48	2
Minhajul Abedin	9	–	43	2
Naimur Rahman	7	–	46	–

Fall of Wickets
1–**171**, 2–**177**, 3–**213**, 4–**284**

Bangladesh

Batsman	Dismissal	Runs
Athar Ali Khan	b Muralitharan	42
Naimur Rahman	c Kalpage, b S.C. de Silva	47
Habibul Bashar	run out	6
Aminul Islam	run out	29
Akram Khan (Capt)	st S.K.L. de Silva, b Chandana	32
Minhajul Abedin	c S.C. de Silva, b Muralitharan	1
Mafizur Rahman	c S.C. de Silva, b P.A. de Silva	6
*Khalid Masud	not out	6
Hasibul Hussain	run out	1
Saiful Islam		
Sheikh Salahuddin		
	b 3, lb 6, w 12, nb 2	23
	46 overs (for 8 wickets)	193

Bowler	O	M	R	W
Liyanage	3	–	10	–
S.C. de Silva	4	–	17	1
P.A. de Silva	9	–	39	1
Ranatunga	2	–	16	–
Muralitharan	10	–	29	2
Chandana	9	–	38	1
Kalpage	9	1	35	–

Fall of Wickets
1–**42**, 2–**95**, 3–**117**, 4–**167**, 5–**177**, 6–**178**, 7–**190**, 8–**193**

Umpires: Salim Badar & S. Venkataraghavan   *Man of the Match:* S.T. Jayasuriy

Sri Lanka won by 103 runs

Match Six – India *v.* Bangladesh
24 July 1997 at Sinhalese Sports Club, Colombo

Bangladesh

Batsman	Dismissal	Runs
Athar Ali Khan	lbw, b Tendulkar	33
Naimur Rahman	lbw, b Kuruvilla	0
Minhajul Abedin	c Karim, b Venkatesh Prasad	3
Aminul Islam	c Kumble, b Singh	30
Akram Khan (Capt)	c Jadeja, b Kumble	11
*Khalid Masud	c Ganguly, b Singh	12
Enamul Hoque	run out	4
Mafizur Rahman	not out	15
Hasibul Hussain	lbw, b Singh	0
Sheikh Salahuddin	not out	3
Zakir Hassan		
	lb 15, w 2, nb 2	19
	43 overs (for 8 wickets)	130

Bowler	O	M	R	W
Venkatesh Prasad	7	1	15	1
Kuruvilla	6	–	28	1
Kumble	10	3	17	1
Ganguly	6	1	24	–
Tendulkar	5	–	18	1
Singh	9	2	13	3

Fall of Wickets
1–**2**, 2–**12**, 3–**57**, 4–**79**, 5–**92**, 6–**100**, 7–**104**, 8–**104**

India

Batsman	Dismissal	Runs
S.C. Ganguly	not out	73
S.R. Tendulkar (Capt)	b Enamul Hoque	28
M. Azharuddin	not out	23
N.S. Sidhu		
R.S. Dravid		
A.D. Jadeja		
R.R. Singh		
*S.S. Karim		
A.R. Kumble		
A. Kuruvilla		
Venkatesh Prasad		
	b 4, lb 1, w 2, nb 1	8
	15 overs (for 1 wicket)	132

Bowler	O	M	R	W
Hasibul Hussain	3	–	25	–
Zakir Hassan	2	–	17	–
Sheikh Salahuddin	3	–	22	–
Enamul Hoque	3	–	34	1
Mafizur Rahman	2	–	16	–
Minhajul Abedin	2	–	13	–

Fall of Wickets
1–**54**

Umpires: K.T. Francis & Mohammad Nazir   *Man of the Match:* S.C. Ganguly

India won by 9 wickets

Asia Cup Final – Sri Lanka v. India
26 July 1997 at Premadasa Stadium, Colombo

India

S.C. Ganguly	c P.A. de Silva, **b** Dharmasena	**34**
N.S. Sidhu	c Muralitharan, **b** S.C. de Silva	**10**
R.S. Dravid	c Mahanama, **b** Vaas	**7**
S.R. Tendulkar (Capt)	c Kalpage, **b** Muralitharan	**53**
M. Azharuddin	c Muralitharan, **b** Dharmasena	**81**
A.D. Jadeja	run out	**22**
R.R. Singh	c P.A. de Silva, **b** Vaas	**9**
A.R. Kumble	not out	**7**
*S.S. Karim	not out	**1**
Venkatesh Prasad		
N.M. Kulkarni		
	b 1, lb **8**, w **5**, nb 1	**15**
	50 overs (for 7 wickets)	**239**

	O	M	R	**W**
Vaas	8	1	32	**2**
S.C. de Silva	9	1	44	**1**
Dharmasena	10	1	54	**2**
Muralitharan	10	1	38	**1**
Jayasuriya	10	–	46	**–**
Kalpage	3	–	16	**–**

Fall of Wickets
1–**32**, 2–**51**, 3–**59**, 4–**168**, 5–**215**, 6–**225**, 7–**234**

Sri Lanka

S.T. Jayasuriya	c Sindhu, **b** Kulkarni	**63**
M.S. Atapattu	not out	**84**
P.A. de Silva	c and **b** Ganguly	**6**
A. Ranatunga (Capt)	not out	**62**
R.S. Mahanama		
*S.K.L. de Silva		
R.S. Kalpage		
H.D.P.K. Dharmasena		
W.P.U.J.C. Vaas		
M. Muralitharan		
S.C. de Silva		
	lb **10**, w **13**, nb **2**	**25**
	36.5 overs (for 2 wickets)	**240**

	O	M	R	**W**
Venkatesh Prasad	4	–	43	**–**
Singh	3	–	26	**–**
Kumble	8	–	54	**–**
Tendulkar	3	–	20	**–**
Kulkarni	10	–	48	**1**
Ganguly	5	–	25	**1**
Jadeja	1.5	–	8	**–**
Dravid	2	–	6	**–**

Fall of Wickets
1–**137**, 2–**144**

Umpires: Salim Nadar & Mohammad Nazir *Man of the Match:* M.S. Atapattu

Sri Lanka won by 8 wickets

First-Class Averages

Batting

	M	Inns	NOs	Runs	HS	Av	100s	50s
P.A. de Silva	4	6	2	483	168	120.75	3	
H.P. Tillekeratne	12	12	4	717	143	89.62	4	2
H.D.P.K. Dharmasena	7	9	4	405	155*	81.00	1	2
R.S. Kaluwitharana	13	18	–	1270	179	70.55	6	3
A. Ranatunga	11	13	2	680	200*	61.81	1	4
T.T. Samaraweera	12	16	8	476	117	59.50	1	3
R.P. Wickramaratne	12	15	3	688	130	57.33	2	4
V.S.K. Waragoda	6	8	–	438	138	54.75	1	3
A.A.W. Gunawardene	10	14	3	599	158*	54.45	2	1
R.S.Mahanama	9	13	3	520	176	52.00	2	1
S. Janaka	7	12	1	560	148	50.90	1	5
G.R.P. Peiris	10	13	1	600	125	50.00	2	3
S.I. Fernando	14	21	3	887	178*	49.27	2	4
U.U. Chandana	9	12	1	537	104*	48.81	2	4
R.S. Kalpage	14	21	6	729	160*	48.60	1	5
Sanjeeva Silva	7	10	–	473	135	47.30	2	1
S.T. Jayasuriya	12	20	1	881	129	46.36	2	5
G. Wijekoon	11	14	2	552	117	46.00	1	4
D.R.M. Jayawardene	12	17	3	644	106*	46.00	2	5
I. Amithakeerthi	11	16	4	547	137*	45.58	2	
C.N. Fernando	7	8	1	317	107	45.28	1	2
M.S. Atapattu	13	19	3	721	135*	45.06	3	3
S.K.L. de Silva	14	25	1	1032	109	43.00	4	5
A. Jayasinghe	13	19	1	773	183	42.94	2	2
A. Gunawardene	12	14	2	499	120*	41.50	2	1
M.N. Nawaz	11	19	1	747	124	41.50	2	3
E.M.I. Galagoda	13	23	1	913	117	41.50	1	5
J. Kulatunga	12	18	2	634	118	39.62	1	4
S.T. Perera	13	21	3	700	102*	38.88	1	5
E.F.M.U. Fernando	9	15	1	540	105	38.57	1	3
R.C. Liyanage	12	22	2	741	86	37.05		6
S. Kumara	11	17	1	589	142	36.81	1	4
A.P.R. Shaman	12	18	4	510	117	36.42	1	2

Batting

	M	Inns	NOs	Runs	HS	Av	100s	50s
S. Ranatunga	16	23	3	720	97	36.00		5
M.C. Mendis	13	20	–	714	131	35.70	2	2
D. Rajapakse	13	22	1	743	101*	35.38	1	5
P.B. Dassanayake	10	15	–	530	119	35.33	1	3
A.P. Dalugoda	8	12	1	377	80	34.27		4
R.P. Arnold	16	23	1	751	131	34.13	3	2
Y.N. Tillakaratne	8	13	1	406	135*	33.83	1	1
D.P. Samaraweera	13	21	1	664	100	33.20	1	3
M.S. Mendis	11	17	1	530	100	33.12	1	4
S. Jayantha	12	23	1	726	97	33.00		3
S.K. Silva	10	16	–	524	111	32.75	1	4
A.S. Wewalwala	12	24	3	667	74	31.76		4
S.P. Herathge	8	10	–	310	60	31.00		2
R.S. Jayawardene	9	13	2	335	89	30.45		3
U.N.K. Fernando	10	12	–	357	92	29.75		3
D.N. Nadarajah	13	17	3	415	102*	29.64	1	2
H. Liyanage	9	16	3	380	82	29.23		3
S.I. de Saram	8	12	–	348	105	29.00	1	1
N. Shirdman	10	18	1	486	103	28.58	1	2
S. Tennekoon	10	16	1	428	62	28.53		3
A. Perera	12	18	1	483	90	28.41		3
M. Perera	8	12	1	310	106	28.18	1	1
D. Ruwan	13	21	2	528	61*	27.78		2
D. Arnolda	10	17	4	359	129*	27.61	1	1
A. Rideegammanagadera	13	22	1	572	100	27.23	1	3
A. Fernando	13	19	2	461	113	27.11	1	2
D. Sudarshana	13	22	1	569	91	27.09		5
D.D. Wickramasinghe	13	21	1	532	103*	26.60	1	3
B.P. Perera	12	19	–	498	110	26.21	1	1
R.R. Wimalasiri	13	22	2	480	66*	24.00		4
N.M. Tillakaratne	12	24	–	569	78	23.70		4
H.S.S. Fonseka	13	26	–	612	91	23.53		3
M. Rajapakse	9	16	–	376	66	23.50		2

First-Class Averages (continued)

Batting

	M	Inns	NOs	Runs	HS	Av	100s	50s
S.M. Faumi	12	19	2	398	46	23.41		
T.M. Dilshan	13	26	–	606	111	23.30	1	4
R.R. Jaymon	12	22	–	507	102	23.04	1	2
D.D. Madurapperuma	13	21	3	414	59*	23.00		1
A. Priyantha	13	22	–	484	79	22.00		3
T.P. Kodikara	13	23	1	479	88	21.77		3
S.N. Liyanage	12	19	1	385	77	21.38		2
S. Kodituwakku	10	17	1	332	74	20.75		2
P. Perera	12	24	–	496	133	20.66	1	2
M. Peiris	11	18	1	345	43	20.29		
I.D. Gunawardene	13	22	2	402	93	20.10		2
R. Kottahachchi	10	20	3	341	52	20.05		1
W.N.M. Soysa	13	23	1	438	73	19.90		3
H. Premasiri	12	23	–	457	71	19.86		2
C. Perera	11	18	1	335	74	19.70		1
C.N. Hettiarachchi	12	24	–	473	68	19.70		2
V. Sittamige	12	19	–	369	62	19.42		2
S. Jayawardene	12	21	–	408	120	19.42	1	
R. Kariyawasam	12	22	1	377	87	17.95		1
A.W. Ekanayake	11	19	1	323	82	17.94		2
M.N.C. Silva	13	21	1	357	58*	17.85		1
P.N. Wanasinghe	13	23	1	389	110	17.68	1	2
T. Achintha	12	23	2	358	47	17.04		
G. Sanjeewa	13	25	1	406	58	16.91		2
W.M.J. Kumudu	12	24	–	318	48	13.25		

(Qualification 300 runs, average 10.00)

Bowling

	Overs	Mds	Runs	Wks	Av	Best	10/m	5/inn
S.D. Anurasiri	325.5	148	474	39	12.15	1/84	1	5
M. Muralitharan	389	101	972	66	14.72	7/55	2	6
B. de Silva	67.4	11	239	16	14.93	6/22	1	2
A. Priyantha	159.2	38	401	29	15.42	6/30		1
B. Ranjith	369	81	1148	70	16.40	9/29	3	7
M. Villavarayan	123.4	32	357	21	17.00	9/15	1	1
C. Bandaratilleke	393.3	77	1001	58	17.25	8/78		4
K.G. Perera	469	156	993	57	17.42	7/49	1	3
S.B. Dodanwela	174	49	526	29	18.13	5/39		1
H.D.P.K. Dharmasena	166.5	55	327	18	18.16	5/27		1
W.P.U.J.C. Vaas	361.5	94	945	51	18.52	6/12		2
P.K. Serasinghe	401.4	87	996	53	18.79	7/55		3
R.S. Kalpage	472.4	119	1147	60	19.11	7/37	2	3
D.N.T. Zoysa	273	58	811	42	19.30	7/58		2
U.C. Hathurusinghe	250.5	68	700	36	19.44	8/29	1	4
T.T. Samaraweera	260.2	67	743	38	19.55	5/8		2
B. Perera	113.1	7	534	27	19.77	4/21		
S.C. de Silva	233.5	48	675	33	20.45	6/48		2
C.D.U.S. Weerasinghe	176.1	24	683	33	20.69	8/77	2	4
S. Madanayake	140.3	18	540	26	20.76	5/36		2
D.L. Liyanage	228	37	800	37	21.62	5/26		2
A.P.R. Shaman	146.5	32	434	20	21.70	4/45		
K.R. Pushpakumara	206.3	34	726	33	22.00	6/43	2	6
A. Rideegammana	392.1	98	1017	46	22.10	5/54		2
M.A.W. Madurasinghe	325.1	91	753	34	22.14	5/49		1

Bowling

	Overs	Mds	Runs	Wks	Av	Best	10/m	5/inn
P.W. Gunaratne	223.4	38	712	32	22.25	6/71	1	1
S. Jayaratne	94	17	388	17	22.82	5/106		1
V. Ranaweera	294.2	51	936	41	22.82	5/39		2
A.W. Ekamayake	361.5	66	1075	47	22.87	5/41		3
K.J. Silva	490.2	134	1287	56	22.98	6/42		3
R.P. Arnold	306.1	69	901	39	23.10	7/84		1
W.K. Jayalath	246.2	62	653	28	23.32	4/26		
G.P. Wickremasinghe	209.5	45	913	39	23.41	6/82		1
P. Perera	292.1	71	824	35	23.54	6/41		3
I. Amithakeerthi	132.3	27	380	16	23.75	5/5		1
K.E.A. Upashantha	220.1	44	769	32	24.03	4/48		
U.U. Chandana	221.5	37	707	29	24.37	6/25		1
R.K.B. Amunugama	123.4	16	420	17	24.70	5/61		1
I.S. Gallage	259.2	49	899	36	24.97	5/72		2
S.H.S.M.K. Silva	158.3	39	459	18	25.50	4/35		
P. Salgado	179.1	35	585	22	26.59	5/42		1
D.D. Madurapperuma	209.5	26	712	26	27.38	6/45		1
R. Kottahachchi	123.5	12	440	16	27.50	5/60		1
M.M. de Silva	371.2	65	1270	46	27.60	6/27	1	4
S.I. Fernando	195.4	51	528	19	27.78	5/45		1
K.C. Silva	125.1	16	511	18	28.38	5/41		1
A.S. Wewalwala	138.2	23	540	19	28.42	5/40		1
R.L. Perera	120	12	427	15	28.46	5/26		1
S. Kumara	283.1	90	608	21	28.95	3/37		
H.S.S. Fonseka	114.2	25	435	15	29.00	3/30		
P.N. Wanasinghe	291.3	44	1017	35	29.05	6/42		2
T.M.C. Boteju	128	21	449	15	29.93	3/41		
A. Perera	251.1	34	937	31	30.22	6/87		2
K. Dharmasena	183.2	50	523	17	30.76	3/41		
M.W. Kumara	309.5	65	982	31	31.67	6/64		1
D. Arnolda	138.2	25	490	15	32.66	3/55		
K.P. Rathnaweera	211.4	48	667	20	33.35	4/59		
R. Kariyawasam	150	24	513	15	34.20	4/95		
S.M. Faumi	279.4	44	924	27	34.22	4/111		
W.N.M. Soysa	277.4	46	805	23	35.00	5/44		1
W.C. Labrooy	180.4	18	915	26	35.19	5/90		1
R. Chandana	123.5	6	604	17	35.52	3/41		
A.P. Dalugoda	287.4	84	642	18	35.66	4/31		
S. Jayawardene	197.2	34	684	19	36.00	5/40		1
C.M. Hathurusinghe	263.2	63	852	23	37.04	6/72		1
P. Silva	236.4	26	1176	28	42.00	4/68		
H.M.L. Sagara	309	59	976	22	44.36	4/131		
S. Sanjeewa	219.1	29	822	15	54.80	3/67		

(Qualification – 15 wickets)

Leading Fielders

45 – S.K.L. Silva (ct 39 / st 6); 40 – E.M.I. Galagoda (ct 35 / st 5); 36 – T.M. Dilshan (ct 30 / st 6) and C.I. Danusinghe (ct 32 / st 4); 35 – R.S. Kaluwitharana (ct 31 /st 4); 32 – N. de Silva (ct 25 / st 7); 30 – M. Perera (ct 25 / st 5); 26 – R.C. Liyanage (ct 23 / st 3) and S.K. Silva (ct 19 / st 7); 23 – S.T. Perera (ct 17 / st 6); 21 – T. Achintha (ct 18 / st 3) and U.N.K. Fernando (ct 17 / st 4); 20 – P.B. Dassanayake (ct 18 / st 2) , C.K. Hewakanne (ct 16 / st 4) and S.N. Liyanage; 19 – E.F.M.U. Fernando (ct 10 / st 9) and N.C. Mendis (ct 17 / st 2); 18 – R.S. Mahanama; 17 – J. Kalatunga, M.N. Nawaz and G. Sanjeewa (ct 16 / st 1); 16 – R.P. Arnold, M Kudagodage (ct 11 / st 5) and V. Sittamige; 15 – N. Amugoda (ct 13 / st 2), D.P. Samaraweera and R.D. Wickramaratne.

India

Indian cricket suffered a loss of prestige in England in 1996. A talented side failed to do themselves justice, and the early departure of

A good start for Sachin Tendulkar as India's captain with victory over Australia in the Test match, triumph in the Titan Cup and a series win over South Africa. (Clive Mason/Allsport)

Sidhu, smarting from his omission from a one-day international, neither aided their cause nor improved their spirits. There were positive gains from the tour, notably the emergence of Ganguly and Dravid, the advance of Venkatesh Prasad and the hint of class suggested by Joshi before his injury.

Australian Tour
South African tour
Titan Cup
Irani Trophy
Duleep Trophy
Ranji Trophy
Independence Cup

In spite of these gains, changes were inevitable. Sachin Tendulkar replaced Mohammad Azharuddin as captain while Madan Lal, highly successful in his work with the under-19 side, was appointed the new coach.

Having played in one-day tournaments in Canada, Kenya and Sri Lanka, India returned home to entertain Australia in one Test, South Africa in a three-match series and engage in one-day competition with both. Limited-over cricket continued to dominate India's international agenda.

Australian Tour

Australia were handicapped by the absence of Shane Warne who was still recovering from surgery on a finger on his bowling hand. His place was taken by fellow leg-spinner Peter McIntyre, and there was also room for Bradley Hogg, the left-hander, who bowls chinamen. The side played one warm-up match before the solitary Test.

5, 6 and 7 October 1996
at Patiala
Australians 358 for 8 dec. (M.G. Bevan 100 not out, R.T. Ponting 58, M.J. Slater 56, D. Ganesh 5 for 103) and 99 for 2
Indian Board President's XI 262 (P. Dharmani 130 not out, M.E. Waugh 6 for 68)
Match drawn

Michael Bevan made a strong claim for a place in the Test side with an accomplished hundred in a match marred by rain. India had cause for optimism in the bowling of Ganesh, a medium-pacer from Karnataka, and the batting of Dharmani, the Punjab wicket-keeper.

Test Match

India v. Australia

India and Australia competed for the Border-Gavaskar Trophy in the first Test match in India for ten years. India selected a party of 14 that, surprisingly, included neither Manjrekar nor Kambli. Srinath was declared unfit, and David Johnson, medium-fast, came in for his first Test. Hirwani and Laxman were omitted from the final eleven. Australia gave a first Test cap to Bradley Hogg and preferred Bevan to Law. Taylor won the toss, and Australia batted.

The pitch proved to be dry, cracked and a nightmare for batting. The opening phase gave no indication of what was to come with Taylor and Slater looking confident enough until the Australian skipper offered no shot at a shooter from Venkatesh Prasad and leg before. Even then, there appeared to be little danger, but, in the last over before lunch, Aashish Kapoor produced a giant off-break that bowled Ponting between bat and pad.

Nayan Mongia drives to the boundary during his mighty innings of 152 against Australia at Dehli. (Clive Mason/Allsport)

In the post-lunch period, Australia declined rapidly. Slater had batted for 130 minutes and hit six fours when he played a poor shot to give Kumble a return catch. The bowler took it well, tumbling as he made the dismissal. Mongia was less assured when he held an inside edge to account for Steve Waugh, but Australia were 94 for 4.

Mark Waugh and Bevan gave a hint of a recovery in a stand of 49, but three wickets then fell for four runs. Joshi was obtaining considerable turn and he trapped Bevan leg before when the left-hander played across the line. In his next over, Joshi accounted for Mark Waugh, and Kumble, finding the control and spinning ability that had deserted him in England, ran through the tail.

India began cautiously and lost Rathore at 13, but Ganguly was quickly into his stride, and India closed on 57 for 1 from 21 overs. Nayan Mongia had opened the Indian innings because Sidhu was serving a 50-day suspension for walking out of the tour of England. The wicket-keeper accepted his responsibility avidly, and he and Ganguly took their second wicket partnership into the afternoon of the second day. They had added 131 in 51 overs when Ganguly, who batted with the fluency he had shown in England, became Hogg's first Test victim. Ganguly should have been stumped by Healy before he had added to his overnight score, but Australia were heartened when Tendulkar edged a leg-break to slip and Azharuddin was bowled by McGrath.

Dravid hit 40 off 54 balls before being caught off a leg-glance by the acrobatic Healy, and Joshi was caught at deep mid-wicket, but the day belonged entirely to India who finished on 319 for 6.

Mongia's first Test century became an innings of 152 on the third morning until, after 497 minutes at the crease, he was bowled by Reiffel. This was a mighty innings, total in its application. It took India to a first innings lead of 179 and made it virtually certain that they would win the match. If Mongia's knock underlined the difference between the two sides then so too did the lack of control and variety shown by McIntyre, Hogg and Mark Waugh, who could not match the class of Kumble, Joshi and Kapoor.

There was early disaster for Australia when they batted again. Slater swished at Johnson, and Azharuddin leaped high to his right to take a stunning catch. It gave Johnson his first Test wicket. Ponting was ill at ease, but played a couple of fine drives before having his stumps wrecked by Venkatesh Prasad.

Mark Waugh and Taylor showed resolution, but the pressure was intense as fieldsmen crowded the bat to the spinners and Mark Waugh was caught off a bottom edge as he cut at Kumble. Taylor, back to lead the side after his operation, was visibly tiring, and it was no surprise when he pushed a catch to short-leg. At 78 for 4, Australia were in despair. Steve Waugh and Michael Bevan played with a determination that shamed others. They added 67 and forced Tendulkar to ring the bowling changes until the return of Kumble brought success, Bevan edging him to slip. Healy smote three boundaries, but Kumble deceived him with a flipper and Mongia confirmed it was his match with a sharp leg-side stumping. Australia closed on 168 for 6.

The Australians held out until 15 minutes after lunch on the fourth day, and for that they were indebted to Steve Waugh who finished unbeaten on 67, which included five fours and occupied 273 minutes. He had faced 221 balls. McIntyre offered brave support, but Kumble's extra pace and bounce were decisive. Venkatesh Prasad quickly captured the last two wickets.

Needing 56 to win, India did not find the task too easy. Mongia fell immediately, but he had long since done enough to be Man of the Match, and Rathore and Tendulkar, with two failures in his first Test as captain, went cheaply before Ganguly and Azharuddin briskly hit off the required runs.

It was India's first Test win over Australia for 15 years, and Australia have now not won in India for 26 years. It was not the best of starts for new coach Geoff Marsh, but the defeat was taken in good grace.

Deposed skipper Mohammad Azharuddin congratulates new cap David Johnson on his first Test wicket, Slater caught at slip for 0 by Azharuddin himself. (Clive Mason/Allsport)

Test Match – India v. Australia
10. 11. 12 and 13 October 1996 at Feroze Shah Kotla Ground, Dehli

Australia

	First Innings		Second Innings	
M.J. Slater	c and b Kumble	44	(2) c Azharuddin, b Johnson	0
M.A. Taylor (Capt)	lbw, b Prasad	27	(1) c Rathore, b Kapoor	37
R.T. Ponting	b Kapoor	14	b Prasad	13
M.E. Waugh	c Dravid, b Joshi	26	c Mongia, b Kumble	23
S.R. Waugh	c Mongia, b Kapoor	0	not out	67
M.G. Bevan	lbw, b Joshi	26	c Azharuddin, b Kumble	33
*I.A. Healy	b Kumble	17	st Mongia, b Kumble	12
G.B. Hogg	c Rathore, b Kumble	1	c Rathore, b Kumble	4
P.R. Reiffel	c Dravid, b Kumble	7	lbw, b Kumble	6
P.E. McIntyre	not out	6	lbw, b Prasad	16
G.D. McGrath	run out	6	c Mongia, b Prasad	0
	b 4, lb 3, nb 1	8	b 9, lb 6, w 1, nb 7	23
		182		**234**

India

	First Innings		Second Innings	
V. Rathore	c Ponting, b Reiffel	5	b Reiffel	14
*N.R. Mongia	b Reiffel	152	lbw, b Reiffel	0
S.C. Ganguly	c M.E. Waugh, b Hogg	66	not out	21
S.R. Tendulkar (Capt)	c M.E. Waugh, b McIntyre	10	b McGrath	0
M. Azharuddin	b McGrath	17	not out	21
R.S. Dravid	c Healy, b S.R. Waugh	40		
S.B. Joshi	c Ponting, b McIntyre	23		
A.R. Kapoor	c Ponting, b M.E. Waugh	22		
A.R. Kumble	lbw, b Reiffel	2		
D. Johnson	not out	0		
Venkatesh Prasad	b McIntyre	3		
	b 10, lb 1, nb 10	21	w 1, nb 1	2
		361	(for 3 wickets)	**58**

	O	M	R	W	O	M	R	W
Venkatesh Prasad	12	4	34	1	13.3	7	18	3
Johnson	4	1	12	–	12	2	40	1
Joshi	23	7	36	2	20	7	52	–
Kumble	24	7	63	4	41	12	67	5
Kapoor	10	3	30	2	22	5	42	1

	O	M	R	W	O	M	R	W
McGrath	29	10	56	1	7	2	30	1
Reiffel	17	7	35	3	6	2	24	2
S.R. Waugh	13	5	25	1				
McIntyre	37.4	7	103	3	0.2	–	4	–
Hogg	17	3	69	1				
M.E. Waugh	18	–	62	1				

Fall of Wickets
1–47, 2–81, 3–93, 4–94, 5–143, 6–144, 7–147, 8–169, 9–170
1–4, 2–25, 3–72, 4–78, 5–145, 6–159, 7–171, 8–191, 9–232

Fall of Wickets
1–13, 2–144, 3–169, 4–199, 5–260, 6–303, 7–341, 8–353, 9–354
1–0, 2–25, 3–26

Umpires: S. Venkataraghavan & P. Willey

India won by 7 wickets

Titan Cup

South Africa joined India and Australia to compete for the Titan Cup. Each side was to play the other three times, and the top two sides from the initial league tournament were to meet in the final.

India named two players new to international cricket in their squad for the first three games: opening batsman Sujith Somasunder of Karnataka and wicket-keeper batsman Pankaj Dharmani of Punjab. Somasunder made his debut in the first match of the series in which South Africa beat India quite convincingly. Gary Kirsten hit 84 off 81 balls, and a seventh wicket stand of 76 between Cronje and McMillan gave India a most difficult target. Cronje won the applause of the 35,000 crowd when he recalled Ganguly after the Indian batsman had been run out. Ganguly had crashed into bowler de Villiers in attempting a quick single, and the collision left him short of his ground. The match marked the 225th appearance of Azharuddin in a limited-over international, an Indian record.

Kirsten won his second individual award in two days when his seventh century in one-day international cricket took South Africa to victory over Australia with 23 balls to spare. Australia had begun well enough with Mark Waugh and Taylor scoring 85 for the first wicket. The side had then stumbled, and only Bevan's 56 off 78 balls had ensured that South Africa would face a reasonable target. The South African fielding, Rhodes in particular, had been outstanding. Hudson and Kirsten hit 118 for the first wicket, and Kirsten went on to score 105 off 139 balls.

Mark Taylor scored a fine century in Bangalore, but Australia still failed to win. Facing a target of 216, India were 42 for 2 when Azharuddin was adjudged leg before by umpire Bansal. The batsman clearly disagreed with the decision, and his show of dissent caused disturbances in the crowd. Bottles were thrown, and the game was held up for more than 20 minutes. Azharuddin was later reprimanded but not fined by referee Reid. India were given hope by Tendulkar and Jadeja who added 79 for the fifth wicket, but, with Tendulkar and Mongia taking India to 157, three wickets fell for seven runs. India looked beaten, but Kumble joined Srinath in a match-winning stand of 52. To add to Australia's woes, Healy pulled a hamstring, and Gilchrist was flown to India to replace him.

South Africa continued their winning ways with victory in Jaipur. Kirsten established a record for the most runs in one-day internationals in a calendar year, but the South African heroes were Cullinan and Cronje, who added 113 for the third wicket. Cullinan played a disciplined innings, for the pitch was not easy, as Ganguly and Tendulkar later discovered when they scored 126 in 31 overs for India's first wicket. There was little support from the middle order, and Azharuddin was left stranded as India fell 28 runs short of their target.

A spell of four wickets for no runs in eight balls by Allan Donald destroyed Australia in the match at Faridabad. Australia lost their last five wickets for three runs. South Africa did not find the task of scoring 216 an easy one, but Cullinan played another responsible innings to steer his side to victory with 16 balls to spare.

The sixth match, scheduled to be played at Cuttack between India and Australia, was abandoned without a ball being bowled because of rain. The abandonment was to provide Australia with their only point of the competition.

A brisk 53 from Srinath, promoted to number three, helped India to reach 105 for 2 in 26 overs, but four wickets then fell for 23 runs in nine overs. Jadeja and Joshi stopped the rot, but the final score was disappointing. Kirsten and Gibbs hit 62 in 14 overs, after which three wickets fell quickly. Cronje and Rhodes shared a determined stand of 63 which brought South Africa in sight of their fifth successive win in the tournament.

Michael Bevan, the only Australian batsman to show consistency in the Titan Cup, hit 79 from 70 balls against South Africa at Guwahati. With Slater scoring a welcome 50 and only Ponting failing, Australia reached a commendable 238 for 6. It proved insufficient to halt South Africa, for whom Klusener hit 88 off 98 deliveries to celebrate his promotion to number three.

India qualified for the final with a thrilling last over win against Australia. Tendulkar was in top form at the outset, and Azharuddin played a brilliant innings of 94. He and Dravid added 110 for the fourth wicket. Facing a formidable target, Australia were well served by skipper Taylor, who hit 78 off 91 balls. Bevan and Slater again batted well, and when the last over arrived Australia were just six short of victory with the last pair together. Hogg was run out off the first ball so that India entered the final.

Qualifying Table

	P	W	L	Nr	Pts
South Africa	6	6	–	–	12
India	6	2	3	1	5
Australia	6	–	5	1	1

Titan Cup Final

India surprised South Africa in the final with a positive, purposeful display, especially in the field. Tendulkar was happy to bat first when he won the toss, and he led the way with a fine 67, but it was a late assault by Jadeja, 43 off 42 balls, that gave the Indian innings impetus. The Indian total was a little disappointing, but their bowlers soon shredded the South African innings. At 96 for 7, a total rout looked likely, but Richardson and Symcox kept hopes alive with a partnership of 88. Well as they batted, the winning score always looked out of reach, and Kumble made sure that India would win the Titan Cup. Not for the first time, South Africa had carried all before them only to lose the match that mattered most. They had some consolation in that Donald was named Man of the Series.

Match One – India v. South Africa
17 October 1996 at Lal Bahadur Shastri Stadium, Hyderabad

South Africa

A.C. Hudson	c Azharuddin, b Venkatesh Prasad	34
G. Kirsten	c Azharuddin, b Kumble	84
P.L. Symcox	b Kumble	3
D.J. Cullinan	c Venkatesh Prasad, b Joshi	16
J.N. Rhodes	c and b Jadeja	10
W.J. Cronje (Capt)	not out	63
D.N. Crookes	b Kumble	2
B.M. McMillan	run out	32
D.J. Richardson	not out	9
P.S. de Villiers		
A.A. Donald		
	lb 4, w 2, nb 2	8
	50 overs (for 7 wickets)	261

	O	M	R	W
Srinath	9	–	45	–
Venkatesh Prasad	10	–	45	1
Joshi	10	–	64	1
Kumble	10	–	42	3
Tendulkar	5	–	28	–
Jadeja	6	–	33	1

Fall of Wickets
1–74, 2–85, 3–128, 4–145, 5–158, 6–166, 7–242

India

S. Somasunder	run out	10
S.R. Tendulkar (Capt)	c Cullinan, b de Villiers	11
R.S. Dravid	c Rhodes, b Crookes	62
M. Azharuddin	c Cullinan, b Crookes	32
S.C. Ganguly	c Symcox, b Donald	31
A. Jadeja	c Cronje, b Donald	15
*N.R. Mongia	run out	3
J. Srinath	not out	16
S.B. Joshi	run out	2
A.R. Kumble	c Hudson, b Donald	9
Venkatesh Prasad	c Crookes, b de Villiers	0
	b 5, lb 14, w 4	23
	46.3 overs	214

	O	M	R	W
de Villiers	8.3	1	26	2
McMillan	8	1	31	–
Donald	9	–	43	3
Cronje	2	–	11	–
Symcox	10	–	43	–
Crookes	9	–	41	2

Fall of Wickets
1–19, 2–30, 3–97, 4–144, 5–171, 6–178, 7–180, 8–188, 9–206

Umpires: H.S. Sekhon & R.C. Sharma   *Man of the Match:* G. Kirsten

South Africa won by 47 runs

Match Two – Australia v. South Africa
19 October 1996 at Nehru Stadium, Indore

Australia

M.E. Waugh	run out	50
M.A. Taylor (Capt)	run out	39
R.T. Ponting	c Richardson, b Donald	35
S.R. Waugh	st Richardson, b Symcox	1
S.G. Law	c and b Crookes	1
M.G. Bevan	b Donald	56
*I.A. Healy	c Riodhes, b Donald	11
G.B. Hogg	not out	11
P.R. Reiffel	not out	6
J.N. Gillespie		
G.D. McGrath		
	lb 4, w 1, nb 4	9
	50 overs (for 7 wickets)	219

	O	M	R	W
de Villiers	10	–	38	–
McMillan	9	–	48	–
Donald	10	–	57	3
Crookes	10	–	39	1
Symcox	10	–	28	1
Cronje	1	–	5	–

Fall of Wickets
1–85, 2–99, 3–103, 4–106, 5–167, 6–197, 7–204

South Africa

A.C. Hudson	c Taylor, b McGrath	53
G. Kirsten	not out	105
D.J. Cullinan	b McGrath	0
W.J. Cronje (Capt)	c Healy, b Gillespie	14
J.N. Rhodes	not out	19
B.M. McMillan		
P.L. Symcox		
*D.J. Richardson		
D.N. Crookes		
P.S. de Villiers		
A.A. Donald		
	b 5, lb 14, w 3, nb 7	29
	46.1 overs (for 3 wickets)	220

	O	M	R	W
McGrath	10	1	42	2
Reiffel	10	1	34	–
Gillespie	10	–	51	1
Hogg	7.1	–	37	–
Law	6	–	23	–
M.E. Waugh	1	–	14	–

Fall of Wickets
1–118, 2–129, 3–175

Umpires: Suresh Deo & Subroto Banerjee   *Man of the Match:* G. Kirsten

South Africa won by 7 wickets

Match Three – India v. Australia
21 October 1996 at Chinnaswamy Stadium, Bangalore

Australia

M.E. Waugh	c Tendulkar, **b** Venkatesh Prasad	4
M.A. Taylor (Capt)	c Azharuddin, **b** Tendulkar	105
M.J. Slater	c Mongia, **b** Venkatesh Prasad	3
S.R. Waugh	c Ganguly, **b** Joshi	41
M.G. Bevan	c Kumble,**b** Venkatesh Prasad	36
S.G. Law	lbw, **b** Kumble	5
*I.A. Healy	c Tendulkar, **b** Kumble	8
G.B. Hogg	not out	3
J.N. Gillespie		
D.W. Fleming		
G.D. McGrath		
	b 1, lb **4**, w **3**, nb **2**	10
	50 overs (for 7 wickets)	**215**

	O	M	R	**W**
Srinath	10	2	35	–
Venkatesh Prasad	10	–	37	3
Kumble	10	–	40	2
Joshi	10	1	42	1
Ganguly	2	–	11	–
Tendulkar	8	–	45	1

Fall of Wickets
1–**9**, 2–**23**, 3–**115**, 4–**197**, 5–**204**, 6–**212**, 7–**215**

India

S. Somasunder	**b** McGrath	7
S.R. Tendulkar (Capt)	lbw, **b** S.R. Waugh	88
R.S. Dravid	lbw, **b** Fleming	6
M. Azharuddin	lbw, **b** Gillespie	1
S.C. Ganguly	run out	4
A. Jadeja	run out	27
*N.R. Mongia	c McGrath, **b** S.R. Waugh	14
S.B. Joshi	**b** Fleming	1
J. Srinath	not out	30
A.R. Kumble	not out	16
Venkatesh Prasad		
	b 1, lb **8**, w **12**, nb **1**	22
	48.5 overs (for 8 wickets)	**216**

	O	M	R	**W**
McGrath	9.5	2	27	1
Fleming	10	–	39	2
Gillespie	10	1	44	1
Hogg	10	–	45	–
S.R. Waugh	9	–	52	2

Fall of Wickets
1–**30**, 2–**41**, 3–**42**, 4–**47**, 5–**126**, 6–**157**, 7–**164**, 8–**164**

Umpires: S.K. Porel & S.K. Bansal   *Man of the Match:* S.R. Tendulkar

India won by 2 wickets

Match Four – India v. South Africa
23 October 1996 at Sawi Mansingh Stadium, Jaipur

South Africa

A.C. Hudson	lbw, **b** Venkatesh Prasad	5
G. Kirsten	c Joshi, **b** Kumble	29
D.J. Cullinan	st Mongia, **b** Kumble	106
W.J. Cronje (Capt)	c and **b** Joshi	58
J.N. Rhodes	lbw, **b** Jadeja	4
D.N. Crookes	lbw, **b** Jadeja	10
B.M. McMillan	not out	19
*D.J. Richardson	not out	8
P.L. Symcox		
P.S. de Villiers		
A.A. Donald		
	b **3**, w **4**, nb **3**	10
	50 overs (for 6 wickets)	**249**

	O	M	R	**W**
Srinath	10	–	45	–
Venkatesh Prasad	9	–	42	1
Kumble	10	–	49	2
Joshi	10	–	41	1
Tendulkar	3	–	22	–
Jadeja	8	–	47	2

Fall of Wickets
1–**5**, 2–**55**, 3–**168**, 4–**180**, 5–**204**, 6–**232**

India

S.C. Ganguly	**b** Donald	54
S.R. Tendulkar (Capt)	c Kirsten, **b** McMillan	64
R.S. Dravid	c Richardson, **b** McMillan	0
M. Azharuddin	not out	56
J. Srinath	c Symcox	4
A.D. Jadeja	**b** McMillan	10
P.K. Dharmani	**b** de Villiers	8
A.R. Kumble	**b** Donald	1
*N.R. Mongia	not out	8
S.B. Joshi		
Venkatesh Prasad		
	b lb **8**, w **9**	17
	50 overs (for 7 wickets)	**222**

	O	M	R	**W**
de Villiers	10	2	28	1
McMillan	9	1	32	3
Donald	10	–	49	2
Symcox	10	–	38	1
Crookes	4	–	32	–
Cronje	7	–	35	–

Fall of Wickets
1–**126**, 2–**126**, 3–**148**, 4–**153**, 5–**191**, 6–**207**, 7–**208**

Umpires: J. Kurushinkal & S. Chaudhary   *Man of the Match:* D.J. Cullinan

South Africa won by 27 runs

Match Five – Australia v. South Africa
25 October 1996 at Mayur Nahar Stadium, Faridabad

Australia

Batsman	Dismissal	Runs
M.A. Taylor (Capt)	c McMillan, b Symcox	42
M.E. Waugh	c Richardson, b McMillan	16
R.T. Ponting	c Richardson, b Symcox	17
S.R. Waugh	c McMillan, b Boje	40
M.G. Bevan	c Hudson, b Boje	12
S.G. Law	run out	52
*A.C. Gilchrist	b Donald	18
G.B. Hogg	lbw, b Donald	0
P.R. Reiffel	b Donald	0
D.W. Fleming	not out	1
G.D. McGrath	c Cronje, b Donald	1
	b 1, lb 8, w 3, nb 4	16
	47.3 overs	215

South Africa

Batsman	Dismissal	Runs
A.C. Hudson	run out	32
G. Kirsten	b Fleming	1
P.L. Symcox	c Bevan, b Reiffel	26
D.J. Cullinan	not out	71
J.N. Rhodes	b Reiffel	42
W.J. Cronje (Capt)	c Gilchrist, b Reiffel	0
B.M. McMillan	run out	21
*D.J. Richardson	c Gilchrist, b Reiffel	5
N. Boje	c S.R. Waugh, b Hogg	6
P.S. de Villiers	not out	0
A.A. Donald		
	lb 9, w 3, nb 2	14
	47.2 overs (for 8 wickets)	218

	O	M	R	W
de Villiers	9	–	35	–
McMillan	9	–	41	1
Cronje	2	–	12	–
Donald	8.3	–	31	4
Symcox	10	–	43	2
Boje	9	–	44	2

	O	M	R	W
Fleming	8.2	–	53	1
Reiffel	10	1	35	4
McGrath	10	1	50	–
Hogg	8	1	23	1
Law	3	–	14	–
M.E. Waugh	8	1	34	–

Fall of Wickets
1–34, 2–72, 3–107, 4–128, 5–162, 6–212, 7–212, 8–212, 9–214

Fall of Wickets
1–3, 2–40, 3–77, 4–142, 5–142, 6–184, 7–205, 8–214

Umpires: B.A. Jamula & M.R. Singh   *Man of the Match:* A.A. Donald

South Africa won by 2 wickets

Match Seven – India v. South Africa
29 October 1996 at Municipal Stadium, Rajkot

India

Batsman	Dismissal	Runs
S.R. Tendulkar (Capt)	lbw, b Donald	28
N.S. Sidhu	run out	2
J. Srinath	c Symcox	53
R.S. Dravid	run out	21
M. Azharuddin	c Richardson, b Boje	9
A.D. Jadeja	b Donald	26
*N.R. Mongia	c and b Boje	3
S.B. Joshi	c Cullinan, b Klusener	20
A.R. Kapoor	lbw, b Klusener	0
A.R. Kumble	b Donald	12
Venkatesh Prasad	not out	1
	lb 4, w 3, nb 3	10
	48.1 overs	185

South Africa

Batsman	Dismissal	Runs
G. Kirsten	c Jadeja, b Joshi	38
H.H. Gibbs	c Tendulkar, b Venkatesh Prasad	35
D.J. Cullinan	c Kumble, b Joshi	6
W.J. Cronje (Capt)	run out	27
J.N. Rhodes	c Jadeja, b Venkatesh Prasad	54
N. Boje	not out	13
*D.J. Richardson	not out	4
P.L. Symcox		
L. Klusener		
P.S. de Villiers		
A.A. Donald		
	lb 7, w 3, nb 1	11
	48.4 overs (for 5 wickets)	188

	O	M	R	W
de Villiers	9	1	19	–
Klusener	9	–	54	2
Donald	9.1	1	31	3
Symcox	10	–	37	1
Bojes	10	–	38	2
Cronje	1	–	2	–

	O	M	R	W
Srinath	8	–	26	–
Venkatesh Prasad	9	–	38	2
Kumble	9.4	1	40	–
Joshi	10	–	32	2
Kapoor	10	–	32	–
Tendulkar	2	–	13	–

Fall of Wickets
1–7, 2–48, 3–105, 4–111, 5–122, 6–128, 7–169, 8–170, 9–172

Fall of Wickets
1–62, 2–72, 3–88, 4–151, 5–184

Umpires: B.S. Rao & V.K. Chopra   *Man of the Match:* J.N. Rhodes

South Africa won by 5 wickets

Match Eight – Australia v. South Africa
1 November 1996 at Nehru Stadium, Guwahati

Australia

M.A. Taylor (Capt)	c Rhodes, b Symcox	38
S.G. Law	c Cullinan, b Klusener	22
S.R. Waugh	c McMillan, b Boje	37
M.G. Bevan	c Symcox, b Donald	79
R.T. Ponting	b Boje	0
M.J. Slater	not out	53
*A.C. Gilchrist	run out	0
G.B. Hogg	not out	0
D.W. Fleming		
P.R. Reiffel		
G.D. McGrath		
	lb 7, w 2	9
	50 overs (for 6 wickets)	238

	O	M	R	W
McMillan	10	2	35	–
Symcox	10	–	32	1
Klusener	7	–	55	1
Donald	9	–	47	1
Boje	10	–	43	2
Cronje	4	–	19	–

Fall of Wickets
1–38, 2–94, 3–113, 4–113, 5–237, 6–237

South Africa

A.C. Hudson	c Hogg, b Law	68
G. Kirsten	b Hogg	27
L. Klusener	not out	88
D.J. Cullinan	not out	43
J.N. Rhodes		
W.J. Cronje (Capt)		
B.M. McMillan		
*D.J. Richardson		
P.L. Symcox		
N. Boje		
A.A. Donald		
	lb 1, w 4, nb 8	13
	45 overs (for 2 wickets)	239

	O	M	R	W
Fleming	7	–	37	–
Reiffel	10	1	51	–
Hogg	8	–	42	1
McGrath	6	–	41	–
S.R. Waugh	4	–	24	–
Law	10	–	43	1

Fall of Wickets
1–60, 2–133

Umpires: K. Murali & K. Parthasarathy *Man of the Match:* P.L. Symcox

South Africa won by 8 wickets

Match Nine – India v. South Africa
3 November 1996 at Punjab C.A. Stadium, Mohali

India

S.R. Tendulkar (Capt)	c Law, b M.E. Waugh	62
N.S. Sidhu	run out	11
J. Srinath	st Healy, b M.E. Waugh	3
M. Azharuddin	b M.E. Waugh, b McGrath	94
R.S. Dravid	c Taylor, b Law	56
R.R. Singh	c Slater, b Law	6
A.D. Jadeja	not out	25
*N.R. Mongia	not out	19
A.R. Kumble		
S.B. Joshi		
Venkatesh Prasad		
	lb 7, w 2, nb 4	13
	50 overs (for 6 wickets)	289

	O	M	R	W
McGrath	10	–	52	1
Reiffel	10	1	52	–
Gillespie	9	–	63	–
M.E. Waugh	9	–	38	2
Law	10	–	65	2
Hogg	2	–	12	–

Fall of Wickets
1–54, 2–75, 3–95, 4–205, 5–217, 6–253

Australia

M.E. Waugh	b Singh	37
M.A. Taylor (Capt)	lbw, b Kumble	78
S.G. Law	c Azharuddin, b Singh	0
S.R. Waugh	st Mongia, b Joshi	33
M.G. Bevan	b Venkatesh Prasad	40
M.J. Slater	lbw, b Srinath	52
*I.A. Healy	run out	2
G.B. Hogg	run out	11
P.R. Reiffel	b Kumble	9
J.N. Gillespie	b Kumble	2
G.D. McGrath	not out	8
	lb 6, w 4, nb 2	12
	49.1 overs	284

	O	M	R	W
Srinath	10	–	62	1
Venkatesh Prasad	10	–	68	1
Kumble	10	–	42	3
Singh	7	–	45	2
Joshi	10	–	50	1
Jadeja	2	–	11	–
Tendulkar	0.1	–	0	–

Fall of Wickets
1–84, 2–84, 3–151, 4–155, 5–241, 6–248, 7–250, 8–265, 9–273

Umpires: A.K. Sharma & A.V. Jayaprakash *Man of the Match:* M. Azharuddin

India won by 5 runs

Titan Cup Final – India v. South Africa
6 November 1996 at Wankhede Stadium, Bombay

India			South Africa		
S.R. Tendulkar (Capt)	c Cronje, b Boje	67	A.C. Hudson	c Azharuddin, b Venkatesh Prasad	7
S.V. Manjrekar	c Richardson, b de Villiers	7	G. Kirsten	c Dravid, b Kumble	23
J. Srinath	c de Villiers, c Donald	5	L. Klusener	c Dravid, b Venkatesh Prasad	7
M. Azharuddin	c Richardson, b Boje	26	D.J. Cullinan	c Azharuddin, b Singh	31
R.S. Dravid	b de Villiers	31	W.J. Cronje (Capt)	c Joshi, b Singh	6
R.R. Singh	run out	5	J.N. Rhodes	c Joshi, b Kumble	6
A.D. Jadeja	not out	43	N. Boje	c Azharuddin, b Joshi	3
*N.R. Mongia	c Boje, b de Villiers	15	*D.J. Richardson	c Singh, b Venkatesh Prasad	43
S.B. Joshi	not out	8	P.L. Symcox	st Mongia, b Kumble	46
A.R. Kumble			P.S. de Villiers	not out	0
Venkatesh Prasad			A.A. Donald	b Kumble	0
	lb 6, w 5, nb 2	13		lb 1, w 1, nb 1	13
	50 overs (for 7 wickets)	220		47.2 overs	185

	O	M	R	W		O	M	R	W
de Villiers	10	3	32	3	Srinath	10	–	45	–
Klusener	4	–	26	–	Venkatesh Prasad	9	–	28	3
Donald	10	1	36	1	Kumble	8.2	–	25	4
Cronje	6	–	27	–	Singh	10	1	40	2
Boje	10	–	51	2	Joshi	10	–	46	1
Symcox	10	–	42	–					

Fall of Wickets
1–34, 2–43, 3–91, 4–137, 5–147, 6–153, 7–204

Fall of Wickets
1–19, 2–29, 3–49, 4–60, 5–84, 6–92, 7–96, 8–184, 9–185

Umpires: S. Vankataraghavan & V.K. Ramaswamy   *Man of the Match:* A.R. Kumble   **India won by 35 runs**

South African Tour

No sooner had the Titan Trophy been completed than South Africa began preparations for their first Test series in India. They had the privilege, not common these days, of playing two first-class matches before the series began in an attempt to get acclimatised.

10, 11 and 12 November 1996
at Kochi
South African XI 243 (R. Ananth 4 for 72) and 233 (A. Katti 4 for 67)
Karnataka 115 (L. Klusener 5 for 38, A.A. Donald 4 for 39) and 117
South African XI won by 244 runs

Victory over Karnataka gave the South Africans much encouragement. They batted responsibly on a pitch that was never easy, and their quick bowlers met with great success.

15, 16 and 17 November 1996
at Motibaug Palace Ground, Baroda
Indian Board President's XI 179 (S.A. Ankola 63, P.S. de Villiers 5 for 46) and 94 (P.S. de Villiers 4 for 37)

South African XI 206 (H.H. Gibbs 74, Venkatapathy Raju 6 for 64) and 70 for 0
South African XI won by 10 wickets

The South African pace bowlers were again in fine form, and the home side would have been totally routed but for Ankola's 63 at number ten. The ninth wicket added 73 runs. South Africa again showed commendable application and well deserved their victory.

First Test Match

India v. South Africa

With Ganguly injured and Sidhu suspended, India gave a first Test cap to Laxman of Hyderabad. Mongia was asked to open the innings and had three different partners in the course of the series. Tendulkar won the toss, and India batted first on a pitch which was expected to crumble and aid the spinners by the third or fourth day. If this were to be the case, India must have been generally disappointed with their first day showing. Mongia was out to a controversial leg before decision, and Dravid also seemed unlucky. Tendulkar looked in fine form, but he became fretful against the off-spin of Symcox and was brilliantly caught by Rhodes when he attempted a big hit over mid-wicket. Rhodes was also instrumental in the dismissal of Azharuddin, the former

Indian captain, who was run out at the non-striker's end when the outstanding South African fielder hit the stumps with a direct throw from cover. India suffered badly in the final session of the day, losing four wickets, three of them to Donald with the second new ball. They closed on 215 for 8.

Donald and de Villiers claimed the last two wickets early on the second morning, but where India had succumbed to pace, South Africa were soon tormented by spin. Joshi – a most improved left-arm bowler who had been unlucky on the tour of England – and Kumble took control. At 119 for 7, South Africa were in dreadful trouble, but de Villiers joined Symcox in a stand that realised 63. The partnership was broken when Joshi deceived Symcox with a most intelligent arm ball. The leg before decision was clear, but this was more than could be said for some of the decisions earlier in the day – the standard of umpiring was severely criticised. Donald and de Villiers took the score to 202 by the close.

By the time Srinath bowled Donald, South Africa had taken a first innings lead. Forty overnight, de Villiers went on to make his highest Test score, being left unbeaten on 67. He had seen his side take a 21-run advantage, which in the context of the match looked as if it might be significant. Indeed, Donald removed both openers before the arrears were wiped off, and when Tendulkar fell to McMillan it seemed South Africa were on course for victory. Dravid, Azharuddin and Joshi all played minor innings, but seven wickets went down for 124, and it was debutant Laxman, in partnership with Kumble, who revived India. Cronje led his players from the field during the final session after Adams had been hit by a stone thrown from the crowd, but they returned after ten minutes and peace was restored.

Leading by 151 at the end of the third day, India were all out within 20 minutes on the fourth day, having added just 18 more runs. This meant that South Africa needed 170 to win, a task that did not seem too difficult in spite of the help that the pitch was now offering to the spinners. It was Srinath, the pace bowler, however, who did the damage. His fifth delivery cut back sharply and trapped Hudson leg before, and with his next ball he clipped the edge of Cullinan's bat and had him caught behind. Kirsten and Cronje attempted to restore some order to the shattered ranks, but the introduction of spin brought an end to Kirsten's innings, and Kumble accounted for McMillan.

Srinath's bowling was inspired. He had Richardson caught behind and Rhodes was too late on the next ball and was leg before. Symcox saved the hat-trick only to be bowled by Kumble who had de Villiers taken at slip. Srinath ended all resistance by clean bowling both Donald and Adams. The last six South African wickets had gone down for nine runs in 22 balls, and the match was over an hour after lunch on the fourth day. Srinath, named Man of the Match, had returned his best figures in Test cricket in an outstanding display of fast bowling.

Azharuddin, the dominant batting force in the series between India and South Africa. In Calcutta, he hit the fourth fastest century in Test cricket and followed it with a majestic unbeaten 163 at Kanpur. (Nigel French/ASP)

Second Test Match

India v. South Africa

Ganguly returned to the Indian side at the expense of Manjrekar, Dravid being moved up to open, while South Africa made two changes, bringing in Gibbs and Klusener for their Test debuts at the expense of Rhodes and de Villiers. Cronje won the toss, and South Africa found Eden Gardens more to their liking than Ahmedabad. By the end of the first day, South Africa were 339 for 2, and, as the score suggests, the batsmen were in total command. Kirsten and Hudson had 98 on the board at lunch, and by tea, the score was 236. Srinath bowled Kirsten in the first over after tea, and Hudson was out an hour before the close. Hudson, in particular, batted with grandeur and authority, but he was dropped before he had scored and again on four, and the Indian fielding remained wretched all day.

With the departure of Kirsten and Hudson, Gibbs and Cullinan enjoyed the pitch and looked totally at ease, but Venkatesh Prasad bowled India back into contention on the second morning. South Africa's last eight wickets fell for 82 runs, and Venkatesh Prasad bowled quite beautifully to finish with 6 for 104, his best performance in Test cricket.

Mongia and Dravid gave India a good start, but three wickets fell for nine runs and suddenly the massive crowd was silent. Azharuddin was forced to retire hurt on six after being struck on the arm by a ball from McMillan, and Donald's pace ripped out Tendulkar and Laxman. Gibbs had

First Test Match – India v. South Africa
20, 21, 22 and 23 October 1996 at Gujarat Stadium, Ahmedabad

India

	First Innings		Second Innings	
S.V. Manjrekar	b Adams	34	c Hudson, b Donald	5
*N.R. Mongia	lbw, b de Villiers	9	c Richardson, b Donald	5
R.S. Dravid	lbw, b Symcox	24	lbw, b Symcox	34
S.R. Tendulkar (Capt)	c Rhodes, b Symcox	42	c Rhodes, b McMillan	7
M. Azharuddin	run out	35	c McMillan, b Donald	24
V.V.S. Laxman	lbw, b Donald	11	lbw, b Adams	51
S.B. Joshi	c Hudson, b Donald	16	c McMillan, b Symcox	13
J. Srinath	c Cullinan, b Donald	14	lbw, b de Villiers	1
A.R. Kumble	c Kirsten, b Donald	17	not out	30
Venkatesh Prasad	c Donald, b de Villiers	9	c McMillan, b Adams	0
N.D. Hirwani	not out	0	c sub (Crookes), b Adams	9
	lb 9, nb 3	12	b 4, lb 4, nb 3	11
		223		**190**

South Africa

	First Innings		Second Innings	
G. Kirsten	st Mongia, b Kumble	17	(2) lbw, b Joshi	20
A.C. Hudson	lbw, b Kumble	23	(1) lbw, b Srinath	0
D.J. Cullinan	lbw, b Joshi	43	c Mongia, b Srinath	0
W.J. Cronje (Capt)	lbw, b Hirwani	1	not out	48
J.N. Rhodes	c Manjrekar, b Joshi	14	(7) lbw, b Srinath	0
B.M. McMillan	b Joshi	8	(5) c Joshi, b Kumble	17
*D.J. Richardson	b Hirwani	4	(6) c Mongia, b Srinath	7
P.L. Symcox	lbw, b Joshi	32	b Kumble	0
P.S. de Villiers	not out	67	c Azharuddin, b Kumble	0
A.A. Donald	b Srinath	17	b Srinath	4
P.R. Adams	c Azharuddin, b Srinath	1	b Srinath	0
	b 7, lb 9, nb 1	17	b 1, lb 3, w 5	9
		244		**105**

	O	M	R	W	O	M	R	W
Donald	27	14	37	4	15	3	32	3
de Villiers	18	5	55	2	17	4	45	1
McMillan	11	4	20	–	9	4	18	1
Cronje	5	3	8	–	7	1	10	–
Adams	17	2	46	1	9.2	4	30	3
Symcox	21	5	48	2	22	8	47	2

	O	M	R	W	O	M	R	W
Srinath	19	7	47	2	11.5	4	21	6
Venkatesh Prasad	9	2	24	–	7	–	18	–
Kumble	31	6	76	2	12	2	34	3
Joshi	24	4	43	4	8	1	28	1
Hirwani	15	3	38	2				

Fall of Wickets
1–22, 2–63, 3–98, 4–129, 5–159, 6–165, 7–193, 8–196, 9–221
1–10, 2–15, 3–38, 4–82, 5–91, 6–123, 7–124, 8–180, 9–180

Fall of Wickets
1–29, 2–46, 3–49, 4–95, 5–102, 6–113, 7–119, 8–182, 9–242
1–0, 2–0, 3–40, 4–65, 5–96, 6–96, 7–100, 8–100, 9–105

Umpires: S.K. Bansal & G. Sharp

India won by 64 runs

earlier run out Mongia, who had not enjoyed a good match behind the stumps, and now ran out Joshi with a brilliant piece of fielding at backward point. India closed on 152 for 6, with Azharuddin injured.

Azharuddin returned to the crease when Donald bowled Srinath on the third morning and by lunch had reached 97. He had hit Klusener for five consecutive boundaries, and he pulled Adams for his 18th boundary to reach his century in the first over after lunch. It had taken him 74 deliveries and was equal fourth fastest in Test cricket. It was a defiant gesture by the deposed captain who no longer seemed at ease with his team-mates and who was the subject of much public criticism for events in his private life. His reaction to the standing ovation by the 70,000 crowd was, to say the least, a little muted. Kumble gave Azharuddin wonderful support in an eighth wicket partnership of 161, and his 88 was his highest Test score. Having been 119 for 6, India had moved to within 99 of South Africa's total.

South Africa still held the advantage, and they were determined to consolidate in spite of the loss of Hudson with an injured thumb. Gibbs fell cheaply, but Kirsten and Cullinan were masterly. They took the score to 160 by the close and they were unrelenting in their destruction of the Indian bowling on the fourth day. They extended their partnership to 212, and Kirsten reached his second century of the match. Cullinan's six-hour innings included 15 fours

and a six, and Cronje was able to declare shortly before tea. If his declaration seemed cautious, it was conditioned by the knowledge that Donald was unfit to bowl. In fact, his part in the tour was over.

Even without him, South Africa had all but clinched victory by the end of the fourth day. India lost three wickets to Klusener, and Symcox captured the most prized scalp of Tendulkar to leave India on 59 for 4.

Azharuddin, unbeaten on 25 overnight, took his score to 52 off 55 balls on the last morning, but all the honours went to the man he had destroyed on the third day, Lance Klusener. The 25-year-old pace bowler became the first South African to take eight wickets in an innings on his Test debut. Five of his victims were caught at slip or behind the wicket, and the other three were bowled. He kept a full length, and all but Azharuddin found him virtually unplayable. India suffered their heaviest defeat; and South Africa claimed their biggest victory in terms of runs.

3, 4 and 5 December 1996
at Vidarbha CA Stadium, Nagpur
South African XI 384 for 5 dec. (H.H. Gibbs 200 not out, D.N. Crookes 76, W.J. Cronje 53) and 492 for 3 dec.
(H.H. Gibbs 171, B.M. McMillan 130, L. Klusener 102 not out)
India 'A' 340 (V.G. Kambli 98, P.R. Adams 5 for 108)
Match drawn

Played in between the second and third Tests, this match brought a feast of runs and records. Gibbs hit the first double century of his career and followed it with 171 in the second innings when he and McMillan put on 313 for the first wicket. Klusener followed his success in the second Test with the second century of his career.

Third Test Match

India v. South Africa

India brought in Raman for Laxman to provide Mongia with his fourth opening partner in four Tests, and off-spinner Kapoor replaced leg-spinner Hirwani. For South Africa, de Villiers returned in place of Donald who had returned home for treatment. Tendulkar won the toss, and India batted.

At first, all went well. Mongia and Raman took the score to 76 at lunch, but five balls into the afternoon Mongia was bowled by McMillan. Raman, the left-hander from Tamil Nadu, had never been able to reproduce his domestic form at Test level, but he hit 11 fours in his 57 before driving at McMillan and edging to gully. Ganguly fell to Cronje, but Tendulkar looked in top form and drove Symcox into the crowd for six. This prompted the recall of Adams, whose first four overs had cost 23 runs. He now found length and turn and removed Dravid, Azharuddin and Joshi in three overs. India had lost four wickets for 33 runs and closed on an unhappy 204 for 6.

Things did not improve on the second morning when India lost their last four wickets and scored only 33 runs. Adams finished with 6 for 55, the best figures of his brief and fascinating career.

The South African bowlers had done all that could have been expected of them, with Adams excelling, and now the batsmen began confidently against the Indian pace men. Kumble broke the opening partnership when he had Hudson leg before, and it was Kumble in harness with Srinath who broke the back of the South African batting. In 31 balls, four wickets fell while only ten runs were scored. The last seven wickets went down to Srinath and Kumble for 56 runs, and India had grabbed a vital and unexpected lead of 60. They immediately lost Raman and were 7 for 1 at the close, but they now held the advantage.

That advantage was enhanced by the batting of Kumble, a most competent night-watchman, who frustrated the South African bowlers on the third morning. The only wicket to fall before lunch was that of Mongia, and Ganguly, batting with a runner because of an injured ankle, hit six fours in his innings of 41. South Africa's disappointment was the inability of Adams to exploit a pitch on which he had bowled well in the first innings and on which Kumble thrived. In contrast, Azharuddin showed his ability as a batsman on any pitch. He drove and pulled serenely and was unbeaten on 88 by the close, 60 of his runs had come in boundaries. Dravid had also batted well, and India were 270 for 5.

Second Test Match – India v. South Africa
27, 28, 29, 30 November and 1 December 1996 at Eden Gardens, Calcutta

South Africa

	First Innings		Second Innings	
A.C. Hudson	b Venkatesh Prasad	146	retired hurt	6
G. Kirsten	b Srinath	102	run out	133
H.H. Gibbs	lbw. b Prasad	31	c Dravid, b Srinath	9
D.J. Cullinan	lbw. b Prasad	43	not out	153
W.J. Cronje (Capt)	c Mongia, b Srinath	4	c and b Kumble	34
B.M. McMillan	lbw, b Prasad	0	not out	17
*D.J. Richardson	not out	36		
L. Klusener	b Venkatesh Prasad	10		
P.L. Symcox	b Venkatesh Prasad	13		
A.A. Donald	c Laxman, b Kumble	0		
P.R. Adams	b Kumble	4		
	b 6, lb 24, nb 9	39	lb 10, w 1, nb 4	15
		428	for 3 wks., dec	**367**

India

	First Innings		Second Innings	
*N.R. Mongia	run out	35	c Cullinan, b Klusener	8
R.S. Dravid	c Hudson, b McMillan	31	b McMillan	23
S.C. Ganguly	b McMillan	6	c Richardson, b Klusener	0
S.R. Tendulkar (Capt)	b Donald	18	c Kirsten, b Symcox	2
M. Azharuddin	c and b Adams	109	(6) c McMillan, b Klusener	52
V.V.S. Laxman	b Donald	14	(5) b Klusener	1
S.B. Joshi	run out	4	c McMillan, b Klusener	1
J. Srinath	b Donald	11	(9) c McMillan, b Klusener	19
A.R. Kumble	run out	88	(8) b Klusener	17
Venkatesh Prasad	c Richardson, b Adams	1	not out	3
N.D. Hirwani	not out	0	b Klusener	0
	lb 5, nb 7	12	lb 2, nb 9	11
		329		**137**

	O	M	R	W	O	M	R	W		O	M	R	W	O	M	R	W
Srinath	37	7	107	2	24	2	97	1	Donald	21.2	4	72	3				
Venkatesh Prasad	35	6	104	6	15	–	63	–	Klusener	14	1	75	–	21.3	4	64	8
Joshi	12	1	48	–	11	–	56	–	Adams	13	1	69	2				
Ganguly	3	–	10	–					McMillan	16	4	52	2	19	8	33	1
Kumble	20.1	1	78	2	33	5	101	1	Cronje	6	3	13	–	7	4	10	1
Hirwani	14	2	51	–	11	1	40	–	Symcox	11	1	43	–	6	1	28	1

Fall of Wickets
1–**236**, 2–**296**, 3–**346**, 4–**361**, 5–**362**, 6–**362**, 7–**379**, 8–**421**
1–**39**, 2–**251**, 3–**306**

Fall of Wickets
1–**68**, 2–**71**, 3–**77**, 4–**114**, 5–**119**, 6–**119**, 7–**161**, 8–**322**, 9–**324**
1–**17**, 2–**17**, 3–**27**, 4–**28**, 5–**88**, 6–**92**, 7–**97**, 8–**132**, 9–**137**

Umpires: B.C. Cooray & V.K. Ramaswamy

South Africa won by 329 runs

Azharuddin and Dravid were not separated until their stand was worth a record 165, and when Tendulkar declared at lunch on the fourth day, Azharuddin was unbeaten on 163. His runs had come off 288 balls and he had hit a six and 25 fours.

Needing an impossible 461 to win, South Africa made a terrible start, losing three wickets for 29. Most disastrously, Cullinan was run out at the non-striker's end when Tendulkar hit the stumps from mid-off. Cronje and Hudson stopped the rot with a stand of 58. The South African skipper hit Joshi for four fours in one over, but the left-arm spinner took his revenge when he had him caught at extra cover. South Africa ended the day on 127 for 5, and India were a breath away from a series victory.

McMillan and Richardson were out within the first 20 minutes of the final day, but Klusener showed admirable defence to take the game into the afternoon. His broad bat to the spinners prompted Tendulkar to take the second new ball. Srinath and Venkatesh Prasad used it well and took the last wickets in four overs so that South Africa suffered their first 'series' defeat since their return to Test cricket.

Azharuddin was named Man of the Match and Man of the Series, but Srinath's 17 wickets deserve the highest praise. He and Venkatesh Prasad have given Indian cricket a new dimension.

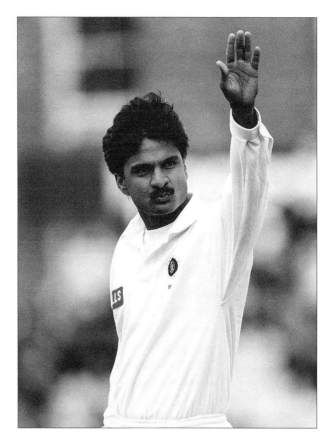

A match-winning 6 for 21 in the first Test and 17 wickets in the three-match series against South Africa for Javagal Srinath. (David Munden/Sportsline)

Third Test Match – India v. South Africa
8, 9, 10, 11 and 12 December 1996 at Green Park, Kanpur

India

	First Innings		Second Innings	
*N.R. Mongia	b McMillan	41	(2) lbw, b Klusener	18
W.V. Raman	c Klusener, b McMillan	57	(1) lbw, b de Villiers	2
S.C. Ganguly	lbw, b Cronje	39	(4) c McMillan, b Symcox	41
S.R. Tendulkar (Capt)	c de Villiers, b Adams	61	(5) c Richardson, b Klusener	36
R.S. Dravid	lbw, b Adams	7	(7) c McMillan, b Adams	56
M. Azharuddin	c and b Adams	5	not out	163
S.B. Joshi	c Klusener, b Adams	0	(8) b Adams	16
A.R. Kumble	b Cronje		(3) c Gibbs, b de Villiers	42
A.R. Kapoor	c de Villiers, b Adams	11	not out	6
J. Srinath	c and b Adams	0		
Venkatesh Prasad	not out	1		
	b 3, lb 6, nb 1	10	b 4, lb 14, nb 2	20
		237	(for 7 wickets, dec.)	400

South Africa

	First Innings		Second Innings	
A.C. Hudson	lbw, b Kumble	15	c sub (Laxman), b Kumble	31
G. Kirsten	c Raman, b Kapoor	43	lbw, b Srinath	7
H.H. Gibbs	b Kapoor	17	b Venkatesh Prasad	5
D.J. Cullinan	c Azharuddin, b Kumble	29	run out	2
W.J. Cronje (Capt)	c sub (Laxman), b Kumble	15	c Tendulkar, b Joshi	50
B.M. McMillan	b Srinath	1	c sub (Laxman), b Joshi	18
*D.J. Richardson	b Srinath	4	lbw, b Srinath	5
L. Klusener	c Dravid, b Srinath	9	not out	34
P.L. Symcox	not out	23	c and b Joshi	11
P.S. de Villiers	lbw, b Kumble	6	b Venkatesh Prasad	2
P.R. Adams	run out	8	c Azharuddin, b Srinath	1
	b 4, lb 3	7	lb 14	14
		177		180

	O	M	R	W	O	M	R	W
de Villiers	15	7	18	–	24	10	58	2
Klusener	17	4	47	–	25	7	72	2
McMillan	18	7	40	2	16	6	36	–
Symcox	21	5	57	–	26	2	101	1
Adams	19.1	6	55	6	20	1	84	2
Cronje	10	5	11	2	15	5	31	–

	O	M	R	W	O	M	R	W
Srinath	16	7	42	3	19	6	38	3
Venkatesh Prasad	14	5	25	–	10	5	25	2
Kumble	27	2	71	4	24	11	27	1
Kapoor	8	2	19	2	13	8	10	–
Joshi	7.3	2	13	–	29	10	66	3

Fall of Wickets
1–76, 2–111, 3–160, 4–185, 5–193, 6–193, 7–214, 8–224, 9–237
1–2, 2–41, 3–91, 4–121, 5–192, 6–357, 7–385

Fall of Wickets
1–34, 2–73, 3–94, 4–121, 5–126, 6–130, 7–131, 8–144, 9–153
1–21, 2–26, 3–29, 4–97, 5–109, 6–127, 7–138, 8–167, 9–179

Umpires: S. Venkataraghavan & D.R. Shepherd

India won by 280 runs

Test Match Averages – India v. South Africa

Batting

	M	Inns	NO	Runs	HS	Av	100s	50s
M. Azharuddin	3	6	1	388	163*	77.60	2	1
A.R. Kumble	3	6	1	199	88	39.80		1
R.S. Dravid	3	6	–	175	56	29.16		1
S.R. Tendulkar	3	6	–	166	61	27.66		1
S.C. Ganguly	2	4	–	86	41	21.50		
N.R. Mongia	3	6	–	116	41	19.33		
V.V.S. Laxman	2	4	–	77	51	19.25		1
J. Srinath	3	5	–	45	19	9.00		
S.B. Joshi	3	6	–	50	16	8.33		
Venkatesh Prasad	3	5	2	14	9	4.66		
N.D. Hirwani	2	4	2	9	9	4.50		

(Played in one Test: W.V. Raman 57 & 2; A.R. Kapoor 11 & 6*; S.V. Manjrekar 34 & 5)

Batting

	M	Inns	NO	Runs	HS	Av	100s	50s
D.J. Cullinan	3	6	1	270	153*	54.00	1	
G. Kirsten	3	6	–	322	133	53.66	2	
A.C. Hudson	3	6	1	221	146	44.20	1	
W.J. Cronje	3	6	1	152	50	20.40		1
L. Klusener	2	3	1	53	34*	26.50		
P.S. de Villiers	2	4	1	75	67*	25.00		1
P.L. Symcox	3	5	1	79	32	19.75		
H.H. Gibbs	2	4	–	62	31	15.50		
D.J. Richardson	3	5	1	56	36*	14.00		
B.M. McMillan	3	6	1	61	17*	12.20		
A.A. Donald	2	3	–	21	17	7.00		
P.R. Adams	3	5	–	14	8	2.80		

(Played in one Test: J.N. Rhodes 14 & 0)

Bowling

	Overs	Mds	Runs	Wks	Av	Best	10/m	5/inn
A.R. Kapoor	21	10	29	2	14.50	2/19		
J. Srinath	127	33	352	17	20.70	6/21		1
A.R. Kumble	147.1	27	387	13	29.76	4/71		
S.B. Joshi	91.3	18	254	8	31.75	4/43		
Venkatesh Prasad	90	18	259	8	32.37	6/104		1
N.D. Hirwani	40	6	129	2	64.50	2/38		

(Bowled in one innings: S.C. Ganguly 3–0–10–0)

Bowling

	Overs	Mds	Runs	Wks	Av	Best	10/m	5/inn
A.A. Donald	63.2	21	141	10	14.10	4/37		
P.R. Adams	78.3	14	284	14	20.28	6/55		1
B.M. McMillan	77.3	16	258	10	25.80	8/64		1
L. Klusener	89	33	199	6	33.16	2/40		
P.S. de Villiers	74	26	176	5	35.20	2/55		
W.J. Cronje	50	21	83	2	41.50	2/11		
P.L. Symcox	107	22	324	6	54.00	2/47		

Leading Fielders

4 – M. Azharuddin, N.R. Mongia (ct 3 / st 1) and V.V.S. Laxman (inc 3 as sub);
2 – R.S. Dravid and S.B. Joshi; 1 – W.V. Raman, S.R. Tendulkar, A.R. Kumble and S.V. Manjrekar

Leading Fielders

8 – B.M. McMillan; 4 – D.J. Richardson; 3 – A.C. Hudson and P.R. Adams; 2 – L. Klusener, G. Kirsten, J.N. Rhodes, D.J. Cullinan and P.S. de Villiers; 1 – H.H. Gibbs, A.A. Donald and D.N. Crookes (sub)

One-Day International

India v. South Africa

Seemingly unsatiated in spite of the Titan Cup, India and South Africa met in another one-day international before South Africa returned home. It was not without incident. Tendulkar won the toss and batted first. He reached his 10th century in limited-over internationals, his 114 came off 126 balls, and he hit 14 boundaries. He was dropped at point when three and was finally stumped by make-shift wicket-keeper Gary Kirsten.

Cronje led his side off the field after crowd disturbances which followed the dismissal of Azharuddin, given out caught behind, seemingly off his pad. There was a 20-minute delay, and Jadeja boosted the Indian innings when play restarted with 54 off 44 balls.

South Africa were never in contention after the early loss of Gary Kirsten. Sachin Tendulkar had enjoyed a promising start to his career as captain.

Irani Trophy

21, 22, 23 and 24 September 1996

at M. Chinnaswamy Stadium, Bangalore
Rest of India 203 (P. Dharmani 84, S.S. Karim 72, D. Ganesh 6 for 84) and 288 (V.V.S. Laxman 78, P. Dharmani 72, G.K. Khoda 67, D. Ganesh 5 for 89)
Karnataka 356 (J. Arun Kumar 93, R. Vijay 93, P.V. Shashikant 69, K. Sriram 54, N.D. Hirwani 6 for 129) and 139 for 5 (S. Shiruguppi 62 not out)
Karnataka won by 5 wickets

Performances in the Irani Trophy match have, by tradition, had an influence on selectors, and both Dharmani and Ganesh were to win international honours within months of the fixture. Doddanarasiah Ganesh had an outstanding match. Fast medium pace, he routed the Rest on the opening day, reducing them to 27 for 4 before Dharmani and Karim added 97. In contrast, Karnataka, Ranji Trophy holders, lost Somasunder for 0 but prospered as Arun Kumar and Vijay added 165. They passed 300 with only four wickets down before Hirwani was rewarded for good bowling. Khoda and Laxman put on 109 for the Rest's second wicket when they batted again, but Karnataka always had control.

One-Day International – India v. South Africa
14 December 1996 at Wankhede Stadium, Bombay

India		
S.R. Tendulkar (Capt)	st Kirsten, b Boje	114
W.V. Raman	c Cronje, b Symcox	29
M. Azharuddin	c Kirsten, b Crookes	22
R.S. Dravid	run out	16
A.D. Jadeja	not out	54
R.R. Singh	c Symcox, b Adams	10
J. Srinath	c Gibbs, b Adams	3
S.B. Joshi	not out	1
*N.R. Mongia		
A.R. Kumble		
Venkatesh Prasad		
	b 1, lb 4, w 12, nb 1	18
	50 overs (for 6 wickets)	267

South Africa		
A.C. Hudson	b Joshi	45
*G. Kirsten	c Azharuddin, b Prasad	1
W.J. Cronje (Capt)	c Singh, b Venkatesh Prasad	10
D.J. Cullinan	c Joshi, b Singh	44
H.H. Gibbs	c Raman, b Venkatesh Prasad	31
D.N. Crookes	run out	18
B.M. McMillan	c Mongia, b Srinath	16
N. Boje	c Venkatesh Prasad, b Kumble	3
P.L. Symcox	not out	3
P.S. de Villiers	b Srinath	0
P.R. Adams	c Mongia, b Venkatesh Prasad	0
	lb 13, w 7, nb 2	22
	46 overs	193

	O	M	R	**W**
de Villiers	5	–	24	–
McMillan	6	–	33	–
Cronje	6	–	36	–
Symcox	10	1	51	1
Boje	10	1	33	1
Crookes	6	–	35	1
Adams	7	–	50	2

	O	M	R	**W**
Srinath	10	1	40	2
Venkatesh Prasad	8	1	27	4
Joshi	7	–	25	1
Singh	6	–	29	1
Kumble	9	1	34	1
Raman	6	1	25	–

Fall of Wickets
1–90, 2–150, 3–188, 4–202, 5–230, 6–249

Fall of Wickets
1–2, 2–35, 3–80, 4–122, 5–161, 6–166, 7–174, 8–188, 9–188

Umpires: S.K. Porel & K. Parthasarathy *Man of the Match:* S.R. Tendulkar

India won by 74 runs

Duleep Trophy

20, 21, 22, 23 and 24 November 1996
at Ferozeshah Kotla Ground, Delhi
East Zone 276 (D. Gandhi 71, P.K. Amre 67, S. Raul 50, R. Sanghvi 5 for 45) and 472 for 9 dec. (S.S. Karim 190, P.K. Amre 95, U. Chatterjee 69)
North Zone 506 (V. Dahiya 134, R. Nayyar 108 not out, A.D. Jadeja 74, A.K. Sharma 67, U. Chatterjee 6 for 115) and 91 for 2
Match drawn

The Duleep Trophy was played under a new format in 1996–97, a straightforward knock-out system replacing the former league programme. This reduced the number of games from ten to four. North Zone won the preliminary round match by virtue of their first innings lead. East Zone squandered the early advantage given them by Amre who hit 67 off 81 balls when they lost their last four wickets for 11 runs. Jadeja gave North Zone a fine start, but it was a sixth wicket stand of 208 between Rajeev Nayyar and the Delhi wicket-keeper Vijay Dahiya that put the match firmly in North Zone's grasp. They batted into the fourth day, and the rest was academic.

Semi-Finals

27, 28, 29, 30 November and 1 December 1996
at Nahar Singh Stadium, Faridabad
North Zone 344 (V. Rathore 150, A.K. Sharma 80, D. Johnson 4 for 82) and 332 (A.D. Jadeja 89, V. Rathore 84, B. Ramprakash 5 for 100)
South Zone 286 (R.R. Singh 84, M.S.K. Prasad 60, W.V. Raman 51, F. Ghayas 4 for 54) and 393 for 5 (S. Ramesh 143 not out, S. Sharath 140)
South Zone won by 5 wickets

at Feroze Shah Kotla Ground, Delhi
Central Zone 503 (C.S. Pandit 189, R.V. Sapru 85, K. Obaid 55) and 500 for 3 dec. (A.R. Khurasiya 126, G.K. Khoda 124, R. Shamshad 120 not out, R.V. Sapru 100 not out)
West Zone 244 (S.S. Bhave 75, H. Prasana 52, K. Obaid 7 for 74) and 280 for 8 (S.S. Bhave 86)
Match drawn

Trailing by 58 runs on the first innings, South Zone brought off a remarkable victory over North Zone. They were bowled back into the match by Kerala off-spinner Bhaskaran Ramprakash and his team-mate leg-spinner Anan Padmanabhan, but a target of 391 looked very demanding. It seemed out of reach when they ended the fourth day on 117 for 4, but Sridharan Sharath and Sandagoppan Ramesh, the Tamil Nadu pair, joined together in a stand of 258 which set up a famous victory.

Chandrakant Pandit, the Central Zone skipper, rescued his side with a fine century after they had slipped to 91 for 4. Medium-pacer Kamal Obaid then produced the best bowling performance of his career to put Central in total command. In the second innings, Pandit adopted the policy of what we have we hold as four batsmen scored centuries. West Zone were happy to bat out for a draw.

Final

4, 5, 6, 7 and 8 December 1996
at Punjab CA Stadium, Mohali
Central Zone 264 (G.K. Khoda 72, B. Ramprakash 5 for 85) and 359 (R.V. Sapru 161, G.K. Khoda 68, J. Gokulkrishnan 4 for 81)
South Zone 225 (M.V. Sridhar 90, Z. Hussain 4 for 68) and 237 (S. Ramesh 77, A. Pathak 58, R.R. Singh 50, Z. Hussain 5 for 88, K. Obaid 4 for 79)
Central Zone won by 161 runs

On a pitch on which batsmen rarely found it easy to score runs, Central Zone regained the Duleep Trophy after a gap of 25 years. They struggled to reach 245 for 7 on the opening day and were all out within half an hour on the second morning. South Zone were soon in trouble and were only saved from humiliation by Hyderabad's Murati Sridhar, a late recruit to the side. The outstanding batsman of the match was Rahul Sapru of Uttar Pradesh, whose century took Central Zone to an impregnable position. Seam bowlers Hussain and Obaid completed an emphatic victory on the last day.

Ranji Trophy

South Zone

25, 26, 27 and 28 October 1996
at Municipal Stadium, Thallassery
Tamil Nadu 397 (S. Sharath 151, R. Paul 84) and 73 for 3
Kerala 330 (A.S. Kudva 82, S.C. Oasis 72, B. Ramprakash 60)
Match drawn
Tamil Nadu 5 pts, Kerala 3 pts

at Gymkhana Ground, Panaji
Goa 346 (V.B. Chandrasekhar 88, R.R. Naik 55, S. Dhuri 51, D. Ganesh 5 for 92)
Karnataka 114 (S. Somasunder 70, J. Gokulkrishnan 7 for 54) and 151 (J. Gokulkrishnan 4 for 60)
Goa won by an innings and 81 runs
Goa 8 pts, Karnataka 0 pts

at Vizianagram Stadium, Vizianagram
Andhra 302 (A. Pathak 123, K.B.S. Naik 55) and 119 for 6 (M.S.K. Prasad 64 not out)
Hyderabad 290 (W.V.S. Laxman 61, Y. Singh 50, H. Ramkishen 4 for 131)
Match drawn
Andhra 5 pts, Hyderabad 3 pts

No play was possible on the last day at Thallassery, but the game always looked to be drawn after Tamil Nadu had crawled to 215 for 5 in 96 overs on the first day. On the second day, Sharath was run out after facing 404 balls for his 151, which included 14 fours and four sixes. Reuben Paul hit six sixes in his belligerent 84.

The season began sensationally for Goa who astounded the Indian cricket world by beating reigning champions Karnataka by an innings. The hero was 23-year-old pace bowler Jayaraman Gokulkrishnan who, unable to hold a regular place in the Tamil Nadu side, had moved to Goa. He returned the best bowling figures for both innings and match and was the dominant force in the famous victory for a side who, the previous season, had mustered one draw and five defeats.

Pathak scored a fine century for Andhra, but overcautious batting cost Hyderabad dearly in a match marred by the weather.

3, 4, 5 and 6 November 1996
at M. Chinnaswamy Stadium, Bangalore
Hyderabad 358 (A. Shetty 75, V.V.S. Laxman 67, N David 65, D. Ganesh 4 for 96) and 227 for 9 dec.

Chandrakant Pandit led Central Zone to success in the Duleep Trophy and enjoyed a fine season with the bat.
(David Munden/Sportsline)

Karnataka 335 (V. Bharadwaj 116, F. Khaleel 76)
Match drawn
Hyderabad 5 pts, Karnataka 3 pts

at Arlem Ground, Margao
Tamil Nadu 326 (H. Badani 94, S. Sharath 86) and 264 for 4 dec. (S. Sharath 94, H. Badani 80 not out)
Goa 253 (S. Dhuri 65, A. Shetty 63) and 80 for 3
Match drawn
Tamil Nadu 5 pts, Goa 3 pts

Karnataka's hopes of retaining the Ranji Trophy suffered a further setback when they surrendered first innings points to Hyderabad who owed much to Shetty and Laxman. The pair added 120 in just over 41 overs for the second wicket on the opening day. Vijay Bharaswaj reached his fourth Ranji Trophy century, and he was ably supported by Fazal Khaleel, but Karnataka lost their last five wickets for 49 runs.

Badani and Sharath rescued Tamil Nadu with a fifth wicket stand of 153. In reply to Tamil Nadu's 326, Goa lost both openers for eight, and, in spite of Arun Shetty's brave knock and a late knock from Dhuri, they were never able to match Tamil Nadu.

10, 11, 12 and 13 November 1996
at Gymkhana Ground, Hyderabad
Kerala 245 (S.C. Oasis 66, S. Shankar 62, Kanwaljit Singh 4 for 72) and 112 (N. David 4 for 33)
Hyderabad 203 (M.V. Sridhar 55, K.N.A. Padmanabhan 4 for 47) and 158 for 4 (M.V. Sridhar 61, V. V.S. Laxman 56)
Hyderabad won by 6 wickets
Hyderabad 6 pts, Kerala 2 pts

Hyderabad redeemed themselves after some shoddy first innings batting that saw them lose their last seven wickets for 38 runs.

17, 18, 19 and 20 November 1996
at Trishna Ground, Ukkunagaram
Andhra 76 (B. Ramprakash 4 for 26) and 159 (A. Pathak 80, C.T.K. Masood 5 for 53)
Kerala 284 (K. Chandrasekhara 72 not out, K.C. Rao 4 for 70)
Kerala won by an innings and 49 runs
Kerala 8 pts, Andhra 0 pts

Andhra never recovered from being skittled out for 76 on the opening day by the end of which Kerala were 69 for 1. The match was finished in three days.

at M.A. Chidambaram Stadium, Madras
Tamil Nadu v. **Karnataka**
Match abandoned
Tamil Nadu 3 pts, Karnataka 3 pts

12, 13, 14 and 15 December 1996
at Gymkhana Ground, Panaji
Goa 371 (V.B. Chandrasekhar 194, H. Ramkishen 7 for 126) and 37 for 0
Andhra 141 (S.V. Kamat 4 for 36) and 265 (R.V.C. Prasad 141 not out, A. Pathak 58, S. Khalid 5 for 54)
Goa won by 10 wickets
Goa 8 pts, Andhra 0 pts

Goa's second win on the season was founded on a splendid knock by skipper Vakkadi Chandrasekhar who hit the 10th century of his career.

19, 20, 21 and 22 December 1996
at Government Victoria College Ground, Palakkad
Goa 276 (J. Gokulkrishnan 104 not out, B.K.P. Misquin 52, B. Ramprakash 5 for 109) and 153 (B. Ramprakash 6 for 34)
Kerala 281 (S.C. Oasis 57, P.J. Rodrigues 4 for 57, S. Khalid 4 for 85) and 153 for 3 (S. Shankar 55 not out)
Kerala won by 7 wickets
Kerala 8 pts, Goa 0 pts

at Gymkhana Ground, Hyderabad
Tamil Nadu 424 (H. Badani 164, R. Paul 100, R.R. Singh 59, Kanwaljit Singh 4 for 74) and 146 for 5 (S. Ramesh 65 not out, S. Sriram 51)
Hyderabad 395 (M.V. Sridhar 94, A. Shetty 93, R. Sridhar 58, S. Subramaniam 5 for 84)
Match drawn
Tamil Nadu 5 pts, Hyderabad 3 pts

at M. Chinnaswamy Stadium, Bangalore
Karnataka 237 (V. Bharadwaj 63) and 290 for 8 dec. (S.B. Joshi 72 not out, V. Bharadwaj 68)
Andhra 120 (S.B. Joshi 5 for 57) and 199 (S.B. Joshi 6 for 97)
Karnataka won by 208 runs
Karnataka 8 pts, Andhra 0 pts

Gokulkrishnan's move to Goa had brought him nothing but success, and he reached another milestone in the game against Kerala when he hit a maiden first-class century. It did not bring victory for Ramprakash's off-spinners turned the game in favour of Kerala, who now looked likely to qualify for the final stages of the competition.

Tamil Nadu recovered from 75 for 4 through the efforts of Hemang Badani and skipper Robin Singh. The 20-year-old Badani was most impressive, and equally impressive on the second day was Reuben Paul who hit 100 off 101 balls. Hyderabad fought tenaciously, but Tamil Nadu claimed first innings points.

The return of Sunil Joshi inspired Karnataka to their first win of the season. He had a fine all-round match.

28, 29, 30 and 31 December 1996

at Gymkhana Ground, Hyderabad
Hyderabad 393 (V. Pratap 94, N.P. Singh 74, N. David 70,
S. Kiran Kumar 59, N. Kalekar 5 for 104, J. Gokulkrishnan
4 for 94) and 305 for 8 dec. (V. Pratap 136, N. David 106)
Goa 192 (R.R. Naik 61, S. Vishnu Vardhan 4 for 51)
and 46 for 0
Match drawn
Hyderabad 5 pts, Goa 3 pts

at M.A. Chidambaram Stadium, Madras
Tamil Nadu 457 (R.R. Singh 150, S. Ramesh 146,
K. Chakradar Rao 4 for 179)
Andhra 162 (A. Pathak 114) and 179 (B.S. Nayak 92,
W.D. Balaji Rao 5 for 47)
Tamil Nadu won by an innings and 16 runs
Tamil Nadu 8 pts, Andhra 0 pts

at Government Victoria College Ground, Palakkad
Karnataka 153 (B. Ramprakash 6 for 52) and 74
(B. Ramprakash 7 for 25)
Kerala 161 (A.S. Kudva 60, S.B. Joshi 5 for 68) and 69 for 4
Kerala won by 6 wickets
Kerala 8 pts, Karnataka 0 pts

Hyderabad clinched a place in the 'super' league by heavily
outscoring Goa, who had enjoyed such a brave season.
Tamil Nadu, too, ensured themselves of a place in the next
round of the competition. They were indebted to skipper
Robin Singh, who hit his first Ranji Trophy for two seasons.
His innings included five sixes.

Winners of the trophy in 1995-96, Karnataka failed to
qualify for the final stages. They were bowled out on the
treacherous pitch at Palakkad where 13 wickets fell on the
first day. The match was a triumph for off-spinner
Ramprakash, who returned the best bowling figures of his
career in the second innings and led Kerala to the South
Zone championship.

Final Table

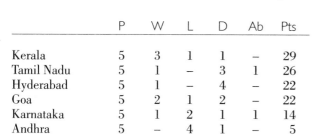

	P	W	L	D	Ab	Pts
Kerala	5	3	1	1	–	29
Tamil Nadu	5	1	–	3	1	26
Hyderabad	5	1	–	4	–	22
Goa	5	2	1	2	–	22
Karnataka	5	1	2	1	1	14
Andhra	5	–	4	1	–	5

Prolific scoring for Punjab in the Ranji Trophy by Vikram Rathore
but still no success at Test level.
(David Munden/Sportsline)

North Zone

24, 25, 26 and 27 October 1996

at Feroze Shah Kotla Ground, Delhi
Services 249 (K.K. Dixit 78, P. Maitreya 51, M. Prabhakar
4 for 31) and 318 (C. Sharma 117, M.V. Rao 56 not out,
J.N. Pandey 52, R. Sanghvi 6 for 75)
Delhi 350 (V. Dahiya 72, A.K. Sharma 56) and 221 for 8
(A.K. Sharma 68, A. Dani 58, M.V. Rao 7 for 59)
Delhi won by 2 wickets
Delhi 8 pts, Services 0 pts

at Gandhi Ground, Amritsar
Punjab 485 (V. Rathore 254, M. Mehra 105, A. Qayyum
4 for 97, A. Gupta 4 for 199)
Jammu and Kashmir 225 (Kanwaljit Singh 97, S. Sharma
55, B. Vij 7 for 55) and 169 (Kanwaljit Singh 63, B. Vij 4 for 23)
Punjab won by an innings and 91 runs
Punjab 8 pts, Jammu and Kashmir 0 pts

at Police Stadium, Chamba
Haryana 456 for 9 dec. (Jitender Singh 230, N.R. Goel 63)
Himachal Pradesh 99 (P. Thakur 6 for 32) and 97
(P. Jain 6 for 25, P. Thakur 4 for 41)
Haryana won by an innings and 260 runs
Haryana 8 pts, Himachal Pradesh 0 pts

A century from Chinmoy Sharma and a career best bowling
performance by medium-pacer Mutyala Rao gave Delhi a
difficult task in their opening North Zone match, and it
needed the steadiness of Ajay Sharma to see them to victory.
Punjab and Haryana, in contrast, enjoyed easy wins.
Vikram Rathore and Manav Mehra shared a fifth wicket
partnership of 235 for Punjab against Jammu and Kashmir

for whom Kanwaljit Singh batted bravely. Rathore hit the highest score of his career, and Bharati Vij returned his best bowling figures.

For Haryana, Jitender Singh hit the first double century of his career.

---

31 October, 1, 2 and 3 November 1996
at Nahar Singh Stadium, Faridabad
Jammu and Kashmir 283 (A. Gupta 99, V. Bhaskar 96, R.P. Singh 4 for 64, P. Thakur 4 for 89) and 268 (A. Gupta 102, R. Gill 79)
Haryana 464 (A.S. Kaypee 135 not out, S. Khan 95, V. Yadav 70) and 89 for 2
Haryana won by 8 wickets
Haryana 8 pts, Jammu and Kashmir 0 pts

at Paddal Stadium, Mandi
Himachal Pradesh 305 (C. Kumar 89, B. Vij 5 for 92) and 268 (R. Nayyar 110 not out, B. Vij 6 for 90)
Punjab 482 (V. Rathore 167, D. Mongia 115, A. Mehra 87, Jaswant Rai 5 for 122) and 92 for 4 (Jaswant Rai 4 for 42)
Punjab won by 6 wickets
Punjab 8 pts, Himachal Pradesh 0 pts

Haryana and Punjab gained their second wins of the season although both were given some frights by weak opposition. Skipper Ashwini Gupta played two heroic innings for Jammu and Kashmir, and Himachal Pradesh's captain Rajiv Nayyar made an unbeaten 110 out of 258 in a vain attempt to save his side. Vikram Rathore hit another century for Punjab and shared an opening stand of 227 with Ajay Mehra. Dinesh Mongia followed with a maiden first-class century.

6, 7, 8 and 9 November 1996
at Gandhi Ground, Amritsar
Haryana 249 (A.S. Kaypee 56) and 307 (R. Puri 64, Jitender Singh 62, N.R. Goel 55, B. Bhushan 4 for 69)
Punjab 222 (V. Rathore 104) and 134 for 5 (Sandeep Dharma 80 not out)
Match drawn
Haryana 5 pts, Punjab 3 pts

at Air Force Sports Complex, Palam
Services 430 (C. Sharma 207, P. Maitreya 60, Jaswant Rai 6 for 126) and 81 for 1
Himachal Pradesh 125 and 377 (R. Nayyar 148, N. Gaur 125)
Services won by 9 wickets
Services 8 pts, Himachal Pradesh 0 pts

Punjab claimed the honours on the first day in Amritsar by restricting Haryana to 249, but they surrendered the initiative on the second day when, in spite of Rathore's third century in as many matches, they failed to gain first innings points. No other batsman in the first nine reached 20, and

Ajay Sharma led Dehli to the Ranji Trophy final and with 1,198 runs, average 99.83, was India's leading run-scorer. (Adrian Murrell/Allsport)

only a last wicket stand of 35 between Chaman Lal and Bharat Bhushan took Punjab past 200. Consistent batting made certain that Haryana maintained their grip on the game.

Chinmoy Sharma's first double century put Services in a strong position against Himachal Pradesh, who fought back bravely when Nischal Gaur and Rajiv Nayyar shared a partnership of 222 for the second wicket in the second innings. Gaur hit a maiden century while Nayyar made his second hundred in successive matches and the highest score of his career.

13, 14, 15 and 16 November 1996
at Air Force Sports Complex, Palam
Haryana 375 (A.S. Kaypee 113, S. Khan 67) and 69 for 2
Services 115 (P. Thakur 4 for 23, Dhanraj Singh 4 for 37) and 325 (C. Sharma 70, Sarabjit Singh 64, M.V. Rao 57)
Haryana won by 8 wickets
Haryana 8 pts, Services 0 pts

at Feroze Shah Kotla Ground, Delhi
Delhi 486 for 5 dec. (A. Dani 215, S. Dogra 101 not out, A.K. Sharma 78, Jaswant Rai 4 for 158)
Himachal Pradesh 188 (R. Nayyar 99 not out) and 143
Delhi won by an innings and 155 runs
Delhi 8 pts, Himachal Pradesh 0 pts

The batting of Armajit Kaypee and the bowling of Thakur and Dhanraj Singh, 7 for 88 in the match, were the reasons for Haryana's dominance of Services. Predictably, Delhi crushed Himachal Pradesh, and Ashu Dani took the chance to make his first double century. Sumeet Dogra followed with a bubbly century on the second morning, and Delhi won in three days.

18, 19, 20 and 21 November 1996
at Air Force Sports Complex, Palam
Services 238 (P. Maitreya 78, B. Vij 6 for 88) and 182 (S. Verma 57, B. Vij 5 for 43)
Punjab 568 for 4 dec. (D. Mongia 207 not out, A. Mehra 84, N.S. Sidhu 81, Bhupinder Singh jnr. 56, R.S. Sodhi 55, M. Mehra 50)
Punjab won by an innings and 148 runs
Punjab 8 pts, Services 0 pts

Having hit his maiden first-class century at the beginning of the month, Dinesh Mongia was quick to follow it with a double century as Punjab overwhelmed Services. Left-arm spinner Bharati Vij again proved to be a match-winner, taking 11 wickets in a game for the third time in the season.

11, 12, 13 and 14 December 1996
at Feroze Shah Kotla Ground, Delhi
Punjab 351 (N.S. Sidhu 132, M. Mehra 77, Robin Singh 6 for 80) and 190 for 5 (Bhupinder Singh jnr. 68)
Delhi 604 for 9 dec. (R. Lamba 250, A. Malhotra 120, V. Dahiya 61 not out, B. Vij 5 for 178)
Match drawn
Delhi 5 pts, Punjab 3 pts

at Indira Stadium, Una
Himachal Pradesh 385 (R. Nayyar 170, C. Kumar 80, Jasminder Singh 61, A. Qayyum 5 for 110)
Jammu and Kashmir 187 (Idrees Singh 63, Surinder Singh 5 for 41, Jaswant Rai 4 for 67) and 156 (S. Chandel 5 for 25)
Himachal Pradesh won by an innings and 42 runs
Himachal Pradesh 8 pts, Jammu and Kashmir 0 pts

A brilliant century from Sidhu on the opening day failed to get the deserved support from his colleagues, and Punjab paid dearly. Delhi replied with the veteran opener Raman Lamba hitting 250 off 429 balls with three sixes and 29 fours. He and Akash Malhotra added 291 for the third wicket, with Malhotra facing 283 balls and hitting 15 fours.

A third century of the season for Nayyar gave Himachal Pradesh control of the game at Una, and they never relinquished command. Nayyar bettered his previous highest score made a month earlier.

24, 25, 26 and 27 December 1996
at Nehru Stadium, Gurgaon
Haryana 268 (Jitender Singh 98, V. Yadasv 68, Robin Singh 5 for 52) and 449 for 6 (A.D. Jadeja 154, N.R. Goel 135, A.S. Kaypee 80 not out)
Delhi 326 (R. Lamba 60, V. Dahiya 51, P. Thakur 4 for 93)
Match drawn
Delhi 5 pts, Haryana 3 pts

Half the Haryana side perished to indiscreet shots for 80 runs before Jitender Singh at last found a reliable partner in skipper Vijay Yadav. The pair added 105, but a score of 268 was of little threat to Delhi. Dani, Lamba and Dahiya gave Delhi a good start, and they reached 184 for 2, but collapse followed and the second day ended with them on 248 for 7. Oniel Wilson was out for the addition of one run on the third morning before Nikhil Chopra and Rahul Sanghvi took first innings points with a stand of 60. Thereafter the match descended into near farce as personal records took precedence over any hope of achieving a result. Jadeja and Goel hit centuries and shared a second wicket stand of 294 while Amarjit Kaypee completed 6,000 runs in Ranji Trophy cricket.

Jammu and Kashmir failed to appear in Delhi or Palam for their final matches. Accordingly, matches in which they had participated were declared null and void as far as league points were concerned, although runs scored and wickets taken were still recorded in the averages.

Final Table

	P	W	L	D	Pts
Delhi	4	2	–	2	26
Haryana	4	2	–	2	24
Punjab	4	2	–	2	22
Services	4	1	3	–	8
Himachal Pradesh	4	–	4	–	0

West Zone

27, 28, 29 and 30 October 1996
at Wankhede Stadium, Mumbai
Mumbai 451 (A.A. Muzumdar 214 not out, P.L. Mhambrey 97, S.V. Manjrekar 50, D.T. Patel 4 for 63)
Gujarat 113 (A. Kuruvilla 5 for 36) and 148
Mumbai won by an innings and 190 runs
Mumbai 8 pts, Gujarat 0 pts

at IPCL Stadium, Vadodara
Vadodara 205 (K.S. More 59, H.J. Parsana 57) and 229 for 9 dec. (A.C. Bedade 76, H.J. Parsana 5 for 64)

Saurashtra 151 (T.B. Arothe 5 for 38) and 168 for 5
Match drawn
Vadodara 5 pts, Saurashtra 3 pts

Mumbai (Bombay) began the season with a resounding victory over Gujarat. The game was significant for Mhambrey's first first-class fifty and for another double century by Anil Muzumdar. The 22-year-old announced his entry into first-class cricket in 1993–94 with a double hundred, and he has scored heavily and consistently since then. It cannot be long before he wins the confidence of the Indian selectors.

Vadodara (Baroda) struggled to 205 at two runs an over against Saurashtra, but, on a painfully slow wicket, this proved to be enough for first innings points.

4, 5, 6 and 7 November 1996
at Municipal Ground, Rajkot
Saurashtra 595 for 4 dec. (S.S. Tanna 141, B.M. Jadeja 132 not out, P.J. Bhatt 123, H.J. Parsana 100 not out, S.H. Kotak 89)
Mumbai 647 for 4 (W. Jaffer 314 not out, S.K. Kulkarni 239, S.V. Bahutule 72)
Match drawn
Mumbai 5 pts, Saurashtra 3 pts

at Pune CC, Pune
Maharashtra 547 for 9 dec. (H.H. Kanitkar 205, S.V. Jedhe 158, S.S. Sugwekar 57, D. Barot 4 for 118)
Gujarat 280 (M.H. Parmar 134, M.S. Kulkarni 4 for 59) and 197 (N.D. Mody 51, S.V. Ranjane 4 for 49, I.R. Siddiqui 4 for 49)
Maharashtra won by an innings and 70 runs
Maharashtra 8 pts, Gujarat 0 pts

Four Saurashtra batsmen scored centuries, and yet their side failed to take first innings points. In a match all too typical of cricket in India, 1,242 runs were scored in four days at Rajkot while only eight wickets fell. Wasim Jaffer and Sukashan Kulkarni scored 459 for Mumbai's first wicket, a record for the state and the second highest in the history of the competition. Both batsmen made career best scores.

Hrishikesh Kanitkar made the first double century of his career and shared a third wicket stand of 279 with Santosh Jedhe as Maharashtra triumphed over Gujarat.

12, 13, 14 and 15 December 1996
at IPCL Stadium, Vadodara
Gujarat 139 (M.H. Parmar 50, S.S. Hazare 5 for 29) and 218 (P.H. Patel 51, R.A. Swarup 5 for 69, Sukbir Singh 4 for 32)
Vadodara 462 (R.A. Swarup 134, J.J. Martin 106 not out, C.C. Williams 62, K.S. More 55, D.T. Patel 4 for 66, B.N. Mehta 4 for 146)
Vadodara won by an innings and 105 runs
Vadodara 8 pts, Gujarat 0 pts

at Nehru Stadium, Pune
Maharashtra 335 (S.S. Bhave 101, R.R. Kanade 81, S.V. Bahutule 4 for 100, A. Kuruvilla 4 for 102) and 304 (S.S. Sugwekar 121, N.M. Kulkarni 5 for 65)
Mumbai 381 (J.V. Paranjpe 165) and 21 for 1
Match drawn
Mumbai 5 pts, Maharashtra 3 pts

Vadodara proved far too strong for Gujarat, who suffered their third defeat in a row, while the might of Mumbai just edged ahead of Maharashtra.

20, 21, 22 and 23 December 1996
at Wankhede Stadium, Mumbai
Vadodara 117 (P.L. Mhambrey 5 for 34) and 189 (K.S. More 79)
Mumbai 283 (S.V. Manjrekar 77, V.G. Kambli 69, R.A. Swarup 6 for 121, Sukhbir Singh 4 for 39) and 24 for 1
Mumbai won by 9 wickets
Mumbai 8 pts, Vadodara 0 pts

at Railway Ground, Rajkot
Saurashtra 208 (S.H. Kotak 93, S.V. Jedhe 5 for 47) and 247 (J. Motivaras 52, S.V. Jedhe 4 for 80)
Maharashtra 482 for 9 dec. (H.H. Kanitkar 121, S.S. Bhave 74, I. Kamtekar 63, S. Shukla 4 for 128)
Maharashtra won by an innings and 27 runs
Maharashtra 8 pts, Saurashtra 0 pts

By the end of the first day at the Wankhede Stadium, Mumbai had passed Vadodara's 117 and had nine wickets standing. Sukhbir Singh bowled the visitors back into contention, but Mumbai won in three days.

Saurashtra were swamped by Maharashtra for whom Kanitkar continued his prolific scoring and Jedhe had a fine match with his off-breaks.

28, 29, 30 and 31 December 1996
at IPCL Stadium, Vadodara
Vadodara 438 (K.S. More 180, T.B. Arothe 99, J.J. Martin 56, I.R. Siddiqui 5 for 99) and 48 for 1
Maharashtra 495 (A.V. Kale 150, S.S. Bhave 87, I. Kamtekar 62 not out, S.S. Hazare 5 for 158)
Match drawn
Maharashtra 5 pts, Vadodara 3 pts

at Sardar Patel Stadium, Ahmedabad
Gujarat 324 (N.D. Mody 106, B.N. Mehta 73, M.H. Parmar 58, H.J. Parsana 5 for 74) and 252 for 9 dec. (T.N. Varsani 109 not out, S. Shukla 4 for 61)
Saurashtra 359 (P.J. Bhatt 101, H.J. Parsana 85, B.N. Mehta 5 for 126) and 103 for 2 (H.J. Parsana 68 not out)
Match drawn
Saurashtra 5 pts, Gujarat 3 pts

Former Test wicket-keeper More set his side a fine example with a fighting innings for Vadodara against Maharashtra. He and Arothe added 186 for the sixth wicket, but Maharashtra scored consistently to take first innings points.

Gujarat posted a reasonable score against Saurashtra who lost their first four wickets for 74 before Bhatt and Parsana added 181.

Final Table

	P	W	L	D	Pts
Mumbai	4	2	–	2	26
Maharashtra	4	2	–	2	24
Vadodara	4	1	1	2	16
Saurashtra	4	–	1	3	11
Gujarat	4	–	3	1	3

East Zone

3, 4, 5 and 6 November 1996
at Keenan Stadium, Jamshedpur
Bihar 474 for 6 dec. (R. Kumar 129 not out, D. Chakraborty 111, S. Kumar 105)
Tripura 150 (K.V.P. Rao 6 for 47) and 295 (R. Sharma 92 not out, S. Lahiri 54, D.K. Singh 5 for 24)
Bihar won by an innings and 29 runs
Bihar 8 pts, Tripura 0 pts

at Eden Gardens, Calcutta
Bengal 188 (N. Haldipur 64, B.D. Mohanty 5 for 52) and 293 for 9 dec. (S.S. Karim 66, R.S. Gavaskar 55, B.D. Mohanty 4 for 91, R.R. Biswal 4 for 109)
Orissa 181 (N.D. Hirwani 6 for 86) and 185 for 5 (S.S. Das 68)
Match drawn
Bengal 5 pts, Orissa 3 pts

Rajiv Kumar, Sunil Kumar and Debjit Chakraborty all hit centuries as Bihar gained their expected triumph over Tripura. The match at Eden Gardens was a more tense affair. Bengal struggled to 152 for 8 in 90 overs on the first day. Chetan Sharma coaxed another 36 runs out of the last two wickets on the second morning, and then Orissa tumbled to Hirwani. They lost their last three wickets for seven runs to give Bengal the first innings points they could not have expected.

12, 13, 14 and 15 November 1996
at Railway Stadium, Guwahati
Assam 162 (U. Chatterjee 5 for 34) and 233 (Sukhbinder Singh 80 not out, S.S. Sawant 53)
Bengal 279 (N. Haldipur 91, P.K. Amre 85, Sukhbinder

Singh 4 for 84) and 117 for 2 (R.S. Gavaskar 52 not out)
Bengal won by 8 wickets
Bengal 8 pts, Assam 0 pts

at Digwadih Stadium, Dhanbad
Orissa 247 (S. Mohanty 56) and 193 (P. Jaychandra 62, S.S. Das 52)
Bihar 369 (Avinash Kumar 139, S. Raul 6 for 106) and 72 for 1
Bihar won by 9 wickets
Bihar 8 pts, Orissa 9 pts

Discarded by the Test selectors, Utpal Chatterjee bowled his left-arm spin to great effect to put Bengal totally in command on the first day in Guwahati. Bengal took complete command on the second day although batting was never easy on a pitch that aided the spinners. Amre hit three sixes and seven fours as he made 85 off 128 balls. He and Haldipur added 149 for the third wicket. Bengal won early on the last day.

Bihar gained their second win in as many matches and owed much to the veteran Avinash Kumar, who hit a maiden first-class hundred after 12 years in the game.

11, 12, 13 and 14 December 1996
at Eden Gardens, Calcutta
Tripura 96 (A. Sarkar 4 for 39) and 151 (A. Verma 4 for 24, U. Chatterjee 4 for 48)
Bengal 282 (A. Sarkar 57 not out, P. Kumar 5 for 85)
Bengal won by an innings and 35 runs
Bengal 8 pts, Tripura 0 pts

at Railway Stadium, Guwahati
Assam 212 (S. Saikia 59, G. Dutta 54 not out) and 262 for 9 dec. (S. Saikia 50)
Orissa 216 (P. Jaychandra 84, Sukhbinder Singh 4 for 54, G. Dutta 4 for 64) and 260 for 2 (P.R. Mohapatra 102 not out, S.S. Das 85, S. Raul 65 not out)
Orissa won by 8 wickets
Orissa 8 pts, Assam 0 pts

Bengal defeated Tripura by an innings inside three days although their batsmen had seemed over confident in playing their shots. Orissa's ninth wicket pair gave their side first innings points against Assam, but eventually outright victory seemed to come easily. Needing 259 to win, Orissa were set on their way by Prasant Mohapatra and Shiv Das who put on 154 for the second wicket. Skipper Sanjay Raul then helped Mohapatra to complete the win. Mohapatra faced 229 deliveries and hit five fours.

20, 21, 22 and 23 December 1996
at PTI Ground, Agartala
Orissa 183 (S.S. Das 72, S. Roy 7 for 50) and 267 (A. Khatua 79, S.S. Das 53, R.R. Parida 50, R. Yadav 7 for 80)

Tripura 123 (S. Lahiri 54, S. Raul 6 for 44) and 139 (S. Mohanty 4 for 35, S. Raul 4 for 44)
Orissa won by 188 runs
Orissa 8 pts, Tripura 0 pts

at Railway Stadium, Guwahati
Bihar 150 (V. Khullar 75, Sukhbinder Singh 5 for 35) and 263 (Avinash Kumar 57, V. Khullar 53, Sukhbinder Singh 7 for 99)
Assam 293 (Sukhbinder Singh 89, V.R. Samant 89, S. Saikia 56, K.V.P. Rao 5 for 63) and 123 for 6 (K.V.P. Rao 4 for 43)
Assam won by 4 wickets
Assam 8 pts, Bihar 0 pts

Orissa beat Tripura in a low scoring match, but Tripura, without a point, could take comfort from the bowling of Sujit Roy, whose off-breaks brought him a career best 7 for 50.

Sukhbinder Singh was Assam's hero in their first ever victory over Bihar and their first win of the season. The left-arm spinner had match figures of 12 for 134 and scored 100 runs for once out. It was Assam's first day form that set up the victory. Thereafter the smell of success put their nerves on edge and they nearly squandered their chance when they lost six wickets for 96 before Dutta and Sukhbinder Singh brought sense and stability.

28, 29, 30 and 31 December 1996
at PTI Ground, Agartala
Assam 524 for 8 dec. (Sukhbinder Singh 167, N. Bordoloi 151 not out, S.S. Sawant 63, D. Bora 50)
Tripura 65 (Sukhbinder Singh 5 for 20) and 132 (R. Choudhury 67, Sukhbinder Singh 5 for 41)
Assam won by an innings and 327 runs
Assam 8 pts, Tripura 0 pts

at Eden Gardens, Calcutta
Bihar 243 (R. Kumar 56, Tariq-ur-Rehman 53, N.D. Hirwani 4 for 57) and 41 for 1
Bengal 750 for 7 dec. (H. Feroze 152 not out, U. Chatterjee 120, N. Haldipur 113, A. Verma 98, P.K. Amre 78, R.S. Gavaskar 70)
Match drawn
Bengal 5 pts, Bihar 3 pts

Sukhbinder Singh and Nishanta Bordoloi established a new record for Assam's seventh wicket when they put on 263 against Tripura. Sukhbinder enjoyed another outstanding all-round match following his career best score with ten wickets.

Ajay Verma and Nikhil Haldipur put on 197 for Bengal's first wicket. Haldipur hit a maiden century, and Utpal Chatterjee and Hamza Feroze emulated him as the match faded to a weary draw.

Final Table

	P	W	L	D	Pts
Bengal	4	2	–	2	26
Orissa	4	2	1	1	19
Bihar	4	2	1	1	19
Assam	4	2	2	–	16
Tripura	4	–	4	–	0

Central Zone

22, 23, 24 and 25 October 1996
at Karnail Singh Stadium, Delhi
Madhya Pradesh 329 (Raja Ali 70, P.K. Dwevedi 61) and 89 for 8 (Zakir Hussain 5 for 31)
Railways 122 (M.S. Majithia 4 for 18, H.S. Sodhi 4 for 46) and 313 (Z. Zuffri 55, D. Sudhakar 51, R.K. Chauhan 5 for 112, S. Pandey 4 for 63)
Match drawn
Madhya Pradesh 5 pts, Railways 3 pts

at Vidarbha CA Ground, Nagpur
Uttar Pradesh 263 for 3 dec. (M.S. Mudgal 81, R. Sharma 60, J.P. Yadav 54, R. Shamshad 54 not out)
Vidarbha 158 for 5 (M. Sabir 68)
Match drawn
Uttar Pradesh 4 pts, Vidarbha 4 pts

By the end of the second day in Delhi, Railways appeared well beaten. Madhya Pradesh had scored consistently, and medium-pacer Harvinder Sodhi and left-arm spinner Manish Majithia had then forced Railways to follow on 207 runs in arrears. In their second innings, Railways had lost Bangar to Chauhan and closed on 2 for 1. The third day saw consistent application ward off an innings defeat, and Railways extended their innings beyond lunch on the last day. Seam bowler Zakir Hussain startled Madhya Pradesh with an inspired spell. Needing 107 to win, they reached 62 for 2, and then lost six wickets for 20 runs. Defeat loomed, but an appeal against the light was upheld, much to the chagrin of Bharatan and his side.

The match in Nagpur was ruined by rain and no result was possible.

30, 31 October, 1 and 2 November 1996
at Nehru Stadium, Indore
Madhya Pradesh 199 (S. Abbas Ali 82, M.S. Dosi 4 for 64) and 281 for 8 dec. (Raja Ali 72, P.K. Hedaoo 5 for 115)
Vidarbha 173 (M.S. Majithia 6 for 59) and 106 for 3
Match drawn
Madhya Pradesh 5 pts, Vidarbha 3 pts

at Mansarover Stadium, Jaipur
Uttar Pradesh 490 (R.V. Sapru 185 not out, G.K. Pandey 101) and 285 for 2 (J.P. Yadav 113, M.S. Mugal retired hurt 101, R. Shamshad 51 not out)
Rajasthan 364 (G.K. Khoda 93, N. Negi 87, K. Obaid 5 for 92)
Match drawn
Uttar Pradesh 5 pts, Rajasthan 3 pts

The Vidarbha spinners played havoc with the Madhya Pradesh batting on the opening day in Indore, but Majithia was again in fine form for the home side and snatched first innings points. A run feast in Jaipur saw Rahul Sapru and Gyanendrakumar Pandey put on 180 for Uttar Pradesh's sixth wicket.

7, 8, 9 and 10 November 1996
at Jayanti Stadium, Bhilai
Rajasthan 227 (R.J. Kanwat 68, V. Joshi 54, R.K. Chauhan 7 for 62) and 333 (V. Joshi 137, G.K. Khoda 52, R.K. Chauhan 5 for 93)
Madhya Pradesh 577 (S. Abbas Ali 198, C.S. Pandit 116, P.K. Dwevedi 80, K.K. Patel 74)
Madhya Pradesh won by an innings and 17 runs
Madhya Pradesh 8 pts, Rajasthan 0 pts

at Karnail Singh Stadium, Delhi
Railways 163 (P.K. Hedaoo 4 for 59) and 172 (U.V. Gandhe 4 for 32)
Vidarbha 130 (M. Karthik 6 for 28) and 95 (M. Suresh Kumar 4 for 21)
Railways won by 110 runs
Railways 8 pts, Vidarbha 0 pts

Rajasthan were totally outplayed by Madhya Pradesh for whom Chauhan bowled excellently and Abbas Ali and Pandit added 204 after five wickets had gone down for 147. No batsman reached 50 in the match in the Karnail Stadium, where Karthik had match figures of 9 for 57.

16, 17, 18 and 19 December 1996
at Green Park, Kanpur
Uttar Pradesh 480 (R. Sharma 98, R.V. Sapru 86, G.K. Pandey 64, R.K. Chauhan 5 for 132) and 92 for 1 (R Shamshad 51 not out)
Madhya Pradesh 330 (J.P. Yadav 94, S. Abbas Ali 62, C.S. Pandit 60)
Match drawn
Uttar Pradesh 5 pts, Madhya Pradesh 3 pts

at Mansarover Stadium, Jaipur
Railways 338 (S.B. Bangar 87, D Sudhakar 69, K. Bharatan 63) and 160 for 4 (S.B. Bangar 72 not out)
Rajasthan 374 (N. Negi 119, P.K. Krishnakumar 110)
Match drawn
Rajasthan 5 pts, Railways 3 pts

Two drawn matches left the qualifying places for the Super League in doubt until the final round of fixtures. The most remarkable achievement came from lowly Rajasthan. Facing a total of 338, they were 105 for 6 when Naveen Negi joined Pudiyangum Krishnakumar. The pair added 218, and Rajasthan snatched first innings points.

24, 25, 26 and 27 December 1996
at Green Park, Kanpur
Uttar Pradesh 267 (J.P. Yadav 79, I.A. Thakur 5 for 84) and 209 (I.A. Thakur 4 for 42)
Railways 343 (Z. Zuffri 86, K. Obaid 5 for 98) and 33 for 0
Match drawn
Railways 5 pts, Uttar Pradesh 3 pts

at Vidarbha CA Ground, Nagpur
Vidarbha 308 (P.K. Hedaoo 74, L.S. Rajput 56, M. Aslam 5 for 95) and 345 for 8 (L.S. Rajput 123, M. Aslam 4 for 104)
Rajasthan 396 (V. Joshi 75 not out, A.S. Parmar 74, G.K. Khoda 60, R.J. Kanwat 52)
Match drawn
Rajasthan 5 pts, Vidarbha 3 pts

Railways and Uttar Pradesh were content with the draw that put both sides into the next stage of the competition.
The first three sides from each zone were placed in one of the three Super Leagues.

Final Table

	P	W	L	D	Pts
Madhya Pradesh	4	1	–	3	21
Railways	4	1	–	3	19
Uttar Pradesh	4	–	–	4	17
Rajasthan	4	–	1	3	13
Vidarbha	4	–	1	3	10

Ranji Trophy
Super League Section A

20, 21, 22 and 23 January 1997
at Punjab CA Stadium, Mohali
Kerala 206 (Harvinder Singh 5 for 71) and 90 (Harvinder Singh 6 for 36, B. Bhushan 4 for 33)
Punjab 176 (Bhupinder Singh jnr 62, S.C. Oasis 4 for 59) and 122 for 3 (N.S. Sidhu 77 not out)
Punjab won by 7 wickets
Punjab 6 pts, Kerala 2 pts

at Nehru Stadium, Pune
Madhya Pradesh 334 (J.P. Yadav 107, C.S. Pandit 96, I.R. Siddiqui 5 for 104) and 274 for 2 (H.S. Sodhi 120 not out, J.P. Yadav 96)

Maharashtra 519 for 5 dec. (S.S. Sugwekar 193,
S.V. Jedhe 144 not out, H.H. Kanitkar 60, S.S. Bhave 52,
N. Dixit 50)
Match drawn
Maharashtra 5 pts, Madhya Pradesh 3 pts

The Indian Board introduced a new system for the Ranji
Trophy in 1996–97. The top teams from the five associations qualified for the Super League section of the competition. The Super League consisted of three sections each
comprising five teams, and from these three sections would
come the quarter-finalists.

In the opening round of matches in Section A, Punjab
came from behind to beat Kerala. They owed a great deal to
medium-pacer Harvinder Singh who returned the best
match bowling figures of his career. The game in Pune was
dominated by the batsmen. Jai Yadav and Chandrakant
Pandit added 177 after Madhya Pradesh had lost their first
three wickets for 46 while the first five Maharashtra
batsmen all reached 50. Sugwekar continued his fine form
with an innings of 193 out of 310.

29, 30, 31 January and 1 February 1997
at Barabati Stadium, Cuttack
Madhya Pradesh 275 (J.P.Yadav 95, Raj Ali 58) and 154
(K.K. Patel 64, S. Raul 5 for 31)
Orissa 156 (R.K. Chauhan 5 for 42) and 155
(R.K. Chauhan 7 for 52)
Madhya Pradesh won by 118 runs
Madhya Pradesh 8 pts, Orissa 0 pts

at Nehru Stadium, Pune
Kerala 133 and 356 (K.N.A. Padmanabhan 161 not out,
S.V. Jedhe 4 for 53)
Maharashtra 447 for 3 dec. (S.S. Bhave 168, H.H. Kanitkar
100, A.V. Kale 72 not out) and 43 for 1
Maharashtra won by 9 wickets
Maharashtra 8 pts, Kerala 0 pts

Off-spinner Rajesh Chauhan is no longer in favour with the
Indian selectors, but he produced a devastating perfor-
mance to take Madhya Pradesh to victory over Orissa.
Maharashtra once again scored heavily at Pune. Bhave and
Sugwekar shared an opening stand of 206, and Bhave and
Kanitkar added 98 for the second wicket. Kanitkar featured
in another large stand as he and Kale put on 143. Victory for
Maharashtra looked certain, but Anantha Padmanabhan hit
a brave maiden century that nearly denied the home side.

7, 8, 9 and 10 February 1997
at Maharani Usharaje Trust Ground, Indore
Madhya Pradesh 439 (S. Abbas Ali 147, K.K. Patel 79,
A.R. Khurasiya 57, Raj Ali 56, C.T.K. Masood 4 for 55)
Kerala 273 (S.C. Oasis 54, H.S. Sodhi 4 for 70) and
226 for 8 (S.C. Oasis 52 not out, K.N. Balasubramaniam 52)

Match drawn
Madhya Pradesh 5 pts, Kerala 3 pts

at Punjab CA Stadium, Mohali
Orissa 312 (S. Raul 64, P.R. Mohapatra 50, B. Bhushan
5 for 72) and 146 for 3 (P.R. Mohapatra 80 not out)
Punjab 434 for 8 dec. (A. Mehra 200 not out)
Match drawn
Punjab 5 pts, Orissa 3 pts

The Trust Cricket Ground at Indore staged a first-class
match for the first time, and the pitch played well. Kerala
were forced to follow on, but they battled well in their
second innings and saved the match, so avoiding defeat in
the Super League for the first time. Ajay Mehra hit a maiden
double century as Punjab drew with Orissa.

16, 17, 18 and 19 February 1997
at Barabati Stadium, Orissa
Kerala 535 for 9 dec. (K.N.A. Padmanabhan 200,
S.C. Oasis 135, Feroze Rashid 63 not out, A.S. Kudva 51,
S. Raul 6 for 143)
Orissa 253 (P. Das 53, K.N.A. Padmanabhan 6 for 99) and
291 for 8 (R.R. Parida 94)
Match drawn
Kerala 5 pts, Orissa 3 pts

at Nehru Stadium, Pune
Maharashtra 417 (S.S. Sugwekar 169, H.H. Kinitkar 159)
and 307 (S.S. Sugwekar 85, Sandeep Sharma 4 for 65)
Punjab 380 (N.S. Sidhu 87, Sandeep Sharma 83, R. Saini
74, Amit Sharma 63) and 85 for 0
Match drawn
Maharashtra 5 pts, Punjab 3 pts

The wonderful all-round cricket of Anantha Padmanabhan
continued. He and Sunil Oasis shared a stand of 290 with
both batsmen making their highest scores in first-class
cricket. Padmanabhan then took 6 for 99 and 2 for 60 with
his leg-breaks and googlies, but Orissa managed a draw.

Shantanu Sugwekar and Hrishikesh Kanitkar put on
309 for Maharashtra's second wicket against Punjab, who
were in danger of having to follow on until Saini and
Sandeep Sharma added 119 for the eighth wicket.

25, 26, 27 and 28 February 1997
at Roop Singh Stadium, Gwalior
Punjab 330 (A. Mehra 79, Bhupinder Singh jnr 55,
M. Mehra 51, R.K. Chauhan 4 for 92) and 326 for 6 (V.
Rathore 98, R. Saini 63, A.R. Kapoor 53 not out, S.S. Lahore
4 for 84)
Madhya Pradesh 396 (C.S. Pandit 111, J.P.Yadav 82,
A.R. Kapoor 5 for 94, B.Vij 4 for 143)
Match drawn
Madhya Pradesh 5 pts, Punjab 3 pts

at Barabati Stadium, Cuttack
Orissa 432 (S. Raul 173, P. Das 67, P. Mullick 64, P.V. Chitale
5 for 102) and 231 for 5 (R.R. Parida 111 not out, S. Raul 55)
Maharashtra 337 (I. Kamthekar 78)
Match drawn
Orissa 5 pts, Maharashtra 3 pts

Madhya Pradesh had to work hard for first innings points
against Punjab. They were 288 for 7 when Pandit at last
found a reliable partner in Chauhan. The pair added 66 and
gained the lead. Throughout the first three-and-a-half-days,
runs came at under three an over.

Orissa surprised all by taking first innings points
against Maharashtra, whose star batsmen failed to flourish.
The outstanding performance came from Sanjay Raul, who
hit the highest score of his career.

Super League Section A Final Table

	P	W	L	D	Pts
Madhya Pradesh	4	1	–	3	21
Maharashtra	4	1	–	3	21
Punjab	4	1	–	3	17
Orissa	4	–	1	3	11
Kerala	4	–	2	2	10

Super League Section B

20, 21, 22 and 23 January 1997
at IPCL Stadium, Vadodara
Vadodara 439 (J.J. Martin 114, K.S. More 82, T.B. Arothe
72, C.C. Williams 64, I.A. Thakur 4 for 89)
Railways 223 (Y. Gowda 77 not out, R.A. Swarup
5 for 68) and 246 for 5 (Y. Gowda 100 not out, S. Yadasav
82)
Match drawn
Vadodara 5 pts, Railways 3 pts

at Feroze Shah Kotla Ground, Delhi
Tamil Nadu 255 (S. Mahesh 82 not out, S. Sharath 60)
and 171 for 6 (S. Sriram 57)
Delhi 413 for 5 dec. (A.K. Sharma 128, V. Dahiya 95,
R. Lamba 64, A. Malhotra 56 not out)
Match drawn
Delhi 5 pts, Tamil Nadu 3 pts

Jacob Martin's century and consistent batting down the
order took Vadodara to a position of strength by the end of
the second day against Railways. Yere Gowda played two
fine innings for the visitors, but he was unable to prevent
them from being forced to follow on.

Delhi's team of seasoned campaigners were too strong
for Tamil Nadu but had to settle for a draw. Tamil Nadu were

117 for 7 in their first innings, but they were saved from
total humiliation by Mahesh.

29, 30, 31 January and 1 February 1997
at Karnail Singh Stadium, Delhi
Delhi 457 (A.K. Sharma 220 not out, R. Lamba 87,
N. Chopra 84, K. Parida 6 for 121)
Railways 205 (S. Yadav 83, N. Chopra 6 for 78,
A.S. Wassan 4 for 47) and 117 (A.S. Wassan 5 for 48)
Delhi won by an innings and 135 runs
Delhi 8 pts, Railways 0 pts

at IPCL Stadium, Vadodara
Vadodara 238 (T.B. Arothe 75, K.S. More 60, A. Sarkar
5 for 50) and 316 for 6 dec. (R.A. Swarup 97, K.S. More 85)
Bengal 181 (P.K. Amre 55, T.B. Arothe 4 for 30, Sukhbir
Singh 4 for 53) and 199 for 5 (D. Gandhi 57, N. Haldipur 50)
Match drawn
Vadodara 5 pts, Bengal 3 pts

Ajay Sharma's services to Delhi and Indian cricket over the
years are incalculable. His one Test appearance is a decade in
the past, yet he continues to score prolifically and has 8,000
first-class runs to his credit. He notched another double
century in Delhi's trouncing of Railways, and he and veteran
Raman Lamba added 163 for the third wicket. With all-
rounder Nikhil Chopra, he put on 167 for the seventh wicket.

Rain severely hampered play on the second day at
Vadodara where home skipper More had a good match.

7, 8, 9 and 10 February 1997
at Feroze Shah Kotla Ground, Delhi
Vadodara 287 (C. Williams 62, J. Martin 51, F. Ghayas
4 for 82) and 242 (T.B. Arother 78, A.S. Wassan 5 for 49)
Delhi 384 (A.K. Sharma 118, R. Lamba 69, N. Chopra 53,
Sukhbir Singh 4 for 100) and 146 for 8 (Sukhbir Singh
4 for 73)
Delhi won by 2 wickets
Delhi 8 pts, Vadodara 0 pts

at M.A. Chidambaram Stadium, The Chepauk, Madras
Bengal 247 (R. Gavaskar 69, A. Verma 51) and 295 for 5
(D. Gandhi 182)
Tamil Nadu 425 for 8 dec. (S. Sharath 131, S. Sriram 99,
H. Badani 62)
Match drawn
Tamil Nadu 5 pts, Bengal 3 pts

Delhi gained a thrilling victory over Vadodara, who had
batted with consistency into the second day. As in the
previous match, Delhi relied heavily on Lamba, Ajay
Sharma and Nikhil Chopra, and they lost six wickets before
taking first innings points. Vadodara's second innings lasted
into the fourth afternoon, and Delhi had 38 overs in which to
score 146 to win. They tended to panic against some tight

bowling, and three batsmen were run out. The last ball arrived with two needed, and Nikhil Chopra became the hero by scoring the winning runs.

There was no such excitement in Madras, where skipper Sharath put Tamil Nadu on top with a century. When Bengal batted a second time, Devang Gandhi made the highest score of his career.

16, 17, 18 and 19 February 1997
at Karnail Singh Stadium, Delhi
Tamil Nadu 157 (J. Zaman 5 for 45, Zakir Hussain 4 for 66) and 135 (J. Zaman 4 for 20, K. Parida 4 for 20)
Railways 357 (S.B. Bangar 122, S. Yadav 108, D.K. Devan and 7 for 74)
Railways won by an innings and 65 runs
Railways 8 pts, Tamil Nadu 0 pts

at Eden Gardens, Calcutta
Bengal 383 (A. Verma 162, A. Das 81, Robin Singh 4 for 107, A.S. Wassan 4 for 111) and 245 for 6 dec. (A. Das 66, D. Gandhi 61, P.K. Amre 55, A.S. Wassan 5 for 73)
Delhi 251 (A. Malhotra 71) and 251 (P. Joshi 67, N.D. Hirwani 6 for 51)
Bengal won by 188 runs
Bengal 8 pts, Delhi 0 pts

Form was turned on its head as Railways trounced Tamil Nadu and Bengal overcame mighty Delhi. Railways won in three days with Bangar and Satyendra Yadav sharing a second wicket partnership of 220. Bengal were well served by Verma and Ajoy Das, who added 217 after five wickets had gone for 120. Hirwani had match figures of 9 for 91. Delhi were without several leading players.

25, 26, 27 and 28 February 1997
at M.A. Chidambaram Stadium, The Chepauk, Madras
Tamil Nadu 415 (S. Sriram 172, J. Ashique Ali 55, M. Kadri 4 for 99) and 180 for 5 (T. Jabbar 59 not out)
Vadodara 193 (R.A. Swarup 93, M. Venkataramana 5 for 63) and 399 for 7 dec. (J. Martin 115, A.C. Bedade 102 not out, M. Kadri 81, K.S. More 61)
Tamil Nadu won by 5 wickets
Tamil Nadu 8 pts, Vadodara 0 pts

at Eden Gardens, Calcutta
Railways 455 for 9 dec. (S. Bhatia 97, Y. Gowda 96, M. Karthik 74, Z. Zuffri 56, S. Yadav 50, S. Muzumdar 4 for 105)
Bengal 244 (U. Chatterjee 52) and 126 for 5
Match drawn
Railways 5 pts, Bengal 3 pts

Vadodara fought back bravely after trailing by 222 runs on the first innings. Centuries by Jacob Martin and Atul Bedade gave More the opportunity to declare, for only victory would have given Vadodara the chance of winning a place in the quarter-finals. However the brave gesture just failed.

In contrast, Bengal needed only a draw and, although forced to follow on, this was achieved without too many problems.

Super Leage Section B Final Table

	P	W	L	D	Pts
Delhi	4	2	1	1	21
Bengal	4	1	–	3	17
Tamil Nadu	4	1	1	2	16
Railways	4	1	1	2	16
Vadodara	4	–	2	2	10

Super League Section C

20, 21, 22 and 23 January 1997
at Keenan Stadium, Jamshedpur
Bihar 161 (N.M. Kulkarni 6 for 51) and 143 (Tariq-ur-Rehman 58 not out, S.V. Bahutule 4 for 35)
Mumbai 318 for 9 dec. (J.V. Paranjpe 84, S.V. Manjrekar 70, W. Jaffer 65, S.V. Bahutule 53, Anil Kumar 4 for 102)
Mumbai won by an innings and 14 runs
Mumbai 8 pts, Bihar 0 pts

Raman Lamba, more than a thousand runs in the season for Dehli. (Adrian Murrell/Allsport)

at *Lal Bahadur Shastri Stadium, Hyderabad*
Hyderabad 343 (V. Pratap 93, A. Shetty 71, S. Pandey
5 for 106)
Haryana 114 (N. David 4 for 26) and 187 (A.R. Kaypee 62)
Hyderabad won by an innings and 42 runs
Hyderabad 8 pts, Haryana 0 pts

Both Mumbai and Hyderabad began their quest for a place
in the final stages of the Ranji Trophy with emphatic and
workmanlike victories. Mumbai bowled out Bihar on the
last day while Hyderabad beat Haryana inside three days.

29, 30, 31 January and 1 February 1997
at *Nahar Singh Stadium, Faridabad*
Uttar Pradesh 345 (R.V. Sapru 118, J.P. Yadav 93) and
267 for 5 (J.P. Yadav 85, R. Shamshad 53 not out)
Haryana 471 for 9 dec. (Jitender Singh 229 not out,
R. Puri 62, A.L. Gera 5 for 133)
Match drawn
Haryana 5 pts, Uttar Pradesh 3 pts

at *Gymkhana Ground, Secunderabad*
Hyderabad 265 (A. Shetty 116) and 279 for 9 dec.
(M.V. Sridhar 81, N. David 65, V. Pratap 60, Avinash Kumar
4 for 84)
Bihar 260 (Sunil Kumar 63, Venkatapathy Raju 4 for 65)
and 172 for 4 (C.M. Jha 60)
Match drawn
Hyderabad 5 pts, Bihar 3 pts

Jitender Singh hit his second double century of the season
as Haryana claimed vital points against Uttar Pradesh. He
batted throughout 160 overs. Hyderabad were much
indebted to Arvind Shetty who held their innings together
with little support.

7, 8, 9 and 10 February 1997
at *KD Singh Babu Stadium, Lucknow*
Mumbai 342 (W. Jaffer 106, A.A. Mazumdar 88,
S.V. Manjrekar 50, K. Obaid 4 for 71) and 27 for 2
Uttar Pradesh 151 (N.M. Kulkarni 4 for 40) and 214
(R.V. Sapru 52, N.M. Kulkarni 5 for 73)
Mumbai won by 8 wickets
Mumbai 8 pts, Uttar Pradesh 0 pts

at *Moin-ul-Haq Stadium, Patna*
Haryana 362 (R. Puri 130, N.R. Goel 86) and
169 for 9 dec. (Avinash Kumar 6 for 42)
Bihar 281 (Tariq-ur-Rehman 82, C. Jha 57, P. Jain 7 for 72)
and 226 (C. Jha 63, Tariq-ur-Rehman 52, P. Jain 5 for 79)
Haryana won by 24 runs
Haryana 8 pts, Bihar 0 pts

The continued excellence of the batting of Wasim Jaffer and
the all round strength of Mumbai was too much for Uttar

Pradesh, while Haryana pulled off a brave victory against
Bihar. Having taken a first innings lead of 81, Haryana set
Bihar a target of 251 at nearly five an over. Bihar went for
the runs, but with Pradeep Jain in devastating form with his
left-arm spin they lost their last five wickets for 34 runs.

16, 17, 18 and 19 February 1997
at *Gymkhana Ground, Secunderabad*
Hyderabad 240 and 218 (V. Pratap 61, N.M. Kulkarni
5 for 87)
Mumbai 540 (S.V. Manjrekar 150, A.A. Muzumdar 138,
V.G. Kambli 111, J.V. Paranjpe 51)
Mumbai won by an innings and 82 runs
Mumbai 8 pts, Hyderabad 0 pts

at *Keenan Stadium, Jamshedpur*
Bihar 329 (Tariq-ur-Rehman 118 not out) and
213 for 5 dec. (Tariq-ur-Rehman 62)
Uttar Pradesh 289 (R. Shamshad 107, S.A. Shukla 51,
Avinash Kumar 4 for 103, K.V.P. Rao 4 for 117) and 194
for 6 (G.K. Pandey 50 not out)
Match drawn
Bihar 5 pts, Uttar Pradesh 3 pts

Mumbai confirmed their domination in stylish fashion with
their three leading batsmen all scoring centuries and
putting them in an unassailable position at the top of Group
C. The left-handed Tariq-ur-Rehman, a few days short of his
23rd birthday, hit the third century of his career as Bihar
drew with Uttar Pradesh.

25, 26, 27 and 28 February 1997
at *Wankhede Stadium, Bombay*
Haryana 303 (Shafiq Khan 84, V. Yadav 80, M.P. Patel
5 for 65) and 234 (A.S. Kaypee 82, Shafiq Khan 64, R. Pawar
5 for 93)
Mumbai 330 (S.K. Kulkarni 126, M.V. Joglekar 80, P. Jain
5 for 67) and 208 for 6 (A.A. Muzumdar 82, V.G. Kambli 71,
P. Thakur 4 for 79)
Mumbai won by 4 wickets
Mumbai 8 pts, Haryana 0 pts

at *Gymkhana Ground, Secunderabad*
Uttar Pradesh 314 (S.A. Shukla 145) and 272 for 5 dec.
(R.V. Sapru 101 not out, M.S. Mudgal 94)
Hyderabad 292 (V. Pratap 78, S.K. Yadav 70, K. Obaid
6 for 120) and 107 for 1 (M.V. Sridhar 56 not out)
Match drawn
Uttar Pradesh 5 pts, Hyderabad 3 pts

Mumbai completed their fourth win in four matches to gain a
place in the semi-finals along with Delhi. Hyderabad gained
the draw they needed to clinch second spot and a place in the
quarter-finals, where they would be joined by the runners up
of the other two groups and the winners of Group A.

Super Leage Section C Final Table

	P	W	L	D	Pts
Mumbai	4	4	–	–	32
Hyderabad	4	1	1	2	16
Haryana	4	1	2	1	13
Uttar Pradesh	4	–	1	3	11
Bihar	4	–	2	2	8

Quarter Finals

17, 18, 19, 20 and 21 March 1997
at Nehru Stadium, Pune
Hyderabad 226 (V. Pratap 76, M.S. Kulkarni 4 for 71) and 230 (N.P. Singh 62, S.K. Yadav 52, V. Pratap 50, I.R. Siddiqui 4 for 46)
Maharashtra 287 (I. Kamtekar 53) and 172 for 3 (S.S. Bhave 86, S.S. Sugwekar 56)
Maharashtra won by 7 wickets

at URT Trust Ground, Indore
Madhya Pradesh 464 (A.R. Khurasiya 209, D.N. Bundela 72 not out) and 425 for 5 dec. (J.P. Yadav 108, D.N. Bundela 102 not out, S. Abbas Ali 75, P.K. Dwevedi 57, R.K. Chauhan 54 not out)
Bengal 420 (R.S. Gavaskar 109, G. Shome jnr 88, N. Haldipur 63) and 54 for 2
Match drawn

A good team performance took Maharashtra into the semi-finals. They bowled and fielded well and remained calm under pressure. Needing 170 to win, they were given an excellent start of 151 by Bhave and skipper Sugwekar. A double century by Amay Khurasiya gave Madhya Pradesh the advantage over Bengal helped by Gavaskar's maiden hundred.

Madhya Pradesh qualified for the semi-final by virtue of their first innings lead.

Semi-Finals

27, 28, 29, 30 and 31 March 1997
at Nehru Stadium, Pune
Delhi 656 (R. Lamba 192, A.K. Sharma 144, V. Dahiya 85, N. Chopra 74 not out, A. Malhotra 61, S.V. Inamdar 4 for 163) and 264 for 2 (R. Lamba 101, V. Dahiya 74, A. Dani 50 not out)
Maharashtra 524 (H.H. Kanitkar 174, A.V. Kale 54, R.R. Kanade 54)
Match drawn

Mumbai won the Ranji Trophy for the 32nd time. For Sanjay Manjrekar, it was a first triumph as captain. (Alain Cozzi)

at URT Trust Ground, Indore
Madhya Pradesh 369 (M.S. Majithia 75, N.M. Kulkarni 5 for 81) and 291 for 7 dec. (S. Abbas Ali 102 not out, H.S. Sodhi 58, S.V. Bahutule 4 for 75)
Mumbai 532 (A.A. Muzumdar 125, S.V. Manjrekar 114, W. Jaffer 65, R.K. Chauhan 6 for 191) and 25 for 0
Match drawn

Massive scores by the two strongest sides in the competition ensured that they would meet in the final by having first innings leads in drawn matches. Raman Lamba hit a century in each innings for Delhi against Maharashtra, for whom Kanitkar hit his fifth century of the season and completed 1,000 runs. Lamba and Dahiya scored 214 for Delhi's first wicket, and Lamba and Ajay Sharma added 198 for the third wicket.

A third wicket stand of 209 between Manjrekar and Muzumdar ended only when Mumbai had drawn level with Madhya Pradesh. Chauhan sent down 93.5 overs to take 6 for 191. He bowled 30 maidens, and Mumbai's innings occupied 230.5 overs.

Ranji Trophy Final

5, 6, 7, 8 and 9 April 1997
at Roop Singh Stadium, Gwalior
Mumbai 630 (A.A. Muzumdar 144, J.V. Paranjpe 111, V.G. Kambli 89, S.V. Manjrekar 78, W. Jaffer 58)
Delhi 559 (A. Dani 178, A.K. Sharma 176, N.M. Kulkarni 4 for 143)
Match drawn

Match One – Pakistan v. New Zealand
9 May 1997 at Punjab CA Stadium, Mohali

New Zealand

B.A. Young	b Abdul Razzaq	59
N.J. Astle	st Moin Khan, b Shahid Afridi	117
M.J. Horne	b Saqlain Mushtaq	45
C.L. Cairns	b Aqib Javed	17
S.P. Fleming (Capt)	c and b Saqlain Mushtaq	9
C.Z. Harris	b Saqlain Mushtaq	4
D.N. Patel	run out	4
*A.C. Parore	not out	16
G.R. Larsen	not out	1
A.C. Penn		
H.T. Davis		
	lb 2, w 9, nb 2	13
	50 overs (for 7 wickets)	285

	O	M	R	W
Abdul Razzaq	7	–	45	1
Aqib Javed	8	–	70	1
Shahid Afridi	10	–	49	1
Saqlain Mushtaq	10	–	38	3
Mohammad Hussain	5	–	36	–
Salim Malik	10	–	45	–

Fall of Wickets
1–155, 2–234, 3–236, 4–256, 5–264, 6–264, 7–282

Pakistan

Saeed Anwar	c Harris, b Penn	17
Shahid Afridi	b Larsen	59
Rameez Raja (Capt)	run out	11
Ijaz Ahmed	lbw, b Astle	50
Salim Malik	c Harris, b Astle	47
Inzamam-ul-Haq	c Harris, b Patel	30
*Moin Khan	c Fleming, b Astle	16
Mohammad Hussain	c Davis, b Larsen	1
Abdul Razzaq	st Parore, b Astle	8
Saqlain Mushtaq	not out	6
Aqib Javeb	not out	6
	lb 2, w 7, nb 3	12
	50 overs (for 9 wickets)	263

	O	M	R	W
Penn	6	–	50	1
Davis	6	–	39	–
Harris	10	2	34	–
Larsen	10	–	46	2
Patel	10	–	49	1
Astle	5	–	43	4

Fall of Wickets
1–45, 2–92, 3–106, 4–187, 5–220, 6–232, 7–242, 8–243, 9–256

Umpires: S. Venktaraghavan & K.T. Francis   *Man of the Match:* N.J. Astle

New Zealand won by 22 runs

Match Two – Pakistan v. Sri Lanka
13 May 1997 at Roop Singh Stadium, Gwalior

Pakistan

Saeed Anwar	st Kaluwitharana, b Muralitharan	36
Shahid Afridi	c Kaluwitharana, b S.C. de Silva	52
Rameez Raja (Capt)	c P.A. de Silva, b S.C. de Silva	49
Ijaz Ahmed	c Mahanama, b Jayasuriya	29
Salim Malik	b Vaas	49
Inzamam-ul-Haq	b S.C. de Silva	22
*Moin Khan	not out	23
Mohammad Hussain	not out	17
Azhar Mahmood		
Saqlain Mushtaq		
Aqib Javeb		
	b 4, lb 3, w 5	12
	50 overs (for 6 wickets)	289

	O	M	R	W
Vaas	10	1	71	1
S.C. de Silva	10	–	59	3
Dharmasena	10	–	54	–
Muralitharan	10	1	39	1
Jayasuriya	10	–	59	1

Fall of Wickets
1–74, 2–112, 3–158, 4–190, 5–219, 6–260

Sri Lanka

S.T. Jayasuriya	lbw, b Aqib Javed	0
*R.S. Kaluwitharana	b Aqib Javed	7
M.S. Atapattu	c Ijaz Ahmed, b Aqib Javed	0
P.A. de Silva	c Ijaz Ahmed, b Aqib Javed	33
A. Ranatunga (Capt)	c Azhar Mahmood, b Salim Malik	58
H.P. Tillekeratne	c Inzamam-ul-Haq, b Salim Malik	29
R.S. Mahanama	c Ijaz Ahmed, b Saqlain Mushtaq	54
H.D.P.K. Dharmasena	lbw, b Saqlain Mushtaq	28
W.P.U.J.C. Vaas	b Aqib Javed	15
M. Muralitharan	c Azhar Mahmood, b Saqlain	7
S.C. de Silva	not out	13
	lb 10, w 1, nb 4	15
	49.5 overs	259

	O	M	R	W
Aqib Javed	10	1	35	5
Azhar Mahmood	5	–	36	–
Saqlain Mushtaq	9.5	–	43	3
Shahid Afridi	8	–	58	–
Salim Malik	10	–	46	2
Mohammad Hussain	7	–	31	–

Fall of Wickets
1–0, 2–0, 3–25, 4–59, 5–134, 6–134, 7–205, 8–229, 9–243

Umpires: S. Venktaraghavan & R.S. Dunne   *Man of the Match:* Aquib Javeb

Pakistan won by 30 runs

Match Three – India v. New Zealand
14 May 1997 at M. Chinnaswamy Stadium, Bangalore

New Zealand

B.A. Young	c Kumle, b Joshi	17
N.J. Astle	b R.R. Singh	92
M.J. Horne	run out	23
S.P. Fleming (Capt)	run out	13
C.L. Cairns	lbw, b R.R. Singh	3
C.Z. Harris	c and b Kumble	3
*A.C. Parore	run out	32
D.N. Patel	run out	10
G.R. Larsen	b Joshi	12
A.C. Penn	not out	7
H.T. Davis	not out	0
	lb 4, w 1, nb 3	8
	50 overs (for 9 wickets)	220

	O	M	R	W
Venkatesh Prasad	10	–	40	–
Kuruvilla	6	1	37	–
Kumble	10	1	30	1
Joshi	10	–	47	2
Tendulkar	7	–	35	–
R.R. Singh	7	–	27	2

Fall of Wickets
1–59, 2–109, 3–136, 4–147, 5–154, 6–166, 7–185, 8–209, 9–219

India

S.C. Ganguly	c Parore, b Larsen	62
S.R. Tendulkar (Capt)	b Astle	117
R.S. Dravid	not out	21
V.G. Kambli	not out	4
A.D. Jadeja		
*N.R. Mongia		
R.R. Singh		
S.B. Joshi		
A.R. Kumble		
Venkatesh Prasad		
A. Kuruvilla		
	lb 1, w 13, nb 3	17
	42.3 overs (for 2 wickets)	221

	O	M	R	W
Penn	8.3	–	59	–
Davis	5	–	54	–
Larsen	8	2	26	1
Harris	7	1	26	–
Patel	7	–	30	–
Astle	7	–	25	1

Fall of Wickets
1–169, 2–216

Umpires: Javed Akhtra & D.L. Orchard *Man of the Match:* S.R. Tendulkar

India won by 8 wickets

Match Four – India v. Sri Lanka
17 May 1997 at Wankhede Stadium, Bombay

India

S. Ganguly	b Vaas	0
S.R. Tendulkar (Capt)	c Dharmasena, b S.C. de Silva	2
R.S. Dravid	b Muralitharan	61
V.G. Kambli	c Tillekeratne, b S.C. de Silva	4
A.D. Jadeja	b Jayasuriya	72
R.R. Singh	b S.C. de Silva	51
*N.R. Mongia	not out	21
A.R. Kumble	c Muralitharan, b Vaas	0
S.B. Joshi		
Venkatesh Prasad		
A.Kuruvilla		
	lb 6, w 7, nb 1	14
	50 overs (for 7 wickets)	225

	O	M	R	W
Vaas	10	3	13	2
S.C. de Silva	10	–	59	3
Muralitharan	10	–	37	1
Dharmasena	10	2	38	–
Jayasuriya	8	–	55	1
P.A. de Silva	2	–	17	–

Fall of Wickets
1–0, 2–4, 3–29, 4–124, 5–182, 6–224, 7–225

Sri Lanka

S.T. Jayasuriya	not out	151
*R.S. Kaluwitharana	c Tendulkar, b Kuruvilla	0
M.S. Atapattu	run out	38
P.A. de Silva	lbw, b Kumble	0
A. Ranatunga (Capt)	c sub (G.K. Khoda), b Kumble	17
H.P. Tillekeratne	c Mongia, b Kuruvilla	6
R.S. Mahanama	not out	4
H.D.P.K. Dharmasena		
W.P.U.J.C. Vaas		
M. Muralitharan		
S.C. de Silva		
	b 4, lb 2, w 7	13
	40.5 overs (for 5 wickets)	229

	O	M	R	W
Venkatesh Prasad	10	1	57	–
Kuruvilla	7	1	22	2
Kumble	10	–	55	2
Joshi	9.5	–	56	–
R.R. Singh	2	–	20	–
Tendulkar	2	–	13	–

Fall of Wickets
1–8, 2–146, 3–151, 4–194, 5–220

Umpires: R.S. Dunne & D.L. Orchard *Man of the Match:* S.T. Jayasuriya

Sri Lanka won by 5 wickets

Match Five – Sri Lanka v. New Zealand
20 May 1997 at Lal Bahadur Shastri Stadium, Hyderabad

Sri Lanka

S.T. Jayasuriya	c Cairns, b O'Connor	4
M.S. Atapattu	run out	41
P.A. de Silva	b O'Connor	9
A. Ranatunga (Capt)	c Parore, b Larsen	15
H.P. Tillekeratne	b Astle	29
R.S. Mahanama	c McMillan, b O'Connor	41
*R.S. Kaluwitharana	c Cairns, b Astle	44
H.D.P.K. Dharmasena	run out	6
W.P.U.J.C. Vaas	b Larsen	0
M. Muralitharan	not out	9
S.C. de Silva	lbw, b Larsen	0
	b 5, lb 6, w 3, nb 2	16
	48.3 overs	214

	O	M	R	W
O'Connor	9	–	44	3
Patel	10	–	37	–
Larsen	9.3	1	43	3
Harris	10	–	30	–
Astle	8	1	37	2
Cairns	2	–	12	–

Fall of Wickets
1–6, 2–23, 3–63, 4–85, 5–126, 6–172, 7–188, 8–194, 9–210

New Zealand

B.A. Young	c Kaluwitharana, b S.C. de Silva	22
N.J. Astle	c Kaluwitharana, b Vaas	9
M.J. Horne	st Kaluwitharana, b Jayasuriya	41
S.P. Fleming (Capt)	lbw, b P.A. de Silva	24
C.L. Cairns	c P.A. de Silva, b Jayasuriya	6
C.D. McMillan	st Kaluwitharana, b P.A. de Silva	10
C.Z. Harris	not out	26
*A.C. Parore	c Tillekeratne, b Dharmasena	9
D.N. Patel	c Muralitharan, b Dharmasena	5
G.R. Larsen	b Muralitharan	1
S.B. O'Connor	c Tillekeratne b Muralitharan	0
	b 1, lb 5, w 2, nb 1	9
	44.5 overs	162

	O	M	R	W
Vaas	6	2	23	1
S.C. de Silva	6	2	13	1
Muralitharan	9.5	1	49	2
Dharmasena	6	–	28	2
P.A. de Silva	10	1	22	2
Jayasuriya	7	1	21	2

Fall of Wickets
1–29, 2–31, 3–97, 4–103, 5–120, 6–120, 7–140, 8–147, 9–152

Umpires: S.K. Bansal & Javed Akhtar   *Man of the Match:* R.S. Kaluwitharana   **Sri Lanka won by 52 runs**

Match Six – India v. Pakistan
21 May 1997 at M.A. Chidambaram Stadium, The Chepauk, Madras

Pakistan

Saeed Anwar	c Ganguly, b Tendulkar	194
Shahid Afridi	c Ganguly, b Kuruvilla	5
Rameez Raja (Capt)	b R.R. Singh	22
Ijaz Ahmed	lbw, b Kumble	39
Inzamam-ul-Haq	not out	39
*Moin Khan	b Tendulkar	9
Mohammad Hussain	not out	7
Salim Malik		
Azhar Mahmood		
Saqlain Mushtaq		
Aqib Javed		
	b 1, lb 8, w 3	12
	50 overs (for 5 wickets)	327

	O	M	R	W
Venkatesh Prasad	9	–	63	–
Kuruvilla	10	2	50	1
Kumble	9	1	58	1
Joshi	4	–	36	–
Tendulkar	9	–	61	2
R.R. Singh	9	–	50	1

Fall of Wickets
1–8, 2–97, 3–213, 4–297, 5–315

India

S.R. Tendulkar (Capt)	c Inzamam-ul-Haq, b Aqib Javed	4
S. Ganguly	b Saqlain Mushtaq, b Aqib Javed	33
R.S. Dravid	c Shahid Afridi, b Aqib Javed	107
V.G. Kambli	c Ijaz, b Mohammad Hussain	65
A.D. Jadeja	c sub (Mohammad Wasim), b Salim	4
R.R. Singh	run out	35
*N.R. Mongia	not out	23
S.B. Joshi	c Moin Khan, b Aqib Javed	2
A.R. Kumble	c and b Saqlain Mushtaq	0
A. Kuruvilla	c Mohammad Hussain, b Aqib Javed	1
Venkatesh Prasad	c Moin Khan, b Saqlain Mushtaq	2
	lb 7, w 8, nb 1	16
	49.2 overs	292

	O	M	R	W
Aqib Javed	10	–	61	5
Azhar Mahmood	4	–	24	–
Saqlain Mushtaq	9.2	–	46	2
Shahid Afridi	10	–	56	–
Salim Malik	6	1	46	1
Mohammad Hussain	10	–	52	1

Fall of Wickets
1–9, 2–61, 3–195, 4–209, 5–247, 6–275, 7–279, 8–281, 9–284

Umpires: K.T. Francis & D.L. Orchard   *Man of the Match:* Saeed Anwar   **Pakistan won by 35 runs**

First Final – Pakistan v. Sri Lanka
24 May 1997 at Punjab CA Stadium, Mohali

Sri Lanka

S.T. Jayasuriya	c sub (Mohammad Wasim),	
	b Mohammad Hussain	96
M.S. Atapattu	lbw, b Mohammad Hussain	53
P.A. de Silva	st Moin Khan, b Saqlain Mushtaq	90
A. Ranatunga (Capt)	st Moin Khan, b Saqlain Mushtaq	80
*R.S. Kaluwitharana	not out	1
D.K. Liyanage	not out	1
R.S. Mahanama		
H.P. Tillekeratne		
W.P.U.J.C. Vaas		
S.C. de Silva		
M. Muralitharan		
	lb 8, w 8, nb 2	18
50 overs (for 4 wickets)		339

	O	M	R	W
Abdul Razzaq	5	–	41	–
Aqib Javed	9	–	64	–
Shahid Afridi	10	–	63	–
Saqlain Mushtaq	10	–	72	2
Mohammad Hussain	10	–	56	2
Salim Malik	6	–	35	–

Fall of Wickets
1–148, 2–184, 3–337, 4–338

Pakistan

Saeed Anwar	c Liyanage, b S.C. de Silva	14
Shahid Afridi	c Atapattu, b S.C. de Silva	18
Mohammad Hussain	b S.C. de Silva	8
Rameez Raja (Capt)	run out	42
Ijaz Ahmed	c sub (U.U. Chandana),	
	b Dharmasena	23
Salim Malik	b P.A. de Silva	29
*Moin Khan	not out	57
Saqlain Mushtaq	c Atapattu, b P.A. de Silva	18
Aqib Javeb	lbw, b Dharmasena	5
Inzamam-ul-Haq	absent injured	–
Abdul Razzaq	absent injured	–
	lb 1, w 8, nb 1	10
43.5 overs		224

	O	M	R	W
Liyanage	6	–	40	–
S.C. de Silva	7	–	40	3
Dharmasena	6.5	–	33	2
Muralitharan	7	–	48	–
P.A. de Silva	10	–	39	2
Jayasuriya	5	–	23	–

Fall of Wickets
1–30, 2–41, 3–49, 4–85, 5–141, 6–143, 7–212, 8–224

Umpires: S. Venktaraghavan & R.S. Dunne   *Man of the Match:* S.T. Jayasuriya

Sri Lanka won by 115 runs

Second Final – Pakistan v. Sri Lanka
27 May 1997 at Eden Gardens, Calcutta

Sri Lanka

S.T. Jayasuriya	c sub (Azar Mahmood),	
	b Arshad Khan	55
M.S. Atapattu	c sub (Hasan Raza),	
	b Arshad Khan	29
*R.S. Kaluwitharana	lbw, b Shahid Afridi	5
P.A. de Silva	b Saqlain Mushtaq	57
A. Ranatunga (Capt)	run out	59
H.P. Tillekeratne	c sub (Hasan Raza), b Salim Malik	38
W.P.U.J.C. Vaas	c Ijaz Ahmed, b Saqlain Mushtaq	3
R.S. Mahanama	b Salim Malik	27
H.D.P.K. Dharmasena	b Saqlain Mushtaq	16
S.C. de Silva	lbw, b Saqlain Mushtaq	0
M. Muralitharan	not out	0
	lb 6, w 13, nb 1	20
49.4 overs		309

	O	M	R	W
Aqib Javed	6	–	49	–
Arshad Khan	10	–	54	2
Shahid Afridi	5	–	40	1
Saqlain Mushtaq	9.4	–	53	4
Mohammad Hussain	9	–	46	–
Salim Malik	10	–	61	2

Fall of Wickets
1–69, 2–90, 3–110, 4–177, 5–250, 6–254, 7–276, 8–304, 9–308

Pakistan

Saeed Anwar	c Muralitharan, b Vaas	6
Shahid Afridi	c P.A. de Silva, b S.C. de Silva	17
Rameez Raja (Capt)	b Dharmasena	76
Ijaz Ahmed	st Kaluwitharana, b Jayasuriya	55
Salim Malik	lbw, b Muralitharan	2
Mohammad Wasim	st Kaluwitharana,	
	b Muralitharan	20
*Moin Khan	c Atapattu, b Muralitharan	2
Mohammad Hussain	not out	18
Saqlain Mushtaq	b P.A. de Silva	0
Arshad Khan	run out	0
Aqib Javed	run out	4
	b 4, lb 8, w 10, nb 2	24
43.1 overs		224

	O	M	R	W
Vaas	7	–	40	1
S.C. de Silva	6	–	41	1
Dharmasena	8.1	–	23	1
Muralitharan	10	–	40	3
Jayasuriya	7	–	42	1
P.A. de Silva	5	–	26	1

Fall of Wickets
1–14, 2–34, 3–132, 4–135, 5–193, 6–195, 7–204, 8–207, 9–207

Umpires: R.S. Dunne & D.L. Orchard   *Man of the Match:* P.A. de Silva

Sri Lanka won by 85 runs

Mumbai (Bombay) won the Ranji Trophy for the 32nd time, and for the first time under the captaincy of Sanjay Manjrekar. Mumbai batted with power and purpose right down the order, and when they ended the second day on 520 for 6 it was obvious that the match would be decided on the first innings and that they had taken a firm grip on the game. When Ashu Dani and Ajay Sharma joined together in a third wicket stand of 313 it looked as if Delhi might pull off a surprise, but once both were caught behind Mumbai regained control.

Ajay Sharma and Lamba both completed 1,000 runs for the season. Left-arm spinner Nilesh Kulkarni took four for 143 and conceded runs at less than two an over.

Independence Cup

The Ranji Trophy final has traditionally marked the end of the Indian season, but, with their insatiable appetite for limited-over cricket, the Indian Board staged the Independence Cup in May. The tournament broke new ground in that matches began at dusk in order to avoid the summer heat and were not completed until after midnight. The result was that huge crowds attended, and floodlit cricket received a further boost. Pakistan entered the tournament at a disadvantage, being without Waqar Younis, Wasim Akram and Mushtaq Ahmed because of their commitments to English counties, although Wasim proved to be unfit to assist Lancashire and had to undergo an operation on his shoulder. Pakistan welcomed the return of Saeed Anwar after illness. India were still without the injured Srinath and chose to drop Azharuddin on the grounds of his indisciplined batting in the Caribbean.

New Zealand won the opening match thanks to a wonderful all-round performance from Nathan Astle, who hit a century and took four wickets to emulate Viv Richards's feat. Pakistan gave Mohammad Hussain his first game in a one-day international but he failed to take a wicket. Consistency brought Pakistan victory over Sri Lanka in the second match, and, in spite of another fine knock from Astle, India trounced New Zealand in Bangalore. Ganguly and Tendulkar scored 169 for India's first wicket with the Indian captain hitting his 12th one-day international hundred, but defeat followed for India at the hands of Sri Lanka. They were savaged by Jayasuriya, who made his highest score in international cricket.

Sri Lanka followed success against India with a very easy win over New Zealand, and this meant that the hosts had to beat Pakistan to qualify for the final. That they failed to do so was due almost entirely to a marvellous innings by Saeed Anwar. The left-hander, 28 years old, had to overcome cramp and batted with a runner for a period as he hit 194 off 147 balls to surpass Viv Richards's record for a one-day international. He struck three sixes in succession off Kumble and, in all, hit five sixes and 22 fours. It was Saeed's 12th one-day international hundred – his first against India – and he received a generous standing ovation from a crowd of 50,000 when he finally pulled a ball from Tendulkar into the hands of fine leg. There was a brave fight by India, and Rahul Dravid scored his first century in a one-day international.

Following the Australian pattern, the final was decided on the best of three matches, but only two games were necessary, Sri Lanka winning outright. Nothing went right for Pakistan. Their bowling was mutilated by Sri Lanka in the first match when they lost Abdul Razzaq with a ruptured blood vessel and Inzamam-ul-Haq with a hairline fracture of his left thumb. Jayasuriya made 96 off 67 balls, and he and Atapattu put on 148 in 20 overs for the first wicket. In the second match, Sri Lanka did not last their full 50 overs, but consistency had taken them to 309, a total Pakistan could not approach. The World Champions claimed yet another trophy.

First-Class Averages

Batting

	M	Inns	NO	Runs	HS	Av	100s	50s
W. Jaffer	7	10	4	692	314*	115.33	2	3
A.K. Sharma	10	13	1	1198	220*	99.83	5	5
Sukhbinder Singh	4	7	2	383	167*	76.60	1	2
V. Joshi	4	5	1	302	137	75.50	1	2
R. Lamba	10	14	–	1034	250	73.00	3	4
Chinmoy Sharma	4	6	–	438	207	73.00	2	1
R.V. Sapru	10	16	3	949	185*	73.00	5	3
R. Nayyar	8	13	3	717	170	71.70	4	1
H.H. Kanitkar	11	16	2	1003	205	71.64	5	1
S.S. Sugwekar	10	14	1	928	193	71.38	3	4
M. Azharuddin	4	8	2	426	163*	71.00	2	1
S. Sharath	8	12	1	774	151	70.36	3	3
R.R. Singh	5	7	1	422	150	70.33	1	3
P. Dharmani	5	8	2	411	130*	68.50	1	2
H. Badani	6	9	2	473	164	67.57	1	3
S.V. Manjrekar	11	11	1	675	150	67.50	2	5
A.A. Muzumdar	12	16	2	942	214*	67.28	4	2
H.J. Parsana	6	11	4	466	100*	66.57	1	3
T.N. Varsania	2	4	1	188	109*	62.66	1	
A.S. Kaypee	8	14	4	619	135*	61.90	2	4
I. Kamtekar	8	8	3	303	78*	60.60		4
P.J. Bhatt	3	4	–	242	123	60.50	2	
A. Das	3	5	1	240	81	60.00		2

Batting

	M	Inns	NO	Runs	HS	Av	100s	50s
C.S. Pandit	12	16	1	873	189	58.20	3	2
Y. Gowda	6	9	2	406	100*	58.00	1	2
V. Rathore	10	17	–	982	254	57.76	4	2
A.D. Jadeja	4	7	–	392	154	56.00	1	2
J. Yadav	5	8	–	442	113	55.25	1	4
K.S. More	8	13	–	714	180	54.92	1	7
S. Abbas Ali	10	15	1	761	198	54.35	3	3
J.V. Paranjpe	8	11	1	541	165	54.10	2	2
A. Dani	10	14	1	696	215	53.53	2	2
V. Dahiya	12	17	3	738	134	52.71	1	6
Tariq-ur-Rehman	7	12	2	526	118*	52.60	1	5
A.V. Mehra	9	14	2	630	200*	52.50	1	3
N. Negi	4	5	–	260	154	52.00	1	1
B.M. Jadeja	4	7	2	260	132*	52.00	1	
V.B. Chandrasekhar	5	7	–	364	194	52.00	1	1
S.S. Bhave	11	16	–	832	168	52.00	2	6
P. Joshi	3	5	2	155	67	51.66		1
G. Dutta	3	5	2	154	54*	51.33		1
Jitender Singh	10	18	2	807	230	50.43	2	2
S.V. Jedhe	10	12	1	553	158	50.27	2	
V. Pratap	10	16	1	754	136	50.26	1	7
S. Sriram	6	10	–	499	172	49.90	1	3
R. Shamshad	10	19	5	694	120*	49.57	2	4

First-Class Averages (continued)

Batting

	M	Inns	NO	Runs	HS	Av	100s	50s
N.S. Sidhu	8	10	1	441	132	49.00	1	3
R.A. Swarup	7	12	1	537	134	48.81	1	2
J.J. Martin	8	13	1	578	115	48.15	3	2
S.K. Kulkarni	10	12	1	524	239	47.63	2	
Kanvaljit Singh	2	4	–	190	97	47.50		2
D. Mongia	8	13	2	521	207*	47.36	2	
N. Haldipur	6	11	–	521	113	47.36	1	4
K.N.A. Padmanabhan	11	18	5	615	200	47.30	2	
T.B. Arothe	7	11	1	470	99	47.00		4
G.K. Khoda	8	13	–	609	124	46.84	1	6
S.S. Raul	9	17	2	698	173	46.53	1	4
S.Y. Dhuri	4	4	–	186	65	46.50		2
A.R. Khurasiya	10	17	–	790	209	46.47	2	2
V.G. Kambli	11	13	–	604	111	46.46	1	4
R.R. Kanade	9	11	2	418	81	46.44		3
R.S. Gavaskar	10	16	2	648	109	46.28	1	4
N. Chopra	9	11	3	357	84	44.62		3
L.S. Rajput	4	7	1	266	123	44.33	1	1
S.S. Sawant	3	5	–	218	63	43.60		2
M.V. Mehra	9	12	3	388	105	43.11	1	3
M.S. Mudgal	8	15	2	555	101*	42.69	1	3
N. David	7	11	1	423	105	42.30	1	3
S.C. Oasis	9	15	1	589	135	42.07	1	5
S.H. Kotak	4	6	1	209	93	41.80		1
M.V. Sridhar	10	16	1	621	94	41.40		6
J.P. Yadav	12	20	1	825	108	41.25	2	4
N.R. Goel	9	16	2	570	135	40.71	1	3
S.S. Karim	6	10	–	407	190	40.70	1	2
G.K. Pandey	8	12	1	445	101	40.75	1	2
P. Das	3	6	1	202	67	40.40		2
A.S. Pathak	6	12	–	482	123	40.16	2	3
P.K. Amre	9	16	1	598	95	39.86		6
S. Mahesh	5	7	3	158	82*	39.50		1
B. Mullick	3	6	1	197	64	39.40		1
P.K. Dwevedi	7	11	–	428	80	38.90		3
S. Ramesh	10	18	1	655	146	38.52	2	3
V. Bhaskar	2	4	–	153	96	38.25		1
S.S. Upadhye	4	8	3	190	45	38.00		
S.S. Das	6	12	–	455	85	37.91		5
N.D. Modi	4	8	–	303	106	37.87	1	1
P.P. Maitrey	4	7	–	265	78	37.85		3
S.B. Saikia	3	5	–	227	59	37.83		3
A. Verma	8	12	1	413	162	37.54	1	2
R.D. Saini	5	7	1	225	74	37.50		2
S.B. Banger	9	16	2	524	122	37.42	1	2
R.R. Parida	8	14	2	447	111*	37.25	1	2
S.K. Yadav	3	5	–	181	70	36.20		2
D.N. Bundela	5	8	2	215	102*	35.83	1	1
R.R. Kumar	8	13	3	356	129*	35.60	1	1
R.J. Kanwat	4	5	–	178	68	35.60		2
C.M. Jha	4	8	–	283	63	35.60		2
K.K. Patel	8	12	1	389	79	35.36		3
Sahfiq Khan	8	15	–	530	95	35.33		4
S.C. Ganguly	3	6	1	173	66	34.60		1
D. Gandhi	9	16	–	549	182	34.31	1	3
A. Malhotra	10	13	1	409	120	34.08	1	3
U. Chatterjee	10	14	3	369	120	33.54	1	2
N.R. Mongia	4	8	–	268	152	33.50	1	
A.R. Kumble	4	7	1	201	88	33.50		1
S.S. Tanna	3	5	–	167	141	33.40	1	
A. Gupta	4	7	–	233	102	33.28	1	1
R. Naik	4	5	–	166	61	33.20		2
R.V.C. Prasad	5	10	2	265	141*	33.12	1	1
G.A. Shetty	10	17	–	563	116	33.11	1	3
R. Paul	8	12	–	397	100	33.08	1	1
H.S. Sodhi	9	13	3	330	120*	33.00	1	1
M.V. Rao	4	7	1	198	57	33.00		2
S.A. Shukla	8	12	–	394	145	32.83	1	3
S. Dogra	8	10	2	259	101*	32.37	1	1
V. Yadav	9	13	–	416	80	32.00		3
M.H. Parmar	4	8	–	256	134	32.00	1	2
J. Gokulkrishnan	6	8	2	192	104*	32.00	1	
H.A. Feroze	7	10	2	254	152*	31.75	1	
A.B. Kumar	8	11	1	317	139	31.70	1	1
B.K.P. Misquin	4	5	–	158	52	31.60		1
W.V.S. Laxman	8	14	–	441	78	31.50		5
S. Yadav	7	12	1	345	83	31.36		1
S.B. Tarun Kumar	7	11	2	282	57	31.33		1
A.V. Kale	12	16	1	470	150	31.33	1	2
N. Gaur	5	9	–	282	125	31.33	1	

Batting

	M	Inns	NO	Runs	HS	Av	100s	50s
S.J. Kalyani	4	6	1	156	35	31.20		
S. Kumar	9	15	1	431	105	30.78	1	1
Bhupinder Singh jnr	9	13	1	367	68	30.58		4
A.S. Kudva	9	15	2	393	82	30.23		3
R.V. Bharadwaj	8	15	–	453	116	30.20	1	3
R. Sharma	8	15	2	392	98	30.15		2
B. Khullar	6	11	2	270	75	30.00		2
R.K. Chauhan	12	17	6	330	54*	30.00		1
K.B.S. Naik	5	10	–	299	92	29.90		2
R. Puri	9	14	–	414	130	29.57	1	2
D. Sudhakar	5	9	1	236	69	29.50		2
A.R. Kapoor	8	10	2	236	53*	29.50		1
S. Sharma	10	13	2	324	83	29.45		2
V.R. Samant	4	7	–	206	89	29.42		1
A.C. Bedade	7	11	1	289	102*	28.90	1	1
C. Kumar	5	9	–	257	89	28.55		2
C.C. Williams	8	14	1	364	54	28.00		3
Raja Ali	6	9	–	252	70	28.00		3
N.P. Singh	10	15	4	306	74	27.81		2
S. Shankar	9	15	1	389	62	27.78		2
Samjay Sharma	2	4	–	109	55	27.28		1
K.K. Dixit	4	8	1	186	78	26.57		1
P.R. Mohapatra	9	18	2	418	102*	26.12	1	2
R.S. Dravid	5	9	–	235	56	26.11		1
R. Gill	3	6	–	156	79	26.00		1
A.J. Parmar	4	5	–	127	74	25.40		1
W.V. Raman	6	10	–	253	57	25.30		2
S.V. Bahutule	10	12	2	253	72	25.30		2
J. Motivaras	2	4	–	101	52	25.25		1
A.N. Kishore	9	15	1	353	47	25.21		
Z. Zuffri	8	13	–	327	108	25.15	1	2
M.S. Sabir	4	7	–	174	68	24.85	1	2
K. Burman	4	8	–	195	48	24.37		
P.S. Rawat	5	8	1	170	56	24.28		1
M. Yadav	4	7	1	144	44	24.00		
R.S. Sodhi	3	5	–	120	55	24.00		1
A. Sarkar	7	8	3	118	57*	23.60		1
J. Arun Kumar	5	9	–	212	93	23.55		1
Narinder Singh	4	8	1	164	37	23.42		
A. Sharma	4	5	–	117	63	23.40		1
P.K. Hedaoo	4	6	–	140	74	23.33		1
K. Bharatan	8	12	1	254	63	23.09		1
K.S.T. Sai	3	6	–	138	48	23.00		
F. Khalil	4	7	–	161	76	23.00		1
P. Jayachandra	8	16	–	358	84	22.37		2
A. Khatua	4	7	–	155	79	22.14		1
S.R. Tendulkar	4	8	–	176	61	22.00		1
I.R. Siddiqui	10	9	2	154	48*	22.00		
Rajib Sharma	3	6	1	109	92*	21.80		1
K.N. Balsubraman	9	15	–	326	52	21.73		1
Z. Hussain	9	13	3	212	97	21.20		1
B.N. Mehta	4	8	–	169	73	21.12		1
M. Prabhakar	5	6	–	125	44	20.33		
S. Verma	4	8	–	165	57	20.62		1
P.H. Patel	4	8	–	165	51	20.62		1
D.V. Kumar	3	6	1	103	32	20.60		
M. Kartik	6	9	–	185	74	20.55		1
R. Sridhar	8	12	–	243	58	20.25		1
M. Aslam	5	6	1	100	30	20.00		
P.K. Krishna Kumar	6	8	–	160	110	20.00	1	
C.A. Balekh	3	6	–	120	45	20.00		
S.A. Somasekhar	6	11	1	199	62*	19.90		1
S.A. Ankola	4	6	–	119	63	19.83		1
P.V. Shashikant	6	11	–	214	69	19.45		1
D. Charkraborty	5	9	–	175	111	19.44	1	1
A.H.M. Malam	3	6	–	115	47	19.16		
R.C.V. Kumar	4	7	–	134	35	19.14		
S. Kiran Kumar	5	7	–	134	59	19.14		1
A.S. Wassan	9	11	1	190	48	19.00		
A. Gera	8	9	2	132	27*	18.85		
M.S.K. Prasad	6	11	–	206	60	18.72		1
S.B. Joshi	7	12	1	206	72*	18.72		1
P. Jain	9	13	1	224	48	18.66		
K. Sriram	5	9	–	167	54	18.55		1
Venkatapathy Raju	9	14	6	146	36*	18.25		
R. Choudhury	4	8	–	144	67	18.00		1
V. Sharma	5	9	–	159	45	17.66		
S. Lahiri	4	8	–	138	54	17.25		2
Dhanraj Singh	8	12	1	187	41	17.00		
S. Manoj	8	13	1	202	47	16.83		

First-Class Averages (continued)

Batting

	M	Inns	NO	Runs	HS	Av	100s	50s
Sarabjit Singh	4	7	–	116	64	16.57		1
S. Subramaniam	8	10	2	132	40*	16.50		
V. Vardhan	6	9	1	131	39	16.37		
S. Mohanty	6	10	2	131	56	16.37		1
G. Gopal	7	11	–	179	48	16.27		
U.V. Gandhe	5	7	–	111	32	15.85		
P.L. Mhambrey	8	9	–	142	97	15.77		1
B. Ramprakasg	11	16	1	235	60	15.66		1
S.M. Kondhalkar	10	10	1	141	37	15.66		
R.L. Sanghvi	12	14	3	170	41	15.45		
F.V Rashid	9	14	1	200	63*	15.38		1
R. Sett	6	10	1	134	37	14.88		
Jaswant Rai	5	9	–	133	31	14.77		
P. Thakur	9	13	1	175	46	14.58		
S.B. Somasunder	8	15	–	218	70	14.53		1
M. Suresh Kumar	7	11	2	129	33	14.33		
M.B. Majithia	9	13	2	157	75	14.27		1
K. Obaid	10	13	–	182	55	14.00		1
V.Z. Yadav	6	11	–	153	37	13.90		
A.M. Raju	5	10	1	125	39	13.88		
H.R. Jadhav	6	9	1	109	32	13.62		
B. Vij	10	10	–	112	32	11.20		

(Qualification: 100 runs, average 10.00) (N. Bordoloi 151 not out, one match)

Bowling

	Overs	Mds	Runs	Wks	Av	Best	10/m	5/inn
J. Zaman	88.5	32	178	16	11.12	5/45		1
K.K. Parida	96	40	204	15	13.60	6/121		1
Sukhbinder Singh	183	51	435	31	14.03	7/99	2	4
T.B. Arothe	147.2	34	331	20	16.55	5/83		1
S.A. Roy	82.3	19	184	11	16.72	7/50		1
M. Prabhakar	117.5	38	271	16	16.93	4/31		
N. David	159.2	44	337	18	18.72	4/26		
I.A. Thakur	113.1	22	303	16	18.93	5/84		1
M. Kartik	175.3	70	310	16	19.37	6/28		1
P. Jain	333.2	79	879	44	19.97	7/72	1	4
D.T. Patel	81.4	19	201	10	20.10	4/63		
J. Srinath	127.3	33	356	17	20.94	6/21		1
J. Gokulkrishnan	266.1	68	594	28	21.21	7/54	1	1
B. Ramprakash	497.1	136	1136	53	21.43	8/25	2	6
Sukhbir Singh	259.2	65	591	27	21.88	4/32		
N.M. Kulkarni	444.3	145	904	41	22.04	6/75		5
A. Katti	196.1	85	464	21	22.09	4/67		
S.S. Raul	345.1	92	845	38	22.23	6/44	1	4
S.B. Joshi	234.4	68	615	27	22.77	6/51	1	3
A.R. Kumble	211.1	45	517	22	23.50	5/67		1
P. Thakur	400.1	60	1133	47	24.10	6/32	1	1
K. Obaid	367.2	86	948	39	24.30	7/74		4
Jaswant Rai	259	63	685	28	24.46	6/126		2
B. Vij	527.1	108	1449	58	24.98	7/55	3	6
N.D. Hirwani	409.1	106	1045	41	25.48	6/51		3
A.S. Wassam	335.4	70	1049	41	25.58	5/48		3
S.C. Oasis	190	50	487	19	25.63	4/59		
U. Chatterjee	459.3	138	1030	40	25.75	6/115		2
A. Kuruvilla	298	64	852	33	25.81	5/36		1
Venkatesh Prasad	116.3	28	311	12	25.91	6/104		1
M. Suresh Kumar	183.4	50	415	16	25.93	4/21		
D. Ganesh	279	38	961	37	25.97	6/84	1	4
G. Dutta	95.5	14	260	10	26.00	4/64		
S.V. Kamat	122	27	316	12	26.33	4/36		
S.T. Banerjee	123	33	264	10	26.40	3/23		
Y.C. Barde	89	13	264	10	26.40	3/60		
R.K. Chaudan	753.3	233	1588	60	26.46	7/52	2	7
C.T.K. Masood	191.5	46	453	17	26.64	5/53		1
B. Bharat	239.4	67	695	26	26.73	5/72		1
R. Ananth	216	60	485	18	26.94	4/72		
Venkatapathy Raju	359	121	767	28	27.39	6/64		1
W.D. Balaji Rao	131.2	24	331	12	27.58	5/47		1
U.V. Gandhe	106.1	24	276	10	27.60	4/32		
M.P. Patel	134.5	36	305	11	27.72	5/65		1
Harvinder Singh	155	40	445	16	27.81	6/36	1	2

Bowling

	Overs	Mds	Runs	Wks	Av	Best	10/m	5/inn
A. Verma	199.2	42	557	20	27.85	4/24		
Z. Hussain	305.5	39	902	32	28.18	5/31		2
A. Qayyum	83	13	284	10	28.40	5/110		1
H. Ramkishen	306.5	74	799	28	28.53	7/126		1
V. Vardan	177.3	38	486	17	28.58	4/51		
K. Chakradhar Rao	255.4	84	572	20	28.60	4/70		
R.A Swarup	324.4	58	832	29	28.68	5/121		3
S. Subramaniam	261	52	717	25	28.68	5/84		1
D. Mohanty	269	70	691	24	28.79	5/52		
K.V.P. Rao	438.1	110	1095	38	28.81	6/47		2
S.S. Hazare	139	26	377	13	29.00	5/29		2
I.R. Siddiqui	337.3	64	960	33	29.09	5/99		2
Sandeep Sharma	360	95	908	31	29.29	4/65		
S.V. Jedhe	298.5	66	734	25	29.36	5/47		1
R.R. Singh	107	18	295	10	29.50	2/26		
S. Mohanty	179.5	34	534	18	29.66	4/35		
D.K. Devenand	172.3	36	445	15	29.66	7/74		1
K.K. Dixit	108.2	22	327	11	29.72	3/51		
H. Yadav	138	28	422	14	30.14	7/80		1
P.K. Hedaoo	164.1	42	484	16	30.25	5/115		1
H.H. Kanitkar	271	60	642	21	30.57	3/41		
Robin Singh	302	58	931	30	31.03	6/89		2
M.V. Rao	106	15	373	12	31.08	7/59		1
N. Kalekar	162.2	32	480	15	32.00	5/104		1
S. Bajpai	160.5	50	386	12	32.16	3/49		
S.B. Banger	165.1	35	451	14	32.21	3/46		
K.N.A. Padmanabhan	415.1	96	1044	32	32.62	6/99		1
A.B. Kumar	502.0	123	1307	40	32.67	6/42		1
P.L. Mhambrey	227.4	53	590	18	32.77	5/34		1
S.A. Ankola	123	27	364	11	33.09	3/101		
Dhanraj Singh	156.4	31	472	14	33.71	4/37		
S.V. Bahutule	503.2	112	1316	39	33.74	4/25		
S. Khalid	216.1	35	473	14	33.78	5/54		1
R. Sridhar	219	61	587	17	34.52	3/155		
M.B. Majithia	337.4	105	727	21	34.61	6/59		1
R.L. Sanghvi	381	89	1114	32	34.81	6/75		2
F.K. Ghayas	199.1	42	664	19	34.94	4/54		
S. Mahesh	193	48	426	12	35.50	3/55		
M. Aslam	239.5	46	685	19	36.05	5/95		1
S. Chandramouli	198.2	50	478	13	36.76	3/46		
S.S. Lahore	430	117	993	27	36.77	4/84		
V.B. Jain	165.3	38	442	12	36.83	3/40		
N.P. Singh	313	72	885	24	36.87	3/66		
S.V. Ranjane	119	27	369	10	36.90	4/49		
M.S. Kulkarni	255.4	56	746	20	37.30	4/59		
A.R. Kapoor	272	52	804	21	38.28	5/94		1
H.S. Sodhi	224.5	31	656	17	38.58	4/46		
S. Pandey	114	19	390	10	39.00	5/106		1
Kanwaljit Singh	308	72	835	21	39.76	4/72		
D.J. Johnson	199.5	31	654	16	40.87	4/82		
A. Gera	212	46	532	13	40.92	5/133		1
A. Sarkar	202.1	42	618	15	41.20	5/50		1
H.J. Parsana	254.4	47	784	19	41.26	5/64		2
R. Pawar	153.1	26	463	11	42.09	5/93		1
P.K. Krishna Kumar	197.3	42	607	14	43.35	3/43		
B.N. Mehta	191	50	538	12	44.83	5/126		1
G.K. Pandey	230.5	64	501	11	45.54	3/27		
N. Chopra	351.3	66	961	21	45.76	6/78		1
Chaman Lal	192.1	37	506	11	46.00	3/93		
H. Patel	171.3	43	486	10	48.60	3/153		
V.N. Buch	233.5	47	690	11	62.72	3/62		

(Qualification: 10 wickets)

Leading Fielders

38 – S.K. Kulkarni (ct 34 / st 4); 35 – M.V. Mehra (ct 29 / st 6); 34 – S.M. Kondhalkar (ct 32 / st 2); 30 – Z. Zuffri (ct 27 / st 3); 28 – V. Dahiya (ct 24 / st 4); 25 – Sunil Kumar (ct 18 / st 7); 23 – H.A. Feroze (ct 17 / st 6), S.S. Karim (ct 16 / st 7) and Yuvraj Singh (ct 22 / st 1); 22 – V. Yadav (ct 18 / st 4); 20 – M.S. Mudgal (ct 17 / st 3); 19 – C.S. Pandit (ct 16 / st 3); 18 – G. Gopal (ct 14 / st 4), K.K. Patel (ct 15 / st 3) and R. Puri; 17 – S. Abbas Ali and K.S. More (ct 15 / st 2); 16 – A.A. Muzumdar; 15 – S.Y. Dhuri (ct 12 / st 3) and D. Gnandi

Pakistan

Within these pages in the last few years we have often suggested that, far from playing too much cricket, first-class cricketers do not play enough. Such a criticism could not be levelled at Pakistan's leading players in 1996-97. They followed a programme so punishing that one is amazed at how successfully they coped. Less than two weeks after the completion of their triumphant tour of England, they were engaged in a one-day series in Canada.

Wasim Akram, 257 not out for Pakistan against Zimbabwe in the first Test. He and Saqlain Mushtaq set a new eighth wicket record for Test cricket with a stand of 313. Wasim's innings was the highest by a number eight in a Test match. (Nigel French/ASP)

Zimbabwe Tour
New Zealand Tour
Quaid-e-Azam Trophy
Patron's Trophy

Seven days after the last of five matches in Toronto, Pakistan started their first game in the four-nation tournament in Kenya. They reached the final, and 11 days later they were entertaining Zimbabwe at Sheikhupura. Five days after the third and final one-day international against Zimbabwe they were in Sharjah for the Singer Champions' Trophy. They beat New Zealand in the final on 15 November and six days later the two teams began a Test match in Lahore.

The last of three one-day internationals against New Zealand was played on 8 December. Four days later, Pakistan arrived in Australia and on 12 December they met the host country in the first of eight qualifying matches in the World Series competition.

If the Pakistani players suffered from indigestion and grew sick of the sight of cricket balls and aeroplanes, they gave no indication of it as one success followed another. Significantly, too, a generation of very young cricketers of exceptional talent began to emerge and to prosper. Sadly, one cricketer of immense potential, fast bowler Barkatullah Khan, died of cancer at the age of 22.

Saqlain Mushtaq shared a record partnership with Wasim Akram, made his highest score in a Test match and took seven wickets in the game against Zimbabwe at Sheikhupura (Nigel French/ASP)

Zimbabwe Tour

12, 13 and 14 October 1996
at Montgomery Biscuit Factory, Sahiwal
Zimbabwe XI 307 for 7 dec. (D.L. Houghton 105, A. Flower 100 not out) and 203 for 8 dec. (G.W. Flower 75, C.B. Wishart 68 not out, Mohammad Hussain 4 for 68)
Pakistan Cricket Board XI 236 for 8 dec. (Azam Khan 70, Hasan Raza 58) and 238 for 9 (Mohammad Hussain 58 not out, A.R. Whittall 5 for 97)
Match drawn

Both teams could take satisfaction from this match. Dave Houghton, having been unavailable for the tour of Sri Lanka, returned to the Zimbabwe side and scored a century. He and Andy Flower shared a fourth wicket stand of 131. Andy Whittall took five second innings wickets with his off-breaks. Azam Khan, 20-year-old left-handed all-rounder Mohammad Hussain, and 15-year-old batsman Hasan Raza did well for the Board XI. Indeed, Hasan Raza displayed his prodigious talent with a 55-ball half-century. International recognition was soon to come his way.

Test Series

Pakistan v. Zimbabwe

Houghton may have returned for Zimbabwe, but their main strike bowler Heath Streak was back in Harare nursing a groin strain, and the attack suffered in his absence. Zimbabwe were welcomed to a new Test venue, Sheikhupura, and by two players new to Test cricket, Azam Khan and Shahid Nazir.

Quick bowler Shahid Nazir had been in the party that toured England, but his international recognition on the tour had been delayed until the last Texaco match. His selection ahead of Aqib Javed did not please the Sheikhupura crowd who were soon to show Wasim Akram their feelings, but Shahid fully justified his selection. When Zimbabwe won the toss and batted he took three wickets and ran out the dangerous Houghton.

The pitch was grassless, and Zimbabwe began confidently. Wasim trapped Dekker leg before at 33, and the 19-year-old Shahid dismissed Campbell with his third ball in Test cricket. Grant Flower, dropped by Moin Khan when 39 and Houghton took Zimbabwe to lunch at an impressive 100 for 2, but four wickets fell for 64 runs in the afternoon session. Having run out Houghton, Shahid Nazir returned to take the wickets of Andy Flower and Wishart with successive deliveries. This achievement rather mocked those spectators who had thrown stones on the outfield and twice held up play in protest at the non-inclusion of Aqib Javed.

At 142 for 6, Zimbabwe were in trouble, but Grant Flower remained calm and was unbeaten at the end of the day on 98, by which time, with the help of Paul Strang, he had taken his side to 240 for 6.

The Flower/Strang partnership was eventually worth 131, and Grant Flower's dedication was rewarded with a century. He hit 12 fours and a six, but his dismissal brought no collapse, although Andy Whittall went for 0. Paul Strang was on 60 when he was joined by his brother Bryan, and the pair added 87 in 18 overs. Twice dropped off the luckless Waqar, Paul Strang was on 99 when Bryan was bowled by Saqlain. Olonga survived three balls with men crowded round the bat, and Paul Strang reached the first century of his career. His unbeaten 106 came off 206 balls and was an innings of thought and sound judgement. Shahid Nazir bowled Olonga to finish with 5 for 54 on his Test debut, but Zimbabwe had reached a highly commendable score.

They were let down by some erratic new ball bowling, and Aamir Sohail and Saeed Anwar gave Pakistan a brisk start. Both fell to Paul Strang. Aamir was caught behind, and Shadab Kabir was spectacularly caught at extra cover off Andy Whittall. The pitch was dry and turning, and Paul Strang posed a threat. It was Olonga, however, who accounted for Ijaz Ahmed. Saeed Anwar was stumped off a googly, and Azam Khan fell to a similar delivery. When Salim Malik was bowled round his legs Pakistan were 183 for 6, and the close came six runs later. Paul Strang had enjoyed a memorable day.

Fortunes changed on the third day. Only one wicket fell before lunch, Moin caught at backward point to give Paul Strang a five-wicket haul to go with his century, but the rest of the day belonged to Wasim Akram and Saqlain Mushtaq. They took Pakistan to 392 without further loss.

Unbeaten on 144 at the end of the third day, Wasim Akram played a masterly innings. He never lapsed in concentration and selected his shots with great wisdom. Light rain delayed the start of the fourth day, but when play began Wasim continued to display watchful defence, and it was not until the score had reached 550 that Saqlain, who had batted with great maturity for his highest score in Test cricket, was bowled by Guy Whittall. Saqlain's 79 had occupied 358 balls, and he and Wasim Akram had established a record partnership for the eighth wicket in Test cricket of 313 in 110 overs. This was an incredible achievement when one considers that Pakistan were in deep trouble when the pair came together.

There were other records. Once he had reached his double century with a six, Wasim cut loose. He created a new Test record by hitting 12 sixes, three of them in one over off Paul Strang. He also hit 22 fours, and his unbeaten 257 was not only his career-best score, but the highest score by a number eight in Test cricket. He faced 370 balls and was at the crease for 489 minutes. His was a towering effort.

Before the close, Saqlain dismissed Dekker, and only two runs were added the next morning before Campbell was adjudged leg before to Waqar. Houghton and Grant Flower steadied the innings, but it was the Flower brothers – Grant 46 in 47 overs and Andy 18 off 120 balls – who made the match safe when the Zimbabwe innings threatened to crumble. Saqlain had a fine match, but Mushtaq Ahmed was much missed. Wasim Akram, inevitably, won the individual award. Never has it been more deserved.

Zimbabwe made two changes for the second Test. Matambanadzo and Mbangwa, both quick bowlers, made their debuts at the expense of Andy Whittall and Olonga. Matambanadzo had been named Everton after the great West Indian batsman, Everton Weekes. Pakistan also brought in two new Test caps, Mohammad Hussain, the left-handed all-rounder from Lahore, and Hasan Raza who, like Shahid Afridi, could only be given an estimated age of around 15

although earlier claims suggested that he was 14 years 227 days old when the match began. This would make him the youngest ever Test player.

Campbell again won the toss and chose to bat, but his judgement proved faulty. The pitch was surprisingly well grassed, and the Pakistan bowlers, Wasim Akram in particular, reaped a rich harvest. The Pakistan captain claimed his first wicket in the seventh over when he knocked back Grant Flower's off stump with a superb delivery. Unwisely, Wishart had been promoted to number three, and his inexperience was all too obvious when he played back to Waqar Younis and was leg before. Houghton now had to face the new ball on a pitch that was giving the home bowlers assistance, and he was bowled round his legs when he moved across his stumps to a Wasim cutter. Dekker lost patience and was out when he tried to hook, and Saqlain, introduced early into the attack, had Campbell caught behind.

After lunch, Wasim Akram returned to knock over Guy Whittall's off stump and to bowl Bryan Strang and Mbangwa with in-swingers. Paul Strang provided Mohammad Hussain with his first Test wicket, and Andy Flower, far too low at number six in this batting line up, was last man out when he attacked as he was running out of partners.

Matambanadzo and Mbangwa both took a wicket in their opening spells to lift Zimbabwe's spirits, but they were erratic in length and direction and Saeed Anwar punished them severely to move to a brisk fifty. Bryan Strang accounted for Salim Malik, and Hasan Raza was at the crease before the end of his first day in Test cricket. He batted with confidence, although troubled by Paul Strang's googly, and finished on 20. Saeed had 69, and, at 114 for 3, Pakistan were in command.

Saeed Anwar became Matambanadzo's second victim when he was caught at the wicket early on the second morning, and Hasan Raza's promising debut came to an end when he was caught at slip off Bryan Strang. Wasim Akram and Moin Khan batted responsibly, and Waqar Younis launched a violent attack at the end of the innings to take Pakistan to a first innings lead of 134.

When Waqar and Wasim reduced Zimbabwe to 23 for 3, it seemed that the match would soon be over, but, in 26 overs, Houghton and Campbell scored 113 to put Zimbabwe two runs ahead at the end of the second day.

Houghton had batted brilliantly, hitting 74 off 101 balls, hooking Wasim for a four and a six in the process, but Zimbabwe's hopes were dashed when he fell to Wasim's first ball of the third day. Campbell, too, failed to add to his overnight score and was caught at the wicket off Shahid Nazir's fourth delivery. Waqar and Wasim wrapped up the innings before lunch, and Saeed Anwar and Aamir Sohail scored the runs needed for victory without any problems.

Wasim Akram, 10 for 106, was named Man of the Match for the second time and was delighted with the positive cricket that his side had played. Pakistan still tend to suffer from lapses in concentration, but, at their best, they are a formidable combination and the equal to any other side in the world.

First Test Match – Pakistan v. Zimbabwe
17, 18, 19, 20 and 21 October 1996 at Sheikhupura Cricket Stadium

Zimbabwe

Batsman	First Innings		Second Innings	
G.W. Flower	c sub (Shahid Afridi), b Saqlain Mushtaq	110	(2) c Shadab Kabir, b Saqlain Mushtaq	46
M.H. Dekker	lbw, b Wasim Akram	14	(1) c Wasim, b Saqlain	13
A.D.R. Campbell (Capt)	lbw, b Shahid Nazir	8	lbw, b Waqar Younis	15
D.L. Houghton	run out	43	b Saqlain Mushtaq	65
*A. Flower	lbw, b Shahid Nazir	11	b Shahid Nazir	18
C.B. Wishart	lbw, b Shahid Nazir	0	b Shahid Nazir	10
G.J. Whittall	c Shadab, b Saqlain	0	c sub (Shahid Afridi), b Saqlain Mushtaq	32
P.A. Strang	not out	106	not out	13
A.R. Whittall	lbw, b Shahid Nazir	0	not out	0
B.C. Strang	b Saqlain Mushtaq	42		
H.K. Olonga	b Shahid Nazir	7		
Extras	b 9, lb 16, w 1, nb 8	34	b 11, lb 10, nb 8	29
Total		375	(for 7 wickets)	241

Pakistan

Batsman	First Innings	
Aamir Sohail	c A. Flower, b P.A. Strang	46
Saeed Anwar	st A. Flower, b P.A. Strang	51
Shadab Kabir	c Houghton, b A.R. Whittall	2
Ijaz Ahmed	lbw, b Olonga	9
Salim Malik	b P.A. Strang	52
Azam Khan	lbw, b P.A. Strang	14
*Moin Khan	c A.R. Whittall, b P.A. Strang	18
Wasim Akram (Capt)	not out	257
Saqlain Mushtaq	b G.J. Whittall	79
Waqar Younis	b G.J. Whittall	0
Shahid Nazir	c Dekker, b A.R. Whittall	0
Extras	b 10, lb 8, w 2, nb 5	25
Total		553

Bowler	O	M	R	W	O	M	R	W
Wasim Akram	28	9	58	1	5	–	16	–
Waqar Younis	22	3	90	–	20	3	60	1
Shahid Nazir	22	3	54	5	19	6	45	2
Saqlain Mushtaq	36.3	–	126	3	40	16	75	4
Aamir Sohail	6	–	22	–	11	6	12	–
Salim Malik					5	1	12	–

Bowler	O	M	R	W
Olonga	19	6	60	1
B.C. Strang	20	2	34	–
A.R. Whittall	45.2	7	146	2
P.A. Strang	69	12	212	5
G.J. Whittall	25	5	73	2
G.W. Flower	10	4	10	–

Fall of Wickets
1–33, 2–41, 3–119, 4–141, 5–141, 6–142, 7–273, 8–274, 9–361
1–13, 2–40, 3–124, 4–159, 5–177, 6–221, 7–232

Fall of Wickets
1–64, 2–77, 3–91, 4–142, 5–176, 6–183, 7–237, 8–550, 9–550

Umpires: Khizar Hayat & D.L. Orchard

Match drawn

Second Test Match – Pakistan v. Zimbabwe
24, 25 and 26 October 1996 at Iqbal Stadium, Faisalabad

Zimbabwe

Batsman	First Innings		Second Innings	
G.W. Flower	b Wasim Akram	15	lbw, b Wasim Akram	0
M.H. Dekker	c Moin Khan, b Wasim	19	lbw, b Waqar Younis	0
C.B. Wishart	lbw, b Waqar Younis	0	c Salim Malik, b Waqar	7
D.L. Houghton	b Wasim Akram	1	lbw, b Wasim Akram	74
A.D.R. Campbell (Capt)	c Moin Khan, b Saqlain	9	c Moin, b Shahid Nazir	51
*A. Flower	c Mohammad, b Shahid	61	c Saeed, b Waqar	23
G.J. Whittall	b Wasim Akram	9	lbw, b Shahid Nazir	0
P.A. Strang	c Salim, b Mohammad	3	b Waqar Younis	9
B.C. Strang	b Wasim Akram	1	not out	13
M. Mbangwa	b Wasim Akram	0	(11) lbw, b Wasim Akram	2
E. Matambanadzo	b Wasim Akram	0	(10) b Wasim Akram	7
Extras	b 4, lb 10, nb 1	15	lb 8, nb 6	14
Total		133		200

Pakistan

Batsman	First Innings		Second Innings	
Saeed Anwar	c A. Flower, b Matambanadzo	81	not out	50
Aamir Sohail	lbw, b Matambanadzo	2	not out	18
Ijaz Ahmed	c A. Flower, c Mbangwa	2		
Salim Malik	c A. Flower b B.C. Strang	18		
Hasan Raza	c Houghton, b B.C. Strang	27		
Wasim Akram (Capt)	b Mbangwa	35		
*Moin Khan	c A. Flower, b B.C. Strang	58		
Mohammad Hussain	run out	0		
Saqlain Mushtaq	not out	15		
Waqar Younis	b G.W. Flower	23		
Shahid Nazir	lbw, b P.A. Strang	1		
Extras	lb 4, nb 1	5	w 1	
Total		267	for no wicket	69

Bowler	O	M	R	W	O	M	R	W
Wasim Akram	20	8	48	6	18.4	4	58	4
Waqar Younis	11	6	13	1	15	3	54	4
Saqlain Mushtaq	15	5	28	1	7	1	33	–
Shahid Nazir	5.5	–	23	1	11	5	25	2
Mohammad Hussain	6	3	7	1	4	1	14	–
Salim Malik					2	–	8	–

Bowler	O	M	R	W	O	M	R	W
Matambanadzo	11	–	62	2	5	–	27	–
Mbangwa	17	1	67	2	7	3	14	–
B.C. Strang	18	6	53	3	4.5	1	20	–
G.J. Whittall	7	4	11	–				
P.A. Strang	24.1	8	66	1	2	–	8	–
G.W. Flower	2	–	4	1				

Fall of Wickets
1–22, 2–33, 3–34, 4–49, 5–55, 6–102, 7–111, 8–118, 9–129
1–0, 2–0, 3–23, 4–136, 5–136, 6–140, 7–169, 8–174, 9–198

Fall of Wickets
1–7, 2–10, 3–67, 4–127, 5–141, 6–194, 7–200, 8–235, 9–264

Umpires: Mahboob Shah & D.B. Cowie

Pakistan won by 10 wickets

One-Day International Series

Pakistan v. Zimbabwe

Hasan Raza, Gavin Rennie and Gary Brent made their first appearance in limited-over internationals in the first of the matches in the series. Zimbabwe elected to bat when they won the toss, and, in his first over, Wasim Akram had Houghton leg before to claim his 300th wicket in one-day internationals. He was the first bowler to achieve this feat. John Rennie and Campbell were soon out, and Zimbabwe were in trouble at 25 for 3. The Flower brothers saved the day with a partnership of 143 and Zimbabwe were able to present a challenging target. Pakistan began briskly, but they lost their way towards the end of their innings, and it was only the steadiness of Salim Malik which brought them victory with five balls to spare.

Pakistan surprisingly omitted Aamir Sohail from the second match and brought in Azam Khan and Abdul Razzak. Like Mbangwa of Zimbabwe, they were both playing in their first one-day internationals. Once again Zimbabwe decided to bat first when they won the toss, and once again they began badly. This time, in spite of Andy Flower's 51, there was no effective recovery. Facing a target of 196, Pakistan got off to a blistering start. Shahid Afridi revived memories of Kenya with eight fours and four sixes in his 66 which came off just 36 balls. He and Saeed Anwar had 100 on the board in 10.2 overs, and Ijaz Ahmed then joined Saeed to take Pakistan to victory in the 29th over.

Matambanadzo and Zahoor Elahi were the debutants in the final match which, sadly, had to be reduced to 40 overs because of crowd disturbances. Winning the toss and batting, Pakistan were 43 for 3 before Ijaz Ahmed and Azam Khan came together and added 151. With Moin hitting hard, Pakistan reached a formidable 264 in their 40 overs. Wasim led his men off the field when Abdul Razzak was struck by a missile, but peace was restored and Zimbabwe's target was reduced to 225 in 34 overs. It mattered little. Batting without skipper Campbell who had been injured while fielding, Zimbabwe lost their last eight wickets for 37 runs and crashed to defeat. Their main destroyer was Saqlain Mushtaq, who became the first spinner to perform the hat-trick in a one-day international. He is only the ninth bowler to have achieved this feat in this type of international, and four of the others have been Pakistanis.

Wasim Akram and Grant Flower were named as Men of the Series, a series totally dominated by Pakistan.

The only century of the limited-over series between Pakistan and Zimbabwe was hit by Ijaz Ahmed.
(David Munden/Sportsline)

16, 17 and 18 November 1996
at Montgomery Biscuit Factory, Sahiwal
New Zealanders 171 (Mohammad Zahid 6 for 54) and 211 for 7 dec. (B.A.Young 73)
Pakistan Cricket Board XI 193 for 7 dec. and 41 for 0
Match drawn

Within days of having met in Sharjah, New Zealand and Pakistan were now arrayed for battle in Pakistan. The New Zealand tour followed the same pattern as that undertaken by Zimbabwe, a warm-up first-class game, two Test matches and three one-day internationals. The match against the Board XI had little to commend it except for the performance of the pace bowler Mohammad Zahid. He had played against England 'A' in 1995–96 and had done well, and he had gone to Kenya to bolster a side hit by injuries. He had match figures of 8 for 94 against the New Zealanders and looked to be a good prospect.

First One-Day International – Pakistan v. Zimbabwe
30 October 1996 at Nawab Akbar Bughti Stadium, Quetta

Zimbabwe

G.W. Flower	c Shahid Afridi, b Salim Malik	91
D. L. Houghton	lbw, b Wasim Akram	0
J.A. Rennie	c Moin Khan, b Shahid Nazir	7
A.D.R. Campbell (Capt)	b Shahid Nazir	7
*A. Flower	c Shahid Nazir, b Saqlain Mushtaq	82
C.B. Wishart	c Wasim Akram, b Shahid Afridi	2
G.J. Whittall	run out	10
G.J. Rennie	run out	0
P.A. Strang	not out	13
G.B. Brent	b Saqlain Mushtaq	1
A.R. Whittall	not out	1
	b 5, lb 7, w 11	23
	50 overs (for 9 wickets)	237

	O	M	R	W
Wasim Akram	10	1	27	1
Shahid Nazir	7	–	28	2
Azhar Mahmood	4	–	17	–
Saqlain Mushtaq	8	–	40	2
Shahid Afridi	8	–	36	1
Aamir Sohail	6	–	40	–
Salim Malik	7	–	37	1

Fall of Wickets
1–1, 2–14, 3–25, 4–168, 5–175, 6–201, 7–206, 8–228, 9–235

Pakistan

Saeed Anwar	st A. Flower, b A.R. Whittall	26
Shahid Afridi	c G.J Rennie, b G.J. Whittall	28
Aamir Sohail	b J.A. Rennie	55
Ijaz Ahmed	c Houghton, b A.R. Whittall	17
Salim Malik	not out	72
Wasim Akram (Capt)	c Houghton, b A.R. Whittall	9
*Moin Khan	b G.J. Whittall	3
Hasan Raza	run out	11
Azhar Mahmood	not out	6
Saqlain Mushtaq		
Shahid Nazir		
	b 1, lb 5, w 6	12
	49.1 overs (for 7 wickets)	239

	O	M	R	W
J.A. Rennie	10	–	54	1
G.J. Whittall	9.1	–	48	2
Brent	5	–	29	–
A.R. Whittall	10	–	36	3
P.A. Strang	10	1	45	–
G.W. Flower	4	–	17	–
Campbell	1	–	4	–

Fall of Wickets
1–45, 2–73, 3–107, 4–160, 5–196, 6–200, 7–224

Umpires: Khizar Hayat & Shakeel Khan *Man of the Match:* Salim Malik

Pakistan won by 3 wickets

Second One-Day International – Pakistan v. Zimbabwe
1 November 1996 at Qaddafi Stadium, Lahore

Zimbabwe

G.W. Flower	b Shahid Nazir	6
M.H. Dekker	b Wasim Akram	18
A.D.R. Campbell (Capt)	lbw, b Shahid Nazir	1
D.L. Houghton	b Abdul Razzak	25
*A. Flower	c Ijaz Ahmed, b Abdul Razzak	51
G.J. Whittall	st Moin Khan, b Saqlain Mushtaq	9
P.A. Strang	run out	17
J.A. Rennie	c Azam Khan, b Saqlain	27
A.R. Whittall	not out	4
B.C. Strang	st Moin Khan, b Saqlain Mushtaq	6
M. Mbangwa	run out	11
	lb 12, w 5, nb 3	20
	49.1 overs	195

	O	M	R	W
Wasim Akram	9.1	2	26	1
Shahid Nazir	9	–	31	2
Abdul Razzak	7.3	1	29	2
Saqlain Mushtaq	10	–	46	3
Shahid Afridi	10	–	38	–
Salim Malik	3.3	–	13	–

Fall of Wickets
1–18, 2–27, 3–33, 4–61, 5–101, 6–127, 7–161, 8–172, 9–184

Pakistan

Saeed Anwar	not out	84
Shahid Afridi	b J.A Rennie	66
Ijaz Ahmed	not out	34
Salim Malik		
Hasan Raza		
Azam Khan		
Wasim Akram (Capt)		
*Moin Khan		
Saqlain Mushtaq		
Shahid Nazir		
Abdul Razzak		
	b 1, lb 9, w 1, nb 1	12
	28.4 overs (for 1 wicket)	196

	O	M	R	W
J.A. Rennie	5	–	29	1
Mbangwa	5.4	–	48	–
P.A. Strang	6	1	44	–
A.R. Whittall	5	–	26	–
G.J. Whittall	3	–	18	–
B.C. Strang	4	1	21	–

Fall of Wickets
1–100

Umpires: Mahboob Shah & Shakoor Rana *Man of the Match:* Shahid Afridi

Pakistan won by 9 wickets

Test Series

Pakistan v. New Zealand

New Zealand were beset with problems before the start of the first Test with Morrison returning home because of a persistent groin strain, and Gavin Larsen also forced home because of strained hamstring. Another New Zealand casualty was manager Earle Cooper, who flew home during the first Test for eye surgery. Pakistan's shock came on the morning of the match when Wasim Akram declared himself unfit due to a nagging shoulder injury. Pakistan gave first Test caps to Zahoor Elahi, who opened in place of Aamir Sohail, and Mohammad Wasim.

Lee Germon won the toss, and New Zealand batted, but, initially, all went the way of Pakistan. Both New Zealand openers were out with only 16 scored, and the one stand of any significance was that of 51 for the third wicket between Parore and Fleming. They were separated, and seven wickets fell for 50 runs before Doull and Patel shared a spirited last wicket stand of 38. It proved to be invaluable.

The pitch presented no problems, but Waqar Younis and Mushtaq Ahmed bowled splendidly, and now it was the turn of Simon Doull to show his prowess and bring New Zealand back into the game. At 21, he bowled Saeed Anwar, the acting captain, and eight runs later, Ijaz Ahmed was leg before to Cairns. Doull then had Inzamam caught at third

slip before accounting for both debutants, Zahoor Elahi and Mohammad Wasim. Pakistan were reeling at 37 for 5 and were thankful that the experience of Salim Malik and Moin Khan prevented any more disasters before play ended ten overs early because of bad light with the score on 52 for 5.

The Salim/Moin partnership had become worth 48 before Salim was caught at slip off Doull. Moin Khan now found another very useful partner in Saqlain Mushtaq, and the pair added 56. Vaughan gained leg before decisions against Moin and Waqar, and Pakisan lunched at 163 for 8. Saqlain and Mushtaq Ahmed hit vigorously in the afternoon before Vaughan finished the innings. Doull and Vaughan both returned their best figures in Test cricket, but Pakistan had a first innings lead of 36.

This began to seem a significant advantage when Mushtaq Ahmed dismissed both openers and Saqlain Mushtaq won a leg before decision against Parore to leave New Zealand on an uncertain 88 for 3 at the close.

Astle did not add to his overnight score, and Greatbatch went cheaply, but there followed a sixth wicket stand that changed the course of the match. The pair added 141 in 34.3 overs. Fleming provided the solidity that, so far, only Moin Khan had managed, while Cairns went on to the attack. He hit 93 off 91 and his innings included 12 fours and three sixes. When he became another leg before victim and Harris went immediately, Fleming was left to nurse the late order and see how many runs could be gathered. Most of his

Third One-Day International – Pakistan v. Zimbabwe

3 November 1996 at Arbab Niaz Stadium, Peshawar

Pakistan

Shahid Afridi	c J.A. Rennie, b Matambanadzo	0
Zahoor Elahi	c Houghton, b Matambanadzo	1
Ijaz Ahmed	c G.W. Flower,	
	b Matambanadzo	117
Hasan Raza	c G.J. Rennie, b Matambanadzo	12
Azam Khan	c P.A. Strang, b J.A. Rennie	72
Wasim Akram (Capt)	run out	1
Moin Khan	c P.A. Strang, b J.A. Rennie	34
Salim Malik	c A. Flower, b G.J. Whittall	0
Saqlain Mushtaq	run out	3
Shahid Nazir	not out	5
Abdul Razzak	not out	0
	lb 4, w 12, nb 3	19
	40 overs (for 9 wickets)	264

	O	M	R	W
Matambanadzo	8	–	32	4
J.A. Rennie	8	–	37	2
G.J. Whittall	8	–	64	1
A.R. Whittall	8	–	62	–
P.A. Strang	4	–	33	–
Dekker	4	–	32	–

Fall of Wickets
1–0, 2–18, 3–43, 4–194, 5–199, 6–231, 7–251, 8–256, 9–263

Zimbabwe

G.W. Flower	c Moin Khan, b Saqlain Mushtaq	77
M.H. Dekker	lbw, b Abdul Razzak	11
P.A. Strang	c Wasim Akram,	
	b Shahid Afridi	29
D.L. Houghton	c Moin Khan, b Shahid Afridi	6
*A. Flower	c Wasim Akram, b Salim Malik	1
G.J. Whittall	run out	0
G.J. Rennie	b Saqlain Mushtaq	6
J.A. Rennie	c Moin Khan, b Saqlain	0
A.R. Whittall	c Salim Malik, b Saqlain	0
E. Matambanadzo	not out	2
A.D.R. Campbell (Capt)	absent hurt	–
	lb 5, w 6, nb 4	15
	32.1 overs	147

	O	M	R	W
Wasim Akram	4	–	20	–
Shahid Nazir	6	–	16	–
Abdul Razzak	5	–	24	1
Saqlain Mushtaq	6.1	–	28	4
Shahid Afridi	7	–	25	2
Salim Malik	4	–	29	1

Fall of Wickets
1–34, 2–95, 3–110, 4–118, 5–119, 6–143, 7–143, 8–143, 9–147

Umpires: Shakoor Rana & Javed Akhtar   *Man of the Match:* Ijaz Ahmed

Pakistan won by 77 runs (target reduced)

Mohammad Wasim – a century on Test debut against New Zealand in Lahore. (Shaun Botterill/Allsport)

support was from Doull, who had an outstanding match, and the last wicket realised 49. Doull was stumped off Mushtaq who finished with 6 for 84 and ten wickets in the match, and Fleming was left unbeaten for a composed and vital 92. He had very much deserved a century.

Pakistan were left with more than two days in which to score 276 to win. By the end of the third day, their hopes of victory had all but disappeared. Simon Doull was their main destroyer. In the space of five balls, he trapped Saeed Anwar leg before and bowled Ijaz Ahmed when he left his leg stump unguarded. Inzamam-ul-Haq was well caught at second slip off Cairns. Night-watchman Saqlain fell to Vaughan without scoring, and Young took a low catch off the bowling of Patel to remove Zahoor Elahi. New Zealand had completed a magnificent day and, with Pakistan on 46 for 5, they were on the brink of a famous victory.

Victory was harder to achieve than had been imagined, especially as Salim Malik was an early victim on the fourth day, caught behind off Doull. New Zealand were held up by an innings of great character from the young Mohammad Wasim, who became only the fourth Pakistani batsman to score a century on the occasion of his Test debut. He and Moin Khan added 75 for the seventh wicket, and

Mushtaq Ahmed stayed while 76 runs were scored for the eighth wicket. From a lunch score of 94 for 6, Pakistan moved to 211 for 8 at tea, and even a win against all the odds seemed possible.

Shortly before tea, Waqar was bowled by Patel, who then claimed the last wicket, that of Shahid Nazir. Mohammad Wasim was left unbeaten on 109. He had reached his century in 198 minutes off 151 deliveries, and he had driven and cut with gusto and assurance. His innings was some consolation to Pakistan who had suffered their first home defeat at the hands of New Zealand for 27 years. Simon Doull was named Man of the Match, as he deserved to be, and both sides were less than pleased with the standard of umpiring, which had upheld 15 leg before appeals in the match and which had lacked consistency.

New Zealand were delighted to name an unchanged side for the second Test, but Pakistan suffered a further blow when Waqar Younis reported unfit. He was replaced by a quick bowler new to Test cricket, the tall 20-year-old Mohammad Zahid who had done so well for the Board XI before the first Test. Pakistan made another change in preferring the medium-pacer Mohammad Akram to off-spinner Saqlain Mushtaq.

Saeed Anwar won the toss and asked New Zealand to bat first. The game was delayed for 20 minutes because no new balls of sufficient standard had been provided, nor, seemingly, did anyone want to take the blame for the oversight. Balls were finally purchased from a local shop. There was to be another hold-up after tea when Germon and Fleming complained that the sun was shining straight into their eyes.

On a flawless pitch, New Zealand lost three wickets before lunch. Two of the wickets went to debutant Mohammad Zahid who, settling after early nerves, bowled with pace and aggression and deceived both Vaughan and Parore with in-swingers. Bryan Young was out when he swept at Mushtaq Ahmed and missed and was clearly leg before. It was Mushtaq's 100th Test victim.

Astle went soon after lunch as Mushtaq weaved his spell and soon New Zealand had plummeted to 111 for 7. They were salvaged by Fleming and Germon who put on 81 for the eighth wicket. Fleming batted with elegance and authority for 109 minutes and hit 11 fours before falling to a Mushtaq googly. New Zealand closed on 215 for 8, with Germon unbeaten on 45.

The ninth wicket partnership was worth 49 before Germon, who hit eight fours, was caught behind off Mohammad Zahid. Patel was last out, the sixth victim of Mushtaq Ahmed, who had now taken 16 wickets in three innings against New Zealand. Mohammad Zahid finished with an impressive and deserved 4 for 64.

By the end of the day, Pakistan, 269 for 2, had taken an iron grip on the game. They had begun badly, losing Zahoor Elahi, caught at slip in the second over, but Saeed Anwar and Ijaz Ahmed came together in a record stand of 262 in which they routed the New Zealand bowling. Ijaz Ahmed reached his century immediately after tea when he cracked boundaries to cover and mid-wicket off Astle and then took the single that brought him to three figures. Runs had come at a brisk pace, and Ijaz's sixth Test hundred had occupied 219 minutes and included a six and 16 fours. He was out in the penultimate over of the day when he was adjudged leg before to Cairns. He seemed to indicate to the umpire that he had touched the ball, with the result that he was fined 50 per cent of his match fee. Saeed Anwar ended the day unbeaten on 130 ,which included 19 fours. He had reached his fourth Test century off 146 balls in 204 minutes.

Saeed was finally out after facing 214 balls in 305 minutes and adding another boundary to his overnight quota. Although Inzamam-ul-Haq went quickly, Mushtaq Ahmed and Salim Malik consolidated Pakistan's strong position with a stand of 84. The New Zealand bowling was tighter and more aggressive than it had been earlier in the innings. Cairns, in particular, performed well, although he became the second player to lose half his match fee when he reacted angrily to umpire Javed Akhtar's decision not to uphold a leg before appeal against Salim Malik when the batsman was on 27.

Inspired bowling by Simon Doull set up New Zealand's victory over Pakistan in Lahore.
(David Munden/Sportsline)

Needing to score 181 to make Pakistan bat again, New Zealand were well served by Young and Vaughan who remained unbeaten at the close with 69 to their credit. The pair seemed untroubled on the fourth morning, but, at 82, Vaughan was leg before to Mohammad Zahid, who hails from the same area as Waqar Younis, and the floodgates opened. By lunch, New Zealand had been reduced to 137 for 6, and the first five of those wickets had gone to Mohammad Zahid, who bowled with passion and intelligence. Parore was trapped by a ball that cut back, and Young, having hit six fours in 174 minutes, slashed to gully. Germon and Astle were deceived by yorkers of genuine pace, and when Greatbatch tried to force Mushtaq off the back foot only to be caught at cover New Zealand's defeat was imminent.

The match was over in less than an hour after lunch. In the first over of the afternoon, Fleming, suffering from gastric influenza, was caught at the wicket, and Cairns was later bowled round his legs. Mohammad Zahid then claimed the 27th and 28th lbw decisions of the two-match series to give Pakistan victory by an innings.

Mohammad Zahid finished with match figures of 11 for 130, an astonishing performance by the 20-year-old debutant. Pakistan had found another star.

First Test Match – Pakistan v. New Zealand
21, 22, 23 and 24 November 1996 at Qaddafi Stadium, Lahore

New Zealand

	First Innings		Second Innings	
J.T.C. Vaughan	lbw, b Shahid Nazir	3	(2) b Mushtaq Ahmed	11
B.A. Young	lbw, b Waqar Younis	8	(1) c Wasim, b Mushtaq	36
A.C. Parore	c Salim, b Saqlain	37	lbw, b Saqlain Mushtaq	15
S.P. Fleming	c Salim, b Mushtaq	19	not out	92
N.J. Astle	lbw, b Mushtaq Ahmed	0	lbw, b Mushtaq Ahmed	3
M.J. Greatbatch	c Wasim, b Waqar	18	b Waqar Younis	1
C.L. Cairns	c Inzamam-ul-Haq, b Mushtaq	4	lbw, b Mushtaq Ahmed	93
C.Z. Harris	b Waqar Younis	16	c Salim, b Mushtaq	0
*L.K. Germon (Capt)	lbw, b Waqar Younis	0	lbw, b Mushtaq Ahmed	11
D.N. Patel	lbw, b Mushtaq Ahmed	26	lbw, b Shahid Nazir	0
S.B. Doull	not out	15	st Moin Khan, b Saqlain	26
	b 4, lb 5	9	b 6, lb 16, nb 1	23
		155		**311**

Pakistan

	First Innings		Second Innings	
Saeed Anwar (Capt)	b Doull	8	lbw, b Doull	0
Zahoor Elahi	c Fleming, c Doull	22	c Young, b Patel	6
Ijaz Ahmed	lbw, b Cairns	3	b Doull	8
Inzamam-ul-Haq	c Astle, b Doull	0	c Young, b Cairns	14
Salim Malik	c Young, b Doull	21	(6) c Germon, b Doull	21
Mohammad Wasim	b Doull	0	(7) not out	109
*Moin Khan	lbw, b Vaughan	59	(8) c Germon, b Astle	38
Saqlain Mushtaq	lbw, b Vaughan	23	(5) c Fleming, b Vaughan	0
Waqar Younis	lbw, b Vaughan	2	(10) b Patel	1
Mushtaq Ahmed	c Germon, b Vaughan	25	(9) c Fleming, b Patel	15
Shahid Nazir	not out	13	c Harris, b Patel	13
	b 5, lb 7, nb 3	15	b 8, lb 8, nb 2	18
		191		**231**

	O	M	R	W	O	M	R	W
Waqar Younis	15	3	48	4	15	6	26	1
Shahid Nazir	8	3	15	1	16	1	84	1
Mushtaq Ahmed	22.1	4	59	4	32	7	84	6
Saqlain Mushtaq	12	3	24	1	22.2	4	95	2

	O	M	R	W	O	M	R	W
Cairns	19	5	79	1	16	5	62	1
Doull	16	3	46	5	16	4	39	3
Harris	1	–	3	–	6	2	20	–
Vaughan	12.5	2	27	4	14	5	48	1
Patel	7	2	24	–	15.1	6	36	4
Astle					4	1	10	1

Fall of Wickets
1–6, 2–16, 3–67, 4–70, 5–73, 6–83, 7–102, 8–102, 9–117
1–46, 2–59, 3–85, 4–88, 5–101, 6–242, 7–242, 8–262, 9–262

Fall of Wickets
1–21, 2–29, 3–34, 4–37, 5–37, 6–85, 7–141, 8–143, 9–164
1–0, 2–8, 3–25, 4–26, 5–42, 6–60, 7–135, 8–211, 9–219

Umpires: Shakoor Rana & R.B. Tiffin

New Zealand won by 44 runs

Second Test Match – Pakistan v. New Zealand
28, 29, 30 November and 1 December 1996 at Pindi Cricket Stadium, Rawalpindi

New Zealand

	First Innings		Second Innings	
B.A. Young	lbw, b Mushtaq	39	c Zahoor, b Zahid	61
J.T.C. Vaughan	lbw, b Mohammad Zahid	12	lbw, b Mohammad Zahid	27
A.C. Parore	lbw, b Mohammad Zahid	3	lbw, b Mohammad Zahid	6
S.P. Fleming	c Moin Khan, b Mushtaq	67	(7) c Moin Khan, b Shahid	4
N.J. Astle	c Moin Khan, b Mushtaq	11	lbw, b Mohammad Zahid	4
M.J. Greatbatch	c Saeed, b Mushtaq	2	c Saeed, b Mushtaq	19
C.L. Cairns	c Wasim, b Mushtaq	9	(8) b Mushtaq Ahmed	11
C.Z. Harris	lbw, b Mohammad Zahid	1	(9) lbw, b Zahid	14
*L.K. Germon (Capt)	c Moin Khan, b Zahid	55	(4) b Mohammad Zahid	0
D.N. Patel	c Ijaz, b Mushtaq	21	lbw, b Mohammad Zahid	0
S.B. Doull	not out	1	not out	4
	b 4, lb 14, nb 10	28	lb 7, w 1, nb 13	21
		249		**168**

Pakistan

	First Innings	
Saeed Anwar (Capt)	c Doull, b Cairns	149
Zahoor Elahi	c Fleming, b Cairns	2
Ijaz Ahmed	lbw, b Cairns	125
Mushtaq Ahmed	lbw, b Harris	42
Inzamam-ul-Haq	c Vaughan, b Harris	1
Salim Malik	b Cairns	78
Mohammad Wasim	b Cairns, b Doull	5
*Moin Khan	lbw, b Doull	2
Shahid Nazir	c and b Cairns	10
Mohammad Zahid	lbw, b Astle	0
Mohammad Akram	not out	0
	lb 14, nb 2	16
		430

	O	M	R	W	O	M	R	W
Mohammad Zahid	21	5	64	4	20	3	66	7
Shahid Nazir	9	3	23	–	7	1	19	1
Mohammad Akram	12	1	48	–	7	2	11	–
Mushtaq Ahmed	30	3	87	6	22	7	52	2
Salim Malik	2	–	9	–	2	–	13	–

	O	M	R	W
Doull	31	7	86	2
Cairns	30.4	2	137	5
Vaughan	17	1	72	–
Astle	9	1	31	1
Patel	15	4	33	–
Harris	24	7	57	2

Fall of Wickets
1–33, 2–43, 3–69, 4–77, 5–87, 6–110, 7–111, 8–192, 9–241
1–82, 2–105, 3–109, 4–112, 5–119, 6–137, 7–137, 8–163, 9–163

Fall of Wickets
1–6, 2–268, 3–290, 4–291, 5–375, 6–394, 7–398, 8–419, 9–420

Umpires: L.H. Barker & Javed Akhtar

Pakistan won by an innings and 13 runs

First One-Day International – Pakistan v. New Zealand
4 December 1996 at Jinnah Municipal Stadium, Gujranwala

Pakistan

Saeed Anwar	run out	27
Zahoor Elahi	c Fleming, b Kennedy	5
Ijaz Ahmed	c Harris, b Doull	3
Inzamam-ul-Haq	c Germon b Astle	14
Salim Malik	not out	73
*Moin Khan	c Fleming, b Cairns	3
Wasim Akram (Capt)	c Patel, b Harris	52
Shahid Afridi	c Patel, b Harris	16
Saqlain Mushtaq	c Young, b Astle	10
Mushtaq Ahmed	not out	3
Waqar Younis		
	b 1, lb 3, w 17, nb 1	22
	46 overs (for 8 wickets)	228

New Zealand

B.A. Young	b Waqar Younis	58
C.M. Spearman	run out	6
A.C. Parore	lbw, b Mushtaq Ahmed	35
S.P. Fleming	st Moin Khan, b Saqlain	36
C.L. Cairns	c Moin Khan, b Waqar Younis	36
N.J. Astle	c Salim Malik, b Saqlain	11
D.N. Patel	st Moin Khan, b Saqlain Mushtaq	0
S.B. Doull	run out	0
C.Z. Harris	c Shahid Afridi, b Saqlain	20
*L.K. Germon (Capt)	c sub (Mohammad Zahid), b Saqlain	2
R.J. Kennedy	not out	0
	lb 2, w 8, nb 3	13
	45.4 overs	217

	O	M	R	W
Doull	9	–	33	1
Kennedy	9	–	47	1
Cairns	10	–	49	1
Astle	9	1	31	2
Harris	6	–	40	2
Patel	3	–	24	–

	O	M	R	W
Wasim Akram	9	–	44	–
Waqar Younis	9	–	48	2
Mushtaq Ahmed	9	–	35	1
Saqlain Mushtaq	9.4	–	44	5
Shahid Afridi	9	–	44	–

Fall of Wickets
1–11, 2–19, 3–60, 4–61, 5–71, 6–162, 7–182, 8–197

Fall of Wickets
1–26, 2–104, 3–117, 4–177, 5–185, 6–185, 7–186, 8–200, 9–213

Umpires: Khizar Hayat & Javed Akhtar   *Man of the Match*: Salim Malik   **Pakistan won by 11 runs**

Second One-Day International – Pakistan v. New Zealand
6 December 1996 at Jinnah Stadium, Sialkot

Pakistan

Saeed Anwar	run out	91
Zahoor Elahi	b Cairns	86
Ijaz Ahmed	c Spearman, b Vaughan	59
Inzamam-ul-Haq	st Germon, b Astle	2
Wasim Akram (Capt)	b Harris	4
Shahid Afridi	b Harris	2
*Moin Khan	c Astle, b Harris	1
Waqar Younis	st Germon, b Harris	0
Saqlain Mushtaq	b Harris	2
Mushtaq Ahmed	not out	5
Salim Malik	not out	1
	lb 8, w 14, nb 2	24
	47 overs (for 9 wickets)	277

New Zealand

B.A. Young	c Moin Khan, b Waqar Younis	5
C.M. Spearman	c Moin Khan, b Wasim Akram	0
A.C. Parore	c Ijaz Ahmed, b Saqlain Mushtaq	37
S.P. Fleming	c and b Shahid Afridi	88
C.L. Cairns	b Saqlain Mushtaq	10
N.J. Astle	c Ijaz Ahmed, b Salim Malik	20
C.Z. Harris	lbw b Wasim Akram	22
*L.K. Germon (Capt)	lbw, b Shahid Afridi	2
J.T.C. Vaughan	c Moin Khan, b Wasim Akram	13
S.B. Doull	c sub (Mohammad Wasim), b Waqar	1
R.J. Kennedy	not out	7
	b 9, lb 3, w 12, nb 2	26
	42.1 overs	231

	O	M	R	W
Doull	8	1	60	–
Kennedy	3	–	24	2
Cairns	8	1	35	1
Vaughan	9	1	55	1
Harris	10	–	42	5
Astle	9	–	53	1

	O	M	R	W
Wasim Akram	8.1	–	43	3
Waqar Younis	6	–	32	2
Saqlain Mushtaq	8	–	54	2
Mushtaq Ahmed	10	–	42	–
Shahid Afridi	7	–	40	2
Salim Malik	2.5	–	8	1
Ijaz Ahmed	0.1	–	0	–

Fall of Wickets
1–177, 2–225, 3–240, 4–247, 5–252, 6–260, 7–261, 8–269, 9–276

Fall of Wickets
1–3, 2–27, 3–125, 4–146, 5–170, 6–190, 7–195, 8–213, 9–216

Umpires: Khizar Hayat & Mahboob Shah   *Man of the Match*: Saeed Anwar   **Pakistan won by 46 runs**

Third One-Day International – Pakistan v. New Zealand
8 December 1996 at National Stadium, Karachi

Pakistan

Saeed Anwar	c Young, b Vaughan	16
Zahoor Elahi	b Hart	51
Inzamam-ul-Haq	st Germon, b Hart	7
Ijaz Ahmed	not out	73
Mohammad Wasim	c and b Harris	8
Wasim Akram (Capt)	not out	66
Shahid Afridi		
*Moin Khan		
Saqlain Mushtaq		
Mushtaq Ahmed		
Mohammad Zahid		
	lb 5, w 5, nb 3	13
	50 overs (for 4 wickets)	234

New Zealand

B.A. Young	c Wasim Akram, b Shahid Afridi	32
N.J. Astle	run out	60
A.C. Parore	c Moin Khan, b Wasim Akram	47
S.P. Fleming	not out	48
C.L. Cairns	not out	25
C.Z. Harris		
M.J. Greatbatch		
*L.K. Germon (Capt)		
M.N. Hart		
J.T.C. Vaughan		
S.B. Doull		
	b 1, lb 10, w 6, nb 6	23
	45.1 overs (for 3 wickets)	235

	O	M	R	W
Doull	4	–	23	–
Vaughan	10	3	59	1
Cairns	9	–	45	–
Astle	8	2	27	–
Hart	10	1	33	2
Harris	9	–	42	1

	O	M	R	W
Wasim Akram	8	–	36	1
Mohammad Zahid	6	–	41	–
Mushtaq Ahmed	10	–	49	–
Saqlain Mushtaq	10	–	43	–
Shahid Afridi	8.1	1	39	1
Ijaz Ahmed	1	–	6	–
Saeed Anwar	2	–	10	–

Fall of Wickets
1–38, 2–62, 3–103, 4–126

Fall of Wickets
1–96, 2–99, 3–183

Umpires: Shakeel Khan & Mahboob Shah   *Man of the Match*: N.J. Astle

New Zealand won by 7 wickets

One-Day Series

Pakistan *v.* New Zealand

Cricket can be as cruel as it can be strange. Having become the first Pakistani cricketer to take ten wickets on his Test debut, Mohammad Zahid was omitted from the side for the first of the one-day internationals. Pakistan elected to play three spinners on a ground that seemed ideally suited to pace bowling. The error was compounded when Wasim Akram who, like Waqar Younis, was returning to the side without having proved his fitness in domestic cricket, decided to bat first on a damp pitch. Kennedy and Doull grasped the opportunity offered them. Zahoor Elahi could do nothing with a delivery that reared and kicked and was caught in the slips as he fended the ball away, and Ijaz was hurried into a shot and was caught at point. Saeed's fine run of form appeared to be continuing until he ran himself out, although it must be said that Harris's pick up and direct hit on the stumps was fielding of the highest quality. Inzamam was upset by the run out and edged Astle to the keeper while Moin fell to the menacing Cairns. At 71 for 5, Pakistan were sinking fast, but Wasim Akram saw no demons in the pitch and blasted three sixes and three fours in his 52 out of a

Mushtaq Ahmed took 18 wickets in two Test matches against New Zealand. (Nigel French/ASP)

partnership of 91 with Salim Malik who, having received valuable assistance from Shahid Afridi and Saqlain Mushtaq, hit Harris for six off the last ball of the Pakistan innings.

New Zealand got away to a brisk start, but Inzamam's magnificent throw shattered the stumps when Spearman backed up too far. Parore and Young, 58 off 93 balls, looked comfortable, and Fleming and Cairns maintained momentum and looked likely to win the match. Cairns hit Waqar and Shahid Afridi for sixes and made 36 off 28 balls before edging to Moin Khan. Now Saqlain Mushtaq drew the profit for his accuracy and composure under fire. He restricted the scoring so that, with three balls remaining, New Zealand needed 11 to win. Harris went for a massive hit that would have carried for six had not Shahid Afridi taken an outstanding running catch just inside the ropes to win the match.

A crowd of 25,000 packed into the Jinnah Stadium in Sialkot for the second match of the series, a sharp contrast to the very poor attendances at the Test matches. Vaughan for Patel was the only change from the sides that had played at Gujranwala. Pakistan took control from the start with Saeed Anwar and Zahoor Elahi scoring 177 for the first wicket. The Pakistan vice-captain adopted a responsible role, while Zahoor was given free rein to play his shots. Ijaz Ahmed gave the innings further impetus with 59 off 57 balls. He hit two sixes and four fours to the delight of his home crowd. The rest were sacrificed in the scramble of quick runs as the overs were running out.

New Zealand began disastrously, but Fleming played with great assurance, adding 118 with Parore. Wasim led his side off the field in protest at the behaviour of part of the crowd. The interruption did not please Germon and certainly disturbed Fleming when he was going well. Fleming showed great flair and hit ten fours, but once he was out at 146, the New Zealand cause was lost. Saqlain followed his best performance in a one-day international in the first match with two vital wickets, Parore and Cairns, in this second game, which gave New Zealand the series.

A near-capacity crowd of close to 50,000 emphasised once again that while interest in Test cricket is waning rapidly, the one-day game reigns supreme. Mohammad Wasim and Mohammad Zahid played in their first limited-over internationals as Waqar Younis and Salim Malik stood down. Greatbatch and Hart replaced Spearman and Kennedy in the New Zealand line-up. Pakistan won the toss and batted.

Zahoor Elahi gave another impressive exhibition of exciting stroke-play, but the real fireworks in the Pakistan innings came in an unbroken partnership of 108 between Ijaz Ahmed and Wasim Akram. They took 68 runs off the last five overs of the innings.

New Zealand responded in kind as Young and Astle shared a thrilling opening stand of 96. Young hit 32 off 38 balls. He was caught off Shahid Afridi, and three balls later Astle was run out after hitting 60 off 69 deliveries with a six and four fours. Parore, Fleming and Cairns maintained the aggression, and New Zealand won with 4.5 overs to spare. Saeed Anwar and Stephen Fleming were named Men of the Series.

Quaid-e-Azam Trophy

4, 5, 6 and 7 October 1996
at National Stadium, Karachi
Lahore 253 (Zahoor Elahi 124, Ali Gohar 6 for 55) and 331 (Shahid Nawaz 62, Shahid Anwar 57, Ali Gohar 4 for 81, Athar Laeeq 4 for 81)
Karachi Blues 379 (Mahmood Hamid 94, Asif Mujtaba 66, Nadeem Khan 59, Shoaib Mohammad 54, Mohammad Hussain 4 for 86) and 218 for 6 (Manzoor Akhtar 62, Azam Khan 56)
Karachi Blues won by 4 wickets
Karachi Blues 12 pts, Lahore 0 pts

at Bahawalpur Stadium, Bahawalpur
Bahawalpur 112 (Aamir Sohail jnr 51, Salman Raza 5 for 13) and 244 (Sher Ali 52, Naeem Tayyab 4 for 55)
Karachi Whites 160 (Murtaza Hussain 4 for 67) and 48 (Murtaza Hussain 4 for 27)
Bahawalpur won by 148 runs
Bahawalpur 10 pts, Karachi Whites 0 pts

Consistent batting in the limited-over series against New Zealand from Zahoor Elahi, and for Lahore. (Shaun Botterill/Allsport)

at KRL Ground, Rawalpindi
Rawalpindi 299 (Asif Mahmood 62, Raja Afaq 52, Aqib
Javed 5 for 51, Bilal Rana 4 for 135)
Islamabad 187 for 6 (Asif Ali 58, Zaheer Abbasi 50 not out)
Match drawn
No points

at Arbab Niaz Stadium, Peshawar
Peshawar 322 (Jahangir Khan snr 77, Wajatullah Wasti 67,
Wasim Yousufi 65, Nadeem Afzal 5 for 69) and 262 for 7
(Wasim Yousufi 100 not out, Saadat Gul 4 for 53)
Faisalabad 258 (Akram Raza 77 not out, Mohammad
Ramzan 51, Kabir Khan 6 for 64)
Match drawn
Peshawar 2 pts, Faisalabad 0 pts

Karachi Blues began the defence of their title in fine form.
Lahore were troubled by Ali Gohar's medium pace in both
innings, and only Zahoor Elahi's 124 off 159 balls saved
them from total disintegration after they had been put in to
bat. Karachi's innings was given substance by Mahmood
Hamid and impetus by Nadeem Khan who, coming in at
number nine, hit 59 off 46 deliveries.

  Bahawalpur brought about a remarkable reversal of
fortune to beat Karachi Whites. They trailed by 48 on the
first innings but won by a huge margin. There was no play
possible on the first day, and 16 wickets fell on the second,
which ended with the Whites on 45 for 6. Their last three
wickets realised 92 runs on the third morning, and
Bahawalpur lost two wickets in clearing off the arrears. At
109 for 7, they looked beaten, but their last three wickets
brought 135 runs with Faisal Elahi making an unbeaten 42
in a last wicket stand of 75. Karachi Whites then crumpled
in under 37 overs.

  Rain totally ruined the match in Rawalpindi and
restricted play to ten overs on the first day in Peshawar. The
teams concentrated on first innings points, but Wasim
Yousufi made the second century of his career off 132 balls.

at CRA Ground, Islamabad
Peshawar 523 (Jahangir Khan snr 147, Akhtar Sarfraz 87,
Wajahatullah 86, Wasim Yousufi 84, Azhar Mahmood
4 for 118)
Islamabad 203 (Raj Hans 106, Kabir Khan 8 for 70) and
277 (Azhar Mahmood 68, Mohammad Nawaz 65,
Bilal Rana 56, Arshad Khan 6 for 74)
Peshawar won by an innings and 43 runs
Peshawar 12 pts, Islamabad 0 pts

at KRL Ground, Rawalpindi
Rawalpindi 148 (Shahid Javed 56 not out, Akram Raza 4
for 48) and 159 (Akram Raza 5 for 49)
Faisalabad 272 (Bilal Ahmed 78, Javed Iqbal 60, Shoaib
Akhtar 5 for 58, Mohammad Riaz 4 for 77) and 36 for 2
Faisalabad won by 8 wickets
Faisalabad 12 pts, Rawalpindi 0 pts

Karachi Blues continued their dominance with a crushing
victory over Bahawalpur. Athar Laeeq, medium pace, took
ten wickets in a match for the second time in his career,
while Mahmood Hamid notched his 17th century.

  Karachi Whites, too, had a resounding win, but the
honours of the match in Lahore went to the home side's all-
rounder Manzoor Elahi. The former Test cricketer returned
the best bowling figures of his career with his medium pace,
8 for 43, and, with four wickets in the second innings, had
his best match figures. He then hit 57 off 63 balls but still
finished on the losing side.

  Jahangir Khan snr and Akhtar Sarfraz began the
match in Islamabad with a stand of 240 for Peshawar's first
wicket. Jahangir hit a maiden first-class century. Left-arm
medium-pacer Kabir Khan made a claim for a Test recall
with the best bowling figures of his career, and the off-
breaks of Arshad Khan proved too much for Islamabad in
the second innings.

  The off-breaks of Test veteran Akram Raza played a
major part in Faisalabad's win over Rawalpindi.

10, 11, 12 and 13 October 1996
at National Stadium, Karachi
Bahawalpur 128 (Athar Laeeq 5 for 35) and 361
(Aamir Sohail jnr 93, Bilal Moin Khilji 83, Saifullah 57,
Athar Laeeq 5 for 86)
Karachi Blues 458 (Mahmood Hamid 157, Asif Mujtaba
63, Murtaza Hussain 5 for 151) and 32 for 0
Karachi Blues won by 10 wickets
Karachi Blues 12 pts, Bahawalpur 0 pts

at Qaddafi Stadium, Lahore
Karachi Whites 224 (Manzoor Elahi 8 for 43) and 283
(Aamer Hanif 82, Manzoor Elahi 4 for 79)
Lahore 102 (Baqar Rizvi 5 for 33) and 226 (Manzoor Elahi
57, Shahid Anwar 52, Aamer Hanif 4 for 53)
Karachi Whites won by 179 runs
Karachi Whites 12 pts, Lahore 0 pts

16, 17, 18 and 19 October 1996
at Karachi CA Stadium, Karachi
Karachi Blues 123 (Salman Fazal 6 for 42) and 187
(Hasan Raza 96, Iqbal Imam 7 for 71)
Karachi Whites 233 (Mohammad Masroor 93 not out,
Nadeem Khan 6 for 79) and 81 for 0
Karachi Whites won by 10 wickets
Karachi Whites 12 pts, Karachi Blues 0 pts

at Bahawalpur Stadium, Bahawalpur
Lahore 219 (Zahoor Elahi 58, Murtaza Hussain 5 for 84,
Mohammad Zahid 4 for 61) and 271 (Shahid Nawaz 94,
Murtaza Hussain 4 for 104)
Bahawalpur 108 (Mohammad Asif 5 for 20,
Mohammad Hussain 5 for 30) and 122 (Bilal Moin Khilji
52 not out, Mohammad Asif 5 for 33, Mohammad Hussain
5 for 86)

Lahore won by 260 runs
Lahore 12 pts, Bahawalpur 0 pts

at CRA Ground, Islamabad
Islamabad 342 (Bilal Rana 69, Raj Hans 63,
Qaiser Mahmood 57, Akram Raza 4 for 71, Naved Nazeer
4 for 106) and 226 (Mohammad Nawaz 62, Ihsan Butt 60)
Faisalabad 205 (Azhar Mahmood 7 for 65) and 210
(Mohammad Saleem 71, Fahad Khan 4 for 63)
Islamabad won by 153 runs
Islamabad 12 pts, Faisalabad 0 pts

at Arbab Niaz Stadium, Peshawar
Peshawar 309 (Akhtar Sarfraz 104 not out,
Shakeel Ahmed 56, Idrees Baig 56, Shoaib Akhtar 4 for 114)
and 164 (Jahangir Khan snr 75, Shoaib Akhtar 5 for 74)
Rawalpindi 260 (Shahid Javed 65, Mohammad Wasim 63,
Kabir Khan 6 for 100)
Match drawn
Peshawar 2 pts, Rawalpindi 0 pts

Karachi Whites caused the first major upset of the season when they beat their sister club, the Blues, in two days. Young Hasan Raza batted splendidly in the Blues' second innings, but Iqbal Imam's off-breaks proved decisive. Mohammad Masroor hit a career best unbeaten 93 off 130 balls.

Mohammad Asif and Mohammad Hussain blended their spin, off-breaks and slow left arm respectively, to capture ten wickets each as Lahore overwhelmed Bahawalpur, while medium-pacer Azhar Mahmood set up Islamabad's win over Faisalabad with the best bowling performance of his career.

Rain limited play on the second day in Peshawar and allowed none at all on the third, but there was time for more good bowling by Kabir Khan. Akhtar Sarfraz made an unbeaten 104 off 115 deliveries.

22, 23, 24 and 25 October 1996
at United Bank Sports Complex, Karachi
Karachi Blues 138 (Aqib Javed 5 for 25, Azhar Mahmood
4 for 40) and 233 (Basit Ali 83, Saeed Azad 66,
Azhar Mahmood 6 for 94, Aqib Javed 4 for 61)
Islamabad 254 (Zaheer Abbasi 69, Mohammad Nawaz
62, Athar Laeeq 4 for 90) and 121 for 7 (Ali Gohar
6 for 70)
Islamabad won by 3 wickets
Islamabad 12 pts, Karachi Blues 0 pts

at Qaddafi Stadium, Lahore
Lahore 285 (Zahoor Elahi 81) and 284 (Manzoor Elahi 75
not out, Mansoor Rana 59, Shoaib Akhtar 5 for 129)
Rawalpindi 252 (Naseer Ahmed 80, Ata-ur-Rehman 5 for
87, Naeem Ashraf 4 for 82) and 252 for 7 (Mohammad
Wasim 100, Naseer Ahmed 58, Ata-ur-Rehman 4 for 72)
Match drawn
Lahore 2 pts, Rawalpindi 0 pts

at Arbab Niaz Stadium, Peshawar
Peshawar 216 (Akhtar Sarfraz 53, Murtaza Hussain 5 for
43, Azhar Shafiq 5 for 83) and 165 (Azhar Shafiq 5 for 61)
Bahawalpur 189 (Sher Ali 53, Kabir Khan 5 for 52) and
197 for 2 (Sher Ali 123 not out)
Bahawalpur won by 8 wickets
Bahawalpur 10 pts, Peshawar 0 pts

at National Stadium, Karachi
Karachi Whites 479 (Iqbal Salim 207, Ali Haider 124,
Nadeem Butt 5 for 108, Naseer Shaukat 5 for 157) and
231 for 5 dec. (Aamer Hanif 80 not out)
Faisalabad 358 (Mohammad Amjad 77, Ijaz Ahmed 63,
Mohammad Nawaz 58, Bilal Ahmed 54, Aamer Hanif 4 for
49) and 238 for 5 (Mohammad Ramzan 66)
Match drawn
Karachi Whites 2 pts, Faisalabad 0 pts

Karachi Blues suffered a second defeat and gave way to the Whites at the top of the table. Azhar Mahmood's second ten-wicket haul in successive matches brought about the destruction of the Blues, who, through Ali Gohar, nearly achieved a remarkable victory.

Set a target of 318 in 63 overs, Rawalpindi fell well short in spite of Mohammad Wasim's maiden first-class century, but Bahawalpur turned the tables on Peshawar thanks to a brilliant unbeaten 123 off 154 balls from Sher Ali. Bahawalpur hit 197 in under 40 overs. Azhar Shafiq's fine medium-pace bowling had brought them back into the game after they trailed on the first innings.

The highlight of the game at the National Stadium was a fifth wicket partnership of 240 between Iqbal Salim and Ali Haider that took Karachi Whites to an impregnable position against Faisalabad. The runs came in 223 minutes. Iqbal's double century was the first of his career, and Ali Haider reached a maiden first-class hundred.

28, 29, 30 and 31 October 1996
at Pindi Cricket Stadium, Rawalpindi
Karachi Blues 303 (Basit Ali 88, Naeem Akhtar 5 for 45)
and 166 (Mohammad Akram 5 for 57, Shoaib Akhtar
4 for 75)
Rawalpindi 253 (Mohammad Wasim 105, Haaris A. Khan
5 for 56) and 218 for 5 (Tassawar Hussain 75,
Mohammad Wasim 66)
Rawalpindi won by 5 wickets
Rawalpindi 10 pts, Karachi Blues 0 pts

at Lahore CA Ground, Lahore
Lahore 493 (Zahoor Elahi 153, Mujahid Jamshed 129,
Shahid Anwar 70, Bilal Rana 6 for 179)
Islamabad 171 (Naveed Ahmed 72, Mushtaq Ahmed 6
for 66) and 183 (Mohammad Nawaz 52, Mushtaq Ahmed
4 for 88)
Lahore won by an innings and 139 runs
Lahore 12 pts, Islamabad 0 pts

Pakistan's new pace bowling star Mohammad Akram.
(Ross Kinnaird/Allsport)

Karachi Whites consolidated their place at the top of the table with an easy win over Peshawar. Aamer Hanif enjoyed a good all-round match and hit the tenth century of his career.

Naseer Shaukat also had a good all-round match and played a major part in Faisalabad's win over Bahawalpur.

3, 4, 5 and 6 November 1996
at National Stadium, Karachi
Peshawar 269 (Akhtar Sarfraz 77, Wajahatullah 51, Imranullah 6 for 75) and 259 (Akhtar Sarfraz 69, Jahangir Khan snr 50 not out, Nadeem Khan 4 for 77)
Karachi Blues 312 (Asif Mujtaba 116, Ahmer Saeed 74, Kabir Khan 5 for 75) and 217 for 5 (Basit Ali 84, Ahmer Saeed 55)
Karachi Blues won by 5 wickets
Karachi Blues 12 pts, Peshawar 0 pts

at Iqbal Stadium, Faisalabad
Faisalabad 226 (Naved Nazir 53, Ata-ur-Rehman 4 for 63, Imran Tahir 4 for 83) and 175 (Naseer Shaukat 56, Ata-ur-Rehman 5 for 56)
Lahore 296 (Intikhab Alam 82, Tahir Mahmood 52, Saeed Ajmal 4 for 72) and 106 for 5
Lahore won by 5 wickets
Lahore 12 pts, Faisalabad 0 pts

at CRA Ground, Islamabad
Bahawalpur 114 (Bilal Rana 6 for 26) and 222 (Saifullah 54, Bilal Rana 5 for 55)
Islamabad 166 (Khalid Butt 4 for 27, Murtaza Hussain 4 for 78) and 172 for 5 (Zaheer Abbasi 52, Mohammad Zahid 4 for 68)
Islamabad won by 5 wickets
Islamabad 12 pts, Bahawalpur 0 pts

at Asghar Ali Shah Stadium, Karachi
Rawalpindi 251 (Shakeel Ahmed 66, Ali Hussain Rizvi 5 for 83) and 162 (Naeem Akhtar 72, Aamer Hanif 4 for 55)
Karachi Whites 190 (Shoaib Akhtar 4 for 46, Shakeel Ahmed 4 for 53) and 103 (Naeem Akhtar 5 for 37)
Rawalpindi won by 121 runs
Rawalpindi 12 pts, Karachi Whites 0 pts

at National Stadium, Karachi
Peshawar 236 (Mohammad Salam 90, Aamer Hanif 5 for 57) and 166 (Ali Hussain Rizvi 4 for 60)
Karachi Whites 289 (Aamer Hanif 134, Ali Haider 59, Kabir Khan 4 for 62) and 114 for 1 (Moin-ul-Atiq 68 not out)
Karachi Whites won by 9 wickets
Karachi Whites 12 pts, Peshawar 0 pts

at Iqbal Stadium, Faisalabad
Faisalabad 244 (Naseer Shaukat 70 not out, Mohammad Ramzan 68, Mohammad Zahid 4 for 48, Azhar Shafiq 4 for 57) and 191 (Ijaz Mahmood 56, Azhar Shafiq 5 for 58)
Bahawalpur 108 (Naseer Shaukat 6 for 51) and 239 (Azhar Shafiq 60)
Faisalabad won by 88 runs
Faisalabad 12 pts, Bahawalpur 0 pts

Karachi Blues suffered their third defeat in a row, losing to Rawalpindi after leading by 50 runs on the first innings. Mohammad Wasim hit his second century in successive innings to keep Rawalpindi in touch, and the Blues then collapsed against Mohammad Akram and Shoaib Akhtar. A third wicket stand of 141 between Mohammad Wasim and Tassawar Hussain put Rawalpindi on the road to victory.

Lahore welcomed the great leg-spinner Mushtaq Ahmed back to their side briefly, and he helped complete victory over Islamabad by taking 10 for 154. Lahore were given a wonderful start by openers Zahoor Elahi and Mujahid Jamshed, who hit 281 in 265 minutes.

The return of Asif Mujtaba brought success back to Peshawar. He hit 116 in 243 minutes and shared a third wicket stand of 192 with Ahmer Saeed. Basit Ali, something of a forgotten figure in Pakistan cricket, hit 84 off 69 balls as the Blues swept to victory on the final day.

Lahore gained a convincing win over Faisalabad and were much indebted to the pace of Ata-ur-Rehman. Needing 106 to win, they reached their target in 17.5 overs.

The left-arm spin of Bilal Rana was the crucial factor in Islamabad's victory over Bahawalpur, while Naeem

Akhtar's all-round cricket brought Rawalpindi a most surprising win over Karachi Whites.

9, 10, 11 and 12 November 1996
at Iqbal Stadium, Faisalabad
Faisalabad 184 (Naseer Shaukat 72, Ali Gohar 5 for 61) and 174 (Fida Hussain 55, Imranullah 4 for 51, Ali Gohar 4 for 72)
Karachi Blues 82 (Naseer Shaukat 5 for 23, Saadat Gul 5 for 35) and 218 (Asif Mujtaba 58, Naseer Shaukat 5 for 43)
Faisalabad won by 58 runs
Faisalabad 12 pts, Karachi Blues 0 pts

at Arbab Niaz Stadium, Peshawar
Lahore 103 (Sohail Idrees 55, Ijaz Elahi 5 for 27, Arshad Khan 4 for 28) and 53 (Kabir Khan 5 for 29, Ijaz Elahi 4 for 23)
Peshawar 319 (Wajatullah 77, Kabir Khan 57, Imanullah 8 for 109)
Peshawar won by an innings and 163 runs
Peshawar 12 pts, Lahore 0 pts

at Bahawalpur Stadium, Bahawalpur
Rawalpindi 188 (Naseer Ahmed 89 not out, Murtaza Hussain 5 for 77) and 281 (Naseer Ahmed 89, Mohammad Wasim 77, Murtaza Hussain 4 for 108)
Bahawalpur 175 (Azhar Shafiq 50, Iftikhar Asghar 4 for 32, Tauqir Hussain 4 for 63) and 151
Rawalpindi won by 144 runs
Rawalpindi 12 pts, Bahawalpur 0 pts

at CRA Stadium, Islamabad
Karachi Whites 181 (Ghulam Abbas 4 for 53) and 215 (Sohail Jaffer 72, Raj Hans 5 for 74)
Islamabad 127 (Rashid Hanif 7 for 36) and 256 (Ahsan Butt 88, Zaheer Abbasi 56, Naeem Tayyab 6 for 88)
Karachi Whites won by 13 runs
Karachi Whites 12 pts, Islamabad 0 pts

Karachi Blues were caught on a bad wicket and succumbed to the bowling of Naseer Shaukat and Saadit Ali in 31.4 overs. In their second innings, they lost their last six wickets for 18 runs.

Lahore, too, were trapped on a crumbling surface and were bowled out in 17.2 overs by Kabir Khan and Ijaz Elahi.

Rawalpindi gained their third win in succession but could not find a way into the semi-finals. Islamabad, on the other hand, qualified for the last four in spite of being beaten by Karachi Whites for whom Rashid Hanif returned his best bowling figures.

Qualifying Table

	P	W	L	D	Pts
Karachi Whites	7	4	2	1	50
Lahore	7	3	3	1	38
Islamabad	7	3	3	1	36
Faisalabad	7	3	2	2	36
Karachi Blues	7	3	4	–	36
Rawalpindi	7	3	1	3	34
Peshawar	7	2	3	2	28
Bahawalpur	7	2	5	–	20

Semi-Finals

16, 17, 18 and 19 November 1996
at Asghar Ali Stadium, Karachi
Karachi Whites 554 (Iqbal Saleem 182, Nasir Ali Khan 167, Rashid Hanif 50, Saeed Ajmal 7 for 220)
Faisalabad 237 (Mohammad Salim 107, Kashif Ibrahim 5 for 29) and 198 (Mohammad Younis 50, Naeem Tayyab 5 for 47, Rashid Hanif 4 for 48)
Karachi Whites won by an innings and 119 runs

at Pindi Cricket Stadium, Rawalpindi
Lahore 301 (Sohail Idrees 55, Bilal Rana 5 for 59) and 38 for 1
Islamabad 299 (Ahsan Butt 77, Bilal Rana 63, Ijaz Khan 4 for 64)
Match drawn
Lahore qualified on first innings lead

Career-best batting performances from Iqbal Saleem and Nasir Ali Khan who shared a fourth wicket stand of 301, put Karachi Whites into a winning position against Faisalabad. Saeed Ajmal bore the brunt of the Faisalabad attack, sending down 65 overs of his off-breaks to capture 7 for 220.

The other semi-final was badly affected by the weather with the third day totally washed out. Bilal Rana battled bravely for Islamabad, and he was last out, caught off Ijaz Khan with just three needed for the first innings lead.

Quaid-e-Azam Trophy Final

23, 24 and 25 November 1996
at Makli Cricket Ground, Thatta
Karachi Whites 242 (Masood Anwar 5 for 81) and 120 (Abdul Razzaq 7 for 51)
Lahore 214 (Shahid Nawaz 75) and 149 for 9 (Shahid Nawaz 81, Kashif Ibrahim 5 for 37)
Lahore won by 1 wicket

The Makli ground had staged no first-class match nor any game of importance until the England 'A' side played there in November 1995, and it proved to be less than suitable for the Quaid-e-Azam final. Shahid Nawaz won the toss and asked Karachi Whites to bat. They lost their third wicket with the score at 100, but no batsman was able to establish himself. Shahid Afridi, batting at number seven, hit a typical 30 off 36 balls, but the innings lacked substance.

Lahore found batting equally difficult with only Shahid Nawaz mastering the conditions, playing a captain's innings. Batting a second time, Karachi struggled against the medium pace of Abdul Razzaq, and only the boldness of Ali Haider, 25 off 24 balls, and Shahid Afridi, 23 off 27, saw them past 100.

Needing 149 to win, Lahore were again splendidly served by Shahid Nawaz, who hit 81 in just over two hours. He found a brave partner in Ahsan Raza who stayed for 108 minutes to score 20 and to help Shahid to add 85 after six wickets had gone for 47. In spite of this, when the ninth wicket fell, Lahore were still four short of victory, and it was Abdul Razzaq who made the winning runs. The game finished with two of its allotted days unused. Shahid Nawaz was named Man of the Match.

Aqib Javed forced his way back into the Pakistan side with some inspired bowling for Allied Bank. He finished the season with 50 wickets at 17.04 runs each.
(David Munden/Sportsline)

Patron's Trophy

16, 17, 18 and 19 November 1996
at Defence Stadium, Karachi
Allied Bank 349 (Manzoor Akhtar 124, Ijaz Ahmed jnr 67, Rameez Raja 53, Sajjad Akbar 4 for 94) and 204 for 9 dec. (Mohammad Nawaz 83, Mohsin Kamal 4 for 43)
PNSC 260 (Mohammad Zahid 4 for 44) and 157 for 9 (Sajid Shah 50)
Match drawn
Allied Bank 2 pts, PNSC 0 pts

at KRL Ground, Rawalpindi
ADBP 146 (Shahzad Butt 5 for 42) and 221 for 6 (Mansoor Rana 76)
United Bank 331 (Saleem Elahi 75, Wasim Yousufi 51, Mohammad Asif 4 for 75)
Match drawn
United Bank 2 pts, ADBP 0 pts

at United Bank Sports Complex, Karachi
PIA 325 (Rizwan-uz-Zaman 91, Asif Mujtaba 83, Shoaib Mohammad 54, Kabir Khan 4 for 83) and 187 for 2 (Ghulam Ali 101 not out, Rizwan-uz-Zaman 50)
Habib Bank 356 (Mujahid Jamshed 102, Tahir Rasheed 73, Shakeel Ahmed 69, Asif Mujtaba 5 for 60)
Match drawn
Habib Bank 2 pts, PIA 0 pts

at National Stadium, Karachi
Customs 341 (Azhar Shafiq 123, Mohammad Javed 4 for 70) and 148 (Azhar Shafiq 52, Shahid Anwar 6 for 2)
National Bank 422 (Shahid Anwar 105, Sajid Ali 69, Shahid Tanvir 64, Mohammad Javed 52, Nadeem Iqbal 4 for 134) and 69 for 3
National Bank won by 7 wickets
National Bank 12 pts, Customs 0 pts

Somewhat perversely the Patron's Trophy began before the Quaid-e-Azam competition had finished. Allied Bank were thwarted by PNSC after dominating the match at the Defence Stadium. Needing 294 to win, PNSC were 66 for 7 before Sajid Shah joined Sajjad Akbar in a stand worth 86. More importantly, Sajid Shah held out for more than two hours and although both he and Sajjad were out within four runs of each other, the final pair had only two balls to survive.

United Bank, too, dominated in Rawalpindi, but were forced to settle for a draw, while Habib Bank narrowly gained a first innings lead against PIA. Rizwan-uz-Zaman and Shoaib Mohammad began PIA's innings with a 145-run partnership, but the batting fell away after Asif Mujtaba's 83. Shakeel Ahmed and Moin-ul-Atiq scored 105 for Habib Bank's first wicket before five wickets fell for two runs. Mujahid Jamshed and Tahir Rasheed halted the slide.

The only outright winners in the first round of matches were National Bank, who owed their victory almost entirely to their skipper Shahid Anwar. He hit 105 off 169 balls and shared an opening stand of 146 with Sajid Ali. In their second innings, Customs had reached 145 for 3 when Shahid began to bowl his medium pace. In 4.5 overs he took six wickets for two runs, and the last seven wickets went down for three runs.

22, 23, 24 and 25 November 1996
at National Stadium, Karachi
ADBP 461 for 7 dec. (Mujahid Hameed 187, Mansoor Rana 117, Manzoor Elahi 66)
PNSC 306 (Majid Saeed 85, Sher Ali 73, Shoaib Akhtar 5 for 90) and 260 for 3 (Majid Saeed 115 not out, Nasir Wasti 84)
Match drawn
ADBP 2 pts, PNSC 0 pts

at United Bank Sports Complex, Karachi
Allied Bank 358 (Ijaz Ahmed jnr 150, Aamer Hanif 52, Shahzad Butt 5 for 114) and 170 for 3 dec. (Aamir Sohail 59, Aamer Hanif 57)
United Bank 235 (Mohammad Ramzan 73, Mohammad Akram 6 for 56) and 219 for 7 (Ata-ur-Rehman 4 for 53)
Match drawn
Allied Bank 2 pts, United Bank 0 pts

at Defence Stadium, Karachi
Customs 184 (Aamer Iqbal 57, Nadeem Ghauri 4 for 39) and 375 (Azam Khan 70, Naved Latif 62, Nadeem Ghauri 4 for 71)
Habib Bank 316 (Mujahid Jamshed 120, Shakeel Ahmed 67, Tahir Rasheed 54, Ali Hussain Rizvi 6 for 123) and 100 for 2
Match drawn
Habib Bank 2 pts, Customs 0 pts

at Asghar Ali Shah Stadium, Karachi
National Bank 203 (Zafar Iqbal 79, Mohammad Zahid 6 for 49) and 131 (Zafar Iqbal 54, Mohammad Zahid 4 for 59)
PIA 289 (Sohail Jaffar 62, Asif Mujtaba 59, Naeem Tayyab 5 for 55) and 66 for 1
PIA won by 9 wickets
PIA 12 pts, National Bank 0 pts

Mujahid Hameed's career best score and a fourth wicket partnership of 209 with Mansoor Rana took ADBP to a declaration against PNSC, who were forced to follow on but saved the game comfortably. United Bank, too, managed a draw with Allied Bank after trailing by 123 runs on the first innings.

Customs trailed by 132 on the first innings but batted consistently at the second attempt to set Habib Bank a target of 244 in 25 overs, an impossible task.

PIA managed an outright victory. They were indebted to the pace bowling of Mohammad Zahid who took ten wickets in a match for the first time, although a few days later he was to perform even more sensationally in a Test match. Their batting owed much to Asif Mujtaba and Sohail Jaffar who added 103 for the fourth wicket. Asif, PIA's captain, remains an enigmatic figure, an outstandingly consistent performer in domestic cricket who has yet to do himself justice at international level.

28, 29, 30 November and 1 December 1996
at Bahawalpur Stadium, Bahawalpur
Allied Bank 113 (Mohammad Asif 4 for 15) and 150 (Ahsan Butt 64)
ADBP 133 (Arshad Khan 5 for 52, Aamer Nazir 4 for 27) and 131 for 3
ADBP won by 7 wickets
ADBP 12 pts, Allied Bank 0 pts

at Quaid-e-Azam Stadium, Sahiwal
PNSC 206 (Mohammad 4 for 51) and 182 (Mohammad Hussain 6 for 81)
United Bank 348 (Basit Ali 100, Saleem Elahi 59, Mohammad Hussain 55 not out) and 41 for 3
United Bank won by 7 wickets
United Bank 12 pts, PNSC 0 pts

at Montgomery Biscuit Factory, Sahiwal
Customs 202 (Haaris A. Khan 50 not out) and 97 (Asif Mujtaba 4 for 30)
PIA 170 (Shahid Ali 5 for 36) and 130 for 4
PIA won by 6 wickets
PIA 12 pts, Customs 0 pts

at Multan CA Stadium, Multan
Habib Bank 299 (Salman Fazal 6 for 62) and 22 for 1
National Bank 76 (Kabir Khan 4 for 16) and 341 (Akhtar Sarfraz 135, Nadeem Ghauri 7 for 101)
Habib Bank won by 9 wickets
Habib Bank 12 pts, National Bank 0 pts

Uncertain pitches brought outright results in all four matches in the third round. In Bahawalpur, 16 wickets fell on the opening day, and the run-rate throughout the match never exceeded two-and-a-half an over. Mohammad Hussain's left-arm spin brought him ten wickets for United Bank against PNSC, and Basit Ali hit a fine century in difficult conditions. He and Saleem Elahi put on 157 after two wickets had gone for 22.

Customs slumped to 97 all out in their second innings, dismissed in 45 overs, after leading PIA by 32 runs on the first innings. Nadeem Ghauri's left-arm spin gave Habib Bank the advantage after National Bank staged a brave fight-back in Multan.

4, 5, 6 and 7 December 1996
at Bohran Wali Ground, Faisalabad
Allied Bank 111 (Nadeem Khan 6 for 35) and 327
(Aamir Sohail 132, Ijaz Ahmed jnr 81, Asif Mujtaba 5 for 74,
Wasim Haider 4 for 27)
PIA 324 (Asif Mujtaba 100, Aamir Sohail 4 for 76) and
117 for 2 (Ghulam Ali 68 not out)
PIA won by 8 wickets
PIA 12 pts, Allied Bank 0 pts

at Sheikhupura Stadium
Habib Bank 391 (Moin-ul-Atiq 129, Tahir Rasheed 70,
Murtaza Hussain 4 for 89) and 286 for 8 (Shakeel Ahmed
123, Shahid Hussain 5 for 83)
PNSC 284 (Sajjad Akbar 110, Kabir Khan 4 for 87)
Match drawn
Habib Bank 2 pts, PNSC 0 pts

at Lahore CA Ground, Lahore
United Bank 168 (Iqbal Imam 71 not out, Athar Laeeq
6 for 57) and 296 (Mohammad Ramzan 112,
Wasim Yousufi 52, Salman Fazal 5 for 102)
National Bank 195 (Shahid Anwar 64) and 119
(Tauseef Ahmed 5 for 36)
United Bank won by 150 runs
United Bank 12 pts, National Bank 0 pts

at Railway Stadium, Lahore
ADBP 177 (Ali Hussain Rivzi 4 for 49, Haaris A. Khan
4 for 56) and 339 for 9 dec. (Atif Rauf 105, Sabih Azhar 65,
Haaris A. Khan 6 for 131)
Customs 113 (Azam Khan 56, Mohammad 5 for 31) and
102 (Mohammad Asif 4 for 28)
ADBP won by 301 runs
ADBP 12 pts, Customs 0 pts

There were fine all-round performances from both Aamir
Sohail and Asif Mujtaba in Faisalabad, but it was the PIA
captain Asif who once more came out on top with 125 runs
for once out and eight wickets for 88 runs in the match.

Habib Bank ran out of time in their efforts to press
home advantage against PNSC, but, in truth, their efforts were
somewhat tardy. The match was marked by several good individual performances. Meanwhile, United Bank came from
behind to beat National Bank. Veteran off-spinner Tauseef
Ahmed had match figures of 8 for 68. ADBP were another side
to make a significant second innings revival. Sabih Azhar and
Atif Rauf added 167 for the third wicket, and Atif's 105 came
in 209 minutes, three minutes quicker than Sabih's 65.

10, 11, 12 and 13 December 1996
at Qaddafi Stadium, Lahore
Habib Bank 354 (Mujahid Jamshed 83, Naved Anjum 83,
Asadullah Butt 64 not out, Mohammad Akram 4 for 114)
and 131 (Aqib Javed 9 for 51)

Allied Bank 188 (Rameez Raja 65, Kabir Khan 4 for 40)
and 286 (Rameez Raja 93, Ijaz Ahmed jnr 88, Shakeel Khan
4 for 80)
Habib Bank won by 11 runs
Habib Bank 12 pts, Allied Bank 0 pts

at Montgomery Biscuit Factory, Sahiwal
PNSC 152 (Zahid Ahmed 5 for 35) and 204
(Zahid Ahmed 6 for 71)
PIA 331 (Ghulam Ali 68, Zahid Ahmed 68, Zahid Fazal 62,
Javed Qadeer 52) and 26 for 0
PIA won by 10 wickets
PIA 12 pts, PNSC 0 pts

at Jinnah Stadium, Sialkot
Customs 198 and 291 (Azhar Shafiq 91, Kashif Ahmed
59, Azhar Mahmood 5 for 81)
United Bank 226 (Mohammad Hussain 78, Saleem Elahi
63, Nadeem Ashraf 5 for 81) and 64 for 0
Match drawn
United Bank 2 pts, Customs 0 pts

at Jinnah Stadium, Gujranwala
National Bank 277 (Aamer Gul 60, Shahid Anwar 58,
Mohammad Ali 4 for 110) and 189 for 6 dec.
ADBP 290 (Bilal Ahmed 53, Maqsood Rana 5 for 76) and
57 for 3
Match drawn
ADBP 2 pts, National Bank 0 pts

The match in Lahore was marked by the number of penalty
runs awarded for slow over-rates, penalties that affected the
result of the game. This was particularly hard on Aqib
Javed, the Test bowler, who took 9 for 51, by far the best
figures of his career, and finished with match figures of 12
for 134, also a best performance.

PIA beat PNSC early on the last day. Left-hander
Zahid Ahmed had an outstanding match. His spin bowling
brought him 11 wickets for 106 runs while he and Javed
Qadeer added 125 after seven wickets had fallen for 189.

Rain shortened the first day in the match between
Customs and United Bank, and the loss of time eventually
denied the Bank victory. Staunch defence by Azhar Shafiq
and Kashif Ahmed in Customs' second innings meant that
United Bank had only 16 overs in which to score 264 to win,
an impossible task. Rain also affected the match in
Gujranwala and a result never looked likely.

16, 17, 18 and 19 December 1996
at KRL Ground, Rawalpindi
National Bank 171 (Aamer Nazir 4 for 51) and 212
(Sajid Ali 54, Aqib Javed 4 for 53, Aamer Nazir 4 for 70)
Allied Bank 476 (Ijaz Ahmed jnr 151, Mohammad Nawaz
83, Aqib Javed 65, Ali Haider 50, Mohammad Javed 5 for 75)
Allied Bank won by an innings and 93 runs
Allied Bank 12 pts, National Bank 0 pts

Brave batting for lowly Customs from Azam Khan.
(David Munden/Sportsline)

at Railway Stadium, Lahore
PNSC 125 (Ali Hussain Rizvi 5 for 38) and 147
(Ali Hussain Rizvi 5 for 59, Haaris A. Khan 4 for 42)
Customs 136 (Sajjad Akbar 4 for 13, Shahid Hussain 4 for
40) and 137 for 7 (Murtaza Hussain 4 for 49)
Customs won by 3 wickets
Customs 12 pts, PNSC 0 pts

at Qaddafi Stadium, Lahore
United Bank 163 (Azhar Mahmood 69, Nadeem Afzal
7 for 70) and 252 (Iqbal Imam 88 not out)
PIA 79 (Hasnain Kazim 4 for 36) and 223 (Asif Mujtaba
96, Wasim Haider 57, Hasnain Kazim 4 for 52)
United Bank won by 113 runs
United Bank 12 pts, PIA 0 pts

at Lahore CA Ground, Lahore
Habib Bank 259 (Asadullah Butt 83, Naved Anjum 77,
Shoaib Akhtar 5 for 89) and 221 (Javed Hayat
6 for 49)
ADBP 298 (Manzoor Elahi 88 not out, Javed Hayat 57,
Akram Raza 5 for 113, Nadeem Ghauri 4 for 129) and 183
for 4 (Akram Raza 4 for 65)
ADBP won by 6 wickets
ADBP 12 pts, Habib Bank 0 pts

The consistent form of Ijaz Ahmed jnr. was to earn him a call to Australia to strengthen the national side, which had been hit by injuries. Against National Bank, he batted for more than six hours for his 151. In contrast, Aqib Javed, who again bowled well, hit the highest score of his career, 65 off 64 balls in 83 minutes batting at number ten. He helped Allied Bank to their first win of the tournament.

Customs also gained their first win of the season although once again their batting proved very frail. In the first innings they lost their last six wickets for 18 runs, and stumbled nervously when they went in search of 137 to win. Azam Khan's unbeaten 39 in 93 minutes did much to see them through.

At the Qaddafi Stadium, 20 wickets fell in 70.4 overs on the first day. Nadeem Afzal routed United Bank with his medium pace, but another medium pacer, Hasnain Kazim, helped bring havoc to PIA's innings. United Bank batted with more certainty in their second innings and looked well on top when they reduced PIA to 66 for 5. Asif Mujtaba and Wasim Haider added 152, only for the last five wickets to go down for five runs.

A seventh wicket stand of 151 between Javed Hayat and Manzoor Elahi regained the initiative for ADBP after earlier batsmen had failed. Javed Hayat had a good all-round match. He claimed six of the last seven second innings wickets to fall and then hit 42 off 46 balls as he and Mansoor Rana took ADBP to victory with an 81-run partnership in 67 minutes.

22, 23, 24 and 25 December 1996
at Arbab Niaz Stadium, Peshawar
Allied Bank 330 (Rameez Raja 100, Aamer Hanif 66, Ali Hussain Rizvi 4 for 107) and 185 (Azhar Ahafiq 6 for 56)
Customs 187 (Murtaza Abbasi 68) and 210 (Aqib Javed 7 for 64)
Allied Bank won by 118 runs
Allied Bank 12 pts, Customs 0 pts

at Pindi Cricket Stadium, Rawalpindi
National Bank 269 (Akhtar Sarfraz 63, Sajid Shah 5 for 89) and 205 for 5 (Sajid Ali 52)
PNSC 259 (Sher Ali 77, Mazhar Qayyum 52, Maqsood Rana 5 for 42)
Match drawn
National Bank 2 pts, PNSC 0 pts

at Jinnah Stadium, Gujranwala
Habib Bank 247 (Shahid Javed 73)
United Bank 224 for 5 (Mansoor Akhtar 101 retired hurt)
Match drawn
No points

at KRL Ground, Rawalpindi
ADBP 264 (Zahoor Elahi 113) and 84 for 2
PIA 356 (Ghulam Ali 142, Sohail Jaffar 70, Mohammad Ali 5 for 89)
Match drawn
ADBP 2 pts, PIA 0 pts

Aqib Javed's magnificent form continued as Allied Bank beat Customs for their second victory in succession, but this late spurt did not find them a place in the semi-finals. Another to star for Allied Bank was skipper Rameez Raja who made a patient century and shared a fifth wicket stand of 138 with Aamer Hanif.

PNSC finished pointless after failing narrowly on the first innings in the rain-affected game in Rawalpindi. They lost their last seven wickets for 47 runs.

It was not even possible to get a first in Gujranwala while the Airlines had to be content with first innings points when rain washed out the last day's play at the KRL ground.

Patron's Trophy Qualifying Table

	P	W	L	D	Pts
Pakistan International Airlines	7	4	1	2	48
Agricultural Development Bank of Pakistan	7	3	–	4	42
United Bank	7	3	–	4	40
Habib Bank	7	2	1	4	30
Allied Bank	7	2	3	2	28
National Bank of Pakistan	7	1	4	2	16
Customs	7	1	4	2	12
Pakistan National Shipping Corporation	7	–	3	4	0

Semi-Finals

28, 29, 30 and 31 December 1996
at Pindi Cricket Stadium, Rawalpindi
United Bank 272 (Basit Ali 84, Nadeem Khan 6 for 63) and 249 (Basit Ali 72, Asif Mujtaba 4 for 47, Nadeem Khan 4 for 97)
PIA 213 (Asif Mujtaba 71, Tauseef Ahmed 4 for 32, Azhar Mahmood 4 for 76) and 256
United Bank won by 52 runs

at National Stadium, Karachi
Habib Bank 343 (Moin-ul-Atiq 112, Mujahid Jamshed 60, Shoaib Akhtar 5 for 110) and 346 for 4 (Moin-ul-Atiq 81, Shahid Javed 58 not out, Shakeel Ahmed 53, Idrees Baig 50)
ADBP 244 (Ghaffar Kazmi 76, Mansoor Rana 51 not out, Akram Raza 4 for 30)
Match drawn
Habib Bank qualify for final on first innings lead

Two brilliant innings from Basit Ali were a feature of the semi-final in Rawalpindi, while left-arm spinner Nadeem Khan of PIA had match figures of 10 for 160. On the last day PIA were faced with a target of 309 in 62 overs. They made a brave attempt but fell short of their objective as they lost their last five wickets for 41 runs in the dash.

In Karachi, Habib Bank were content that their first innings lead should take them into the final. A six-hour innings by Moin-ul-Atiq, who put on 158 for the second wicket with Mujahid Jamshed, helped to take Habib Bank to a strong position. In reply, Ghaffar Kazmi made a brisk 76, but the tail was long, and ADBP never looked like equalling Habib's score. Batting a second time, Habib Bank indulged themselves on a placid wicket. On the strength of his two fifties in this match and his generally consistent form, Mujahid Jamshed found himself flying to Australia along with Ijaz Ahmed jnr as reinforcement for the national side.

ADBP's captain Mansoor Rana and his colleague Javed Hayat received hefty fines from referee Iqbal Qasim after being reported by umpire Salim Badar.

Patron's Trophy Final

4, 5, 6, 7 and 8 January 1997
at Qaddafi Stadium, Lahore
United Bank 338 (Shehzad Butt 88, Saleem Elahi 78) and 294 (Basit Ali 74, Mohammad Ramzan 70, Asadullah Butt 5 for 77)
Habib Bank 145 (Hasnain Kazim 6 for 41) and 181 (Naved Anjum 92, Hasnain Kazim 5 for 87, Azhar Mahmood 4 for 56)
United Bank won by 306 runs

The start of play was delayed for 105 minutes due to poor visibility, and Akram Raza asked United Bank to bat first when he won the toss. Mohammad Ramzan and Saleem Elahi responded positively with 113 in 246 minutes. Six wickets then fell for 68 runs before Shehzad Butt brought relief to United Bank, who were helped to 338 by 50 extras.

The pitch aided seam bowling, but it was by no means difficult. Medium-pacer Hasnain Kazim returned the best figures of his career, exploiting the conditions intelligently while Habib Bank's batsmen failed to apply themselves. With a healthy lead United Bank were able to bat in a relaxed manner, and Mohammad Ramzan and Saleem Elahi again began with a century stand, 109. Basit Ali, who had done so much to take United to the final, played a charming innings of 74, and one cannot believe that his international career is behind him.

Habib Bank faced an impossible task in that they began batting late on the fourth day needing 488 to win. They were handicapped further by the absence of Shakeel Ahmed, who retired at the end of the fourth day because of a family bereavement. Tauseef Ahmed set attacking fields,

and Husnain Kazim, Man of the Match, again bowled splendidly. Habib Bank slipped to 62 for 6, and with Shakeel absent, it seemed that they would not reach 100. That they did so was due entirely to Naved Anjum who smashed 92 off 93 balls with a six and 17 fours. He dominated a last wicket stand of 76 off 80 balls with Shakeel Khan before falling leg before to Azhar Mahmood.

The game was over ten minutes before tea, and United Bank had won the Patron's Trophy for the first time.

The Pentagular Tournament was not played in 1997.

First-Class Averages

Batting

	M	Inns	NO	Runs	HS	Av	100s	50s
Wasim Akram	2	2	1	292	257*	292.00	1	
Saeed Anwar	4	6	1	339	149	67.80	1	3
Nasir Ali Khan	2	3	–	196	167	65.33	1	
Asif Mujtaba	11	19	3	913	116	57.06	1	7
Mohammad Wasim	8	14	2	630	109*	52.50	3	3
Mujahid Jamshed	10	16	1	771	129	51.40	3	4
Mujahis Hameed	5	8	2	291	187	48.50	1	
Aamir Sohail	5	9	1	377	132	47.12	1	1
Manzoor Elahi	13	19	3	730	113	45.62	1	4
Ghulam Ali	10	19	5	636	142	45.42	2	2
Iqbal Saleem	9	14	1	573	207	44.07	2	
Zahoor Elahi	8	14	1	571	153	43.92	2	2
Jahangir Khan	7	12	–	522	147	43.50	1	2
Hasan Raza	3	5	–	217	96	43.40		2
Naseer Ahmed Mughal	7	12	1	474	89*	43.09	1	1
Ijaz Ahmed jnr	13	23	1	911	151	41.40	2	4
Naved Anjum	7	11	1	410	92	41.00		3
Majid Saeed	7	12	1	445	115*	40.45	1	2
Saqlain Mushtaq	3	4	1	117	79	39.00		1
Saleem Elahi	9	16	1	546	78	39.00		4
Salim Malik	4	5	–	190	78	38.00		2
Basit Ali	12	21	–	784	100	37.33	1	6
Moin Khan	5	6	–	221	59	36.83		2
Akram Raza	12	16	6	365	77*	36.50		1
Wasim Yousufi	14	23	3	724	100*	36.20	1	4
Shahid Nawaz	9	16	–	576	94	36.00		4
Moin-ul-Atiq	11	20	3	611	129	35.94	2	2
Akhtar Sarfraz	12	22	2	700	135	35.00	2	5
Mansoor Rana	13	21	3	619	117	34.38	1	3
Mahmood Hamid	11	15	1	474	157	33.85	1	1
Rameez Raja	7	12	–	405	100	33.75	1	3
Rashid Hanif	3	5	2	101	50	33.66		1
Naseer Shaukat	7	12	1	369	72	33.54		3
Sajjad Akbar	7	12	2	332	110	33.20	1	
Javed Hayat	12	21	7	404	57	33.14		1
Azam Khan	9	17	1	529	70	33.06		4
Ahmar Saeed	4	7	–	231	74	33.00		2
Abdul Salam	4	7	–	229	90	32.71		1
Asadullah Butt	8	13	4	291	83	32.33		2
Mohammad Salim	4	8	–	258	107	32.25	1	1
Aamer Hanif	13	24	1	735	134	31.95	1	5
Mohammad Ramzan	14	25	2	731	112	31.78	1	5
Shahid Javed	13	21	4	538	73	31.64		4
Sohail Jaffar	11	17	–	537	72	31.58		3
Wajahatullah	7	11	–	345	86	31.36		4
Shoaib Mohammad	5	9	2	219	54	31.28		2
Sher Ali	10	18	1	528	123*	31.05	1	4
Zaheer Abbasi	8	14	2	372	69	31.00		4
Ijaz Mahmood	2	4	–	123	56	30.75		1
Shakeel Ahmed	14	25	1	716	123	29.83	1	4
Nasir Wasti	3	5	–	148	84	29.60		1
Ijaz Ahmed	4	5	–	147	125	29.40	1	
Naeem Akhtar	6	10	2	232	72	29.00		1
Shahid Anwar	12	23	1	630	105	28.63	1	5
Ali Haider	11	20	–	572	124	28.60	1	2
Tahir Mahmood jnr	7	12	1	311	52	28.27		1
Mohammad Hussain	13	20	4	451	78	28.18		3
Muzaffar Abbasi	3	6	–	169	68	28.16		1
Tahir Rasheed	10	15	1	394	73	28.14		3
Yousuf Youhana	2	4	–	109	48	27.25		
Zafar Iqbal	9	17	2	407	79	27.13		2
Ahsan Butt	10	18	1	460	88	27.05		4

Batting

	M	Inns	NO	Runs	HS	Av	100s	50s
Mohammad Nawaz snr	12	22	–	587	83	26.68		6
Azhar Shafiq	14	27	1	689	123	26.50	1	4
Saeed Azad	5	9	–	235	66	26.11		1
Mushtaq Ahmed	3	4	–	103	42	25.75		
Mohammad Masroor	5	8	1	172	93*	24.57		1
Atif Rauf	8	14	2	294	105	24.50	1	
Manzoor Akhtar	8	15	–	363	124	24.20	1	1
Asif Mahmood	4	6	–	144	62	24.00		1
Ghaffar Kazmi	8	13	–	311	76	23.92		1
Sohail Idrees	4	8	–	191	55	23.87		1
Bilal Rana	12	20	3	402	69	23.64		3
Amjad Ali	4	8	–	186	77	23.25		1
Sajid Ali	11	22	1	479	69	22.80		3
Mazhar Qayyum	4	6	–	136	52	22.66		1
Iqbal Imam	15	25	2	520	88*	22.60		2
Mohammad Nawaz jnr	7	14	2	267	58	22.25		1
Naeem Ashraf	4	7	–	154	44	22.00		
Sabih Azhar	8	15	1	304	65	21.71		1
Mansoor Akhtar	8	14	2	260	101*	21.66	1	
Kashif Ahmed	8	16	1	303	59	21.64		1
Anwar Miandad	3	5	–	108	49	21.60		
Raj Hans	7	12	–	255	106	21.25	1	1
Shadab Kabir	6	10	–	205	46	20.50		
Rizwan-uz-Zaman	8	15	1	283	91	20.21		2
Wasim Haider	5	6	1	101	57	20.20		1
Aamer Gul	5	10	–	202	60	20.20		1
Intikhab Alam jnr	4	8	1	141	82	20.14		1
Sajjad Ali	5	8	–	159	40	19.87		
Azhar Mahmood	11	19	1	355	69	19.72		2
Shakeel Ahmed	6	9	2	138	66	19.71		1
Javed Sami Khan	5	10	–	197	46	19.70		
Saifullah	7	14	1	256	57	19.69		2
Javed Qadir	8	11	1	196	52	19.60		1
Tahir Shah	6	12	1	212	43	19.27		
Bilal Moin Khilji	9	17	1	307	83	19.18		1
Shahzad Butt	7	11	1	188	88	18.80		1
Bilal Ahmed	12	17	1	300	78	18.75		3
Naveed Ahmed	7	12	–	223	72	18.58		1
Saadat Gul Khan	4	6	–	111	44	18.50		
Rashid Latif	7	13	2	200	38	18.18		
Naveed Latif	7	14	1	233	62	17.92		1
Zahid Fazal	7	12	–	215	62	17.91		1
Javed Iqbal	5	9	–	160	60	17.77		1
Idrees Baig	9	16	–	273	56	17.06		2
Qaiser Mehmood	6	7	–	119	57	17.00		1
Maisam Hasnain	5	9	1	136	44	17.00		
Tassawar Hussain	4	8	–	135	75	16.87		1
Murtaza Hussain	13	21	3	302	42*	16.77		
Aqib Javed	10	15	4	183	65	16.63		1
Haaris A. Khan	9	17	4	214	50*	16.46		1
Aamer Iqbal	6	12	1	181	57	16.45		1
Aamir Sohail	8	15	–	233	93	15.53		2
Nadeem Khan	13	18	1	261	59	15.35		1
Asif Ali Saeed	7	12	–	183	58	15.25		1
Tahir Mahmood snr	4	7	–	101	41	14.42		
Naeem Tayyab	9	16	4	173	47*	14.41		
Mohammad Zahid	8	15	5	143	27	14.30		
Naved Nazir	7	11	4	100	53	14.28		1
Shahid Hussain	7	12	2	142	43	14.20		
Naveed Ashraf	6	10	–	139	28	13.90		
Sajid Shah	9	14	1	179	50	13.76		1
Wasim Arif	6	11	1	136	36	13.60		

First-Class Averages

Batting

	M	Inns	NO	Runs	HS	Av	100s	50s
Kamran Haider	6	12	1	146	47	13.27		
Nasir Jam	7	13	1	159	37	13.25		
Mohammad Javed	8	14	1	168	52	12.92		1
Shahid Saeed	4	8	–	102	26	12.75		
Nadeem Hussain	10	16	–	200	41	12.50		
Mohammad Asif	12	15	5	119	31	11.90		
Arshad Khan	12	20	–	222	32	11.10		
Shoaib Akhtar	12	16	4	126	23	10.50		
Athar Laeeq	9	14	2	122	22	10.16		

(Qualification: 100 runs, average 10.00)

Bowling

	Overs	Mds	Runs	Wks	Av	Best	10/m	5/inn
Kashif Ibrahim	74.3	20	164	15	10.93	5/29		2
Mohammad Zahid	166.3	34	440	35	12.57	7/66	2	3
Asif Mujtaba	198.3	76	342	26	13.15	5/60		2
Zahid Ahmed	97.5	26	220	15	14.66	6/71	1	2
Hasnain Kazim	107	15	369	25	14.76	6/41	1	2
Shahid Anwar	50	12	150	10	15.00	6/2		1
Mushtaq Ahmed	157.1	36	436	28	15.57	6/66	2	3
Aamer Hanif	195.5	48	488	30	16.26	5/57		1
Wasim Akram	71.4	21	180	11	16.36	6/48	1	1
Aqib Javed	282.2	49	852	50	17.04	9/51	2	4
Naeem Akhtar	172.2	35	428	25	17.12	5/37		2
Ata-ur-Rehman	138.2	23	431	25	17.24	5/56		2
Azhar Mahmood	393.5	106	1031	59	17.47	7/65	2	3
Azhar Shafiq	218.1	30	756	43	17.58	6/56	1	4
Mohammad Asif	432.2	86	959	53	18.09	5/20	1	3
Ijaz Elahi	78.4	16	272	15	18.13	5/27		1
Akram Raza	373.3	96	967	51	18.96	5/49		2
Ghulam Abbas	65	10	232	12	19.33	4/53		
Rashid Hanif	110.5	30	292	15	19.46	7/36		1
Kabir Khan	456	101	1404	71	19.77	8/70		6
Ali Hussain Rizvi	387.1	64	1090	54	20.18	6/123	1	4
Saadat Gul Khan	86.1	12	285	14	20.35	5/35		1
Salman Fazal	352.5	83	808	39	20.71	6/42		1
Tauseef Ahmed	239.3	80	438	21	20.85	5/36		1
Mohammad Hussain	448.1	158	1015	48	21.14	6/81	2	3
Shahid Nazir	115.3	26	339	16	21.18	5/53		1
Imranullah	80.2	18	286	13	22.00	6/75		1
Naseer Shaukat	189.1	29	664	30	22.13	6/51	1	4
Murtaza Hussain	528.3	129	1441	64	22.51	5/43		4
Shoaib Akhtar	426.4	58	1633	69	23.66	5/58		6

Bowling

	Overs	Mds	Runs	Wks	Av	Best	10/m	5/inn
Shakeel Ahmed	130.4	31	357	15	23.80	4/53		
Iqbal Imam	219.1	39	550	23	23.91	7/71		1
Ali Gauhar	415.3	96	1244	52	23.92	6/55	1	3
Nadeem Khan	552.3	149	1308	54	24.22	6/35	1	3
Arshad Khan	347.4	69	878	36	24.38	6/74		2
Baqar Rizvi	118.5	25	344	14	24.57	5/33		1
Nadeem Ghauri	246.3	62	639	26	24.57	7/101	1	1
Haaris A. Khan	330.3	77	836	34	24.58	6/131	1	2
Athar Laeeq	306.5	68	935	38	24.60	5/57	1	3
Mohammad Zahid	267.3	64	723	29	24.93	4/48		
Manzoor Elahi	262.5	64	699	28	24.96	8/43	1	1
Maqsood Rana	139.4	15	483	19	25.42	5/42		2
Nadeem Afzal	239	44	776	30	25.86	7/70	1	2
Naeem Tayyab	321.4	67	808	31	26.06	6/88		3
Waqar Younis	98	25	291	11	26.45	4/48		
Ijaz Ahmed jnr	101.4	18	270	10	27.00	3/36		
Mohammad Akram	175.2	27	621	23	27.00	6/56		2
Sajjad Akbar	206.1	42	542	20	27.10	4/13		
Kashif Elahi	70	6	271	10	27.10	3/38		
Bilal Rana	392	102	984	36	27.33	6/26	1	4
Aamer Nazir	205.3	30	767	28	27.39	4/27		
Shakeel Khan	93.3	15	330	12	27.50	4/80		
Saeed Ajmal	86.4	5	307	11	27.90	7/220		1
Javed Hayat	261.1	56	546	18	30.33	6/49		1
Shahzad Butt	158.1	21	584	19	30.73	5/42		2
Naved Nazir	176.1	30	454	14	32.42	4/106		
Sajid Shah	244	46	782	24	32.58	5/89		1
Mohsin Kamal	98.2	13	398	12	33.16	4/43		
Saqlain Mushtaq	133.2	31	383	11	34.81	4/75		
Shahid Hussain	244.2	50	715	20	35.75	5/83		1
Mohammad Ali	170.3	27	543	15	36.20	5/89		1
Mohammad Javed	170	27	534	14	38.14	5/75		1
Raj Hans	140.2	23	421	11	38.27	5/74		1
Asadullah Butt	196.5	36	647	16	40.43	5/77		1
Zafar Iqbal	123	13	469	10	46.90	3/35		

(Qualification: 10 wickets)

Leading Fielders

42 – Wasim Yousufi (ct 38 / st 4); 41 – Tahir Rasheed (ct 40 / st 1); 36 – Javed Qadir (ct 30 / st 6); 30 – Iqbal Saleem; 28 – Bilal Ahmed (ct 25 / st 3); 24 – Rashid Latif (ct 23 / st 1); 23 – Ahsan Raza (ct 21 / st 2) and Pervez-ul-Hasan (ct 21 / st 2); 21 – Saifullah (ct 16 / st 5); 20 – Ijaz Ahmed jnr; 19 – Ali Haider; 18 – Shakeel Ahmed; 17 – Qaiser Mehmood (ct 15 / st 2) and Wasim Arif (ct 16 / st 1); 13 – Mohammad Asif and Azhar Mahmood; 12 – Kamran Haider, Naseer Ali Mughal, Naveed Ahmed, Sajid Ali and Shahid Nawaz

Australia

Although Sri Lanka had proved themselves to be World Champions in the limited-over game, Australia entered the 1996–97 season generally recognised as the leading nation in Test cricket. They had beaten West Indies and destroyed England and all-comers, yet, by November, 1996, they were beset by uncertainty. Simpson's reign as national coach had ended, and he had been replaced by Geoff Marsh.

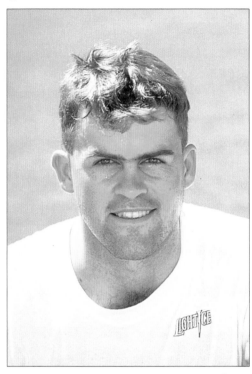

Jamie Cox, Tasmania's opening batsman, the only player to pass a thousand runs during the season. Cox hit five centuries, including a career best double century against the Pakistanis.
(Stephen Laffer/Sportsline)

Australia's saviour in the first Test. Ian Healy drives a boundary during his outstanding innings of 161 not out at Brisbane. (Shaun Botterill/Allsport)

Shane Warne had undergone a finger operation and had been unavailable for the short tour of India. Without him, Australia had fared disastrously in both the Test match and in the limited-over series. There was further concern in that others had shown a disturbing loss of form, particularly the once mighty opening partnership of Taylor and Slater. The highly talented Ponting, too, had performed indifferently, Law had shown poor form after the brilliance he had displayed with Essex, and Hogg and McIntyre had failed to grasp the chances offered them.

The first rays of sun appeared as the West Indians began their tour. Shane Warne captained Victoria against New South Wales, sent down 45 overs and appeared to be fully recovered from his operation. Australia breathed a sigh of relief.

West Indies Tour

No longer the dominant force of yore, the West Indians arrived in Australia to face a testing examination of their character and ability. Internal strife, indiscipline and home defeat at the hands of the Australians had led to a complete overhaul of West Indian cricket which had resulted in Pat Rousseau, a highly successful business man, becoming the dynamic leader of the West Indies Cricket Board and to Clive Lloyd and Malcolm Marshall becoming manager and coach of the national side. Courtney Walsh, much respected, continued as captain in the wake of the demise of Richie Richardson.

In spite of the success of spinners in domestic cricket in the Caribbean, West Indies still put all their faith in a pace attack, and Thompson, McLean, Bishop, Ambrose and Kenny Benjamin joined Walsh in the tour party while spin was left in the hands of Adams and Hooper, neither of them front rank. West Indies faced a gruelling challenge.

4 November 1996
at Lilac Hill, Perth
West Indians 256 for 9 (B.C. Lara 66)
Australian Cricket Board Chairman's XI 258 for 7 (B.P. Julian 96 not out, T.M. Moody 66, I.R. Bishop 4 for 44)
Australian Cricket Board Chairman's XI won by 3 wickets

In the opening match of their tour, the West Indians faced a side that included veterans Lillee, Thomson, Border and Rackemann, and fell foul of a violent assault by Brendon Julian who hit 96 of the last 163 runs scored. Jimmy Adams was hit for 33 in two overs.

---

6 November 1996
at WACA Ground, Perth
West Indians 127 for 8
Western Australia 128 for 1 (R.J. Campbell 64 not out, D.R. Martyn 51 not out)
Western Australia won by 9 wickets

In a match reduced to 31 overs, the state side reached their target in 19.2 overs. Campbell and Martyn shared an unbroken second wicket stand of 85.

---

7 November, 1996
at WACA Ground, Perth
Western Australia 235 for 6 (J.L. Langer 79, M.E. Hussey 56)
West Indians 237 for 9 (S. Chanderpaul 91, C.L. Hooper 51)
West Indians won by 1 wicket

When last man McLean joined Bishop, eight runs were needed for victory, and this was achieved with two balls of the match remaining. Chanderpaul and Hooper had earlier added 92 for the third wicket. Hussey and Langer had scored 128 for Western Australia's second wicket, but West Indies were happy to claim their first win of the tour.

8, 9 and 10 November 1996
at WACA Ground, Perth
Western Australia 293 for 6 dec. (A.C. Gilchrist 108 not out, M.P. Lavender 51) and 170 (C.L. Hooper 4 for 59)
West Indians 442 for 5 dec. (S. Chanderpaul 135, R.G. Samuels 96, C.L. Hooper 84, R.I.C. Holder 68) and 26 for 1
West Indians won by 9 wickets

Adam Gilchrist blazed 108 off 101 balls on the first day, including three sixes and 14 fours. In their opening first-class fixture, West Indies batted impressively with Samuels and Chanderpaul sharing a second wicket stand of 207.

Hooper made 84 and had match figures of 7 for 123 to set up a comfortable West Indian victory.

---

12 November 1996
at Traeger Park, Alice Springs
West Indians 218 for 8 (J.C. Adams 67, C.O. Browne 50)
Northern Territory Invitation XI 170 (A.C. Gilchrist 64 not out)
West Indians won by 48 runs

Jimmy Adams and Courtney Browne put on 98 for the sixth wicket to revive West Indian fortunes at Alice Springs. Earlier, the Tasmanian left-arm spinner Mark Hatton had caused concern by sending back Campbell, Lara and Holder at a personal cost of 24 runs in ten overs. Only Adam Gilchrist offered positive resistance to the West Indian bowlers.

15, 16, 17 and 18 November 1996
at Bellerive Oval, Hobart
Australian XI 544 for 4 dec. (M.L. Hayden 224, M.T.G. Elliott 158, G.S. Blewett 89 not out) and 28 for 0
West Indians 317 (C.O. Browne 93 not out, A.J. Bichel 4 for 61, A.M. Stuart 4 for 104) and 251 (S. Chanderpaul 77, B.C. Lara 63, G.S. Blewett 5 for 29)
Australian XI won by 10 wickets

A chilly first day in Hobart became colder for the West Indians as Hayden and Elliott, both contenders for a place in the Australian Test side, scored 316 without being separated. Elliott was bowled by Bishop on the second morning when only another seven runs had been added, but Blewett then joined Hayden in a stand worth 127. Facing a massive 544, the tourists lost seven wickets for 179 runs. Browne battled bravely, but the West Indians were forced to follow on and began the last day 125 runs in arrears with eight wickets standing. They seemed set to save the game, but on the last afternoon Blewett took five for 12 in 5.5 overs to make possible an easy victory for an Australian XI who emphasised the strength in depth of the national side. Blewett's 5 for 29 represented his best bowling figures in first-class cricket.

First Test Match

Australia v. West Indies

Australia introduced two players to Test cricket: Matthew Elliott, the left-handed Victorian opener, and Michael Kasprowicz, the Queensland fast bowler and a prolific wicket-taker over the past two seasons. Jason Gillespie was the unlucky player from the original party of twelve while Griffith was twelfth man for West Indies. The most significant selection for either side was that of Shane Warne, who had declared himself fit enough to return to Test cricket so giving Australia a distinct psychological advantage.

West Indies won the toss and fielded. Walsh's decision brought instant success, with Elliott failing to score on his debut and being caught behind in the fourth over. Ponting, brimming with confident aggression, joined his captain to take Australia to lunch without further disaster, although both batsmen faced problems in the first hour. Taylor hung on grimly, and, by lunch, he had battled to 19 out of 82, an innings of determination for a man palpably out of form. Ponting was on 56 at the first interval.

Taylor appeared to have negotiated his bad patch and had produced his famous square cut to good effect when he bottom edged a pull and dragged the ball into his stumps. He had faced 136 balls and batted for five minutes under three hours. Australia seemed secure, but Ponting's eloquent innings came to an abrupt end when he pulled a ball from Benjamin into the hands of mid-on. Ponting had batted beautifully, hitting a six and ten fours and suggesting that Test bowlers worldwide would suffer at his hands over the next decade.

Mark Waugh became the third batsman to succumb to the pull shot. He hit a brisk 38, adding 50 with his twin brother, before getting a bottom edge that Browne, who kept well, took with expert ease. Next ball, Walsh moved a ball of full length across Bevan, who jabbed to slip so that, at 196 for 5, and all the front-line batsmen except Steve Waugh gone, Australia were in some difficulties.

It is, perhaps, insulting to Healy not to regard him as a front-line batsman. He has a healthy Test average and two Test centuries to his credit, and by the end of the day he was on his way to a third, scoring at almost a run a ball. He finished with 47 to Steve Waugh's 48 as Australia closed on a happier 282 for 5.

Healy's belligerence was unabated on the second day. His stand with Steve Waugh was broken before lunch, but it had produced 142 match-winning runs, and the West Indian pace men, prone to bowl short at Steve Waugh, had been blunted and were bereft of ideas. They failed to remove Reiffel who stayed for 83 minutes while 69 were added, and Warne played his part in a 62-minute stand that realised 61 runs. McGrath did not survive, but by the time he was

The vital dismissal of Brian Lara for 44, caught in the gully by Mark Waugh off Reiffel. (Shaun Botterill/Allsport)

McGrath had a fine series, capturing 26 wickets. He brings victory closer for Australia in the first Test when he bowls Chanderpaul. (Shaun Botterill/Allsport)

bowled by the inconsistent Benjamin, Australia had scored 479 and were in an impregnable position.

The hero and Man of the Match was, of course, Ian Healy. He hit 20 fours, faced 250 balls and batted for 356 minutes. He had taken the attack to the enemy and routed them. His unbeaten 161 was his third Test century, the highest by an Australian wicket-keeper. He reached his fifty off 68 balls, but his second fifty had taken him 95 balls as he played with a determination that the tail should produce as many runs as possible. Indeed, the last four wickets brought 141 runs to the Australian score.

Healy's contribution was far from over. Samuels edged a McGrath cutter to him, and Campbell was then taken at slip. Lara and Hooper took the score to 61, but the day had belonged to Australia, a team united in the field – with this unity emphasised in that all wore their green caps.

Lara had added only seven to his overnight score when, in the eighth over of the third morning, he edged a pull to Mark Waugh. There then followed a tense partnership between Hooper and Chanderpaul. They were confronted by bowling which far outshone that produced by West Indies. Both batsmen played with discipline and determination, although both enjoyed good fortune in their partnership of 172. Hooper hit ten fours and pulled Warne for 6. He reached his sixth Test hundred, but as soon as he was out West Indies collapsed.

Hooper fell to a magnificent diving catch at mid-wicket, and the flood gates opened. The last seven West Indian wickets went down for 28 runs in 12 overs, and Taylor could have invoked the follow-on. He chose to bat again, and eight runs were added before the close.

The opening pair had scored 55 before Elliott was bowled between bat and pad. Taylor was caught behind when he cut at Benjamin, while Ponting leg-glanced to the keeper. Mark Waugh played a fluent innings before cutting at a wider delivery, and Bevan, dropped first ball, was slow to settle. He appeared to have established confidence when he hoisted Ambrose to square-leg.

Once again it was Healy who provided the panache. He cut and drove with relish, and when Reiffel ran himself out Taylor was able to declare and set West Indies a target of 420. They began confidently enough, but Warne was soon introduced into the attack, and he quickly had Samuels taken at slip. Lara responded with aggression, and the day ended with West Indies on 89 for 1, with an enthralling last day in prospect.

Lara's blast soon ended on the last morning when he drove at Reiffel and edged to slip. Warne imposed fear and restraint, and others prospered. Bevan's impressive wrist spin had Hooper in two minds and Chanderpaul fell to McGrath, a bowler of intelligence and aggression, after lunch. Warne had Adams leg before, and West Indies were sinking fast. Browne batted boldly before becoming McGrath's second victim, and Bevan claimed the crucial wicket of Campbell, who had played resolutely for 407 minutes. The tail was now open, and Bevan and McGrath quickly brought Australia victory.

Second Test Match

Australia v. West Indies

Australia had been without the services of Steve Waugh for the last two days of the first Test because he was suffering from a groin strain. The injury prevented him playing at Sydney, and Blewett replaced him. Australia surprisingly chose Gillespie ahead of Reiffel who was relegated to twelfth man. West Indies were unchanged. Taylor won the toss and elected to bat.

The start of the day did not go well. Elliott and Taylor scored 54 in 78 minutes, but four wickets fell for 40 runs, and when Bevan, whose batting lacked conviction, nibbled outside the off stump as Taylor and Elliott had done, Australia were 131 for 5. It was Blewett and Healy who staged a revival. Bristling with confidence, Healy hit hard and often, and Blewett displayed a maturity of technique and temperament which halted the West Indian advance. By the close, Australia were 224 for 5.

Sydney Cricket Ground, the second Test. Jimmy Adams falls to a catch on the boundary. (Shaun Botterill/Allsport)

Australia's secret weapon – the bowling of Michael Bevan. Bevan captures the wicket of Carl Hooper in the second innings of the second Test. The ball was diverted from Healey to Taylor who kicked it up as he lay on the ground and held it as it dropped. (David Munden/Sportsline)

Healy was taken at slip without addition to the score on the second morning, and when Blewett was taken at short-leg Australia's future looked uncertain. Blewett had batted with considerable flair, and his loss was grievous as the tail was considered to be long and weak. Warne and Kasprowicz set out to prove otherwise, attacking with relish, but the real surprise came in a last wicket stand of 43

between Gillespie and McGrath. McGrath, a world famous rabbit, passed 20 for the first time in his career, and Australia reached 331.

McGrath's contribution to the day was far from over. Campbell and Samuels began confidently, and Ponting dropped a simple chance offered by Samuels. The advent of Warne curbed the scoring, and the tension heightened. Samuels fell to McGrath when he offered no shot, and a magnificent delivery from the New South Wales fast bowler took the edge of Lara's bat on its way to the wicket-keeper. Taylor rang the bowling changes, and Blewett responded by removing the impressive Campbell with an in-swinging yorker. Hooper and Chanderpaul moved unsteadily to 156 for 3 at the close.

Hooper faced 33 balls on the third morning without adding to his score before falling leg before to Warne. Adams was deceived by McGrath's slower ball, and the same bowler sent back Browne fourth ball. Chanderpaul's 196-minute innings was brought to an end by Warne's guile, and Gillespie took his first wickets in Test cricket to give Australia a first innings lead of 27.

First Test Match – Australia v. West Indies
22, 23, 24, 25 and 26 November 1996 at Woolloongabba, Brisbane

Australia

	First Innings		Second Innings	
M.A. Taylor (Capt)	b Walsh	43	(2) c Browne, b Benjamin	36
M.T.G. Elliott	c Browne, b Ambrose	0	(1) b Bishop	21
R.T. Ponting	c Walsh, b Benjamin	88	c Browne, b Bishop	9
M.E. Waugh	c Browne, b Walsh	38	c Browne, b Bishop	57
S.R. Waugh	c Lara, b Bishop	66		
M.G. Bevan	c Samuels, b Walsh	0	(5) c sub (Griffith), b Ambrose	20
I.A. Healy	not out	161	(6) not out	45
P.R. Reiffel	c and b Walsh	20	(7) run out	11
S.K. Warne	c and b Bishop	24		
M.S. Kasprowicz	c Benjamin, b Bishop	6		
G.D. McGrath	b Benjamin	0		
	lb 8, w 3, nb 22	33	b 1, lb 3, nb 14	18
		479	(for 6 wickets), dec.	217

	O	M	R	W	O	M	R	W
Ambrose	34	4	93	1	18	2	47	1
Walsh	35	6	112	4	17	1	58	–
Benjamin	33	6	97	2	15	1	52	1
Bishop	30	2	105	3	13	2	49	3
Hooper	19	3	64	–	2	–	7	–

Fall of Wickets
1-4, 2-130, 3-146, 4-196, 5-196, 6-338, 7-407, 8-468, 9-477
1-55, 2-74, 3-82, 4-137, 5-189, 6-217

West Indies

	First Innings		Second Innings	
S.L. Campbell	c Warne, b Reiffel	18	lbw, b Bevan	113
R.G. Samuels	c Healy, b McGrath	10	c Taylor, b Warne	29
B.C. Lara	c M.E. Waugh, b McGrath	26	c M.E. Waugh, b Reiffel	44
C.L. Hooper	c Ponting, b S.R. Waugh	102	c Healy, b Bevan	23
S. Chanderpaul	c M.E. Waugh, b Reiffel	82	b McGrath	14
J.C. Adams	lbw, b Ponting	0	lbw, b Warne	2
*C.O. Browne	c Healy, b Reiffel	4	c Healy, b McGrath	20
I.R. Bishop	lbw, b Warne	0	c Ponting, b Bevan	24
C.E.L. Ambrose	c sub (Gillespie), b Reiffel	0	c Warne, b McGrath	7
K.C.G. Benjamin	lbw, b Warne	9	c Healy, b McGrath	1
C.A. Walsh (Capt)	not out	0	not out	1
	lb 8, w 1, nb 17	26	b 8, lb 3, nb 7	18
		277		296

	O	M	R	W	O	M	R	W
McGrath	21	7	32	2	29.5	12	60	4
Reiffel	24.1	6	58	4	9	–	58	1
Kasprowicz	22	5	60	–	13	2	29	–
Warne	27	3	88	2	41	16	92	2
S.R. Waugh	8.1	1	15	1				
M.E. Waugh	4	1	16	–				
Ponting	1.5	1	0	1				
Bevan					14	3	46	3

Fall of Wickets
1-30, 2-43, 3-77, 4-249, 5-255, 6-267, 7-268, 8-268, 9-277
1-54, 2-118, 3-154, 4-187, 5-202, 6-242, 7-281, 8-293, 9-293

Umpires: C.J. Mitchley & S.G. Randell

Australia won by 123 runs

Second Test Match – Australia v. West Indies
29, 30 November, 1, 2 and 3 December 1996 at Sydney Cricket Ground

Australia

	First Innings		Second Innings	
M.A. Taylor (Capt)	c Chanderpaul, b Bishop	27	(2) c Lara, b Bishop	16
M.T.G. Elliott	c Lara, b Bishop	29	(1) retired hurt	78
R.T. Ponting	c Samuels, b Walsh	9	c Browne, b Bishop	4
M.E. Waugh	c Lara, b Walsh	19	c Browne, b Ambrose	67
M.G. Bevan	c Hooper, b Benjamin	16	c Browne, b Benjamin	52
G.S. Blewett	c Adams, b Walsh	69	not out	47
*I.A. Healy	c Lara, b Walsh	44	not out	22
S.K. Warne	c Browne, b Bishop	28		
M.S. Kasprowicz	c Campbell, b Walsh	21		
J.N. Gillespie	not out	16		
G.D. McGrath	lbw, b Adams	24		
	lb 10, w 1, nb 18	29	b 4, lb 10, w 3, nb 9	26
		331	(for 4 wickets), dec.	**312**

West Indies

	First Innings		Second Innings	
S.L. Campbell	b Blewett	77	lbw, b McGrath	15
R.G. Samuels	lbw, b McGrath	35	b Warne	16
B.C. Lara	c Healy, b McGrath	2	c Healy, b McGrath	11
C.L. Hooper	lbw, b Warne	27	c Taylor, b Bevan	57
S. Chanderpaul	c and b Warne	48	b Warne	71
J.C. Adams	c Bevan, b McGrath	30	c Blewett, b McGrath	5
*C.O. Browne	c Blewett, b McGrath	0	not out	25
I.R. Bishop	c Elliott, b Warne	48	run out	0
C.E.L. Ambrose	b Gillespie	9	b Bevan	0
K.C.G. Benjamin	b Gillespie	6	c Taylor, b Warne	4
C.A. Walsh (Capt)	not out	2	c McGrath, b Warne	18
	b 4, lb 6, nb 10	20	lb 2, nb 1	3
		304		**215**

	O	M	R	W	O	M	R	W
Ambrose	25	5	73	–	20	2	66	1
Walsh	30	6	98	5	19	5	36	–
Benjamin	22	4	69	1	16	4	46	1
Hooper	14	6	15	–	27	7	75	–
Bishop	25	5	55	3	20	6	54	2
Adams	5.5	1	11	1	4	–	21	–

	O	M	R	W	O	M	R	W
McGrath	31	9	82	4	17	6	36	3
Kasprowicz	13	2	37	–				
Warne	35.2	13	65	3	27.4	6	95	4
Gillespie	23	5	62	2	7	2	27	–
Bevan	11	–	35	–	14	2	40	2
Blewett	4	–	13	1				
M.E. Waugh					4	–	15	–

Fall of Wickets
1–54, 2–68, 3–73, 4–94, 5–131, 6–224, 7–245, 8–283, 9–288
1–51, 2–67, 3–209, 4–274   Australia (2) M.T.G. Elliott retired hurt at 143 for 2

Fall of Wickets
1–92, 2–108, 3–136, 4–166, 5–229, 6–229, 7–243, 8–286, 9–298
1–33, 2–33, 3–35, 4–152, 5–157, 6–176, 7–176, 8–176, 9–183

Umpires: D.B. Hair & D.R. Shepherd

Australia won by 124 runs

Third Test Match – Australia v. West Indies
26, 27 and 28 December 1996 at Melbourne Cricket Ground

Australia

	First Innings		Second Innings	
M.A. Taylor (Capt)	b Ambrose	7	(2) c Hooper, b Walsh	10
M.L. Hayden	c Hooper, b Ambrose	5	(1) b Ambrose	0
J.L. Langer	run out	12	c Hooper, b Ambrose	0
M.E. Waugh	lbw, b Ambrose	0	lbw, b Walsh	19
S.R. Waugh	c Murray, b Bishop	58	b Benjamin	37
G.S. Blewett	run out	62	c Murray, b Walsh	7
*I.A. Healy	c Hooper, b Ambrose	36	b Benjamin	0
P.R. Reiffel	c Samuels, b Benjamin	0	lbw, b Benjamin	8
S.K. Warne	c Campbell, b Bishop	10	c Adams, b Ambrose	18
J.N. Gillespie	not out	4	lbw, b Ambrose	2
G.D. McGrath	c Hooper, b Ambrose	0	not out	5
	lb 8, nb 17	25	lb 4, w 1, nb 11	16
		219		**122**

West Indies

	First Innings		Second Innings	
S.L. Campbell	lbw, b McGrath	7	c Hayden, b McGrath	0
R.G. Samuels	c Taylor, b Warne	17	lbw, b McGrath	13
S. Chanderpaul	c and b McGrath	58	b Reiffel	40
B.C. Lara	c Warne, b McGrath	2	c Hayden, b McGrath	2
C.L. Hooper	run out	7	not out	27
J.C. Adams	not out	74	not out	
*J.R. Murray	c Reiffel, b McGrath	53		
I.R. Bishop	lbw, b McGrath	0		
C.E.L. Ambrose	b Warne	8		
K.C.G. Benjamin	b Reiffel	11		
C.A. Walsh (Capt)	c M.E. Waugh, b Warne	4		
	b 4, lb 7, nb 3	14	nb 4	4
		255	(for 4 wickets)	**8**

	O	M	R	W	O	M	R	W
Ambrose	24.5	7	55	5	12	4	17	4
Bishop	11	1	31	2	10	2	26	–
Benjamin	19	2	64	1	12.5	5	34	3
Walsh	14	–	43	–	11	4	41	3
Adams	1	–	4	–				
Hooper	5	1	14	–				

	O	M	R	W	O	M	R	W
McGrath	30	11	50	5	9	1	41	3
Reiffel	29	8	76	1	9	2	16	–
Warne	28.1	3	72	3	3	–	17	–
Gillespie	3	2	5	–				
Blewett	9	3	19	–	2.5	–	13	–
S.R. Waugh	10	5	22	–				

Fall of Wickets
1–5, 2–26, 3–26, 4–27, 5–129, 6–195, 7–200, 8–203, 9–217
1–0, 2–3, 3–28, 4–47, 5–64, 6–65, 7–76, 8–107, 9–113

Fall of Wickets
1–12, 2–62, 3–71, 4–86, 5–107, 6–197, 7–197, 8–215, 9–230
1–0, 2–25, 3–32, 4–82

Umpires: P.D. Parker & S. Venkataraghavan

West Indies won by 6 wickets

Back with a vengeance. Shane Warne traps Jimmy Adams leg before for 2. (Shaun Botterill/Allsport)

Bishop bowled as admirably at the start of Australia's second innings as he had done in the first, and he had the luckless Taylor taken at first slip. Ponting, too, looked out of sorts and edged Bishop to Browne so that Australia ended the day on 77 for 2.

The fourth day saw a transformation. West Indies bowled and, in particular, fielded dreadfully. Browne seemed to have no understanding with his slips and could not lift his side. One mishap allowed Mark Waugh to escape and to go on to make 67. West Indies' one 'success' came when Elliott, who had shown composure and style, collided with partner Mark Waugh and was carried off the field with a torn cartilage in the right knee. Bevan was able to find more assurance than he had done in previous innings, and Blewett blossomed once more against a lacklustre attack and embarrassing fielding. Taylor was able to declare and set a target of 340.

West Indies had scored 27 by the end of the fourth day, and 30 minutes into the last morning they had added eight runs and lost three wickets. Campbell had gone leg before, and Samuels was beaten by Warne's quicker ball. Lara attempted to hook a short ball, then tried to withdraw his bat and toe-ended low to Healy. Hooper and Chanderpaul counter-attacked, and Chanderpaul raced to 50 off 38 balls. Warne had been withdrawn, but he was brought back shortly before lunch and with the penultimate delivery before the break he turned the ball viciously out of the rough and hit Chanderpaul's leg stump.

In the afternoon, Adams gave a catch to mid-off, and Hooper, who had gone into his shell, was eventually caught by Taylor off Bevan. The ball had been deflected to Taylor by Healy, and the captain dropped the chance only to knock up the ball with his feet as he was lying on the ground and hold the catch at the second attempt. The rest succumbed quickly and quietly to Warne and Bevan. Australia were two up in the series, and Shane Warne had re-established himself as the batsman's nightmare.

Fourth Test Match – Australia v. West Indies
25, 26, 27 and 28 January 1997 at Adelaide Oval

West Indies

	First Innings		Second Innings	
S.L. Campbell	c Healy, b McGrath	0	c Taylor, b Bevan	24
A.F.G. Griffith	lbw, b Bichel	13	c S.R. Waugh, b McGrath	1
S. Chanderpaul	c Taylor, b Warne	20	c Taylor, b Bevan	8
B.C. Lara	c Blewett, b Warne	9	c Healy, b Warne	78
C.L. Hooper	c M.E. Waugh, b McGrath	17	lbw, b Warne	45
J.C. Adams	c and b Warne	10	c M.E. Waugh, b Bevan	0
*J.R. Murray	c Blewett, b Bevan	34	(8) c Taylor, b Bevan	25
I.R. Bishop	c Healy, b Bevan	1	(7) c Bevan, b Warne	0
C.A. Walsh (Capt)	c Healy, b Bevan	0	c S.R. Waugh, b Bevan	1
C.E. Cuffy	c Healy, b Bevan	2	not out	3
P.I.C. Thompson	not out	10	c Hayden, b Bevan	6
	b 4, lb 1, nb 9	14	b 2, lb 5, nb 6	13
		130		**204**

Australia

	First Innings	
M.A. Taylor (Capt)	lbw, b Bishop	14
M.L. Hayden	st Murray, b Hooper	125
J.L. Langer	c Murray, b Cuffy	19
M.E. Waugh	c Murray, b Hooper	82
S.R. Waugh	c Hooper, b Chanderpaul	26
G.S. Blewett	b Cuffy	99
M.G. Bevan	not out	85
*I.A. Healy	c Lara, b Thompson	12
S.K. Warne	c Hooper, b Bishop	9
A.J. Bichel	c Lara, b Walsh	7
G.D. McGrath	b Walsh	1
	b 2, lb 15, w 4, nb 20	41
		517

	O	M	R	W	O	M	R	W
McGrath	12	4	21	2	17	4	31	1
Bichel	10	1	31	1	8	4	16	–
Bevan	9.5	2	31	4	22.4	3	82	6
Warne	16	4	42	3	20	4	68	3
Blewett					2	2	0	–

	O	M	R	W
Walsh	37.3	6	101	2
Bishop	34	6	92	2
Cuffy	33	4	116	2
Thompson	16	–	80	1
Hooper	31	7	86	2
Adams	8	–	23	–
Chanderpaul	3	1	2	1

Fall of Wickets
1–11, 2–22, 3–45, 4–58, 5–72, 6–113, 7–117, 8–117, 9–119
1–6, 2–22, 3–42, 4–138, 5–145, 6–154, 7–181, 8–192, 9–196

Fall of Wickets
1–35, 2–78, 3–242, 4–288, 5–288, 6–453, 7–475, 8–494, 9–507

Umpires: S.G. Randell & D.R. Shepherd

Australia won by an innings and 183 runs

Mark Taylor, the Australian captain, suffered a wretched series and season with the bat. Curtly Ambrose bowled him for 7 in the third Test.
(Shaun Botterill/Allsport)

10 December 1996
at Manuka Oval, Canberra
Prime Minister's XI 258 for 8 (I.J. Harvey 55 not out, D.F. Hills 52)
West Indians 200 (B.E.Young 4 for 46)
Prime Minister's XI won by 58 runs

With the World Series bringing a break in the Test series, West Indies, having suffered two defeats in the first two one-day internationals, struggled to find some form. Lara showed some improvement in an innings of 32, but the tail again proved long and ineffective.

13 December 1996
at Melbourne Cricket Ground
West Indians 217 for 8 (S. Chanderpaul 72)
Australia 'A' 218 for 4 (I.J. Harvey 67 not out, D.S. Lehmann 63 not out)
Australia 'A' won by 6 wickets

West Indies suffered their seventh successive defeat on the tour as Ian Harvey and Darren Lehmann shared an unbroken partnership of 132 to take Australia 'A' to victory with 32 balls to spare. Only Chanderpaul showed any glimpse of form. Twelfth man for the Australian side was Andrew Symonds who had severed his connection with Gloucestershire and declared himself an Australian player. Australia is the country in which he learned his cricket.

19, 20, 21 and 22 December 1996
at Wangaratta
Victoria 354 (G.R.Vimpani 133, D.S. Berry 50, N.A.M. McLean 5 for 45) and 197
West Indians 336 (B.C. Lara 86, S.L. Campbell 80, J.C. Adams 52, I.J. Harvey 5 for 56) and 219 for 4 (S.L. Campbell 112 not out)
West Indians won by 6 wickets

There was comfort for West Indies on the eve of the third Test. Victoria had dominated the first day with Vimpani scoring a confidently aggressive hundred, but the tourists fought back. McLean quickly wrapped up the tail, Campbell continued with his impressive form and Lara gave further indication that he was regaining his touch. Batting a second time, Victoria crumbled against the West Indian pace bowlers, and Campbell stroked his side to a comfortable victory. He and Lara added 105 for the second wicket.

Third Test Match

Australia v. West Indies

Australia made four changes from the side that had won the second Test. Matthew Hayden, the 26-year-old Queensland left-hander, replaced the injured Elliott while Steve Waugh and Paul Reiffel returned at the expense of Bevan and Kasprowicz. Justin Langer was preferred to Ricky Ponting. West Indies made one change, Murray replacing Browne behind the stumps.

Australia chose to bat first and were soon in deep trouble. Taylor was bowled by Ambrose after taking 23 balls to get off the mark, and Hayden was caught low at second slip. Langer pulled Benjamin for six and was then run out when he hesitated as Steve Waugh called for a sharp single. Mark Waugh had already gone first ball so Australia were 27 for 4. They were victims of Ambrose, who had bowled poorly on the tour but now seemed rejuvenated in pace and attitude.

Steve Waugh found an able and willing partner in Blewett, and the pair added 102. With the first ball of a new spell, Bishop induced the faintest of edges to account for Steve Waugh, but Healy maintained the revival with some belligerent cricket. His dismissal, caught at slip off Ambrose, heralded a decline as three wickets fell in successive overs. Samuels went immediately, and Blewett's fine knock came to an end when he was run out from mid-wicket. Warne offered temporary resistance before he and McGrath were out in quick succession.

McGrath, bowling with pace, fire and accuracy trapped Campbell leg before, and West Indies closed on 29 for 1. By the end of the second day they led by 14 runs and had just one wicket remaining. Samuels had gone to a brilliant slip catch by Taylor off the bowling of Warne, and Lara again failed, caught at fourth slip driving at the outstanding McGrath, who then ran out Hooper. Chanderpaul had survived this increasing carnage, but he fell to an astonishing

one-handed reaction catch by McGrath off his own bowling. West Indies were in desperate need of salvation, and it came in the form of Adams and Murray. In 30 overs, they added 90 to bring their side back into contention.

The stand was broken when Murray top-edged an intended hook to long leg, and in his next over McGrath had Bishop leg before. Warne and Reiffel struck in turn, but on the third morning Walsh stayed with Adams longer than had been expected, and West Indies took a 36 run lead.

The Australian second innings was immediately undermined. Hayden offered no shot at Ambrose's fifth delivery and was bowled middle and off. Langer also failed to score, caught at slip off thigh pad and the back of his bat. Either side of lunch Walsh produced a high class spell of bowling that accounted for Taylor, Mark Waugh and Blewett, crucial wickets. Benjamin gave admirable support by dismissing the dangerous Healy and Reiffel. Australia's innings was in shreds, and although Warne offered Steve Waugh some help in the resistance, Ambrose, in the same fine form he had shown in the first innings, returned to send back Gillespie and the leg-spinner. Steve Waugh's heroics were ended by Benjamin, and West Indies needed 87 to win.

They began the task uneasily after tea. McGrath accounted for Campbell, hooking, in the first over, and he trapped Samuels leg before and had Lara caught at cover in quick succession. Chanderpaul stayed serene as danger threatened, and by the time he was bowled by Reiffel victory had been assured. The bowling of Ambrose had seen to that.

7 January 1997
at Toowoomba, Queensland
West Indians 275 for 7 (S. Chanderpaul 123, S.L. Campbell 65)
Australian Country XI 239 (M. Robinson 50 not out)
West Indians won by 36 runs

The World Series limited-over competition occupied much of the time between the third and fourth Tests, and West Indies were restricted to an up-country 50-over game in which Chanderpaul confirmed that he was the major success of the tour.

Fourth Test Match

Australia v. West Indies

Kenny Benjamin had returned to the Caribbean due to injury and Cameron Cuffy had replaced him while Curtly Ambrose was unable to play because of a hamstring strain. West Indies brought in Patterson Thompson and replaced Samuels with Adrian Griffith, who was making his Test debut.

Australia made two changes from the side that lost the third Test, Bevan and Bichel replacing Reiffel and Gillespie. Pace bowler Andrew Bichel had enjoyed an outstanding season for Queensland and deserved his first Test cap. Indeed, Australia were looking for some inspiration. In spite of being two-one up in the series, they faced an air of crisis for having failed to reach the final of the World Series. By the end of the first day, any hint of crisis had evaporated.

West Indies won the toss and batted. Campbell pondered for 15 balls before touching the 16th to Healy. Once more McGrath had struck early. Bichel was soon to claim his first Test wicket, trapping fellow debutant Griffith leg before. Lara appeared to play himself in, hit two fours and then attempted to hit Warne's second ball out of the ground. He was caught at mid-on, a grotesque dismissal.

Chanderpaul and Adams batted with greater sense, but Warne deceived Chanderpaul with a delivery from wide of the crease and had him caught at slip, and he beat Adams in the flight to make the batsman offer a simple return catch. It was then Bevan who took centre stage. His wrist spin, still in its formative years, proved too subtle for the West Indian tail. He took 4 for 1 in 28 balls, and West Indies were all out for 130. By the close, Australia, having lost Taylor, his rhythm still awry, and Langer, weakly cutting a wide delivery to the keeper, had a lead of nine runs, and Hayden and Mark Waugh appeared to be in full flow.

They took total command on the second morning. Hayden reached a maiden Test century in six hours, and Mark Waugh batted with that blissful serenity that is unequalled by any other batsman in the world. There were no setbacks until after lunch when, with the stand worth 164, Mark Waugh, having hit ten fours and a six, nicked an essayed cut to the keeper. Hayden, 15 fours and a six, tried to hit another six and missed to leave himself stranded. The dismissal of Steve Waugh without a run added suggested mid-innings crisis, but Bevan and Blewett quickly re-established supremacy. By the end of the day, Australia were 434 for 5 and Blewett was only nine short of his century.

Blewett was to be denied a century, falling to the generally unimpressive Cuffy on 99. Bevan, not so convincing as Blewett, whose runs came off 154 balls, stayed to the end and saw Australia to a lead of 387.

Brian Lara is caught behind off Warne for 78, and Australia are close to winning the series.
(Shaun Botterill/Allsport)

McGrath attacked with relish, and Griffith fended a catch to gully in the bowler's second over. Taylor produced two splendid slip catches to remove Chanderpaul and Campbell, both victims of Bevan who had been brought on as first change. Hooper joined Lara in a stand worth 96, but he pulled across the line at Warne and was leg before. Adams and Bishop fell in quick succession to undermine

totally the work that Lara and Hooper had done, and West Indies ended the third day on 154 for 6, defeat in match and series imminent.

On 28 January 1997, Mark Taylor became the first Australian captain to lead the side to two series wins over West Indies. Lara, having played his first responsible innings of the series, fell to Warne, and the other three wickets went to Bevan, whose chinamen gave him match figures of 10 for 113, his best in any form of cricket. West Indies suffered their third heaviest loss in their Test history, and Australia, with new talent emerging month by month, were indisputably top of the world.

Fifth Test Match

Australia v. West Indies

Australia brought back Reiffel for Langer. West Indies returned Samuels as opener in place of Griffith, Browne as wicket-keeper for Murray and Ambrose returned for Cuffy. Simmons bolstered the side at the expense of Thompson.

West Indies had won their four previous Tests at the WACA, and they were to make it five out of five, winning in three days on a dreadful pitch. Choosing to bat, Australia fell apart on the first morning, and only a fifth wicket partnership of 120 between Mark Waugh and Bevan saved

Fifth Test Match – Australia v. West Indies
1, 2 and 3 February 1997 at WACA Ground, Perth

Australia

	First Innings		Second Innings	
M.L. Hayden	c Lara, b Ambrose	0	(2) lbw, b Hooper	47
M.A. Taylor (Capt)	run out	2	(1) c Browne, b Ambrose	1
G.S. Blewett	c Browne, b Simmons	17	b Ambrose	0
M.E. Waugh	c Campbell, b Ambrose	79	c Browne, b Walsh	9
S.R. Waugh	c Browne, b Ambrose	1	c Hooper, b Walsh	0
M.G. Bevan	not out	87	c Simmons, b Walsh	15
*I.A. Healy	b Ambrose	7	c Chanderpaul, b Walsh	29
P.R. Reiffel	c Simmons, b Ambrose	0	c Adams, b Walsh	5
S.K. Warne	c Browne, b Bishop	9	c Simmons, b Bishop	30
A.J. Bichel	c Browne, b Bishop	15	c Samuels, b Bishop	18
G.D. McGrath	c Ambrose, b Bishop	0	not out	2
	lb 10, w 2, nb 14	26	b 2, lb 8, w 6, nb 22	38
		243		**194**

	O	M	R	**W**	O	M	R	**W**
Ambrose	18	5	43	**5**	9	2	50	2
Bishop	18	5	54	**3**	12.3	1	44	2
Walsh	9	–	29	**–**	20	4	74	5
Simmons	20	5	58	**1**	3	–	9	–
Hooper	15	1	49	**–**	3	–	7	1

Fall of Wickets
1–0, 2–7, 3–45, 4–49, 5–169, 6–186, 7–186, 8–216, 9–243
1–7, 2–17, 3–43, 4–48, 5–84, 6–105, 7–110, 8–133, 9–189

West Indies

	First Innings		Second Innings	
S.L. Campbell	c Healy, b Reiffel	21	not out	14
R.G. Samuels	c M.E. Waugh, b Warne	76	not out	35
S. Chanderpaul	c Reiffel, b McGrath	3		
B.C. Lara	c Healy, b Warne	132		
C.L. Hooper	c Healy, b Reiffel	57		
J.C. Adams	c Healy, b McGrath	18		
P.V. Simmons	c M.E. Waugh, b Reiffel	0		
*C.O. Browne	c Warne, b Reiffel	0		
I.R. Bishop	c Taylor, b Reiffel	13		
C.E.L. Ambrose	run out	15		
C.A. Walsh (Capt)	not out	5		
	b 5, lb 10, w 1, nb 28	44	b 2, w 1, nb 3	6
		384	for no wickets	**57**

	O	M	R	**W**	O	M	R	**W**
McGrath	30	5	86	2	4	1	14	–
Bichel	18	1	79	–	1.2	–	17	–
Reiffel	26	6	73	5	5	–	24	–
Warne	19	8	55	2				
Blewett	6	2	19	–				
Bevan	5	–	31	–				
S.R. Waugh	7	1	26	–				

Fall of Wickets
1–30, 2–43, 3–251, 4–275, 5–331, 6–332, 7–332, 8–359, 9–367

Umpires: D.B. Hair & P. Willey

West Indies won by 10 wickets

hem from total humiliation. Mark Waugh again looked in ublime form, but again he disappointed when he steered Ambrose to slip shortly after tea as a century seemed his for he taking. Bevan gave further demonstration of his esource with an unbeaten 87 off 164 balls, and if there are ome who doubt his quality as a Test batsman, none can leny his immense all-round contribution to Australia's riumph in this series.

The man of the day, and eventually of the match, lowever, was Ambrose, who relished bowling on this pitch and vas mainly responsible for blowing Australia away for 243.

Campbell had made a brisk start on the first evening, but he soon fell to Reiffel on the second morning, and with McGrath inevitably claiming a scalp, West Indies were a roubled 43 for 2. Lara was now to play a redeeming innings, but sadly far too late to influence the outcome of the series. Playing his best Test innings for two years, he made 132 off 185 balls with a six and 22 fours. In partnership with Samuels, he put on 208, and the runs came in 223 minutes. Samuels was an admirable partner for the great man before ne, like Lara, fell to Warne.

There was the customary late order collapse with Reiffel the beneficiary, but West Indies, 353 for 7 at the end of the second day, took a first innings lead of 141. They might have hoped for more, but it proved ample. The Australian second innings was soon in shreds, and Walsh, suffering from a hamstring injury, bowled unchanged for 20 overs to record figures of 5 for 74. Warne and Bichel added 56 in nine overs for the ninth wicket, but this was a dying gesture of defiance, and West Indies completed their fifth win in five Tests at Perth.

Ambrose was named Man of the Match, McGrath Man of the Series. In spite of his century, Lara won few friends on this tour, and his relationship with his opponents marred what was generally an amicable series. He will have to question himself severely, for he will soon become captain of a West Indian side that is in serious decline. Ambrose and Walsh are close to retirement. Bishop does not look the force of yore. There is a lack of quality spin, glaring weaknesses in batting, and the standard of fielding against Australia was appalling. Defeated at Perth, Australia could still purr contentedly.

Test Match Averages – Australia v. West Indies

Australia Batting

	M	Inns	NO	Runs	HS	Av	100s	50s
A. Healy	5	9	3	356	161*	59.33	1	
M.G. Bevan	4	7	2	275	87*	55.00		2
G.S. Blewett	4	7	1	301	99	50.16		3
M.T.G. Elliott	2	4	1	128	78*	42.66		1
M.E. Waugh	5	9	–	370	82	41.11		4
M.L. Hayden	3	5	–	177	125	35.40	1	
S.R. Waugh	4	6	–	188	66	31.33		2
R.T. Ponting	2	4	–	110	88	27.50		1
J.N. Gillespie	2	3	2	22	16*	22.00		
S.K. Warne	5	7		128	30	18.28		
M.A. Taylor	5	9	–	153	43	17.00		
M.S. Kasprowicz	2	2	–	27	21	13.50		
A.J. Bichel	2	3	–	40	18	13.33		
J.L. Langer	2	3	–	31	19	10.33		
P.R. Reiffel	3	6	–	44	20	7.33		
G.D. McGrath	5	7	2	32	24	6.40		

West Indies Batting

	M	Inns	NO	Runs	HS	Av	100s	50s
C.L. Hooper	5	9	1	362	102	45.25	1	2
S. Chanderpaul	5	9	–	344	82	38.22		2
J.R. Murray	2	3	–	112	53	37.33		1
R.G. Samuels	4	8	1	231	76	33.00		1
B.C. Lara	5	9	–	296	132	32.88	1	1
S.L. Campbell	5	10	1	291	113	32.33	1	1
J.C. Adams	5	9	2	140	74*	20.00		1
C.O. Browne	3	5	1	49	25*	12.25		
I.R. Bishop	5	8	–	86	48	10.75		
C.A. Walsh	5	8	4	31	18	7.75		
C.E.L. Ambrose	4	6	–	39	15	6.50		
K.C.G. Benjamin	3	5	–	31	11	6.20		

Played in one Test: A.F.G. Griffith 13 & 1; P.V. Simmons 0; C.E. Cuffy 2 & 3*; P.I.C. Thompson 10* & 6

Australia Bowling

	Overs	Mds	Runs	Wks	Av	Best	10/m	5/inn
G.D. McGrath	200.5	60	453	26	17.42	5/50		1
M.G. Bevan	76.3	10	265	15	17.66	6/82	1	1
P.R. Reiffel	102.1	22	305	12	25.41	5/73		1
S.K. Warne	217.1	57	594	22	27.00	4/95		
J.N. Gillespie	33	9	94	2	47.00	2/62		
S.R. Waugh	25.1	7	63	1	63.00	1/15		
G.S. Blewett	23.5	7	64	1	64.00	1/13		
A.J. Bichel	37.2	6	143	1	143.00	1/31		
M.E. Waugh	8	1	31	–	–			
M.S. Kasprowicz	48	9	126	–	–			

Bowled in one innings: R.T. Ponting 1.5–1–10–1

West Indies Bowling

	Overs	Mds	Runs	Wks	Av	Best	10/m	5/inn
C.E.L. Ambrose	160.5	31	444	19	23.36	5/74		2
I.R. Bishop	173.3	30	510	20	25.50	3/49		
C.A. Walsh	192.3	32	592	19	31.15	5/74		2
K.C.G. Benjamin	117.5	22	362	9	40.22	3/34		
J.C. Adams	18.5	1	59	1	59.00	1/11		
P.V. Simmons	23	5	67	1	67.00	1/58		
C.L. Hooper	116	25	317	3	105.66	2/86		

Bowled in one innings: C.E. Cuffy 33 – 4 – 116 – 2; P.I.C. Thompson 16 – 0 – 80 – 1; S. Chanderpaul 3 – 1 – 2 – 1

Australia Fielding Figures

15 – I.A. Healy; 9 – M.A. Taylor; 8 – M.E. Waugh; 6 – S.K. Warne; 4 – G.S. Blewett; 3 – M.L. Hayden; 2 – M.G. Bevan, S.R. Waugh, R.T. Ponting, P.R. Reiffel and G.D. McGrath; 1 – M.T.G. Elliott and sub (J.N. Gillespie)

Fielding Figures

15 – C.O. Browne; 9 – C.L. Hooper; 8 – B.C. Lara; 5 – J.R. Murray (ct 4 / st 1); 4 – R.G. Samuels; 3 – P.V. Simmons, S.L. Campbell and J.C. Adams; 2 – C.A. Walsh and S. Chanderpaul; 1 – I.R. Bishop, C.E.L. Ambrose, K.C.G. Benjamin and sub (A.F.G. Griffith)

Pakistan Tour

13 December 1996
at Adelaide Oval
Australian Cricket Academy 248 for 5
(M. Dighton 62)
Pakistanis 236 (Zahoor Elahi 61, Saeed Anwar 56)
Australian Cricket Academy won by 12 runs

Arriving in Australia four days after completing a Test and one-day series against New Zealand, the Pakistan touring side had one 50-over match in preparation for the World Series. They lost four middle order wickets for 15 runs and were narrowly beaten.

19, 20 and 21 December 1996
at Bellerive Oval, Hobart
Pakistanis 299 (Shahid Afridi 80, Mushtaq Ahmed 65, S. Young 7 for 64) and 67 (J.M. Saint 4 for 10)
Tasmania 435 (J. Cox 200, Mushtaq Ahmed 4 for 97)
Tasmania won by an innings and 69 runs

Pakistan's one first-class encounter of the tour proved to be a disaster. They were salvaged by batsmen eight and nine in their first innings and bowled out for 67 in their second. Pace bowler Mohammad Zahid had four stitches in his hand after catching Boon and could not bat in the second innings. James Cox registered the first double century of his career and Shaun Young returned his best bowling figures as Tasmania completed their first victory over an international side for 18 years.

26 December 1996
at Woolloongabba, Brisbane
Queensland 186 for 8
Pakistanis 123 (A.C. Dale 5 for 28)
Queensland won by 63 runs

Pakistan's run of defeats continued when they were bowled out in 38.2 overs in Brisbane. Hero of the match was Adam Dale who shared an unbeaten stand of 76 with Andrew Bichel after three wickets had fallen at 110 and then captured 5 for 28 in his ten overs.

28 December 1996
at Sydney Cricket Ground
Australia 'A' 292 for 7 (S.G. Law 76, D.S. Lehmann 69, M.J. DiVenuto 63)
Pakistanis 293 for 7 (Ijaz Ahmed 123, Inzamam-ul-Haq 59)
Pakistanis won by 3 wickets

Ricky Ponting is run out in Adelaide as Australia crash to Pakistan. (Shaun Botterill/Allsport)

Stuart Law and Michael DiVenuto scored 115 for the Australians' first wicket from 131 balls, and Darren Lehmann maintained the aggression, but Andrew Symonds did not score and failed to take a wicket on his debut for the 'A' side. Ijaz Ahmed hit 123 from 129 balls, and he and Inzamam-ul-Haq added 147 runs off 163 balls for the fourth wicket. The visitors claimed their first win outside the World Series with one ball to spare.

30 December 1996
at Newcastle
Pakistanis 186 for 9 (Zahoor Elahi 69, Inzamam-ul-Haq 55, G. Geise 5 for 20)
Hunter Invitation XI 161 (Saqlain Mushtaq 5 for 28)
Pakistanis won by 25 runs

Rain reduced the match to 32 overs, and Pakistan were indebted to Zahoor Elahi and Inzamam-ul-Haq who added 117 in 61 minutes before wickets tumbled. George Geise, a medium-pacer, took three wickets in his second over and five in 16 balls.

5 January 1997
at Northern Tasmania C.A. Ground, Launceston
Tasmania 235 for 6 (S. Young 59 not out)
Pakistanis 236 for 7 (Zahoor Elahi 89)
Pakistanis won by 3 wickets

In spite of a middle order collapse when five wickets went down for 17 runs, Pakistan gained an encouraging win with one over to spare. They faced the final stages of the World Series with growing confidence.

A new fast bowler on the scene for Australia. Andrew Bichel enjoyed a memorable season and won Test caps in Adelaide and Perth. (David Munden/Sportsline)

Carlton and United World Series

Australia began the mammoth one-day competition as firm favourites. They had beaten West Indies in two Test matches and were at the top of their form. West Indies' morale was low with Lara suffering a run of failures and their pace attack beginning to look tired and jaded and aged. None of the newcomers suggested they were of international standard.

Pakistan were also beset with problems. Australia was the sixth leg of a punishing schedule. Salim Malik declared himself unfit as the party was about to leave for the tournament, and within the next few weeks Aamir Sohail, Moin Khan, Wasim Akram, Waqar Younis, Inzamam-ul-Haq and, most seriously, Saeed Anwar were all to suffer illness or injury. Saeed, plagued by a mysterious fatigue syndrome, was forced to return to Pakistan for treatment, and Mujahid Jamshed, the 25-year-old from Rawalpindi, and Ijaz Ahmed junior joined the party as reinforcements.

The opening match of the series went as expected. Australia beat West Indies with some ease. They had recalled Tom Moody after an absence of four years, and he bowled an impeccable line to help restrict West Indies to 172 on a lively pitch. Moody also claimed the wicket of Brian Lara whose wretched form continued when he clipped the ball into the hands of mid-wicket. With a desperately slow outfield a handicap, only Chanderpaul showed the necessary authority for West Indies, who had given one-day international debuts to McLean and Samuels.

Australia began confidently, but they stuttered in mid-innings and needed 82 from the last 18 overs. Blewett made an unbeaten 57 off 90 deliveries and steered them to victory with eight balls to spare. A crowd of 42,000 was treated to bursts of music between overs.

The music continued in Sydney where West Indies were totally outplayed. West Indies introduced Griffith to international cricket, but he was no more successful than his colleagues, and the last seven wickets fell for 37 runs. Warne virtually decided the match when he took five wickets in 15 balls. Lara received another hostile reception from a crowd who were no longer prepared to tolerate his tantrums and who had been angered by his clash with Healy when he was given caught behind in the second Test. Mark Waugh passed 4000 runs in one-day internationals as he took Australia to a resounding win.

Pakistan's victory over Australia in the third match surprised people. Aamir Sohail and Mohammad Wasim scored 102 for the second wicket before Warne again wrought havoc. Australia reached 192 for 5 only to lose their last five wickets for 19 runs with Saqlain Mushtaq taking top honours.

West Indies' morale was boosted by a massive victory over Pakistan in the fourth match, a day/night game at Adelaide. Both Ambrose and Lara showed improved form, but Jimmy Adams was the surprise as his spin brought him 5 for 37, his best figures in a one-day international. Junior Murray then hit 86 off 78 balls, and West Indies won with 13.5 overs to spare.

For Pakistan, Zahoor Elahi had made a patient 51 before being smartly run out by Lara. For West Indies, victory had come after manager Clive Lloyd had threatened to introduce fresh faces if form and attitudes did not improve.

On New Year's Day, Pakistan bounced back to form and beat Australia for the second time. Saqlain Mushtaq was again a potent force with his off-breaks, and he ran out Moody as well as taking three wickets. Australia generally batted badly, but credit should be given to the Pakistan bowlers for their enthusiasm. Shahid Afridi, in particular, deserves special mention.

He showed equal enthusiasm in his batting. Opening in place of the sick Saeed Anwar, who had returned to Pakistan, he hit 34 off 27 balls in an opening stand of 54. Reiffel pulled a hamstring after bowling three balls in his fourth over, and the last three balls were bowled by Blewett. Shahid hit each of them for four. Warne brought his end and dismissed Zahoor two balls later. Law, too, bowled his leg-breaks commendably, but Pakistan were not to be denied.

The crowd's behaviour was an unfortunate aspect of this match, causing pitch invasions and arrests.

Two days later, Pakistan suffered defeat in Brisbane, at the hands of West Indies. Pakistan had a dreadful start,

A highly successful experiment by West Indies was to use Junior Murray as opener in the one-day series. He crashes a ball from Mushtaq Ahmed to the boundary. Moin Khan is the wicket-keeper. (Stephen Laffer/Sportsline)

losing four wickets for 47 runs. Ijaz Ahmed and Mohammad Wasim stopped the rot, and Moin Khan hit 43 off 52 balls, but Pakistan's score never looked sufficient. With Lara suggesting better form, and Hooper and Adams batting well, West Indies won with 13 balls to spare.

West Indies' star continued to ascend when they overcame an imposing Australian total in the second match at Brisbane. Australia introduced two pace bowlers to international cricket, Bichel of Queensland and Stuart of New South Wales, but the day belonged to the batsmen. All seemed set for an Australian victory when Mark Waugh hit a sparkling century and shared a second wicket stand of 145 with Law, who hit an impressive 93.

Bichel was rewarded with an early wicket on his debut, and Stuart had to wait only a few overs more, but Lara and Hooper then dominated in scoring 154 off 167 balls. Lara hit two sixes and eight fours, and when he was out Hooper took command to bring victory with seven balls to spare.

Defeat in Hobart left Australia facing the unwelcome fact that they were in danger of not reaching the final. The pitch was difficult, but none could have expected the astonishing turnaround after Pakistan's first three batsmen all went without scoring. Two of Pakistan's younger players, Mohammad Wasim and Mujahid Jamshed, making his international debut, helped to revive their side's fortunes. Mujahid also bowled four tight overs of off-breaks and took the vital wicket of Law as Australia struggled against a below strength attack. Bevan was top scorer, but his 24 occupied 81 balls, and, in truth, Australia never looked like reaching their moderate target. Shahid Afridi took the last two wickets to bring merciful release.

The biggest problem confronting Australia was the total lack of form shown by skipper Mark Taylor who was struggling for runs in all types of cricket. In contrast, Brian Lara confirmed his return to the heights with his second century in successive limited-over internationals, which helped West Indies to romp to victory over Pakistan.

Pakistan scored a formidable 257, and Ijaz Ahmed was mainly responsible for this score. Mohammad Wasim struggled for 53 off 105 balls as Hooper and Adams initially imposed a tight control on the Pakistani batsmen. West Indies gave a one-day international debut to Thompson, but it was the spinners who provided the greatest threat to Pakistan. In desperation, Ijaz Ahmed went down the pitch to Adams and missed. Luckily for the batsman, Murray missed the simple stumping, and Ijaz celebrated with an innings of 94, hitting a cascade of boundaries in the closing overs.

Murray made amends for his error by hitting 62 off 66 balls before, ironically, being stumped, but the honours went to Lara, who played delightfully for his 103 from 113 balls. This was vintage Lara, joyful to see.

By beating Australia at the WACA Ground, West Indies ensured that the home side would not qualify for the final for the first time since 1979–80. None could doubt that Mark Waugh did all he could to keep alive Australia's hopes. He hit a sparkling 92 and led his side to a formidable 267, but Murray made 56 off 67 balls, again proving himself a useful quick fire opener. Chanderpaul played well, but three wickets fell for 14 runs, and Australia were on top. Samuels provided Lara with the help he needed, and the pair added 86 off 51 balls to bring West Indies to the brink of victory.

Lara, having been dropped by McGrath off the bowling of Bevan when 22, was caught at long-on off Warne on the last ball of the 49th over. Two balls later, Samuels hit the winning boundary. West Indies had needed 66 from the last seven overs, but Lara took 14 and 11 off two overs from Warne to make victory possible.

The last two qualifying matches had no meaning as West Indies and Pakistan were already set for the final. West Indies rested Walsh, Ambrose and Lara and were trounced by Pakistan, while Australia gave their supporters some encouragement by claiming victory over Pakistan in the final encounter. Anthony Stuart, the New South Wales pace bowler who was playing in his third one-day international reduced Pakistan to 29 for 5 with a spectacular hat-trick. He sent back Ijaz Ahmed and Mohammad Wasim caught behind and had Moin Khan caught at slip. Wasim Akram struck back for Pakistan, but Michael Bevan took Australia to victory with three balls to spare.

Qualifying Table

	P	W	L	Pts
West Indies	8	5	3	10
Pakistan	8	4	4	8
Australia	8	3	5	6

to 123 for 7. Holder and Bishop added 53 in 16 overs, but a final total of 179 was scant consolation for a crowd in excess of 32,000.

With Aamir Sohail suspended for disciplinary reasons, Shahid Afridi moved up to open. He seemed undaunted by the early loss of Inzamam and Zahoor and cracked his way to 53 out of 93, routing the pace men in the process. When he was out, caught by Walsh who covered much ground to reach the ball, Ijaz Ahmed took over, and he and the reliable Moin added 71 for the fifth wicket, which took Pakistan to the brink of victory.

Pakistan survived a poor start to beat West Indies with considerable ease at Melbourne and so win the World Series for the first time in six attempts. With McLean and Kenny Benjamin on their way back to the Caribbean, West Indies still had enough pace power to cause problems, but Ijaz Ahmed and Mohammad Wasim brought a revival, and, inevitably, Moin Khan made a valuable contribution. Nevertheless, a total of 165 hardly looked a winning score. It took on massive proportions when West Indies were reduced to 42 for 7. Wasim Akram bowled a fine spell in spite of a hamstring injury, and Waqar Younis and Shahid Nazir were equally effective. Holder and Ambrose staged a recovery, and as Saqlain Mushtaq walked back to bowl the second ball of the 35th over, with West Indies 85 for 7, the lights went out. The crowd of over 23,000 remained calm during the stoppage which lasted 24 minutes. When power was restored Pakistan quickly brought the game to an end.

Shahid Afridi was named Man of the Finals. Brian Lara was named Player of the Series.

A hat-trick for pace bowler Stuart of Australia in the match against Pakistan in Melbourne. (Shaun Botterill/Allsport)

Finals

Pakistan v. West Indies

The finals proved to be rather disappointing. The first match promised more. Invited to bat first on a pitch that offered help to spin, West Indies raced to 99 in 25 overs with Murray and Campbell hitting the ball cleanly and often. Waqar Younis had conceded 29 runs in his first four overs and had been banished from the attack. It seemed to matter little when Murray offered Mushtaq Ahmed a simple return catch, but it did matter when Lara immediately offered Shahid Afridi another simple return catch from a careless shot. Shahid then bowled Campbell with his quicker ball, and suddenly West Indies were 117 for 3. Waqar was brought back and immediately burst through Chanderpaul's defence. One run later, Phil Simmons, who had flown from South Africa to bolster the West Indian party, was too late on his shot and palpably leg before. Samuels went the same way, and when Shahid Afridi accounted for Jimmy Adams West Indies had disintegrated

Player of the Finals Shahid Afridi hits Curtly Ambrose for 4. (Stephen Laffer/Sportsline)

Match One – Australia v. West Indies
6 December 1996 at Melbourne Cricket Ground

West Indies

S.L. Campbell	c Healy, b Gillespie	31
R.G. Samuels	c M.E. Waugh, b Gillespie	7
B.C. Lara	c Warne, b Moody	5
S. Chanderpaul	c Healy, b Blewett	54
C.L. Hooper	run out	7
J.C. Adams	lbw, b Moody	5
*J.R. Murray	c Blewett, b Warne	24
N.A.M. McLean	c and b M.E. Waugh	7
K.C.G. Benjamin	b Warne	8
C.E.L. Ambrose	run out	2
C.A. Walsh (Capt)	not out	8
	lb 10, w 1, nb 3	14
	49.2 overs	172

	O	M	R	W
Reiffel	10	2	26	–
Gillespie	10	–	39	2
Blewett	10	1	25	2
Blewett	6.2	–	27	1
Warne	10	–	34	2
M.E. Waugh	3	–	11	1

Fall of Wickets
1–11, 2–38, 3–64, 4–73, 5–81, 6–120, 7–135, 8–150, 9–153

Australia

M.A. Taylor (Capt)	b McLean	29
M.E. Waugh	c Murray, b Benjamin	27
R.T. Ponting	lbw, b McLean	5
G.S. Blewett	not out	57
M.G. Bevan	st Murray, b Hooper	3
S.G. Law	b Hooper	21
T.M. Moody	not out	3
*I.A. Healy		
P.R. Reiffel		
S.K. Warne		
J.N. Gillespie		
	lb 17, w 3, nb 8	28
	48.4 overs (for 5 wickets)	173

	O	M	R	W
Ambrose	10	3	19	–
Walsh	9	–	34	–
Benjamin	9.4	–	43	1
McLean	10	1	33	2
Hooper	10	–	27	2

Fall of Wickets
1–59, 2–70, 3–78, 4–90, 5–161

Umpires: S.G. Randell & P.D. Parker *Man of the Match:* G.S. Blewett

Australia won by 5 wickets

Match Two – Australia v. West Indies
8 December 1996 at Sydney Cricket Ground

West Indies

S.L. Campbell	Lbw, b Blewett	38
A.F.G. Griffith	c Taylor, b Reiffel	1
B.C. Lara	c Healy, b Moody	26
C.L. Hooper	c Healy, b Reiffel	41
J.C. Adams	c Healy, b Blewett	22
R.I.C. Holder	b Warne	7
*J.R. Murray	c Bevan, b Warne	8
N.A.M. McLean	c Reiffel, b Warne	0
K.C.G. Benjamin	lbw, b Warne	3
C.E.L. Ambrose	not out	5
C.A. Walsh (Capt)	b Warne	0
	lb 4, w 1, nb 5	10
	48.3 overs	161

	O	M	R	W
McGrath	9	1	26	–
Reiffel	10	1	26	2
Moody	10	–	38	1
Warne	9.3	1	33	5
Blewett	10	–	34	2

Fall of Wickets
1–8, 2–62, 3–91, 4–124, 5–142, 6–147, 7–147, 8–155, 9–155

Australia

M.A. Taylor (Capt)	c Holder, b Ambrose	17
M.E. Waugh	not out	83
R.T. Ponting	b Walsh	44
G.S. Blewett	not out	12
S.G. Law		
M.G. Bevan		
T.M. Moody		
*I.A. Healy		
P.R. Reiffel		
S.K. Warne		
G.D. McGrath		
	w 1, nb 5	6
	42 overs (for 2 wickets)	162

	O	M	R	W
Walsh	8	–	30	–
Benjamin	10	1	38	–
Ambrose	8	1	27	1
McLean	7	–	27	–
Hooper	5	–	24	–
Adams	4	1	16	–

Fall of Wickets
1–39, 2–137

Umpires: D.B. Hair & T.A. Prue *Man of the Match:* S.K. Warne

Australia won by 8 wickets

Match Three – Australia v. Pakistan
15 December 1996 at Adelaide Oval

Pakistan

Aamir Sohail	c Healy, b Bevan	67
Zahoor Elahi	run out	21
Mohammad Wasim	c Taylor, b Bevan	44
Ijaz Ahmed	c Taylor, b Blewett	18
Inzamam-ul-Haq	c Blewett, b McGrath	34
Wasim Akram (Capt)	st Healy, b Warne	7
*Moin Khan	st Healy, b Warne	7
Shahid Afridi	c Warne, b McGrath	6
Saqlain Mushtaq	c M.E. Waugh, b Warne	3
Waqar Younis	b Warne	2
Mushtaq Ahmed	not out	0
	lb 3, w 6, nb 5	14
	49.5 overs	223

	O	M	R	W
McGrath	10	2	45	2
Reiffel	7	1	34	–
Moody	10	1	38	–
Warne	9.5	1	52	4
Blewett	5	–	19	1
Bevan	8	–	32	2

Fall of Wickets
1–39, 2–141, 3–142, 4–170, 5–191, 6–205, 7–213, 8–220, 9–223

Australia

M.A. Taylor (Capt)	c Moin Khan, b Saqlain	28
M.E. Waugh	b Waqar Younis	24
R.T. Ponting	run out	19
S.R. Waugh	c Mohammad Wasim, b Saqlain	57
G.S. Blewett	b Shahid Afridi	12
M.G. Bevan	b Wasim Akram	30
T.M. Moody	st Moin Khan, b Saqlain	8
*I.A. Healy	c Mohammad Wasim, b Saqlain	4
P.R. Reiffel	run out	1
S.K. Warne	c Ijaz Ahmed, b Saqlain	11
G.D. McGrath	not out	0
	lb 5, w 11, nb 1	17
	47.5 overs	211

	O	M	R	W
Wasim Akram	10	1	44	1
Waqar Younis	8	1	33	1
Saqlain Mushtaq	8.5	–	29	5
Mushtaq Ahmed	9	–	43	–
Shahid Afridi	10	–	49	1
Aamir Sohail	2	–	8	–

Fall of Wickets
1–39, 2–76, 3–81, 4–106, 5–175, 6–192, 7–194, 8–195, 9–211

Umpires: D.J. Harper & R. Emerson *Man of the Match*: Saqlain Mushtaq

Pakistan won by 12 runs

Match Four – West Indies v. Pakistan
17 December 1996 at Adelaide Oval

Pakistan

Aamir Sohail	c Adams, b Benjamin	11
Zahoor Elahi	run out	51
Ijaz Ahmed	c Ambrose	16
Inzamam-ul-Haq	c Chanderpaul, b Adams	12
Mohammad Wasim	lbw, b Ambrose	37
Shahid Afridi	c Campbell, b Adams	3
Wasim Akram	c Hooper, b Adams	3
*Moin Khan	b Adams	23
Saqlain Mushtaq	b Adams	6
Mushtaq Ahmed	run out	1
Waqar Younis	not out	2
	lb 8, w 3	11
	48.4 overs	176

	O	M	R	W
Walsh	8	2	24	–
Benjamin	8	–	42	1
McLean	2	–	13	–
Ambrose	9.4	3	16	2
Adams	10	–	37	5
Chanderpaul	4	–	13	–
Hooper	7	1	23	–

Fall of Wickets
1–21, 2–66, 3–93, 4–97, 5–102, 6–105, 7–143, 8–163, 9–171

West Indies

S.L. Campbell	c Aamir, b Mushtaq Ahmed	24
*J.R. Murray	lbw, b Shahid Afridi	86
S. Chanderpaul	c Aamir, b Shahid Afridi	21
B.C. Lara	not out	31
C.L. Hooper	not out	10
J.C. Adams		
R.G. Samuels		
K.C.G. Benjamin		
C.E.L. Ambrose		
N.A.M. McLean		
C.A. Walsh (Capt)		
	lb 3, w 1, nb 1	5
	36.1 overs (for 3 wickets)	177

	O	M	R	W
Wasim Akram	5	1	27	–
Waqar Younis	5	–	28	–
Saqlain Mushtaq	5	–	43	–
Mushtaq Ahmed	10	–	32	1
Shahid Afridi	8.1	1	31	2
Aamir Sohail	3	–	13	–

Fall of Wickets
1–69, 2–128, 3–137

Umpires: D.J. Harper & T.A. Prue *Man of the Match*: J.R. Murray

West Indies won by 7 wickets

Match Five – Australia v. Pakistan
1 January 1997 at Sydney Cricket Ground

Australia

M.A. Taylor (Capt)	run out	11
*M.E. Waugh	c Moin Khan, b Wasim Akram	12
S.G. Law	c Zahoor, b Mushtaq Ahmed	23
S.R. Waugh	b Saqlain Mushtaq	42
M.G. Bevan	c and b Shahid Afridi	27
G.S. Blewett	b Aamir Sohail	33
T.M. Moody	run out	4
*I.A. Healy	not out	22
P.R. Reiffel	c and b Aamir Sohail	3
S.K. Warne	c Ijaz Ahmed, b Saqlain	11
G.D. McGrath	c Aamir Sohail, b Saqlain	1
	lb 7, w 2, nb 1	10
47.1 overs		**199**

	O	M	R	W
Wasim Akram	8	1	35	1
Shahid Nazir	7	–	31	–
Aamir Sohail	9	–	33	2
Saqlain Mushtaq	7.1	2	23	3
Mushtaq Ahmed	7	–	38	1
Shahid Afridi	9	–	32	1

Pakistan

Aamir Sohail	lbw, b Warne	52
Shahid Afridi	c Blewett, b Warne	34
Zahoor Elahi	c and b Warne	0
Ijaz Ahmed	c Bevan, b Law	58
Inzamam-ul-Haq	b Warne	8
Mohammad Wasim	not out	16
Wasim Akram (Capt)	st Healy, b Law	11
*Moin Khan	not out	17
Saqlain Mushtaq		
Mushtaq Ahmed		
Shahid Nazir		
	lb 5, w 2	7
45.3 overs (for 6 wickets)		**203**

	O	M	R	W
McGrath	10	1	41	–
Reiffel	3.3	2	18	–
Blewett	0.3	–	12	–
M.E. Waugh	5.3	1	27	–
Warne	10	1	37	4
Moody	2	–	6	–
Bevan	10	–	35	–
Law	4	–	22	2

Fall of Wickets
1–24, 2–24, 3–75, 4–96, 5–154, 6–156, 7–165, 8–173, 9–191

Fall of Wickets
1–54, 2–54, 3–129, 4–153, 5–160, 6–180

Umpires: S.G. Randell & R.A. Emerson *Man of the Match*: S.K. Warne

Pakistan won by 4 wickets

Match Six – West Indies v. Pakistan
3 January 1997 at Wooloongabba, Brisbane

Pakistan

Aamir Sohail	c Murray, b Walsh	9
Shahid Afridi	c Griffith, b Walsh	2
Zahoor Elahi	c McLean, b Bishop	14
Ijaz Ahmed	c Murray, b Walsh	59
Inzamam-ul-Haq	c McLean, b Ambrose	1
Mohammad Wasim	run out	34
Wasim Akram	run out	1
*Moin Khan	c Samuels, b Bishop	43
Saqlain Mushtaq	c Murray, b Bishop	4
Shahid Nazir	c Ambrose, b Bishop	8
Mohammad Zahid	not out	0
	lb 9, w 6, nb 7	22
49.5 overs		**197**

	O	M	R	W
Walsh	10	1	40	3
Bishop	9.5	1	38	4
Ambrose	10	–	26	1
McLean	4	–	21	–
Hooper	10	–	38	–
Adams	6	–	25	–

West Indies

S.L. Campbell	b Saqlain Mushtaq	35
*J.R. Murray	b Wasim Akram	15
A.F.G. Griffith	run out	2
B.C. Lara	c Moin, b Mohammad Zahid	48
C.L. Hooper	not out	54
J.C. Adams	not out	33
R.G. Samuels		
N.A.M. McLean		
C.E.L. Ambrose		
I.R. Bishop		
C.A. Walsh (Capt)		
	lb 7, w 2, nb 2	11
48.1 overs (for 4 wickets)		**198**

	O	M	R	W
Wasim Akram	9	–	30	1
Mohammad Zahid	10	2	29	1
Shahid Nazir	8	–	37	–
Saqlain Mushtaq	10	2	38	1
Shahid Afridi	6.1	–	39	–
Aamir Sohail	5	–	18	–

Fall of Wickets
1–12, 2–12, 3–45, 4–47, 5–120, 6–124, 7–157, 8–184, 9–192

Fall of Wickets
1–27, 2–36, 3–78, 4–124

Umpires: R.A. Emerson & D.J. Harper *Man of the Match*: C.L. Hooper

West Indies won by 6 wickets

Match Seven – Australia v. West Indies
5 January 1997 at Wooloongabba, Brisbane

Australia

M.A. Taylor (Capt)	c Murray, b McLean	26
M.E. Waugh	run out	102
S.G. Law	c Lara, b Bishop	93
S.R. Waugh	run out	6
M.G. Bevan	not out	18
G.S. Blewett	not out	18
T.M. Moody		
*I.A. Healy		
S.K. Warne		
A.J. Bichel		
A.M. Stuart		
	lb 7, w 3, nb 8	18
	50 overs (for 4 wickets)	281

	O	M	R	W
Bishop	10	2	33	1
Walsh	8	–	50	–
Ambrose	9	–	53	–
Hooper	7	–	52	–
McLean	6	–	23	1
Chanderpaul	2	–	16	–
Adams	8	–	47	–

Fall of Wickets
1–57, 2–202, 3–227, 4–253

West Indies

S.L. Campbell	c Healy, b Bichel	6
*J.R. Murray	c Moody, b Stuart	21
B.C. Lara	c Bevan, b Stuart	102
C.L. Hooper	not out	110
J.C. Adams	not out	34
R.G. Samuels		
S. Chanderpaul		
I.R. Bishop		
N.A.M. McLean		
C.E.L. Ambrose		
C.A. Walsh (Capt)		
	b 4, lb 4, w 3	11
	48.5 overs (for 3 wickets)	284

	O	M	R	W
Bichel	10	1	57	1
Stuart	10	–	48	2
Moody	6.5	–	50	–
Warne	9	–	51	–
Bevan	10	–	46	–
S.R. Waugh	3	–	24	–

Fall of Wickets
1–21, 2–45, 3–199

Umpires: S.G. Randell & P.D. Parker *Man of the Match*: C.L. Hooper

West Indies won by 7 wickets

Match Eight – Australia v. Pakistan
7 January 1997 at Bellerive Oval, Hobart

Pakistan

Aamir Sohail	c Healy, b McGrath	0
Zahoor Elahi	lbw, b Bichel	0
Ijaz Ahmed	c S.R. Waugh, b Bichel	0
Inzamam-ul-Haq	c McGrath, b Blewett	10
Mohammad Wasim	c Taylor, b Warne	54
Mujahid Jamshed	c S.R. Waugh, b Bichel	23
*Moin Khan	not out	33
Wasim Akram (Capt)	st Healy, b Warne	1
Shahid Afridi	c Blewett, b Stuart	3
Saqlain Mushtaq	run out	2
Mohammad Zahid	run out	1
	lb 10, w 12	22
	45.2 overs	149

	O	M	R	W
McGrath	8	1	21	1
Bichel	10	3	17	3
Stuart	10	1	35	1
Blewett	10	2	31	1
Warne	7.2	–	35	2

Fall of Wickets
1–4, 2–4, 3–7, 4–28, 5–78, 6–116, 7–121, 8–132, 9–136

Australia

M.A. Taylor (Capt)	c Moin Khan, b Wasim Akram	6
M.E. Waugh	c Moin Khan, b Ijaz Ahmed	18
S.G. Law	c Ijaz, b Mujahid Jamshed	21
S.R. Waugh	b Wasim Akram	5
M.G. Bevan	lbw, b Wasim Akram	24
G.S. Blewett	c Mohammad Wasim, b Mohammad Zahid	9
*I.A. Healy	c Wasim Akram, b Saqlain	2
S.K. Warne	c Zahoor, b Mohammad Zahid	4
A.J. Bichel	lbw, b Shahid Afridi	2
A.M. Stuart	b Shahid Afridi	1
G.D. McGrath	not out	0
	lb 6, w 9, nb 13	28
	41.5 overs	120

	O	M	R	W
Wasim Akram	8	2	13	3
Mohammad Zahid	10	1	53	2
Ijaz Ahmed	10	–	28	1
Mujahid Jamshed	4	1	6	1
Saqlain Mushtaq	8	1	13	1
Shahid Afridi	1.3	–	1	2

Fall of Wickets
1–29, 2–38, 3–52, 4–68, 5–93, 6–102, 7–115, 8–118, 9–120

Umpires: S.G. Randell & T.A. Prue *Man of the Match*: Mohammad Wasim

Pakistan won by 29 runs

155

Match Nine – Pakistan v. West Indies
10 January 1997 at WACA Ground, Perth

Pakistan

Aamir Sohail	c Hooper, b Walsh	9
Zahoor Elahi	c Griffith, b Adams	32
Mohammad Wasim	c Lara, b Chanderpaul	53
Ijaz Ahmed	run out	94
Shahid Afridi	st Murray, b Hooper	29
Wasim Akram (Capt)	c Adams, b Thompson	10
*Moin Khan	c Adams, b Walsh	5
Mujahid Jamshed	not out	3
Ijaz Ahmed jnr	not out	3
Saqlain Mushtaq		
Mohammad Zahid		
	lb 7, w 8, nb 4	19
	50 overs (for 7 wickets)	257

	O	M	R	W
Walsh	10	2	38	2
Bishop	9	1	60	–
Hooper	10	1	38	1
Thompson	9	1	46	1
Adams	9	1	52	1
Chanderpaul	3	–	16	1

Fall of Wickets
1–14, 2–71, 3–151, 4–200, 5–245, 6–247, 7–252

West Indies

S.L. Campbell	b Wasim Akram	21
*J.R. Murray	st Moin Khan, b Aamir Sohail	62
B.C. Lara	not out	103
C.L. Hooper	b Saqlain Mushtaq	3
S. Chanderpaul	st Moin Khan, b Ijaz Ahmed jnr	35
J.C. Adams	run out	8
R.G. Samuels	not out	7
A.F.G. Griffith		
I.R. Bishop		
C.A. Walsh (Capt)		
P.I.C. Thompson		
	b 2, lb 13, w 2, nb 2	19
	48.4 overs (for 5 wickets)	258

	O	M	R	W
Wasim Akram	10	1	39	1
Mohammad Zahid	10	–	41	–
Saqlain Mushtaq	10	–	45	1
Aamir Sohail	10	–	53	1
Shahid Afridi	6	–	52	–
Ijaz Ahmed jnr	2	–	9	1
Ijaz Ahmed	0.2	–	4	–

Fall of Wickets
1–60, 2–93, 3–102, 4–219, 5–242

Umpires: R.A. Emerson & D.J. Harper *Man of the Match:* B.C. Lara

West Indies won by 5 wickets

Match Ten – Australia v. West Indies
12 January 1997 at WACA Ground, Perth

Australia

M.E. Waugh	c Adams, b Chanderpaul	92
M.A. Taylor (Capt)	b Ambrose	18
S.G. Law	c and b Adams	14
S.R. Waugh	c Griffith, b Chanderpaul	29
T.M. Moody	c Adams, b Hooper	0
M.G. Bevan	c Griffith, b Ambrose	35
G.S. Blewett	run out	29
*I.A. Healy	not out	16
S.K. Warne	not out	10
A.J. Bichel		
G.D. McGrath		
	lb 8, w 7, nb 9	24
	50 overs (for 7 wickets)	267

	O	M	R	W
Walsh	10	–	53	–
Bishop	9	–	49	–
Ambrose	10	–	53	2
Adams	9	–	53	1
Hooper	8	–	35	1
Chanderpaul	4	–	16	2

Fall of Wickets
1–63, 2–92, 3–147, 4–148, 5–181, 6–217, 7–251

West Indies

S.L. Campbell	c Taylor, b Warne	15
*J.R. Murray	c Law, b Bevan	56
B.C. Lara	c Law, b Warne	90
S. Chanderpaul	run out	49
J.C. Adams	c S.R. Waugh, b Moody	0
C.L. Hooper	c McGrath, b Moody	8
R.G. Samuels	not out	36
A.F.G. Griffith	not out	0
I.R. Bishop		
C.E.L. Ambrose		
C.A. Walsh (Capt)		
	b 1, lb 11, w 3	15
	49.2 overs (for 6 wickets)	269

	O	M	R	W
McGrath	10	–	37	–
Bichel	7.2	–	52	–
Warne	10	1	46	2
Law	6	–	31	–
Bevan	10	–	45	1
Moody	6	–	46	2

Fall of Wickets
1–60, 2–80, 3–165, 4–168, 5–179, 6–265

Umpires: T.A. Prue & D.B. Hair *Man of the Match:* B.C. Lara

West Indies won by 4 wickets

Match Eleven – Pakistan v. West Indies
14 January 1997 at Sydney Cricket Ground

West Indies

S.L. Campbell	c Inzamam, b Waqar Younis	3
*J.R. Murray	c Ijaz Ahmed jnr, b Saqlain	22
S. Chanderpaul	c Wasim, b Mushtaq Ahmed	72
A.F.G. Griffith	c Aamir Sohail, b Saqlain	47
R.I.C. Holder	lbw, b Saqlain Mushtaq	2
J.C. Adams	b Saqlain Mushtaq	11
R.G. Samuels	lbw, b Waqar Younis	3
C.L. Hooper (Capt)	c Aamir Sohail, b Waqar Younis	1
I.R. Bishop	not out	2
N.A.M. McLean	run out	1
P.I.C. Thompson	b Wasim Akram	2
	b 6, lb 4, w 5	15
	47.3 overs	181

	O	M	R	W
Wasim Akram	8.3	1	17	1
Waqar Younis	10	1	35	3
Saqlain Mushtaq	9	–	17	4
Mushtaq Ahmed	9	–	51	1
Aamir Sohail	8	–	35	–
Ijaz Ahmed jnr	3	–	16	–

Fall of Wickets
1–10, 2–50, 3–156, 4–159, 5–160, 6–165, 7–169, 8–176, 9–179

Pakistan

Aamir Sohail	b Adams	55
Inzamam-ul-Haq	c Murray, b Thompson	42
Zahoor Elahi	not out	31
Ijaz Ahmed	not out	43
Wasim Akram (Capt)		
Mujahid Jamshed		
*Moin Khan		
Ijaz Ahmed jnr		
Mushtaq Ahmed		
Saqlain Mushtaq		
Waqar Younis		
	b 1, w 7, nb 4	12
	39.2 overs (for 2 wickets)	183

	O	M	R	W
Bishop	7	–	20	–
Thompson	10	1	64	1
McLean	5	–	28	–
Hooper	6	–	21	–
Adams	8	2	30	1
Chanderpaul	3.2	–	19	–

Fall of Wickets
1–90, 2–125

Umpires: P.D. Parker & S.G. Randell *Man of the Match:* Saqlain Mushtaq

Pakistan won by 8 wickets

Match Twelve – Australia v. Pakistan
16 January 1997 at Melbourne Cricket Ground

Pakistan

Aamir Sohail	c Lehmann, b Stuart	6
Inzamam-ul-Haq	c Stuart, b Bevan	64
Zahoor Elahi	c Bichel, b Stuart	1
Ijaz Ahmed	c Healy, b Stuart	2
Mohammad Wasim	c Healy, b Stuart	0
*Moin Khan	c Taylor, b Stuart	0
Wasim Akram (Capt)	run out	33
Shahid Afridi	c Stuart, b Bevan	29
Saqlain Mushtaq	not out	30
Mushtaq Ahmed	st Healy, b Bevan	9
Waqar Younis	not out	1
	lb 1, w 3, nb 2	6
	50 overs (for 9 wickets)	181

	O	M	R	W
Bichel	8	2	31	–
Stuart	10	1	26	5
McGrath	10	–	40	–
Warne	10	2	37	–
Bevan	10	1	36	3
Lehmann	2	–	10	–

Fall of Wickets
1–19, 2–20, 3–29, 4–29, 5–29, 6–92, 7–130, 8–146, 9–171

Australia

M.A. Taylor (Capt)	lbw, b Wasim Akram	8
G.S. Blewett	c Moin Khan, b Wasim Akram	2
S.R. Waugh	c Wasim Akram, b Saqlain	20
M.G. Bevan	not out	79
S.G. Law	c Mohammad Wasim, b Waqar	28
D.S. Lehmann	lbw, b Wasim Akram	10
*I.A. Healy	b Wasim Akram	0
S.K. Warne	lbw, b Shahid Afridi	2
A.J. Bichel	not out	16
A.M. Stuart		
G.D. McGrath		
	lb 7, w 9, nb 1	17
	49.3 overs (for 7 wickets)	182

	O	M	R	W
Wasim Akram	10	1	25	4
Waqar Younis	10	–	36	1
Saqlain Mushtaq	10	–	37	1
Mushtaq Ahmed	10	–	28	–
Shahid Afridi	9	–	48	1
Aamir Sohail	0.3	–	1	–

Fall of Wickets
1–9, 2–14, 3–54, 4–110, 5–139, 6–139, 7–148

Umpires: P.D. Parker & D.B. Hair *Man of the Match:* A.M. Stuart

Australia won by 3 wickets

First Final – Pakistan v. West Indies
18 January 1997 at Sydney Cricket Ground

West Indies

S.L. Campbell	**b** Shahid Afridi	52
*J.R. Murray	**c and b** Mushtaq Ahmed	48
B.C. Lara	**c and b** Shahid Afridi	0
S. Chanderpaul	**b** Waqar Younis	11
P.V. Simmons	lbw, **b** Waqar Younis	0
J.C. Adams	lbw, **b** Shahid Afridi	2
R.G. Samuels	lbw, **b** Waqar Younis	1
R.I.C. Holder	run out	32
I.R. Bishop	not out	18
C.E.L. Ambrose	lbw, **b** Waqar Younis	0
C.A. Walsh (Capt)	not out	2
	b **1**, lb **7**, w **2**, nb **3**	13
	50 overs (for 9 wickets)	**179**

	O	M	R	**W**
Wasim Akram	10	–	23	–
Waqar Younis	10	1	43	4
Saqlain Mushtaq	10	1	32	–
Mushtaq Ahmed	10	–	40	1
Shahid Afridi	10	–	33	3

Fall of Wickets
1–**99**, 2–**100**, 3–**117**, 4–**120**, 5–**121**, 6–**123**, 7–**123**, 8–**176**, 9–**176**

Pakistan

Inzamam-ul-Haq	**c** Chanderpaul, **b** Walsh	5
Shahid Afridi	**c** Walsh, **b** Bishop	53
Zahoor Elahi	**c** Murray, **b** Ambrose	4
Ijaz Ahmed	**c** Adams, **b** Walsh	60
Mohammad Wasim	run out	3
*Moin Khan	not out	38
Mujahid Jamshed	**b** Chanderpaul	1
Wasim Akram (Capt)	not out	1
Saqlain Mushtaq		
Mushtaq Ahmed		
Waqar Younis		
	b **4**, lb **7**, w **3**, nb **6**	20
	38.2 overs (for 6 wickets)	**185**

	O	M	R	**W**
Ambrose	9	1	35	1
Walsh	10	1	29	2
Bishop	8	–	36	1
Simmons	5	–	34	–
Adams	3	–	19	–
Chanderpaul	3.2	–	21	1

Fall of Wickets
1–**13**, 2–**40**, 3–**93**, 4–**99**, 5–**170**, 6–**171**

Umpires: S.G. Randell & D.B. Hair

Pakistan won by 4 wickets

Second Final – Pakistan v. West Indies
20 January 1997 at Melbourne Cricket Ground

Pakistan

Aamir Sohail	**c** Lara, **b** Cuffy	16
Shahid Afridi	**c** Lara, **b** Walsh	0
Zahoor Elahi	**c** Lara, **b** Walsh	0
Ijaz Ahmed	**c** Murray, **b** Simmons	45
Inzamam-ul-Haq	run out	5
Mohammad Wasim	**c** Adams, **b** Ambrose	41
Wasim Akram (Capt)	run out	3
*Moin Khan	**c** Simmons, **b** Adams	26
Saqlain Mushtaq	**c** Murray, **b** Cuffy	4
Waqar Younis	**b** Ambrose	4
Shahid Nazir	not out	0
	lb **12**, w **4**, nb **5**	21
	48.3 overs	**165**

	O	M	R	**W**
Ambrose	9.3	2	17	2
Walsh	9	1	24	2
Cuffy	9	1	33	2
Hooper	10	–	35	–
Simmons	9	2	30	1
Adams	2	–	14	1

Fall of Wickets
1–**2**, 2–**6**, 3–**38**, 4–**53**, 5–**96**, 6–**102**, 7–**137**, 8–**154**, 9–**159**

West Indies

S.L. Campbell	hit wicket, **b** Wasim Akram	0
*J.R. Murray	lbw, **b** Waqar Younis	0
B.C. Lara	**c** Moin Khan, **b** Shahid Nazir	19
S. Chanderpaul	**c** Moin Khan, **b** Wasim Akram	10
C.L. Hooper	**c** Shahid Afridi, **b** Wasim Akram	0
J.C. Adams	**c** Moin Khan, **b** Shahid Nazir	1
P.V. Simmons	**b** Shahid Nazir	0
R.I.C. Holder	**b** Shahid Afridi	20
C.E.L. Ambrose	not out	31
C.A. Walsh (Capt)	**b** Saqlain Mushtaq	0
C.E. Cuffy	**b** Waqar Younis	4
	b **1**, lb **7**, w **10**	18
	40.3 overs	**103**

	O	M	R	**W**
Wasim Akram	7	2	17	3
Waqar Younis	6.3	1	17	2
Shahid Nazir	10	3	14	3
Saqlain Mushtaq	10	–	26	1
Shahid Afridi	7	–	21	1

Fall of Wickets
1–**3**, 2–**3**, 3–**31**, 4–**31**, 5–**32**, 6–**41**, 7–**42**, 8–**89**, 9–**90**

Umpires: S.G. Randell & P.D. Parker   *Man of the Finals*: Shahid Afridi

Pakistan won by 62 runs

England 'A' Tour

Tours by 'A' sides have become fashionable in recent years, and that they have some value in providing experience for younger players is unquestionable. The problem is that countries like England and Australia find it increasingly difficult to offer suitable opposition within their already crowded fixture lists. The England 'A' tour of Australia before Christmas 1996 was no exception. The team engaged in only three matches which were accorded first-class status, and limited-over games against moderate opposition is hardly suitable grounding for potential Test cricketers.

The England side was managed by David Graveney, later to become chairman of selectors, and Mike Gatting acted as coach when Gooch withdrew from the position because of his father's illness. Adam Hollioake, who had shown impressive qualities of leadership with Surrey when Stewart was on international duty, captained the party.

There were some interesting selections in the England side, notably Shah, the young Middlesex batsman, Harris, the Derbyshire pace bowler, and Giles, the left-arm spinner from Warwickshire, a bowler of great promise. Less enterprising choices were seen in the inclusion of Hegg and Such, both of whom, one felt, were sufficiently experienced and mature as to be wasted on an 'A' tour where younger players would have benefitted more.

31 October, 1, 2 and 3 November 1996
at Tamworth
England 'A' 155 (O.A. Shah 76, S.C.G. MacGill 4 for 43) and 217 (O.A. Shah 79, M.A. Butcher 52, S.C.G. MacGill 5 for 84)
New South Wales XI 330 (S.M. Thompson 90, C.A. Glassock 84, A.F. Giles 5 for 110) and 43 for 1
New South Wales XI won by 9 wickets

What was in fact a New South Wales 2nd XI proved far too strong for England 'A' in the opening match of the tour. Spinners MacGill and Freedman held the England batsmen in a vice-like grip from which only Owais Shah, taking leave from his 'A' Level studies, was able to break free. He batted

Johnson is caught by Hollioake off the bowling of Headley in England 'A's victory over South Australia. (Shaun Botterill/Allsport)

impressively in both innings. Ashley Giles took four wickets as New South Wales slipped to 102 for 5, but Craig Glassock and Scott Thompson batted into the third day as they added 141 for the sixth wicket. Thompson was particularly severe on Such, whom he hit for three sixes. When the tourists batted again Mark Butcher showed good form against pace, but, like all except Shah, floundered against the spin. England held out until mid-afternoon with Such batting an hour for five and Giles scoring 11 in 69 minutes, but MacGill's leg-spin was the decisive factor.

6 November 1996
at Adelaide Oval No 2
South Australia 203 for 7 (D.S. Lehmann 61 not out)
England 'A' 204 for 4 (M.A. Butcher 76)
England 'A' won by 6 wickets

Lehmann's 61 off 59 balls boosted South Australia after Adam Hollioake had restricted them with 3 for 44 in his ten overs. Facing a full strength side, England lost Vaughan at 50 before Butcher and McGrath took them to 117 in 27 overs. Three wickets then fell for 29 runs until White and Hollioake stood firm and brought the tourists victory with 31 balls to spare.

8, 9, 10 and 11 November 1996
at Adelaide Oval
England 'A' 294 (M.A. Butcher 73, W.K. Hegg 69, C. White 61, M.A. Harrity 4 for 61) and 151 (P.E. McIntyre 4 for 43)
South Australia 276 (J.D. Siddons 101, D.W. Headley 6 for 60) and 157 (J.C. Scuderi 55, D.W. Headley 5 for 38)
England 'A' won by 12 runs

England 'A' won their opening first-class match and owed much to Dean Headley who had performed splendidly for the 'A' side in Pakistan a year earlier only to miss the beginning of the England season and the chance of a place in the Test side because of injury. England had begun disastrously, losing four wickets for 45. White and Butcher added 109, but the real bonus came from Warren Hegg, who dominated a last wicket stand of 76 with Headley.

It was Headley who bowled England to a creditable first innings lead of 18. Jamie Siddons' century had taken South Australia to 220 for 5 before Headley brought about a collapse. England, in turn, collapsed as, once again, they floundered against leg-spin.

Needing 164 to win, South Australia plunged to 59 for 5, with Headley the architect of their destruction once again. Scuderi and Young added 70, but Giles dismissed Young and Headley accounted for Gillespie and McIntyre with successive deliveries. Giles bowled Harrity, and England claimed an unexpected victory although they were fortunate that Darren Lehmann was unable to bat for South Australia because of his commitment to play against the West Indies.

*Adam Smith is run out by Vaughan as England 'A' beat the
Australian Cricket Academy. (Shaun Botterill/Allsport)*

15, 16, 17 and 18 November 1996
at Marist Park, Mt Gambier
Australian Cricket Academy 258 (M. Dighton 72,
S. Craig 61, A.F. Giles 4 for 63) and 175 (J. Cassell 69,
A.J. Harris 5 for 61)
England 'A' 272 (M.A. Butcher 81, A.J. Hollioake 62,
D. Nash 7 for 66) and 165 for 3 (M.P. Vaughan 70)
England 'A' won by 7 wickets

The Australian Academy side had embarrassed the full
England team the previous season, but they were brushed
aside by the 'A' eleven though only 17 overs were possible on
the third day. Ashley Giles again bowled most impressively,
and Andy Harris enjoyed his best game of the tour. England
overcame the loss of six middle innings wickets for 19 runs
in ten overs in their first knock to win comfortably. Hollioake
and Harris added 66 for the ninth wicket.

21, 22, 23 and 24 November 1996
at Optus Oval (formerly Carlton)
England 'A' 438 (C. White 99, M.A. Ealham 78,
A.J. Hollioake 58, M.A. Butcher 55)
Victoria 211 (L.D. Harper 63, G. Chapple 4 for 43) and
219 (G.R. Vimpani 53, D.J. Saker 51 not out)
England 'A' won by an innings and 8 runs

England 'A' made it two wins in two first-class matches
when they beat Victoria by an innings, although they were
once more aided in that the state side batted without
Dodemaide and Fleming, both injured, in their second
innings. A fifth wicket stand of 102 between White and
Hollioake gave substance to the England innings. White
was within one run of his century when he edged Fleming to
slip. The Yorkshireman, who had learned his cricket in
Victoria, had lost concentration after exchanging heated
words with Saker. Ealham continued the run spree as the
last three wickets added a violent 133. Bowling and fielding
with passion and joy, England 'A' dismissed Victoria for 211

and were in total control when they captured the home side's
seventh second innings wicket at 124. Saker then joined
Vimpani in a stand which occupied nearly two hours and
produced 95 runs. It ended when Vimpani went to pull
Chapple and dragged the ball into his stumps, giving
England 'A' victory with just 11.4 overs remaining.

28 November 1996
at Manuka Oval, Canberra
Australian Capital Territory 198 for 7 (P.J. Solway 68)
England 'A' 201 for 3 (M.A. Butcher 72)
England 'A' won by 7 wickets

England 'A's fifth victory in succession came with 7.3 of
their 50 overs unused. It gave further evidence of the side's
confidence, ability and exemplary spirit.

30 November, 1, 2 and 3 December 1996
at Manuka Oval, Canberra
Canberra 216 (P.J. Solway 59, P.M. Such 5 for 29)
and 320 (I.A. Garrity 90, M.R.J. Veletta 68, A.J. Hollioake
4 for 27)
England 'A' 408 (A. McGrath 108, G. Chapple 59 not out,
C. White 53, B.J. Smith 5 for 91) and 123 for 5
Match drawn

The winning sequence of the England side came to an end,
but only after a brave and dramatic bid failed narrowly.
Such, who did not appear in any of the first-class matches,
dominated the first Canberra innings, conceding only 29
runs in 32.3 overs as he took five wickets. On the second
day, Anthony McGrath hit the first century of the tour and
took England 'A' to a comfortable lead, which was enhanced
by some brisk batting in the tail. Mike Veletta, once of
Australia, and Evans began Canberra's second innings with
a stand of 106, but the home side closed the third day on
140 for 4, still 52 runs adrift of England.

Garrity held up England on the final day, and the
home side extended their innings by 72 overs. England 'A'
were left 15 overs in which to score 129 to win. Butcher,
Shah and Vaughan all made valiant efforts, and Hegg, too,
took up the chase, but, with six needed off the last ball, the
Lancashire wicket-keeper swung and missed.

5 December 1996
at SCG, Sydney
New South Wales 243 for 6 (S. Lee 113, C.J. Richards 55)
England 'A' 244 for 8 (A.J. Hollioake 51, G.R. Robertson
4 for 46)
England 'A' won by 2 wickets

Giles and Headley scored the last 42 runs and brought their
side a fine victory with three balls to spare. England 'A' had
earlier survived a blistering century from Lee.

Marist Park, Mount Gambier, a beautiful setting for the match between England 'A' and the Australian Cricket Academy. (Shaun Botterill/Allsport)

Mercantile Mutual Cup

Australia's one-day competition, rather awkwardly balanced within the domestic programme, continues to expand with Australian Capital Territory due to enter the tournament in 1997–98. There were several cricketers who found places in state elevens for the one-day games but did not appear in the Sheffield Shield. Prominent among them were Dean Waugh and Trevor Bayliss of New South Wales.

7 December 1996
at North Dalton Park, Wollongong
England 'A' 154 for 6 (S. Lee 4 for 35)
v. **New South Wales**
Match abandoned

Rain caused the abandonment of the match after 30.4 of the 50 overs of the England 'A' innings had been bowled.

10, 11, 12 and 13 December 1996
at Woolloongabba, Brisbane
England 'A' 230 (M.A. Butcher 72, B.N. Creevey 6 for 70) and 106 for 4
Queensland 298 (M.P. Mott 73, T.J. Dixon 62, C. White 6 for 66)
Match drawn

England 'A' ended their tour with a first-class match against Queensland. Law won the toss and asked the visitors to bat. With Mark Butcher again producing the rescue act, England made 170 for 7 on a first day shortened by a tropical storm. Brendan Creevey, a medium-pacer making his first-class debut, took two more wickets on the second morning to finish with an impressive 6 for 70.

England were handicapped in the field, losing Ealham with a broken finger and Headley with what was feared to be a recurrence of his hip problem. Queensland reached 154 for 4 when bad light ended play prematurely. Only 85 minutes play was possible on the third day when Queensland advanced their score to 195 for the loss of Cassell. As the game petered out to a draw Craig White had the satisfaction of claiming the best bowling figures of his career and being summoned to Zimbabwe to bolster the England side, which had been hit by injury to Irani.

So ended a highly successful tour. The England party had performed well on the field and had won many friends off it. They had played cricket with a zest and joyful commitment that gained the highest admiration. Messrs Graveney and Gatting deserved much praise for what they had achieved and for the way in which the team had carried itself.

12 October 1996
at Adelaide Oval
Victoria 238 for 4 (D.M. Jones 93 not out, B.J. Hodge 50)
South Australia 208 for 9 (G.S. Blewett 61)
Victoria (2 pts) won by 30 runs

13 October 1996
at North Sydney Oval
New South Wales 242 for 7 (C.J. Richards 109)
Western Australia 246 for 6 (A.C. Gilchrist 61 not out, J.L. Langer 54)
Western Australia (2 pts) won by 4 wickets

A stand of 88 for the third wicket between Dean Jones and Brad Hodge gave substance to the Victorian innings. Jones also shared a stand of 72 with Ian Harvey for the fourth wicket. South Australia were never in touch with the required rate.

Corey Richards scored his first century for New South Wales in any form of cricket but still finished on the losing side. Langer and Campbell scored 92 for Western Australia's first wicket, and Gilchrist took them to victory with 3.2 overs to spare.

18 October 1996
at Woolloongabba, Brisbane
New South Wales 169
Queensland 173 for 5 (M.L. Hayden 75 not out, A.M. Stuart 4 for 22)
Queensland (2 pts) won by 5 wickets

New South Wales lost their last four wickets for seven runs, while Queensland owed much to Hayden, who stayed calm through 45.2 overs when Stuart threatened to wreck the home side's innings.

27 October 1996
at Optus Oval
Victoria 250 for 4 (D.M. Jones 100 not out, M.T.G. Elliott 59)
Tasmania 192 (D.C. Boon 52, S.K. Warne 5 for 35)
Victoria (2 pts) won by 58 runs

at Woolloongabba, Brisbane
Queensland 214 (M.L. Hayden 64, K.M. Harvey 4 for 37)
Western Australia 218 for 6 (M.P. Lavender 75,
D.R. Martyn 53)
Western Australia (2 pts) won by 4 wickets

Dean Jones was unbeaten for a match-winning score for the
second time while Shane Warne took five wickets in a
domestic one-day game for the first time. Australia sighed
with relief.

2 November 1996
at Sydney Cricket Ground
Tasmania 173 (B.E. McNamara 6 for 25)
New South Wales 174 for 3 (S. Lee 63, K.J. Roberts
55 not out)
New South Wales (2 pts) won by 7 wickets

3 November 1996
at Adelaide Oval
South Australia 134
Queensland 138 for 3 (M.L. Love 58 not out)
Queensland (2 pts) won by 7 wickets

Bradley McNamara produced his best bowling figures in
limited-over cricket. They were among the best ever
recorded in the competition.

10 November 1996
at Woolloongabba, Brisbane
Queensland 275 for 5 (J.P. Maher 91)
Tasmania 235 (M.J. DiVenuto 78)
Queensland (2 pts) won by 40 runs

Stuart Law was back to captain Queensland who trounced
Tasmania, without a victory in three matches. Geoff Foley
took the individual award for his rumbustious unbeaten 46
and two economical wickets.

18 December 1996
at WACA Ground, Perth
Western Australia 210 for 9 (T.M. Moody 102 not out)
South Australia 171 (T.M. Moody 4 for 30)
Western Australia (2 pts) won by 39 runs

Western Australia approached the Christmas break with a
one hundred per cent record. They owed a vast amount to

*Adam Dale enjoyed a fine season for Queensland in all forms of
cricket and took the bowling prize in the Mercantile Mutual Cup.
(Stephen Laffer/Sportsline)*

skipper Tom Moody who, coming in at 24 for 4, hit an
unbeaten 102 and followed it with his best bowling
performance in limited-over domestic cricket.

17 January 1997
at WACA Ground, Perth
Victoria 143 (R.P. Larkin 61)
Western Australia 146 for 5
Western Australia (2 pts) won by 5 wickets

Western Australia claimed their fourth victory in as many
matches and clinched first place in the qualifying table.

19 January 1997
at Manuka Oval, Canberra
South Australia 297 for 9 (J.D. Siddons 75, G.S. Blewett
53, D.S. Lehmann 52)
Australian Capital Territory 139 (G.S. Blewett 4 for 20)
South Australia won by 158 runs

This was a rehearsal for Canberra's entry into the
competition in 1997–98. They did not fare well as Greg
Blewett had an outstanding all-round match.

8 February 1997
at Bellerive Oval, Hobart
Western Australia 222 (M.E. Hussey 82, M.W. Ridgway
4 for 37)
Tasmania 196 (R.T. Ponting 64)
Western Australia (2 pts) won by 26 runs

at Adelaide Oval
New South Wales 178 (B.E. McNamara 63)
South Australia 179 for 6
South Australia (2 pts) won by 4 wickets

9 February 1997
at Melbourne Cricket Ground
Queensland 240 for 6 (J.P. Maher 111 not out,
G.I. Foley 52)
Victoria 162 for 7
Queensland (2 pts) won by 78 runs

Victory in Hobart gave Western Australia a clean sweep
over other states in the qualifying rounds. South Australia,
in contrast, gained their first win in the competition.
Queensland made sure of second spot as Jimmy Maher hit
his first limited-over century.

15 February 1997
at Sydney Cricket Ground
New South Wales 152 for 9
Victoria 129 for 8
New South Wales (2 pts) won by 23 runs

16 February 1997
at Bellerive Oval, Hobart
Tasmania 260 for 5 (M.J. DiVenuto 129 not out,
S. Young 64)
South Australia 145 (D.S. Lehmann 65, P.J. Hutchison
5 for 27)
Tasmania (2 pts) won by 115 runs

With the top four positions already settled, the final
matches had only academic interest. DiVenuto hit his first
century in the competition while Paul Hutchison, once of
South Australia, returned his best bowling figures.

Qualifying Table

	P	W	L	Pts
Western Australia	5	5	–	10
Queensland	5	4	1	8
New South Wales	5	2	3	4
Victoria	5	2	3	4
Tasmania	5	1	4	2
South Australia	5	1	4	2

Semi-Finals

22 February 1997
at Woolloongabba, Brisbane
Queensland 265 for 5 (S.G. Law 93, G.I. Foley 66)
New South Wales 248 for 9 (R. Chee Quee 52,
A.C. Dale 4 for 48)
Queensland won by 17 runs

23 February 1997
at WACA Ground, Perth
Victoria 191 for 8
Western Australia 193 for 7 (R.J. Campbell 50,
D.R. Martyn 50)
Western Australia won by 7 wickets

Stuart Law hit 93 off 98 balls to set up Queensland's victory
over New South Wales. He and Foley added 158 for the
fourth wicket. The visitors responded bravely. Richard
Chee Quee hit 52 off 78 balls and New South Wales reached
129 for three. Prestwidge claimed two wickets as three men
were out while eight were scored. Emery, 49 off 51 balls,
and Robertson, 33 off 39 balls, rallied their side, but they
fell short of their target.

Facing a moderate target at the WACA Ground,
Western Australia were boosted by Ryan Campbell whose
50 off 32 balls was the fastest of the season and won him
five thousand dollars. Brendon Julian square cut Ian
Harvey for the winning boundary with 7.1 overs remaining.

Final

Western Australia v. Queensland

Western Australia won the Mercantile Mutual Cup with 15
overs to spare. This was the ninth time they had taken the
title. Queensland batted poorly, and although Western
Australia lost Hussey for 0, Campbell and Martyn added
65 for the second wicket with Campbell hitting two sixes
and seven fours in his 43-ball 50. He was named Man of
the Final. Martyn, 48, and Moody, 37, stroked Western
Australia to victory after Campbell's departure at 74.

The Man of the Series award went to Queensland's
Geoff Foley. He scored 238 runs, average 79.33, and
captured three wickets with bowling that was always
economical. His team-mate, Adam Dale, won five
thousand dollars for bowling the most victims. The award
for the best new talent went to Kade Harvey of Western
Australia who captured 18 wickets at 13.50 runs each in
seven matches.

Others deserving of mention are Michael DiVenuto
who scored 274 runs in five matches, and the veteran
Dean Jones, 193 runs in two matches without being
dismissed.

Sheffield Shield

Like domestic competitions in other parts of the world, Australia's famous Sheffield Shield suffered because of the ever increasing number of international matches. All but two matches in the Shield coincided with international fixtures, and state sides had to face other problems. The match between New South Wales and Queensland in November, for example, was scheduled for the Sydney Cricket Ground, but it had to be switched to Bankstown Oval because Michael Jackson had booked the SCG for a concert.

South Australia began as favourites to retain the Shield, but with May and Nobes retiring and Webber having to undergo knee surgery, the odds on them lengthened.

Queensland lost Rowell because of a foot injury, and Tasmania lost Tucker who retired. Greg Matthews, rather surprisingly, was appointed captain of New South Wales whose chances of winning the Shield were seen as slight because of the inevitable demands of international cricket.

Dean Jones was deposed as captain of Victoria and replaced by Shane Warne, who was to be available only for the first two matches. The country held its breath while he proved his fitness following his finger operation. So much depends upon the leg-spinner.

6, 7, 8 and 9 November 1996
at Woolloongabba, Brisbane
Tasmania 168 (M.J. DiVenuto 66, D.F. Hills 60, A.J. Bichel 6 for 63) and 176 (S.A. Muller 4 for 35, A.C. Dale 4 for 44)
Queensland 244 (G.I. Foley 82 not out) and 101 for 1
Queensland won by 9 wickets
Queensland 6 pts, Tasmania 0 pts

8, 9, 10 and 11 November 1996
at Sydney Cricket Ground
New South Wales 264 (M.G. Bevan 79) and 353 for 8 dec. (M.G. Bevan 150 not out, M.J. Slater 69, B.A. Williams 4 for 63)
Victoria 161 (W.G. Ayres 55, A.M. Stuart 5 for 63) and 398 (M.T.G. Elliott 187, D.S. Berry 148, S.C.G. MacGill 4 for 72)
New South Wales won by 58 runs
New South Wales 6 pts, Victoria −0.3 pts

Queensland started the season brightly. With Law, Healy and Kasprowicz absent, they were led by Hayden who, as in the Mercantile Mutual Cup, showed admirable tactical awareness. He asked Tasmania to bat first when he won the toss and was well served by his pace bowlers Bichel and Dale. Dale, 28 years old, was making his first-class debut, having appeared in one-day matches the previous season. He had Cox caught off the fourth ball he bowled. Hills and DiVenuto added 121, but Tasmania lost their last nine wickets for 47 runs. Six of these wickets fell to Andrew Bichel, who returned career-best figures. One of his victims

Geoff Foley, Man of the Series in the limited-over competition. (Shaun Botterill/Allsport)

was Daniel Marsh, son of Rodney and formerly of South Australia, who was playing his first game for Tasmania.

Queensland did not find run-getting easy but were lifted by Geoff Foley's unbeaten 82 off 138 balls. Batting a second time, Tasmania fell to Dale and Muller who was another to return career-best bowling figures. Dale finished with match figures of 7 for 73 on his debut.

The main interest at the SCG centred on the return of Shane Warne. He could claim a satisfactory rather than inspiring come-back, bowling 45 overs in the match and taking the wickets of Stuart and MacGill at a personal cost of 115 runs. The important fact was that he bowled intelligently within himself, and his fitness was not in doubt. His team was less successful. A middle order collapse against the pace of Stuart, who claimed his first five-wicket haul, saw them surrender first innings points. Michael Bevan then hit a fine century. His 150 included 16 fours, and Matthew's declaration left Victoria a day and a half in which to get 457 to win. At the end of the third day, they were 100 for 5 and all looked lost. Wicket-keeper Darren Berry had other ideas. He reached the first century of his career and shared a record sixth wicket stand of 290 with Elliott, who, after batting for 440 minutes, was finally bowled by leg-spinner MacGill, formerly of Western Australia. Berry was out two runs later, having batted for 283 minutes, and Victoria's brave challenge was at an end.

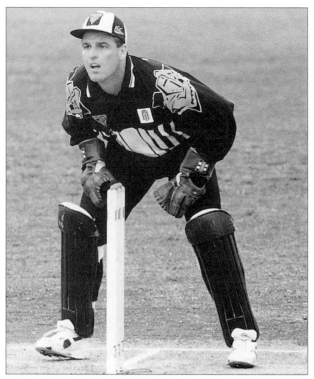

Darren Berry of Victoria hit a maiden first-class century in the opening Shield match of the season and followed this with eight wicket-keeping dismissals in the first innings of the match against South Australia. (Stephen Laffer/Sportsline)

15, 16, 17 and 18 November 1996
at Melbourne Cricket Ground
Victoria 345 for 9 dec. (D.M. Jones 152, I.J. Harvey 70) and 38 for 1
South Australia 84 (D.J. Saker 4 for 22) and 298 (G.R. Parker 112, B.A. Johnson 52, I.J. Harvey 7 for 44)
Victoria won by 9 wickets
Victoria 6 pts, South Australia 0 pts

at WACA Ground, Perth
Tasmania 473 for 6 dec. (M.J. DiVenuto 130, D.F. Hills 111, R.T. Ponting 67, J. Cox 62) and 252 for 4 dec. (J. Cox 116, D.F. Hills 68)
Western Australia 326 for 4 dec. (J.L. Langer 143 not out, T.M. Moody 114) and 258 (M.E. Hussey 90, D.R. Martyn 70, C.R. Miller 4 for 48)
Tasmania won by 141 runs
Tasmania 6 pts, Western Australia 0 pts

at Bankstown Oval, Sydney
New South Wales 296 (S.R. Waugh 106, M.A. Taylor 53, M.S. Kasprowicz 5 for 110) and 141
Queensland 330 (A. Symonds 111, T.J. Barsby 79) and 108 for 3 (T.J. Barsby 68)
Queensland won by 7 wickets
Queensland 6 pts, New South Wales 0 pts

Victoria's win over South Australia was significant for a number of remarkable individual performances. Ex-Victorian Geoff Parker hit a maiden first-class hundred on his debut for South Australia, while Dean Jones scored the 51st century of his career and added 129 with Ian Harvey after four wickets had gone for 71. Harvey produced the best bowling figures of his career in the second innings and took the last four South Australian wickets in 16 balls as only five runs were scored. Victorian wicket-keeper Darren Berry equalled Wally Grout's record of eight dismissals in an innings, seven caught and one stumped. He took three more catches in the second innings to fall one short of Don Tallon's record for dismissals in a match in Australia.

Rain delayed the start of the game in Perth, but Tom Moody must have regretted asking Tasmania to bat when he won the toss as the visitors' first three wickets all realised century partnerships. Langer and Moody put on 231 after the home state had lost three wickets for 64, and Moody conceded first innings points. Tasmania again showed their batting strength, and Western Australia found a target of 400 well beyond them.

Queensland gained their second Shield victory of the season, and it was marked by Andrew Symonds' first Shield century. He hit 111 off 99 balls with 16 fours and three sixes. He scored 103 during the last session of the second day. Queensland's varied attack, well handled by Healy, was too much for New South Wales.

29, 30 November, 1 and 2 December 1996
at Woolloongabba, Brisbane
Victoria 162 (A.J. Bichel 5 for 42) and 277 (W.G. Ayres 56, B.J. Hodge 51, A.J. Bichel 5 for 69)
Queensland 305 (A. Symonds 77, T.J. Barsby 59) and 137 for 2 (M.L. Hayden 73 not out)
Queensland won by 8 wickets
Queensland 6 pts, Victoria 0 pts

at Bellerive Oval, Hobart
New South Wales 403 for 9 dec. (B.E. McNamara 137 not out, M.J. Slater 76, P.J.S. Alley 54 not out) and 225 for 3 dec. (S. Lee 101 not out, K.J. Roberts 54)
Tasmania 327 for 9 dec. (S. Young 108 not out, M.J. DiVenuto 50, B.E. McNamara 4 for 72) and 268 for 9 (D.C. Boon 77, J. Cox 67, P.J.S. Alley 4 for 69)
Match drawn
New South Wales 1.8 pts, Tasmania 0 pts

at Adelaide Oval
South Australia 277 (J.C. Scuderi 55, B.P. Julian 4 for 77) and 325 (J.A. Brayshaw 96, G.R. Parker 80, B.P. Julian 5 for 98, M.S. Garnaut 4 for 81)
Western Australia 318 (J.L. Langer 116, D.R. Martyn 96, J.C. Scuderi 4 for 42) and 288 for 5 (T.M. Moody 89 not out)
Western Australia won by 5 wickets
Western Australia 6 pts, South Australia 0 pts

Six first innings dismissals and one catch in the second innings made Berry the most successful wicket-keeper in Victorian history with 266 dismissals for the state, but it could not prevent Queensland from gaining their third victory in as many matches. Bichel was again the star with ten wickets in a match for the first time.

New South Wales followed Victoria in losing a fraction of a point as the second team to be fined for a slow over rate. This was rather unfortunate as they had battled well in the earlier part of the game in Hobart. Slater held together their top order, but, at 178 for 6, they were struggling. Brad McNamara then hit the second and highest century of his career and shared an unbroken last wicket stand of 138, the highest tenth wicket partnership ever recorded against Tasmania and the fourth highest in Shield history. Alley hit the highest score of his career, and McNamara followed his batting with some fine bowling. The left-handed Shaun Young kept Tasmania in contention with the seventh century of his career. On the last morning, Shane Lee hit a hundred before lunch, and Matthews set Tasmania a target of 302 in 81 overs. Initially, the home side went for the runs, but wickets fell and Ridgway and Atkinson, the last pair, held out for a quarter of an hour to bring a draw.

Brendon Julian bowled well in Western Australia's win in Adelaide. Western Australia were 8 for 2 in their first innings before Langer, in fine form, and Martyn added 155. Langer's 116 came off only 117 balls with 19 fours.

Brad McNamara hit the highest score of his career, 137 not out, New South Wales v. Tasmania in Hobart and finished the season with 385 runs and 33 wickets. (Stephen Laffer/Sportsline)

6, 7, 8 and 9 December 1996
at Bellerive Oval, Hobart
Tasmania 481 for 8 dec. (M.J. DiVenuto 119, D.C. Boon 118, S. Young 113) and 311 for 3 dec. (J. Cox 132, D.F. Hills 124 not out)
Victoria 431 for 9 dec. (D.M. Jones 145, L.D. Harper 77, D.J. Saker 66 not out) and 204 for 3 (I.J. Harvey 62 not out, W.G. Ayres 56)
Match drawn
Tasmania 2 pts, Victoria 0 pts

Jones and Young scored their second centuries in successive matches in this run feast in Hobart. Hard-hitting David Saker made the highest score of his career, and Hills and Cox scored 215 for Tasmania's first wicket in the second innings. The first five Taswegian batsmen made centuries in the match.

19, 20, 21 and 22 December 1996
at Woolloongabba, Brisbane
New South Wales 190 (S.R. Waugh 55, A.J. Bichel 6 for 56) and 445 for 9 (S.R. Waugh 186 not out, M.E. Waugh 159)
Queensland 549 (S.G. Law 144, J.P. Maher 91, I.A. Healy 88, A.J. Bichel 58, A. Symonds 50)
Match drawn
Queensland 2 pts, New South Wales 0 pts

20, 21, 22 and 23 December 1996
at WACA Ground, Perth
South Australia 258 (J.A. Brayshaw 73, D.S. Lehmann 52) and 381 for 7 (J.D. Siddons 81, G.S. Blewett 66, J.N. Gillespie 58, G.R. Parker 52 not out)
Western Australia 560 for 8 dec. (J.L. Langer 274 not out, D.R. Martyn 104, J.N. Gillespie 5 for 64)
Match drawn
Western Australia 2 pts, South Australia 0 pts

Queensland had lost the services of Martin Love for the rest of the season. The very promising 22-year-old batsman had torn ligaments during training. In spite of this, Queensland took total control over New South Wales in the first two days at the 'Gabba. Andrew Bichel's *annus mirabilis* continued with the best bowling figures of his career, and Maher and Law shared a third wicket stand of 244 with Law hitting his first century of the season. Healy and Bichel added 88 for the seventh wicket, and Queensland took a first innings lead of 359. Slater and Taylor were dismissed for 67, but this brought together the Waugh twins who saved the match with a partnership worth 273. Steve Waugh defied the Queensland bowlers for nine-and-a-half hours.

In Perth, Justin Langer and Damien Martyn were again the backbone of the Western Australian batting. They shared a third wicket stand of 238, with Langer, in majestic form, making the highest score of his career. However, South Australia batted through 136 overs to save the game.

A return to the Australian side for Justin Langer who hit 274 not out for Western Australia against South Australia at Perth. (Mike Hewitt/Allsport)

3, 4, 5 and 6 January 1997
at Adelaide Oval
New South Wales 415 (C.J. Richards 76, G.R.J. Matthews 58, B.E. McNamara 50) and 173 for 3 dec. (R.J. Davison 67 not out, S. Lee 67)
South Australia 137 (S.M. Thompson 4 for 56) and 308 (D.S. Lehmann 97, B.E. Young 92 not out, M.P. Faull 68, P.J.S. Alley 5 for 89)
New South Wales won by 143 runs
New South Wales 6 pts, South Australia 0 pts

at WACA Ground Perth
Victoria 332 (R.P. Larkin 104, I.J. Harvey 55) and 283 (G.R. Vimpani 88, D.M. Jones 75)
Western Australia 495 (M.E. Hussey 147, D.R. Martyn 108, R.J. Campbell 74, A.C. Gilchrist 67, A.I.C. Dodemaide 4 for 67, B.J. Stacey 4 for 122) and 121 for 3 (M.E. Hussey 50)
Western Australia won by 7 wickets
Western Australia 6 pts, Victoria 0 pts

South Australia's hopes of retaining the Sheffield Shield were diminishing match by match and defeat at the hands of New South Wales left them pointless after four matches. In contrast, Western Australia's challenge seemed to be gaining momentum, and their strong batting helped to overcome Victoria in Perth. Leg-break bowler Brad Stacey captured four wickets, his best performance in first-class cricket, but this was scant consolation for Victoria, who were continuing to struggle.

9, 10, 11 and 12 January 1997
at Melbourne Cricket Ground
Tasmania 359 for 7 dec. (D.J. Marsh 97, D.C. Boon 75, M.N. Atkinson 50 not out, S. Young 50) and 264 for 4 dec (R.T. Ponting 94 not out, D.C. Boon 52)
Victoria 284 for 9 dec. (G.R. Vimpani 62) and 340 for 9 (G.R. Vimpani 113, R.P. Larkin 70, D.S. Berry 50 not out)
Victoria won by 1 wicket
Victoria 6 pts, Tasmania 2 pts

at Sydney Cricket Ground
New South Wales 126 (J. Angel 4 for 20, M.S. Garnaut 4 for 51) and 337 (R.J Davison 99)
Western Australia 244 (G.B. Hogg 59, B.E. McNamara 5 for 75) and 220 for 1 (M.E. Hussey 81 not out, J.L. Langer 70 not out, R.J. Campbell 50)
Western Australia won by 9 wickets
Western Australia 6 pts, New South Wales 0 pts

10, 11, 12 and 13 January 1997
at Adelaide Oval
South Australia 527 for 6 dec. (D.S. Lehmann 265, T.J. Nielsen 110 not out, J.D. Siddons 61, M.P. Faull 50, M.S. Kasprowicz 4 for 93) and 51 for 1
Queensland 227 (W.A. Seccombe 59, P.E. McIntyre 6 for 64) and 350 (G.I. Foley 72, M.L. Hayden 69, B.E. Young 4 for 111, P.E. McIntyre 4 for 133)
South Australia won by 9 wickets
South Australia 6 pts, Queensland 0 pts

Tasmania's hopes of challenging Queensland at the top of the table received a setback when they were dramatically beaten by Victoria at the MCG. With Daniel Marsh making the highest score of his career, Tasmania took first innings points, and Boon's declaration set Victoria a target of 340. Vimpani led the chase with a brisk 113, and Larkin and Harper shared a fifth wicket stand of 79. When Larkin was sixth out the score was 301 and three more wickets went down as 22 runs were added so that Fleming, the last man, joined Berry with 17 runs needed for victory. Fleming stood firm with seven, and Berry reached 50 to win the match.

Meanwhile, Western Australia beat New South Wales and drew level with Queensland at the top of the table. Robert Davison, who has played much club cricket in England, was caught one short of his century, and there was a later flurry from Alley, whose batting had improved considerably. However, Langer and Hussey rushed Western Australia to victory with an unbroken stand of 139.

Queensland suffered a surprise defeat at the hands of South Australia. The home side lost Johnson and Parker for seven before Faull and Lehmann added 96. Siddons then helped Lehmann in a stand of 117, and although Vaughan went for 0, Kasprowicz's fourth victim, Nielsen joined Lehmann in a sixth wicket partnership that realised 260. Nielsen had been out of form with the bat, but he reached the third century of his career, and Lehmann made his third and highest double century. Seen as a new Bradman, Darren Lehmann has never quite fulfilled his potential in a career blighted by serious injury, but he remains a fine player. Queensland fell to the leg-spin of McIntyre and had to follow on. They fought hard in their second innings, but defeat was inevitable.

23, 24, 25 and 26 January 1997
at Sydney Cricket Ground
South Australia 154 and 117 (B.E. McNamara 5 for 19)
New South Wales 440 for 6 dec. (K.J. Roberts 119, G.R.J. Matthews 109 not out, M.J. Slater 102)
New South Wales won by an innings and 169 runs
New South Wales 6 pts, South Australia 0 pts

24, 25, 26 and 27 January 1997
at Bellerive Oval, Hobart
Tasmania 314 (J. Cox 96, M.J. di Venuto 65, J. Angel 4 for 71) and 175 (J. Cox 51, T.M. Moody 7 for 41)
Western Australia 312 (M.E. Hussey 83, R.J. Campbell 78, M.W. Ridgway 6 for 88) and 180 for 3 (M.E. Hussey 87)
Western Australia won by 7 wickets
Western Australia 6 pts, Tasmania 2 pts

A maiden century from Kevin Roberts, a first hundred for six years from Greg Matthews, and a most welcome first of the season for Michael Slater were significant reasons for New South Wales's total destruction of South Australia. McNamara again bowled well, but South Australia's fragile batting was much in evidence.

For the second time, Tasmania took a first innings lead, albeit a narrow one, and lost the match. The veteran Mark Ridgway bowled them to two points after Western Australia had at one time been 210 for 1. In their second innings, Tasmania collapsed against the medium pace of Tom Moody, who has matured considerably as a bowler in recent years.

30, 31 January, 1 and 2 February 1997
at Woolloongabba, Brisbane
Queensland 179 and 412 (T.J. Barsby 107, J.P. Maher 76, S.G. Law 56)
Western Australia 183 (A.C. Dale 5 for 43) and 273 for 5 (T.M. Moody 136, S.M. Katich 65 not out)
Match drawn
Western Australia 2 pts, Queensland 0 pts

at Melbourne Cricket Ground
New South Wales 290 (M.J. Slater 71, B.E. McNamara 69, C.J. Richards 58, D.W. Fleming 4 for 66, D.J. Saker 4 for 71) and 264 for 8 dec. (R.J. Davison 88, P.J.S. Alley 56)
Victoria 164 (B.E. McNamara 5 for 30) and 391 for 8 (G.R. Vimpani 161, I.J. Harvey 88, M.T.G. Elliott 65)
Victoria won by 2 wickets
Victoria 6 pts, New South Wales 2 pts

A maiden first-class century for Queensland's admirable wicket-keeper Wade Seccombe. (Stephen Laffer/Sportsline)

1, 2, 3 and 4 February 1997
at Adelaide Oval
South Australia 293 (D.S. Lehmann 76, B.E. Young 56 not out, J.D. Siddons 55) and 142 (S. Young 5 for 26)
Tasmania 425 (J. Cox 94, D.F. Hills 59, M.N. Atkinson 58, D.J. Marsh 58) and 11 for 0
Tasmania won by 10 wickets
Tasmania 6 pts, South Australia 0 pts

Western Australia edged ahead of Queensland at the top of the Sheffield Shield table when Mulder scored all seven runs of a last wicket first innings stand to claim two points. Defending a modest 179, Queensland had looked likely to concede a large first innings lead when Western Australia reached 160 for 5, but Dale and Kasprowicz took four wickets as 16 were scored. Batting a second time, Queensland were well served by all their batsmen. Barsby and Maher scored 98 for the second wicket, and Law was in good form so that Western Australia were left a target of 409. At 53 for 4, they were in great trouble, but skipper Moody and Katich put on 209 to save the game.

Victoria pulled off another remarkable victory to dispose of New South Wales. Slater gave further indication of a return of confidence, and there was more good all-round cricket from McNamara so that New South Wales led by 126 on the first innings. A solid second innings performance enabled Matthews to set a target of 391. Vimpani made the highest score of his career, and with Elliott restored after injury and Ian Harvey continuing his excellent form, Victoria struck out confidently. There was a scare when they went from 362 for 4 to 382 for 8, but Dodemaide steadied the nerves and won the match.

Tasmania kept alive their Shield hopes by crushing South Australia. Hills and Cox proved themselves a most reliable opening pair with a stand of 158.

5, 6, 7 and 8 February 1997
at Melbourne Cricket Ground
Queensland 229 (W.A. Seccombe 103, I.J. Harvey 5 for 45) and 355 for 4 dec. (M.P. Mott 150, J.P. Maher 95)
Victoria 191 (R.P. Larkin 52, B.N. Creevey 5 for 32) and 213 for 8
Match drawn
Queensland 2 pts, Victoria 0 pts

Wade Seccombe rescued Queensland from the depths of 84 for 7 with the first century of his career. The wicket-keeper came in at 68 for 6 and made 103 out of the last 161 runs scored. Creevey was mainly responsible for Queensland taking a first innings lead of 38, and Mott and Maher then shared a second wicket stand of 180 to make possible Law's declaration. Mott's 150 was the highest score of his career. Victoria hung on grimly for 100 overs to save the match.

11, 12, 13 and 14 February 1997
at Bellerive Oval, Hobart
South Australia 387 (B.A. Johnson 91, J.C. Scuderi 70, T.J. Nielsen 64, M.P. Faull 62, J.P. Marquet 4 for 107) and 209 for 5 dec. (G.R. Parker 68 not out, M.P. Faull 65)
Tasmania 248 (R.T. Ponting 126, J.C. Scuderi 5 for 43) and 351 for 5 (R.T. Ponting 145 not out, J. Cox 57)
Tasmania won by 5 wickets
Tasmania 6 pts, South Australia 0 pts

14, 15, 16 and 17 February 1997
at WACA Ground, Perth
Western Australia 414 (M.W. Goodwin 127, D.R. Martyn 62, R.J. Campbell 53, S.A. Muller 5 for 76) and 320 for 8 (M.W. Goodwin 77, R.J. Campbell 55)
Queensland 400 (M.P. Mott 90, J.P. Maher 56, G.I. Foley 53, T.M. Moody 4 for 73)
Match drawn
Western Australia 2 pts, Queensland 0 pts

Discarded by the Australian selectors, Ricky Ponting responded with a century in each innings for Tasmania against South Australia. An opening stand of 165 between Faull and Johnson put South Australia in a strong position, which was consolidated by Scuderi and Nielsen's sixth wicket partnership of 122. At 172 for 7, Tasmania were in danger of having to follow on, but Ponting rallied the tail, and the last three wickets realised 76 runs. South Australia still had a commanding lead of 139, which they added to briskly. Facing a daunting target of 349 at more than four runs an over, Tasmania lost Hills and DiVenuto, but Ponting played a glorious innings that brought his side victory and gave them every chance of reaching the Shield final.

The leaders in the Shield produced a more dour struggle. Goodwin, who hit a maiden first-class hundred, and Martyn put on 157 for Western Australia's third wicket to help their side to 414. Queensland responded in slow but determined fashion, but Moody thwarted them in their attempt to gain first innings points.

7, 8, 9 and 10 March 1997
at WACA Ground, Perth
New South Wales 89 (B. Mulder 5 for 2) and 217 (B. Mulder 6 for 65)
Western Australia 228 (A.C. Gilchrist 66, R.J. Campbell 64, B.P. Julian 51, G.R.J. Matthews 6 for 66) and 80 for 1
Western Australia won by 9 wickets
Western Australia 6 pts, New South Wales 0 pts

at Adelaide Oval
South Australia 216 and 449 for 9 dec. (D.S. Lehmann 167, B.E. Young 70 not out, M.P. Faull 54, J.D. Siddons 51)
Victoria 241 (I.J. Harvey 73, B.J. Hodge 50, P.E. McIntyre 4 for 90) and 263 (R.P. Larkin 56, L.D. Harper 52, P.E. McIntyre 5 for 88)
South Australia won by 161 runs
South Australia 6 pts, Victoria 2 pts

at Bellerive Oval, Hobart
Tasmania 408 (R.T. Ponting 159, S. Young 92, D.J. Marsh 52) and 263 for 9 dec. (J. Cox 74, M.J. DiVenuto 56, P.W. Jackson 5 for 85, M.S. Kasprowicz 4 for 70)
Queensland 283 (G.I. Foley 77, M.P. Mott 74, M.W. Ridgway 4 for 76) and 198 for 4 (S.G. Law 74 not out, T.J. Barsby 59)
Match drawn
Tasmania 2 pts, Queensland 0 pts

Fine all-round cricket for Victoria from Ian Harvey, 491 runs and 35 wickets. (Stephen Laffer/Sportsline)

In his 100th first-class match, the New South Wales keeper Phil Emery hit his maiden century and ended Tasmania's hopes of reaching the Shield final. (Stephen Laffer/Sportsline)

13, 14, 15 and 16 March 1997
at Woolloongabba, Brisbane
Queensland 277 and 218 (M.P. Mott 60, S.G. Law 50)
South Australia 160 (J.D. Siddons 82, M.S. Kasprowicz 5 for 64, A.C. Dale 4 for 40) and 198 (M.P. Faull 64, M.S. Kasprowicz 4 for 55)
Queensland won by 137 runs
Queensland 6 pts, South Australia 0 pts

at Sydney Cricket Ground
Tasmania 463 for 7 dec. (J. Cox 143, M.J. DiVenuto 65, R.T. Ponting 64, D.C. Boon 52) and 290 for 5 dec. (J. Cox 125, D.F. Hills 75, S.C.G. MacGill 4 for 78)
New South Wales 449 (P.A. Emery 100 not out, M.J. Slater 87, J.L. Arnberger 71, G.R.J. Matthews 56) and 305 for 4 (M.J. Slater 79, S. Lee 75 not out, R.J. Davison 63, J.L. Arnberger 57)
New South Wales won by 6 wickets
New South Wales 6 pts, Tasmania 2 pts

at Melbourne Cricket Ground
Victoria 205 (S.A. Craig 90, J. Angel 4 for 32) and 224 (L.D. Harper 100 not out, B.P. Julian 7 for 48)
Western Australia 458 for 9 dec. (M.E. Hussey 138, R.J. Campbell 113, M.W. Goodwin 90, D.W. Fleming 4 for 85)
Western Australia won by an innings and 29 runs
Western Australia 6 pts, Victoria 0 pts

The game in Perth was over in two days. New South Wales lost their last seven wickets for four runs, collapsing before the spin of Mulder, who returned the remarkable figures of 5 for 2 in six overs. Western Australia did not find batting much easier and were 95 for 6 with Greg Matthews enjoying the conditions. Gilchrist and Julian added 101, and although New South Wales batted with more determination in their second innings, Mulder again thrived. The home state romped to victory and confirmed their place in the Shield final.

The two most inconsistent sides in the competition, Victoria and South Australia, were true to form in Adelaide. Victoria's last two wickets, marshalled by the admirable Ian Harvey, took them to first innings points, but Lehmann transformed the game with a mighty knock of 167. Young and Nielsen hit lustily to add 65 for the seventh wicket, and Siddons was able to set a target of 424. With McIntyre turning the ball viciously, Victoria never looked like saving the match.

Ricky Ponting hit his third century in three innings and led Tasmania to a strong position in the vital match against Queensland after three wickets had fallen for 31. Young helped Ponting to add 190 for the fifth wicket, and Marsh and Atkinson made valuable contributions. Queensland batted inconsistently and lost their last six wickets for 68 runs to concede a first innings lead of 125. Tasmania pressed for quick runs, but they were thwarted in their bid for victory. The results from this penultimate round of matches meant that Tasmania, 26 points, Queensland and New South Wales, each 22 points, all had a chance of qualifying to meet Western Australia in the final.

Queensland's victory over South Australia earned them a place in the Sheffield Shield final by virtue of a superior run quotient. Queensland batted with consistent application to reach 277, and by the end of the first day they were well on top having captured three South Australian wickets for 26. Siddons, 82 off 117 balls, and Nielsen, 34, were the only batsmen to reach double figures, but the score was boosted by 21 extras. Conditions were not easy, but Law and Mott consolidated Queensland's position of supremacy, and with Dale and Kasprowicz again in top form, the match was over after five runs had been scored on the fourth morning.

Tasmania had seemed set to reach the final when they scored 370 for 6 on the first day against New South Wales. Hills was out for 0, but Cox and DiVenuto added 145, and Cox and Ponting 103. Cox faced 286 balls for his 143 and became the only batsman to pass a thousand runs for the season. New South Wales batted consistently in reply, but it looked as if Tasmania would claim a significant first innings lead until Phil Emery came in at 263 for 5. In 191 minutes, Emery, playing his 100th first-class match in a decade as New South Wales's wicket-keeper, hit a maiden first-class century. He was close to not reaching three figures, as an appeal for run out came when he took his 100th run, but the third umpire showed the green light. His effort took his side to within 14 runs of Tasmania. The visitors closed the third day on 135 without loss, and on the last morning they hit 155 before lunch, with Cox scoring his second century of the match. New South Wales had two sessions in which to score 305 to win at nearly five runs an over. Slater and Davison hit 151 in 123 minutes for the first wicket to set the pace, and Arnberger, Lee and Roberts maintained the momentum to give New South Wales a rousing victory and to deny Tasmania a place in the final.

Western Australia emphasised their superiority with an innings win in Melbourne. Craig hit the highest score of his career, but this was overshadowed by Ryan Campbell who hit an explosive maiden first-class century, 113 off 106 balls out of an opening stand of 144 with Hussey. Campbell, a graduate of the Cricket Academy, had made his debut at the beginning of the season as wicket-keeper when Gilchrist was absent, but his violent batting had won him a regular place in the side. Hussey and Goodwin added 148, and Victoria's only consolation was to be a maiden first-class century from Laurie Harper. Julian's 7 for 48 was a career best, and he returned match figures of 10 for 86, also a career best.

Sheffield Shield Final

Western Australia v. Queensland

Winning the toss and batting, Queensland were given an ideal start by Barsby and Mott who put on 100 with Barsby, first out, the dominant partner. Maher went cheaply, but Law and Mott added 115 in 144 minutes, Law making 70 of the runs. Finishing the first day on 266 for four, Queensland lost wickets cheaply on the second morning, but by the end of the day, they were in total command. Adam Dale capped a wonderful season with the best bowling figures of his career, and Western Australia were struggling on 164 for nine. Barsby's century and Law's positive 72 put Queensland in a virtually impregnable position, and by the end of the fourth day, with Western Australia 166 for 5, Law's men had a grip on the Shield.

Tom Moody battled bravely for 434 minutes and faced 234 balls. While he remained Western Australia had a hope of saving the game and so claiming the Shield, but he was ninth out, caught off the highly impressive Kasprowicz who then had Garnaut taken at slip. The match was over with three hours to spare.

Queensland became the first away side in 15 years to win the Shield, their second success in three years. Dale's match figures of 9 for 84 equalled Holdsworth's record for the final.

Sheffield Shield Final Table

	P	W	L	D	Pts	R/Q
Western Australia	10	6	1	3	42	1.328
Queensland	10	4	1	5	28	1.190
New South Wales	10	4	4	2	28	1.078
Tasmania	10	3	4	3	28	1.061
Victoria	10	3	5	2	19.7	0.768
South Australia	10	2	7	1	14	0.728

Sheffield Shield Final – Western Australia v. Queensland
21, 22, 23, 24 and 25 March 1997 at WACA Ground, Perth

Queensland

	First Innings		Second Innings	
T.J. Barsby	c Garnaut, b Mulder	67	(2) c Gilchrist, b Garnaut	111
M.P. Mott	c Campbell, b Angel	86	(1) c Goodwin, b Garnaut	1
J.P. Maher	c Gilchrist, b Julian	8	c Moody, b Mulder	10
S.G. Law (Capt)	c Garnaut, b Hogg	70	c Gilchrist, b Moody	72
A. Symonds	c Julian, b Moody	27	run out	30
G.I. Foley	c Gilchrist, b Moody	17	c Gilchrist, b Julian	2
*W.A. Seccombe	c Gilchrist, b Julian	3	c Gilchrist, b Moody	10
B.N. Creevey	lbw, b Moody	0	(9) c Gilchrist, b Moody	0
P.W. Jackson	not out	6	(8) not out	22
A.C. Dale	c Julian, b Moody	15	c Martyn, b Angel	0
M.S. Kasprowicz	b Goodwin, b Angel	1	c Angel, b Moody	26
	lb 7, w 1, nb 12	20	lb 16, w 1, nb 8	25
		320		**309**

	O	M	R	W	O	M	R	W
Angel	18	7	56	2	19	8	40	1
Garnaut	9	1	36	–	13	2	46	2
Julian	31	6	74	2	18	7	36	1
Moody	27	8	75	4	23.4	4	76	4
Mulder	18	4	41	1	18	2	62	1
Hogg	6	–	27	1	7	–	24	–
Martyn	2	–	4	–	5	1	9	–

Fall of Wickets
1–100, 2–112, 3–227, 4–258, 5–281, 6–296, 7–296, 8–296, 9–317
1–20, 2–56, 3–187, 4–236, 5–238, 6–241, 7–275, 8–275, 9–276

Western Australia

	First Innings		Second Innings	
M.E. Hussey	lbw, b Dale	5	b Dale	5
R.J. Campbell	c Seccombe, b Dale	0	c Barsby, b Dale	0
M.W. Goodwin	lbw, b Dale	63	lbw, b Jackson	5
D.R. Martyn	c Maher, b Kasprowicz	7	c Foley, b Kasprowicz	0
T.M. Moody (Capt)	c Law, b Jackson	23	c Symonds, b Kasprowicz	152
G.B. Hogg	lbw, b Kasprowicz	1	c Seccombe, b Kasprowicz	30
*A.C. Gilchrist	c Barsby, b Dale	23	c Barsby, b Kasprowicz	48
B.P. Julian	c Law, b Dale	0	c Seccombe, b Dale	8
J. Angel	c Law, b Dale	28	c Maher, b Jackson	13
M.S. Garnaut	not out	2	c Law, b Kasprowicz	7
B. Mulder	c Maher, b Kasprowicz	6	not out	4
	b 5, lb 2	7	b 5, lb 11, w 2, nb 14	32
		165		**304**

	O	M	R	W	O	M	R	W
Kasprowicz	20.1	9	42	3	41.3	14	83	5
Dale	22	9	38	6	27	9	46	3
Creevey	10	1	37	–	17	3	58	–
Jackson	16	3	41	1	29	6	74	2
Law	2	–			2	–	3	–
Foley					6	2	24	–

Fall of Wickets
1–2, 2–5, 3–16, 4–51, 5–74, 6–101, 7–101, 8–152, 9–157
1–2, 2–9, 3–10, 4–18, 5–99, 6–185, 7–216, 8–246, 9–300

Umpires: D.B. Hair & P.D. Parker

Queensland won by 160 runs

First-Class Averages

Batting

	M	Inns	NO	Runs	HS	Av	100s	50s
J.L. Langer	8	14	4	771	274*	77.10	3	1
M.T.G. Elliott	5	10	2	577	187	72.12	2	2
J. Cox	11	21	1	1349	200	67.45	5	7
M.G. Bevan	7	12	3	561	150*	62.33	1	4
M.W. Goodwin	5	9	2	428	127	61.14	1	3
R.T. Ponting	10	18	2	960	159	60.00	3	4
M.P. Mott	6	10	–	590	150	59.00	1	5
I.A. Healy	7	11	3	452	161*	56.50	1	1
S.R. Waugh	7	12	1	609	186*	55.36	2	3
M.L. Hayden	8	14	2	648	224	54.00	2	2
D.S. Lehmann	11	19	1	960	255	53.33	2	3
G.R. Vimpani	8	15	–	752	161	50.13	3	3
T.M. Moody	9	14	1	621	152	47.76	3	1
S.G. Law	10	16	3	617	144	47.46	1	5
G.S. Blewett	7	12	2	473	99	47.30		5
M.E. Hussey	12	22	2	928	147	46.40	2	5
P.J.S. Alley	8	12	7	228	56	45.60		2
S.M. Katich	2	4	1	131	65*	43.66		1
M.E. Waugh	7	13	–	564	159	43.38	1	4
T.J. Barsby	11	19	1	765	111	42.50	2	5
R.J. Davison	7	13	2	464	99	42.18		4
D.M. Jones	7	13	–	521	152	40.07	2	1
M.J. DiVenuto	11	20	–	799	130	39.95	2	5
B.E. Young	9	17	5	475	91*	39.58		3
A.C. Gilchrist	12	17	2	591	108*	39.40	1	2
S. Young	11	18	4	548	113	39.14	2	2
B.E. McNamara	8	12	2	385	137*	38.50	1	2
R.J. Campbell	11	19	1	672	113	37.33	1	6
M.J. Slater	10	19	–	703	102	37.00	1	5
D.C. Boon	11	17	–	628	118	36.94	2	4
D.R. Martyn	12	20	1	701	108	36.89	2	3
D.F. Hills	11	21	2	701	124*	36.89	2	4
M.L. Love	3	5	–	179	46	35.80		
D.J. Marsh	11	19	5	500	97	35.71		3
A. Symonds	11	18	1	604	111	35.52	1	2
K.J. Roberts	7	13	1	424	119	35.33	1	2
R.P. Larkin	6	12	–	423	104	35.25	1	3
G.I. Foley	11	17	3	483	82*	34.50		4
S. Lee	9	17	2	506	101*	33.73	1	2
S.A. Craig	2	4	–	132	90	33.00		1
L.D. Harper	10	19	2	543	100*	31.94	1	3
J.P. Maher	11	19	2	532	95	31.29		4
D.S. Berry	11	20	1	590	148	31.05	1	2
T.J. Dixon	5	9	–	271	62	30.11		1
J.D. Siddons	11	21	–	631	101	30.04	1	5
M.N. Atkinson	11	15	4	328	58	29.81		2
W.A. Seccombe	10	14	1	386	103	29.69	1	1
G.R. Parker	10	19	2	500	112	29.41	1	3
J.C. Scuderi	7	14	2	352	70	29.33		2
J.A. Brayshaw	4	8	–	234	96	29.25		2
T.J. Nielsen	11	20	2	521	110*	28.94	1	1
G.R.J. Matthews	10	15	1	403	109*	28.78	1	1
M.P. Faull	8	16	–	459	68	28.68		6
P.A. Emery	10	17	3	390	100*	27.85	1	
C.J. Richards	6	11	–	292	76	26.54		2
D.J. Saker	11	20	6	365	66*	26.07		2
B.A. Johnson	7	14	1	331	91	25.46		2
I.J. Harvey	11	21	1	491	88	24.55		5
W.G. Ayres	8	16	1	364	56	24.26		3
J.N. Gillespie	5	7	2	120	58	24.00		1
G.B. Hogg	10	11	1	226	59	22.60		1
P.W. Jackson	10	13	6	152	49	21.71		
B.J. Hodge	7	14	–	282	51	20.14		2
B.P. Julian	9	11	2	178	51	19.77		1
J. Angel	8	9	3	117	28	19.50		
M.P. Lavender	4	7	–	126	51	18.00		1
C.R. Miller	10	13	3	172	41	17.20		
A.J. Bichel	6	6	–	103	58	17.16		1
M.A. Taylor	8	15	–	252	53	16.80		1
S.K. Warne	7	10	–	159	30	15.90		
R.M. Baker	5	9	2	111	48	15.85		
A.I.C. Dodemaide	7	13	5	114	41*	14.25		
B.N. Creevey	7	10	2	113	48*	14.12		
M.R. Foster	6	12	1	151	32	13.72		
D.W. Fleming	9	16	6	136	36	13.60		
A.C. Dale	10	14	–	180	31	12.85		
M.S. Kasprowicz	11	15	3	154	26	12.83		
P.R. Reiffel	6	11	2	115	24*	12.77		
B.J. Stacey	7	12	2	115	32	11.50		

(Qualification 100 runs, average 10.00)

(J.L. Arnberger – one match, 71 & 57)

Bowling

	Overs	Mds	Runs	Wks	Av	Best	10/m	5/inn
J.C. Scuderi	130.4	32	399	23	17.34	5/43		1
G.D. McGrath	229.5	66	567	29	19.55	5/50		1
M.G. Bevan	97.3	14	336	16	21.00	6/82	1	1
A.J. Bichel	239.1	64	650	30	21.66	6/56	1	4
A.C. Dale	454.5	170	927	42	22.07	6/38		2
J. Angel	274.5	81	685	31	22.09	4/20		
B.E. McNamara	235.2	53	741	33	22.45	5/19		1
T.M. Moody	357.4	94	926	38	24.36	7/41		1
B. Mulder	242.2	60	578	23	25.13	6/65	1	2
P. Wilson	202.4	73	456	18	25.33	3/44		
M.S. Kasprowicz	466.4	131	1226	48	25.54	5/64		3
B.P. Julian	318	78	908	35	25.94	7/48	1	2
B.N. Creevey	198.1	45	588	22	26.72	6/70		1
J.M. Saint	84	24	270	10	27.00	4/10		
I.J. Harvey	315.4	81	965	35	27.57	7/44		3
P.J.S. Alley	194.5	40	641	23	27.86	5/89		1
S.K. Warne	314.4	88	795	27	29.44	4/95		
K.M. Harvey	113	23	354	12	29.50	3/30		
P.R. Reiffel	225.1	59	596	20	29.80	5/73		1
A.M. Stuart	186.1	40	643	21	30.61	5/63		1
S.A. Muller	216.3	43	645	21	30.71	5/76		1
S. Young	366.5	102	1096	35	31.31	7/64		2
P.W. Jackson	351.2	111	789	23	34.30	5/85		1
G.R.J. Matthews	263.1	77	620	18	34.44	6/66		
M.W. Ridgway	298.3	64	978	28	34.92	6/88		1
C.R. Miller	433.3	113	1143	32	35.71	4/48		
S. Lee	127.5	17	438	12	36.50	3/15		
S.C.G. MacGill	190.3	41	592	16	37.00	4/72		
D.J. Saker	426	119	1210	32	37.81	4/22		
A.I.C. Dodemaide	234.1	69	618	16	38.62	4/67		
B.E. Young	303.1	67	903	23	39.26	4/111		
P.E. McIntyre	492.5	114	1413	35	40.37	6/64	1	2
D.A. Freedman	145	31	487	12	40.58	3/92		
J.P. Marquet	289.2	59	1028	25	41.12	4/107		
M.S. Garnaut	319	81	953	23	41.43	4/51		
M.A. Harrity	230.4	57	708	17	41.64	4/61		
D.W. Fleming	318.4	72	979	23	42.56	4/66		
B.A. Williams	122	30	432	10	43.20	4/63		
D.J. Marsh	352	89	955	22	43.40	3/55		
G.B. Hogg	235.4	43	814	16	50.87	3/73		
S.P. George	209.5	41	768	14	54.85	3/70		
B.J. Stacey	168.3	26	691	12	57.58	4/122		

(Qualification 10 wickets)

Leading Fielders

62 – A.C. Gilchrist (ct 60 / st 2); 45 – D.S. Berry (ct 40 / st 5); 39 – W.A. Seccombe (ct 35 / st 4); 36 – M.N. Atkinson (ct 33 / st 3); 35 – T.J. Nielsen; 26 – P.A. Emery (ct 25 / st 1); 23 – I.A. Healy; 18 – J.D. Siddons; 17 – J.P. Maher; 15 – G.I. Foley and S.G. Law; 14 – T.M. Moody and R.J. Campbell (ct 13 / st 1); 13 – T.J. Barsby and M.A. Taylor; 12 – M.E. Waugh; 11 – D.R. Martyn; 10 – M.J. DiVenuto, D.J. Marsh and R.T. Ponting

South Africa

One begins to have some sympathy for the international cricketer. The South Africans engaged in a triangular one-day series and three

A rising star – Adam Bacher. Bacher won his first Test caps and was the only batsman to score a thousand runs in the South African season. (Mike Hewitt/Allsport)

Test matches in India and within ten days of their return home they were to begin another three-Test series against India, followed by another triangular limited-over series. The Australians were to arrive for a Test and one-day series, and, in all, the South African public were to be treated to 17 one-day internationals in 1996–97.

Indian Tour and Tests
Standard Bank Triangular Series –
    South Africa, India and Zimbabwe
Supersport Series
UCBL Bowl
Australian Tour, Tests and One-Day Internationals

Before their own season began, South African cricketers had already been asked to play in 12 one-day internationals. Surely there is a danger of a surfeit of delights.

In the Republic, optimism and enthusiasm remained high, but, in India, South Africa had suffered their first *series* defeat since their return to Test cricket and it was apparent that there was a need for the younger generation of players to establish themselves firmly in international cricket.

Indian Tour

For India, the tour of South Africa was the second leg of a long, hard year, which would continue in the Caribbean and end with the Independence Cup in India and the Asia Cup in Sri Lanka.

Tendulkar led a party of 16, which included four seamers and two spinners. There were three uncapped players in the party – wicket-keeper Syed Karim of Bengal; batsman Pankaj Dharmani of Punjab; and medium-pacer Doddanarasiah Ganesh of Karnataka.

21, 22 and 23 December 1996
at St George's Park, Port Elizabeth
Indians 335 for 6 dec. (S.C. Ganguly 97, V. Rathore 71, S.R. Tendulkar 62)
Eastern Province 322 for 4 dec. (K.C. Wessels 103 not out, P.G. Amm 81)
Match drawn

The Indian tourists were granted only one match before the beginning of the Test series, and that match was badly disrupted by rain. The pitch was never easy, but the visitors batted with some flourish. Rathore hit three sixes and 12 fours. The final day saw the veteran Wessels hit his 61st first-class century.

First Test Match

South Africa v. India

South Africa welcomed back both Donald and Pollock. Shaun Pollock had missed the tour of India because of an ankle injury. South Africa left Kallis and Adams out of the party of 13 chosen for the Test and gave a first cap to Adam Bacher, who was enjoying an outstanding domestic season and had made 210 and 112 not out for Transvaal against Griqualand West a few weeks earlier.

India decided upon one spinner and named Johnson as the third seamer. They entrusted the responsibility of opening the innings to Rathore and Raman but, in the continued absence of Sidhu, this remained an area in which they seemed particularly vulnerable.

Tendulkar won the toss and asked South Africa to bat first on a pitch that was hard and green and was to prove difficult for batsmen throughout the match because of its

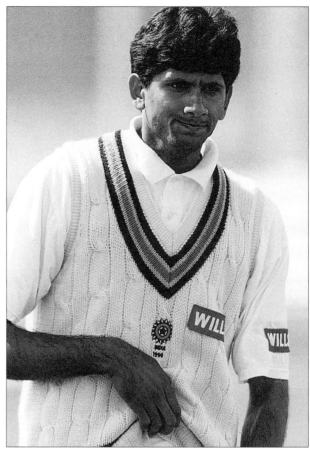

Venkatesh Prasad took ten wickets in a Test match for the first time and still ended on the losing side, South Africa v. India, first Test at Kingsmead, Durban. (David Munden/Sportsline)

high bounce. In the fourth over of the innings, Venkatesh Prasad knocked over Kirsten's off stump, but Bacher and Hudson took the home side to 70 by lunch. Srinath trapped Bacher leg before with the first ball after the interval, and Cullinan, Cronje and Gibbs were out in quick succession. Had chances offered by Hudson been taken, South Africa would have been in a parlous state. As it was, Hudson held the innings together before falling to Ganguly, who had been pressed into service when Tendulkar was forced to leave the field with an injury.

Venkatesh Prasad bowled quite splendidly, as did Srinath, and his swing and deceptive changes of pace earned just reward with five wickets. Mongia held five catches behind the stumps, testimony to the movement that the bowlers produced, and South Africa were bowled out for 235. Raman and Rathore negotiated two hostile overs before the close and scored two.

If India had taken the honours on the first day, the second belonged entirely to South Africa in general and to Donald in particular. Pollock made the initial breakthrough, but Donald thrived in the conditions. He had Rathore taken at slip and uprooted Tendulkar's stumps with a magnificent delivery. South Africa's strength was that they could offer

First Test Match – South Africa v. India

26, 27 and 28 December 1996 at Kingsmead, Durban

South Africa

	First Innings		Second Innings	
A.C. Hudson	c Mongia, b Ganguly	80	c Tendulkar, b Kumble	52
G. Kirsten	b Venkatesh Prasad	2	c Dravid, b Prasad	2
A.M. Bacher	lbw, b Srinath	25	c Tendulkar, b Kumble	55
D.J. Cullinan	c Mongia, b Prasad	1	c Mongia, b Prasad	3
W.J. Cronje (Capt)	c Mongia, b Prasad	15	c Mongia, b Prasad	17
H.H. Gibbs	c Mongia, b Johnson	0	lbw, b Srinath	25
B.M. McMillan	lbw, b Johnson	34	not out	51
S.M. Pollock	not out	23	c Rathore, b Prasad	2
*D.J. Richardson	b Venkatesh Prasad	24	b Srinath	4
L. Klusener	c Mongia, b Srinath	1	c Mongia, b Srinath	4
A.A. Donald	c Rathore, b Prasad	5	c Rathore, b Prasad	26
	b 4, lb 10, nb 11	25	b 7, lb 6, nb 5	18
		235		**259**

	O	M	R	W	O	M	R	W
Srinath	20	7	36	2	23	5	80	3
Venkatesh Prasad	19	6	60	5	25	4	93	5
Johnson	15	2	52	2	9	1	39	–
Tendulkar	2.4	2	0	–				
Kumble	20.2	3	61	–	11	3	26	2
Ganguly	9	4	12	1	2	–	8	–

India

	First Innings		Second Innings	
V. Rathore	c Hudson, b Donald	7	c Richardson, b Donald	2
W.V. Raman	b Pollock	0	b Donald	1
S.C. Ganguly	c Klusener, b Pollock	16	b Donald	0
S.R. Tendulkar (Capt)	b Donald	15	c Kirsten, b Pollock	4
M. Azharuddin	c Bacher, b McMillan	15	c Klusener, b Pollock	8
R.S. Dravid	lbw, b McMillan	7	not out	27
*N.R. Mongia	c Richardson, b Donald	4	c Cronje, b Klusener	4
A.R. Kumble	not out	13	c Hudson, b Klusener	2
J. Srinath	c Cullinan, b Donald	0	run out	7
D. Johnson	c Bacher, b Donald	3	c Klusener, b Pollock	5
Venkatesh Prasad	c Richardson, b Klusener	4	c Hudson, b Donald	1
	b 4, lb 3, w 7, nb 2	16	lb 2, nb 3	5
		100		**66**

	O	M	R	W	O	M	R	W
Donald	16	5	40	5	11.1	4	14	4
Pollock	8	2	18	2	12	4	25	3
Klusener	7.1	2	8	1	8	2	16	2
McMillan	8	2	27	2	2	–	9	–

Fall of Wickets

1–8, 2–70, 3–71, 4–99, 5–113, 6–162, 7–190, 8–229, 9–230
1–4, 2–115, 3–120, 4–120, 5–164, 6–164, 7–171, 8–181, 9–185

Fall of Wickets

1–2, 2–22, 3–36, 4–52, 5–68, 6–74, 7–74, 8–74, 9–89
1–2, 2–2, 3–7, 4–15, 5–20, 6–25, 7–40, 8–51, 9–59

Umpires: D.L. Orchard & R.S. Dunne

South Africa won by 328 runs

Donald first-class support in attack and in the field, and India were powerless in their attempts to stem the aggression. In contrast, India offered the admirable Venkatesh Prasad and Srinath scant support. Hudson and Bacher added 111 for the second South African wicket, and Hudson reached his second 50 of the match. Bacher made 55 with nine fours on his Test debut, and South Africa finished the second day on 164 for 4, a lead of 299, which, in the conditions, appeared to put them in a match-winning position.

So it proved. The game was all over within half an hour after tea on the third day. South Africa lost three wickets quickly to slip to 185 for 9, but Donald and McMillan, a most valuable cricketer, added 74 in 11 overs for the last wicket. This had a crushing effect on the Indian morale, which had never been high. Venkatesh Prasad claimed his second five-wicket haul in the match to finish with 10 for 153, the first time he had taken ten wickets in a Test. He is a very good and ever-improving bowler.

The game was decided by Donald's opening burst in the second innings. Bowling at great pace, he sent back Rathore, Raman and Ganguly at a personal cost of ten runs in six overs. Pollock and Klusener supported him well, and but for Dravid's unbeaten 27 in over two hours, India would have been dismissed for their lowest score in Test cricket. As it was, in any case, 66 was the lowest score ever made against South Africa.

Allan Donald, 9 for 54, was named Man of the Match.

Second Test Match

South Africa v. India

Adams replaced Gibbs in the South African side for the match at Newlands, while India brought in Ganesh for his Test debut at the expense of Johnson and replaced Rathore by Laxman, using Dravid as yet another makeshift opener. Cronje won the toss, and South Africa batted. The pitch at Newlands was slower than that at Kingsmead had been, but the Indian fielding was just as fallible. Venkatesh Prasad again bowled splendidly, and he soon accounted for Hudson, but Kirsten was dropped twice off his bowling before reaching double figures. The left-hander was to make India pay dearly for these lapses. He lost Bacher, who looked a fine prospect, just after lunch, but this was India's only success in the second session.

Kirsten batted with grace and style for 290 minutes and hit eight fours. He and Cullinan shared a joyful partnership. They added 114 runs, and Cullinan's 77 included a six and six fours. Srinath and Venkatesh Prasad bowled manfully, but again the support was limited. It looked as if Kirsten and Cullinan might bat for ever, but Azharuddin fielded a ball at square-leg and Kirsten, committed to the run, was sent back by Cullinan. Even though Azharuddin's return was to the keeper, Mongia was still able to beat Kirsten at the bowler's end. Cullinan then fell to a fine leg-side catch by Mongia, and South Africa closed on 280 for 4.

Srinath and Venkatesh Prasad struck quickly on the second morning, sending back Cronje and Pollock. McMillan, watchful defence and uninhibited aggression, found a good ally in Richardson, and the pair added 83 before Richardson hooked Srinath to long leg. This brought in Klusener, who immediately began to whack the ball. He was soon catching up McMillan who had had a four-hour start on him, but it was McMillan who was first to three figures. Klusener's century followed a quarter-of-an-hour later. He hit two sixes and 13 fours, and his 102 came off 100 balls. He was appearing in only his fourth Test match, and so far it had been roses all the way.

Cronje declared as soon as Klusener reached his hundred, but the all-rounder's contribution to the day was far from over. Klusener bats left and bowls right, and, as a batsman, he had shared a record eighth wicket stand of 147. Now he bowled Dravid and ran out Raman. Adams bowled night-watchman Venkatesh Prasad, and India ended the day on 29 for 3. A capacity crowd had thoroughly enjoyed themselves.

Klusener was to be brought back to earth on the third day. Ganguly and Laxman were soon gone, and India were 58 for 5, the result of lapses in concentration and application. India's last hopes rested with the captain and

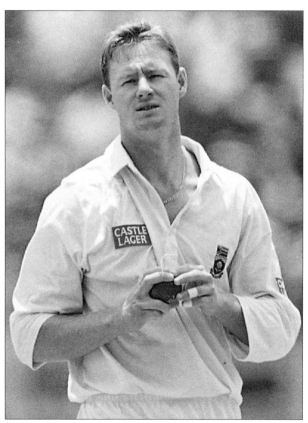

Lance Klusener took eight wickets on his Test debut in India and hit 102 off 100 balls in his second Test in South Africa. He and McMillan shared an unbroken eighth wicket stand of 147. (Mike Hewitt/Allsport)

the deposed captain, Tendulkar and Azharuddin. They did not disappoint. They played dazzling cricket in a glorious partnership which brought 222 in 40 overs. Rarely has Test cricket seen batting of this quality. They put South Africa to the sword. After lunch, Azharuddin went from 50 to 100 in 42 balls, and his 115 came off 110 deliveries. He hit a six and 19 fours, and it was his third hundred in four Tests. Two of these centuries had been of exceptional merit.

In one spell, Klusener was hit for 60 runs in six overs as Tendulkar and Azharuddin ran riot. Azharuddin bats now as if he is batting against the rest of the world, and the rest of the world is losing. He was out when he went for a run for which there had been no call.

Tendulkar, having saved the follow-on in the company of Srinath, reached his century just before Azharuddin and was last out for 169, an innings that included 26 sizzling fours. It was hard to believe that this innings had been played at a time of crisis.

India trailed by 170, but Ganesh captured his first Test wicket when he accounted for Kirsten, and Srinath trapped Bacher to leave South Africa 24 for 2 at the close. That was the high point for India. Thereafter they lost their way.

Venkatesh Prasad was indisposed and could bowl little on the fourth day so that a weak attack was further depleted. Srinath and Kumble carried a huge burden, and Srinath struck early when he had Klusener caught off a mis-hook, but the remainder of the South Africans batted with consummate ease. Cronje declared and set India a target of 427, or, more realistically, gave his bowlers a minimum of 118 overs in which to bowl out the visitors. Mongia immediately fell to a superb ball from Donald, and Raman, who lived dangerously, and Dravid both fell to catches behind.

Beginning the final day on 52 for 3, India lost Tendulkar and Azharuddin by the end of the fifth over, and with their departures went the match. A record attendance for the game of 74,577 had seen South Africa triumph once again, and many of those people had been fortunate enough to see one of the passages in Test history, the batting of Tendulkar and Azharuddin on the third day.

11, 12 and 13 January 1997
at Springbok Park, Bloemfontein
Free State 320 for 7 dec. (H.H. Dippenaar 96, C.F. Craven 76, J.F. Venter 54 not out, D.J. Johnson 5 for 78) and 259 for 2 dec. (G.F.J. Liebenberg 133 not out, D. Jordaan 66)
Indians 296 for 6 dec. (V. Rathore 115, V.V.S. Laxman 56 not out, S.S. Karim 53 not out) and 185 for 6 (V. Rathore 50)
Match drawn

Between the second and third Tests, the tourists played a first-class match against Free State. Rathore's century earned him a recall to the Test side in place of Raman, but Johnson's five-wicket haul brought no recognition.

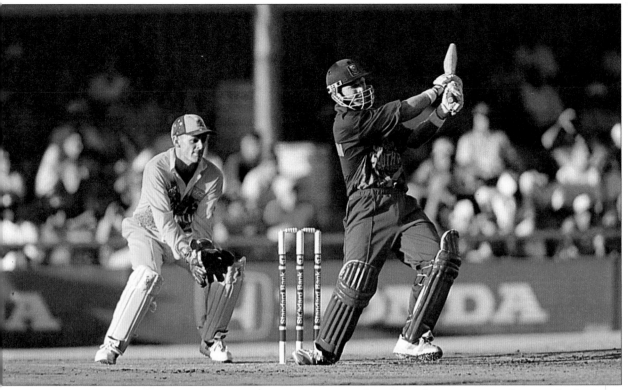

A match-saving century by Darryl Cullinan in the third Test against India was followed by Cullinan's major contributions to South African victories in the one-day series against both India and Australia. (Mike Hewitt/Allsport)

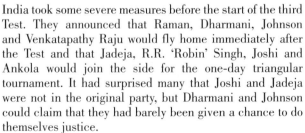

Third Test Match

South Africa v. India

India took some severe measures before the start of the third Test. They announced that Raman, Dharmani, Johnson and Venkatapathy Raju would fly home immediately after the Test and that Jadeja, R.R. 'Robin' Singh, Joshi and Ankola would join the side for the one-day triangular tournament. It had surprised many that Joshi and Jadeja were not in the original party, but Dharmani and Johnson could claim that they had barely been given a chance to do themselves justice.

The first day of the final Test was a strange affair. India scored at under two runs an over until tea. The pitch posed some problems for the batsmen but was not as quick as expected. Tendulkar was very well caught at slip some 20 minutes before tea, but after the break Dravid and Ganguly virtually doubled the score by adding 116 to the 117 that the first two sessions had produced.

Overnight rain delayed the start of the second day, and Klusener quickly brought an end to Ganguly's delightful innings. He also had Azharuddin taken at slip and broke Laxman's finger. In spite of this, the Indian batting did not capitulate, and Dravid reached a maiden Test century. It was a slow innings, 362 balls and nine hours at the crease, but it was full of charm, and Dravid is an

elegant driver on the off. South Africa had two balls at the end of the day before play was called off.

India seemed to take a grip on the game on the third day when Venkatesh Prasad and Srinath reduced South Africa to 147 for 5. The strength of the late middle order then became apparent as Pollock and McMillan added 112. Any thought of the follow-on was extinguished but, thanks to Srinath's second five-wicket haul in Test cricket, India led by 89 on the first innings.

Dravid and Ganguly contributed another scintillating century partnership to the Indian cause, and Tendulkar was able to declare and set South Africa a target of 356. They had the last day and five overs of the fourth day in which to get the runs, and Kumble, introduced for the last over of the penultimate day, bowled Hudson with his fifth delivery.

When play belatedly began on the final morning Venkatesh Prasad had Kirsten caught at slip without addition to the overnight score. The Indian bowlers were well on top, and, having reduced South Africa to 95 for 7, India seemed certain of victory. Cullinan at last found a capable partner in Klusener, and the pair saved the game with a stand of 127. Cullinan was outstanding in an innings of high quality, and Klusener confirmed his reputation as being the thorn in India's side throughout the series. These two held India at bay, but the tourists could also claim that they were deprived of their consolation win by the vagaries of the weather and the tardiness of the ground staff.

Second Test Match – South Africa v. India
2, 3, 4, 5 and 5 January 1996 at Newlands, Cape Town

South Africa

Batsman	First Innings		Second Innings	
A.C. Hudson	c Mongia, b Prasad	16	b Srinath	55
G. Kirsten	run out	103	lbw, b Ganesh	0
A.M. Bacher	c Mongia, b Srinath	25	lbw, b Srinath	0
D.J. Cullinan	c Mongia, b Prasad	77	(5) b Kumble	55
W.J. Cronje (Capt)	c Mongia, b Srinath	41	(6) c Dravid, b Kumble	18
B.M. McMillan	not out	103	(7) not out	59
S.M. Pollock	c Tendulkar, b Prasad	1	(8) not out	40
*D.J. Richardson	c Dravid, b Srinath	39		
L. Klusener	not out	102	(4) c Dravid, b Srinath	12
A.A. Donald				
P.R. Adams				
Extras	b 5, lb 9, nb 8	22	b 4, lb 12, w 1	17
Total	(for 7 wickets, dec.)	529	(for 6 wickets, dec.)	256

India

Batsman	First Innings		Second Innings	
W.V. Raman	run out	5	c Richardson, b Pollock	16
R.S. Dravid	b Klusener	2	(3) c Richardson, b Adams	12
S.C. Ganguly	c McMillan, b Donald	23	(4) c McMillan, b Pollock	30
Venkatesh Prasad	b Adams	0	(10) st Richardson, b Adams	15
S.R. Tendulkar (Capt)	c Bacher, b McMillan	169	c Klusener, b McMillan	9
W.V.S. Laxman	c Richardson, b Pollock	5	(7) not out	35
M. Azharuddin	run out	115	(6) c Hudson, b Donald	2
*N.R. Mongia	lbw, b Adams	5	(2) b Donald	2
A.R. Kumble	c Richardson, b Donald	2	(8) c Richardson, b Adams	14
J. Srinath	b Pollock	11	absent hurt	–
D. Ganesh	not out	2	(9) b Donald	1
Extras	lb 9, nb 11	20	b 1, w 2, nb 5	8
Total		359		144

	O	M	R	W	O	M	R	W
Srinath	38	8	130	3	18	5	78	3
Venkatesh Prasad	36	1	114	3	7	1	16	–
Ganesh	23.5	6	93	–	10	3	38	1
Kumble	51	7	136	2	25	4	58	2
Ganguly	9	1	24	–	2	–	5	–
Raman	5	1	18	–	10	–	45	–
Donald	24	4	99	2	18	5	40	3
Pollock	23	2	76	2	12	2	29	2
Adams	18	5	49	2	16.2	4	45	3
Klusener	12	1	88	1	9	3	13	–
McMillan	6.2	–	22	1	11	4	16	1
Cronje	9	5	16	–				

Fall of Wickets
1–37, 2–89, 3–203, 4–251, 5–291, 6–299, 7–382
1–6, 2–7, 3–33, 4–127, 5–133, 6–155

Fall of Wickets
1–7, 2–24, 3–25, 4–33, 5–58, 6–280, 7–298, 8–315, 9–340
1–7, 2–26, 3–44, 4–59, 5–61, 6–87, 7–115, 8–121, 9–144

Umpires: D.B. Hair & R.E. Koertzen

South Africa won by 282 runs

Third Test Match – South Africa v. India
16, 17, 18, 19 and 20 January 1997 at Wanderers, Johannesburg

India

Batsman	First Innings		Second Innings	
V. Rathore	c Richardson, b Adams	13	lbw, b Donald	44
*N.R. Mongia	b Donald	21	c McMillan, b Donald	50
R.S. Dravid	c Pollock, b Cronje	148	c Cullinan, b Adams	81
S.R. Tendulkar (Capt)	c McMillan, b Cronje	35	c Richardson, b Cronje	9
S.C. Ganguly	c McMillan, b Klusener	73	b Adams	60
M. Azharuddin	c Hudson, b Klusener	18	lbw, b Pollock	2
W.V.S. Laxman	retired hurt	0		
A.R. Kumble	c Richardson, b Klusener	29	(7) b Adams	6
J. Srinath	c Hudson, b Donald	41	(8) lbw, b Donald	4
D. Ganesh	c Cullinan, b Donald	1	(9) not out	0
Venkatesh Prasad	not out	2	(10) not out	1
Extras	lb 15, w 5, nb 9	29	b 3, w 4, nb 2	9
Total		410	(for 8 wickets, dec.)	266

South Africa

Batsman	First Innings		Second Innings	
A.C. Hudson	c Azharuddin, b Kumble	18	b Kumble	3
G. Kirsten	b Venkatesh Prasad	29	c Rathore, b Prasad	1
A.M. Bacher	lbw, b Srinath	13	b Venkatesh Prasad	23
D.J. Cullinan	c sub (Dharmani), b Srinath	33	not out	122
W.J. Cronje (Capt)	c Mongia, b Srinath	43	not out	6
B.M. McMillan	lbw, b Ganguly	47	c sub (Dharmani), b Srinath	2
S.M. Pollock	c Mongia, b Srinath	79	b Srinath	
*D.J. Richardson	c Azharuddin, b Ganguly	13	c Azharuddin, b Kumble	7
L. Klusener	not out	22	c Dravid, b Kumble	49
A.A. Donald	b Venkatesh Prasad	4	not out	0
P.R. Adams	c Dravid, b Srinath	2		
Extras	b 2, lb 7, w 1, nb 8	18	b 1, lb 13, nb 1	15
Total		321	(for 8 wickets)	228

	O	M	R	W	O	M	R	W
Donald	32.1	9	88	3	18	6	38	3
Pollock	30	11	55	–	11	–	28	1
McMillan	21.5	4	50	–	11	–	48	–
Klusener	27	6	75	3	13	1	41	–
Adams	24	6	88	1	21	1	80	3
Cronje	16.3	5	39	2	8	3	24	1
Bacher					1	–	4	–
Srinath	25.1	5	104	5	24	6	89	2
Venkatesh Prasad	20	2	83	2	15	1	59	2
Kumble	25	5	63	1	23	7	40	3
Ganesh	7	1	26	–	2	–	8	–
Ganguly	12	2	36	1	2	2	0	–
Tendulkar					2	2	18	–

Fall of Wickets
1–25, 2–46, 3–100, 4–245, 5–266, 6–327, 7–403, 8–408, 9–410
1–90, 2–109, 3–124, 4–232, 5–235, 6–256, 7–265, 8–265

Fall of Wickets
1–36, 2–64, 3–73, 4–139, 5–147, 6–259, 7–285, 8–303, 9–318
1–4, 2–4, 3–49, 4–71, 5–76, 6–78, 7–95, 8–222

Umpires: C.J. Mitchley & P. Willey

Match drawn

Test Match Averages – South Africa v. India

South Africa Batting

	M	Inns	NOs	Runs	HS	Av	100s	50s
B.M. McMillan	3	6	3	296	103*	98.66	1	2
D.J. Cullinan	3	6	1	291	122*	58.20	1	2
L. Klusener	3	6	2	190	102*	47.50	1	
A.C. Hudson	3	6	–	224	80	37.33		3
S.M. Pollock	3	6	2	145	79	36.25		1
A.M. Bacher	3	6	–	141	55	23.50		1
W.J. Cronje	3	6	–	140	43	23.33		
G. Kirsten	3	6	–	137	103	22.83	1	
D.J. Richardson	3	5	–	87	39	17.40		
A.A. Donald	3	4	1	35	26	11.66		

Played in two Tests: P.R. Adams 2
Played in one Test: H.H. Gibbs 25

India Batting

	M	Inns	NOs	Runs	HS	Av	100s	50s
R.S. Dravid	3	6	1	277	148	55.40	1	1
S.R. Tendulkar	3	6	–	241	169	40.16	1	
V.V.S. Laxman	2	3	2	40	35*	40.00		
S.C. Ganguly	3	6	–	202	73	33.66		2
M. Azharuddin	3	6	–	160	115	26.66	1	
V. Rathore	2	4	–	66	44	16.50		
N.R. Mongia	3	6	–	86	50	14.33		1
A.R. Kumble	3	6	1	66	29	13.20		
J. Srinath	3	5	–	63	41	12.60		
Venkatesh Prasad	3	6	2	23	15	5.75		
W.V. Raman	2	4	–	22	16	5.50		
D. Ganesh	2	4	2	4	2*	2.00		

Played in one Test – D.J. Johnson 5 & 3

South Africa Bowling

	Overs	Mds	Runs	Wks	Av	Best	10/m	5/inn
A.A. Donald	119.2	32	319	20	15.95	5/40		1
S.M. Pollock	96	21	231	10	23.10	3/25		
W.J. Cronje	33.3	13	79	3	26.33	2/39		
P.R. Adams	79.2	16	262	9	29.11	3/45		
L. Klusener	76.1	15	241	7	34.42	3/75		
B.M. McMillan	60.1	10	172	4	43.00	2/27		

Bowled in one innings: A.M. Bacher 1–0–4–0

India Bowling

	Overs	Mds	Runs	Wks	Av	Best	10/m	5/inn
Venkatesh Prasad	122	15	425	17	25.00	5/60	1	2
S.C. Ganguly	36	9	85	3	28.33	2/36		
J. Srinath	148.1	36	517	18	28.72	5/104		1
D.J. Johnson	24	3	91	2	45.50	2/52		
A.R. Kumble	155.2	29	384	8	48.00	3/40		
D. Ganesh	42.5	10	165	1	165.00	1/38		
S.R. Tendulkar	4.4	2	18	–	–			
W.V. Raman	15	1	63	–	–			

South Africa Fielding Figures

12 – D.J. Richardson (ct 11 / st 1); 6 – A.C. Hudson; 5 – B.M. McMillan; 4 – L. Klusener; 3 – D.J. Cullinan and A.M. Bacher; 1 – S.M. Pollock, W.J. Cronje and G. Kirsten

Fielding Figures

14 – N.R. Mongia; 6 – R.S. Dravid; 4 – V. Rathore; 3 – S.R. Tendulkar and M. Azharuddin; 2 – sub (P. Dharmani)

Standard Bank Triangular Series

The one-day competition was totally dominated by South Africa. Eight of the ten matches were played as day/night games, and each side met the others three times. South Africa won all six of their qualifying matches while India and Zimbabwe, having tied in their first encounter, each won one game. India qualified for the final by virtue of their better run rate.

South Africa gave a first international cap to Rudi Bryson, once of Surrey, and to Adam Bacher, who had already won a Test cap, while India introduced wicket-keeper Karim. Mongia had combined the tour with his honeymoon.

Klusener's success continued with five wickets in the opening match, but Rhodes took the individual award for his 57 off 39 balls at a time when South Africa were lagging.

Grant Flower hit a stirring 90 in the second game, and Zimbabwe reduced South Africa to 43 for 4, but Cullinan thwarted Zimbabwe just as he had thwarted India in the Test series.

The third match brought the excitement. The Boland Park outfield was sluggish, and it was not easy to find the boundary. Zimbabwe started badly and just as Grant Flower was effecting a recovery he played on to Ankola, the ball trickling on to the stumps. Campbell played a captain's innings, and Strang, promoted, hit four fours. Evans added lustre with three sixes and two fours. Needing 237 to win, India slumped to 176 for 7, but 'Robin' Singh hit a valiant 48 before being run out on the fifth ball of the last over. The ball was, in fact, called wide, but Singh went for a run when he could have stayed and faced another delivery.

Zimbabwe twice brought about batting recoveries against South Africa but were still beaten, and Kallis took two wickets and made his highest one-day score against India at St George's Park. Ganguly had his highest one-day score in the next match and shared an opening stand of 117 with Dravid, but South Africa still triumphed with four balls to spare.

Zimbabwe gained their solitary victory in the eighth match. Rain interrupted play, and Zimbabwe's target was reduced to 171 in 34 overs. They slipped to 78 for 6 before Evans and Strang added 71. Streak then hit nine off the first four balls of the last over to win the match. This result meant that India had to win the last game and reach their target inside 40 overs in order to qualify for the final. This they achieved thanks to Tendulkar at last finding his true form. Brandes, who had enjoyed a fine tournament, was battered

Match One – South Africa v. India
23 January 1997 at Springbok Park, Bloemfontein

South Africa

A.C. Hudson	c Tendulkar, b Venkatesh Prasad	15
G. Kirsten	c Singh, b Venkatesh Prasad	73
L. Klusener	run out	15
D.J. Cullinan	c Jadeja, b Kumble	51
J.N. Rhodes	not out	57
W.J. Cronje (Capt)	not out	44
S.M. Pollock		
*D.J. Richardson		
P.L. Symcox		
C.R. Matthews		
A.A. Donald		
	lb 6, w 7, nb 2	15
	50 overs (for 4 wickets)	270

	O	M	R	W
Srinath	10	–	50	–
Venkatesh Prasad	10	1	63	2
Ankola	10	–	45	–
Kumble	9	–	44	1
Singh	8	–	40	–
Jadeja	3	–	22	–

Fall of Wickets
1–36, 2–54, 3–165, 4–168

India

S.C. Ganguly	c Rhodes, b Donald	40
S.R. Tendulkar (Capt)	b Pollock	0
J. Srinath	c Cullinan, b Klusener	37
M. Azharuddin	b Klusener	52
R.A. Dravid	c Symcox	8
A. Jadeja	c Richardson, b Cronje	1
R.R. Singh	b Symcox	0
*S.S. Karim	b Klusener	55
S.A. Ankola	b Klusener	3
A.R. Kumble	c Richardson, b Klusener	7
Venkatesh Prasad	not out	10
	b 1, lb 3, w 10, nb 4	18
	47.4 overs	231

	O	M	R	W
Pollock	8	–	46	1
Matthews	5	–	31	–
Donald	9	–	43	1
Symcox	10	–	38	2
Klusener	8.4	–	42	5
Cronje	7	1	27	1

Fall of Wickets
1–14, 2–87, 3–107, 4–128, 5–129, 6–136, 7–179, 8–183, 9–211

Umpires: S.B. Lambson & C.J. Mitchley *Man of the Match:* J.N. Rhodes

South Africa won by 39 runs

Match Two – South Africa v. Zimbabwe
25 January 1997 at Centurion Park, Centurion

Zimbabwe

G.W. Flower	c Hudson, b Donald	90
A.C. Waller	c Cullinan, b Pollock	0
A.D.R. Campbell (Capt)	c Kirsten, b Cullinan	15
*A. Flower	c Richardson, b Cronje	16
C.B. Wishart	c Donald, b Cronje	8
D.L. Houghton	c Cullinan, b Klusener	8
G.J. Whittall	c Richardson, b Donald	13
P.A. Strang	b Donald	39
H.H. Streak	b Donald	9
E.A. Brandes	run out	2
J.A. Rennie	not out	0
	lb 4, w 6, nb 1	11
	48.5 overs	211

	O	M	R	W
Pollock	10	–	33	1
Matthews	0.1	–	4	–
Cronje	8.5	–	34	2
Klusener	9	–	38	1
Donald	9.5	–	37	4
Symcox	10	–	54	–
Cullinan	1	–	7	1

Fall of Wickets
1–1, 2–53, 3–85, 4–99, 5–110, 6–157, 7–171, 8–203, 9–211

South Africa

A.C. Hudson	lbw, b Brandes	0
G. Kirsten	c Campbell, b Rennie	4
L. Klusener	b Rennie	1
D.J. Cullinan	c A. Flower, b Streak	73
J.N. Rhodes	c G.W. Flower, b Streak	16
W.J. Cronje (Capt)	not out	87
S.M. Pollock	not out	20
P.L. Symcox		
C.R. Matthews		
*D.J. Richardson		
A.A. Donald		
	lb 1, w 5, nb 5	11
	46.1 overs (for 5 wickets)	212

	O	M	R	W
Brandes	8	2	31	1
Rennie	7	1	28	2
Streak	10	–	51	2
Whittall	8	–	42	–
Strang	10	–	43	–
G.W. Flower	3.1	–	16	–

Fall of Wickets
1–0, 2–5, 3–7, 4–43, 5–166

Umpires: D.F. Becker & C.J. Mitchley *Man of the Match:* D.J. Cullinan

South Africa won by 5 wickets

Match Three – India v. Zimbabwe
27 January 1997 at Paarl CC, Paarl

Zimbabwe

.W. Flower	b Ankola	28
.C. Waller	b Venkatesh Prasad	6
A. Flower	run out	7
A. Strang	c Kumble, b Venkatesh Prasad	47
.D.R. Campbell (Capt)	c Jadeja, b Srinath	61
.L. Houghton	c Venkatesh Prasad, b Kumble	13
.J. Whittall	c and b Whittall	9
.N. Evans	b Kumble	40
.H. Streak	not out	4
.A. Brandes		
A. Rennie		
	lb 8, w 9, nb 4	21
	50 overs (for 8 wickets)	211

	O	M	R	W
rinath	10	–	34	1
enkatesh Prasad	10	1	49	3
.R. Singh	7	2	33	–
nkola	8	1	32	1
umble	10	–	58	2
endulkar	5	–	22	–

Fall of Wickets
-17, 2–32, 3–51, 4–145, 5–172, 6–179, 7–211, 8–236

India

S.R. Tendulkar (Capt)	c Campbell, b Brandes	6
S.C. Ganguly	c G.W. Flower, b Evans	38
J. Srinath	b Brandes	8
M. Azharuddin	b Brandes	6
R.S. Dravid	run out	23
A. Jadeja	b Brandes	32
*S.S. Karim	c and b Strang	38
R.R. Singh	run out	48
A.R. Kumble	b Brandes	4
S.A. Ankola	run out	9
Venkatesh Prasad	not out	1
	b 3, lb 9, w 11	23
	49.5 overs	236

	O	M	R	W
Brandes	9.5	1	41	5
Rennie	3	–	17	–
Whittall	7	–	28	–
Streak	10	–	52	–
Evans	10	–	48	1
Strang	10	–	38	1

Fall of Wickets
1–10, 2–22, 3–40, 4–85, 5–110, 6–166, 7–176, 8–204, 9–228

Umpires: W.A Diedricks & R.E. Koertzen   *Man of the Match:* E.A. Brandes

Match tied

Match Four – South Africa v. Zimbabwe
29 January 1997 at Newlands, Cape Town

Zimbabwe

.W. Flower	b Pollock	0
.C. Waller	b Bryson	52
A. Flower	run out	13
A. Strang	c Rhodes, b Symcox	11
.N. Evans	c and b Pollock	19
.D.R. Campbell (Capt)	c Rhodes, b Cronje	30
.L. Houghton	not out	57
.J. Whittall	not out	26
.H. Streak		
.A. Brandes		
A. Rennie		
	b 1, lb 4, w 5, nb 8	18
	50 overs (for 6 wickets)	226

	O	M	R	W
ollock	10	–	50	2
ryson	10	–	41	1
onald	10	–	44	–
lusener	10	–	38	–
ymcox	4	–	16	1
ronje	6	–	32	1

Fall of Wickets
-0, 2–49, 3–77, 4–100, 5–125, 6–176

South Africa

A.C. Hudson	c Strang, b Brandes	26
G. Kirsten	run out	55
L. Klusener	c G.W. Flower, b Rennie	19
D.J. Cullinan	c Campbell, b Whittall	33
J.N. Rhodes	not out	36
W.J. Cronje (Capt)	b Rennie	22
S.M. Pollock	not out	26
*D.J. Richardson		
P.L. Symcox		
R.E. Bryson		
A.A. Donald		
	lb 4, w 5, nb 3	12
	47 overs (for 5 wickets)	229

	O	M	R	W
Brandes	10	–	51	1
Rennie	10	1	51	2
Streak	8	–	34	–
Whittall	8	–	42	1
Strang	7	–	26	–
Evans	4	–	21	–

Fall of Wickets
1–50, 2–84, 3–131, 4–154, 5–187

Umpires: R.E. Koertzen & D.L. Orchard   *Man of the Match:* D.L. Houghton

South Africa won by 5 wickets

Match Five – South Africa v. Zimbabwe
31 January 1997 at Wanderers, Johannesburg

Zimbabwe

G.W. Flower	b Cronje	62
A.C. Waller	c and b Donald	1
*A. Flower	c Richardson, b Donald	0
C.B. Wishart	c Richardson, b Pollock	24
A.D.R. Campbell (Capt)	run out	5
D.L. Houghton	c Rhodes, b Symcox	57
G.J. Whittall	c Pollock, b Donald	41
P.A. Strang	not out	40
H.H. Streak	b Donald	12
E.A. Brandes	not out	1
E. Matambanadzo		
	lb 5, w 7, nb 1	13
	50 overs (for 8 wickets)	256

	O	M	R	W
Donald	10	1	46	4
Bryson	8	1	44	–
Pollock	10	1	43	1
Klusener	7	–	39	–
Symcox	10	–	55	1
Cronje	5	1	24	1

Fall of Wickets
1–6, 2–6, 3–51, 4–61, 5–154, 6–168, 7–231, 8–247

South Africa

A.C. Hudson	lbw, b Brandes	1
G. Kirsten	lbw, b Brandes	7
L. Klusener	c Whittall, b Brandes	5
D.J. Cullinan	b Whittall	30
J.N. Rhodes	c Campbell, c Matambanadzo	34
W.J. Cronje (Capt)	not out	70
S.M. Pollock	b Streak	75
*D.J. Richardson	not out	11
P.L. Symcox		
R.E. Bryson		
A.A. Donald		
	lb 10, w 16, nb 10	26
	48.3 overs (for 6 wickets)	259

	O	M	R	W
Brandes	10	1	45	3
Streak	9	–	44	1
Whittall	9	–	47	1
Matambanadzo	8.3	–	53	1
Strang	10	–	48	–
G.W. Flower	2	–	12	–

Fall of Wickets
1–4, 2–15, 3–16, 4–72, 5–102, 6–239

Umpires: D.F. Becker & S.B. Lambson   *Man of the Match:* W.J. Cronje   **South Africa won by 4 wickets**

Match Six – South Africa v. India
2 February 1997 at St George's Park, Port Elizabeth

India

S.C. Ganguly	run out	0
R.S. Dravid	c Cronje, b Donald	50
J. Srinath	c Richardson, b Kallis	3
S.R. Tendulkar (Capt)	b Donald	1
M. Azharuddin	c Rhodes, b Donald	57
A.D. Jadeja	lbw, b Kallis	15
*S.S. Karim	c Bacher, b Adams	8
R.R. Singh	c Donald, b Pollock	18
A.R. Kumble	not out	11
S.A. Ankola	run out	8
Venkatesh Prasad		
	lb 3, w 4, nb 1	8
	50 overs (for 9 wickets)	179

	O	M	R	W
Pollock	10	1	37	1
Kallis	8	2	23	2
Donald	10	2	40	3
Klusener	8	–	28	–
Adams	10	1	31	1
Cronje	4	–	17	–

Fall of Wickets
1–0, 2–7, 3–11, 4–116, 5–118, 6–132, 7–147, 8–168, 9–179

South Africa

A.M. Bacher	b Kumble	13
G. Kirsten	c Azharuddin, b Venkatesh Prasad	6
J.H. Kallis	c Ankola, b Singh	79
D.J. Cullinan	c Jadeja, b Singh	21
J.N. Rhodes	not out	29
W.J. Cronje (Capt)	not out	20
S.M. Pollock		
L. Klusener		
*D.J. Richardson		
A.A. Donald		
P.R. Adams		
	lb 9, w 1, nb 2	12
	45.1 overs (for 4 wickets)	180

	O	M	R	W
Srinath	7.1	2	24	–
Venkatesh Prasad	9	–	41	1
Kumble	9	–	30	1
Ankola	10	–	42	–
Singh	10	–	34	2

Fall of Wickets
1–8, 2–47, 3–89, 4–152

Umpires: R.E. Koertzen & D.L. Orchard   *Man of the Match:* J.H. Kallis   **South Africa won by 6 wickets**

Match Seven – South Africa v. India
4 February 1997 at Buffalo Park, East London

India

S.C. Ganguly	run out	83
R.S. Dravid	run out	53
S.R. Tendulkar (Capt)	c Cullinan, b Klusener	14
M. Azharuddin	b Donald	13
A.D. Jadeja	c Cronje, b Klusener	19
R.R. Singh	not out	32
*S.S. Karim	not out	7
S.B. Joshi		
A.R. Kumble		
J. Srinath		
Venkatesh Prasad		
	lb 7, w 3, nb 1	11
	50 overs (for 5 wickets)	232

	O	M	R	W
Pollock	10	2	26	–
Kallis	6	–	34	–
Klusener	10	–	58	2
Donald	10	1	38	1
Cronje	9	1	37	–
Adams	5	–	32	–

Fall of Wickets
1–117, 2–150, 3–171, 4–176, 5–216

South Africa

G. Kirsten	c Kumble, b Venkatesh Prasad	82
A.M. Bacher	c Dravid, b Kumble	14
D.J. Cullinan	st Karim, b Joshi	32
J.H. Kallis	not out	52
J.N. Rhodes	lbw, b Srinath	22
W.J. Cronje (Capt)	not out	21
S.M. Pollock		
L. Klusener		
*D.J. Richardson		
A.A. Donald		
P.R. Adams		
	b 1, lb 7, w 2, nb 3	13
	49.2 overs (for 4 wickets)	236

	O	M	R	W
Srinath	10	–	50	1
Venkatesh Prasad	9.2	1	43	1
Kumble	10	–	36	1
Singh	6	–	31	–
Joshi	10	–	48	1
Tendulkar	3	–	17	–
Jadeja	1	–	3	–

Fall of Wickets
1–44, 2–134, 3–142, 4–200

Umpires: W.A. Diedricks & D.L. Orchard   Men of the Match: S.C. Ganguly & G. Kirsten

South Africa won by 6 wickets

Match Eight – India v. Zimbabwe
7 February 1997 at Centurion Park, Centurion

India

S.C. Ganguly	c Strang, b Whittall	31
R.S. Dravid	c A. Flower, b Rennie	12
J. Srinath	c Evans, b Streak	9
S.R. Tendulkar (Capt)	c Waller, b Campbell	41
M. Azharuddin	st A. Flower, b Strang	44
A.D. Jadeja	run out	36
R.R. Singh	run out	11
*S.S. Karim	run out	10
A.R. Kumble	c A. Flower, b Brandes	7
S.A. Ankola	c Campbell, b Brandes	0
Venkatesh Prasad	not out	0
	lb 6, w 9	15
	48.4 overs	216

	O	M	R	W
Brandes	9.4	–	44	2
Rennie	8	1	26	1
Streak	10	2	42	1
Whittall	5	–	20	1
Strang	9	–	43	1
Evans	2	–	13	–
Campbell	2	–	8	1
G.W. Flower	3	–	14	–

Fall of Wickets
1–25, 2–46, 3–67, 4–137, 5–161, 6–195, 7–198, 8–216, 9–216

Zimbabwe

G.W. Flower	b Ankola	28
A.C. Waller	c Ganguly, b Venkatesh Prasad	2
*A. Flower	c Karim, b Singh	9
G.J. Whittall	run out	4
A.D.R. Campbell (Capt)	run out	10
D.L. Houghton	c Kumble, b Singh	13
C.N. Evans	c Azharuddin, b Kumble	43
P.A. Strang	not out	31
H.H. Streak	not out	11
E.A. Brandes		
J.A. Rennie		
	lb 8, w 7, nb 5	20
	33.4 overs (for 7 wickets)	171

	O	M	R	W
Srinath	7	–	32	–
Venkatesh Prasad	6.4	–	39	1
Kumble	7	–	31	1
Ankola	5	–	32	1
Singh	7	1	18	2
Tendulkar	1	–	11	–

Fall of Wickets
1–16, 2–46, 3–53, 4–55, 5–77, 6–78, 7–149

Umpires: D.F. Becker & C.J. Mitchley   Men of the Match: C.N. Evans & P.A. Strang

Zimbabwe won on faster scoring rate

Match Nine – India v. Zimbabwe
9 February 1997 at Willowmore Park, Benoni

Zimbabwe

G.W. Flower	c Jadeja, b Joshi	40
S.V. Carlisle	c Mongia, b Srinath	3
A.D.R. Campbell (Capt)	b Srinath	86
G.J. Whittall	c Dravid, b Kumble	20
*A. Flower	b Joshi	35
D.L. Houghton	c Kumble, b Joshi	1
C.N. Evans	not out	17
P.A. Strang	c Azharuddin, b Kumble	6
H.H. Streak	b Srinath	3
E.A. Brandes	not out	8
J.A. Rennie		
	b 3, lb 6, w 10, nb 2	21
	50 overs (for 8 wickets)	240

	O	M	R	W
Srinath	10	–	35	3
Venkatesh Prasad	10	1	45	–
Singh	5	–	31	–
Kumble	10	–	53	2
Joshi	10	1	40	3
Tendulkar	3	–	16	–
Ganguly	2	–	11	–

Fall of Wickets
1–18, 2–79, 3–128, 4–191, 5–195, 6–212, 7–219, 8–225

India

S.C. Ganguly	c Carlisle, b Rennie	12
S.R. Tendulkar (Capt)	c Campbell, b Evans	104
M. Azharuddin	b Rennie	2
R.S. Dravid	b Whittall	17
A.D. Jadeja	not out	56
R.R. Singh	not out	38
*N.R. Mongia		
J. Srinath		
A.R. Kumble		
S.B. Joshi		
Venkatesh Prasad		
	lb 2, w 6, nb 4	12
	39.2 overs (for 4 wickets)	241

	O	M	R	W
Brandes	5.2	–	50	–
Rennie	9	–	36	2
Streak	9	–	62	–
Whittall	6	–	36	1
Strang	5	–	30	–
Evans	5	–	25	1

Fall of Wickets
1–19, 2–34, 3–119, 4–158

Umpires: D.F. Becker & W.A. Diedricks   *Man of the Match:* S.R. Tendulkar

India won by 6 wickets

Final – South Africa v. India
13 February 1997 at Kingsmead, Durban

South Africa

A.C. Hudson	c Karim, b Srinath	19
G. Kirsten	c Dravid, b Singh	51
J.H. Kallis	lbw, b Singh	49
D.J. Cullinan	b Kumble	60
J.N. Rhodes	b Tendulkar	41
W.J. Cronje (Capt)	b Venkatesh Prasad	10
S.M. Pollock	lbw, b Venkatesh Prasad	0
L. Klusener	b Kumble	16
*D.J. Richardson	not out	15
R.E. Bryson	not out	2
A.A. Donald		
	lb 8, w 3, nb 4	15
	50 overs (for 8 wickets)	278

	O	M	R	W
Srinath	10	–	50	1
Venkatesh Prasad	10	1	43	2
Kumble	10	–	45	2
Ankola	7	–	50	–
Singh	10	–	63	2
Tendulkar	3	–	19	1

Fall of Wickets
1–44, 2–130, 3–130, 4–221, 5–242, 6–242, 7–244, 8–266

India

S.C. Ganguly	c Donald, b Pollock	5
S.R. Tendulkar (Capt)	c Bryson, b Cronje	45
R.S. Dravid	c Kirsten, b Klusener	84
M. Azharuddin	c Rhodes, b Pollock	45
A.D. Jadeja	c Hudson, b Klusener	18
R.R. Singh	run out	15
*S.S. Karim	b Donald	3
J. Srinath	c Cullinan, b Donald	1
S.A. Ankola	b Donald	0
A.R. Kumble	run out	6
Venkatesh Prasad	not out	2
	b 1, lb 4, w 2, nb 3	10
	39.2 overs	234

	O	M	R	W
Pollock	6	–	39	2
Bryson	7	–	47	–
Donald	7.2	–	48	3
Cronje	8	–	35	1
Klusener	8	–	42	2
Kallis	3	–	18	–

Fall of Wickets
1–18, 2–84, 3–165, 4–198, 5–210, 6–224, 7–224, 8–224, 9–230

Umpires: R.E. Koertzen & C.J. Mitchley   *Man of the Match:* R.S. Dravid

South Africa won on faster scoring rate

o all parts of the field, and Jadeja and Singh shared an unbroken stand of 83 to win the game.

The final was originally scheduled for 12 February, but this match was ruined by rain and abandoned with South Africa 42 for 1 in 14.3 overs in reply to India's 191 for 9. There was more rain the next day and India's target was reduced to 251 in 40 overs after South Africa had made 278 for 8 in their full quota of 50 overs. Cronje won the toss for the first time, and his side began well with 44 in 11 overs before Hudson fell to Srinath. Kirsten and Kallis added 86. Kirsten hit 51 off 65 deliveries before being caught in the deep, and Kallis was out next ball. Cullinan and Rhodes scored at a brisk rate, hitting 91 off 81 balls, and the only curb to the South African avalanche of runs came in the 44th over when Venkatesh Prasad dismissed Cronje and Pollock with successive deliveries.

Tendulkar, Dravid and Azharuddin gave the Indian innings the momentum it needed, but once they were dismissed the cause was lost.

Cronje was named as Man of the Series.

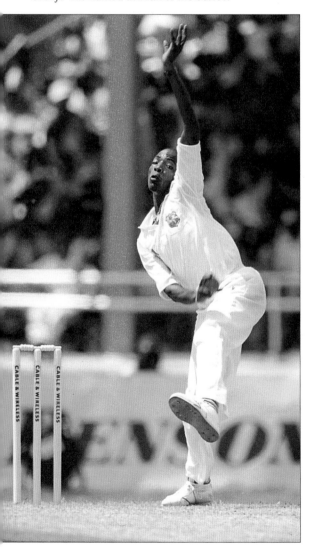

Supersport Series

1, 2, 3 and 4 November 1996
at Boland Park, Paarl
Boland 268 (L.D. Ferreira 127, C.V. English 5 for 65) and 260 (K.C. Jackson 70, A.C. Kuiper 63)
Griqualand West 250 (P.H. Barnard 64) and 83 (R. Telemachus 6 for 21)
Boland won by 195 runs
Boland 16 pts, Griqualand West 6 pts

at Kingsmead, Durban
Natal 332 (D.M. Beckenstein 129 not out, M.L. Bruyns 73, S.M. Pollock 66, V.C. Drakes 8 for 59) and 257 (S.M. Pollock 77, D.J. Watson 75)
Border 205 and 385 for 6 (P.N. Kirsten 90, F.J.C. Cronje 67, P.C. Strydom 61)
Border won by 4 wickets
Border 14 pts, Natal 8 pts

at Newlands, Cape Town
Western Province 220 (J.B. Commins 81 not out, H.D. Ackerman 51, R.E. Bryson 4 for 64) and 399 (S.G. Koenig 97, D.L. Haynes 71, E.O. Simons 61)
Northern Transvaal 355 (R.F. Pienaar 95, R.B. Richardson 56) and 226
Western Province won by 38 runs
Western Province 14 pts, Northern Transvaal 8 pts

The former Currie Cup and Castle Cup became the Supersport Series in 1996–97, and Griqualand West joined the elite. Boland included the Leicestershire pace bowler David Millns in their side for the opening match, but their heroes were Lloyd Ferreira, who hit a maiden first-class century and medium-pacer Roger Telemachus, whose second innings bowling figures were the best of his career.

Vasbert Drakes had match figures of 11 for 101 for Border against Natal, and he captured eight wickets in an innings for the first time. Skipper Dale Benkenstein's century and fine knocks from Bruyns and Pollock, recovering from an ankle injury, put Natal on top, but consistently fine batting in the second innings took Border to a remarkable victory. None contributed more than 41-year-old Peter Kirsten.

Another veteran in good form was Desmond Haynes, who featured in Western Province's win over Northern Transvaal. The visitors took a first innings lead of 135 with Roy Pienaar, once of Kent, and skipper Richie Richardson, once of West Indies, adding 112 for the third wicket, but in the second innings they collapsed against a varied attack.

Vasbert Drakes returned the best bowling figures of his career and of the the season when he took 8 for 59 for Border against Natal who suffered their only defeat of the season. (Ben Radford/Allsport)

A happy return to cricket with Natal and to the Test side for Shaun Pollock who recovered from the ankle injury that kept him out of the tour of South Africa. (Mike Hewitt/Allsport)

14, 15, 16 and 17 November 1996
at Newlands, Cape Town
Boland 239 (P.R. Adams 4 for 68) and 205 (A.C. Dawson 5 for 30)
Western Province 509 for 7 dec. (J.B. Commins 148 not out, S.G. Koenig 119, H.D. Ackerman 65, A.C. Dawson 64)
Western Province won by an innings and 65 runs
Western Province 18 pts, Boland 4 pts

15, 16, 17 and 18 November 1996
at Buffalo Park, East London
Border 261 (M.V. Boucher 51)
Eastern Province 338 for 5 (P.G. Amm 81 not out, D.J. Callaghan 74, K.C. Wessels 70, L.J. Koen 64)
Match drawn
Eastern Province 8 pts, Border 5 pts

at Centurion Park, Centurion
Free State 349 (L.J. Wilkinson 87, J.F. Venter 76, R.E. Bryson 5 for 84)
Northern Transvaal 190 (R.F. Pienaar 60) and 154 (F.D. Stephenson 4 for 21)
Free State won by an innings and 5 runs
Free State 18 pts, Northern Transvaal 4 pts

at Kimberley Country Club, Kimberley
Transvaal 440 for 6 dec. (A.M. Bacher 210, N.D. McKenzie 84, D.R. Laing 80) and 194 for 4 dec. (A.M. Bacher 112 not out)

Griqualand West 327 (P.H. Barnard 93, M.I. Gidley 52, C.E. Eksteen 4 for 105) and 214 (R.A. Koster 74, C.E. Eksteen 4 for 72)
Transvaal won by 93 runs
Transvaal 17 pts, Griqualand West 3 pts

Western Province made two wins in as many matches when they demolished Boland. Skipper John Commins had begun the season in top form and hit an unbeaten century. It was the tenth of his career, and the left-handed 23-year-old Sven Koenig hit the third century of his most promising career. Western Province's attack had variety and penetration.

There was no play on the last two days at Buffalo Park while Free State won in three days at Centurion. Louis Wilkinson hit 87 off 98 balls and dominated a third wicket stand of 141 with Gerhadus Liebenberg after two wickets had fallen for one run. Franklyn Stephenson had match figures of 7 for 82.

Adam Bacher won a place in the Test side with innings of 210 and 112 not out as Transvaal began the campaign with a win over Griqualand West. His double century included three sixes and 24 fours. Left-arm spinner Clive Eksteen took the bowling honours.

29 and 30 November, 1 and 2 December 1996
at St George's Park, Port Elizabeth
Eastern Province 476 for 6 dec. (L.J. Koen 186, D.J. Callaghan 102, M.W. Rushmere 63) and 185 for 3 dec. (K.C. Wessels 64 not out)
Griqualand West 266 (M.I. Gidley 86, E.A.E. Baptiste 5 for 60) and 306 (B.M. Benkenstein 68, W.M. Dry 56, G.T. Love 4 for 38, T.G. Shaw 4 for 67)
Eastern Province won by 89 runs
Eastern Province 19 pts, Griqualand West 4 pts

at Centurion Park, Centurion
Natal 360 (E.L.R. Stewart 78, N.C. Johnson 69, S. Elworthy 4 for 71) and 261 for 9 dec. (D.M. Benkenstein 87)
Northern Transvaal 121 (G.M. Gilder 5 for 57, T. Bosch 4 for 19) and 214 (R.B. Richardson 68, M.J.R. Rindel 60, S.M. Pollock 5 for 48)
Natal won by 286 runs
Natal 19 pts, Northern Transvaal 4 pts

at Springbok Park, Bloemfontein
Western Province 446 (J.H. Kallis 143, D.B. Rundle 81 not out, A.C. Dawson 59)
Free State 274 (G.F.J. Liebenberg 90, M.W. Pringle 4 for 61, A. Martyn 4 for 76) and 483 for 2 (H.H. Dippenaar 151 not out, L.J. Wilkinson 139 not out, G.F.J. Liebenberg 91, D. Jordaan 80)
Match drawn
Western Province 7 pts, Free State 4 pts

at Wanderers, Johannesburg
Transvaal 308 (N.D. McKenzie 80, D.R. Laing 76,
A.M. Bacher 58, C.W. Henderson 5 for 107, R. Telemachus
4 for 71)
Boland 146 (C.E. Eksteen 4 for 38) and 159 (R.E. Veenstra
4 for 48)
Transvaal won by an innings and 3 runs
Transvaal 17 pts, Boland 3 pts

Louis Koen hit 186 off 229 balls with four sixes and 25 fours
and David Callaghan hit 102 off 134 balls with 13 fours to
set up Eastern Province's win over Griqualand West, who
batted consistently and defiantly.

Natal notched their first win of the season, while Free
State, forced to follow on against Western Province, battled
back to draw. Jordaan and Liebenberg began their second
innings with a stand of 161, and Dippenaar, who hit a career
best 151 not out, and Wilkinson shared an unbroken third
wicket partnership of 300, a Free State record.

Transvaal beat Boland in three days with Eksteen
again among the wickets.

12, 13, 14 and 15 December 1996
at Kingsmead, Durban
Boland 133 (S.M. Pollock 4 for 22, G.M. Gilder 4 for 36)
and 201 (G.M. Gilder 5 for 60)
Natal 198 (D.M. Benkenstein 50, H.S. Williams
6 for 57, D.J. Millns 4 for 64) and 137 for 2 (D.J. Watson
51 not out)
Natal won by 8 wickets
Natal 15 pts, Boland 4·pts

13, 14, 15 and 16 December 1996
at Kimberley Country Club, Kimberley
Free State
 493 (B.T. Player 133 not out, C.F. Craven 109, L.J. Wilkinson
75, H.H. Dippenaar 50)
Griqualand West 340 (J.M. Arthur 57, M.I. Gidley 52,
P.H. Barnard 52, B.T. Player 4 for 41) and 222 for 6
(M.I. Gidley 76)
Match drawn
Griqualand West 6 pts, Free State 4 pts

at Wanderers, Johannesburg
Transvaal 334 (D.R. Laing 128, A.J. Hall 60, E.A.E. Baptiste
4 for 65) and 272 for 3 dec. (A.M. Bacher 114,
N.D. McKenzie 53 not out)
Eastern Province 261 (G. Morgan 65 not out,
K.C. Wessels 51, R.E. Veenstra 5 for 36) and 185 (L.J. Koen
75, C.E. Eksteen 4 for 74)
Transvaal won by 160 runs
Transvaal 18 pts, Eastern Province 6 pts

at Newlands, Cape Town
Border 210 (M.V. Boucher 71) and 185 (M.V. Boucher 68,
B.N. Schultz 5 for 69, M.W. Pringle 4 for 26)

Western Province 290 (D.L. Haynes 99, C.R. Matthews
96, M. Ntini 6 for 49) and 106 for 2
Western Province won by 8 wickets
Western Province 17 pts, Border 6 pts

Kingsmead proved as difficult for Boland and Natal as it
was to prove for South Africa and India and the match was
over in three days with left-arm medium pacer Gildes
particularly enjoying the pitch, and right-arm medium pace
bowler Henry Williams returning the best figures of his
career.

Griqualand West again displayed remarkable
tenacity in avoiding defeat as they frustrated Free State.
Brad Player hit the second and higher century of his career
as he and Craven added 146 for the eighth wicket. Player's
133 came off 189 balls and included eight sixes and 11
fours. He followed this with 4 for 41 in 26 overs, but he
could not bring Free State victory.

Dean Laing made the highest score of his career and
saved a tottering Transvaal. Bacher was again in splendid
form in Transvaal's second innings, and Eksteen brought his
total of wickets to 20 in three matches as he helped bowl the
home side to victory on the final day.

Having bowled out Border for 210, Western Province
stumbled to 116 for 7. Desmond Haynes then found a
capable partner in Craig Matthews. The pair added 144, of
which Matthews made 96 off 127 balls with 14 fours.
Haynes was last out, leg before to fast bowler Makhaya Ntini
whose 6 for 49 was the best performance of a brief career.
Boucher was aggressively defiant for Border in both
innings, but Western Province won in three days.

26, 27, 28 and 29 December 1996
at Boland Park, Paarl
Boland 170 (A.P. Kuiper 74) and 179 (K.C. Jackson 62,
M.J.G. Davis 6 for 80)
Northern Transvaal 117 (H.S. Williams 4 for 31)
and 177
Boland won by 55 runs
Boland 15 pts, Northern Transvaal 4 pts

29, 30, 31 December 1996 and 1 January 1997
at Buffalo Park, East London
Transvaal 291 (R.E. Veenstra 135 not out, A.J. Hall 78,
P.J. Botha 5 for 38) and 162 (M.R. Benfield 53, P.J. Botha
4 for 47)
Border 319 for 8 dec. (P.N. Kirsten 106, I.L. Howell
102 not out, E.W. Kidwell 4 for 97) and 135 for 5
Border won by 5 wickets
Border 18 pts, Transvaal 6 pts

3, 4, 5 and 6 January 1997
at St George's Park, Port Elizabeth
Western Province 401 for 2 dec. (D.L. Haynes
202 not out, J.H. Kallis 94) and 228 for 6 dec.
(H.D. Ackerman 102 not out, J.H. Kallis 79)

Makhaya Ntini took a career best 6 for 49 for Border against Western Province. A member of South Africa's Under-19 side, Ntini made a considerable advance during the season and is a fast bowler of immense promise. (Neal Simpson/EMPICS)

Eastern Province 300 for 9 dec. (L.J. Koen 128, M.W. Rushmere 74, M.W. Pringle 4 for 79) and 331 for 5 (K.C. Wessels 179, D.J. Callaghan 88)
Eastern Province won by 5 wickets
Eastern Province 14 pts, Western Province 9 pts

at Kingsmead, Durban
Natal 282 (D.M. Benkenstein 100, N.C. Johnson 50) and 349 for 7 dec. (J.N. Rhodes 156 not out, D.N. Crookes 52)
Free State 160 (H.H. Dippenaar 81) and 312 for 9 (H.H. Dippenaar 93, D. Jordaan 81, P.J.L. Radley 58 not out, D.N. Crookes 7 for 114)
Match drawn
Natal 7 pts, Free State 5 pts

A low scoring game in Paarl was over in three days with Boland's Williams enjoying another good match and off-spinner Mark Davis thriving for Northern Transvaal.

Ross Veenstra hit a maiden first-class hundred and Andrew Hall made his highest score when they lifted Transvaal from 62 for 6 to 210 before they were separated, and it seemed that their efforts would be well rewarded when Border were reduced to 130 for 7. Peter Kirsten was then joined by Ian Howell, and the pair established a new Border eighth wicket record with a stand of 153. Peter

Kirsten was finally out after five-and-a-half hours which brought him his 56th first-class hundred. Howell reached three figures for the fifth time. Botha, Drakes and Ntini bowled out Transvaal in under 59 overs, and Boucher and Strydom stroked Border to victory after some early hiccups.

St George's Park was full of runs. Desmond Haynes and Jacques Kallis put on 205 for Western Province's second wicket, and Haynes went on to make an unbeaten 202 off 333 balls with four sixes and 21 fours. It was the 61st and last century of Haynes's distinguished career, for the great West Indian announced his retirement from first-class cricket two months later. Louis Koen responded with 128 off 154 balls for the home side, and Wessels declared 101 in arrears. Ackerman became the game's third centurion, and Matthews declared, setting Eastern Province to make 330 at nearly four an over. They were 67 for 3, but Wessels and Callaghan put on 241 in 204 minutes. Wessels made 179 off 235 balls with three sixes and 25 fours and led his side to victory.

Jonty Rhodes made the highest score of his career in Durban, but Natal's bid for victory was thwarted by Free State's last pair who survived the final two overs.

10, 11, 12 and 13 January 1997
at Centurion Park, Centurion
Northern Transvaal 334 for 7 dec. (B.J. Sommerville 62, D.J. van Zyl 57, S. Elworthy 51) and 155 (A.J. Seymore 58, P.J. Botha 5 for 35)
Border 271 for 5 dec. (P.J. Botha 62, P.C. Strydom 52 not out) and 220 for 4 (P.J. Botha 77, B.M. White 63)
Border won by 6 wickets
Border 16 pts, Northern Transvaal 6 pts

Strydom's enterprising captaincy was rewarded with victory for Border over Northern Transvaal. He owed much to the all-round cricket of Peterus Botha, who had match figures of 7 for 121 and shared a second innings opening partnership of 121 with White.

17, 18, 19 and 20 January 1997
at Buffalo Park, East London
Border 331 (S.C. Pope 103, P.C. Strydom 100, H.S. Williams 4 for 74) and 201 for 4 dec. (M.V. Boucher 68 not out, B.M. White 54)
Boland 277 (W.S. Truter 95, A.R. Wylie 74) and 219 for 7 (K.C. Jackson 90 not out, L.D. Ferreira 53)
Match drawn
Boland 6 pts, Border 5 pts

at St George's Park, Port Elizabeth
Eastern Province 265 (K.C. Wessels 61, D.N. Crookes 4 for 62) and 118 (P.L. Symcox 4 for 26)
Natal 429 (E.L.R. Stewart 138, J.N. Rhodes 108)
Natal won by an innings and 46 runs
Natal 18 pts, Eastern Province 4 pts

at Kimberley Country Club, Kimberley
Griqualand West 298 (M.I. Gidley 117, C.V. English 51,
C.R. Matthews 4 for 44) and 167 (B.N. Schultz 5 for 49)
Western Province 470 for 5 dec. (J.B. Commins
200 not out, D.L. Haynes 91)
Western Province won by an innings and 5 runs
Western Province 19 pts, Griqualand West 4 pts

at Springbok Park, Bloemfontein
Free State 251 (C.F. Craven 64, D. Jordaan 57,
E.W. Kidwell 4 for 54) and 246 (D. Jordaan 66, J.F. Venter 57)
Transvaal 197 (N. Pothas 100 not out) and 108
(N.W. Pretorius 4 for 26)
Free State won by 192 runs
Free State 17 pts, Transvaal 5 pts

A century stand between Pope and Strydom revived Border
against Boland. Pope, a nephew of Ken McEwan, reached his
maiden first-class century. Boland were eventually set a
target of 256, and Border looked set for victory until rain and
Jackson intervened. Natal, rapidly emerging as the strongest
side in the competition, overwhelmed Eastern Province.
Crookes bowled well in both innings, and Steward and
Rhodes added 235 for the third wicket, beating the 60-year
old record of Siedle and Dudley Nourse. Martyn Gidley, once
of Leicestershire, made the fifth century of his career, but
Griqualand West were beaten in three days by Western
Province. John Commins hit the first double century of his
career, and the visitors scored at four-and-a-half runs an over.

Nic Pothas's second first-class hundred could not
save Transvaal at Springbok Park. Free State produced a
strong team performance.

1, 2, 3 and 4 February 1997
at Kingsmead, Durban
Griqualand West 91 (T. Bosch 5 for 15) and 166
(D.N. Crookes 5 for 43)
Natal 423 for 3 dec. (D.N. Crookes 128 not out,
D.M. Benkenstein 101 not out, E.L.R. Stewart 82,
D.J. Watson 52)
Natal won by an innings and 156 runs
Natal 20 pts, Griqualand West 1 pt

at Springbok Park, Bloemfontein
Border 367 for 9 dec. (P.J. Botha 136, P.N. Kirsten 56,
M.V. Boucher 53, H.C. Bakkes 6 for 43) and 205 for 5 dec.
(S.C. Pope 68 not out)
Free State 251 (J.F. Venter 101, D. Jordaan 68) and 282 for
9 (D. Jordaan 117, H.H. Dippenaar 54, P.C. Strydom 4 for 52)
Match drawn
Free State 7 pts, Border 7 pts

2, 3, 4 and 5 February 1997
at Boland Park, Paarl
Boland 204 (K.C. Jackson 120) and 237 (A.P. Kuiper 82,
A.R. Wylie 61)

Eastern Province 262 (M.W. Rushmere 89 not out,
G. Morgan 64, J.D. Albanie 4 for 37) and 181 for 4
(M.G. Beamish 76)
Eastern Province won by 6 wickets
Eastern Province 16 pts, Boland 5 pts

Natal maintained their pressure at the top of the league with
a three-day win over Griqualand West. Derek Crookes made
a career-best 128 not out and shared an unbroken fourth
wicket partnership of 197 with Dale Benkenstein. The runs
came in 152 minutes. Peterus Botha hit a career-best 136
for Border but the game in Bloemfontein ended in
stalemate. Eastern Province eased to victory over Boland.

7, 8, 9 and 10 February 1997
at Kimberley Country Club, Kimberley
Northern Transvaal 363 (A.J. Seymore 132, M. van
Jaarsveld 109, G.A. Roe 4 for 74) and 185
Griqualand West 541 for 6 dec. (P.H. Barnard 212,
W.M. Dry 74, B.N. Benkenstein 62 not out, M.I. Gidley 51)
and 10 for 0
Griqualand West won by 10 wickets
Griqualand West 16 pts, Northern Transvaal 4 pts

at Wanderers, Johannesburg
Transvaal 371 (N.D. McKenzie 139, S. Jacobs 85, B.N. Schultz
5 for 64) and 263 for 8 dec. (K.R. Rutherford 126 not out)
Western Province 227 (E.O. Simons 80, P. Kirsten 50,
C.E. Eksteen 4 for 65) and 352 for 7 (H.D. Ackerman 122,
H.H. Gibbs 103, E.O. Simons 58 not out)
Match drawn
Transvaal 8 pts, Western Province 5 pts

*Veteran Peter Kirsten was a tower of strength for Border throughout
the season. (David Munden/Sportsline)*

Griqualand West won their first match in the top flight. They owed much to Pieter Barnard, who hit the first double century of his career. Northern Transvaal's first innings was marked by a fifth wicket partnership of 171 between Seymore and van Jaarsveld, both of whom made the highest scores of their careers. For van Jaarsveld it was a maiden first-class century.

Western Province's failure in Johannesburg left Natal clear at the top of the table. McKenzie and Rutherford, long out of touch, hit their first centuries of the season, but the heroes were Gibbs and Ackerman who made hundreds after Western Province, chasing a target of 408, had lost both openers for 24.

A farewell double century for the great Desmond Haynes, Western Province v. Eastern Province, Port Elizabeth, 3 January 1997. (Steve Lindsell)

14, 15, 16 and 17 February 1997

at Boland Park, Paarl
Free State 254 (J.F. Venter 59, H.S. Williams 5 for 48) and 264 (W.J. Cronje 52)
Boland 264 (B.C. Baguley 77, J.F. Venter 6 for 96) and 256 for 5 (A.P. Kuiper 117 not out, A. Wessels 56 not out, J.F. Venter 4 for 109)
Boland won by 5 wickets
Boland 17 pts, Free State 7 pts

at Buffalo Park, East London
Border 400 (P.N. Kirsten 173 not out) and 192 for 5 dec. (P.J. Botha 90 not out)
Griqualand West 253 (P.H. Barnard 79) and 299 (W. Bossenger 82, J.M. Arthur 67, M. Ntini 4 for 73)
Border won by 40 runs
Border 18 pts, Griqualand West 4 pts

at St George's Park, Port Elizabeth
Eastern Province 432 for 9 dec. (L.J. Koen 87, M.W. Rushmere 66, K.C. Wessels 58, E.A.E. Baptiste 50, S. Elworthy 4 for 95) and 161 for 2 dec. (L.J. Koen 75, C.C. Bradfield 50 not out)
Northern Transvaal 272 (R.B. Richardson 69, G. Dros 54, E.A.E. Baptiste 5 for 56) and 115 (E.A.E. Baptiste 5 for 37)
Eastern Province won by 206 runs
Eastern Province 16 pts, Northern Transvaal 4 pts

at Wanderers, Johannesburg
Natal 407 (J.N. Rhodes 137, C.E. Eksteen 5 for 83) and 241 for 8 dec. (C.E. Eksteen 4 for 75)
Transvaal 241 (K.R. Rutherford 88, S.M. Pollock 4 for 58, L. Klusener 4 for 61) and 262 (D.J. Cullinan 78, S.M. Pollock 4 for 61, P.L. Symcox 4 for 76)
Natal won by 145 runs
Natal 19 pts, Transvaal 5 pts

Adrian Kuiper turned back the clock to take his side Boland to a great victory over Free State. Needing 255 to win, Boland were 91 for 5. Kuiper, well assisted by Andrew Wessels, hit nine sixes and eight fours to change the course of the match and take the individual award. All this was hard on off-break bowler Jacobus Venter who had the best bowling figures of his career in the first innings and took ten wickets in a match for the first time.

Another veteran, Peter Kirsten, was prominent as Border beat Griqualand West, and Eldine Baptiste, a fortnight short of his 37th birthday took the individual award for a fine all-round performance as Eastern Province beat Northern Transvaal. Natal succeeded where Western Province had failed, and their win at Wanderers virtually assured them of the title. Their Test players all performed well. Jonty Rhodes hit his third century of the summer, and Shaun Pollock had match figures of 8 for 119.

7, 8, 9 and 10 March 1997

at Centurion Park, Centurion
Transvaal 201 for 6 dec. (A.M. Bacher 102) and 71 for 1
Northern Transvaal 164 (R.F. Pienaar 55, E.W. Kidwell 4 for 58)
Match drawn
Transvaal 6 pts, Northern Transvaal 3 pts

at Springbok Park, Bloemfontein
Free State 178 (A. Badenhorst 4 for 39) and 275 (G.F.J. Liebenberg 85, T.G. Shaw 4 for 81)
Eastern Province 198 (L.J. Koen 57, K.C. Wessels 57, S.A. Cilliers 5 for 69) and 181
Free State won by 74 runs
Free State 15 pts, Eastern Province 5 pts

at Newlands, Cape Town
Western Province 433 for 3 dec. (H.H. Gibbs 163 not out, J.H. Kallis 138, D.L. Haynes 83) and 222 (C.R. Matthews 64, B.M. McMillan 63)
Natal 359 (D.N. Crookes 96, N.C. Johnson 52) and 55 for 1
Match drawn
Western Province 6 pts, Natal 4 pts

Bacher hit his fourth century of the season in the rain-ruined game in Centurion, while Free State recovered to beat Eastern Province, who lost Wessels with an injury in their second innings.

The two leading sides met at Newlands, and Gibbs made his highest score in South Africa as he and Kallis established a new Western Province third wicket record with a stand of 257. Natal responded with consistent application to reduce the first innings deficit to 74. The draw confirmed Natal as champions.

Supersport Series Final Table

	P	W	L	D	Bat	Bwl	Pts
Natal	8	5	1	2	32	28	110
Western Province	8	4	1	3	28	27	95
Border	8	4	1	3	25	25	90
Eastern Province	8	4	3	1	25	23	88
Transvaal	8	3	3	2	24	28	82
Free State	8	3	1	4	22	25	77
Boland	8	3	4	1	14	26	70
Griqualand West	8	1	6	1	18	16	44
Northern Transvaal	8	–	7	1	15	22	37

(Bonus Pts: Bat, Bwl)

Friendly Matches

25, 26 and 27 March 1997
at Kingsmead, Durban
Leicestershire 252 (V.J. Wells 61, D.L. Maddy 50) and 250 (J.J. Whitaker 105, P.A. Nixon 51)
Natal 503 for 5 dec. (D.J. Watson 200 not out, D.N. Crookes 110, D.M. Benkenstein 89)
Natal won by an innings and 1 run

11, 12 and 13 April 1997
at Wanderers, Johannesburg
Nottinghamshire 240 (P.R. Pollard 79, D.J. Terbrugge 4 for 54) and 218 for 4 dec. (P. Johnson 88 not out, C.M. Tolley 51 not out)
Transvaal 185 and 210 for 7 (D. Gain 88, N. Pothas 50, M.N. Bowen 4 for 56)
Match drawn

Leicestershire and Nottinghamshire undertook pre-season tours of South Africa, and the reigning champions of England and the Republic met in Durban. The match went emphatically in favour of Natal who were without their Test players. Doug Watson hit the first double century of his career off 375 balls with a six and 16 fours. In Johannesburg, Transvaal gave a first-class debut to pace bowler Terbrugge, and he had match figures of 6 for 86.

United Cricket Board of South Africa Bowl

31 October, 1 and 2 November 1996
at Wanderers, Johannesburg
Transvaal 'B' 277 (G.A. Pollock 115) and 247 (M.R. Benfield 122, D. Gain 62, A. Birrell 5 for 62)
Eastern Province 'B' 401 for 4 dec. (M.G. Beamish 164, P.G. Amm 105, G.C. Victor 95) and 125 for 4 (G.C. Victor 69 not out)
Eastern Province 'B' won by 6 wickets
Eastern Province 'B' 19 pts, Transvaal 'B' 5 pts

1, 2 and 3 November 1996
at Willowmore Park, Benoni
Easterns 290 for 7 dec. (C.R. Norris 75, T. Blake 64 not out, M.J. Lavine 4 for 58) and 302 for 6 dec. C.M.J. Mitchley 55, C.R. Norris 55, T.A. Marsh 52 not out)
North West 290 (M.J. Lavine 107, M. Strydom 87, C.R. Norris 4 for 72) and 122 (C.R. Norris 4 for 14)
Easterns won by 180 runs
Easterns 18 pts, North West 6 pts

The Bowl was split into two grades in 1996–97 with only the first grade accorded first-class status. Phil Amm and Michael Beamish began the season with a record opening partnership of 220 for Eastern Province 'B' in the win over Transvaal 'B'. Easterns, who had not won a match in 1995–96 and whose season had been marked by discord, began with a convincing victory. They were indebted to some fine all-round cricket by much travelled left-hander Craig Norris.

14, 15 and 16 November 1996
at Kingsmead, Durban
Natal 'B' 251 for 6 dec. (N. Parsons 84, J. Buxton-Foreman 70) and 178 for 5 (C.B. Sugden 85 not out)
Western Province 'B' 277 (F. Davids 65, G.M. Gilder 4 for 66)
Match drawn
Natal 'B' 6 pts, Western Province 'B' 6 pts

15, 16 and 17 November 1996
at Wanderers, Johannesburg
North West 160 (A.J. Hall 4 for 29) and 254 (S. Nicolson 70, L.P. Vorster 69)
Transvaal 'B' 247 for 8 dec. (D. Gain 82, D. Rossouw 5 for 61) and 53 for 3
Match drawn
Transvaal 'B' 8 pts, North West 4 pts

Natal 'B' laboured through their first innings against Western Province 'B', although Buxton-Foreman and

Parsons gave them a good start with a partnership of 135. It was rain rather than slow scoring that decided the game in Johannesburg.

28, 29 and 30 November 1996
at Kingsmead, Durban
Natal 'B' 225 (J. Buxton-Foreman 60, U.H. Goedeke 52, A.V. Birrell 4 for 46, A.J. Badenhorst 4 for 51) and 203 (G.S. Katz 54, L.D. Botha 6 for 59)
Eastern Province 'B' 174 (K.G. Storey 5 for 51, R.B. MacQueen 4 for 44) and 255 for 3 (A.G. Prince 125 not out, G.C. Victor 51)
Eastern Province 'B' won by 7 wickets
Eastern Province 'B' 15 pts, Natal 'B' 6 pts

29 and 30 November and 1 December 1996
at Newlands, Cape Town
Easterns 304 for 9 dec. (M.J. Mitchley 201 not out, C.R. Norris 50) and 96 (D.G. Payne 5 for 26)
Western Province 'B' 191 (G. de Kock 50, J.R. Meyer 6 for 48) and 214 (C.R. Norris 4 for 47)
Easterns won by 28 runs
Easterns 18 pts, Western Province 'B' 6 pts

Lodewikus Botha's career-best bowling performance and Ashwell Prince's maiden first-class century brought Eastern Province a fine victory in Durban. Like Eastern Province, Easterns made it two wins in two matches. They owed a vast amount to left-hander Mark Mitchley, who carried his bat through 88.5 overs to reach the first double century of his career. Opening partner Norris made 50 in a stand of 162, but nobody else got to 20. Medium-pacer Jon Meyer followed Mitchley's fine knock with a career-best bowling performance.

12, 13 and 14 December 1996
at Old Grey Ground, Kemsley Park, Port Elizabeth
Eastern Province 'B' 241 (M.G. Beamish 108) and 178 (A.G. Prince 78)
Western Province 'B' 298 (H. Pangarkar 92, F. Davids 52 not out, S. Hofmeyr 51) and 123 for 0 (R. Maron 65 not out, F.B. Touzel 52 not out)
Western Province 'B' won by 10 wickets
Western Province 'B' 18 pts, Eastern Province 'B' 6 pts

at Witrand Stadium, Potchefstroom
Natal 'B' 299 for 8 dec. (U.H. Goedeke 102 not out, B.A. Nash 64) and 142 (G.S. Katz 58, M. Strydom 6 for 55)
North West 210 (G.M. Hewitt 52, K.G. Storey 7 for 58) and 73 for 2
Match drawn
North West 7 pts, Natal 'B' 7 pts

Eastern Province 'B' suffered their first defeat of the season while, at the Witrand Stadium, fortunes fluctuated. Wicket-

keeper Udo Goedeke hit an unbeaten 102 off 121 balls with a six and 17 fours and then took five catches as Keith Storey returned the best bowling figures of his career. Natal seemed well on top, but off-break bowler Morne Strydom took five wickets in an innings for the first time, ended with 6 for 55, and the match was drawn.

13, 14 and 15 December 1996
at Willowmore Park, Benoni
Easterns 340 (M.J. Mitchley 119, T.A. Marsh 61, S. Jacobs 5 for 63) and 274 for 7 dec. (P.V. Simmons 102)
Transvaal 'B' 301 for 5 dec. (H.A. Manack 137 not out, G. Brophy 68) and 129 for 3 (Z. de Bruyn 70 not out)
Match drawn
Transvaal 'B' 8 pts, Easterns 7 pts

Another fine innings from Mitchley and a typical 102 off 112 balls by West Indian Phil Simmons could not bring Easterns victory over Transvaal, for whom Hussein Manack made a career-best unbeaten 137.

10, 11 and 12 January 1997
at St George's Park, Port Elizabeth
Easterns 231 (C.R. Norris 61, G.T. Love 4 for 51) and 282 for 9 (A.G. Pollock 56 not out, A.V. Birrell 8 for 134)
Eastern Province 'B' 350 for 3 dec. (C.C. Bradfield 163, M.G. Beamish 105)
Match drawn
Eastern Province 'B' 8 pts, Easterns 4 pts

In the vital top of the table match, Eastern Province had much the better of the draw and moved ahead of Easterns. Michael Beamish and Carl Bradfield scored 193 for the home side's first wicket with the left-handed Bradfield, four days short of his 22nd birthday, hitting a maiden first-class hundred. Left-arm spinner Adrian Birrell, who had been out of the game for two years, returned the best bowling figures of his career for innings and match. He had 11 for 210.

16, 17 and 18 January 1997
at Kingsmead, Durban
Transvaal 'B' 249 (G.L. Brophy 67, K.G. Storey 4 for 65)
Natal 'B' 253 for 8 (C.B. Sugden 71)
Match drawn
Natal 'B' 8 pts, Transvaal 'B' 7 pts

at Newlands, Cape Town
North West 116 (D.G. Payne 5 for 20) and 221 (M. Strydom 91)
Western Province 'B' 193 (M. van Schalkwyk 4 for 17) and 117 (D. Rossouw 4 for 30, F. Baird 4 for 33)
North West won by 27 runs
North West 15 pts, Western Province 'B' 6 pts

Rain ruined the match in Durban, while North West won inside two days at Newlands where only Morne Strydom, three sixes and nine fours in his 91, mastered the vagaries of the pitch.

5, 6 and 7 February 1997
at Newlands, Cape Town
Transvaal 'B' 385 for 7 dec. (H.A. Manack 173) and 256 (R.P. Snell 52)
Western Province 'B' 350 for 8 dec. (H. Pangarkar 144, G. de Kock 67, Z. de Bruyn 6 for 120)
Match drawn
Transvaal 'B' 7 pts, Western Province 'B' 6 pts

Batsmen thrived in the drawn match at Newlands with Manack improving on the career-best score made two months earlier.

13, 14 and 15 February 1997
at Fanie du Toit Stadium, Potchefstroom
Eastern Province 'B' 300 for 9 dec. (G.C. Victor 63, A.G. Prince 51) and 273 (G.C. Victor 79)
North West 373 for 8 dec. (M. Strydom 129, B.D. Esterhuysen 58) and 162 for 8 (S. Nicolson 57, A.V. Birrell 4 for 75)
Match drawn
North West 8 pts, Eastern Province 'B' 6 pts

at Willowmore Park, Benoni
Natal 'B' 227 (B.A. Nash 51, A.G. Pollock 4 for 52) and 244 for 1 dec. (M.L. Bruyns 103, P.J.R. Steyn 100 not out)
Easterns 149 (K.G. Storey 4 for 39) and 146 (A.G. Botha 4 for 52)
Natal 'B' won by 176 runs
Natal 'B' 17 pts, Easterns 5 pts

Although Eastern Province were denied victory by North West, they claimed the championship because Easterns crashed at home to Natal. Natal had been rooted to the bottom of the table, but they twice bowled out Easterns with left-arm spinner Tony Botha having match figures of 7 for 67, while Mark Bruyns and Phil Steyn began their second innings with a record partnership of 176.

UCB Bowl Final Table

	P	W	L	D	Pts
Eastern Province 'B'	5	2	1	2	54
Easterns	5	2	1	2	52
Natal 'B'	5	1	1	3	44
Western Province 'B'	5	1	2	2	42
North West	5	1	1	3	40
Transvaal 'B'	5	–	1	4	35

Australian Tour

13 February 1997
at Randjesfontein
Australians 284 for 7 (M.T.G. Elliott 91, S.R. Waugh 72 retired, M.L. Hayden 60)
N. Oppenheimer's XI 265 (N.D. McKenzie 133)
Australians won by 19 runs

It has become the tradition for touring sides to begin their programme with a match against Nicky Oppenheimer's Invitation XI at Randjesfontein. Twenty-one-year-old Neil McKenzie grasped his opportunity with an impressive century after four wickets had fallen for 73. The Australians presented a strong test for South Africa. They arrived with a seasoned party of 14, and one could only wonder at the talent left at home, for no place had been found for Ponting, Law and others who would have claimed a spot in most national sides.

Ian Healy catches Cullinan off McGrath for 27 to leave South Africa on 78 for 4 on the opening day of the first Test. McGrath broke the back of the South African batting. (Mike Hewitt/Allsport)

15, 16 and 17 February 1997

at Newlands, Cape Town
Australians 439 for 4 dec. (M.L. Hayden 112, M.A. Taylor 85, M.T.G. Elliott 74, S.R. Waugh 69) and 175 for 6 dec. (G.S. Blewett 86, J.H. Kallis 4 for 46)
Western Province 261 for 5 dec. (J.B. Commins 59 not out) and 321 (H.H. Gibbs 80, J.B. Commins 51, A.J. Bichel 5 for 62)
Australians won by 32 runs

Australian skipper Mark Taylor had experienced a very lean time in the series against West Indies and in the Sheffield Shield, so he was delighted to begin the tour of South Africa with his highest score of the year as he and Hayden scored 194 for the first wicket. All the Australian batsmen scored well in this match, one of two first-class games before the first Test. Commins kept the match alive by declaring 178 runs in arrears, and Kallis bowled his medium pace to such good effect that the visitors were reduced to 74 for 4 at the end of the second day. Taylor's declaration eventually set the home province a target of 354. The South Africans went about their task eagerly with Gibbs hitting 80 off 92 balls, but Bichel destroyed the middle order, and Bevan bowled his longest spell since being used as a front-line spinner. The Australians snatched an exciting victory.

19 February 1997

at Boland Park, Paarl
Australians 319 for 3 (M.E. Waugh 101 retired, M.G. Bevan 80 not out, J.L. Langer 57, M.A. Taylor 56)
Boland 269
Australians won by 50 runs
Mark Waugh hit six sixes and four fours as he made 101 off 93 balls in this day/night match.

21, 22 and 23 February 1997

at Kingsmead, Durban
Natal 335 (M.L. Bruyns 105, D.M. Benkenstein 103, J.N. Gillespie 4 for 71) and 112 (M.G. Bevan 4 for 35)
Australians 370 for 9 dec. (M.E. Waugh 124, M.G. Bevan 52, P.L. Symcox 4 for 117) and 81 for 2
Australians won by 8 wickets

With the first Test a week away, the Australians continued their winning run and Mark Waugh hit his second century in consecutive matches. He hit four sixes and 13 fours in his 152-ball innings. Bevan again impressed with his left-arm spin.

25 February 1997

at Soweto
Australians 261 for 7 (M.T.G. Elliott 69, J.L. Langer 63, A.J. Hall 4 for 49)
Transvaal XI 182
Australians won by 79 runs

First Test Match

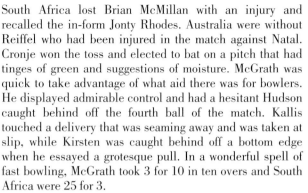

South Africa v. Australia

South Africa lost Brian McMillan with an injury and recalled the in-form Jonty Rhodes. Australia were without Reiffel who had been injured in the match against Natal. Cronje won the toss and elected to bat on a pitch that had tinges of green and suggestions of moisture. McGrath was quick to take advantage of what aid there was for bowlers. He displayed admirable control and had a hesitant Hudson caught behind off the fourth ball of the match. Kallis touched a delivery that was seaming away and was taken at slip, while Kirsten was caught behind off a bottom edge when he essayed a grotesque pull. In a wonderful spell of fast bowling, McGrath took 3 for 10 in ten overs and South Africa were 25 for 3.

Cullinan struggled against Warne and was dropped, one of four catches to go down, but he survived until after lunch. He was out when he played back to McGrath and held his bat out. Cronje offered the first respite, batting with unrelenting application as those around him fell. He took 33 minutes to get off the mark, but he played a determined and authoritative role.

Rhodes looked set until he played back to Gillespie, and Pollock hit eight fours and made 35 out of a stand of 50 before being caught at backward point. The crisis point came when Cronje was out just after tea, and South Africa were 195 for 8. The crisis was met by Dave Richardson, a luxury at number nine for any side. He, Donald and Adams cajoled 107 from the last two wickets. The last wicket stand between Richardson and Adams realised a frustrating 72, and when Adams was finally deceived by Warne to bring an end to the innings and the day South Africa had reached a highly satisfactory 302.

The South African bowlers did not take advantage of conditions at the start of the second day, but Australia contrived to lose wickets with some regularity. The shining exception to some rather careless batting was the left-handed Matthew Elliott, who added a brisk 95 with Hayden for the second wicket. Elliott batted with positive grace and ease and when he pulled Donald over mid-wicket for six he reached his best Test score. He hit 12 fours and was out when he again attempted to pull Donald over mid-wicket. He mistimed the shot and looped a catch to Adams. This was, in fact, Donald's second wicket in three balls, for he had Mark Waugh caught behind with the last ball of his previous over. That was the end of South Africa's joy until two days later and by then they were a beaten side. Greg Blewett and Steve Waugh came together 25 minutes before tea, and when play was called off for the day shortly after the interval Waugh was on 14, Blewett on 3, and the score was 191 for 4.

At the close of play on the third day, Australia were 479 for 4. Steve Waugh had reached 137 and Greg Blewett had outstripped his senior partner to move to 156. The pair were not separated until shortly before lunch on the fourth

First Test Match – South Africa v. Australia
28 February, 1, 2, 3 and 4 March 1997 at Wanderers, Johannesburg

South Africa

	First Innings		Second Innings	
A.C. Hudson	c Healy, b McGrath	0	run out	31
G. Kirsten	c Healy, b McGrath	9	b Warne	8
J.H. Kallis	c M. Waugh, b McGrath	6	b Warne	39
D.J. Cullinan	c Healy, b McGrath	27	c Healy, b Warne	0
W.J. Cronje (Capt)	c M. Waugh, b Warne	76	c Healy, b S. Waugh	22
J.N. Rhodes	c Healy, b Gillespie	22	lbw, b Warne	8
S.M. Pollock	c S. Waugh, b Bevan	35	not out	14
L. Klusener	c Taylor, b Bevan	9	c Hayden, b Bevan	0
*D.J. Richardson	not out	72	c Hayden, b Bevan	2
A.A. Donald	c Healy, b Gillespie	21	b Bevan	0
P.R. Adams	lbw, b Warne	15	b Bevan	0
	b 1, lb 13, w 3, nb 3	10	b 4, lb 2	6
		302		130

Australia

	First Innings	
M.A. Taylor (Capt)	b Pollock	16
M.L. Hayden	c Cullinan, b Pollock	40
M.T.G. Elliott	c Adams, b Donald	85
M.E. Waugh	c Richardson, b Donald	26
S.R. Waugh	c Richardson, b Kallis	160
G.S. Blewett	c Adams, b Klusener	214
M.G. Bevan	not out	37
*I.A. Healy	c Kirsten, b Adams	11
S.K. Warne	b Cronje	9
J.N. Gillespie		
G.D. McGrath		
	b 1, lb 15, w 4, nb 10	30
	(for 8 wickets, dec.)	628

	O	M	R	W	O	M	R	W
McGrath	26	8	77	4	10	5	17	–
Gillespie	17	6	66	2	11	4	24	–
Warne	27.4	9	68	2	28	15	43	4
Bevan	17	1	64	2	15	3	32	4
Blewett	4	–	23	–				
S.R. Waugh					4	1	4	1
M.E. Waugh					1	–	4	–

	O	M	R	W
Donald	33	7	136	2
Pollock	32	3	105	2
Klusener	37	10	122	1
Kallis	21	4	54	1
Adams	52	7	163	1
Cronje	16.4	5	32	1

Fall of Wickets
1–0, 2–15, 3–25, 4–78, 5–115, 6–165, 7–183, 8–195, 9–253
1–36, 2–41, 3–46, 4–90, 5–108, 6–127, 7–128, 8–130, 9–130

Fall of Wickets
1–33, 2–128, 3–169, 4–174, 5–559, 6–577, 7–613, 8–628

Umpires: C.J. Mitchley & S. Venkataraghavan

Australia won by an innings and 196 runs

morning when Steve Waugh was caught behind off Kallis. Waugh had batted for 502 minutes, faced 366 deliveries and hit 22 fours in his 12th Test century. His partnership with Blewett was worth 385, a record for any wicket against South Africa. One cannot over-praise the quality of the batting. It was mentally and technically secure and positive in every aspect.

In the afternoon session, Australia scored briskly. Blewett had reached the highest score made by an Australian in South Africa when, in search of quick runs, he sliced Klusener into the deep. It was the first chance he had offered after 520 minutes at the crease, during which time he faced 421 balls and hit 34 boundaries. It was a truly magnificent innings, and it underlined the immense quality and depth of the Australian batting.

Taylor declared at 628 for 8, the highest score in Tests between the two countries, and by the end of the day South Africa, 99 for 4, were in total despair. Ten balls after tea, Kirsten was bowled when he tried to cut a ball from Warne that turned in to him. Disaster struck 17 balls later when Kallis called Hudson for an unwise single, and Steve Wasugh hit the stumps from 30 yards. Warne had Cullinan caught behind off a bottom edge to give himself figures of 2 for 7 off eight overs. He was ultimately replaced by Steve Waugh, who had Cronje caught chasing a wide ball with his third delivery.

Spinners Warne and Bevan duly completed Australia's task before lunch on the last day. It was the first

The record breakers confer. Steve Waugh and Greg Blewett who shared a fifth wicket partnership of 385 for Australia in the Test at Wanderers. Blewett's 214 was the highest score made by an Australian in South Africa. (Mike Hewitt/Allsport)

time South Africa had suffered an innings defeat for 33 years. Steve Waugh and Greg Blewett shared the individual award of Man of the Match.

7, 8 and 9 March 1997

at Buffalo Park, East London
Border 117 (J.N. Gillespie 7 for 34) and 148 (P.C. Strydom 55)
Australians 370 for 9 dec. (G.S. Blewett 112, M.E. Waugh 62)
Australians won by an innings and 105 runs

Greg Blewett maintained his appetite for runs and Jason Gillespie returned career-best bowling figures as the tourists won inside two days. Reiffel showed no signs of his recent injury in taking four wickets.

11 March 1997

at St George's Park, Port Elizabeth
Australians 243 for 4 (M.L. Hayden 68, J.L. Langer 56)
Eastern Province XI 228 for 8 (L.J. Koen 78, M.G. Bevan 4 for 37)
Australians won by 15 runs

Australia entered the second Test with a hundred per cent record.

Second and Third Test Matches

South Africa v. Australia

Not surprisingly, Australia stuck to a winning team, but South Africa chose to drop Hudson and Rhodes and to bring in Bacher and Gibbs. McMillan returned after injury, and Klusener was relegated to twelfth man.

Jason Gillespie bowls Herschelle Gibbs in the midst of his first five-wicket haul in Test cricket, second Test, Port Elizabeth.
(Mike Hewitt/Allsport)

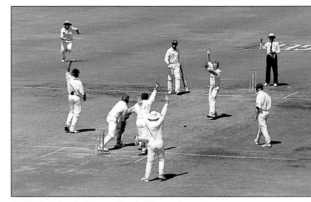

Pollock is leg before to Shane Warne for seventeen.
(Mike Hewitt/Allsport)

Mark Taylor won the toss and asked South Africa to bat first on a grassy pitch. His decision paid instant dividends. In his first five overs, Gillespie had both Kirsten and Kallis caught close in on the leg side from lifting deliveries, and when McGrath had Bacher taken at gully and saw Cronje play on South Africa were 22 for 4. Cullinan and Gibbs survived until lunch but, in the afternoon, Gillespie claimed three wickets in three overs. Cullinan was taken in the gully off a poor stroke. Gibbs was bowled, and Pollock was leg before first ball. McMillan and Richardson, the first batsmen of the day to offer sense and discipline, added 85 in 28 overs. Australia dropped catches, the slip pair of Mark Waugh and Mark Taylor proving unusually unreliable. Warne took the last three wickets, and Gillespie finished with a well deserved first five-wicket haul in Test cricket. Having dismissed South Africa for 209, Australia could be well satisfied, although the score should have been less.

Australia had to endure 13 very hostile overs before the close and lost Hayden, caught at slip, and scored ten. The second day produced some extraordinary cricket as South Africa climbed into what appeared to be a position of great strength. Taylor was soon gone, nibbling at a ball from Pollock who then retired with a hamstring problem and did not bowl again in the series. On a slow pitch, Elliott and Mark Waugh laid the foundations of a stand, but the advent of Cronje accounted for Mark Waugh, adjudged leg before as he played across the line. Steve Waugh defended doggedly, and Elliott was looking a good player until, trying to risk a single, he was sent back and run out. This waste was followed by the departure of Steve Waugh who pushed at an away-swinger. Unable to play their shots against tight bowling and a dead pitch, Australia were succumbing to frustration. Blewett was bowled by a fine delivery, Donald's one reward for a fine, sustained spell, and Healy lost patience. In nearly 71 overs, Australia were all out for 108. By the close, South Africa were 83 without loss.

It seemed that the home side was poised to level the series, but two hours and 20 minutes into the third day, South Africa had been bowled out for 168. They had lost all ten wickets for 85 runs in 44 overs. Once again, Gillespie

Mark Waugh acknowledges the applause of the crowd as he reaches one of the finest of Test centuries that brought Australia a famous victory at Port Elizabeth. (Mike Hewitt/Allsport)

A pull too far. Matthew Elliot hooks Donald into the hands of Schultz. Third Test. (Mike Hewitt/Allsport)

started the collapse with a spell of 3 for 13, and Bevan followed with three wickets in ten overs. Needing 270 to win, Australia lost both openers for 30 before Elliott, a positive and confident batsman, and Mark Waugh added 88 in 23 overs. Adams took a return catch to dismiss Elliott, and the Waugh twins took Australia to 145 for 3 at the close. The game was still in the balance, and the pitch was deteriorating rapidly.

The Waugh twins settled comfortably, and the score had advanced to 167 on the fourth morning when Steve Waugh drove at Kallis and was brilliantly caught by Cronje. Blewett was yorked by Adams, and Australia went to lunch at 204 for 5. Much rested on the shoulders of Mark Waugh, and he did not let his country down. He remains one of the five best batsmen in world cricket, and in the opinion of many, he has no superior. He faced 228 balls and hit a six, a five (off the fielding helmet) and 17 fours. He and Bevan added 66 off 21 overs to take Australia to the brink of victory. With the promised land in sight, Mark Waugh was bowled by Kallis between bat and pad. The crowd stood to one of the greatest of Test innings and one for which, in the particular context of the match, no praise could be too high.

Australia lost two more wickets in the next three overs, Bevan caught at slip and Warne leg before, and suddenly the match was in the balance again. Gillespie joined Healy, and only the noted 'rabbit' McGrath was to come. Gillespie blocked as men crowded him. In the next over, Cronje overpitched, and Healy, the ideal man for the moment, hit the ball over long leg for six and a famous victory.

For the final Test, Australia retained the 11 players who had already won the series. South Africa brought in Schultz for the injured Pollock, and Klusener and veteran off-spinner Symcox replaced Gibbs and Adams, who had been erratic in the dramatic second Test.

Brett Schultz celebrated his return to the South African side with four wickets that sent Australia tumbling to 227 all out after they had been put in. Three of his wickets came in a ten-over spell which helped send Australia crashing from 190 for 4. Steve Waugh was the first victim in this spell, given out caught down the leg side after hitting nine fours in an innings of 67. Bevan and Warne were out in the space of three balls. Donald had dismissed Elliott and Mark Waugh earlier in the day so that when he had Healy caught down the leg side he claimed his 150th Test wicket.

South Africa took a grip on the game on the second day. Kirsten provided Healy with his 300th victim in Test

A fine return to Test cricket for Brett Schultz. He captured six wickets and fielded well to his own bowling, as in this instance when he stops a drive from Matthew Hayden. (Mike Hewitt/Allsport)

Second Test Match – South Africa v. Australia
14, 15, 16 and 17 March 1997 at St George's Park, Port Elizabeth

South Africa

	First Innings		Second Innings	
G. Kirsten	c Hayden, b Gillespie	0	b Gillespie	43
A.M. Bacher	c Elliott, b McGrath	11	c McGrath, b Gillespie	49
J.H. Kallis	c Blewett, b Gillespie	0	run out	2
D.J. Cullinan	c Warne, b Gillespie	34	lbw, b Gillespie	2
W.J. Cronje (Capt)	b McGrath	0	c Healy, b Bevan	27
H.H. Gibbs	b Gillespie	31	c M. Waugh, b McGrath	7
B.M. McMillan	c S. Waugh, b Warne	55	lbw, b Bevan	2
S.M. Pollock	lbw, b Gillespie	0	lbw, b Warne	17
*D.J. Richardson	c McGrath, b Warne	47	not out	3
A.A. Donald	c and b Warne	9	c Warne, b Bevan	7
P.R. Adams	not out	5	c Taylor, b Warne	1
	b 8, lb 8, w 1	17	b 1, lb 5, nb 2	8
		209		**168**

	O	M	R	W	O	M	R	W
McGrath	22	7	66	2	13	3	43	1
Gillespie	23	10	54	5	18	4	49	3
Warne	23.4	5	62	3	17.4	7	20	2
Blewett	4	2	3	–	7.3	4	16	–
Bevan	2	–	8	–	13	3	18	3
S.R. Waugh					4.3	–	16	–

Australia

	First Innings		Second Innings	
M.L. Hayden	c Cullinan, b Pollock	0	(2) run out	14
M.A. Taylor (Capt)	c Richardson, b Pollock	8	(1) lbw, b McMillan	13
M.T.G. Elliott	run out	23	c and b Adams	44
M.E. Waugh	lbw, b Cronje	20	b Kallis	116
S.R. Waugh	c Richardson, b McMillan	8	c Cronje, b Kallis	18
G.S. Blewett	b Donald	13	b Adams	7
M.G. Bevan	c Richardson, b McMillan	0	c Cullinan, b Cronje	24
*I.A. Healy	c Bacher, b Cronje	5	not out	10
S.K. Warne	lbw, b Adams	18	lbw, b Kallis	3
J.N. Gillespie	not out	1	not out	0
G.D. McGrath	c Richardson, b Kallis	0		
	b 1, lb 7, w 2, nb 2	12	b 11, lb 8, w 3	22
		108	(for 8 wickets)	**271**

	O	M	R	W	O	M	R	W
Donald	23	13	18	1	26	6	75	–
Pollock	6	3	6	2				
Adams	4	–	5	1	21	4	66	2
McMillan	14	2	32	2	21	5	46	1
Cronje	14	7	21	2	9.3	1	36	1
Kallis	9.4	2	18	1	16	7	29	3

Fall of Wickets
1–13, 2–17, 3–21, 4–22, 5–70, 6–95, 7–95, 8–180, 9–204
1–87, 2–98, 3–99, 4–100, 5–122, 6–137, 7–152, 8–156, 9–166

Fall of Wickets
1–1, 2–13, 3–48, 4–64, 5–66, 6–70, 7–85, 8–86, 9–106
1–23, 2–30, 3–113, 4–167, 5–192, 6–258, 7–258, 8–265

Umpires: R.E. Koertzen & S. Venkataraghavan

Australia won by 2 wickets

Third Test Match – South Africa v. Australia
21, 22, 23 and 24 March 1997 at Centurion Park, Centurion

Australia

	First Innings		Second Innings	
M.A. Taylor (Capt)	c Richardson, b Klusener	38	c Richardson, b Donald	5
M.L. Hayden	b Schultz	10	lbw, b Schultz	0
M.T.G. Elliott	c Schultz, b Donald	18	b Donald	12
M.E. Waugh	b Donald	5	b Symcox	42
S.R. Waugh	c Richardson, b Schultz	67	not out	60
G.S. Blewett	c Richardson, b Symcox	37	b Donald	0
M.G. Bevan	lbw, b Schultz	6	b Symcox	5
*I.A. Healy	c Richardson, b Donald	19	c Richardson, b Schultz	12
S.K. Warne	lbw, b Schultz	0	lbw, b Donald	12
J.N. Gillespie	not out	0	b Donald	0
G.D. McGrath	b Klusener	0	b Klusener	11
	b 1, lb 4, w 7, nb 9	21	b 2, lb 6, w 4, nb 14	26
		227		**185**

	O	M	R	W	O	M	R	W
Donald	20	5	60	3	18	5	36	5
Schultz	20	4	52	4	17	4	39	2
Cronje	5	3	5	–				
Klusener	14.5	4	23	2	14.4	1	40	1
Symcox	23	4	62	1	19	5	49	2
Kallis	7	2	20	–	5	1	13	–

South Africa

	First Innings		Second Innings	
G. Kirsten	c Healy, b McGrath	16	c Taylor, b Blewett	6
A.M. Bacher	lbw, b McGrath	96	c Elliott, b Gillespie	5
B.M. McMillan	c Hayden, b M. Waugh	55	not out	7
D.J. Cullinan	b McGrath	47	not out	7
P.L. Symcox	c Blewett, b Gillespie	16		
J.H. Kallis	c S. Waugh, b McGrath	2		
W.J. Cronje (Capt)	not out	79		
*D.J. Richardson	b McGrath	0		
L. Klusener	b Gillespie	30		
A.A. Donald	c Healy, b Gillespie	8		
B.N. Schultz	c Healy, b McGrath	2		
	b 11, lb 16, w 1, nb 5	33	w 1, nb 1	2
		384	(for 2 wickets)	**32**

	O	M	R	W	O	M	R	W
McGrath	40.4	15	86	6				
Gillespie	31	13	75	3	3.4	–	19	1
Blewett	5	–	19	–	3	–	13	1
Warne	36	11	89	–				
Bevan	15	3	54	–				
M.E. Waugh	7	1	34	1				

Fall of Wickets
1–23, 2–60, 3–72, 4–110, 5–190, 6–197, 7–212, 8–212, 9–226
1–5, 2–10, 3–28, 4–94, 5–99, 6–108, 7–131, 8–164, 9–164

Fall of Wickets
1–26, 2–128, 3–229, 4–252, 5–255, 6–262, 7–262, 8–330, 9–367
1–11, 2–15

Umpires: C.J. Mitchley & M.J. Kitchen

South Africa won by 8 wickets

Test Match Averages – South Africa v. Australia

South Africa Batting

	M	Inns	NOs	Runs	HS	Av	100s	50s
W.J. Cronje	3	5	1	204	79*	51.00		2
D.J. Richardson	3	5	2	124	72*	41.00		1
A.M. Bacher	2	4	–	161	96	40.25		1
B.M. McMillan	2	4	1	119	55	39.66		2
D.J. Cullinan	3	6	1	122	47	24.40		
S.M. Pollock	2	4	1	66	35	22.00		
G. Kirsten	3	6	–	82	43	13.66		
L. Klusener	2	3	–	39	30	13.00		
J.H. Kallis	3	5	–	49	39	9.80		
A.A. Donald	3	5	–	45	21	9.00		
P.R. Adams	2	4	1	21	15	7.00		

Played in one Test: H.H. Gibbs 31 & 7; P.L. Symcox 16; B.N. Schultz 2; A.C. Hudson 0 & 31; J.N.Rodhes 22 & 8

Australia Batting

	M	Inns	NOs	Runs	HS	Av	100s	50s
S.R. Waugh	3	5	1	313	160	78.25	1	2
G.S. Blewett	3	5	–	271	214	54.20	1	
M.E. Waugh	3	5	–	209	116	41.80	1	
M.T.G. Elliott	3	5	–	182	85	36.40		1
M.G. Bevan	3	5	1	72	37*	18.00		
M.A. Taylor	3	5	–	80	38	16.00		
I.A. Healy	3	5	1	57	19	14.25		
M.L. Hayden	3	5	–	64	40	12.80		
S.K. Warne	3	5	–	42	18	8.40		
J.N. Gillespie	3	4	3	7	6*	7.00		
G.D. McGrath	3	3	–	11	11	3.66		

South Africa Bowling

	Overs	Mds	Runs	Wks	Av	Best	10/m	5/inn
B.N. Schultz	37	8	91	6	15.16	4/52		
W.J. Cronje	45.1	16	94	4	23.50	2/21		
B.M. McMillan	35	7	78	3	26.00	2/32		
J.H. Kallis	58.4	16	134	5	26.80	3/29		
S.M. Pollock	38	6	111	4	27.75	2/6		
A.A. Donald	122	36	325	11	29.54	5/36		1
P.L. Symcox	42	9	111	3	37.00	2/49		
L. Klusener	66.3	15	185	4	46.25	2/23		
P.R. Adams	77	11	234	4	58.50	2/66		

India Bowling

	Overs	Mds	Runs	Wks	Av	Best	10/m	5/inn
M.G. Bevan	62	10	176	9	19.55	4/32		
S.R. Waugh	8.3	1	30	1	20.00	1/4		
J.N. Gillespie	103.4	37	287	14	20.50	5/54		1
G.D. McGrath	111.4	38	289	13	22.23	6/86		1
S.K.Warne	133	47	282	11	25.63	4/43		
M.E. Waugh	8	1	38	1	38.00	1/34		
G.S. Blewett	23.3	6	74	1	74.00	1/13		

South Africa Fielding Figures

12 – D.J. Richardson; 3 – P.R Adams and D.J. Cullinan; 1 – W.J. Cronje, A.M. Bacher, G. Kirsten and B.N. Shultz

Fielding Figures

11 – I.A. Healy; 4 – M.L. Hayden; 3 – S.R. Waugh, M.A. Taylor, M.E. Waugh and S.K. Warne; 2 – G.S. Blewett, M.T.G. Elliott and G.D. McGrath

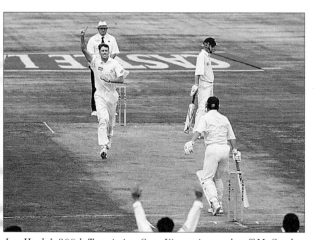

Ian Healy's 300th Test victim. Gary Kirsten is caught off McGrath for 16. (Mike Hewitt/Allsport)

cricket before Bacher and McMillan added 102. Cullinan and Bacher then added 101 before Cullinan edged the second new ball into his stumps. Bacher remained unperturbed, ending the day six short of a maiden Test century, with his side on 240 for 3.

At the start of the third day, night-watchman Symcox became over-ambitious and fell to Gillespie. Kallis could only fend off a rising ball from McGrath and the same

bowler ended Bacher's seven-and-a-half hour innings and denied the young man his century. Richardson was out second ball to McGrath, who bowled beautifully for his sixth five-wicket haul in Test cricket, and South Africa were 262 for 7, the initiative lost.

What handicapped Australia was the lack of a third quality pace bowler on a pitch which nullified spin. Cronje is a cricketer of resolution, and he and Klusener added 68 in 16 overs. It was this positive approach in a critical situation that turned the game decisively in South Africa's favour. The home side took a first innings lead of 157, and when Taylor, Hayden and Elliott fell in the first 13 overs of Australia's second innings, South Africa sensed victory. The Waugh twins put on 66 and while they remained Australia lived, but Mark Waugh was bowled off an inside edge when he tried to drive Symcox, and Australia were 96 for 4 at the close.

Donald bowled Blewett three runs into the fourth morning, and although Steve Waugh stood firm, Donald struck with two wickets in three balls immediately after lunch, and a South African victory was an inevitability. Healy was given out caught behind by umpire Mitchley when he clearly got nowhere near the ball, and the batsman reacted angrily. Referee Subba Row suspended Healy for the first two one-day internationals. That punishment was right and inevitable, but it could not disguise the fact that a fine series had been marred by dreadful umpiring.

Limited-Over International Series

South Africa v. Australia

Australia sent home Elliott, Langer, Hayden and McGrath before the beginning of the one-day series and recruited diVenuto, Law, Dale, Julian and Gilchrist. McGrath returned to Australia to rest before the 'Ashes' tour, and Gilchrist arrived to keep wicket in the first two matches in place of the suspended Healy. Dale and diVenuto were to make their international debuts during the series as was Louis Koen who had had a fine season for Eastern Province.

The first game was turned in favour of South Africa by some brilliant fielding. Law and Steve Waugh were scoring freely after Australia had made an uncertain start, but Waugh was thrillingly run out by Gibbs and Law was splendidly caught by Kallis. Cronje ran out Blewett, and Rhodes ran out Gilchrist as five wickets went down for 15 runs. Dale and Bevan equalled the record for Australia's last wicket in a one-day international when they added 45 off 64 balls, but the total of 223 was well short of what had been expected. South Africa stuttered to 50 for 3 before Cullinan joined Kallis in a stand of 122, and victory eventually came with three overs to spare.

Australia's one-day form had been poor, but they gained a crushing victory in the second encounter when Mark Waugh hit an unbeaten 115 off 125 balls with three

Day/night cricket. Newlands under floodlights.
(Mike Hewitt/Allsport)

sixes and eight fours. He and his twin Steve scored the last 107 runs to take their side to victory with five overs to spare. Put in, South Africa had struggled against some fine seam bowling. Adam Dale took 3 for 5 in 24 deliveries, and although Kallis and Rhodes effected a recovery, Gillespie

---

First One-Day International – South Africa v. Australia
29 March 1997 at Buffalo Park, East London

Australia				South Africa		
M.A. Taylor (Capt)	c Rhodes, b Pollock	7		A.M. Bacher	c Warne, b Reiffel	27
M.J. DiVenuto	c Cullinan, b Pollock	23		H.H. Gibbs	c Gilchrist, b Dale	10
S.G. Law	c Kallis, b Symcox	50		J.H. Kallis	st Gilchrist, b Warne	63
S.R. Waugh	run out	50		L. Klusener	b Warne	0
G.S. Blewett	run out	14		D.J. Cullinan	not out	85
M.G. Bevan	not out	51		J.N. Rhodes	not out	24
*A.C. Gilchrist	run out	1		S.M. Pollock		
S.K. Warne	c Cullinan, b Donald	4		W.J. Cronje (Capt)		
P.R. Reiffel	b Klusener	1		*D.J. Richardson		
J.N. Gillespie	c Cullinan, b Klusener	0		P.L. Symcox		
A.C. Dale	not out	15		A.A. Donald		
	lb 1, w 6	7			b 4, lb 7, w 5, nb 2	18
	50 overs (for 9 wickets)	223			47 overs (for 4 wickets)	227

	O	M	R	W		O	M	R	W
Pollock	10	1	36	1	Reiffel	10	1	44	1
Kallis	8	–	42	1	Dale	10	–	55	1
Donald	10	–	37	1	Warne	10	–	36	2
Klusener	6	1	29	2	Gillespie	7	–	36	–
Symcox	10	–	53	1	Bevan	10	–	45	–
Cronje	6	–	25	–					

Fall of Wickets
1–**26**, 2–**32**, 3–**129**, 4–**134**, 5–**163**, 6–**169**, 7–**176**, 8–**178**, 9–**178**

Fall of Wickets
1–**31**, 2–**48**, 3–**50**, 4–**172**

Umpires: C.J. Mitchley & D.L. Orchard *Man of the Match:* D.J. Cullinan

South Africa won by 6 wickets

Second One-Day International – South Africa v. Australia
31 March 1997 at St George's Park, Port Elizabeth

South Africa

A.M. Bacher	c Bevan, b Dale	3
L.J. Koen	c M.E. Waugh, b Dale	0
J.H. Kallis	b Gillespie	82
D.J. Cullinan	b Dale	0
J.N. Rhodes	c Reiffel, b Bevan	57
W.J. Cronje (Capt)	b Gillespie	31
S.M. Pollock	c Dale, b Warne	9
L. Klusener	not out	27
*D.J. Richardson	run out	1
P.L. Symcox	not out	0
A.A. Donald		
	b 1, lb 4, w 3, nb 3	11
	50 overs (for 8 wickets)	221

	O	M	R	W
Reiffel	9	–	33	–
Dale	7	3	18	3
Blewett	10	1	42	–
Gillespie	10	–	51	2
Warne	6	–	39	1
Bevan	8	–	33	1

Fall of Wickets
1–2, 2–4, 3–16, 4–120, 5–181, 6–183, 7–212, 8–215

Australia

M.E. Waugh	not out	115
M.A. Taylor (Capt)	c Cullinan, b Donald	17
S.G. Law	c Rhodes, b Symcox	33
S.K. Warne	b Symcox	0
S.R. Waugh	not out	50
G.S. Blewett		
M.G. Bevan		
*A.C. Gilchrist		
P.R. Reiffel		
A.C. Dale		
J.N. Gillespie		
	lb 2, w 2, nb 3	7
	45 overs (for 3 wickets)	222

	O	M	R	W
Pollock	8	–	39	–
Kallis	5	–	21	–
Donald	9	1	22	1
Cronje	5	–	25	–
Symcox	10	–	65	2
Klusener	8	1	48	–

Fall of Wickets
1–47, 2–115, 3–115

Umpires: R.E. Koertzen & C.J. Mitchley   Man of the Match: M.E. Waugh

Australia won by 7 wickets

Third One-Day International – South Africa v. Australia
2 April 1997 at Newlands, Cape Town

South Africa

L.J. Koen	c DiVenuto, b Dale	22
H.H. Gibbs	b Gillespie	28
J.H. Kallis	b Warne	23
D.J. Cullinan	run out	12
J.N. Rhodes	not out	83
W.J. Cronje (Capt)	b Blewett	3
D.N. Crookes	c Healy, b Gillespie	18
S.M. Pollock	lbw, b Warne	21
*D.J. Richardson	run out	4
R.E. Bryson	not out	17
A.A. Donald		
	lb 11, w 2, nb 1	14
	50 overs (for 8 wickets)	245

	O	M	R	W
Reiffel	10	–	47	–
Dale	10	1	26	1
Gillespie	10	1	39	2
Warne	10	–	64	2
Blewett	6	–	30	1
Bevan	4	–	28	–

Fall of Wickets
1–52, 2–53, 3–80, 4–101, 5–106, 6–176, 7–216, 8–222

Australia

G.S. Blewett	b Pollock	6
M.J. DiVenuto	run out	13
S.G. Law	c Richardson, b Bryson	4
S.R. Waugh	b Bryson	0
M.G. Bevan	c Kallis, b Pollock	82
*I.A. Healy (Capt)	c and b Crookes	25
S.K. Warne	run out	23
P.R. Reiffel	run out	6
A.C. Dale	not out	12
J.N. Gillespie	c Gibbs, b Donald	17
M.E. Waugh	absent ill	–
	lb 4, w 6, nb 1	11
	44.5 overs	199

	O	M	R	W
Pollock	8	–	35	2
Bryson	9	–	34	2
Donald	7.5	1	25	1
Cronje	4	–	29	–
Crookes	10	–	42	1
Kallis	6	–	30	–

Fall of Wickets
1–14, 2–25, 3–25, 4–25, 5–94, 6–136, 7–157, 8–170, 9–199

Umpires: R.E. Koertzen & D.L. Orchard   Man of the Match: J.N. Rhodes

South Africa won by 46 runs

Fourth One-Day International – South Africa v. Australia
5 April 1997 at Kingsmead, Durban

Australia

M.J. DiVenuto	run out	14
G.S. Blewett	c Crookes, b Bryson	53
S.G. Law	c Kallis, b Pollock	0
S.R. Waugh	c Crookes, b Donald	1
M.G. Bevan	run out	0
A.C. Gilchrist	c Cronje, b Pollock	77
*I.A. Healy (Capt)	c Richardson, b Pollock	19
S.K. Warne	b Bryson	12
A.J. Bichel	lbw, b Pollock	17
A.C. Dale	not out	10
J.N. Gillespie	not out	5
	lb 2, nb 1	3
	50 overs (for 9 wickets)	211

	O	M	R	W
Pollock	10	2	33	4
Bryson	10	–	47	2
Donald	10	–	37	1
Kallis	7	–	34	–
Crookes	10	–	40	–
Cronje	3	–	18	–

Fall of Wickets
1–30, 2–40, 3–48, 4–50, 5–83, 6–129, 7–153, 8–195, 9–198

South Africa

A.M. Bacher	lbw, b Warne	45
H.H. Gibbs	c S.R. Waugh, b Dale	0
D.J. Cullinan	c and b Warne	38
J.H. Kallis	run out	1
J.N. Rhodes	b Gillespie	1
W.J. Cronje (Capt)	b Bichel	28
D.N. Crookes	b Bichel	17
S.M. Pollock	not out	41
*D.J. Richardson	lbw, b Bichel	0
R.E. Bryson	c Warne, b Blewett	9
A.A. Donald	run out	6
	lb 6, w 4	10
	48.1 overs	196

	O	M	R	W
Dale	10	2	22	1
Bichel	10	1	43	3
Gillespie	9	3	30	1
Law	3	–	16	–
Warne	8.1	1	36	2
S.R. Waugh	5	–	25	–
Blewett	3	–	18	1

Fall of Wickets
1–1, 2–81, 3–88, 4–89, 5–89, 6–126, 7–143, 8–143, 9–165

Umpires: W.A. Diedricks & D.L. Orchard   *Man of the Match*: S.M. Pollock

Australia won by 15 runs

Fifth One-Day International – South Africa v. Australia
8 April 1997 at Wanderers, Johannesburg

Australia

G.S. Blewett	c Richardson, b Cronje	36
M.J. DiVenuto	lbw, b Donald	89
S.G. Law	c Crookes, b Cronje	10
J.N. Gillespie	c Gibbs, b Donald	26
S.R. Waugh	b Bryson	20
M.G. Bevan	c Cullinan, b Donald	32
A.C. Gilchrist	b Pollock	26
*I.A. Healy (Capt)	not out	3
S.K. Warne	not out	6
A.J. Bichel		
A.C. Dale		
	b 1, lb 6, w 1, nb 2	10
	50 overs (for 7 wickets)	258

	O	M	R	W
Pollock	10	1	48	1
Bryson	9	–	47	1
Donald	10	–	67	3
Kallis	1	–	10	–
Crookes	10	–	37	–
Cronje	10	1	42	2

Fall of Wickets
1–93, 2–109, 3–160, 4–167, 5–202, 6–244, 7–248

South Africa

A.M. Bacher	c S.R. Waugh, b Bichel	6
H.H. Gibbs	lbw, b Dale	22
D.N. Crookes	run out	0
D.J. Cullinan	b Blewett	53
J.H. Kallis	c S.R. Waugh, b Gillespie	55
J.N. Rhodes	c Law, b Gillespie	10
W.J. Cronje (Capt)	not out	40
S.M. Pollock	c Law, b Warne	40
*D.J. Richardson	b Bichel	8
R.E. Bryson	not out	4
A.A. Donald		
	lb 6, w 4, nb 2	12
	50 overs (for 8 wickets)	250

	O	M	R	W
Dale	10	1	40	1
Bichel	10	–	55	2
Warne	10	–	45	1
Gillespie	10	–	46	2
Bevan	3	–	22	–
Blewett	7	–	36	1

Fall of Wickets
1–27, 2–31, 3–31, 4–132, 5–149, 6–154, 7–227, 8–240

Umpires: D.F. Becker & S.B. Lambson   *Man of the Match*: M.J. DiVenuto

Australia won by 8 runs

Sixth One-Day International – South Africa v. Australia
10 April 1997 at Centurion Park, Centurion

South Africa

A.M. Bacher	b Dale	15
H.H. Gibbs	c Healy, b Gillespie	33
W.J. Cronje (Capt)	run out	80
D.J. Cullinan	c M.E. Waugh, b Warne	89
J.H. Kallis	st Healy, b Warne	3
J.N. Rhodes	run out	10
S.M. Pollock	c Dale, b Bichel	33
D.N. Crookes	not out	4
*D.J. Richardson	not out	0
R.E. Bryson		
A.A. Donald		
	lb 12, w 4, nb 1	17
	50 overs (for 7 wickets)	284

	O	M	R	W
Dale	10	–	44	1
Bichel	9	–	50	1
Warne	10	1	52	2
Gillespie	9	–	45	1
Blewett	5	–	41	–
Bevan	7	–	40	–

Fall of Wickets
1–52, 2–77, 3–226, 4–232, 5–232, 6–261, 7–283

Australia

M.E. Waugh	c Rhodes, b Pollock	0
G.S. Blewett	c Crookes, b Pollock	21
S.G. Law	b Cronje	31
S.R. Waugh	lbw, b Pollock	89
M.G. Bevan	lbw, b Bryson	103
A.C. Gilchrist	not out	20
*I.A. Healy (Capt)	not out	9
S.K. Warne		
A.C. Dale		
A.J. Bichel		
J.N. Gillespie		
	lb 5, w 7, nb 2	14
	49 overs (for 5 wickets)	287

	O	M	R	W
Pollock	10	–	40	3
Bryson	10	–	63	1
Donald	10	1	59	–
Cronje	7	–	46	1
Crookes	6	–	37	–
Kallis	6	–	37	–

Fall of Wickets
1–0, 2–36, 3–58, 4–247, 5–262

Umpires: D.F. Becker & S.B. Lambson   *Man of the Match*: M.G. Bevan   **Australia won by 5 wickets**

Seventh One-Day International – South Africa v. Australia
13 April 1997 at Springbok Park, Bloemfontein

South Africa

L. Klusener	c Blewett, b Julian	92
H.H. Gibbs	c Gilchrist, b Julian	29
P.L. Symcox	run out	26
W.J. Cronje (Capt)	c Dale, b Law	69
D.J. Cullinan	not out	57
J.H. Kallis	b Bichel	10
J.N. Rhodes	c Blewett, b Bichel	0
S.M. Pollock	not out	8
D.N. Crookes		
*D.J. Richardson		
A.A. Donald		
	lb 4, w 10, nb 5	19
	50 overs (for 6 wickets)	310

	O	M	R	W
Dale	8	1	70	–
Reiffel	10	–	46	–
Julian	8	–	53	2
Bevan	5	–	35	–
Bichel	10	–	50	2
M.E. Waugh	3.3	–	16	–
Law	5.3	–	36	1

Fall of Wickets
1–61, 2–109, 3–218, 4–246, 5–290, 6–290

Australia

M.J. DiVenuto	b Klusener	11
M.E. Waugh	c Richardson, b Klusener	3
B.P. Julian	b Pollock	0
S.G. Law	c Klusener, b Cronje	17
S.R. Waugh (Capt)	b Donald	91
M.G. Bevan	c Klusener, b Symcox	29
G.S. Blewett	c Crookes, b Kallis	18
*A.C. Gilchrist	b Symcox	3
P.R. Reiffel	c Richardson, b Donald	10
A.J. Bichel	b Klusener	0
A.C. Dale	not out	1
	lb 7, w 8, nb 3	18
	37 overs	201

	O	M	R	W
Pollock	8	1	26	1
Klusener	7	1	41	3
Cronje	2	–	9	1
Donald	7	–	37	2
Symcox	9	–	60	2
Kallis	4	–	21	1

Fall of Wickets
1–17, 2–18, 3–18, 4–52, 5–100, 6–139, 7–153, 8–186, 9–201

Umpires: W.A. Diedriks & R.E. Koertzen   *Man of the Match*: L. Klusener   **South Africa won by 109 runs**

blunted the charge in the 45th over when he dismissed Kallis and Cronje in the space of three deliveries.

South Africa took the lead in the series with a comfortable win in the third match. Put in to bat, South Africa slipped to 106 for 5, but Rhodes hit 83 off 77 balls to take them to a challenging total. With Mark Waugh unable to bat because of a hand injured while attempting to take a slip catch, Australia were never in touch. In the eighth over of their innings, they lost three wickets and, in spite of Bevan's brave knock, they never truly recovered.

Australia levelled the series by winning the tense fourth encounter. They came back into the game through Adam Gilchrist who was played as a batsman. When Healy had returned for the third game after suspension Mark Taylor had decided to stand down for the rest of the series, and Gilchrist was one of those to benefit from the captain's decision. His 77 came off 88 balls. South Africa laboured as they attacked a small target, and it was not until the arrival of Pollock that they were in contention. He and Donald put on 31 for the last wicket, and 16 were needed from the last two overs. Pollock tried to steal a single, and both batsmen ended up at the same wicket.

The fifth match saw Australia win by a small margin. They scored consistently and powerfully with Michael

Michael Bevan hit a maiden one-day international century to lead Australia to victory at Centurion Park. (Mike Hewitt/Allsport)

Allan Donald bowls Steve Waugh and leaps in joy as South Africa win the last match in the one-day series. (Mike Hewitt/Allsport)

First-Class Averages

Batting

	M	Inns	NOs	Runs	HS	Av	100s	50s
J.B. Commins	7	10	4	598	200*	99.66	2	3
J.L. Howell	8	9	5	300	102*	75.00	1	
L.J. Wilkinson	5	7	1	396	139*	66.00	1	2
J.N.Rhodes	7	11	2	589	156*	65.44	3	
K.C.Wessels	9	14	2	736	179	61.33	2	6
B.M. McMillan	7	13	5	490	103*	61.25	1	5
C.R. Matthews	6	5	2	183	96	61.00		2
A.M. Bacher	10	19	2	1012	210	59.52	4	3
D.M. Benkenstein	10	15	1	806	129	57.57	4	3
H. Pangarkar	4	6	–	345	144	57.50	1	1
L.J. Koen	9	16	1	859	186	57.26	2	5
H.H. Gibbs	6	11	1	553	163*	55.30	2	1
H.D. Ackerman	9	14	3	573	122	52.09	2	2
M. Strydom	5	10	1	464	129	51.55	1	2
M.J. Miethley	5	10	1	462	201*	51.33	2	1
D.N. Crookes	7	10	1	453	128*	50.33	2	2
D.L. Haynes	8	13	1	600	202*	50.00	1	4
P.G. Amm	5	8	1	340	105	48.57	1	2
R.P. Snell	3	5	1	192	52	48.00		1
H.H. Dippenaar	9	16	1	716	151*	47.73	1	5
M.W. Rushmere	9	15	4	521	89*	47.36		4
M.V. Boucher	9	17	5	566	71	47.16		5
J.H. Kallis	10	16	2	656	143	46.85	2	2
A.C. Dawson	5	7	2	230	64	46.00		2
U.H. Goedeke	5	8	2	275	102*	45.83	1	1
D. Jordaan	9	16	–	703	117	43.93	1	6
D.J. Watson	10	16	3	571	200*	43.92	1	3
P.H. Barnard	8	15	–	652	212	43.46	1	4
M.G. Beamish	8	15	–	633	164	42.20	3	1
B.A. Nash	3	4	–	168	64	42.00		2
S.C. Pope	8	13	3	417	103	41.70	1	1
P.N. Kirsten	9	17	1	666	173*	41.62	2	3
G.F.J. Liebenberg	9	16	1	618	133*	41.20	1	3
O.Gain	6	11	1	408	88	40.80		3
M.I. Gidley	8	16	2	559	117	39.92	1	4
G.C. Victor	6	12	1	439	95	39.90		5
P.J. Botha	9	17	1	636	136	39.75	1	3
A.P. Kuiper	7	14	1	514	117*	39.53	1	3
D.J.Cullinan	8	15	2	512	122*	39.38	1	3
E. Davids	6	7	1	233	65	38.83		2
S.G. Koenig	8	13	–	496	119	38.15	1	2
C.B. Sugden	7	10	3	265	85*	37.85		2
H.A. Manack	7	13	2	414	173	37.63	2	
C.F. Craven	5	7	–	263	109	37.57	1	2
L. Klusener	6	11	3	300	102*	37.50	1	
P.J.R. Steyn	4	7	1	222	100*	37.00	1	
A.G. Prince	6	10	1	333	125*	37.00	1	2
A.C. Hudson	6	12	1	398	80	36.18		3
K.C. Jackson	8	16	1	542	120	36.13	1	3
E.L.R Stewart	10	17	1	576	138	36.00	1	2
J.M. Arthur	8	16	1	539	86	35.93		3
J.F. Venter	9	14	1	464	101	35.69	1	4
P.L. Symcox	6	9	4	175	45*	35.00		
E.O. Simons	7	9	1	278	80	34.75		3
M. van Wyk	2	3	–	104	49	34.66		
W.J. Cronje	9	17	2	520	79*	34.66		3
D.R. Laing	7	13	1	410	128	34.16	1	2
N.D. McKenzie	9	17	2	511	139	34.06	1	3
P.C. Strydom	9	16	3	442	100	34.00	1	3
C.C. Bradfield	7	13	2	371	163	33.72	1	1
S.M. Pollock	9	17	3	471	79	33.64		2
T.A. Marsh	5	10	2	269	61	33.62		2
G.S. Katz	3	5	–	168	58	33.50		2
R.F. Pienaar	6	11	–	367	95	33.36		3
C.R. Norris	5	10	–	331	75	33.10		4
D.G. Payne	5	7	3	131	41*	32.75		
M.L. Bruyns	9	15	–	490	105	32.66	2	1
P.J.L. Radley	9	13	5	261	58*	32.62		1
D.J. Callaghan	9	16	2	445	102	31.78	1	2
A.G. Pollock	5	9	3	187	56*	31.16		1
J. Buxton-Foreman	4	7	–	213	70	30.42		2
G. Morgan	8	11	2	273	65*	30.33		2
T.G. Shaw	9	9	3	178	40	29.66		
A.J. Hall	8	13	2	322	78	29.27		2
C.N. du Plessis	4	6	1	145	45	29.00		
R. Maron	6	10	1	257	65*	28.55		1
R.A. Koster	5	10	–	284	74	28.40		1
R.E. Veenstra	8	12	3	252	135*	28.00	1	
D.J. Richardson	7	11	2	252	72*	28.00		1

Batting

	M	Inns	NOs	Runs	HS	Av	100s	50s
B.T. Player	7	10	2	221	133*	27.62	1	
P.V. Simmons	4	8	–	220	102	27.50	1	
A.J. Seymore	8	15	–	409	132	27.26	1	1
M.R. Benfield	9	17	–	459	122	27.00	1	1
G. de Kock	5	7	–	187	67	26.71		2
N. Pothas	9	15	2	344	100*	26.46	1	1
L.D. Ferreira	8	16	–	409	127	25.56	1	1
W.M. Dry	6	11	–	280	74	25.45		2
N.C. Johnson	10	15	1	356	69	25.42		3
S. Jacobs	7	9	2	178	85	25.42		1
M.J. Levine	5	9	–	227	107	25.22	1	
N. Parsons	2	4	–	100	84	25.00		1
D.J. van Zyl	5	10	–	249	57	24.90		1
K.R. Rutherford	8	14	1	322	126*	24.76	1	1
J.S. Lerm	3	6	–	142	38	23.66		
B.N. Benkenstein	7	13	3	232	68	23.20		2
M. van Jaarsveld	7	13	–	301	109	23.15	1	
K.A. Forde	10	12	2	231	38	23.10		
R.B. Richardson	6	11	–	254	69	23.09		3
L.P. Vorster	5	9	–	206	69	22.88		1
E.A.E. Baptiste	8	11	2	201	50	22.33		1
B.C. Baguley	3	6	–	134	77	22.33		1
G.A. Pollock	5	9	–	199	115	22.11	1	
G. Myburgh	5	10	–	221	45	22.10		
C.V. English	8	15	–	326	51	21.73		1
S. Nicolson	5	10	–	215	70	21.50		2
Z. de Bruyn	6	11	1	215	70*	21.50		1
D.J. Millns	5	10	1	193	44	21.44		
B.D. Esterhuysen	3	5	–	106	58	21.20		1
V.C. Drakes	6	8	2	127	41	21.16		
A.R. Wylie	5	10	–	210	74	21.00		2
S. Elworthy	8	15	–	324	51	20.93		1
B.J. Sommerville	3	6	–	125	62	20.83		1
A.V. Birrel	6	8	2	125	34	20.83		
A.V. Eksteen	9	12	3	187	32	20.77		
F.J.C. Cronje	4	7	–	145	67	20.71		1
A.Wessels	3	6	1	103	56*	20.60		1
F.C. Brooker	4	7	–	143	45	20.42		
A.G. Botha	7	9	3	122	41*	20.33		
S. Hofmeyr	4	6	–	119	51	19.83		1
W.S. Truter	7	14	–	276	95	19.71		1
D. Rossouw	4	7	1	118	49	19.66		
M.J.R. Rindel	6	12	–	230	60	19.16		1
P. Kirsten	8	10	2	153	50	19.12		1
G. Kirsten	8	16	–	305	103	19.06	1	
H.C. Bakkes	7	11	–	202	43	18.36		
B.M. White	9	17	–	312	63	18.35		2
W. Bossenger	8	15	2	236	82	18.15		1
R. Telemachus	3	6	–	107	29	17.83		
M. Badat	3	6	–	107	45	17.83		
F.B. Touzel	5	8	1	124	52*	17.71		1
C.W. Henderson	7	14	3	191	29	17.36		
N. Boje	6	11	–	189	34	17.18		
R.E. Bryson	7	12	4	137	22	17.12		
D.B. Rundle	7	9	1	134	81*	16.75		1
G.L. Brophy	5	7	–	116	68	16.57		1
E.G. Poole	5	9	2	112	43	16.00		
J.M. Henderson	4	7	–	112	30	16.00		
M.T. Solomons	6	8	–	125	32	15.62		
M.J.G. Davis	7	13	3	149	38*	14.90		
M.C. Venter	5	10	1	126	46	14.00		
I. Pistorius	8	15	3	151	33	12.58		
G.M. Hewitt	5	10	–	107	52	10.70		1

(Qualification 100 runs, average 10.00)

Bowling

	Overs	Mds	Runs	Wks	Av	Best	10/m	5/inn
J.R. Meyer	74.2	21	197	11	17.90	6/43		1
D.G. Payne	182.5	49	434	24	18.08	5/20		2
S.M. Pollock	269	62	660	36	18.33	5/48		1
R. Telemachus	99.3	27	222	12	18.50	6/21		1
G. de Kock	97.3	20	288	15	19.20	3/8		
F.D. Stephenson	91	28	213	11	19.36	4/21		
K.G. Storey	280.4	60	741	38	19.50	7/58		2
D. Rossouw	105	26	332	17	19.52	5/61		1

First-Class Averages (continued)

Bowling

	Overs	Mds	Runs	Wks	Av	Best	10/m	5/inn
E.A.E. Baptiste	327.3	87	753	38	19.81	5/37	1	3
C.R. Norris	127	22	363	18	20.16	4/14		
H.S. Williams	220.3	61	511	25	20.44	6/57		2
R.E. Veenstra	239.3	60	680	33	20.60	5/36		1
A.A. Donald	241.2	68	644	31	20.77	5/36		2
P.J. Botha	283.3	70	698	33	21.15	5/35		2
A.J. Hall	166.5	55	455	21	21.66	4/29		
A.G Botha	172.1	37	464	21	22.03	4/52		
C.E. Eksteen	393.2	107	904	40	22.60	5/83		1
G.M. Gilder	314.5	72	868	38	22.84	5/57		2
T. Bosch	218.1	67	470	20	23.50	5/15		1
M.J. Levine	150	32	434	18	24.11	4/58		
D.J. Callaghan	132	37	291	12	24.25	2/11		
J.H. Kallis	143.2	34	414	17	24.35	4/46		
A. Martyn	122.3	32	317	13	24.38	4/76		
B.T. Player	204.3	46	588	24	24.50	4/41		
A. Badenhorst	171.1	52	472	19	24.84	4/39		
S.S. Cilliers	217.2	48	672	27	24.84	4/39		
D.N. Crookes	229	58	625	25	25.00	7/114		2
V.C. Darkes	201.3	34	552	22	25.09	8/59	1	1
N.W. Pretorius	124.1	27	405	16	25.31	4/26		
A.V. Birrell	252.4	43	812	32	25.37	8/134	1	2
C. Vorster	116.1	24	362	14	25.85	3/44		
A.C. Dawson	189.3	52	494	19	26.00	5/30		1
B.N. Schultz	352	62	1113	42	26.50	5/49		3
M. Strydom	137	28	401	15	26.73	6/55		1
S. Jacobs	220.2	63	527	19	27.73	5/63		1
A.G. Pollock	117.3	22	333	12	27.75	4/52		
R.E. Bryson	222.2	46	642	23	27.91	5/84		1
P. Joubert	103.3	29	286	10	28.60	3/52		
J.F. Venter	256.3	71	718	25	28.72	6/96	1	1
N.C. Johnson	205.3	50	575	20	28.75	3/52		
H.C. Bakkes	165	44	492	17	28.94	6/43		1
D. Taljard	111.5	18	320	11	29.09	3/33		
P.L. Symcox	246.2	48	678	22	30.81	4/26		
C.W. Henderson	322.2	85	779	25	31.16	5/107		1
L.D. Botha	176.5	30	545	17	32.05	6/59		1

Bowling

	Overs	Mds	Runs	Wks	Av	Best	10/m	5/inn
L.D. Botha	176.5	30	545	17	32.05	6/59		1
G.T. Love	251.3	86	521	16	32.56	4/38		
E.W. Kidwell	320.4	66	1044	32	32.62	4/54		
Q. Ferreira	198	42	593	18	32.94	3/64		
L. Klusener	194.2	45	536	16	33.50	4/61		
S. Elworthy	258.2	67	804	24	33.50	4/71		
M. Ntini	222.1	26	847	25	33.88	6/49		1
P.R. Adams	205.2	45	618	18	34.33	4/68		
D.Q. MacHelm	170.1	42	490	14	35.00	3/76		
Z. de Bruyn	96	13	386	11	35.09	6/120		1
M.W. Pringle	345.1	68	1057	30	35.23	4/26		
M.J.G. Davis	222.3	40	622	17	36.58	6/80		1
C.V. English	183.5	31	668	18	37.11	5/65		1
C.R. Matthews	167.1	35	564	15	27.60	4/44		
D.J. Millns	118	23	399	10	39.90	4/64		
T.G. Shaw	358	115	807	19	42.47	4/67		
G.A. Roe	299.3	56	901	21	42.90	4/74		
M.I. Gidley	156.4	29	526	11	47.81	3/59		
N. Boje	188	48	532	11	48.36	3/60		
D.B. Rundle	231	42	720	14	51.42	3/42		
I.L. Howell	247.5	63	571	11	51.90	3/46		
V.A. Walsh	301	47	1002	19	52.73	3/58		
M. Hayward	202	33	680	12	56.66	2/62		
B.N. Benkenstein	228.1	45	711	10	71.10	3/35		

(Qualification – 10 wickets)

Leading Fielders

41 – K.A. Forde (ct 39 / st 2); 36 – M.V. Boucher (ct 33 / st 3) and N. Pothas (ct 30 / st 6); 34 – P. Kirsten (ct 33 / st 1); 30 – P.J.L. Radley (ct 28 / st 2); 26 – D.J. Richardson (ct 25 / st 1); 24 – I. Pretorius; 21 – W. Bessenger (ct 19 / st 2); 20 – G. Morgan (ct 18 / st 2); 18 – M.T. Solomons (ct 17 / st 1); 16 – B.N. White, G.L. Brophy, L.J. Koen and L. Masikazana (ct 14 / st 2); 15 – N.C. Johnson and E.G. Poole (ct 12 / st 3); 14 – F.C. Brooker (ct 13/ st 1), E.L.R. Stewart and G. Rothman (ct 13 / st 1); 13 – K.R. Rutherford; 12 – U.H. Goedeke; 11 – D. Jordaan and D.B. Rundle; 10 – N. Boje, M.L. Bruyns, D.J. Cullinan, S. Nicolson and C.B. Sugden

diVenuto taking his first award in international cricket. South Africa lost two early wickets and could never approach the required run rate.

By winning their third match in succession, Australia established a winning margin in the series. South Africa set a daunting target in spite of another impressive bowling performance by Adam Dale who enjoyed an excellent series. Cronje and Cullinan shared a third wicket stand of 149, and when Australia were reduced to 58 for 3 it seemed South Africa were on course for victory. Steve Waugh was then joined by Michael Bevan, and the pair added 189, an Australian fourth wicket record in limited-over cricket. Bevan reached his first century in a one-day international, and Australia's 287 was the highest winning score by a side batting second in a limited-over international in South Africa.

With the series won, Australia rested some of their top players for the final game, and Steve Waugh led the side for the first time. He was last man out for 91, but South Africa won convincingly.

The series threw up some interesting questions. Both Hudson and Kirsten were dropped, suggesting that South Africa's consistently successful opening pair may be nearing the end of their international careers. The home side reverted to a left/right opening partnership in the last match when Klusener was promoted to go in with Gibbs but, eminently profitable as this was on the day, it hardly looks a long-term solution.

Leading wicket-taker for Australia was Shane Warne who remains a most potent force in world cricket. In the fifth match, he bowled the final over to Cronje, well set, with 14 needed. Only six were scored.

Sharjah

Cricket in Sharjah has long been a lucrative source of income for some of the world's leading players both old and new. Talat Ali, Sadiq Mohammad and Ijaz Ahmed were the beneficiaries from the Singer Trophy, and there was prize money in excess of 50,000 dollars for those who took part in the competition. Sadly, in organisation and interest, this tournament fell short of the standards which have been associated with Sharjah in the past.

Saeed Anwar, scorer of two centuries in the Champions' Trophy, receives congratulations from a young admirer. (David Munden/Sportsline)

The Singer Champions' Trophy
Sharjah Cup

The publicity and enthusiasm which have attended previous contests in the United Arab Emirates were missing, and the management reduced prices and opened the grandstand in an attempt to attract the public, but fewer than a thousand people watched the opening match between New Zealand and Sri Lanka, and it was apparent that the absence of India had a debilitating effect upon the competition. There were also indications that the management and control which have made Sharjah an exemplary venue over the years were not as they had been, and crowd invasions wasted time and affected players' concentration in several matches.

The tournament, which was spread over a period of nine days, began with New Zealand gaining a surprise victory over Sri Lanka. They were much indebted to Chris Cairns who hit 71 off 91 balls and took two wickets, but much credit was also due to Chris Harris who was outstanding in a brilliant fielding side and captured two vital wickets.

Sri Lanka regained their composure the following day with an emphatic win over Pakistan whose batting was depressingly ragged in comparison to the consistency of Sri Lanka. Wasim Akram bowled splendidly, but it was the left-arm spin of Jayasuriya which finally tilted the game in

The outstanding fielder in Sharjah, 1996 and 1997, Roshan Mahama of Sri Lanka. (David Munden/Sportsline)

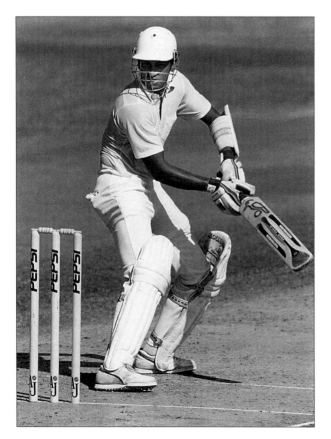

Muttiah Muralitharan walks away dejectedly as New Zealand celebrate his dismissal and the achievement of a remarkable tie. (David Munden/Sportsline)

favour of Sri Lanka. Pakistan's last four wickets fell for the addition of only five runs.

In the third match of the tournament, New Zealand did well to reach 197 after losing their first three wickets for five runs. Adam Parore was their saviour, but even his efforts proved to be insufficient. Pakistan were in some trouble at 86 for five, but Saeed Anwar took them to victory with his tenth century in one-day internationals. Pakistan's win meant that all three sides were level after the first round of matches.

The second meeting between New Zealand and Sri Lanka provided the most exciting match of the series. With only Astle and Greatbatch showing any form, New Zealand were restricted to 169 in their 50 overs, and, at 98 for 4, Sri Lanka looked set for victory. Two wickets fell at that total, but Ranatunga and Chandana added 42 to keep Sri Lanka on course. It was Danny Morrison who brought about a dramatic change with three wickets in two overs. He had Ranatunga caught behind, bowled Sajeeva de Silva with the scores level and then had Muralitharan caught at slip to tie the match.

Sri Lanka's chances of reaching the final were hit the following day when they were crushed by Pakistan. Needing 190 to win, Pakistan were given a roistering start as Saeed Anwar and Aamir Sohail put on 173 in 39.1 overs for the first wicket. Saeed Anwar hit 112 off 125 balls while Aamir Sohail's 65 came off 126 balls. Saeed's century was his 11th in one-day internationals.

The qualifying part of the competition ended in chaos. Another brave innings by Adam Parore saved New Zealand from total humiliation after Waqar Younis had wrecked the top order. Parore and Germon put on 115 for the seventh wicket, and Pakistan were asked to score 193 to win. This they did with nine balls to spare although their batting again had passages of uncertainty.

The referee, M.J.K. Smith, declared that Sri Lanka would now meet Pakistan in the final of the Singer Trophy by virtue of their superior run rate over New Zealand, but the New Zealand management then sought clarification of the rules. Talks with the ICC and the United Cricket Board

Match One – New Zealand v. Sri Lanka
7 November 1996 at Sharjah C.A. Stadium

New Zealand

C.M. Spearman	c Chandana, b S.C. de Silva	39
N.J. Astle	c and b S.C. de Silva	0
A.C. Parore	lbw, b Vaas	0
S.P. Fleming	c Tillekeratne, b Vaas	1
C.L. Cairns	c Kaluwitharana, b Chandana	71
M.J. Greatbatch	c and b Muralitharan	23
C.Z. Harris	not out	34
L.K. Germon (Capt)	c S.C. de Silva, b Vaas	20
D.N. Patel	b Vaas	0
S.B. Doull	not out	1
D.K. Morrison		
	b 1, lb 6, w 6, nb 4	17
	50 overs (for 8 wickets)	206

	O	M	R	W
Vaas	9	1	22	4
S.C. de Silva	8	1	37	2
Dharmasena	7	–	31	–
Muralitharan	10	–	37	1
Jayasuriya	7	–	39	–
Chandana	9	–	33	1

Fall of Wickets
1–7, 2–7, 3–25, 4–48, 5–92, 6–165, 7–205, 8–205

Sri Lanka

S.T. Jayasuriya	c Astle, b Doull	15
*R.S. Kaluwitharana	lbw, b Doull	16
A.P. Gurusinha	c Doull, b Patel	27
P.A. de Silva	c Harris, b Morrison	47
A. Ranatunga (Capt)	b Harris	3
H.P. Tillekeratne	c Doull, b Morrison	41
U.U. Chandana	c Cairns, b Harris	4
H.D.P.K. Dharmasena	b Astle	7
W.P.U.J.C. Vaas	c Harris, b Cairns	1
M. Muralitharan	b Cairns	3
S.C. de Silva	not out	0
	lb 7, w 6	13
	49.1 overs	177

	O	M	R	W
Morrison	9	–	28	2
Doull	7	1	29	2
Cairns	9.1	–	39	2
Astle	6	1	20	1
Patel	10	2	26	1
Harris	8	–	28	2

Fall of Wickets
1–23, 2–40, 3–83, 4–88, 5–131, 6–142, 7–158, 8–162, 9–175

Umpires: I.D. Robinson & G. Sharp *Man of the Match:* C.L. Cairns   **New Zealand won by 29 runs**

Match Two – Pakistan v. Sri Lanka
8 November 1996 at Sharjah C.A. Stadium

Sri Lanka

S.T. Jayasuriya	c Ijaz Ahmed, b Wasim Akram	33
R.S. Kaluwitharana	c Waqar Younis, b Wasim Akram	12
A.P. Gurusinha	lbw, b Shahid Afridi	32
P.A. de Silva	c Salim Malik, b Waqar Younis	4
A. Ranatunga (Capt)	c Saqlain Mushtaq, b Salim Malik	23
R.S. Mahanama	c Aamir Sohail, b Saqlain Mushtaq	37
W.P.U.J.C. Vaas	c Shahid Afridi, b Salim Malik	14
H.P. Tillekeratne	c Ijaz Ahmed, b Saqlain Mushtaq	20
H.D.P.K. Dharmasena	lbw, b Wasim Akram	1
M. Muralitharan	b Wasim Akram	4
S.C. de Silva	not out	1
	lb 6, w 16, nb 3	25
	49.3 overs	206

	O	M	R	W
Wasim Akram	10	–	42	4
Shahid Nazir	7	–	38	–
Waqar Younis	8	–	21	1
Saqlain Mushtaq	9.3	–	32	2
Shahid Afridi	9	–	37	1
Salim Malik	6	–	30	2

Fall of Wickets
1–25, 2–64, 3–79, 4–119, 5–133, 6–158, 7–191, 8–194, 9–204

Pakistan

Saeed Anwar	c Kaluwitharana, b S.C. de Silva	7
Shahid Afridi	c Mahanama, b S.C. de Silva	7
Aamir Sohail	c Kaluwitharana, b Muralitharan	14
Ijaz Ahmed	run out	49
Azam Khan	c Jayasuriya, b Muralitharan	15
Salim Malik	c Kaluwitharana, b S.C. de Silva	6
Wasim Akram (Capt)	b Jayasuriya	12
*Moin Khan	c and b Jayasuriya	10
Saqlain Mushtaq	c and b P.A. de Silva	1
Waqar Younis	b Jayasuriya	2
Shahid Nazir	not out	1
	w 6, nb 1	7
	36 overs	131

	O	M	R	W
Vaas	6	1	12	–
S.C. de Silva	10	–	48	3
Muralitharan	7	1	33	2
Ranatunga	3	–	15	–
Jayasuriya	5	1	15	3
P.A. de Silva	5	2	8	1

Fall of Wickets
1–11, 2–29, 3–38, 4–48, 5–93, 6–109, 7–126, 8–127, 9–129

Umpires: G. Sharp & S.K. Bansai *Man of the Match:* S.T. Jayasuriya   **Sri Lanka won by 75 runs**

Match Three – Pakistan v. New Zealand
10 November 1996 at Sharjah C.A. Stadium

New Zealand

C.M. Spearman	c Moin Khan, b Wasim Akram	0
N.J. Astle	b Waqar Younis	0
A.C. Parore	run out	93
S.P. Fleming	lbw, b Waqar Younis	1
C.L. Cairns	c Saqlain Mushtaq, b Mushtaq	26
M.J. Greatbatch	c Waqar Younis, b Mushtaq	10
C.Z. Harris	run out	23
*L.K. Germon (Capt)	b Saqlain Mushtaq	7
D.N. Patel	b Saqlain Mushtaq	7
S.B. Doull	st Moin Khan, b Saqlain Mushtaq	14
D.K. Morrison	not out	1
	lb 3, w 9, nb 3	15
	50 overs	**197**

	O	M	R	W
Wasim Akram	10	1	57	1
Waqar Younis	10	–	38	2
Saqlain Mushtaq	10	1	31	3
Mushtaq Ahmed	10	–	30	2
Shahid Nazir	10	–	38	–

Fall of Wickets
1–**0**, 2–**0**, 3–**5**, 4–**56**, 5–**73**, 6–**135**, 7–**162**, 8–**176**, 9–**189**

Pakistan

Saeed Anwar	not out	104
Aamir Sohail	c Germon, b Morrison	6
Shahid Anwar	b Cairns	20
Ijaz Ahmed	c Germon, b Cairns	4
Salim Malik	c Fleming, b Astle	7
Azam Khan	run out	4
*Moin Khan	st Germon, b Astle	15
Wasim Akram (Capt)	not out	28
Waqar Younis		
Saqlain Mushtaq		
Mushtaq Ahmed		
	lb 3, w 7	10
	46.3 overs (for 6 wickets)	**198**

	O	M	R	W
Morrison	7	–	44	1
Doull	8	1	30	–
Cairns	8.3	–	33	2
Astle	9	1	25	2
Patel	10	–	41	–
Harris	4	–	22	–

Fall of Wickets
1–**15**, 2–**45**, 3–**53**, 4–**67**, 5–**86**, 6–**135**

Umpires: I.D. Robinson & S.K. Bansai *Man of the Match:* Saeed Anwar

Pakistan won by 4 wickets

Match Four – New Zealand v. Sri Lanka
11 November 1996 at Sharjah C.A. Stadium

New Zealand

C.M. Spearman	c Mahanama, b S.C. de Silva	2
N.J. Astle	c Mahanama, b Muralitharan	66
A.C. Parore	c Kaluwitharana, b S.C. de Silva	0
S.P. Fleming	b S.C. de Silva	13
C.L. Cairns	run out	11
M.J. Greatbatch	c Vaas, b P.A. de Silva	35
C.Z. Harris	st Kaluwitharana, b P.A. de Silva	13
*L.K. Germon (Capt)	not out	11
D.N. Patel	run out	3
S.B. Doull	not out	0
D.K. Morrison		
	B 3, lb 4, w 8	15
	50 overs (for 8 wickets)	**169**

	O	M	R	W
Vaas	10	1	25	–
S.C. de Silva	8	2	18	3
Muralitharan	10	2	22	1
Ranatunga	2	–	20	–
Chandana	4	–	17	–
Jayasuriya	9	–	32	–
P.A. de Silva	7	–	28	2

Fall of Wickets
1–**8**, 2–**8**, 3–**29**, 4–**61**, 5–**136**, 6–**144**, 7–**160**, 8–**167**

Sri Lanka

S.T. Jayasuriya	run out	53
*R.S. Kaluwitharana	c Germon, b Morrison	0
M.S. Atapattu	c and b Morrison	16
P.A. de Silva	b Doull	1
H.P. Tillekeratne	c Germon, b Cairns	22
A. Ranatunga (Capt)	c Germon, b Morrison	34
R.S. Mahanama	lbw, b Cairns	0
U.U. Chandana	c Germon, b Astle	14
W.P.U.J.C. Vaas	not out	17
S.C. de Silva	b Morrison	0
M. Muralitharan	c Fleming, b Morrison	0
	B 1, lb 5, w 4, nb 2	12
	48 overs	**169**

	O	M	R	W
Morrison	10	–	34	5
Doull	9	2	37	1
Cairns	10	1	44	2
Harris	10	1	24	–
Patel	6	–	16	–
Astle	3	–	8	1

Fall of Wickets
1–**1**, 2–**31**, 3–**39**, 4–**82**, 5–**98**, 6–**98**, 7–**140**, 8–**159**, 9–**169**

Umpires: I.D. Robinson & G. Sharp *Man of the Match:* D.K. Morrison

Match tied

Match Five – Pakistan v. Sri Lanka
12 November 1996 at Sharjah C.A. Stadium

Sri Lanka

S.T. Jayasuriya	c Moin Khan, b Waqar Younis	1
R.S. Kaluwitharana	run out	12
M.P. Atapattu	run out	58
P.A. de Silva	lbw, b Wasim Akram	0
H.P. Tillekeratne	c Moin, b Mushtaq Ahmed	34
A. Ranatunga (Capt)	c Wasim Akram, b Waqar	27
W.P.U.J.C. Vaas	c Shahid Afridi, b Salim Malik	0
R.S. Mahanama	not out	31
U.U. Chandana	c Moin Khan, b Saqlain	0
S.C. de Silva	c Aamir Sohail, b Waqar	3
M. Muralitharan	c Wasim Akram, b Saqlain	1
	lb 10, w 11, nb 1	221

50 overs		189

	O	M	R	W
Wasim Akram	7	1	31	1
Waqar Younis	10	–	28	3
Saqlain Mushtaq	10	1	36	2
Mushtaq Ahmed	10	–	39	1
Shahid Afridi	9	–	34	–
Salim Malik	4	–	11	1

Fall of Wickets
1–3, 2–29, 3–30, 4–105, 5–132, 6–132, 7–166, 8–166, 9–182

Pakistan

Saeed Anwar	not out	112
Aamir Sohail	c S.C. de Silva, b Jayasuriya	65
Hasan Raza	c Chandana, b Muralitharan	5
*Moin Khan	not out	4
Ijaz Ahmed		
Salim Malik		
Shahid Afridi		
Wasim Akram (Capt)		
Saqlain Mushtaq		
Waqar Younis		
Mushtaq Ahmed		
	w 4, nb 3	7

46.4 overs (for 2 wickets)		193

	O	M	R	W
Vaas	8	1	23	–
S.C. de Silva	10	–	36	–
Muralitharan	8.4	–	57	1
P.A. de Silva	6	–	18	–
Jayasuriya	9	1	35	1
Chandana	5	–	24	–

Fall of Wickets
1–173, 2–188

Umpires: S.K. Bansai & G. Sharp *Man of the Match:* Saeed Anwar

Pakistan won by 8 wickets

Match Six – New Zealand v. Pakistan
13 November 1996 at Sharjah C.A. Stadium

New Zealand

B.A. Young	lbw, b Shahid Nazir	2
C.M. Spearman	c Moin Khan, b Shahid Nazir	2
A.C. Parore	c Shahid Afridi, b Waqar	78
N.J. Astle	c Moin Khan, b Waqar Younis	6
C.L. Cairns	b Waqar Cairns	18
M.J. Greatbatch	lbw, b Waqar Younis	0
C.Z. Harris	lbw, b Waqar Younis	1
L.K. Germon (Capt)	run out	52
D.N. Patel	b Waqar Younis	2
S.B. Doull	not out	3
D.K. Morrison	c Salim Malik, b Saqlain	0
	lb 5, w 20, nb 3	28

50 overs		192

	O	M	R	W
Waqar Younis	10	1	44	6
Shahid Nazir	7	1	35	2
Mushtaq Ahmed	10	–	30	–
Saqlain Mushtaq	10	1	30	1
Shahid Afridi	7	1	26	–
Salim Malik	6	–	22	–

Fall of Wickets
1–2, 2–7, 3–28, 4–57, 5–57, 6–60, 7–175, 8–187, 9–191

Pakistan

Saeed Anwar (Capt)	c Greatbatch, b Harris	54
Aamir Sohail	c Parore, b Cairns	25
Ijaz Ahmed	c Germon, b Astle	16
Salim Malik	c Germon, b Morrison	41
Hasan Raza	lbw, b Cairns	1
*Moin Khan	not out	37
Shahid Afridi	b Cairns	3
Saqlain Mushtaq	not out	5
Waqar Younis		
Mushtaq Ahmed		
Shahid Nazir		
	lb 3, w 9, nb 2	14

48.3 overs (for 6 wickets)		196

	O	M	R	W
Morrison	8	–	46	1
Doull	0.2	–	7	–
Astle	9.4	–	29	1
Patel	10	2	60	–
Harris	10	1	27	1
Cairns	10	2	18	3
Spearman	0.3	–	6	–

Fall of Wickets
1–66, 2–101, 3–109, 4–113, 5–181, 6–187

Umpires: I.D. Robinson & S.K. Bansai *Man of the Match:* Waqar Younis

Pakistan won by 4 wickets

of South Africa resulted in New Zealand being declared finalists as they had beaten and tied with Sri Lanka in the qualifying league.

Qualifying League Table

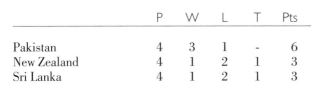

	P	W	L	T	Pts
Pakistan	4	3	1	-	6
New Zealand	4	1	2	1	3
Sri Lanka	4	1	2	1	3

Final

A disappointing batting display by Pakistan was redeemed by the bowlers. New Zealand were cruelly hit by injuries and took the field in the final without their opening attack of Doull and Morrison. In spite of this, they bowled out Pakistan for 160 in 48.5 overs. They even looked as if they might win when Greatbatch and Parore were together, but once these two were separated the side fell apart and the last eight wickets went down for 38 runs.

Waqar Younis was declared Man of the Series, and there were awards for Saeed Anwar for the fastest 50 and for Mahanama as the best fielder.

Sharjah Cup

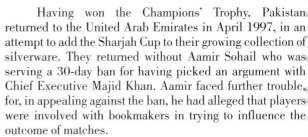

Having won the Champions' Trophy, Pakistan returned to the United Arab Emirates in April 1997, in an attempt to add the Sharjah Cup to their growing collection of silverware. They returned without Aamir Sohail who was serving a 30-day ban for having picked an argument with Chief Executive Majid Khan. Aamir faced further trouble, for, in appealing against the ban, he had alleged that players were involved with bookmakers in trying to influence the outcome of matches.

This was forgotten as Sri Lanka enjoyed a total triumph against Zimbabwe in the opening game of the tournament. Put in to bat, Zimbabwe were restricted to 187 for 9, mainly because of some fine bowling by Vaas. Sri Lanka were undaunted by the early loss of Kaluwitharana as Jayasuriya hit 56 off 74 balls in a stand of 79 with Atapattu who enjoyed his best form in international cricket in this tournament. He offered the solidity as Aravinda de Silva attacked the bowling to bring Sri Lanka victory with 26 balls to spare. In the process de Silva became the first Sri Lankan to pass 6000 runs in limited-over international cricket.

The following day, Sri Lanka virtually made sure of a place in the final when they gained a dramatic victory over Pakistan. They lost both openers with only four scored, but

Singer Champions' Trophy Final – Pakistan v. New Zealand
15 November 1996 at Sharjah C.A. Stadium

Pakistan

Saeed Anwar	c Fleming, b Vaughan	1
Aamir Sohail	st Germon, b Patel	16
Shahid Afridi	c Greatbatch, b Larsen	21
Ijaz Ahmed	c Fleming, b Astle	10
Salim Malik	lbw, b Cairns	40
Azam Khan	c Greatbatch, b Harris	22
*Moin Khan	lbw, b Cairns	32
Wasim Akram (Capt)	c Vaughan, b Patel	0
Saqlain Mushtaq	lbw, b Harris	0
Waqar Younis	run out	0
Mushtaq Ahmed	not out	4
	lb 12, w 2	14
	48.5 overs	160

	O	M	R	W
Vaughan	8	–	33	1
Larsen	9	1	22	1
Cairns	9.5	–	24	2
Astle	3	–	7	1
Harris	9	2	32	2
Patel	10	2	30	2

Fall of Wickets
1-4, 2-32, 3-51, 4-63, 5-116, 6-120, 7-120, 8-138, 9-145

New Zealand

B.A. Young	b Wasim Akram	5
M.J. Greatbatch	c Ijaz Ahmed, b Mushtaq Ahmed	52
A.C. Parore	lbw, b Saqlain Mushtaq	22
N.J. Astle	c Mushtaq Ahmed, b Saqlain	8
S.P. Fleming	lbw, b Waqar Younis	4
C.L. Cairns	lbw, b Wasim Akram	8
C.Z. Harris	c Shahid Afridi, b Mushtaq Ahmed	2
*L.K. Germon (Capt)	lbw, b Wasim Akram	5
D.N. Patel	lbw, b Shahid Afridi	1
J.T.C. Vaughan	not out	1
G.R. Larsen	b Shahid Afridi	0
	w 5, nb 6	11
	36.5 overs	119

	O	M	R	W
Wasim Akram	8	1	20	3
Waqar Younis	8	–	22	1
Saqlain Mushtaq	8	–	32	2
Shahid Afridi	2.5	–	14	2
Mushtaq Ahmed	10	–	31	2

Fall of Wickets
1-7, 2-66, 3-81, 4-98, 5-102, 6-111, 7-114, 8-117, 9-119

Umpires: G. Sharp & S.K. Bansai *Man of the Match:* Wasim Akram

Pakistan won by 41 run

Match One – Sri Lanka v. Zimbabwe
3 April 1997 at Sharjah C.A. Stadium

imbabwe

W. Flower	b Zoysa	12
B. Wishart	run out	32
D.R. Campbell (Capt)	lbw, b Vaas	2
P. Viljoen	st Kaluwitharana, b Dharmasena	17
A. Flower	b Muralitharan	38
V. Carlisle	c Tillekeratne, b Muralitharan	6
A. Strang	b Vaas	38
H. Streak	run out	11
A. Brandes	not out	10
R. Whittall	c Kaluwitharana, b Vaas	4
Matambanadzo	not out	0
	b 3, lb 7, w 4, nb 3	17
	50 overs (for 9 wickets)	**187**

	O	M	R	**W**
aas	10	2	25	3
oysa	10	–	46	1
uralitharan	10	1	39	2
A. de Silva	10	–	34	–
harmasena	10	–	33	1

all of Wickets
31, 2–34, 3–65, 4–77, 5–100, 6–139, 7–169, 8–180, 9–186

Sri Lanka

S.T. Jayasuriya	c Wishart, b P.A. Strang	56
*R.S. Kaluwitharana	c Wishart, b Brandes	0
M.S. Atapattu	not out	52
P.A. de Silva	c P.A. Strang, b G.W. Flower	60
A. Ranatunga (Capt)	not out	0
R.S. Mahanama		
H.P. Tillekeratne		
H.D.P.K. Dharmasena		
W.P.U.J.C. Vaas		
N. Zoysa		
M. Muralitharan		
	b 6, lb 3, w 11	20
	45.4 overs (for 3 wickets)	**188**

	O	M	R	**W**
Brandes	7	–	33	1
Matambanadzo	7	–	38	–
A.R. Whittall	10	–	30	–
Streak	7	1	22	–
P.A. Strang	10	–	41	1
G.W. Flower	4.4	–	15	1

Fall of Wickets
1–1, 2–80, 3–187

Umpires: R.S. Dunne & D.B. Cowie *Man of the Match:* P.A. de Silva

Sri Lanka won by 7 wickets

Match Two – Sri Lanka v. Pakistan
4 April 1997 at Sharjah C.A. Stadium

ri Lanka

T. Jayasuriya	lbw, b Waqar Younis	3
R.S. Kaluwitharana	lbw, b Wasim Akram	0
S. Atapattu	c Mushtaq Ahmed, b Salim	94
A. de Silva	st Moin Khan, b Saqlain	97
Ranatunga (Capt)	c Rameez Raja, b Saqlain	20
S. Mahanama	c Waqar Younis, b Wasim	3
P.U.J.C. Vaas	b Saqlain Mushtaq	0
P. Tillekeratne	run out	1
D.P.K. Dharmasena	not out	3
Muralitharan	not out	4
C. de Silva		
	lb 6, w 12	18
	50 overs (for 8 wickets)	**243**

	O	M	R	**W**
asim Akram	10	1	52	2
aqar Younis	7	1	34	1
aqlain Mushtaq	10	–	47	3
ushtaq Ahmed	10	–	44	–
hahid Afridi	9	1	39	–
alim Malik	4	–	21	1

all of Wickets
3, 2–4, 3–188, 4–222, 5–232, 6–232, 7–233, 8–238

Pakistan

Rameez Raja	b S.C. de Silva	6
Shahid Afridi	c S.C. de Silva, b Jayasuriya	67
Ijaz Ahmed	c S.C. de Silva, b Dharmasena	18
Salim Malik	lbw, b Muralitharan	51
Inzamam-ul-Haq	c Kaluwitharana, b Jayasuriya	9
Mohammad Wasim	c Tillekeratne, b Muralitharan	17
*Moin Khan	not out	30
Wasim Akram (Capt)	st Kaluwitharana, b Muralitharan	0
Mushtaq Ahmed	run out	1
Saqlain Mushtaq	run out	1
Waqar Younis	not out	9
	lb 7, w 4, nb 5	16
	50 overs (for 9 wickets)	**224**

	O	M	R	**W**
Vaas	8	–	45	–
S.C. de Silva	7	–	24	1
Muralitharan	10	–	38	3
Dharmasena	7	–	39	1
Jayasuriya	10	–	42	2
P.A. de Silva	8	1	29	–

Fall of Wickets
1–21, 2–84, 3–111, 4–140, 5–173, 6–190, 7–190, 8–190, 9–197

Umpires: C.J. Mitchley & R.S. Dunne *Man of the Match:* P.A. de Silva

Sri Lanka won by 19 runs

Match Three – Pakistan v. Zimbabwe
6 April 1997 at Sharjah C.A. Stadium

Pakistan

Rameez Raja	c A. Flower, b Streak	20
Shahid Afridi	c Carlisle, b Matambanadzo	1
Ijaz Ahmed	c Streak, b Matambanadzo	1
Salim Malik	b P.A. Strang	33
Inzamam-ul-Haq	c and b G.J. Whittall	46
Mohammad Wasim	c Streak, b G.J. Whittall	27
*Moin Khan	c Brandes, b Streak	11
Wasim Akram (Capt)	b Streak	5
Saqlain Mushtaq	run out	3
Mushtaq Ahmed	not out	16
Waqar Younis	run out	10
	lb 6, w 7, nb 1	14
50 overs		187

	O	M	R	W
Brandes	8	–	24	–
Matambanadzo	8	–	25	2
Streak	10	1	37	3
P.A. Strang	10	2	29	1
A.R. Whittall	4	–	29	–
G.W. Whittall	10	–	37	2

Fall of Wickets
1–6, 2–9, 3–58, 4–67, 5–128, 6–143, 7–157, 8–157, 9–164

Zimbabwe

C.B. Wishart	run out	29
G.W. Flower	run out	14
E.A. Brandes	b Wasim Akram	2
A.D.R. Campbell (Capt)	c and b Saqlain Mushtaq	8
G.J. Whittall	c Ijaz Ahmed, b Waqar Younis	1
*A. Flower	not out	21
S.V. Carlisle	c Wasim Akram, b Mushtaq Ahmed	4
P.A. Strang	c Ramees Raja, b Shahid Afridi	8
H.H. Streak	run out	1
A.R. Whittall	lbw, b Mushtaq Ahmed	0
E. Matambanadzo	run out	0
	lb 1, w 5	6
31.4 overs		94

	O	M	R	W
Wasim Akram	7	–	25	1
Waqar Younis	6	1	14	1
Mushtaq Ahmed	7	–	20	2
Saqlain Mushtaq	5	–	23	1
Shahid Afridi	6.4	1	11	1

Fall of Wickets
1–39, 2–47, 3–57, 4–58, 5–61, 6–78, 7–87, 8–90, 9–93

Umpires: C.J. Mitchley & D.B. Cowie *Man of the Match:* Inzamam-ul-Haq

Pakistan won by 93 run

Match Four – Sri Lanka v. Pakistan
7 April 1997 at Sharjah C.A. Stadium

Sri Lanka

S.T. Jayasuriya	c Waqar Younis, b Salim Malik	67
*R.S. Kaluwitharana	lbw, b Waqar Younis	3
M.S. Atapattu	lbw, b Waqar Younis	0
P.A. de Silva	c Waqar Younis, b Saqlain	134
A. Ranatunga (Capt)	c Wasim Akram, b Salim Malik	1
R.S. Mahanama	c Moin Khan, b Shahid Afridi	12
H.P. Tillekeratne	c and b Saqlain Mushtaq	13
H.D.P.K. Dharmasena	not out	10
W.P.U.J.C. Vaas		
M. Muralitharan		
S.C. de Silva		
	b 1, lb 5, w 3, nb 2	11
50 overs (for 7 wickets)		251

	O	M	R	W
Wasim Akram	7	–	34	–
Waqar Younis	8	–	60	2
Saqlain Mushtaq	10	–	42	2
Mushtaq Ahmed	6	–	37	–
Shahid Afridi	10	–	30	1
Salim Malik	9	–	42	2

Fall of Wickets
1–3, 2–11, 3–137, 4–138, 5–171, 6–193, 7–251

Pakistan

Sajid Ali	c Kaluwitharana, b S.C. de Silva	15
Shahid Afridi	c sub (Kalpage), b Vaas	7
Rameez Raja	c Jayasuriya, b Muralitharan	47
Salim Malik	c and b Muralitharan	8
Inzamam-ul-Haq	c Tillekeratne, b Muralitharan	62
*Moin Khan	c Mahanama, b Dharmasena	19
Wasim Akram (Capt)	c Kaluwitharana, b Dharmasena	27
Mohammad Wasim	c Kaluwitharana, b Jayasuriya	1
Mushtaq Ahmed	run out	2
Saqlain Mushtaq	not out	4
Waqar Younis	c Mahanama, b Dharmasena	3
	lb 1, w 3, nb 1	5
45.4 overs		200

	O	M	R	W
Vaas	6	–	21	1
S.C. de Silva	7	–	28	1
Muralitharan	9	1	47	3
Dharmasena	9.4	–	27	3
P.A. de Silva	5	–	30	–
Jayasuriya	9	–	46	1

Fall of Wickets
1–9, 2–29, 3–49, 4–126, 5–156, 6–186, 7–187, 8–192, 9–196

Umpires: R.S. Dunne & D.B. Cowie *Man of the Match:* P.A. de Silva

Sri Lanka won by 51 run

Match Five – Sri Lanka v. Zimbabwe
8 April 1997 at Sharjah C.A. Stadium

Zimbabwe

.W. Flower	lbw, **b** Kalpage	28
*.B. Wishart	**c** Mahanama, **b** Pushpakumara	0
A. Flower	**c** Chandana, **b** Kalpage	42
.A. Strang	**c** Tillekeratne, **b** Kalpage	11
..D.R. Campbell (Capt)	**c** Atapattu, **b** Muralitharan	30
.J. Whittall	**c** and **b** Muralitharan	44
.P. Viljoen	**st** Kaluwitharana, **b** Chandana	22
.H. Streak	**c** Mahanama, **b** Chandana	14
.A. Brandes	not out	2
.R. Whittall	lbw, **b** S.C. de Silva	3
..Matambanadzo	**c** Mahanama, **b** S.C. de Silva	1
	lb **2**, w **3**, nb **1**	6
	49.5 overs	203

	O	M	R	**W**
?ushpakumara	7	–	34	1
..C. de Silva	6.5	–	12	2
Kalpage	9	1	38	3
Muralitharan	10	–	39	2
.tapattu	9	–	41	–
..handana	8	–	37	2

Fall of Wickets
?–3, 2–68, 3–73, 4–91, 5–157, 6–164, 7–197, 8–198, 9–201

Sri Lanka

R.S. Mahanama	**c** and **b** P.A. Strang	42
*R.S. Kaluwitharana	**c** Streak, **b** Matambanadzo	4
M.S. Atapattu	run out	14
P.A. de Silva	**c** G.W. Flower, **b** Brandes	32
A. Ranatunga (Capt)	**c** A. Flower, **b** P.A. Strang	0
H.P. Tillekeratne	**c** Viljoen, **b** G.J. Whittall	36
R.S. Kalpage	**c** Matambanadzo, **b** A.R. Whittall	7
U.U. Chandana	**b** A.R. Whittall	0
M. Muralitharan	**b** Streak	1
K.R. Pushpakumara	not out	2
S.C. de Silva	lbw, **b** Streak	0
	b **1**, lb **2**, w **11**, nb **1**	15
	46.1 overs	153

	O	M	R	**W**
Brandes	6	–	24	1
Matambanadzo	5	1	18	1
Streak	8.1	2	12	2
P.A. Strang	7	3	16	2
G.W. Whittall	10	–	42	1
A.R. Whittall	10	–	38	2

Fall of Wickets
1–14, 2–59, 3–69, 4–69, 5–131, 6–148, 7–149, 8–151, 9–151

Umpires: C.J. Mitchley & R.S. Dunne *Man of the Match:* G.J. Whittall **Zimbabwe won by 50 runs**

Match Six – Zimbabwe v. Pakistan
9 April 1997 at Sharjah C.A. Stadium

Pakistan

.nzamam-ul-Haq	run out	14
..ajid Ali	**c** Matambanadzo	4
..jaz Ahmed	**c** A.R. Whittall, **b** Brandes	19
..alim Malik	**c** A. Flower, **b** Brandes	0
.Iohammad Wasim	lbw, **b** Streak	3
Wasim Akram (Capt)	**c** P.A. Strang, **b** Matambanadzo	1
Moin Khan	**c** A.R. Whittall, **b** Streak	61
.hahid Afridi	**b** Streak	5
.aqlain Mushtaq	**c** G.W. Flower, **b** Streak	20
.Iushtaq Ahmed	not out	5
Waqar Younis	not out	8
	b **1**, lb **6**, w **4**	11
	50 overs (for 9 wickets)	151

	O	M	R	**W**
Brandes	10	4	39	2
Matambanadzo	8	–	27	2
Streak	10	2	18	4
?.A. Strang	10	–	32	–
..J. Whittall	8	1	18	–
..R. Whittall	4	1	10	–

Fall of Wickets
?–8, 2–34, 3–34, 4–40, 5–41, 6–43, 7–51, 8–128, 9–140

Zimbabwe

C.B. Wishart	**b** Waqar Younis	5
G.W. Flower	**c** Ijaz Ahmed, **b** Waqar Younis	1
*A. Flower	**b** Mushtaq Ahmed	28
P.A. Strang	**b** Saqlain Mushtaq	26
A.D.R. Campbell (Capt)	**b** Saqlain Mushtaq	0
G.J. Whittall	**c** Moin Khan, **b** Mushtaq Ahmed	0
D.P. Viljoen	run out	25
H.H. Streak	lbw, **b** Waqar Younis	20
E.A. Brandes	**st** Moin Khan, **b** Mushtaq Ahmed	0
A.R. Whittall	**c** Wasim Akram, **b** Mushtaq Ahmed	0
E. Matambanadzo	not out	5
	lb **5**, w **4**	9
	40.1 overs	119

	O	M	R	**W**
Wasim Akram	7	1	11	–
Waqar Younis	5.1	2	14	3
Saqlain Mushtaq	9	1	37	2
Shahid Afridi	9	1	25	–
Mushtaq Ahmed	10	–	27	4

Fall of Wickets
1–5, 2–14, 3–57, 4–57, 5–58, 6–76, 7–94, 8–94, 9–94

Umpires: C.J. Mitchley & D.B. Cowie *Man of the Match:* Moin Khan **Pakistan won by 32 runs**

Sharjah Cup Final – Pakistan v. Sri Lanka
11 April 1997 at Sharjah C.A. Stadium

Pakistan

Rameez Raja	c Ranatunga, b S.C. de Silva	12
Sajid Ali	c Tillekeratne, b Muralitharan	28
Ijaz Ahmed	b Jayasuriya	33
Salim Malik	b Muralitharan	58
Inzamam-ul-Haq	run out	61
*Moin Khan	c Mahanama, b Muralitharan	1
Wasim Akram (Capt)	b Dharmasena	3
Shahid Afridi	b Vaas	8
Waqar Younis	c P.A. de Silva, b Vaas	2
Saqlain Mushtaq	c Mahanama, b S.C. de Silva	1
Mushtaq Ahmed	not out	0
	b 1, lb 1, w 5, nb 1	8
	49.2 overs	214

	O	M	R	W
Vaas	9.2	1	32	2
S.C. de Silva	9	–	35	2
Muralitharan	10	–	42	3
Dharmasena	9	1	30	1
Jayasuriya	5	–	31	1
P.A. de Silva	7	–	42	–

Fall of Wickets
1–**19**, 2–**68**, 3–**87**, 4–**185**, 5–**187**, 6–**195**, 7–**208**, 8–**210**, 9–**212**

Sri Lanka

S.T. Jayasuriya	lbw, b Waqar Younis	13
*R.S. Kaluwitharana	c Ijaz Ahmed, b Wasim Akram	0
M.S. Atapattu	lbw, b Mushtaq Ahmed	29
P.A. de Silva	not out	87
A. Ranatunga (Capt)	c and b Salim Malik	28
R.S. Mahanama	c Mushtaq Ahmed, b Saqlain	31
H.P. Tillekeratne	c Ijaz Ahmed, b Saqlain	7
H.D.P.K. Dharmasena	not out	3
W.P.U.J.C. Vaas		
M. Muralitharan		
S.C. de Silva		
	lb 11, w 2, nb 4	17
	49.2 overs (for 6 wickets)	215

	O	M	R	W
Wasim Akram	10	1	30	1
Waqar Younis	8	–	43	1
Saqlain Mushtaq	9.2	–	41	2
Mushtaq Ahmed	10	–	41	1
Shahid Afridi	5	–	24	–
Salim Malik	7	–	25	1

Fall of Wickets
1–**1**, 2–**35**, 3–**67**, 4–**133**, 5–**193**, 6–**204**

Umpires: R.S. Dunne & C.J. Mitchley *Man of the Match:* P.A. de Silva

Sri Lanka won by 4 wickets

Atapattu and Aravinda equalled Sri Lanka's highest wicket stand in a one-day international when they put on 184 and helped take their side to a commendable 243 for 8, but this seemed inadequate as Pakistan reached 173 for 4 by the 38th over. Shahid Afridi had given the innings impetus with 67 off 55 balls. Pakistan suffered an unexpected collapse against the spinners, and five wickets went down for 24 runs to leave Moin Khan and Waqar Younis with a hopeless task.

Having bowled and fielded well to restrict Pakistan in the third match in the competition, Zimbabwe threw away any chance of victory with a series of insane run-outs. Wishart and Grant Fowler scored 39 for the first wicket before both being run out, and needless sacrifices followed.

Sri Lanka sailed into the final on the back of a brilliant century by Aravinda de Silva who once again was dominating a limited-over tournament with his thrilling batting. Undeterred by coming to the crease at 11 for 2, he hit 134 off 131 balls. He and Jayasuriya added 126 after which de Silva put the Pakistan attack to rout. Only Rameez Raja and Inzamam-ul-Haq offered any serious resistance to the Sri Lankan bowlers.

Zimbabwe kept alive their faint hopes of reaching the final when they beat a below strength Sri Lankan side. Zimbabwe batted consistently, but it was determined bowling and electric fielding that brought them success.

Their bowling and fielding were again most impressive when they met Pakistan the following day, and when they had reduced their opponents to 51 for 7 Zimbabwe looked set for victory. Moin Khan and Saqlain Mushtaq added 77, but, facing a modest target of 152 Zimbabwe should have won with ease. They failed miserably. Waqar Younis made the early inroads, and when Dirk Viljoen, having his first taste of international cricket in this tournament, and Heath Streak suggested a fight back Mushtaq Ahmed quickly wrapped up the tail.

Sri Lanka had looked the best of the three sides in the Sharjah Cup, and they deservedly took the trophy when Aravinda de Silva guided them to victory over Pakistan with four balls to spare. Once more, Sri Lanka had to overcome a poor start, but de Silva's class and dominance were decisive. He brought his total number of runs in the tournament to 410, average 102.50. There was no challenge for the title of Man of the Series.

Qualifying Table

	P	W	L	Pts
Sri Lanka	4	3	1	6
Pakistan	4	2	2	4
Zimbabwe	4	1	3	2

ICC Trophy

The inaugural ICC Trophy was played in England in 1979. Fifteen nations competed. They were divided into three groups, and the

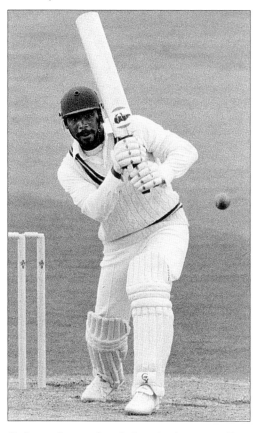

matches were played at the end of May and the beginning of June on club grounds in the West Midlands. There were rich prizes for the winners, Sri Lanka, and the runners-up, Canada, for both gained entry to the World Cup competition played in England later in the summer.

No longer the most feared of opening batsmen in Test cricket, but now the coach who helped Bangladesh to their most memorable triumph in Malaysia, Gordon Greenidge. (Neal Simpson/ASP)

By the time of the second competition, 1982, Sri Lanka were a Test nation, and the second winners of the Trophy, Zimbabwe, were also to gain Test status.

In 1997, Malaysia hosted the sixth ICC Trophy, and there were 22 competing countries, but, sadly and unexpectedly, the weather was to play an important part in deciding who was to progress to the World Cup in England in 1999.

There were some familiar names in the tournament. The United States side included D.I. Kallicharran and S.F.A. Bacchus, rich in experience in West Indies and South Africa. They were coached by Roger Harper. Bobby Simpson guided Bermuda, and Gordon Greenidge managed Bangladesh. Ireland were coached by Mike Hendrick, and Denmark's most famous player, Ole Mortensen, the former Derbyshire fast bowler, is now in charge of the national side.

The 22 countries were divided into four sections, and the top two in each section qualified for the next stage of the competition. The winners of each group were Kenya, Bangladesh, Holland and Scotland. The runners-up who accompanied them into the last eight were Ireland, Denmark, Canada and Hong Kong. These eight teams were now divided into two groups while the countries who had been eliminated competed for the Plate and to determine overall rankings.

Group E

1 April
Scotland 164 (G. Salmond 59, P. Jensen 4 for 25)
Denmark 122
Scotland won by 44 runs

Kenya 303 for 6 (M. Odumbe 148 not out, S. Tikolo 93)
Canada 126 for 7
Kenya won on faster scoring rate

2 April
Kenya 33 for 4
v. **Denmark**
Match abandoned

Canada 87 for 4
v. **Scotland**
Match abandoned

4 April
Kenya 153
Scotland 37 for 3
Kenya won on faster scoring rate

Denmark 126
Canada 119 (T. Hansen 5 for 51)
Denmark won by 7 runs

Final Positions

	P	W	L	NR	Pts
Kenya	3	2	–	1	5
Scotland	3	1	1	1	3
Denmark	3	1	1	1	3
Canada	3	–	2	1	1

Scotland qualified for the semi-final ahead of Denmark because they had beaten Denmark when the two nations met. Thomas Hansen produced one of the best bowling performances of the competition in the win over Canada.

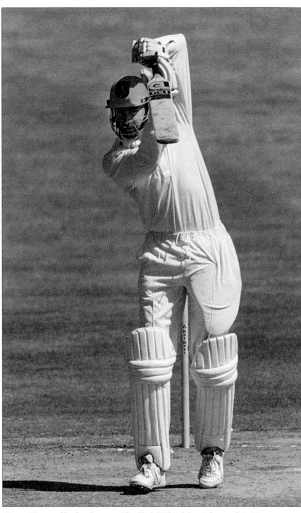

Peter Cantrell, the former Sheffield Shield cricketer, hit 53 not out for Holland against Ireland, but his side were dogged by rain and failed to reach the semi-finals. (Paul Sturgess/Sportsline)

Earlier in the competition, he had returned from hospital with five stitches in a hand injury and scrambled a run off the last ball to bring Denmark victory over United Arab Emirates who had been qualifiers in the last World Cup. Maurice Odumbe hit an unbeaten 148 for Kenya in the victory over Canada and was later named Man of the Series.

Group F

1 April
Holland 211 for 8 (P.E. Cantrell 53 not out)
Ireland 91 for 3
Ireland won on faster scoring rate

Hong Kong 145
Bangladesh 148 for 3 (Aminul Islam 53 not out)
Bangladesh won by 7 wickets

2 April
Ireland 129
Bangaldesh 24 for 0
Match abandoned

Hong Kong 170
Holland 16 for 0
Match abandoned

4 April
Ireland 223 for 7 (A.R. Dunlop 54)
Hong Kong 172 (S. Brew 50)
Ireland won by 51 runs

Holland 171
Bangladesh 141 for 6
Bangladesh won on faster scoring rate

Final Positions

	P	W	L	NR	Pts
Bangladesh	3	2	–	1	5
Ireland	3	2	–	1	5
Holland	3	–	2	1	1
Hong Kong	3	–	2	1	1

Holland, who had performed so well in the last World Cup finals, could consider themselves desperately unlucky in that all three of their matches were marred by the weather, and they suffered two defeats when their opponents reached revised and reduced targets.

Semi-Finals

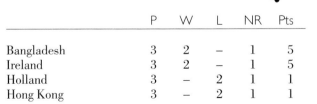

6 and 7 April
at Tenga Sports Ground, Kuala Lumpur
Kenya 215 for 8 (M. Odumbe 67, K. Otieno 51, P. McCrum 4 for 51)
Ireland 208 for 9 (D. Heasley 51, Asif Karim 4 for 28)
Kenya won by 7 runs

9 April
at Tenga Sports Ground, Kuala Lumpur
Bangladesh 243 for 7 (Khaled Masud 70, Aminul Islam 57)
Scotland 171 (Mohammad Rafique 4 for 25)
Bangladesh won by 72 runs

One of the prizes for reaching the semi-final stage of the ICC Trophy was qualification for the Commonwealth Games in Kuala Lumpur in 1998 when, for the first time, cricket will be included in the programme. Rain again struck and took the first semi-final into a second day. Despite the closeness of the score, Kenya always seemed to have the edge. Four quick wickets by Mohammad Rafique proved decisive in the other match.

Third Place Play-off

10 and 11 April
at Tenga Sports Ground, Kuala Lumpur
Scotland 187 for 8
Ireland 141 (K.L.P. Sheridan 4 for 24)
Scotland won on faster scoring rate

Scotland and Ireland have been regular cricket adversaries over the years, but never have they met in a more important match than the one which decided who would go forward to the World Cup finals. Ireland could complain that rain pursued them to the last. It caused the match to be reduced to 45 overs, and Ireland, under the Duckworth-Lewis method, faced a revised target of 192. They were bowled out in 39 overs for 141.

Final

Kenya v. Bangladesh

Rain haunted the competition to the very end. The final went into a second day, and even then Bangladesh faced a revised target of 166 in 25 overs. In spite of a damp outfield and the loss of three wickets for 38 runs, Kenya batted with exciting power and aggression. Stephen Tikolo gave a dazzling display and won the individual award for his 147.

Bangladesh had a dreadful start when Marin Suji bowled Naimur Rahman in the first over, but there were consistently brisk contributions from most of the batsmen. Mohammad Rafique and Minhajul Abedin added 50 in seven overs, and Akram Khan and Aminul Islam put on 53 in nine overs for the fourth wicket. With six overs remaining, 50 were needed, and 11 were wanted from the last over. This came down to one from the last ball bowled by Suji. It hit Hasibul on the pad, and the batsmen scampered the winning leg-bye.

ICC Trophy Rankings 1997

1. Bangladesh
2. Kenya
3. Scotland
4. Ireland
5. Denmark
6. Holland
7. Canada
8. Hong Kong
9. Bermuda
10. United Arab Emirates
11. Fiji
12. U.S.A.
13. Papua New Guinea
14. Singapore
15. Namibia
16. Malaysia
17. East and Central Africa
18. West Africa
19. Gibraltar
20. Argentina
21. Israel and Italy

The importance of these rankings cannot be over-emphasised, for the next ICC Trophy will see countries split into two divisions, and the top 12 in the above list will form the first division.

ICC Trophy Final – Kenya v. Bangladesh
12 and 13 April at Tenga Sports Ground, Kuala Lumpur

Kenya

Asif Karim	b Saiful Islam	0
S. Gupta	c and Khalid Mahmood	16
*K. Otieno	lbw, b Saiful Islam	2
S. Tikolo,	c Saiful Islam,	
	b Khalid Mahmood	147
M. Odumbe (Capt)	st Khaled Masud, b M. Rafique	43
T. Odoyo	c Mohammad Rafique	1
H. Modi	not out	12
A. Ondek	st Khaled Masud, b M. Rafique	1
D. Tikolo		
B. Patel		
M. Suji		
	b 1, lb 9, nb 9	19
	50 overs (for 7 wickets)	241

	O	M	R	W
Saiful Islam	9	–	39	2
Hasibul	6	–	15	–
Athar Ali Khan	5	–	22	–
Kahlid Mahmood Sujan	7	1	31	2
Emanul Haq	10	–	41	–
Naimur Rahman	4	–	21	–
Mohammad Rafique	6	1	40	3
Akram Khan	3	1	22	–

Fall of Wickets
1–0, 2–15, 3–38, 4–196, 5–212, 6–230, 7–241

Bangladesh

Naimur Rahman	b Suji	0
Mohammad Rafique	c Odumbe, b Ondek	26
Minhajul	c Patel, b Odoyo	26
Aminul Islam	b Asif Karim	37
Athar Ali Khan	c Odoyo, b Odumbe	22
Emanul Haq	c Gupta, b Asif Karim	5
Saiful Islam	c Odumbe, b Asif Karim	14
*Khaled Masud	not out	15
Kahlid Mahmood	st Otieno, b Odumbe	5
M. Hasibul	not out	4
Akram Khan (Capt)		
	b 3, lb 4, w 5	12
	25 overs (for 8 wickets)	166

	O	M	R	W
Suji	4	–	28	1
D. Tikolo	4	–	29	–
Odoyo	5	–	27	1
Ondek	5	–	26	1
Asif Karim	4	–	31	3
Odumbe	3	–	18	2

Fall of Wickets
1–0, 2–50, 3–63, 4–116, 5–118, 6–123, 7–139, 8–151

Umpires: D.B. Hair & S. Venkataraghavan   *Man of the Match:* S. Tikolo

Bangladesh won by 2 wickets

West Indies

There has been a crisis in West Indian cricket. In 1996–97, a new administration sought to address the problems that have seen

the decline in standards and the failures of the West Indian side in Test series and one-day internationals. Defeat in Australia, where the side also failed against Pakistan in the final of the World Series, only seemed to confirm the belief that a radical restructuring of cricket in the Caribbean was necessary.

West Indies new pace bowler Franklyn Rose who captured 71 wickets in the season including six in one innings on his Test debut.(Gordon Brook/Sportsline)

Indian Tour
Red Stripe Cup
Sri Lankan Tour

It had long been thought that there was a desperate need for the leading West Indian players to be seen more regularly in domestic cricket. Many were contracted to English counties and South African associations, and their appearances in the Caribbean had often been restricted solely to international engagements. To counter this, it had been stipulated that cricketers must appear in the Red Stripe Cup in order to gain selection for the Test side. In 1996–97, further steps were taken in that the number of matches in the Red Stripe were doubled with each side meeting each other home and away. As well as this, the season was extended to become the longest in West Indian history, with the two-Test series against Sri Lanka stretching to the end of June. West Indian cricketers faced the busiest season they had known.

The West Indian Cricket Board began the season by electing three new selectors – Wes Hall, Joey Carew and Michael Findlay – and by appointing Christopher Dehring as Chief Marketing Executive on a three-year contract. He was formerly president of an investment bank.

The Shell/Sandals one-day tournament was played in the first fortnight in October 1996 before the West Indian party left for Australia. Canada and Bermuda were invited to join the competition, and the eight sides played in two groups, each side meeting the other twice. Guyana and Trinidad and Tobago finished at the top of the groups and met in the final at Bourda. Phil Simmons hit 80 off 67 balls as Trinidad made 236 for 4 off their 50 overs, and Guyana were bowled out for 227 to give Lara's side victory by nine runs. Leg-spinner Dhanraj took 4 for 16 in 9.3 overs. Dhanraj was the leading bowler in the competition while the batting honours went to Lara and to Chanderpaul, who averaged 157 and made 88 off 93 balls for Guyana in the final.

Free State became the first South African provincial team to visit West Indies when they undertook a two-week tour of Barbados in September. They played four one-day matches and met Barbados in a first-class fixture.

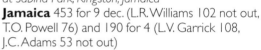

23, 24, 25 and 26 September 1996
at Kensington Oval, Bridgetown, Barbados
Barbados 163 (R.I.C. Holder 76, S.G. Cronje 5 for 43) and 356 for 5 (A.F.G. Griffith 123, R.O. Hurley 122, F.L. Reifer 56)
Free State 322 (G.F.J. Liebenberg 131, H.H. Dippenaar 111)
Match drawn

No play was possible on the fourth day so that an interesting match was drawn. Liebenberg and Dippenaar added 240 for Free State's second wicket.

Rose bowls Laxman in the first Test against India at Sabina Park. It was Rose's first wicket in Test cricket. (Gordon Brooks/Sportsline)

Indian Tour

India named only one newcomer in the 16-man squad to tour the Caribbean, Abey Kuruvilla, a quick bowler from Mumbai. They also recalled Navjot Singh Sidhu, the experienced opening batsman who had been suspended following his walk-out on the tour of England. The tour started disastrously for the Indians. Srinath suffered a recurrence of a shoulder injury during net practice and flew to Johannesburg for treatment from orthopeadic surgeon Mark Ferguson who advised that the only cure was a two-month rest. So India were deprived of their main strike bowler before a ball was bowled. He was replaced by off-spinner Noel David who had no international experience.

28, February, 1, 2 and 3 March 1997
at Sabina Park, Kingston, Jamaica
Jamaica 453 for 9 dec. (L.R. Williams 102 not out, T.O. Powell 76) and 190 for 4 (L.V. Garrick 108, J.C. Adams 53 not out)
Indians 323 (V.V.S. Laxman 98, R.S. Dravid 86, S.C. Ganguly 82 not out, C.A. Walsh 4 for 44)
Match drawn

The tourists' only match before the first two Test matches saw them reduce Jamaica to 285 for 7, at which point fast-medium pacer Laurie Williams came in and hit his maiden first-class century. The Indians batted unevenly with only four men reaching double figures. Newcomer Leon Garrick made a century on the last day.

First Test Match

West Indies v. India

There were three debutants in the first Test of the series, the two pace bowlers Rose and Kuruvilla, and the West Indian batsman Roland Holder. Holder had played the first of his one-day internationals four years earlier, but he was 29 years old before he won his first Test cap. West Indies also brought in Stuart Williams for the first time since the tour of England in 1995, while India restored Sidhu as opener. Walsh won the toss, and West Indies batted.

The pitch was slow and any movement was minimal. Venkatesh Prasad was uncharacteristically wayward, but Kuruvilla settled well to Test cricket. He was accurate and used the slower ball intelligently. Six feet six inches tall, he soon captured his first Test wicket when he bowled Williams. Campbell fell to left-arm spinner Joshi, and when Chanderpaul was dismissed by a fine delivery from Venkatesh Prasad, the ball coming back at him sharply, West Indies were 143 for 3 in mid-afternoon.

Runs were not easily scored, and Lara was initially patient, but he and Hooper used their feet admirably against the spinners and shared a delightful partnership of 147 in 37 overs. The final session brought 130 runs, and Lara looked set for a century until he leg-glanced Kuruvilla to the wicket-keeper shortly before the close. He had faced 141 balls and hit ten fours. Hooper was unbeaten on 87, and West Indies ended a good day on 300 for 4.

Anil Kumble had been wicketless on the first day, but he struck back for India on the second after Hooper and night-watchman Bishop had made their partnership worth 67 before Bishop drove Kumble to mid-off. Hooper had reached his seventh Test hundred before losing Bishop, and he became Kuruvilla's third victim when he, too, was caught at mid-off. He never quite recaptured the smoothness and elegance of the first day, but 129 off 212 balls with 17 fours was an innings of great charm. Kumble worked quietly and efficiently through the remaining batsmen to finish with his eighth five-wicket haul in Test cricket.

Sidhu was rooted in his crease and was quickly leg before to Bishop, but Laxman reached a confident 54 before the close. With Dravid gaining power after a cautious start, India were 108 for 1.

It was the introduction of Rose on the second morning that changed the character of the game. He had made no impact when he had bowled on the Friday, but he now found grace, rhythm and pace. In his first over, he bowled Laxman with an off-cutter, and he sent back Dravid, Tendulkar and Azharuddin in successive overs. Tendulkar was beaten by a ball that kept low, and Azharuddin was taken at first slip. Had Murray not dropped Ganguly, Rose would have had five wickets in seven overs. By the time Ganguly was taken at first slip in the first over after tea, he and Mongia had saved the follow-on.

Bishop bowled Kumble, but Mongia found a resolute partner in Joshi, and India closed on 308 for 7.

Mongia added only four to his overnight score before lobbing a catch to square-leg. He had batted for over five hours and had done much to save India. Joshi, too, did well for 196 minutes and was last out. Rose, the local hero, finished with six wickets, a most impressive Test debut which was to win him the individual award.

A draw began to look inevitable when there were two breaks for rain, and it looked even more inevitable when Chanderpaul and Campbell became bogged down so that when Lara arrived Kumble had 2 for 8 in ten overs. Lara immediately hit Kumble for 12 in an over and made 78 off 83 balls with eight fours and a six before he was caught behind cutting at Kumble.

Walsh delayed his declaration until the close of play on the fourth day, and persistent rain prevented any play until shortly before tea on the last day so that a draw became inevitable.

Second Test Match

West Indies v. India

Ian Bishop strained a hamstring muscle during the first Test and reported unfit for the match in Port-of-Spain. The selectors called up Ottis Gibson, but Gibson had gone to England with his sick wife, and West Indies turned to Mervyn Dillon, the Trinidad pace man, who made his Test debut. Walsh again won the toss, and West Indies batted on another slow pitch.

Kumble caused problems on the opening day, taking five wickets as West Indies crawled to 239 for 7. Walsh had debated long before deciding to bat, and his concern was soon to be justified as Kumble removed both openers in successive overs. Lara was never at ease on his home ground and struggled for 65 minutes before edging Joshi to slip just before lunch. When Holder joined Hooper in the early afternoon the score was 99 for 4. The pair added 50 before Hooper was taken at slip off Kumble, who soon

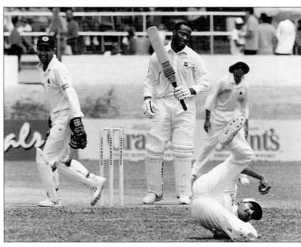

Azharuddin pulls off a spectacular catch to dismiss Lara in the first innings of the second Test. (Gordon Brooks/Sportsline)

First Test Match – West Indies v. India
6, 7, 8 9 and 10 March 1997 at Sabina Park

West Indies

Batsman	First Innings		Second Innings	
S.L. Campbell	c Mongia, b Joshi	40	b Kumble	43
S.C. Williams	b Kuruvilla	23	b Kumble	26
S. Chanderpaul	c Mongia, b Prasad	52	c Tendulkar, b Kuruvilla	48
B.C. Lara	c Mongia, b Kuruvilla	83	c Mongia, b Kumble	78
C.L. Hooper	c Prasad, b Kuruvilla	129	not out	12
I.R. Bishop	c Joshi, b Kumble	24		
R.I.C. Holder	c Azharuddin, b Kumble	17	(6) not out	21
*J.R. Murray	lbw, b Kumble	1		
C.E.L. Ambrose	c Ganguly, b Kumble	23		
F.A. Rose	not out	14		
C.A. Walsh (Capt)	b Kumble	4		
	lb 9, nb 8	17	b 4, lb 9	13
		427	(for 4 wickets, dec.)	241

	O	M	R	W	O	M	R	W
Venkatesh Prasad	28	5	104	1	15	2	46	–
Kuruvilla	30	6	82	3	17	2	56	1
Kumble	42.4	5	120	5	23	6	76	3
Joshi	27	6	81	1	6	1	27	–
Ganguly	7	1	17	–				
Laxman	3	–	14	–	3	–	14	–
Tendulkar					2	–	9	–

India

Batsman	First Innings		Second Innings	
V.V.S. Laxman	b Rose	64	c Holder, b Rose	27
N.S. Sidhu	lbw, b Bishop	10	c Holder, b Walsh	0
R.S. Dravid	c Murray, b Rose	43	not out	51
S.R. Tendulkar (Capt)	b Rose	7	not out	15
S.C. Ganguly	c Lara, b Rose	42		
M. Azharuddin	c Lara, b Rose	5		
*N.R. Mongia	c Holder, b Walsh	78		
A.R. Kumble	b Bishop	7		
S.B. Joshi	b Bishop	43		
A. Kuruvilla	b Rose	0		
Venkatesh Prasad	not out	10		
	b 5, lb 9, nb 23	37	lb 1, nb 5	6
		346	(for 2 wickets)	99

	O	M	R	W	O	M	R	W
Ambrose	25	10	35	–	6	3	7	–
Bishop	24.5	4	62	3				
Rose	33	7	100	6	9	1	23	1
Walsh	32	6	73	1	8	3	7	1
Hooper	21	9	40	–	16	6	27	–
Chanderpaul	11	4	22	–	6	–	18	–
Lara					3	–	16	–

Fall of Wickets
1–41, 2–96, 3–143, 4–290, 5–357, 6–368, 7–370, 8–408, 9–423
1–68, 2–81, 3–203, 4–203

1–32, 2–127, 3–140, 4–145, 5–153, 6–234, 7–248, 8–315, 9–320
1–6, 2–68

Umpires: S.A. Bucknor & M.J. Kitchen

Match drawn

Second Test Match – West Indies v. India
14, 15, 16, 17 and 18 March 1997 at Queen's Park Oval, Port-of-Spain, Trinidad

West Indies

Batsman	First Innings		Second Innings	
S.L. Campbell	c Prasad, b Kumble	8	lbw, b Kuruvilla	4
S.C. Williams	c Dravid, b Kumble	18	c Kumble, b Joshi	128
S. Chanderpaul	c Mongia, b Prasad	42	c Azharuddin, b Joshi	79
B.C. Lara	c Azharuddin, b Joshi	14	c Azharuddin, b Kumble	19
C.L. Hooper	c Azharuddin, b Kumble	40	c Laxman, b Kumble	14
R.I.C. Holder	b Joshi	91	c Laxman, b Joshi	9
J.R. Murray	c and b Kumble	11	not out	12
C.E.L. Ambrose	c Dravid, b Kumble	16	not out	10
F.A. Rose	c Dravid, b Joshi	34		
C.A. Walsh (Capt)	b Mongia, b Ganguly	0		
M. Dillon	not out	0		
	lb 20, nb 2	22	b 8, lb 13, nb 3	24
		296	(for 6 wickets)	299

	O	M	R	W	O	M	R	W
Venkatesh Prasad	26	9	54	1	20	7	38	–
Kuruvilla	22	9	36	–	23	6	47	1
Kumble	39	8	104	5	40	9	109	2
Joshi	22.3	2	79	3	36	11	57	3
Ganguly	5	3	3	1	3	–	6	–
Laxman					9	3	21	–

India

Batsman	First Innings	
V.V.S. Laxman	lbw, b Ambrose	0
N.S. Sidhu	b Ambrose	201
R.S. Dravid	b Ambrose	57
S.R. Tendulkar (Capt)	run out	88
S.C. Ganguly	c Chanderpaul, b Rose	6
M. Azharuddin	b Ambrose	1
*N.R. Mongia	b Dillon	17
A.R. Kumble	not out	12
S.B. Joshi	c Walsh, b Ambrose	24
A. Kuruvilla	c Murray, b Dillon	2
Venkatesh Prasad	c Lara, b Dillon	0
	b 9, lb 11, nb 8	28
		436

	O	M	R	W
Ambrose	41.4	10	87	5
Walsh	36	11	71	–
Rose	35	6	93	1
Dillon	35	6	92	3
Hooper	28	9	53	–
Chanderpaul	8	1	20	–

Fall of Wickets
1–26, 2–29, 3–59, 4–99, 5–149, 6–169, 7–220, 8–289, 9–290
1–25, 2–201, 3–244, 4–252, 5–271, 6–273

1–0, 2–171, 3–345, 4–370, 5–371, 6–382, 7–401, 8–420, 9–420

Umpires: L.H. Barker & S.G. Randell

Match drawn

added Murray and Ambrose to his victims. Holder had stood firm and was unbeaten on 71 at the close.

Rose gave Holder positive support in a stand of 69, and Holder looked sure to reach a maiden Test century until he played all over a yorker from Joshi. He had defied India for 293 minutes.

Ambrose trapped Laxman leg before with the second ball of the Indian innings, but it was West Indies' last success until the third ball of the following morning when Ambrose hit Dravid's off stump with a ball that kept low. By that time, Dravid and Sidhu had added 171 in 268 minutes, and Sidhu had 102 to his credit. The only other wicket to fall on the third day was that of Sachin Tendulkar who helped Sidhu to add a record 174 in 306 minutes. Tendulkar was brilliantly run out by Walsh's direct hit on the stumps late in the evening session. Sidhu finished the day on 196, which was the same number of runs that had been scored in the three sessions. The first had brought 48 off 29 overs; the second 68 off 27 overs. Another draw loomed large.

India had a firm base, but no one was able to force the pace on the fourth day. The last seven wickets added 69 runs off 28.4 overs. Ganguly and Azharuddin were soon out,

and Sidhu was at last bowled by Ambrose. He had faced 491 balls and hit a six and 19 fours in the highest score of his Test career. His innings lasted for just under 11 and a quarter hours.

The ball was turning, but the wicket had not deteriorated as expected. West Indies were 118 for the loss of Campbell at the end of the fourth day, but Stuart Williams and Chanderpaul added 176 for the second wicket, and Williams batted for seven and a half hours for his maiden Test century, which earned West Indies a draw.

22, 23 and 24 March 1997
at Kensington Oval, Bridgetown, Barbados
Indians 210 (A.D. Jadeja 50, D.K. Marshall 6 for 62) and 166 for 5 (S.C. Ganguly 73 not out)
Barbados 338 for 4 dec. (S.L. Campbell 97, P.A. Wallace 69)
Match drawn

In the drawn game between the second and third Tests, the Indian bowlers suffered a hard time. Wallace and Campbell put on 135 for Barbados' first wicket.

Third Test Match

West Indies v. India

For the first time in the series, a pitch was prepared heavily grassed and lively. It was to produce the only result in the five Tests. Sensibly, West Indies brought in Browne for Murray, who had not kept well in the first two Tests, and Bishop returned in place of Walsh, who was injured. Lara led West Indies for the first time. India played a third seam bowler, Ganesh, in place of spinner Joshi. Tendulkar won the toss and asked West Indies to bat.

There was immediate reward when Venkatesh Prasad, who well deserved his five wickets for some fine bowling, had Campbell taken low at second slip. Chanderpaul now began a long vigil that was to last into the second day. Chanderpaul was ideally suited to the role he was forced to play. As senior players like Lara and Hooper, men eager to excite with their strokes, fell to the moving ball, Chanderpaul exercised caution and patience. He stood firm while those around him capitulated. Just before tea, with the score on 131 for 5, the front line batsmen gone, he was joined by Browne. The pair added 56 in 94 minutes before Browne skied Kumble to square leg. The first five wickets had all gone to catches off the outside edge.

Bishop went quickly, but Ambrose gave Chanderpaul valiant support, and shortly before the close, the young left-hander, playing his 30th innings in Test cricket, reached his first Test hundred. It was an emotional moment.

Fifty runs were added on the second morning before the West Indian innings closed, and Chanderpaul was left unbeaten on 137 off 284 balls in just under seven and a half hours. He did not offer a chance.

Sidhu is embraced by Mongia after reaching the first double century of his Test career, India v. West Indies, second Test. (Gordon Brooks/Sportsline)

Ambrose soon accounted for Laxman, and Sidhu fell to Rose, but Tendulkar gave a masterly exhibition. He displayed his full range of strokes and punctured the attacking fields with some gloriously aggressive drives, pulls and cuts. He hit two sixes and 14 fours before being well caught at deep gully. He faced 147 balls, and his partnership with Dravid, an admirable supporting player, realised 170. India ended the day on 249 for 3 and seemed in total command.

India disappointed in the morning session of the third day. They lost Ganguly, Dravid and Mongia while only 41 were scored. Early in the afternoon, Azharuddin was caught behind off Rose, and the innings soon folded with India just 21 runs ahead, far fewer than had been anticipated. The constant failures of Azharuddin in the series after the glories he had shown against South Africa were a crucial factor in India's tendency to fail to capitalise on strong positions.

By the end of the third day, however, in spite of the batting disappointments, India were in the strongest of positions. Kuruvilla, the young fast bowler, performed outstandingly well, and he was most ably supported by Venkatesh Prasad and Ganesh. A fierce 45 from Lara was all that stood in the way of the pace trio routing West Indies totally. When the ninth wicket fell the home side were 107, a lead of 86. Dillon swung his bat gleefully and hit a six and three fours as he made 21 off 27 balls. He and Ambrose put on 33 for the last wicket. It seemed a joyful irrelevance, but it was to prove crucial.

Sidhu scored two runs before the close so that India began the fourth day needing another 118 to win, and six sessions in which to get the runs. It was Franklyn Rose who first undermined the Indian batting. Sidhu parried a ball

Chanderpaul acknowledges the applause of the crowd as he reaches his maiden Test hundred during the victory at Bridgetown. He was named man of the Test and one-day series.
(Gordon Brooks/Sportsline)

that reared throat high and was taken at third slip. Dravid sparred at a lifter outside off stump and was caught behind, and Laxman, half forward, fell to a leg-cutter.

It was Bishop who delivered the crucial blow. A well pitched out-swinger caught Tendulkar in two minds and Lara took a low catch at slip. Their inspiration gone, the Indian batsmen surrendered. Ganguly was bowled between bat and pad, and Azharuddin was late on a ball that kept low. There was devilry in the pitch, and the bowling was hostile and accurate and well supported in the field, but the collapse came too easily. The promised land had been in sight, but India could not manage the last few yards. They were out for 81, their lowest score in a Test in the Caribbean.

Fourth Test Match

West Indies v. India

Walsh was back for Dillon, and Jadeja and Joshi replaced Sidhu and Ganesh, but it mattered not a jot. No play was possible on the first three days because of heavy rain, a wet outfield and primitive drying operations.

West Indies, who won the toss, scored 252 for 7 when play did get under way. Brian Lara entertained the crowd with a six and 11 fours in his 103. On the last day, Jadeja made his highest score in Test cricket. He hit two sixes and seven fours.

11, 12, 13 and 14 April 1997

at Bourda, Georgetown, Guyana
Indians 341 (A.D. Jadeja 106, S.C. Ganguly 90, M. Azharuddin 57, R.R. Singh 54, R.D. King 7 for 82) and 277 for 4 dec. (N.S. Sidhu 103, S.C. Ganguly 81)
Guyana 300 (S. Chanderpaul 176 not out, S.B. Joshi 5 for 98) and 227 (M.V. Nagamootoo 56, Z.A. Haniff 51, S.B. Joshi 4 for 74)
Indians won by 91 runs

In spite of another fine innings by Chanderpaul, captain of Guyana, India gained their one first-class victory of the tour. Jadeja and Ganguly shared a second wicket stand of 143 in India's first innings, and Joshi bowled admirably.

Fifth Test Match

West Indies v. India

The final Test suffered the same fate as the fourth Test. India, having won the toss, made 194 for 2 on a curtailed first day. There was no play on the second and third days, and the Indian score had advanced to 241 for 4 on a brief fourth day. Dravid and Tendulkar shared a third wicket stand of 163 with some more most impressive batting. On the last day, Williams, Lara and Chanderpaul entertained the crowd by scoring 145 in 30 overs.

Third Test Match – West Indies v. India

27, 29, 30 and 31 March 1997, at Kensington Oval, Bridgetown, Barbados

West Indies

	First Innings		Second Innings	
S.L. Campbell	c Azharuddin, b Prasad	6	c Mongia, b Ganesh	18
S.C. Williams	c Laxman, b Ganesh	24	b Venkatesh Prasad	0
S. Chanderpaul	not out	137	lbw, b Kuruvilla	3
B.C. Lara (Capt)	c Tendulkar, b Prasad	19	c Azharuddin, b Prasad	45
C.L. Hooper	c Mongia, b Ganesh	19	lbw, b Ganesh	4
R.I.C. Holder	c Azharuddin, b Prasad	5	c Mongia, b Prasad	13
*C.O. Browne	c Tendulkar, b Kumble	24	c Mongia, b Kuruvilla	1
I.R. Bishop	b Venkatesh Prasad	4	lbw, b Kuruvilla	6
C.E.L. Ambrose	c Tendulkar, b Kuruvilla	37	not out	18
F.A. Rose	run out	11	c Ganguly, b Kuruvilla	4
M. Dillon	lbw, b Venkatesh Prasad	0	b Kuruvilla	21
	lb 5, nb 7	12	lb 5, nb 2	7
		298		**140**

India

	First Innings		Second Innings	
V.V.S. Laxman	b Ambrose	6	b Rose	19
N.S. Sidhu	c Browne, b Rose	26	c Williams, b Rose	3
R.S. Dravid	b Bishop	78	c Browne, b Rose	2
S.R. Tendulkar (Capt)	c Campbell, b Bishop	92	c Lara, b Bishop	4
S.C. Ganguly	c Browne, b Dillon	22	b Ambrose	8
M. Azharuddin	c Browne, b Rose	17	b Ambrose	9
*N.R. Mongia	c Williams, b Bishop	1	b Bishop	5
A.R. Kumble	not out	23	c Holder, b Bishop	1
A. Kuruvilla	b Ambrose	0	(10) c Holder, b Ambrose	9
D. Ganesh	c Browne, b Rose	8	(9) not out	6
Venkatesh Prasad	c Holder, b Rose	0	b Bishop	0
	b 2, lb 12, w 2, nb 30	46	b 2, lb 2, nb 11	15
		319		**81**

	O	M	R	W	O	M	R	W
Venkatesh Prasad	31.4	9	82	5	18	6	39	3
Kuruvilla	28	4	88	1	21	5	68	5
Ganesh	21	2	70	2	6	1	28	2
Kumble	16	1	44	1				
Ganguly	2	1	9	–				

	O	M	R	W	O	M	R	W
Ambrose	29	8	74	2	15	3	36	3
Bishop	28	6	70	3	11.5	4	22	4
Dillon	19	5	56	1				
Rose	22	4	77	4	9	2	19	3
Hooper	8	1	28	–				

Fall of Wickets

1–**10**, 2–**40**, 3–**88**, 4–**118**, 5–**131**, 6–**187**, 7–**193**, 8–**258**, 9–**290**

1–**9**, 2–**18**, 3–**37**, 4–**65**, 5–**86**, 6–**87**, 7–**91**, 8–**95**, 9–**107**

Fall of Wickets

1–**23**, 2–**42**, 3–**212**, 4–**253**, 5–**273**, 6–**275**, 7–**295**, 8–**296**, 9–**319**

1–**3**, 2–**16**, 3–**32**, 4–**32**, 5–**45**, 6–**51**, 7–**57**, 8–**66**, 9–**80**

Umpires: L.H. Barker & S.G. Randell

West Indies won by 38 runs

Fourth Test Match – West Indies v. India

4, 5, 6, 7 and 8 April 1997 at Recreation Ground, St John's, Antigua

West Indies

	First Innings	
S.L. Campbell	run out	10
S.C. Williams	c Tendulkar, b Kuruvilla	0
S. Chanderpaul	c Laxman, b Kumble	24
B.C. Lara	c Mongia, b Venkatesh Prasad	103
C.L. Hooper	c Azharuddin, b Joshi	26
R.I.C. Holder	c Mongia, b Kumble	56
*C.O. Browne	not out	39
I.R. Bishop	c Dravid, b Joshi	17
C.E.L. Ambrose	c Mongia, b Kuruvilla	22
C.A. Walsh (Capt)	c Dravid, b Joshi	21
F.A. Rose	absent ill	–
	b 1, lb 5, nb 9	15
		333

India

	First Innings	
A.D. Jadeja	run out	96
V.V.S. Laxman	c Browne, b Walsh	56
R.S. Dravid	not out	37
S.B. Joshi	not out	10
S.R. Tendulkar (Capt)		
S.C. Ganguly		
M. Azharuddin		
*N.R. Mongia		
A.R. Kumble		
A. Kuruvilla		
Venkatesh Prasad		
	lb 3, nb 10	13
	(for 2 wickets)	**212**

	O	M	R	W
Venkatesh Prasad	24	4	65	1
Kuruvilla	24	1	69	2
Kumble	36	14	93	2
Joshi	23.4	7	76	3
Ganguly	3	–	24	–

	O	M	R	W
Ambrose	9	1	26	–
Bishop	16	3	47	–
Walsh	15	3	37	1
Hooper	15	4	40	–
Chanderpaul	11	–	40	–
Williams	3	–	19	–

Fall of Wickets

1–**0**, 2–**32**, 3–**40**, 4–**82**, 5–**224**, 6–**230**, 7–**252**, 8–**295**, 9–**333**

Fall of Wickets

1–**97**, 2–**198**

Umpires: S.A. Bucknor & B.C. Cooray

Match drawn

Fifth Test Match – West Indies v. India
17, 18, 19, 20 and 21 April 1997 at Bourda, Georgetown, Guyana

India

First Innings		
A.D. Jadeja	c Browne, **b** Bishop	8
N.S. Sidhu	c Hooper, **b** Walsh	36
R.S. Dravid	c Hooper, **b** Rose	92
S.R. Tendulkar (Capt)	c and **b** Bishop	83
M. Azharuddin	c Browne, **b** Rose	31
*N.R. Mongia	c Hooper, **b** Rose	39
A.R. Kumble	c Walsh, **b** Hooper	15
S.B. Joshi	c Browne, **b** Chanderpaul	7
D. Ganesh	c Browne, **b** Hooper	7
A. Kuruvilla	c Bishop, **b** Hooper	5
Venkatesh Prasad	not out	0
	b **8**, lb **8**, w **3**, nb **13**	32
		355

West Indies

First Innings		
S.C. Williams	lbw, **b** Kumble	44
S. Chanderpaul	not out	58
B.C. Lara	c Sidhu, **b** Joshi	30
C.L. Hooper	run out	1
*C.O. Browne	not out	0
R.I.C. Holder		
S.L. Campbell		
I.R. Bishop		
C.E.L. Ambrose		
F.A. Rose		
C.A. Walsh (Capt)		
	b **72**, lb **2**, w **1**, nb **2**	12
	(for 3 wickets)	**145**

	O	M	R	**W**
Ambrose	29	14	36	–
Bishop	31	9	61	2
Rose	33.1	7	90	3
Walsh	28.2	8	62	1
Hooper	18	7	34	3
Chanderpaul	29	7	56	1

	O	M	R	**W**
Venkatesh Prasad	7	–	37	–
Kuruvilla	7	1	34	–
Ganesh	7	2	24	–
Kumble	4	1	30	1
Joshi	5	1	11	1

Fall of Wickets
1–**32**, 2–**68**, 3–**231**, 4–**241**, 5–**280**, 6–**303**, 7–**320**, 8–**343**, 9–**355**

Fall of Wickets
1–**72**, 2–**127**, 3–**145**

Umpires: E. Nicholls & G. Sharp

Match drawn

Test Match Averages – West Indies v. India

West Indies Batting

	M	Inns	NOs	Runs	HS	Av	100s	50s
S. Chanderpaul	5	8	2	443	137*	73.83	1	3
B.C. Lara	5	8	1	391	103	48.87	1	2
R.I.C. Holder	5	7	1	212	91	35.33		2
C.L. Hooper	5	8	1	245	129	35.00	1	
S.C. Williams	5	8	–	263	128	32.87	1	
C.O. Browne	3	4	2	64	39*	32.00		
C.E.L. Ambrose	5	6	2	126	37	31.50		
F.A. Rose	5	4	1	63	54	21.00		
S.L. Campbell	5	7	–	129	43	18.42		
I.R. Bishop	4	4	–	51	24	12.75		
J.R. Murray	2	3	1	24	12*	12.00		
M. Dillon	2	3	1	21	21	10.50		
C.A. Walsh	4	3	–	25	21	8.33		

India Batting

	M	Inns	NOs	Runs	HS	Av	100s	50s
R.S. Dravid	5	7	2	360	92	72.00		4
S.R. Tendulkar	5	6	1	289	92	57.80		3
A.D. Jadeja	2	2	–	104	96	52.00		1
N.S. Sidhu	4	6	–	276	210	46.00	1	
V.V.S. Laxman	4	6	–	172	64	28.66		2
N.R. Mongia	5	5	–	140	78	28.00		1
S.B. Joshi	4	4	1	84	43	21.00		
S.C. Ganguly	4	4	–	78	42	19.50		
A.R. Kumble	5	5	2	58	23*	19.33		
M. Azharuddin	5	5	–	63	31	12.60		
D. Ganesh	2	3	1	21	8	10.50		
Venkatesh Prasad	5	5	2	10	10*	3.33		
A. Kuruvilla	5	5	–	16	9	3.20		

Bowling

	Overs	Mds	Runs	Wks	Av	Best	10/m	5/inn
I.R. Bishop	110.4	26	262	12	21.83	4/22		
F.A. Rose	141.1	27	402	18	22.33	6/100		1
C.E.L. Ambrose	154.4	49	301	10	30.10	5/87		
M. Dillon	54	11	148	4	37.00	3/92		
C.A. Walsh	119.2	31	250	4	62.50	1/7		
C.L. Hooper	106	36	222	3	74.00	3/34		
S. Chanderpaul	65	12	156	1	156.00	1/56		

bowled in one innings – B.C. Lara 3 – 0 – 16 – 0;
S.C. Williams 3 – 0 – 19 – 0

Bowling

	Overs	Mds	Runs	Wks	Av	Best	10/m	5/inn
S.B. Joshi	120.1	28	331	11	30.09	3/57		
A.R. Kumble	200.4	44	576	19	30.31	5/104		2
D. Ganesh	34	5	122	4	30.50	2/28		
A. Kuruvilla	172	34	480	13	36.92	5/68		1
Venkatesh Prasad	169.4	42	465	11	42.27	5/82		1
S.C. Ganguly	20	5	59	1	59.00	1/3		
V.V.S. Laxman	15	3	49	–				

bowled in one innings – S.R. Tendulkar 2 – 0 – 9 – 0

Fielding Figures

10 – C.O. Browne; 6 – R.I.C. Holder; 4 – B.C. Lara; 3 – C.L. Hooper; 2 – S.C. Williams, I.R. Bishop, J.R. Murray and C.A. Walsh; 1 – S.L. Campbell and S. Chanderpaul

Fielding Figures

13 – N.R. Mongia; 9 – M. Azharuddin; 5 – R.S. Dravid and S.R. Tendulkar; 4 – V.V.S. Laxman; 2 – S.C. Ganguly, A.R. Kumble and Venkatesh Prasad; 1 – N.S. Sidhu and S.B. Joshi

One-Day Series

West Indies v. India

24 April 1997

at Queen's Park Oval, Port-of-Spain, Trinidad
Indians 274 for 6 (S.C. Ganguly 101, N.S. Sidhu 70)
University of West Indies Vice Chancellor's XI 242
(S.Chanderpaul 66, B.C. Lara 57, S.B. Joshi 4 for 36)
Indians won by 32 runs

In a warm-up match before the one-day series, Ganguly and Sidhu scored 150 for the first wicket. The home side included Ntini, the black South African fast bowler.

The rain that had ruined the fourth and fifth Tests returned to haunt the one-day series. India chose to bat first on a lively pitch, and Tendulkar gave them a fine start with 44 off 43 balls with nine fours. He was adjudged caught behind although the ball seemed to come off his shoulder, and once he had departed no one could get the innings moving. Ambrose bowled well, and Rose, in his first one-day international, was outstanding.

Rain caused a lengthy delay when West Indies began their innings, and their target was reduced to 146 in 33 overs. Chanderpaul continued with his blissful form, 83 off 87 balls with 12 fours, and West Indies won with ease.

Mongia was injured in the first match and gave way to Karim for the rest of the series. Noel David came in for his international debut and made an excellent impression, but the chief honours went to Kuruvilla who, as a newcomer, had been the major success of the tour. Venkatesh Prasad and Kuruvilla removed five of the top six West Indian batsmen for 32 after Tendulkar had asked West Indies to bat first. The wickets went down inside 12 overs, and there was no real recovery. Rain again interfered, and India's target was reduced to 113 in 40 overs. Tendulkar hit 65 off 70 balls, and the target was reached with 16.5 overs remaining.

The third match saw India panic just as they had the game in their grasp. West Indies' 249 was a good score but by no means daunting, and with Ganguly and Dravid shrugging off the early loss of Tendulkar to add 130 in 29 overs for the second wicket, India were well placed. The pair had been particularly severe on Gibson, who gained some revenge when he bowled Dravid. Azharuddin and Ganguly kept the score moving so that when Ganguly fell to Rose 65 were needed off 68 balls, a seemingly simple task with so much batting to come. What followed was mindless running and wild heaves so that, in all, the last eight wickets went down for 46 runs in 55 deliveries. The three run-outs tell their own story.

India were totally annihilated in the final match. Walsh won the toss for the first time in four matches and asked India to bat first on a pitch that gave early assistance to the pace bowlers. The loss of Tendulkar and Ganguly was a grievous blow, but Jadeja restored some pride with an innings of 68 off 78 balls. He hit four fours but was adept at stealing the singles. India's 199 was better than they might

First One-Day International – West Indies v. India

26 April 1997 at Queen's Park Oval, Port-of-Spain, Trinidad

India

S.R. Tendulkar (Capt)	c Browne, b Ambrose	44
N.S. Sidhu	lbw, b Ambrose	5
R.S. Dravid	c Hooper, b Rose	17
M. Azharuddin	b Rose	3
A.D. Jadeja	c Browne, b Rose	19
*N.R. Mongia	b Ambrose	29
R.R. Singh	c Williams, b Bishop	2
A.R. Kumble	c Hooper, b Adams	13
S.B. Joshi	b Ambrose	8
A. Kuruvilla	not out	3
Venkatesh Prasad	run out	5
	lb 6, w 20, nb 5	31
	43.3 overs	179

	O	M	R	W
Ambrose	9.3	–	36	4
Bishop	7	–	37	1
Walsh	8	–	34	–
Rose	10	2	25	3
Hooper	10	1	33	–
Adams	4	1	8	1

Fall of Wickets
1–40, 2–65, 3–71, 4–86, 5–119, 6–123, 7–154, 8–171, 9–172

West Indies

S.C. Williams	c Venkatesh Prasad, b Kumble	14
S. Chanderpaul	c Kuruvilla, b Venkatesh Prasad	83
B.C. Lara	not out	25
C.L. Hooper	not out	9
J.C. Adams		
R.I.C. Holder		
*C.O. Browne		
I.R. Bishop		
C.E.L. Ambrose		
F.A. Rose		
C.A. Walsh (Capt)		
	b 8, lb 1, w 8, nb 1	18
	27.5 overs (for 2 wickets)	149

	O	M	R	W
Venkatesh Prasad	7	1	35	1
Kuruvilla	4.5	–	27	–
Kumble	4	–	23	1
Singh	5	–	25	–
Joshi	4	–	19	–
Tendulkar	3	–	11	–

Fall of Wickets
1–43, 2–132

Umpires: E. Nicholls & C.E. Cumberbatch *Man of the Match*: S. Chanderpaul

West Indies won on faster scoring rate

Second One-Day International – West Indies v. India
27 April 1997 at Queen's Park Oval, Port-of-Spain, Trinidad

West Indies

S.C. Williams	lbw, **b** Venkatesh Prasad	3
S. Chanderpaul	c Karim, **b** Kuruvilla	12
B.C. Lara	c Karim, **b** Venkatesh Prasad	0
C.L. Hooper	c Ganguly, **b** Kuruvilla	14
J.C. Adams	not out	35
R.I.C. Holder	c Karim, **b** Kuruvilla	0
*C.O. Browne	c and Kumble	7
I.R. Bishop	c Venkatesh Prasad, **b** David	31
C.E.L. Ambrose	c Sidhu, **b** David	4
F.A. Rose	**b** David	5
C.A. Walsh (Capt)	c Karim, **b** Kumble	3
	b 1, lb **2**, w **4**	7
	43.5 overs	121

	O	M	R	**W**
Venkatesh Prasad	8	1	22	2
Kuruvilla	10	2	23	3
Kumble	8.5	3	22	2
Ganguly	8	1	26	–
David	8	–	21	3
Tendulkar	1	–	4	–

India

S.R. Tendulkar (Capt)	not out	65
S.C. Ganguly	not out	39
N.S. Sidhu		
M. Azharuddin		
R.S. Dravid		
A.D. Jadeja		
*S.S. Karim		
N. David		
A.R. Kumble		
A. Kuruvilla		
Venkatesh Prasad		
	b **4**, lb **3**, w **3**, nb **2**	12
	23.1 overs (for no wicket)	116

	O	M	R	**W**
Ambrose	6	1	21	–
Rose	7	1	32	–
Walsh	6	1	17	–
Bishop	4	–	35	–
Hooper	0.1	–	4	–

Fall of Wickets
1–**5**, 2–**5**, 3–**32**, 4–**32**, 5–**32**, 6–**44**, 7–**100**, 8–**107**, 9–**116**

Fall of Wickets

Umpires: C.E. Cumberbatch & E. Nicholls *Man of the Match:* A. Kuruvilla

India won on faster scoring rate

Third One-Day International – West Indies v. India
30 April 1997 at Arnos Vale, Kingstown, St Vincent

West Indies

S.C. Williams	c Singh, **b** Tendulkar	76
S. Chanderpaul	lbw, **b** Kuruvilla	5
B.C. Lara	**b** Singh	33
J.C. Adams	c Dravid, **b** David	9
C.L. Hooper	c and **b** Kumble	48
R.I.C. Holder	c Karim, **b** Venkatesh Prasad	16
O.D. Gibson	run out	3
C.E.L. Ambrose	**b** Venkatesh Prasad	13
*C.O. Browne	not out	10
F.A. Rose	run out	9
C.A. Walsh (Capt)	not out	0
	b **4**, lb **15**, w **2**, nb **6**	27
	50 overs (for 9 wickets)	249

	O	M	R	**W**
Venkatesh Prasad	10	–	53	2
Kuruvilla	10	1	34	1
Kumble	10	1	46	1
Singh	7	–	46	1
David	10	1	38	1
Tendulkar	3	–	13	1

India

S.R. Tendulkar (Capt)	**b** Walsh	9
S.C. Ganguly	c Ambrose, **b** Rose	79
R.S. Dravid	**b** Gibson	74
M. Azharuddin	c Hooper, **b** Gibson	24
A.D. Jadeja	**b** Gibson	9
R.R. Singh	c Adams, **b** Ambrose	4
*S.S. Karim	c Lara, **b** Gibson	6
A.R. Kumble	run out	0
N. David	not out	8
A. Kuruvilla	run out	0
Venkatesh Prasad	run out	0
	lb **11**, w **3**, nb **4**	18
	48.2 overs	231

	O	M	R	**W**
Walsh	9.2	2	26	1
Ambrose	9	1	34	1
Rose	8	–	41	1
Gibson	10	–	61	4
Hooper	8	–	36	–
Adams	4	–	22	–

Fall of Wickets
1–**11**, 2–**71**, 3–**86**, 4–**170**, 5–**193**, 6–**197**, 7–**214**, 8–**228**, 9–**248**

Fall of Wickets
1–**27**, 2–**157**, 3–**185**, 4–**201**, 5–**214**, 6–**217**, 7–**219**, 8–**224**, 9–**230**

Umpires: L.H. Barker & S.A. Bucknor *Man of the Match:* S.C. Williams

West Indies won by 18 runs

Fourth One-Day International – West Indies v. India
3 May 1997 at Kensington Oval, Bridgetown, Barbados

India

S.R. Tendulkar (Capt)	c Lara, b Walsh	1
S.C. Ganguly	b Ambrose	4
R.S. Dravid	c Chanderpaul, b Rose	30
M. Azharuddin	c Browne, b Chanderpaul	40
A.D. Jadeja	b Walsh	68
R.R. Singh	c sub (Garrick), b Gibson	29
*S.S. Karim	run out	14
A.R. Kumble	not out	8
N. David	not out	1
A. Kuruvilla		
Venkatesh Prasad		
	lb 1, nb 3	4
	50 overs (for 7 wickets)	199

	O	M	R	W
Walsh	9	3	26	2
Ambrose	10	1	33	1
Gibson	8	–	48	1
Rose	10	1	32	1
Chanderpaul	8	–	36	1
Hooper	5	1	23	–

Fall of Wickets
1–**4**, 2–**6**, 3–**62**, 4–**93**, 5–**168**, 6–**187**, 7–**194**

West Indies

S.C. Williams	not out	78
S. Chanderpaul	not out	109
B.C. Lara		
C.L. Hooper		
J.C. Adams		
R.I.C. Holder		
*C.O. Browne		
O.D. Gibson		
C.E.L. Ambrose		
F.A. Rose		
C.A. Walsh (Capt)		
	lb 9, w 1, nb 3	13
	44.4 overs (for no wicket)	200

	O	M	R	W
Venkatesh Prasad	9	–	44	–
Kuruvilla	6	2	15	–
Kumble	10	2	33	–
David	6	–	38	–
Singh	2	–	7	–
Ganguly	4	–	26	–
Tendulkar	5	–	22	–
Jadeja	2.4	–	6	–

Fall of Wickets

Umpires: L.H. Barker & S.A. Bucknor *Man of the Match*: S. Chanderpaul

West Indies won by 10 wickets

have expected, but Williams and Chanderpaul reduced it to nothing. Chanderpaul followed his first Test century with his first limited-over international century as West Indies won by ten wickets. Chanderpaul was named Man of the Match, Man of the Series, and Man of the Test Series. He is 22 years old and has matured into a very fine cricketer. Confidence grows with every match.

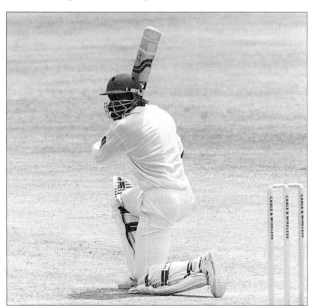

Red Stripe Cup

24, 25, 26 and 27 January 1997
at Kensington Oval, Bridgetown, Barbados
Guyana 156 (O.D. Gibson 4 for 58) and 294 (C.B. Lambert 145, A.R. Percival 91)
Barbados 448 for 8 dec. (F.L. Reifer 151 not out, P.A. Wallace 74, T.E. Rollock 53) and 4 for 0
Barbados won by 10 wickets
Barbados 16 pts, Guyana 0 pts

at Queen's Park Oval, Port-of-Spain
Trinidad & Tobago 302 (D. Williams 53) and 80 for 6
Windward Islands 140 (R. Dhanraj 4 for 18) and 238 (J.A.R. Sylvester 66, B.M. Watt 57, M. Persad 4 for 55)
Trinidad & Tobago won by 4 wickets
Trinidad & Tobago 16 pts, Windward Islands 0 pts

Floyd Reifer – record-breaking
exploits with Barbados won him his first Test cap.
(Gordon Brooks/Sportsline)

at Webster Park, Anguilla
Jamaica 332 (F.A. Rose 96, D.S. Morgan 63)
and 199 for 5
Leeward Islands 234 (B.S. Murphy 5 for 85)
Match drawn
Jamaica 8 pts, Leeward Islands 4 pts

With the Test team still operating in Australia, younger players had the opportunity to forward their claims for recognition. Floyd Reifer was quick to take his chance, hitting the highest score of his career and winning the individual award at Bridgetown. The left-hander was to win his first Test cap later in the year. Returning to Guyana as captain, Clayton Lambert hit a century and shared a third wicket stand of 167 with Andre Percival, but only one other batsman reached double figures, Semple, 19.

Trinidad were consistent in their middle order batting, and Dhanraj's leg-spin forced Windwards to follow on, but the home side made rather a hash of chasing a small target on the last day.

Rain restricted play on the first day in Anguilla and a draw became inevitable. Rose returned to the fray with the highest score of his career. The fast bowler was to enjoy an outstanding season.

31 January, 1, 2 and 3 February 1997
at Albion, Berbice, Guyana
Guyana *v.* **Leeward Islands**
Match abandoned
Guyana 4 pts, Leeward Islands 4 pts

at Mindoo Phillip Park, Castries
Jamaica 77 and 184 (M.J. Morgan 4 for 33,
R.N. Lewis 4 for 37)
Windward Islands 104 and 126 (F.A. Rose
4 for 25)
Jamaica won by 31 runs
Jamaica 16 pts, Windward Islands 5 pts

at Kensington Oval, Bridgetown, Barbados
Trinidad & Tobago 165 (L.A. Roberts 52,
T.E. Rollock 6 for 15) and 253
Barbados 238 (F.L. Reifer 50) and 186 for 3
(S.N. Proverbs 112 not out)
Barbados won by 7 wickets
Barbados 16 pts, Trinidad & Tobago 0 pts

No play in Guyana or on the second day in Castries was possible, but Rose turned the game at Phillip Park in favour of Jamaica. The strength in depth of Barbados was again apparent as they won with ease against Trinidad. Newcomer Terry Rollock was the star performer, and there was a century for Stanton Proverbs, who was to lose his place once the West Indian party returned from Australia.

7, 8, 9 and 10 February 1997
at Recreation Ground, St John's, Antigua
Leeward Islands 352 (R.D. Jacobs 107, D.R.E. Joseph 66,
D. Ramnarine 4 for 90)
Trinidad & Tobago 26 for 2
No result
Leeward Islands 4 pts, Trinidad & Tobago 4 pts

at Everest, Guyana
Guyana *v.* **Jamaica**
Match abandoned
Guyana 4 pts, Jamaica 4 pts

at Queen's Park, Grenada
Barbados 161 (M.J. Morgan 4 for 32) and 167
Windward Islands 166 (R.N. Lewis 55 not out,
O.D. Gibson 4 for 56) and 111
Barbados won by 51 runs
Barbados 16 pts, Windward Islands 5 pts

Rain continued to haunt the competition with limited play in Antigua and none at all in Guyana. Ridley Jacobs hit a century for Leeward Islands and injured Dhanraj. The leg-spinner damaged the ring finger of his right hand in attempting to take a return catch and was out for eight weeks. Barbados beat Windward Islands inside three days. It was their third victory in succession.

14, 15, 16 and 17 February 1997
at Guaracara Park, Pointe-à-Pierre, Trinidad
Jamaica 349 (L.V. Garrick 138, J.C. Adams 66)
and 201 for 5 dec. (J.C. Adams 67, L.V. Garrick 64)
Trinidad & Tobago 256 (B.C. Lara 135) and 118 for 5
(S. Ragoonath 54)
Match drawn
Jamaica 8 pts, Trinidad & Tobago 4 pts

at Kensington Oval, Bridgetown, Barbados
Leeward Islands 339 (S.C. Williams 141,
W.E. Reid 4 for 59) and 117 for 2 (S.C. Williams
50 not out)
Barbados 141 (R.I.C. Holder 53) and 311
(R.I.C. Holder 111, W.D. Phillip 6 for 78)
Leeward Islands won by 8 wickets
Leeward Islands 16 pts, Barbados 0 pts

at Bourda, Georgetown, Guyana
Guyana *v.* **Windward Islands**
Match abandoned
Guyana 4 pts, Windward Islands 4 pts

With the West Indian side back from Australia, there was much debate in Barbados as to whether or not a winning team should be disturbed. It was, and Barbados lost their first match of the season in spite of Holder's heroics.

Campbell, like Simmons of Trinidad, was out first ball. Both men had played in the last Test in Australia. Lara began his season with a century, and there was a fine maiden hundred for the 20-year-old Leon Garrick. Small in stature and promoted to open the innings, Garrick was one of the few positive discoveries of the season and was asked to join the Test party in order to gain 'atmospheric' experience.

There was more rain in Guyana.

21, 22, 23 and 24 February 1997

at Kaiser SC, Discovery Bay, Jamaica
Barbados 184 (R.I.C. Holder 58, F.L. Reifer 50, D.S. McKenzie 4 for 35) and 223 (R.I.C. Holder 54, F.A. Rose 5 for 62)
Jamaica 180 (H.R. Bryan 4 for 42) and 106
Barbados won by 121 runs
Barbados 16 pts, Jamaica 0 pts

at Queen's Park Oval, Port-of-Spain, Trinidad
Trinidad & Tobago 305 (P.V. Simmons 78, L.A. Roberts 65, N.C. McGarrell 7 for 84) and 204 for 9 dec. (B.C. Lara 72, N.C. McGarrell 4 for 63)
Guyana 241 (S. Chanderpaul 60, N.A. de Groot 53, D. Ramnarine 5 for 69) and 3 for 0
Match drawn
Trinidad & Tobago 8 pts, Guyana 4 pts

at Webster Park, Anguilla
Leeward Islands 168 (R.D. Jacobs 50 not out, C.A. Davis 4 for 30) and 236 (K.L.T. Arthurton 95, C.A. Davis 5 for 43)
Windward Islands 199 and 203 (J.R. Murray 52)
Leeward Islands won by 2 runs
Leeward Islands 16 pts, Windward Islands 5 pts

Walsh and Ambrose had yet to return to the fray because of injury, but Rose continued to impress although his side was well beaten by Barbados, who remained well in front at the top of the table. This was the first first-class match to be played at Kaiser Sports Club in Discovery Bay, and Jamaica's Brian Murphy celebrated by hitting left-arm spinner Winston Reid for four sixes in one over. Another left-arm spinner, Neil McGarrell of Guyana, returned the best bowling figures of his career for both innings and match as his side drew in Trinidad.

There was an exciting finish in Anguilla where Leewards won by two runs. Last man McNeil Morgan played a ball to mid-wicket and moved forward. He slipped and was run out, and as the players left the field torrential rain fell.

---

28 February, 1, 2 and 3 March 1997

at Windsor Park, Dominica
Windward Islands 199 (J.R. Murray 100) and 214 (J.A.R. Sylvester 70)

Trinidad & Tobago 370 for 9 dec. (S. Ragoonath 120, R.A.M. Smith 62, B.C. Lara 53) and 44 for 0
Trinidad & Tobago won by 10 wickets
Trinidad & Tobago 16 pts, Windward Islands 0 pts

at Bourda, Georgetown, Guyana
Barbados 240 (C.O. Browne 78, P.A. Wallace 62, C.L. Hooper 5 for 52) and 211 for 5 dec. (P.A. Wallace 69, S.L. Campbell 58)
Guyana 164 (O.D. Gibson 5 for 57) and 263 for 7 (C.L. Hooper 101)
Match drawn
Barbados 8 pts, Guyana 4 pts

Barbados gave up the chase at Bourda when within 25 runs of victory because Nagamootoo was injured and unable to bat. No play had been possible on the first day. Trinidad gained their second win of the season but, with four matches to go, Barbados were 24 points clear at the top of the table.

20, 21, 22 and 23 March 1997

at Chedwin Park, St Catherine, Jamaica
Jamaica 156 (C.E.L. Ambrose 4 for 16) and 337 for 9 dec. (M.D. Ventura 96, J.C. Adams 73, L.V. Garrick 50, W.D. Phillip 7 for 104)
Leeward Islands 145 (F.A. Rose 6 for 63) and 97 (F.A. Rose 5 for 36)
Jamaica won by 251 runs
Jamaica 16 pts, Leeward Islands 0 pts

at Albion, Berbice, Guyana
Guyana 281 (C.L. Hooper 119, C.B. Lambert 55, I.R. Bishop 5 for 82) D. Ramnarine 4 for 80) and 263 for 2 (C.B. Lambert 159, N.A. de Groot 63)
Trinidad & Tobago 413 (P.V. Simmons 116, D. Ganga 54, I.R. Bishop 50)
Match drawn
Trinidad & Tobago 8 pts, Guyana 4 pts

Walsh returned to lead Jamaica, but bowled only in the first innings when he took three wickets. Rose, 11 for 99 in the match, was again the star for the home side.

Captain and captain earlier in the season, Hooper and Lambert scored centuries to save the day for Guyana in Berbice.

10, 11, 12 and 13 April 1997

at Warner Park, Basseterre, St Kitts
Barbados 275 (R.I.C. Holder 107, F.L. Reifer 61) and 165 for 7 dec. (R.I.C. Holder 57)
Leeward Islands 152 (H.R. Bryan 5 for 39) and 254 (S.C. Williams 118, D.K. Marshall 4 for 70)
Barbados won by 81 runs
Barbados 16 pts, Leeward Islands 0 pts

at Kaiser SC, Discovery Bay, Jamaica
Windward Islands 117 (L.R. Williams 6 for 26)
and 161 (C.A. Walsh 5 for 49)
Jamaica 276 (R.G. Samuels 69, C.A. Davis 7 for 58)
and 4 for 0
Jamaica won by 10 wickets
Jamaica 16 pts, Windward Islands 0 pts

Leg-spinner Dave Marshall took three wickets in four balls in the penultimate over of the match to give Barbados a sensational victory over Leeward Islands. Marshall was playing his first Red Stripe Cup match for three years. The win put Barbados in an impregnable position at the top of the table.

Fast bowler Casper Davis took 7 for 58 for Windward Islands against Jamaica. These were the best bowling figures of the season, but he finished on the losing side.

9, 10, 11 and 12 May 1997

at Sabina Park, Kingston, Jamaica
Jamaica 206 (J.C. Adams 52, R.D. King 4 for 47) and 251 (D.S. Morgan 51, R.D. King 5 for 56)
Guyana 271 (C.L. Hooper 73, N.A. de Groot 61, B.S. Murphy 4 for 43) and 116 for 1 (S. Chanderpaul 56 not out)
Match drawn
Guyana 8 pts, Jamaica 4 pts

at Queen's Park Oval, Port-of-Spain, Trinidad
Barbados 394 (S.L. Campbell 109, A.F.G. Griffith 60, M. Dillon 4 for 94) and 288 (W.E. Reid 54 not out, I.R. Bishop 4 for 51)
Trinidad & Tobago 361 (S. Ragoonath 128, I.R. Bishop 111, W.E. Reid 4 for 72) and 99 for 1 (S. Ragoonath 73)
Match drawn
Barbados 8 pts, Trinidad & Tobago 4 pts

at Arnos Vale, St Vincent
Leeward Islands 390 (S.C. Williams 111, J. Mitchum 89, K.L.T. Arthurton 78, C.A. Davis 5 for 70) and 107 for 4 (R.D. Jacobs 56 not out)
Windward Islands 158 and 337 (K. Martin 65, B.M. Watt 64, K.K. Sylvester 56)
Leeward Islands won by 6 wickets
Leeward Islands 16 pts, Windward Islands 0 pts

The draw at Sabina Park was due mainly to the fact that only 125 runs were scored off 88.2 overs on the third day, the fewest made in a first-class match in the West Indies. Campbell was forced to retire hurt on 93 but returned to complete his century, while Williams and Mitchum set up Leewards' victory at Arnos Vale with an opening stand of 186.

16, 17, 18 and 19 May 1997
at Sabina Park, Kingston, Jamaica
Trinidad & Tobago 160 and 245 (D. Williams 55, F.A. Rose 4 for 89)
Jamaica 226 (R. Dhanraj 4 for 65) and 134 (R.G. Samuels 55)
Trinidad & Tobago won by 45 runs
Trinidad & Tobago 16 pts, Jamaica 5 pts

at Grove Park, Charlestown, Nevis
Guyana 257 (R.R. Sarwan 77) and 264 (Z.A. Haniff 71, A. Haniff 62, W.D. Phillip 5 for 108)
Leeward Islands 221 (K.L.T. Arthurton 61, R.M. Powell 51, M.V. Nagamootoo 4 for 88) and 129 for 1 (A. Adams 69 not out)
Match drawn
Guyana 8 pts, Leeward Islands 4 pts

at Kensington Oval, Bridgetown, Barbados
Windward Islands 82, (P.T. Collins 4 for 36) and 161
Barbados 434 for 9 dec. (F.L. Reifer 200, P.A. Wallace 121, R.L. Hoyte 50 not out, R.N. Lewis 5 for 160)
Barbados won by an innings and 191 runs
Barbados 16 pts, Windward Islands 0 pts

Barbados celebrated their triumph in the Red Stripe Cup with an innings victory inside two days over Windwards. This was the first time for 58 years that a regional match had been completed in two days. Philo Wallace and Floyd Reifer established a Barbadian third wicket record in regional cricket with a stand of 275.

23, 24, 25 and 26 May 1997
at Kensington Oval, Bridgetown, Barbados
Barbados 258 (F.L. Reifer 59) and 180 (P.A. Wallace 53, C.A. Walsh 6 for 39)
Jamaica 282 (W.W. Hinds 84, D.S. Morgan 54, O.D. Gibson 4 for 57) and 157 for 2 (R.G. Samuels 90 not out, J.C. Adams 50 not out)
Jamaica won by 8 wickets
Jamaica 16 pts, Barbados 0 pts

at Queen's Park Oval, Port-of-Spain, Trinidad
Leeward Islands 208 (K.L.T. Arthurton 70) and 95 (D. Ramnarine 4 for 28)
Trinidad & Tobago 110 (W.K.L. Quinn 4 for 39) and 138 (B.C. Lara 52, M. Mills 5 for 33)
Leeward Islands won by 55 runs
Leeward Islands 16 pts, Trinidad & Tobago 0 pts

at Tanteen, St George's, Grenada
Windward Islands 446 (J.R. Murray 218, B.M. Watt 50, M.V. Nagamootoo 4 for 104) and 177 for 9 dec. (R.D. King 5 for 43, M.V. Nagamootoo 4 for 67)

Guyana 315 (N.C. McGarrell 73, Z.A. Haniff 66, R.R. Sarwan 54, R.N. Lewis 4 for 104) and 120 for 8
Match drawn
Windward Islands 8 pts, Guyana 4 pts

Brian Lara equalled the regional record with five catches in Leewards' second innings in the match at Queen's Park Oval. Tanteen became the latest first-class ground when it staged the match between Windward Islands and Guyana. Junior Murray marked the occasion with the highest score of his career and the highest score of the season. It was also the first double century by a Windward Islands batsman in the Red Stripe Cup.

Red Stripe Cup Final Table

	P	W	L	D	NR	Pts
Barbados (5)	10	6	2	2		112
Jamaica (3)	10	4	2	3	1	93
Leeward Islands (2)	10	4	2	2	2	80
Trinidad & Tobago (1)	10	3	2	4	1	76
Guyana (6)	10	–	1	6	3	44
Windward Islands (4)	10	–	8	1	1	27

(1996 positions in brackets)

Sri Lankan Tour

4 June 1997
at Guaracara Park, Pointe-à-Pierre, Trinidad
Sri Lankans 226 for 8 (M.S. Atapattu 55, R. Dhanraj 4 for 59)
Trinidad & Tobago 215 for 7 (S. Ragoonath 110 not out, I.R. Bishop 53)
Trinidad & Tobago won on faster scoring rate

The Sri Lankans suffered the same misfortune as the Indians had done in that they lost their main strike bowler, Vaas, on the eve of the tour. Vaas was deemed unfit and did not travel to the Caribbean for the short tour. The one-day game in Trinidad was marred by rain. The home side's target was reduced to 215 in 41 overs, and they won with seven balls to spare. Ian Bishop was used as an opening batsman, and he and Ragoonath put on 105.

One-Day International

West Indies v. Sri Lanka

Sri Lanka continued to be unfortunate. The new, young fast bowler Zoysa was diagnosed as having a stress fracture of the lower vertebra and did not play after the opening match.

One-Day International – West Indies v. Sri Lanka
6 June 1997 at Queen's Park Oval, Port-of-Spain, Trinidad

West Indies

S.C. Williams	c Liyanage, b Jayasuriya	90
*J.R. Murray	c Muralitharan, b S.C. de Silva	2
F.A. Rose	c Dharmasena, b P.A. de Silva	7
B.C. Lara	c Liyanage, b Jayasuriya	67
C.L. Hooper	c Kaluwitharana, b Jayasuriya	25
F.L. Reifer	c Atapattu, b Jayasuriya	9
R.I.C. Holder	not out	41
L.R. Williams	c Dharmasena, b Jayasuriya	14
C.E.L. Ambrose	not out	9
D. Ramnarine		
C.A. Walsh (Capt)		
	lb **12**, w **4**, nb **3**	19
	49 overs (for 7 wickets)	**283**

	O	M	R	W
Liyanage	9	1	36	–
S.C. de Silva	7	–	58	1
P.A. de Silva	3	–	20	1
Muralitharan	10	1	58	–
Dharmasena	10	–	41	–
Jayasuriya	10	–	58	**5**

Fall of Wickets
1–**11**, 2–**46**, 3–**170**, 4–**183**, 5–**211**, 6–**220**, 7–**254**

Sri Lanka

S.T. Jayasuriya	c S.C. Williams, b L.R. Williams	44
M.S. Atapattu	c Hooper, b Walsh	1
P.A. de Silva	c Hooper, b Ambrose	7
A. Ranatunga (Capt)	c Ambrose, b Ramnarine	53
H.P. Tillekeratne	c Reifer, b L.R. Williams	2
R.S. Mahanama	c Rose, b Ramnarine	14
*R.S. Kaluwitharana	c Hooper	9
H.D.P.K. Dharmasena	not out	51
D.K. Liyanage	c and b L.R. Williams	43
M. Muralitharan	not out	5
S.C. de Silva		
	lb **9**, w **8**, nb **2**	19
	49 overs (for 8 wickets)	**248**

	O	M	R	W
Ambrose	7	1	19	1
Walsh	8	1	27	1
L.R. Williams	8	–	56	**3**
Rose	6	–	45	–
Hooper	10	1	40	1
Ramnarine	10	–	52	**2**

Fall of Wickets
1–**6**, 2–**19**, 3–**39**, 4–**89**, 5–**121**, 6–**139**, 7–**150**, 8–**241**

Umpires: E. Nicholls & L.H. Barker   *Man of the Match*: S.C. Williams   **West Indies won by 35 runs**

Kalpage flew from Sri Lanka as replacement. Chanderpaul, West Indies' outstanding player against India, was ruled out of the series against Sri Lanka because of a neck injury sustained in the last Red Stripe Cup match.

Floyd Reifer, the left-handed batsman who had enjoyed a fine season, Laurie Williams, the Jamaican medium-pacer, and Dinanath Ramnarine, Trinidad's leg-spinner, all earned places in the West Indian one-day side, as did Junior Murray following his double century for Windward Islands.

West Indies lost two early wickets, but Stuart Williams, 90 off 105 balls, and Brian Lara, two sixes and six fours in his 67 off 68 balls, added 124. Holder hit 41 off 30 balls towards the end of the innings, and Jayasuriya picked up five wickets in the final slog.

Sri Lanka were never really in the hunt, and the 91-run stand between Dharmasena and Liyanage came too late to influence the result.

8, 9 and 10 June 1997
at Recreation Ground, St John's, Antigua
Sri Lankans 192 for 6 dec. (R.S. Mahanama 65) and 398 for 4 dec. (R.P. Arnold 158, M.S. Atapattu 118, P.A. de Silva 80)
Leeward Islands 148 (M. Muralitharan 4 for 34) and 128 for 0 (A. Adams 68 not out, J. Mitchum 50 not out)
Match drawn

The Sri Lankans drew their only first-class match outside the Tests. The dominating feature of the game was a second wicket stand of 242 between Arnold and Atapattu.

Tillekeratne leaves the field with a broken arm in the first Test. (Gordon Brooks/Sportsline)

Test Series

West Indies v. Sri Lanka

West Indies relied on the side that had been successful against India with Reifer, a new cap, replacing the injured Chanderpaul. Walsh won a vital toss and asked Sri Lanka to bat first on a very moist pitch. The rapid fall of wickets was inevitable. Mahanama touched an Ambrose leg-cutter to the keeper, and Arnold prodded the same bowler to third slip. Aravinda de Silva made an unwise slash to cover so that Sri Lanka were 23 for 3 in the sixth over, all three wickets to Ambrose.

Jayasuriya and Ranatunga batted with courage and determined technical application to add 110. The two left-handers showed remarkable determination in spite of being struck about the body on numerous occasions. Sadly it was a misunderstanding that separated them. Ranatunga hit a no-ball from Walsh to mid-off and set out on a run to which his partner did not respond. He attempted to regain his ground too late and was beaten by Ambrose's throw to the keeper. Six runs later, Tillekeratne, having faced five balls, was struck on the arm by a ball from Walsh. He was wearing no arm-guard, and the arm was broken. His tour was over, and Sri Lanka had suffered another misfortune.

Jayasuriya, who is ever keen to punish the loose ball and hit two sixes and nine fours, was deceived by Hooper's quicker ball and bowled. His value as a one-day player is well known, but Jayasuriya is now a Test cricketer of maturity and substance. Kaluwitharana and Dharmasena offered defiance which took Sri Lanka past 200. Ambrose returned to round off the innings and when Sajeewa de Silva skied to cover the tall fast bowler had claimed his 300th wicket in Test cricket.

West Indies lost Williams, caught at mid-on, but they began the second day on 53 for 1.

Pushpakumara caused problems on the second morning. He had both Lara and Reifer caught behind, and Sajeewa de Silva accounted for Campbell so that four wickets were down at lunch. Off-spinner Muralitharan now took over. He sent back Hooper and Holder in successive overs, and the last six West Indian wickets went down for 21 runs in 50 minutes.

Sri Lanka had a lead of 34, and it had been well earned, but Ambrose now gnawed into their advantage. He had Jayasuriya taken at slip third ball, and Arnold, looking uncertain, and Mahanama fell to catches by the wicket-keeper. Aravinda de Silva counter-attacked, hitting a six and seven fours as he made 47 off 52 balls, but Bishop dismissed both him and Ranatunga in the same over. Dharmasena brought some stability to the lower order, but the absence of Tillekeratne was a dreadful blow, and Sri Lanka ended the day on 151 for 8. They added just one run the following morning, and West Indies had three days in which to score 187 to win.

An opening stand of 160 between Williams and Campbell, who seem to have solved West Indies' opening

problem, assured victory. Williams hit sixes off Muralitharan and Jayasuriya, but Muralitharan's off-spin impressed the West Indians. The margin of victory seemed comfortable, and the game was over half an hour before tea on the third day, but none of the luck had gone to Sri Lanka, and they pressed West Indies far harder than the score would suggest.

Ambrose was named Man of the Match.

West Indies were unchanged for the second game, and Sri Lanka replaced the injured Tillekeratne with Sanjeeva Ranatunga who has two Test hundreds to his credit. The match was played at Arnos Vale, which became Test cricket's 78th different venue. Sri Lanka won the toss and asked West Indies to bat on a pitch that offered pace and bounce.

The first day belonged entirely to Sri Lanka. In the second over, Williams gloved a catch to the keeper and Reifer was leg before first ball. Three overs later, Lara gave Sajeewa de Silva a simple return catch, and West Indies were 5 for 3. Campbell and Hooper repaired some of the damage, but a mixture of good bowling and cavalier batting saw West Indies all out for 147 in 44.4 overs.

Jayasuriya gave Sri Lanka just the start they needed. The West Indian bowlers provided him with width to play his strokes, and he raced to 50 off 62 balls. He lost Mahanama, Atapattu and, crucially, Aravinda de Silva

Sajeewa de Silva skies to cover, and Ambrose captures his 300th Test wicket. (Gordon Brooks/Sportsline)

First Test Match – West Indies v. Sri Lanka
13, 14, 15, 16, and 17 June 1997 at Recreation Ground, St John's, Antigua

Sri Lanka

	First Innings		Second Innings	
S.T. Jayasuriya	b Hooper	85	c Hooper, b Ambrose	0
R.S. Mahanama	c Browne, b Ambrose	1	c Browne, b Ambrose	14
R.P. Arnold	c Williams, b Ambrose	0	c Browne, b Ambrose	12
P.A. de Silva	c Walsh, b Ambrose	0	c Browne, b Bishop	47
A. Ranatunga (Capt)	run out	42	c Rose, b Bishop	13
H.P. Tillekeratne	retired hurt	1	absent hurt	–
*R.S. Kaluwitharana	hit wkt, b Bishop	23	(6) c Browne, b Walsh	16
H.D.P.K. Dharmasena	c Browne, b Ambrose	29	(7) c Walsh, b Rose	31
K.R. Pushpakumara	c Reifer, b Bishop	1	(8) c Williams, b Rose	8
S.C. de Silva	c Reifer, b Ambrose	6	(9) not out	2
M. Muralitharan	not out	6	(10) c Williams, b Rose	0
	b 4, lb 11, nb 14	29	lb 2, nb 7	9
		223		**152**

	O	M	R	W	O	M	R	W
Ambrose	13.1	3	37	5	9	–	41	3
Bishop	15	3	44	2	7	–	29	2
Walsh	11	–	46	–	10	–	37	1
Rose	10	2	32	–	9	1	43	3
Hooper	19	2	49	1				

West Indies

	First Innings		Second Innings	
S.L. Campbell	c Muralitharan, b S.C. de Silva	50	c Mahanama, b Muralitharan	79
S.C. Williams	c Arnold, b Pushpakumara	21	c sub (D.K. Liyanage), b Muralitharan	83
F.L. Reifer	c Kaluwitharana, b Pushpakumara	29	b Dharmasena	1
B.C. Lara	c Kaluwitharana, b Pushpakumara	0	c sub (D.K. Liyanage), b Muralitharan	4
C.L. Hooper	lbw, b Muralitharan	27	not out	6
R.I.C. Holder	c and b Dharmasena	28	not out	0
*C.O. Browne	c Jayasuriya, b Muralitharan	0		
I.R. Bishop	b Muralitharan	5		
C.E.L. Ambrose	not out	11		
F.A. Rose	b Muralitharan	0		
C.A. Walsh (Capt)	b Muralitharan	0		
	b 4, lb 6, nb 8	18	b 4, lb 2, w 1, nb 9	16
		189	(for 4 wickets)	**189**

	O	M	R	W	O	M	R	W
S.C. de Silva	13	1	56	1	9	2	35	–
Pushpakumara	15	2	62	3	8	–	38	–
Dharmasena	8	4	19	1	7	2	21	1
Muralitharan	23.4	13	34	5	21.2	5	72	3
Jayasuriya	1	–	8	–	4	–	17	–

Fall of Wickets
1–19, 2–19, 3–23, 4–133, 5–171, 6–206, 7–210, 8–216, 9–223
1–0, 2–17, 3–41, 4–85, 5–91, 6–113, 7–140, 8–151, 9–152

Fall of Wickets
1–40, 2–94, 3–97, 4–122, 5–168, 6–168, 7–172, 8–189, 9–189
1–160, 2–178, 3–182, 4–183

Umpires: L.H. Barker & R.S. Dunne

West Indies won by 6 wickets

Second Test Match – West Indies v. Sri Lanka
20, 21, 22, 23 and 24 June 1997 at Arnos Vale, Kingstown, St Vincent

West Indies

	First Innings		Second Innings	
S.L. Campbell	c Mahanama, b Dharmasena	20	b Pushpakumara	33
S.C. Williams	c Kaluwitharana, b Pushpakumara	0	c Jayasuriya, b Muralitharan	46
F.L. Reifer	lbw, b Pushpakumara	0	(4) c Kaluwitharana, b Pushpakumara	18
B.C. Lara	c and b S.C. de Silva	1	(3) c Jayasuriya, b Dharmasena	115
C.L. Hooper	c Atapattu, b Pushpakumara	81	c Kaluwitharana, b Dharmasena	34
R.I.C. Holder	c Atapattu, b Muralitharan	16	hit wkt, b Muralitharan	34
I.R. Bishop	b Muralitharan	11	lbw, b Muralitharan	0
*C.O. Browne	lbw, b Pushpakumara	0	lbw, b Muralitharan	0
C.E.L. Ambrose	b Pushpakumara	7	c Kaluwitharana, b S.C. de Silva	31
F.A. Rose	b Muralitharan	1	not out	0
C.A. Walsh (Capt)	not out	1	b Muralitharan	0
	b 3, lb 3, nb 3	9	b 4, lb 21, nb 7	32
		147		**343**

Sri Lanka

	First Innings		Second Innings	
S.T. Jayasuriya	lbw, b Hooper	90	b Walsh	17
R.S. Mahanama	c Browne, b Rose	28	c Browne, b Bishop	29
M.S. Atapattu	c Hooper, b Rose	7	b Walsh	10
P.A. de Silva	c Lara, b Hooper	35	b Walsh	78
A. Ranatunga (Capt)	c Lara, b Walsh	13	not out	72
S. Ranatunga	c Hooper, b Walsh	9	run out	2
*R.S. Kaluwitharana	c Browne, b Ambrose	7	hit wkt, b Walsh	2
H.D.P.K. Dharmasena	b Hooper	10	c Browne, b Ambrose	7
K.R. Pushpakumara	c Browne, b Hooper	0		
S.C. de Silva	not out	4	not out	1
M. Muralitharan	c Reifer, b Hooper	4	(9) c Holder, b Ambrose	0
	b 2, lb 3, nb 10	15	lb 3, nb 14	17
		222 (for 8 wickets)		**233**

	O	M	R	W	O	M	R	W
S.C. de Silva	13	2	46	1	17	1	62	1
Pushpakumara	12.4	1	41	5	19	2	81	2
Dharmasena	7	1	26	1	25	4	62	2
Muralitharan	12	1	28	3	41	13	113	5

	O	M	R	W	O	M	R	W
Ambrose	9	1	34	1	15	1	51	2
Walsh	22	3	62	2	24	2	73	4
Rose	12	1	44	2	6	1	24	–
Bishop	7	–	51	–	14	1	61	1
Hooper	13.4	5	26	5	9	3	21	–

Fall of Wickets
1–**2**, 2–**2**, 3–**5**, 4–**92**, 5–**126**, 6–**133**, 7–**140**, 8–**145**, 9–**147**
1–**62**, 2–**92**, 3–**143**, 4–**240**, 5–**272**, 6–**276**, 7–**286**, 8–**339**, 9–**343**

Fall of Wickets
1–**63**, 2–**75**, 3–**151**, 4–**178**, 5–**185**, 6–**196**, 7–**211**, 8–**211**, 9–**215**
1–**26**, 2–**55**, 3–**118**, 4–**189**, 5–**193**, 6–**208**, 7–**231**, 8–**231**

Umpires: S.A. Bucknor & D.B. Cowie

Match drawn

Pushpakumara leaps in joy as Lara is caught behind for 0 in the first Test. (Gordon Brooks/Sportsline)

shortly before the close, by which time Sri Lanka had a lead of ten and Jayasuriya was on 80.

The second day was a disappointment. An hour was lost to rain at the start, and progress was slow as Hooper bowled with intelligent variation. Conditions were not easy for batting, and for the second time in as many matches, Jayasuriya was denied the century he had deserved. Sri Lanka lost their last seven wickets for 44 in 15 overs, and their lead was restricted to 75. Hooper finished with his career-best bowling figures. Campbell and Williams scored 19 after another two hours had been lost to rain.

Four more hours were lost on the third day, which ended with Reifer and Lara in partnership and the score on 128 for 2. Lara batted with disciplined aggression and became the 11th West Indian batsman to score 4,000 runs in Test cricket. This was Lara at his responsible best. It was his tenth Test century and he hit 11 fours and a six. Having taken punishment from Lara, Muralitharan returned to wrap up the tail and claim his second five-wicket haul in the series. The discussion over his action in Australia has tended to obscure his quality as a bowler. The West Indians have no doubt as to his quality.

Sri Lanka needed 269 to win, and by the end of the fourth day they were 97 for 2 with Aravinda de Silva in full flow. He had cut, pulled and driven Bishop for 18 runs in one over, and the scoring rate overall was five an over.

Mahanama was out in the first hour of the last day which saw Walsh put in a yeoman spell of bowling. Arjuna Ranatunga and Aravinda de Silva, the Sri Lankan seniors, added 71, and the visitors were within 80 runs of victory when Walsh produced a magnificent yorker to hit de Silva's off stump. In between the rain, neither the younger Ranatunga nor Kaluwitherana could cope with the situation, and when, after a third break for rain, Ambrose removed Dharmasena first ball and Muralitharan third the game swung towards West Indies. Then the gloom descended, and Ranatunga, sensibly if reluctantly, accepted the draw.

It had been an unlucky tour for Sri Lanka, but they acquitted themselves well in adversity. West Indies' extended season had produced little. Rose had emerged, but the rest of the bowling was ageing, and the batting in the Red Stripe Cup had been generally poor. There was no sign of an immediate challenge to Australia's supremacy.

First-Class Averages

Batting

	M	Inns	NOs	Runs	HS	Av	100s	50s
C.B. Lambert	4	8	1	454	159	64.85	2	1
S. Chanderpaul	11	18	4	815	176*	58.21	2	5
S. Ragoonath	8	14	3	625	128	56.81	2	2
J.C. Adams	8	15	2	572	73	44.00		6
C.L. Hooper	12	20	2	791	129	43.94	3	2
B.C. Lara	13	22	–	965	135	43.86	3	5
F.L. Reifer	14	25	2	940	200	40.86	2	5
P.V. Simmons	4	6	1	200	116	40.00	1	1
J.R. Murray	8	15	1	547	218	39.07	2	1
R.D. Jacobs	10	15	3	464	107	38.66	1	2
S.C. Williams	16	26	1	964	141	38.56	4	2
A. Adams	3	6	2	153	69*	38.25		2
R.I.C. Holder	15	26	2	908	111	37.83	2	7
P.A. Wallace	12	21	–	787	121	37.47	1	5
K.L.T. Arthurton	9	15	1	488	95	34.85		4
L.V. Garrick	10	20	1	640	138	33.68	2	2
S.L. Campbell	15	25	1	790	109	32.91	1	4
Z.A. Haniff	4	7	–	229	71	32.71		3
D. Williams	9	13	1	360	55	30.00		
S.N. Proverbs	5	9	2	210	112*	30.00		2
R.G. Samuels	8	16	2	417	90*	29.78		3
R.O. Hurley	4	6	–	176	122	29.33	1	
R.N. Lewis	9	18	5	366	55*	28.15		1
R.L. Hoyte	5	8	2	167	50*	27.83		1
L.A. Roberts	8	13	1	319	65	26.58		2
A.F.G. Griffith	8	13	–	339	123	26.07	1	1
A.R. Percival	4	8	1	182	91	26.00		1
A. Haniff	3	5	–	128	62	25.60		1
L.R. Williams	10	17	4	331	102*	25.46	1	
M.D. Ventura	6	10	1	229	96	25.44		1
N.C. McGarrell	8	14	3	279	73	25.36		1
B.S. Murphy	10	17	5	299	43*	24.91		
J. Mitchum	5	10	1	224	89	24.88		2
D.S. Morgan	9	15	1	343	63	24.50		3
J.A.R. Sylvester	7	14	–	332	70	23.71		3
B.M. Watt	9	18	–	422	64	23.44		3
N.A. de Groot	8	15	1	328	63	23.42		3
R.M. Powell	7	10	–	228	51	22.80		1
M.D. Liburd	4	6	–	134	40	22.33		
H.R. Bryan	11	16	5	239	42*	21.72		
L.C. Weekes	6	9	2	150	38*	21.42		

Batting

	M	Inns	NOs	Runs	HS	Av	100s	50s
R.A.M. Smith	9	14	1	277	62	21.30		1
T.O. Powell	8	15	–	317	76	21.13		1
M. Bodoe	4	6	–	121	49	20.16		
W.E. Reid	10	17	5	240	54*	20.00		
C.E.L. Ambrose	10	13	3	189	37	18.90		
V. Nagamootoo	7	11	1	186	36	18.60		
I.R. Bishop	13	17	–	315	111	18.52	1	1
S.G.B. Ford	10	15	2	231	44	17.76		
D.R.E. Joseph	10	16	2	248	66	17.71		1
R.R. Sarwan	7	12	–	210	77	17.50		2
S.C.F. Joseph	7	12	–	197	49	16.41		
R.A. Marshall	9	18	–	295	46	16.38		
K. Martin	4	8	–	129	65	16.12		1
C.A. Davis	9	18	7	175	27*	15.90		
O.D. Gibson	11	17	–	268	49	15.76		
K.A. Mason	5	7	–	110	49	15.71		
F.A. Rose	16	20	3	263	96	15.47		1
M.V. Nagamootoo	7	11	1	154	56	15.40		1
C.O. Browne	12	20	4	245	78	15.31		1
D. Ganga	6	11	2	137	54	15.22		1
H.A.G. Anthony	6	9	1	117	29	14.62		
T.O. Rollock	7	11	1	137	53	13.70		1
V. Pope	6	12	–	161	34	13.41		
N.O. Perry	5	9	–	115	41	12.77		
D. Ramnarine	10	14	2	151	43	12.58		
D. Thomas	6	12	2	119	33*	11.90		

(qualification: 100 runs, average 10.00)

Bowling

	Overs	Mds	Runs	Wks	Av	Best	10/m	5/inn
M. Mills	57	11	138	10	13.80	5/33		1
F.A. Rose	420.5	84	1306	71	18.39	6/63	1	4
L.R. Williams	252.3	60	648	33	19.63	6/26		1
D.K. Marshall	100.1	27	295	15	19.66	6/62		1
C.E.L. Ambrose	268.3	75	575	29	19.82	5/37		2
W.K.L. Quinn	123.1	38	283	14	20.21	4/39		
W.E. Reid	348	109	812	40	20.30	4/72		

First-Class Averages (continued)

Bowling

	Overs	Mds	Runs	Wks	Av	Best	10/m	5/inn
T.O. Rollock	91	26	266	13	20.46	6/15		1
R.D. King	185.4	35	542	26	20.84	7/82		3
C.A. Davis	202.1	42	613	29	21.13	7/58		3
O.D. Gibson	322.4	64	990	46	21.52	5/57		1
R.A. Marshall	273.4	59	654	30	21.80	3/15		
D. Thomas	141.4	29	328	15	21.86	3/21		
H.R. Bryan	266.1	61	820	37	22.16	5/39		1
D. Ramnarine	365.1	89	848	38	22.31	5/69		1
C.A. Walsh	365.2	78	883	39	22.64	6/39		2
R. Dhanraj	164	32	417	18	23.16	4/18		
I.R. Bishop	360.3	71	1006	43	23.39	5/82		1
B.S. Murphy	203.2	49	496	21	23.61	5/85		1
M.J. Morgan	180.2	34	628	24	26.16	4/32		
P.T. Collins	114.1	14	423	16	26.43	4/36		
R.M. Powell	283	70	655	23	28.47	3/31		
D.S. McKenzie	76	14	292	10	29.20	4/35		
W.D. Phillip	452.2	123	1024	35	29.25	7/104		3
M. Dillon	324.1	56	1068	36	29.66	4/94		
M.V. Nagamootoo	321.5	80	872	29	30.06	4/59		
L.C. Weekes	134.5	23	393	13	30.23	3/46		

Bowling

	Overs	Mds	Runs	Wks	Av	Best	10/m	5/inn
R.N. Lewis	286.2	37	899	27	33.29	5/160		1
H.A.G. Anthony	138	23	401	12	33.41	3/32		
N.B Francis	129.1	15	436	13	33.53	2/37		
N.C. McGarrell	387.2	111	924	27	34.22	7/84	1	1
C.L. Hooper	258.1	83	539	15	35.93	5/26		2
P.I.C. Thompson	111	16	447	11	40.63	3/27		
C.E.L. Stuart	177	26	616	13	47.38	2/29		

(Qualification: 10 wickets)

Leading Fielders

42 – C.O. Browne (ct 40 / st 2); 36 – S.G.B. Ford (ct 35 / st 1); 27 – D. Williams (ct 20 / st 7); 26 – R.D. Jacobs (ct 21 / st 5); 19 – J.R. Murray (ct 16 / st 3); 17 – B.C. Lara; 16 S.C. Williams; 15 – V. Pope (ct 12 / st 3); 14 – P.A. Wallace, R.I.C. Holder and M.V. Magamootoo (ct 10 / st 4); 13 - R.L. Hoyte; 12 – C.L. Hooper and D. Ramnarine; 11 – L.V. Garrick, O.D. Gibson, D.S. Morgan and L. Reifer; 10 – R.N. Lewis

England

The England and Wales Cricket Board replaced the Test and County Cricket Board, and 1997 began with the game in England facing a revolutionary restructuring. There was to be much debate and discussion, and not everyone would be happy by the end of September, but initially there was the thrill of the Ashes Series. The Australians were coming, and, momentarily at least, talk of revolution was postponed.

The happy hopeful shape of the summer to come.
The England crowd at Headingley.
(George Herringshaw/ASP)

Oxford and Cambridge in first-class cricket
Benson and Hedges Cup
Australian Tour, Test and Texaco Series
Pakistan 'A' tour
NatWest Trophy
AXA Life League
The Britannic Assurance County Championship
First-class averages
Form Charts

It had been a revolutionary close season. A winter of discontent at Sussex had seen the chairman resign, the administration redesigned and former players, Tony Pigott and Robin Marlar, take control. It was Pigott who had brought about the revolution, and he and the much respected Robin Marlar, a former captain of the club sought to revitalise Sussex.

The troubles had started with the dismissal of Alan Wells as captain. Wells later moved to Kent, but by then the club had already lost Salisbury to Surrey, Speight to Durham and Danny Law to Essex.

Problems bubbled below the surface at Derbyshire where Chris Adams made his annual plea to move. One sympathises with Adams, a fine player who has not received the recognition he is due, but one wonders why he had signed a five-year contract presented to him the previous season. That all was not well at Derbyshire had been apparent from committee resignations, but few expected what happened some weeks into the season when Dean Jones relinquished the captaincy and left the club citing a lack of commitment from several players as his reason. The reasons have never been fully explained, but Geoffrey Boycott forwarded the view that Jones was a hard taskmaster, determined to win and horrified by the apathy and lack of ambition which seems to be the attitude of too many cricketers in England. It should not be forgotten that Jones had driven Derbyshire to second place in the County Championship in 1996.

The Australian David Boon took over the captaincy at Durham, and Gloucestershire were led by Mark Alleyne.

The extension of the West Indian season into June had meant that it was necessary for three or four counties to reassess their position with regard to their overseas player. The extension deprived Gloucestershire of the services of Courtney Walsh, their captain, and they offered the post to 'Jack' Russell. Russell could not agree terms with the county and they turned to Mark Alleyne as captain and Shaun Young, the Tasmanian all-rounder, as overseas player. These proved to be wise decisions.

Hampshire were able to engage Matthew Hayden when he was not selected in the Australian party, while Kent, denied Carl Hooper, signed Paul Strang of Zimbabwe. Strang is not only an excellent leg-spin bowler, but a very fine, totally committed cricketer in every sense. He will serve the game with refreshing vigour for many years.

Kent also made a shrewd move in appointing the former New Zealand Test player John Wright as manager and coach. He is a man of wisdom, charm and humility with a profound knowledge of the game.

Lancashire, too, started the season under new management, having wooed Davenall Whatmore from Sri Lanka. In spite of limited-over successes, the Lancashire faithful had voiced their disquiet at the county's miserable showing in the first-class game. Whatmore hoped to silence the critics, but he was not aided when it became obvious that Lancashire would be without Wasim Akram for most of the season because of a shoulder injury.

The reigning champions, Leicestershire, fought hard to acquire the services of the South African Neil Johnson when they learned that Phil Simmons was contracted to remain in the Caribbean, and Middlesex turned to another South African, the highly talented Jacques Kallis, when Greg Blewett was named in the Australian party. Surrey had to make a hasty readjustment when Brendon Julian was unexpectedly chosen and turned to Saqlain Mushtaq, the Pakistani off-spinner, a young cricketer of world class.

Northamptonshire chose Pakistani pace bowler Mohammad Akram, and Nottinghamshire contracted the fast bowling prodigy Mohammad Zahid only to discover that he was unfit and unable to play. They found an excellent replacement in Nathan Astle, the New Zealand all-rounder, an outstanding team-player of the utmost determination.

Michael Bevan had made a great impact at Yorkshire who had to face life without him when he was selected for the Australian party to tour England. They turned again to Australia and to Darren Lehmann who had seemed destined for an outstanding Test career until injury and eye problems intervened. He was to prove a more than adequate replacement for Bevan.

A new panel of England selectors was in place – Graveney, Gatting and Gooch. Gatting was soon to hand over the captaincy of Middlesex to Ramprakash, but he was to continue to play. No man has served a county better Gooch, as we shall see, felt that he had gone a season too far and was to retire in July. For the moment, however, expectation was high, the season had arrived, and we turned, inevitably, to Fenner's and The Parks.

The season begins. Lewis and Collingwood leave the pavilion at Oxford to open the innings for Durham. They shared a stand of 290. Both batsmen reached the highest scores of their careers with Jonathan Lewis making a double century on his debut for Durham. (Mark Thompson/Allsport)

Oxford and Cambridge Universities

15, 16 and 17 April
at Cambridge
Cambridge University 195 (E.T. Smith 85) and 156
(R.O. Jones 57 not out, K.J. Dean 4 for 39)
Derbyshire 363 for 7 dec. (A.S. Rollins 79, D.M. Jones 58,
V.P. Clarke 57, J.W.O. Freeth 4 for 101)
Derbyshire won by an innings and 12 runs

at Oxford
Durham 353 for 2 dec. (J.J.B. Lewis 210 not out,
P.D. Collingwood 107) and 144 for 3 dec.
(D.C. Boon 58)
Oxford University 153 (A.P. Scrini 58 not out,
I.A.G. Fulton 54, M.M. Betts 6 for 51) and 247 (C. Patel 50,
S.J.E. Brown 4 for 35)
Durham won by 97 runs

Two Australians led their counties to victories in the
opening matches of the season. Derbyshire fielded two
players who had previously appeared for two other counties,
Andy Hayhurst, Lancashire and Somerset, who had been
engaged primarily to look after the Second XI, and Vince
Clarke, Somerset and Leicestershire, who hit a maiden first-
class fifty. Kevin Dean returned his best bowling figures and
took three wickets in six balls.

Durham paraded four new players – skipper Boon,
Speight from Sussex, Speak from Lancashire, and Lewis
from Essex. Jonathan Lewis had made a century on the
occasion of his first-class debut for Essex. He improved on
that with a double century for Durham as he and
Collingwood shared an opening stand of 290 on the first day.
There was also a career-best bowling performance from the
promising but erratic pace man Melvyn Betts.

18, 19 and 20 April
at Cambridge
Leicestershire 451 for 3 dec. (A. Habib
175 not out, J.M. Dakin 103 not out, I.J Sutcliffe 99)
and 222 for 2 dec. (J.J. Whitaker 100 not out,
V.J. Wells 74)
Cambridge University 333 for 7 dec. (E.T. Smith 190)
and 51 for 1
Match drawn

18, 19 and 21 April
at Oxford
Oxford University 243 for 9 dec. (P.G. Morgan 60) and
193 for 7 (A.D. Mascarenhas 5 for 63)
Hampshire 415 for 5 dec. (J.P. Stephenson 140, M. Keech
127, K.D. James 53, J.M.M. Averis 5 for 98)
Match drawn

The wicket at Fenner's was a batsman's dream, and
Whitaker decided to allow the reigning champions some
practice. Dakin, an underused cricketer, made the highest
score of his career as did the mightily impressive Edward
Smith. A batsman of real quality, Smith had played once for
Kent at the end of the 1996 season.

Hampshire were encouraged by the form of the
medium pace bowler Dimitri Mascarenhas who had taken 16
wickets in two county matches during his previous, debut,
season. The honours really went to James Averis, who had
played in the Sunday League for Gloucestershire and who
took five wickets in what was his second first-class match.

23, 24 and 25 April
at Cambridge
Middlesex 359 for 2 dec. (M.W. Gatting 160 retired hurt,
P.E. Wellings 128 not out) and 160 for 2 (P.N. Weekes 101)
Cambridge University 235
Match drawn

at Oxford
Yorkshire 335 for 2 dec. (D. Byas 126 not out, A. McGrath
105 not out, M.D. Moxon 53) and 275 for 2 (B. Parker 138
not out, M.P. Vaughan 109)
Oxford University 114
Match drawn

Peter Wellings, playing his fifth first-class match for
Middlesex at the age of 27, hit a maiden century and laid
claim to a regular place in the side. He was one of three
centurions at Fenner's. There were four at Oxford, all to
Yorkshire for the loss of only four wickets in a match where
no play was possible on the third day.

7, 8 and 9 May
at Cambridge
Cambridge University 285 for 9 dec. (A. Singh 134,
E.T. Smith 72, D.R. Law 5 for 93) and 91 for 6
Essex 403 for 5 dec. (S.D. Peters 102 not out, D.R. Law 81,
P.J. Prichard 72, D.D.J. Robinson 59)
Match drawn

at Oxford
Oxford University 129 (G. Welch 4 for 39) and 115
(D.R. Brown 4 for 24)
Warwickshire 297 for 7 dec. (A.F. Giles 69 not out,
N.M.K. Smith 55 not out, D.P. Ostler 51)
Warwickshire won by an innings and 53 runs

Anurag Singh, the Cambridge captain, also of
Warwickshire, hit 134, and Danny Law had his first five-

A return to form and favour for James Hindson? Eight wickets for Nottinghamshire against Oxford University. (David Munden/Sportsline)

wicket haul for Essex. Stephen Peters made his second first-class hundred. Both of the England Under-19 batsman's centuries have come against Cambridge.

Bowlers thrived in the rain-scarred game in the Parks. Chetan Patel performed the hat-trick to reduce Warwickshire to 174 for 7, but Giles and Neil Smith added 123 in 12.5 overs.

14, 15 and 16 May
at Cambridge
Cambridge University 280 for 9 dec. (W.J. House 68, R.O. Jones 60, E.T. Smith 59, J.F. Brown 4 for 50) and 61 for 3
Northamptonshire 367 for 8 dec. (R.J. Bailey 105, A.L. Penberthy 56)
Match Drawn

at Oxford
Worcestershire 359 for 2 dec. (G.A. Hick 164 not out, W.P.C. Weston 119) and 192 for 8 dec. (V.S. Solanki 128 not out)
Oxford University 281 for 8 dec. (M.A. Wagh 64, R.D. Hudson 62) and 135 for 7
Match drawn

Graeme Hick hit the 91st century of his career in the match at Oxford. The former England player had declined to appear for the Duke of Norfolk's XI against the Australians at Arundel, preferring instead to try to restore form and favour in a first-class game. He and Philip Weston added 235 in 49 overs for the second wicket. Hick hit four sixes and 17 fours, and his 164 came off 179 balls. Rain was to end the match early, but not before Vikram Solanki had reached a maiden first-class hundred with three sixes and 18 fours. Solanki is a man of grace and charm and a young cricketer of immense potential.

---

17 May
at Cambridge

Cambridge University 297 for 6 (E.T. Smith 86, J. Ratledge 79, A. Singh 57)
Oxford University 224 (R.D. Hudson 79, C.G.R. Lightfoot 58, R.O. Jones 4 for 57)
Cambridge University won by 73 runs

The 50-over competition for the Johnson Fry Trophy was won for the second time in three years by Cambridge. Cambridge had retained eight blues from last year's side as opposed to Oxford's one, skipper Wagh. Ratledge and Smith took the light blues past 100 in the 30th over and scored 164 for the first wicket. Then came acceleration with Singh hitting 57 off 34 balls. Oxford were never in touch, and Robin Jones took three wickets in the 44th over. The innings ended in the 48th.

30, 31 May and 2 June
at Oxford
Oxford University 234 for 8 dec. (J.A.G. Fulton 50) and 190 (J.J. Bates 4 for 47, C.J. Batt 4 for 56)
Sussex 203 for 5 dec. (T.A. Radford 58 not out) and 222 for 1 (R.K. Rao 83 not out, T.A. Radford 83 not out)
Sussex won by 9 wickets

Led by Neil Lenham, Sussex fielded three debutants and four others with little experience of first-team cricket, but they contained Oxford on a beautiful wicket on the opening day and eventually won. Two of the debutants, off-break bowler Bates and left-arm medium pacer Batt, brought about an Oxford second innings collapse with the last eight wickets falling for 83 runs. Radford and Rao shared an unbeaten second wicket stand of 154.

5, 6 and 7 June
at Oxford
Glamorgan 422 for 2 dec. (M.J. Powell 200 not out, G.P. Butcher 101 not out, P.A. Cottey 83) and 137 for 2 dec.
Oxford University 284 for 9 dec. (M.A. Wagh 116, P.G. Morgan 63, S.D. Thomas 5 for 95) and 278 for 5 (M.A. Wagh 101, C. Patel 63 not out)
Oxford University won by 5 wickets

Oxford University beat a county side for the first time in four years in a match studded with fine individual performances. On the opening day Michael Powell, 20 years old and making his first-class debut, hit 200 off 213 balls with a six and 31 fours. He became only the third batsman this century to score a double century in English cricket on his debut. He and Butcher savaged 171 in 18 overs in an unbroken third wicket partnership. Mark Wagh kept Oxford in touch with a century and when the University were set a target of 276 in three hours ten minutes plus 20 overs Wagh hit his second century of the match and his side won off the penultimate ball.

4, 15 and 16 June
at Cambridge
Durham 288 for 2 dec. (N.J. Speak 124 not out,
D.C. Boon 105 not out) and 32 for 0
Cambridge University 188 for 2 dec.
(E.T. Smith 99)
Match drawn

4, 16 and 17 June
at Oxford
Nottinghamshire 324 for 4 dec. (P.R. Pollard 115
retired hurt, A.A. Metcalfe 78, G.F. Archer 50 not out)
and 166 for 4 dec. (R.T. Robinson 51 not out,
N.A. Gie 50)
Oxford University 124 (J.E. Hindson 4 for 28) and
248 for 6 (C. Patel 51 not out, J.A.G. Fulton 51,
E. Hindson 4 for 97)
Match drawn

Speak and Boon put on 203 for Durham's third wicket at
Fenner's, while Nottinghamshire welcomed a return to form
by left-arm spinner James Hindson. Hindson, once seen as
a potential England player, had suffered a period of decline,
but he is still only 23 years old.

20, 21 and 22 June
at Chelmsford
Oxford University 120 (N.F. Williams 5 for 55)
Essex 34 for 0
Match drawn
Under 64 overs were bowled in the match due to rain.

28, 29 and 30 June
at Canterbury
Kent 245 (M.J. Walker 62, E.J. How 5 for 59) and 193 for 5
(N.J. Llong 99, D.P. Fulton 57)
Cambridge University 187 (E.T. Smith 54,
J.B.D. Thompson 4 for 58)
Match drawn

at Taunton
Oxford University 241 for 8 dec. (M.A. Wagh 125 not
out) and 186 (R.W. Sladdin 5 for 60)
Somerset 473 for 7 dec. (S.C. Ecclestone 133, P.D. Bowler
123, M. Burns 56)
Somerset won by an innings and 46 runs

The Universities engaged in their last county matches
before the Varsity game, but rain deprived Cambridge of the
final day at Canterbury. Wagh hit his third hundred of the
season but damaged his left hand in attempting to take a
return catch when Somerset batted. He went in at number
eleven in the second innings in a brave but vain attempt to
stave off defeat. Somerset included the former Derbyshire
left-arm spinner Sladdin in their side.

Varsity Match

2, 3 and 4 July
at Lord's
Cambridge University 358 for 8 dec. (W.J. House 94,
A. Singh 91, R.O. Jones 58, C. Patel 6 for 110) and
239 for 4 dec. (J. Ratledge 100 not out)
Oxford University 272 (M.A. Wagh 82, J.A.G. Fulton 78,
P.S. Jones 6 for 67) and 249 for 8 (C.G.R. Lightfoot 61,
A.N. Janisch 4 for 71)
Match drawn

The 152nd Varsity Match will be remembered for the fact
that the two captains, Anurag Singh of Cambridge and Mark
Wagh of Oxford, were from the same school, King Edward's,
Birmingham, and were both on the Warwickshire staff.
Singh's light blues started as favourites, and even the loss of
Smith and Ratledge for 48 did not lessen their power. Singh
and Robin Jones added 138 in 34 overs before both fell to
the worthy Patel, who claimed a career-best six wickets.
Will House hit two sixes and 14 fours as he made 94 off 90
balls, and Singh declared at 358 for 8, made in 80 overs.
How dismissed Lightfoot before the close, and Cambridge
ended the first day very much on top.

Within 12 overs of the second morning, Oxford were
87 for 4. Wagh found an ally in Fulton, and the pair added
103 runs in 28 overs of quality batting. The turning point
came when Steffan Jones knocked back Wagh's middle
stump. The medium-pacer quickly mopped up the tail to
emulate Patel with a career-best six wickets.

Cambridge led by 86 runs, and a declaration at lunch
on the last day would have given them a fine chance of
victory, but Singh delayed and allowed Ratledge to reach
his century. Oxford were left a daunting target of 326 in 20
minutes under two sessions. They made a brave attempt, but
Cambridge finished just two wickets short of victory – the
price of sentiment?

*Michael Powell of Glamorgan hit 200 off 213 balls on the occasion
of his first-class debut v. Oxford University in The Parks, 5 June.
(Clive Mason/Allsport)*

Cambridge University First-Class Matches Batting, 1997

Player	M	Inns	NO	Runs	100	HS	Av
J. Radledge	8	12	1	268	—	100*	24.36
E.T. Smith	8	12	2	683	2	190	68.30
A. Singh	8	11	1	354	1	134	35.40
W.J. House	8	11	1	293	1	94	29.30
R.O. Jones	8	12	3	325	—	60	36.11
Q.J. Hughes	8	12	3	197	—	47*	21.88
M.W. Dawson	4	7	2	35	—	23	5.00
P.S. Jones	7	8	2	116	—	36	19.33
D.R.H. Churton	7	7	—	177	—	44	29.50
J.W.O. Freeth	7	5	2	9	—	7*	3.00
E.J. How	8	4	—	0	—	0	0.00
Imram Mohammad	1	1	—	12	—	12	12.00
P. Schaffer	3	1	—	12	—	12	12.00
A.N. Janiseh	4	3	1	18	—	11	6.00
M.R.K. Bailey	—	1	—	6	—	6*	—

Team match totals

Match	Total	Wickets	Result
v. Derbyshire (Cambridge) 15–17 April	195 / 156	10 / 10	L
v. Leicestershire (Cambridge) 18–20 April	333 / 51	7 / 1	D
v. Middlesex (Cambridge) 23–25 April	235	10	D
v. Essex (Cambridge) 7–9 May	285 / 91	9 / 6	D
v. Northamptonshire (Cambridge) 14–16 May	280 / 61	9 / 3	D
v. Durham (Cambridge) 14–16 June	188	2	D
v. Kent (Canterbury) 28–30 June	187	10	D
Varsity Match (Lord's) 2–4 July	358 / 239	8 / 4	D

Extras (Byes / Leg-byes / Wides / No-balls) recorded per innings.

Fielding figures
10 – W.J. House and D.R.H. Churton (ct 9 / st 1)
4 – R.O. Jones
3 – A. Singh
2 – J.W.O. Freeth and E.T. Smith
1 – E.J. How, M.W. Dawson, Q.J. Hughes, M.R.K. Bailey and sub

Cambridge University First-Class Matches Bowling

Match	P.S. Jones	E.J. How	M.W.W. Dawson	J.W.O. Freeth	W.J. House	R.O. Jones	Q.J. Hughes	P. Schaffer	A. Singh	A.N. Janisch	Byes	Leg-byes	Wides	No-balls	Total	Wkts
v. Derbyshire (Cambridge) 15–17 April	27-3-76-1	11-1-43-0	17-0-55-0	22-1-101-4	5-1-14-0	14-3-39-1					23	12	2		363	7
v. Leicestershire (Cambridge) 18–20 April	11.4-0-51-1	20-1-98-1 / 8-1-40-0	12.2-1-64-0 / 3-0-24-0	13-0-78-0 / 7-1-33-1	22-3-78-0 / 9-2-24-0	18-1-70-1 / 13.1-1-77-1					5	7		8	451 / 222	3 / 2
v. Middlesex (Cambridge) 23–25 April		18-5-70-1 / 10.4-2-58-1		26-2-110-0 / 8-0-31-1	10-0-61-0 / 3-0-20-0	10-0-51-0 / 7-2-25-0	4-0-23-0	20-5-58-1 / 8-3-19-0			4	5	8		359 / 160	2 / 2
v. Essex (Cambridge) 7–9 May	16-3-49-1	13-5-25-0	11-2-56-0	27-3-101-2	4-0-21-0	17-1-66-0	16.2-3-73-2		1-0-5-0		5	4	4	4	403	5
v. Northamptonshire (Cambridge) 14–16 May	15-1-48-0	22-5-59-2	16-3-41-0		6-1-17-0	32-5-116-3	8-3-18-1		2-1-5-0	14.5-2-43-2	3	4			367	8
v. Durham (Cambridge) 14–16 June	22-6-70-2	21-3-71-0 / 7-4-10-0		10-0-60-0	12-3-27-0	12-3-27-0	6-1-9-0			6-0-46-0 / 7-2-0-0	6	14	6	8	288 / 32	2 / 0
v. Kent (Canterbury) 28–30 June	19-0-87-1	15-2-59-5 / 13-3-36-0		9-4-21-1 / 8-2-28-2	3-2-12-0 / 3-0-11-0 / 1-0-2-0	2.3-0-12-1 / 10-1-47-1 / 5-0-23-0	1-0-5-0			13-4-43-2 / 5-1-17-0	4 / 7	1 / 2	2	10	245 / 195	10 / 5
v. Varsity Match (Lord's) 2–4 July	16.3-4-45-2 / 28.4-10-67-6 / 21-7-81-3	25-6-74-1 / 10-2-42-1		11-2-30-0 / 8-1-16-0			35.2-7-128-3		3-1-10-0	9-0-59-1 / 15-1-71-4	9 / 8	5 / 8	14 / 12	2 / 10	272 / 249	10 / 8

Bowler's average:
- P.S. Jones: 176.5-34-574-17, 33.76
- E.J. How: 193.4-40-685-12, 57.08
- M.W.W. Dawson: 59.2-6-240-0, —
- J.W.O. Freeth: 149-16-609-11, 55.36
- W.J. House: 66-9-260-0, —
- R.O. Jones: 148.4-17-580-9, 64.44
- Q.J. Hughes: 35.2-7-128-3, 42.66
- P. Schaffer: 28-8-77-1, 77.00
- A. Singh: 3-1-10-0, —
- A.N. Janisch: 79.5-10-299-9, 33.22

Fielding figures
13 – A.P.Scrini
7 – M.A.Wagh
6 – J.A.G.Fulton
4 – P.G.Morgan
2 – C.Patel, C.G.R.Lightfoot and R.D.Hudson
1 – N.E.F.Laughton, L.G.Buchanan, J.M.M.Averis and C.M.Battarbee

Oxford University First-Class Matches Batting, 1997

Batsman	M	Inns	NO	Runs	HS	Av
R.D.Hudson	11	20	2	202	62	11.22
J.E.Haynes	2	4	1	13	9	3.25
C.G.R.Lightfoot	11	16	–	289	61	18.06
B.W.Byrne	11	20	–	354	49	17.70
J.J.Bull	3	5	1	49	30	12.25
J.A.G.Fulton	10	19	–	451	78	23.73
N.E.F.Laughton	1	2	–	6	5	3.00
C.Patel	11	20	4	411	63*	25.68
A.P.Scrini	11	15	6	253	58*	21.08
J.M.M.Averis	9	15	4	276	42	25.09
D.F.Mather	2	3	1	10	5*	5.00
M.A.Wagh	10	18	1	684	125*	40.23
P.G.Morgan	10	18	1	444	63	26.11
L.G.Buchanan	10	14	4	168	43*	16.80
G.J.Wright	3	2	–	0	0*	0.00
C.M.Battarbee	7	8	6	29	10*	14.50
N.G.Pirihi	7	3	–	15	15	5.00
J.R.Cockcroft	7	1	–	1	1	1.00

Match columns (left to right): v. Durham 15–17 April (Oxford); v. Hampshire 18–21 April (Oxford); v. Yorkshire 23–25 April (Oxford); v. Warwickshire 7–9 May (Oxford); v. Worcestershire 14–16 May (Oxford); v. Sussex 30 May–2 June (Oxford); v. Glamorgan 5–7 June (Oxford); v. Nottinghamshire 14–17 June (Oxford); v. Essex 20–22 June (Chelmsford); v. Somerset 28–30 June (Taunton); v. Varsity Match 2–4 July (Lord's).

Match results / totals:

	Durham	Hampshire	Yorkshire	Warwickshire	Worcestershire	Sussex	Glamorgan	Nottinghamshire	Essex	Somerset	Varsity
Total	153	243/193	114	129/115	281/135	234/190	284/278	248	120	241/186	272/249
Wickets	10	9/7	10	10/10	8/7	10/10	9/5	6	10	8/10	10/8
Result	L	D	D	L	D	L	W	D	D	L	D

Oxford University First-Class Matches Bowling

Bowler	Overs–Mdns–Runs–Wkts (season)	Average
C.Patel	309–48–1261–27	46.70
J.M.M.Averis	255.2–36–1028–16	64.25
D.P.Mather	45–7–190–2	95.00
B.W.Byrne	99–11–439–3	146.33
R.D.Hudson	41.5–184–0	–
C.G.R.Lightfoot	21–2–126–0	–
M.A.Wagh	194–36–669–6	111.50
C.M.Battarbee	150.4–21–627–11	57.00
G.J.Wright	46–7–246–1	246.00
J.A.G.Fulton	5–0–18–0	–

Bowling match list: v. Durham 15–17 April (Oxford); v. Hampshire 18–21 April; v. Yorkshire 23–25 April; v. Warwickshire 7–9 May; v. Worcestershire 14–16 May; v. Sussex 30 May–2 June; v. Glamorgan 5–7 June; v. Nottinghamshire 14–17 June (Oxford); v. Essex 20–22 June (Chelmsford); v. Somerset 28–30 June (Taunton); v. Varsity Match 2–4 July (Lord's).

Benson and Hedges Cup

Of the 18 first-class counties, Durham, Glamorgan and Sussex began the 1997 season never having won the trophy. They may well have looked in envy at Lancashire, the holders, who had won the cup on four occasions, a record, and were strongly tipped to win again in 1997.

28 April
at Chelmsford
Glamorgan 210 (H. Morris 67)
Essex 211 for 5 (R.C. Irani 82 not out)
Essex (2 pts) won by 5 wickets
(Gold Award: R.C. Irani)

at Bristol
Gloucestershire 281 for 6 (N.J. Trainor 62, S. Young 52, R.S.C. Martin-Jenkins 4 for 57)
British Universities 159 (T.M.B. Bailey 52, M.C.J. Ball 4 for 23)
Gloucestershire (2 pts) won by 122 runs
(Gold Award: S. Young)

at Leicester
Leicestershire 371 for 6 (D.L. Maddy 97, I.J. Sutcliffe 59)
Scotland 193 for 6
Leicestershire (2 pts) won by 178 runs
(Gold Award: D.L. Maddy)

at The Oval
Surrey 257 (A.J. Stewart 51, M.V. Fleming 5 for 54)
Kent 262 for 6 (M.J. Walker 56)
Kent (2 pts) won by 4 wickets
(Gold Award: M.V. Fleming)

Irish wicket-keeper Andy Patterson is exuberant after stumping Dutch. Patterson also hit 24 off 15 balls to play a vital part in Ireland's famous victory. (Inpho/Allsport)

Decker Curry and Hansie Cronje celebrate Ireland's triumph over Middlesex. (Inpho/Allsport)

at Hove
Sussex 232 for 7 (C.W.J. Athey 66)
Hampshire 183 (J.P. Stephenson 65)
Sussex (2 pts) won by 49 runs
(Gold Award: P.W. Jarvis) .

at Worcester
Worcestershire 96 (D.R. Brown 5 for 31)
Warwickshire 97 for 4
Warwickshire (2 pts) won by 6 wickets
(Gold Award: D.R. Brown)

28 and 29 April
at Dublin (Castle Avenue)
Ireland 281 for 4 (W.J. Cronje 94 not out, J.D. Curry 75)
Middlesex 235
Ireland (2 pts) won by 46 runs
(Gold Award: J.D. Curry)

at Old Trafford
Yorkshire 203
Lancashire 154 (N.H. Fairbrother 64 not out)
Yorkshire (2 pts) won by 49 runs
(Gold Award: C.E.W. Silverwood)

at Lakenham
Minor Counties 256 for 7 (R.N. Dalton 76, M.A. Fell 67)
Derbyshire 260 for 4 (C.J. Adams 138)
Derbyshire (2 pts) won by 6 wickets
(Gold Award: C.J. Adams)

at Trent Bridge
Durham 230 for 5 (D.C. Boon 64 not out)
Nottinghamshire 234 for 5 (G.F. Archer 111 not out)
Nottinghamshire (2 pts) won by 5 wickets
(Gold Award: G.F. Archer)

The first round of zonal matches in the Benson and Hedges Cup suffered from rain interruptions, but all games were completed and surprises abounded.

Glamorgan had seemed set for a big score against Essex, reaching 140 for 2 in the 28th over with Morris and Maynard going strongly. They were blunted by Irani and Grayson and some excellent Essex fielding. Robert Rollins, who had seemed destined to miss most of the season through injury, made two stumpings and held three catches. Essex were reduced to 95 for 4, with Hussain unable to bat because of a ricked neck. He was not needed. Irani, having taken three wickets in his ten overs, hit a powerful unbeaten 82, and Essex won with 6.5 overs to spare.

At Bristol, the Australian all-rounder Shaun Young took the Gold Award on his first appearance in the competition. He hustled the score along with his left-handed batting and bowled four economic overs. The Universities bowled well, with Robin Martin-Jenkins taking four prime wickets with his medium pace.

Scotland's ICC Trophy successes were a distant memory as Leicestershire hit the highest score since the competition had been reduced to 50 overs. Maddy and

Hampshire captain John Stephenson bowls Neil Taylor of Sussex, but Sussex win the opening match at Hove by 49 runs. This was one of Taylor's rare failures in the competition. The former Kent batsman has now scored more Benson and Hedges Cup centuries than any other player with the exception of Graham Gooch. (Laurence Griffiths/Allsport)

Sutcliffe made 159 in 25 overs for the first wicket. Scotland adopted batting practice.

Surrey made a rather frenetic 257 in 49.5 overs against Kent, but their bowlers showed greater calm. Salisbury was particularly impressive and took the wicket of top-scorer Walker at a cost of 31 runs in his ten overs. Kent arrived at the last over needing seven to win, which was reduced to one off the last ball. Mark Ealham settled the matter by hitting Ben Hollioake over mid-wicket for six.

Sussex put their woes behind them to beat Hampshire even though they were without Lewry and Kirtley, both injured. They were admirably served by three Yorkshire exiles, Athey, Robinson, who bowled tidily, and Jarvis who made an unbeaten 42 off 38 balls and took 3 for 30 in nine overs.

Put in to bat on a damp pitch, Worcestershire were destroyed by Dougie Brown whose 5 for 31 were his best figures in limited-over cricket. Worcestershire were 56 for 9 before Lampitt and Newport added 36 for the last wicket.

The great surprise was in Dublin. Put in to bat, Ireland were given a rollicking start by Decker Curry, who hit debutant Simon Cooke for two sixes in his 75 off 93 balls. Gatting had to turn to his spinners for containment, but his bowlers had little respite as the South African captain Hansie Cronje, playing and coaching in Ireland, made a splendidly crafted, unbeaten 94 off 82 balls. Facing a daunting target of 282, Middlesex needed one batsman to make a big innings, but, although many got started, none progressed past 34. When rain ended play on the Monday, Middlesex were 134 for 6 from 32.2 overs. All the main batsmen, save Brown, were gone, and when he was out on Tuesday Middlesex were beaten in spite of Fraser's brave efforts.

Only 10.5 overs were possible on the Monday at Old Trafford, and Yorkshire made 43 without loss. They lost wickets regularly on the Tuesday and were all out in 48 overs. Silverwood, Gough and Hartley struck early when Lancashire batted before Fairbrother and Austin shared a fifth wicket stand of 67. Silverwood returned to dismiss Austin and Hegg, and the tail failed to support Fairbrother. One could not imagine a worse start for the holders than to lose at home to Yorkshire.

When Jones won the toss and asked Minor Counties to bat and they subsided to 31 for 3, Larkins among the fallen, it seemed that a predictable rout was on the way. The rallying point came in a fifth wicket stand of 76 in ten overs between Dalton and Fell. Richard Dalton, once of Northamptonshire now of Bedfordshire, made 76 off 59 balls, and Derbyshire had to chase 257 at five runs an over. Chris Adams got his side off to a whirlwind start and was perched on 95 with the score on 166 for 2 from 32 overs when rain fell. His hundred came off 91 balls, and Derbyshire won with 11 balls to spare.

Nottinghamshire, too, were taken to a second day by the weather, and their victory, with three balls to spare, came thanks to Graeme Archer's first century in limited-over cricket. His unbeaten 111 came off 125 balls.

---

30 April

at Cambridge
British Universities 217 for 6
Sussex 198 (V.C. Darkes 58, M.J. Chilton 5 for 26)
British Universities (2 pts) won by 19 runs
(Gold Award: M.J Chilton)

at Chester-le-Street
Durham 225 for 6 (D.C. Boon 103)
Northamptonshire 161 (R.J. Bailey 62, S.J.E. Brown 6 for 30)
Durham (2 pts) won by 64 runs
(Gold Award: S.J.E. Brown)

at Bristol
Gloucestershire 280 for 7 (R.J. Cunliffe 113, S. Young 67)
Surrey 282 for 7 (B.C. Hollioake 69, A.D. Brown 66)
Surrey (2 pts) won by 3 wickets
(Gold Award: R.J. Cunliffe)

at Canterbury
Hampshire 207 (M.V. Fleming 5 for 27)
Kent 211 for 8 (M.J. Walker 83, N.J. Llong 55)
Kent (2 pts) won by 2 wickets
(Gold Award: M.V. Fleming)

at Old Trafford
Lancashire 223 (J.E.R. Gallian 52)
Derbyshire 225 for 4 (K.J. Barnett 112 not out)
Derbyshire (2 pts) won by 6 wickets
(Gold Award: K.J. Barnett)

at Leicester
Leicestershire 295 for 7 (D.L. Maddy 101, V.J. Wells 70)
Nottinghamshire 218
Leicestershire (2 pts) won by 77 runs
(Gold Award: D.L. Maddy)

at Lord's
Middlesex 226 for 8 (M.R. Ramprakash 77, J.C. Pooley 50 not out)
Essex 227 for 9 (S.G. Law 53)
Essex (2 pts) won by one wicket
(Gold Award: M.C. Ilott)

at Taunton
Somerset 258 for 9 (M.N. Lathwell 77, R.J. Harden 68)
Glamorgan 117
Somerset (2 pts) won by 141 runs
(Gold Award: M.N. Lathwell)

at Edgbaston
Warwickshire 261 for 7 (D.R. Brown 62, A.J. Moles 60)
Minor Counties 106 (G.C. Small 5 for 23)
Warwickshire (2 pts) won by 155 runs
(Gold Award: G.C. Small)

at Leeds
Worcestershire 199 for 9
Yorkshire 187 for 7 (P.J. Newport 4 for 37)
Worcestershire (2 pts) won by 12 runs
(Gold Award: P.J. Newport)

Four counties claimed their second win in two matches and so began to look optimistically towards the quarter-finals. Five counties suffered their second defeat and faced elimination. Among the five were Lancashire, the holders, who were resoundingly beaten by Derbyshire. Winners for the past two seasons, Lancashire never truly recovered from being reduced to 29 for 4. Gallian and Fairbrother added 93, and, at 122 in the 24th over, the Red Rose still looked set for a big score. Both batsmen missed straight balls from inexperienced spinner Glenn Roberts, and Graham Lloyd, a player very much in form, seemed wasted at number seven as his side were bowled out in 44 overs. Kim Barnett launched Derbyshire's challenge with a century off 136 balls and when 67 were needed from the last ten overs Krikken, 42 not out, batted with calm and authority to bring victory with nine balls to spare.

British Universities gained their fourth win against county opposition in ten years when they bowled out Sussex at Fenner's inside 49 overs. The students had batted steadily to score 217, and Greenfield and Drakes began Sussex's reply with an 87-run partnership. The university bowlers maintained relentless pressure, P.S. Jones took one for 22 in 10 overs, and the last eight wickets went down for 74 runs. Medium-pacer Mark Chilton of Durham University and Lancashire had the remarkable figures of 6.3-0-26-5 to take the Gold Award.

David Boon made his first century for Durham in a most welcome victory over Northamptonshire. Durham's new captain did not take the individual award. That went, for the first time, to Simon Brown who bowled splendidly for his six wickets and also held two catches.

Choosing to bat first on a flat pitch, Gloucestershire lost Lynch in the second over, but Cunliffe's century helped towards a formidable score. He and Young put on a county record 169 for the third wicket. Surrey lost the services of Stewart as wicket-keeper from the 31st over. He hurt a hand, and Shahid had to take over. This gave some benefit to the home side in the closing overs of the innings, but Stewart was fit to open the Surrey innings when Butcher strained a groin muscle after crashing into boundary boards when fielding. Stewart made only seven, but Surrey got off to a flying start with Brown hitting 12 fours and Ben Holioake hitting a six and eight fours. Adam Holioake and Chris Lewis maintained the momentum and victory came with four balls to spare.

Matthew Fleming gained his second Gold Award in three days for his best bowling figures in the competition, but Kent had no easy passage. They were 116 for 5 on a pitch of uneven bounce before Walker, 83 off 106 balls, and Llong, 72, staged a recovery. Then three wickets fell for seven runs. Paul Strang halted the decline and made the winning hit with 26 balls to spare.

Leicestershire made the highest score of the round for the second time running, and, like Fleming, Maddy won his second Gold Award in three days. He made 101 off 93 deliveries, and he and Wells added 122 in 18 overs for the second wicket after Whitaker had retired hurt. Johnson, who had arrived from South Africa only a few hours before the match, took 2 for 38 on his debut, and Notting-hamshire were never in the hunt.

Essex made very hard work of beating Middlesex. Their bowlers did a reasonable job in restricting Middlesex to 226, with Ilott capturing 3 for 28. Essex looked set for a comfortable win when they needed 52 from the last 15 overs with seven wickets standing, but there was some unin-

Durham's Simon Brown, 6 for 30, in the victory over Northamptonshire. (Nigel French/ASP)

telligent and intemperate middle-order batting, and the last over arrived with four runs needed and three wickets standing. Rollins and Ilott were run out off the first and fifth balls, and Cowan was left to score two off the last ball. A hit to deep mid-off and a slight misfield by debutant Blanchett gave Essex their narrow win. Tight bowling by Dutch and Weekes had done much to put Middlesex back in the game.

Glamorgan rued dropped catches against Somerset, and they were never in contention once Caddick had produced an opening spell of 3 for 20 in seven overs. Glamorgan were 96 for 9, and it was Parkin and Watkin who gave some respectability.

Gladstone Small won his first Gold Award as Warwickshire overwhelmed Minor Counties, but Yorkshire and Worcestershire had a tense battle at Headingley. The pitch was slow, hardly suitable for a one-day game, and batsmen struggled. It transpired that when the last Worcestershire pair, Lampitt and Brinkley, took 19 from White's last over of the innings they won the match. Lehmann, making his debut for Yorkshire, was one of four batsmen to fall to Newport. Vaughan and McGrath added 80 for the fourth wicket, but the run-rate flagged, and 21 off the last over was a requirement beyond the powers of Hartley and Gough.

Matthew Fleming, Kent medium-pace bowler and hard-hitting opening batsman, won the Gold Award in the first two rounds of zonal matches and was the leading wicket-taker in the competition. (George Herringshaw/ASP)

2 May

at Derby
Yorkshire 260 for 7 (M.D. Moxon 52)
Derbyshire 260 for 7 (K.J. Barnett 88)
Yorkshire (2 pts) won on higher score after 25 overs
(Gold Award: R.D. Stemp)

at Cardiff
Glamorgan 252 for 7 (A. Dale 100, H. Morris 76, K.P. Dutch 4 for 42)
Middlesex 245 (J.H. Kallis 72)
Glamorgan (2 pts) won by 7 runs
(Gold Award: A Dale)

at Southampton
Gloucestershire 263 for 9 (M.A. Lynch 87)
Hampshire 261 for 9 (R.A. Smith 92, S. Young 4 for 54)
Gloucestershire (2 pts) won by 2 runs
(Gold Award: M.A. Lynch)

at Canterbury
Sussex 152 (P.W. Jarvis 63, P.A. Strang 4 for 27)
Kent 154 for 4 (M.J. Walker 69)
Kent (2 pts) won by 6 wickets
(Gold Award: D.W. Headley)
at Trent Bridge

Nottinghamshire 218 for 9 (M.P. Dowman 92, Mohammad Akram 4 for 47)
Northamptonshire 221 for 2 (R.J. Bailey 73 not out, D.J. Capel 68)
Northamptonshire (2 pts) won by 8 wickets
(Gold Award: D.J. Capel)

at Forfar
Scotland 150 for 8 (M.J. Smith 55 not out)
Durham 154 for 2 (M.J. Foster 73 not out)
Durham (2 pts) won by 8 wickets
(Gold Award: M.J. Smith)

at Taunton
Somerset 349 for 7 (S.C. Ecclestone 92)
Ireland 128 (Mushtaq Ahmed 7 for 24)
Somerset (2 pts) won by 221 runs
(Gold Award: Mushtaq Ahmed)

at The Oval
British Universities 198 (W.J. House 93)
Surrey 199 for 4 (A.J. Stewart 86 not out)
Surrey (2 pts) won by 6 wickets
(Gold Award: W.J. House)

at Edgbaston
Lancashire 208 for 8 (Wasim Akram 52 not out, A.A. Donald 5 for 25)
Warwickshire 208 (G. Welch 55 not out, T.L. Penney 55)
Lancashire (2 pts) won on losing fewer wickets with scores level
(Gold Award: Wasim Akram)

at Worcester
Minor Counties 177 (R.N. Dalton 69, D.A. Leatherdale 4 for 13)
Worcestershire 181 for 6 (T.M. Moody 50)
Worcestershire (2 pts) won by 4 wickets
(Gold Award: R.N. Dalton)

The positions in Group A became extremely tense after two of the closest possible finishes were to leave the group with four counties tied on four points each from three matches. At Derby, Yorkshire chose to bat first and were well placed at 150 for 2, but the later order failed to capitalise fully on the position. The significant factor, however, was that Yorkshire reached 116 for 2 after 25 overs. Barnett kept Derbyshire up with the required rate, but he was caught at long-on after making 88 off 130 balls, and Stemp frustrated the middle order. The last over arrived with 11 needed, and when Silverwood yorked Krikken with the second ball the odds were much in favour of Yorkshire. With six needed off the last ball, Yorkshire seemed to have won when DeFreitas could manage only two, but umpire Constant had called 'no-ball' for a delivery above waist height so that Derbyshire had four runs to their credit and another ball off which to score two. DeFreitas could get just a single from a delivery of full length. The scores were level, the number of wickets lost were the same, but after 25 overs Derbyshire had scored 103 for 2, so Yorkshire were the winners.

At Edgbaston, Lancashire looked set for elimination from the competition when Warwickshire began the 48th over needing six to win. Welch, having reached his first Benson and Hedges fifty, hit the first ball for a single, but Wasim Akram's next five deliveries were straight and quick and Donald could only defend. The last over, bowled by Ian Austin, saw Lloyd dive to save Welch's powerful drive off the first ball, and a single to Welch from the next ball brought Donald on strike, and he was bowled. Small entered with two runs needed from two balls. He could do nothing with the first, but he hit the last to cover. One run was easy; two were not, and he was run out by feet. The scores were level, but Warwickshire had lost ten wickets to Lancashire's eight and so had lost the match.

The third match in Group A saw Worcestershire win comfortably against Minor Counties, but not before Richard Dalton had given another exhilarating exhibition, with 69 off 47 balls.

In Group B, Durham gained a second victory. Foster made his highest Benson and Hedges score and finished the game with a six out of the ground. Northamptonshire kept hopes alive with an emphatic win at Trent Bridge. The home side were given a good start by Matthew Dowman, but they lost their way dreadfully. Mohammad Akram captured four wickets, and Snape and Emburey had such an hypnotic effect that only one boundary was scored in the last 28 overs. In response, Capel opened and made 68 from 69 balls and Bailey hit an unbeaten 73 off 71 balls. Victory came with 8.2 overs unused.

Kent took a firm grip on Group C with their third win in as many matches. Headley helped reduce Sussex to 82 for 7, and although there was a recovery, Kent won with nearly 23 overs to spare. Surrey moved into second place in the group with a most decisive victory over the Universities. Will House's gallant 98 off 92 balls raised the students from 30 for 4 to 198 all out, but Alec Stewart walloped two sixes and 11 fours, and Surrey, watched by the ex-Prime Minister John Major on the first day after losing the election, raced to their target in 25.2 overs.

Also in this group were Gloucestershire, who kept abreast of Surrey with a narrow win at Southampton. Lynch hit seven fours and three sixes in his dynamic 87, but Robin Smith kept Hampshire in the game with a brilliant 92, which included two sixes and nine fours. His dismissal brought decline, and 30 were needed from three overs. This came down to 15 from three balls, and Hampshire were given new life when Smith bowled a no-ball, but it was not to be their day, or their year.

Somerset's highest Benson and Hedges score was much aided by Ireland's inability to hold their catches. The Irish were then routed by the leg-spin of Mushtaq Ahmed who returned his best figures in the competition.

Glamorgan registered their first win with a narrow victory over Middlesex, for whom new overseas signing Jacques Kallis made an impressive start. A second wicket stand of 112 between Morris and Dale was the basis of the Glamorgan innings, and Dale later produced a spell of 3 for 1 in six balls.

5 May
at Chelmsford
Somerset 269 for 8 (M. Burns 91, R.J. Harden 64)
Essex 270 for 2 (P.J. Prichard 114, S.G. Law 88)
Essex (2 pts) won by 8 wickets
(Gold Award: P.J. Prichard)

at Southampton
Surrey 228 for 9 (A.J. Hollioake 80, N. Shahid 52, S.J. Renshaw 6 for 25)
Hampshire 63 (J.E. Benjamin 4 for 19)
Surrey (2 pts) won by 165 runs
(Gold Award: A.J. Hollioake)

Mohammad Akram claimed four wickets in Northamptonshire's victory over Nottinghamshire. Chris Tolley is bowled to become one of his victims. (Ross Kinnaird/Allsport)

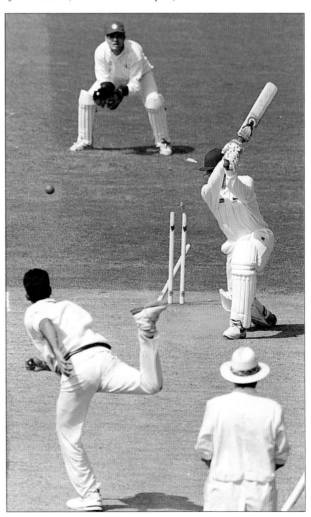

at Canterbury
British Universities 223 for 8 (T.P. Hodgson 60, A. Singh 53 not out, M.J. McCague 4 for 41)
Kent 225 for 6 (N.J. Llong 75, M.V. Fleming 63)
Kent (2 pts) won by 4 wickets
(Gold Award: N.J. Llong)

at Hove
Sussex 273 for 4 (N.R. Taylor 116, M. Newell 87)
Gloucestershire 239 (R.C. Russell 66)
Sussex (2 pts) won by 34 runs
(Gold Award: N.R. Taylor)

---

5 and 6 May
at Derby
Derbyshire 231 (K.J. Barnett 59, V.P. Clarke 52, D.A. Leatherdale 4 for 33)
Worcestershire 211 (T.M. Moody 77)
Derbyshire (2 pts) won by 30 runs
(Gold Award: V.P. Clarke)

at Cardiff
Ireland 202 for 9 (W.J. Cronje 85)
Glamorgan 203 for 4 (M.P. Maynard 50)
Glamorgan (2 pts) won by 6 wickets
(Gold Award: W.J. Cronje)

Hampshire's medium-pace bowler Simon Renshaw established a record for the county when he took 6 for 25 against Surrey, but he still finished on the losing side. (Graham Chadwick/Allsport)

at Walsall
Lancashire 210 for 7 (N.H. Fairbrother 62, W.K. Hegg 54 not out)
Minor Counties 175
Lancashire (2 pts) won by 35 runs
(Gold Award: N.H. Fairbrother)

at Northampton
Scotland 160 for 9 (D. Follett 4 for 39)
Northamptonshire 164 for 5
Northamptonshire (2 pts) won by 5 wickets
(Gold Award: M.B. Loye)

at Edgbaston
Warwickshire 233 for 8 (N.M.K. Smith 57)
Yorkshire 237 for 5 (M.P. Vaughan 88, D.S. Lehmann 67)
Yorkshire (2 pts) won by 5 wickets
(Gold Award: M.P. Vaughan)

---

6 May
at Chester-le-Street
Leicestershire 287 for 4 (A. Habib 111, V.J. Wells 90)
Durham 263 for 9 (J.E. Morris 62, N.J. Speak 59)
Leicestershire (2 pts) won on faster scoring rate
(Gold Award: A. Habib)

Essex qualified for the quarter-finals with an outstanding victory over Somerset, who chose to bat first when they won the toss. Burns anchored the Somerset innings while others were sent in to clout runs, a ploy devised by new coach Dermot Reeve. Kerr was dropped twice off successive balls and helped Burns to add 46 in seven overs, while Richard Harden was principally responsible for the 55 runs garnered from the last six overs. Essex faced a daunting target of 270, and they were well aware that at least one batsman had to make a big score, but none could have expected what followed. In 29 overs of exotic stroke-play, Paul Prichard and Stuart Law scored 204 for the first wicket. Law's 88 came off 89 balls, but he was for once upstaged by Prichard who made 114 off 102 balls. After 11 overs, Essex had 63 on the board, and the introduction of Mushtaq Ahmed did nothing to stem the scoring. He went for 31 in three overs. Eventually caught behind in the 36th over for his highest one-day score, Prichard hit 17 fours. Gooch and Hussain were left the easiest of tasks, taking Essex to victory with 32 balls to spare.

Medium-pacer Simon Renshaw established a Hampshire record in the competition when he took 6 for 25 against Surrey, but he finished on the losing side. Surrey had been 22 for 4, but Shahid and Adam Hollioake added 138. Hampshire disintegrated before the Surrey pace attack with only three batsmen reaching double figures. The victory gave Surrey every chance of reaching the quarter-finals. Kent assured themselves of a place in the last eight by beating the Universities, while Sussex dented the hopes of Gloucestershire with a win at Hove. Sussex were indebted to Neil Taylor whom they had signed in the winter after he had given many years service to Kent. Taylor hit his sixth hundred in the competition off 101 balls and shared a stand of 208 for the third wicket with Mark Newell, who made his highest score in the Benson and Hedges Cup. The partnership broke the Sussex record for any wicket in the competition.

In the matches that were taken into a second day because of bad weather, Derbyshire kept on course for a place in the last eight, and Waqar Younis made his first appearance for Glamorgan in their victory over Ireland.

Lancashire had something of a fright at Walsall when they were 41 for 5. Their main redemption came through Hegg and Fairbrother, who put on 101 for the seventh wicket. Minor Counties roared away through Dean and Larkins, who scored 60 in the first nine overs, but then they fell apart.

Northamptonshire suffered some discomforts in beating Scotland, but Yorkshire had an accomplished win over Warwickshire. Neil Smith hit 57 off 61 balls, and Giles and Donald scored 39 for the ninth wicket in the last six overs. On the Tuesday, Vaughan and Lehmann put on 117 after Byas had fallen at 17, and Hartley and McGrath played positively to assure Yorkshire of victory and almost certainly a place in the same quarter-finals.

There was no play at Chester-le-Street and a flurry of snow gave Durham a revised target of 283 in 48 overs, which proved beyond them. Habib made his highest one-day score off 117 balls, and Leicestershire were assured of a place in the quarter-finals.

12 May
at Oxford
British Universities 284 for 8 (T.P. Hodgson 113, U.B.A. Rashid 82)
Hampshire 287 for 3 (M.L. Hayden 120 not out, G.W. White 56)
Hampshire (2 pts) won by 7 wickets
(Gold Award: M.L. Hayden)

at Old Trafford
Lancashire 274 for 6 (N.H. Fairbrother 75 not out, J.E.R. Gallian 59)
Worcestershire 274 for 8 (T.M. Moody 92)
Lancashire (2 pts) won by losing fewer wickets with the scores level
(Gold Award: T.M. Moody)

at Northampton
Northamptonshire 238 for 8
Leicestershire 186 for 8 (N.C. Johnson 58, J.N. Snape 5 for 32)
Northamptonshire (2 pts) won by 52 runs
(Gold Award: J.N. Snape)

at The Oval
Surrey 310 for 8 (G.P. Thorpe 78, A.J. Stewart 72, P.W. Jarvis 4 for 60)

Sussex 299 (N.R. Taylor 67, R.K. Rao 61, M. Newell 60, I.D.K. Salisbury 4 for 53)
Surrey (2 pts) won by 11 runs
(Gold Award: I.D.K. Salisbury)

at Leeds
Yorkshire 309 for 5 (A. McGrath 109 not out, D. Byas 72)
Minor Counties 125 (S.J. Dean 56)
Yorkshire (2 pts) won by 184 runs
(Gold Award: A. McGrath)

12 and 13 May
at Bristol
Kent 239 for 7 (G.R. Cowdrey 77)
Gloucestershire 50 for 1
No Result
Gloucestershire 1 pt, Kent 1 pt

at Lord's
Somerset 287 for 6 (P.D. Bowler 79, R.J. Harden 66, M. Burns 54)
Middlesex 260 (P.N. Weekes 77, S.P. Moffat 60)
Somerset (2 pts) won by 27 runs
(Gold Award: P.D. Bowler)

13 May
at Derby
Derbyshire 216 for 8 (C.J. Adams 61)
Warwickshire 217 for 9 (N.V. Knight 69, D.R. Brown 58, V.P. Clarke 4 for 49)
Warwickshire (2 pts) won by 1 wicket
(Gold Award: G.C. Small)

at Glasgow (Titwood)
Match abandoned
Scotland 1 pt, Nottinghamshire 1 pt

at Downpatrick
Match abandoned
Ireland 1 pt, Essex 1 pt

At Oxford, Tim Hodgson, Durham University and Essex, hit a fine century off 137 balls and shared a second wicket stand of 168 with Middlesex's Umar Rashid. The pair had to be content with these personal achievements, for Matthew Hayden's first hundred for Hampshire won the game for the county side.

Lancashire were engaged in another close finish. Hick and Moody put on 131 in 17 overs, and with Moody hitting two sixes and 11 fours in his 83-ball innings, Worcestershire seemed to be cruising to victory. The turning point came when Hick and Moody were dismissed within the space of three balls from Martin. Panic set in, and the last ball arrived with one run needed for a Worcestershire victory, but Newport was caught by Green off Wasim. In

Gladstone Small had never won the Gold Award before 1997 when he was twice chosen. He took 15 wickets in six matches and hit a six off the penultimate ball to beat Derbyshire and give Warwickshire a place in the quarter-finals. (Alan Cozzi)

spite of this win, Lancashire failed to qualify for the quarter-finals for the first time since 1988.

Northamptonshire qualified by beating Leicestershire. Snape took three wickets in eight balls when the visitors were going strong.

Surrey were given a magnificent start at The Oval where Stewart and Brown scored 101 in 17 overs for the first wicket. Thorpe and Butcher maintained the momentum, but Surrey lost their way over the last ten overs and settled for 310. Taylor, shrugging off his reputation as a tortoise, hit 67 off 66 balls, and Mark Newell made 60 off 60 – and this after Rao and Greenfield had scored 93 in the first 15 overs. At 268 for 3 in the 45th over, Sussex were set for victory, but the return of Salisbury changed the game. He stemmed the flow of runs, bowled Mark Newell and Athey and dismissed Phillips and Khan to leave his old county 11 short of the Surrey score. Surrey had qualified for the last eight.

Yorkshire finished top of Group A by beating Minor Counties in resounding fashion. Anthony McGrath made his

first limited-over hundred. Who would accompany Yorkshire into the quarter-finals from Group A was not known until the Tuesday. Derbyshire were restricted to 216 for 8, but they seemed to have won the match when they reduced Warwickshire to 193 for 9, four wickets having fallen for two runs, and 12 were needed from the final over. Donald and Small pushed and ran to take six off the first four balls bowled by Malcolm. Small met the fifth with a full swing of the bat and sent the ball over long-off for six, victory and a place ahead of Derbyshire on run rate and so into the last eight.

Kent's abandonment had no bearing on final places nor did the abandonments in soggy Ireland and Scotland. Somerset's win over a lacklustre Middlesex gave them second place in Group D.

Final Zone Tables

Group A	P	W	L	NR	Pts	RR
Yorkshire	5	4	1	–	8	16.13
Warwickshire	5	3	2	–	6	15.21
Derbyshire	5	3	2	–	6	2.68
Lancashire	5	3	2	–	6	−1.50
Worcestershire	5	2	3	–	4	−3.90
Minor Counties	5	–	5	–	0	−28.56

Group B	P	W	L	NR	Pts	RR
Leicestershire	4	3	1	–	6	18.15
Northamptonshire	4	3	1	–	6	9.20
Durham	4	2	2	–	4	14.74
Nottinghamshire	4	1	2	1	2	−13.07
Scotland	4	–	3	1	1	−51.27

Group C	P	W	L	NR	Pts	RR
Kent	5	4	–	1	9	9.84
Surrey	5	4	1	–	8	21.19
Gloucestershire	5	2	2	1	5	7.06
Sussex	5	2	3	–	4	−0.51
Hampshire	5	1	4	–	2	−15.50
British Universities	5	1	4	–	2	−18.57

Group D	P	W	L	NR	Pts	RR
Essex	4	3	–	1	7	8.54
Somerset	4	3	1	–	6	29.88
Glamorgan	4	2	2	–	4	−6.83
Ireland	4	1	2	1	3	−32.62
Middlesex	4	–	4	–	0	−6.75

Quarter-Finals

27 May
at Chelmsford
Essex 214 (N. Hussain 52)
Surrey 215 for 4 (G.P. Thorpe 73, A.D. Brown 71)
Surrey won by 6 wickets
(Gold Award: M.P. Bicknell)

at Canterbury
Warwickshire 304 for 8 (N.M.K. Smith 125, M.V. Fleming 4 for 58)
Kent 306 for 6 (M.J. Walker 117)
Kent won by 4 wickets
(Gold Award: M.J. Walker)

at Leicester
Leicestershire 197 (B.F. Smith 61, J.J. Whitaker 51, H.R.J. Trump 4 for 51)
Somerset 177
Leicestershire won by 20 runs
(Gold Award: D.J. Millns)

at Leeds
Yorkshire 253 for 9 (M.P. Vaughan 85, B. Parker 58, D.J. Capel 5 for 51)
Northamptonshire 254 for 3 (R.J. Bailey 70 not out, D.J. Capel 67)
Northamptonshire won by 7 wickets
(Gold Award: D.J. Capel)

A feature of Kent's thrilling semi-final win over Northamptonshire was their brilliant fielding. Paul Strang catches David Follett to end the match. (Graham Chadwick/Allsport)

Essex had won six of the last seven encounters with Surrey in the Benson and Hedges Cup, but they gave a dreadful performance when the sides met in the 1997 quarter-final. Put in to bat, they slammed 31 in three overs, but, having reached 34 in 5, they lost their top three batsmen, Prichard, Stuart Law and Gooch, for three runs. Gooch was bowled off his pads for 0, and was a trifle unlucky, but Prichard and Law fell to extravagant shots that saw them caught behind. Hussain and Irani built a stand of 71 in 12 overs, but too few of Hussain's runs were in front of the wicket, and with Martin Bicknell moving the ball menacingly, Essex were always struggling.

Grayson tried manfully to hold the late order together and made an unbeaten 49, but there were some woeful shots against some accurate bowling. A score of 214 in 45.5 overs seemed grossly inadequate, and so it proved even though Stewart fell in Ilott's first over. The Essex fielding matched their batting. Thorpe was not at his best but was twice dropped, and once Brown began clouting the home side appeared to surrender. It was difficult to judge how good Surrey were; Essex were so bad.

At Canterbury, life was very different, and the match was pulsating. Kent have had the better of Warwickshire in the Benson and Hedges Cup, but on this occasion they were forced to fight to the end. The visitors' innings was founded on a highest one-day score by Neil Smith whose 125 came off 119 balls. He and Ostler added 103 for the fourth wicket, and with Warwickshire's capacity for finding runs from anywhere in the order, Kent faced a hard target of 306. Walker and Fleming set about their task briskly. They put on 84, but they had some help. Allan Donald hobbled off with a back strain after conceding 16 runs, 14 of them leg-side wides, in two overs. Substitute fielder Sheikh dropped Walker, who went on to score a magnificent 117 from 119 balls. It was the left-hander's first limited-over hundred and

Graham Cowdrey is bowled by Chris Lewis and Kent are sinking fast. (Ben Radford/Allsport)

was a pugnacious innings of considerable character and style. He laid the foundation for victory, and Cowdrey, 39 off 26 balls, and Llong kept the runs flowing so that the target was reached with three balls to spare.

It was the bowlers who dominated at Leicester. Rose dismissed both the home side's openers for ducks, and Leicestershire were in dire straits at 14 for 3. Whitaker and Smith added 102, and Habib batted well. A target of 198 had seemed within easy reach for Somerset, but Millns and Mullally swept away their top order, and they crumbled to 73 for 6. A stand of 60 for the ninth wicket between Turner and Caddick was valiant but never came close to altering the course of the match.

Northamptonshire beat Yorkshire with surprising ease. David Capel tore the heart out of the home side's innings with a spell of 4 for 3 in nine balls; one of his victims being Lehmann, who was just beginning to build a big innings. Capel then opened the Northamptonshire innings and scored 67 off 59 balls with two sixes and nine fours as he and Montgomerie put on 90. Skipper Bailey was able to follow with a calm and calculated innings that took his side into the semi-finals with four overs to spare.

Semi-Finals

10 June
at Canterbury
Kent 206 for 8 (T.R. Ward 78)
Northamptonshire 140 (P.A. Strang 4 for 29)
Kent won by 66 runs

at The Oval
Surrey 308 for 8 (A.J. Stewart 87, G.P. Thorpe 79, A.J. Hollioake 63)
Leicestershire 178 (P.A. Nixon 53, M.P. Bicknell 4 for 41)
Surrey won by 130 runs

Kent had batted strongly on their way to the semi-final so that, at 63 for 4 and the front-line batsmen gone, they faced a crisis. It was met by Trevor Ward and Mark Ealham who added 100 by scampering singles and batting with unrelenting energy. In spite of their efforts and the unexpected slowness of the pitch, Kent could not be satisfied with their score of 206, 36 of which had come in an unbroken ninth wicket stand between Marsh and McCague. They had been used to scores in excess of 300. It proved more than adequate. Headley uprooted Warren's middle stump with his third ball, and he soon accounted for Loye and Curran. The Kent bowling was relentlessly hostile

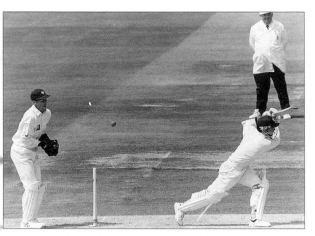

A brave effort by Paul Strang ends when he is beaten by Salisbury's intended googly. (David Munden/Sportsline)

and accurate, and the fielding was dynamic. Northamptonshire were under constant pressure, attacked by bowlers and fielders, and they succumbed. Once Bailey, top scorer with 33, fell to a fine outswinger by McCague the end was near, and Kent were at Lord's.

At The Oval, Leicestershire's challenge lasted for little more than two overs. They put Surrey in to bat, and Mullally found the edge of Brown's bat with his fourth ball. With the first ball of his next over, he had Ben Hollioake taken at mid-on. This brought together Stewart and Thorpe who added 138 in 32 overs. They were followed by skipper Adam Hollioake, who hit 63 off 40 balls. Leicestershire kept up their spirits as their bowlers, Johnson in particular, were being put to the sword, but those spirits soon sagged as, with Martin Bicknell again in excellent form and moving the ball appreciably, they subsided to 96 for 8. Nixon offered a gesture, but the issue had long since been decided.

Chris Lewis of Surrey is run out in the semi-final against Leicestershire at The Oval, but Surrey were easy winners. (Laurence Griffiths/Allsport)

Benson and Hedges Cup Final

Kent v. Surrey

Lord's basked in the sun, but the cricket itself never quite matched the weather. Kent decided to bat when they won the toss, which they had intended to do in 1995 only to have a late change of mind. Walker and Fleming punched boundaries in the opening overs, and Martin Bicknell was swinging the ball extravagantly and conceding wides so that the Kent majority in the stadium erupted ecstatically. The joy was short-lived. Within four overs, both openers were back in the pavilion. Walker dragged a widish delivery onto his stumps, and Fleming pushed half-forward to Lewis, who greeted the wicket with ill-mannered gestures. When Wells fell to a ball that nipped back at him Kent were 23 for 3 in seven overs, and the initiative that batsmen are intended to seize in the first 15 overs of the innings had gone.

Ward was uncharacteristically subdued as he attempted to save something from the debris, but he and Llong added 45 in 11 overs. It was the biggest stand of the innings. Ward was deceived by a slower ball from the elder Hollioake, and when Llong was caught at extra cover just as he was finding his touch Kent were 106 for 5 in the 30th over and looking doomed.

Graham Cowdrey had been doubtful for the final because of injury, but if he were fit, it was hard to understand why he was batting as low as number seven. He never looked at ease and faced 20 balls before playing down the wrong line to Lewis.

Ealham had batted well without ever taking command, and it was Paul Strang who was really the first to lift the Kent supporters. He was severe on Salisbury and raced to 23 off 25 balls with refreshing urgency before missing an intended googly that did not turn.

McCague clouted the admirable Saqlain to mid-on in the 49th over, and, with Ealham having departed the previous over for 52 off 88 balls, Marsh and Headley gathered what they could as the innings closed. As the capacity crowd was roasted by the sun, it was apparent that 212 was not a winning score.

There was one cheer left for Kent. Brown fell in the first over, very well caught at point off a fierce cut, but this brought in Ben Hollioake, Man of the Moment. He had not bowled well, but he batted with the joyful exuberance of youth. After 15 overs, Surrey had raced to 80, and Ben Hollioake's fifty came off 49 balls. He and Stewart had added 159 in 33 overs when Hollioake attempted to hit over mid-on and was caught. His 98 had come off 113 balls and included 15 fours. It was no surprise when he was named Gold Award winner.

Something might still have been saved had Marsh adopted a more positive approach. In 1983, Gatting had pulled off an amazing victory when he jettisoned one-day field-placings and played the game as if it were a championship match. Marsh took no such gamble, and Surrey strolled to victory with five overs to spare.

Skipper Adam Hollioake and ex-skipper Alec Stewart stand each side of Surrey hero Ben Hollioake and display the Benson and Hedges Cup. (Dave Pinegar/ASP)

Gold Award winner Ben Hollioake crashes a ball to the boundary during his innings of 98. (Ben Radford / Allsport)

PRIZE STRUCTURE

£160,750 of the £824,457 Benson and Hedges sponsorship of this event will go in prize money for teams or individuals.

The breakdown is as follows:

- The Champions will win £42,000 (and hold, for one year only, the Benson and Hedges Cup)
- For the Runners-up £21,000
- For the losing Semi-finalists £10,500
- For the losing Quarter-finalists £5,250

ADDITIONAL TEAM AWARDS

The winners of all matches in the Group stages of the Cup received £800.

INDIVIDUAL GOLD AWARDS

There is a Benson and Hedges Gold Award for the outstanding individual performance at all matches throughout the Cup.

These are:

In the Group matches	£250
In the Quarter-finals	£375
In the Semi-finals	£425
In the Final	£900

SPECIAL ACHIEVEMENT AWARDS

First batsman to score 450 runs	£1,000
First bowler to take 20 wickets	£1,000
First wicket-keeper to equal the Benson and Hedges record of 8 dismissals in an innings	£1,000

BENSON and HEDGES CUP 1997

MARYLEBONE CRICKET CLUB

50p

FINAL
KENT v. SURREY

at Lord's Ground, Saturday, July 12th 1997

Any alterations to teams will be announced over the public address system

KENT

1	M. V. Fleming	lbw b Lewis	7
2	M. J. Walker	b Bicknell	6
3	T. R. Ward	lbw b A. Hollioake	15
4	A. P. Wells	lbw b Bicknell	5
7	N. J. Llong	c Butcher b Mushtaq	42
6	M. A. Ealham	c Brown b Lewis	52
5	G. R. Cowdrey	b Lewis	8
8	P. A. Strang	b Salisbury	23
†*9	S. A. Marsh	not out	24
10	M. J. McCague	c Thorpe b Mushtaq	0
11	D. W. Headley	not out	3
	B 1, l-b 7, w 17, n-b 2,		27
	Total ....(50 overs)		212

FALL OF THE WICKETS

1...15 2...15 3...23 4...68 5...106 6...135 7...170 8...194 9...198 10...

Bowling Analysis	O.	M.	R.	W.	Wd.	N-b.
Bicknell	8	0	33	2	6	1
Lewis	10	3	39	3	2	...
A. Hollioake	7	0	31	1	2	...
B. Hollioake	6	0	28	0	2	...
Mushtaq	9	1	33	2	1	...
Salisbury	10	0	40	1	1	...
	...	...	...	...	...	...

SURREY

1	A. D. Brown	c Fleming b McCague	2
*2	A. J. Stewart	not out	75
3	B. C. Hollioake	c Strang b Ealham	98
4	G. P. Thorpe	not out	17
†5	A. J. Hollioake		
6	M. A. Butcher		
7	C. C. Lewis		
8	J. D. Ratcliffe		
9	M. P. Bicknell		
10	I. D. K. Salisbury		
11	Saqlain Mushtaq		
	B , l-b 11, w 6, n-b 6,		23
	Total ....(45 overs)		215

FALL OF THE WICKETS

1...2 2...161 3... 4... 5... 6... 7... 8... 9... 10...

Bowling Analysis	O.	M.	R.	W.	Wd.	N-b.
McCague	8	0	45	1	1	...
Headley	10	0	53	0	...	3
Fleming	7	1	29	0	1	...
Ealham	6	0	31	1	3	...
Strang	10	1	31	0	1	...
Llong	4	0	15	0	...	...
	...	...	...	...	...	...

†Captain *Wicket-keeper
Umpires—G. Sharp & D. R. Shepherd
Scorers—K. R. Booth & J. C. Foley

Toss won by—Kent
RESULT—Surrey won by 8 wickets

The playing conditions for the Benson and Hedges Cup Competition are printed on the back of this score card.

Total runs scored at end of each over :—

Kent	1	2	3	4	5	6	7	8	9	10	11	12	13	14	15	16	17	18	19	20
	21	22	23	24	25	26	27	28	29	30	31	32	33	34	35	36	37	38	39	40
	41	42	43	44	45	46	47	48	49	50										
Surrey	1	2	3	4	5	6	7	8	9	10	11	12	13	14	15	16	17	18	19	20
	21	22	23	24	25	26	27	28	29	30	31	32	33	34	35	36	37	38	39	40
	41	42	43	44	45	46	47	48	49	50										

The Australian Tour

The Australians arrived in England in mid-May, some weeks later than had been the custom. They had been engaged in demanding Test series against West Indies at home and against South Africa in the Republic. Both series had been won, and they were undisputed 'world champions' of Test cricket, yet doubts existed about the composition of their side.

Controversy surrounded the retention of Mark Taylor as captain. None argued with Taylor's qualities and expertise as a leader, but his form, internationally and domestically, had been wretched for the best part of a year, and there was an opinion that he was no longer worth his place in the side. It had been the Australian tradition to name a party, and then to select a captain from within the best available players. To name a man simply on his experience and worth as a captain was to break with that tradition.

The retention of Taylor caused other selection problems in that Slater was recalled as cover for the captain should he fail as an opening batsman. The recall of Slater meant the exclusion of Stuart Law from the final squad, which was astonishing to those who had seen him in England. This was a luxury that the England selectors must have envied, for Law's Australian colleagues were of the opinion that had he been English, Law would have replaced any of the first six in the England batting order on merit and ability.

In the bowling department, Australia relied on the genius of Warne and the recently emerging talent of Bevan as spinners. The pace attack was headed by McGrath with the very promising and already proven Gillespie as his main lieutenant. Kasprowicz and Bichel, who had done splendidly for Queensland, were in support. There was more controversy in the choice of Julian ahead of Reiffel, but the selectors had doubts as to the Victorian's fitness.

Neither of the Waugh twins was fully fit to bowl although both would cause England enough problems with the bat it was feared. Steve Waugh had been named as vice-captain ahead of Ian Healy, who had done the job admirably. Healy remained the best wicket-keeper in the world, and his deputy, Gilchrist, was a good keeper and a fine left-handed batsman.

Elliott, Langer, Ponting and Blewett were young batsmen of immense talent, yet the belief persisted that this Australian side was vulnerable and that the 'Ashes' could be recaptured. We live in hope.

The captain go forth. Michael Atherton of England and Mark Taylor of Australia. (Dave Pinegar/ASP)

opposition were amiable, but, with the Texaco Trophy only a week away and the first Test less than a month away, the Australians had to apply themselves more seriously than was generally the case. Mark Waugh and Mark Taylor scored 101 for the first wicket, and Slater hit three sixes in his 50 off 53 balls. Three Zimbabwe Test players, the Flower brothers and Andy Whittall, were in the Duke's side, but the game followed its natural course. The fixture had previously been played on a Sunday, but the pressures of the schedule caused it to be played on a Thursday in 1997. It did not affect the attendance as some 9,000 people thronged this picnic paradise.

15 May
at Arundel
Australians 235 for 5 (M.J. Slater 50 not out)
Duke of Norfolk's XI 122 (J.N. Gillespie 4 for 21)
Australians won by 113 runs

The tour began with the gentle fixture at the beautiful Arundel ground, a place that seems to ease away care. The

17 May
at Northampton
Australians 232 (M.A. Taylor 76)
Northamptonshire 134 for 5 (M.B. Loye 65 not out)
Australians won on faster scoring rate

The Duckworth-Lewis method was applied when rain stopped the Northamptonshire innings after 35 overs. The Australians were judged winners by 17 runs.

18 May
at Worcester
Australians 121 (D.A. Leatherdale 5 for 10)
Worcestershire 123 for 5
Worcestershire won by 5 wickets

Worcestershire chose to field first, for the pitch, due to moisture, was difficult for batting. The Australians succumbed to the Worcestershire medium pacers in 47.4 overs. It took the county 36.5 overs to reach their target. For the Australians this was scant preparation for the Texaco Trophy.

20 May
at Chester-le-Street
Durham v. **Australians**
Match abandoned

The ultimate disaster for the Australians was that their third and final warm-up game was rained off.

Adams Gilchrist hits out during his innings of 53 at The Oval. His tour was to end early through injury.
(David Munden/Sportsline)

The Texaco Trophy

The new England selectors caused both surprise and elation when they named the squad for the three Texaco Trophy matches. There was surprise at the retention of Knight after injury and little practice and the recall of DeFreitas earned little applause. Lloyd had begun the season in fine form and was preferred to vice-captain Hussain, and Giles, the left-arm spinner from Warwickshire, had worked hard to earn some recognition. The general elation came at the inclusion of the Hollioake brothers. Adam, now captain of Surrey, had appeared in the Texaco matches against Pakistan the previous season, but Ben was a member of the England Under-19 side and held no regular place in the Surrey eleven. Both were essentially one-day cricketers.

Giles, Silverwood, Crawley and Ben Hollioake were omitted for the first match, while the Australians chose Slater ahead of Ponting or Langer. Atherton won the toss and asked Australia to bat. The day was dull and cloudy, and it was apparent that batting would not be easy. So it proved.

Gough bowled a tight opening spell, and in the fourth over, Taylor moved bat but not feet and edged to the wicket-keeper. The Waugh twins were held in check by good bowling and tigerish fielding. In the 15th over, with the score only 39, Mark Waugh played across the line to

England find a hero – Ben Hollioake smashes a ball to the boundary during his innings of 63. (Adrian Murrell/Allsport)

Headley and was bowled. In the next over, Steve was leg before to Ealham. At the end of what should have been the prosperous period, Australia was 43 for 3.

Bevan and Blewett showed the first positive batting of the match and added 63 in 17 overs. The partnership was broken when Bevan called for an unwise single to Thorpe and was run out. Gough knocked out Blewett's middle stump with an in-swinging yorker next ball, and the game was firmly in England's grasp. Slater and Healy worked hard, but Hollioake's accuracy accounted for Healy and Warne, while Slater fell to a spectacular caught and bowled. Kasprowicz hit 17 off 18 balls, but England were well content to restrict Australia to 170.

Atherton and Knight were troubled by the pace of McGrath, but it was Kasprowicz who broke through, having the England captain taken low on the leg side. The unhappy Knight was leg before to McGrath in the fifth over, and Stewart was out in the same manner six overs later. When Lloyd, sent back by Thorpe, was run out by Blewett, England was 40 for 4 in the 14th over and were in a worse plight than Australia had been.

Adam Hollioake began uneasily and edged Warne dangerously past Healy. Then he settled, and with Thorpe assured, the complexion of the game, if not the weather,

changed completely. The pair took England to victory with an unbroken stand of 135 in 27 overs. Hollioake hit two sixes and five fours and made his 66 off 84 balls.

At The Oval, England brought in Giles for Headley and Australia played Gilchrist for Blewett, but the result was the same. England again won the toss and again asked Australia to bat.

The pitch was flat and hard and the weather an improvement on Headingley, but the Australians had a death wish. Both openers were run out, as was Slater, beaten by DeFreitas's direct hit on the stumps. With Steve Waugh playing onto Croft, Australia were 98 for 4 before sanity prevailed. Gilchrist calmed the situation, and he and fellow left-hander Bevan added 113. It was Adam Hollioake who broke the stand, and Healy became the fourth run out of the innings before Bevan reached his second one-day international century within a matter of weeks.

Knight was once more at a loss against the opening attack, but Atherton and Stewart mounted an onslaught on the bowling. Stewart went down the pitch to Warne and hit 40 off as many deliveries before being bowled off his pads. It was the leg-spinner's only wicket of the series.

England were 92 for 2 off 20 overs with Atherton in dominant mood. He lost Thorpe at 104 and Lloyd 54 runs later, but Hollioake again batted with remarkable confidence and maturity, hitting 53 off 41 balls as England won with 10 balls to spare. Atherton, Man of the Match, was unbeaten on 113, which came off 149 balls with 10 fours.

With the Trophy won and lost, Mark Taylor stood down at Lord's and Matthew Elliott replaced him. Justin Langer came in for Slater, and England found places for the players who had not featured in the earlier games – Crawley, Ben Hollioake and Silverwood. The toss went again to England, who again elected to field. The sun shone, and England thrived.

Gough had Elliott taken at second slip in the opening over. Mark Waugh looked totally at ease as he and his brother added 50, but no one else was able to match his serenity. He had scored more than half of his side's runs, 95 off 96 balls, when he was beaten by Gough's off-cutter. Gilchrist and Healy showed urgency, and Kasprowicz clouted 28 off 26 balls towards the close, but Australia's 269 was less than might reasonably have been expected.

Stewart began in roaring fashion, but he lost Atherton in the sixth over. This brought in Ben Hollioake, who straight-drove the third ball he received for four. He hit in the air often, but he hit with confidence and purpose. He swung Warne over mid-wicket for six and he reached 50 off 37 balls. When, at 113, he fell to Steve Waugh, he had made 63 off 48 balls with 11 fours as well as his six, and Stewart's score had advanced by 15 in the same period. It was Boys' Own Paper stuff.

Stewart, Crawley and Thorpe all scored merrily, and England won with more comfort than one over suggests. There was a state of euphoria. England was the greatest! The Ashes and all else beckoned. The real world lay around the corner.

Match One – England v. Australia
22 May 1997 at Headingley, Leeds

Australia		
M.A. Taylor (Capt)	c Stewart, b Gough	7
M.E. Waugh	b Headley	11
S.R. Waugh	lbw, b Ealham	19
M.G. Bevan	run out	30
G.S. Blewett	b Gough	28
M.J. Slater	c and b Ealham	17
*I.A. Healy	c Atherton, b A.J. Hollioake	17
S.K. Warne	c Thorpe, b A.J. Hollioake	4
M.S. Kasprowicz	not out	17
J.N. Gillespie	not out	3
G.D. McGrath		
	lb 7, w 9, nb 1	17
	50 overs(for 8 wickets)	170

England		
N.V. Knight	lbw, b McGrath	12
M.A. Atherton (Capt)	c Healy, b Kasprowicz	4
*A.J. Stewart	lbw, b McGrath	7
G.P. Thorpe	not out	75
G.D. Lloyd	run out	0
A.J. Hollioake	not out	66
M.A. Ealham		
P.A.J. DeFreitas		
R.D.B. Croft		
D. Gough		
D.W. Headley		
	b 1, w 6, nb 4	11
	40.1 overs (for 4 wickets)	175

	O	M	R	W
DeFreitas	9	1	35	–
Gough	10	2	33	2
Ealham	8	3	21	2
Headley	8	–	36	1
Croft	10	1	16	–
A.J. Hollioake	5	–	22	2

	O	M	R	W
McGrath	10	2	34	2
Kasprowicz	7	–	27	1
Gillespie	8.1	1	39	–
Warne	10	–	46	–
M.E. Waugh	2	–	16	–
Blewett	3	–	12	–

Fall of Wickets
1–8, 2–39, 3–43, 4–106, 5–106, 6–140, 7–140, 8–157

Fall of Wickets
1–18, 2–20, 3–32, 4–40

Umpires: R. Julian & P. Willey *Man of the Match:* A.J. Hollioake

England won by 6 wickets

27, 28 and 29 May
at Bristol
Australians 249 (S.R. Waugh 92, M.E. Waugh 66, J.J. Lewis 4 for 89) and 354 for 4 dec. (J.L. Langer 152 not out, M.T.G. Elliott 124)
Gloucestershire 350 (N.J. Trainor 121, R.J. Cunliffe 61, S.K. Warne 4 for 97)
Match drawn

Justin Langer is run out in the third Texaco Trophy match at Lord's. (Clive Mason/Allsport)

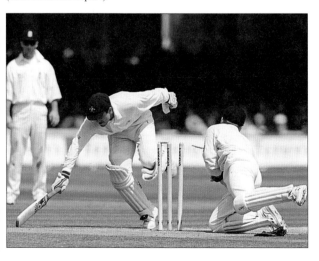

The Australians passage towards the first Test continued to be an uneasy one. Batting first at Bristol, they lost their first three batsmen, including Taylor for 0, for 21 runs. The Waugh twins put on 96, but the batting as a whole lacked conviction. The attack, comprising the four front-line bowlers expected to play in the first Test, was equally unimpressive. The pitch was much like a pudding, and Gloucestershire were far happier on it than the tourists. Nick Trainor and Robert Cunliffe put on 130 for the third wicket, and the 21-year old Trainor reached a maiden first-class century. Batting a second time 101 runs in arrears, the Australians lost Taylor for 30. Elliott and Langer then shared a stand worth 192 and enjoyed the practice as they became the first first-class centurions of the tour.

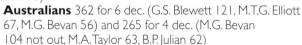

31 May, 1 and 2 June
at Derby
Australians 362 for 6 dec. (G.S. Blewett 121, M.T.G. Elliott 67, M.G. Bevan 56) and 265 for 4 dec. (M.G. Bevan 104 not out, M.A. Taylor 63, B.P. Julian 62)
Derbyshire 257 for 9 dec. (M.R. May 67) and 371 for 9 (C.J. Adams 91, A.S. Rollins 66, D.M. Jones 57, S.K. Warne 7 for 103)
Derbyshire won by 1 wicket

The limited first-class programme before the first Test meant that neither Ponting, a young batsman of rare talent, nor Slater had any chance to stake a claim for a place in the

Match Two – England v. Australia
24 May 1997 at The Oval

Australia

M.E. Waugh	run out	25
M.A. Taylor (Capt)	run out	11
S.R. Waugh	b Croft	24
M.G. Bevan	not out	108
M.J. Slater	run out	1
A.C. Gilchrist	lbw, b A.J. Hollioake	53
*I.A. Healy	run out	7
S.K. Warne	not out	11
M.S. Kasprowicz		
J.N. Gillespie		
G.D. McGrath		
	lb 8, nb 1	9
	50 overs (for 6 wickets)	249

	O	M	R	W
DeFreitas	8	–	47	–
Gough	10	3	42	–
Ealham	9	2	40	–
Giles	9	–	48	–
Croft	10	2	39	1
A.J. Hollioake	4	–	25	1

Fall of Wickets
1–35, 2–37, 3–94, 4–98, 5–211, 6–226

England

N.V. Knight	lbw, b Kasprowicz	4
M.A. Atherton (Capt)	not out	113
*A.J. Stewart	b Warne	40
G.P. Thorpe	c S.R. Waugh, b Bevan	7
G.D. Lloyd	c Warne, b McGrath	22
A.J. Hollioake	not out	53
M.A. Ealham		
R.D.B. Croft		
P.A.J. DeFreitas		
A.F. Giles		
D. Gough		
	lb 5, w 8, nb 1	14
	48.2 overs (for 4 wickets)	253

	O	M	R	W
McGrath	9	1	46	1
Kasprowicz	9.2	–	58	1
Gillespie	8	1	42	–
Warne	10	–	39	1
Bevan	9	–	43	1
S.R. Waugh	3	–	20	–

Fall of Wickets
1–6, 2–77, 3–104, 4–158

Umpires: J.H. Hampshire & D.R. Shepherd *Man of the Match:* M.A. Atherton

England won by 6 wickets

Match Three – England v. Australia
25 May 1997 at Lord's

Australia

M.T.G. Elliott	c A.J. Hollioake, b Gough	1
M.E. Waugh	lbw, b Gough	95
S.R. Waugh (Capt)	c Thorpe, b Gough	17
M.G. Bevan	c sub (Knight), b Gough	8
J.L. Langer	run out	29
A.C. Gilchrist	lbw, b Ealham	33
*I.A. Healy	c Lloyd, b Croft	27
S.K. Warne	c Stewart, b Ealham	5
M.S. Kasprowicz	not out	28
J.N. Gillespie	c Thorpe, b Gough	6
G.D. McGrath	st Stewart, b A.J. Hollioake	1
	b 2, lb 10, w 5, nb 2	19
	49.2 overs	269

	O	M	R	W
Gough	10	–	44	5
Silverwood	6	–	44	–
Ealham	10	–	47	2
Croft	10	–	51	1
B.C. Hollioake	7	–	36	–
A.J. Hollioake	6.2	–	35	1

Fall of Wickets
1–2, 2–52, 3–63, 4–142, 5–184, 6–218, 7–228, 8–242, 9–268

England

M.A. Atherton (Capt)	lbw, b Kasprowicz	1
*A.J. Stewart	c Langer, b M.E. Waugh	79
B.C. Hollioake	c S.R. Waugh, b Gillespie	63
J.P. Crawley	run out	52
G.P. Thorpe	not out	45
A.J. Hollioake	not out	4
G.D. Lloyd		
M.A. Ealham		
R.D.B. Croft		
C.E.W. Silverwood		
D. Gough		
	lb 9, w 13, nb 4	26
	49 overs (for 4 wickets)	270

	O	M	R	W
McGrath	9	2	45	–
Kasprowicz	8	1	40	1
Warne	9	–	44	–
Gillespie	10	–	55	1
Bevan	3	–	27	–
S.R. Waugh	4	–	22	–
M.E. Waugh	6	–	28	1

Fall of Wickets
1–21, 2–113, 3–193, 4–253

Umpires: M.J. Kitchen & G. Sharp *Man of the Match:* D. Gough

England won by 6 wickets

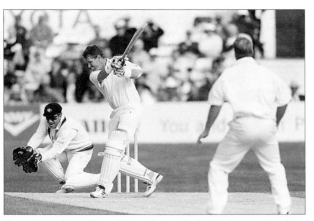

Dean Jones drives Shane Warne during Derbyshire's sensational victory over the Australians. Jones, a former Australian Test batsman, was to leave Derbyshire within weeks of this match. (Clive Mason/Allsport)

Australian side, for they were given no opportunity to play an innings. Against Derbyshire, Australia encountered another problem in that Bichel broke down after bowling five overs. He was to take no further part in the tour. Shortly after the first Test he returned to Australia and Paul Reiffel, the controversial omission, was summoned as replacement.

In spite of the loss of Taylor for 5, the Australians enjoyed a good first day at Derby. The county side had been asked to rest Malcolm, but DeFreitas reduced the tourists to 16 for 2. Elliott and Blewett put on 131, and with Steve Waugh, Bevan and Healy batting positively, Taylor declared at 362 for 6, and Rollins fell to Julian before the close. Michael May resisted solidly on the Sunday when there was a most unfortunate incident concerning Chris Adams. He was adjudged leg before to Warne, although television evidence suggested that he had played a leg glance off the full face of the bat. Adams remonstrated with umpire and players for several minutes to no avail. He was later fined £750 by Derbyshire but initially refused to accept the punishment.

Australia were cheered by Taylor's second innings of 63 and by Bevan's century, and Taylor's declaration left the county 69 overs in which to score 371 to win. This seemed a most difficult task, but Adams, still smarting with a sense of injustice, hit a six and 19 fours and partnered Rollins in a second wicket stand worth 142 in 28 overs. Jones maintained momentum, and there were useful contributions from Clarke, Krikken and DeFreitas. Bichel and Gillespie were both out of the Australian attack with injuries, while Warne was restricted in his repertoire for fear of aggravating his shoulder injury before the Test. The last over arrived with five runs needed and one wicket standing. Aldred hit a single and Dean made two from an overthrow when he could have been run out. The next ball was steered through the covers, and, to much jubilation, Derbyshire had won.

It had been many years since Australia approached a first Test in England with such a poor record behind them. English euphoria continued unabated.

First Test Match
England v. Australia

England named a squad of 13 players and omitted Tufnell and Adam Hollioake in their final selection. Australia played the eleven that had been virtually determined since their arrival three weeks earlier.

The Edgbaston Test was Mike Atherton's 68th for England, and, in leading his country 41 times, he equalled Peter May's record. None would suggest that Atherton is the equal of May either as a batsman or as a captain, but his is a remarkable achievement and one of which to be proud. He did not win the toss, but in view of what followed it did not matter.

Taylor chose to bat, but by the end of the day he must have wondered at the decision. Gough's first ball seemed to go right through the Australian captain, who suffered the same fate at the other end when he faced Malcolm. The Derbyshire bowler was quick and controlled and was able to bring the ball back sharply at the two left-handers. Gough was a little disconcerted by the left-handed pairing and bowled two wides when he essayed the outswinger. It was not until the fifth over that Australia registered a boundary. Elliott edged Gough through the slips, but next ball Gough brought a delivery back to hit middle and off. In the next over, Taylor drove Malcolm through the covers with a shot of great splendour. He tried to repeat the shot to the next delivery, but his bat was too far from his body and he succeeded only in edging to second slip where the debutant Mark Butcher took the catch.

After nine overs, with a score on 24 for 2, Caddick replaced Malcolm, but it was Gough who claimed the prize scalp of Mark Waugh. The Yorkshireman beat Waugh with an inswinger that hit off stump. The bowler was aided by a big gap between bat and pad. Gough also bowled Blewett with a no-ball, but he made amends immediately when Blewett seemed to slice the ball to third slip off the middle of the bat. After an hour, Australia were 28 for 4, and Gough had 3 for 16 from seven overs. He and Malcolm had totally undermined the Australian innings.

There was plenty of lift and movement for the bowlers, who were also producing prodigious swing. Steve Waugh cover drove a four and was caught behind next ball. Healy was more obviously caught at the wicket first ball, and Australia were 48 for 6. Malcolm had returned in place of Gough and was bowling to four slips and two gullies. Bevan edged to the first of the gullies, and three wickets had gone down with the score on 48.

Such was the surprise, so great the debacle, that record books were being scoured to discover Australia's lowest score against England and grave doubts were being cast as to the pedigree of the pitch. The doubts increased when Gillespie was leg before to Caddick, and Australia were 54 for 8.

Warne adopted the once traditional method of how Australian batsmen meet a crisis. He faced fire with fire, hit three fours and a three in his opening salvo and was

Mark Butcher, making his Test debut, catches Taylor at slip off Malcolm. (David Munden/Sportsline)

unbeaten on 31 at lunch when Australia, having left the indignity of the lowest score ever behind them, were 92 for 8. In all, Warne faced 46 balls and hit eight fours before skying Caddick to third man. Kasprowicz had already been taken at slip, so that Australia were all out six overs into the afternoon for a paltry 118.

The concern regarding the pitch grew when Atherton was caught off a ball that lifted and left him, and Kasprowicz had his first Test wicket when he slanted a ball across Butcher's body. Stewart batted as if in a frenzy, following Warne's pattern, and it was no surprise when an attempted pull simply skied the ball to Elliott. Hussain and Thorpe were more disciplined. At tea, England were 74 for 3. By the close, they were 200 for 3, Hussain 80, Thorpe 83. The Surrey left-hander should have been caught at square-leg by Bevan, but otherwise it had been a faultless display.

Australia had lost Gillespie with a hamstring problem and Warne looked listless as he bowled a series of long hops. McGrath could not find the right line or length and was at war with himself. Hussain and Thorpe were still together at lunch on the second day, by which time England led by 217 runs and the pair had beaten the fourth wicket record against Australia previously held by Hammond and Paynter.

Thorpe had added only three runs to his lunchtime score when he looped a catch to mid-wicket. He had batted for six minutes under five hours, faced 219 balls and hit 19 fours in his third century in his last four Tests. Crawley was out quickly, and just before tea, Hussain was out when he touched a ball from Warne to the keeper. No praise can be too high for the Essex man who had come to the wicket when England were 16 for 2 and had answered the call with the first double century of his career. He drove magnificently, and he produced late cuts which were a reminder of a lost art. He was 440 minutes at the crease, faced 337 balls and hit 38 fours. Since being reinstated in the England side he had become the most dependable of batsmen, one who could wed flair and solidity.

Having finished the second day on 449 for 6, England added another 29 on the third morning before Atherton

declared at the fall of Caddick's wicket. Kasprowicz persevered nobly for his wickets, but Australia were below par and did not enjoy the best of luck. From any criticism of their out-cricket, one man must be excepted. One cannot remember seeing a wicket-keeper give a more perfect display of his art than Ian Healy. It was not that he held six catches, but that his whole technique and commitment were of such a standard as to be an aesthetic pleasure in themselves.

Elliott and Taylor began the task of restoration with determination, good sense and no lack of positivity. In 37 overs, they scored 133 for the first wicket and were not parted until Elliott, who hit 12 fours, played inside a straight ball from Croft. Taylor had raced to 50, but he was a little more circumspect in moving to his hundred after more than five hours at the crease. It was not only Australia but Taylor who had needed restoration, and courageously the Australian captain had almost accomplished both within one innings. He had suffered severe criticism from many quarters, and his hold on his position had been tenuous. He had responded in the only way possible. By the end of the day, Taylor had 108, Blewett, neat and purposeful in all he did, was 61, and Australia were 256 for 1. This was a brave effort, but England still led by 104 runs, and Mark Waugh had been taken ill with stomach pains, which were initially feared to be the result of appendicitis. Waugh recovered, but Australia still had a mountain to climb.

Blewett reached his third century in three Tests against England with eight fours in the first hour of the fourth day. His off-drives were of such fluency that makes batting seem such a simple thing, and, in all, he treated us to 19 fours and a six. He and Taylor had added 194 when

Darren Gough begins the rout of Australia. Matthew Elliott is bowled for 6. (David Munden/Sportsline)

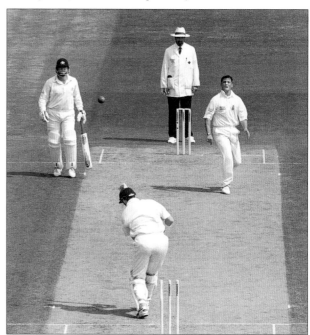

Taylor, deceived in the flight perhaps, gave Croft the easiest of return catches. Croft also accounted for the admirable Blewett, caught bat and pad, and it was apparent that Australia needed another big innings if they were to be saved. Steve Waugh was resolute for two-and-a-quarter hours, but Gough, who had a fine match, caused Bevan, who had suggested a blend of aggression and determination, to fend the ball to gully and, crucially, he caused Mark Waugh to glove to the wicket-keeper.

When Steve Waugh was sixth out, pinned back on his stumps by Gough, Australia led by only 71. Ealham now proved what the old pros believed – that it is not how you bowl but when you bowl that matters. He bowled quite dreadfully, but Healy, perhaps in frustration, slashed the first ball of his second over, wide and short, into the hands of the gully. Two balls later, Kasprowicz nudged a better delivery to slip, and, in his third over, Gillespie's runner was run out and Warne gave an inexplicably simple return catch.

England needed 118 to win. Butcher hit two fours to leg but never looked assured. He faced only 10 balls and was leg before to Kasprowicz. Atherton and Stewart were prepared for no nonsense. They raced to a jubilant victory, hitting the last 90 runs in 72 minutes.

Hussain was named Man of the Match. Euphoria had become something close to hysteria, and there were some unwise predictions that were hard to justify on the evidence of one match in which Australia had begun to show their true mettle on the second and third days.

The England heroes, record-breakers Nasser Hussain and Graham Thorpe. (Clive Mason/Allsport)

England could justifiably be proud of their triumph. They had seized the day, and one must enjoy the moments when they happen. They do not come that often.

First Cornhill Test Match – England v. Australia
5, 6, 7 and 8 June 1997 at Edgbaston, Birmingham

Australia

	First Innings			Second Innings		
M.A. Taylor (Capt)	c Butcher, b Malcolm	7	(2) c and b Croft			129
M.T.G. Elliott	b Gough	6	(1) b Croft			66
G.S. Blewett	c Hussain, b Gough	7	c Butcher, b Croft			125
M.E. Waugh	b Gough	5	(6) c Stewart, b Gough			1
S.R. Waugh	c Stewart, b Caddick	12	(4) lbw, b Gough			33
M.G. Bevan	c Ealham, b Malcolm	8	(5) c Hussain, b Gough			24
*I.A. Healy	c Stewart, b Caddick	0	c Atherton, b Ealham			30
J.N. Gillespie	lbw, b Caddick	4	(10) run out			0
S.K. Warne	c Malcolm, b Caddick	47	(8) c and b Ealham			32
M.S. Kasprowicz	c Butcher, b Caddick	17	(9) c Butcher, b Ealham			0
G.D. McGrath	not out	1	not out			0
	w 2, nb 2	4	B 18, lb 12, w 2, nb 5			37
		118				**477**

	O	M	R	**W**	O	M	R	**W**
Gough	10	1	43	**3**	35	7	123	**3**
Malcolm	10	2	25	**2**	21	6	52	–
Caddick	11.5	1	50	**5**	30	6	87	–
Croft					43	10	125	**3**
Ealham					15.4	3	60	**3**

England

	First Innings			Second Innings		
M.A. Butcher	c Healy, b Kasprowicz	8	lbw, b Kasprowicz			14
*A.J. Stewart	c Healy, b McGrath	2	not out			57
M.A. Atherton (Capt)	c Elliott, b Gillespie	18	not out			40
N. Hussain	c Healy, b Warne	207				
G.P. Thorpe	c Bevan, b McGrath	138				
J.P. Crawley	c Healy, b Kasprowicz	1				
M.A. Ealham	not out	53				
R.D.B. Croft	c Healy, b Kasprowicz	24				
D. Gough	c Healy, b Kasprowicz	0				
A.R. Caddick	lbw, b Bevan	0				
D.E. Malcolm						
	B 4, lb 7, w 1, nb 15	27	b 4, lb 4			8
	(for 9 wickets, dec.)	**478**	(for 1 wicket)			**119**

	O	M	R	**W**	O	M	R	**W**
McGrath	32	8	107	**2**	7	1	42	–
Kasprowicz	39	8	113	**4**	7	–	42	**1**
Gillespie	10	1	48	**1**				
Warne	35	8	110	**1**	7.3	–	27	–
Bevan	10.4	–	44	**1**				
S.R. Waugh	12	2	45	–				

Fall of Wickets
1–11, 2–15, 3–26, 4–28, 5–48, 6–48, 7–48, 8–54, 9–110
1–133, 2–327, 3–354, 4–393, 5–399, 6–431, 7–465, 8–465, 9–477

Fall of Wickets
1–8, 2–16, 3–50, 4–338, 5–345, 6–416, 7–460, 8–463, 9–478
1–29

Umpires: P. Willey & S.A. Bucknor

England won by 9 wickets

The England collapse. Atherton is taken low down at first slip by Taylor off McGrath. (David Munden/Sportsline)

11, 12 and 13 June
at Trent Bridge
Nottinghamshire 239 (N.J. Astle 99, G.D. McGrath 4 for 63)
Australians 398 for 5 (M.T.G. Elliott 127, S.R. Waugh 115, M.G. Bevan 75 not out)
Match drawn

No play was possible on the first day, and the Australians were denied the practice they wanted and needed. Paul Reiffel played his first match since arriving from Australia to replace Bichel. Bowling well within himself, he took 3 for 15 in 10 overs. New Zealand Test player Nathan Astle played a delightful innings for the county, while Elliott confirmed his solid form and Steve Waugh hit 115 off 137 balls for the tourists.

14, 15 and 16 June
at Leicester
Australians 220 for 8 dec. (R.T. Ponting 64, J. Ormond 6 for 54) and 105 for 3 dec. (M.A. Taylor 57)
Leicestershire 62 for 4 dec. and 179 (S.K. Warne 5 for 42)
Australians won by 84 runs

The Australians gratefully claimed their first first-class win of the season. It came on the eve of the second Test and was brought about by generous declarations after much play had been lost on the first two days. The Australian first innings was built around Ponting, Healy and 46 extras, and Reiffel increased his chances of playing at Lord's when he took 3 for 12 in Leicestershire's brief first innings. Reiffel took three more wickets in the second innings when he and Warne reduced the county side from 155 for 5 to 179 all out. For Leicestershire, the most encouraging feature of the game was the bowling of 19-year-old fast medium pace bowler Jimmy Ormond, who took a career best 6 for 54.

Second Test Match

England v. Australia

The Lord's Test is one of the greatest events of the cricketing calendar, and it was sad that the eagerly anticipated Ashes encounter in 1997 should be ruined by rain. Reiffel had replaced the injured Gillespie in the Australian side, while England, to no-one's surprise, fielded an unchanged eleven. No play was possible on the first day, and only 21 overs, 92 minutes were played before lunch on the second day. During that time Australia did enough to quieten some of the Edgbaston hysteria.

Taylor won the toss again and asked England to bat. Neither Atherton nor Butcher looked at ease against McGrath and Reiffel, and it was little surprise when, in the seventh over, having edged McGrath over slips for four, Butcher turned a lifting ball into the hands of short-leg off bat and pad. In McGrath's next over, Atherton edged low to first slip where Taylor took a good catch, and when McGrath pounded in again for his sixth over of the innings Stewart shouldered arms and allowed the ball to hit off stump. England were 13 for 3 in 11 overs.

Matters could have been worse. Before he had scored, Thorpe edged McGrath, and Healy, diving forward, scooped the ball up. The umpires meditated, but Healy ran forward to explain he had taken the ball on the half-volley. The world's finest wicket-keeper had set a model that some England fielders could well have imitated later in the series. With Thorpe on 13 and Hussain on 10, England were 38 for 3 when the rain returned to end play for the day.

What happened on the Saturday morning took all by surprise. Five overs into the morning, Reiffel, bowling from the Nursery End, had Thorpe taken at short-leg off a simple lob from bat and pad. It was Reiffel's third delivery of the day, most of the rest of which belonged to McGrath. Crawley looked far from at ease before edging low to Healy's right. Hussain had looked composed, but when he played across

McGrath strikes again. Crawley is caught by Healy for 1. (David Munden/Sportsline)

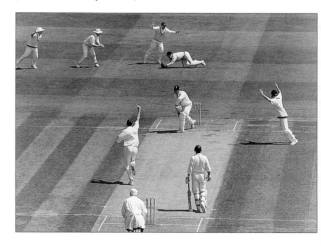

the line to McGrath England were 62 for 6 in the 35th over. Perhaps Hussain's concentration had been disturbed by a brief shower, for he fell to the first ball after the resumption.

McGrath was irresistible. He gave a magnificent display of fast bowling. He ran in smoothly from the Pavilion End, used his height and his intelligence, got close to the stumps and moved the ball devastatingly late. He was to finish with 8 for 38, the best figures ever recorded by an Australian bowler in a Lord's Test, and they did not flatter him.

Croft slashed at Reiffel and was dropped at slip, so he slashed at McGrath and was caught at the wicket. Gough clouted two fours and then lofted an attempted hook to Healy. Ealham lobbed to mid-on after more than 50 painful minutes, and Caddick played across the line. England were out for 77. They were more the victims of great bowling than bad batting, but there was a feeling that we had returned to the real world.

Stewart had back spasms so Crawley kept wicket. Taylor played on to Gough in the fifth over, but chances went begging and England's out-cricket was generally poor. Blewett was taken at slip, but when play ended Australia were 131 for 2, and the day was very much theirs.

A soggy Sunday allowed no play until 5.40, and Australia used what time was available, 17.4 overs, to press home their advantage. They advanced their score to 213 for 7 with Matthew Elliott making an admirable maiden Test

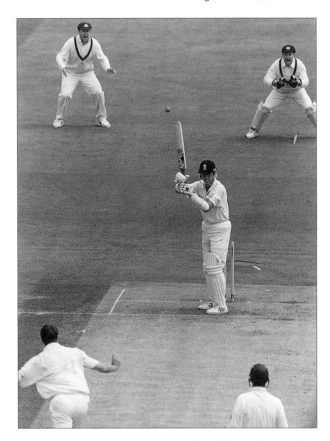

Stewart offers no shot at a ball from McGrath and is bowled.
(David Munden/Sportsline)

Second Cornhill Test Match – England v. Australia
19, 20, 21, 22 and 23 June 1997 at Lord's

England

	First Innings		Second Innings	
M.A. Butcher	c Blewett, b McGrath	5	b Warne	87
M.A. Atherton (Capt)	c Taylor, b McGrath	1	hit wkt, b Kasprowicz	77
*A.J. Stewart	b McGrath	1	c Kasprowicz, b McGrath	13
N. Hussain	lbw, b McGrath	19	c and b Warne	0
G.P. Thorpe	c Blewett, b Reiffel	21	not out	30
J.P. Crawley	c Healy, b McGrath	1	not out	29
M.A. Ealham	c Elliott, b Reiffel	7		
R.D.B. Croft	c Healy, b McGrath	2		
D. Gough	c Healy, b McGrath	10		
A.R. Caddick	lbw, b McGrath	1		
D.E. Malcolm	not out	0		
	B 4, nb 5	9	b 8, lb 14, w 1, nb 7	30
		77	(for 4 wickets)	266

Australia

	First Innings	
M.A. Taylor (Capt)	b Gough	1
M.T.G. Elliott	c Crawley, b Caddick	112
G.S. Blewett	c Hussain, b Croft	45
M.E. Waugh	c Malcolm, b Caddick	33
S.K. Warne	c Hussain, b Gough	0
S.R. Waugh	lbw, b Caddick	0
M.G. Bevan	c Stewart, b Caddick	4
*I.A. Healy	not out	13
P.R. Reiffel	not out	1
M.S. Kasprowicz		
G.D. McGrath		
	b 1, lb 3	213
	(for 7 wickets, dec.)	118

	O	M	R	W	O	M	R	W
McGrath	20.3	8	38	8	20	5	65	1
Reiffel	15	9	17	2	13	5	29	–
Kasprowicz	5	1	9	–	15	3	54	1
Warne	2	–	9	–	19	4	47	2
Bevan					8	1	29	–
S.R. Waugh					4	–	20	–

	O	M	R	W
Gough	20	4	82	2
Caddick	22	6	71	4
Malcolm	7	1	26	–
Croft	12	5	30	1

Fall of Wickets
1–11, 2–12, 3–13, 4–47, 5–56, 6–62, 7–66, 8–76, 9–77
1–162, 2–189, 3–197, 4–202

Fall of Wickets
1–4, 2–73, 3–147, 4–147, 5–147, 6–159, 7–212

Umpires: S. Venkataraghavan & D.R. Shepherd

Match drawn

Glenn McGrath leaves the field in triumph having taken 8 for 38. (David Munden/Sportsline)

dropped by Taylor at slip off the simplest of chances. The Surrey left-hander was on two at the time, and had Taylor held the catch, his Test carrer, at least temporarily, would have been at an end. As it was, he and Atherton scored 162 for the first wicket, and he faced 210 balls and hit 14 fours in his 87, which ended when he was deceived by Warne.

So the match trickled to the draw that four days of bad weather had made inevitable. England stll led one-nil in the series, but the bowling of McGrath and the batting of Elliott had jerked the host nation out of the land of dreams.

28, 29 and 30 June
at Southampton
Hampshire 156 and 176 (J.N. Gillespie 5 for 33)
Australians 465 for 8 dec. (M.E. Waugh 173, M.A. Taylor 109, M.T.G. Elliott 61, S.J. Renshaw 4 for 107)
Australians won by an innings and 133 runs

century. He pulled and drove with relish, and his three-hour innings included 20 fours. Caddick produced a spell of 4 for 30 as Australia sought quick runs, but, in the gloom, Elliott, 55 on Saturday evening and last out on the Sunday, was very much the hero.

England needed some good fortune if they were to survive on the Monday, and they had it when Butcher was

The tourists had lost the whole of their scheduled three-day match against British Universities to rain and were thankful for a resounding victory over Hampshire with Mark Waugh and Taylor finding form and Gillespie proving his fitness.

A failure for Mark Taylor, bowled by Gough for 1. (David Munden/Sportsline)

Third Test Match

England v. Australia

England chose 14 players for the Old Trafford Test and once more left out Tufnell. Malcolm was also omitted from the final eleven because of fitness doubts, and the other player to miss out was Mike Smith, the Gloucestershire left-arm pace bowler, who was having a highly successful season. Smith had not appeared in Test cricket, but Dean Headley was luckier, winning his first cap as replacement for Malcolm. Australia brought back Gillespie for Kasprowicz. Taylor won the toss for the thrid time, and Australia batted.

The decision to bat first was seen as something of a risk in doubtful weather on an uncertain pitch, and Taylor may have rued his decision when he was caught at first slip in the sixth over to give Headley his first Test wicket. Five overs later, Blewett chopped a ball from Gough into his stumps. Mark Waugh, too, went before lunch. Ealham bowled two rank long hops, and Mark Waugh seemed so surprised by a ball of good length that he sliced it to the wicket-keeper.

Elliott showed great resolve, and Steve Waugh was the cool head and master in a situation which threatened disaster, but Elliott was adjudged caught behind and Bevan, his place in jeopardy, was all nerves before being squared up by a beautiful ball from Headley which he touched to the keeper. Healy gloved a ball down the leg side, and Warne fell to a straight forward so that Australia were 162 for 7 at tea, and England were very much on top.

The day had been punctuated by rain and play was extended by an hour, but in those 14 overs Steve Waugh and Paul Reiffel redressed the balance. Waugh, supreme in command of temperament and of the technique demanded by the pitch and the conditions, reached a masterly century. He hit 12 fours and never suggested anything but permanence. By the close, Australia were 224 for 7, Waugh 102, Reiffel 26.

It was something of a surprise that the pair did not add more on the Friday morning, but Gough did well to account for them both. He yorked Reiffel and bowled Waugh with a ball of full length which took the inside edge. Gillespie gave Stewart his sixth catch of the innings, and Headley finished with a most respectable 4 for 72 on his debut.

England needed to get to lunch unscathed, but Atherton fell in the ninth over when he was taken down the leg side by Healy. At the interval, England were 37 for 1, and Butcher and Stewart appeared settled.

There were some alarms in the afternoon, but there were no disasters until Warne pitched a ball on leg stump that turned sharply across Stewart's body and caught the outside edge to be taken well at slip. Butcher had reached his second Test fifty when he became the victim of a piece of utmost brilliance by Healy. Bevan bowled a full toss down the leg side. It should have gone for four, but the left-hander over-balanced slightly, Healy whipped off the bails before the batsman could take another breath. This was wicket-

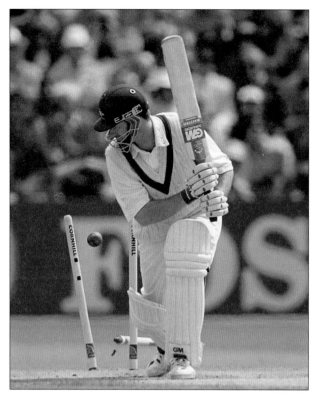

Steve Waugh is bowled by Gough for 108. Steve Waugh batted outstandingly in difficult conditions and hit a century in each innings. (Clive Mason/Allsport)

keeping of a class that only men like Tallon, Evans and Knott have reached in the years since the war.

Thorpe, too, was out before tea. He swept at Warne and got a bottom edge onto his pad, from whence it flew to slip. Without a run added after the break, Hussain fell to Warne's leg-spinner, and four passive overs later Crawley suffered the same fate. The combination of the world's best leg-break bowler and the world's best wicket-keeper was once again proving far too lethal a weapon for England,

Shane Warne again proves to be England's tormentor. Crawley is caught behind for 4. (Adrian Murrell/Allsport)

Croft swatted McGrath to mid-off, a shot which denied him the right to be called an all-rounder, and Gough offered no shot at Warne once too often. Ealham was something of an anonymous figure in the England side, but he was still there on 23 at the close, and the more robust Caddick was 15. England trembled at 161 for 8.

Ealham and Caddick had hinted at recovery on the Friday evening, but Caddick was taken at silly point to the fourth ball he received from Warne on the Saturday morning, and Headley was yorked by the first ball he received from McGrath, whose pace and probing accuracy were the perfect foil and aid to Warne.

Headley quickly had Taylor taken at slip when Australia batted a second time, but Gough was wayward, and Atherton soon summoned Croft. Blewett drove at the off-spinner and edged to slip, where Hussain dived forward, juggled with the ball and claimed the catch. There was more than an element of doubt, and the umpires conferred long and hard before giving Blewett out.

It was not a claim nor a judgement that the Australians welcomed, and it was to fester with them for the rest of the series. Elliott was caught at second slip, and England could now have seized the initiative, but they lost their way. Croft and Gough both presented leg side offerings which were punished, and ominously the Waugh twins took control.

It could have been worse. They had increased the score by 92 when Ealham surprised Mark with a change of pace and bowled him. Bevan immediately fended limply to gully, but Healy was the man for the moment, the ideal partner for the resilient Steve Waugh. He drove and square-cut viciously and he scampered runs. When he clouted Croft to mid-wicket, 88 had been scored in 24 overs, and Australia were disappearing over the horizon.

The last hour of the day brought another 52 runs, 33 of them to Warne who hit a six and two fours. Steve Waugh, unbeaten on 82 after five hours at the crease, stood like the sword of Damocles above England's head. Australia were 335 ahead, and Warne on a deteriorating pitch in the fourth innings loomed in the near distance.

The torment continues. Alec Stewart is totally deceived and bowled by Warne for 1 in the second innings (Laurence Griffiths/Allsport)

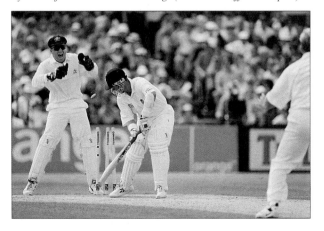

Far from collapsing early, the Australians lost only two more wickets on the fourth day while adding another 133 runs. Warne reached a second Test half century, an innings full of gusto, before receiving a ball that bounced disconcertingly. Steve Waugh reached his second century of the match a few moments later. He was finally caught behind off Headley, but by then he had hit 10 fours, batted for 382 minutes, faced 271 balls and put the match way beyond England's reach.

Even the departure of Steve Waugh did not end England's misery. Reiffel and Gillespie shared a merry stand of 62 in as many minutes, and Taylor's declaration left England a target of 469. Survival was all that England could hope for.

That prospect became unlikely when, in the 17th over of the innings, Gillespie, having switched to the Stretford End, trapped Atherton leg before. In the next over, Warne's third of the innings, Stewart was comprehensively beaten by a ball that appeared to spin right through him and leave him floundering with bat and legs divorced.

After tea Gillespie forced Hussain back on his stumps and beat him with a ball of full length. He then dropped one short to Butcher, who obligingly pulled to fine-leg where McGrath took the catch low down. Gillespie had claimed three of England's top batsmen in the space of 19 balls.

Worse was to follow. Thorpe was frustrated and suddenly cut at a ball from Warne that span wide. He edged to the incomparable Healy. With attacking fields to pierce, Crawley hit seven fours and ran to 53 before the close. Ealham was on 5, and England were 130 for 5 and sinking fast.

They might have sunk even faster than they did, but Blewett put down Crawley at short-leg off Warne early on the last day. It was McGrath who made the breakthrough. As soon as he was able to bowl at Ealham he produced a quicker ball which moved late and took the edge of the bat to be superbly caught one-handed, low to his right, by Healy. Croft, bitterly disappointing with the bat, was taken at leg gully when he flinched and fended. Crawley's valiant innings ended four overs later when he went back too far onto his stumps and dislodged a bail. Gough attempted some swashbuckling before McGrath knocked back his off stump. It was McGrath's fourth wicket in 31 balls at a personal cost of 15 runs.

Caddick took liberties with Warne, hitting him far and wide, but the leg-spinner had him taken at mid-on to end the game and to bring his match figures to 11 for 111. The series was level, but the problem was that so convincing had been Australia's victory, so great was the gap between the two sides, that it felt as if Australia were already ahead.

9 July
at Jesmond
Australians 290 for 7 (B.P. Julian 106)
Minor Counties 281 for 9 (I. Cockbain 82)
Australians won by 9 runs

Third Cornhill Test Match – England v. Australia
3, 4, 5, 6 and 7 July 1997 at Old Trafford, Manchester

Australia

	First Innings		Second Innings	
M.A. Taylor (Capt)	c Thorpe, b Headley	2	(2) c Butcher, b Headley	1
M.T.G. Elliott	c Stewart, b Headley	40	(1) c Butcher, b Headley	11
G.S. Blewett	b Gough	8	c Hussain, b Croft	19
M.E. Waugh	c Stewart, b Ealham	12	b Ealham	55
S.R. Waugh	b Gough	108	c Stewart, b Headley	116
M.G. Bevan	c Stewart, b Headley	7	c Atherton, b Headley	0
*I.A. Healy	c Stewart, b Caddick	9	c Butcher, b Croft	47
S.K. Warne	c Stewart, b Ealham	3	c Stewart, b Caddick	53
P.R. Reiffel	b Gough	31	not out	45
J.N. Gillespie	c Stewart, b Headley	0	not out	28
G.D. McGrath	not out	0		
	b 8, lb 4, nb 3	15	b 1, lb 13, nb 6	20
		235		395

	O	M	R	W	O	M	R	W
Gough	21	7	52	3	20	3	62	–
Headley	27.3	4	72	4	29	4	104	4
Caddick	14	2	52	1	21	–	69	1
Ealham	11	2	34	2	13	3	41	1
Croft	4	–	13	–	39	12	105	2

Fall of Wickets
1–9, 2–22, 3–42, 4–85, 5–113, 6–150, 7–160, 8–230, 9–235
1–5, 2–33, 3–39, 4–131, 5–132, 6–210, 7–298, 8–333

England

	First Innings		Second Innings	
M.A. Butcher	st Healy, b Bevan	51	c McGrath, b Gillespie	28
M.A. Atherton (Capt)	c Healy, b McGrath	5	lbw, b Gillespie	21
*A.J. Stewart	c Taylor, b Warne	30	b Warne	1
N. Hussain	c Healy, b Warne	13	lbw, b Gillespie	1
G.P. Thorpe	c Taylor, b Warne	3	c Healy, b Warne	7
J.P. Crawley	c Healy, b Warne	4	hit wkt, b McGrath	83
M.A. Ealham	not out	24	c Healy, b McGrath	9
R.D.B. Croft	c S. Waugh, b McGrath	7	c Reiffel, b McGrath	7
D. Gough	lbw, b Warne	1	b McGrath	6
A.R. Caddick	c M. Waugh, b Warne	15	c Gillespie, b Warne	17
D.W. Headley	b McGrath	0	not out	0
	b 4, lb 3, nb 2	9	b 14, lb 4, w 1, nb 1	20
		162		200

	O	M	R	W	O	M	R	W
McGrath	23.4	9	40	3	21	4	46	4
Reiffel	9	3	14	–	2	–	8	–
Warne	30	14	48	6	30.4	8	63	3
Gillespie	14	3	39	–	12	4	31	3
Bevan	8	3	14	1	8	2	34	–

Fall of Wickets
1–8, 2–74, 3–94, 4–101, 5–110, 6–111, 7–122, 8–123, 9–161
1–44, 2–45, 3–50, 4–55, 5–84, 6–158, 7–170, 8–177, 9–188

Umpires: G. Sharp & S. Venkataraghavan

Australia won by 268 runs

Injury again struck the tourists as Gilchrist was forced to return home and was replaced by Berry, the Victorian wicket-keeper. Meanwhile, the Australians entered their mid-term leisure period.

12 July
at Edinburgh (The Grange)
Australians 278 for 9 (M.J. Slater 95, K.L.P. Sheridan 5 for 65)
Scotland 95 for 6
Match abandoned

A thunderstorm caused the game to be abandoned after 21.5 overs of Scotland's innings.

14 July
at Wormsley
Australians 267 for 5 dec. (M.T.G. Elliott 95, M.G. Bevan 54)
J. Paul Getty's XI 237 for 4 (M.D. Crowe 115 not out, R.A. Smith 57, M.G. Bevan 4 for 85)
Match drawn

The social event of the tour in the beautiful Oxfordshire countryside. The Australians made their runs off 44 overs, leaving Getty's XI 37 overs in which to score 268 runs. Bevan took all four wickets but conceded 85 runs in his nine overs.

16, 17 and 18 July
at Cardiff
Australia 369 for 4 dec. (R.T. Ponting 126 not out, M.A. Taylor 71, G.S. Blewett 54, J.L. Langer 50 not out) and 217 for 7 dec. (P.R. Reiffel 56, G.S. Blewett 50 not out)
Glamorgan 254 (S.P. James 91, P.R. Reiffel 5 for 61) and 211 for 3 (S.P. James 79)
Match drawn

With Glamorgan resting their three main bowlers, Waqar, Watkin and Croft, this match, played on the most tranquil of surfaces was always destined to be drawn. Ponting hit a stylish century to press his claims for a recall to the Test side. On the final day, Steve James became the first batsman in the country to reach 1,000 runs.

19, 20 and 21 July
at Lord's
Middlesex 305 (M.W. Gatting 85, M.R. Ramprakash 76, G.D. McGrath 4 for 61) and 201 for 6
Australians 432 for 7 dec. (M.E. Waugh 142 not out, M.T.G. Elliott 83, S.R. Waugh 57)
Match drawn

A gentle warm-up before the fourth Test brought encouragement to the Australians through Mark Waugh's century.

Fourth Test Match

England v. Australia

Hot upon the heels of the defeat at Old Trafford, the England selectors had named an unchanged squad, saying that they had total faith in their men. Ultimately they made one change, Mike Smith winning his first Test cap in place of Caddick. As expected, Ponting replaced Bevan in the Australian side.

The Australian management lodged a complaint when it was found that the pitch had been changed from that originally designated, and that the chairman of the England selectors was believed to have some part in bringing about this change.

Australia won the toss and asked England to bat. Only four overs were possible before lunch and only another five balls before tea was taken. Play began in earnest shortly before five, and two hours in the evening sunshine did not prove to be the happiest time for England. Atherton and Butcher added 29 runs to the 14 they had gathered in the two brief sessions before Reiffel, who had been switched to the football stand end, had Butcher taken at short-leg. The

Jason Gillespie celebrates one of his seven wickets at Headingley. (David Munden/Sportsline)

batsman turned the ball off his legs quite forcefully but at waist height, and Blewett clutched it to his midriff. Some suggested that Butcher was unlucky; the more knowing recalled the old pros view that if you hit the ball in the air in a Test match, you were likely to be caught.

Stewart was not having a good series. His wicket keeping was far below international standard, and his batting was all at sea. He flayed and missed at his first ball and after an unhappy half hour he was caught at short-leg off the shoulder of the bat. Hussain looked assertive and hit four boundaries, but three overs from the end of the day he was caught at first slip off McGrath. Atherton looked calm and dependable, but England were 106 for 3.

The second day was a sad one for England. By the end of it, Australia led by 86 runs with six wickets still standing. There was no indication of how the day would go when, in the first 45 minutes, Headley batted with such sound judgement as to make one forget that he was a night watchman. He had hit two fours and had made a happy 22 before driving at Gillespie's first ball of the morning and edging high to the gully where Steve Waugh took the catch. This was the encouragement that Gillespie needed. It was the beginning of a spell that wrecked England, but it was McGrath who struck the next, vital blow.

He bowled a bouncer to Atherton who helped it into the hands of the hands of Gillespie at fine-leg. In the next over, Thorpe pulled at Gillespie and chopped the ball grotesquely into his stumps. Crawley turned a ball from Gillespie firmly to Blewett. It struck the fielder on the boot and his reactions were sharp enough to allow him to grab the chance. Croft played a lifting ball to leg gully; Gough and Smith each lasted two balls before having their stumps scattered. Gillespie's morning spell had brought him 6 for 23 in 7.4 overs. England's last seven wickets had gone down for 34 runs.

In the early afternoon, it seemed as if England would still take the honours. Taylor was cruelly unlucky when he ducked a bouncer that might have touched glove and certainly touched forearm. Blewett drove rashly at a wide delivery and was caught behind while Mark Waugh pushed Headley a return catch. With his score on 29, Elliot touched Smith's away swinger to Thorpe at slip. It was face high, but it was the simplest of offerings. Thorpe dropped it. It was Smith's third over in Test cricket.

When Steve Waugh was caught at short-leg in the next over one felt that Thorpe's miss might not matter. It did. Elliott was dropped again, on 63, in the gully by Atherton. By the end of the day he had hit three sixes and 17 fours and had given a splendid exhibition of pulling and driving in his unbeaten 134. If anything, Ponting was even more immaculate and stood 14 short of a maiden Test century. The England out-cricket had been poor, with the captaincy often diffident. Ealham had bowled six overs, and one wondered why he was in the side.

There was no play after lunch on the Saturday, but Australia, scoring at nearly four runs an over, took their score to 373 for the loss of Ponting. The Tasmanian had

The crucial miss. Elliott is out down by Thorpe at slip off the bowling of Smith. (Clive Mason/Allsport)

completed a truly delightful century. He is handsome and classical in style, and he hits the ball very hard as his 19 fours and a six testify. He is, surely, a batsman destined for greatness. He romped to his hundred without any sign of nerves, but he should have been stumped off Croft when he had reached three figures. Stewart is not a Test wicket-keeper, and the yawning gap between him and Healy was in many ways symbolic of the chasm that separated the two sides. Ponting was out when he skied Gough and was caught at point by Ealham, who remained anonymous in the field, seemingly unknown to his captain. Healy began with a flurry of boundaries, and Elliott moved to 164.

Healy added another four before being beaten by Ealham on the fourth morning. Warne also fell to the Kent all-rounder, but Reiffel proved harder to dislodge, and Elliott was the next to go.

He had batted more than seven and a half hours, hit three sixes and 23 fours and faced 351 balls when he was beaten by Gough's yorker. He was one run short of a double century. He had enjoyed some fortune, but he has that rare quality of composure which never allows him to think about the last ball, nor is he simply a rock, for Australia's success in this Test was founded on the speed with which they scored their runs.

Gough bowled Gillespie to claim five wickets in the innings, but Reiffel and McGrath batted merrily for 37 minutes to add 40 and to take the score past 500.

Despair soon gripped England. McGrath, bowling round the wicket, had Butcher caught behind and Atherton taken at slip. Hussain could have been run out by yards first ball. He pushed to cover and ran in a frenzy. Ponting's throw

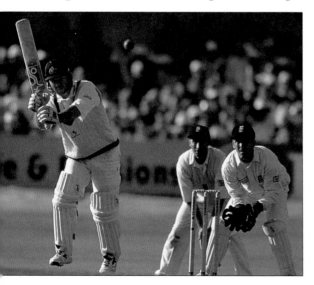

Ricky Ponting on his way to a most attractive maiden Test century. (David Munden/Sportsline)

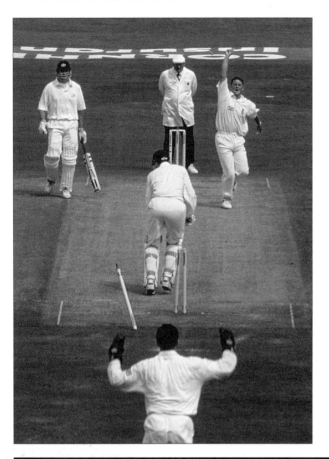

shaved the wicket and went for four overthrows. Stewart was beaten by Reiffel's low bounce, and Thorpe, having been missed at gully, was taken at second slip by Mark Waugh after Healy had parried the ball.

In spite of these disasters, Hussain batted with flair. He punished anything loose and offered a square on defence to anything that suggested trouble. Crawley exuded more confidence than of late, and England were still alive on 212 for 4 at the end of the day. Hussain had reached his second century of the series.

Warne had done little in the Test, which Australia had dominated since the first day, but in the fifth over of the final day he struck the decisive blow. He deceived Hussain in the flight and had him caught at mid-off. One end was now open to Australia, and in the hour before lunch they rushed to victory. Crawley was virtually becalmed, and Ealham looked happy to escape to the non-striker's end in order to avoid Gillespie's pace. Escape proved to be no sanctuary for him. He slashed at Reiffel, and Mark Waugh took an astonishing right-handed catch at second slip, clutching the ball when it appeared to be behind him.

Reiffel knocked back Crawley's off stump, and Headley was palpably leg before. This brought in Smith for four balls before lunch. He pushed an easy single which, incredibly, Croft refused so he hit Gillespie through the off side for four. The first ball after the break saw Croft fend limply to Healy. It

The end of Elliott, yorked by Gough for 199.
(David Munden/Sportsline)

Fourth Cornhill Test Match – England v. Australia
24, 25, 26, 27 and 28 July 1997 at Headingley, Leeds

England

First Innings		Second Innings	
M.A. Butcher	c Blewett, b Reiffel	24	c Healy, b McGrath	19
M.A. Atherton (Capt)	c Gillespie, b McGrath	41	c Warne, b McGrath	2
*A.J. Stewart	c Blewett, b Gillespie	7	b Reiffel	16
N. Hussain	c Taylor, b McGrath	26	c Gillespie, b Warne	105
D.W. Headley	c S. Waugh, b Gillespie	22	(8) lbw, b Reiffel	3
G.P. Thorpe	b Gillespie	15	(5) c M. Waugh, b Gillespie	15
J.P. Crawley	c Blewett,b Gillespie	2	(6) b Reiffel	72
M.A. Ealham	not out	8	(7) c M. Waugh, b Reiffel	4
R.D.B. Croft	c Ponting, b Gillespie	6	c Healy, b Reiffel	5
D. Gough	b Gillespie	0	c M. Waugh, b Gillespie	0
A.M. Smith	b Gillespie	0	not out	4
	b 4, lb 4, w 1, nb 12	21	b 6, lb 4, nb 13	23
		172		**268**

	O	M	R	**W**	O	M	R	**W**
McGrath	22	5	67	**2**	22	5	80	**2**
Reiffel	20	4	41	**1**	21.1	2	49	**5**
Gillespie	13.4	1	37	**7**	23	8	65	**2**
Blewett	3	–	17	**–**				
Warne	1	–	2	**–**	21	6	53	**1**
S.R. Waugh					4	1	11	**–**

Fall of Wickets
1–**43**, 2–**58**, 3–**103**, 4–**138**, 5–**154**, 6–**154**, 7–**163**, 8–**172**, 9–**172**
1–**23**, 2–**28**, 3–**57**, 4–**89**, 5–**222**, 6–**252**, 7–**256**, 8–**263**, 9–**264**

Australia

First Innings		
M.A. Taylor (Capt)	c Stewart, b Gough	0
M.T.G. Elliott	b Gough	199
G.S. Blewett	c Stewart, b Gough	1
M.E. Waugh	c and b Headley	8
S.R. Waugh	c Crawley, b Headley	4
R.T. Ponting	c Ealham, b Gough	127
*I.A. Healy	b Ealham	31
S.K. Warne	c Thorpe, b Ealham	0
P.R. Reiffel	not out	54
J.N. Gillespie	b Gough	3
G.D. McGrath	not out	20
	b 9, lb 10, nb 35	54
	(for 9 wickets, dec.)	**501**

	O	M	R	**W**
Gough	36	5	149	**5**
Headley	25	2	125	**2**
Smith	23	2	89	**–**
Ealham	19	3	56	**2**
Croft	18	1	49	**–**
Butcher	2	–	14	**–**

Fall of Wickets
1–**0**, 2–**16**, 3–**43**, 4–**50**, 5–**318**, 6–**382**, 7–**383**, 8–**444**, 9–**461**

Umpires: M.J. Kitchen & C.J. Mitchley

Australia won by an innings and 61 runs

was a humiliation compounded by his refusal to take the run and the responsibility offered by Smith.

England had been beaten in what amounted to little more than three days. The defeat was total.

1, 2, 3 and 4 August

at Taunton

Somerset 284 (K.A. Parsons 71, R.J. Turner 58, S.K. Warne 5 for 57) and 147 for 3 (R.J. Turner 65 not out)
Australians 323 (B.P. Julian 71, S.R. Waugh 62, A.R. Caddick 5 for 54)
Match drawn

Fourteen wickets fell on the first day while 466 runs were scored. Somerset went off at a whirlwind pace, and they averaged four runs an over. The tourists made 182 for 4 in 32 overs before the close. A stand of 106 for the seventh wicket between Healy and Julian put the Australians in command on the Saturday, but rain prevented any play on the last two days.

In spite of the general excitement of the cricket, this was an unfortunate match. Sections of the crowd hurled abuse at the Australian players, and at one point the police were called to calm the situation. This disease had started during the first Test at Edgbaston when obscene songs were chanted at Shane Warne. Roger Knight, the MCC secretary, had read the riot act before the rain-ruined game at Lord's, but there had been incidents at Headingley and Old Trafford where Warne was booed. As the leg-spinner's only offence was to take English wickets, one presumes that Warne was abused because he is so good. English cricket is disgraced by these actions, and one would suggest that they are not the actions of the members but those who visit a ground once a year – for a Test match.

Croft is caught behind off Reiffel on the first ball after lunch on the fifth day, and Australia take a 2–1 lead in the series.
(David Munden/Sportsline)

Fifth Cornhill Test Match

England v. Australia

England had to win the fifth Test match in order to keep alive any hope of regaining the Ashes. Chairman of Selectors David Graveney announced that what was believed would be a winning side would be chosen. Caddick and Malcolm returned at the expense of Smith and Gough, who was injured. Butcher was dropped and Stewart resumed as Atherton's opening partner while he still kept wicket. Crawley moved up to number three, and the Hollioake brothers were brought in with Ealham omitted. Croft was again preferred to Tufnell. Australia were unchanged.

The selection of the Hollioake brothers was as puzzling as the enthusiasm with which it was greeted. Adam Hollioake is not one of the six best batsmen in England, and he cannot be considered as a Test all-rounder. He entered the match with 462 first-class runs to his credit in 14 completed innings. He had nine wickets and had only twice bowled as many as ten overs in an innings. Brother Ben, although very promising, did not hold a regular place in the Surrey side. He had two fifties to his credit and had 11 first-class wickets, which included four in the 'A' team at the start of the season. In spite of this, with a passion to ignore the facts, the two were seen as England's saviours. Adam was talked of as captain before he had set foot on the field; and Ben was Young Cricketer of the Year. The brothers received press coverage of which the Spice Girls would have been envious. It is likely that the Hollioakes, who learned their cricket in Australia, will have very good careers, Ben in particular, but to cast them as saviours when they are untried and untested does a disservice to them and to the game itself.

The sun shone brightly at Trent Bridge, and a capacity crowd, well-mannered in every way, were roasted. So, too, were the England bowlers by the Australian batsmen. Having won the toss, Australia were 84 for 0 at lunch. Two wickets went down in the afternoon session while 97 runs were added. The first wicket to fall was that of Elliott, who got an inside edge to a ball from Headley ten overs into the afternoon.

Taylor looked set for a century, and he had passed 6,000 runs in Test cricket when Caddick beat and bowled him as he attempted to drive. The only other wicket to fall was that of Blewett. He had hit seven fours and was relishing the drive, but he tried to run Ben Hollioake to third man and was caught behind. Ben Hollioake's first spell had been a disaster, three overs of varied length and direction had given the Australians 23 runs. Brother Adam might also have had a wicket when Mark Waugh over-balanced, but Stewart missed the stumping. Mark Waugh finished on 60, Steve on 38, and Australia on 302.

In the morning session of the second day, Australia scored 103 runs from 26 overs. They lost the wickets of Mark Waugh, leg before to Caddick as he pushed half forward; Ponting, playing on as he got in a tangle with

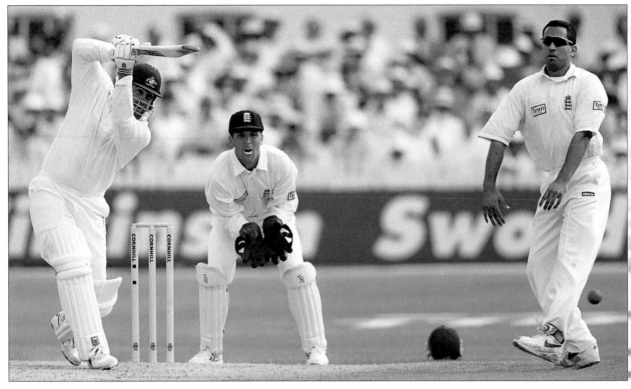

Headley; Healy, edging a drive to slip; and, crucially, Steve Waugh, beaten for pace by a ball which knocked back off stump. A revitalised Malcolm took 3 for 14 in 20 balls, and England did well to take five wickets in a session, but the Australian run-rate was close to four an over.

Reiffel and Gillespie added 33 for the ninth wicket before Headley returned to bring the innings to a close. England went off at a storming rate. Stewart batted as never before in the series, cracking the ball through the off side with an air of contempt. He had 52 out of 76 off 19 overs at

Mark Taylor – a century at Edgbaston, innings of 76 and 45 at Trent Bridge and intelligent captaincy as Australia retained the Ashes. (Clive Mason/Allsport)

tea. In the evening the balance again tilted very much in favour of Australia. In the 27th over of the innings, Atherton angled Warne to Healy for a routine catch. Six overs later, Stewart, who hit 14 fours in his 87 and faced 107 balls, drove at Warne as the ball turned sharply. Healy could only parry the ball as it flew at him, but he spun round and took the catch one-handed as he dived. This was as thrilling as it was magnificent.

Hussain was strangely ill at ease and was bowled by a Warne leg-break. Crawley gloved a ball from McGrath down the leg side to the wicket-keeper, and had Thorpe been given run out when Gillespie hit the stumps from mid-on as television replays suggest he should have been, England would have ended the day in a worse plight than 188 for 4.

On the Saturday, Thorpe and Adam Hollioake added another 55 runs before the Surrey captain was taken at first slip by Taylor. It was an exceptional catch, as Taylor was unsighted by second slip diving in front of him. Thorpe was out in the next over, taken at short-leg off pad and glove. Ben Hollioake played some positive shots, and Croft hit Warne for a straight six, but McGrath had long since devised a way of dimissing Croft and had him taken at short-leg. Ben Hollioake, possibly a Test cricketer of tomorrow but not of today, was taken at second slip, and the rapturous

Atherton is caught behind by Healy off Warne for 27.
(David Munden/Sportsline)

reception he received for his 28 shows only the state of desperation to which English cricket had come.

Caddick became Healy's fourth victim, and Malcolm lifted the crowd with three fours before having his stumps shattered by McGrath. England trailed by 114 runs.

Taylor and Elliott again went off at lightning speed. Elliott had scored 37 off 39 balls with seven fours, and it seemed that the 40th ball would produce an eighth four when he pulled a bouncer from Caddick, But Crawley sprinted round the boundary and held a wonderful catch at square-leg. It was a valuable wicket, but the younger Hollioake had again conceded the luxury of five runs an over.

Mark Waugh had had a generally disappointing series, and it was not to be redeemed now as he struggled for more than half an hour before missing a ball from Headley. Blewett was, as ever, in a hurry. He drove majestically through the covers, but an ambitious pull caused him to glove to the wicket-keeper. Steve Waugh and Ponting moved casually to the close at 167 for 4. Australia had a lead of 281, and England's hopes of regaining the Ashes had all but been vanquished.

Suddenly, on the Sunday morning, spirits were lifted again, but all too briefly. Steve Waugh crashed the first ball to the boundary. The second, Caddick made rear menacingly and Waugh could only fend to slip. Healy drove wildly at his first ball; the second, he square-cut viciously to the fence. This signalled the end of England. For reasons beyond comprehension, the bowlers maintained a short-pitch attack, and Healy and Ponting plundered 50 runs in the next 35 minutes. The batting was glorious to watch; the bowling lacked all discipline. The stand between Ponting and Healy lasted for 25 overs and realised 105 runs. It took the game out of England's reach. Throughout the series Healy had displayed wicket-keeping of unparalleled excellence, now he batted with style and panache that was refreshing in attitude and design. His 63 included nine fours and came off 78 balls, and he was out when he touched a gentle outswinger to the keeper.

Ponting should have been stumped off Croft, and Stewart also fumbled a run out chance. The choice of the Surrey man as wicket-keeper continues to anger and amaze. Relieved of the duties for which he is so obviously ill-suited, he would have provided a belligerent opening partner for Atherton, and a specialist keeper – Nixon, Rollins, Russell – would have scored as many runs as any who batted at number seven for England in this series.

Ponting became Adam Hollioake's second Test victim, and Warne clouted Croft for six and then gave the Welshman a long-awaited wicket when he drove to extra cover. Gillespie sliced to slip, and Reiffel was taken off Croft. England had more than four sessions in which to score 451 runs to win – or to survive.

There were nine overs before tea, and Atherton perished in the last of them, victim of a vicious lifter from McGrath that touched the glove. Stewart fell to Reiffel's first ball after tea, a lazy edge to gully. Hussain, two centuries behind him in the series, was strangely hesitant and ill at

Alec Stewart's exciting innings of 87 is ended by a spectacular catch by Man of the Match Ian Healy. (David Munden/Sportsline)

ease. He despatched two loose balls to the boundary, but there was a touch of frenzy about him, and it was no surprise when Gillespie bowled him.

Gillespie was engaged in a bizarre spell. With a very attacking field, Thorpe, in particular, was able to claim a boundary from anything wayward, and Gillespie conceded eight runs an over. But he took wickets. Crawley gloved the ball down the leg side, and Adam Hollioake went back and was palpably leg before. Ben Hollioake offered no stroke at Warne, who took the wicket of Croft, caught at mid-on after hitting a six.

The extra half hour was claimed, and Caddick was trapped in front for his second 0 of the match. Headley offered defiance for 35 minutes before he was quite brilliantly caught by Healy diving to his right in front of and beyond first slip. Thorpe had played entertainingly, but his innings was almost an irrelevance, and he never really took on the responsibility that was his. He was happy to take a single and leave Malcolm to deal with three balls over a McGrath over. McGrath had dismissed Malcolm in the first innings with a slow yorker that the batsman had jumped over, both feet in the air. Now he sliced the second ball he received to Mark Waugh at second slip who took the catch nonchalantly even though it had come to him at great speed.

The Australians immediately embraced in a tight circle in the middle of the wicket, as united physically as they had been as a team throughout the series. Their cricket was bred of pure passion, self-belief and total commitment to each other. In technique and temperament they had outclassed England, and the margin of their victories in no way flattered them. They had accomplished their mission and retained the Ashes.

Fifth Cornhill Test Match – England v. Australia
7, 8, 9 and 10 August 1997 at Trent Bridge, Nottingham

Australia

	First Innings			Second Innings	
M.T.G. Elliott	c Stewart, b Headley	69	(2) c Crawley, b Caddick	37
M.A. Taylor (Capt)	b Caddick	76	(1) c Hussain, b B. Hollioake	45
G.S. Blewett	c Stewart, b B. Hollioake	50	c Stewart, b Caddick	60
M.E. Waugh	lbw, b Caddick	68	lbw, b Headley	7
S.R. Waugh	b Malcolm	75	c A. Hollioake, b Caddick	14
R.T. Ponting	b Headley	9	c Stewart, b A. Hollioake	45
*I.A. Healy	c A. Hollioake, b Malcolm	16	c Stewart, b A. Hollioake	63
S.K. Warne	c Thorpe, b Malcolm	0	c Thorpe, b Croft	20
P.R. Reiffel	c Thorpe, b Headley	26	c B. Hollioake, b Croft	22
J.N. Gillespie	not out	18	c Thorpe, b Headley	4
G.D. McGrath	b Headley	1	not out	1
	b 4, nb 10, w 1, nb 4	19	b 1, lb 11, nb 6	18
		427		**336**

	O	M	R	W	O	M	R	W
Malcolm	25	4	100	3	16	4	52	–
Headley	30.5	7	87	4	19	3	56	2
Caddick	30	4	102	2	20	2	85	3
B.C. Hollioake	10	1	57	1	5	1	26	1
Croft	19	7	43	–	26.5	6	74	2
A.J. Hollioake	7	–	24	–	12	2	31	2

England

	First Innings			Second Innings	
M.A. Atherton (Capt)	c Healy, b Warne	27	c Healy, b McGrath	8
*A.J. Stewart	c Healy, b Warne	87	c S. Waugh, b Reiffel	16
J.P. Crawley	c Healy, b McGrath	18	c Healy, b Gillespie	33
N. Hussain	b Warne	2	b Gillespie	21
G.P. Thorpe	c Blewett, b Warne	53	not out	82
A.J. Hollioake	c Taylor, b Reiffel	45	lbw, b Gillespie	2
B.C. Hollioake	c M. Waugh, b Reiffel	28	lbw, b Warne	2
R.D.B. Croft	c Blewett, b McGrath	18	c McGrath, b Warne	6
A.R. Caddick	c Healy, b McGrath	0	lbw, b Warne	0
D.W. Headley	not out	10	c Healy, b McGrath	4
D.E. Malcolm	b McGrath	12	c M. Waugh, b McGrath	0
	b 2, lb 6, nb 5	13	b 6, lb 2, nb 4	12
		313		**186**

	O	M	R	W	O	M	R	W
McGrath	29.5	9	71	4	13.5	4	36	3
Reiffel	21	2	101	2	11	3	34	1
Gillespie	11	3	47	–	8	–	65	3
Warne	32	8	86	4	16	4	43	3

Fall of Wickets
1–117, 2–160, 3–225, 4–311, 5–325, 6–355, 7–363, 8–386, 9–419
1–51, 2–105, 3–134, 4–156, 5–171, 6–276, 7–292, 8–314, 9–326

Fall of Wickets
1–106, 2–129, 3–135, 4–141, 5–243, 6–243, 7–272, 8–290, 9–290
1–25, 2–25, 3–78, 4–99, 5–121, 6–144, 7–150, 8–166, 9–186

Umpires: C.J. Mitchley & D.R. Shepherd

Australia won by 264 runs

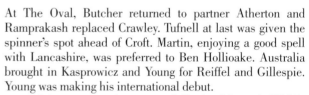

16, 17 and 18 August
at Canterbury
Kent 201 (M.V. Fleming 67, S. Lee 4 for 27, Kasprowicz 4 for 72) and 343 (M.A. Ealham 85, T.R. Ward 68, A.P. Wells 65, S. Lee 4 for 86)
Australians 315 (S.R. Waugh 154, M.G. Bevan 55) and 231 for 4 (R.T. Ponting 56 not out)
Australians won by 6 wickets

With the Ashes retained, the Australians could afford to be in a relaxed mood in their last match against a county side. They did face problems. Reiffel returned to Australia to be with his wife who was having a difficult pregnancy, while it was learned that Gillespie would not play in the final Test because of a back injury. It was decided to call upon Shaun Young who had been enjoying a very good season with Gloucestershire and Shane Lee who had done well with Somerset in 1996 and was now playing in the Lancashire League. Both played at Canterbury, and Lee took eight wickets, but it was Young who was to play at The Oval.

The Kent innings was remarkable in that the first three and the last three batsmen all failed to score. The tourists had an uneasy start when they lost four wickets for 40, three of them to Igglesden, but Steve Waugh, leading the side, revived them with a fine century. Mark Ealham batted in his old, welcome, aggressive style when Kent batted a second time, but the Australians won with ease.

Sixth Test Match
England v. Australia

At The Oval, Butcher returned to partner Atherton and Ramprakash replaced Crawley. Tufnell at last was given the spinner's spot ahead of Croft. Martin, enjoying a good spell with Lancashire, was preferred to Ben Hollioake. Australia brought in Kasprowicz and Young for Reiffel and Gillespie. Young was making his international debut.

Atherton won the toss and England batted. Within seven overs both openers were back in the pavilion. Butcher pulled at a ball outside his off stump and dragged it onto his wicket, and Atherton fell to a ball that darted back at him and took the inside edge on its way through to the keeper. Both were victims of McGrath, who bowled a fine opening spell, but Hussain and Stewart calmed nerves and went to lunch at 97 for 2.

Young bowled a frustrating spell in which he kept a line outside off stump and had Hussain flailing widely for much of the time, but it was Stewart who was next out. He fell to the first ball he received after lunch, stuck at his crease. A pairing of Hussain and Thorpe offered hope, but Hussain drove at McGrath when he was off balance and was taken at mid-on. Ramprakash with a meagre Test record behind him, was transparently nervous and lasted only eight balls before nudging the ball into the hands of short-leg, but by then Thorpe and Hollioake were out. They both surrendered to

incredibly inept lapses in technique. McGrath went round the wicket to the left-handed Thorpe and knocked over the left-hander's leg stump, which was left totally unguarded. As if this was not the depths of inadequacy, Hollioake lifted his bat to a ball from Warne, offered no stroke and saw his middle and off-stumps sent askew. On a village green, it might have caused mirth; in a Test match it was deeply embarrassing.

Caddick and Martin offered some light relief with some bold and agressive shots. They both hit sixes before Martin became McGrath's seventh victim and Tufnell lobbed Warne gently to short-leg. Malcolm was leg before first ball, and England were out inside 57 overs for 180.

The England new-ball attack of Malcolm and Martin was as bad as the batting had been. After eight overs, 38 runs were on the board. In the 12th, with the advent of Tufnell, Elliott drove extravagantly at a ball that turned expansively out of the rough and was bowled. In his next over, Tufnell had Taylor caught at short-leg. Australia ended the day on 77 for 2, and England were still alive.

Showers caused a hesitant start on the Friday, but Tufnell was soon extracting turn and testing the batsmen. Mark Waugh was his only victim in the brief first session, caught at silly point, and Australia were 125 for 3 at lunch. In the fifth over of the afternoon, Caddick, who kept a tight line and aided Tufnell greatly, trapped Steve Waugh leg before. Ten runs later, Blewett swept at Tufnell and got an edge onto his front pad that Stewart caught well as he dived to his left.

The destroyers of England receive mementoes of their successes before the match at The Oval – Shane Warne, Glenn McGrath and Jason Gillespie in the company of former England wicket-keeper Bob Taylor, representing Cornhill Insurance.
(David Munden/Sportsline)

McGrath strikes again. Martin is bowled for 20 to give the Australian fast bowler seven wickets in the innings.
(David Munden/Sportsline)

Above: Total embarrassment. Adam Hollioake offers no shot at a straight ball from Warne and is bowled. (Clive Mason/Allsport)

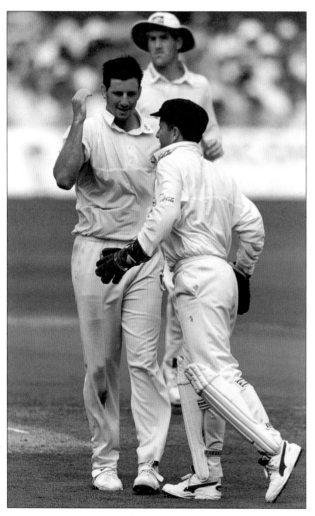

Healy was not his usual bubbling self, but he was most unfortunate to be out. He edged a delivery from Tufnell that Stewart failed to take, but the ball lodged between the keeper's pads. Young was out third ball. He tried to cut against the spin and simply plopped the ball up to Stewart.

The procession halted when Warne joined Ponting. In six overs, the score advanced by 41, with Warne hitting a six and three fours as he made 30 off 34 balls. A shower brought the tea break at 188 for 7, and Warne was bowled by Caddick three overs into the final session. Kasprowicz was out first ball, and Ponting launched a last virile attack which was brought to an end when Tufnell turned a ball sharply to find the edge of his bat. Australia led by 40 runs, but England had a hero on whom they could focus – Phil Tufnell. The left-arm spinner had given an outstanding display.

The joy was short-lived as England lost three wickets before they cleared the arrears. Atherton was caught in the gully off a good delivery from Kasprowicz who then had a rather jumpy Stewart leg before. Butcher missed a full toss from Mark Waugh who was having his first bowl of the series, and Hussain and Thorpe took England unsteadily to the close at 52 for 3. Hussain had scored two in an hour; Thorpe 22 in that time.

On the third morning, it transpired that Warne had a groin strain, the severity of which became all too apparent when he began to bowl. Limply and obligingly, Hussain cut the third ball of the day into the hands of point. This brought in Ramprakash for his most difficult examination. He passed it well if not with flying colours. In an hour and a half he and Thorpe added 79.

Thorpe was guilty of underestimating the worth of Kasprowicz and drove at him recklessly to be well caught at slip by Taylor. Hollioake was fortunate to score four from a quick single which brought three overthrows. He was then most positively leg before, trapped on his crease. Nothing we had seen in two Tests gave any hint that he was a Test cricketer. England lunched at 145 for 6.

Ramprakash became frustrated, too eager to reach 50. He charged down the pitch at Warne and was stumped by a yard. Kasprowicz then brought an abrupt end to the England innings by taking three wickets in five balls. He finished with the remarkable figures of 7 for 36, but his period of glory was to be cruelly brief.

Australia began their innings at 2.30, needing 124 to win. On the Friday evening, they had expressed doubts regarding the pitch and were adamant that the game would be over in three days, but few could have expected what was to follow. Malcolm bowled his customary loose delivery which went for four, and then he trapped Elliott leg before in his first over. Malcolm and Martin, a sub-standard fielder, were soon removed from the attack, and Tufnell and Caddick employed.

Taylor seemed assured, but he fell leg before to Caddick. Tufnell produced a beautiful delivery to have

Seven wickets in a Test series for Mark Kasprowicz. Healy offers his congratulations. (David Munden/ Sportsline)

Mark Ramprakash, stumped Healy, bowled Warne for 48.
(Adrian Murrell/Allsport)

Mark Waugh taken at slip. Next there came a controversial and decisive decision. Blewett drove outside a ball from Caddick which hit his pad and was caught by the tumbling Stewart. There was a vociferous appeal, and umpire Barker raised his finger. It appeared to be a dreadful decision. One remembers that it was Mr Barker who gave Robert Bailey out caught off his hip at Bridgetown in 1990. On that occasion he succumbed to haranguing from Viv Richards. This time he was swayed by the histrionics of Stewart and the England fielders.

Australia were 50 for 4 at tea, and their target seemed to be getting ever more out of reach. When Steve steered Caddick to first slip just after the resumption England were firm favourites for a famous victory. Ponting and Healy represented Australia's last hope, and they added 34 before Ponting was caught on the back foot. Healy is always a fighter, and he square cut Caddick venomously for four. He attempted to drive the next ball through the covers but was late on his shot and gave the bowler a return catch which he held after a juggling act.

Warne limped in with a runner, and, if anything, his reduced powers as a batsman were more of a handicap to Australia than the restrictions that his injury had placed on his bowling. He attempted a big hit and Martin judged the skier well. Kasprowicz pushed the ball into the hands of extra cover, and Young at last drove Caddick for four.

Man of the Match Phil Tufnell leaps in celebration as England win. Tufnell had match figures of 11 for 93. (Allsport)

Young's innings had been difficult to comprehend. He tried to leave or play everything from Tufnell with his pad while wickets tumbled around him. He batted for 42 minutes and faced 24 balls when the situation cried out for a more positive approach.

McGrath drove at Tufnell but succeeded only in getting a leading edge which flew to mid-off. England were jubilant.

One wishes to take nothing away from the praise of this fine victory, which was very much a triumph of character, but the euphoria that followed obscured the reality of what had happened in the summer. England had been outclassed in every department in four out of the six Tests, and it would be a disservice to the game to allow one victory when the rubber was dead to hide that fact.

Sixth Cornhill Test Match – England v. Australia

21, 22 and 23 August 1997 at The Oval, Kennington

England

	First Innings		Second Innings	
M.A. Butcher	b McGrath	5	lbw, b M. Waugh	13
M.A. Atherton (Capt)	c Healy, b McGrath	8	c S. Waugh, b Kasprowicz	8
*A.J. Stewart	lbw, b McGrath	36	lbw, c Kasprowicz	3
N. Hussain	c Elliott, b McGrath	35	c Elliott, b Warne	2
G.P. Thorpe	b McGrath	27	b Kasprowicz	62
M.R. Ramprakash	c Blewett, b McGrath	4	st Healy, b Warne	48
A.J. Hollioake	b Warne	0	lbw, b Kasprowicz	4
A.R. Caddick	not out	26	not out	0
P.J. Martin	b McGrath	20	c and b Kasprowicz	3
P.C.R. Tufnell	c Blewett, b Warne	1	c Healy, b Kasprowicz	0
D.E. Malcolm	b Kasprowicz	0	b Kasprowicz	0
	b 2, lb 6, nb 10	18	b 6, lb 10, nb 4	20
		180		**163**

	O	M	R	W	O	M	R	W
McGrath	21	4	76	7	17	5	33	–
Kasprowicz	11.4	2	56	1	15.5	5	36	7
Warne	17	8	32	2	26	9	57	2
Young	7	3	8	–	1	–	5	–
M.E. Waugh					7	3	16	1

Fall of Wickets
1–18, 2–24, 3–07, 4–128, 5–131, 6–132, 7–132, 8–158, 9–175
1–20, 2–24, 3–26, 4–52, 5–131, 6–138, 7–170, 8–163, 9–163

Australia

	First Innings		Second Innings	
M.T.G. Elliott	b Tufnell	12	(2) lbw, b Malcolm	4
M.A. Taylor (Capt)	c Hollioake, b Tufnell	38	(1) lbw, b Caddick	18
G.S. Blewett	c Stewart, b Tufnell	47	c Stewart, b Caddick	19
M.E. Waugh	c Butcher, b Tufnell	19	c Hussain, b Tufnell	1
S.R. Waugh	lbw, b Caddick	22	c Thorpe, b Caddick	6
R.T. Ponting	c Hussain, b Tufnell	40	lbw, b Tufnell	20
*I.A. Healy	c Stewart, b Tufnell	2	c and b Caddick	14
S. Young	c Stewart, b Tufnell	0	not out	4
S.K. Warne	b Caddick	30	c Martin, b Tufnell	4
M.S. Kasprowicz	lbw, b Caddick	0	c Hollioake, b Caddick	4
G.D. McGrath	not out	1	c Thorpe, b Tufnell	1
	lb 3, w 1, nb 5	9	b 3, lb 4, w 1, nb 2	10
		220		**104**

	O	M	R	W	O	M	R	W
Malcolm	11	2	37	–	3	–	15	1
Martin	15	5	38	–	4	–	13	–
Caddick	19	4	76	3	12	2	42	5
Tufnell	34.3	16	66	7	13.1	6	27	4

Fall of Wickets
1–49, 2–54, 3–94, 4–140, 5–150, 6–164, 7–164, 8–205, 9–205
1–5, 2–36, 3–42, 4–49, 5–54, 6–88, 7–92, 8–95, 9–99

Umpires: L.H. Barker & P. Willey

England won by 19 runs

Test Match Averages – England v. Australia

England Batting

	M	Inns	NO	Runs	HS	Av	100s	50s
G.P. Thorpe	6	11	2	453	138	50.33	1	3
N. Hussain	6	11	–	431	207	39.18	2	
M.A. Ealham	4	6	3	105	53*	35.00		1
J.P. Crawley	5	9	1	243	83	30.37		2
M.A. Butcher	5	10	–	254	87	25.40		2
A.J. Stewart	6	12	1	268	87	24.36		1
M.A. Atherton	6	12	1	257	77	23.36		2
A.J. Hollioake	2	4	–	51	45	12.75		
A.R. Caddick	5	8	2	59	26*	9.83		
D.W. Headley	3	6	2	39	22	9.75		
R.D.B. Croft	5	8	–	75	24	9.37		
D.E. Malcolm	4	5	1	12	12	3.00		
D. Gough	4	7	–	17	10	2.83		

Played in one Test: M.R. Ramprakash 4 & 48; B.C. Hollioake 28 & 2; A.M. Smith 0 & 4*; P.C.R. Tufnell 1 & 0; P.J. Martin 20 & 3

Australia Batting

	M	Inns	NO	Runs	HS	Av	100s	50s
P.R. Reiffel	4	6	3	179	54*	59.66		1
M.T.G. Elliott	6	10	–	556	199	55.60	2	2
R.T. Ponting	3	5	–	241	127	48.20	1	
S.R. Waugh	6	10	–	390	116	39.00	2	1
G.S. Blewett	6	10	–	381	125	38.10	1	2
M.A. Taylor	6	10	–	317	129	31.70	1	1
I.A. Healy	6	10	–	225	63	22.50		1
M.E. Waugh	6	10	–	209	68	20.90		2
S.K. Warne	6	10	–	188	53	18.80		1
G.D. McGrath	6	8	6	25	20*	12.50		
J.N. Gillespie	4	7	2	57	28*	11.40		
M.G. Bevan	3	5	–	43	24	8.60		
M.S. Kasprowicz	3	4	–	21	17	5.25		

Played in one match: S. Young 0 & 4*

Bowling

	Overs	Mds	Runs	Wks	Av	Best	10/m	5/inn
P.C.R. Tufnell	47.4	22	93	11	8.45	7/66	1	1
M.A. Ealham	58.4	11	191	8	23.87	3/60		
A.R. Caddick	179.5	27	634	24	26.41	5/50		2
A.J. Hollioake	19	2	55	2	27.50	2/31		
D.W. Headley	131.2	20	444	16	27.75	4/72		
D. Gough	142	27	511	16	31.93	5/149		1
B.C. Hollioake	15	2	83	2	41.50	1/26		
D.E. Malcolm	93	19	307	6	51.16	3/100		
R.D.B. Croft	161.5	41	439	8	54.87	3/125		
P.J. Martin	19	5	51	–	–	–		

Bowled in one innings: M.A. Butcher 2 – 0 – 14 – 0; A.M. Smith 23 – 2 – 89 – 0.

Bowling

	Overs	Mds	Runs	Wks	Av	Best	10/m	5/inn
G.D. McGrath	249.5	67	701	36	19.47	8/38		2
J.N. Gillespie	91.4	20	332	16	20.75	7/37		1
M.S. Kasprowicz	93.3	19	310	14	22.14	7/36		1
S.K. Warne	237.1	69	577	24	24.04	6/48		1
P.R. Reiffel	112.1	28	293	11	26.63	5/49		1
M.G. Bevan	34.4	6	121	2	60.50	1/14		
S. Young	8	3	13	–	–	–		
S.R. Waugh	20	3	76	–	–	–		

Bowled in one innings: G.S. Blewett 3 – 0 – 17 – 0; M.E. Waugh 7 – 3 – 16 – 1.

Fielding Figures

23 – A.J. Stewart; 8 – N. Hussain, G.P. Thorpe and M.A. Butcher; 4 – A.J. Hollioake; 3 - M.A. Ealham and J.P. Crawley; 2 – M.A. Atherthon and D.E. Malcolm; 1 – B.C. Hollioake, P.J. Martin, A.R. Caddick, D.W. Headley and R.D.B. Croft.

Fielding Figures

27 – I.A. Healy (ct 25 / st 2); 9 – G.S. Blewett; 6 – M.E. Waugh and M.A. Taylor; 4 – M.T.G. Elliott and S.R. Waugh; 3 – J.N. Gillespie; 2 – G.D. McGrath, S.K. Warne and M.S. Kasprowicz; 1 – R.T. Ponting, P.R. Reiffel and M.G. Bevan.

Fielding figures

- 43 – I.A. Healy (ct 39 / st 4)
- 17 – G.S. Blewett
- 11 – M.E. Waugh
- 10 – D.S. Berry (ct 9 / st 1)
- 9 – S.R. Waugh
- 8 – M.S. Kasprowicz and M.A. Taylor
- 7 – M.T.G. Elliott and R.T. Ponting
- 6 – M.G. Bevan
- 5 – J.N. Gillespie, S.K. Warne and J.L. Langer
- 4 – B.P. Julian and G.D. McGrath
- 3 – A.C. Gilchrist, M.J. Slater and subs
- 2 – P.R. Reiffel
- 1 – S. Lee

Australians in England, 1997 — First-Class Matches — Batting

Matches 1–10

Batting	v. Gloucestershire (Bristol) 27–29 May	v. Derbyshire (Derby) 31 May–2 June	First Test Match (Edgbaston) 5–9 June	v. Nottinghamshire (Trent Bridge) 11–13 June	v. Leicestershire (Leicester) 14–16 June	Second Test Match (Lord's) 19–23 June	v. Hampshire (Southampton) 28–30 June	Third Test Match (Old Trafford) 3–7 July	v. Glamorgan (Cardiff) 16–18 July	v. Middlesex (Lord's) 19–21 July	M	Inns	NO	Runs	HS	Av
M.A. Taylor	0, 30	5, 63	7, 129	127	57	112	109	40, 11	71	27	12	19	1	680	129	35.78
M.T.G. Elliott	124	67, 4	6, 66	—	—	—	61	—	26, 37	83	12	19	0	1091	199	57.42
J.L. Langer	152*	1	—	—	9*	—	—	12	50*, 10	142*	6	10	3	312	152*	44.57
M.E. Waugh	66	—	5	29	6, 16*	33, 0	173	0	54	—	13	20	3	746	173	43.88
S.R. Waugh	92	18	8, 24	115	11, 34	4	11, 24	108, 116	126*	—	13	17	3	924	154	54.35
M.G. Bevan	—	104*	8, 30	75*	—	13*, 0	29*	7, 0	—	39	11	16	3	463	104*	35.61
I.A. Healy	30*	40*, 2*	47, 32	—	34, 20	—	38	9, 47	—	16	12	16	4	407	63	33.91
S.K. Warne	16	—	17, 0	—	—	—	6*	3, 53	—	—	12	17	2	293	53	18.31
M.S. Kasprowicz	3	—	4, 0	—	—	—	—	0, 28*	—	—	10	8	3	56	17	11.20
J.N. Gillespie	—	—	1*	—	5	—	2	0*, 19	—	—	8	9	2	67	28*	9.57
G.D. McGrath	—	—	7	—	—	—	—	8	—	—	11	12	6	25	20*	6.25
G.S. Blewett	—	121	—	—	—	45	—	—	—	40	11	18	1	686	125	40.35
B.P. Julian	—	12*	—	14	16	—	—	—	26, 28*	—	5	5	1	162	71	40.50
A.J. Bichel	—	62	—	19	64	—	—	—	—	—	—	—	—	—	—	—
M.J. Slater	—	—	125	9*	6*	—	—	31, 45*	56	—	5	8	1	159	47	19.87
R.T. Ponting	—	—	—	—	—	—	—	31, 45*	—	40	8	12	3	571	127	63.44
A.C. Gilchrist	—	—	—	—	—	1*	—	—	—	5	—	—	—	9	9*	—
P.R. Reiffel	—	—	—	9*	6*	—	—	—	—	—	8	9	4	242	56	48.40
D.S. Berry	—	—	—	12, 0	—	—	—	—	—	—	3	2	0	21	12	10.50
S. Young	—	—	—	—	4*	—	1	—	—	—	2	3	1	4	4*	2.00
S. Lee	—	—	—	—	—	—	—	—	—	—	2	2	1	1	1	1.00
Byes	3	5	18	3	23	1	8	8	4	2						
Leg-byes	6	2	12	3	14	3	—	4	8	10						
Wides	2	—	2	4	7	—	—	—	2	—						
No-balls	4	10, 12	2, 5	4	4	—	2	6	2	10						
Total	249, 354	362, 265	118, 477	398	220, 105	213	465	235, 395	369, 217	432						
Wickets	10, 4	6, 4	10, 10	5	8, 3	7	8	10, 8	4, 7	7						
Result	D	L	L	D	W	D	W	W	D	D						

Matches 11–15

Batting	Fourth Test Match (Leeds) 24–28 July	v. Somerset (Taunton) 1–4 August	Fifth Test Match (Trent Bridge) 7–11 August	v. Kent (Canterbury) 16–18 August	Sixth Test Match (The Oval) 21–25 August	M	Inns	NO	Runs	HS	Av
M.A. Taylor	0	—	76, 69	—	38, 18	12	19	1	680	129	35.78
M.T.G. Elliott	199	—	45, 37	—	12	12	19	0	1091	199	57.42
J.L. Langer	—	30	—	20, 22	19	6	10	3	312	152*	44.57
M.E. Waugh	8	37	68, 75	154, 55	19, 6	13	20	3	746	173	43.88
S.R. Waugh	4	62	16	55	2, 30	13	17	3	924	154	54.35
M.G. Bevan	—	16	16, 20	—	2, 30	11	16	3	463	104*	35.61
I.A. Healy	31	33	18*, 4	12*	0, 4	12	16	4	407	63	33.91
S.K. Warne	—	1*	18*, 4	—	1*, 0	12	17	2	293	53	18.31
M.S. Kasprowicz	3	—	—	—	—	10	8	3	56	17	11.20
J.N. Gillespie	20*	—	—	—	—	8	9	2	67	28*	9.57
G.D. McGrath	—	20	50, 60	0	47, 19	11	12	6	25	20*	6.25
G.S. Blewett	—	71	50, 60	18	47	11	18	1	686	125	40.35
B.P. Julian	—	18	—	47, 56*	20	5	5	1	162	71	40.50
A.J. Bichel	—	—	—	—	—	—	—	—	—	—	—
M.J. Slater	—	—	—	—	—	5	8	1	159	47	19.87
R.T. Ponting	127	9	9, 45	—	40	8	12	3	571	127	63.44
A.C. Gilchrist	—	26	—	—	—	—	—	—	9	9*	—
P.R. Reiffel	54*	—	26	—	—	8	9	4	242	56	48.40
D.S. Berry	—	—	—	12, 0	—	3	2	0	21	12	10.50
S. Young	—	—	—	—	—	2	3	1	4	4*	2.00
S. Lee	—	—	—	—	0, 4*	2	2	1	1	1	1.00
Byes	9	—	4	7	3						
Leg-byes	10	2	10	2	4						
Wides	—	—	1	—	1						
No-balls	35	32	6	4	5						
Total	501	323	427, 336	315, 231	220, 104						
Wickets	10	D	10, 10	W, W	10, 10						
Result	W	D	W	W	L						

Australians in England, 1997 First-Class Matches, Bowling

Match	M.S. Kasprowicz	G.D. McGrath	S.K. Warne	J.N. Gillespie	M.G. Bevan	M.E. Waugh	B.P. Julian	S.R. Waugh	M.T.G. Elliott	P.R. Reiffel	R.T. Ponting	G.S. Blewett	Byes	Leg-byes	Wides	No-balls	Total	Wkts
v. Gloucestershire (Bristol) 27–29 May	21–2–101–3	19–11–31–1	35.2–10–97–4	20–4–66–2	12–1–45–0								4	6		20	350	10
v. Derbyshire (Derby) 31 May–2 June			14–3–45–2 / 23–2–103–7	17.3–62–2 / 5–0–35–0	9–4–21–2 / 10–0–60–0 / 10.4–0–44–1		20–6–88–3 / 21.3–1–126–2	1–0–8–0 / 12–2–45–0					7	6	3 / 2	34 / 16	257 / 371	9 / 9
First Test Match (Edgbaston) 5–9 June	39–8–113–4 / 7–0–42–1	32–8–107–2 / 7–1–42–0	35–8–110–1 / 7.3–0–27–0	10–1–48–1					8–0–35–0				4	7	1	15	478	9
v. Nottinghamshire (Trent Bridge) 11–13 June	17–4–54–1	18.1–4–63–4			7–1–32–0		18–1–70–2			10–3–15–3			4 / 1	4		22	119 / 239	1 / 10
v. Leicestershire (Leicester) 14–16 June	5–1–9–0 / 15–3–54–1	12–2–24–0 / 14–5–40–1	5–1–20–1 / 16.4–2–42–5		1–0–11–0		3.3–2–2–0 / 8–1–35–1			10–6–12–3 / 12–3–49–3			2	2 / 1		6 / 10	62 / 179	4 / 10
Second Test Match (Lord's) 19–23 June		20.3–8–38–8 / 20–5–65–1	2–0–9–0 / 19–4–47–2	16–2–65–2 / 13–6–33–5	8–1–29–0			4–0–20–0		15–9–17–2 / 13–5–29–0			4 / 8	14 / 10		5 / 7	77 / 266	10 / 4
v. Hampshire (Southampton) 28–30 June	11.1–2–33–3 / 14.4–1–69–3		15–4–30–3 / 19–3–26–1	14–3–39–0 / 12–4–31–3	7–3–15–0 / 8–3–14–1 / 8–2–34–0					7–1–17–2 / 8–1–27–1			4 / 14	3 / 4		24 / 14	156 / 176	10 / 10
Third Test Match (Old Trafford) 3–7 July	18–5–56–2 / 15–2–63–1	23.4–9–40–3 / 21–4–46–4	30–14–48–6 / 30.4–8–63–3		20–2–73–3 / 16–1–74–2					9–3–14–0 / 2–0–8–0			4	17 / 2	1	2 / 1	162 / 200	10 / 10
v. Glamorgan (Cardiff) 16–18 July	13–2–47–2 / 6–1–10–1		23–4–76–1 / 16.4–55–3			12–0–36–0 / 7–1–37–1	9–2–34–0 / 9–1–26–0			18.3–5–61–5 / 11–2–46–0	3–0–9–0			6	1 / 5	24 / 8	254 / 211	10 / 3
v. Middlesex (Lord's) 19–21 July		21.4–7–61–4 / 11–3–37–0		23–2–67–2 / 13–6–32–0				5–2–13–1				5–1–12–0			3	2	305	10
Fourth Test Match (Leeds) 24–28 July		22–5–67–2 / 22–5–80–2	1–0–2–0 / 21–6–53–1	13.4–1–37–7 / 23–8–65–2				4–1–11–0	1–0–8–0	20–4–41–1 / 21.1–2–49–5		3–0–17–0	4 / 6	4	1	12 / 13	172 / 268	10 / 10
v. Somerset (Taunton) 1–4 August	14–2–95–2 / 5–2–11–0	11.2–3–31–2 / 7–1–24–1	18.3–7–57–5 / 11–3–26–1			9–1–31–1	14–2–52–1 / 5–1–22–0					4–0–33–0	10	4		42 / 2	284 / 147	10 / 3
Fifth Test Match (Trent Bridge) 7–11 August		29.5–9–71–4 / 13.5–4–36–3	32–8–86–4 / 16–4–43–3	11–3–47–0 / 8–4–65–3	8–2–39–0					21–2–101–2 / 11–3–34–1			2 / 6	6 / 2		5 / 4	313	10
v. Kent (Canterbury) 16–August	15–4–72–4 / 24–4–89–3	21–4–76–7 / 17–5–33–0			11–1–49–1 / 17–2–66–1	12–5–30–1						3–1–5–0 / 5–2–26–0	4 / 2	2 / 2		26 / 12	186 / 201	10 / 10
Sixth Test Match (The Oval) 21–2 August	11.4–2–56–1 / 15.5–5–36–7		17–8–32–2 / 26.9–57–2			7–3–16–1							6 / 6	6 / 10		10 / 4	343 / 180	10 / 10
Bowler's average	267.2–50– 1010–39 25.89	363.4–102– 1012–49 20.65	433.4–112– 1154–57 20.24	198.4–43– 692–29 23.86	152.4–23– 606–11 55.09	47–10– 150–4 37.50	108–17– 455–9 50.55	26–5– 97–1 97.00	9–0– 43–0 —	188.4–49– 520–28 18.57	3–0– 9–0 —	20–4– 93–0 —						

A A.J. Bichel 5–1–28–0
B S. Lee 10.3–4–27–4, 25–7–86–4; S. Young 11–3–46–1, 15–7–40–1;
C S. Young 7–3–8–0, 1–0–5–0

Pakistan 'A' Tour

The Pakistan 'A' side that undertook a seven-week tour of England in 1997 must be one of the youngest groups ever to make a major tour. Led by Mohammad Wasim, the party of 15 had an average age of 17, with vice-captain Mujahid Jamshed the only player over 25. Two of the party had no experience of first-class cricket, but four had played at international level. One of these was Hasan Raza, who, a few months earlier, had become the youngest player to appear in Test cricket.

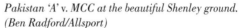

2, 3 and 4 July
at Trent Bridge
Nottinghamshire 298 for 9 dec. (G.F. Archer 81, Shoaib Akhtar 4 for 71) and 107 for 8 dec.
Pakistan 'A' 150 (Azhar Mahmood 50 not out)
Match drawn

The tour began in rather unpleasant weather, and the first day was curtailed by bad light. The tourists provided a dreadfully slow over rate, and, in attempting to save the follow-on, which they did, they scored at barely two runs an over. Nottinghamshire were content to use the remaining time for batting practice.

5, 6 and 7 July
at Derby
Pakistan 'A' 169 (Hasan Raza 56) and 201 (Hasan Raza 96)
Derbyshire 148 (A.S. Rollins 51, Azhar Mahmood 4 for 34) and 223 for 3 (M.R. May 107 not out, A.S. Rollins 77)
Derbyshire won by 7 wickets

Pakistan 'A' v. MCC at the beautiful Shenley ground. (Ben Radford/Allsport)

The Pakistanis suffered their first defeat of the tour in a match which changed character. They led narrowly on the first innings, and the precocious talent of Hasan Raza was much in evidence. Eventually, however, Derbyshire ran out comfortable winners. Michael May, 25 years old but without a regular place in the county side, had enjoyed a good match against the Australians earlier in the season. Against the Pakistanis he hit a maiden first-class hundred, and he and Rollins set up victory with an opening partnership of 154.

9, 10 and 11 July
at Shenley
Pakistan 'A' 119 (Salim Elahi 53, H.A.G. Anthony 6 for 34) and 257 (Ali Naqvi 114, H.A.G. Anthony 4 for 79)
MCC 362 (K.L.T. Arthurton 200 not out, G.W. Flower 78, Shoaib Akhtar 5 for 64, Azhar Mahmood 4 for 90) and 18 for 0
MCC won by 10 wickets

The young tourists were opposed by an MCC side with a rich international flavour. Choosing to bat first, the Pakistanis fared badly against the West Indian pace bowler Hamish Anthony, once of Glamorgan. MCC's reply was founded upon a second wicket stand of 186 between the West Indian Keith Arthurton and Zimbabwe's Grant Flower. The last four wickets went down for seven runs, but MCC's 362 came off just over 86 overs. The pitch at Shenley Park, the Compton Ground, is now as beautiful as the lovely ground itself. When Pakistan batted a second time there was a most impressive century from Ali Naqvi, who was playing in only

Scottish all-rounder Douglas Brown had a memorable match for the ECB XI in their victory over Pakistan 'A' at Chelmsford. The Warwickshire player's second innings 8 for 89 was a career best bowling performance. (Dave Pinegar/ASP)

his fifth first-class match. He batted for more than six hours and played some shots of great charm.

13 July
at Walsall
English Cricket Board XI 145
Pakistan 'A' 147 for 0 (Ali Naqvi 80 not out, Salim Elahi 58 not out)
Pakistan 'A' won by 10 wickets

The ECB XI, composed of Minor County cricketers, was bowled out in 47.1 overs and Pakistan 'A' raced to victory with 29.3 of their 50 overs unused.

16, 17 and 18 July
at Worcester
Worcestershire 265 (G.R. Haynes 65, G.A. Hick 55, Ali Hussain Rizvi 5 for 68) and 338 for 4 (G.A. Hick 144)
Pakistan 'A' 489 for 9 dec. (Salim Elahi 229, Mohammad Wasim 64, Farhan Adil 50)
Match drawn

Graeme Hick captaining Worcestershire for the first time in a first-class match, hit a very brisk 50 and then was caught

at long-off to become one of five victims claimed by the young leg-spinner Ali Hussain Rizvi. The second day belonged to Salim Elahi, who reached a maiden double century in first-class cricket. He hit 35 fours and two sixes. With dropped catches abounding and spirits drooping in consequence, Hick reached the 93rd hundred of his career as the game moved to a draw.

19, 20 and 21 July
at Taunton
Somerset 213 (S.C. Ecclestone 102) and 244 (M.N Lathwell 60)
Pakistan 'A' 227 (Salim Elahi 70, Mujahid Jamshed 59, K.J. Shine 6 for 74) and 231 for 5 (Ali Naqvi 96)
Pakistan 'A' won by 5 wickets

Pakistan 'A' recorded their first first-class win of the tour when they disposed of Somerset less than an hour after lunch on the third day at Taunton. Somerset had fielded four new players, one of whom was the Australian leg-spinner Macgill, but it was Simon Ecclestone who grasped the opportunity offered with his maiden first-class century. Pakistan bowled consistently well, and they raced to victory at nearly five an over with Ali Naqvi, one of the tour's successes, hitting 96 off 101 balls.

22 July
at Cheltenham
Pakistan 'A' 279 for 7 (Salim Elahi 66, Rana Qayyum 56)
Gloucestershire 230
Pakistan 'A' won by 49 runs

The tourists showed their aptitude for the 50-over game with some positive batting in a convincing victory.

24, 25, 26 and 27 July
at Hove
Pakistan 'A' 306 (Rana Qayyum 75, Azhar Mahmood 63) and 248 (Rana Qayyum 97, Abdul Razzak 62, A.D. Edwards 5 for 34)
Sussex 331 (K. Greenfield 108, R.K. Rao 71) and 90 for 7
Match drawn

No play was possible on the third day, and, ultimately, Sussex were left a target of 224 from 28 overs. The county side's decision to attempt to score the runs nearly brought disaster.

29 July
at Southampton
Hampshire 167
Pakistan 'A' 168 for 4
Pakistan 'A' won by 6 wickets

Paul Hutchison played his first first-class game for Yorkshire in England against Pakistan 'A' and took 11 for 102 in the match. Hutchison had previously played for the county in Zimbabwe and for a Rest of England side against England 'A'. His performance against Pakistan 'A' sparked an outstanding run of success in August. (Paul Chadwick/Allsport)

Rana Qayyum's unbeaten 47 took Pakistan to victory with 31 balls to spare.

1, 2, 3 and 4 August
at Bristol
Gloucestershire 167 (T.H.C. Hancock 50, M.C.J. Ball 50, Shoaib Akhtar 5 for 62, Abdul Razzak 4 for 33) and 204 for 5 (N.J. Trainor 64, M.J. Church 53)
Pakistan 'A' 220 (Hasan Raza 63, Javed Qadir 61, M.W. Alleyne 4 for 56)
Match drawn

Fifteen wickets fell on the first day at Bristol, but thereafter weather was the winner with the Pakistanis again frustrated as no play was possible on the last day.

7, 8, 9 and 10 August
at Leeds
Yorkshire 243 (D. Byas 84, Azhar Mahmood 5 for 66) and 378 (M.D. Moxon 155, Abdul Razzak 5 for 106)
Pakistan 'A' 365 (Mohammad Wasim 155, Javed Qadir 61, P.M. Hutchison 4 for 64, G.M. Hamilton 4 for 95) and 187 (Salim Elahi 89, P.M. Hutchison 7 for 38)
Yorkshire won by 69 runs

The tourists were not happy about the pitch on which they were asked to play at Headingley, and certainly it deterio-

rated rapidly. Skipper Mohammad Wasim hit a fine century, and Martyn Moxon was pleased to get runs in Yorkshire's second innings, but the outstanding performance of the match came from Paul Hutchison. A left-arm medium-pace bowler, Hutchison was appearing in his first first-class match of the season and his first for Yorkshire in England. His previous three first-class games had brought him 12 wickets, and he almost doubled that against the Pakistanis with match figures of 11 for 102. It was to be the beginning of an outstanding run for the 20-year-old.

12 August
at Northampton
Northamptonshire 300 for 5 (R.J. Bailey 153 not out, R.R. Montgomerie 81)
Pakistan 'A' 240 (Mohammad Wasim 59)
Northamptonshire won by 60 runs

That Pakistan 'A' suffered their only one-day defeat of the tour was due mainly to Robert Bailey's unbeaten 153 off 113 balls. The Northamptonshire captain hit 15 fours and five sixes. Salim Elahi and Mujahid Jamshed made 53 in six overs, but once they were separated the task was too daunting.

15, 16, 17 and 18 August
at Chelmsford
Pakistan 'A' 227 (P.M. Such 5 for 74) and 318 (Azhar Mahmood 92, Hasan Raza 57, Abdul Razzak 55, D.R. Brown 8 for 89)
England and Wales Cricket Board XI 439 (A.F. Giles 81, A.P. Grayson 77, G. Welch 62, D.L. Hemp 53) and 109 for 5
ECB XI won by 5 wickets

The Board XI was chosen from players who were not engaged in championship matches. Rather surprisingly, Paul Grayson, who had done well for Essex since his move from Yorkshire, was named as captain of the side, but he did a fine job in quickly welding the eleven into a unit that showed commitment and ambition. Such, still regarded by many as the best off-spinner available to England, dominated the first day, but there were some fine individual performances. The Warwickshire trio of Brown, Welch and Giles batted with such strength in the lower order as to put the Board XI in a commanding position, and Dougie Brown, enjoying a fine August, produced the best bowling performance of his career to emphasise his side's superiority. Azhar Mahmood led a strong fight back with a fiercely struck 92, but the Board won early afternoon on the fourth day.

The Pakistanis were disappointed that they had had no fixture against an England 'A' side, but they were content that their young cricketers had gained much from the tour. Salim Elahi was the leading run-scorer with 625 runs, average 48.07, while Azhar Mahmood captured 40 wickets (average 20.72) and hit 379 runs, average 31.58.

NatWest Bank Trophy

First Round

24 June

at Beaconsfield
Essex 327 for 7 (N. Hussain 78, R.J. Rollins 67 not out,
P.J. Prichard 58, A.P. Grayson 56, K.L.T. Arthurton 4 for 53)
Bukinghamshire 238 for 7 (N.D. Burns 51)
Essex won by 89 runs
(Man of the Match: R.A. Rollins)

at Wisbech
Hampshire 321 for 4 (R.A. Smith 126,
M.L. Hayden 90)
Cambridgeshire 82 (J.P. Stephenson 5 for 34)
Hampshire won by 239 runs
(Man of the Match: R.A. Smith)

at Barrow
Northamptonshire 223 (A.L. Penberthy 57,
D.J.G. Sales 53)
Cumberland 187 for 9 (A.D. Mawson 77, A.L. Penberthy
5 for 56)
Northamptonshire won by 36 runs
(Man of the Match: A.L. Penberthy)

at Exmouth
Leicestershire 225 for 8 (I.J. Sutcliffe 103 not out)
Devon 172 for 9
Leicestershire won by 53 runs
(Man of the Match: I.J. Sutcliffe)

at Cardiff
Bedfordshire 179 for 9
Glamorgan 182 for 3 (R.D.B. Croft 64)
Glamorgan won by 7 wickets
(Man of the Match: R.D.B. Croft)

at Bristol
Gloucestershire 351 for 2 (A.J. Wright 177,
N.J. Trainor 143)
Scotland 250 for 9 (B.M.W. Patterson 77, M.J. Smith 73,
T.H.C. Hancock 6 for 58)
Gloucestershire won by 101 runs
(Man of the Match: A.J. Wright)

at Old Trafford
Lancashire 351 for 7 (G.D. Lloyd 96,
M.E. Harvey 86)
Berkshire 182 for 5 (J.S. Hodgson 53 not out)
Lancashire won by 169 runs
(Man of the Match: M.E. Harvey)

at Lincoln Lindum
Lincolnshire 116 (P. Aldred 4 for 30)
Derbyshire 121 for 2 (C.J. Adams 71 not out)
Derbyshire won by 8 wickets
(Man of the Match: C.J. Adams)

at Lord's
Kent 225 (N.J. Llong 68, R.L. Johnson 5 for 50)
Middlesex 227 for 7 (M.R. Ramprakash 72)
Middlesex won by 3 wickets
(Man of the Match: M.R. Ramprakash)

at Trent Bridge
Staffordshire 95
Nottinghamshire 96 for 0
Nottinghamshire won by 10 wickets
(Man of the Match: N.J. Astle)

at Taunton
Somerset 367 for 5 (S.C. Ecclestone 101,
P.C.L. Holloway 90, P.D. Bowler 87)
Herefordshire 136 (Mushtaq Ahmed 4 for 27)
Somerset won by 231 runs
(Man of the Match: S.C. Ecclestone)

at The Oval
Durham 247 for 7 (J.E. Morris 75, D.C. Boon 57,
M.J. Foster 56 not out)
Surrey 251 for 5 (A.J. Stewart 90 not out)
Surrey won by 5 wickets
(Man of the Match: A.J. Stewart)

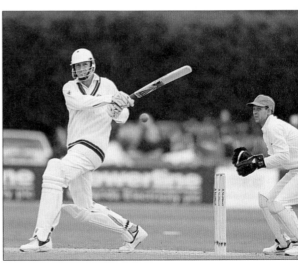

*Tom Moody on his way to a first round century against Holland.
(Mike Hewitt/Allsport)*

at Hove
Shropshire 116 (R.J. Kirtley 5 for 39)
Sussex 119 for 0 (K. Greenfield 89 not out)
Sussex won by 10 wickets
(Man of the Match: R.J. Kirtley)

at Edgbaston
Warwickshire 207 (A.F. Giles 69, A.J. Moles 64,
P.G. Newman 4 for 23)
Norfolk 127 (A.F. Giles 5 for 21)
Warwickshire won by 80 runs
(Man of the Match: A.F. Giles)

at Worcester
Worcestershire 336 for 6 (T.M. Moody 108, K.R. Spiring 53)
Holland 225 (B. Zuiderent 99)
Worcestershire won by 111 runs
(Man of the Match: B. Zuiderent)

at Leeds
Yorkshire 249 (P.J. Hartley 83, C. White 63)
Ireland 53 (D. Gough 7 for 27)
Yorkshire won by 196 runs
(Man of the Match: D. Gough)

The first round of the match in the NatWest Trophy saw the predictable slaughter of the innocents, but several were slain only after the bravest of fights.

Essex were opposed by their former wicket-keeper Neil Burns, now captain of Buckinghamshire. He had at his disposal the former West Indian Test cricketer Keith Arthurton, who took four wickets. Robert Rollins arrived with Essex on 232 for 6 and hit 67 off 26 balls to win his first Man of the Match award. Burns and Bowyer took Buckinghamshire to 117 for 1 with Burns hitting Irani for five fours in one over, but Bowyer and Arthurton fell to Greyson, and Burns was bowled by Stuart Law and the Minor County side was beaten.

Hampshire crushed Cambridgeshire with Hayden and Robin Smith, who took his eighth individual award, putting on 176 for the second wicket.

Cumberland pressed Northamptonshire hard. With former Nottinghamshire pace bowler Pennett taking three wickets, they bowled out the visitors in 56.4 overs, and, at one time, Northamptonshire were 68 for 5. Sales and Penberthy saved the day with a stand of 84 in 25 overs. Andrew Mawson hit 77, and he and skipper Simon Dutton put on 66 in 28 overs for the fourth wicket. However, the asking rate became more than the lower order could manage.

In spite of Peter Roebuck's economic bowling, Leicestershire, 99 for 6 at one time, were taken to victory by Iain Sutcliffe's patient century at Exmouth. He was at the crease in the second over and was there at the end. Vitally, he and Millns hit 44 runs in the last four overs. Croft had a good all-round match as Glamorgan beat Bedfordshire with nearly half their 60 overs unused. Croft won his first Man of the Match award.

At Bristol, Tony Wright and Nick Trainor put on 311 for Gloucestershire's first wicket, the highest partnership record for any wicket in the 60-over competition. Wright's 177, which included a six and 19 fours, was the highest score made by a Gloucestershire batsman in the NatWest Trophy. Scotland batted with flair, but the gap between the sides was enormous.

Lancashire, the holders, were indebted to Lloyd and Harvey for their victory over Berkshire. The pair added 176 for the fourth wicket.

Lincolnshire were routed by Derbyshire, who took only 19 overs to hit off the required runs, and Nottinghamshire were equally destructive in defeating Staffordshire. They ambled to a ten-wicket win in 31.5 overs.

One of the most important contests was at Lord's, where Middlesex and Kent, both fancied to win the Trophy, locked horns. Kent, the Benson and Hedges Cup finalists, elected to bat first and lost their first four wickets for 64 runs, all to catches by wicket-keeper Brown. Llong, Ealham and Fleming effected a recovery, but Kent looked to be some 30 runs short of a winning score. Middlesex soon lost Kellis, but Ramprakash batted with authoritative calm until he was bowled by a ball from Fleming that kept low in the 44th over. Kent was handicapped by the loss of McCague with a hamstring injury, but Headley and Llong performed admirably, and when Hewitt joined Shah, 29 were needed in six overs with three wickets standing so that the game was in the balance. The two young men showed no sign of nerves, and Hewitt hit Llong over mid-off for the winning four with four balls remaining.

Simon Ecclestone hit a century off 60 balls as Somerset crushed Herefordshire, and Sussex meandered to a ten-wicket victory over Shropshire. Runs came at barely two an over in this game.

Durham joined Kent as the other first-class county to depart in the first round. They had recovered reasonably well after losing their openers for 26, and they dismissed Butcher and Thorpe for ducks, but Ratcliffe, Brown, Adam Hollioake and Stewart were in forceful form. Stewart hit 90 off 118 balls and victory for Surrey came with 67 balls to spare.

The near sensation of the day was at Edgbaston. The game was barely an hour old when Warwickshire, having been put into bat, were 25 for 6. The bowler who did the damage was the Norfolk skipper Paul Newman, once of Derbyshire. Bradshaw had also bowled well, but the attack lacked depth, and Giles and Moles, who batted 58 overs for his 64, put on 137 in 38 overs. Norfolk's moment had passed. Giles took four wickets in 12 balls, and the margin of victory for Warwickshire was 80 runs, but that was as flattering as it was misleading.

Zuiderent saw that Holland went down fighting at Worcester, and Darren Gough established a new Yorkshire record for the competition when he took 7 for 27 including the hat-trick. Yorkshire had been 55 for 6 before Hartley and White added 100. Ireland were all out in 18.5 overs.

Second Round

9 July
at Derby
Derbyshire 324 for 7 (K.J. Barnett 111, C.J. Adams 101)
Northamptonshire 180 (A.L. Penberthy 62,
J.N. Snape 54, D.E. Malcolm 7 for 35)
Derbyshire won by 144 runs
(Man of the Match: D.E. Malcolm)

at Chelmsford
Worcestershire 286 for 9 (G.A. Hick 146)
Essex 287 for 3 (S.G. Law 100, A.P. Grayson 82 not out,
R.C. Irani 79 not out)
Essex won by 7 wickets
(Man of the Match: R.C. Irani)

at Southampton
Hampshire 302 for 6 (R.A. Smith 119)
Glamorgan 304 for 8 (A. Dale 71, S.P. James 69, H. Morris 53)
Glamorgan won by 2 wickets
(Man of the Match: S.P. James)

at Leicester
Yorkshire 310 for 5 (C. White 96 not out,
M.D. Moxon 74, B. Parker 69)
Leicestershire 182 (I.J. Sutcliffe 90, R.D. Stemp 4 for 54)
Yorkshire won by 128 runs
(Man of the Match: C. White)

at Uxbridge
Gloucestershire 277 for 9 (M.A. Lynch 100,
J.H. Kallis 4 for 47)
Middlesex 280 for 6 (J.H. Kallis 100, J.C. Pooley
79 not out)
Middlesex won by 4 wickets
(Man of the Match: J.H. Kallis)

at The Oval
Nottinghamshire 176 (N.J. Astle 56)
Surrey 154
Nottinghamshire won by 22 runs
(Man of the Match: N.J. Astle)

at Hove
Lancashire 283 for 6 (J.P. Crawley 113 not out,
I.D. Austin 97)
Sussex 286 for 3 (K. Greenfield 129, M. Newell 75 not out)
Sussex won by 7 wickets
(Man of the Match: K. Greenfield)

at Edgbaston
Warwickshire 220 (D.P. Ostler 54)
Somerset 209 (S.C. Ecclestone 87, A.A. Donald 4 for 54)
Warwickshire won by 11 runs
(Man of the Match: S.C. Ecclestone)

The second round of the NatWest Trophy produced some surprises in that both the holders and the favourites were eliminated. Derbyshire overwhelmed Northamptonshire with Devon Malcolm continuing his outstanding season with his best figures in the competition. It was not a record for the county – Michael Holding took eight wickets against Sussex nine years ago. A Derbyshire record was established in the match against Northamptonshire, Adams and Barnett adding 183 for the third wicket.

Essex seemed to be facing a stiff task at Chelmsford. Neil Williams bowled a fine opening spell and removed Moody, but Hick was in majestic form and hit five sixes and ten fours in his 146. He shared a stand of 91 with Curtis and a stand of 121 with Spiring. He took 26 off one over from Grayson. It looked as if Worcestershire would exceed 300, but Hick was caught at long-on off Cowan, and six wickets went down for 17 runs. Essex soon lost Prichard and Hussain, but Stuart Law gave another outstanding display. He made 100 out of 151. His 100 came off 89 balls with two sixes and 11 fours, but he got out when there was still work to be done. Irani batted with much sense in helping Law in a stand worth 132, and he and Grayson then took Essex to victory with 15 balls to spare.

Glamorgan won a fine contest at Southampton with just two balls to spare. Robin Smith made his seventh NatWest century, and Hampshire then dismissed Croft for 0. Morris and Dale righted matters with a second wicket stand of 128, but the middle order began to crumble, and a seventh wicket stand of 76 between James and Shaw was vital. Waqar Younis hit Connor for the winning boundary.

Leicester gave a surprisingly listless display against Yorkshire, whom they asked to bat first. Mullally could find no sort of line and conceded an abundance of wides. McGrath, Byas and Lehmann went fairly cheaply, but the

An outstanding all-round performance from Jacques Kallis brought Middlesex a second round victory over Gloucestershire. Kallis took 4 for 47 and hit 100 off 138 balls to take his first Man of the Match Award. (Laurence Griffiths/Allsport)

The sensation of the second round was Sussex's victory over the holders Lancashire. The hero was Keith Greenfield, 129.
(John Gichigi/Allsport)

steadfast Moxon and White added 94, and White and Parker salvaged 129 for the fifth wicket. The home county were 51 for 5, and although Sutcliffe showed resolution, he never gave the hint that Leicestershire could win.

Monte Lynch inspired a Gloucestershire recovery at Uxbridge, but the cricket of South African all-rounder Kallis brought victory to Middlesex with three balls to spare. He faced 138 balls and hit three sixes and six fours. His 96-run partnership with Pooley for the fourth wicket turned the game in favour of the home side. Pooley made his highest score in the competition and steered Middlesex to victory.

There was an astonishing result at The Oval where the favourites and Benson and Hedges Cup finalists, Surrey, were beaten by Nottinghamshire. Surrey appeared to have done all that was necessary when they sent back four Notts batsmen for 41 runs. Tolley gave Astle solid support in a stand worth 68, but the visitors were bowled out in 55.1 overs and seemed to be well short of a winning score. Ratcliffe went early, but Butcher and Stewart batted positively and took the score to 72, at which point the Surrey innings fell apart. Thorpe was out third ball to a wretched shot, and with Astle bowling ten overs for 12 runs and the wicket of Ben Hollioake, Surrey collapsed to 132 for 9. Martin Bicknell and Saqlain Mushtaq offered defiance, but they could not prevent the inevitable.

Even more surprising was the demise of the holders Lancashire at Hove. They had early worries when, electing to bat, they lost four wickets for 38 runs. Crawley and Watkinson stopped the rot with a partnership of 67, which was followed by a stand of 178 between Crawley and Austin, which ended when Austin was caught off the last ball of the innings. His 97 had come off 104 balls. Athey and Greenfield gave Sussex a solid start with 85 for the first wicket and, although Taylor went cheaply, Mark Newell and Greenfield made victory appear possible with a stand of 128. Badly dropped by Crawley when 81, Greenfield made his highest score in the competition, facing 173 balls and hitting 12 fours. He was out with 54 still needed, but he had done his job, and Mark Newell and Lenham took Sussex to their target with 15 balls to spare. In the middle of such a traumatic season this was a wonderful boost for the southern county.

The former Warwickshire hero Dermot Reeve returned to Edgbaston as coach of Somerset, but it was his old love rather than the new that won the day. On a pitch of variable pace and bounce, Warwickshire struggled and were out in 58.1 overs. The batting lacked authority, and the over-rate was appalling. Simon Ecclestone was in prime form for Somerset, and with 20 overs remaining, Somerset were 86 short of victory with eight wickets standing. Small then produced a spell of 3 for 6 in 21 balls, and Donald returned to maul the tail as Somerset fell apart.

Quarter-Finals

29 July
at Derby
Derbyshire 327 for 8 (C.J. Adams 129 not out, V.C. Drakes 4 for 62)
Sussex 329 for 5 (R.K. Rao 158)
Sussex won by 5 wickets
(Man of the Match: R.K. Rao)

at Cardiff
Yorkshire 236 for 8 (D.S. Lehmann 105)
Glamorgan 237 for 9 (M.P. Maynard 62, R.D.B. Croft 55, D. Gough 4 for 36)
Glamorgan won by 1 wicket
(Man of the Match: Waqar Younis)

at Lord's
Warwickshire 286 for 6 (D.L. Hemp 112, D.P. Ostler 51)
Middlesex 258 for 9 (M.R. Ramprakash 98, K.R. Brown 50)
Warwickshire won by 28 runs
(Man of the Match: D.L. Hemp)

at Trent Bridge
Nottinghamshire 288 for 5 (P. Johnson 106, R.T. Robinson 52)
Essex 289 for 7 (N. Hussain 89 not out)
Essex won by 3 wickets
(Man of the Match: N. Hussain)

Sussex's victory over Lancashire had been the shock of the second round. Their win over Derbyshire in the quarter-finals must rank as one of the most remarkable in the history of the competition. Electing to bat and with Cork back in their side, Derbyshire made their highest score against first-class opposition in their 34 years in the tournament. Their innings rested firmly on another magnificent knock by Chris Adams, whose unbeaten 129 came off 148 balls with a six and eight fours. No side had ever reached a target of 328 to win a match in the 60-over competition, and the

More sensations for Sussex in the quarter-finals, a stunning victory over Derbyshire with Rajesh Rao scoring 158 of the 328 runs needed. (John Gichigi/Allsport)

suspected weakness of the Sussex batting and the potential strength of the Derbyshire bowling did not suggest that that fact would now change. Greenfield, hero of the second round, was bowled by Malcolm's third ball. However, the experienced Athey was joined by Rajesh Rao, a late replacement for the injured Lenham and making his NatWest Trophy debut, and the pair added 101 in 21 overs. The pitch was cracked and conducive to spin, but that department is not the strength of Derbyshire's attack. Athey was out for 30, but Rao had raced to 50 off 47 balls with nine fours, and he now set his eyes on a century. He and Mark Newell put on 67 before Newell was run out in the 37th over, and 160 were still needed. Taylor's previous successes in this competition were now of immense value to both Rao and to Sussex. He made 48 off 54 balls and, vitally, the pair added 110 in 16 overs. They were both out by the 54th over, and the closing overs were tense as 15 were still required off the last two, But Keith Newell and Moores saw Sussex to a famous victory with four balls to spare.

There was equal tension at Cardiff. Yorkshire were 72 for 4 before Darren Lehmann hit a pugnacious century that took his side to a respectable total. At 140 for 2, Glamorgan were cruising to victory with 97 needed at less than four runs an over. Seven wickets fell for 69, three of them to Gough, and Cosker joined Waqar Younis with 28 required from six overs. Waqar skied to mid-on and was dropped. He relished the escape, farmed the bowling intelligently and took his side to victory with an over to spare. He made 39.

The loss of Neil Smith in the opening over failed to disturb Warwickshire. Hemp and Ostler put on 130 for the third wicket, and Hemp played a masterly innings of 112 off 182 balls. It was his highest NatWest score and it took his side to a challenging total on a pitch that was never easy. Warwickshire were aided, too, by the Middlesex attack, Fraser apart, which conceded 20 wides and 11 no-balls. Warwickshire outshone Middlesex in the field, and Penney,

who ran out Shah, took a fine running and diving catch to dismiss Ramprakash, with whom went Middlesex's last hope of victory.

Essex were without Ilott and Williams at Trent Bridge and gave Cousins his first game for more than a year. In spite of fielding a depleted attack, Essex chose to field first. Cowan was steady, but Irani and Danny Law were wayward. Irani was fortunate to dismiss Dowman, a very promising cricketer, who edged a wide delivery into his stumps. Robinson and Johnson settled into a 91 stand in 15 overs, which was helped by Hussain spilling two easy chances. Hussain dropped another catch with Such this time the sufferer, but Such and Grayson, the Essex spinners, exerted some control on the batsmen. Hussain redeemed himself. Robinson and Astle had added 72 and looked like taking the game out of the reach of Essex when Hussain ran out Astle with a direct hit on the stumps. Having made 106 off 110 balls, Johnson was bowled off his pads by Stuart Law, and the later batsmen failed to improve the score as well as they should have done. Essex began at a terrific rate with Prichard and Stuart Law scoring 81 off the first 12 overs. Law had hit 49 off 33 balls when he mistimed a pull off Franks and skied the ball. Hussain provided the rock as those around him promised more than they achieved. Tolley, in particular, bowled well, and the run-rate began to look more daunting until Robert Rollins took 14 in an over off Franks. Cowan kept up the momentum and was indebted to Johnson, who sportingly signalled he had taken a 'catch' on the half-volley. Hussain had steered Essex to victory, hitting 89 off 133 balls with ten judicious fours, with ten overs to spare. He batted with intelligence and discipline and more than compensated for his errors in the field.

Paul Johnson on his way to a valiant century for Nottinghamshire against Essex at Trent Bridge, but the captain's effort did not bring victory to his side. (Laurence Griffiths/Allsport)

Semi-Finals

12 and 13 August
at Chelmsford
Glamorgan 301 for 8 (S.P. James 109, P.A. Cottey 56)
Essex 303 for 9 (S.G. Law 90, D.D.J. Robinson 62,
R.C. Irani 51, S.D. Thomas 5 for 74)
Essex won by 1 wicket
(Man of the Match: S.G. Law)

13 and 14 August
at Edgbaston
Warwickshire 342 for 3 (D.L. Hemp 111 not out,
N.M.K. Smith 72, D.P. Ostler 58, A.J. Moles 56)
Sussex 237 (M. Newell 79, A.A. Donald 5 for 37)
Warwickshire won by 105 runs
(Man of the Match: D.L. Hemp)

For the first time, the two semi-finals were scheduled for different days, but rain took both matches into a second day.

The game at Chelmsford was one of the most exciting and certainly one of the most emotionally charged the NatWest Trophy has known, and it was decided by the narrowest of margins. Essex were without skipper Paul Prichard because of a hamstring injury, and they were intelligently led by Nasser Hussain. Their attack was at full strength with the return of Mark Ilott. Hussain won the toss and asked Glamorgan to bat. He also made an astute field change, which saw Morris caught at gully just before the first shower. James and Dale added 102 to put Glamorgan back on course, and James, the most prolific batsman in the country, gave his side the basis they needed with 109 off 157 balls. He was the calm in the storm, and this was a very worthy innings. The Essex fielding was not at its best, with the usually impressive Rollins below par, but there were three run outs. The most valuable of these for Essex was Maynard, always capable of running riot. Cottey, a busy little cricketer, hit a brisk 56, but Glamorgan's 301 was tantalisingly on the brink. It was not clearly a winning score, but it was defendable.

It did not seem defendable once Stuart Law began. Waqar Younis, the greatest menace, had to be withdrawn from the attack after his first three overs cost 24 runs. In the 12th over, with 77 on the board, Thomas hit Law on the upper arm with a beamer. His apology was no more than a perfunctory gesture, while the Australian reacted angrily, throwing down bat and gloves and engaging in some verbal encounters with neighbouring fielders. It took him some time to recover his composure, after which he began belting the Glamorgan attack to all parts of the field again. Robinson was a sensible partner, and after 20 overs the score was 122. Four overs later, Law, having hit Butcher for a straight six, attempted to repeat the shot but failed to follow through and was caught at long-off by Waqar Younis. His 90 had come off 73 balls, and Essex were 150.

Hussain and Robinson kept the score moving until Hussain dabbed Watkin and was caught at slip, and

Robinson slashed to cover in Watkin's next over. Irani, playing with pain-killing injections because of a rib injury, and Grayson halted the Glamorgan advance while not allowing the run rate to falter. At 256 for 4, Essex held the upper hand, and Danny Law emphasised this when he faced Waqar who had been recalled in the gathering gloom. He put the first delivery over long-on for six, and the third and fourth in the same direction for fours. He was yorked by Thomas for 16, but this was an invaluable contribution, for any pressure regarding run-rate had been eradicated.

Rollins did not last long, but Essex needed only 16 at less than two runs an over. Irani was playing well and had refused the offer of bad light, and Essex were strolling to victory when suddenly he and Cowan were seen at the same end. Cowan trudged back to the pavilion, and next ball Irani was leg before to Thomas. The bowler danced down the pitch with his back to the batsman. When the umpire's finger was slowly raised he swung round in delight and felled the oncoming Irani with a right hook as good as any delivered by Frank Bruno. Irani took the main force of the blow on his helmet, but was not amused, even less so when, getting to his feet, he learned he was out. Words were exchanged in an atmosphere that was now highly charged. Irani had batted splendidly, 51 off 64 balls, but, like Stuart Law, he was to be reprimanded for his verbal outburst.

Robert Rollins runs out Robert Croft in the highly competitive and emotional semi-final at Chelmsford. Rollins won his first Man of the Match award in the opening round at Beaconsfield.
(Laurence Griffiths/Allsport)

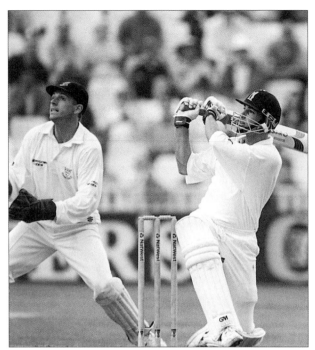

David Hemp hits another mighty blow in his second century in successive NatWest matches, and Warwickshire are on their way to the final. (Laurence Griffiths/Allsport)

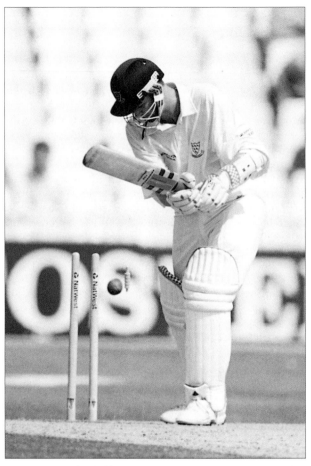

Peter Moores is bowled by Allan Donald, and the Sussex fairy tale is at an end. (Laurence Griffiths/Allsport)

It was 8.10 on a cloudy evening. It was now impossible for spectators to follow the ball. Waqar was recalled and his first ball shaved the left-handed Hodgson's off stump. Ilott immediately spoke to the umpires who conceded that the light was too bad to continue, and that life and limb could be endangered. While the umpires were debating, Ilott and Croft, great friends off field, engaged in an altercation that resulted in pushing and shoving. It was an unhappy end to a highly competitive and fiery day, and both men were fined £1000. They also received suspended sentences.

Play began late on the Wednesday with Essex needing six runs to win, two wickets standing and 6.5 overs remaining. The sun was now shining, and the tension had eased a little when Hodgson, the Durham University student playing his first NatWest game, pushed Waqar throught the offside for a single. Two more singles followed so that Essex now needed three more to win.

With the first ball of the next over, Thomas had Hodgson caught behind. This brought in last man Such, by no means the worst number 11 in county cricket. Thomas bowled four deliveries of full length, each of which Such met firmly in the middle of the bat. The last ball of the over was slightly over-pitched and outside off stump. Such hit it past mid-off for four, and Essex had won an enthralling, if somewhat bad-tempered, game.

There was not the same excitement at Edgbaston, where Sussex's fairy tale did not have a happy ending. They asked Warwickshire to bat first and suffered a mauling. Jarvis could find neither line nor length and was sav-

aged mercilessly. Robinson and Drakes did well to stem the tide, but the support bowling was inadequate. The pair conceded 72 runs in 24 overs; their colleagues conceded 261 in 36. On top of this, the Sussex fielding was ragged. Moles and Neil Smith began with 130 in 29 overs before Smith skied a ball from Keith Newell. He had hit ten fours. Moles was the rock on which all else was founded, and when he went at 150, Hemp and Ostler took over. In 22 overs, they added 142. Hemp took 24 off one over from the leg-spinner Khan. In all he hit five sixes and his unbeaten 111 came off 93 balls. He and Penney scored 50 from the last five overs.

Rain had delayed the start and Sussex had 11 overs to negotiate before the close. They lost Greenfield, needlessly run out in the first over, and Rao, caught off Welch for 0. The heroes against Lancashire and Derbyshire were gone, and Sussex, 43 for 2, began the second day with little hope.

They were soon 73 for 4. Athey was bowled by Donald in the third over in the day, and as the run rate soared Taylor was run out by Penney. Mark Newell and Moores, 45, gave a hint of respectability, but it was always Warwickshire who were going to meet Essex at Lord's, where they would start as favourites.

NatWest Trophy Final

Essex v. Warwickshire

Due to the funeral of Diana, Princess of Wales, the NatWest Trophy Final was put back 24 hours and played on the Sunday. Rarely can a side have started such strong favourites as Warwickshire. Their all-round ability with strength in depth in both batting and bowling contrasted sharply with Essex, who had always to improvise in finding 12 overs from a 'fifth' bowler and now had doubts as to the fitness of Irani. The all-rounder had a rib injury that had occasioned visits to a Munich clinic for treatment, and there were strong doubts, eventually unfounded, as to whether he would be able to bowl. In batting, too, since the retirement of Gooch, Essex looked increasingly vulnerable. Much depended on Stuart Law.

Prichard won the toss, and, following accepted Essex policy, he asked Warwickshire to bat. There were immediate dividends. Cowan's third ball was a wide. His third legitimate delivery nipped back at Knight, who offered no shot and was clearly lbw. The NatWest Final has not been a happy show piece for Knight, whose technical limitations have been cruelly exposed by the camera.

Four leg-byes came in Ilott's first over, but it was not until the last ball of the third over that runs first came from the bat. The last ball of the fourth over produced the first boundary when Smith pushed Ilott through the covers. In spite of this, the batsmen looked very ill at ease. On a pitch of uncertain pedigree and under a cloudy sky, the ball was moving and Cowan and Ilott were sustaining accuracy and venom. Smith's technique was sadly deficient in coping with the moving ball, and he was constantly being turned square by Cowan, while Hemp was playing and missing with monotonous regularity. After six overs Warwickshire had just 12 runs on the board, and it came as no surprise when Smith edged the third ball of the next over low to first slip. The ball from Cowan had moved only slightly, but it had moved enough to beat Smith's tentative push.

It was not until the 13th over that Hemp hit the second boundary of the match, but Cowan was still able to retire after a seven-over spell with figures of 2 for 13. Ilott had been equally demanding, and his seven overs had cost just seven runs.

Irani immediately settled into rhythm and line which taxed the batsmen, and Stuart Law, arguably the weak link in the Essex attack, gave nothing away. There were three maiden overs in succession before Hemp broke loose with an off-drive and a pull off Law that produced boundaries in the 18th over. In the next over, Ostler edged Irani to second slip where Cowan put down a comfortable chance. The score was 35, and Ostler was on three.

The sun shone for a brief period, and Ostler looked the most assured of the Warwickshire batsmen. Even so, on the advice of his wicket-keeper, Prichard brought in a slip when Law was bowling to Ostler, and with 22 overs gone, Warwickshire's run rate was exactly two an over.

Now came further disaster – Ostler slipped, Hemp hesitated, and Grayson's under-arm throw hit the stumps with Hemp so short of his line that no reference to the third umpire was needed.

Ostler was driving quite sweetly, but Penney could find no sort of timing. Prichard recalled Cowan shortly before lunch and brought on Such, whose mean spell was everything that could be expected of him. Law and Irani had retired from the attack having conceded 34 runs between them in 16 overs. For Essex, this was the decisive bonus. With his fifth ball of the last over before the interval, Cowan took the edge of Penney's bat with an outswinger, and Warwickshire were 75 for 4 in 35 overs.

Gradually, Ostler and Brown tried to increase the momentum, But Ostler was over-ambitious. He swung Irani high to the square-leg boundary where Danny Law caught the ball, dropped it, tried to hug it to his chest from which it rebounded and finally held it as he dived forward. The Essex fielding had been well disciplined, but this catch tested the nerves.

Warwickshire were 90 for 5 in the 41st over, and three overs and six runs on they lost their sixth wicket. This was brought about by a piece of sheer brilliance from Such, who fell to his right to hold a fierce drive from Welch.

The hundred was posted in the 46th over, but there was an astonishing lack of urgency in the Warwickshire cricket. The running between the wickets lacked ambition and bordered on lethargy. It was not until the 49th over that the second boundary of the afternoon was registered.

As had been anticipated, Warwickshire's strength was in their lower order, and Brown and Giles put together the best stand of the innings as the clouds dispersed and the sun shone. The partnership was worth 51 when, on the first ball of the 56th over, there was another crime of hesitancy, and Grayson's throw from square-leg to the wicket-keeper left Giles well short of the line.

The eighth wicket fell in the 58th over when Brown was very well caught at extra cover off a sumptuous drive. It was testimony to the excellence of Essex's display in the field and to the sustained excellence of their bowlers that the last over of the innings cost only two runs. Warwickshire's

Ashley Cowan gains his second wicket as Stuart Law catches Neil Smith at slip. (Adrian Murrel/Allsport)

Danny Law does a juggling act before catching Dominic Ostler on the square-leg boundary. (David Munden/Sportsline)

170 had an air of respectability, and there were many pundits who insisted that the pitch was no better than it had been in 1996, and that the Midland county had amassed a winning score. This proved to be far from the truth.

The pitch was not good, but it was far better than the dreadful strip of the previous year. Soon, all the debates regarding the pitch were silenced.

Welch opened the bowling for Warwickshire from the Nursery End. Prichard edged his second ball short of slip who dived over it and let it through for two. It was the last false short we were to see from an Essex batsman. Brown bowled three wides, and in Welch's second over, Law asserted his authority. He drove the first ball for four, the next was driven through the covers for four, the fifth ball produced a magnificent straight drive to the boundary, and the last was pulled past square-leg for another boundary. Ten runs came off the next over. Essex were 34 after four overs, and Warwickshire's tactic of keeping back their main strike bowlers, Donald and Small, was in tatters.

Small replaced Welch and conceded 11 in his first over. Donald took over from Brown and went for 12. By the end of the sixth over, Essex had 57 on the board, and when nine runs came in the next over they had hit as many boundaries, 11, as Warwickshire had hit in the whole of their innings.

There were early signs of disintegration in the field, so devastating was the assault. Prichard went to his 50 off 40 balls in the 13th over. He had hit seven fours, and the last ball of the over he pulled over mid-wicket for six to

bring up the hundred. Three balls later, he went back to Donald and was leg before, but he had helped launch Essex with an array of scintillating strokes.

Stuart Law reached his 50 with the help of an overthrow; it had come off 39 balls. He hooked Giles for six and produced on-drives of breath-taking splendour. Hussain was quickly in the mood with four fours and a six.

If Neil Smith could be accused of a lack of imagination in response to the situation, it must be said that Warwickshire, who wilted visibly, were overtaken by events. Stuart Law's violent attack on the bowling was launched before anyone could draw breath, and the stream of magnificent drives and pulls could only be greeted with gasps of wonder. Tea was taken after 25 overs, and Essex were 152 for 1.

It took only nine balls after tea to finish the game. Fifteen came from the first over, 11 of them to Law. Smith surrendered and brought on Penney. The third ball he bowled was driven square on the off side to the Mound Stand boundary. Essex had won with 33.1 overs and nine wickets to spare. Law, a six and 10 fours, made 80 off 71 balls.

The discussion now raged at the inadequacy of the pitch (far better than last year's offering), the value of winning the toss, the early start that handicapped the side batting first because of the low cloud, and the necessity, after 34 years, of playing the final earlier. Warwickshire supporters, the paying

NatWest Trophy Final – Essex v. Warwickshire
7 September 1997 at Lord's

Warwickshire

N.V. Knight	lbw, **b** Cowan	0
N.M.K. Smith (Capt)	c S.G. Law, **b** Cowan	5
D.L. Hemp	run out	21
D.P. Ostler	**c** D.R. Law, **b** Irani	34
T.L. Penney	c Rollins, **b** Cowan	5
D.R. Brown	**c** D.R. Law, **b** Ilott	37
G. Welch	c and **b** Such	2
A.F. Giles	run out	21
*K.J. Piper	not out	15
A.A. Donald	not out	3
G.C. Small		
	b **5**, lb **15**, w **5**, nb **2**	27
	60 overs (for 8 wickets)	**170**

Essex

P.J. Prichard (Capt)	lbw, **b** Donald	57
S.G. Law	not out	80
N. Hussain	not out	25
R.C. Irani		
A.P. Grayson		
D.D.J. Robinson		
D.R. Law		
*R.J. Rollins		
A.P. Cowan		
M.C. Ilott		
P.M. Such		
	b **1**, lb **4**, w **4**	9
	26.3 overs (for one wicket)	**171**

	O	M	R	**W**
Cowan	12	3	29	**3**
Ilott	12	3	29	**1**
Irani	12	4	22	**1**
S.G. Law	12	4	38	**–**
Such	12	1	32	**1**

	O	M	R	**W**
Welch	5	–	34	**–**
Brown	4	–	29	**–**
Small	7	–	43	**–**
Donald	6	–	36	**1**
Giles	4	1	20	**–**
Penney	0.3	–	4	**–**

Fall of Wickets
1–**12**, 2–**12**, 3–**45**, 4–**75**, 5–**90**, 6–**96**, 7–**147**, 8–**156**

Fall of Wickets
1–**109**

Umpires: M.J. Kitchen & P. Willey *Man of the Match*: S.G. Law

Essex won by 9 wickets

customer, so often so much closer to the game than the critics, were honest in their appraisal. Warwickshire played badly, and Essex outclassed them in every department of the game. They had exorcised the nightmare of the 1996 final and had won the game before 5.20.

The match had been preceded by a minute's silence in memory of Diana, Princess of Wales. It ended with respectful silence for the presentation party and Sir Gary Sobers. The great West Indian gave the Man of the Match Award to Stuart Law. If only he were English.

Men of the Moment. Stuart Law and Paul Prichard hold the NatWest Trophy. Essex owed much to the pair for a dynamic batting display that routed the Warwickshire attack. Prichard's positive captaincy earned considerable praise. Law took the individual award. (Adrian Murrell/Allsport)

Peter Such falls backward and tosses the ball in the air in triumph after pulling off a magnificent caught and bowled to dismiss Welch. (David Munden/Sportsline)

AXA Life League
(and minor limited-over competitions)

27 April
at Chelmsford
Hampshire 198 for 5 (W.S. Kendall 55, M. Keech 52)
Essex 202 for 7
Essex (4 pts) won by 3 wickets

at Cardiff
Warwickshire 147 for 7 (S.L. Watkin 4 for 15)
Glamorgan 81 for 3
Glamorgan (4 pts) won on faster scoring rate

at Canterbury
Derbyshire 184 for 8 (G.A. Khan 71 not out)
Kent 185 for 4 (M.J. Walker 80, A.P. Wells 56 not out)
Kent (4 pts) won by 6 wickets

at Old Trafford
Lancashire 268 for 6 (G.D. Lloyd 134, J.P. Crawley 83)
Durham 211 for 5 (M.A. Roseberry 91 not out)
Lancashire (4 pts) won by 57 runs

A fine acquisition for Essex, Danny Law was particularly successful in the one-day game. He moved to Essex from Sussex in the close season. (Andrew Budd/ Alan Cozzi)

at Leicester
Gloucestershire 236 for 8
Leicestershire 125 for 9
Gloucestershire (4 pts) won by 111 runs

at Trent Bridge
Nottinghamshire 183 for 8
Worcestershire 184 for 3 (T.M. Moody 89)
Worcestershire (4 pts) won by 7 wickets

at The Oval
Somerset 180 (R.J. Harden 53)
Surrey 181 for 7 (C.C. Lewis 68 not out)
Surrey (4 pts) won by 3 wickets

at Hove
Sussex 160 (K. Greenfield 58, J.N. Snape 4 for 31)
Northamptonshire 162 for 1 (A.L. Penberthy 74 not out, M.B. Loye 68)
Northamptonshire (4 pts) won by 9 wickets

Robinson and Cowan scored nine runs off the final over to bring Essex victory, but history was made at Cardiff where the Duckworth-Lewis system was used for the first time to determine the winner of a limited-over game interrupted by rain. Graham Lloyd's purple patch continued with an innings of 134 against Durham, which equalled the highest ever made by a Lancashire player in the Sunday League. Gloucestershire hit 61 off the last five overs at Grace Road where Gordon Parsons conceded 46 runs in three overs.

The Oval saw the introduction of music accompanying the batsmen, the county calling themselves the Lions and a commentator telling you what you could see. There was some cricket, too.

4 May
at Derby
Lancashire 262 for 7 (G.D. Lloyd 81, N.H. Fairbrother 74)
Derbyshire 217 for 9 (D.M. Jones 58)
Lancashire (4 pts) won by 35 runs

at Chelmsford
Essex 256 (S.G. Law 79, D.R. Law 55, P.N. Weekes 4 for 38)
Middlesex 190 (A.P. Cowan 4 for 31)
Essex (4 pts) won by 66 runs

at Southampton
Yorkshire 227 (D.S. Lehmann 75, R.J. Maru 4 for 29)
Hampshire 156
Yorkshire (4 pts) won by 71 runs

at Canterbury
Kent 193 for 8 (G.R. Cowdrey 82, A.J. Hollioake 5 for 38)
Surrey 181 for 8 (A.D. Brown 52, D.W. Headley 4 for 27)
Kent (4 pts) won by 12 runs

at Taunton
Glamorgan 207 (P.A. Cottey 61)
Somerset 210 for 4 (M.N. Lathwell 73, R.J. Harden 50 not out)
Somerset (4 pts) won by 6 wickets

at Hove
Sussex 160 for 7 (K. Greenfield 69 not out, K.P. Evans 4 for 26)
Nottinghamshire 162 for 4 (P. Johnson 60,
R.T. Robinson 51)
Nottinghamshire (4 pts) won by 6 wickets

at Edgbaston
Northamptonshire 173 for 9
Warwickshire 145 for 5
Warwickshire (4 pts) won by 5 wickets

Graham Lloyd continued his batting dominance as Lancashire won again. Derbyshire's target was reassessed as 253 in 38 overs. Lehmann starred in his first Sunday League game for Yorkshire, and Kent had the better of Surrey in a 25-over match at Canterbury even though Adam Hollioake produced his best Sunday League bowling figures. Sussex and Nottinghamshire played a 28-over game, and Warwickshire reached a revised target of 145 in 30 overs. Neil Smith emulated his father when he captained Warwickshire for the first time.

11 May
at Derby
Match abandoned
Derbyshire 2 pts, Surrey 2 pts

at Hartlepool
Durham 155 for 8
Nottinghamshire 157 for 1 (P. Johnson 74 not out)
Nottinghamshire (4 pts) won by 9 wickets

at Bristol
Gloucestershire 139 for 5 (M.A. Lynch 88 not out)
v. **Hampshire**
No result
Gloucestershire 2 pts, Hampshire 2 pts

at Lord's
Sussex 131 for 9
Middlesex 132 for 3 (M.R. Ramprakash 57)
Middlesex (4 pts) won by 7 wickets

at Northampton
Match abandoned
Northamptonshire 2 pts, Somerset 2 pts

at Worcester
Leicestershire 98 for 6
Worcestershire 92 for 9
Leicestershire (4 pts) won by 6 runs

at Leeds
Glamorgan 192 for 6 (P.A. Cottey 59)
Yorkshire 193 for 3 (D. Byas 83)
Yorkshire (4 pts) won by 7 wickets

Wretched weather devastated the third Sunday League programme. Two games were abandoned without a ball being bowled, and, at Bristol, the match was reduced to 16 overs, in which the home county scored 139. Lynch, 88 off 51 balls, and Alleyne hit 97 in four overs for the fourth wicket, but it was all in vain. The rain returned to prevent Hampshire from batting.

There was a 23-over match at Hartlepool, but Nottinghamshire needed only 18.4 overs to reach their target. Middlesex put a painful restraint on Sussex, who could make only 131 in 40 overs. Angus Fraser took 3 for 10 in his eight overs. Sussex were 92 for 9 before Robinson and Khan shared an unbroken record last wicket stand. Middlesex romped to victory in 27 overs.

Worcestershire and Leicestershire played a 16-over game at New Road, and the visitors, Parsons in particular, bowled tightly enough to defend a score of 98. A delayed start at Headingley reduced the game to 32 overs, but, inspired by skipper Byas, Yorkshire won with 33 balls to spare.

18 May
at Chelmsford
Durham 208 for 8 (J.E. Morris 110, A.P. Grayson 4 for 63)
Essex 210 for 8 (D.R. Law 82, M.J. Saggers 4 for 35)
Essex (4 pts) won by 2 wickets

at Southampton
Leicestershire 231 for 6 (N.C. Johnson 54, B.F. Smith 51 not out)
Hampshire 193 (K.D. James 50)
Leicestershire (4 pts) won by 38 runs

at Canterbury
Kent 238 for 9 (M.A. Ealham 61)
Glamorgan 230 (A. Dale 65, R.D.B. Croft 50, M.A. Ealham 5 for 41)
Kent (4 pts) won by 8 runs

at Old Trafford
Nottinghamshire 139
Lancashire 141 for 8 (J.E.R. Gallian 54 not out)
Lancashire (4 pts) won by 2 wickets

at Lord's
Derbyshire 178 (C.J. Adams 52)
Middlesex 179 for 6 (M.W. Gatting 82 not out)
Middlesex (4 pts) won by 4 wickets

at Taunton
Sussex 109 (A.R. Caddick 4 for 19)
Somerset 111 for 4 (M.N. Lathwell 53 not out)
Somerset (4 pts) won by 6 wickets

at The Oval
Gloucestershire 176 for 9 (M.W. Alleyne 58)
Surrey 177 for 5
Surrey (4 pts) won by 5 wickets

at Edgbaston
Yorkshire 185 for 9 (A.A. Donald 4 for 32)
Warwickshire 186 for 6
Warwickshire (4 pts) won by 4 wickets

Essex made it three wins out of three when their self-belief got the better of Durham. John Morris hit seven sixes in a magnificent 110 off 96 balls, but he was poorly supported, and the tail fell away against Grayson, who had earlier taken a pounding. At 38 for 4, Essex looked well beaten, but Danny Law drove with tremendous power for 82 off 75 balls. He was given sensible support, but when he was out in the 37th over Essex were still 24 short of their target. Ilott and Cowan rose to the occasion and won the match with eight balls to spare.

Neil Johnson's bold hitting at the top of the order in an opening stand of 88 set Leicestershire on the path to a good score against Hampshire, who laboured in response.

At Canterbury, Kent won their third match in succession, a victory that owed much to the all-round talents of Mark Ealham. He was Kent's top scorer, but Glamorgan were given a rousing start by Croft and looked set for a victory at 218 for 4. Collapse followed as Ealham had a personal triumph with 5 for 1 in his last nine balls.

Lancashire joined Kent and Essex at the top of the table with a stuttering win over Nottinghamshire. The pitch was difficult, and only Metcalfe and Gallian got beyond 20. Lancashire won with 13 balls to spare.

Having crushed Derbyshire in the championship match, Middlesex had a narrower win in the AXA Life game. Gatting and Nash added 62 for the sixth wicket when 79 were needed from the last 10 overs. Nash was out, but Gatting steered his side home with one ball to spare.

Somerset, mainly through Andy Caddick, bowled out Sussex in 31.4 overs and strolled to their target in 23.2 overs. At The Oval, Surrey won off the last ball. Gloucestershire fielded tigerishly to defend a moderate total, and Surrey needed 26 from the last three overs. It came down to two off the last over, but only one was managed off the first five balls.

Allan Donald spearheaded a comfortable Warwickshire win over Yorkshire at Edgbaston.

Bill Athey hit 109 not out as Sussex caused a surprise by beating Kent at Horsham. Athey retired in August, and this proved to be the last Sunday League hundred of a long career. (Nigel French/ASP)

25 May
at Chester-le-Street
Worcestershire 177 for 6 (D.A. Leatherdale 53 not out)
Durham 180 for 3 (M.P. Speight 61)
Durham (4 pts) won by 7 wickets

at Cardiff
Hampshire 180 for 8
Glamorgan 181 for 4 (A. Dale 53)
Glamorgan (4 pts) won by 6 wickets

at Gloucester
Gloucestershire 139
Essex 142 for 5 (S.G. Law 58)
Essex (4 pts) won by 5 wickets

at Old Trafford
Lancashire 241 for 6 (J.E.R. Gallian 101 not out)
Northamptonshire 166 (R.J. Bailey 67, P.J. Martin 5 for 21)
Lancashire (4 pts) won by 75 runs

at Leicester
Leicestershire 234 for 7
Surrey 238 for 5 (A.D. Brown 157 not out)
Surrey (4 pts) won by 5 wickets

at Trent Bridge
Nottinghamshire 280 for 6 (P. Johnson 117, G.F. Archer 104 not out)
Derbyshire 248 for 7 (C.J. Adams 121)
Nottinghamshire (4 pts) won by 32 runs

at Taunton
Somerset 260 for 7 (R.J. Harden 81, P.D. Bowler 61)
Yorkshire 261 for 3 (D.S. Lehmann 76, M.P. Vaughan 66)
Yorkshire (4 pts) won by 7 wickets

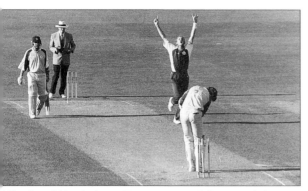

Allan Donald bowls Angus Fraser as Warwickshire overwhelm Middlesex in the AXA Life League match at Edgbaston, 25 May. (Philip Wilcox)

at Horsham
Kent 220 for 9 (M.J. Walker 60, A.A. Khan 5 for 40)
Sussex 224 for 6 (C.W.J. Athey 109 not out)
Sussex (4 pts) won by 4 wickets

at Edgbaston
Warwickshire 222 for 5 (D.P. Ostler 68 not out, N.M.K. Smith 53)
Middlesex 114 (G.C. Small 5 for 26)
Warwickshire (4 pts) won by 108 runs

Durham claimed their first Sunday League win of the season. Speight hit 61 off 66 balls, and skipper David Boon steered his side home with 5.2 overs to spare. He was unbeaten on 49. Waqar Younis took three wickets in four balls as Glamorgan beat Hampshire. It was Hampshire's fourth defeat in five matches.

Essex kept up their winning sequence, racing to victory in 26.5 overs against Gloucestershire while Lancashire stayed level with them at the top by beating Northamptonshire. Gallian made his best ever Sunday League score, and Peter Martin returned his best Sunday bowling figures. His opening spell brought him 3 for 14 and virtually ended the visitors' challenge.

Alistair Brown broke his own Surrey record for the Sunday League when he hit 157 off 117 balls at Leicester. His innings included three sixes and 15 fours. Facing a target of 235, he and Mark Butcher put on 107 in 15 overs for Surrey's first wicket. Butcher's contribution was 16. Ratcliffe Shahid and Ward went cheaply, but Surrey won with 20 balls to spare.

There were three centuries at Trent Bridge. Archer's was his first in the competition, and he and skipper Johnson put on 200 for the third wicket. It was the first time that two Nottinghamshire batsmen had scored hundreds in the same Sunday League match. Chris Adams, still inexplicably ignored by the England selectors, replied for Derbyshire with customary belligerence, but the only support he received came from Dean Jones. The pair scored 117 in 20 overs for the first wicket.

Yorkshire crushed Somerset at Taunton. Lehmann and Vaughan scored 134 in 18 overs for Yorkshire's second wicket.

The surprise of the day came at Horsham, where Sussex gained their first win of the season and Kent sustained their first loss. Leg-spinner Amer Khan provided the biggest surprise with a Sunday display of 5 for 40. Athey and Greenfield put on 100 for the home county's second wicket, and Athey won the match with three balls to spare when he hit 109 off 112 balls.

Warwickshire overwhelmed Middlesex to move within four points of the leaders.

1 June
at Ilford
Essex 262 for 9
Yorkshire 264 for 6 (D. Byas 72, M.P. Vaughan 66, D.S. Lehmann 58 not out)
Yorkshire (4 pts) won by 4 wickets

at Pontypridd
Durham 183 for 8 (N.J. Speak 74 not out)
Glamorgan 184 for 4
Glamorgan (4 pts) won by 6 wickets

at Southampton
Hampshire 278 for 4 (M.L. Hayden 118, G.W. White 67, S.D. Udal 50 not out)
Warwickshire 264 (D.P. Ostler 70, A.F. Giles 57, N.M.K. Smith 52, J.N.B. Bovill 4 for 44)
Hampshire (4 pts) won by 14 runs

at Leicester
Leicestershire 258 for 5 (D.L. Maddy 85, J.J. Whitaker 74)
Lancashire 259 for 5 (J.E.R. Gallian 104, N.H. Fairbrother 50 not out)
Lancashire (4 pts) won by 5 wickets

at Lord's
Northamptonshire 198 for 7 (K.M. Curran 66, A.L. Penberthy 53)
Middlesex 131 (J.C. Pooley 55, K.M. Curran 4 for 36)
Northamptonshire (4 pts) won by 67 runs

at Trent Bridge
Kent 252 for 7 (G.R. Cowdrey 81 not out, M.J. Walker 78)
Nottinghamshire 206 for 9 (N.A. Gie 75 not out)
Kent (4pts) won by 46 runs

at Worcester
Worcestershire 262 for 4 (G.A. Hick 119 not out)
Somerset 177 (R.J. Turner 67)
Worcestershire (4 pts) won by 85 runs

Essex completed a bad few days with their first defeat in the Sunday League. Knocked out of the Benson and Hedges Cup, on the brink of their first championship defeat, they batted consistently to reach a good score

Centuries on successive Sundays for Lancashire's Jason Gallian.
(David Munden/Sportsline)

against Yorkshire only to see Byas and Vaughan blast 146 in 17 overs for Yorkshire's first wicket. The visitors won with 19 balls to spare.

Glamorgan and Northamptonshire had comfortable wins, while Hampshire claimed their first victory of the summer when they surprisingly overcame Warwickshire. Their win was founded on an innings of 118 off 90 balls by Matthew Hayden. He dominated an opening stand of 185 with White.

Leicestershire's batting gave hope with a third wicket stand of 144 in 19 overs between Maddy and Whitaker, both of whom played attractively. When Parsons dismissed Atherton and Crawley with successive deliveries the home county were very much on top, but the bowling wavered dreadfully. Johnson, Pierson and Maddy were savaged by Lloyd's reverse sweep. Jason Gallian hit his second AXA Life League hundred in succession, 104 off 100 balls, and Lancashire went top of the table against a mediocre attack.

Graham Cowdrey gave a violent display of hitting, 81 off 43 balls, and tore a hamstring as Kent reasserted their challenge with victory at Trent Bridge, while Graeme Hick made 119 off 91 balls as Worcestershire beat Somerset. It was Hick's first limited-over hundred since his unbeaten 102 for England against Holland in the World Cup in February 1996.

8 June
at Chesterfield
Hampshire 170 for 7
Derbyshire 182 for 6
Derbyshire (4 pts) won on faster scoring rate

at Chester-le-Street
Durham 216 for 6 (D.C. Boon 76, J.J.B. Lewis 69 not out)
Sussex 57 for 4
Durham (4 pts) won on faster scoring rate

at Tunbridge Wells
Kent 177 (T.R. Ward 59, D.R. Brown 4 for 42)
Warwickshire 145
Kent (4 pts) won by 32 runs

at Lord's
Middlesex 196 for 4 (J.C. Pooley 52 not out)
Leicestershire 198 for 4 (D.L. Maddy 82, N.C. Johnson 80 not out)
Leicestershire (4pts) won on faster scoring rate

at Milton Keynes
Northamptonshire 222 for 5 (R.J. Bailey 52 not out)
Nottinghamshire 204 for 9 (N.J. Astle 75, J.E. Emburey 4 for 28)
Northamptonshire won on faster scoring rate

at Taunton
Lancashire 141 for 8
Somerset 107 for 5
Somerset (4 pts) won on faster scoring rate

at The Oval
Surrey 176 (J.D. Ratcliffe 69, A.P. Cowan 4 for 36)
Essex 185 for 4 (D.R. Law 55 not out)
Essex (4 pts) won on faster scoring rate

at Leeds
Gloucestershire 252 for 3 (S. Young 146 not out, R.J. Cunliffe 56)
Yorkshire 206 for 8 (R.J. Blakey 56)
Gloucestershire (4 pts) won on faster scoring rate

With rain prevalent, the Duckworth-Lewis method was employed in every match save the one at Tunbridge Wells. Targets were raised and lowered as the weather cut into the numbers of overs. Essex found themselves in the bizarre position of bowling out Surrey in 34.3 overs for 176 and then facing a revised target of 184 in 35 overs. They won with seven balls to spare.

The outstanding performance of the day came from Shaun Young. The Tasmanian all-rounder established a Gloucestershire Sunday League record with an innings of 146 not out off 105 balls. He hit nine sixes and nine fours in a magnificent display.

15 June
at Cardiff
Middlesex 185 for 6
Glamorgan 186 for 4 (M.P. Maynard 71 not out)
Glamorgan (4 pts) won by 6 wickets

at Bristol
Gloucestershire 177 (R.J. Cunliffe 50, S.R. Lampitt 4 for 49)
Worcestershire 176 for 7 (D.A. Leatherdale 51)
Gloucestershire (4 pts) won by 1 run

at Basingstoke
Somerset 175
Hampshire 169 for 9 (J.I.D. Kerr 4 for 28)
Somerset (4 pts) won by 6 runs

at Old Trafford
Lancashire 172 for 3 (M.A. Atherton 90 not out)
Kent 155 (T.R. Ward 53)
Lancashire (4 pts) won by 17 runs

at The Oval
Yorkshire 198 for 9 (D.S. Lehmann 56)
Surrey 199 for 5 (G.P. Thorpe 100 not out)
Surrey (4 pts) won by 5 wickets

at Hove
Sussex 216 for 6 (R.K. Rao 60, K. Greenfield 58 not out)
Essex 220 for 2 (S.G. Law 123, P.J. Prichard 68)
Essex (4 pts) won by 8 wickets

at Edgbaston
Warwickshire 201 for 6 (N.M.K. Smith 60, D.R. Brown 57)
Derbyshire 93
Warwickshire (4 pts) won by 108 runs

There were some close finishes in the eighth round of matches in the AXA Life League. Worcestershire, playing only their fifth game, restricted Gloucestershire to a meagre 177, but then lost their first four wickets for 16 runs. They recovered, but Leatherdale was caught off the third ball of the last over with six runs needed. Young bowled tightly, and Gloucestershire clinched a thrilling victory.

Kerr and Mushtaq Ahmed frustrated Hampshire and gave Somerset a close win at Basingstoke, while joint-leaders Lancashire got the better of close rivals Kent in a low scoring game at Old Trafford. The match was restricted to 35 overs, and Lancashire owed much to Atherton's first substantial Sunday score of the season. He hit an unbeaten 90 off 102 balls. Lancashire welcomed back Wasim Akram for the first time in three weeks. He took 2 for 18 in seven overs and led the side well. Kent, gifted 18 wides by their hosts, lost their last six wickets for 40 runs.

The match at The Oval did not finish until 7.40, the teams having been presented to the Yorkshire patron, the Duchess of Kent. Thorpe and Ben Hollioake took Surrey

to victory with an unbroken sixth wicket stand of 103 in 16 overs.

Essex raced to victory at Hove, winning with nearly 10 overs to spare to stay level at the top of the league with Lancashire. Stuart and Paul Prichard put Essex on the way to success with 199 for the first wicket. Law hit three sixes and 16 fours in his highest Sunday League score.

Derbyshire were dismembered at Edgbaston. They were bowled out in 16.5 overs.

22 June
at Derby
Match abandoned
Derbyshire 2 pts, Sussex 2 pts

at Darlington
Kent 141 (J. Wood 4 for 17, A. Walker 4 for 18)
Durham 125
Kent (4 pts) won by 16 runs

at Bristol
Gloucestershire 232 for 6 (S. Young 89 not out, M.A. Lynch 53)
Middlesex 177 for 6 (O.A. Shah 65 not out)
Gloucestershire (4 pts) won by 55 runs

at Old Trafford
Match abandoned
Lancashire 2 pts, Glamorgan 2 pts

at Northampton
Hampshire 159 for 2 (M.L. Hayden 54, J.S. Laney 53)
Northamptonshire 174 for 6 (R.J. Bailey 50)
Northamptonshire (4 pts) won on faster scoring rate

at Trent Bridge
Nottinghamshire 169 for 4 (A.A. Metcalfe 70 not out)
Yorkshire 78 for 5
Nottinghamshire (4 pts) won on faster scoring rate

at Bath
Leicestershire 166 for 8
Somerset 30 for 1
Leicestershire (4 pts) won on faster scoring rate

at Worcester
Surrey 149 (M.P. Bicknell 57 not out, G.R. Haynes 4 for 13)
Worcestershire 150 for 3
Worcestershire (4 pts) won by 7 wickets

The rain caused two abandonments, and the Duckworth-Lewis method was employed at Northampton, where the home side's target was raised, Trent Bridge and Bath. The Durham bowlers performed nobly at Darlington with Wood and Walker both producing their Sunday bests, but the batsmen fared miserably in ever darkening conditions. With Morris leading the assault, Durham were 58 for 2 in the 13th over. Two wickets fell quickly, and the home side never recovered against some accurate Kent bowling.

Middlesex suffered their sixth defeat in eight matches and paid a high price for their slow over rate. They were fined £660 and had two overs deducted from their quota so that they were never in the hunt against an ebullient Gloucestershire side for whom Young and Lynch added 115 in 17 overs for the third wicket.

Worcestershire beat Surrey with 8.3 overs to spare. Surrey were 59 for 8 before Martin Bicknell and Saqlain Mushtaq saved them from total humiliation with a stand of 83.

26 June
at The Oval
Match abandoned
Surrey 2 pts, Nottinghamshire 2 pts

The first scheduled floodlit match in England was abandoned because of torrential rain.

29 June
at Southend
Essex 205 for 7 (R.C. Irani 52)
Derbyshire 121 for 7
Essex (4 pts) won on faster scoring rate

at Swansea
Sussex 135 (C.W.J. Athey 60, Waqar Younis 4 for 14)
Glamorgan 136 for 2 (H. Morris 66 not out)
Glamorgan (4 pts) won by 8 wickets

at Leicester
Leicestershire 115 for 8
Warwickshire 117 for 2
Warwickshire (4 pts) won by 8 wickets

at Luton
Match abandoned
Northamptonshire 2 pts, Gloucestershire 2 pts

at Worcester
Worcestershire 235 for 7 (G.A. Hick 86, V.S. Solanki 58)
Lancashire 121
Worcestershire (4 pts) won by 114 runs

at Leeds
Middlesex 173 for 8 (J.C. Pooley 61, P.N. Weekes 53 not out)
Yorkshire 175 for 4
Yorkshire (4 pts) won by 6 wickets

The Duckworth-Lewis method caused confusion to spectators at Southend. Essex had their full quota of overs, but rain arrived when Derbyshire were 56 for 0 from 12 overs. The revised target allowed Derbyshire another 11 overs in which to score 66 more runs. They arrived at the last over with eight needed with six wickets standing. Grayson captured two wickets, and Aldred needed to hit two off the last ball. He was run out attempting a second run so that the scores were level, but under the Duckworth-Lewis system a tie is not possible, and Essex were winners by one run.

The win took them clear at the top of the table, for Lancashire gave a wretched batting display at Worcester, where they were bowled out in 28.1 overs.

Glamorgan beat Sussex with 12 overs in hand, and Leicestershire came off the worse in a 15-over slog against Warwickshire, who won with eight balls to spare.

The Middlesex misery continued when Yorkshire passed their inadequate score with 4.1 overs remaining.

6 July
at Chester-le-Street
Durham 162 for 9 (J.J.B. Lewis 51 not out, J.P. Stephenson 4 for 28)
Hampshire 163 for 4
Hampshire (4 pts) won by 6 wickets

at Chelmsford
Essex 209 for 9
Somerset 211 for 6 (M. Burns 83)
Somerset (4 pts) won by 4 wickets

at Swansea
Gloucestershire 236 for 7 (A.J. Wright 69, T.H.C. Hancock 57)
Glamorgan 219 for 7 (S.P. James 75 not out, M.C.J. Ball 4 for 26)
Gloucestershire (4 pts) won by 17 runs

at Maidstone
Kent 209 for 8
Northamptonshire 207 for 9 (R.J. Bailey 54)
Kent (4 pts) won by 2 runs

at Leicester
Leicestershire 298 for 9 (D.L. Maddy 70, J.J. Whitaker 66, V.J. Wells 51, A.C. Morris 4 for 49)
Yorkshire 298 for 9 (C. White 148)
Match tied
Leicestershire 2 pts, Yorkshire 2 pts

at Uxbridge
Middlesex 197 (J.C. Pooley 73)
Lancashire 197 for 9 (N.H. Fairbrother 70)
Match tied
Middlesex 2 pts, Lancashire 2 pts

at Arundel
Worcestershire 207 for 3 (K.R. Spiring 58 not out,
D.A. Leatherdale 58 not out)
Sussex 158
Worcestershire (4 pts) won by 49 runs

at Edgbaston
Warwickshire 231 for 6 (D.P. Ostler 58)
Surrey 183 for 9 (A.J. Hollioake 50)
Warwickshire (4 pts) won by 48 runs

Another disappointing batting display set Durham on the road to defeat by Hampshire while Essex gave a generally inept performance against Somerset. They slipped from 109 for 2 to 181 for 9, and Somerset, with Burns hitting his highest Sunday League score, won with 16 balls to spare.

Essex maintained a joint-leadership at the top, and Gloucestershire moved to within four points of the leaders with a fine victory over Glamorgan. Wright and Hancock shared an opening stand of 107 for Gloucestershire.

Kent moved level with Essex with a thrilling win over Northamptonshire. Once again they had to defend a moderate score, and Northamptonshire reached the last over needing 10 to win with two wickets standing. Snape and Taylor managed seven before Snape was brilliantly run out by Fleming off the penultimate ball of the match.

The game at Leicester was even closer. The home county posted an impressive 298, but Craig White led Yorkshire to the brink of a fine victory. His 148, which included five sixes and 10 fours, was made off 114 balls and was the highest score for Yorkshire in a Sunday League match. The last over, bowled by Parsons, arrived with five runs needed, but three wickets fell, including that of Stemp who was run out off the last ball going for the second run, which would have won the match.

Astonishingly, there was also a tie at Uxbridge, Lancashire needed 13 from the last over, which was bowled by Richard Johnson. Hegg took eight off the first two balls. Both Hegg and Martin were run out, and the last ball arrived with two needed. Middlesex restricted Lancashire to a bye, and the match was tied, taking Lancashire level with Kent and Essex.

Such excitement was not to be experienced at Arundel or Edgbaston.

13 July
at Derby
Derbyshire 259 for 2 (C.J. Adams 109 not out,
V.P. Clarke 77 not out)
Yorkshire 145
Derbyshire (4 pts) won by 114 runs

at Chester-le-Street
Durham 174 for 2 (M.P. Speight 64 not out, S. Hutton 57)
Warwickshire 137 for 5 (D.L. Hemp 50)
Warwickshire (4 pts) won on faster scoring rate

at Southampton
Hampshire 232 for 4 (M. Keech 53 not out,
S.D. Udal 52 not out)
Worcestershire 145 (J.P. Stephenson 6 for 33)
Hampshire (4 pts) won by 87 runs

at Trent Bridge
Somerset 227 for 6 (M. Burns 60, K.A. Parsons 52
not out, C.M. Tolley 4 for 24)
Nottinghamshire 197 for 7 (P.R. Pollard 87)
Somerset (4 pts) won by 30 runs

at Hove
Gloucestershire 141 for 9
Sussex 142 for 9 (K. Greenfield 62)
Sussex (4 pts) won by 1 wicket

Cricket at Arundel. Robin Martin-Jenkins bowling for Sussex against Worcestershire. It was a traumatic season for Sussex, but all-rounder Martin-Jenkins is one who gives hope for the future. (Ben Radford/Allsport)

With the three leading clubs idle, Warwickshire moved level on points, when they beat Durham under the Duckworth-Lewis system. Their target was revised to 137 in 17 overs, and with Hemp battering 50 at the top, they won with three balls to spare. Earlier they had been deprived of the bowling services of Gladstone Small, who was removed from the attack after three warnings for running on the pitch.

Chris Adams gave the England selectors another reminder with 109 from 110 balls as he batted through the innings in the victory over Yorkshire. He and Clarke shared an unbroken third wicket stand of 158 to take Derbyshire to their highest score against Yorkshire in the 28 years of the Sunday League.

John Stephenson, the Hampshire captain, finished off the Worcester innings and won the match with wickets off consecutive deliveries. His 6 for 33 represented his best bowling figures in limited-over cricket.

Somerset had a comfortable win at Trent Bridge to go within two points of the leaders, while Sussex, a model of inconsistency, cut things very close. They needed one run off the last over to beat Gloucestershire. Alleyne bowled Keith Newell with the first ball and had Robinson stumped off the second, which was down the leg side. Umpire Jones, however, had signalled a wide so the wicket stood, but Sussex gained the run that won the match.

At Guildford, 20 July, Alistair Brown became the first batsman to hit a double century in the Sunday League, 203 for Surrey against Hampshire. (Phil Cole/Allsport)

20 July

at Cheltenham
Derbyshire 246 for 9 (K.J. Barnett 99)
Gloucestershire 247 for 3 (S. Young 85, M.A. Lynch 54 not out)
Gloucestershire (4 pts) won by 7 wickets

at Canterbury
Leicestershire 258 for 7 (V.J. Wells 69, J.J. Whitaker 60)
Kent 225 (N.J. Llong 52)
Leicestershire (4 pts) won by 33 runs

at Old Trafford
Sussex 170 for 9
Lancashire 171 for 2 (J.E.R. Gallian 80 not out)
Lancashire (4 pts) won by 8 wickets

at Northampton
Northamptonshire 198 for 8 (R.J. Bailey 75, D.J. Capel 54)
Essex 199 for 8 (A.P. Grayson 69 not out)
Essex (4 pts) won by 2 wickets

at Trent Bridge
Nottinghamshire 229 for 8 (R.T. Robinson 56, G.F. Archer 53)
Warwickshire 142 (D.R. Brown 68, M.N. Bowen 4 for 29)
Nottinghamshire (4 pts) won by 87 runs

at Guildford
Surrey 344 for 5 (A.D. Brown 203)
Hampshire 276 (S.D. Udal 78)
Surrey (4 pts) won by 68 runs

at Worcester
Worcestershire 242 for 3 (T.S. Curtis 93, G.R. Haynes 64 not out)
Glamorgan 197
Worcestershire (4 pts) won by 45 runs

at Scarborough
Yorkshire 259 for 7 (D.S. Lehmann 77, C. White 64, A. McGrath 51 not out)
Durham 121 (C. White 4 for 18)
Yorkshire (4 pts) won by 138 runs

Alistair Brown became the first person to hit a double century in a Sunday League match when he made 203 off 119 balls as Surrey beat Hampshire at Guildford. His innings included 11 sixes and 19 fours. He totally dominated the match. He reached 50 off 20 deliveries, and Stewart made only 14 in an opening partnership of 90. Connor and Bovill were the main sufferers, both conceding more than 10 runs an over.

Gloucestershire had a fine win over Derbyshire, for whom Barnett performed nobly before being out to the last ball of the innings. Hancock and Wright scored 72 for the home county's first wicket, and Young hit 85 of 61 balls with seven sixes and five fours. He was winning matches and many hearts in Gloucestershire with his dynamic cricket.

Kent were never in contention against Leicestershire, and Lancashire romped to victory over Sussex with 31 balls to spare. Worcestershire and Yorkshire also won with ease.

Essex narrowly held on to top place with Lancashire when they beat Northamptonshire off the last ball. They began the last over needing nine to win. Grayson batted admirably, and although he ran out Cowan, he kept the strike and pushed runs through the gaps in the field. He hit Emburey's last ball for two to win the game.

At Trent Bridge, Warwickshire's run of four consecutive Sunday victories came to an end. Nottinghamshire had lost their first three wickets for 39 before Archer and Robinson added 94. From that point on, Warwickshire were never in contention.

23 July
at Edgbaston
Warwickshire 224 for 5 (A. Singh 86, N.M.K. Smith 59)
Somerset 189 (P.D. Bowler 57)
Warwickshire (4 pts) won by 35 runs

Warwickshire brought forward their Sunday League match to the Wednesday, the first scheduled day of the championship match, and staged the first competitive floodlit game in England. The match lasted from 6.10 to 11.37 and was watched by a crowd of 16,000 who were delighted by the home side's success. Singh and Smith scored 112 for the first wicket.

27 July
at Chesterfield
Glamorgan 103 (D.G. Cork 6 for 21)
Derbyshire 106 for 2
Derbyshire (4 pts) won by 8 wickets

at Chelmsford
Worcestershire 217 (T.M. Moody 59, S.G. Law 4 for 37)
Essex 217
Match tied
Essex 2 pts, Worcestershire 2 pts

at Cheltenham
Durham 226 for 7 (J.J.B. Lewis 102)
Gloucestershire 230 for 5 (R.C. Russell 59 not out, T.H.C. Hancock 50)
Gloucestershire (4 pts) won by 5 wickets

at Southampton
Hampshire 210 for 9 (M.L. Hayden 55)
Lancashire 214 for 6 (N.H. Fairbrother 88)
Lancashire (4 pts) won by 4 wickets

at Leicester
Leicestershire 252 for 9 (J.J. Whitaker 73)
Nottinghamshire 165
Leicestershire (4 pts) won by 87 runs

at Lord's
Middlesex 151 for 8 (K.P. Dutch 58)
Kent 152 for 2 (T.R. Ward 68 not out, A.P. Wells 56)
Kent (4 pts) won by 8 wickets

at Northampton
Surrey 206 for 7 (J.D. Ratcliffe 82, Mohammad Akram 4 for 19)
Northamptonshire 208 for 5 (A.L. Penberthy 81 not out)
Northamptonshire (4 pts) won by 5 wickets

England's missing man Dominic Cork, having lost more than three-quarters of the season through injury, was back

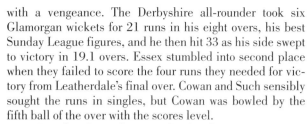

with a vengeance. The Derbyshire all-rounder took six Glamorgan wickets for 21 runs in his eight overs, his best Sunday League figures, and he then hit 33 as his side swept to victory in 19.1 overs. Essex stumbled into second place when they failed to score the four runs they needed for victory from Leatherdale's final over. Cowan and Such sensibly sought the runs in singles, but Cowan was bowled by the fifth ball of the over with the scores level.

Jonathan Lewis hit a maiden Sunday League century but could not stop Durham from being well beaten by Gloucestershire. Durham remained rooted to the bottom of the table, and Hampshire were not far above them. Fairbrother hit 88 off 104 balls and Ian Austin offered some lusty blows as Lancashire beat Hampshire with three balls to spare and went two points clear at the top of the table.

James Whitaker reached 5,000 Sunday League runs and led his side to victory over Nottinghamshire while Middlesex's batting, without the injured Ramprakash, flopped again. Kent used nearly their full quota of overs in getting the runs but won with ease. Surrey's hopes of retaining their title virtually disappeared at Northampton where Mohammad Akram bowled with accuracy and devil, and Penberthy and Fordham scored 104 for the home side's first wicket.

3 August
at Chester-le-Street
Derbyshire 181 for 9
Durham 185 for 5
Durham (4 pts) won by 5 wickets

at Colchester
Leicestershire 225 for 9 (D.L. Maddy 75)
Essex 190
Leicestershire (4 pts) won by 30 runs

at Colwyn Bay
Nottinghamshire 228 for 8 (M.P. Dowman 71, N.J. Astle 63)
Glamorgan 208 (A.R. Oram 4 for 45)
Nottinghamshire (4 pts) won by 20 runs

at Lord's
Surrey 74 for 7
v. **Middlesex**
Match abandoned
Middlesex 2 pts, Surrey 2 pts

at Edgbaston
Sussex 162 for 9
Warwickshire 102 for 3
Warwickshire (4 pts) won on faster scoring rate

at Worcester
Worcestershire 117 for 3
v. **Kent**
Match abandoned
Worcestershire 2 pts, Kent 2 pts

at Leeds
Yorkshire 239 for 9 (A. McGrath 63, C. White 57)
Northamptonshire 201 (K.M. Curran 57)
Yorkshire (4 pts) won by 38 runs

Without Dominic Cork, Derbyshire could not overcome Durham, whose third win of the season took them off the bottom. That place was filled by Sussex, who lost at Edgbaston on the Duckworth-Lewis method. The win for Warwickshire took them level on points at the top of the table with Lancashire, who had a game in hand. Essex slipped back when they were crushed by Leicestershire. Nottinghamshire and Yorkshire had comfortable victories.

10 August
at Canterbury
Kent 223 for 7 (G.R. Cowdrey 80, M.A. Ealham 50)
Essex 106
Kent (4 pts) won by 117 runs

at Old Trafford
Warwickshire 219 for 9 (T.L. Penney 57, D.P. Ostler 53)
Lancashire 198 for 9 (N.H. Fairbrother 79)
Warwickshire (4 pts) won by 21 runs

at Lord's
Hampshire 216 for 7 (M.L. Hayden 89)
Middlesex 200 (J.C. Pooley 94 not out)
Hampshire (4 pts) won by 16 runs

at Northampton
Northamptonshire 207 for 9
Worcestershire 208 for 8
Worcestershire (4 pts) won by 2 wickets

at Taunton
Somerset 267 for 8 (P.C.L. Holloway 117)
Gloucestershire 194 (M. Burns 4 for 39)
Somerset (4 pts) won by 73 runs

at The Oval
Durham 189 for 9 (M.A. Roseberry 55 not out, M.P. Bicknell 4 for 28)
Surrey 190 for 3 (M.A. Butcher 81)
Surrey (4 pts) won by 7 wickets

at Eastbourne
Leicestershire 184 (B.F. Smith 71)
Sussex 140 (D. Williamson 5 for 32)
Leicestershire (4 pts) won by 44 runs

Essex's hopes of winning the AXA Life League disappeared at Canterbury where Kent rounded off a fine week with a resounding victory. Kent were 52 for 4 before Cowdrey and Ealham added 89. Graham Cowdrey's 80 came off 79 balls and then he took a low catch at long-off to get rid of Stuart

Law, Essex's key man. With Irani run out without facing a ball, Essex's day of misery was complete.

The win took Kent to second place, two points behind Warwickshire and with a game in hand. The Midland county won the vital match at Old Trafford. Warwickshire's strength is their all-round capability in depth. Ostler and Penney added 82 for the fifth wicket, but they have so many players like Welch, Brown and Giles who are always making a contribution in one area of the game. Lancashire reached 162 for 3, but when Fairbrother was out in the 34th over the innings fell apart. Beaten by Hampshire, Middlesex moved closer to the bottom with only Sussex propping them up. Sussex fell victim to Dominic Williamson, the young medium pace bowler, who returned his best figures for Leicestershire in any form of cricket.

Somerset played positive cricket to beat Gloucestershire with Piran Holloway making his first century in a limited-over game. His 117 came off 107 balls, and he and Simon Ecclestone put on 107 for the second wicket.

24 August
at Chester-le-Street
Match abandoned
Durham 2 pts, Middlesex 2 pts

at Cardiff
Match abandoned
Glamorgan 2 pts, Northamptonshire 2 pts

at Bristol
Lancashire 41 for 3
v. **Gloucestershire**
Match abandoned
Gloucestershire 2 pts, Lancashire 2 pts

at Leicester
Match abandoned
Leicestershire 2 pts, Derbyshire 2 pts

at Trent Bridge
Match abandoned
Nottinghamshire 2 pts, Essex 2 pts

at Taunton
Somerset 89 for 7
Kent 81 for 6
Kent (4 pts) won on faster scoring rate

at Worcester
Warwickshire 151 for 8
Worcestershire 87 for 5
Warwickshire (4 pts) won on faster scoring rate

at Scarborough
Match abandoned
Yorkshire 2 pts, Sussex 2 pts

The drought and the heat wave gave way to rain, and, remarkably, the only two fixtures where a result could be achieved involved the two leading counties. Even in these matches, the Duckworth-Lewis system had to be employed. At Taunton, the match was reduced to 18 overs, but more rain brought Kent a revised target of 78 in 13 overs. They won with four balls to spare.

Warwickshire had 25 overs at Worcester, but the home county's target was revised to 95 off 16, which they failed to reach.

27 August
at Hove
Sussex 151 (R.K. Rao 58, C.C. Lewis 4 for 21)
Surrey 152 for 5
Surrey (4 pts) won by 5 wickets

Another venture into the twilight zone saw Sussex move their game against Surrey to the Wednesday and stage it under floodlights. The visitors won with ease, bowling Sussex out in 37.3 overs and reaching their target in 27.3 overs, but the Sussex club could point to the fact that, although they were bottom of the table and the earlier poor weather caused four overs to be lopped off the match, the attendance was approximately 4,000, larger than the average Sunday attendance.

31 August
at Derby
Match abandoned
Derbyshire 2 pts, Somerset 2 pts

at Chelmsford
Warwickshire 255 for 5 (D.L. Hemp 70 not out, N.M.K. Smith 57)
Essex 108 (A.A. Donald 5 for 10)
Warwickshire (4 pts) won by 147 runs

at Bristol
Match abandoned
Gloucestershire 2 pts, Nottinghamshire 2 pts

at Portsmouth
Hampshire 175
Kent 179 for 4 (E.T. Smith 72 not out)
Kent (4 pts) won by 6 wickets

at Old Trafford
Lancashire 93 for 6
Yorkshire 62 for 8
Lancashire (4 pts) won by 31 runs

at Leicester
Match abandoned
Leicestershire 2 pts, Glamorgan 2 pts

at Worcester
Match abandoned
Worcestershire 2 pts, Middlesex 2 pts

The tragic death of Diana, Princess of Wales, led to the match between Northamptonshire and Durham being postponed until 8 September, while rain wiped out all the other games save the three games involving the top three sides. Warwickshire massacred Essex to maintain their lead at the head of the table and to maintain their superior run-rate over Kent, who won comfortably at Portsmouth. Warwickshire's win at Chelmsford had a double significance, for the two sides were to meet in the NatWest Final a week later. Essex were not at full strength, but Donald's 5 for 10 in 5.5 overs was a frightening portent for them.

The match at Old Trafford was a 10-over slog in which Yorkshire were very much second best.

7 September
at Derby
Derbyshire 145 for 9 (J.A.R. Blain 5 for 24)
Northamptonshire 146 for 3
Northamptonshire (4 pts) won by 7 wickets

at Canterbury
Gloucestershire 136 for 9
Kent 139 for 1 (E.T. Smith 54 not out, T.R. Ward 54)
Kent (4 pts) won by 9 wickets

at Leicester
Leicestershire 252 for 8 (I.J. Sutcliffe 96, D.L. Maddy 70, J. Boiling 4 for 46)
Durham 146
Leicestershire (4 pts) won by 106 runs

Floodlight cricket at Hove. Sussex v. Surrey, 27 August.
(Laurence Griffiths/Allsport)

Michael Burns – a consistently quick scorer for Somerset with a century against Middlesex in the penultimate match of the season. (George Herringshaw/ASP)

at Trent Bridge
Nottinghamshire 209 for 9
Hampshire 206 for 8 (M.L. Hayden 100, J.S. Laney 69, C.M. Tolley 4 for 39)
Nottinghamshire (4 pts) won by 3 runs

at Taunton
Somerset 237 for 7 (M. Burns 115 not out)
Middlesex 219 for 6 (M.R. Ramprakash 90)
Somerset (4 pts) won by 18 runs

at The Oval
Glamorgan 242 for 8 (M.P. Maynard 132 not out)
Surrey 243 for 8 (A.D. Brown 64, A.J. Hollioake 63, J.D. Ratcliffe 54, O.T. Parkin 4 for 45)
Surrey (4 pts) won by 2 wickets

at Leeds
Worcestershire 220 for 6 (T.M. Moody 67)
Yorkshire 182 (A. Sheriyar 4 for 18)
Worcestershire (4 pts) won by 38 runs

With Warwickshire engaged in the NatWest Trophy final, Kent moved to the top of the table with a resounding victory over Gloucestershire, who lost three wickets with the score on 114. Kent only needed 27.4 overs to reach their target. The game was the last in the Sunday League for Paul Strang

who led Kent out to a tremendous ovation. The Zimbabwe all-rounder had been a very fine and most popular acquisition for the hop county, who now needed only to win their final game to take the title.

Leicestershire moved into third place with victory over Durham, while neither Middlesex, Hampshire nor Derbyshire could improve their positions. Morale at Derbyshire was particularly low, with Adams having been released from his contract and the news that DeFreitas would not be considered for the captaincy in 1998. They fell foul of Scottish seamer John Blain, who returned his best figures for Northamptonshire.

Gordon Parsons led out Leicestershire and received a standing ovation on his last appearance for the county.

8 September
at Northampton
Durham 185 for 6 (D.C. Boon 54 not out)
Northamptonshire 186 for 5 (R.R. Montgomerie 86 not out)
Northamptonshire (4 pts) won by 5 wickets

Not for the first time Durham lost a match that they looked like winning. Northamptonshire were 118 for 5 before Walton joined Montgomerie to score 68 in 10 overs.

9 September
at Old Trafford
Essex 230 for 8 (P.J. Prichard 103, P.J. Martin 5 for 41)
Lancashire 233 for 4 (M. Watkinson 66, J.P. Crawley 51)
Lancashire (4 pts) won by 6 wickets

Paul Prichard hit a celebratory century after Essex's success in the NatWest Trophy, but he was overshadowed by Peter Martin, whose five wickets took him past Wasim Akram's Sunday League of 29 in a season. Lancashire won with two overs to spare.

14 September
at Chester-le-Street
Durham 205 for 8 (J.J.B. Lewis 57, M.P. Speight 50)
Somerset 211 for 3 (S.C. Ecclestone 96 not out, M.N. Lathwell 57 not out)
Somerset (4 pts) won by 7 wickets

at Cardiff
Glamorgan 168 (A. Dale 62, P.M. Such 5 for 29)
Essex 169 for 4 (S.G. Law 59)
Essex (4 pts) won by 6 wickets

at Southampton
Sussex 181 (M. Newell 60, J.P. Stephenson 4 for 41)
Hampshire 184 for 8 (S.D. Udal 70)
Hampshire (4 pts) won by 2 wickets

Leading wicket-taker in the AXA Life League – Peter Martin of Lancashire, 31 wickets. (David Munden/Sportsline)

at Lord's
Middlesex 231 for 4 (O.A. Shah 66 not out, P.N. Weekes 53, M.R. Ramprakash 52)
Nottinghamshire 230 for 7 (P. Johnson 100, G.E. Welton 68, P.N. Weekes 4 for 51)
Middlesex (4 pts) won by 1 run

at Northampton
Leicestershire 179 for 9 (J.F. Brown 4 for 26)
Northamptonshire 181 for 5 (K.M. Curran 78 not out, R.R. Montgomerie 69)
Northamptonshire (4 pts) won by 5 wickets

at The Oval
Lancashire 206 for 8 (N.H. Fairbrother 54)
Surrey 210 for 5 (A.J. Stewart 67 not out, B.C. Hollioake 61)
Surrey (4 pts) won by 5 wickets

at Edgbaston
Warwickshire 221 for 6 (N.V. Knight 102)
Gloucestershire 150 (A.A. Donald 4 for 24, A.F. Giles 4 for 25)
Warwickshire (4 pts) won by 71 runs

at Worcester
Worcestershire 215 for 3 (T.M. Moody 112)
Derbyshire 216 for 5 (V.P. Clarke 69 not out)
Derbyshire (4 pts) won by 5 wickets

at Leeds
Kent 185 for 8
Yorkshire 187 for 3 (D.S. Lehmann 78 not out)
Yorkshire (4 pts) won by 7 wickets

As in the Benson and Hedges Cup, Kent fell at the last hurdle. Paul Strang had been given special permission to remain in England until after the vital AXA Life League game at Headingley, and he gave the Kent innings a much needed boost from the depths of 124 for 7, but 185 hardly looked like a winning score. McGrath was caught off Igglesden for nine to leave Yorkshire on 14 for 1, but Lehmann took over. He and Vaughan added 125, and Yorkshire went on to win with more than 10 overs to spare. Lehmann ended as second leading run-scorer in the league behind fellow Australian Hayden. Another Australian, Stuart Law, was third.

Meanwhile, at Edgbaston, Warwickshire overwhelmed Gloucestershire to take the title for the second time in four years. Nick Knight put behind him a disappointing summer in which he had suffered two broken fingers and missed much cricket to reach his century in the 36th over and give Warwickshire the comfort of a score in excess of 200. Dawson and Hancock began well enough for Gloucestershire, but soon they were undermined by Donald, whose four wickets brought him to just one behind Peter Martin. There should be a word of praise for Gladstone Small, whose eight overs cost only 25 runs. He had played in the Warwickshire side that first won the Sunday League in 1980.

Warwickshire win the AXA Life League.
(Dave Tyrell/Allsport)

AXA Life League
Final Table

	P	W	L	T	NR	Pts	RR
Warwickshire (4)	17	13	4	0	0	52	14.14
Kent (10)	17	12	4	0	1	50	7.70
Lancashire (9)	17	10	4	1	2	46	1.89
Leicestershire (12)	17	9	5	1	2	42	7.11
Surrey (1)	17	9	5	0	3	42	1.06
Somerset (5)	17	9	6	0	2	40	4.31
Essex (17)	17	9	6	1	1	40	-2.38
Worcestershire (8)	17	8	6	1	2	38	6.87
Northamptonshire (6)	17	8	6	0	3	38	2.78
Yorkshire (3)	17	8	7	1	1	36	5.24
Gloucestershire (16)	17	7	6	0	4	36	1.01
Nottinghamshire (2)	17	7	7	0	3	34	-0.19
Glamorgan (13)	17	5	9	0	3	26	-4.01
Derbyshire (11)	17	4	9	0	4	24	-3.04
Hampshire (15)	17	5	11	0	1	22	-4.73
Middlesex (7)	17	3	10	1	3	20	-8.28
Durham (18)	17	3	13	0	1	14	-12.27
Sussex (14)	17	2	13	0	2	12	-16.72

(1996 positions in brackets)

Costcutter Cup

at Harrogate

9 June
Yorkshire 305 for 4 (D. Byas 82, C. White 72,
D.S. Lehmann 63 not out)
Gloucestershire 308 for 5 (N.J. Trainor 113,
M.A. Lynch 61)
Gloucestershire won by 5 wickets
(Man of the Match: N.J. Trainor)

10 June
Scotland 222 for 7 (B.M.W. Patterson 97)
Durham 226 for 2 (M.A. Roseberry 102 not out,
P.D. Collingwood 64)
Durham won by 8 wickets
(Man of the Match: J. Boiling)

The Harrogate Festival saw two fine games of cricket. The
55-over Costcutter Cup had Gloucestershire and Durham
qualifying for the final. Nick Trainor hit 113 off 126 balls to
set up victory over Yorkshire while Durham owed much to
Boiling's economical spell of 2 for 18 in 11 overs.
Unfortunately, rain prevented any play in the final on 11
June, and Durham won the trophy on the toss of a coin.

Scarborough Festival

Northern Electric Trophy

12 July
Durham 292 for 7 (J.J.B. Lewis 100, N.J. Speak 61)
Yorkshire 294 for 5 (A. McGrath 67, D. Byas 63,
M.D. Moxon 61, C. White 56 not out)
Yorkshire won by 5 wickets

McCain Challenge

13 July
Leicestershire 247 for 7 (B.F. Smith 69, J.M. Dakin
50 not out)
Essex 246 for 6 (D.D.J. Robinson 93 not out, R.C. Irani 68,
S.G. Law 51)
Leicestershire won by 1 run

Tetley Bitter Festival Trophy

14 July
President's XI 168 for 9 (D.C. Boon 59, R.J. Sidebottom
5 for 27)
Yorkshire 169 for 5 (A. McGrath 52, M.D. Moxon 51,
C.Z. Harris 4 for 26)
Yorkshire won by 5 wickets

The Scarborough Festival has changed much over the years
and in 1997 consisted of three one-day matches. The first
and third were 50-over contests while the McCain
Challenge was 40 overs. Yorkshire won their matches with
three balls and 9.1 overs to spare, and only Essex can say
how they contrived not to beat Leicestershire when the
game was comfortably in their grasp.

Friendly Match

21 July
at Old Trafford
Lancashire 239 for 8 (N.H. Fairbrother 108
not out)
Yorkshire 226 (D.S. Lehmann 63, C. White 55)
Lancashire won by 13 runs

This was an experimental match played under floodlights. It followed a pattern tried in Australia in which
one side bats for 25 overs and then the second side bats
for 25 overs before the first side completes its quota of
50 overs.

AXA Life League Averages

Derbyshire

Batting

	M	Inns	NO	Runs	HS	Av	100s	50s	ct/st
C.J. Adams	11	11	1	427	121	42.70	2	1	9
K.J. Barnett	8	7	–	297	99	42.42		1	1
D.M. Jones	5	5	–	189	58	37.80		1	1
A.S. Rollins	8	8	2	212	36	35.33			3
G.A. Khan	7	6	1	124	71*	24.80		1	1
V.P. Clarke	13	12	2	238	77*	23.80		2	4
D.G. Cork	3	3	–	67	33	22.33			
K.M. Krikken	12	11	2	153	39	19.12			11/3
P.A.J. DeFreitas	12	10	1	140	45	15.55			4
I.D. Blackwell	4	4	–	54	29	13.50			
T.A. Tweats	4	4	1	40	16	13.33			2
M.E. Cassar	4	3	–	36	33	12.00			2
J.E. Owen	2	2	1	11	6*	11.00			
P. Aldred	10	6	1	53	17	10.60			1
A.N. Hayhurst	2	2	–	20	12	10.00			
A.J. Harris	13	7	4	27	10*	9.00			2
S.J. Lacey	3	1	–	9	9	9.00			
M.J. Vandrau	3	2	–	16	10	8.00			1
G.M. Roberts	6	5	2	19	9	6.33			1
K.J. Dean	10	3	2	2	1*	2.00			3

Played 1 in match: B.L. Spendlove 4; D.E. Malcolm 3; S.P. Griffiths did not bat (ct 1)

Bowling

	Overs	Mds	Runs	Wks	Av	Best	4/inn
K.J. Barnett	2	1	20	2	10.00	2/20	
D.G. Cork	17	1	80	6	13.33	6/21	1
A.N. Hayhurst	7	–	37	2	18.50	2/37	
A.J. Harris	88.2	2	479	21	22.80	4/22	2
P.A.J. DeFreitas	63.5	6	309	10	30.90	3/19	
M.J. Vandrau	10	–	63	2	31.50	2/32	
V.P. Clarke	52	2	292	9	32.44	2/28	
K.J. Dean	69.3	4	329	10	32.90	3/24	
P. Aldred	55	1	290	7	41.42	3/40	
M.E. Cassar	11	1	85	2	42.50	1/15	
D.E. Malcolm	8	–	51	1	51.00	1/51	
S.J. Lacey	11	–	62	1	62.00	1/38	
C.J. Adams	10	–	85	1	85.00	1/49	

Also bowled: A.S. Rollins 2–0–15–0; D.M. Jones 4–0–45–0; G.M. Roberts 32.3–0–195–0

Durham

Batting

	M	Inns	NO	Runs	HS	Av	100s	50s	ct/st
M.A. Roseberry	7	6	4	202	91*	101.00		2	3
J.J.B. Lewis	16	15	4	469	102	42.63	1	3	4
D.C. Boon	16	16	3	448	76	34.46		2	3
M.P. Speight	16	16	1	407	64*	27.13		3	10/1
S. Hutton	7	7	–	188	57	26.85		1	3
J.E. Morris	15	15	–	376	110	25.06	1		4
N.J. Speak	9	9	1	192	74*	24.00		1	4
A. Walker	16	5	3	25	11	12.50			4
M.M. Betts	6	5	2	35	21	11.66			1
J. Boiling	16	10	5	54	19*	10.80			8
R.M.S. Weston	2	2	–	19	13	9.50			1
P.D. Collingwood	8	7	–	63	19	9.00			3
M.J. Foster	10	8	–	66	18	8.25			1
J. Wood	8	6	1	27	11*	5.40			2
S.J.E. Brown	12	8	1	25	8	3.57			5
N. Killeen	7	4	1	2	1*	0.66			

M.J. Saggers 5* (4 matches, ct 1); M.J. Symington 7 (1 match, ct 1)

Bowling

	Overs	Mds	Runs	Wks	Av	Best	4/inn
M.J. Saggers	28	–	141	6	23.50	4/35	1
N. Killeen	47.4	3	259	11	23.54	4/46	1
J. Wood	58	5	278	11	25.27	4/17	1
S.J.E. Brown	82.3	3	420	13	32.30	2/34	
P.D. Collingwood	20.4	–	104	3	34.66	1/2	
A. Walker	103	5	538	14	38.42	4/18	1
M.M. Betts	40	2	193	5	38.60	3/22	
M.J. Foster	50	–	315	8	39.37	3/52	
J. Boiling	101.3	1	530	11	48.18	3/33	
M.J. Symington	7	–	51	1	51.00	1/51	

Also bowled: J.E. Morris 1–0–1–0; D.C. Boon 7–0–46–0

Essex

Batting

	M	Inns	NO	Runs	HS	Av	100s	50s	ct/st
S.G. Law	16	16	–	574	123	35.87	1	3	7
D.R. Law	15	14	3	339	82	30.81		3	4

Essex (continued)

Batting

	M	Inns	NO	Runs	HS	Av	100s	50s	ct/st
P.J. Prichard	12	12	–	349	103	29.08	1	1	3
R.C. Irani	15	15	3	321	52	26.75		1	3
P.M. Such	16	7	6	25	15*	25.00			3
D.D.J. Robinson	14	14	2	300	38	25.00			7
A.P. Grayson	16	15	1	333	69*	23.78		1	4
N. Hussain	12	12	2	206	45*	20.60			4
A.P. Cowan	16	12	4	113	22	14.12			5
R.J. Rollins	12	9	–	124	38	13.77			9/7
M.C. Ilott	12	8	3	65	15*	13.00			
S.J.W. Andrew	2	2	1	12	7	12.00			
S.D. Peters	3	2	1	17	15	8.50			
G.R. Napier	3	2	–	17	12	8.50			1
B.J. Hyam	4	2	1	4	3	4.00			6
J.C. Powell	5	3	1	4	2	2.00			

Played in 1 match: G.A. Gooch 28; T.P. Hodgson 12; D.M. Cousins 1

Bowling

	Overs	Mds	Runs	Wks	Av	Best	4/inn
D.D.J. Robinson	0.5	–	7	1	7.00	1/7	
S.J.W. Andrew	14	–	42	3	14.00	3/20	
R.C. Irani	88.2	3	421	20	21.05	3/23	
P.M. Such	99.2	–	459	21	21.85	5/29	1
A.P. Cowan	109.2	4	560	23	24.34	4/31	2
S.G. Law	56.5	–	298	10	29.80	4/37	1
A.P. Grayson	100	1	572	19	30.10	4/63	1
J.C. Powell	11	1	63	2	31.50	2/10	
D.M. Cousins	8	1	42	1	42.00	1/42	
M.C. Ilott	84	1	342	9	48.00	2/10	
D.R. Law	22	–	139	2	69.50	2/29	
G.R. Napier	11	–	79	–	–		

Glamorgan

Batting

	M	Inns	NO	Runs	HS	Av	100s	50s	ct/st
M.P. Maynard	12	12	2	426	132	42.60	1	1	7
S.P. James	11	10	4	230	75*	38.33		1	5
A. Dale	13	13	1	400	65	33.33		3	2
P.A. Cottey	13	12	2	327	61	32.70		2	3
M.J. Powell	3	3	–	85	42	28.33			
R.D.B. Croft	10	9	–	230	50	25.55		1	3
G.P. Butcher	13	10	2	192	47	24.00			1
H. Morris	10	10	1	180	66*	20.00		1	4
A.W. Evans	7	6	1	70	25	14.00			1
W.L. Law	2	2	–	23	15	11.50			1
A.D. Shaw	14	9	2	73	48	10.42			7/1
S.D. Thomas	10	7	–	53	15	7.57			3
S.L. Watkin	11	4	1	22	15	7.33			4
Waqar Younis	9	4	2	12	11*	6.00			
D.A. Cosker	7	2	–	5	5	2.50			2
O.T. Parkin	8	5	3	2	1*	1.00			1

A.P. Davies 3 (1 match)

Bowling

	Overs	Mds	Runs	Wks	Av	Best	4/inn
A.P. Davies	8	–	25	2	12.50	2/25	
Waqar Younis	58	3	285	14	20.35	4/14	1
A. Dale	66.5	6	350	13	26.92	2/18	
S.D. Thomas	62.1	2	307	10	30.70	3/30	
S.L. Watkin	77	3	348	10	34.80	4/15	1
O.T. Parkin	46	3	262	7	37.42	4/45	1
D.A. Cosker	52	3	250	6	41.66	2/40	
R.D.B. Croft	76	1	339	8	42.37	2/31	
G.P. Butcher	40.4	–	305	6	50.83	2/28	
P.A. Cottey	22	–	127	2	63.50		

Also bowled: M.P. Maynard 0.4–0–2–0

Gloucestershire

Batting

	M	Inns	NO	Runs	HS	Av	100s	50s	ct/st
S. Young	14	14	2	457	146*	38.00	1	2	4
M.A. Lynch	14	13	2	356	88*	32.36		3	5
M.W. Alleyne	15	14	3	339	58	30.81		1	10
R.J. Cunliffe	9	9	1	225	56	28.12		2	
R.I. Dawson	8	6	1	131	45	26.20			1
T.H.C. Hancock	15	15	–	332	57	25.53		2	8
A.J. Wright	12	12	–	236	69	19.66		1	5
R.C. Russell	13	10	1	156	59*	17.33		1	13/1
N.J. Trainor	3	2	–	26	22	13.00			1
R.P. Davis	6	4	2	24	12*	12.00			3

AXA Life League Averages (continued)

Gloucestershire (continued)

Batting

	M	Inns	NO	Runs	HS	Av	100s	50s	ct/st
A.M. Smith	14	8	4	46	10	11.50			1
K.P. Sheeraz	5	3	2	9	7*	9.00			
J.J. Lewis	12	5	3	16	8	8.00			2
M.C.J. Ball	15	10	2	54	12	6.75			3
M.G.N. Windows	5	2	–	13	8	6.50			

J.M.M. Averis did not bat (2 matches); R.C.J. Williams 0 (1 match); D.R. Hewson did not bat (1 match); C.W.W. Read 0 (1 match)

Bowling

	Overs	Mds	Runs	Wks	Av	Best	4/inn
A.M. Smith	89	13	386	16	24.12	2/14	
J.M.M. Averis	9	–	53	2	26.50	2/43	
M.W. Alleyne	81.1	5	430	16	26.87	3/24	
J.J. Lewis	83	3	389	14	27.78	3/39	
R.P. Davis	17	–	139	5	27.80	2/29	
K.P. Sheeraz	19.5	1	87	3	29.00	2/34	
S. Young	80	2	444	15	29.60	3/32	
M.C.J. Ball	86	–	402	12	33.50	4/26	1
T.H.C. Hancock	20.4		94	2	47.00	1/22	

Also bowled: N.J. Trainor 4–0–12–0

Hampshire

Batting

	M	Inns	NO	Runs	HS	Av	100s	50s	ct/st
M.L. Hayden	16	15	–	654	118	43.60	2	3	7
M. Keech	11	11	3	295	53*	36.87		2	1
S.D. Udal	17	14	3	342	78	31.09		4	5
J.P. Stephenson	16	13	4	251	38*	27.88			7
J.S. Laney	14	14	–	371	69	26.50		2	4
G.W. White	7	7	–	154	67	22.00		1	
S.J. Renshaw	17	12	7	104	25	20.80			1
K.D. James	8	3	–	57	50	19.00		1	
W.S. Kendall	16	13	–	235	55	18.07		1	15
R.A. Smith	14	13	–	229	49	17.61			4
A.N. Aymes	17	11	4	107	30	15.28			14/6
D.A. Masceranhas	3	2	–	17	10	8.50			1
R.J. Maru	7	4	2	15	6*	7.50			5
P.R. Whitaker	3	2	–	6	6	3.00			1
C.A. Connor	8	3	2	1	1*	1.00			
S.M. Milburn	4	3	1	1	1	0.50			

J.N.B. Bovill 2 (4 matches, ct 1); L. Savident 7* & 1* (3 matches, ct 1); C. Patel did not bat (1 match, ct 1); S.R.G. Francis did not bat (1 match)

Bowling

	Overs	Mds	Runs	Wks	Av	Best	4/inn
S.R.G. Francis	8	–	31	2	15.50	2/31	
L. Savident	19.1	–	104	6	17.33	3/41	
M. Keech	6	–	40	2	20.00	2/29	
S.D. Udal	126	4	590	29	20.34	3/26	
J.P. Stephenson	100.5	3	544	24	22.66	6/33	3
K.D. James	40	3	221	8	27.60	3/16	
S.J. Renshaw	115	1	621	22	28.22	3/45	
R.J. Maru	45	–	231	7	33.00	4/29	1
S.M. Milburn	27	–	137	4	34.25	1/27	
J.N.B. Bovill	25	–	180	5	36.00	4/44	1
M.L. Hayden	13.3	–	78	2	39.00	2/38	
C.A. Connor	55.5	2	300	6	50.00	2/35	
P.R. Whitaker	12	–	54	1	54.00	1/37	

Also bowled: G.W. White 2–0–14–0; W.S. Kendall 2–0–22–0; C. Patel 4–0–25–0; D.A. Masceranhas 11–0–96–0

Kent

Batting

	M	Inns	NO	Runs	HS	Av	100s	50s	ct/st
E.T. Smith	4	3	2	146	72*	146.00		2	2
G.R. Cowdrey	13	11	2	354	82	39.33		3	2
T.R. Ward	17	16	1	566	68*	37.73		4	5
M.J. Walker	13	13	–	374	80	28.76		3	2
A.P. Wells	16	15	2	321	56*	24.69		2	10
M.A. Ealham	12	10	1	201	61	22.33		2	3
S.A. Marsh	16	12	6	107	39*	17.83			10/1
M.V. Fleming	17	14	2	192	40	16.00			2
P.A. Strang	17	12	1	165	40	15.00			5
N.J. Llong	15	9	–	123	52	13.66		1	4
J.B.D. Thompson	11	5	3	27	18*	13.50			1
D.P. Fulton	3	3	–	19	9	6.33			
D.W. Headley	5	3	1	12	7*	6.00			
M.J. McCague	12	8	1	41	11	5.85			3

A.P. Igglesden did not bat (6 matches); T.N. Wren did not bat (3 matches, ct 1); B.J. Phillips 2* (2 matches, ct 2); W.J. House 0 (1 match); S.C. Willis did not bat (1 match, st 1)

Kent (continued)

Bowling

	Overs	Mds	Runs	Wks	Av	Best	4/inn
B.J. Phillips	10	1	34	2	17.00	1/17	
G.R. Cowdrey	8	–	35	2	17.50	2/35	
D.W. Headley	59	6	220	12	18.33	4/27	1
M.V. Fleming	107.5	5	530	26	20.38	3/14	
A.P. Igglesden	43	1	195	9	21.66	3/29	
M.A. Ealham	62.2	3	280	12	23.33	5/41	1
M.J. McCague	72.2	1	377	14	26.92	3/50	
J.B.D. Thompson	70.4	2	322	11	29.27	3/17	
N.J. Llong	26.4	–	162	5	32.40	1/1	
P.A. Strang	111.3	5	531	16	33.18	3/31	

Also bowled: T.N. Wren 17–0–96–0

Lancashire

Batting

	M	Inns	NO	Runs	HS	Av	100s	50s	ct/st
J.E.R. Gallian	10	10	3	424	104	60.57	2	2	5
N.H. Fairbrother	15	15	5	491	88	49.10		5	3
G.D. Lloyd	15	14	–	516	134	36.85	1	2	4
M.A. Atherton	10	10	1	260	90*	28.88		1	2
G. Yates	16	10	7	85	18	28.33			4
J.P. Crawley	11	11	1	267	83	26.70		2	3
G. Chapple	11	4	3	26	13*	26.00			3
A. Flintoff	4	4	–	83	31	20.75			2
M. Watkinson	12	11	–	162	66	17.67		1	6
W.K. Hegg	15	11	3	141	31*	17.62			18/8
Wasim Akram	3	2	–	29	28	14.50			2
I.D. Austin	16	13	4	119	27*	13.22			2
M.J. Chilton	3	3	–	31	22	10.33			
P.C. McKeown	4	4	–	39	37	9.75			2
P.J. Martin	16	5	2	17	11*	5.66			3
D.J. Shadford	7	3	2	3	2	3.00			3

R.J. Green did not bat (5 matches, ct 1); M.E. Harvey 8 (2 matches); G. Keedy did not bat (1 match)

Bowling

	Overs	Mds	Runs	Wks	Av	Best	4/inn
P.J. Martin	96.2	8	392	31	12.64	5/21	2
Wasim Akram	23	1	89	6	14.83	3/39	
D.J. Shadford	41.5	2	246	11	22.36	3/30	
I.D. Austin	105.5	7	432	19	22.73	3/25	
R.J. Green	26	–	150	6	25.00	3/18	
M.J. Chilton	16	–	80	3	26.66	2/27	
M. Watkinson	38	–	224	8	28.00	3/23	
G. Yates	92	2	455	15	30.33	3/29	
J.E.R. Gallian	28	1	144	4	36.00	1/23	
G. Chapple	67	2	382	10	38.20	3/22	

Also bowled: G. Keedy 5.1–0–47–0

Leicestershire

Batting

	M	Inns	NO	Runs	HS	Av	100s	50s	ct/st
A. Habib	6	6	3	114	45*	38.00			2
G.J. Parsons	11	6	4	70	41*	35.00			3
G.L. Maddy	15	15	–	515	85	34.33		5	4
I.J. Sutcliffe	7	7	1	182	96	30.33		1	2
N.C. Johnson	11	11	1	299	79*	29.90		2	6
J.J. Whitaker	14	14	–	400	74	28.57		4	8
V.J. Wells	15	15	–	376	69	25.06		2	3
B.F. Smith	12	12	1	275	71	25.00		2	4
J. Ormond	8	7	4	70	18	23.33			1
J.M. Dakin	14	13	2	224	41*	20.36		1	
P.A. Nixon	15	14	2	181	33	15.08			11/3
D. Williamson	5	4	2	28	4*	14.00			3
T.J. Mason	10	9	4	56	17*	11.20			1
G.I. Macmillan	4	4	–	34	15	8.50			3
D.I. Stevens	2	2	–	7	6	3.50			1

A.D. Mullally 6 (6 matches, ct 1), M.T. Brimson 12* (6 matches, ct 2); D.J. Millns 3* & 3* (3 matches); A.R.K. Pierson did not bat (1 match)

Bowling

	Overs	Mds	Runs	Wks	Av	Best	4/inn
D. Williamson	32.4	–	147	8	18.37	5/32	1
J. Ormond	39	1	167	9	18.55	3/30	
D.L. Maddy	30.4	–	184	9	20.44	3/11	
N.C. Johnson	47.2	–	325	14	23.21	3/37	
J.M. Dakin	56	1	330	13	25.38	3/38	
M.T. Brimson	39	3	201	7	28.71	3/37	
A.D. Mullally	38	–	207	7	29.57	3/36	
V.J. Wells	69.5	4	366	12	30.50	3/33	
T.J. Mason	43.4	–	247	8	30.87	2/15	

AXA Life League Averages (continued)

Leicestershire (continued)

Bowling	Overs	Mds	Runs	Wks	Av	Best	4/inn
D.J. Millns	18	1	67	2	33.50	1/9	
G.J. Parsons	76	3	345	8	43.12	2/9	

Also bowled: A.R.K. Pierson 1–0–11–0

Middlesex

Batting	M	Inns	NO	Runs	HS	Av	100s	50s	ct/st
J.C. Pooley	13	12	3	438	94*	48.66		5	5
O.A. Shah	7	7	2	201	66*	40.20		2	1
M.R. Ramprakash	12	11	1	329	90	32.90		3	3
P.N. Weekes	15	14	1	306	53*	23.53		2	4
K.R. Brown	13	12	4	159	44*	19.87			11/2
M.W. Gatting	11	10	1	164	82*	18.22		1	5
J.P. Hewitt	14	6	2	69	32*	17.25			2
K.P. Dutch	14	10	3	114	58	16.28		1	1
S.P. Moffat	6	5	–	77	29	15.40			1
R.L. Johnson	10	7	2	72	29	14.40			
J.H. Kallis	11	10	–	140	24	14.00			4
D.C. Nash	6	5	–	69	23	13.80			5
A.R.C. Fraser	14	7	2	65	33	13.00			1
A.J. Strauss	2	2	–	7	4	3.50			1
I.N. Blanchett	5	2	1	2	1*	2.00			2

T.F. Bloomfield 1 (6 matches); R.A. Fay did not bat (2 matches); P.C.R. Tufnell 7 (2 matches);
P.E. Wellings 12 (1 match, ct 1), N.D. Martin did not bat (1 match)

Bowling	Overs	Mds	Runs	Wks	Av	Best	4/inn
R.A. Fay	16	1	50	3	16.66	2/23	
A.R.C. Fraser	108	9	430	20	21.50	3/10	
P.N. Weekes	73	2	369	17	21.70	4/38	2
J.H. Kallis	34.2	1	124	5	24.80	2/19	
J.P. Hewitt	102	1	431	17	25.35	2/24	
M.R. Ramprakash	4.3	–	28	1	28.00	1/26	
N.D. Martin	6	–	29	1	29.00	1/29	
R.L. Johnson	63	1	366	12	30.50	3/35	
T.F. Bloomfield	39	1	198	6	33.00	2/8	
K.P. Dutch	75.5	–	375	10	37.50	2/19	
P.C.R. Tufnell	16	–	103	1	103.00	1/56	
I.N. Blanchett	28	–	188	1	188.00	1/51	

Also bowled: P.E. Wellings 1–0–9–0; A. Shah 2–0–29–0

Northamptonshire

Batting	M	Inns	NO	Runs	HS	Av	100s	50s	ct/st
R.R. Montgomerie	5	5	1	204	86*	51.00		2	2
K.M. Curran	12	12	2	440	78*	44.40		3	3
R.J. Bailey	13	12	1	381	75	38.10		5	3
J.P. Taylor	13	4	3	33	20	33.00			2
R.J. Warren	9	8	3	144	33	28.80			9/2
A.L. Penberthy	14	14	2	317	81*	26.41		3	
M.B. Loye	6	6	–	151	68	25.16		1	1
J.N. Snape	9	6	2	95	33	23.75			2
A. Fordham	5	5	–	114	43	22.80			2
D.G.J. Sales	10	10	1	168	42*	18.66			2
T.C. Walton	13	11	1	163	42	16.30			1
D.J. Capel	7	6	–	79	54	13.16		1	2
D. Ripley	3	3	–	35	20	11.66			1
J.E. Emburey	11	7	2	25	8	5.00			3
D. Follett	4	2	1	2	1*	2.00			2
G.P. Swann	4	2	1	0	0*	0.00			

Mohammad 2*, 1* & 0* (5 matches, ct 1); K.J. Innes 19* & 7* (4 matches, ct 1);
J.R. Blain did not bat (3 matches, ct 1), T.M.B. Bailey did not bat (3 matches, ct 4 / st 1);
J.F. Brown did not bat (1 match)

Bowling	Overs	Mds	Runs	Wks	Av	Best	4/inn
J.F. Brown	7	–	26	4	6.50	4/26	1
J.R. Blain	24	–	110	7	15.71	5/24	1
A.L. Penberthy	69	1	307	16	19.18	3/32	
Mohammad Akram	34	3	141	6	23.50	4/19	1
G.P. Swann	32		128	5	25.60	2/28	
J.E. Emburey	72.3	2	350	13	26.92	4/28	1
D. Follett	26	–	138	5	27.60	2/28	
J.N. Snape	52	3	261	9	29.00	4/31	1
K.M. Curran	49	–	292	9	32.44	4/36	1
D.J. Capel	32		195	5	39.00	2/42	
R.J. Bailey	21		121	3	40.33	1/18	
J.P. Taylor	86	5	369	9	41.00	2/13	

Also bowled: K.J. Innes 4–0–36–0

Nottinghamshire

Batting	M	Inns	NO	Runs	HS	Av	100s	50s	ct/st
G.F. Archer	11	10	3	319	104*	45.57	1	1	4
P. Johnson	12	12	1	467	117	42.45	2	2	7
R.T. Robinson	7	7	1	240	58	40.00		2	2
A.A. Metcalfe	5	5	1	133	70*	33.25		1	
M.J. Astle	6	6	–	192	75	32.00		2	3
N.A. Gie	8	6	1	149	75*	29.80		1	3
P.R. Pollard	6	5	–	129	87	25.80		1	4
C.M. Tolley	11	10	2	196	43	24.50			4
G.E. Welton	5	5	–	96	68	19.20		1	2
W.M. Noon	13	10	5	89	31	17.80			10/5
M.P. Dowman	13	13	–	222	71	17.07		1	3
P.J. Franks	4	2	1	15	8	15.00			
M.N. Bowen	11	6	3	44	14	14.66			2
U.Afzaal	2	2	–	29	20	14.50			
L.N.P. Walker	2	2	–	24	22	12.00			
K.P. Evans	12	10	2	74	20	9.25			3
R.T. Bates	13	9	1	32	9	4.00			1

A.R. Oram 0* & 0* (9 matches); R.A. Pick 8 (3 matches, ct 1); J.E. Hindson 38 (1 match)

Bowling	Overs	Mds	Runs	Wks	Av	Best	4/inn
C.N. Tolley	64	1	328	15	21.86	4/24	2
N.J. Astle	39	3	203	9	22.55	3/22	
M.N. Bowen	66.2	–	429	17	25.23	4/29	1
A.R. Oram	58.5	–	283	10	28.30	4/45	1
G.F. Archer	9	–	70	2	35.00	1/28	
K.P. Evans	86	2	436	12	36.33	4/26	1
R.T. Bates	67.5	1	349	9	38.77	3/33	
P.J. Franks	27	1	163	4	40.75	2/42	
M.P. Dowman	44.5	–	254	4	63.50	2/31	
R.A. Pick	17.5	1	67	1	67.00	1/30	

Also bowled: P. Johnson 0.1–0–1–0; U. Afzaal 2–0–21–0

Somerset

Batting	M	Inns	NO	Runs	HS	Av	100s	50s	ct/st
R.J. Harden	8	8	2	244	85	40.66		3	7
P.C.L. Holloway	11	10	2	267	117	33.37	1		3
P.D. Bowler	14	13	2	353	61	32.09		2	5
K.A. Parsons	11	7	3	125	52*	31.25		1	7
M. Burns	15	14	1	362	115*	27.84	1	2	5
J.I.D. Kerr	12	6	3	75	33	25.00			2
M.N. Lathwell	15	15	1	316	72	24.80		3	4
S.C. Ecclestone	12	11	1	236	96*	23.60		1	1
G.D. Rose	15	13	5	181	37*	22.62			6
R.J. Turner	14	12	1	220	67	20.00		1	13/1
M.E. Trescothick	5	4	1	50	28	16.66			2
Mushtaq Ahmed	12	5	2	15	7*	5.00			3
A.R. Caddick	10	3	–	13	9	4.33			4

K.J. Shine 3 (5 matches); H.R.J. Trump 0 (2 matches, ct 1);
S. Herberg did not bat (2 matches, ct 1); P.S. Jones did not bat (1 match, ct 1);
B.J. Trott did not bat (1 match)

Bowling	Overs	Mds	Runs	Wks	Av	Best	4/inn
A.R. Caddick	74	3	374	21	17.80	4/19	1
G.D. Rose	113.4	5	436	24	18.16	3/15	
M.Burns	58.1	–	324	13	24.92	4/39	1
Mushtaq Ahmed	89.1	8	348	12	29.00	3/36	
B.J. Trott	4		29	1	29.00	1/29	
J.I.D. Kerr	81.5	1	485	16	30.31	4/28	1
K.J. Shine	30.2	–	182	6	30.33	2/25	
S. Herzberg	5	–	37	1	37.00	1/37	
K.A. Parsons	64		301	7	43.00	2/18	
P.D. Bowler	7	–	56	1	56.00	1/33	

Also bowled: P.S. Jones 2–0–19–0; M.E. Trescothick 7–0–52–0; H.R.J. Trump 10–0–70–0

Surrey

Batting	M	Inns	NO	Runs	HS	Av	100s	50s	ct/st
M.P. Bicknell	14	7	5	107	57*	53.50		1	4
G.P. Thorpe	6	6	1	225	100*	45.00	2	2	1
I.D.K. Salisbury	10	5	4	43	23*	43.00			5
A.D. Brown	14	14	1	558	203	42.92	2	2	1
C.C. Lewis	12	11	5	182	68*	30.33		1	2
J.D. Ratcliffe	13	10	–	290	82	29.00		3	5
D.J.Bicknell	4	4	1	79	49*	26.33			1
M.A. Butcher	10	10	1	227	81	25.22		1	6

AXA Life League Averages (continued)

Surrey (continued)

Batting

	M	Inns	NO	Runs	HS	Av	100s	50s	ct/st
A.J.Hollioake	12	12	–	288	63	24.00	2	3	
B.C. Hollioake	11	10	1	213	61	23.66		1	1
Saqlain Mushtaq	9	4	1	61	29*	20.33			2
A.J. Stewart	8	8	1	141	67*	20.14		1	7/2
N. Shahid	9	8	2	97	34*	16.16			1
I.J. Ward	10	9	3	81	31	13.50			1
J.E. Benjamin	12	3	1	18	13*	9.00			1
J.A. Knott	4	3	–	23	22	7.66			5
J.N. Batty	4	3	1	15	8	7.50			1

A.J. Tudor did not bat (2 matches, ct 2); R.M. Amin did not bat (1 match, ct 1)

Bowling

	Overs	Mds	Runs	Wks	Av	Best	4/inn
R.M. Amin	8	–	34	2	17.00	2/34	
C.C. Lewis	79.3	1	345	16	21.56	4/21	1
M.P. Bicknell	84	1	389	18	21.61	4/28	1
Saqlain Mushtaq	55.3	1	276	12	23.00	3/31	
A.J. Hollioake	58	2	375	16	23.43	5/38	1
A.J. Tudor	9	–	49	2	24.50	1/23	
I.D.K. Salisbury	56	–	310	10	31.00	3/56	
B.C. Hollioake	77	–	444	13	34.15	3/47	
M.A. Butcher	8	–	35	1	35.00	1/24	
J.E. Benjamin	69	1	321	7	45.85	2/40	
J.D. Ratcliffe	19	–	92	2	46.00	1/16	

Sussex

Batting

	M	Inns	NO	Runs	HS	Av	100s	50s	ct/st
J.R. Carpenter	2	2	1	35	18*	35.00			
K. Greenfield	15	15	2	426	69*	32.76		4	3
C.W.J Athey	9	9	1	252	109*	31.50	1	1	
R.K. Rao	12	12	–	266	60	22.16		2	5
M. Newell	13	13	1	258	60	21.50		1	4
N.R. Taylor	8	8	1	139	47	19.85			3
N.J. Lenham	4	4	–	71	41	17.75			
P. Moores	15	15	1	182	26	13.00			10/1
K. Newell	13	12	–	152	35	12.66			4
M.A. Robinson	14	10	6	39	9*	9.75			2
V.C. Drakes	9	8	2	48	12*	8.00			
N.C. Phillips	5	4	–	31	21	7.75			
J.P. Pyemont	4	4	1	23	18*	7.66			1
R.J. Kirtley	7	4	2	14	7	7.00			2
A.A. Khan	13	9	2	48	22*	6.85			2
P.W. Jarvis	11	11	–	51	14	4.63			1
J.J. Bates	3	3	1	8	5*	4.00			1
A.D. Edwards	4	4	1	11	9*	3.66			1
R.S.C. Martin-Jenkins	2	2	–	5	3	2.50			

Played in 1 match: M.T.E. Peirce 7; M.R. Strong

Bowling

	Overs	Mds	Runs	Wks	Av	Best	4/inn
N.J. Lenham	2	–	14	1	14.00	1/14	
A.D. Edwards	17.5	1	82	3	27.33	2/44	
P.W. Jarvis	73.2	2	355	12	29.58	3/32	
A.A. Khan	90.5	3	474	15	31.60	5/40	1
K. Newell	53	2	222	7	31.71	2/22	
V.C. Drakes	57	5	282	7	40.28	2/21	
M.A. Robinson	90	3	365	9	40.55	1/15	
R.J. Kirtley	48.1	–	300	7	42.85	2/36	
J.J. Bates	10	–	53	1	53.00	1/24	
N.C. Phillips	16	1	79	1	79.00	1/17	
R.S.C. Martin-Jenkins	16	–	90	1	90.00	1/32	

Also bowled: J.R. Carpenter 1–0–15–0; M.R. Strong 3–0–23–0; R.K. Rao 5–0–34–0; K. Greenfield 7–0–38–0

Warwickshire

Batting

	M	Inns	NO	Runs	HS	Av	100s	50s	ct/st
D.P. Ostler	17	16	4	466	70	38.83		4	3
N.V. Knight	8	8	–	252	102	31.50	1		3
N.M.K. Smith	17	17	–	532	60	31.29		5	10
D.L. Hemp	17	17	4	370	70*	28.46		2	7
G. Welch	17	15	8	195	32*	27.85			3
A.F. Giles	15	9	3	159	57	26.50		1	2
D.R. Brown	17	17	1	374	68	23.37		2	4
A. Singh	5	5	–	112	86	22.40		1	1
T.L. Penney	17	15	3	268	57	22.33		1	4
K.J. Piper	10	4	–	53	29*	17.66			13/1
M.D. Edmond	5	3	–	34	19	17.00			1
G.C. Small	15	3	2	11	9*	11.00			3

Warwickshire (continued)

Batting

	M	Inns	NO	Runs	HS	Av	100s	50s	ct/st
W.G. Khan	3	3	–	33	27	11.00			
T. Frost	7	2	1	2	2*	2.00			7

A.A. Donald 2* & 3* (14 matches, ct 4); M.A. Sheikh 1 (2 matches); A.J. Moles 19 (1 match)

Bowling

	Overs	Mds	Runs	Wks	Av	Best	4/inn
A.A. Donald	85.5	4	336	30	11.20	5/10	3
M.D. Edmond	30.5	–	146	9	16.22	2/4	
G.C. Small	95.5	5	462	21	22.00	5/26	1
A.F. Giles	76.1	2	398	18	22.11	4/25	1
D.R. Brown	96	4	432	17	25.41	4/42	1
N.M.K. Smith	70	2	329	10	32.90	3/20	
G. Welch	97.5	–	439	12	36.58	2/18	

Worcestershire

Batting

	M	Inns	NO	Runs	HS	Av	100s	50s	ct/st
S.R. Lampitt	15	8	5	130	38*	43.33			5
D.A. Leatherdale	15	12	5	301	58*	43.00		3	9
G.R. Haynes	13	12	3	355	64*	39.44		1	1
G.A. Hick	16	16	2	549	119*	39.21	1	1	7
K.R. Spiring	13	12	6	235	58*	39.16		1	5
T.S. Curtis	5	5	–	195	93	39.00		1	3
T.M. Moody	15	15	–	529	112	39.26	1	3	7
V.S. Solanki	16	13	1	239	58	19.91		1	5
S.J. Rhodes	16	7	4	38	19	12.66			20/4
W.P.C. Weston	14	11	1	93	28	9.30			2
A. Sheriyar	12	2	1	1	1	1.00			1
R.J. Chapman	9	2	–	0	0	0.00			

P.J. Newport 7 (5 matches); R.K. Illingworth 2* (4 matches); M.M. Mirza did not bat (4 matches, ct 1); M.J. Rawnsley 2* (2 matches); J.E. Brinkley 7 (1 match); I. Dawood 1 (1 match)

Bowling

	Overs	Mds	Runs	Wks	Av	Best	4/inn
P.J. Newport	30	3	107	8	13.37	3/18	
D.A. Leatherdale	58.3	2	315	18	17.50	3/13	
V.S. Solanki	4	–	18	1	18.00	1/9	
M.J. Rawnsley	15	–	83	4	20.75	2/29	
G.R. Haynes	72	3	326	15	21.73	4/13	1
S.R. Lampitt	91	–	460	21	21.90	4/49	1
A. Sheriyar	49.5	2	272	11	24.72	4/18	1
G.A. Hick	48.4	–	251	9	27.88	2/12	
T.M. Moody	53	3	241	8	30.12	2/29	
R.J. Chapman	49	2	214	7	30.57	3/27	
R.K. Illingworth	27	–	119	3	39.66	2/29	
M.M. Mirza	16	–	113	1	113.00	1/31	

Also bowled: J.E. Brinkley 3–0–26–0;

Yorkshire

Batting

	M	Inns	NO	Runs	HS	Av	100s	50s	ct/st
D.S. Lehmann	16	16	3	643	78*	49.46		6	5
A. McGrath	13	11	3	281	63	35.12		2	5
M.P. Vaughan	9	9	–	309	66	34.33		2	2
C. White	15	13	–	408	148	31.38	1	2	9
D. Byas	16	16	–	409	83	25.56		2	7
A.C. Morris	10	7	2	102	35	20.40			2
P.J. Hartley	14	12	2	200	48*	20.00			7
R.J. Blakey	16	15	3	231	56	19.25		1	18/4
D. Gough	9	7	3	69	23*	17.25			2
B. Parker	16	14	2	193	42	16.08			1
M.D. Moxon	2	2	–	14	13	7.00			
C.E.W. Silverwood	14	8	4	21	7*	5.25			2
R.D. Stemp	13	6	2	13	9*	3.25			1

G.M. Hamilton 18* 9* & 1* (6 matches); R.J. Sidebottom did not bat (3 matches, ct 1); I.D. Fisher did not bat (2 matches); R.A. Kettleborough 9 (1 match); A.G. Wharf did not bat (1 match)

Bowling

	Overs	Mds	Runs	Wks	Av	Best	4/inn
I.D. Fisher	16	–	47	4	11.75	2/23	
D.S. Lehmann	12.4	–	85	4	21.25	3/43	
C. White	90	–	462	20	23.10	4/18	1
D. Gough	63	1	325	14	23.21	3/21	
A.C. Morris	34	–	209	9	23.22	4/49	1
R.D. Stemp	88	1	437	18	24.27	3/29	
C.E.W. Silverwood	89.3	4	452	14	32.28	3/12	
M.P. Vaughan	35	–	229	7	32.71	3/48	
P.J. Hartley	85.4	4	490	12	40.83	3/42	
G.M. Hamilton	31	–	222	5	44.40	3/33	
R.J. Sidebottom	19	2	103	1	103.00	1/41	

Also bowled: A.G. Wharf 3–0–34–0

The Britannic Assurance County Championship
and other first-class matches

16, 17, 18 and 19 April
at Leeds
Yorkshire 289 (B. Parker 85 not out, M.J. Wood 81, G. Yates 4 for 46) and 298 (C.A. Chapman 80, P.J. Martin 4 for 53)
Lancashire 482 (G.D. Lloyd 225, I.D. Austin 83) and 106 for 4
Lancashire won by 4 wickets

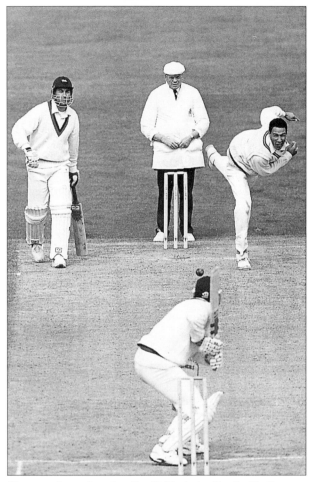

The advent of the four-day game and the reduction of the number of matches played in the county championship has prompted the establishment of an alternative Roses Match as the curtain-raiser to each season. With three players from each county engaged in the game at Edgbaston, both sides gave experience to lesser known cricketers. Yorkshire fielded as many as seven young hopefuls. One of them, reserve wicket-keeper Colin Chapman, hit a maiden first-class fifty in what was his ninth first-class match in eight seasons with the club. The honours went very much to Lancashire in spite of Chapman's performance and good efforts from Matthew Wood on his debut and Brad Parker. Graham Lloyd made 225 from 151 deliveries with 10 sixes and 25 fours. Lloyd and Austin set up a record for Lancashire's seventh wicket with 248 in 41 overs.

18, 19, 20 and 21 April
at Edgbaston
England 'A' 453 for 4 dec. (M.A. Butcher 153, J.E.R. Gallian 106, A.J. Hollioake 70) and 173 for 8 dec. (A. McGrath 62, S.J.E. Brown 4 for 50)
The Rest 350 for 6 dec. (M.R. Ramprakash 108 not out, R.J. Warren 50) and 9 for 0
Match drawn

Honours were even at Edgbaston where the successful England 'A' side, led by Surrey's new captain Adam Hollioake, took on The Rest, an eleven that included a few surprises. Mark Ramprakash was made to believe that he had not been forgotten by the selectors when he was named captain of The Rest, and Derbyshire's Chris Adams was another to realise he was not being neglected. There was an interesting opening partnership in Maddy and Laney, and developing cricketers in Silverwood, Solanki, Ben Hollioake, who had been a member of England's Under-19 side, and Tudor, who had played no first-class matches in 1996, were all recognised. The major controversy concerned the inclusion of Warren as wicket-keeper. A most promising bat, Warren had neither relished nor distinguished himself when asked to take on the keeper's role for Northamptonshire, but as we were to learn throughout the summer, wicket-keeping was not an art the selectors took seriously.

The season's curtain-raiser. Ben Hollioake bowling for The Rest against England 'A' at Edgbaston. Adam Hollioake is at the non-striker's end. (Graham Chadwick/Allsport)

Ramprakash asked England 'A' to bat first, and Gallian and Mark Butcher responded with a partnership of 237. Butcher's innings was an accomplished affair, but few realised at the time the effect it was to have on the three selectors in attendance. Ramprakash, who was to share the Tetley Man of the Match £500 award with Butcher, batted with his usual elegance. The Rest were set a target of 277 in 52 overs, but after nine balls came the rain.

23, 24, 25 and 26 April
at Chelmsford
Essex 246 (P.J. Prichard 65, C.A. Connor 7 for 46) and 442 for 8 dec. (R.C. Irani 123 not out, S.G. Law 78, P.J. Prichard 56)
Hampshire 161 (A.P. Cowan 5 for 49) and 64 for 2
Match drawn
Essex 8 pts, Hampshire 7 pts

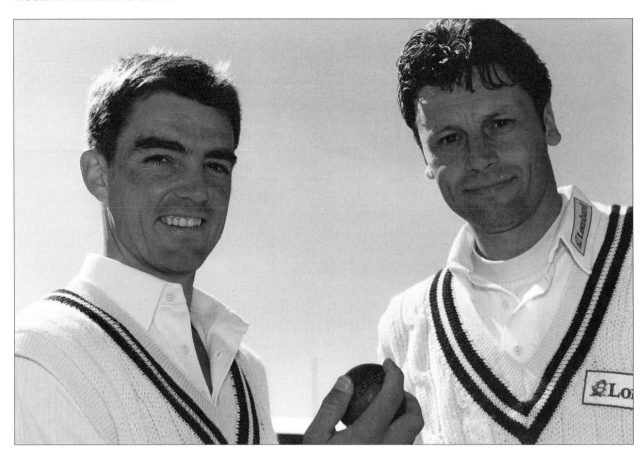

at Cardiff
Warwickshire 151 (S.D. Thomas 4 for 62) and 77 for 3
Glamorgan 551 for 3 dec. (H. Morris 233 retired hurt,
A. Dale 106, S.P. James 83)
Match drawn
Glamorgan 11 pts, Warwickshire 3 pts

at Canterbury
Kent 251 (M.A. Ealham 72 not out, S.A. Marsh 57,
D.E. Malcolm 6 for 74) and 333 (T.R. Ward 95, P.A. Strang 69,
M.J. McCague 53 not out, P.A.J. DeFreitas 7 for 64)
Derbyshire 248 (K.M. Krikken 61, M.J. McCague 5 for 75,
D.W. Headley 4 for 81) and 248 for 3 (C.J. Adams 108,
D.M. Jones 99 not out)
Match drawn
Kent 9 pts, Derbyshire 8 pts

at Old Trafford
Lancashire 506 (G.D. Lloyd 102, P.J. Martin 78 not out,
J.E.R. Gallian 78, G. Chapple 66, M. Watkinson 51)
Durham 201 for 6 (D.C. Boon 85 not out)
Match drawn
Lancashire 9 pts, Durham 8 pts

at Leicester
Gloucestershire 245 (S. Young 59, R.C. Russell 57,
A.D. Mullally 5 for 52) and 8 for 0

Paul Strang, Zimbabwe's leading all-rounder, is welcomed to Kent by skipper Steve Marsh. Leg-spinner Strang had an outstanding season and became a great favourite with the Kent crowd. (Steve Lindsell/Sportsline)

Leicestershire 307 (D.L. Maddy 80, P.A. Nixon 77 not out)
Match drawn
Leicestershire 10 pts, Gloucestershire 8 pts

at Trent Bridge
Worcestershire 417 (T.S. Curtis 113, T.M. Moody 70,
W.P.C. Weston 52, M.N. Bowen 5 for 99)
Nottinghamshire 196 for 3 (P.R. Pollard 81,
R.T. Robinson 80)
Match drawn
Worcestershire 8 pts, Nottinghamshire 5 pts

at The Oval
Somerset 463 (R.J. Harden 136 not out, P.D. Bowler 63,
S. Herzberg 56, M.N. Lathwell 50)
Surrey 209 for 8
Match drawn
Somerset 10 pts, Surrey 7 pts

at Hove
Northamptonshire 315 (R.R. Montgomerie 68, D.J. Capel
57, J.N. Snape 55, M.A. Robinson 6 for 78) and 41 for 0

Sussex 411 for 7 dec. (N.R. Taylor 127, K. Newell 107 not
out, P.W. Jarvis 64, C.W.J. Athey 50)
Match drawn
Sussex 11 pts, Northamptonshire 9 pts

There is a sense of inevitability that the first round of matches
in the county championship should be disrupted by rain, and
1997 was true to tradition. Neither of the debutants at
Chelmsford, Matthew Hayden for Hampshire and Danny Law
for Essex, both of whom, of course, were experienced cricketers, had much to cheer them. The one to draw pleasure from
a game which was ended by rain after 21 overs on the last day
was Ronnie Irani, who made the highest score of his career.
Irani had reshaped his stance in an effort to reclaim the all-
rounder's spot in the England side. The weight was pushed
further forward, and if the posture was ugly, it seemed to bring
good results. The young fast bowler Ashley Cowan had a fine
start to the season with his best bowling figures, and Cardigan
Connor launched his benefit year in magnificent style with
seven wickets on the opening day.

In these pages last year, we suggested that Glamorgan
should be considered a good bet for the title, and, even
though Waqar was yet to join them, they began their quest in
a positive manner. Having shot out Warwickshire, who won
the toss, in under 40 overs, they raced into the lead as
James and Morris made 190 for the first wicket. Hugh
Morris went on to make the highest score of his career
before being hit on the head by a Donald bouncer and being
forced to retire to hospital. He and Dale put on 242 for the
third wicket, and Warwickshire conceded 71 extras. The
game was ruined by rain with little play possible on the
third day and none on the fourth.

Warwickshire included David Hemp, the very
promising left-hander who had missed much of the previous
season with a serious injury and who had demanded terms
from Glamorgan with which they could not agree.
Warwickshire, it seems, were more acquiescent.

Glamorgan had taken a pre-season decision to play
Shaw instead of Metson as wicket-keeper in an attempt to
strengthen batting. Shaw held five catches.

Paul Strang marked his debut for Kent with an
innings of 69, but this game was again spoiled by rain.
Needing 337 to win, Derbyshire were within 89 of their target with 26 overs remaining when rain ended play. Chris
Adams and Dean Jones had scored 202 for the third wicket,
and Jones was stranded one short of his century by the rain.
Min Patel, Kent's England left-arm spinner, had his season
virtually ended by injury after this match.

Graham Lloyd followed his double century in the
friendly Roses match with 102 off 80 balls against Durham.
He and Watkinson added 90 in eight overs for the fifth
wicket. Chapple and Martin scored 146 for the last wicket.
David Boon had reached 85 at the end of the second day, the
highest championship score by a Durham skipper, but there
was no more play thereafter.

At Leicester, the last two days were also barren.
Gloucestershire had been 84 for 5 on the opening day and

The Britannic Assurance County Championship Trophy.
(Nigel French/ASP)

owed much to new import Shaun Young who put on 112 with
'Jack' Russell.

Somerset included Burns, formerly of Warwickshire,
at The Oval, and they also gave a first game to the much-
travelled spinner Herzberg, who has appeared for Kent,
Worcestershire, Western Australia and Tasmania. Certainly
all the honours went to Somerset, whose total included 86
extras. Surrey were thankful that only 16 overs were possible on the third day and none on the fourth. Ian Salisbury
took 3 for 107 on his debut for Surrey.

There were early season concerns that Sussex had
lost so many players that they might not be able to field an
eleven. They answered the jokers in emphatic fashion. They
included three new signings, Neil Taylor from Kent, Amer
Khan, a leg-spinner from Middlesex, and Mark Robinson,
the former Yorkshire and Northamptonshire seamer.
Robinson had a dream debut with three wickets in five balls
in his return of 6 for 78, while Taylor became the first batsman for 60 years to score a hundred on his debut for the
county. Perhaps even more encouraging for Sussex was the
batting of 25-year-old Keith Newell who hit the third century of his career. As in so many places, there was little play
on the third day and none on the fourth.

The first round of matches in the championship. Gloucestershire's 'Jack' Russell is bowled by David Millns of Leicestershire. Both players went on to have excellent seasons. (Alex Livesey/Allsport)

7, 8, 9 and 10 May

at Derby
Surrey 267 (G.P. Thorpe 83, M.P. Bicknell 74, D.E. Malcolm 4 for 95)
Derbyshire 156 for 3 (G.A. Khan 62 not out)
Match drawn
Derbyshire 7 pts, Surrey 6 pts

at Hartlepool
Nottinghamshire 170 (C.M. Tolley 54, A. Walker 7 for 56) and 200 for 6 (R.T. Robinson 69)
Durham 331 (N.J. Speak 93, D.C. Boon 68)
Match drawn
Durham 10 pts, Nottinghamshire 7 pts

at Bristol
Hampshire 316 (S.D. Udal 58, R.A. Smith 52, A.M. Smith 4 for 61) and 145 (A.M. Smith 6 for 45)
Gloucestershire 403 (S. Young 73, R.C. Russell 66, M.A. Lynch 62, M.W. Alleyne 62, J.P. Stephenson 4 for 81) and 59 for 4 (S.J. Renshaw 4 for 30)

Gloucestershire won by 6 wickets
Gloucestershire 24 pts, Hampshire 6 pts

at Lord's
Middlesex 490 for 9 dec. (M.R. Ramprakash 145, K.R. Brown 144 not out, A.A. Khan 5 for 137)
Sussex 187 (C.W.J. Athey 60 not out, J.P. Hewitt 4 for 60) and 119 for 6 (J.P. Hewitt 4 for 24)
Match drawn
Middlesex 11 pts, Sussex 5 pts

at Northampton
Northamptonshire 185 (K.M. Curran 73, A.R. Caddick 6 for 65) and 122 for 5
Somerset 290 (G.D. Rose 109 not out, M. Burns 82, Mohammad Akram 5 for 72)
Match drawn
Somerset 9 pts, Northamptonshire 7 pts

at Worcester
Worcestershire 257 (K.R. Spiring 55, A.D. Mullally 4 for 86)
Leicestershire 69 (P.J. Newport 7 for 37) and 141 for 4 (N.C. Johnson 87 not out)
Match drawn
Worcestershire 9 pts, Leicestershire 7 pts

at Leeds
Glamorgan 336 (S.P. James 109, R.D.B. Croft 57, H. Morris 55, D. Gough 5 for 56) and 166 for 2 dec. (H. Morris 96, S.P. James 52)
Yorkshire 200 for 9 dec. (D.S. Lehmann 54, R.D.B. Croft 4 for 58)
Match drawn
Glamorgan 10 pts, Yorkshire 8 pts

Cold and wet greeted the championship in May. It was far from cricket weather. There was no play on the first two days at Derby, and the equivalent of about five sessions were lost at Hartlepool where Nottinghamshire had edged into a narrow lead with only four wickets standing when rain brought a halt shortly after lunch on the last afternoon. The most noteworthy aspect of the match was the bowling of 34-year-old Alan Walker. The former Northamptonshire medium-pacer had played little in 1996, but he had forced his way back into the championship side at Durham with consistent performances in limited-over matches, and his 7 for 56 wrecked Nottinghamshire on the opening day. No Durham bowler has ever done better on home soil.

Time was lost at Bristol, but Gloucestershire played with such positivity as to be the only county to gain an outright victory. The match saw the return to first-class cricket of David Lawrence, the Gloucestershire pace bowler who had not been seen since the terrible knee injury he suffered in New Zealand in 1992. A passionately committed cricketer, Lawrence, now 34, was endeavouring to make a comeback. He captured two wickets, but he was to play very little during the season. The hero was his pace-bowling colleague Mike Smith. The left-armer took 10 wickets in the match, and with Lynch hitting 50 off 44 balls, and Russell, Young and Alleyne showing urgency, the home county compensated for lost time. On the last day, with rain clouds threatening, they hit the runs they needed in under 13 overs. Simon Renshaw, an unlucky career-best performer in the Benson and Hedges Cup, suffered the same fate in a first-class match. He returned his best bowling figures, and his side lost.

Rain saved Sussex at Lord's. There were interruptions on three days, but Ramprakash and Brown savaged the Sussex attack, and Hewitt twice bettered his previous best bowling performance. There was also a fire in the restaurant at Lord's which saw the arrival of four fire engines behind the Warner Stand. The game went on, but in the end it was water that dampened Middlesex's hopes of a convincing victory.

There was snow at Northampton where Rose warmed spectators with a 138-ball century. He hit a six and 12 fours after Caddick had bowled Somerset into a good position. The weather won.

Leicestershire came close to defeat at Worcester where nearly half the playing time was lost over the first three days, and there was no play at all on the fourth. Worcestershire's tail wagged well, and by the close of the second day Leicestershire were on 42 for 5. They were all out on the Friday for 69, the lowest score of the season to

Worcestershire's skipper Tom Moody falls victim to Leicestershire's new signing Neil Johnson who raises his arms in celebration, New Road, 7 May.
(Graham Chadwick/Allsport)

date. Their innings lasted 34.2 overs, and Newport and Sheriyar bowled unchanged. Following on, the reigning champions were 14 for 3 with Vince Wells, captaining the county in a championship match for the first time, out for a 'pair'. Neil Johnson revived hopes of salvation with a vigorous 87, dominating a stand of 118 in 27 overs with Maddy for the fourth wicket. Then the rain returned, and there was no play on the last day.

Glamorgan were 213 for 1 from 66 overs at the end of a truncated first day at Headingley, but no play was possible on the second day so that a draw became inevitable. Waqar Younis had a quiet championship debut for Glamorgan and took one wicket. Yorkshire were set a target of 303 in 64 overs, but the rain returned before they could begin their attempt.

Darren Lehmann of Yorkshire is missed at slip by Andy Moles of Warwickshire, Edgbaston, 14 May. Lehmann, the Australian, became a prolific scorer for Yorkshire. (David Munden/Sportsline)

14, 15, 16 and 17 May

at Chelmsford
Essex 237 (A.P. Grayson 76, S.G. Law 63, N. Killeen 4 for 50, S.J.E. Brown 4 for 54) and 366 for 9 dec. (S.G. Law 118 not out, P.J. Prichard 80, N. Hussain 67, M.J. Foster 4 for 94)
Durham 291 (P.D. Collingwood 62, M.P. Speight 53, A.P. Cowan 4 for 73) and 187 (J.E. Morris 76, P.M. Such 6 for 55)
Essex won by 125 runs
Essex 21 pts, Durham 6 pts

at Southampton
Hampshire 285 (K.D. James 56 not out, A.D. Mullally 4 for 69) and 182 (A.R.K. Pierson 4 for 58)
Leicestershire 349 (D.J. Millns 114 not out, A. Habib 77, S.D. Udal 4 for 118) and 119 for 5
Leicestershire won by 5 wickets
Leicestershire 23 pts, Hampshire 6 pts

at Canterbury
Glamorgan 279 (M.J. McCague 6 for 75) and 193 (S.P. James 54, M.V. Fleming 4 for 28, P.A. Strang 4 for 59)
Kent 154 (R.D.B. Croft 5 for 33) and 231 (A.P. Wells 85, D.A. Cosker 4 for 64)
Glamorgan won by 87 runs
Glamorgan 22 pts, Kent 4 pts

at Old Trafford
Lancashire 125 (J.P. Crawley 51 not out, K.P. Evans 6 for 40) and 357 (J.P. Crawley 101, M.A. Atherton 68, G.D. Lloyd 62)
Nottinghamshire 263 (U. Afzaal 70 not out, P. Johnson 66, I.D. Austin 4 for 44) and 233 for 4 (P. Johnson 87 not out, U. Afzaal 77 not out)
Nottinghamshire won by 6 wickets
Nottinghamshire 22 pts, Lancashire 4 pts

at Lord's
Middlesex 146 (P.A.J. DeFreitas 5 for 46, D.E. Malcolm 5 for 50) and 262 (K.R. Brown 76, J.H. Kallis 52, D.E. Malcolm 6 for 75)
Derbyshire 178 (D.M. Jones 53) and 99 (R.L. Johnson 4 for 26)
Middlesex won by 131 runs
Middlesex 20 pts, Derbyshire 4 pts

at Taunton
Sussex 241 (Mushtaq Ahmed 6 for 70) and 259 for 5 (C.W.J. Athey 138 not out)
Somerset 409 (G.D. Rose 191, R.J. Harden 103, P.W. Jarvis 5 for 122)
Match drawn
Somerset 11 pts, Sussex 8 pts

at The Oval
Surrey 115 (S. Young 4 for 26) and 269 (G.P. Thorpe 81, M.W. Alleyne 6 for 64)
Gloucestershire 371 (R.C. Russell 59, A.J. Tudor 6 for 101) and 15 for 1)
Gloucestershire won by 9 wickets
Gloucestershire 24 pts, Surrey 4 pts

at Edgbaston
Yorkshire 233 (D.S. Lehmann 62, M.P. Vaughan 56, A.F. Giles 4 for 54, A.A. Donald 4 for 55) and 154
Warwickshire 140 (T.L. Penney 57, D. Gough 4 for 62) and 249 for 6 (D.R. Brown 65 not out, D. Gough 4 for 65)
Warwickshire won by 4 wickets
Warwickshire 20 pts, Yorkshire 5 pts

Essex gained their first championship win of the season, but much of the game was rather desultory. Choosing to bat, Essex were 27 for 4 and were revived only by the middle order batting of Stuart and Danny Law and Paul Grayson. Durham's response to a mediocre Essex total was initially positive, but by the end of a miserable second day on which 57 overs were lost, they had advanced slowly and were still one run short of the Essex total with five wickets standing. They stumbled at the last, and Stuart Law made an invigorating century against an attack lacking the injured Simon Brown.

Prichard's declaration came 80 minutes before lunch on the final day and left Durham a target of 313. They lost only Lewis before lunch, and Collingwood and Morris appeared to be batting purposefully, but in the afternoon Peter Such took over. Four wickets fell for 12 runs in mid-innings, and the last four went down for five runs after Boiling and Speight had offered resistance. Essex won with eight overs remaining.

The champions claimed their first win of the season, but conceded 56 extras in Hampshire's first innings, 30 of them in no-balls. This seemed particularly rash when, on the second day, Leicestershire were reduced to 157 for 7 by the Hampshire spinners. The home side's progress was arrested by David Millns, a pace bowler good enough for England and an increasingly aggressively successful batsman. He hit the second and higher century of his career, and, with the help of Habib and Brimson took his side to a valuable lead. Hampshire were offered another 41 extras in the second innings, but the visitors were able to afford such extravagance and won with ease.

Bowled out for 279 on the opening day at Canterbury, Glamorgan confirmed their championship challenge with a decisive win over Kent in spite of the loss of much of the second day to rain. The spinners Croft and Cosker were the architects of the victory rather than the formidable new-ball pairing of Waqar and Watkin.

It was the medium pace of Kevin Evans that saw Lancashire destroyed in 36 overs at Old Trafford. They were 52 for 9 before Crawley at last found a reliable partner in Martin, who scored 32 as the pair added 73. Nottinghamshire were 37 for 4, but Johnson and Afzaal gave the innings substance. The top scorer was extras, 71 of them of which 28 were wides. Lancashire regained some strength and composure when they batted a second time, but even so they lost their last five wickets for 41 runs. Martin took three wickets, and it seemed that Lancashire might pull off an improbable victory when Nottinghamshire slipped to 63 for 4, but Johnson and Afzaal again came to the rescue. It was in this match that Wasim Akram's shoulder began troubling him again, and his season was doomed.

Middlesex beat Derbyshire in three days. Fifteen wickets fell on the first day, and Derbyshire were handicapped by the fact that Barnett injured a hand fielding and could bat in neither innings. Defeat was hard on Devon Malcolm, who continued his outstanding start to the season with match figures of 11 for 125, and to Karl Krikken who held six catches in the match, five in Middlesex's second innings. Derbyshire's second innings lasted only 35.4 overs.

Facing a Sussex total of 241, Somerset were 67 for 6 when Rose joined Harden. The pair established a new record for the county with a partnership worth 279. The durable Harden reached the 27th hundred of his career while Rose hit 28 fours in his 251-ball innings, which was the highest of his career. He remains a more than useful all-rounder, capable of swinging the ball effectively and of batting with great power. The weak and inexperienced Sussex side showed considerable determination, and, aided a little by rain, they saved the game through a defiant unbeaten century from Athey, who passed 25,000 runs in first-class cricket.

As at Lord's, so at The Oval, where 15 wickets fell on the first day. Young was proving a most useful acquisition for Gloucestershire and star-studded Surrey, much beloved by selectors and choosing to bat first, were continuing in their role as great under-achievers. Tudor returned the best bowling figures of his young career, but Gloucestershire took a big first innings lead. Batting a second time, Surrey lost two early wickets to Lawrence, but it was Mark Alleyne, impressive in his capacity as captain, who brought about their demise with the best bowling performance of his career. The match was over inside three days, and Gloucestershire were top of the table.

The match at Edgbaston also ended in three days and saw considerable changes in fortune. Bowled out for 233 by Giles and Donald on the first day, Yorkshire struck back by capturing four Warwickshire wickets for 22. Penney and Brown offered middle order resistance, but the last five wickets fell in 20 deliveries for two runs. Yorkshire failed to build on their considerable first innings advantage, and only Lehmann and Parker batted with conviction against Donald, Giles and Brown. Needing 248 to win, Warwickshire ended the second day on 76 for 3. They soon lost two more wickets and Penney retired hurt on the third morning. Brown, Welch and Giles proved their considerable abilities as middle-order batsmen of reliability and worth, and Warwickshire claimed victory on a pitch which many considered to be sub-standard.

21, 22, 23 and 24 May

at Chester-le-Street
Worcestershire 351 for 6 dec. (G.R. Haynes 67, T.M. Moody 61) and 113 for 8 (M.J. Saggers 5 for 57)
Durham 132 (P.J. Newport 4 for 33, A. Sheriyar 4 for 53) and 332 (M.J. Foster 58, D.C. Boon 57, J.J.B. Lewis 52, A. Sheriyar 5 for 54)
Match drawn
Worcestershire 16 pts, Durham 5 pts

at Cardiff
Hampshire 309 for 4 dec. (R.A. Smith 94, K.D. James 85, M.L. Hayden 57) and 0 for 0 dec.
Glamorgan 0 for 0 dec. and 287 for 8 (S.P. James 76, G.P. Butcher 58)
Match drawn
Hampshire 8 pts, Glamorgan 6 pts

at Gloucester
Gloucestershire 290 (R.C. Russell 91 not out, T.H.C. Hancock 62, M.C. Ilott 4 for 82) and 64 for 3
Essex 310 (S.G. Law 84, A.P. Grayson 81)
Match drawn
Essex 10 pts, Gloucestershire 9 pts

at Old Trafford
Northamptonshire 479 (K.M. Curran 108, D. Ripley 79 not out, T.C. Walton 60, R.J. Bailey 58) and 232 for 6 dec. (R.J. Bailey 63, M.B. Loye 61, T.C. Walton 50 not out)
Lancashire 415 for 9 dec. (I.D. Austin 95, N.H. Fairbrother 83, J.P. Taylor 4 for 101) and 114 for 0 (J.E.R. Gallian 56 not out)
Match drawn
Northamptonshire 7 pts, Lancashire 6 pts

Warwickshire v. Middlesex at Edgbaston, 21–24 May.
Jacques Kallis of Middlesex is bowled by Mohammad Sheikh
who was making his debut for Warwickshire.
(Philip Wilcox)

at Leicester
Surrey 278 (M.A. Butcher 59, A.R.K. Pierson 4 for 47,
D.J. Millns 4 for 64) and 166 for 5
Leicestershire 340 (D.L. Maddy 103, P.A. Nixon 64 not
out, V.J. Wells 56, C.C. Lewis 4 for 64)
Match drawn
Leicestershire 10 pts, Surrey 9 pts

at Trent Bridge
Derbyshire 319 (D.M. Jones 77, V.P. Clarke 50, M.N. Bowen
7 for 75) and 117 (M.N. Bowen 4 for 34, K.P. Evans 4 for 40)
Nottinghamshire 192 (P. Johnson 60, U. Azfaal 52,
D.E. Malcolm 4 for 42) and 248 for 8 (W.M. Noon 63,
P.J. Franks 50, D.E. Malcolm 4 for 91)
Nottinghamshire won by 2 wickets
Nottinghamshire 20 pts, Derbyshire 7 pts

at Taunton
Yorkshire 306 (D.S. Lehmann 177, A.R. Caddick 6 for
103) and 237 for 6 dec. (D. Byas 103 not out)
Somerset 203 for 5 dec. (S.C. Ecclestone 79 not out)
and 200 (R.J. Harden 50 not out, P.J. Hartley 5 for 34)
Yorkshire won by 140 runs
Yorkshire 21 pts, Somerset 5 pts

at Horsham
Kent 245 (T.R. Ward 67, K. Newell 4 for 61) and 440
(S.A. Marsh 142, T.R. Ward 83, B.J. Phillips 65 not out,
V.C. Drakes 4 for 152)
Sussex 264 (M. Newell 56, P.W. Jarvis 55, B.J. Phillips 5
for 47) and 317 (K. Newell 112, M. Newell 57,
M.J. McCague 7 for 82)
Kent won by 104 runs
Kent 21 pts, Sussex 6 pts

at Edgbaston
Middlesex 221 and 132 (M.R. Ramprakash 50,
G. Welch 5 for 46)
Warwickshire 158 and 198 for 2 (A.J. Moles 67 not out,
N.M.K. Smith 60)
Warwickshire won by 8 wickets
Warwickshire 20 pts, Middlesex 5 pts

No play was possible on the first day at Chester-le-Street, Leicester and Edgbaston, and very little play was possible at Cardiff and Taunton. Durham were beset by injuries, and their second-string attack, with Lugsden returning from a long lay off, suffered when Boon put Worcestershire in. Forced to follow on, Boon's men batted solidly in spite of losing three mid-innings wickets for six runs. Worcestershire faced a target of 114 in 25 overs. Durham bowled far better than they had done in the first innings, and Saggers took the first five wickets. Walker also bowled well and was entrusted with the last over when nine were needed. He conceded seven off the first three balls before Weston took a wild swing and was bowled by the fourth. Haynes was run out next ball, and Rhodes was run out off the last ball attempting a second run which would have won the match. Worcestershire gained eight points for batting second in a game where the scores finished level.

Little play on the first two days and none on the third doomed the game at Cardiff to a draw, although forfeitures were made in an attempt to keep the game alive. Glamorgan were set a target of 310 in 78 overs, but, having lost five wickets for 190, they were happy to settle for a draw.

The top of the table clash between Gloucestershire and Essex was also badly disrupted by the weather. With Mark Ilott in good form, Essex reduced the home county to 84 for 7 before Russell and Hancock added 108. Russell and Ball then added 98. Essex, too, started badly, but Stuart Law and Grayson put on 105 for the fifth wicket.

It was slow batting rather than rain which was the problem at Old Trafford. A placid pitch offered little entertainment or joy to anybody. A barren first day blighted the match at Grace Road where James Knott, son of the famous Alan, made his championship debut, and Darren Maddy gave further evidence of his talent with an accomplished century.

Nottinghamshire made a remarkable comeback to beat local rivals Derbyshire at Trent Bridge. Dean Jones and Vince Clarke, showing good form with his third county, put on 112 for the visitors' fifth wicket, but the last six wickets went down for 49 runs. Wayne Noon held six catches behind the stumps to equal the Nottinghamshire record. The game seemed very much in Derbyshire's favour when they captured the first eight Nottinghamshire wickets for 128 with the knowledge that Tim Robinson had a damaged hand and was down at number 11. Afzaal and Franks saved the follow-on in a stand of 64, and Bowen dismissed Rollins before the end of the second day. Bowen had had a career best of 7 for 75 in the first innings, and he now took ten or more wickets in a match for the first time as Derbyshire were bowled out for 117. The odds were still on Derbyshire, for, needing 245 to win, Nottinghamshire ended the penultimate day on 122 for 5, with Dowman having retired hurt and Pollard having damaged a finger. Robinson was unlikely to bat. Noon and Franks extended their stand until it was worth 94 in 40 overs, at which point Noon was caught in the gully after batting for nearly four hours. Dowman returned, but he was out at 211. Nine runs later, young Paul Franks, having reached the first fifty of his career, was leg before to Aldred, but Bowen offered solid defence at one end while Pollard steered his side to a brave victory.

There was little play on the first two days at Taunton, but Darren Lehmann enlivened the match with his first century for Yorkshire. Bowler made a result possible when he declared Somerset's innings closed 103 runs in arrears. On the last day he offered some 'friendly' bowling, of which Byas took advantage with a 97-ball century. Byas was not so friendly in his declaration, which gave Somerset 77 overs in which to score 341 to win. With Hartley taking three wickets in four balls, Somerset collapsed to 123 for 8 before Mushtaq Ahmed and Kevin Shine suggested some respectability in defeat.

There was an active opening day at Horsham when Kent chose to bat first and lost Fulton to the second ball of the match when he was struck on the elbow. He retired hurt but returned later. Kent raced to 100 in 18 overs as Trevor Ward smashed 67 off 85 balls, but the middle order crumbled, and Keith Newell returned the best bowling figures of his career with his medium-pacers. His brother Mark and Paul Jarvis were the main reasons for Sussex taking a first innings lead. They added 92 for the ninth wicket, aided by a plethora of dropped catches. Ward now batted with more restraint to bring Kent back into the game, but the sensation came in the last wicket stand of 183 between Marsh and Phillips who both made their highest scores in first-class cricket. To their credit, Sussex showed much character and did not wilt after being subjected to this partnership. The Newell brothers added 138 in 41 overs for the fifth wicket, but the last five wickets fell for 23 as the tail succumbed to McCague, who bowled his side to victory with less than nine overs to spare. McCague's bowling was impressive, hostile and accurate.

Much time was lost at Edgbaston, but, after trailing on the first innings, Warwickshire gained a surprisingly comfortable victory. Welch's career-best bowling performance and the batting of Sheikh, on his debut, and Frost in the first innings helped make a Warwickshire victory possible. In the second innings, needing 196 in 57 overs, Warwickshire were indebted to Smith's 50 off 61 balls.

29, 30, 31 May and 2 June
at Ilford
Essex 297 (R.J. Rollins 60, D. Gough 5 for 74) and 312 (R.C. Irani 100, S.G. Law 76, R.D. Stemp 6 for 77)
Yorkshire 334 (M.P. Vaughan 161, R.J. Blakey 92, P.M. Such 6 for 121) and 277 for 8 (D. Byas 89, D.S. Lehmann 81, P.M. Such 5 for 94)
Yorkshire won by 2 wickets
Yorkshire 23 pts, Essex 6 pts

at Cardiff
Glamorgan 597 for 8 dec. (S.P. James 153, H. Morris 135, M.P. Maynard 134 not out, A. Dale 73)
Durham 345 (M.J. Foster 129, D.C. Boon 66, S.L. Watkin 4 for 73) and 244 (J.E. Morris 149, Waqar Younis 4 for 56)
Glamorgan won by an innings and 8 runs
Glamorgan 24 pts, Durham 4 pts

at Southampton
Warwickshire 631 for 7 dec. (A.J. Moles 168, D.L. Hemp
138, T.L. Penney 86 not out, N.V. Knight 81, G. Welch 75)
and 252 for 1 dec. (N.V. Knight 119 not out, D.L. Hemp
114 not out)
Hampshire 549 for 6 dec. (M.L. Hayden 235 not out,
S.D. Udal 117 not out, W.S. Kendall 76, G. Welch 4 for 119)
and 274 for 9 (M.L. Hayden 119, D.R. Brown 5 for 106)
Match drawn
Warwickshire 9 pts, Hampshire 7 pts

at Leicester
Lancashire 373 (G.D. Lloyd 82, G. Chapple 63, W.K. Hegg
58, A.D. Mullally 5 for 79) and 425 for 5 dec. (M.A. Atherton
108, G.D. Lloyd 100 not out, J.E.R. Gallian 99, J.P. Crawley 61)
Leicestershire 468 (N.C. Johnson 150, P.A. Nixon 96,
V.J. Wells 95) and 247 for 5 (V.J. Wells 107)
Match drawn
Leicestershire 11 pts, Lancashire 10 pts

at Lord's
Middlesex 531 (J.H. Kallis 121, M.R. Ramprakash 111,
M.W. Gatting 108, K.R. Brown 61 not out, J.P. Taylor 4 for 99)
Northamptonshire 216 (K.M. Curran 89 not out,
J.P. Hewitt 5 for 59) and 258 (D. Ripley 58 not out,
P.C.R. Tufnell 4 for 64)
Middlesex won by an innings and 57 runs
Middlesex 24 pts, Northamptonshire 3 pts

at Trent Bridge
Nottinghamshire 216 (U. Azfaal 54, M.V. Fleming 5
for 51) and 119 (M.J. McCague 4 for 33)
Kent 440 (M.A. Ealham 122, D.P. Fulton 94, P.A. Strang 73)
Kent won by an innings and 105 runs
Kent 24 pts, Nottinghamshire 4 pts

at Worcester
Worcestershire 303 (T.S. Curtis 101, G.R. Haynes 70,
A.R. Caddick 5 for 64) and 316 for 7 dec. (W.P.C. Weston
65, D.A. Leatherdale 57, G.R. Haynes 52)
Somerset 343 (R.J. Turner 83 not out, P.C.L. Holloway 61,
D.A. Leatherdale 5 for 56) and 185 for 5 (P.D. Bowler 61
not out)
Match drawn
Worcestershire 10 pts, Somerset 10 pts

Essex had a bad week. Knocked out of the Benson and
Hedges Cup at the quarter-final stage, they suffered their first
defeat in the championship in a nail-biting finish at Ilford.
They chose to bat first, but Gough was in prime form and they
were reduced to 184 for 8. Rollins and Cowan restored credibility by adding 84 in 13 overs. Yorkshire lost five wickets for
67 before Blakey joined Vaughan in a stand worth 189.
Vaughan reached the eighth century of his career, and
Yorkshire led by 37 runs. Irani continued his fine start to the
season with his second century of the campaign, but Stemp
ran through the tail, and Yorkshire had more than a day in

Middlesex pace bowler James Hewitt had a fine season.
(George Herringshaw/ASP)

which to score 276. They lost Moxon and Vaughan for 25, but
Byas and Lehmann added 139. At 229 for 3, they were cruising to victory, at which point the Essex spinners captured four
wickets for six runs. Gough brought resolution, but the eighth
wicket went down at 266, and the game went into a fourth day
with Essex needing two wickets and Yorkshire six runs. The
match was over after eight balls on the Monday morning.

James and Morris put on 229 for Glamorgan's first
wicket against Durham. James reached his century before
lunch when the score was 169. Maynard added the third
century of the innings on the second day and declared when
his county had made their highest total in first-class cricket.
Durham battled bravely, and Michael Foster hit his maiden
first-class century, but he and Boon could not prevent the
follow-on. Morris, scoring more than 60% of Durham's runs
when they batted a second time took the game into a fourth
day, but he could not stop the inevitable.

Southampton provided a match beloved of statisticians
but not so popular with paying customers. Moles shared an
opening partnership of 154 with Knight and a second wicket
stand of 184 with Hemp before being caught off Kenway's
third ball in first-class cricket. Facing a total in excess of 600,
Hampshire lost three wickets for 79 before Hayden was joined
by Kendall in stand worth 206. Hayden and Udal shared an
unbroken partnership of 205 for the seventh wicket, with Udal
reaching a maiden first-class hundred and Hayden surpassing

his previous highest score. The fourth morning saw Hemp and Knight gifted centuries from 'friendly' bowling. Hemp reached three figures for the second time in the match, and Hampshire were set the task of scoring 335 in 72 overs. Their attempts to score nearly brought disaster in spite of Hayden equalling Mead's record of a double century and a century in the same match for Hampshire. Brown and Welch bowled well, and Bovill and Kenway had to survive 43 balls to save the game.

There was a similar pattern to the game at Leicester although there was no such excitement in the draw. Lancashire's first innings had a sting in the tail with the last four wickets producing 194 runs. Johnson and Nixon gave substance to Leicestershire's innings with a sixth wicket stand of 199. The South African Johnson made the highest score of his career. There were two notable centuries in Lancashire's second innings – Atherton made his first championship century since 1995, and Lloyd hit 100 off 73 balls, the fastest of the season. Vince Wells hit the fourth century of the game in which there were also three nineties as the home county settled for a draw.

There were three centurions at Lord's, where Middlesex raced to 400 on the opening day. Northamptonshire followed on on the Saturday, and the last four wickets of their second innings fell on the Monday morning.

Kent disposed of Nottinghamshire in three days. Batting first, they were troubled by Matthew Fleming, who took three wickets in eight balls and finished with career-best bowling figures. Kent were 250 for 8 when Paul Strang joined Mark Ealham, who hit the second first-class hundred of his career. The pair added 171 and established a record for Kent's ninth wicket. Nottinghamshire surrendered meekly when they batted a second time.

There was a certain amount of tedium at Worcester, where Curtis batted six hours for his century. Neither side seemed able to seize the initiative, and Somerset declined to chase a target of 277 in 55 overs.

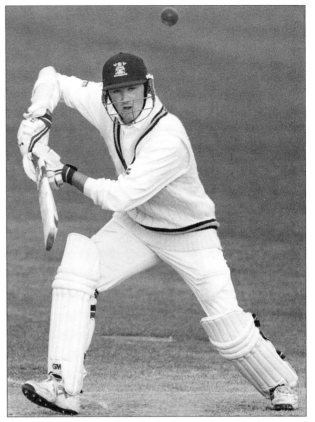

An exciting emerging talent, Nottinghamshire's opening batsman Matthew Dowman. (Dave Pinegar/ASP)

4, 5, 6 and 7 June

at Chesterfield
Derbyshire 523 (A.S. Rollins 210, P. Aldred 83, C.J. Adams 79, S.J. Renshaw 5 for 110) and 208 for 4 dec. (K.J. Barnett 101, A.S. Rollins 51)
Hampshire 422 for 7 dec. (R.A. Smith 154, J.S. Laney 61, K.D. James 51) and 310 for 3 (M.L. Hayden 136 not out, J.S. Laney 93, R.A. Smith 52)
Hampshire won by 7 wickets
Hampshire 23 pts, Derbyshire 6 pts

at Chester-le-Street
Sussex 373 (N.J. Lenham 93, P. Moores 60, S.J.E. Brown 5 for 115) and 271 (N.R. Taylor 109, C.W.J. Athey 50, A. Walker 6 for 68)
Durham 338 (J.J.B. Lewis 89, M.J. Foster 56, V.S. Drakes 4 for 90) and 269 for 8 (J.E. Morris 124)
Match drawn
Sussex 11 pts, Durham 10 pts

at Tunbridge Wells
Warwickshire 314 (T.L. Penney 84, J.B. Thompson 5 for 89) and 280 (D.L. Hemp 117)
Kent 379 (D.P. Fulton 73, A.P. Wells 70, J.B. Thompson 59 not out) and 216 for 6 (A.P. Wells 62 not out, N.M.K. Smith 4 for 68)
Kent won by 4 wickets
Kent 23 pts, Warwickshire 6 pts

at Lord's
Leicestershire 280 (J.J. Whitaker 110, A.R.C. Fraser 6 for 77) and 462 for 7 dec. (V.J. Wells 224, D.L. Maddy 103)
Middlesex 395 (M.R. Ramprakash 97, M.W. Gatting 94, J.C. Pooley 55, G.J. Parsons 4 for 22)
Match drawn
Middlesex 11 pts, Leicestershire 9 pts

at Northampton
Northamptonshire 235 (D. Ripley 77, M.N. Bowen 5 for 57) and 337 for 6 dec. (R.J. Bailey 117 not out, J.N. Snape 66, M.N. Bowen 4 for 128)
Nottinghamshire 272 (W.M. Noon 83, K.M. Curran 4 for 61) and 301 for 7 (M.P. Dowman 111, N.J. Astle 64, P. Johnson 57, J.P. Taylor 7 for 87)
Nottinghamshire won by 2 wickets
Nottinghamshire 22 pts, Northamptonshire 5 pts

Devon Malcolm bowled himself back into the England side with consistently high quality fast bowling. (George Herringshaw/ASP)

at Taunton
Lancashire 88 (K.J. Shine 7 for 43) and 164 (K.J. Shine 4 for 54)
Somerset 189 (P.D. Bowler 53, P.J. Martin 4 for 29) and 66 for 3
Somerset won by 7 wickets
Somerset 20 pts, Lancashire 4 pts

at The Oval
Essex 347 (D.D.J. Robinson 98, R.J. Rollins 56) and 302 (A.P. Grayson 105, G.A. Gooch 56)
Surrey 280 (A.D. Brown 109, A.P. Cowan 5 for 58) and 222 (B.C. Hollioake 72, J.D. Ratcliffe 53)
Essex won by 147 runs
Essex 23 pts, Surrey 6 pts

at Leeds
Gloucestershire 205 (M.A. Lynch 60) and 388 (A.J. Wright 79, M.A. Lynch 64, M.W. Alleyne 52)
Yorkshire 183 (R.J. Blakey 51 not out, A.M. Smith 6 for 58) and 246 (B. Parker 64, M.D. Moxon 63, S. Young 4 for 41, A.M. Smith 4 for 74)
Gloucestershire won by 164 runs
Gloucestershire 21 pts, Yorkshire 4 pts

There are few counties able to score 523 in their first innings and then contrive to lose by seven wickets as Derbyshire did against Hampshire. Andrew Rollins made his second and higher double century and shared a second wicket stand of 124 with Chris Adams. The tail wagged very strongly, and Aldred joined Rollins in an eighth wicket stand worth 149. Aldred's 83 was the first score he had made above 33. The Hampshire response was positive. Laney and Hayden began with a partnership of 110, and James and Robin Smith put on 109 for the third wicket. Smith shared another century stand with Stephenson and went on to make 154 off 215 balls with two sixes and 23 fours. It was the type of innings he was wont to play in his early days with Hampshire, thoroughly entertaining. Barnett made the 50th century of his career, and Hampshire was set a target of 310 in 65 overs. Six were lost to rain, but Laney and Hayden, a tower of strength in the southern county's batting, scored 213 for the first wicket, just the start that was needed. Smith and Hayden hit 88 in 14 overs, and victory came with 19 balls to spare. Hayden's century was his third in four championship innings, and a Sunday League hundred was wedged in between them.

It was honours even for Durham and Sussex. Neil Taylor revived Sussex in their second innings, and Durham were set a target of 307 in 83 overs. Jarvis was unable to bowl because of Achilles tendon trouble, and Durham began well enough with Morris hitting his second century of the week. They reached 244 for 7 with 13.3 overs remaining when rain robbed them of three overs. They could not regain the momentum on the resumption and were happy to draw in the end. They were aided by some unintelligent bowling by Vasbert Drakes, who bowled an excess of bouncers at Simon Brown.

The unexpected strength of Kent's late order batting was again in evidence in the victory over Warwickshire, who were bowled out for 314 on the first day at Tunbridge Wells. Thompson had taken five wickets, and on the second and third days he was to emerge as a batsman. He hit a maiden first-class fifty in what was his first match of the season, and he and Phillips put on 109 for the ninth wicket. The pair then took three wickets each as Warwickshire were bowled out for 280, with Hemp making his third century in four innings. Wells and Fulton batted purposefully for the second time in the match, and with Marsh playing an essential role as support for Wells, Kent won impressively.

Lord's provided disappointing fare. On the first day, Whitaker scored his first first-class hundred at Lord's, and Ben Smith had a finger broken by a ball from Johnson. Gus

Fraser had his best championship bowling return for four seasons, and Middlesex took a first innings lead. Play did not begin until after lunch on the Saturday, and Leicestershire batted out with Vince Wells making his career best score. He and the so promising Maddy put on 173 for the first wicket.

Nottinghamshire included their new overseas signing, Nathan Astle, for the first time, but the early honours went to Mark Bowen, who was enjoying the best period of form of his career. He took five wickets on the opening day against his old county, for whom John Emburey was playing his last first-class match before retiring from first-class cricket. Nottinghamshire took a narrow first innings lead thanks to Noon, another former Northamptonshire player. Forceful batting from Bailey and Snape set up a declaration which left the visitors 77 overs in which to make 301. They began badly, but Dowman and Astle added 156 for the third wicket. Paul Taylor was playing a lone hand for Northamptonshire and took all seven wickets to fall. He sent down 25 overs and with steadier support he might well have snatched the game for his side, but Dowman hit 20 fours in his career best 111 and, with fine support from Johnson, made it possible for Nottinghamshire to win with three balls to spare.

The match at Taunton saw 21 wickets fall on the first day. Lancashire chose to bat first and were all out in 22.1 overs. Bowling unchanged, Kevin Shine took seven wickets. Watkinson scored 33, and he and Hegg added 28 for the seventh wicket. Somerset took the lead for the loss of one wicket, but their last six wickets went down for 41 runs. Lancashire fared only marginally better in their second innings than they had done in their first. Gallian was forced to retire hurt after being struck on the finger, and Shine took ten or more wickets in a match for the second time. Van Troost was also impressively fiery. Lancashire's resistance was woefully weak, beaten in two days.

Essex returned to their winning ways with a comfortable win at The Oval. Darren Robinson gave them a solid start, but they were again indebted to the late order of Rollins, Cowan and Ilott. Surrey lost their first six wickets for 107 runs before Brown and acting captain Lewis added 85. Joey Benjamin hit 22 at number 11. When Essex batted a second time Gooch hit his first 50 of the season and Grayson, promoted to number three, hit 15 fours in his first century of the season off 139 balls. Essex went from 222 for 3 to 250 for 8 before Ilott and Cowan made a spirited rally. Surrey faced a target of 370 and had more than a day in which to get the runs. They lost Darren Bicknell and Kennis before the close of the third day, and even though Ilott was unable to bowl on the final day, they never looked like winning. Surrey's one consolation was Ben Holliake's maiden first-class 50.

Gloucestershire maintained their good form under Mark Alleyne's imaginative leadership with victory at Headingley. Sixteen wickets fell on the first day and Vaughan was forced to retire when a ball from Smith, the Yorkshireman in exile, cracked a bone in his left wrist.

Pressing for a place as an England opener, Darren Maddy of Leicestershire.
(David Munden/Sportsline)

Blakey engineered some sort of recovery on the second day, but by the end of it, with Lynch again batting positively, Gloucestershire were in firm control. Alleyne and the lower order made significant contributions on the third morning, and Yorkshire were left more than one day in which to score 411. Their last six wickets went down for 34 runs and the game was over in 75 minutes on the last morning. Gloucestershire were top of the table, five points ahead of Kent with Nottinghamshire, to the surprise of all, in third place.

Brad Parker established a regular place in the Yorkshire side with consistently positive cricket. (Nigel French/ASP)

12, 13, 14 and 16 June

at Cardiff
Glamorgan 281 (R.D.B. Croft 82, M.P. Maynard 59, A.R.C. Fraser 4 for 68) and 31 (J.P. Hewitt 6 for 14, A.R.C. Fraser 4 for 17)
Middlesex 319 (J.H. Kallis 96, M.R. Ramprakash 63, S.L. Watkin 4 for 43, S.D. Thomas 4 for 52)
Middlesex won by an innings and 7 runs
Middlesex 23 pts, Glamorgan 6 pts

at Bristol
Worcestershire 250 (S.J. Rhodes 78, S.R. Lampitt 52, K.R. Spiring 52, M.W. Alleyne 5 for 41) and 350 for 4 dec. (T.S. Curtis 137, G.A. Hick 137)

Gloucestershire 229 and 276 (R.C. Russell 65)
Worcestershire won by 95 runs
Worcestershire 22 pts, Gloucestershire 5 pts

at Basingstoke
Hampshire 204 and 189 (M.L. Hayden 63, G.D. Rose 5 for 53)
Somerset 159 (P.C.L. Holloway 73 not out, K.D. James 5 for 44) and 225 (K.A. Parsons 74, P.C.L. Holloway 59, K.D. James 8 for 49)
Hampshire won by 9 runs
Hampshire 21 pts, Somerset 4 pts

at Old Trafford
Kent 373 (B.J. Phillips 100 not out, A.P. Wells 65) and 217 for 9 dec. (D.J. Shadford 4 for 67)
Lancashire 285 (G.D. Lloyd 122, P.A. Strang 7 for 118) and 247 (J.P. Crawley 91, P.A. Strang 4 for 68)
Kent won by 58 runs
Kent 24 pts, Lancashire 6 pts

at The Oval
Surrey 549 (A.J. Stewart 271 not out, A.J. Hollioake 69, B.C Hollioake 53) and 153 (C.E.W. Silverwood 5 for 49)
Yorkshire 387 (D.S. Lehmann 100, D. Byas 59, M.D. Moxon 57, R.J. Blakey 53 not out, A.J. Hollioake 4 for 22, Saqlain Mushtaq 4 for 118) and 115 for 4 (D.S. Lehman 57 not out)
Match drawn
Surrey 11 pts, Yorkshire 10 pts

at Hove
Sussex 140 (A.P. Cowan 5 for 45, N.F. Williams 4 for 29) and 356 (R.K. Rao 89, N.J. Lenham 60, A.P. Cowan 4 for 78)
Essex 384 (R.C. Irani 110, R.J. Rollins 82) and 115 for 0 (P.J. Prichard 54 not out, G.A. Gooch 51 not out)
Essex won by 10 wickets
Essex 24 pts, Sussex 4 pts

at Edgbaston
Derbyshire 200 (V.P. Clarke 99, D.R. Brown 4 for 33, N.M.K. Smith 4 for 37) and 229 for 3 dec. (A.S. Rollins 59, K.J. Barnett 54)
Warwickshire 340 (A.J. Moles 83, T.L. Penney 73, D.L. Hemp 60, D.E. Malcolm 5 for 85)
Match drawn
Warwickshire 10 pts, Derbyshire 8 pts

Meetings between Middlesex and Glamorgan have tended to produce strange events, but few have been stranger than that which occurred at Cardiff on 14 June. Glamorgan's first innings had stuttered along and rain took it briefly into the second day. Middlesex, with Ramprakash and Kallis putting on 160 for the second wicket, took a first innings lead of 38, which seemed slight enough. It proved to be sufficient for an innings victory. Fraser and Hewitt bowled unchanged, and Glamorgan were out for 31 in 16 overs. Cottey was the only man to reach double figures, 12, and Jamie Hewitt returned career best figures of 6 for 14. Glamorgan were dazed, for there seemed to be no logical reason for what had happened. The game ended on the Saturday afternoon.

Gloucestershire's stay at the top was brief. They reduced Worcestershire to 65 for 6 on the opening day, but acting skipper Rhodes and Lampitt added 124 for the eighth wicket. Gloucestershire, too, relied on their tail, and Ball and Lewis put on 67 for the last wicket. When Worcestershire batted again Hick and Curtis shared a second wicket stand of 227. Hick's 137 was his first championship hundred of the season. Needing 372 to win, Gloucestershire lost Trainor for 0, and on the Monday they slipped to 38 for 4. Lynch, Young, Alleyne, Russell and Hancock all showed great determination, but Worcestershire claimed their first championship win of the season with 27 overs remaining.

The match at Basingstoke ended in three days. Hampshire's hero was Kevan James, who had enjoyed a fine season in 1996. He claimed ten or more wickets in a match for the first time, and his 8 for 49 in the second innings rep-resented the best bowling performance of his career. The Lancashire agony continued. A first day cut short by rain saw Phillips go in as night-watchman when Kent were 135 for 5. He finished the day on 3, but on the Friday he completed the first century of a career which had begun with three matches the previous season. A faltering Lancashire were rescued by Graham Lloyd, and the home county seemed right back in the game when Kent were 81 for 4 at the close of play on Saturday. It was an illusion. Strang, Marsh, Phillips and Thompson batted well enough on the Monday morning to allow a declaration. Lancashire, wanting 306 in 58 overs, made a bid for victory, but their last six wickets fell for 44 runs, and Kent went 11 points clear of Middlesex at the top of the championship.

Alec Stewart's 271 not out was his second double century, his first century for Surrey since 1995 and the highest score of his career. It was also the highest score made against Yorkshire this century. He hit 36 fours and three sixes and batted with a stylish authority that can make him one of the most attractive batsmen in the game. In spite of Lehmann's century, Yorkshire fell short of saving the follow-on. It did not matter, for Adam Hollioake did not impose it. He may well have regretted his decision, for Surrey were bowled out in 46.1 overs, and rain brought an abrupt close on the Monday.

Put in to bat at Hove, Sussex were bowled out for 140 by Ashley Cowan and Neil Williams who was standing in for the injured Ilott. By the end of the day, Essex led by 92 runs and had five wickets standing. Irani drove and pulled with vigour to reach his third hundred of the season, and Rollins made another spectacular contribution with 82 off 104 balls to take Essex to maximum bonus points. Lenham and Rao breathed hope into the Sussex cause with a second innings opening partnership of 116, and there was late violence from Vasbert Drakes, but Essex had nearly two days in which to score 113 to win. They needed only 23.2 overs.

It was events off field rather than those on which dominated the game at Edgbaston. The resignation and departure of Dean Jones as captain of Derbyshire had shocked the cricket world, and DeFreitas, leading the side in his stead, could have had little joy from a first day which saw the county bowled out for 200. They were 16 for 4 before Vince Clarke's best championship score brought some relief. Moles and Hemp laid a solid foundation for Warwickshire in what limited play there was on the second and third days. The rain helped Derbyshire to save the match, but most attention was focused on the fact that coach Les Stillman had been given a vote of no confidence by the senior players and that Dominic Cork, out of the side through injury, was strongly criticised by Geoffrey Boycott in a television interview. One recalled, too, that previous overseas players, including Azharuddin, had left Derbyshire in less than happy circumstances and that Adams wanted to leave the club.

Ben Phillips of Kent, a maiden century against Lancashire, 13 June, and a regular flow of wickets.
(Andrew Budd/Alan Cozzi)

18, 19, 20 and 21 June
at Derby
Sussex 200 for 9 dec.
Derbyshire 233 for 9 (V.P. Clarke 65 not out, C.J. Adams 53, V.C. Drakes 4 for 44 , R.J. Kirtley 4 for 98)
Match drawn
Derbyshire 8 pts, Sussex 8 pts

at Darlington
Durham 251 (J.J.B. Lewis 158 not out, M.V. Fleming 5 for 55) and 183 for 8 dec. (M.P. Speight 73 not out, M.V. Fleming 4 for 34)
Kent 167 (M.M. Betts 7 for 29) and 132 (S.J.E. Brown 4 for 57)
Durham won by 135 runs
Durham 22 pts, Kent 4 pts

at Bristol
Middlesex 237 (K.P. Dutch 79, M.R. Ramprakash 73, A.M. Smith 5 for 23) and 124 for 8 dec. (J. Lewis 6 for 50)
Gloucestershire 99 (R.L. Johnson 4 for 27) and 218 (M.W. Alleyne 75)
Middlesex won by 44 runs
Middlesex 21 pts, Gloucestershire 4 pts

at Liverpool
Glamorgan 272 for 1 dec. (S.P. James 152 not out, A. Dale 78 not out) and 0 for 0 dec.
Lancashire 0 for 0 dec. and 51 (Waqar Younis 7 for 25)
Glamorgan won by 221 runs
Glamorgan 18 pts, Lancashire 0 pts

at Northampton
Hampshire 405 for 8 dec. (M.L. Hayden 150, R.A. Smith 74, K.D. James 56, J.P. Taylor 6 for 91) and 0 for 0 dec.
Northamptonshire 86 for 2 dec. and 297 for 9 (M.B. Loye 86)
Match drawn
Hampshire 7 pts, Northamptonshire 5 pts

at Trent Bridge
Yorkshire 364 (D. Byas 128, D.S. Lehmann 62, M.D. Moxon 60, K.P. Evans 6 for 91)
Nottinghamshire 148 for 7 (C. White 4 for 51)
Match drawn
Yorkshire 10 pts, Nottinghamshire 7 pts

at Bath
Leicestershire 442 for 6 dec. (J.J. Whitaker 133 not out, I.J. Sutcliffe 112, V.J. Wells 70, D.L. Maddy 58)
Somerset 256 (R.J. Turner 66, D.J. Millns 6 for 61) and 146 for 3 (K.A. Parsons 56 not out)
Match drawn
Leicestershire 11 pts, Somerset 7 pts

at Worcester
Surrey 452 for 9 dec. (J.D. Ratcliffe 135, A.D. Brown 121, S.R. Lampitt 4 for 104)
Worcestershire 81 for 1
Match drawn
Worcestershire 7 pts, Surrey 7 pts

The rain that ruined the Lord's Test was no kinder to the championship matches. At Derby, the Jones affair rather than the cricket dragged on. Barnett was fined £1,500 for making unauthorised statements to the media. There was very little play on the second and third days and none at all on the fourth.

The shock came at Darlington where Durham gained their first championship win for two seasons. Jon Lewis carried his bat through the 115 overs of the Durham innings in making his first championship century for his new county. Crucially, he and Boiling added 110 for the eighth wicket. Kent lost their last six first innings wickets for 27 runs as Melvyn Betts returned the best bowling figures of his career. Durham's second innings followed a pattern similar to their first, being redeemed by an eighth wicket stand of 92 between Speight and Boiling. Kent went in search of 268 in 64 overs on a shortened last day, and they were soon reduced to 41 for 5 by Brown and Betts. There seemed little chance of Kent winning, but there seemed every chance that Durham would be thwarted by the weather. Boon was forced to withdraw his quick bowlers because of the light, and he took on the responsibility himself, bowling his off-breaks. He had Marsh taken at slip, and McCague was caught bat and pad at silly mid-off with just 5.3 overs remaining.

The pitch at Bristol came under scrutiny from the ECB after 25 wickets fell in under two days. A suspended sentence was imposed on Gloucestershire of a 10-point penalty. It was as well that it was suspended, for the western county's title aspirations suffered another blow when they were defeated by Middlesex, who leapt over Kent to the top of the table. They recovered from 47 for 5 on the opening day, but there was no recovery for Gloucestershire on the second day when their last seven wickets went down for 37 runs and Middlesex fell to 78 for 6 in their second innings. A blank third day forced Ramprakash to be bold, and he set the home county a target of 263. This proved way beyond them. Nine wickets went down for 169 runs before Smith and Lewis scored 49 in nine overs on a pitch where cracks were giving encouragement to the medium-pace bowlers. Less than seven overs were left when Lewis was taken at slip off Johnson.

Lancashire continued their journey through the valley of doom. At Liverpool, Glamorgan made 173 for 1 in 50.2 overs on the first day, and rain left James suspended on 99. There was no more play until the Saturday when 'friendly' bowling encouraged the Welsh county to score 99 more runs in 10 overs. Forfeitures followed, and Lancashire were left 60 overs in which to score 273, which was most generous. They lasted for 14 overs. Waqar and Watkin bowled unchanged, and Waqar returned the best bowling figures of his career and performed the hat-trick, his victims being Chilton, who was making his debut, Hegg and Yates.

Hampshire and Northamptonshire came to an agreement in an effort to get a result. Hayden hit his fourth first-class hundred of the season, but there was little play on the second and third days. Northamptonshire's eventual target was one of 320 at just over three and a half runs an over. Loye, almost a forgotten man, batted superbly in making 86 off 116 balls, but the home county lost five wickets for 41 runs in 39 balls as they tried to maintain the run-rate. Boswell and Hughes survived the last 17 balls to secure a draw.

Little play on the second and third days and none on the fourth was the diet at Trent Bridge, where the two captains had different fortunes. Byas of Yorkshire scored a hundred; Johnson of Nottinghamshire broke a finger.

Ian Sutcliffe hit a maiden championship century for Leicestershire, who spoiled the celebrations of Somerset's Shine and van Troost, both of whom were awarded their county caps before the start of the match at Bath. Sutcliffe and Whitaker added 192 for the third wicket. Somerset succumbed to Millns and were forced to follow-on, but too much time was lost to rain for a result to be realistically possible.

Jason Ratcliffe made the highest score of his career and his first championship century for Surrey when he and Alistair Brown put on 179 for the fourth wicket, but rain prevented any play at Worcester on the third and fourth days.

26, 27, 28 and 30 June
at Southend
Derbyshire 142 (M.C. Ilott 7 for 59) and 86 (P.M. Such 5 for 27)
Essex 373 for 8 dec. (S.G. Law 157, P.J. Prichard 106)
Essex won by an innings and 145 runs
Essex 24 pts, Derbyshire 3 pts

at Swansea
Glamorgan 172 (R.J. Kirtley 6 for 60) and 183 for 9 dec. (S.P. James 82 not out, M.P. Maynard 61, M.A. Robinson 4 for 42)
Sussex 54 (Waqar Younis 8 for 17) and 67 (S.D. Thomas 5 for 24)
Glamorgan won by 234 runs
Glamorgan 20 pts, Sussex 4 pts

at Leicester
Match abandoned
Leicestershire 3 pts, Warwickshire 3 pts

at Luton
Gloucestershire 180 for 7 dec. (K.M. Curran 4 for 69)
Northamptonshire 58 for 6
Match drawn
Northamptonshire 3 pts, Gloucestershire 3 pts

at Worcester
Worcestershire 100 for 7 dec. and 135 for 0 dec. (T.S. Curtis 77 not out)
Lancashire 0 for 0 dec. and 237 for 7 (A. Flintoff 70, W.K. Hegg 54 not out)
Lancashire won by 3 wickets
Lancashire 19 pts, Worcestershire 0 pts

at Leeds
Middlesex 150 for 3 (M.R. Ramprakash 76 not out)
v. **Yorkshire**
Match drawn
Yorkshire 4 pts, Middlesex 3 pts

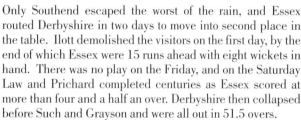

27, 28, 29 and 30 June
at The Oval
Surrey 201 for 9 dec. (P.J. Franks 4 for 47) and 123 for 6 dec.
Nottinghamshire 73 for 1 dec. and 120 (I.D.K. Salisbury 6 for 19)
Surrey won by 131 runs
Surrey 17 pts, Nottinghamshire 4 pts

Only Southend escaped the worst of the rain, and Essex routed Derbyshire in two days to move into second place in the table. Ilott demolished the visitors on the first day, by the end of which Essex were 15 runs ahead with eight wickets in hand. There was no play on the Friday, and on the Saturday Law and Prichard completed centuries as Essex scored at more than four and a half an over. Derbyshire then collapsed before Such and Grayson and were all out in 51.5 overs.

The only other ground on which there was play on the scheduled first day was Swansea, where Glamorgan scored 114 for 5 in 30.4 overs. Kirtley, a bowler of much promise for Sussex and England, returned the best bowling figures of his career, but he was overshadowed by Waqar Younis. Twenty-four wickets fell on the second day as Sussex were destroyed in 22.5 overs with Waqar improving on the career-best bowling figures he had set in the previous match. His astonishing 8 for 17 came from 11.5 overs. Maynard declared shortly before the close, leaving Sussex two days and four overs in which to score 302. They did not lose a wicket that evening, but on the Saturday they went from 45 for 2 to 67 all out. Waqar was wicketless, but Thomas obtained the best bowling figures of his career. Life was hard for Sussex.

Rain devastated the games at Leicester, Luton and Leeds. There was no play on the first three days at Luton, and attempts to finish the stipulated one innings match were thwarted. There was play only briefly on the second day at Headingley.

No play on the first day at Worcester and little on the second and third led to arranged declarations, and Lancashire reached their target of 236 with just under 12 overs to spare. It was Lancashire's first championship win of the season, and they owed a debt to Flintoff, who made his highest first-class score off 101 balls.

A hope for Durham, Michael Foster, now with his third county, played some excellent all-round cricket and helped bring stability to the north-eastern county. (Mark Thompson/Allsport)

There was no play on the first two days at The Oval, but, with generosity on both sides, Surrey managed a victory with five balls to spare. Ian Salisbury won the match with his best bowling performance for his new county.

2, 3, 4 and 5 July

at Chester-le-Street
Match abandoned
Durham 3 pts, Hampshire 3 pts

at Chelmsford
Essex 280 (D.D.J. Robinson 78, P.J. Prichard 51, J.D. Kerr 4 for 83) and 129 (S.G. Law 55, K.J. Shine 5 for 72)
Somerset 389 (P.C.L. Holloway 90, M.N. Lathwell 87, R.J. Turner 80 not out) and 22 for 0
Somerset won by 10 wickets
Somerset 24 pts, Essex 6 pts

at Swansea
Glamorgan 400 for 5 dec. (H. Morris 173, M.P. Maynard 98, P.A. Cottey 76 not out) and 52 for 0
Gloucestershire 214 and 233 (D.A. Cosker 4 for 87)
Glamorgan won by 10 wickets
Glamorgan 24 pts, Gloucestershire 3 pts

at Maidstone
Kent 306 (N.J. Llong 57, P.A. Strang 55, Mohammad Akram 4 for 56) and 99 for 2 dec.
Northamptonshire 84 for 0 dec. and 322 for 9 (R.J. Bailey 83, R.J. Warren 74, D.J.G. Sales 59)
Northamptonshire won by 1 wicket
Northamptonshire 20 pts, Kent 3 pts

at Leicester
Yorkshire 268 (D. Byas 88, A.D. Mullally 5 for 103) and 309 for 3 dec. (D.S. Lehmann 163 not out, M.D. Moxon 63)
Leicestershire 406 for 8 dec. (D.L. Maddy 94, J.J. Whitaker 87, P.A. Nixon 77 not out)
Match drawn
Leicestershire 11 pts, Yorkshire 8 pts

at Uxbridge
Middlesex 118 (P.J. Martin 8 for 32) and 245 (J.H. Kallis 62, P.J. Martin 5 for 47, G. Yates 4 for 89)
Lancashire 417 for 9 dec. (N.H. Fairbrother 97, S.P. Titchard 79, I.D. Austin 69, N.T. Wood 67, P.C.R. Tufnell 5 for 90)
Lancashire won by an innings and 54 runs
Lancashire 23 pts, Middlesex 1 pt

at Arundel
Worcestershire 255 (S.J. Rhodes 98 not out)
Sussex 71 (A. Sheriyar 6 for 19) and 149 (S.R. Lampitt 5 for 39, A. Sheriyar 4 for 44)
Worcestershire won by an innings and 35 runs
Worcestershire 22 pts, Sussex 4 pts

at Edgbaston
Surrey 193 (G. Welch 4 for 62, A.A. Donald 4 for 64) and 144 (J.D. Ratcliffe 59, A.A. Donald 6 for 55)
Warwickshire 306 (T.L. Penney 99, N.M.K. Smith 69 not out, D.R. Brown 66, M.P. Bicknell 4 for 96) and 34 for 5
Warwickshire won by 5 wickets
Warwickshire 23 pts, Surrey 4 pts

It appeared that life at the top carried with it the threat of impending disaster. Put in to bat at Chelmsford, Essex endured a mid-innings crisis and were restored by a last wicket stand of 66 between Cowan and Such. Ilott claimed wickets with the first two balls of the Somerset innings, but there the Essex joy ended. On an abbreviated second day, Lathwell and Holloway added 147 for the third wicket, and on the third day, the sky fell in on Essex. Turner, Rose and Kerr pepped up the scoring rate, and Somerset led by 109 runs. In a totally wretched batting display, Essex surrendered to Shine, Rose and Kerr in 37.3 overs. Only Gooch, Stuart Law and extras reached double figures. The match was over on the third evening.

In spite of this defeat, Essex remained in second place, but Glamorgan jumped above them with a most impressive win over Gloucestershire, for whom nothing had gone right since their brief stay at the top. There was much rain at Swansea over the first two days, and the Glamorgan innings went into the third day. It was founded on a third wicket stand of 223 between Morris and Maynard. Waqar, Watkin and Cosker bowled with control and menace to dismiss the visitors for 214 and force them to follow on. Cosker then broke through again to account for Wright. The tremendous spirit in the Glamorgan side was evident on the Saturday when they overcame stiff resistance to gain their fifth championship win of the season. All the bowlers made vital contributions, but there was particular pleasure in the development and success of Darren Thomas.

Bailey and Marsh had to manipulate a result at Maidstone where Alan Igglesden appeared in the Kent side for the first time in two years. The final equation gave Northamptonshire a target of 322 in 96 overs. The pitch was grassy and slow, and this was a challenging but fair target. Kent never ceased to attack, and Strang bowled from before lunch until the close of play. A second wicket stand of 137 between Warren and Bailey gave Northamptonshire the necessary base, and at tea they were 173 for 3. Sales maintained the desired run rate in a good innings of 59, and Snape hit Strang for a six and a four off consecutive balls. Ripley and Mohammad Akram were run out, and with the last pair, Boswell and Snape together, 15 were needed. When the final over arrived 7 were needed. Phillips, the bowler, conceded three runs off the first five balls, but Snape touched the last ball past a diving long-leg, and Northamptonshire had their first championship win of the season.

The loss of much of the first two days could not be overcome at Leicester, where Lehmann batted with brutal splendour in the second innings to save Yorkshire from embarrassment. He hit an unbeaten 163 off 146 balls, an innings that included five sixes, and he dominated a stand of 160 for the fourth wicket with Parker, who contributed 15.

Lancashire suddenly reappeared in the sunlight after recent traumas. They asked Middlesex to bat first at Uxbridge and bowled them out in 39.5 overs, with Peter Martin claiming eight wickets in an innings for the first time. By the end of the first day, they were already eight runs ahead and had not lost a wicket. Consistent batting took them to a commanding lead, and the game was over before lunch on the Saturday. Martin finished with match figures of 13 for 79, the first time he had captured ten wickets in a match.

Sheriyar was another to take ten wickets in a match for the first time. He played a decisive role in Worcestershire's win at Arundel, where Sussex gave another sorry showing. Worcestershire plunged to 34 for 3 on a restricted first day. Spiring, Moody, Rhodes and Newport all helped effect a recovery. Sussex were soon in trouble, and only Peirce and Mark Newell reached double figures. Following on, they fared little better, and the match was over in three days.

Put in to bat, Surrey were 157 for 6 from 50 overs at the end of the first day at Edgbaston. They were out for 193 on the second, and Warwickshire lost their first four

wickets, three of them to Martin Bicknell, for 55 runs. Trevor Penney and Dougie Brown brought about a recovery with a stand of 131 which spread into the third day. Trailing by 113, Surrey collapsed from 87 for 1 to 144 all out, losing eight wickets before they had cleared off the arrears. Bizarre events followed as Warwickshire sought the 32 they needed to win. Anxious perhaps to have a day off, they scored 23 from nine overs but lost four wickets. They lost a fifth on the last morning, but the match was decided after 11 balls. Sadly for Warwickshire, Nick Knight broke a finger while fielding.

16, 17, 18 and 19 July
at Cheltenham
Derbyshire 120 (K.J. Barnett 58, A.M. Smith 6 for 47) and 329 (K.J. Barnett 94, M.J. Vandrau 54, A.M. Smith 4 for 59)
Gloucestershire 484 (S. Young 237, M.W. Alleyne 97, T.H.C. Hancock 54, D.E. Malcolm 4 for 102)
Gloucestershire won by an innings and 35 runs
Gloucestershire 24 pts, Derbyshire 4 pts

at Canterbury
Kent 498 for 9 dec. (M.A. Ealham 139, S.A. Marsh 98 not out, P.A. Strang 82, T.R. Ward 51, J. Ormond 5 for 107) and 26 for 0 dec.
Leicestershire 160 for 4 dec. (N.C. Johnson 72 not out) and 367 for 4 (B.F. Smith 121 not out, N.C. Johnson 117 not out)
Leicestershire won by 6 wickets
Leicestershire 19 pts, Kent 5 pts

at Old Trafford
Lancashire 561 for 8 dec. (N.H. Fairbrother 132, J.P. Crawley 112, I.D. Austin 78 not out, M. Watkinson 75)
Sussex 307 (N.R. Taylor 82, K. Newell 74) and 236 (C.W.J. Athey 53, G. Yates 5 for 59)
Lancashire won by an innings and 18 runs
Lancashire 24 pts, Sussex 5 pts

at Northampton
Northamptonshire 364 (D.J. Roberts 117, A.P. Grayson 4 for 53) and 216 (D.J.G. Sales 63, A.P. Cowan 4 for 54)
Essex 275 (N. Hussain 77, P.J. Prichard 50, K.M. Curran 4 for 32) and 290 (P.J. Prichard 75, A.P. Grayson 62, J.N. Snape 4 for 46)
Northamptonshire won by 15 runs
Northamptonshire 24 pts, Essex 6 pts

at Trent Bridge
Warwickshire 344 (D.L. Hemp 70, D.P. Ostler 65, P.J. Franks 4 for 84, N.J. Astle 4 for 92) and 95 for 4
Nottinghamshire 133 (G. Welch 4 for 26, D.R. Brown 4 for 37) and 415 (N.J. Astle 100, M.P. Dowman 96, A.A. Donald 5 for 98)
Match drawn
Warwickshire 10 pts, Nottinghamshire 7 pts

The youngest Nottinghamshire bowler to perform the hat-trick in the county championship, Paul Franks, v. Warwickshire, Trent Bridge, 16 July.
(David Munden/Sportsline)

at Guildford
Surrey 477 (A.J. Stewart 98, G.P. Thorpe 84, C.C. Lewis 76, A.J. Hollioake 75, M.A. Butcher 69) and 78 for 1
Hampshire 303 (M.L. Hayden 58, M.P. Bicknell 4 for 88) and 251 (A.N. Aymes 96 not out, S.J. Renshaw 56, M.P. Bicknell 5 for 34)
Surrey won by 9 wickets
Surrey 24 pts, Hampshire 7 pts

at Scarborough
Durham 152 (J.J.B. Lewis 50, D. Gough 4 for 37) and 164
Yorkshire 372 (D.S. Lehmann 86, B. Parker 74 not out, A. McGrath 57)
Yorlrshire won by an innings and 56 runs
Yorkshire 24 pts, Durham 4 pts

Gloucestershire's depressing run ended with a victory over Derbyshire in the Cheltenham Festival. The match had an extraordinary start in which the visitors, having chosen to bat first, were bowled out before lunch. Mike Smith, on the eve of an England debut, took six wickets and caused Vandrau to retire when he hit the batsman under the jaw with a lifting delivery. Malcolm produced a three-wicket burst while Gloucestershire scored only 16, but Hancock and Young added 139 before Young took total command with the highest score of his career. He and Alleyne put on 244 for the fifth wicket, and the left-handed Young was finally leg before to DeFreitas for 237, an innings that included two sixes and 37 fours. The Tasmanian also took wickets with consecutive balls when Derbyshire batted a second time. He accounted for top-scorers Barnett and Vandrau, and he finished with 3 for 25. Smith returned match figures of 10 for 106, and the game was over in three days.

Kent's efforts to gain comfort from rain-affected matches again floundered when they were savaged by Leicestershire at Canterbury. They were 162 for 6 before Mark Ealham shared stands of 145 with Strang and 146 with Marsh. Ealham made the highest score of his career and his first hundred on home soil, but the Kent innings had been spread over two days by the weather, and connivance was needed to bring a result. Kent's second innings lasted only five overs, and Leicestershire were left just over a day in which to score 365. At 142 for 4, a win for the visitors looked improbable, but Jonson and Smith shared an unbeaten stand of 225, and the reigning champions notched their second victory of the season.

Lancashire's new-found confidence was again in evidence when they crushed Sussex at Old Trafford. It was their first championship win at their headquarters for two years. Moores's decision to ask Lancashire to bat first seemed totally justified given that the pitch was damp and the weather overcast. Sussex might well have gained rich dividends had Crawley been caught before he had scored as he should have been. In the event, he and Fairbrother put on 243 for the third wicket in 58 overs. The Lancashire innings stretched into the second day, by which time only one result looked possible. Sussex did not capitulate easily, but the match was over shortly after lunch on the fourth day.

Essex suffered their third defeat in four matches but still held on to second place. For Northamptonshire, it was two wins in a row. They had decided that David Roberts would be given an extended period as an opening batsman, and he responded with a maiden first-class century in his second championship match of the season. The pitch was good, and many of his colleagues looked set for big scores only to throw their wickets away. Essex batted somewhat frenetically. Gooch hit the first and sixth balls of the innings for six, but he was leg before for 24, and it was at the end of this game that the news broke that he was to retire. The Essex batting disappointed once more, and the home county took a first innings lead of 89. There was still hope for Essex when Cowan, Williams and Grayson worked hard to bowl Northamptonshire out for 216, leaving Essex 92 overs in which to score 306. Prichard batted well for the second time in the match, and Stuart Law hit a rapid 45. Essex looked well set, but five wickets fell for 42 runs. Williams joined Grayson, who batted with admirable composure, in a ninth wicket stand of 52. The end came when Bailey caught Williams and ran out Grayson.

The main attraction at Trent Bridge was 18-year-old Paul Franks, the Nottinghamshire seam bowler, who became the youngest player from his county to perform the hat-trick. He claimed a formidable trio, Penney, Brown and Welch, but Warwickshire had the upper hand, and Nottinghamshire were forced to follow on. They were saved by Dowman and Astle, who batted outstandingly well in the knowledge that neither Johnson nor Pollard was likely to bat because of injury. Johnson did continue normally, and Pollard came in at number eleven to finish 0 not out to thwart Warwickshire and help draw the match.

Butcher and Stewart added 174 for Surrey's second wicket, but the whole side batted consistently to reach 457 for 9 on the opening day at Guildford. Hampshire fought well but were obliged to follow on. They were 71 for 7 in their second innings when Aymes found a reliable partner in Renshaw, and the pair put on 123. Milburn also offered resistance, but the match was won by Surrey shortly after lunch on the fourth day.

Yorkshire beat Durham before lunch on the third day at Scarborough where the pitch was not to the liking of everyone and on which no batsmen felt easy. The Yorkshire seam bowlers took a grip on the game on the first day and never relinquished it.

23, 24, 25 and 26 July
at Chesterfield
Derbyshire 513 for 6 dec. (A.S. Rollins 148, M.R. May 116, V.P. Clarke 76 not out) and 35 for 0
Glamorgan 364 for 8 dec. (A. Dale 142 not out)
Match drawn
Derbyshire 10 pts, Glamorgan 9 pts

at Chelmsford
Worcestershire 394 (K.R. Spiring 150, V.S. Solanki 60) and 250 for 5 dec. (G.A. Hick 107 not out, D.A. Leatherdale 59 not out)
Essex 451 (D.D.J. Robinson 148, P.J. Prichard 120)
Match drawn
Essex 8 pts, Worcestershire 8 pts

at Cheltenham
Durham 86 (M.W. Alleyne 5 for 14) and 357 (J.J.B. Lewis 81, D.C. Boon 66)
Gloucestershire 471 for 6 dec. (M.W. Alleyne 165, R.C. Russell 103 not out, M.G.N. Windows 75, S. Young 52)
Gloucestershire won by an innings and 28 runs
Gloucestershire 24 pts, Durham 2 pts

at Southampton
Lancashire 569 for 8 dec. (M. Watkinson 135, A. Flintoff 117, G.D. Lloyd 90, N.T. Wood 82, I.D. Austin 69 not out) and 255 for 9 dec. (W.K. Hegg 77 not out, J.N.B. Bovill 4 for 62)
Hampshire 412 for 4 dec. (M. Keech 101 not out, J.S. Laney 95, M.L. Hayden 94)
Match drawn
Hampshire 10 pts, Lancashire 8 pts

Chris Tolley, good all-round cricket for Nottinghamshire and a hat-trick against Leicestershire, at Leicester, 23–26 July. (Nigel French/ASP)

Chelmsford, 23–26 July, Goodbye to All That. Graham Gooch leaves the field after his last innings in first-class cricket. (Ben Radford/Allsport)

at Leicester
Nottinghamshire 342 (M.P. Dowman 149) and 182 (A.D. Mullally 5 for 62)
Leicestershire 267 (D.L. Maddy 103, N.C. Johnson 76 not out, C.M. Tolley 6 for 61) and 217 for 9 (V.J. Wells 59, A.R. Oram 4 for 69)
Match drawn
Nottinghamshire 10 pts, Leicestershire 9 pts

at Lord's
Kent 208 (A.P. Wells 63) and 157 (J.H. Kallis 5 for 54)
Middlesex 105 (M.J. McCague 7 for 50) and 256 (M.R. Ramprakash 113 not out, P.A. Strang 6 for 88)
Kent won by 4 runs
Kent 21 pts, Middlesex 4 pts

at Northampton
Surrey 581 for 7 dec. (A.D. Brown 170 not out, D.J. Bicknell 162, A.J. Hollioake 81)
Northamptonshire 401 (A.L. Penberthy 96, R.J. Warren 72, A. Fordham 72, J.N. Snape 52, C.C. Lewis 4 for 82) and 241 for 2 dec. (A. Fordham 82 not out, R.J. Bailey 62 not out)
Match drawn
Surrey 10 pts, Northamptonshire 9 pts

24, 25, 26 and 27 July
at Edgbaston
Warwickshire 336 (A.F. Giles 97, T. Frost 56, Mushtaq Ahmed 5 for 66) and 198 for 5 dec. (D.L. Hemp 65 not out, M.A. Wagh 57, G.D. Rose 4 for 75)
Somerset 304 for 6 dec. (P.C.L. Holloway 106, M.E. Trescothick 57) and 134 for 6
Match drawn
Somerset 10 pts, Warwickshire 8 pts

Rollins and May scored 247 for Derbyshire's first wicket against Glamorgan. Rollins reached his century before lunch, moving to three figures off 97 balls. In all, he hit 29 fours. May staked further claim to a regular place in the side with his maiden championship century. Dale's unbeaten 142 gave Glamorgan maximum batting points but weather disrupted the third day, and only 13 balls were bowled on the fourth.

The match at Chelmsford marked Graham Gooch's farewell to first-class cricket. Sadly, it was not an occasion to remember. Worcestershire won the toss and batted. Gooch led Essex on to the field on his 44th birthday. Worcestershire were 166 for 5 before two young men of promise, Spiring and Solanki, put on 151. Spiring went on to make the highest score of his career. Gooch was bowled for 11, but Prichard and Robinson added 182 for the second wicket. Robinson made the highest score of his career and was awarded his county cap. Law fell cheaply, and Rollins hit brightly before being caught off left-arm spinner Rawnsley. Irani seemed inhibited and at odds with the world. He and Robinson had the simplest of tasks to collect a fourth batting point but failed miserably. Essex took a first innings lead of 57 and captured five Worcestershire second innings wickets for 99, but they did not capture another one on the last morning when Hick batted attractively. It rained at lunch, and Gooch's career came to a soggy end.

Cheltenham was agreeing with Gloucestershire. Fifteen wickets fell on the first day when Durham lost their last eight wickets for 25 runs. The home side lost their first three wickets for 28 but then raced into the lead. Alleyne and Russell put on 205 for the sixth wicket. Consistent application saw Durham through the third day, and they held out even when Gloucestershire claimed the extra half-hour. It seemed that the weather might save them, but their last three wickets went down in 41 minutes on the Saturday morning. Shortly after the game had finished came the deluge.

The pitch at Southampton provided a paradise for batsmen. England Under-19 captain Andy Flintoff hit the first first-class century of his career, and Keech made the second of his career. Laney and Hayden began Hampshire's innings with a partnership of 200, and Hayden became the second batsman in the country to reach 1,000 runs.

Whitaker won the toss and asked Nottinghamshire to bat at Grace Road. They took their innings into the second day as Dowman continued his most impressive run of form. The young left-hander made the highest score of his career. He was aided by Oram, who stayed while 48 were added for the last wicket. Another young batsman of immense potential, Maddy, reached his third century of the summer for Leicestershire before being leg before to Tolley. Next ball, Ben Smith was caught down the leg side by wicket-keeper Noon, and Nixon was brilliantly caught at slip by Astle to give Tolley his hat-trick. It was the second hat-trick by a Nottinghamshire bowler in successive matches, and Tolley finished with the best bowling figures of his career. Mullally, Ormond and Millns bowled Leicestershire back into contention, and the home side faced a target of 258 in more than a day. They had an uneasy passage, losing seven wickets for 143. They also lost 28 overs to rain, and in the end they were thankful to Mullally and Ormond, who survived the last 13 balls to earn a draw.

A fascinating game at Lord's saw Kent win in three days. Choosing to bat first, Kent were 24 for 4 as Gus Fraser took 3 for 10 in 19 balls. Fleming responded in typical fashion with 44 of 43 balls, while Alan Wells and Steve Marsh did a more careful repair job. In the evening session,

The leading batsman in the country, 1997, and the first to 1,000 runs, Stephen James of Glamorgan. (David Munden/Sportsline)

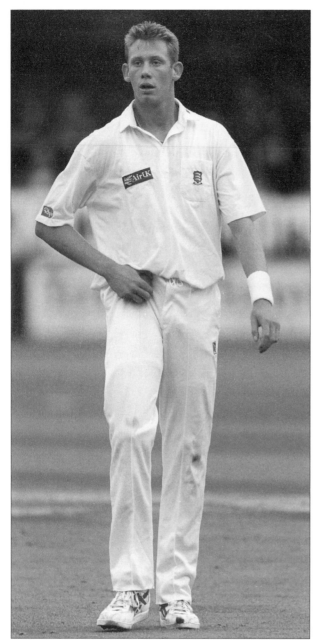

A pace bowler of immense promise, Ashley Cowan of Essex won a place in the England party to tour West Indies. (David Munden/Sportsline)

Middlesex lost nine wickets for 103 runs, six of them to McCague, so that 19 wickets had fallen in the day. The pitch was duly reported. Gatting deputised for Brown behind the stumps when Kent batted a second time and held four catches. Fleming and Marsh were very much involved in another rescue act, and Middlesex had more than two days in which to score 261 to win. Ramprakash opened with Weekes and was unbeaten on 69 at close of play on the second day when his side were 134 for 5. Crucially, Kallis was out at 156 and Brown a run later on the third morning, but Johnson

stood firm and positive with Ramprakash while 57 were added. Fraser also batted well, but when he became Strang's fifth victim Middlesex were still 25 short of their target. Ramprakash had already reached his fourth century of the season, and Tufnell was watchful so that Middlesex lunched 11 short of victory. Four overs after the break, Tufnell was exposed to a full over from Strang. The leg-spinner needed only two deliveries to induce a chance which Ward took inches from the bat. Ramprakash could only look on, having faced 200 balls to carry out his bat for 113.

Darren Bicknell was recalled to the Surrey side and showed his county the error of their ways in having omitted him. He made 162 with 24 fours in a match saturated with runs. Brown had 24 fours and two sixes in his 170. Northamptonshire made 401 and still could not save the follow-on, but they were never in danger of losing.

Only 11 balls were possible on the first day at Edgbaston, and although Warwickshire batted with zest, a draw always looked likely. Giles and Frost shared a ninth wicket stand of 141 after Mushtaq had had a spell of 5 for 3 in 39 balls. Eventually Somerset faced a target of 231 in 47 overs. They crashed to 82 for 6 and were indebted to Parsons and Rose for saving the game.

31 July, 1, 2 and 4 August

at Chester-le-Street
Derbyshire 254 (C.J. Adams 107, S.J.E. Brown 4 for 63) and 176 (M.R. May 64, S.J.E. Brown 5 for 58)
Durham 174 (P.A.J. DeFreitas 5 for 37) and 257 for 4 (J.J.B. Lewis 160 not out, J. Boiling 62)
Durham won by 6 wickets
Durham 20 pts, Derbyshire 6 pts

at Colchester
Essex 533 for 8 dec. (S.G. Law 175, N. Hussain 128, A.P. Grayson 81, R.C. Irani 76)
Leicestershire 515 for 9 dec. (B.F. Smith 131 not out, I.J. Sutcliffe 130, N.C. Johnson 91, D.J. Millns 55, P.M. Such 4 for 94)
Match drawn
Essex 9 pts, Leicestershire 7 pts

at Colwyn Bay
Nottinghamshire 202 (M.P. Dowman 62) and 239 for 8 (C.M. Tolley 73 not out)
Glamorgan 363 for 6 dec. (S.P. James 162)
Match drawn
Glamorgan 11 pts, Nottinghamshire 6 pts

at Edgbaston
Warwickshire 227 (M.A. Wagh 57, M.A. Robinson 4 for 53, V.C. Drakes 4 for 84) and 41 for 1
Sussex 63 (A.A. Donald 4 for 11) and 203 (C.W.J. Athey 67, A.A. Donald 4 for 40)
Warwickshire won by 9 wickets
Warwickshire 21 pts, Sussex 4 pts

at Worcester
Worcestershire 422 (D.A. Leatherdale 129 not out, V. S. Solanki 61, T.M. Moody 60) and 174 for 3 dec. (G.A. Hick 56 retired hurt, D.A. Leatherdale 51)
Kent 276 (M.A. Ealham 56) and 158 for 4 (T.R. Ward 52)
Match drawn
Worcestershire 11 pts, Kent 9 pts

at Leeds
Yorkshire 166 (J.P. Taylor 6 for 45) and 322 (C. White 67, R.J. Blakey 51, R.J. Bailey 4 for 10)
Northamptonshire 286 (K. M. Curran 63, R.J. Bailey 61, C.E.W. Silwerwood 4 for 62) and 176 (C. White 5 for 31)
Yorkshire won by 36 runs
Yorkshire 20 pts, Northamptonshire 6 pts

Chris Adams is a man for lost causes. A brilliant century in the NatWest Trophy had not prevented his side from losing to Sussex, and a hundred before lunch for Derbyshire against Durham was soon to be overshadowed as his side lost in three days. Sixteen wickets fell on the first day; 17 on the second, which ended with Durham, chasing 257 to win, struggling on 46 for 3. Boiling had come in as night-watch-man with the score on 28. When he was caught off Harris, Durham had reached 232. The stand of 204 with Lewis established a new Durham record for the fourth wicket, and Boiling's 62 was his highest championship score. The Man of the Match, however, was Jonathan Lewis, whose move from Essex had seen him prosper mightily. His 160 came off 234 balls and contained 25 fours. It brought Durham their second championship win of the season.

Essex and Leicestershire contested a dire game at Colchester. Essex gave a debut to young off-spinner Jonathan Powell, later to be a surprise selection for the England 'A' tour. Prichard won the toss, and Essex lost both openers for nine before Stuart Law raced to a century on a day severely truncated by rain. He and Hussain put on 317 for the third wicket with Hussain scoring his first century of the season for Essex. Having scored at four runs an over, Essex declared on the second evening and captured the wickets of both Leicestershire openers before the close. That was virtually the end of the entertainment. Sutcliffe scored a good century on the Saturday, but Whitaker declined to accept a target of 225 in 55 overs because he had batsmen who were not fully fit. The visitors batted throughout the Saturday and Monday, and Peter Such established a record for county cricket when he bowled more balls and more six-ball overs than any bowler had managed before. His figures tell the tale: 86 overs, 49 maidens, 94 runs, 4 wickets.

Rain ruined the match at Colwyn Bay, with no play on the first day and only 52 overs bowled on the second. Nottinghamshire's first innings lasted into the third day, and Glamorgan forced the pace with some exciting batting. The country's leading scorer Stephen James led the charge as runs came at more than four an over, but too much time had been lost to bring a result. There were scares for the visitors when they slipped to 74 for 5, but Tolley, having a

fine season, held firm. Glamorgan's 11 points took them to the top of the table.

In contrast, Sussex, beaten in three days by Warwick-shire, were adrift at the bottom without a win to their credit. There was very little play on the first day, although Moles did damage a finger. There was some encouragement for Sussex in the bowling of Alex Edwards of Loughborough University on his championship debut, but the batting offered no comfort.

Kent's championship ambitions suffered a minor set-back when they had the worst of the draw at Worcester. Maneer Mirza, brother of the late Parvaz Mirza, made his championship debut and bowled well, but the rain was the only winner. Only 16 overs were bowled on the first day, and rain returned when Kent went in search of a target of 321 off 80 overs.

There was curtailment at Headingley, but in 51 overs on the first day, Yorkshire were reduced to 163 for 9. Had Taylor been better supported in the field, Northamptonshire would have thrived even more. As it was, they batted unevenly on the second day but still took a first innings lead of 120. This was due mainly to a third wicket stand of 115 between Bailey and Roberts and some positive batting by Curran. Yorkshire fought back strongly. McGrath and Vaughan scored 90 for the first wicket, and White and

Somerset's Simon Ecclestone, an exciting batsman at last given an extended run in the county side. He prospered.
(Graham Chadwick/Allsport)

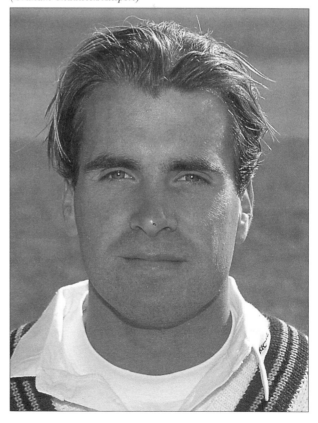

A tower of strength in the Worcestershire attack, Alamgir Sheriyar. (David Munden/Sportsline)

Blakey put on 102 for the sixth. Then the last five wickets fell for 25 runs as Bailey captured 4 for 10 with his occasional off-breaks. Northamptonshire had more than a day in which to score 213, and they ended Saturday on 78 for 1. Gough was unable to bowl through injury, but Yorkshire did not need him. Craig White returned his best bowling figures in the championship, Snape could not bat because of a badly broken thumb, and Northamptonshire lost their last eight wickets for 91.

6, 7, 8 and 9 August
at Canterbury
Kent 525 for 9 dec. (M.V. Fleming 138, A.P. Wells 109, M.A. Ealham 58, P.A. Strang 55, G.R. Cowdrey 53)
Essex 156 (R.C. Irani 50, M.J. McCague 4 for 81) and 361 (P.J. Prichard 224, P.A. Strang 5 for 119)
Kent won by an innings and 8 runs
Kent 24 pts, Essex 2 pts

at Blackpool
Warwickshire 139 (P.J. Martin 6 for 46, I.D. Austin 4 for 45) and 310 (A.F. Giles 72, D.R. Brown 53, D.J. Shadford 5 for 80)
Lancashire 362 (G.D. Loyd 75, I.D. Austin 68, N.H. Fairbrother 60, G. Welch 6 for 115) and 91 for 7 (G. Welch 5 for 25)
Lancashire won by 3 wickets
Lancashire 24 pts, Warwickshire 4 pts

at Lord's
Middlesex 442 for 8 dec. (M.R. Ramprakash 190, O.A. Shah 77) and 178 for 1 dec. (J.H. Kallis 102 not out, M.W. Gatting 69 not out)
Hampshire 306 for 5 dec. (M. Keech 78 not out, G.W. White 62) and 97 (A.R.C. Fraser 5 for 38)
Middlesex won by 217 runs
Middlesex 22 pts, Hampshire 5 pts

at Northampton
Worcestershire 551 (W.P.C. Weston 205, D.A. Leatherdale 110, S.J. Rhodes 55, S.A.J. Boswell 5 for 94) and 272 for 7 dec. (K.R. Spiring 84, G.R. Haynes 50)
Northamptonshire 403 for 5 dec. (R.J. Warren 174 not out, A. Fordham 57) and 319 (R.J. Bailey 115, R.J. Warren 67, K.M. Curran 55, T.M. Moody 5 for 148)
Worcestershire won by 101 runs
Worcestershire 22 pts, Northamptonshire 6 pts

at Taunton
Gloucestershire 350 for 8 dec. (S. Young 83, M.W. Alleyne 70, G.D. Rose 4 for 55) and 178 for 3 dec. (T.H.C. Hancock 100 not out)
Somerset 252 for 5 dec. (M.N. Lathwell 95, P.D. Bowler 73) and 138 for 9 (G.D. Rose 67 not out, M.C.J. Ball 4 for 15, A.M. Smith 4 for 60)
Match drawn
Gloucestershire 9 pts, Somerset 8 pts

at The Oval
Surrey 350 (J.D. Ratcliffe 76, I.J. Ward 56, J. Wood 4 for 73) and 64 for 1
Durham 136 (Saqlain Mushtaq 5 for 17) and 274 (J.E. Morris, M.P. Speight 51, Saqlain Mushtaq 5 for 111)
Surrey won by 9 wickets
Surrey 24 pts, Durham 4 pts

at Eastbourne
Sussex 330 for 6 dec. (N.R. Taylor 122 not out, K. Newell 64, P.W. Jarvis 55) and 0 for 0 dec.
Leicestershire 0 for 0 dec. and 292 (N.C. Johnson 74 not out, B.F. Smith 74, D.L. Maddy 61, P.W. Jarvis 5 for 44)
Sussex won by 38 runs
Sussex 19 pts, Leicestershire 2 pts

9, 10 and 11 August
at Dublin (Malahide)
Ireland 270 for 9 dec. (K. McCallan 65, J. Davy 51 not out, K. Sheridan 4 for 43) and 192 for 5 dec. (J.D.R. Benson 61 not out)
Scotland 189 for 3 dec. (D. Lockhart 77 not out) and 247 for 9 (G. Salmond 89, B.M.W. Patterson 83)
Match drawn

Any hopes that Essex still nourished about winning the championship disappeared at Canterbury where Kent overwhelmed them. Wells scored a century, his first for Kent, on a first day halved by rain. The ball moved appreciably, but the Essex attack was well below strength. The second day saw Matthew Fleming hit a career best 138 off 195 balls. He and Strang put on 92 in 10 overs with Fleming hitting four sixes. McCague scythed into the Essex batting, taking four wickets as they ended the day on 89 for 5. They duly followed on, and Prichard played an heroic captain's innings. A hamstring injury caused the Essex captain to bat with a runner after he had reached 69, but he went on to score 224 from 295 balls, just failing to carry out his bat. Prichard fell to McCague, but Kent's last day star was Paul Strang, totally committed to cricket and the county. Kent won 25 minutes before lunch, and they took a 12-point lead at the top of the table.

After their early season disasters Lancashire continued their recuperation with their fourth win in the championship. They bowled out Warwickshire on the first day at Blackpool and were 55 runs ahead by the close. Peter Martin was once more the cutting force in the Lancashire attack. Austin followed some good bowling with some lusty batting, and Lancashire looked set for an innings victory when the inexperienced Shadford struck to reduce Warwickshire to 98 for 6 in their second innings. Brown and Welch stopped the slide, but it was Giles and Frost who led the counterattack with 107 in 17 overs for the ninth wicket. The partnership was broken when Shadford took an excellent return catch off Frost to claim his first five-wicket haul in first-class cricket. Lancashire appeared to have a simple task but they tottered alarmingly to 67 for 7 before Hegg and Yates restored sanity. Victory came in three days.

Middlesex and Hampshire were hit by rain, but Stephenson's desire to keep the game alive brought a result, although not the one he would have wished for. Ramprakash batted with attractive fluency for Middlesex, who were also encouraged by the batting of Shah, promoted to number five and looking a very good player. Since touring Australia with the England 'A' side little had been heard of him, mainly because of the demands of the examination room. Kallis showed his technical accomplishment and power that will make him the scourge of England and other nations over the next decade, and Hampshire were set a target of 315 in 77 overs. They lasted under 27 as Angus Fraser, 32 the previous day, opened with a spell of 4 for 5 in 10 balls.

Batsmen prospered on a docile pitch at Northampton. Philip Weston hit the first double century of his career and

One of the country's leading wicket-takers and a batsman of considerable ability, adaptable to any situation, Douglas Brown of Warwickshire. (Dave Pinegar/ASP)

Russell Warren batted with patience and sense. There was another century for David Leatherdale, who had reclaimed a regular place in the Worcestershire side and was displaying the form which had drawn so much attention when he had made his debut at the age of 21 nine years previously. The game looked destined to be drawn when Moody set Northamptonshire a target of 421 off 90 overs. Northamptonshire had never reached such heights before, but, with Bailey going strong and the score 290 for 5 with 25 overs remaining, it looked likely that they would make history. A late collapse in which four wickets went down in three overs for one run changed the picture and gave Worcestershire a comfortable win with 13.2 overs unused. Their hero was skipper Tom Moody who, in the absence of a front-line spinner, bowled off-breaks with considerable success.

Gloucestershire lost ground on the leaders with their failure to beat Somerset. There was no play at Taunton on the first day and only 40 overs on the second. Young and Alleyne scored briskly on the third morning, and Young's 83

Somerset wicket-keeper Robert Turner enjoyed a good season behind the stumps and was converted into an opening batsmen with great success. (Steve White/ASP)

occupied only 79 balls. Somerset, too, wasted no time, and the final demand was that they should score 277 from a minimum of 45 overs if they wanted to win. Any hopes of victory ended immediately after tea when they were 38 for 6. Missed chances proved decisive, and Rose batted for two and a half hours, eventually in the company of last man Shine, to save the match. That Gloucestershire were able to set a target was due to Hancock's 100 off 90 balls, and that they came so close to victory owed much to Ball's three wickets in four deliveries.

The loss of half the first day at The Oval caused Surrey few problems and they beat Durham before lunch on the fourth day. The key to their success was the bowling of Saqlain Mushtaq, 10 for 128 in the match and surely with no superior in the world among off-break bowlers. There was also a most impressive debut by left-arm spinner Rupesh Amin who took 3 for 58 in 36 overs in the second innings.

At Eastbourne, Sussex gained their first win of the season and Leicestershire suffered their first defeat. No play was possible on the first two days, and a century from Taylor and some 'friendly' bowling by Leicestershire enabled Sussex to reach 330 on the third. The last day was given over to Leicestershire. They looked well set at one time and entered the last hour as favourites, but Paul Jarvis returned his best figures of the season and Neil Johnson was left stranded as the last four wickets fell for nine runs.

15, 16, 17 and 18 August

at Derby
Derbyshire 411 (P.A.J. DeFreitas 96, K.J. Barnett 86, K.M. Krikken 72, P.J. Martin 4 for 77)
Lancashire 118 (D.E. Malcolm 6 for 23) and 256 (J.P. Crawley 133, D.E. Malcolm 4 for 42, D.G. Cork 4 for 48)
Derbyshire won by an innings and 37 runs
Derbyshire 24 pts, Lancashire 4 pts

at Portsmouth
Yorkshire 501 for 8 dec. (D.S. Lehmann 182, R.J. Blakey 75, M.P. Vaughan 74)
Hampshire 281 (R.A. Smith 110, M.L. Hayden 88, P.M. Hutchison 7 for 50) and 471 for 9 dec. (G.W. White 145, J.P. Stephenson 114, J.S. Laney 81, G.M. Hamilton 5 for 89)
Match drawn
Yorkshire 11 pts, Hampshire 8 pts

at Lord's
Middlesex 205 (M.W. Gatting 54, Saqlain Mushtaq 5 for 50) and 201 (J.C. Pooley 72, Saqlain Mushtaq 5 for 66)
Surrey 531 for 9 dec. (A.J. Hollioake 182, M.A. Butcher 79, B.C. Hollioake 76, A.D. Brown 70)
Surrey won by an innings and 125 runs
Surrey 24 pts, Middlesex 4 pts

at Trent Bridge
Somerset 337 (P.C.L. Holloway 72, M. Burns 72, R.J. Turner 55, A.R. Oram 4 for 53) and 338 for 6 dec. (M.E. Trescothick 81, S.C. Ecclestone 65)
Nottinghamshire 356 (A.A. Metcalfe 79) and 305 for 9 (M.P. Dowman 124, N.J. Astle 60)
Match drawn
Nottinghamshire 11 pts, Somerset 10 pts

at Hove
Gloucestershire 320 (R.I. Dawson 98, M.A. Robinson 5 for 66) and 331 for 7 dec. (T.H.C. Hancock 84, M.W. Alleyne 77, R.C. Russell 69 not out)
Sussex 324 (N.R. Taylor 74, M.T.E. Peirce 73, P. Moores 65, R.P. Davis 4 for 35) and 161 (N.R. Taylor 62, M.T.E. Peirce 54, M.C.J. Ball 5 for 66, R.P. Davis 4 for 35)
Gloucestershire won by 166 runs
Gloucestershire 23 pts, Sussex 7 pts

at Worcester
Worcestershire 476 for 9 dec, (T.S. Curtis 160, G.A. Hick 65) and 295 (W.P.C. Weston 114, R.D.B. Croft 4 for 98)
Glamorgan 398 (M.P. Maynard 161 not out, S.P. James 69) and 319 (S.P. James 130)
Worcestershire won by 54 runs
Worcestershire 24 pts, Glamorgan 6 pts

At the 12th attempt Derbyshire won their first championship match of the season. They destroyed Lancashire in two days with Devon Malcolm giving a fine display of fast bowling in what for him, if not for his county, had been a very good season. He twice dismissed Atherton for 4 and 5, and the England captain had the indignity of being jeered by the Derbyshire crowd. The game had not begun well for the home side, who lost their first three wickets for 46. Barnett and Krikken steadied the innings, and DeFreitas hit 96, his best of the season, off 80 balls to take Derbyshire to a formidable score. Lancashire were bowled out in under 28 overs, followed on, and, in spite of Crawley's century, lost inside two days.

Yorkshire amassed a huge score at Portsmouth with the Australian left-hander Darren Lehmann playing another innings of power and authority. Such had been his form that Yorkshire had made known their intention of re-signing him as their overseas player in 1998 even though Michael Bevan was available. Hampshire lost Laney and White for 15 before Matthew Hayden, another eminently successful Australian, and Robin Smith added 184. The last seven Hampshire wickets went down for 41 runs as Paul Hutchison, who had made his mark against the Pakistan 'A' side, gave a fine display of left-arm medium-pace bowling. Following on, Hampshire lost Hayden and Smith cheaply and a Yorkshire win looked inevitable. Giles White changed matters with a maiden championship century, and John Stephenson hit his first championship hundred for two years to earn an honourable draw.

Surrey crushed Middlesex in three days at Lord's. Adam Hollioake hit his first century of the season, a career-best 182, but the real Surrey hero was once more the Pakistan off-spinner Saqlain Mushtaq. For the second successive match he captured ten wickets and bowled his side to an innings victory. His achievement was enriched by the fact that he claimed a first innings hat-trick when he sent back Brown, Johnson and Hewitt with successive deliveries. Middlesex lost seven wickets for 20 in 13 overs.

At Trent Bridge, Nottinghamshire and Somerset engaged in an enthralling draw. Somerset relied heavily on their later order, and Nottinghamshire were particularly well served by their tail. On the last day, the home county were left to make 320 in 76 overs, and once more Matthew Dowman rose to the occasion. The 23-year old has the virtues of both temperament and ability, and he also marked the 1997 season with consistency. He set a pattern that should have won Nottinghamshire the match with 124 from 188 balls. He was one of four batsmen who were out as 44 runs were scored, and when Metcalfe was caught at mid-off Nottinghamshire needed 42 from seven overs with four wickets standing. Noon marshalled 31 runs from the next 29 balls, but Afzaal and Franks were run out, and Evans was leg before to Caddick for 0 so that Nottinghamshire were suddenly 305 for 9 with seven balls remaining. Noon negotiated the last tense over with customary calm.

Gloucestershire bounded back into title contention with an emphatic win over Sussex. Dawson at last played an innings of which all knew he was capable, but Sussex grittily got their noses in front on the first innings. They ultimately faced a target of 328. They reached 109 for 1, but then the spin of Davis and Ball took over, and with fielders clustered round the bat, nine wickets went down for 52

runs. The win took Gloucestershire ten points clear at the top of the table, but the nearest rivals, Kent and Glamorgan, both had a game in hand.

Glamorgan lost their chance to go top by losing to Worcestershire, who were enjoying a good run. Tim Curtis, on the eve of retirement, hit 160 on the opening day, and the Worcestershire tail wagged strongly to seize the initiative. Glamorgan responded dynamically, scoring at six an over. James hit 69 off 76 balls, but it was Maynard who stole the show with a glittering display. The final session of 32 overs brought 212 runs as Maynard gave a reminder of an immense talent that has never been able to translate itself to the international stage. Weston's second century in successive matches left Glamorgan with the daunting task of scoring 374 in 81 overs. James gave them a bright start with his fifth championship hundred of the summer, but the loss of Maynard first ball was a terrible blow. To their credit, perhaps unwisely, Glamorgan maintained the chase to the very end, but the brave death meant sacrificing the three points that they might have earned for a draw.

20, 21, 22 and 23 August

at Chester-le-Street
Durham 343 (D.C. Boon 110, M.J. Foster 70, J.H. Kallis 4 for 98) and 78 for 0
Middlesex 251 (D.C. Nash 94, M.J. Foster 4 for 58)
Match drawn
Durhan 10 pts, Middlesex 9 pts

at Abergavenny
Northamptonshire 330 (K.M. Curran 159, Waqar Younis 4 for 78) and 219 (D.J.G. Sales 103, D. Ripley 58, Waqar Younis 6 for 56)
Glamorgan 354 for 6 dec. (S.P. James 103, A. Dale 71, M.P. Maynard 58) and 197 for 4 (S.P. James 113)
Glamorgan won by 6 wickets
Glamorgan 24 pts, Northamptonshire 5 pts

at Leicester
Leicestershire 486 (V.J. Wells 190, G.J. Parsons 69 not out, J.J. Whitaker 61, P.A.J. DeFreitas 5 for 120) and 281 for 2 dec. (V.J. Wells 93, D.L. Maddy 66, I.J. Sutcliffe 59 not out, B.F. Smith 55 not out)
Derbyshire 366 for 2 dec. (A.S. Rollins 171 not out, K.J. Barnett 147 not out) and 238 (M.R. May 88, A.R.K. Pierson 6 for 56)
Leicestershire won by 163 runs
Leicestershire 20 pts, Derbyshire 8 pts

at Worksop
Essex 440 for 7 dec. (S.G. Law 115, D.R. Law 59) and 183 for 7 dec.
Nottinghamshire 351 for 3 dec. (R.T. Robinson 143 not out, N.J. Astle 100)
Match drawn
Nottinghamshire 9 pts, Essex 8 pts

at Taunton
Somerset 375 (R.J. Turner 144, S.C. Eccleston 123,
B.J. Phillips 5 for 86) and 234 (S.C. Eccleston 94,
P.A. Strang 6 for 72)
Kent 449 (M.A. Ealham 106, G.R. Cowdrey 101,
E.T. Smith 56, M.V. Fleming 53, Mushtaq Ahmed 4 for 114)
and 160 for 6 (A.P. Wells 57)
Match drawn
Kent 16 pts, Somerset 11 pts

at Edgbaston
Warwickshire 252 (M.M. Mirza 4 for 51) and 341 for 5
(N.V. Knight 116 not out)
Worcestershire 448 (G.A. Hick 122, R.K. Illingworth 112,
T.M. Moody 108, D.R. Brown 5 for 118)
Match drawn
Worcestershire 10 pts, Warwickshire 7 pts

at Scarborough
Sussex 157 (M. Newell 62 not out, N.R. Taylor 57,
P.M. Hutchison 5 for 48, C.E.W. Silverwood 4 for 27) and
137 (P.W. Jarvis 51, C.E.W. Silverwood 5 for 59)
Yorkshire 282 (D.S. Lehmann 67, M.A. Robinson 4 for 61,
P.W. Jarvis 4 for 82) and 13 for 1
Yorkshire won by 9 wickets
Yorkshire 22 pts, Sussex 4 pts

Durham had the better of the draw with Middlesex but rain allowed only nine overs on the last day. The all-round cricket of Foster and the continued positive leadership of Boon gave Durham cause for satisfaction, while the Middlesex decision to include reserve wicket-keeper David Nash and play him as a batsman paid handsome dividends. In his first championship innings, he scored 94 off 180 balls at a time when his side were in decay at 133 for 7.

Glamorgan's fine win over Northamptonshire at Abergavenny took them two points ahead of Kent at the top of the table. Northamptonshire batted into the second day as Kevin Curran made the highest score of his career. On a dull second day, Stephen James shone through the gloom with his sixth championship century of his wonderful season. He and Dale put on 116 for the second wicket. There was a splendid urgency in the Glamorgan batting with Powell and Maynard, 58 in 64 balls, claiming the fourth batting point at four runs an over. When Northamptonshire batted a second time they lost five wickets for 61 before Sales and Ripley added 131. Maynard had injured a finger, and acting captain Waqar Younis ensured that Glamorgan would not face too stiff a target when he completed a ten-wicket haul for the match. His efforts were complemented by James, who hit his second century of the match on this beautiful ground as Glamorgan won with 21 overs to spare.

The trials and tribulations of Derbyshire continued unabated. Dropped by Cork off his own bowling, Vince Wells batted more than six hours for his 190, and Gordon Parsons thumped a rousing fifty on the second morning to take Leicestershire to a formidable score. Derbyshire responded encouragingly with Rollins and Barnett sharing an unbroken partnership of 316, a Derbyshire record for any wicket against Leicestershire, after two wickets had gone for 50. The bat had dominated for three days, and the four Leicestershire batsmen who got to the crease in the second innings all scored fifties, so that Whitaker's demand that Derbyshire score in excess of 400 if they wanted to win did not seem unreasonable. They reached 161 for 1, and then lost nine wickets for 77 runs in 20 overs as Pierson's off-spin, beautifully and intelligently delivered, transformed the game.

A Stuart Law century on the opening day, and a second wicket stand for Nottinghamshire of 193 between Robinson and Astle could not save the game at Worksop from a draw. Rain captured the best part of two days.

There was a thrilling finish at Taunton where Kent strove to maintain their title challenge. The game began sensationally when McCague was ordered out of the attack in his third over for an excessive use of the bouncer and a beamer. Umpire Whitehead had no option under Law 42. Wicket-keeper Turner, used as an opener, hit 20 fours in his career-best score, and Simon Eccleston, leading Somerset in the absence of Bowler and Harden, made his maiden first-class hundred. Kent stumbled to 121 for 4 before Cowdrey and Ealham added 185. Cowdrey reached his first hundred of the season while Ealham, only one century to his credit before 1997, made his third championship hundred of the season. When Somerset batted a second time Simon Eccleston, whose knee problem has hampered his career, gave another fluent exhibition with 94 off 149 balls. His approach was the reason for Kent facing a target of 161 in 26 overs. Trevor Ward and Ed Smith put on 50 for the first wicket, but the asking rate increased. Wells hit two sixes and Cowdrey another to lift spirits, and 16 were needed from the last two overs. Wells, 57 off 43 balls, was out, and seven runs were needed off the last over. Four singles were scored, but Fleming was caught behind off Burns's fifth ball. Marsh could manage only two from the last, and the match was drawn with Kent gaining five points for being the side batting second in a game where the scores finished level.

Mirza and Sheriyar bowled out Warwickshire on the opening day at Edgbaston, and Worcestershire took total command when night-watchman Richard Illingworth, returned to the side after a long injury, made the fourth century of his career and shared a third wicket stand of 239 with Hick. Moody became the third centurion of the innings, but time was lost to rain. Knight, appointed captain of Warwickshire in championship matches for the rest of the season – Smith was to lead in the one-day competitions – steered his side to safety on a last day shortened by rain.

Routed in 51.2 overs on the opening day, Sussex succumbed to the youthful power of Silverwood and Hutchison and were beaten in three days. Silverwood had match figures of 9 for 86, and Hutchison, his amazing run of success continuing, had 7 for 92.

27, 28, 29 and 30 August

at Derby
Derbyshire 323 (M.E. Cassar 78, P.A.J. DeFreitas 58, S.J. Lacey 50, A.R. Caddick 4 for 96) and 97 for 2 (D.G. Cork 55 not out)
Somerset 251 for 5 dec. (M.E. Trescothick 83 not out, M. Burns 50)
Match drawn
Somerset 9 pts, Derbyshire 8 pts

at Chelmsford
Essex 178 (S.G. Law 54, A.A. Donald 5 for 50) and 101
Warwickshire 237 (T.L. Penney 77 not out, P.M. Such 6 for 94) and 43 for 2
Warwickshire won by 8 wickets
Warwickshire 23 pts, Essex 4 pts

at Bristol
Nottinghamshire 294 (W.M. Noon 60, R.T. Robinson 56, M.P. Dowman 52, A.M. Smith 6 for 83) and 228 for 5 dec. (P. Johnson 96 not out, C.M. Tolley 52 not out)
Gloucestershire 262 (M.W. Alleyne 71, S. Young 56, N.J. Astle 5 for 46) and 239 (T.H.C. Hancock 68, N.J. Astle 4 for 40)
Nottinghamshire won by 21 runs
Nottinghamshire 22 pts, Gloucestershire 6 pts

at Portsmouth
Hampshire 406 (S.D. Udal 91, J.P. Stephenson 76, B.J. Phillips 4 for 64, D.W. Headley 4 for 105)
Kent 350 for 8 dec. (E.T. Smith 102, D.P. Fulton 75, T.R. Ward 66, S.J. Renshaw 4 for 61)
Match drawn
Kent 10 pts, Hampshire 9 pts

at Old Trafford
Yorkshire 419 for 9 dec. (M.P. Vaughan 105, D. Byas 61, C.E.W. Silverwood 58, C. White 52) and 176 for 5 (A. McGrath 76)
Lancashire 277 for 8 dec. (W.K. Hegg 50 not out)
Match drawn
Yorkshire 10 pts, Lancashire 9 pts

at Leicester
Glamorgan 226 (A. Dale 69) and 67 for 3
Leicestershire 175 (J.J. Whitaker 62, S.L. Watkin 7 for 41)
Match drawn
Glamorgan 8 pts, Leicestershire 7 pts

at Northampton
Northamptonshire 144 (M.M. Betts 9 for 64) and 309 for 9 dec. (A. Fordham 83, R.R. Montgomerie 73, M.M. Betts 4 for 79)
Durham 376 (D.C. Boon 117, S. Hutton 95, Mohammad Akram 5 for 100)
Match drawn
Durham 11 pts, Northamptonshire 6 pts

The best bowling performance of his career and for the season by Melvyn Betts, Durham v. Northamptonshire, Northampton, 27–30 August. (David Munden/Sportsline)

at Kidderminster
Middlesex 252 (A. Sheriyar 5 for 55) and 317 for 1 dec. (J.H. Kallis 172 not out, M.R. Ramprakash 123 not out)
Worcestershire 251 for 5 dec. (D.A. Leatherdale 88 not out, S.J. Rhodes 59 not out) and 149 (W.P.C. Weston 74)
Middlesex won by 169 runs
Middlesex 20 pts, Worcestershire 6 pts

28, 29, 30 and 31 August
at Hove

Sussex 137 (C.C. Lewis 5 for 42) and 162 (I.D.K. Salisbury 5 for 66)

Surrey 400 for 7 dec. (G.P. Thorpe 106 not out, A.J. Hollioake 87, M.A. Butcher 61, A.D. Edwards 4 for 94)

Surrey won by an innings and 101 runs
Surrey 24 pts, Sussex 3 pts

As the championship moved into its vital final fortnight the rain wreaked havoc with the fixture list. There was little play at Derby on the first day and none at all on the fourth. Sadly, Rollins suffered a damaged knee which ended his season. The fine that had been imposed on Barnett was lifted, but the departure of Adams became increasingly likely when he did not figure in the Derbyshire side.

There was only time for 35 overs on the first day at Chelmsford, but Warwickshire still managed to beat Essex on the third day. The home side were shattered by Donald and when they seemed to be clawing their way back into the game, first Penney and Piper, and then Giles and Donald staged a rearguard action. In their second innings, Essex lost their first three wickets for one run, and the end was not long in coming.

Playing his last game for Nottinghamshire before joining the New Zealand side, Nathan Astle returned the best bowling figures of his career and severely blighted Gloucestershire's championship chances. The Nottinghamshire innings on the first day was a strange affair. Dowman and Robinson scored 101 for the first wicket, but the middle order collapsed, and it was left to Noon and Bowen to revitalise the innings. Mike Smith produced another top-class bowling performance. Gloucestershire kept in touch through a fifth wicket stand of 95 between Young and Alleyne, but Johnson and Tolley set a fair challenge with an unbroken sixth wicket partnership of 136. Johnson unselfishly denied himself a century in order to ask Gloucestershire to make 261 runs in 60 overs. Windows and Hancock scored 73 in 22 overs for the first wicket, and Russell and Alleyne made 67 for the fifth wicket, but Astle took four wickets in 18 balls to win the game for Nottinghamshire and to leave Gloucestershire as Cinderella for yet another season.

Kent's aspirations suffered dreadfully from the weather, but Smith and Fulton made 170 for their first wicket with Ed Smith getting his first hundred for the county. Kent took maximum batting points on the last day and Renshaw bowled well for Hampshire as six wickets went down for 41 runs in mid-innings.

There was no play on the last day at Old Trafford, nor at Leicester where there had also been a barren first day. Glamorgan lodged a complaint that the square at Grace Road had not been covered on the third evening.

Only five overs were possible on the first day at Northampton. On the second Mel Betts became the first bowler during the season to take nine wickets in an innings

Graeme Hick, 303 not out for Worcestershire in the last game of the season. He shared a third wicket stand of 438 with Tom Moody, a record for the championship. (David Munden/Sportsline)

and the first Durham bowler to take nine wickets in an innings since the county attained first-class status. Betts has a reputation for being an erratic bowler, but he has matured in control, pace and movement, and his advance contributed much to Durham's improved performances. The improvement owed much, too, to David Boon, who hit his second successive championship century. Northamptonshire batted out the last day of the rain-ruined match.

Rain also restricted play at Kidderminster, where Moody kept the game alive with a first innings declaration. When Middlesex batted a second time Pooley fell for 0, but Kallis and Ramprakash then added 317 at more than four runs an over, although some of the bowling was ultimately of a friendly variety. In contrast to the Middlesex innings, Worcestershire's run chase never got started. They tumbled to Hewitt, Fraser and Kallis, a thrilling all-round cricketer, and Middlesex's faint hopes of winning the title were kept alive.

Rain reduced the game at Hove, but Surrey managed to beat Sussex in what amounted to little more than two days. Having bowled out Sussex for 137, Surrey raced to 400 in 75 overs with Thorpe hitting 106 off 138 balls. Sussex were soon in trouble again at 90 for 7, and the game was over inside three hours on the Saturday.

2, 3, 4 and 5 September
at Derby
Derbyshire 192 and 189 (D.G. Cork 53, M.K. Davies 5 for 46)
Northamptonshire 334 (K.M. Curran 86, A. Fordham 72, D.E. Malcolm 4 for 82) and 51 for 1
Northamptonshire won by 9 wickets
Northamptonshire 23 pts, Derbyshire 4 pts

at Chester-le-Street
Warwickshire 412 (M.A. Wagh 124, N.V. Knight 92, S.J.E. Brown 4 for 135)
Durham 118 and 195 (D.C. Boon 81, D.R. Brown 4 for 39)
Warwickshire won by an innings and 99 runs
Warwickshire 23 pts, Durham 3 pts

at Canterbury
Kent 305 (A.P. Wells 77) and 432 for 4 dec. (T.R. Ward 161 not out, A.P. Wells 94, M.J. Walker 51)
Gloucestershire 256 (R.I. Dawson 110, R.C. Russell 55, B.J. Phillips 4 for 44) and 209 (M.G.N. Windows 84, D.W. Headley 5 for 92)
Kent won by 272 runs
Kent 23 pts, Gloucestershire 6 pts

at Old Trafford
Essex 389 (S.G. Law 155, R.J. Rollins 60 not out, G. Keedy 4 for 98) and 0 for 0 dec.
Lancashire 39 for 0 dec. and 324 (M.A. Atherton 56, W.K. Hegg 55, R.J. Green 51, I.D. Austin 50, P.M. Such 4 for 103, A.P. Grayson 4 for 143)
Essex won by 26 runs
Essex 20 pts, Lancashire 4 pts

at Trent Bridge
Nottinghamshire 291 (M.P. Dowman 74, J.P. Stephenson 6 for 54) and 253 for 4 dec. (P. Johnson 93 not out, M.P. Dowman 62)
Hampshire 260 for 6 dec. (M.L. Hayden 74, J.S. Laney 59, S.D. Udal 54 not out) and 114 for 2
Match drawn
Hampshire 9 pts, Nottinghamshire 7 pts

at Taunton
Somerset 241 (R.J. Turner 71, G.D. Rose 56 not out, P.C.R. Tufnell 4 for 53) and 295 for 8 dec. (M.E. Trescothick 65)
Middlesex 236 (J.H. Kallis 100, Mushtaq Ahmed 5 for 66, A.R. Caddick 4 for 71) and 187 for 5 (J.H. Kallis 52, Mushtaq Ahmed 4 for 71)
Match drawn
Somerset 8 pts, Middlesex 8 pts

at The Oval
Surrey 204 (A.D. Brown 60) and 487 (G.P. Thorpe 222, A.J. Hollioake 65, M.P. Bicknell 53)
Glamorgan 438 (M.P. Maynard 76, S.D. Thomas 75 not out, A. Dale 72, R.D.B. Croft 53) and 107 for 3
Match drawn
Glamorgan 11 pts, Surrey 8 pts

at Leeds
Yorkshire 501 for 7 dec. (C. White 172 not out, A. McGrath 141, D. Byas 53, D.S. Lehmann 51) and 83 for 4 dec.
Worcestershire 313 for 6 dec. (G.R. Haynes 62, G.A. Hick 57) and 205 (T.M. Moody 67)
Yorkshire won by 66 runs
Yorkshire 22 pts, Worcestershire 5 pts

For Derbyshire misery on the field and off the field. They were totally outplayed by lowly Northamptonshire, whose victory was achieved in spite of the loss of a day to rain. The most encouraging aspect of the victory for Northamptonshire was the performance of the slow left-arm bowler Michael Davies, 21 years old and in his first season. Given an extended run in the side, he bowled consistently well and claimed his first five-wicket haul.

David Boon must have regretted putting Warwickshire in when he won the toss, for Wagh, who made a maiden championship century, and Knight put on 206 for the first wicket. Durham struggled from that point on and suffered an innings defeat early on the fourth day.

Gloucestershire's title hopes were brought to an end at Canterbury where they were heavily beaten by Kent, who took over at the top of the table. Gloucestershire began well enough, capturing Kent's first three wickets for 51, but Wells, hitting the ball crisply and often, and Walker added 117. The visitors could still take satisfaction from the opening day, but their batting failed miserably on the second. Phillips and Ealham reduced them to 61 for 5 before Dawson and Russell stopped the rot with a stand of 116. Ball also hit well, but the main honours went to Dawson, who has never quite fulfilled his promise and had only recently won back a place in the Gloucestershire side. Kent now batted Gloucestershire out of the match with some sumptuous stroke-play, Ward and Wells sharing a highly entertaining stand of 193. Gloucestershire lost four wickets on the Friday evening, and only Windows and Alleyne offered serious resistance to the bowling of Headley and Strang.

Rain brought forfeiture and declaration at Old Trafford. Stuart Law played another of his magnificent innings on the first day, 155 off 131 balls made out of 199 while he was at the wicket. There was no play on the second day, and Lancashire were allowed ample time in which to score 351 to win. They were 213 for 6 on the Thursday, and Grayson, Such and Cowan completed the Essex victory on the Friday after stern resistance from Hegg and Green.

Paul Johnson again unselfishly denied himself a century when he declared against Hampshire, but the rain

Chris Silverwood dented Kent's championship hopes with a career-best bowling performance for Yorkshire, at Headingley, 10–13 September. (David Munden/Sportsline)

thwarted both sides, but Nottinghamshire were well clear of the wooden spoon to which they had come perilously close in 1996. Youngsters like Dowman, Franks and Oram had boosted the side.

There was little play on the second day at Taunton where Middlesex were indebted to Kallis for bringing them close to parity with Somerset. The wiles of Mushtaq bemused most of his colleagues.

Glamorgan lost ground at the top and went into the last two matches 12 points behind Kent. Initially, all had gone well at The Oval for the Welsh county. They bowled out Surrey for 204 and consistent batting took them to a commanding lead on a shortened second day. Darren Thomas's career best unbeaten 75 emphasised their superiority. When Surrey batted a second time they lost their first four wickets for 95. Thorpe and Adam Hollioake added 120, but still the edge was with Glamorgan until Martin Bicknell joined Thorpe. In a frustrating eighth wicket stand, the pair added 110 and occupied valuable time. Thorpe finished with 222, the highest score of his career, and Glamorgan faced a target of 254 at five and a half an over. They started to chase the target, sending in both Shaw and Croft in an attempt to clout early runs, but, surprisingly,

they called off the race. Maynard feared defeat and settled for three points the draw would bring. It seemed faint-hearted, but Glamorgan argued that they had lost points against Worcestershire by chasing a target beyond the moment of reality. Title aspirants like Kent owed Thorpe a debt of gratitude.

A resounding victory over Worcestershire kept alive Yorkshire's faint hope of taking the title. They were 18 points behind Kent and six behind Glamorgan. McGrath, who made a career-best 141, Byas and Lehmann laid the foundation, and Craig White launched a pulsating attack on the bowling to make 172 off 167 balls. He hit seven sixes and 20 fours. It seemed that Yorkshire had no interest in making Worcestershire follow on, but Byas's tactics proved correct. He asked the visitors to make 272 in 71 overs. Hutchison and Silverwood made immediate inroads into the Worcestershire batting, and it was only Moody's 67 off 94 balls that gave any hope. When he was well caught by Stemp to give Hutchison his third wicket there could be but one winner.

10, 11, 12 and 13 September
at Chester-le-Street
Durham 230 (J.E. Morris 79) and 135 (J.J.B. Lewis 50, A.R. Caddick 4 for 60)
Somerset 217 (M.N. Lathwell 57) and 152 for 2 (S.C. Ecclestone 54 not out)
Somerset won by 8 wickets
Somerset 21 pts, Durham 5 pts

at Cardiff
Glamorgan 361 (H. Morris 82, M.P. Maynard 71, D.R. Law 4 for 69) and 150 for 3 (M.P. Maynard 75 not out)
Essex 169 (S.G. Law 85) and 340 (A.P. Grayson 98 not out, N. Hussain 53, P.J. Prichard 51, R.C. Irani 50, S.L. Watkin 5 for 68)
Glamorgan won by 7 wickets
Glamorgan 24 pts, Essex 4 pts

at Southampton
Sussex 114 (S.D. Udal 4 for 17, S.M. Milburn 4 for 38) and 390 (M.T.E. Peirce 104, J.R. Carpenter 63, N.R. Taylor 52, A.A. Khan 52)
Hampshire 245 (G.W. White 80, P.R. Whitaker 73, R.J. Kirtley 4 for 41, A.A. Khan 4 for 79) and 260 for 3 (J.S. Laney 76, G.W. White 75 not out)
Hampshire won by 7 wickets
Hampshire 21 pts, Sussex 4 pts

at Lord's
Middlesex 430 for 8 dec. (O.A. Shah 104 not out, J.C. Pooley 98, M.R. Ramprakash 55) and 12 for 0
Nottinghamshire 210 (P.C.R. Tufnell 5 for 61, J.H. Kallis 4 for 38) and 228
Middlesex won by 10 wickets
Middlesex 23 pts, Nottinghamshire 3 pts

Promise fulfilled, a maiden first-class century for Owais Shah, Middlesex against Nottinghamshire, Lord's, 10–13 September. (Paul Sturgess/Sportsline)

Future hope, a light in a dark season for Sussex, a maiden first-class century for Toby Peirce v. Hampshire, 12 September. (John Gichigi/Allsport)

at Northampton
Northamptonshire 332 (D. Ripley 92, A. L. Penberthy 65, J. Ormond 6 for 68) and 278 for 9 (D. Ripley 83 not out, R.R. Montgomerie 56)
Leicestershire 557 (J.M. Dakin 190, D.J. Millns 121, I. J. Sutcliffe 61, M. K. Davies 4 for 118)
Match drawn
Leicestershire 11 pts, Northamptonshire 9 pts

at The Oval
Lancashire 592 for 4 dec. (N.T. Wood 155, M.A. Atherton 149, N.H. Fairbrother 112 not out, G.D. Lloyd 65 not out, J.P. Crawley 64)
Surrey 270 (D.J. Bicknell 74, A.J. Stewart 73, G. Keedy 4 for 94) and 267 (J.D. Ratcliffe 90, M.A. Butcher 52, G. Keedy 6 for 79)
Lancashire won by an innings and 55 runs
Lancashire 24 pts, Surrey 3 pts

at Edgbaston
Warwickshire 418 (N.M.K. Smith 148, D.R. Brown 79, N.V. Knight 71, D.L. Hemp 66, J.J. Lewis 6 for 89, A.M. Smith 4 for 70)
Gloucestershire 113 (N.M.K. Smith 4 for 32) and 224 (R.C. Russell 67, A.A. Donald 4 for 63)
Warwickshire won by an innings and 81 runs
Warwickshire 24 pts, Gloucestershire 4 pts

at Worcester
Worcestershire 554 for 8 dec. (W.P.C. Weston 188, T.M. Moody 101, D.A. Leatherdale 93) and 72 for 0 (K.R. Spiring 50 not out)
Derbyshire 223 (M.E. Cassar 76 not out) and 402 (K.J. Barnett 86, T.W. Tweats 83, E.M. Krikken 65, G.A. Hick 4 for 70, A. Sheriyar 4 for 84)
Worcestershire won by 10 wickets
Worcestershire 24 pts, Derbyshire 2 pts

Pillars of strength in a determined and highly talented Glamorgan side, skipper Matthew Maynard... (David Pinegar/ASP)

at Leeds
Yorkshire 312 (D.S. Lehmann 87, D. Byas 59, D. Gough 58, M.A. Ealham 4 for 62, A.P. Igglesden 4 for 67) and 301 (D. Byas 74, D.S. Lehmann 68, M.A. Ealham 4 for 47)
Kent 374 (S.A. Marsh 84, T.R. Ward 56, M.V. Fleming 53, C.E.W. Silverwood 7 for 93) and 147 for 5 (M.V. Fleming 50 not out, C.E.W. Silverwood 5 for 55)
Match drawn
Kent 11 pts, Yorkshire 10 pts

The penultimate round of matches in the Britannic Assurance County Championship left the cricket world in suspense. By beating Essex and taking maximum points, Glamorgan moved to the top of the table just one point ahead of Kent, who were held to a draw at Headingley. Glamorgan won the toss, and, in spite of a rare failure by James, they batted solidly enough to

take four batting points. A second wicket stand of 138 in two hours between Morris and Dale gave the innings a firm foundation, and a fourth wicket stand of 127 between Maynard and Cottey, captain and vice-captain, gave a necessary impetus on a slow pitch. In 15 overs on the second morning, the tail, Thomas and Waqar Younis in particular, scored an invaluable 64. When Essex batted Waqar quickly accounted for Prichard and Hussain, and Stuart Law stood alone as the spirited Glamorgan attack ripped through his colleagues. By the end of the second day, Essex were 59 for 1 in the second innings. Hussain and Prichard added 102 as Essex showed more resilience on the third day, shortened by bad light, and there was an innings of character from Grayson. He was well supported by Hyam and Cowan, but resistance was finally broken on the fourth morning with Grayson left unbeaten but two short of a century he richly deserved. Glamorgan needed 149 to win and had ample time in which to get the runs, but they displayed worrying signs of nerves. Morris flashed wildly and was caught behind off Cowan, who also bowled James. Dale fell to Such, and the score was 24 for 3. Maynard asserted himself immediately. Cottey was as busy as ever, and victory was achieved without any more fuss. The promised land was in sight. Now it needed nerve and continued good form.

Kent faced a stiffer task at Headingley, for Yorkshire were not devoid of title ambitions themselves. Runs flowed quickly, but Yorkshire suffered a middle-order collapse and slipped to 137 for 6. Lehmann then found an admirable partner in Gough, returning to the side after injury. Three wickets had fallen in seven balls, but Lehmann and Gough added 117 in 19 overs. Silverwood also made useful runs, but Yorkshire were once more indebted to Lehmann who batted quite brilliantly. As the season moved to its close we had the sobering thought that neither he nor Stuart Law could get into the Australian side. Kent lost Smith, but finished the first day on 79 for 1. They, too, suffered their mid-innings crisis. When Cowdrey fell to Silverwood's first ball after lunch Kent were 202 for 7, and four wickets had gone down for nine runs. Now Marsh joined Fleming and, with the authority of a captain, restored order where there had been panic. They added 83 before Fleming edged Silverwood to slip. Paul Strang, an astonishing luxury at number ten, helped Marsh to see the score past the third and fourth batting points and remained unbeaten on 29 with Kent in command, particularly as Gough had been forced to retire from the attack with a leg injury. Rain reduced the third day, but McGrath and Vaughan gave Yorkshire a brisk start. Byas and Lehmann then wrested the advantage for Yorkshire with a third wicket partnership of 115 before Ealham struck back with four wickets. Yorkshire were out on the last morning, and Kent faced a target of 240 from 89 overs although nine of these were lost to rain after tea. Silverwood had produced the best bowling figures of his career in the first innings, and he now gave another fine display of fast bowling to claim ten wickets in a match for the first time. He left the Kent innings in ruins at 48 for 5, and Yorkshire sensed victory. Ealham and Fleming, abandoning their usual aggressive approaches, dug in to save the match.

... and bowler Steve Watkin. (David Munden/Sportsline)

Kent scored at less than two runs an over, but Yorkshire failed to press as they should have done, and the match was drawn. Kent's hopes lived on.

Other games had less significance. Durham led on the first innings but lost easily in three days to Somerset.

Sussex fought back bravely against Hampshire, but they still suffered their tenth defeat of the season. They trailed by 131 on the first innings, but showed commendable spirit when they batted a second time. Toby Peirce hit a maiden first-class century, batting for nearly six and a half hours, and James Carpenter and Amer Khan both made career-best scores. Hampshire had more than a day in which to make 260 to win, and, even without Robin Smith who needed an operation on his injured finger, they were comfortably equal to the task.

Lord's also witnessed a maiden first-class century. Owais Shah batted for five hours and hit a six and 13 fours in his unbeaten 104 and confirmed that he has an admirable temperament to accompany his undoubted ability. Middlesex went on to beat Nottinghamshire with ease.

Once again the pitch at Northampton proved a paradise for batsmen, although the home county lost their first five wickets for 105 on the opening day. They were saved by Penberthy and Ripley, whose batting advanced greatly in 1997. The pair added 155. They were overshadowed by Leicestershire's Dakin and Millns, both of whom made the highest scores of their careers in sharing a seventh wicket stand of 205. We have described Dakin elsewhere as an under-used cricketer, and he confirmed that standing with his second century in a season which had seen him play in only three first-class matches. Leicestershire looked set for victory before Bailey, batting with a broken finger at

number eleven, stayed with Ripley for the last 20 overs to save the match.

Lancashire totally demolished Surrey at The Oval. Wood, who made the first century of his career, and Atherton put on 259 for the first wicket. Fairbrother, the third centurion of the innings, and Lloyd shared an unbroken stand of 133 for the fifth wicket. Runs came at four and a half an over. Ben Hollioake was severely savaged, and brother Adam appeared to lose the reins of captaincy and self-control. The match was over in three days with left-arm spinner Gary Keedy producing best bowling performances for innings and match.

Warwickshire beat Gloucestershire in three days in spite of some fine bowling by Lewis and Smith. Neil Smith hit his first hundred of the summer and took his side into third place. Warwickshire were finishing strongly, but Gloucestershire's season, which had promised so much, was ending in smoke. It had been announced that Walsh would return as overseas player, a surprise in that Young had done well, was very popular, an all-rounder and eight years younger than Walsh. One wondered, too, if selection of more experienced players like Lynch might not have served Gloucestershire better in the closing weeks of the season.

Derbyshire's dreadful plight continued with a heavy defeat at Worcester. They fought back bravely, but the club seemed sick at heart. It was announced that Adams, their best batsman, would be leaving, that DeFreitas was not being considered as captain and that Cork would lead the side in 1997.

18, 19, 20 and 21 September

at Derby
Yorkshire 267 (R.J. Blakey 76, D. Byas 56, P.A.J. DeFreitas 4 for 74) and 267 (B. Parker 73, P.A.J. DeFreitas 6 for 98)
Derbyshire 473 for 3 dec. (K.J. Barnett 210 not out, T.A. Tweats 189) and 64 for 1
Derbyshire won by 9 wickets
Derbyshire 24 pts, Yorkshire 3 pts

at Chelmsford
Essex 271 (A.P. Cowan 77, S.G. Law 63, T.F. Bloomfield 5 for 77) and 301 for 8 dec. (D.D.J. Robinson 134, N. Hussain 104, J.P. Hewitt 4 for 31)
Middlesex 306 (D.C. Nash 100, J.P. Hewitt 75, M.C. Ilott 4 for 63) and 139 for 5 (O.A. Shah 54 not out)
Match drawn
Middlesex 10 pts, Essex 9 pts

at Bristol
Gloucestershire 262 (S. Young 100, I.D. Austin 4 for 44) and 228 for 8 dec. (M.W. Alleyne 82 not out)
Lancashire 203 (M.A. Atherton 69, N.H. Fairbrother 61, J.J. Lewis 5 for 55) and 245 for 9 (J.P. Crawley 78, I.D. Austin 53)
Match drawn
Gloucestershire 9 pts, Lancashire 8 pts

at Southampton
Worcestershire 538 for 2 dec. (G.A. Hick 303 not out,
T.M. Moody 180 not out) and 88 for 1
Hampshire 312 (S.D. Udal 66, G.W. White 62,
R.K. Illingworth 7 for 79) and 313 (M.L. Hayden 77)
Worcestershire won by 9 wickets
Worcestershire 24 pts, Hampshire 3 pts

at Canterbury
Surrey 124 (J.B.D. Thompson 4 for 33) and 371
(A.J. Stewart 170, D.J. Bicknell 130)
Kent 220 (M.A. Ealham 52, B.C. Hollioake 4 for 54) and
276 for 5 (D.P. Fulton 110)
Kent won by 5 wickets
Kent 21 pts, Surrey 4 pts

at Leicester
Leicestershire 241 (J.J. Whitaker 93, S.J.E. Brown 5 for 67,
M.M. Betts 4 for 68) and 219 (A.R.K. Pierson 59,
S.J.E. Brown 5 for 74)
Durham 133 (D.J. Millns 4 for 49) and 310 (D.C. Boon 93,
J.E. Morris 84, D.J. Millns 6 for 81)
Leicestershire won by 17 runs
Leicestershire 21 pts, Durham 4 pts

at Taunton
Somerset 252 (P.D. Bowler 63, M.N. Lathwell 62,
Waqar Younis 4 for 41) and 285 (G.D. Rose 67,
A.R. Caddick 56 not out, S.D. Thomas 5 for 38)
Glamorgan 527 (H. Morris 165, M.P. Maynard 142,
R.D.B. Croft 86, A.D. Shaw 53 not out, A.R. Caddick
4 for 132) and 11 for 0
Glamorgan won by 10 wickets
Glamorgan 24 pts, Somerset 6 pts

at Hove
Nottinghamshire 454 for 9 dec. (G.E. Welton 95,
U. Afzaal 80, P. Johnson 74, R.T. Robinson 63, J.J. Bates 5
for 89) and 215 for 3 dec. (P. Johnson 59 not out)
Sussex 314 for 5 dec. (P. Moores 102 not out,
M. Newell 100) and 287 for 7 (M.T.E. Peirce 90, K. Newell 75)
Match drawn
Nottinghamshire 9 pts, Sussex 8 pts

at Edgbaston
Northamptonshire 371 (A.J. Swann 136,
R.R. Montgomerie 58, D.R. Brown 5 for 62) and 150 for 0
dec. (A. Fordham 85 not out, K.M. Curran 57 not out)
Warwickshire 251 for 8 dec. (M.A. Wagh 70) and 246
for 8 (A.F. Giles 73 not out, D.P. Ostler 58)
Match drawn
Northamptonshire 8 pts, Warwickshire 7 pts

'Glamorgan have recruited Waqar Younis for 1997. They
have a balanced and keen side, and one would not bet
against them winning the championship.' These were the
closing sentences of last year's *Benson and Hedges Cricket

Year. And so it came to pass. By triumphing over Somerset
in three days at Taunton, Glamorgan took the title for the
first time since 1969. It was a success hard earned and
richly deserved. There was a rather unnecessary public
comment on the Welsh county by the Surrey coach David
Gilbert on the eve of the last round of matches. He still
seemed to be smarting from Glamorgan's unwillingness to
chase the target that had been set them at The Oval a fortnight earlier, but, as it transpired, Maynard's decision was
proved correct. By settling for the draw against Surrey, they
claimed three points, and the margin that ultimately separated them from Kent was four points.

At Taunton, Maynard won the toss and asked
Somerset to bat. Waqar gave the champions elect just the
start they needed to steady any nerves. He bowled Holloway
and had Ecclestone taken at slip. Turner had gone off at a
rush, but he fell to Watkin. Lathwell and Bowler both threatened to hold up Glamorgan, but the first was finally bowled
by Waqar while the Somerset skipper was taken at slip off
Watkin. The Glamorgan attack, most ably supported in the
field, had done all that could have been asked, and
Somerset were bowled out for 252 in 68.4 overs.

Glamorgan had entered the match knowing that it was
essential that they took maximum points, only then could
they be sure that Kent would not overtake them. They
quickly lost James and Dale, but Morris, former captain,
and Maynard, captain, settled into a stand that was to prove
decisive and which was to touch the heights of brilliance. By
the end of the day, after 35 overs, the score was 159 for 2.

Rain frustrated Glamorgan on the second day, and
play did not begin until ten to four, and even then it was
damp and dark. This did not seem to trouble Morris and
Maynard, who unleashed a glorious array of strokes. Runs
came at seven an over, and they extended their partnership
until it was worth 235 in under three hours. In the 33 overs
allowed by the weather on the second day, Glamorgan added
194 runs. Morris and Maynard reached outstanding centuries, and Croft and Shaw continued the onslaught on the
third morning when conditions had improved. Glamorgan
were finally dismissed for 527, but the runs had occupied
only 99.4 overs. This was champagne cricket. It had the
bubble of champions.

Turner again went off briskly, and Waqar was severely
punished. This time it was Darren Thomas who made the
vital breakthrough, having Holloway caught behind. Thomas
moved the ball sufficiently to disconcert all batsmen, and
wickets fell regularly until Somerset were reduced to 166 for
7. Rose and Caddick held up the advance with a stand of 95,
which was ended when Watkin had Rose caught behind. The
same bowler accounted for Shine, and when young Cosker
trapped Trott leg before Glamorgan knew that the title was
theirs. They needed 11 runs to win, and it took James and
Morris just eight balls to get them. James, batsman of the
year, thumped Rose for four, and the celebrations began.

It was a very different story at Canterbury where 19
wickets fell on the first day and Kent were given a suspended ten-point deduction for an under-prepared pitch.

Glamorgan jubilation as the title draws closer.
(Craig Prentis/Allsport)

Put in to bat, Surrey were shot out in 27 overs, but the visitors' own under-strength attack had bowled out Kent after six balls on the second day. This meant that Kent now had to rely on Glamorgan failing to win if they were to take the title. The Surrey second innings showed a complete change of pattern. Darren Bicknell, wrongly omitted from the side for much of the season, and Alec Stewart shared a third wicket stand of 219 and scored resounding centuries. Their colleagues failed to give adequate support, and the innings collapsed on the third morning. Needing 276 to win, Kent were given a firm foundation by Fulton's first century of the season, and after minor shocks, Ealham and Fleming saw them home comfortably. All in vain, they had been runners-up in the Benson and Hedges Cup, runners-up in the Sunday League and now they were runners-up in the championship. It was not a treble to be envied.

The other matches were of less significance, but produced some vintage cricket. Derbyshire ended the year with their second win, surprisingly beating Yorkshire, who had hoped for third place. The victory was brought about by a second wicket stand of 417 between Kim Barnett and Tim Tweats whose 189 was his maiden first-class century. The partnership was Derbyshire's highest for any wicket in their 127 years of existence.

At Chelmsford, Ashley Cowan made the highest score of his career as he and Ilott put on 113 for the ninth wicket, and Bloomfield took five wickets in an innings for the first time. Then Nash hit the first century of his career, and

Hewitt made his best score in a stand of 169 for Middlesex's seventh wicket. Robinson and Hussain scored centuries on the last day of the drawn match and put on 213 for Essex's second wicket.

At Bristol, Young signed off with a century and Russell claimed his 1000th dismissal when he caught Atherton, but Lancashire held out to deny Gloucestershire victory.

The sensation was at Southampton where Hick and Moody added an unbroken 438 for Worcestershire's third wicket. It was the highest stand for that wicket recorded in the championship, and it was a record for any Worcestershire wicket. Hick's 303 not out was the highest individual score of the season, and it was the second time in his career that he had passed 300. Richard Illingworth showed his recovery after injury was complete by taking seven wickets, and Worcestershire's win over Hampshire took them to a surprising third in the championship.

A day was lost to rain at Leicester where the home side were 87 for 7 in their second innings before Pierson and Brimson made career-best scores. Needing 328 to win, Durham batted valiantly but failed narrowly. Nevertheless, there is a hint that more steel is coming into Durham's cricket, thanks to Boon, and that the Cinderella days may be nearing their end. Both Simon Brown, a most willing worker and fine bowler, and David Millns captured ten wickets in the match.

Rain hampered the game at Hove, where the efforts of the two captains could not bring a result. There was comfort for Sussex. Peirce played another good innings, Bates took five wickets and Moores and Mark Newell hit centuries. Welton came within five runs of a maiden century for Nottinghamshire.

Alec Swann did reach a maiden century for Northamptonshire, for whom Fordham scored an unbeaten 85 in his last innings for the county. Warwickshire had to settle for a draw in a match badly affected by rain.

Wales had voted for its own Assembly, and Glamorgan had won the championship, both by narrow margins, but both bringing much joy to many people.

Britannic Assurance County Championship

Final Table

	P	W	L	T	Bt	Bl	Pts
Glamorgan (10)	17	8	2	7	50	57	256
Kent (4)	17	8	4	5	44	60	252
Worcestershire (7)	17	6	3	8	49	54	228
Middlesex (9)	17	7	4	6	33	56	219
Warwickshire (8)	17	7	2	8	32	51	219
Yorkshire (6)	17	6	3	8	41	54	215
Gloucestershire (13)	17	6	6	5	35	60	206
Surrey (3)	17	5	5	7	39	52	192
Essex (5)	17	5	6	6	39	55	192
Leicestershire (1)	17	4	1	12	37	54	191
Lancashire (15)	17	5	6	6	34	54	186
Somerset	17	3	3	11	38	64	183
Nottinghamshire (17)	17	4	3	10	26	55	175
Hampshire (14)	17	3	5	9	42	41	158
Northamptonshire (16)	17	3	5	9	33	48	156
Derbyshire (2)	17	2	9	6	32	59	141
Durham (18)	17	2	8	7	22	56	131
Sussex (12)	17	1	10	6	24	57	115

Last season's positions in brackets.
Worcestershire and Kent's records include eight points as the side batting last in a match in which the scores finished level.

First-Class Averages

Batting

	M	Inns	NO	Runs	HS	Av	100s	50s
R.K. Illingworth	5	4	2	157	112	78.50	1	
J.M. Dakin	4	5	1	311	190	77.75	2	
G.A. Hick	18	28	6	1524	303*	69.27	6	4
S.P. James	18	30	4	1775	162	68.26	7	8
S.D. Peters	3	3	1	135	102*	67.50	1	
T.A. Radford	2	4	2	131	69*	65.50		2
M.P. Maynard	18	25	7	1170	161*	65.00	3	7
N.C. Johnson	12	18	5	819	150	63.00	2	5
D.S. Lehmann	17	27	2	1575	182	63.00	4	10
G.P. Thorpe	14	23	4	1160	222	61.05	3	6
M.J. Powell	5	8	3	286	200*	57.20	1	
S.G. Law	17	28	2	1482	175	57.00	5	8
M.R. Ramprakash	19	30	4	1453	190	55.88	6	7
D.C. Nash	6	8	2	332	100	55.33	1	1
A.J. Swann	2	3	–	162	136	54.00	1	
T.A. Tweats	7	13	2	590	189	53.63	1	1
M.L. Hayden	17	30	3	1446	235*	53.55	4	7
M.A. Ealham	18	30	10	1055	139	52.75	3	6
H. Morris	17	28	4	1262	233*	52.58	4	3
D.A. Leatherdale	17	25	8	886	129	52.11	2	5
R.J. Turner	17	28	7	1069	144	50.50	1	7
K.J. Barnett	15	24	3	1055	210*	50.23	3	5
G.D. Rose	18	26	9	852	191	50.11	2	3
J.P. Crawley	16	25	2	1141	133	49.60	3	7
W.P.C. Weston	17	29	5	1190	205	49.58	4	3
N.V. Knight	11	17	3	689	119*	49.21	2	3
G.D. Lloyd	16	24	2	1073	225	48.77	4	5
T.M. Moody	14	21	1	973	180*	48.65	3	4
P.J. Prichard	17	27	2	1184	224	47.36	3	9
J.H. Kallis	16	25	3	1034	172*	47.00	4	4
K.M. Curran	15	26	4	1032	159	46.90	2	6
R.C. Russell	19	29	6	1049	103*	45.60	1	8
D. Byas	20	33	4	1319	128	45.48	3	9
G.W. White	10	17	2	681	145	45.40	1	4
S.C. Ecclestone	13	23	2	951	133	45.28	3	4
A. Fordham	9	17	2	673	85*	44.86		6
J.J.B. Lewis	18	32	4	1252	210*	44.71	3	5
B.F. Smith	13	19	5	624	131*	44.57	2	2
V.J. Wells	18	27	–	1200	224	44.44	3	6
R.J. Warren	10	17	2	664	174*	44.26	1	4
P.A. Nixon	19	25	9	708	96	44.25		4
A.S. Rollins	17	29	3	1142	210	43.92	3	6
R.J. Harden	7	11	2	395	136*	43.88	2	1
J.J. Whitaker	16	23	2	919	133*	43.76	3	4
M. Keech	10	16	4	518	127	43.16	2	1
R.J. Bailey	17	30	5	1078	117*	43.12	3	5
E.T. Smith	18	30	3	1163	190	43.07	2	6
D. Ripley	17	24	6	772	92	42.88		6
P. Johnson	16	27	5	942	96*	42.81		8
A.D. Brown	14	21	1	848	170*	42.40	3	2
D.C. Boon	18	30	3	1144	117	42.37	3	8
R.A. Smith	14	23	1	918	154	41.72	2	4
D.M. Jones	7	12	1	458	99*	41.63		5
A.J. Stewart	15	26	2	994	271*	41.41	2	3
S. Herzberg	7	8	3	207	56	41.40		1
T.L. Penney	16	24	5	784	99	41.26		6
D.L. Hemp	18	31	4	1107	138	41.00	3	5
A.P. Grayson	19	28	3	1022	105	40.88	1	6
M.W. Alleyne	19	30	4	1059	169	40.73	1	8
I.J. Sutcliffe	13	20	2	727	130	40.38	2	3
N.H. Fairbrother	16	24	2	887	132	40.31	2	4
N.J. Astle	10	16	–	644	100	40.25	2	3
P.R. Pollard	10	17	5	480	115*	40.00	1	1
M.A. Waugh	18	31	2	1156	125*	39.86	4	5
S.A. Marsh	18	27	6	837	142	39.85	1	3
A. Habib	9	14	4	397	175*	39.70	1	1
D.J. Bicknell	9	15	–	594	162	39.60	2	1
I.D. Austin	17	25	4	825	95	39.28		8
M.R. May	9	17	2	588	116	39.20	2	3
O.A. Shah	11	16	2	548	104*	39.14	1	2
A.F. Giles	16	20	4	624	97	39.00		5
M.W. Gatting	19	29	2	1053	160*	39.00	2	4
N. Hussain	16	28	–	1081	207	38.60	4	3
N.R. Taylor	16	28	1	1033	127	38.25	3	5
R.J. Blakey	18	24	6	680	92	37.77		6
A. Dale	19	27	4	860	142*	37.39	2	5
A.P. Wells	18	31	1	1120	109	37.33	1	9
A.J. Hollioake	16	25	1	891	182	37.12	1	6
T.S. Curtis	13	21	1	742	160	37.10	4	1
D.P. Fulton	16	29	3	953	110	36.65	1	4
S. Young	19	31	4	985	237	36.48	2	5
K.A. Parsons	10	15	3	437	74	36.41		3
R.O. Jones	8	11	2	325	60	36.11		3
D.L. Maddy	19	30	1	1047	103	36.10	3	5
G.R. Haynes	17	25	3	794	70	36.09		6
N.T. Wood	10	15	2	469	155	36.07	1	2
C.W.J. Athey	12	21	2	682	138*	35.89	1	5
V.P. Clarke	19	30	6	847	99	35.29		5
K.R. Spiring	17	28	3	876	150	35.04	1	4
D.D.J. Robinson	14	22	1	735	148	35.00	2	3
J.E. Morris	17	30	1	1009	149	34.79	2	4
C.A. Chapman	2	4	–	139	80	34.75		1
A. McGrath	15	25	1	832	141	34.66	2	3
D.J. Millns	15	15	2	449	121	34.53	2	1
R.C. Irani	16	24	1	793	123*	34.47	3	3
S.J. Rhodes	18	23	6	584	78	34.35		4
M.P. Loye	8	15	3	412	86	34.33		2
M.P. Dowman	19	33	1	1091	149	34.09	3	5
J.P. Stephenson	17	26	3	784	140	34.08	2	1
T.R. Ward	18	32	2	1018	161*	33.93	1	8
N.M.K. Smith	15	22	3	642	148	33.78	1	3
R.R. Montgomerie	10	18	3	504	73	33.60		4
M.P. Vaughan	15	27	2	839	161	33.56	3	2
A.J. Moles	12	22	3	635	168	33.42	1	2
P.R. Whitaker	3	5	1	132	73	33.00		1
G.P. Butcher	11	11	2	296	101*	32.88	1	1
M.A. Atherton	16	28	2	853	149	32.80	2	5
M.D. Moxon	12	18	–	589	155	32.72	1	5
J.S. Laney	15	27	1	848	95	32.61		6
R.T. Robinson	17	29	4	812	143*	32.48	1	5
M.E. Cassar	7	8	1	227	78	32.42		2
M.A. Butcher	19	34	1	1068	153	32.36	1	7
S.J. Lacey	6	8	4	129	50	32.25		1
B. Parker	19	30	5	806	138*	32.24	1	4
C.J. Adams	15	25	1	767	108	31.95	2	3
J.D. Ratcliffe	15	26	2	759	135	31.62	1	4
T.H.C. Hancock	19	31	3	854	100*	30.50	1	5
A. Flintoff	5	8	–	243	117	30.37	1	
P.C.L. Holloway	19	34	4	905	106	30.16	1	5
K.R. Brown	19	29	9	601	144*	30.05	1	2
J.E.R. Gallian	11	19	2	506	106	29.76	1	3
D.J. Roberts	7	13	–	385	117	29.61	1	
D.R.H. Churton	7	7	1	177	44	29.50		
G.R. Cowdrey	9	15	–	442	101	29.46	1	1
M.V. Fleming	18	31	4	790	138	29.25	1	4
C. White	17	24	2	639	172*	29.04	1	2
M. Watkinson	12	19	1	520	135	28.88	1	2
S.D. Udal	18	24	3	600	117*	28.57	1	4
K. Newell	17	31	2	827	112	28.51	2	3
V.S. Solanki	14	18	1	478	128*	28.11	1	2
P.A. Cottey	17	21	4	475	83	27.94		2
S.R. Lampitt	15	17	7	277	52	27.70		1
M.N. Lathwell	20	34	1	912	95	27.63		6
K.D. James	10	15	2	359	85	27.61		5
D.J.G. Sales	14	21	1	548	103	27.40	1	2
A. Singh	10	14	1	355	134	27.30	1	1
G.E. Welton	6	11	–	295	95	26.81		1
U. Afzaal	17	29	2	720	80	26.66		5
P.D. Bowler	16	26	1	666	123	26.64	1	5
C.M. Tolley	12	22	4	479	73*	26.61		3
B.C. Hollioake	14	22	1	559	76	26.61		3
J.I.D. Kerr	5	6	1	133	35	26.60		
M.J. Vandrau	5	8	1	186	54	26.57		1
P.D. Collingwood	8	13	1	316	107	26.33	1	1
A.L. Penberthy	13	19	–	499	96	26.26		3
P.G. Morgan	10	18	1	444	63	26.11		2
R.D.B. Croft	18	26	1	652	86	26.08		4
M.A. Lynch	12	19	1	465	64	25.83		3
W.M. Noon	18	25	4	542	83	25.80		3
T.C. Walton	7	10	1	231	60	25.66		2
J.R. Carpenter	3	6	–	153	63	25.50		1
I.J. Ward	3	4	–	102	56	25.50		1
M. Burns	14	21	4	510	82	25.50		3
W.J. House	10	14	1	331	94	25.46		2
W.K. Hegg	17	23	5	456	77*	25.33		1
R.J. Rollins	13	19	1	452	82	25.11		4
J.M.M. Averis	10	15	4	276	42	25.09		
B.J. Phillips	13	19	4	376	100*	25.06	1	1

Batting

	M	Inns	NO	Runs	HS	Av	100s	50s
M.T.E. Peirce	12	23	–	576	104	25.04	1	3
Saqlain Mushtaq	8	10	4	149	41*	24.83		
C. Patel	12	22	5	420	63*	24.70		3
M.G.N. Windows	8	15	–	369	84	24.60		2
P.A. Strang	17	26	2	590	82	24.58		5
M.C.J. Ball	18	27	3	587	50	24.45		1
S.P. Moffat	4	6	1	122	47	24.40		
J.R. Ratledge	8	12	1	268	100*	24.36	1	
A.D. Shaw	18	21	5	389	53*	24.31		1
W.S. Kendall	12	19	2	413	76	24.29		1
K.M. Krikken	19	27	4	558	72	24.26		3
N.J. Lenham	7	12	–	290	93	24.16		2
D.R. Brown	17	24	3	504	79	24.00		4
D.G. Cork	6	9	1	192	55*	24.00		2
M.J. Foster	14	24	–	575	129	23.95	1	3
A.A. Metcalfe	9	12	1	262	79	23.81		2
J.A.G. Fulton	10	19	–	451	78	23.73		4
G. Chapple	11	14	4	237	66	23.70		2
N.J. Speak	12	21	3	426	124*	23.66	1	1
J.N. Snape	11	16	3	306	66	23.53		3
R.I. Dawson	8	14	–	329	100	23.50	1	1
P.W. Jarvis	11	18	2	374	64	23.37		4
A.N. Aymes	18	23	4	442	96*	23.26		1
G.A. Gooch	10	17	1	369	56	23.06		2
J.C. Pooley	18	28	1	619	98	22.92		3
M.P. Speight	17	28	3	573	73*	22.92		3
C.C. Lewis	13	19	2	389	76	22.88		1
G. Welch	18	26	6	453	75	22.65		2
G.J. Parsons	6	6	1	113	69*	22.60		1
P.C. McKeown	4	6	–	135	46	22.50		
M. Newell	12	22	1	471	100	22.42	1	3
S.J. Renshaw	13	19	7	259	56	22.41		1
A.P. Cowan	16	26	6	447	77	22.35		1
P. Aldred	8	8	2	133	83	22.16		1
A.J. Wright	13	22	3	416	79	21.89		1
Q.J. Hughes	8	12	3	197	47*	21.88		
A.J. Tudor	9	11	6	109	35*	21.80		
M.E. Trescothick	13	19	1	390	83*	21.66		4
P.J. Franks	14	19	6	280	50	21.53		1
S. Hutton	7	13	1	258	95	21.50		1
S.D. Thomas	18	19	5	301	75*	21.50		1
C.E.W. Silverwood	18	23	6	365	58	21.47		1
P. Moores	17	31	4	571	102*	21.14	1	2
A.P. Scrini	11	18	6	253	58*	21.08		1
P.A.J. DeFreitas	19	24	1	484	96	21.04		2
R.J. Cunliffe	9	14	1	273	61	21.00		1
W.G. Khan	3	5	–	102	43	20.40		
M.P. Bicknell	15	20	5	305	74	20.33		2
N.J. Trainor	14	25	1	484	121	20.16	1	1
A.A. Donald	11	13	6	140	29	20.00		
D.J. Capel	4	7	–	140	57	20.00		1
S.P. Titchard	6	9	–	180	79	20.00		1
D.P. Ostler	15	22	1	419	65	19.95		3
R.K. Rao	11	20	1	375	89	19.73		3
K.P. Dutch	7	9	2	138	79	19.71		1
J.A. Knott	5	9	3	118	27*	19.66		
M.J. Walker	10	19	–	369	62	19.42		2
G. Yates	11	13	3	194	39	19.40		
M.C. Ilott	13	20	5	290	47	19.33		
G.F. Archer	12	22	2	375	81	18.75		2
P.J. Martin	17	19	4	281	78*	18.73		1
P.N. Weekes	15	24	–	439	101	18.29	1	
N.J. Llong	8	14	–	256	99	18.28		2
Waqar Younis	16	17	1	289	47	18.06		
C.G.R. Lightfoot	9	16	–	289	61	18.06		1
N. Shahid	7	11	–	198	34	18.00		
A.R. Caddick	18	22	4	321	56*	17.83		1
K. Greenfield	11	21	–	372	108	17.71	1	
B.W. Byrne	11	20	–	354	49	17.70		
T. Frost	9	11	2	158	56	17.55		1
J.J. Lewis	15	19	8	193	30	17.54		
M.J. McCague	11	17	6	190	53*	17.27		1
G.M. Hamilton	11	16	2	240	49	17.14		
R.M.S. Weston	5	8	–	137	36	17.12		
D.R. Law	19	29	–	492	81	16.96		2
J.E. Benjamin	11	15	6	152	35	16.88		
T.P. Hodgson	3	6	–	101	44	16.83		
L.G. Buchanan	8	14	4	168	43*	16.80		
A.R.K. Pierson	16	16	–	266	59	16.62		1

Batting

	M	Inns	NO	Runs	HS	Av	100s	50s
J.J. Bates	7	9	2	113	47	16.14		
J.P. Hewitt	18	21	4	264	75	15.52		1
A.A. Khan	15	24	5	291	52	15.31		1
J. Boiling	17	26	4	334	62	15.18		1
D.J. Shadford	8	10	3	106	30	15.14		
J.B.D. Thompson	9	10	3	106	59*	15.14		1
A.R.C. Fraser	19	23	6	244	35	14.35		
P.S. Jones	10	13	3	142	36	14.20		
R.L. Johnson	18	24	1	320	39	13.91		
K.J. Piper	8	11	3	111	34*	13.87		
D.W. Headley	12	17	5	166	40	13.83		
S.A.J. Boswell	9	12	3	122	35	13.55		
D. Gough	12	16	1	196	58	13.06		1
A.C. Morris	7	9	–	117	37	13.00		
V.C. Drakes	10	18	1	221	48	13.00		
J.P. Taylor	16	21	4	216	36	12.70		
Mushtaq Ahmed	14	16	2	174	33	12.42		
K.P. Evans	15	18	1	208	47	12.23		
P.J. Hartley	9	10	–	121	39	12.10		
M.M. Betts	13	19	1	207	35	11.50		
R.P. Davis	9	12	–	135	39	11.25		
R.D. Hudson	11	20	2	202	62	11.22		1
M.N. Bowen	15	19	6	145	32	11.15		
R.D. Stemp	17	20	6	154	33*	11.00		
S.L. Watkin	17	16	3	138	39	10.61		
I.D.K. Salisbury	13	17	2	159	30*	10.60		

(Qualification: 100 runs; average 10.00)

Also scored 100 runs:
two matches: P.E. Wellings 128* & 13
one match: K.L.T. Arthurton 200; G. Salmond 89 & 46; B.M.W. Patterson 83 & 32; W.K. McCallan 65 & 47; M.J. Wood 81 & 21

Bowling

	Overs	Mds	Runs	Wks	Av	Best	10/m	5/inn
H.A.G. Anthony	42	11	113	10	11.30	6/34	1	1
A.A. Donald	387.5	123	938	60	15.63	6/55	1	3
A.M. Smith	512.2	125	1464	83	17.63	6/45	3	5
K.D. James	161.1	37	504	27	18.66	8/49	1	2
D.R. Brown	521.3	135	1560	81	19.25	8/80	1	4
Saqlain Mushtaq	254.5	75	617	32	19.28	5/17	2	4
T.F. Bloomfield	85	17	258	13	19.84	5/77		1
B.J. Phillips	282.1	73	877	44	19.93	5/47		2
P.M. Hutchison	233.1	56	741	37	20.02	7/38	1	3
J.H. Kallis	234.3	61	655	32	20.46	5/54		1
P.C.R. Tufnell	560.5	174	1205	55	21.90	7/66	1	3
M.C. Ilott	332	95	946	43	22.00	7/59		1
M.M. Betts	329	77	1085	49	22.14	9/64	1	3
Waqar Younis	441.4	83	1551	68	22.80	8/17	1	3
S.L. Watkin	508.2	143	1393	61	22.83	7/41		2
A.D. Edwards	103.2	19	389	17	22.88	5/34		1
P.J. Martin	474.2	136	1342	58	23.13	8/32	1	3
P.J. Hartley	170	39	532	23	23.13	5/34		1
J.P. Hewitt	439	97	1393	60	23.21	6/14		2
P.J. Newport	177.2	56	444	19	23.36	7/37		1
M.J. McCague	312.4	55	1125	48	23.43	7/50		4
D.E. Malcolm	526.1	81	1761	75	23.48	6/23	2	5
N.J. Astle	209	44	523	22	23.77	5/46		1
R.K. Illingworth	206.1	79	442	18	24.55	7/79	1	1
G.D. Rose	486.5	124	1563	63	24.80	5/53		1
G. Welch	540.5	150	1625	65	25.00	6/115	1	3
A. Sheriyar	445.5	94	1575	62	25.40	6/19	1	3
A.P. Cowan	420	106	1334	52	25.65	5/45		3
N.F. Williams	101	16	336	13	25.84	5/55		1
J.J. Lewis	418.5	98	1401	54	25.94	6/50		3
M.W. Alleyne	360.1	89	1148	44	26.09	6/64		1
J.E. Hindson	96.4	24	287	11	26.09	4/28		
A.R. Oram	226.4	55	684	26	26.30	4/53		
P.M. Such	725.1	218	1739	66	26.34	6/55	1	6
C.E.W. Silverwood	478.4	108	1531	58	26.39	7/93	1	4
J. Ormond	345.3	72	1162	44	26.40	6/54		3
A.R. Caddick	702.4	139	2156	81	26.61	6/55		6
M.P. Bicknell	385.2	99	1174	44	26.68	5/34		1
D. Gough	334.4	70	1149	43	26.72	5/56		3
P.A.J. DeFreitas	574.1	132	1810	67	27.01	7/64	2	5

Bowling

	Overs	Mds	Runs	Wks	Av	Best	10/m	5/inn
I.D. Austin	448.3	131	1218	45	27.06	4/44		
S.D. Thomas	405.3	58	1444	53	27.24	5/24		3
D.J. Millns	408.4	87	1341	49	27.36	6/61	1	2
R.D.B. Croft	666.1	159	1698	62	27.38	5/33		1
J.J. Bates	227.2	71	525	19	27.63	5/89		1
S.J.E. Brown	590.3	126	1855	67	27.68	5/58	1	4
S. Herzberg	102	25	281	10	28.10	4/26		
Mushtaq Ahmed	513	146	1407	50	28.14	6/70		3
G.R. Haynes	287.1	68	875	31	28.22	3/46		
J.P. Taylor	455.4	81	1532	54	28.37	7/87	1	3
K.P. Evans	457.5	103	1277	45	28.37	6/40		2
R.L. Johnson	427.2	79	1425	50	28.50	4/26		
D.A. Leatherdale	219.3	46	742	26	28.53	5/56		1
J.B.D. Thompson	223.2	30	890	31	28.70	5/89		1
C.M. Tolley	363	87	1005	35	28.71	6/61		1
K.J. Dean	234.4	47	811	28	28.96	4/39		
M.K. Davies	234.2	71	674	23	29.30	5/46		1
C.C. Lewis	291.4	72	970	33	29.39	5/42		1
M.A. Robinson	448.2	87	1426	48	29.70	6/78		2
K.M.Curran	215.2	57	715	24	29.79	4/32		
A.P. Igglesden	152	23	538	18	29.88	4/67		
C. White	353.4	58	1236	41	30.14	5/31		1
K.J. Shine	443.3	89	1678	55	30.50	7/43	1	3
A.J. Holliaoke	132.4	23	458	15	30.53	4/22		
P.A. Strang	733.1	211	1929	63	30.61	7/118	1	4
D.W. Headley	425.2	75	1419	46	30.84	5/92		1
M.V. Fleming	398.2	97	1145	37	30.94	5/51		2
M.A. Ealham	407.4	80	1238	40	30.95	4/47		
A.R.C. Fraser	571.5	155	1460	47	31.06	6/77		2
I.D.K. Salisbury	314.1	65	936	30	31.23	6/19		2
D.R. Law	270.3	51	969	31	31.25	5/93		1
P.S. Jones	207.5	37	739	23	32.13	6/67		1
A. Walker	341.1	87	1063	33	32.21	7/56		2
A.F. Giles	506.1	155	1225	38	32.23	4/54		
J.F. Brown	203.4	39	651	20	32.55	4/50		
M.M. Mirza	152.4	25	620	19	32.63	4/51		
R.D. Stemp	473	111	1379	42	32.83	6/77		1
C.A. Connor	122.5	23	430	13	33.07	7/46		1
G. Yates	302.3	57	963	29	33.20	5/59		1
G. Chapple	275.5	45	900	27	33.33	4/80		
G.M. Hamilton	241	53	907	27	33.59	5/89		1
V.C. Drakes	300	60	1043	31	33.54	4/55		
G. Keedy	292.4	60	917	27	33.96	6/79	1	1
B.C. Holliaoke	214.2	42	782	23	34.00	4/54		
M.N. Bowen	467.2	107	1394	41	34.00	7/75	1	3
M.J. Foster	275.4	55	1027	30	34.23	4/58		
S. Young	396.3	111	1104	32	34.50	4/26		
S.J. Renshaw	355.3	63	1278	37	34.54	5/110		1
A.D. Mullally	383.1	89	1302	37	35.18	5/52		4
R.J. Kirtley	276.3	48	1094	31	35.29	6/60		1
A.J. Tudor	160.3	27	607	17	35.70	6/101		1
R.P. Davis	241	76	607	17	35.70	4/35		
A.P. Grayson	394.5	112	1009	28	36.03	4/53		

Bowling

	Overs	Mds	Runs	Wks	Av	Best	10/m	5/inn
R.J. Chapman	103.3	18	470	13	36.15	3/26		
P.W. Jarvis	318.5	46	1091	30	36.36	5/44		2
R.J. Bailey	112.3	19	367	10	36.70	4/10		
S.R. Lampitt	334.4	70	1302	35	37.20	5/39		1
J.I.D. Kerr	103	20	374	10	37.40	4/83		
P. Aldred	181	52	454	12	37.83	3/28		
Mohammad Akram	287	43	1135	30	37.83	5/72		2
D.A. Cosker	375.2	88	1100	29	37.93	4/64		
G.J. Parsons	182.2	48	500	13	38.46	4/22		
P.J. Franks	372.4	63	1158	30	38.60	4/47		
R.C. Irani	261.5	73	695	18	38.61	3/51		
G.P. Butcher	114.1	27	466	12	38.83	3/87		
A.R.K. Pierson	499.1	104	1478	38	38.89	6/56		1
J.N.B. Bovill	233.4	37	902	23	39.21	4/62		
V.J. Wells	204	47	671	17	39.47	2/8		
K. Newell	138.1	35	436	11	39.63	4/61		
J.P. Stephenson	428.5	66	1480	37	40.00	6/54		1
M. Watkinson	231.4	41	805	20	40.25	3/35		
N.M.K. Smith	318.2	77	930	23	40.43	4/32		
M.T. Brimson	170.5	48	451	11	41.00	3/49		
D.J. Shadford	149	8	786	19	41.36	5/80		1
D.G. Cork	132	28	457	11	41.54	4/48		
A.A. Khan	444.3	100	1397	33	42.33	5/137		1
T.M. Moody	231.4	42	829	19	43.63	5/148		1
M.C.J. Ball	479.2	129	1271	29	43.82	5/66		
J. Boiling	336	98	925	21	44.04	3/21		
J.N. Snape	253.1	60	724	15	48.26	4/46		
A.J. Harris	481.3	98	1694	35	48.40	3/66		
C. Patel	327	51	1326	27	49.11	6/110		1
J. Wood	112	14	541	11	49.18	4/73		
U. Afzaal	199.1	40	689	14	49.21	4/79		
S.M. Milburn	332	56	1127	22	51.22	4/38		
S.A.J. Boswell	185.5	26	769	15	51.26	5/94		1
R.T. Bates	225.4	51	576	11	52.36	3/89		
S.D. Udal	627	155	1810	34	53.23	4/17		
J.W.O. Freeth	149	16	609	11	55.36	4/101		
C.M. Batterbee	150.4	21	627	11	57.00	2/56		
E.J. How	193.4	40	685	12	57.08	5/59		1
J.E. Benjamin	211	38	759	13	58.38	3/52		
V.P. Clarke	223.4	48	835	13	64.23	3/47		
J.M.M. Averis	272.2	40	1104	16	69.00	5/98		1

(Qualification: 10 wickets)

Leading Fielders

63 – S.A. Marsh (ct 61 / st 2); 61 – P.A. Nixon (ct 57 / st 4); 57 – R.C. Russell (ct 52 / st 5);
54 – M.P. Speight and A.D. Shaw (ct 52 / st 2); 53 – R.J. Blakey (ct 49 / st 4) and R.J. Turner (ct 51 / st 2);
50 – K.R. Brown (ct 47 / st 3); 47 – S.J. Rhodes (ct 44 / st 3); 42 – A.N. Aymes (ct 35 / st 7);
39 – W.K. Hegg (ct 37 / st 2) and A.J. Stewart; 38 – W.M. Noon (ct 34 / st 4); 37 – D. Ripley (ct 30 / st 7);
36 – P. Moores; 30 – T. Frost (ct 28 / st 2) and T.R. Ward; 29 – D.P. Ostler; 28 – M.A. Butcher;
26 – R.J. Rollins (ct 24 / st 2); 25 – K.J. Piper (ct 24 / st 1); 24 – D. Byas; 23 – M.W. Gatting, D.P. Fulton
and M.C.J. Ball; 21 – M.P. Maynard and J.C. Pooley; 20 – A.P. Grayson, G.A. Hick, P.D. Bowler

Derbyshire CCC First-Class Matches Batting

Player	M	Inns	NO	Runs	HS	Av
D.M. Jones	7	12	3	458	99*	41.63
A.S. Rollins	17	29	3	1142	210	43.92
C.J. Adams	14	24	1	723	108	31.82
A.N. Hayhurst	2	2	–	6	6	3.00
M.J. Vandrau	5	8	1	186	54	26.57
V.P. Clarke	19	30	6	847	99	35.20
K.M. Krikken	19	27	4	558	72	24.26
PA.J. DeFreitas	19	24	1	484	96	21.04
G.M. Roberts	2	3	1	45	30*	22.50
K.J. Dean	10	9	2	79	21*	11.28
D.E. Malcolm	15	19	8	80	21*	7.27
K.J. Barnett	15	24	3	1055	210*	50.23
D.G. Cork	6	9	1	192	55*	24.00
G.A. Khan	3	5	1	95	62*	23.75
M.E. Cassar	6	8	1	227	78	32.42
A.J. Harris	17	24	4	171	36	8.55
P. Aldred	8	8	2	133	83	22.16
M.R. May	9	17	2	588	116	39.20
I. Blackwell	4	7	2	51	42	10.20
T.A. Tweats	7	13	2	590	189	53.63
J.E. Owen	5	8	2	83	22	13.83
S.J. Lacey	2	6	2	129	50	32.25
B.J. Spendlove	6	3	2	27	15*	1.00
S.P. Griffiths	2	1	–	–	–	–
S. Stubbings	1	2	–	27	22	13.50
T. Smith	1	–	–	–	–	–

Derbyshire CCC First-Class Matches — Bowling

Matches

1. v. Cambridge University (Cambridge) 15–17 April
2. v. Kent (Canterbury) 23–26 April
3. v. Surrey (Derby) 7–10 May
4. v. Middlesex (Lord's) 14–17 May
5. v. Nottinghamshire (Trent Bridge) 21–24 May
6. v. Australians (Derby) 31 May–2 June
7. v. Hampshire (Chesterfield) 4–7 June
8. v. Warwickshire (Edgbaston) 12–16 June
9. v. Sussex (Derby) 18–21 June
10. v. Essex (Southend) 26–30 June
11. v. Pakistan 'A' (Derby) 5–8 July
12. v. Gloucestershire (Cheltenham) 16–19 July
13. v. Glamorgan (Chesterfield) 23–26 July
14. v. Durham (Chester-le-Street) 31 July–4 August
15. v. Lancashire (Derby) 15–18 August
16. v. Leicestershire (Leicester) 20–23 August
17. v. Somerset (Derby) 27–30 August
18. v. Northamptonshire (Derby) 2–5 September
19. v. Worcestershire (Worcester) 10–13 September
20. v. Yorkshire (Derby) 18–21 September

Bowling figures by bowler

Bowler	Innings figures	Total	Average
D.E. Malcolm	14.4-1-59-1; 16-3-54-3; 27-4-74-6; 20.4-0-112-1; 21-1-95-4; 19-6-50-5; 22.3-5-75-6; 23-7-42-4; 30-4-91-4; 29-5-85-5; 8-0-36-0; 17-2-49-2; 12-4-30-3; 28.3-2-102-4; 23-2-84-1; 14-3-30-2; 21-3-55-2; 9.3-2-23-6; 12.4-2-42-4; 10-1-31-0; 23.4-2-82-4; 4-0-18-1; 23-3-117-1; 4-0-18-0	433.1-62-1454-69	21.07
P.A.J. DeFreitas	17-3-53-3; 8-4-21-2; 21-10-35-3; 16-4-53-1; 19.1-4-46-5; 25-4-88-1; 14-2-61-3; 10-3-31-0; 22-4-76-0; 18-1-76-0; 31-6-88-2; 28-5-63-3; 15-1-55-0; 18-8-37-2; 21-8-33-3; 28-5-99-3; 24-3-86-3; 15-3-37-5; 15-2-56-0; 9-2-28-3; 41-16-120-5; 16-1-69-1; 11-3-44-0; 23-6-39-1; 3-0-7-0; 22-3-85-1; 5-0-31-0; 27-9-74-4; 22-5-98-6	574.1-132-1810-67	27.01
K.J. Dean	9-2-22-1; 9-1-39-4; 12-2-44-0; 12.5-4-21-3; 16-5-51-3; 16-6-37-1; 16-1-76-1; 10-0-45-2; 18-2-86-1; 15.5-0-86-2; 25-11-49-2; 14-4-40-3; 18-7-48-3; 17-1-73-0; 7-0-31-0; 8-0-20-0	234.4-47-811-28	28.96
M.E. Cassar	6-0-22-0; 4-0-22-0; 11-2-31-3; 15-3-50-2; 6.1-0-31-2; 10-1-68-1	52.1-6-224-8	28.00
V.P. Clarke	16-4-47-3; 7-1-23-1; 8-2-35-0; 6-0-53-0; 10-4-14-1; 4.5-1-18-0; 4-0-13-1; 1-0-3-0; 13-3-34-1; 6-0-45-0; 4-1-8-0; 26-5-100-1; 13-3-29-1; 10-6-10-1; 5-0-20-0; 5.1-5-0-1; 14-2-44-1; 10-1-60-0; 5-0-25-0; 3-1-7-0; 2-0-19-0; 11-5-20-0; 8-1-33-1; 4-0-26-0; 18.4-3-98-0; 2-0-8-0; 1-1-0-0	223.4-48-835-13	64.23
M.J. Vandrau	1-1-0-0; 13-0-78-3; 7-1-17-0; 21-5-68-1; 3-0-19-0	45.7-182-4	45.50
D.G. Cork	21-6-52-1; 19.5-5-50-0; 5-0-35-1; 13-4-48-4; 25-3-120-1; 6-0-14-0; 9-1-37-2; 11-1-38-1; 23-8-63-1	132-28-457-11	41.54
D.M. Jones	4-0-20-0; 2-2-0-0	6.2- / 20-0	—
A.J. Harris	16-3-73-1; 6-2-23-0; 24-5-72-2; 21-5-55-0; 17-7-32-0; 18-2-70-1; 16-3-49-1; 29-5-95-2; 12-0-81-1; 36.3-11-109-2; 25-9-40-2; 22-5-87-2; 24-4-124-3; 17.5-4-61-2; 21-1-72-3; 24-4-89-2; 4-0-26-0; 9-0-59-1; 24.3-5-98-3; 6-0-44-0; 10-1-27-1; 25-4-75-1; 4-0-12-0; 13-3-47-1; 4-1-8-0; 23-7-56-1; 16.4-3-66-3	468.3-94-1650-35	47.14
S.J. Lacey	21-0-97-3; 23-8-34-0; 2.4-1-10-0; 28-7-60-2; 4.4-1-14-0; 14.4-2-76-2	94-19-291-7	41.57
P. Aldred	16.1-3-28-3; 21-9-34-1; 12-3-26-0; 15-1-65-1; 18-5-40-3; 4-0-16-0; 15.5-9-10-1; 13-1-29-1; 18-9-43-0; 10-3-30-0; 23-6-83-1; 15-3-50-1	181-52-454-12	37.83
I. Blackwell	15-1-57-1; 9-1-49-0; 6-2-13-0; 7-2-27-1; 9-4-24-0; 6-0-57-0	52-10-227-2	113.50

The label at the foot of the D.E. Malcolm / P.A.J. DeFreitas columns reads **Bowler's average**.

Innings totals and extras (Byes / Leg-byes / Wides / No-balls / Total / Wkts)

Byes	Leg-byes	Wides	No-balls	Total	Wkts	Group
		2	2	195	10	A
	1			156	10	
4	7		6	251	10	B
	9			333	10	
2	9		2	267	10	
	1	8	8	146	10	C
9	9	2	8	262	8	
9	11	2	4	192	8	
5	2	2	6	248	6	
2	4		10	362	4	D
	3		12	265	7	
	8	2	4	422	3	
7	9		14	310	3	
	9			340	10	
9	19	2	12	200	9	
		2	8	373	8	
10	4	1	8	169	10	
1	2		4	201	10	
1	8		22	484	10	
2	8		10	364	8	E
	4	2	14	174	10	
	9		12	257	10	
4	2			118	10	
	4			256	10	
4	17		32	486	5	F
			6	281	10	
2	12		10	251	1	
4	5	4	14	334	8	
	4	2		51	0	
14	20		16	554	10	G
	1		2	72		
5	16	2	2	267		
4	7			267		

Footnotes

A A.N. Hayhurst 4–1–12–1, 5–1–18–0
B A.S. Rollins 1–0–9–0
C G.M. Roberts 6–1–8–0
D A.S. Rollins 2–0–12–0
E M.R. May 0.1–0–2–0
F M.R. May 4–0–48–0; C.J. Adams 2.5–0–16–0
G T. Smith 11–4–27–1, 7–2–24–0

Fielding Figures

- 54 – M.P.Speight
- 19 – D.C. Boon
- 13 – J. Boiling
- 10 – J.J.B. Lewis
- 7 – J.E. Morris
- 6 – N.J. Speak
- 5 – R.M.S. Weston
- 4 – J. Wood
- 3 – M.A. Roseberry
- 2 – N. Killeen, M.J. Foster, S.J.E. Brown, J.A. Daley M.J. Saggers and sub
- 1 – S. Hutton, D.M. Cox and M.M. Betts

Durham CCC First-Class Matches — Batting (season averages)

Batting	M	Inns	NO	Runs	HS	Av
J.J.B. Lewis	17	30	4	1244	210*	47.84
P.D. Collingwood	8	13	1	316	107	26.33
J.E. Morris	17	30	1	1009	149	34.79
N.J. Speak	12	21	3	426	124*	23.66
D.C. Boon	18	30	3	1144	117	42.37
M.P. Speight	17	28	3	573	73*	22.92
M.M. Betts	13	19	1	207	35	11.50
J. Boiling	17	26	4	334	62	15.18
D.M. Cox	4	3	0	46	24	15.33
N. Killeen	3	3	2	24	15	24.00
S.J.E. Brown	16	24	5	121	30	6.36
J. Wood	6	8	2	72	21*	18.00
C.L. Campbell	14	24	4	575	129	23.95
M.J. Foster	12	20	8	92	16	7.66
A. Walker	3	2	0	14	10*	7.00
M.J. Saggers	4	4	—	14	14	4.00
S. Lugsden	4	8	—	97	45	13.85
M.A. Roseberry	2	2	—	46	39	23.00
A. Pratt	—	—	—	—	—	—
J.A. Daley	—	—	—	—	—	—
S. Hutton	7	13	—	258	95	21.50
R.M.S. Weston	5	8	—	137	36	17.12

Durham CCC First-Class Matches
Bowling

	S.J.E. Brown	M.M. Betts	N. Killeen	J. Boiling	D.M. Cox	P.D. Collingwood	M.J. Saggers	J. Wood	C.L. Campbell	A. Walker	M.J. Foster	D.C. Boon	Byes	Leg-byes	Wides	No-balls	Total	Wkts	
v. Oxford University (Oxford) 15–17 April	15-5-33-2 / 22-9-35-4	17.3-5-51-6 / 21-7-43-0	7-1-20-1 / 13-1-46-0	11-3-28-0 / 20.1-8-21-3	8-4-12-1 / 11-5-41-1	6-0-26-1 / 12-2-46-3							6 / 8	3 / 13	2	2	153 / 247	10 / 10	
v. Lancashire (Old Trafford) 23–26 April	26-5-93-2	20.2-2-114-2		17-3-82-1				13-1-70-1	12-0-92-1				2	7		10	506	10	A
v. Nottinghamshire (Hartlepool) 7–10 May	19-5-61-2 / 22-7-57-1		6-3-8-0 / 13-2-24-1	1-1-0-0 / 21.1-12-32-2		1-0-6-0 / 6-0-24-0				17-5-56-7 / 10-2-50-1	6-0-32-1 / 5-0-21-1	3-1-7-0		13 / 3	6	4 / 2	170 / 200	10 / 6	B
v. Essex (Chelmsford) 14–17 May	17.1-1-54-4 / 9-1-35-0		12-2-50-4 / 13-2-57-1	1-0-8-0 / 23-5-80-2		4-0-18-0 / 6-1-26-1				15-4-51-2 / 17.3-4-73-1	13-5-43-0 / 22-2-94-4	1-0-3-0	5 / 2	7 / 4	2	6 / 9	237 / 366	9 / 9	
v. Worcestershire (Chester-le-Street) 21–24 May				23-3-62-0			14-3-28-1 / 12-2-57-2			25-8-61-2 / 13-1-48-1	19-3-69-1			12 / 8	24 / 2	4	351 / 113	6 / 8	
v. Glamorgan (Cardiff) 29 May–2 June	33-4-113-1			33-5-117-1	15.3-2-72-3	11-1-51-1				26-4-112-1	22-4-122-1		3	7	6	6	597	8	
v. Sussex (Chester-le-Street) 4–7 June	37.5-5-115-5 / 23-2-76-3	15-0-51-5 / 18-2-61-1					24-5-56-1 / 8-3-19-0			27-8-82-1 / 26.3-4-68-6	18-8-53-2 / 8-1-43-0		1	16 / 3	18 / 6	4 / 6	373 / 271	10 / 10	
v. Cambridge University (Cambridge) 14–16 June		14-2-52-0		24-11-27-1	6-1-17-1		6-2-17-0	10-1-65-0						10		6	188	2	
v. Kent (Darlington) 18–21 June	18-2-85-1 / 22-8-57-4	16-7-29-7 / 22-3-25-2		2-1-3-0 / 11-8-10-2		2-0-6-0				13-6-18-1 / 8-3-16-0	6-4-16-1	5.2-2-18-2	1 / 4	9 / 2	12	19 / 8	167 / 132	10 / 10	
v. Hampshire (Chester-le-Street) 2–5 July	23-5-70-1	10.1-1-58-2		19-3-58-2				25-7-97-1		26-5-97-2	26-3-78-2		4	7			372	Ab	
v. Yorkshire (Scarborough) 16–19 July	29-7-120-4			19-3-78-0						27.1-7-109-1	11-1-53-0			12	2	14	471	6	
v. Gloucestershire (Cheltenham) 23–26 July	20.1-2-63-4 / 15-5-58-5	10-0-48-2 / 9-2-20-1		3-0-20-0 / 8-3-19-0				14-1-77-2 / 12-2-42-1			7-0-42-1 / 11.4-3-33-2			4 / 4		19	254 / 176	10 / 10	
v. Derbyshire (Chester-le-Street) 31 July–4 August	30.3-4-101-0 / 7-2-17-0	22-8-58-1 / 5-0-22-0		11-2-45-1 / 0.5-0-7-1				17-0-73-4 / 2-0-16-0			20-7-52-3		4	17 / 1	10	6	350 / 64	9 / 1	
v. Surrey (The Oval) 6–9 August	21-10-51-2			21.5-3-72-3						18-6-48-1	19-4-58-4	2-0-9-0	4	9	6	16	251	10	
v. Middlesex (Chester-le-Street) 20–23 August	13-5-43-1 / 30-15-52-2	22-7-64-9 / 15-0-79-4		1-0-3-0 / 32-16-67-1	29-6-60-1						8-1-18-0 / 8-1-30-1		1 / 4	15 / 12	2 / 7	4 / 2	144 / 309	10 / 9	C
v. Northamptonshire (Northampton) 27–30 August	40.2-5-135-4	20-6-43-1		27-7-70-1						32-11-52-2	21-4-85-2		4	23	4	2	412	10	D
v. Warwickshire (Chester-le-Street) 2–5 September	27.1-6-69-3	19-4-56-2 / 5-1-21-0		4-1-10-0 / 1-0-4-0				11-1-66-0 / 8-1-35-2		13-4-37-2 / 6-1-24-0	14-3-37-2 / 11-1-48-2		3	14 / 4	5	2	217 / 152	10 / 2	
v. Somerset (Chester-le-Street) 10–13 September	10-0-52-0 / 21.3-5-67-5	18-3-68-4		1-0-2-0						13-4-35-1				1			241	10	
v. Leicestershire (Leicester) 18–21 September	20-2-74-5	19-5-71-2		1-0-4-0						8-0-35-1			1	3		2	219	10	
Bowler's average	550.4-117- / 1735-63 / 27.53	329-77- / 1085-49 / 22.14	64-14- / 205-7 / 29.28	336-98- / 925-21 / 44.04	69.3-18- / 202-7 / 28.85	48-4- / 203-6 / 33.83	64-15- / 177-7 / 25.28	112-14- / 541-11 / 49.18	12-0- / 92-1 / 92.00	341.1-87- / 1063-33 / 32.12	275.4-55- / 1027-30 / 34.23	12.2-3- / 39-2 / 19.50							

A N.J. Speak 4-0-14-0
B S. Lugsden 16.5-2-88-1
C R.M.S. Weston 1-0-5-0
D J.E. Morris 1-0-1-0

Fielding Figures

26 – R.J. Rollins (ct 24 / st 2)
19 – S.G. Law
16 – A.P. Grayson
15 – B.J. Hyam
13 – G.A. Gooch and D.D.J. Robinson
11 – D.R. Law
10 – P.J. Prichard
7 – N. Hussain
6 – A.P. Cowan
5 – P.M. Such
4 – N.F. Williams
3 – R.C. Irani, S.D. Peters and A.J. Hibbert
2 – sub
1 – M.C. Ilott and D.G. Wilson

Essex First-Class Matches — Batting Averages

Batting	M	Inns	NO	Runs	HS	Av
G.A. Gooch	10	17	—	369	56	23.06
P.J. Prichard	17	27	1	1184	224	47.36
N. Hussain	10	17	—	650	128	38.23
S.G. Law	17	28	2	1482	175	57.00
R.C. Irani	16	24	2	793	123*	34.47
D.D.J. Robinson	14	22	1	735	148	35.00
D.R. Law	19	29	0	492	81	16.96
B.J. Hyam	7	10	2	79	26	9.87
M.C. Ilott	13	20	5	290	47	19.33
A.P. Cowan	16	26	6	447	77	22.35
P.M. Such	19	21	11	58	14	5.27
S.D. Peters	3	3	—	135	102*	67.50
A.J.E. Hibbert	1	1	0	17	17	17.00
A.P. Grayson	18	26	3	914	105	39.73
D.G. Wilson	2	—	—	—	—	—
G.R. Napier	2	2	—	39	35*	9.00
S.J.W. Andrew	3	3	1	27	24	—
R.J. Rollins	13	19	4	452	82	25.11
N.F. Williams	4	5	1	66	23	16.50
J.C. Powell	1	1	—	4	4*	—
T.P. Hodgson	3	6	—	101	44	16.83
I.N. Flanagan	2	3	—	72	40	36.00

Match results and team totals — first half

Match	Total	Wickets	Result	Points
v. Hampshire (Chelmsford) 23–26 April	246 & 442	10 & 8	D	8
v. Cambridge University (Cambridge) 7–9 May	403	5	D	—
v. Durham (Chelmsford) 14–17 May	237 & 366	10 & 9	W	21
v. Gloucestershire (Gloucester) 21–24 May	310	10	D	10
v. Yorkshire (Ilford) 29 May–2 June	297 & 312	10 & 10	L	6
v. Surrey (The Oval) 4–7 June	347 & 302	10 & 10	W	23
v. Sussex (Hove) 12–16 June	384 & 115	10 & 0	W	24
v. Oxford University (Chelmsford) 20–22 June	34	10	D	—
v. Derbyshire (Southend) 26–30 June	373	8	W	24
v. Somerset (Chelmsford) 2–5 July	280 & 129	10 & 10	L	6

Match results and team totals — second half

Match	Total	Wickets	Result	Points
v. Northamptonshire (Northampton) 16–19 July	275 & 290	10 & 10	L	6
v. Worcestershire (Chelmsford) 23–26 July	451	10	D	8
v. Leicestershire (Colchester) 31 July–4 August	533	8	D	9
v. Kent (Canterbury) 6–9 August	156 & 361	10 & 10	L	2
v. Nottinghamshire (Worksop) 20–23 August	440 & 183	7 & 8	D	8
v. Warwickshire (Chelmsford) 27–30 August	178 & 101	10 & 4	L	4
v. Lancashire (Old Trafford) 2–5 September	389	10	W	20
v. Glamorgan (Cardiff) 10–13 September	169 & 340	10 & 10	L	4
v. Middlesex (Chelmsford) 18–21 September	271 & 301	10 & 9	D	9

Essex CCC First-Class Matches

Bowling

	M.C. Ilott	A.P. Cowan	R.C. Irani	D.R. Law	S.J.W. Andrew	P.M. Such	A.P. Grayson	D.G. Wilson	G.R. Napier	J.C. Powell	S.G. Law	N.F. Williams	Byes	Leg-byes	Wides	No-balls	Total	Wkts	
v. Hampshire (Chelmsford)	15.1–2–37–2	21–6–49–5	15–7–23–2	9–2–42–1									2	8		8	161	10	
23–26 April	8–3–13–1	7–0–27–0	3–1–10–1	4–1–13–0										1		4	64	2	
v. Cambridge University				19–1–93–5	17–2–76–0	28–12–41–2	18–7–33–1	4.3–0–36–1						6		12	285	9	
(Cambridge) 7–9 May					5–1–16–1	8–5–8–2	5–3–4–0	11–2–31–1	9–3–25–2				1	5	4		91	6	A
v. Durham (Chelmsford)	25.3–10–53–2	33–14–73–4	22–7–52–1	18–3–81–3		9–4–14–0							5	13	4	23	291	10	
14–17 May	19–7–48–2	17.5–9–33–1	9–3–25–1	2–0–8–0		29–15–55–6					3–0–8–0		4	6		4	187	10	
v. Gloucestershire (Gloucester)	27–7–82–4	25–9–47–2	20–7–49–2	5.3–0–34–2		23–5–57–0	3–0–10–0						1	10	2	2	290	10	
21–24 May	7–4–22–2	6–6–0–0		5–2–29–0		5–0–7–1	3–2–3–0				3–2–1–0			2		4	64	3	
v. Yorkshire (Ilford)	19–6–69–2	9–0–35–0	2–0–23–0			37.2–7–121–6	24–2–65–1				4–0–14–0		1	6	4	10	334	10	
29 May–2 June	10–3–30–2	6–1–30–0				34.2–7–94–5	22–0–79–1				5–2–23–0		4	17	4		277	8	
v. Surrey (The Oval)	11.5–1–58–1	20–4–58–5	11–0–49–1	9.4–1–40–1		19.1–3–66–2								9		2	280	10	
4–7 June	2–1–2–0	18–2–75–3	23.2–8–51–3	11–3–20–1		18–3–40–2					7–2–20–0		5	9	2	2	222	9	B
v. Sussex (Hove)		14.2–2–45–5	7–3–16–0	4–0–31–1							7–4–13–0	11–2–29–4	5	1	2	16	140	10	
12–16 June		29–11–78–4	19.3–7–50–2			23–9–40–1	25–7–56–1				12–1–42–0	22–2–77–1	6	7	10	18	356	10	
v. Oxford University (Chelmsford)	15–6–22–3		5–2–13–0	11.5–3–22–2		8–5–7–0						18–5–55–5		1			120	10	
20–22 June																			
v. Derbyshire (Southend)	19–9–59–7	18.4–5–46–3	5–0–18–0			5–0–13–0							1	5	2	2	142	10	
26–30 June	9–1–16–2	5–2–8–0				20.5–7–27–5	17–9–20–3						7	8			86	10	
v. Somerset (Chelmsford)	22.4–7–70–3	22–3–99–2	18–5–41–0	19–1–72–3		27–9–56–0	19–7–42–2						4	5	4	6	389	10	
2–5 July	2.4–0–13–0	2–0–9–0													2		22	0	
v. Northamptonshire		24–5–98–3	16–4–37–0	23–5–70–2		13–3–41–1	19–6–53–4					19–4–58–0	1	6		17	364	10	
(Northampton) 16–19 July		19–9–54–4	16–6–44–1	12.3–1–31–1		3–2–1–0	23–11–21–2					18–3–52–2	9	4	2	12	216	10	
v. Worcestershire (Chelmsford)		9–0–49–0	22–2–69–1	21–6–54–0	18–7–26–1	36–9–103–3	20–5–54–2				12–4–27–3			12	4	16	394	10	
23–26 July		8–0–40–0	11–4–20–0		5–0–18–1	35–11–70–2	13–4–30–0				11–1–56–2		4	9	6	4	250	5	C
v. Leicestershire (Colchester)		14–2–59–1	9–1–25–1	17–1–94–0		86–49–94–4	38–16–81–2			39–5–109–1	7–0–26–0		17	10		14	515	9	
31 July–4 August																			
v. Kent (Canterbury)			28–6–80–2	25.2–6–77–2	23–7–87–1	26–5–117–2	9–1–44–1				18–7–49–0	13–0–65–1	1	5	6	4	525	9	
6–9 August																			
v. Nottinghamshire (Worksop)	16–6–49–0	13–3–59–1		2–0–10–0		26.3–4–78–1	24–5–71–0		8–3–40–1		10–3–28–0		4	12	14	10	351	3	
20–23 August																			
v. Warwickshire (Chelmsford)	14–4–42–1	20–1–76–2				30–4–94–6	5.5–1–12–1						7	6		8	237	10	
27–30 August	3–0–19–0	4–1–21–0				1–1–0–2	0.4–0–2–0							1		2	43	2	
v. Lancashire (Old Trafford)	4–2–9–0			4–2–8–0		3–1–3–0	4–0–17–0							2		6	39	0	
2–5 September	8–1–25–0	8–1–22–1		4–1–17–1		42–15–103–4	38.2–12–143–4						6	8	18	4	324	10	
v. Glamorgan (Cardiff)	22–4–65–3	5–1–26–0		24.4–6–69–4		31–6–82–0	33–7–84–2				4–0–16–0		5	14	5	6	361	10	
10–13 September	13.1–2–43–0	11–4–14–2		4–0–19–0		12–2–35–1	4–0–23–0						4	12		8	150	3	
v. Middlesex (Chelmsford)	28–8–63–4	26.1–5–84–3		13–5–31–1		23–2–65–2	18–2–42–0				5–4–1–0		7	13	2	2	306	10	
18–21 September	11–1–37–2	5–0–20–1		2–1–4–1		9–3–16–0	9–5–20–1				8–2–32–0		4	6	4		139	5	
	332–95–	420–106–	261.5–73–	270.3–51–	68–17–	671.1–207–	394.5–112–	15.3–2–	17–6–	39–5–	116–30–	101–16–							
	946–43	1334–52	695–18	969–31	223–4	1548–60	1009–28	67–2	65–3	109–1	356–5	336–13							
Bowler's average	22.00	25.65	38.61	31.25	55.75	25.80	36.03	33.50	21.66	109.00	71.20	25.84							

A A.J.E. Hibbert 1–0–1–0
B A.D. Brown absent hurt
C G.A. Gooch 2–1–3–0

Fielding Figures

54 – A.D. Shaw (ct 52 / st 2)
21 – M.P. Maynard
15 – P.A. Cottey
14 – S.P. James
13 – R.D.B. Croft
8 – S.D. Thomas
6 – A. Dale
4 – C.D. Metson (ct 3 / st 1) and D.A. Cosker
3 – S.L. Watkin, Waqar Younis and sub
1 – P. Warren, G.P. Butcher, A.W. Evans, O.T. Parkin and M.J. Powell

Glamorgan CCC First-Class Matches Batting

Batting	v. Warwickshire (Cardiff) 23–26 April	v. Yorkshire (Leeds) 7–10 May	v. Kent (Canterbury) 14–17 May	v. Hampshire (Cardiff) 21–24 May	v. Durham (Cardiff) 29 May–2 June	v. Oxford University (Oxford) 5–7 June	v. Middlesex (Cardiff) 12–16 June	v. Lancashire (Liverpool) 18–21 June	v. Sussex (Swansea) 26–30 June	v. Gloucestershire (Swansea) 2–5 July	M	Inns	NO	Runs	HS	Av
S.P. James	83	109 / 52	46 / 54	76	153	—	3 / 2	152* / 24	48 / 1	8 / 26*	18	30	4	1775	162	68.26
H. Morris	233*	55 / 96	18 / 25	21	135	—	16	24	1 / 3	173	17	28	4	1262	233*	52.58
S.L. Watkin	18*	18*	39	—	—	—	4	—	0	0	17	16	3	138	39	10.61
A. Dale	106	44	—	1	73	83	0	78*	15	98	19	27	4	860	142*	37.39
M.P. Maynard	20*	3 / 0*	12 / 5	34	134*	101*	59 / 9	—	0	16*	18	25	7	1170	161*	65.00
P.A. Cottey	20*	—	17	34 / 58	15	—	21	—	15	76*	17	21	4	475	83	27.94
G.P. Butcher	—	—	—	35	—	—	—	—	34* / 24	—	8	11	2	296	53*	32.88
A.D. Shaw	—	0	0 / 30	—	33 / 29	—	82 / 11*	—	— / 0*	16*	13	18	2	389	101*	24.31
R.D.B. Croft	57	—	39	2*	—	17*	—	—	—	—	18	19	2	577	86	33.94
S.D. Thomas	—	—	46 / 0*	—	7	—	26	78*	—	—	15	18	4	301	75*	21.50
D.A. Cosker	—	—	—	—	—	37	2	2	0* / 5	—	6	9	5	16	7	4.00
Waqar Younis	—	12	47	—	—	16	—	—	—	—	16	17	1	289	47	18.06
A.W. Evans	—	—	—	—	—	14 / 200*	—	—	—	—	2	6	3	61	31	20.33
M.J. Powell	—	—	—	—	—	200*	—	—	—	—	5	8	3	286	200*	57.20
W.L. Law	—	—	5*	—	38*	38*	—	—	—	—	2	3	1	38	38*	—
P. Warren	—	—	10	—	—	—	—	—	—	—	—	—	—	—	—	—
G.J.M. Edwards	—	—	—	—	—	—	—	—	—	—	—	—	—	—	—	—
C.P. Metson	0	—	—	—	—	—	—	—	—	0	—	2	1	0	0	0.00
O.T. Parkin	0*	—	—	—	—	—	—	—	—	—	—	1	1	0	0*	—
Byes	6	4	1	0	3	4	19	8	2	4						
Leg-byes	27	12	4	10	7	4	7	6	2	12						
Wides	2	2	4	2	1	4	8	6	18	10						
No-balls	36	4	10	14	6	16	6	2	12							
Total	551	336 / 166	279 / 193	287	597	422 / 137	281 / 31	272	172 / 183	400						
Wickets	3	10 / 2	10 / 10	8	8	2 / 10	10 / 10	1	10 / 9	5						
Result	D	D	W	D	W	L	L	W	W	W						
Points	11	10	22	4	24	—	6	18	20	24						

Batting

Batting	v. Australians (Cardiff) 16–18 July	v. Derbyshire (Chesterfield) 23–26 July	v. Nottinghamshire (Colwyn Bay) 31 July–4 August	v. Worcestershire (Worcester) 15–18 August	v. Northamptonshire (Abergavenny) 20–23 August	v. Leicestershire (Leicester) 27–30 August	v. Surrey (The Oval) 2–5 September	v. Essex (Cardiff) 10–13 September	v. Somerset (Taunton) 18–21 September	M	Inns	NO	Runs	HS	Av
S.P. James	91 / 79	25	162	69 / 130	103 / 113	14 / 21	23 / 28	2 / 4	8 / 9*	18	30	4	1775	162	68.26
H. Morris	13 / 42	11*	12	4 / 37	113	8 / 23*	16 / 9	82	165	17	28	4	1262	233*	52.58
S.L. Watkin	0	0	20	9 / 13	71 / 58	69 / 13	72 / 26*	49 / 71	5 / 8	17	16	3	138	39	10.61
A. Dale	20*	142*	0	161*	36	0 / 6*	76 / 46	75* / 35*	142 / 13	19	27	4	860	142*	37.39
M.P. Maynard	45*	43	48* / 31*	18 / 33	—	25	76 / 34	6	—	18	25	7	1170	161*	65.00
P.A. Cottey	22	14	—	15 / 33	15	0 / 35	8 / 36*	16	53*	17	21	4	475	83	27.94
G.P. Butcher	23	38	31	27 / 25	19	1*	53 / 7	—	86	8	11	2	296	53*	32.88
A.D. Shaw	—	—	—	44*	—	28	0	17	—	13	18	2	389	101*	24.31
R.D.B. Croft	10 / 15	31	—	46 / 0	9	3	15	—	5	18	19	2	577	86	33.94
S.D. Thomas	2	—	—	0 / 8	31 / 41*	—	—	—	7	15	18	4	301	75*	21.50
D.A. Cosker	—	—	—	—	0	3	—	—	5	6	9	5	16	7	4.00
Waqar Younis	24	8	—	46 / 0	—	—	—	—	—	16	17	1	289	47	18.06
A.W. Evans	—	—	—	—	—	—	—	—	—	2	6	3	61	31	20.33
M.J. Powell	—	—	—	—	—	—	—	—	—	5	8	3	286	200*	57.20
W.L. Law	—	—	—	—	—	—	—	—	—	2	3	1	38	38*	—
P. Warren	—	—	—	—	—	—	—	—	—	—	—	—	—	—	—
G.J.M. Edwards	—	—	—	—	—	—	—	—	—	—	—	—	—	—	—
C.P. Metson	0	—	—	—	—	—	—	—	—	—	2	1	0	0	0.00
O.T. Parkin	0*	—	—	—	—	—	—	—	1	—	1	1	0	0*	—
Byes	4	2	14	11	1	2	8	5	7						
Leg-byes	17	8	12	7	13	10	15	14	—						
Wides	5	—	4	4	5	2	4	6	—						
No-balls	24	10	6	22	2	22	20	8	16						
Total	254	364	353	398	354	226	438	361	527						
Wickets	10	8	6	10	6	10	10	10	10						
Result	D	D	D	L	W	D	D	W	W						
Points	—	9	11	6	24	8	11	24	24						

Glamorgan CCC First-Class Matches — Bowling

Bowling analyses are given as overs–maidens–runs–wickets. Where two figures are shown for a match, they represent the two innings bowled.

Match	S.L.Watkin	S.D.Thomas	R.D.B.Croft	A.Dale	G.P.Butcher	Waqar Younis	D.A.Cosker	P.A.Cottey	M.P.Maynard	P.Warren	G.J.M.Edwards	O.T.Parkin	Total	Wkts
v. Warwickshire (Cardiff) 23–26 April	11-4-32-3 / 12-3-15-0	12-1-62-4 / 12.5-3-31-2	13-1-37-2 / 7-4-10-1	1-0-2-0	2.4-0-14-1 / 3-0-21-0								151 / 77	10 / 3
v. Yorkshire (Leeds) 7–10 May	12-4-34-1	5-0-32-1	16.2-3-58-4	4-0-21-0	5-1-11-2	12-1-42-1							200	9
v. Kent (Canterbury) 14–17 May	14-5-46-1 / 9-1-35-0	11-4-13-3 / 7-1-23-0	18.4-5-33-5 / 18-4-54-3			10-3-49-1 / 14.1-0-52-3							154 / 231	10 / 10
v. Hampshire (Cardiff) 21–24 May	24-2-70-1	12-0-52-0		6.1-2-10-0	5-2-16-0	16-5-39-1		1.3-0-17-0	3.5-1-30-0				309	4
v. Durham (Cardiff) 29 May–2 June	28.2-10-73-4 / 18-7-31-3	20-7-59-2 / 9-1-28-1	25-8-51-1 / 33-10-81-2	3-2-5-0 / 5-2-10-0		22-4-98-3 / 20-7-56-4	12-4-41-0 / 8-2-26-0						345 / 244	10 / 10
v. Oxford University (Oxford) 5–7 June	27-12-43-4		27-3-90-1		14.3-3-56-1 / 11-2-52-1		29.1-0-68-3 / 17.5-4-89-2	1-0-2-0 / 1-1-0-0	3-0-10-0 / 4-0-17-0	14-5-45-0 / 5-2-15-0	5-2-18-0 / 4-0-31-0		284 / 278	9 / 5
v. Middlesex (Cardiff) 12–16 June						22-2-89-1							319	0
v. Lancashire (Liverpool) 18–21 June	7-3-21-3 / 3-2-4-0					7-1-25-7 / 11.5-4-17-8							0 / 51	0 / 10
v. Sussex (Swansea) 26–30 June	8-2-13-2	9.4-3-24-5 / 7.4-1-26-1	8-2-25-2 / 8-5-9-3			7-2-17-0							54 / 67	10 / 10
v. Gloucestershire (Swansea) 2–5 July	17-5-61-3	18-4-40-3		4-1-9-0 / 13-2-49-0	1-0-2-0 / 13-1-52-2	16.1-3-40-2	18-1-59-3 / 27-8-87-4						214 / 233	10 / 10
v. Australians (Cardiff) 16–18 July	22-8-46-1	16-1-73-0 / 14-3-42-3		9-1-43-0 / 8.2-33-0	10-1-36-0 / 9-3-36-0		24-5-95-2 / 17-3-36-1						369 / 217	4 / 7
v. Derbyshire (Chesterfield) 23–26 July	33-5-131-3 / 6-2-11-0	15-2-84-0				28-3-132-2 / 5-0-17-0	38-14-79-1 / 3.1-1-4-0						513 / 35	6 / 0
v. Nottinghamshire (Colwyn Bay) 31 July–4 August	12-3-46-2 / 18-8-27-1	11.1-2-37-2 / 12-2-55-1	24-8-46-3 / 30-5-52-3			18-3-66-3 / 19-3-62-1			2-0-8-0				202 / 239	10 / 8
v. Worcestershire (Worcester) 15–18 August	33-11-82-0	21.3-1-92-2	39-11-80-3 / 42-10-98-4	8-1-30-0	9-2-18-2 / 20-4-87-3	25-7-86-1 / 20.5-6-50-3	15-5-31-0 / 11-0-40-0		1-0-1-0				476 / 295	9 / 10
v. Northamptonshire (Abergavenny) 20–23 August	24-7-49-2	11-1-38-0	28-5-68-3	4-0-17-0	6-1-44-0	22.2-6-78-4	11-5-18-0						330 / 219	10 / 10
v. Leicestershire (Leicester) 27–30 August	22-6-49-1 / 21-6-41-2	4-0-24-0	21-5-54-2 / 16-5-35-2	3-0-23-0		13-3-53-1							175	0
v. Surrey (The Oval) 2–5 September	19.4-6-41-7 / 16-6-42-2	11.2-3-36-3 / 24-2-79-1	23-5-54-3 / 37-4-128-2			16-3-55-2 / 23-4-79-2	5-1-14-0 / 23.4-2-107-3						204 / 487	10 / 10
v. Essex (Cardiff) 10–13 September	22-1-78-1 / 14-2-68-3	8-0-48-2	8.2-2-10-1 / 31-6-86-2			11-2-31-3 / 22-2-82-2	2-1-4-0 / 11-3-25-0					19-4-78-0	169 / 340	0 / 10
v. Somerset (Taunton) 18–21 September	26.4-9-68-5 / 13.4-2-61-3 / 15-1-75-3	16-2-53-0 / 15-2-38-5	13-1-49-1 / 18-5-51-1			12-3-41-4 / 11-0-84-0	11-3-42-2 / 11.4-3-34-1					15-3-38-3	252 / 285	10 / 10
Bowler's average	508.2-143-1393-61 / 22.83	405.3-58-1444-53 / 27.24	504.2-118-1259-54 / 23.31	71.1-14-261-0 / —	114.1-21-466-12 / 38.83	441.4-83-1551-68 / 22.80	343.2-80-1024-28 / 36.57	3.3-1-19-0 / —	13.5-1-66-0 / —	19-7-60-0 / —	9-2-49-0 / —	34-7-116-3 / 38.66		

A M.J. Powell 1-0-3-0

Fielding Figures

57 – R.C. Russell (ct 52 / st 5)
24 – M.C.J. Ball
14 – M.W. Alleyne
11 – A.J. Wright
10 – S. Young and T.H.C. Hancock
9 – M.A. Lynch and R.P. Davis
7 – M.G.N. Windows
4 – R.J. Cunliffe and A.M. Smith
3 – N.J. Trainor, R.I. Dawson and D.R. Hewson
2 – J.J. Lewis
1 – J.M.M. Averis and D.V. Lawrence

†M.A. Lynch absent hurt   ‡D.R. Hewson absent

Gloucestershire CCC First-Class Matches Batting — Season Summary

Batsman	M	Inns	NO	Runs	HS	Av
N.J. Trainor	14	25	1	484	121	20.16
A.J. Wright	13	22	3	416	79	21.89
R.J. Cunliffe	9	14	1	273	61	21.00
M.A. Lynch	12	19	1	465	64	25.83
S. Young	17	28	3	981	237	39.24
M.W. Alleyne	19	30	4	1059	169	40.73
R.C. Russell	19	29	6	1049	103*	45.60
T.H.C. Hancock	19	31	3	854	100*	30.50
M.C.J. Ball	18	27	3	587	50	24.45
A.M. Smith	17	24	8	161	41*	10.06
J.J. Lewis	15	19	8	193	30	17.54
D.V. Lawrence	9	6	2	32	23*	10.66
R.P. Davis	9	12	1	135	39	11.25
K.P. Sheeraz	8	2	1	25	12*	
R.I. Dawson	8	14	0	329	100	23.50
M.G.N. Windows	8	15	0	369	84	24.60
J.M.M. Averis	1	2	–	73	53	18.25
M.J. Church	2	4	–	56	42	14.00
D.R. Hewson	3	4				

Matches (first half of season):
- v. Leicestershire (Leicester) 23–26 April
- v. Hampshire (Bristol) 7–10 May
- v. Surrey (The Oval) 14–17 May
- v. Essex (Gloucester) 21–24 May
- v. Australians (Bristol) 27–29 May
- v. Yorkshire (Leeds) 4–7 June
- v. Worcestershire (Bristol) 12–16 June
- v. Middlesex (Bristol) 18–21 June
- v. Northamptonshire (Luton) 26–30 June
- v. Glamorgan (Swansea) 2–5 July

Matches (second half of season):
- v. Derbyshire (Cheltenham) 16–19 July
- v. Durham (Cheltenham) 23–26 July
- v. Pakistan 'A' (Bristol) 1–4 August
- v. Somerset (Taunton) 6–9 August
- v. Sussex (Hove) 15–18 August
- v. Nottinghamshire (Bristol) 27–30 August
- v. Kent (Canterbury) 2–5 September
- v. Warwickshire (Edgbaston) 10–13 September
- v. Lancashire (Bristol) 18–21 September

Gloucestershire CCC — First-Class Matches — Bowling

Match	A.M. Smith	J.J. Lewis	S. Young	M.C.J. Ball	M.W. Alleyne	T.H.C. Hancock	N.J. Trainor	D.V. Lawrence	R.P. Davis	M.G.N. Windows	K.P. Sheeraz	J.M.M. Averis	Byes	Leg-byes	Wides	No-balls	Total	Wkts	
v. Leicestershire (Leicester) 23–26 April	24.1-8-62-2	23-3-76-2	20-5-56-0	17-4-36-2	20-11-29-3	5-1-24-1	3-2-1-0						12	11		4	307	10	A
v. Hampshire (Bristol) 7–10 May	28-8-61-4		26.3-1-143-3	22-8-89-0	14-4-47-1	10-2-39-1		18-1-78-1					5	9	2	6	316	10	
	22-5-45-6		21-8-48-0	8-3-16-1	8-2-14-1			8-3-15-1						2	8	2	145	9	
v. Surrey (The Oval)	12.5-4-35-3		12-4-26-4		7-2-18-1		2-0-1-0	7-0-35-2					2		6	8	115	10	
v. Essex (Gloucester) 14–17 May	20-5-44-1	19-2-89-4	15-2-26-0	16-7-35-1	16.4-3-64-6	4-0-20-0		13-1-58-2	22-8-63-2				2	9		8	261	10	
	22-3-68-3		16-4-34-1	28-3-65-0	13-4-41-2	6.5-0-28-1							4	7		2	310	10	
v. Australians (Bristol) 21–24 May	11-3-26-2	18-5-59-1	2-0-5-0	17.4-3-56-3	7-2-26-0	8-1-29-0			11-3-20-1				6	3		4	249	10	
	13-5-18-2	9-3-22-0	11-3-35-0	28-9-89-1	8-2-25-0	5-0-26-0	3-2-8-0		29-6-101-0				4	2	1		354	9	B
v. Yorkshire (Leeds) 27–29 May	22.1-6-58-6	18-4-58-2		1-0-4-0	5-2-1-1	3-0-11-0	2-1-4-0							5	4	2	183	9	C
v. Worcestershire (Bristol) 4–7 June	20.4-7-74-4	9-3-22-0		10-2-32-0	13-0-55-0	3-2-13-0							4		4	6	246	10	
	20-1-46-2	22-5-68-2	18.4-5-55-1	15-5-32-0	20.5-7-41-5	9-2-23-0								12	6	4	250	4	
v. Middlesex (Bristol) 12–16 June	13-4-34-1	13-4-34-1	24-6-65-2	28-3-11-1	16-7-37-2	9-2-30-0							8	4	2	4	350	10	
	17.5-9-23-5	16-0-72-1	13-1-49-1	5-1-14-0	1-0-4-0									2			237	8	
v. Northamptonshire (Luton) 18–21 June	10-2-42-1	12.5-1-50-6	8-0-26-1											1		4	124	8	
	10-3-36-3	9.3-6-21-3												2			58	6	
v. Glamorgan (Swansea) 26–30 June		26-3-87-3	18-4-59-1	19-1-76-1	17-1-61-1				15.3-0-70-0		7-0-40-0		4	3	12	10	400	5	
		4-1-12-0	5-1-18-0	3-2-4-0					4.5-1-18-0						2		52	0	
v. Derbyshire (Cheltenham) 2–5 July	12-1-47-6	7-0-36-2	7-1-19-1		2-0-11-0	1-0-8-0								7	2	6	120	10	
v. Durham (Cheltenham) 16–19 July	21.4-5-59-4	20-4-57-1	10-4-9-3	29-5-80-0	18-4-70-2		5-1-27-0					5-2-22-0	6	3		2	329	10	D
		12-4-35-2			8.2-2-14-5					1-1-0-0		12-2-54-0		6		6	86	10	
v. Pakistan 'A' (Bristol) 23–26 July	14-4-50-1	19-5-51-1	30-8-91-3	28-9-58-1	22.2-6-69-4	10-4-31-1			27-11-31-0	1-0-4-0				3	2	4	357	10	
		16-5-42-1		14.5-3-44-3	16-5-46-4									3			220	10	
v. Somerset (Taunton) 1–4 August	17-5-60-3	17-4-84-1	9-1-32-1	10-3-30-0	10-2-43-0									3		6	252	5	
v. Sussex (Hove) 6–9 August	15-4-60-4	5-1-24-1	5-1-15-0	17-11-15-4	3-0-24-0				23.4-10-35-4				1	5	6	16	138	10	
	22-3-88-2	24-4-81-3		16-10-17-0	25-3-80-1				29-13-35-4				2	3		6	324	10	
v. Nottinghamshire (Bristol) 15–18 August	5-1-11-0	8-2-34-1	13-1-43-0	30-7-66-5	13-2-42-2	10-4-17-0	6-1-38-0	13-2-42-0		5-0-47-0			4	11		6	294	10	E
	25.3-4-83-6	21-4-63-2	5-2-13-0	9-5-6-0	4-1-14-0			6-0-28-2							6	6	161	5	
v. Kent (Canterbury) 27–30 August	8-1-18-0	10-4-42-3	21-8-59-1	5-3-7-0	12-2-48-2	3-1-19-0		15-2-50-0	18-8-29-1				6	10		18	228	10	
	20-7-46-3		8-3-43-0	10.5-0-43-3	6-1-42-0	4-0-31-1		6-0-53-0	26-9-86-0					5		21	305	4	
v. Warwickshire (Edgbaston) 2–5 September	9-2-35-0	24-5-89-6		27.2-12-6-3	12-2-48-2	4-1-21-0			6-0-22-0					8		10	432	4	
	20.3-2-70-4		12-0-70-0	29-10-69-0	17-3-69-0								1		2		418	4	F
v. Lancashire (Bristol) 10–13 September	20-7-35-3	22.3-9-55-5		15-5-33-0	6-2-17-1	5-2-16-0			10-1-38-1				2	7			203	10	
	12-4-41-2	14-4-45-1		21-5-68-1	5-0-21-0				19-6-59-3					10		4	245	9	

| Bowler's average | 489.2-123-1375-83 | 418.5-98-1401-54 | 362.3-98-1005-30 | 479.2-129-1271-29 | 360.1-89-1148-44 | 99.5-22-386-5 | 21-7-89-0 | 86-9-359-8 | 241-76-607-17 | 7-1-51-0 | 7-0-40-0 | 17-4-76-0 | | | | | | | |
| | 16.56 | 25.94 | 33.50 | 43.82 | 26.09 | 77.20 | – | 44.87 | 35.70 | – | – | – | | | | | | | |

A M. Keech absent hurt
B R.C. Russell 3-0-15-0
C M.P. Vaughan retired hurt, absent hurt
D M.J. Vandrau retired hurt
E R.I. Dawson 2-0-21-0
F R.I. Dawson 1-0-1-0

Fielding Figures

42 – A.N. Aymes (ct 45 / st 7)
13 – M.L. Hayden
10 – M. Keech
8 – G.W.White
7 – J.P. Stephenson
6 – W.S. Kendall, J.S. Laney and R.J. Maru
5 – K.D. James and J.N.B. Bovill
4 – R.A. Smith
3 – S.J. Renshaw, S.D. Udal and sub
1 – P.R. Whitaker, L. Savident, S.M. Milburn and D.A. Kenway

Hampshire CCC First-Class Matches Batting — Season Aggregates

Batting	M	Inns	NO	Runs	HS	Av
G.W.White	10	17	2	681	145	45.40
J.P.Stephenson	17	26	3	784	140	34.08
M.Keech	10	16	4	518	127	43.16
K.D.James	10	15	2	359	85	27.61
W.S.Kendall	12	19	2	413	76	24.29
P.R.Whitaker	3	5	1	132	73	33.00
A.N.Aymes	18	23	4	442	96*	23.26
S.D.Udal	18	24	3	600	117*	28.57
A.D.Mascarenhas	6	7	1	50	21	8.33
C.A.Connor	5	4	2	34	12*	17.00
S.M.Milburn	8	7	1	90	23	15.00
M.L.Hayden	11	30	3	1446	235*	53.55
J.S.Laney	14	25	—	844	95	33.76
R.A.Smith	13	23	1	918	154	41.72
S.J.Renshaw	9	19	7	269	56	22.41
R.J.Maru	—	9	—	67	36*	9.28
J.N.B.Bovill	3	4	—	65	20*	22.33
D.A.Kenway	—	2	—	22	6	22.00
L.Savident	—	4	—	15	6	5.00
C.Patel	—	2	—	9	—	9.00
T.M.Hansen	—	2	—	31	19	31.00
S.R.G.Francis	—	2	—	8	4	4.00

Match columns (left page, chronological):
v. Oxford University (Oxford) 18–21 April;
v. Essex (Chelmsford) 23–26 April;
v. Gloucestershire (Bristol) 7–10 May;
v. Leicestershire (Southampton) 14–17 May;
v. Glamorgan (Cardiff) 21–24 May;
v. Warwickshire (Southampton) 25 May–2 June;
v. Derbyshire (Chesterfield) 4–7 June;
v. Somerset (Basingstoke) 12–16 June;
v. Northamptonshire (Northampton) 18–21 June;
v. Australians (Southampton) 28–30 June.

Match columns (right page, chronological):
v. Durham (Chester-le-Street) 2–5 July;
v. Surrey (Guildford) 16–19 July;
v. Lancashire (Southampton) 23–26 July;
v. Middlesex (Lord's) 6–9 August;
v. Yorkshire (Portsmouth) 15–18 August;
v. Kent (Portsmouth) 27–30 August;
v. Nottinghamshire (Trent Bridge) 2–5 September;
v. Sussex (Southampton) 10–13 September;
v. Worcestershire (Southampton) 18–21 September.

†M.Keech absent

Hampshire CCC First-Class Matches — Bowling

Bowling figures are given as Overs–Maidens–Runs–Wickets. Where a bowler bowled in two innings the figures are separated by " / ".

Bowling	C.A. Connor	S.M. Milburn	J.P. Stephenson	A.D. Mascarenhas	S.D. Udal	K.D. James	R.A. Smith	S.J. Renshaw	M.L. Hayden	J.N.B. Bovill	R.J. Maru	M. Keech
v. Oxford University (Oxford) 18–21 April	16-2-57-2	18-8-35-3	10-2-29-0	13-3-35-0	18-11-26-1	16-6-36-3						
v. Essex (Chelmsford) 23–26 April	4-1-9-0 / 18-4-46-7	16-4-24-1 / 11-1-51-0	5-1-13-0 / 5-0-21-2	20-3-63-5 / 11-0-53-1	24.5-12-33-0 / 3-0-20-0	13-2-25-1 / 14-2-40-0						
v. Gloucestershire (Bristol) 7–10 May	12-0-66-0	11-0-75-0	20-3-74-3 / 23.1-1-81-4	15-2-48-1 / 1.4-0-8-0	16-2-55-1 / 19-2-59-0	22-0-106-3						
v. Leicestershire (Southampton) 14–17 May	28-9-93-3		8-1-25-0 / 9-3-24-2		48-12-118-4 / 23-7-52-1	8-2-25-2		25-2-73-2 / 6-0-30-4	8-0-28-0 / 5-0-20-0	18.3-0-61-2 / 7-1-30-2		
v. Glamorgan (Cardiff) 21–24 May	21.5-4-58-1 / 23-3-101-0	11-1-47-0	12-0-55-2					16-4-53-0				
v. Warwickshire (Southampton) 29 May–2 June					13-4-31-0 / 49-9-132-2	3-0-20-1 / 18-5-52-1				17-3-65-3 / 33-4-154-3	29-13-60-2 / 8-7-1-0	
v. Derbyshire (Chesterfield) 4–7 June			28-4-99-2 / 6-0-34-0	20-1-96-0	35-14-71-0 / 15-1-63-1	18-5-58-2	3-0-36-0	32-6-110-5 / 17-1-80-2	3-0-19-0 / 2-0-36-0	22-3-76-1 / 6-0-23-0	42-3-137-0	
v. Somerset (Basingstoke) 12–16 June			7.4-1-27-3 / 16-6-42-0	4-2-12-0 / 3-2-2-0	2-0-15-0 / 12-4-27-1	18-5-44-5 / 22.1-9-49-8	2-0-38-0	17-3-36-2 / 9-0-34-0		5-2-23-0 / 11-2-40-1		
v. Northamptonshire (Northampton) 18–21 June		7-1-27-0 / 9-2-42-0	1-0-6-0 / 6-0-33-0 / 27-3-82-2		2-0-15-0 / 12-4-27-1	9-1-49-1		6-2-13-2 / 14-2-55-2 / 27-5-107-4		11-1-40-3 / 26-7-87-0		
v. Australians (Southampton) 28–30 June		21.3-3-96-0										
v. Durham (Chester-le-Street) 2–5 July		26-1-97-3 / 5-2-17-0	28-1-110-3		17-2-69-3 / 20-1-85-1			15-3-86-0 / 3-1-1-0		24.1-4-116-3 / 8-3-19-0	10-2-52-0 / 17-4-56-1	4-0-12-1
v. Surrey (Guildford) 16–19 July		36-7-135-2 / 20-4-35-2	33-7-103-1 / 13-3-30-1		13-1-43-0 / 6-0-29-1		0.1-0-1-0			28-5-106-1		2-0-17-0
v. Lancashire (Southampton) 23–26 July		34.3-6-112-3 / 6-2-16-0	25-4-84-1 / 25-9-98-2		24-3-142-0 / 12-2-47-0					17-2-62-4		
v. Middlesex (Lord's) 6–9 August				19-7-35-0	20-1-72-2			28-8-98-1 / 13-2-55-1	4-0-23-1			1-1-0-0 / 5-0-22-0
v. Yorkshire (Portsmouth) 15–18 August			12-0-61-1		41-10-134-3			23-4-101-1	2-0-11-0			
v. Kent (Portsmouth) 27–30 August		10-0-44-0			41-14-96-2			19-3-61-4				
v. Nottinghamshire (Trent Bridge) 2–5 September		31.3-7-78-1 / 10-0-52-0	27-11-54-6 / 14-1-48-0		34-15-38-2 / 13-3-37-2 / 15.1-7-17-4			13-1-57-1 / 11-1-52-1 / 5-2-8-1	6-0-17-2 / 3-0-12-0		21-6-30-0	
v. Sussex (Southampton) 10–13 September		17-4-38-4	25-5-78-1 / 18-1-76-0		44-12-98-0			27.3-10-52-3				
v. Worcestershire (Southampton) 18–21 September		32-3-106-3	3-0-9-0		31-4-125-1 / 12-1-32-0			29-3-106-1				
Bowler's average	122.5-23- / 430-13 / 33.07	382-56- / 1127-22 / 51.22	428.5-70- / 1410-37 / 40.00	126.4-22- / 417-8 / 52.12	627-156- / 1810-34 / 53.23	161.1-37- / 504-27 / 18.66	5.1-0- / 75-0 / —	355.3-63- / 1278-37 / 34.54	33-0- / 166-3 / 55.33	233.1-47- / 902-23 / 39.21	127-35- / 336-3 / 112.00	12-1- / 51-1 / 51.00

Match totals (Byes, Leg-byes, Wides, No-balls, Total, Wkts):

Match	Byes	Leg-byes	Wides	No-balls	Total	Wkts	Note
v. Oxford University	7	18	12	4	243	9	A
v. Essex		15		4	246	10	
v. Gloucestershire	2	16	2	24	442	8	B
v. Leicestershire	2	2	6	2	403 / 59	8 / 4	C
v. Glamorgan	2	5			249 / 119	5 / 5	D
v. Warwickshire	4	4	8	14	0 / 287	/ 8	
v. Derbyshire	4	1	8	8	631 / 252	7 / 1	
v. Somerset		1	4	1	523 / 208	10 / 4	
v. Northamptonshire	5	13	4	16	159 / 225	10 / 10	
v. Australians		3	6	4	86 / 297	2 / 9	I
v. Durham		3			465 / 477	9 / 10	E
v. Surrey	12	2		4	78 / 569	/ 8	
v. Lancashire		19			255 / 442	9 / 8	F
v. Middlesex	6	3		10	178		G
v. Yorkshire		8	1	2	501	8	
v. Kent		7			350	8	H
v. Nottinghamshire	1	20	26	12	291 / 253	10 / 4	
v. Sussex		10	4	20	114 / 390	6 / 10	
v. Worcestershire	4 / 3	5 / 4	2 / 2	6 / 4	538 / 88	10 / 1	

Ab = abandoned

A P.R.Whitaker 1-1-0-0, 1.4-0-16-0
B G.W.White 1-0-4-0
C G.W.White 5-0-16-0
D A.N.Aymes 9-0-76-0; D.A.Kenway 1-0-5-1, 8-2-53-1; W.S.Kendall 5-0-46-0
E J.S.Laney 5-2-19-0
F L.Savident 23-7-86-2; C.Patel 18-3-65-0
G L.Savident 10-0-64-1; P.R.Whitaker 1.5-0-17-0
H L.Savident 15-2-43-0, 8-0-54-1
I G.White 3-0-12-0; T.M.Hansen 24-10-61-0, 2-0-14-0; S.R.G.Francis 19-1-97-0; P.R.Whitaker 9-1-42-0, 13-2-31-1

Fielding Figures

63 – S.A. Marsh (ct 61 / st 2)
30 – T.R. Ward
23 – D.P. Fulton
17 – P.A. Strang
16 – A.P. Wells
9 – M.A. Ealham and N.J. Llong
7 – G.R. Cowdrey
5 – M.J. Walker, M.V. Fleming and E.T. Smith
3 – M.J. McCague and J.B.D. Thompson
2 – D.W. Headley
1 – M.M. Patel, S.C. Willis, W.J. House, A.P. Igglesden and sub

Kent CCC First-Class Matches — Batting

Batting	v. Derbyshire (Canterbury) 23–26 April	v. Glamorgan (Canterbury) 14–17 May	v. Sussex (Horsham) 21–24 May	v. Nottinghamshire (Trent Bridge) 29 May–2 June	v. Warwickshire (Tunbridge Wells) 4–7 June	v. Lancashire (Old Trafford) 12–16 June	v. Durham (Darlington) 18–21 June	v. Cambridge University (Canterbury) 26–30 June	v. Northamptonshire (Maidstone) 2–5 July	v. Leicestershire (Canterbury) 16–19 July	M	Inns	NO	Runs	HS	Av
D.P. Fulton	43	19	34	94	46	19		57 & 99	35*	19*	16	29	3	953	110	36.65
N.J. Llong	5	6 & 15	9 & 0		13 & 11	22	3	17	57	26	8	14	1	256	99	18.28
T.R. Ward	6 & 96		67 & 83	7	3 & 11	16 & 65	17 & 0	99	26 & 8	51	18	32	2	1018	161*	33.93
A.P. Wells	36	31 & 85	20 & 3	35	70 & 62*	0	7 & 43*	49	12	16	18	31	1	1120	109	37.33
M.V. Fleming		14	14 & 20	11	5 & 33	19	27 & 14		8	139	13	22	4	790	138	29.25
M.A. Ealham	72*	15 & 20*		122	12	0	7		12	82	17	26	6	924	139	57.75
P.A. Strang	57	7 & 3	17 & 142	73	12 & 5	43 & 24	0		55 & 32	98*	18	27	6	590	82	24.58
S.A. Marsh	5	12 & 4	6	14*	16	5 & 8*	0 & 0*	5		14*	11	17	6	837	142	39.85
M.J. McCague	8	4*				26	6		6			10	1	190	53*	17.27
D.W. Headley				8	11	18	6	62	47	31	10	8	1	104	40	14.85
M.M. Patel		32	40	28	41			8 & 0	11		9	2		38	30	19.00
M.J. Walker		35	65*	7	59*	10	8	19 & 18*	0*			19		369	62	19.42
B.J. Phillips	30	29				23*		8				15	4	442	101	29.46
G.R. Cowdrey								32*		31	14	19	4	376	100*	25.06
J.B.D. Thompson								11*		5*	9	10	3	106	59*	15.14
S.C. Willis													1	37	19	37.00
N.W. Preston													1	8	8	8.00
E.J. Stanford												8		32	32	32.00
T.N. Wren	0*								0*	5*	6	18		–	11*	–
A.P. Igglesden		3									10	3		6	3	1.20
E.T. Smith		45						36	31					480	102	28.23
W.J. House											2			38	20	12.66
Byes	4	4	1	14	2	8	1	7	4	8						
Leg-byes	7	9	8		9	6	9	4	6	12						
Wides		2	10	8	10	10	19	2	24	8						
No-balls	6		6	2	20	12	8	10	2							
Total	251	154	245	440	379	373	167	245	306	498						
Wickets	10	10	10	10	10	10	10	10	10	9						
Result	D	L	W	W	W	W	L	D	L	L						
Points	9	4	21	24	23	24	4		3	5						

Batting	v. Middlesex (Lord's) 23–26 July	v. Worcestershire (Worcester) 31 July–4 August	v. Essex (Canterbury) 6–9 August	v. Australians (Canterbury) 16–18 August	v. Somerset (Taunton) 20–23 August	v. Hampshire (Portsmouth) 27–30 August	v. Gloucestershire (Canterbury) 2–5 September	v. Yorkshire (Leeds) 10–13 September	v. Surrey (Canterbury) 18–21 September	M	Inns	NO	Runs	HS	Av
D.P. Fulton	4 & 45	14	35	0 & 0	16		7 & 44	21	0 & 110	16	29	3	953	110	36.65
N.J. Llong	0 & 14	52	109	68 & 65	19 & 57	66 & 20	161* & 94	56 & 7	9 & 12	8	14	1	256	99	18.28
T.R. Ward	63 & 21	24 & 43	138	67 & 30	17	20	77 & 46	53 & 50*	48 & 41*	18	32	2	1018	161*	33.93
A.P. Wells	44	20 & 0*	58	85 & 5	53 & 3*	8 & 43*	31 & 16*	29* & 44*	12 & 18*	18	31	1	1120	109	37.33
M.V. Fleming	12 & 17	58	55	30	105 & 18	0	14	84	16	13	22	4	790	138	29.25
M.A. Ealham	3	47	7*	35*	20*		28	29*	52	17	26	6	924	139	57.75
P.A. Strang		17			101 & 0		1*			18	27	6	590	82	24.58
S.A. Marsh		25				38		40	16	11	17	6	837	142	39.85
M.J. McCague	8	32	53	25	56	11	7	4	7 & 22*		10	1	190	53*	17.27
D.W. Headley	12	7*		0		4*			0	10	8	1	104	40	14.85
M.M. Patel			7*	0 & 3	18		11	36	26	9	2		38	30	19.00
M.J. Walker	0*	3	5	0	34	102	29	0	16		19		369	62	19.42
B.J. Phillips											15	4	442	101	29.46
G.R. Cowdrey										14	19	4	376	100*	25.06
J.B.D. Thompson				2* & 46				13	3	9	10	3	106	59*	15.14
S.C. Willis		19		16	27	14	21	2	30			1	37	19	37.00
N.W. Preston												1	8	8	8.00
E.J. Stanford											8		32	32	32.00
T.N. Wren				20						6	18		–	11*	–
A.P. Igglesden										10	3		6	3	1.20
E.T. Smith													480	102	28.23
W.J. House									23	2			38	20	12.66
Byes	2	2	5	2	8	7	10	2	3						
Leg-byes	3		6	2	6		5	13							
Wides	4	32	4	26	4	14	28	4	30						
No-balls	4	8		12	27		21	2	23						
Total	208	276	525	201	449	350	305	374	220						
Wickets	10	10	10	10	10	10	10	10	10						
Result	W	D	W	L	D	D	W	D	W						
Points	24	10	24		8	6	23	5	5						

Kent CCC First-Class Matches — Bowling

Bowling	M.J. McCague	D.W. Headley	M.A. Ealham	P.A. Strang	M.V. Fleming	M.M. Patel	B.J. Phillips	N.J. Llong	A.P. Wells	J.B.D. Thompson	T.N. Wren	A.P. Igglesden	Byes	Leg-byes	Wides	No-balls	Total	Wkts
v. Derbyshire (Canterbury) 23–26 April	20.1-2-75-5	26-3-81-4	3-0-20-0	15-7-37-0	7-0-22-0								4	9		12	248	10
	18-2-91-1	8-1-26-2	14-1-45-0	11-0-50-0	4-0-11-0								4	9		4	248	3
v. Glamorgan (Canterbury) 14–17 May	20.4-5-75-6	25.4-7-74-2	15-5-64-1	21-6-51-1	3-0-10-0								1	4		4	279	10
	12-2-54-1	7-1-31-0	5-3-12-0	23.5-5-59-4	14-4-28-4											12	193	10
v. Sussex (Horsham) 21–24 May	23-1-71-1				17-4-42-1		19-5-47-5		3-0-17-0				5	8		4	264	10
	27.3-8-82-7			42-14-102-2	15-4-41-0		13-4-33-1	8-1-33-0						9	10	8	317	10
v. Nottinghamshire (Trent Bridge) 29 May–2 June	16-3-46-2	20-6-54-2		14-4-33-0	28.5-9-51-5		11-6-21-1						1	10	2	2	216	10
	17-7-33-4	15-6-23-1		21-11-21-2	10-4-29-1		6.5-1-9-2	8-3-33-2					2	8	2		119	10
v. Warwickshire (Tunbridge Wells) 4–7 June	5-0-20-0			34-11-65-1	14-5-44-1		16-5-49-1	4-2-16-0		22.2-4-89-5			2	8		4	314	10
				38.2-10-109-3	20-7-43-1		12-2-48-3			25-6-48-3			8	8			280	10
v. Lancashire (Old Trafford) 12–16 June	21-4-70-1	12-0-38-1		37-12-118-7	6-0-31-1		8-4-21-1			10-2-33-0			3	2		8	285	10
	15.5-4-61-3	4-0-16-0		17-6-68-4	23-4-55-5		10-1-47-2			4-0-15-0			4	5	3	2	247	10
v. Durham (Darlington) 18–21 June	19-3-45-1	26-7-60-1		31-10-48-2	19-5-34-4		16-6-37-1						4	2			251	10
	9-1-35-0	11-1-27-1		24-11-45-2			6-1-21-1							17	2		183	8
v. Cambridge University (Canterbury) 28–30 June		14-2-63-1					7-3-11-0	4-2-4-0		14-2-58-4	8.4-1-22-2			2		10	187	10
v. Northamptonshire (Maidstone) 2–5 July	8-2-26-0	10-0-42-0		3-1-11-0	13-3-36-0		21-1-5-0	5-1-19-0	3-2-2-0	10-2-28-0		10-5-18-0		1		4	84	0
	11-1-62-1	12-0-43-0		36-9-84-3	6-1-22-1		8-1-32-1	12-2-48-1		15-1-65-2		12-0-42-0	5	10		8	322	9
v. Leicestershire (Canterbury) 16–19 July	15.3-4-50-7			3-1-16-0	6-1-22-1			11.3-0-47-1		15-3-54-3			2	8		2	160	4
	21-4-72-2			39-9-103-1	16-5-50-1					11-1-52-0			12	4		2	367	4
v. Middlesex (Lord's) 23–26 July				6-2-8-0	6-3-10-0		4-2-8-1					7-0-23-2	5	8			105	10
		29.2-6-102-4		27.2-2-88-6	14-2-49-3		7-0-31-0					14-3-47-2	7	6	2	16	256	10
v. Worcestershire (Worcester) 31 July–4 August	17-0-81-4	6-0-21-1	22-4-60-0	22-6-63-1	3-0-14-0				3-2-2-0	9-0-56-0		23-8-81-2	7	1	3	6	422	3
	13.5-2-54-2		4-0-23-2	11-2-32-0	10-6-25-1							4-1-23-0	4	2		8	174	10
v. Essex (Canterbury) 6–9 August		8.3-2-14-3	8.3-2-14-3	36-13-119-5	5-0-27-0		15-1-57-3			9-0-23-3			4	9		4	156	10
		18-4-49-1	14-3-63-1	20-1-44-1	11-2-22-1		6-2-36-0			25-3-105-1			7		1	8	361	10
v. Australians (Canterbury) 16–18 August			14-3-63-1	26-8-78-0	25-2-83-2		25.3-7-86-5		6-2-18-0	11-1-61-1		16-2-56-3		2		6	315	10
v. Somerset (Taunton) 20–23 August	2.1-0-22-0	29.5-5-84-3	29.5-5-84-3	28.3-9-72-6	21-1-1-54-1		19-4-47-2			12-3-58-2		5-0-28-0	1	3	6	2	231	10
		16-3-49-1	16-3-49-1	22-4-82-0	24-4-86-0		24.5-7-64-4							7		8	375	10
v. Hampshire (Portsmouth) 27–30 August	36-9-105-4	26-11-50-2	26-11-50-2		13-3-42-0		14-5-44-1						10	9		8	234	10
v. Gloucestershire (Canterbury) 2–5 September	25-3-72-1	18-4-43-2	18-4-43-2	25.2-6-50-2			12-3-46-1					19-3-67-4	4	5	2	20	406	10
	23.4-4-92-5	11-5-23-1	11-5-23-1	28-14-40-3	16-3-54-1							14-0-55-2		4		18	256	10
v. Yorkshire (Leeds) 10–13 September	17-1-83-1	20.4-2-62-4	20.4-2-62-4	12-2-45-0	18-5-56-1				1-0-5-0			14-0-55-2	5	11		10	312	10
v. Surrey (Canterbury) 18–21 September	13-1-67-0	16-0-47-4	16-0-47-4	16.4-3-55-3	2-0-15-1	3-0-12-0	2-0-19-2		2-0-11-0	10-4-112-3		10-4-55-2	4	8	2		301	10
		5-0-28-1	5-0-28-1		14.3-1-59-1		18-2-58-3			23-1-112-3		18-2-81-1	1	10			124	10
		12-2-39-2	12-2-39-2														371	10
Bowler's average	312.4-55-1121-48 / 23.43	267-46-904-27 / 33.48	336-67-1010-32 / 31.56	733.1-211-1929-63 / 30.61	398.2-97-1145-37 / 30.94	3-0-12-0 / –	282.1-73-877-44 / 19.93	52.3-11-200-4 / 50.00	18-6-55-0 / –	223.2-30-890-31 / 28.70	8.4-1-22-2 / 11.00	152-23-538-18 / 29.88						

A E.J. Stanford 5-2-10-1; N.W. Preston 8-2-21-1
B G.R. Cowdrey 5-0-31-0; E.T. Smith 2-0-22-0; T.R. Ward 4-0-30-0
C W.J. House 2.5-0-24-0

Fielding Figures

37 – W.K. Hegg (ct 35 / st 2)
19 – N.H. Fairbrother
17 – G.D. Lloyd
12 – J.J. Haynes
11 – J.E.R. Gallian
7 – G. Yates and J.P. Crawley
6 – I.D. Austin
5 – M.A. Atherton and D.J. Shadford
4 – A. Flintoff
2 – P.J. Martin, M. Watkinson, N.T. Wood, P.E. Keown and S.P. Titchard
1 – M.E. Harvey, Wasim Akram, G. Chapple, G. Keedy and sub

Lancashire CCC First-Class Matches Batting

	M	Inns	NO	Runs	HS	Av
S.P. Titchard	6	9	–	180	79	20.00
P.C. McKeown	4	6	–	135	46	22.50
J.J. Haynes	2	3	–	41	21	13.66
A. Flintoff	5	8	–	243	117	30.37
N.H. Fairbrother	16	24	2	887	132	40.31
G.D. Lloyd	16	24	2	1073	225	48.77
M. Watkinson	12	19	1	520	135	28.88
I.D. Austin	17	25	4	825	95	39.28
G. Yates	13	13	3	194	39	19.40
R.J. Green	4	5	3	93	51	31.00
P.J. Martin	16	17	4	258	78*	19.84
J.E.R. Gallian	10	17	1	394	99	26.26
M.A. Atherton	10	16	1	596	149	39.73
J.P. Crawley	11	16	1	898	133	59.86
W.K. Hegg	16	22	1	455	77*	26.76
G. Chapple	10	13	3	214	66	21.40
Wasim Akram	2	3	1	16	13	8.00
N.T. Wood	10	15	2	469	155	36.07
G. Keedy	8	8	7	11	6*	11.00
D.J. Shadford	8	10	3	106	30	15.14
P.M. Ridgway	2	2	1	0	0*	0.00
M.J. Chilton	1	1	–	9	9	9.00
M.E. Harvey	2	4	–	49	25	12.25

Match columns (left table): v. Yorkshire (Leeds) 16–19 April; v. Durham (Old Trafford) 23–26 April; v. Nottinghamshire (Old Trafford) 14–17 May; v. Northamptonshire (Old Trafford) 21–24 May; v. Leicestershire (Leicester) 29 May–2 June; v. Somerset (Taunton) 4–7 June; v. Kent (Old Trafford) 12–16 June; v. Glamorgan (Liverpool) 18–21 June; v. Worcestershire (Worcester) 26–30 June; v. Middlesex (Uxbridge) 2–5 July

Match columns (right table): v. Sussex (Old Trafford) 16–19 July; v. Hampshire (Southampton) 23–26 July; v. Warwickshire (Blackpool) 6–9 August; v. Derbyshire (Derby) 15–18 August; v. Yorkshire (Old Trafford) 27–30 August; v. Essex (Old Trafford) 2–5 September; v. Surrey (The Oval) 10–13 September; v. Gloucestershire (Bristol) 18–21 September

†J.E.R. Gallian retired hurt

Lancashire CCC First-Class Matches — Bowling

	P.J. Martin	R.J. Green	I.D. Austin	G. Yates	M. Watkinson	C.D. Lloyd	S.P. Titchard	G. Chapple	J.E.R. Gallian	Wasim Akram	G. Keedy	D.J. Shadford	Byes	Leg-byes	Wides	No-balls	Total	Wkts
v. Yorkshire (Leeds) 16–19 April	17.2-3-58-2	18-2-71-0	14-3-70-2	14-2-46-4	17-3-38-2								3	3		6	289	10
	30-9-53-4	24-8-77-1	25.3-8-65-2	14-4-41-0	10-3-32-1								2	14	4	2	298	10
v. Durham (Old Trafford) 23–26 April	20-9-31-1		14.1-6-28-1	10-4-19-1	4.5-1-10-1		2-0-3-0						5	1		2	201	6
v. Nottinghamshire (Old Trafford) 14–17 May	21-8-44-0		22-6-44-4		5-1-17-0			28.2-2-95-2	2-0-12-0					26	28	16	263	10
	14-3-52-3		17-4-38-1		10-2-35-0								1	2		4	223	4
v. Northamptonshire (Old Trafford) 21–24 May	25-8-81-1		21-4-43-0	32.3-5-86-2				21-6-49-3	1-0-8-0	27-6-74-3	57-13-149-3			5	6	2	479	10
				16-2-70-3				10-0-47-0	6.1-2-36-0	9-4-12-0	20-4-85-1		10	1			232	6
v. Leicestershire (Leicester) 29 May–2 June	23-6-84-1		23-7-65-2	28-5-93-1				29-3-77-3	2-0-11-0		17-2-90-0		8	6			468	6
	9-3-34-0		6-2-15-0	21-4-92-2				4-1-3-0	4-0-27-0		26-7-66-3			7			247	5
v. Somerset (Taunton) 4–7 June	16-5-29-4		16.2-5-33-2					20-4-79-3	14.1-3-51-3		1-0-6-0			2	2		189	10
	9-4-21-2		7-1-16-0					18-1-80-4	2-0-10-0		1.2-0-10-0			2			66	3
v. Kent (Old Trafford) 12–16 June			24.3-7-58-3		4-1-21-0		4-0-11-1	4-0-17-1	6-0-22-0			20-1-110-3	8	6	12	12	373	10
			16-4-50-1					28-7-86-3				12-0-67-4		10		12	217	9
v. Glamorgan (Liverpool) 18–21 June	14-3-32-0		15-7-41-1	1-0-8-0		5-0-59-0		15-2-44-2			5-1-26-0		8	6	2		272	1
								12-2-31-0									0	–
v. Worcestershire (Worcester) 26–30 June	17-7-30-3		7.1-4-1-1			6.5-0-42-0		9-3-27-0				13-1-31-3		1	4	2	100	7
	9-1-23-0		8-3-15-0									8-1-51-0		3	4	14	135	0
v. Middlesex (Uxbridge) 2–5 July	14.5-4-32-8		12-4-36-2	1-1-0-0							5-3-5-0	7-0-43-0		2		14	118	0
	23.2-9-47-5		1-0-10-0	30-7-89-4							15-2-40-1	11-0-47-0	8	4	2		245	10
v. Sussex (Old Trafford) 16–19 July	23-7-61-3		18-6-36-3	30.5-8-59-5	19.5-3-79-3				5-2-10-1			11-1-54-0	9	1		8	307	10
	12-3-25-0		18-7-34-3	31-6-84-1	32-8-73-1				9-1-39-1			6-1-17-0		1		9	236	10
v. Hampshire (Southampton) 23–26 July	14-5-41-1		17-5-61-0		19-2-99-1							13-2-80-0	4	4			412	4
v. Warwickshire (Blackpool) 6–9 August	19-5-46-6		18.4-3-45-4		3-0-11-0				8-2-30-0			4-0-17-0		1		4	139	10
	26-7-110-2	20-6-46-1	23.2-5-78-3		18-1-69-1				6-2-24-0			11-1-80-5		7	2	12	310	10
v. Derbyshire (Derby) 15–18 August	21-6-77-4		24-7-71-2		13-0-60-1				7-0-29-1			15-0-108-1	1	10		16	411	10
v. Yorkshire (Old Trafford) 27–30 August	25-6-69-1	25.2-7-66-3	23-4-77-2	2-1-89-1	13-0-60-1				7-0-48-1		34-6-98-4		5	5		18	419	9
	5-0-38-0	15-2-60-0	6-0-39-0	5.1-0-45-3	4-0-49-2									6			176	5
v. Essex (Old Trafford) 2–5 September	16-1-63-2		17-2-81-2	29-4-85-1									1	1	2	6	389	10
																	0	0
v. Surrey (The Oval) 10–13 September	12.5-4-42-3				25-7-75-3	5-1-30-0		7-2-18-0			35-11-94-4	7-0-50-2	5	6		2	270	0
	17-3-58-1				16-0-53-2	2-0-14-0		11-1-48-1			29.4-6-79-6	7-0-31-1	4	12			267	10
v. Gloucestershire (Bristol) 18–21 September			22-9-44-4		18-7-40-0			22-4-50-2			25.4-5-68-2		3	4	13		262	10
			12-6-14-0		10-2-35-3			14-1-40-1			21-0-101-3		1	6			228	8
Bowler's average	459.1-131-1129-58 — 22.25	102.2-25-320-5 — 64.00	448.4-131-1218-45 — 27.06	302.3-57-963-29 — 33.20	231.4-41-805-20 — 40.25	11-0-101-0 — –	15-1-47-3 — 15.66	255.2-39-816-25 — 32.64	79.2-12-357-7 — 51.00	36-10-86-3 — 28.66	292.4-60-917-27 — 33.96	149-8-786-19 — 41.36						

A A. Flintoff 10-6-11-1
B P.M. Ridgway 19-4-73-0, 13-1-46-2
C M. Chilton 4-0-23-0; N.T. Wood 4.1-0-38-0
D M.A. Atherton 1-0-7-0

Fielding Figures

- 53 – P.A. Nixon (ct 50 / st 3)
- 14 – L.D. Maddy
- 13 – N.C. Johnson
- 9 – V.J. Wells
- 8 – A.R.K. Pierson
- 7 – I.J. Sutcliffe
- 5 – J.J. Whitaker
- 4 – A. Habib
- 3 – G.I. Macmillan, M.T. Brimson and B.F.Smith
- 2 – D.J. Millns, J.M. Dakin, A.D. Mullally and J. Ormond
- 1 – G.J. Parsons, T.J. Mason, D.I. Stevens and sub

Leicestershire First-Class Matches — Batting

Season averages:

Batting	M	Inns	NO	Runs	HS	Av
V.J. Wells	18	27	2	1200	224	44.44
I.J. Sutcliffe	13	20	4	727	130	40.38
A. Habib	9	14	4	397	175*	39.70
D.I. Stevens	2	2	–	35	27	17.50
J.M. Dakin	4	5	1	311	190	77.75
J.J. Whitaker	16	23	2	919	133*	43.76
P.A. Nixon	18	23	8	656	96	43.73
D.J. Millns	15	15	2	449	121	34.53
J. Ormond	12	7	2	65	35	7.22
M.T. Brimson	7	6	–	59	30*	11.80
G.J. Parsons	17	26	6	113	69*	22.60
D.L. Maddy	16	16	–	987	103	37.96
A.R.K. Pierson	16	7	1	266	59	16.62
G.I. Macmillan	13	5	–	99	34	16.50
A.D. Mullally	13	7	5	43	13*	7.16
N.G. Johnson	12	18	5	819	150	63.00
B.F. Smith	13	19	5	624	131*	44.57
T.J. Mason	–	–	–	4	4	4.00
D. Williamson	–	–	–	3	3	3.00

Matches (first half of season):
v. Cambridge University (Cambridge) 18-20 April; v. Gloucestershire (Leicester) 23-26 April; v. Worcestershire (Worcester) 7-10 May; v. Hampshire (Southampton) 14-17 May; v. Surrey (Leicester) 21-24 May; v. Lancashire (Leicester) 29 May-2 June; v. Middlesex (Lord's) 4-7 June; v. Australians (Leicester) 14-16 June; v. Somerset (Bath) 18-21 June; v. Warwickshire (Leicester) 26-30 June.

Matches (second half of season):
v. Yorkshire (Leicester) 2-5 July; v. Kent (Canterbury) 16-19 July; v. Nottinghamshire (Leicester) 23-26 July; v. Essex (Colchester) 31 July-4 August; v. Sussex (Eastbourne) 6-9 August; v. Derbyshire (Leicester) 20-23 August; v. Glamorgan (Leicester) 27-30 September; v. Northamptonshire (Northampton) 10-13 September; v. Durham (Leicester) 18-21 September.

Leicestershire CCC First-Class Matches
Bowling

Matches (in order read):

1. v. Cambridge University (Cambridge) 18–20 April
2. v. Gloucestershire (Leicester) 23–26 April
3. v. Worcestershire (Worcester) 7–10 May
4. v. Hampshire (Southampton) 14–17 May
5. v. Surrey (Leicester) 21–24 May
6. v. Lancashire (Leicester) 29 May–2 June
7. v. Middlesex (Lord's) 4–7 June
8. v. Australians (Leicester) 14–16 June
9. v. Somerset (Bath) 18–21 June
10. v. Warwickshire (Leicester) 26–30 June
11. v. Yorkshire (Leicester) 2–5 July
12. v. Kent (Canterbury) 16–19 July
13. v. Nottinghamshire (Leicester) 21–26 July
14. v. Essex (Colchester) 31 July–4 August
15. v. Sussex (Eastbourne) 6–9 August
16. v. Derbyshire (Leicester) 20–23 August
17. v. Glamorgan (Leicester) 27–30 August
18. v. Northamptonshire (Northampton) 10–13 September
19. v. Durham (Leicester) 18–21 September

Bowling analyses and season totals (O–M–R–W):

Bowler	Analyses (read in match order)	Season total	Avge
D.J. Millns	13-3-55-1, 15-2-47-3, 1.1-0-5-0, 18.2-6-53-3, 23-4-38-3, 14-4-34-3, 26-7-64-4, 7-0-17-1, 19-2-75-1, 8-3-32-0, 22.3-6-61-6, 8-4-24-2, 15-1-60-0, 8-0-45-0, 30-5-106-1, 22-3-91-2, 7.4-2-21-2, 28-8-97-2, 11-1-64-1, 13-2-41-0, 16-3-58-3, 6-2-20-0, 22-4-58-1, 11-1-45-0, 11-1-49-4, 33-13-81-6	408.4-87-1341-49	27.36
G.J. Parsons	17-4-59-2, 4-1-16-0, 22-9-38-0, 14-6-27-2, 33-4-125-2, 13.2-5-22-4, 24-8-43-2, 14-2-53-0, 17-5-41-0, 27-9-63-1, 26-9-49-3, 8-3-12-0	182.2-48-500-13	38.46
M.T. Brimson	36-12-93-1, 3-2-1-1, 8-4-20-0, 12.5-3-23-1, 2-0-4-1, 16-1-62-1, 32-5-124-2	170.5-48-451-11	41.00
J. Ormond	23-5-53-2, 5-1-12-0, 15-3-61-0, 20-7-54-6, 8-0-36-1, 19-1-69-3, 7-1-21-1, 6-2-19-1, 19-7-45-2, 28-4-107-5, 3-0-13-0, 24.5-8-61-3, 20-1-55-3, 9-2-38-0, 17-0-110-1, 10-1-40-2, 15-4-64-2, 6-3-16-0, 24.5-5-68-6, 24-10-55-2, 8.5-0-31-2, 13-6-33-1	325.3-71-1061-44	24.11
J.M. Dakin	10-1-39-1, 6-4-13-0, 6-1-8-0, 5-1-9-0, 6-1-14-1, 5-1-12-2, 30-8-109-1	68-17-204-5	40.80
V.J. Wells	8-1-26-0, 15-5-46-1, 6-3-10-0, 7-2-16-0, 8-2-19-1, 4-0-17-1, 1-1-0-0, 6-0-22-0, 3-0-17-0, 8-0-46-1, 9-3-24-1, 2-0-6-0, 8-0-45-2, 9-1-29-1, 3-0-14-0, 1-0-9-0, 9-4-16-1, 5-1-24-0, 7-3-35-0, 12-4-32-0, 12-4-18-0, 8-1-39-2, 12-2-52-2, 4-1-8-2, 10-0-32-0, 4-3-4-0, 7-0-27-2, 16-7-38-1	204-47-671-17	39.47
A.D. Mullally	20.5-9-52-5, 1-0-3-0, 28-3-86-4, 23-8-69-4, 16-5-44-1, 19-3-75-0, 14-2-48-1, 24.3-5-79-5, 8-3-26-0, 23-7-75-2, 14-1-55-0, 20-3-90-1, 10-1-39-0, 25.5-8-103-5, 14-1-57-0, 30-5-116-1, 34-10-99-2, 19.2-6-62-5, 33-7-114-1, 6-1-10-0	383.1-89-1302-37	35.18
A.R.K. Pierson	7-0-25-0, 10-3-34-1, 4-0-33-0, 2-2-0-0, 9-1-29-0, 14-6-30-2, 19-2-109-0, 32-11-79-2, 27-11-36-1, 1-0-1-0, 29-2-109-3, 42-10-122-3, 17-0-52-0, 15.4-2-56-6, 5-0-23-0, 27-4-84-1, 41-8-118-3, 3-0-7-0	499.1-104-1478-38	38.89
N.C. Johnson	21-4-61-3, 14-2-59-1, 7-1-19-1, 16-0-76-2, 8-0-25-0, 12-1-48-0, 3-0-18-0, 2-0-3-0, 20-6-56-0, 6-3-17-1, 7-1-38-0	116-18-420-8	52.50
D.L. Maddy	1-0-5-0, 5-0-29-0, 7-1-15-0, 7-1-13-0, 3-1-10-0, 9-1-20-0, 4-0-17-0, 0.2-0-0-0, 3-2-2-1, 8-4-11-1	47.2-10-122-2	61.00
T.J. Mason	1-0-1-0, 4.4-0-21-2	5.4-0-22-2	11.00
G.I. MacMillan	11-1-41-0	11-1-41-0	–

Extras and innings totals (in innings order):

Byes	Leg-byes	Wides	No-balls	Total	Wkts
4	8			333	7
3	5		12	51	1
	1	2	6	245	10
	1			8	0
6	8	6	20	257	10
20	4	2	30	285	10
14	9	6	12	182	10
	15	6	12	278	10
6	6	2	32	166	5
6	5	2	12	373	5
	12		12	425	5
11	16			395	10
23	14	7	4	220	8
	2			105	3
5	13	8	10	256	10
11	1		16	146	3
5	6	6	20	268	10
5	5	4	16	309	3
8	12	8	8	498	9
				26	0
9	13	6	24	342	10
13	6		10	182	0
	15	6	22	533	8
8	7	8	4	330	6
				0	0
8	7	16	6	366	10
7	17	4	4	238	2
4	2	10	22	226	10
	8			67	2
5	2		8	332	9
12	1	4	8	298	10
4	10	4	2	133	0
5	14	8	8	310	10

Footnotes (other bowlers):

A I.J. Sutcliffe 1-0-12-0
B J.J. Whitaker 0.2-0-0-0
C B.F. Smith 1-0-4-0
D P.A. Nixon 2-0-4-0; D.I. Stevens 2-1-5-1
E A. Habib 4-0-37-0
F D. Williamson 9.5-3-19-3, 8-2-21-1

Fielding Figures

- 50 – K.R. Brown (ct47 / st 3)
- 23 – M.W. Gatting
- 21 – J.C. Pooley
- 18 – P.N. Weekes
- 15 – J.H. Kallis
- 14 – O.A. Shah
- 8 – M.R. Ramprakash
- 6 – J.P. Hewitt, D.C. Nash and R.L. Johnson
- 4 – P.C.R. Tufnell and A.R.C. Fraser
- 3 – K.P. Dutch
- 2 – S.P. Moffat and T.F. Bloomfield
- 1 – P.E. Wellings and sub

Middlesex CCC First-Class Matches Batting — Averages

Batting	M	Inns	NO	Runs	HS	Av
P.N. Weekes	15	24	–	439	101	18.29
P.E. Wellings	2	2	–	141	128*	141.00
M.W. Gatting	19	29	2	1053	160*	39.00
J.C. Pooley	18	28	1	619	98	22.92
K.R. Brown	19	29	9	601	144*	30.05
D.C. Nash	6	8	2	332	100	55.33
R.L. Johnson	18	24	1	320	39	13.91
J.P. Hewitt	18	21	4	264	75	15.52
K.P. Dutch	7	9	2	138	79	19.71
A.R.C. Fraser	19	23	6	244	35	14.35
P.C.R. Tufnell	16	19	6	100	21	7.69
J.H. Kallis	17	25	3	1034	172*	47.00
M.R. Ramprakash	16	27	3	1293	190	53.87
S.P. Moffat	4	6	1	122	47	24.40
T.F. Bloomfield	4	3	2	–	4	4.00
O.A. Shah	11	16	2	548	104*	39.14

Middlesex CCC First-Class Matches — Bowling

Match / Date	A.R.C. Fraser	R.L. Johnson	P.C.R. Tufnell	J.P. Hewitt	P.N. Weekes	P.E. Wellings	K.P. Dutch	J.H. Kallis	M.R. Ramprakash	M.W. Gatins	T.F. Bloomfield	D.C. Nash	Byes	Leg-byes	Wides	No-balls	Total	Wkts
v. Cambridge University (Oxford) 23–25 April	11-2-37-0	17-1-89-2	2-1-6-1	13-6-38-3	15-5-35-2	3-0-18-0	4.1-2-3-2						3	6	2	4	235	10
v. Sussex (Lord's) 7–10 May	19-5-53-1	14-1-56-3	15-10-8-2	17-4-60-4	1-0-5-0			10.3-5-16-2					4	1	2	12	187	10
	11.3-2-33-0	9-2-24-0	6-1-19-1	15-5-24-4	1-0-2-1			6-2-15-0					3	6	4	2	119	6
v. Derbyshire (Lord's) 14–17 May	20-6-45-2	10.4-2-35-3	1-1-0-0	21-6-56-2	5-2-17-1			9-3-14-0						4	8	6	178	9 A
	7-1-12-0	8.4-1-26-4	11-1-44-2	4-0-13-0				10-2-26-3						5	6	2	99	9
v. Warwickshire (Edgbaston) 29 May–2 June	12-5-30-2	16.1-6-40-2	11-1-42-0	17-4-38-3	4.3-0-23-0									7	2	11	158	10
	15-3-34-0	12-0-66-2	11-1-42-0	5-1-26-0	8-2-33-0			9-3-20-2					3	5		6	198	2
v. Northamptonshire (Lord's) 29 May–2 June	15-6-30-0	20-8-55-2	14-4-22-2	20-5-59-5	16-2-37-0									7	10	2	216	10
	21-6-35-1	18-2-4-0	39.5-16-64-4	12-3-33-1	10-2-16-1								3	1		4	258	10
v. Leicestershire (Lord's) 4–7 June	31.2-7-77-6	12-2-51-1	26-13-32-1	27-8-63-2	24-0-97-0								10	12	6	6	280	10
	23-6-60-0	20-5-55-2	46-15-92-3	17-2-64-1					6.2-1-30-1				19	7	12	2	462	7
v. Glamorgan (Cardiff) 12–16 June	24-4-68-4		14-4-3-1	23-3-88-3			9-2-13-0	2-2-0-0						7	8	6	281	10
	8-2-17-4			8-4-14-6							7-2-13-2		3	7			31	1
v. Gloucestershire (Bristol) 18–21 June	10-3-18-2	17.2-6-27-4		12-2-31-0	5-0-13-0					7-1-46-1	13-1-43-2		4	2	8	8	99	9 B
	25-11-40-2	22.2-5-88-3		17-6-28-3													218	10 Ab
v. Yorkshire (Leeds) 26–30 June	30-5-105-1	24-6-64-0	40-10-90-5	35-8-79-2	8-2-16-0			17-4-51-1					5	7	12	10	417	9
v. Lancashire (Uxbridge) 2–5 July	29-5-115-0	17-2-63-1	38-8-106-2				15-3-79-3				17-1-57-1		2	10	1	10	432	7
v. Australians (Lord's) 19–21 July	14-2-45-3	12-3-29-1	12-5-21-3	13-4-41-2	9.3-0-28-1			12-2-40-0						4	4	4	208	10
	12-3-30-2	8.5-2-26-2	13-6-20-1	5-0-22-0				16-3-54-5						10			157	10
v. Kent (Lord's) 23–26 July	15-2-38-0	13-1-10-2		17-2-70-2			29-6-94-2	12-3-22-1					2		8		306	5
	10-1-38-5			7-1-27-3				6-1-19-0						3		8	97	10
v. Hampshire (Lord's) 6–9 August	26-5-106-2	22-2-79-3	36.3-16-106-1	21-0-126-1			12-0-47-1	8-0-31-0	4-0-15-0				3	18	4	6	531	9
v. Surrey (Lord's) 15–18 August	26-7-56-2	21.3-4-53-3		15-2-69-0	9-3-21-0		16-2-34-1	21-6-98-4					7	5	2	18	343	10
	7-2-8-0	4-0-20-0					3-0-19-0						1		4		78	0
v. Durham (Chester-le-Street) 20–23 August	26-8-55-2	14.5-4-51-0	13-2-42-0	17-8-36-2				19-3-58-1	1-0-3-0			2-0-11-0	4	6	6	4	251	10 C
	12-7-16-2	6.3-0-33-2	7-3-7-0	13-1-48-3				12-3-39-3	1-1-0-0				8	5	6	4	149	10
v. Worcestershire (Kidderminster) 27–30 August	15-6-34-0	13-2-44-1	24.4-8-53-4	13-1-63-2				13-5-34-3	1-1-0-0					8	2	8	241	8
v. Somerset (Taunton) 2–5 September	18-4-46-1	17-3-52-2	30-9-90-2	6-0-23-1				9-1-21-0	11-1-58-1		4-1-12-0			5	2	4	295	8
v. Nottinghamshire (Lord's) 10–13 September	14-7-24-0		32.1-6-61-5	7-1-25-0				18-5-39-4	6-3-18-0		17-6-33-3		7	8		12	210	9 D
	20-10-34-1		40-15-57-1					25-6-58-3	6-4-2-0		21-5-77-5			2	2	2	228	9
v. Essex (Chelmsford) 18–21 September	25-4-69-2	13-2-37-1	12-1-36-0	13-3-50-1										2		4	271	10
	20-5-52-0	18-1-62-1	29-6-63-2	12-2-31-4	11-0-53-0						6-1-23-0	1-0-8-1	5	4	10	2	301	8
Bowler's average	571.5-155-1460-47 / 31.06	427.2-79-1425-50 / 28.50	513.1-152-1112-44 / 23.27	439-97-1393-60 / 23.21	143-21-432-6 / 72.00	3-0-18-0 / –	88.1-15-289-9 / 32.11	234.3-61-655-32 / 20.46	35.2-10-126-2 / 63.00	7-1-46-1 / 46.00	85-17-258-13 / 19.84	3-0-19-1 / 19.00						

A K.J. Barnett absent hurt
B M.A. Lynch absent hurt
C O.A. Shah 2-0-19-0
D M.N. Bowen retired hurt

Fielding Figures

37 – D. Ripley (ct 30 / st 7)
18 – R.J. Bailey
11 – R.J. Warren
9 – A. Fordham and J.N. Snape
7 – A.L. Penberthy, J.P. Taylor and K.M. Curran
5 – R.R. Montgomerie
3 – D.J.G. Sales
1 – M.B. Loye and S.A.J. Boswell
1 – D.J. Roberts, T.C. Walton, J.E. Emburey, M.K. Davis, J.F. Brown, Mohammad Akram and J.A.R. Blain

Northamptonshire CCC First-Class Matches Batting — Season Averages

Batting	M	Inns	NO	Runs	HS	Av
R.R. Montgomerie	10	18	3	504	73	33.60
M.B. Loye	8	15	3	412	86	34.33
R.J. Bailey	17	30	5	1078	117*	43.12
K.M. Curran	15	26	4	1032	159	46.90
A.L. Penberthy	13	19	0	499	96	26.26
D.J. Capel	4	7	0	140	57	20.00
R.J. Warren	9	16	2	614	174*	43.85
J.N. Snape	8	16	3	306	66	23.53
J.E. Emburey	3	4	1	39	39	13.00
Mohammad Akram	11	14	2	116	28	9.66
J.P. Taylor	16	21	4	216	36	12.70
D. Ripley	17	24	7	772	92	42.88
S.A.J. Boswell	7	13	4	122	35	13.55
D.J. Roberts	7	13	3	385	117	29.61
D.J.G. Sales	9	19	1	520	103	28.88
A. Fordham	9	17	2	673	85*	44.86
K.J. Innes	2	8	4	25	16*	6.25
J.F. Brown	6	–	–	8	8*	–
J.G. Hughes	7	10	4	231	60	25.66
T.C. Walton	1	1	–	3	3	1.50
D. Follett	6	6	1	49	17	9.80
M.K. Davies	1	1	–	0	0	–
J.A.R. Blain	2	3	–	162	136	54.00
A.J. Swann						

Left-hand match record (v. Sussex, Hove 23–26 April; v. Somerset, Northampton 7–10 May; v. Cambridge University, Cambridge 14–16 May; v. Lancashire, Old Trafford 21–24 May; v. Middlesex, Lord's 29 May–2 June; v. Nottinghamshire, Northampton 4–7 June; v. Hampshire, Northampton 18–21 June; v. Gloucestershire, Luton 26–30 June; v. Kent, Maidstone 2–5 July; v. Essex, Northampton 16–19 July).

Right-hand match record (v. Surrey, Northampton 23–26 July; v. Yorkshire, Leeds 31 July–4 August; v. Worcestershire, Northampton 6–9 August; v. Glamorgan, Abergavenny 20–23 August; v. Durham, Northampton 27–30 August; v. Derbyshire, Derby 2–5 September; v. Leicestershire, Northampton 10–13 September; v. Warwickshire, Edgbaston 18–21 September).

†J.N. Snape absent

Northamptonshire CCC — First-Class Matches — Bowling

Match	Mohammad Akram	J.P. Taylor	K.M. Curran	J.N. Snape	J.E. Emburey	D.J. Capel	A.L. Penberthy	S.A.J. Boswell	J.G. Hughes	M.K. Davies	J.F. Brown	R.J. Bailey	Byes	Leg-byes	Wides	No-balls	Total	Wkts	Note
v. Sussex (Hove) 23–26 April	22-2-118-3	20-7-52-2	9-2-32-0	16-4-55-0	14-2-39-1	13-1-57-1	11-1-49-0						2	7		30	411	7	
v. Somerset (Northampton) 7–10 May	20.4-3-72-5	22-3-71-3		9-1-21-1		7-2-23-0	4-1-13-0	14-1-83-1						7		14	290	10	
v. Cambridge University (Cambridge) 14–16 May		36-9-101-4 / 3-2-9-0		22-9-33-3 / 6-4-10-1	49-18-115-1 / 1-0-2-0				18-4-60-1 / 6-1-15-2		19-6-50-4 / 6-1-18-0		9 / 1	8 / 4	2 / 2	4 / 14	280 / 61	9 / 3	A, B
v. Lancashire (Old Trafford) 21–24 May			7-0-27-0 / 23-5-67-2	12-3-40-0		6-0-22-1 / 4-0-16-0 / 9-1-62-0	15-2-75-0 / 15-3-52-2 / 3-1-1-0					2-0-14-0		10 / 12	/ 12	14 / 15	415 / 114	9 / 0	C
v. Middlesex (Lord's) 29 May–2 June		41-13-99-4		15-2-60-0			24-3-80-1					7-0-28-0					531	10	
v. Nottinghamshire (Northampton) 4–7 June	20-3-79-1 / 16-4-66-0	20.4-2-54-3	23-9-61-4 / 6-1-32-0	13-5-24-0	25-11-36-2 / 21.3-8-67-0								4 / 8	14 / 11	2 / 4	16 / 4	272 / 301	10 / 7	
v. Hampshire (Northampton) 18–21 June		25-5-87-7 / 32.4-7-91-6	16-7-49-0	8-0-34-0 / 21-5-44-0				21-3-101-1	22-6-66-1			6-0-13-0					405 / 0	8 / 0	D
v. Gloucestershire (Luton) 26–30 June	14-4-30-2	12-1-40-0	15-3-69-4				3-0-19-0	10-5-14-0					4	4	2	6	180	7	
v. Kent (Maidstone) 2–5 July	21.3-6-56-4 / 3-1-3-0	26-2-95-3	15-6-32-1	23-8-47-2 / 9-0-45-1				16-0-66-0 / 2-1-3-0				10-0-48-1 / 1-0-1-0	4	6	3	24 / 2	306 / 99	10 / 2	
v. Essex (Northampton) 16–19 July	19-3-91-3 / 16-3-72-1	19-3-82-1	11.2-2-32-4	3-0-23-1				14-2-41-1 / 13-3-55-0						5 / 8	8 / 8	12 / 4	275 / 290	10 / 10	
v. Surrey (Northampton) 23–26 July	25.5-2-112-0	17.2-2-72-3 / 24-4-112-1	7-1-33-0	19-4-46-4 / 35-4-133-1			20-4-73-1	23-2-107-2				13-2-29-0	15	12		24	581	7	
v. Yorkshire (Leeds) 31 July–4 August	14-5-28-1 / 21-1-94-2	16-3-45-6 / 18-1-98-1	7-2-22-1				6-2-18-0 / 11-0-38-1	9-1-45-2 / 13-2-55-0		28-9-89-0		11.1-5-10-4	5 / 8	8 / 7	6	18 / 14	166 / 332	10 / 10	E
v. Worcestershire (Northampton) 6–9 August		18-1-98-1	10-1-22-2 / 17-4-52-2				24-3-126-1	26.5-3-94-5 / 5-0-16-0		37-10-95-3		24-5-72-0 / 32.1-7-121-3	1	1 / 13		28 / 2	551 / 272	10 / 7	
v. Glamorgan (Abergavenny) 20–23 August	12-1-57-0	13-1-49-0 / 6-0-21-0	2-0-20-0							29-5-109-2 / 13.1-0-59-2	24-3-90-1 / 18-3-68-2	2.2-0-18-2		13 / 2	2	2	354 / 197	6 / 4	
v. Durham (Northampton) 27–30 August	11-2-46-0 / 24.5-2-100-5	31-4-96-1	9-4-17-0				16-4-40-1			34-14-68-1	18-1-47-2		15	10	5	6	376	10	
v. Derbyshire (Derby) 2–5 September	16-2-60-3 / 11-0-51-0	17-4-50-3 / 13-5-31-1	13-5-34-1 / 8-2-25-1				11-2-31-1 / 4-1-5-0			0.5-0-4-2 / 22-8-46-5	3-1-11-0 / 12-4-23-3	1-0-1-0	5	2 / 7		2	192 / 189	10 / 10	
v. Leicestershire (Northampton) 10–13 September		17-0-82-1	7-0-49-0				12-0-48-0	19-3-89-2		34-9-118-4	52.3-14-142-3	3-0-12-0	5	12		24	557	10	
v. Warwickshire (Edgbaston) 18–21 September		14-0-68-2 / 12-3-27-2	4-0-15-1 / 6-2-25-1				5-0-35-0 / 6-2-10-1			21-13-29-2 / 15-3-57-2	26-4-79-3 / 24.5-2-123-2	1-0-1-0 / 3-0-12-0	4	4 / 4		4 / 2	251 / 246	8 / 8	F
Bowler's average	287-43-1135-30 — 37.83	455.4-81-1532-54 — 28.37	215.2-57-715-24 — 29.79	253.1-60-724-15 — 48.26	110.3-39-259-4 — 64.75	39-4-180-2 — 90.00	190-29-722-9 — 80.22	185.5-26-769-15 — 51.26	46-11-141-4 — 35.25	234-71-674-23 — 29.30	203.4-39-651-20 — 32.55	112.3-19-367-10 — 36.70							

A K.J. Innes 14-5-33-0, 6-1-16-0; D.J.G Sales 5-2-12-0; R.R. Montgomerie 1-0-1-0; A. Fordham 2-1-1-0
B T.C. Walton 2-0-7-0
C D. Follett 24.3-1-123-2
D T.C. Walton 4-0-23-0
E J.A.R. Blain 24.5-5-87-1, 6-3-18-1; A. Fordham 1-0-1-0; D.G. Sales 3-0-16-0
F A. Fordham 1.3-0-6-0; T.C. Walton 2-0-15-0

Nottinghamshire CCC First-Class Matches Batting

Batting	v. Worcestershire (Trent Bridge) 23–26 April		v. Durham (Hartlepool) 7–10 May		v. Lancashire (Old Trafford) 14–17 May		v. Derbyshire (Trent Bridge) 21–24 May		v. Kent (Trent Bridge) 29 May–2 June		v. Northamptonshire (Northampton) 4–7 June		v. Australians (Trent Bridge) 11–13 June		v. Oxford University (Oxford) 14–17 June		v. Yorkshire (Trent Bridge) 18–21 June		v. Surrey (The Oval) 27–30 June		M	Inns	NO	Runs	HS	Av
P.R. Pollard	81	–	28	5	2	15	5	23*							115*	–	26	–	37*	33	10	17	5	480	115*	40.00
R.T. Robinson	80	–	15	69	7	–	0*	–							2	51*	18	–	7	10	17	29	4	812	143*	32.48
G.F. Archer	4	–	6	20	0	4	0	10	49	0	11	4			50*	1	10*	–			12	22	2	375	81	18.75
R.T. Bates	6*	–	0	–					0	8	21	2*			–	4					8	12	5	69	21	9.85
A.A. Metcalfe	6*	–					7	7	7	8					78	–			–	4	9	12	1	262	79	23.81
P. Johnson	–	–	10	34	66	87*	60	3	0	2	41	57	6	–			14*	–			16	27	5	942	96*	42.81
M.P. Dowman	–	–	19	10			23	7	21	7	21	111	22	–	4	13	15	–	24*	11	19	33	1	1091	149	34.09
W.M. Noon	–	–	11	13*	5	–	0	63	14	30	83	9*	0	–			6	–	–	7	18	25	4	542	83	25.80
K.P. Evans	–	–	0	–	11	–	5	47	26	5			21	–			5*	–	–	4	15	18	1	208	47	12.23
M.N. Bowen	–	–	4	7	9	–	1	5*	0	4*	32	–					10	–	–	0	15	19	6	145	32	11.15
P.J. Franks	–	–	0*	–	3	–	20	50	21*	6			1	–	–	–			–	1*	14	19	6	280	50	21.53
C.M. Tolley			54	37*	15	25					12	20									12	22	4	479	73*	26.61
N.A. Gie					4	8			9	7					7	50					3	6	–	85	50	14.16
U. Afzaal					70*	77*	52	5	54	36	4	11	34	–			6	–	–	12	17	29	2	720	80	26.66
G.E. Welton											3	0	16	–							6	11	–	295	95	26.81
N.J. Astle											0	64	99	–			28	–	–	11	10	16	–	644	100	40.25
R.A. Pick											8*	–	7	–	–	–	–	–			4	2	1	15	8*	15.00
L.N.P. Walker													5	–	42*	–					4	5	2	97	42*	32.33
A.R. Oram													0*	–							8	9	5	14	5*	3.50
J.E. Hindson															–	6*			–	6	3	4	2	54	42*	27.00
Byes	4				1	1	4	9	1	2	4	4	1		10	4				12						
Leg-byes	3		13	3	26	2	9	11	10	2	14	11	4		4	3	4		1	5						
Wides	6		6		28		2	2	2	2	2	4	1		4	26										
No-balls	6		4	2	16	4	4	6	2		16	4	22		8	8	6		4	4						
Total	196		170	200	263	223	192	248	216	119	272	301	239		324	166	148		73	120						
Wickets	3		10	6	10	4	10	8	10	10	10	7	10		4	4	7		1	10						
Result	D		D		W		W		L		W		D		D		D		L							
Points	5		7		22		20		4		22		–		–		7		4							

Batting

Batting	v. Pakistan 'A' (Trent Bridge) 2–4 July		v. Warwickshire (Trent Bridge) 16–19 July		v. Leicestershire (Leicester) 23–26 July		v. Glamorgan (Colwyn Bay) 31 July–4 August		v. Somerset (Trent Bridge) 15–18 August		v. Essex (Worksop) 20–23 August		v. Gloucestershire (Bristol) 27–30 August		v. Hampshire (Trent Bridge) 2–5 September		v. Middlesex (Lord's) 10–13 September		v. Sussex (Hove) 18–21 September		M	Inns	NO	Runs	HS	Av
P.R. Pollard	10	15	29	0*															43	13*	10	17	5	480	115*	40.00
R.T. Robinson	18	4	10	4	32	13	8	4	32	30	143*	–	56	6	32	0	35	19	63	44*	17	29	4	812	143*	32.48
G.F. Archer	81	1	3	6	30	35	10	40													12	22	2	375	81	18.75
R.T. Bates	13	1															8*	6*	0*	–	8	12	5	69	21	9.85
A.A. Metcalfe	39	–							79	2	–	–	11	14							9	12	1	262	79	23.81
P. Johnson			8	38			1	6	38	20	41	–	6	96*	37	93*	1	44	74	59*	16	27	5	942	96*	42.81
M.P. Dowman	3	3	19	96	149	19	62	6	43	124	27	–	52	1	74	62	28	13	0	2	19	33	1	1091	149	34.09
W.M. Noon			21	30	3	7	29*	17	17	21*	–	–	60	–	25	–	39	7	25	–	18	25	4	542	83	25.80
K.P. Evans							1	0	25	0	–	–	23	–	0	–	13	14	8	–	15	18	1	208	47	12.23
M.N. Bowen	0*	0*			4	0	19	–			–	–	31*	–	13	–	3	3*			15	19	6	145	32	11.15
P.J. Franks	29*	5	7	32	6	10*			42*	0							1	19	27	–	14	19	6	280	50	21.53
C.M. Tolley	2	19	0	49	26	10	10	73*	19	4	–	–	0	52*	0	8*	42	2			12	22	4	479	73*	26.61
N.A. Gie																					3	6	–	85	50	14.16
U. Afzaal	17	31	5	21	22	0	3	10	5	11	–	–	23	14	35	16	14	21	80	31	17	29	2	720	80	26.66
G.E. Welton					0	21									12	40	14	47	95	47	6	11	–	295	95	26.81
N.J. Astle			11	100	13	38	47	13	21	60	100	–	0	39							10	16	–	644	100	40.25
R.A. Pick																					4	2	1	15	8*	15.00
L.N.P. Walker	34	12*													4	–					4	5	2	97	42*	32.33
A.R. Oram			0*	4	5*	0			0	0*	–	–	5	–	0*	–			–	–	8	9	5	14	5*	3.50
J.E. Hindson							0	42*													3	4	2	54	42*	27.00
Byes	2		2	16	9	13	1	14	2	14	4		4		1			7								
Leg-byes	4	3	4	7	13	6	6	10	17	13	12		11		20	10	8	12	10	9						
Wides		1	6	6	6			2	10	2	14		6	4	26	4		2	2							
No-balls	46	12	8	6	24	10	5	2	6	4	10		6	2	12	20	4	12	27	10						
Total	298	107	133	415	342	182	202	239	356	305	351		294	228	291	253	210	228	454	215						
Wickets	9	8	10	10	10	10	10	8	10	9	3		10	5	10	4	10	9†	9	3						
Result	D		D		D		D		D		D		W		D		L		D							
Points	–		7		10		6		11		9		22		7		3		9							

†M.N. Bowen retired hurt

Fielding Figures

38 – W.N. Noon (ct 34 / st 4)
15 – G.F. Archer
12 – P. Johnson
11 – N.J. Astle and M.P. Dowman
9 – U. Afzaal
8 – P.R. Pollard
7 – R.T. Robinson and P.J. Franks
6 – R.T. Bates, C.M. Tolley, K.P. Evans and A.R. Oram
5 – M.N. Bowen
4 – A.A. Metcalfe and N.A. Gie
2 – J.E. Hindson and sub
1 – G.E. Welton and L.N.P. Walker

Nottinghamshire CCC — First-Class Matches Bowling

Match	K.P. Evans	P.J. Franks	M.N. Bowen	G.F. Archer	R.T. Bates	M.P. Dowman	C.M. Tolley	U. Afzaal	R.A. Pick	N.J. Astle	A.R. Oram	J.E. Hindson	Byes	Leg-byes	Wides	No-balls	Total	Wkts
v. Worcestershire (Trent Bridge) 23–26 April	38-11-89-3	30-7-77-0	31.5-7-99-5	21-5-56-1	13-1-33-1	11-2-32-0							8	23	14	12	417	10
v. Durham (Hartlepool) 7–10 May	29.2-5-81-1	20-3-62-1	22-9-62-2		20-5-33-1		29-6-80-3						1	12	12	10	331	10
v. Lancashire (Old Trafford) 14–17 May	16-6-40-6	10-0-37-1	2-0-8-0				8-0-35-3							5	2	6	125	10
	26-9-63-1	25-3-86-2	31-8-70-2			9-2-33-0	11-5-26-0	21.5-3-79-3						9	8	24	357	10
v. Derbyshire (Trent Bridge) 21–24 May	29-6-68-1	20-2-52-1	28.4-6-75-7	6-1-24-1				7-2-15-0					4	16	2	6	319	10
	17.2-6-40-2	14-2-28-2	20-9-34-4	14-2-60-1		3-0-14-0		1-0-4-0						7	12	26	117	10
v. Kent (Trent Bridge) 29 May–2 June	35-4-115-3	29.4-4-94-1	35-9-103-3		30-8-89-3	3-0-14-0							14	11	8	2	440	10
v. Northamptonshire (Northampton) 4–7 June	15-1-51-1		33-11-57-5	2-1-9-0	8-2-29-0	2-1-8-0	27-9-46-2	2-1-3-0	21.2-6-55-2	13-7-19-1			5	4	2		235	10
		18-3-54-0	25.3-2-128-4		6-0-22-0	16-0-78-2	11-0-47-0	5-0-14-0	23-4-85-0	16-4-33-2			4	4	4	2	337	6
v. Australians (Trent Bridge) 11–13 June	15-1-51-1							15.2-1-96-1	13-0-62-1	13-1-37-0			3	3	4		398	5
v. Oxford University (Oxford) 14–17 June		13-7-11-2			15-6-37-1	7-2-13-1			14-7-23-2			18.2-7-28-4	2	10			124	10
		11-2-23-1			32-6-74-1				8-2-29-0			34-8-97-4	7	3	2	2	248	6
v. Yorkshire (Trent Bridge) 18–21 June	24.3-2-91-6		22-5-84-2	3-0-15-0		3-0-15-0		6-0-31-0	18-3-53-0	20-5-58-1			2	6	8	4	364	10
				7-0-24-1														
v. Surrey (The Oval) 27–30 June	21-9-35-2	18-4-47-4	18-4-56-1							5-1-26-0	5-1-14-0	16.2-6-30-1	3	4		4	201	9
	8-0-20-2	9-3-30-2	9.2-1-34-1									8-3-31-1	8	2	2	2	123	6
v. Pakistan 'A' (Trent Bridge) 2–4 July		15-3-32-1	16-3-49-0		11-3-23-1	10-4-10-3	16-6-32-3						2				150	
v. Warwickshire (Trent Bridge) 16–19 July		25-7-84-4	20-1-80-0			5-1-12-0	33-10-92-4	5-3-11-0		18-4-47-0	25-4-81-2		7	10	14	8	344	10
		7-0-31-1					6-1-17-1			3-0-10-0	10-1-29-2		8	6		10	95	4
v. Leicestershire (Leicester) 23–26 July	17-1-52-2	5-2-9-0	16-4-44-1				25-8-61-6	3-1-7-0		20-2-50-2	20-8-49-2		8	3	2	4	267	10
							21-6-40-2	2-0-18-0		16-6-27-2	16-2-69-4		12	7	4	6	217	9
v. Glamorgan (Colwyn Bay) 31 July–4 August			10-1-48-0				13-3-44-0	13-4-43-1		10-1-39-2		20-0-101-1	14	12			353	6
v. Somerset (Trent Bridge) 15–18 August	27.4-7-70-2	28-4-84-2	26-6-84-0				21-6-48-1	8-1-36-0		14-2-35-1	19-6-53-4		1	9	2	4	337	10
	15-3-70-0	12-1-57-1	11-4-23-0				22-2-79-3	18-2-62-1		8-0-17-0	15-4-46-1		6	6	2		338	7
v. Essex (Worksop) 20–23 August	23-8-48-2					4-0-20-0	30-7-102-2	17-4-64-1		15-4-29-1	22-8-71-1		14	8	4	6	440	6
							16-5-21-2	30-10-83-3		7-3-10-1	4-3-2-1		8	8	4		183	7
v. Gloucestershire (Bristol) 27–30 August	18-3-59-2		22-7-45-2				12-4-45-0			20.3-4-46-5	17-4-55-1		2	10	2	2	262	10
	15-2-67-3		14-1-65-0				7-0-29-1			10.3-0-40-4	12-2-29-2		2	7	4	7	239	6
v. Hampshire (Trent Bridge) 2–5 September	17-2-56-2		9-3-11-0			4-0-11-0	18-3-58-1	5-1-11-0			17.4-1-62-2		4	9	2	2	260	6
	5-2-13-1							10-3-13-0			8-1-24-1			7			114	8
v. Middlesex (Lord's) 10–13 September	33-10-70-1	25-4-95-1	25-4-75-1		42-11-80-1		14-2-33-0	12-2-29-2					5	6		28	430	8
							23-4-70-1										12	
v. Sussex (Hove) 18–21 September	16-3-45-0	20-0-102-1			30-8-77-2	7-3-14-0		4-0-23-0			17-5-48-2			5	2	26	314	5
	12-3-34-0	18-3-63-2			18.4-1-79-0			14-2-47-2			19-5-52-1			12	2	16	287	7
Bowler's average	457.5-103-1277-45 / 28.37	372.4-63-1158-30 / 38.60	467.2-107-1394-41 / 34.00	53-9-188-4 / 47.00	225.4-51-576-11 / 52.36	81-15-260-6 / 43.33	363-87-1005-35 / 28.71	199.1-40-689-14 / 49.21	97.2-22-307-5 / 61.40	209-44-523-22 / 23.77	226.4-55-684-26 / 26.30	96.4-24-287-11 / 26.09						

A P. Johnson 13-5-32-0
B P. Johnson 1-0-2-0
C W.M. Noon 1-0-12-0

Fielding figures

- 53 – R.J.Turner (ct 51 / st 2)
- 20 – P.D.Bowler
- 12 – S.C.Ecclestone, K.A.Parsons and P.C.L.Holloway
- 11 – M.N.Lathwell
- 9 – M.Burns (ct 8 / st 1)
- 7 – G.D.Rose
- 6 – M.E.Trescothick
- 5 – L.D.Sutton and K.J.Shine
- 4 – A.R.Caddick
- 3 – R.J.Harden and P.S.Jones
- 2 – Mushtaq Ahmed and S.Herzberg
- 1 – R.W.Sladdin, J.I.D.Kerr and B.J.Trott

Somerset CCC First-Class Matches Batting

Season batting summary:

Batting	M	Inns	NO	Runs	HS	Av
M.N.Lathwell	20	34	–	912	95	27.63
M.E.Trescothick	13	19	–	390	83*	21.66
P.D.Bowler	16	26	1	666	123	26.64
R.J.Harden	11	11	2	395	136*	43.88
P.C.L.Holloway	19	34	4	905	106	30.16
M.Burns	14	21	1	510	82	25.50
R.J.Turner	17	28	7	1069	144	50.90
G.D.Rose	18	26	9	852	191	50.11
A.R.Caddick	13	14	3	262	56*	21.83
S.Herzberg	7	8	3	207	56	41.40
K.J.Shine	18	20	5	96	18	6.40
J.I.D.Kerr	6	6	1	133	35	26.60
Mushtaq Ahmed	14	16	–	174	33	12.42
K.A.Parsons	10	15	3	437	74	36.41
S.C.Ecclestone	13	23	2	951	133	45.28
M.Dimond	–	1	–	4	4	4.00
A.P.van Troost	6	8	3	20	12*	4.00
R.W.Sladdin	–	–	–	–	–	–
B.J.Trott	2	2	1	15	1*	1.00
N.R.Boulton	2	2	–	17	14*	7.50
L.D.Sutton	2	2	–	17	17	17.00
S.C.G.Macgill	2	2	–	32	25	16.00
P.S.Jones	3	5	–	26	13	6.50

First-Class match fixtures (first part):

- v. Surrey (The Oval) 23–26 April
- v. Northamptonshire (Northampton) 7–10 May
- v. Sussex (Taunton) 14–17 May
- v. Yorkshire (Taunton) 21–24 May
- v. Worcestershire (Worcester) 29 May–2 June
- v. Lancashire (Taunton) 4–7 June
- v. Hampshire (Basingstoke) 12–16 June
- v. Leicestershire (Bath) 18–21 June
- v. Oxford University (Taunton) 26–30 June
- v. Essex (Chelmsford) 2–5 July

First-Class match fixtures (second part):

- v. Pakistan 'A' (Taunton) 19–21 July
- v. Warwickshire (Edgbaston) 24–27 July
- v. Australians (Taunton) 1–4 August
- v. Gloucestershire (Taunton) 6–9 August
- v. Nottinghamshire (Trent Bridge) 15–18 August
- v. Kent (Taunton) 20–23 August
- v. Derbyshire (Derby) 27–30 August
- v. Middlesex (Taunton) 2–5 September
- v. Durham (Chester-le-Street) 10–13 September
- v. Glamorgan (Taunton) 18–21 September

Each match column records Byes, Leg-byes, Wides, No-balls, Total, Wickets, Result and Points beneath the individual batting entries.

Bowling

Match / Dates	A.R. Caddick	K.J. Shine	G.D. Rose	S. Herzberg	M. Burns	Mushtaq Ahmed	J.I.D. Kerr	K.A. Parsons	P.D. Bowler	P.S. Jones	M.E. Trescothick	A.P. van Troost	Byes	Leg-byes	Wides	No-balls	Total	Wkts	
v. Surrey (The Oval) 23–26 April	26-2-94-2	9-2-41-1	18-7-35-3	18-9-25-2	5-3-3-0								2	9	4	8	209	8	
v. Northamptonshire (Northampton) 7–10 May	22.4-6-65-6 / 17-2-70-2	7-2-29-2 / 6-2-8-1	20-5-60-2 / 10-4-17-2			4-1-21-0 / 4-2-9-0	4-1-10-0	4-0-1-1	3-1-5-0				4	6 / 4		5	185 / 122	10 / 5	A
v. Sussex (Taunton) 14–17 May	21-5-43-0 / 30-6-59-1	20-2-75-2 / 13-1-66-1	13-3-41-1 / 8-2-19-1			31-12-70-6 / 34.1-16-67-1		5-2-12-0 / 4-0-21-0						10 / 9		12 / 10	241 / 259	10 / 5	
v. Yorkshire (Taunton) 21–24 May	30.3-3-103-6 / 7.2-1-6-1	16-1-54-2 / 8-1-34-0	9-2-30-1		10-2-40-1	22-6-91-1 / 8-0-42-1							5 / 3	13 / 4		8 / 4	306 / 237	6 / 6	
v. Worcestershire (Worcester) 29 May–2 June	29.2-10-64-5 / 31-6-86-3	19-4-42-1 / 14-4-59-1	20-6-44-3 / 17-5-57-0			27-10-66-0 / 42-10-97-3			5-1-48-2 / 2-2-0-0 / 4-3-2-0				4	21 / 7		2 / 4	303 / 316	9 / 10	
v. Lancashire (Taunton) 4–7 June		11.1-3-43-7 / 17-2-54-4	4-3-11-2 / 5-0-15-1			7.3-6-7-1		7-3-10-1 / 3-0-10-1				7-0-27-1		7 / 9	8 / 4		7 / 16	88 / 164	9 / 10	B C
v. Hampshire (Basingstoke) 12–16 June	21-10-42-1 / 13-3-36-0	10-3-41-1 / 19-8-37-3	15-5-26-3 / 21.1-8-53-5			11-3-28-2 / 17-5-46-1						14-1-79-3 / 6-1-43-1		14 / 7	13	20 / 2	204 / 189	10 / 10	
v. Leicestershire (Bath) 18–21 June		26.4-4-92-1	30-7-82-3			15.3-6-32-1	12-1-37-0 / 14-3-41-1	17-5-44-0	9.3-5-18-0			9.2-1-69-0	15		4	14	442	6	
v. Oxford University (Taunton) 28–30 June		23.4-8-73-3 / 19-5-72-5	24-8-79-3 / 10.3-3-23-3	27-8-48-2 / 23-6-61-2	6-1-30-1		23.4-4-83-4	14-3-34-2 / 3.5-1-4-2	2-0-5-0					2 / 13		6	241 / 280	8 / 10	D
v. Essex (Chelmsford) 3–6 July		24-3-74-6 / 20-5-57-2		1-0-1-0		31-9-66-5 / 16-4-43-0	8-3-34-2 / 10-3-33-2	13-3-27-0		14-1-66-0 / 3-1-18-1			1	1		14	129 / 227	10 / 10	
v. Pakistan 'A' (Taunton) 19–21 July		23-6-61-0					8-1-46-0	4-0-23-0 / 2-1-4-0	0.5-0-11-0		4-1-18-0		4	2 / 10	2 / 1	10	231 / 336	5 / 5	E
v. Warwickshire (Edgbaston) 24–27 July	30-8-92-3 / 11-4-33-1	6-0-42-0	19.4-8-81-2 / 15-1-75-4							5-1-32-2				5 / 2		10 / 32	198 / 323	5 / 8	
v. Australians (Taunton) 1–4 August	16-2-54-5		14-3-50-1	5-0-36-0				2-0-4-0			2-0-13-0	15.3-0-132-2		2			350	8	
v. Gloucestershire (Taunton) 6–9 August	32-7-74-2 / 20-5-57-1	15-3-79-2 / 2-1-4-0	22.3-8-55-4 / 4.1-0-34-0		4-2-4-0 / 2-0-7-0	26-5-98-1 / 7-1-31-0			5-3-6-0 / 5-1-24-0	2-0-19-0 / 7-0-30-3	3-0-18-1 / 6-2-20-0	16-2-69-0 / 4-0-27-0	4 / 2	17	4 / 10	24 / 2	178 / 356	3 / 10	
v. Nottinghamshire (Trent Bridge) 15–18 August		24-7-79-2 / 12-0-70-0	21-5-83-2 / 16-0-67-2		8-1-39-0	38.4-6-97-3 / 29-3-88-3						7-0-50-0	14	13	2	4	305 / 449	9 / 6	
v. Kent (Taunton) 20–23 August	36-11-96-4 / 8-0-19-0	10-0-48-0	22-5-60-3	22-1-100-3	8-3-36-0	37.1-10-114-4 / 12-1-78-3							8	8	4	27	323	10	
v. Derbyshire (Derby) 27–30 August	23-4-71-4 / 18-2-68-0	22-5-80-2 / 8-0-48-1	20-5-79-3 / 5-1-23-1	1-0-2-1		11-4-23-0								6 / 3	4	6	160 / 97	2 / 10	
v. Middlesex (Taunton) 2–5 September	22-2-83-1 / 21-7-60-4	12-2-64-0 / 4-0-17-1	12-2-26-0			19.4-2-66-5 / 23.2-7-71-4			1-1-0-1				1 / 4	7 / 6	4	4 / 6	236 / 187	5 / 10	F
v. Durham (Chester-le-Street) 10–13 September	34.4-5-132-4	6-0-26-1	15.4-4-40-3	2-4-6-0 / 3-1-2-0	9-1-24-1	21-4-49-2			6-3-17-0 / 1-0-9-0				4	8 / 7	6	10	230 / 135	9 / 10	
v. Glamorgan (Taunton) 18–21 September	1-0-5-0	17-3-88-2	13.5-2-43-3 / 0.2-0-5-0		7-0-65-0	13-10-4-3								7 / 1	12	16	527 / 11	10 / 0	G
Bowler's average	522.5-112-1522-57 = 26.70	443.3-89-1678-55 = 30.50	486.5-124-1563-63 = 24.80	102-25-281-10 = 28.10	62-13-266-5 = 53.20	513-146-1407-50 = 28.14	103-20-374-10 = 37.40	78.5-18-204-7 = 29.14	44.2-20-145-3 = 48.33	31-3-165-6 = 27.50	15-3-69-1 = 69.00	78.5-5-496-7 = 70.85							

A M.N. Lathwell 5-0-60-1
B M. Dimond 9-2-26-0, 2-1-4-0
C J.E.R. Gallian retired hurt
D B.J. Trott 13-2-40-2, 3-0-14-0; R.W. Sladdin 13-1-45-1, 25-9-60-5
E S.C.G. Macgill 17-8-49-2, 19-3-74-2
F S.C. Ecclestone 1-1-0-0
G B.J. Trott 11-0-74-3

Fielding figures

19 – M.A.Butcher
16 – A.J.Stewart
11 – A.D.Brown
10 – C.C.Lewis, B.C.Hollioake and A.J.Hollioake
9 – g.p.Thorpe and J.A.Knott (ct 8 /st 1)
8 – M.P.Bicknell and J.N.Batty (ct 7 /st 1)
7 – I.D.K.Salisbury
6 – I.J.Ward
4 – N.Shahid
3 – J.D.Ratcliffe and G.J.Kennis
2 – R.M.Amin and sub
1 – R.M.Pearson, D.J.Bicknell and Saqlain Mushtaq

†A.D.Brown absent hurt

Surrey CCC First-Class Matches — Batting (season summary)

Batting	M	Inns	NO	Runs	HS	Av
D.J.Bicknell	13	15	—	594	162	39.60
M.A.Butcher	13	22	1	659	79	31.38
A.J.Stewart	9	14	1	726	271*	55.84
G.P.Thorpe	8	12	2	707	222	70.70
N.Shahid	7	11	—	198	34	18.00
A.J.Hollioake	13	19	—	731	182	38.47
C.C.Lewis	13	19	2	389	76	22.88
I.D.K.Salisbury	13	17	2	159	30*	10.60
M.P.Bicknell	15	20	5	305	74	20.33
A.J.Tudor	8	15	6	109	35	21.80
J.E.Benjamin	12	15	—	152	35	16.88
B.C.Hollioake	12	19	—	483	76	25.42
J.D.Ratcliffe	15	26	—	759	135	31.62
A.D.Brown	14	21	—	848	170*	42.40
J.A.Knott	3	5	—	118	27*	19.66
R.M.Pearson	3	3	—	—	4*	1.00
G.J.Kennis	3	5	—	49	24	9.80
Saqlain Mushtaq	8	10	4	149	41*	24.83
I.J.Ward	3	4	—	102	56	25.50
J.N.Batty	3	3	—	54	23*	27.00
R.M.Amin	4	6	3	11	4*	3.66

First half of season — match-by-match

Batting	v.Somerset (The Oval) 23–26 April	v.Derbyshire (Derby) 7–10 May	v.Gloucestershire (The Oval) 14–17 May	v.Leicestershire (Leicester) 21–24 May	v.Essex (The Oval) 4–7 June	v.Yorkshire (The Oval) 12–16 June	v.Worcestershire (Worcester) 18–21 June	v.Nottinghamshire (The Oval) 27–30 June	v.Warwickshire (Edgbaston) 2–5 July
D.J.Bicknell	48	4	24	18 / 59	5	45 / 0	—	—	—
M.A.Butcher	46	0	— / 15	—	—	271*	—	7 / 10	31 / 5
A.J.Stewart	6	12	— / 81	14	12	—	18	3 / 34	— / 0
G.P.Thorpe	29	32 / 9	34 / 8	31	40 / 5	69 / 6	24	2 / 7	31 / 24
N.Shahid	0	0	4	22	—	6 / 11	—	48 / 33*	9 / —
A.J.Hollioake	3	6	—	34* / 5	—	15	9 / 4	12 / —	— / 5
C.C.Lewis	30*	2*	16 / 16	— / 5	—	21 / 10	31*	21* / —	— / 24
I.D.K.Salisbury	13	74 / 17	— / 1*	36 / 1	22 / 17	53 / 43	135 / 121	44 / 9	1* / 4
M.P.Bicknell	3*	—	— / 3*	21 / —	31 / 109	8 / 0	26	27 / 10	3*
A.J.Tudor	—	1*	— / 1*	14 / —	—	—	—	—	59
J.E.Benjamin	—	—	29 / 19	— / 6*	27* / 6	4	24* / 24	7*	5 / 1
B.C.Hollioake	—	—	—	1	0	9*	—	—	9 / 46 / 21
G.J.Kennis	—	—	—	—	—	—	—	16 / 7 / 18	—
A.D.Brown	—	—	—	—	—	—	—	—	—

	Somerset	Derbyshire	Gloucestershire	Leicestershire	Essex	Yorkshire	Worcestershire	Nottinghamshire	Warwickshire
Byes	2	2	1	3	5	8	5	3	4 / 5
Leg-byes	9	9	— / 8	15	9	11	9	4	— / 1
Wides	4	2	—	6	9	—	—	4	—
No-balls	8	2	8	12	2	2	12	4	14
Total	209	267	115 / 269	278	280 / 222	549	452	201 / 123	193 / 144
Wickets	7	10	10 / 4	10	10 / 6	10	9	9 / 7	10 / 4
Result	D	D	L	D	L	W	D	W	L
Points	7	6	4	9	6	10	7	17	4

Second half of season — match-by-match

Batting	v.Hampshire (Guildford) 16–19 July	v.Northamptonshire (Northampton) 23–26 July	v.Durham (The Oval) 6–9 August	v.Middlesex (Lord's) 15–18 August	v.Sussex (Hove) 27–30 August	v.Glamorgan (The Oval) 2–5 September	v.Lancashire (The Oval) 10–13 September	v.Kent (Canterbury) 18–21 September
D.J.Bicknell	69	162	33 / 24	—	20 / 13	74	0 / 38	0 / 130
M.A.Butcher	98	—	29 / 27*	61 / 34	7 / 222	49 / 73	30 / 4	30 / 170
A.J.Stewart	84 / 26*	—	—	106*	2 / —	—	—	—
G.P.Thorpe	—	—	32	—	—	—	—	8
A.J.Hollioake	75	81	— / 24	87 / 7	22	14 / —	27 / —	— / 15
C.C.Lewis	76 / —	9	15	—	8* / 17	1 / 14*	—	—
I.D.K.Salisbury	11	—	5	— / 2*	53	—	—	—
M.P.Bicknell	0 / 35*	2*	35	—	3 / —	0	17*	—
A.J.Tudor	—	—	—	76 / 19	1* / 14	18 / 8	2	0
J.E.Benjamin	—	49	—	13 / 19	31* / 41	90 / 47	0	2
B.C.Hollioake	—	31 / 170*	76 / 7	70 / 37	60 / —	—	0	4
J.D.Ratcliffe	7 / 23	—	41* / 56 / 8 / 4*	— / 9 / 23* / 0*	21 / —	2 / —	4 / —	1*
G.J.Kennis	—	—	—	—	—	—	—	—

	Hampshire	Northamptonshire	Durham	Middlesex	Sussex	Glamorgan	Lancashire	Kent
Byes	3	3	4	6	1	5	8	1
Leg-byes	10	12	17	6	5	6	4	—
Wides	4	8	10	4	2	2	0	—
No-balls	24	24	6	14	6	2	10	—
Total	477	581	350 / 64	400	204 / 487	270 / 267	124 / 371	—
Wickets	10	7	9 / 7	7	10 / 9	10 / 10	10 / 10	—
Result	W	D	W	W	D	L	L	—
Points	24	10	24	24	8	2	4	—

Bowling

Match	Date	M.P. Bicknell	C.C. Lewis	A.J. Tudor	J.E. Benjamin	I.D.K. Salisbury	A.J. Hollioake	N. Shahid	R.M. Amin	D.J. Bicknell	B.C. Hollioake	J.D. Ratcliffe	Saqlain Mushtaq	Byes	Leg-byes	Wides	No-balls	Total	Wkts	
v. Somerset (The Oval)	23–26 April	25-13-6-1-1	28.4-9-109-2	24-3-83-2	6.2-1-28-0	34.3-10-107-3	20-8-30-2	3-0-9-0		1-0-2-0				10	16	8	52	463	10	A
v. Derbyshire (Derby)	7–10 May	8-1-38-2	6-0-25-0	2-0-20-0	11.4-3-29-1	9-2-23-0	3-0-12-0				18-6-45-0	3-0-13-0			11		18	158	3	
v. Gloucestershire (The Oval)	14–17 May	24-6-65-2 / 2-0-7-1	20-4-64-4	23.3-2-101-6 / 2-0-8-0	23-5-72-0		11-1-57-2	1-0-1-0		2-0-11-0 / 5-1-13-0					6		34	371 / 15	10 / 1	B
v. Leicestershire (Leicester)	21–24 May	19-2-58-1		18-4-62-3	16-4-35-0			1-0-4-0				5-2-14-1 / 11-1-35-0	45-11-118-4 / 6.1-2-16-1 / 1-0-8-0	7	1	8	40	340	1	C
v. Essex (The Oval)	4–7 June		17-4-57-1 / 13.1-3-39-2	21-3-77-2 / 6-2-18-0	16-4-52-3 / 17-6-60-2	22-5-78-2 / 24-4-79-3	4.5-1-22-4 / 2-0-6-0				18-5-53-1 / 14-3-53-1 / 3-0-19-0 / 4-0-26-0 / 3-0-11-0	1-0-1-0 / 4-1-0-0		2	12 / 12	4 / 2	16 / 9	347 / 302	10 / 10	
v. Yorkshire (The Oval)	12–16 June	20-7-67-1 / 11-3-32-3	8-2-22-0		8-0-49-0 / 3-0-14-0	22-4-83-1 / 1-0-6-0	4-1-7-0 / 1-0-4-0 / 14-1-60-0							2	7 / 6	2	30 / 4	387 / 115	10 / 4	
v. Worcestershire (Worcester)	18–21 June	5-0-44-1	10-8-7-0	6-2-18-0			2-0-7-0						8-2-15-0				16	81	1	
v. Nottinghamshire (The Oval)	27–30 June	5-1-10-0 / 11-3-30-1	7-2-20-1 / 7-1-20-1			4-1-19-0 / 18.1-11-19-6	6-1-31-1				5-1-11-1 / 5-2-14-1	1-0-1-0 / 4-1-0-0	26-13-34-2 / 13.4-3-34-1	12 / 5	5 / 12	2	4 / 10	73 / 120	1 / 5	D
v. Warwickshire (Edgbaston)	2–5 July	30-3-96-4 / 5.5-1-24-3	15-3-40-3 / 5-3-9-2	11-1-49-2		32.3-7-83-3 / 16-0-40-0	2-0-7-0				10-1-31-1 / 2-0-7-0	9-2-24-0 / 2-0-5-0			1		4	306 / 34	10	
v. Hampshire (Northampton)	16–19 July	30-5-88-4 / 18.3-10-34-5	15.5-3-31-2 / 14-2-66-1	8-0-46-0 / 6-0-44-1		32.4-8-85-2 / 9-0-31-0	9-1-36-0 / 2-0-18-0					15-3-35-0		15 / 3	7 / 7		12 / 9	303 / 251	10 / 10	
v. Northamptonshire (Northampton)	23–26 July	31-8-111-2 / 13-4-43-0	25.3-7-82-4 / 13-3-34-1		16-6-41-1 / 8-0-31-1				17-4-27-0 / 36-11-58-3				14-6-17-5 / 43.2-14-111-5	3 / 3	7 / 5		40 / 6	401 / 241	10 / 2	D
v. Durham (The Oval)	6–9 August	14-5-37-3 / 10-4-24-1	6-1-23-0 / 6-2-17-0		7-1-22-2 / 10-1-34-1				18.3-5-55-2			2-0-11-0	14-2-50-5	3	8 / 7	6 / 12	12	136 / 274	6 / 10	
v. Middlesex (Lord's)	15–18 August	7-3-14-1 / 21-6-53-3	12-1-44-0 / 14-2-43-1			8-2-20-1 / 23-8-66-5	6.5-1-24-1				13-4-23-3 / 3-0-14-0		27-6-66-5	4	2		19	205 / 201	10 / 10	
v. Sussex (Hove)	27–30 August	9-4-24-2	20-8-42-5 / 8-2-43-2			14-1-51-1 / 11-2-31-2	3-1-3-0				8-1-1-1 / 2-1-3-0		12.3-7-18-1 / 31-8-96-2	4	4 / 15	2	14	137 / 162	10 / 10	
v. Glamorgan (The Oval)	2–5 September	30-4-93-2 / 11-1-32-1			13-0-72-0 / 4-0-22-0		2-0-12-2 / 1-0-2-0				25-3-91-3		5-0-19-0	8		4	20	438 / 107	10 / 3	
v. Lancashire (The Oval)	10–13 September	14-3-56-0			22-3-77-0	20-2-77-0	17-2-61-1		28-5-135-1	4-0-12-1	18-2-101-0	3-1-11-0		4	1	12	24	592	4	F
v. Kent (Canterbury)	18–21 September	8-0-54-1 / 13.2-0-79-0			17-3-45-1 / 13-2-56-1	14-2-38-1			12-5-21-1 / 11-1-31-0		18.2-5-54-4 / 8-1-38-0	3-0-18-0	254.5-75-617-32	1 / 8	3	6	30 / 23	220 / 276	10 / 5	G
Bowler's average		385.2-99-1174-44 / 26.68	291.4-72-970-33 / 29.39	127.3-17-526-16 / 32.87	211-39-759-13 / 58.38	314.1-65-936-30 / 31.20	108.4-19-388-13 / 29.84	5-0-14-0 / —	134.3-35-348-8 / 43.50	12-1-38-1 / 38.00	169.2-34-594-17 / 34.94	58-10-177-1 / 177.00	254.5-75-617-32 / 19.28							

A   G.P.Thorpe 3-0-8-0
B   M.A.Butcher 2-0-10-0; R.M.Pearson 26-4-90-2
C   G.J.Kennis 1-0-4-0
D   A.D.Brown 15-4-24-0; J.N.Batty 4-0-9-0
E   G.P.Thorpe 1-0-5-0
F   M.A.Butcher 8-1-23-1; A.D.Brown 1-0-13-0
G   M.A.Butcher 16-6-24-3, 13-1-26-3

Fielding figures

36 – P. Moores
12 – K. Greenfield
10 – M.T.E. Peirce
9 – C.W.J. Athey and M. Newell
7 – V.C. Drakes
6 – J.J. Bates, R.K. Rao and S. Humphries
5 – P.W. Jarvis and A.D. Edwards
4 – A.A. Khan, M.A. Robinson and R.J. Kirtley
3 – N.R. Taylor and T.A. Radford
2 – N.J. Lenham, J.P. Pyemont, K. Newell, J.R. Carpenter, R.S.C.
Martin – Jenkins and sub
1 – M.J. Thursfield and C.J. Batt

Sussex CCC First-Class Matches — Batting (season summary)

Batting	M	Inns	NO	Runs	HS	Av
K. Greenfield	11	21	—	372	108	17.71
N.J. Lenham	7	12	1	290	93	24.16
N.R. Taylor	16	28	1	1033	127	38.25
C.W.J. Athey	12	21	2	682	138*	35.89
K. Newell	17	31	2	827	112	28.51
V.C. Drakes	10	18	1	221	48	13.00
P. Moores	17	31	4	571	102*	21.14
P.W. Jarvis	10	18	2	374	64	23.37
N.C. Phillips	2	2	1	7	6	7.00
A.A. Khan	15	24	5	291	52	15.31
M.A. Robinson	17	25	9	114	27	7.12
M.T.E. Peirce	12	23	—	576	104	25.04
R.K. Rao	12	20	1	375	89	19.73
M.J. Thursfield	2	4	2	32	32*	32.00
T.A. Radford				131	69*	22.42
M. Newell				471	100	65.50
J.P. Pyemont				22	22	22.00
S. Humphries				52	52	26.00
J.J. Bates				113	41*	16.14
C.J. Batt					47	
R.J. Kirtley				49	15*	5.44
R.S.C. Martin-Jenkins				77	36*	15.40
A.D. Edwards				66	20	8.25
J.R. Carpenter				153	63	25.50

Match schedule — first half of season (left table columns)

- v. Northamptonshire (Hove) 23–26 April
- v. Middlesex (Lord's) 7–10 May
- v. Somerset (Taunton) 14–17 May
- v. Kent (Horsham) 21–24 May
- v. Oxford University (Oxford) 30 May–2 June
- v. Durham (Chester-le-Street) 4–7 June
- v. Essex (Hove) 12–16 June
- v. Derbyshire (Derby) 18–21 June
- v. Glamorgan (Swansea) 26–30 June
- v. Worcestershire (Arundel) 2–5 July

Match schedule — second half of season (right table columns)

- v. Lancashire (Old Trafford) 16–19 July
- v. Pakistan 'A' (Hove) 24–27 July
- v. Warwickshire (Edgbaston) 31 July–4 August
- v. Leicestershire (Eastbourne) 6–9 August
- v. Gloucestershire (Hove) 15–18 August
- v. Yorkshire (Scarborough) 20–23 August
- v. Surrey (Hove) 27–30 August
- v. Hampshire (Southampton) 10–13 September
- v. Nottinghamshire (Hove) 18–21 September

Bowling

Opponent (venue) / Date	V.C. Drakes	P.W. Jarvis	M.A. Robinson	A.A. Khan	K. Newell	N.C. Phillips	K. Greenfield	J.J. Bates	A.D. Edwards	R.K. Rao	R.S.C. Martin-Jenkins	R.J. Kirtley	Byes	Leg-byes	Wides	No-balls	Total	Wkts
v. Northamptonshire (Hove) 23–26 April	26-5-88-0; 5-0-21-0	22-5-51-3; 4-0-16-0	19.5-8-78-6	19-7-27-0	14-6-41-1	3-0-13-0							4; –	13; 4	–; –	15; –	315; 41	10[A]; 0
v. Middlesex (Lord's) 7–10 May	6-1-21-0	39.5-8-126-1	30-7-87-1	37-5-137-5	9-2-35-1		1-0-15-0			5-1-14-1			6	10	6	10	490	9[B]
v. Somerset (Taunton) 14–17 May		31-1-122-5	23-7-80-2	30-6-73-2	6-1-26-0	10-2-39-0	5-1-12-0						7	12	–	26	409	10
v. Kent (Horsham) 21–24 May	21-5-69-3; 39-4-152-4	17-3-61-3; 24-3-75-1	12-2-45-0; 32-11-82-3	26-8-62-1	15.3-4-61-4; 12.4-2-46-1								1; 8	8; –	4; 10	24; 6	245; 440	10[C]; 8
v. Oxford University (Oxford) 30 May–2 June						10-0-47-1; 3-1-15-0		21-7-50-1; 16.2-3-47-4		8-1-19-1; 6-0-35-0		11-3-34-2	–; –	6; 1	4; 4	6; 24	234; 190	8; 10[D]
v. Durham (Chester-le-Street) 4–7 June	27-5-90-4; 26-4-93-3	28-7-97-2	14-2-46-3; 19.5-4-47-5	20-3-54-1; 37-6-117-3	9-1-34-0								6; –	1; 1	–; –	24; 30	338; 269	8; 8
v. Essex (Hove) 12–16 June	22-6-86-2; 8-0-34-0		25-2-101-3; 3-0-16-0	21-5-70-2; 5.2-1-28-0	5-3-12-0					1-0-7-0		20-2-112-2; 6-0-28-0	3; –	–; 2	6; 2	21; 2	384; 115	0; 0
v. Derbyshire (Derby) 18–21 June	22-6-55-4		11-3-41-1		6-1-22-0							20.1-4-98-4	4	13	–	16	233	9
v. Glamorgan (Swansea) 26–30 June	16-3-56-1; 11-2-47-2		15-0-54-3; 15-4-42-4	12-2-44-1; 11-2-33-0	1-0-10-0; 12-4-20-2							22.5-4-60-6; 9-1-37-0	–; –	2; 3	2; 2	18; 12	172; 183	10; 9
v. Worcestershire (Arundel) 2–5 July	20-8-33-3		22-5-48-1		8-1-25-0		4-1-18-0			7-1-18-0	14-3-51-2	24-9-59-2		11	4	2	255	10
v. Lancashire (Old Trafford) 16–19 July	30-6-114-1		32-4-142-3									30-6-125-2		15	2	32	561	8
v. Pakistan 'A' (Hove) 24–27 July	21-5-84-4		14-0-53-4	28.2-12-88-2; 18-3-65-1				18-10-20-1; 20-9-35-3	15-3-71-2; 13-3-34-5		13-3-26-3; 8-0-31-0	18-2-99-2; 20-2-80-1	1; 1	1; 2	–; 2	2; 18	306; 248	10; 10
v. Warwickshire (Edgbaston) 31 July–4 August									14-4-37-2; 2-0-20-0			10-0-50-0; 2.5-0-20-1	–	1; 3	–	–	227; 41; 0	1; 0; –
v. Leicestershire (Eastbourne) 6–9 August		17-2-44-5; 25-4-88-0	9-2-29-0; 29.2-9-66-5	36-8-108-3; 17-5-59-3	1-0-1-0; 8-3-11-0			30.2-8-75-2; 13-3-29-0	4-1-9-0; 19-3-55-2				16	10	4	2; 22	292; 320	10; 7
v. Gloucestershire (Hove) 15–18 August		11-1-42-2	14-1-61-4	37.4-8-126-1	7-3-9-1			15-1-48-0	10-1-39-0				9	5	–	12	331	7
v. Yorkshire (Scarborough) 20–23 August		22-4-82-4	19-3-80-2	3.3-2-7-0	9-3-27-1			14-3-40-0	7.2-1-24-1; 4-2-6-1			19-3-89-1	2	5	–	12; 14	282; 13	1; –
v. Surrey (Hove) 27–30 September			10-4-17-0	15-0-90-0	7-0-35-0				15-1-94-4				6	6	2		400	7
v. Hampshire (Southampton) 10–13 September		16-1-71-1; 13-2-32-0	12-1-41-1	27.4-6-79-4; 28-6-89-1	8-1-21-0			15-6-31-1; 11-3-38-1			14-3-49-0; 8-1-27-0	15-3-41-1; 14-4-34-0	4	6; 3	6	14; 20	245; 260	10[E]; 9
v. Nottinghamshire (Hove) 18–21 September		19-3-67-1; 2-0-13-0	29-2-85-0; 8.2-1-32-0					42.4-14-89-5; 11-4-23-1				30-4-115-3; 4.4-1-13-1		10; 9	2	27; 10	454; 215	3[F]; 3
Bowler's average	300-60-1043-31 **33.64**	318.5-46-1091-30 **36.36**	448.2-87-1426-48 **29.70**	444.3-100-1397-33 **42.33**	138.1-35-436-11 **39.63**	26-3-114-1 **114.00**	10-2-45-0 **–**	227.2-71-525-19 **27.63**	103.2-19-389-17 **22.88**	28-3-100-2 **50.00**	57-10-184-5 **36.80**	276.3-48-1094-31 **35.29**						

A C.W.J. Athey 6-0-17-0; M.T.E. Peirce 7-0-22-0
B M.J. Thursfield 3.3-0-38-0
C C.W.J. Athey 1-0-4-0
D C.J. Bett 21-7-44-2, 19-4-56-4; M.J. Thursfield 15-2-34-1, 11-3-36-2
E J.R. Carpenter 3-0-13-0; M.T.E. Peirce 1.1-0-6-0
F J.R. Carpenter 3-4-18-0, 9.3-1-50-1; M.T.E. Peirce 12-2-48-0

Fielding Figures

- 30 – T. Frost (ct 28 / st 2)
- 29 – D.P. Ostler
- 25 – K.J. Piper (ct 24 / st 1)
- 11 – T.L. Penney
- 10 – A.J. Moles
- 9 – D.L. Hemp
- 8 – D.R. Brown
- 7 – M.A. Wagh
- 6 – N.V. Knight, N.M.K. Smith and sub
- 5 – A.A. Donald
- 3 – G. Welch
- 2 – A. Singh, M.J. Powell and A.F. Giles
- 1 – G.C. Small, W.G. Khan, M.D. Edmond and M.A.V. Bell

Warwickshire CCC First-Class Matches Batting

Player	v. Glamorgan (Cardiff) 23–26 April	v. Oxford University (Oxford) 7–9 May	v. Yorkshire (Edgbaston) 14–17 May	v. Middlesex (Edgbaston) 21–24 May	v. Hampshire (Southampton) 29 May–2 June	v. Kent (Tunbridge Wells) 4–7 June	v. Derbyshire (Edgbaston) 12–16 June	v. Leicestershire (Leicester) 26–30 June	v. Surrey (Edgbaston) 2–5 July	v. Nottinghamshire (Trent Bridge) 16–19 July	M	Inns	NO	Runs	HS	Av
A.J. Moles	9 40*	43	6 33	1 67*	168 138	42 12	83		9	20	12	22	3	635	168	33.42
W.G. Khan	6 0	5		24 29*							3	5	0	102	43	20.40
D.L. Hemp	9 0	51	0 1	37 29*	36	117 19	60		14 70	37	17	29	4	1013	138	40.52
D.P. Ostler	14 –		– 37	18 –	86*	9 40	33		10 65	65	15	24	2	419	65	19.95
T.L. Penney	16 –	7* 10	67 26*	9		9	73		99 25	31*	16	24	5	784	99	41.26
K.J. Piper	– –				6	14 40	12				8	11	3	111	34*	13.87
N.M.K. Smith	36 3	55* 0	15 17	9 4	75 2*	15 27	26 9		69* 6	11*	15	22	3	642	148	33.78
G. Welch	3 35	0	0 38*	3*			9 8		6 0	–	15	25	6	391	75	20.57
A.F. Giles	29 0	69*	2* –		81 119*	11 36			2 –	42 22*	15	19	6	543	97	36.20
A.A. Donald	20* 0		8 9	8		8					13	13	6	140	29	20.00
G.C. Small	0 –	12 0			8 –	14* 21	13				3	4	1	13	11	4.33
N.V. Knight		20	26 4	2 8		2* 30	2		66 0	0 6	11	17	3	689	119*	49.21
M.J. Powell			65* 4	24		6 0	5*			4 –	16	22	2	448	79	22.40
D.R. Brown					119*	2 9					9	11	2	158	56	17.55
T. Frost	56 22	30*							25 30		3	3	1	35	29	17.50
M.D. Edmond	23 57	–									2	3	1	24	24	24.00
D.A. Altree				24												
M.A. Wagh											8	13	1	472	124	39.33
M.A.V. Bell		0									3	3	1	30	30	15.00
A. Singh		–			–					–	2	3	–	1	1	0.33
Byes	4	9	2	1	4	4	7		5	7						
Leg-byes	2	2	7 1	5 3	4 8	10 4	9		12 4	2 6						
Wides	–	2	7		8 8	2			1	14 8						
No-balls	2	22	16 2	8 20	8	4		Ab	10	4 2						
Total	151 77	297	140 249	158 198	631 252	314 280	340	3	306 34	344 95						
Wickets	10 3	7	10 6	10 2	7	10 6	10		10 5	10 4						
Result	D	W	W	W	D	L	D		W	D						
Points	3	–	20	20	9	6	10		23	10						

Batting (continued)

Player	v. Somerset (Edgbaston) 24–27 July	v. Sussex (Edgbaston) 31 July–4 August	v. Lancashire (Blackpool) 6–9 August	v. Worcestershire (Edgbaston) 20–23 August	v. Essex (Chelmsford) 27–30 August	v. Durham (Chester-le-Street) 2–5 September	v. Gloucestershire (Edgbaston) 10–13 September	v. Northamptonshire (Edgbaston) 18–21 September	M	Inns	NO	Runs	HS	Av
A.J. Moles	38	31	15 35	25	0 20*	13		11 15	12	22	3	635	168	33.42
W.G. Khan	49 65*	15 0*	35 12	25	18 0	18	66	20 58	3	5	0	102	43	20.40
D.L. Hemp	4 –		20	9	0* –	40	– 13	27	17	29	4	1013	138	40.52
D.P. Ostler	22 –	17* 10	12	0 42	77*	34*	148	6 0	15	24	2	419	65	19.95
T.L. Penney		38 12	24 38	4* 40	21 17	23	1* 9	35 0	16	24	5	784	99	41.26
K.J. Piper	0	4 23	27 72	27 20	14	7 29	0 –	19* 0*	8	11	3	111	34*	13.87
N.M.K. Smith	97 19*		6 0*	40	19			45 73*	15	22	3	642	148	33.78
G. Welch				20		29			15	25	6	391	75	20.57
A.F. Giles			42 6*	20 8	48 0	92	71	28* 3	15	19	6	543	97	36.20
A.A. Donald	0	6			20*	1	79	45	13	13	6	140	29	20.00
G.C. Small	56	57	6 4	32 0	0	124	10 –	70 18	3	4	1	13	11	4.33
N.V. Knight				116* 16					11	17	3	689	119*	49.21
M.J. Powell									16	22	2	448	79	22.40
D.R. Brown									9	11	2	158	56	17.55
T. Frost									3	3	1	35	29	17.50
M.D. Edmond									2	3	1	24	24	24.00
D.A. Altree														
M.A. Wagh									8	13	1	472	124	39.33
M.A.V. Bell									3	3	1	30	30	15.00
A. Singh									2	3	–	1	1	0.33
Byes	4	3	1 7	4 8	7 6	4 23	8	4						
Leg-byes	10 5	2	2 2	8 10	6 2	2		4 2						
Wides	2 4	1 18	4 12	20 15	8	2	10							
No-balls														
Total	336 198	227 41	139 310	252 241	237 43	412	418	251 246						
Wickets	10 5	10 1	10 10	10 5	10 2	10	10	8 8						
Result	D	W	L	D	W	W	W	D						
Points	8	21	4	7	21	23	24	7						

Warwickshire CCC First-Class Matches — Bowling

Match	A.A. Donald	G.C. Small	G. Welch	A.F. Giles	N.M.K. Smith	D.L. Hemp	D.R. Brown	M.D. Edmond	M.A. Wagh	M.A. Sheikh	D.A. Altree	M.A.V. Bell	Byes	Leg-byes	Wides	No-balls	Total	Wkts
v. Glamorgan (Cardiff) 23–26 April	93-12-62-1	22-3-80-0	33-8-135-1	38-11-116-1	26-3-97-0	2-0-28-0							6	27	2	36	551	3
v. Oxford University (Oxford) 7–9 May			10.3-0-39-4	21-8-44-2	11-3-23-0		8-4-9-2	9-2-26-2					6	5	6	6	129	10
v. Yorkshire (Edgbaston) 14–17 May	19-5-55-4 / 13.3-3-33-3	9-2-27-0	14-7-15-3 / 16-4-46-0	21-11-27-3 / 24-6-54-4			14.3-4-24-4 / 10-4-23-2	6-3-14-0					2 / 17	10 / 1	2	10 / 6	115 / 233	10 / 10
v. Middlesex (Edgbaston) 21–24 May	22-4-38-2 / 14.1-5-24-1		9-1-25-1 / 22-4-75-3	17-4-45-3	5-0-11-0		9-2-36-3 / 28-9-54-3						11 / 17	1 / 16	2	2 / 16	154 / 221	10 / 10
v. Hampshire (Southampton) 29 May–2 June			16-5-46-5 / 31-6-119-4	44-10-112-0 / 22-7-64-2	30-3-120-0 / 10-3-25-0	3-0-24-0	15-4-43-2 / 18-4-54-0				22-3-108-2 / 3-0-11-0		1 / 6	4 / 6	14 / 2	38 / 14	132 / 549	6 / 6
v. Kent (Tunbridge Wells) 4–7 June			15-6-58-2 / 39-8-136-1		30.2-8-68-2 / 27.5-5-68-4		22-3-106-5 / 25-5-73-3	18-7-40-1 / 10-0-43-1									274 / 379	9 / 6
v. Derbyshire (Edgbaston) 12–16 June		19-7-51-3	19-3-67-1	23.2-5-86-2	29-10-61-0		6-1-34-0 / 9-2-33-4	6-1-18-0 / 9-1-34-0									216 / 200	6 / 10
v. Leicestershire (Leicester) 26–30 June			14-2-50-2	26-12-47-1		5-2-13-0	5-2-14-0										229	3
v. Surrey (Edgbaston) 2–5 July	23-5-64-4 / 17.4-4-55-6		28-13-62-4 / 14-4-22-1	2-4-8-0 / 1-1-0-0	1-0-10-0 / 8-2-25-1		13-6-40-1 / 15-5-39-2										193 / 144	10 / 10
v. Nottinghamshire (Trent Bridge) 16–19 July	19-4-52-1		12-4-26-4	22-5-55-0	9-2-36-0		23-3-37-4		2-2-0-0			8.3-3-12-1					133	10
v. Somerset (Edgbaston) 24–27 July	37.4-11-98-5 / 16-4-47-0		27-4-95-2 / 12-3-38-0	32.5-4-113-3 / 11-2-32-1	11-7-14-2		32-9-95-5 / 15-1-65-3		1-1-0-0			21-3-49-1					415 / 304	6 / 10
v. Sussex (Edgbaston) 31 July–4 August	14-1-52-2 / 10.2-5-11-1		12-7-22-2			5-1-9-0	9-3-31-1 / 4-0-30-3										134 / 63	6 / 10
v. Lancashire (Blackpool) 6–9 August	16.1-7-40-4 / 25-7-52-2		15-2-63-3 / 30.1-7-115-6	9-4-20-0 / 6-2-21-0		8-1-46-0	14-4-58-2 / 29-3-106-2										203 / 362	10 / 7
v. Worcestershire (Edgbaston) 6–9 August	16-6-40-1		34.1-9-96-2	38-10-77-3	11-2-44-0		7.1-2-22-1 / 38-7-118-5					27-4-101-0					91 / 448	10
v. Essex (Chelmsford) 20–23 August	23.1-9-50-5 / 7.4-4-7-3		10-5-15-2 / 5-1-8-1	14-6-43-2 / 10-6-24-3	8-1-30-1		19-3-60-1 / 10-2-30-2										178 / 101	10 / 10
v. Durham (Chester-le-Street) 27–30 August	14.4-7-33-3 / 20-10-38-3		9-4-16-1 / 6-2-22-0	13-5-29-3 / 22-6-29-1	20.3-5-57-1		10-3-28-3 / 23-9-39-4										118 / 195	10 / 9
v. Gloucestershire (Edgbaston) 2–5 September	10-4-24-2		10-2-37-2 / 4-1-17-1	19-6-48-2	11-3-32-4 / 14-2-57-2		9-5-20-1 / 16-7-23-0			9.3-5-10-1 / 5-2-14-2		23-4-70-1					113 / 224	9 / 9
v. Northamptonshire (Edgbaston) 18–21 September	15.5-6-63-4		19-9-43-0	39-14-63-1	35.4-9-115-2		28-7-62-5										371 / 150	10 / 0
Bowler's average	387.5-123- 938-60 / 15.63	50-12- 158-3 / 52.66	511.5-139- 1555-63 / 24.68	475.1-145- 1157-37 / 31.27	318.2-77- 930-23 / 40.43	23-4- 120-0 / –	483.4-131- 1406-70 / 20.08	58-14- 175-4 / 43.75	3- 0-0 / –	14.3-7- 24-3 / 8.00	25-3- 119-2 / 59.50	79.3-14- 232-3 / 77.33						

A   W.G. Khan 1-1-0-0
B   D.R. Hewson absent
C   D.P. Ostler 7-0-75-0; N.V. Knight 6-0-71-0

Fielding Figures

47 – S.J.Rhodes (ct 44 / st 3)
20 – G.A. Hick
16 – S.R. Lampitt
15 – D.A. Leatherdale
14 – T. Moody
10 – T.S. Curtis
8 – V.S. Solanki
7 – K.R. Spiring and W.P.C. Weston
5 – G.R. Haynes
3 – A. Sheriyar and I. Dawood (ct / st 2)
2 – R.K. Illingworth and sub
1 – M.M. Mirza and R.J. Chapman

Worcestershire First-Class Matches Batting

Season Summary

Batsman	M	Inns	NO	Runs	HS	Av
T.S. Curtis	13	21	1	742	160	37.10
W.P.C. Weston	17	29	5	1190	205	49.58
G.A. Hick	17	28	6	1524	303*	69.27
K.R. Spiring	17	28	3	876	150	35.04
T.M. Moody	14	21	1	973	180*	48.65
V.S. Solanki	13	17	1	473	128*	29.56
S.J. Rhodes	18	23	6	584	78	34.35
S.R. Lampitt	15	17	7	277	52	27.70
P.J. Newport	8	6	—	91	45	15.16
A. Sheriyar	4	13	4	94	21	10.44
M. Rawnsley	17	5	2	71	26	23.66
G.R. Haynes	6	25	3	794	70	36.09
R.J. Chapman	2	3	—	3	3	1.00
D.A. Leatherdale	1	25	8	886	129	52.11
P.A. Thomas	6	2	1	16	16*	16.00
I. Dawood	5	2	1	10	10*	10.00
M.M. Mirza	—	7	4	17	10*	5.66
R.K. Illingworth	—	4	2	157	112	78.50

Matches — Part 1

Batsman	v. Nottinghamshire (Trent Bridge) 23–26 April	v. Leicestershire (Worcester) 7–10 May	v. Oxford University (Oxford) 14–16 May	v. Durham (Chester-le-Street) 21–24 May	v. Somerset (Worcester) 29 May–2 June	v. Gloucestershire (Bristol) 12–16 June	v. Surrey (Worcester) 18–21 June	v. Lancashire (Worcester) 26–30 June	v. Sussex (Arundel) 2–5 July	v. Pakistan 'A' (Worcester) 16–18 July
T.S. Curtis	113	4	—	43 / 9	101	1 / 137	0	0 / 77*	3	8 / 20*
W.P.C. Weston	52	11	119	42	13	14	17*	11	4	55 / 14
G.A. Hick	4	9	164*	39 / 8	14	12 / 137	48*	46*	36	35 / 13
K.R. Spiring	48	55	28*	32 / 9	24	52 / 33*	—	2	43	6
T.M. Moody	70	8	22 / 128*	61 / 5	—	—	—	26	—	38
V.S. Solanki	15	24	—	—	28 / 8	78 / 52	—	2 / 0*	58*	—
S.J. Rhodes	26*	39	—	14*	9 / 41*	—	—	—	45	—
S.R. Lampitt	2	4	—	1 / 7	0 / 27*	6*	—	—	0	2
P.J. Newport	21	13	—	—	70	24	—	38*	—	—
A. Sheriyar	9	47*	7*	67	52	0 / 5	16	13	34	34
M. Rawnsley	—	3	24	18	57	12*	—	—	2	6 / 9*
G.R. Haynes	—	—	8	0*	—	—	—	—	—	16* / 0
R.J. Chapman	—	—	0	47*	—	—	—	—	—	—
Byes	8	6	3	2	21	4	4	1	11	5 / 10
Leg-byes	23	8	6	12	7	4	4	3	1	7 / 18
Wides	14	6	17	24	8	6	6	4	4	13
No-balls	12	20	2	4	2	6	2	4	2	18
Total	417	257	359	351	303	250	81	100	255	265 / 338
Wickets	10	10	2	6	10	10	1	7	10	10 / 4
Result	D	D	D	D	D	W	D	L	W	D
Points	8	9	—	14	10	22	7	0	22	—

Matches — Part 2

Batsman	v. Essex (Chelmsford) 23–26 July	v. Kent (Worcester) 31 July–4 August	v. Northamptonshire (Northampton) 6–9 August	v. Glamorgan (Worcester) 15–18 August	v. Warwickshire (Edgbaston) 20–23 August	v. Middlesex (Kidderminster) 27–30 August	v. Yorkshire (Leeds) 2–5 September	v. Derbyshire (Worcester) 10–13 September	v. Hampshire (Southampton) 18–21 September
T.S. Curtis	33	25	1	160	6	4	48	188	4
W.P.C. Weston	2	10	205	17	2	0	57	19*	303*
G.A. Hick	14 / 107*	46 / 56*	35	65 / 31	122	23	11	31	34*
K.R. Spiring	150 / 14	5	84	42	108	0	67	50*	28*
T.M. Moody	45 / 41	60 / 0	26	14	—	32	10	101	24
V.S. Solanki	60	61	47 / 10	4 / 5	41	59*	20	20	180*
S.J. Rhodes	5* / 4	11	55 / 20	33 / 27	7	—	46*	24	—
S.R. Lampitt	4	—	5 / 6*	49 / 18*	—	—	12*	14*	—
P.J. Newport	0	23	0*	2*	3	29	12	—	—
A. Sheriyar	26	—	17	9	—	2	27	—	—
M. Rawnsley	4	35 / 0	8	45	16	88*	20	6	—
G.R. Haynes	21	59*	110	23	—	—	—	93	—
R.J. Chapman	—	0*	—	1* / 0	—	0* / 5	33*	7*	—
Byes	12	5	8	5	2	6	8	14	3
Leg-byes	4	7	7	14	10	2	4	4	4
Wides	6	6	—	13	6	6	26	20	2
No-balls	16	16	28	10	10	4	6	16	—
Total	394	422	551	476	448	251	313	554	538
Wickets	10	10	10	9	10	5	6	8	2
Result	D	D	W	W	D	L	L	W	W
Points	8	11	22	24	10	6	5	24	24

Worcestershire CCC — First-Class Matches — Bowling

Bowling analyses are given as Overs–Maidens–Runs–Wickets. Where a match had two innings, the two analyses are separated by " / ". Total and Wkts are likewise given per innings.

Match	P.J. Newport	A. Sheriyar	T.M. Moody	S.R. Lampitt	M. Rawnsley	R.J. Chapman	G.R. Haynes	R.K. Illingworth	D.A. Leatherdale	V.S. Solanki	G.A. Hick	M.M. Mirza	Byes	Leg-byes	Wides	No-balls	Total	Wkts
v. Nottinghamshire (Trent Bridge) 23–26 April	12-1-40-0	12-1-45-1	4-1-5-0	18-3-59-1	13-1-40-1								4	3	6	6	196	3
v. Leicestershire (Worcester) 7–10 May	17.2-5-37-7 / 11-6-20-1	17-5-26-3 / 9-1-30-0											2	6 / 4	2 / 6	2 / 8	69 / 143	10 / 4
v. Oxford University (Oxford) 14–16 May [A]		16-4-40-1 / 9-3-17-2	2-1-5-0			9.4-2-44-1 / 14.5-3-54-2	11-1-43-2 / 8-4-17-1			6-2-15-0 / 2-0-10-0	6-1-26-0		4 / 7	10 / 3		6	281 / 135	8 / 7
v. Durham (Chester-le-Street) 21–24 May [B]	15.2-4-33-4	17-5-53-4		6-2-13-1		10-2-26-3	9-1-32-1		7-1-15-1		15-6-30-0		2	7	4	26	132	10
v. Somerset (Worcester) 29 May–2 June	21.4-6-48-2 / 15-8-22-0	25-9-54-5 / 22-9-90-2		18-4-69-1 / 28.4-11-80-3			7-2-21-1 / 17-4-44-1		1-0-1-0 / 19-5-62-1	5-1-22-0 / 4-1-10-0	5-2-12-0		2	5		33 / 16	332 / 343	10 / 10
v. Gloucestershire (Bristol) 12–16 June		9-0-57-1		13-4-55-1 / 18-6-53-3			19-4-54-0 / 11-2-33-2		20-5-56-5 / 10-1-30-1	1-0-7-0 / 3-0-15-0			4 / 5	1 / 6	4	10	185 / 229	5 / 10
v. Surrey (Worcester) 18–21 June		15-5-28-1 / 16-3-62-0		16-2-63-3 / 28-7-104-4		16-2-69-2 / 17-5-72-1	12-4-19-2 / 10-2-24-1		14-3-50-2 / 9-2-28-2		6-2-7-0 / 3-0-20-0		2	9	4	16 / 12	276 / 452	10 / 9
v. Lancashire (Worcester) 26–30 June	15-3-53-2	27-2-118-3	4-0-20-0	14-3-46-2 / 4-0-15-0	20-4-55-0 / 2.5-0-11-0		24.1-10-46-1		20-4-78-0 / 11.1-0-70-2				1 / 1	1 / 8	3		0 / 237	0 / 7
v. Sussex (Arundel) 2–5 July	14-7-22-1	8-0-47-1 / 16-9-19-6	3-2-4-0	15-5-39-5					6.2-4-12-3 / 12-4-32-1				2	4 / 7		12 / 8	71 / 149	10 / 10
v. Pakistan 'A' (Worcester) 16–18 July [C]	8-2-21-0	14.3-3-44-4		31.4-10-67-3	31.4-10-67-3				17-2-53-0	13-3-61-0	34-9-79-0	27-2-136-3			2		489	9
v. Essex (Chelmsford) 23–26 July	16-4-58-1	17-0-80-3	12-2-50-2	14-4-54-1	19-8-45-2	14-2-87-1	20-5-53-2		7-1-35-0	31-6-98-1		19.3-6-56-2 / 9-2-22-1	4	1	6	22	451	10
v. Kent (Worcester) 31 July–4 August	14-4-33-1 / 14-5-43-0	11-2-28-2 / 18-1-77-0	8-1-32-2	17-1-97-0		5-0-30-0	11-6-17-1 / 8-2-31-1		10-2-25-3				4	7	2 / 4	32 / 8	276 / 158	10 / 4
v. Northamptonshire (Northampton) 6–9 August	4-1-14-0	11-3-72-1 / 6-2-12-0	12-3-40-1 / 19-7-67-0	8-0-44-2 / 11-0-82-2			20-7-58-2 / 7-2-11-2				5-0-27-0 / 12-3-38-0		11 / 4	12 / 1	8 / 10	28 / 22	403 / 319	5 / 10
v. Glamorgan (Worcester) 15–18 August [D]		15-3-48-3 / 13-6-47-0	34.4-3-148-5 / 3-1-9-0	5-0-36-0 / 17-3-60-2		3-0-21-0	11-1-46-3 / 12-1-34-2		15-5-29-3 / 6-2-19-0			17.4-1-95-3 / 13.3-1-53-3	5	8 / 3	4	22	398 / 319	10 / 10
v. Warwickshire (Edgbaston) 20–23 August [E]		18-3-55-5 / 11-2-34-1	22-3-105-2 / 16-4-56-1	8-1-21-0 / 16-4-49-1				3-0-12-0 / 17-4-34-1	10-0-55-1 / 6-0-23-1			16-4-51-4 / 11-2-58-1	1	10	6	20 / 15	252 / 241	10 / 5
v. Middlesex (Kidderminster) 27–30 August [F]		28.4-2-126-1 / 5.1-0-40-3	21.5-5-57-3 / 7-4-11-0	7-0-45-0 / 19-5-58-0			18-2-57-3 / 9-1-43-0	20-7-41-0 / 39-13-118-3	2-0-13-0 / 4-0-14-0		1-0-2-0	18-4-70-1 / 5-0-23-0	7	7 / 15		10	252 / 317	7 / 4
v. Yorkshire (Leeds) 2–5 September		8-1-36-3	9-2-40-0 / 4-0-21-0	5-0-42-1 / 7-1-22-0			21-3-81-1				6-1-37-0 / 5-1-26-0	16-3-56-1	7 / 4	5	2 / 4		501 / 83	10 / 10
v. Derbyshire (Worcester) 10–13 September		21-8-84-4 / 11-1-44-0	3-0-13-1 / 5-0-30-0	10-1-55-0 / 8-2-27-1			8-2-30-2 / 9-1-63-0	16.5-12-39-2 / 26-8-51-2	13-5-42-0		20-6-71-1 / 20-6-70-4		4	3 / 1	2	10 / 6	223 / 402	10 / 10
v. Hampshire (Southampton) 18–21 September		6.3-0-39-2	9-1-46-1 / 16-2-70-0	4-1-14-1		5-1-17-0	5-1-17-0	42.2-14-79-7 / 42-21-68-3			25-3-94-1 / 24-6-90-3		4	7			312 / 313	10 / 10
Bowler's average	177.2-56-444-19 — 23.36	445.5-94-1575-62 — 25.40	213.4-42-829-19 — 43.63	334.4-70-1302-35 — 37.20	86.3-23-218-6 — 36.33	103.3-18-470-13 — 36.15	287.1-68-875-31 — 28.22	206.1-79-442-18 — 24.55	219.3-46-742-26 — 28.53	65-13-238-1 — 238.00	193-46-629-9 — 69.88	152.4-25-620-19 — 32.63						

A P.A. Thomas 17-3-43-3, 9-1-36-1; W.P.C. Weston 2-0-6-0
B T.S. Curtis 1-0-10-0
C P.A. Thomas 17-2-87-0
D W.P.C. Weston 3-0-27-0
E T.S. Curtis 11-1-55-1
F W.P.C. Weston 4-0-36-0; K.R. Spiring 2-0-10-0

Fielding Figures

- 53 – R.J. Blakey (ct 49 / st 4)
- 24 – D. Byas
- 17 – C. White
- 8 – D.S. Lehmann
- 7 – R.D. Stemp
- 6 – B. Parker
- 4 – A. McGrath, A.C. Morris and C.A. Chapman (ct 3 / st 1)
- 3 – M.D. Moxon, P.J. Hartley and M.P. Vaughan
- 2 – P.M. Hutchison, G.M. Hamilton and R.A. Kettleborough
- 1 – M.J. Wood, A.G. Wharf and sub

Yorkshire CCC First-Class Matches Batting

Season batting averages (summary columns common to both tables):

Batting	M	Inns	NO	Runs	HS	Av
M.D. Moxon	12	18	1	589	155	32.72
M.J. Wood	2	2	–	102	81	51.00
D. Byas	20	33	4	1319	128	45.48
R.A. Kettleborough	3	5	2	22	10	4.40
B. Parker	19	30	5	806	138*	32.24
C.A. Chapman	2	4	–	139	80	34.75
A.G. Wharf	1	3	2	19	14	6.33
G.M. Hamilton	11	16	2	240	49	17.14
G.J. Batty	1	2	–	18	18	9.00
R.D. Stemp	17	20	6	154	33*	11.00
M.J. Hoggard	1	2	1	2	1*	2.00
M.P. Vaughan	14	25	–	828	161	36.00
A. McGrath	17	24	1	724	141	32.90
C. White	18	24	2	639	172*	29.04
R.J. Blakey	8	10	6	680	92	19.88
D. Gough	9	18	1	179	58	12.10
P.J. Hartley	17	22	1	121	39	19.88
C.E.W. Silverwood	17	27	2	321	58	19.88
D.S. Lehmann	7	9	2	1575	182	63.00
A.C. Morris	7	7	6	117	37	13.00
R.J. Sidebottom	2	2	1	–	2*	–
I.D. Fisher	2	4	–	75	37	18.75
P.M. Hutchison	7	8	7	29	15*	29.00

Match list (left table)

- v. Lancashire (Leeds) 16–19 April
- v. Oxford University (Oxford) 23–25 April
- v. Glamorgan (Leeds) 7–10 May
- v. Warwickshire (Edgbaston) 14–17 May
- v. Somerset (Taunton) 21–24 May
- v. Essex (Ilford) 29 May–2 June
- v. Gloucestershire (Leeds) 4–7 June
- v. Surrey (The Oval) 12–16 June
- v. Nottinghamshire (Trent Bridge) 18–21 June
- v. Middlesex (Leeds) 26–30 June

Innings totals (left table):

	Byes	Leg-byes	Wides	No-balls	Total	Wickets	Result	Points
v. Lancashire	3	14	4	6	289	10	L	–
v. Oxford University	2	13	4	14	335	2	D	–
v. Glamorgan	–	–	–	6	200	9	D	8
v. Warwickshire	1	1	–	6	233	10	L	5
v. Somerset	5	13	–	8	306	10	W	21
v. Essex	–	6	17	10	334	10	W	23
v. Gloucestershire	4	2	4	2	183	9	L	4
v. Surrey	7	6	–	4	387	10	D	10
v. Nottinghamshire	2	6	–	4	364	10	D	10
v. Middlesex	–	–	–	–	–	–	D	3

Match list (right table)

- v. Leicestershire (Leicester) 2–5 July
- v. Durham (Scarborough) 16–19 July
- v. Northamptonshire (Leeds) 31 July–4 August
- v. Pakistan 'A' (Leeds) 7–10 August
- v. Hampshire (Southampton) 15–18 August
- v. Sussex (Scarborough) 15–18 August
- v. Lancashire (Old Trafford) 27–30 August
- v. Worcestershire (Leeds) 2–5 September
- v. Kent (Leeds) 10–13 September
- v. Derbyshire (Derby) 18–21 September

Innings totals (right table):

	Byes	Leg-byes	Wides	No-balls	Total	Wickets	Result	Points
v. Leicestershire	5	6	6	20	268	10	D	8
v. Durham	4	6	4	16	372	10	W	24
v. Northamptonshire	8	6	14	18	166	10	W	20
v. Pakistan 'A'	11	2	12	10	243	10	W	20
v. Hampshire	2	5	–	16	282	10	W	12
v. Sussex	2	12	–	10	501	7	W	22
v. Lancashire	5	6	18	12	419	9	D	2
v. Worcestershire	15	10	–	10	501	10	W	7
v. Kent	–	1	2	10	312	10	W	10
v. Derbyshire	5	16	7	10	267	10	L	10

Yorkshire CCC First-Class Matches — Bowling

Note: this is a large rotated statistical grid. Bowler figures are given as Overs–Maidens–Runs–Wickets. Innings totals and extras are listed per innings where two figures appear for a match.

Match	A.G. Wharf	G.M. Hamilton	A.C. Morris	P.M. Hutchison	D.S. Lehmann	R.D. Stemp	C.E.W. Silverwood	D. Gough	P.J. Hartley	C. White	M.P. Vaughan	A. McGrath	Byes	Leg-byes	Wides	No-balls	Total	Wkts	Note
v. Lancashire (Leeds) 16–19 April	15-2-61-1	18.4-3-97-3				13-1-65-3	9-4-24-2	11-1-40-2	7-1-21-0	4-1-14-1	2.1-1-3-2		1	16	2		482	10	A
	10-1-37-2	4-2-9-0				4-1-5-3					4-2-6-0			3		8	106	4	
v. Oxford University (Oxford) 23–25 April		21-6-63-0					23-3-80-3	23-9-56-5		13-0-62-0	10-1-50-1	2-0-9-0		7		4	114	0	
		3-0-17-0					5-0-27-0	6-0-31-0				0.5-0-6-0	4	12	2	14	336	10	
v. Glamorgan (Leeds) 7–10 May		10.5-5-23-3				16.4-2-44-1	8-3-28-1	17-5-62-4	11-3-39-2	11-1-37-1	4-2-3-0			4		4	166	2	
		7-1-18-0				16-5-35-1	16.4-4-53-0			6-2-16-0	4-0-25-1		2	7	6		140	2	
v. Warwickshire (Edgbaston) 14–17 May		10-1-54-0				9-2-18-2	6-0-33-0	24-7-65-4	12-4-34-5	8.2-1-28-3				16	2		249	10	
		10-1-44-1				19-5-57-1	5-0-12-1		2-0-15-0	11-3-54-2			4	8		10	203	5	
v. Somerset (Taunton) 21–24 May	6-1-23-1					11-4-36-0	12-3-38-1	15.5-3-74-5		16-1-82-3	4-0-20-0			11		6	200	10	
	12-1-34-0			1-1-0-0		11-3-52-1	20-2-96-3	18-1-78-0		14.5-6-50-2	8-0-44-0			4		12	297	10	
v. Essex (Ilford) 29 May–2 June						22-4-79-3	23-7-83-1		11-4-22-2	25-2-88-2	1-1-0-0		9	7		14	312	10	
				1-0-5-0		31.2-8-77-6	13.1-2-49-5		11-2-31-0	27.5-2-137-2					10		205	10	
v. Gloucestershire (Leeds) 4–7 June		8-2-48-2	12-3-62-2			11-3-41-2	7-2-21-1		27-4-103-2	8-2-13-0					4		388	10	
		16.4-3-56-0	9-3-32-0			36-8-108-3			8-0-36-2	13.1-5-51-4			8	3		2	549	10	
v. Surrey (The Oval) 12–16 June						46-8-148-3			15-5-40-2	6-0-44-1				8		6	153	10	
						17-3-44-3		12-2-36-0						1			148	7	
v. Nottinghamshire (Trent Bridge) 18–21 June			5-0-18-1				8-3-13-1		10-1-39-0					4		7	150	3	B
v. Middlesex (Leeds) 26–30 June						33-11-90-1	27-4-86-0	18.5-7-37-4	22-7-63-3	15-0-70-1			2	14	4	10	406	8	
v. Leicestershire (Leicester) 2–5 July				23.2-5-64-4		3-1-3-0	17-7-32-1			12-2-42-1			8	1		10	152	10	C
				12.3-4-38-1	0.4-0-0-1	3-0-0-0	13-4-40-3			5-2-14-0			8	8	2		164	10	D
v. Durham (Scarborough) 16–19 July			9-1-50-0		1-0-5-0	15-3-43-3	23-10-62-4	18-4-51-3	14-4-29-3	17.4-0-61-3			12	5		18	286	10	
						27-4-59-2	14-3-32-1	17-3-50-0	16-4-34-2	12.3-1-31-5			4	6	2	16	176	9	
v. Northamptonshire (Leeds) 31 July–4 August		26-8-95-4	9-2-29-0	20-4-50-7	3-1-14-0		27-8-73-2				15-2-40-1		11	5	4	17	365	9	E
v. Pakistan 'A' (Leeds) 7–10 August		12-4-52-2	6-1-18-1	30-6-95-2	5-1-6-1	13-2-45-0	10-3-24-0			16.2-2-51-2	17-4-53-0			6	3	2	187	10	
		11-1-49-0	13-4-24-0			30-10-81-0	15-3-27-4			21-5-65-1	10-1-41-0		4	5	3	6	281	10	
v. Hampshire (Southampton) 15–18 August		27-5-89-5		13.2-5-48-5	3-1-14-0	4-1-4-0	13.2-4-59-5			6-0-20-1	16-0-92-0			11	8	14	471	9	
		5-0-12-0		13-1-44-2	5-1-6-1		14.3-1-47-1			9-1-18-2				1		2	157	10	
v. Sussex (Scarborough) 20–23 August		2-1-2-0		21-5-67-3		13-2-44-2	16-3-50-0			12-3-32-1			1	10			137	10	
v. Lancashire (Old Trafford) 27–30 August		11-2-35-1					17-4-61-3	12-1-56-0		7-0-42-0	7-0-42-0			9	8	4	277	8	
v. Worcestershire (Leeds) 2–5 September		15-3-50-2		9-3-31-1	2-0-8-0	25-6-74-2	29.3-8-93-7			17-2-55-0	8-0-33-0		8	4		26	313	6	F
		8.5-2-27-2		12-1-38-3		9-1-39-0	22-6-55-5			13-5-36-2	5-0-35-0		1	1		6	205	10	
v. Kent (Leeds) 10–13 September				28-8-91-1		10-1-32-0	21-3-77-1			20-4-52-1	7-0-35-0	3-0-10-0	2	13	2	20	374	10	
				20-10-22-0		13-6-18-0	5-0-28-1			13-5-13-0		3-0-19-1		4		10	147	5	
v. Derbyshire (Derby) 18–21 September		14-3-67-0	15-3-56-0	27-4-130-2	6-0-21-0						14-3-48-0		10	25	2	8	473	3	
				4-0-23-0	1.2-0-12-0									1			64	1	
Bowler's average	43.5– 155-4 38.75	241.5-3– 907-27 33.59	78-17– 289-4 72.25	233.1-56– 741-37 20.02	21-3– 71-2 35.50	473-111– 1379-42 32.83	440.1-104– 1393-57 24.43	192.4-43– 638-27 23.62	170-39– 532-23 23.13	353.4-58– 1236-41 30.14	147.1-17– 619-5 123.80	8.5-0– 44-1 44.00							

A M.J. Hoggard 20-4-110-1, 7-0-45-1; R.J.Batty 5-0-59-1, 6-0-11-1; R.A.Kettleborough 13-3-74-1
B R.J. Sidebottom, 16.4-4-4-71-3
C J.N. Snape absent hurt
D I.D. Fisher 12-2-38-0, 6-0-26-1
E B. Parker 1-0-3-0
F I.D. Fisher 20-4-39-0, 1-1-0-0